GIAMBATTISTA TIEPOLO

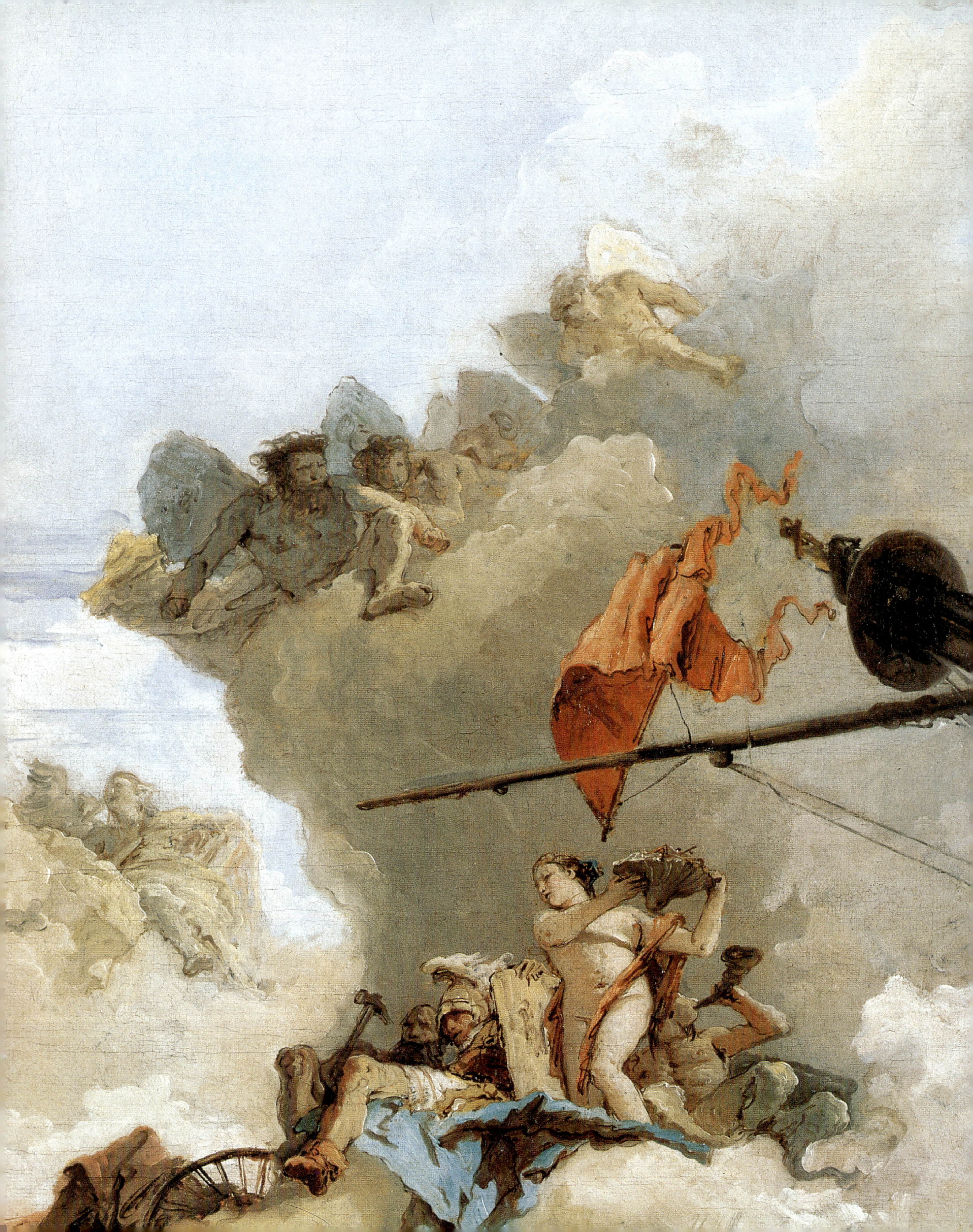

GIAMBATTISTA
TIEPOLO
1696–1770

EDITED BY KEITH CHRISTIANSEN

THE METROPOLITAN MUSEUM OF ART, NEW YORK

Distributed by Harry N. Abrams Inc., New York

This publication is issued in conjunction with the exhibition "Giambattista Tiepolo, 1696–1770," presented on the three-hundredth anniversary of the artist's birth. It was organized by the Soprintendenza ai Beni Artistici e Storia di Venezia, the Assessorato alla Cultura del Comune di Venezia, and The Metropolitan Museum of Art, New York, and held at the Museo del Settecento Veneziano, Ca' Rezzonico, Venice, from September 5 to December 9, 1996, and The Metropolitan Museum of Art, New York, from January 24 to April 27, 1997.

The exhibition is made possible in part by the Italian Trade Commission, the National Endowment for the Arts, and the Samuel H. Kress Foundation. An indemnity has been granted by the Federal Council on the Arts and the Humanities.

Published by The Metropolitan Museum of Art, New York

John P. O'Neill, Editor in Chief
Carol Fuerstein, Editor
Bruce Campbell, Designer
Gwen Roginsky, Matthew Pimm, and Christopher Zichello, Production
Barbara Cavaliere, Production Editor
Robert Weisberg, Computer Specialist

New photography at The Metropolitan Museum of Art by Katherine Dahab, Oi-Cheong Lee, Bruce Schwarz, and Eileen Travell, the Photograph Studio, The Metropolitan Museum of Art, New York

Set in Poetica Chancery and Dante
Printed on R400 matt satin 150 gsm
Separations by Professional Graphics, Rockford, Illinois
Printed and bound by Amilcare Pizzi S.p.A.–arte grafiche, Milan

Translations from the Italian of the essay by Giandomenico Romanelli by Keith Christiansen; the essay by Filippo Pedrocco by Alberto Curotto; the essay by Adriano Mariuz by Stephen Sartarelli; and the entries by Egidio Martin, Filippo Pedrocco, and Giuseppe Maria Pilo by Keith Christiansen and Stephen Sartarelli

Jacket/cover illustration: Detail, *Rinaldo Abandoning Armida*, no. 17c
Frontispiece: Detail, *The Wealth and Benefits of the Spanish Monarchy*, no. 53

Library of Congress Cataloging-in-Publication Data
Tiepolo, Giovanni Battista, 1696–1770.
Giambattista Tiepolo, 1696–1770 / edited by Keith Christiansen.
p. cm.
Catalog of an exhibition opening at the Museum of Ca' Rezzonico, Venice, on Sept. 5, 1996, and on view at the Metropolitan Museum of Art, New York, from Jan. 24 through Apr. 27, 1997.
Includes bibliographical references and index.
ISBN 0-87099-811-0. — ISBN 0-87099-812-9 (pbk.). — ISBN 0-8109-6505-4 (Abrams)
1. Tiepolo, Giovanni Battista, 1696–1770—Exhibitions. I. Christiansen, Keith. II. Museo del Settecento veneziano. III. Metropolitan Museum of Art (New York, N.Y.). IV. Title.
ND623.T5A4 1996
759.5—dc20 96-21058
CIP

Contents

ORGANIZING COMMITTEE

ANDREA BAYER
Research Associate
The Metropolitan Museum of Art

KEITH CHRISTIANSEN
Jayne Wrightsman Curator
The Metropolitan Museum of Art

MONICA DA CORTÀ FUMEI
Assessorato alla Cultura
Comune di Venezia

GIOVANNA NEPI SCIRÈ
Soprintendente per i
Beni Artistici e Storici di Venezia

FILIPPO PEDROCCO
Soprintendente al
Museo di Ca' Rezzonico

GIANDOMENICO ROMANELLI
Direttore
Civici Musei Veneziani d'Arte e di Storia

CONSULTATIVE COMMITTEE

Bernard Aikema
Filippa Aliberti Gaudioso
William L. Barcham
Alessandro Bettagno
Diane De Grazia
Massimo Gemin
George Knox
Adriano Mariuz
Giuseppe Pavanello
Terisio Pignatti
Giuseppe Maria Pilo
Donald Posner
Lionello Puppi
Francesco Valcanover
Catherine Whistler

Lenders to the Exhibition

AUSTRIA
Vienna
Gemäldegalerie der Akademie der Bildenden Künste 47a
Kunsthistorisches Museum 34

CANADA
Montreal, Montreal Museum of Fine Arts 11

DENMARK
Copenhagen, Statens Museum for Kunst 21c

FRANCE
Angers, Musée des Beaux-Arts 52
Paris, Musée Cognacq-Jay 19

GERMANY
Augsburg
Staatsgalerie am Shaezler-Palais, Städtische Kunstsammlungen Augsburg 21d
Berlin, Gemäldegalerie, Staatliche Museen, Preussischer Kulturbesitz 38
Hamburg, Kunsthalle 33
Munich, Bayerische Verwaltung der Staatlichen Schlösser, Gärten und Seen 22a, b
Stuttgart, Staatsgalerie 57b

HUNGARY
Budapest, Szépmüvészeti Múzeum 37

ITALY
Camerino, Museo Diocesano 32
Milan, Pinacoteca del Castello Sforzesco 36b
Rampazzo, Parish Church of S. Maria Maddalena 39
Rome, Galleria Nazionale d'Arte Antica 17e
Rovigo, Pinacoteca dell'Accademia dei Concordi 43

Venice
Sacristy of the Canons, Basilica of S. Marco 28
Church of S. Alvise 31
Church of SS. Apostoli 36a
Church of S. Maria della Consolazione (della Fava) 29
Church of S. Maria dei Derelitti (the Ospedaletto) 2a, b, 5
Church of S. Maria del Rosario (the Gesuati) 35
Gallerie dell'Accademia 1, 6a, b, 48a
Museo del Settecento Veneziano, Ca' Rezzonico 13, 20, 25a, b
Palazzo Ducale 24
Pinacoteca della Fondazione Scientifica Querini Stampalia 46
Scuola Grande Arciconfraternità di San Rocco 27

Verona, Museo di Castelvecchio 10
Vicenza, Museo Civico 18

PORTUGAL
Lisbon, Museu Nacional de Arte Antiga 57c

RUSSIA
Saint Petersburg, The Hermitage Museum 12a–d

SPAIN
Madrid
Fundación Colección Thyssen-Bornemisza 23
Museo del Prado 40b, 41b
Pedrola, Duquesa de Villahermosa 55, 56

SWEDEN
Stockholm, The Stockholm University Art Collection 15

UNITED KINGDOM
County Durham, The Bowes Museum, Barnard Castle 47b
Edinburgh, The National Gallery of Scotland 16a

Foreword

Work on this exhibition began in earnest three years ago, when the Metropolitan Museum, the Soprintendenza ai Beni Artistici e Storici di Venezia, the Assessorato alla Cultura del Comune di Venezia, and the Direzione dei Musei Civici Veneziani agreed to collaborate on a joint venture celebrating the three-hundredth anniversary of the birth of Giambattista Tiepolo, the greatest painter of eighteenth-century Venice and, excepting only Goya and David, of eighteenth-century Europe. A monographic exhibition to commemorate the two-hundredth anniversary of Tiepolo's death was mounted at Villa Passariano, near Udine, in 1971, but not since 1951 has an undertaking approaching the ambition and scope of this project been attempted in Venice, and, astonishingly, a full-scale exhibition devoted to him has never been realized outside Italy. The Metropolitan Museum was especially keen to participate in this enterprise, for New York collectors have long evinced a special admiration for this supremely gifted painter. So assiduously have they amassed his drawings, prints, and paintings that New York can claim to possess the richest holdings of his art outside Venice, with the Metropolitan as the city's primary repository.

Our ambition was simple albeit arduous: to show Tiepolo as one of the presiding geniuses of the European imagination. This is not an easy task, for much of his work was carried out in fresco in places as distant as Würzburg and Madrid and must be viewed in situ. Moreover, many of his greatest canvases are of a scale that prohibits moving them. The organizers accepted these peculiar difficulties as a challenge rather than as an insurmountable limitation. The exhibition has been organized not as a chronological survey but as a demonstration of Tiepolo's achievement and the enormous variety within his oeuvre. Following a section devoted to his formation and early career, the contours of which have assumed greater clarity through research accomplished during the last two decades, there are sections treating various aspects of his production. For those who know Tiepolo only as a decorative artist—the genial magician who casts an enchanted and enchanting spell with his poetic tales culled from Ariosto and Tasso—the seriousness of his religious painting will come as a revelation. Not since Titian and Tintoretto had Venice seen a like talent for transforming the laconic stories of the Bible and of the saints into dramatic narrative. The richness and diversity of Tiepolo's imagination have long seemed to many the most modern aspects of his genius, and the last section of this exhibition has been conceived as a celebration of these traits.

In Venice the works are installed in the dazzling eighteenth-century setting of the Ca' Rezzonico, which contains two splendid frescoed ceilings by Tiepolo commissioned from Giambattista Rezzonico. Complementary itineraries to churches, palaces, and villas will allow visitors to further experience firsthand Tiepolo's frescoes in and around the city. A number of altarpieces have purposely been left in situ so that they can be seen in their architectural settings. Some of these altarpieces will travel to New York, where the exhibition will be augmented by the Metropolitan's three monumental canvases from the Ca' Dolfin and a stunning series of oil sketches for Tiepolo's major fresco commissions. Throughout, only pictures of the most outstanding quality have been selected, and the result is a survey of the artist operating at the highest level.

The success of any exhibition is directly dependent on the generosity of lenders, both institutional and private. To them our heartfelt thanks are extended. Of signal importance in realizing our goals has been the support of the Ministero per i Beni Culturali e Ambientali and of the Comune di Venezia under its mayor, Massimo Cacciari, and its Assessore alla Cultura, Gianfranco Mossetto. Two individuals in Venice deserve to be singled out: Filippo Pedrocco, author of the most authoritative monograph on the artist and a key participant in conceiving the exhibition, and Monica Da Cortà Fumei, who undertook in admirable fashion all aspects of the project related to its complicated organization in Venice. In New York, Keith

Christiansen and Andrea Bayer served as coorganizers, contributing with enthusiasm and irreproachable professionalism to every aspect of the project.

The exhibition in Venice has been sponsored by SKIRA. In New York it has been made possible in part by the Italian Trade Commission, the National Endowment for the Arts, and the Samuel H. Kress Foundation. To these agencies we offer profound thanks.

Philippe de Montebello
Director
The Metropolitan Museum of Art

Giovanna Nepi Scirè
Soprintendente per i
Beni Artistici e Storici di Venezia

Giandomenico Romanelli
Direttore
Civici Musei Veneziani d'Arte e di Storia

Preface and Acknowledgments

For someone whose first area of interest is the quattrocento—the century of Fra Angelico, Piero della Francesca, Andrea Mantegna, and Giovanni Bellini—it seems only fitting to begin by confessing to what some of my colleagues might, a century and a half after Ruskin, still consider a private vice: I have long harbored a deep love of the art of Tiepolo. It has been based on no specialized knowledge of the period or any particular interest in eighteenth-century painting but on an innate response to his frescoes and paintings as strong as that experienced before the work of his more universally adulated predecessors: to those visions of angels whose densely feathered wings and freshly starched draperies rustle almost audibly in the vast expanses of humid skies streaked by a low-hanging sun; to the magnificently garbed (and sometimes magnificently ungarbed) heroines who alternately enslave or enchant their suitors with a look of calm superiority or tender surrender (for Tiepolo is one of those artists who found the female protagonist more interesting than the male); to those martyr saints who, seen across the luminous spaces of a Venetian church, illuminated by light refracted through bottle-glass windows and animated by the reflections of a nearby canal, meet their tragic ends with unimpaired dignity, their gestures communicating a radiantly spiritual release—"a richness of sanctity that is almost profane," to appropriate Henry James's description of Bellini's work; to those Virgins who, in their reserve and aristocratic beauty, proclaim descent from the noble creations of Veronese and Titian yet also manage to retain a hint of the human frailty of a Madonna by Bellini or Cima da Conegliano; and to that sublime union of real architectural space and the space of pictorial fiction—the legacy of Renaissance painting to which Tiepolo laid legitimate claim as the last great master.

In the best Venetian tradition, Tiepolo did not subscribe to the neo-Platonic fallacy that to be great, art must aspire to be erudite and accessible only to the initiate. He sought to please, and his unsurpassed gifts as a draftsman and a colorist were for him tools of seduction. They admit the viewer into an enchanted garden: a place that, on casual inspection, can appear merely beautiful but that, on closer examination, reveals itself to be scented with irony and, at times, overcast with dark tragedy. We know that Tiepolo gave serious thought to the function of art and the way it could work on the emotions and that through his friendship with the worldly wise Francesco Algarotti he had access to the latest aesthetic theories. But he never committed his own ideas to paper, and his paintings, however marked by wit and fantasy, show no overriding attachment to erudition. For Tiepolo, as for generations of Venetian artists before him, art was as much a craft as an intellectual activity—a family enterprise to which his sons Giandomenico and Lorenzo were introduced at an early age. His ideal client may have been a member of the old Venetian oligarchy, a high-ranking ecclesiastic, or a king, but he was most at ease with people of his own class and profession, and at Würzburg he preferred to eat with his fellow workers than to sit with men of knightly rank. The sheer quantity of his drawings and paintings testifies to an indefatigable commitment to his profession.

There are many lenses through which Tiepolo's work can be viewed. One of the most revealing is that provided by the theatrical conventions of eighteenth-century opera and contemporary critical debates about dramatic presentation on the stage. Equally, his art can be examined by reference to its many visual sources, for Tiepolo's imagination fed off the past in much the same manner that Rubens's did. What has been seen as a dependence on the work of Veronese is, in fact, part of a larger cultural phenomenon in eighteenth-century Venice, especially evident in architecture: a revival of cinquecento style that, like a carnival mask, can disguise profound originality. There is something of De Chirico in the way Tiepolo generates a feeling of malaise and enigma with his arbitrary combinations of costume and juxtapositions of seemingly disconnected elements in a composition. And there is something of Matisse in his serious pursuit of the pleasurable. A willful ambivalence characterizes much of his work. Indeed, the authors of a recent book on his breathtaking frescoes above the staircase of the Residenz in Würzburg have commented on "a tart sort of moral after-taste. . . . There seems a diffused meaning . . . that condenses only *after having seen* the picture." This occurs not only because the ceiling in question is too large and complex to be taken in at a glance—

as modern aesthetic experience requires—but also because Tiepolo continually plays off the world of the imagination against the world of nature; his is an art of allusion rather than statement. In this lies its modernity.

During the past three years I have incurred debts from many quarters, and I would like to take this opportunity to thank the numerous people who have offered advice, provided information, arranged for me to see works of art, or helped to trace hard-to-locate pictures. In addition to those on the consultative committee whose names are listed in these pages, the staff members of lending institutions who have patiently answered my queries and the parish priests and bishops who have generously allowed works in their churches to travel to New York, special mention should be made of Lisa Ackerman, Plácido Arango, Joseph Baillio, Dr. Franco Barbieri, Charles Beddington, Catherine Bindman, Beverly Brown, David Bull, David Ekserdjian, Florian Fiedler, Eric Gordon, William Griswold, Nicholas Hall, Peter Krückmann, Douglas Lewis, Stefane Loire, Pietro Marani, Marilyn Perry, Aileen Ribeiro, Andrew Robison, Antonio Romagnolo, Pierre Rosenberg, Paul Taylor, Aidan Weston-Lewis, John Winter, and Linda Wolk-Simon. I have especially fond memories of a trip to out-of-the-way churches in the Veneto, kindly arranged by Filippa Aliberti Gaudioso, and an excursion in the company of Diane De Grazia and Bill Barcham to Würzburg to view the marvelous exhibition mounted there last winter and spring. Earlier in 1996 Werner Rescher and Ingrid Stümmer kindly spent a day with me examining the frescoes over the staircase in Würzburg from a scaffold, and in Venice, Ottorino Nonfarmale generously discussed with me his observations on Tiepolo's fresco technique. Nothing could have been accomplished without my colleagues in Venice, and I would like to single out especially Filippo Pedrocco, who has worked on the project from its inception, and Monica Da Cortà Fumei, who has guided it through delicate negotiations and a complex bureaucracy.

At the Metropolitan, Andrea Bayer has acted as my right hand, critic, and collaborator; without her the exhibition simply would not have taken place. Philippe de Montebello and Everett Fahy lent the project their full and enthusiastic support. Mahrukh Tarapor, Associate Director for Exhibitions, worked tirelessly to help procure loans. As always, the Department of Paintings Conservation under Hubert von Sonnenburg has stood ready to help. I have been fortunate to have been assisted at different stages of research by three gifted students, Lisa Rotmil, Kelley Helmstutler, and Ashley Thomas.

The skillful editing, design, and production of the catalogue are the result of the coordinated efforts of Carol Fuerstein, Bruce Campbell, and Gwen Roginsky, with Jean Wagner, Barbara Cavaliere, Matthew Pimm, Christopher Zichello, and Robert Weisberg, working under the guidance of John P. O'Neill and Barbara Burn. Barbara Bridgers and her staff in the Photograph Studio made time for new photography in the face of competing commitments. Further thanks are due to Aileen Chuk, who had the gargantuan task of overseeing transport and insurance; Emily Kernan Rafferty, Vice President for Development and Membership; Linda M. Sylling, Assistant Manager for Operations; Stephanie Oratz Basta, Assistant Counsel; David Harvey, Exhibition Designer; Sue Koch, Senior Graphic Designer; and Zack Zanolli, Lighting Designer, for their extraordinary efforts on behalf of the exhibition.

Finally, I would like to acknowledge Jayne Wrightsman, who has had no direct involvement in this exhibition but whose love of the art of Tiepolo and whose generous gifts of paintings by him have added immeasurably to the Metropolitan's collection and to the enjoyment of its many visitors. To her I would like to dedicate this catalogue.

Keith Christiansen
Jayne Wrightsman Curator
Department of European Paintings
The Metropolitan Museum of Art

Notes to the Reader

Abbreviated references are used throughout. For full listings, see the bibliography.

Pictures exhibited only in Venice are indicated by *; pictures exhibited only in New York are indicated by †.

Unless otherwise stated, the medium is oil on canvas. Measurements are given in centimeters and inches. Height precedes width.

Unless otherwise stated, works illustrated are by Tiepolo.

Entries are signed with authors' initials, which are listed in the following key.

WLB	William L. Barcham
AB	Andrea Bayer
KC	Keith Christiansen
DDG	Diane De Grazia
EM	Egidio Martini
FP	Filippo Pedrocco
GMP	Giuseppe Maria Pilo
CW	Catherine Whistler

THE ART OF TIEPOLO

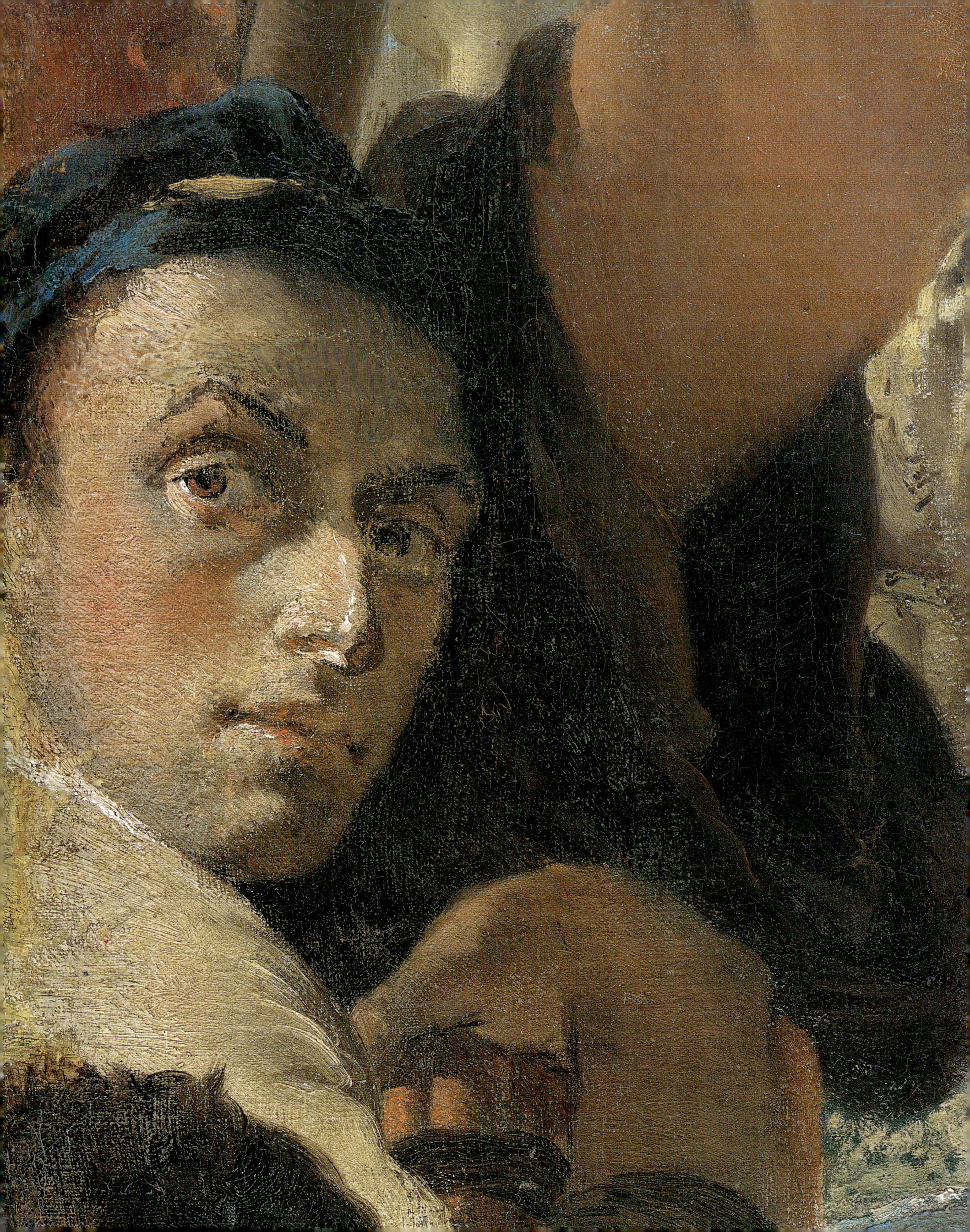

Giambattista Tiepolo: "Painting's True Magician"

ADRIANO MARIUZ

For Marcel Proust the name Tiepolo was associated with a color: an unmistakable tone of pink—the pink of one of the dressing gowns that Odette Swann used to wear in the privacy of her home and which enhanced her charms. One might say that Proust thought of Tiepolo as an ingenious couturier who knew how to bring out the very best in a person's beauty, especially a woman's, by highlighting sensual attractions with apparel and fabrics. And there is no doubt that his costumes, reinventions of cinquecento and Oriental models that always feature some touch of eccentricity—those brocades, those cascades of silk and satin draped over lovely limbs and billowing in midair and in light—are a fundamental ingredient of Tiepolo's spectacle and part of his charm (they conform, moreover, to a manner peculiar to the Venetian school, with precedents in Carpaccio and Veronese). The proof of his brilliance as a costume designer attentive to subtle erotic appeals lies not so much in the gowns and headdresses of queens, princesses, and pages but in the toilettes of his angels: those tunics revealing a bare shoulder or parting at the hip, unveiling a thigh; or those wonderfully inventive belts with grotesque masks for buckles, thrust crosswise, pressing against radiant flesh. Such costumes, like a bird's plumage or a butterfly's wings, seem a natural part of the people wearing them and convey to the viewer a pleasure at once visual and virtually tactile.

During those years in the late nineteenth century when Odette was parading Tiepolo-pink dressing gowns, the Venetian artist had become fashionable again. He had remained in the shadows for nearly a century, for, with a few exceptions, both Neoclassical and Romantic tastes had viewed him critically, as too "artificial" and even as a mad, whimsical genius.[1] Now, however, his praises were everywhere being sung and his works rescued from oblivion. Such was the case with the frescoes in Villa Valmarana (see figs. 9, 44, 45), to which the young art historian Pompeo Molmenti had drawn attention in an article published in 1879 in the review *L'Art* and later in a richly illustrated volume.[2] No less significant was the fact that an avant-garde painter such as Degas, who was also a habitué of museums, could recommend to a friend visiting Venice that he go to see, for Degas's sake, the Tiepolo frescoes in the Palazzo Labia (see frontis., p. 28; fig. 38).[3]

Just a few years later Parisians would have the chance to appreciate Giambattista's incomparable gifts as a fresco painter in their own city. In 1893 Édouard André had the fresco cycle removed from the Villa Contarini-Pisani at Mira and installed in his sumptuous eighteenth-century-style Parisian mansion (unfortunately altering the original order, which was fundamental to its meaning and charm). In this work Tiepolo depicted the reception of Henry III of France, an event that had taken place in that same villa some 150 years earlier, rendered suddenly present through the magic of painting, as if it were happening here and now, with the spectators of that bygone era looking out from the balconies and balustrade ringing the ceiling: a true theater within a theater (see fig. 108).[4]

The Belle Époque rediscovered Tiepolo and made him its own, seeing him above all as a brilliant decorator and the creator of a kind of beauty suffused with sensuality, whose conceptions "have the sort of languor that follows voluptuous indulgence of the flesh and that delicate epicureans prefer to pleasure itself."[5] While artists such as Degas must have been attracted by his lively style and the bold solutions he found for certain exquisitely pictorial problems, most saw him as the principal interpreter of the eighteenth-century Venetian belle époque: an Italian equivalent of Boucher, in short, who had staged his sumptuous spectacle to fulfill the need for escape felt by a frivolous, opulent society by then irreversibly on the road to decadence. A sunset light seemed to radiate from his painting; and in the eyes of his heroines, beneath those heavy lids, one seemed to perceive, together with the promise of pleasure, a shadow of boredom and melancholy.

Today, more than one hundred years after his return to the limelight, and three hundred years after his birth, it is much more difficult to establish exactly who Tiepolo is for us. Over the course of a century, a great mass of studies has accumulated. Under philological scrutiny his work has proved to be more varied, more diversified in its multiple aspects, than ever. For example, the young Tiepolo—experimental, inspired, nuanced in language and mood, "all spirit and fire," in the judgment of

Self-portrait (detail, *The Triumph of Marius*, no. 12e)

his contemporaries[6]—has come to assume increasing prominence, especially in the wake of recent attributions.[7] On another level, on the basis of content as much as style, the more widespread perception of Tiepolo as an artist of predominantly secular inspiration has begun to give way to a recognition of him as the last great painter of sacred visions, someone who, for the sublimity of his achievements in this specific area, can be compared only to such composers of his day as Handel, Vivaldi, and even Bach.[8]

In any case, despite the savage criticisms leveled at him by Roberto Longhi (but this was the aftermath of World War II,[9] when Neorealism was at its height and anything that might seem rhetorical was suspect)—criticisms that, given the authority of the source, have carried perhaps too much weight among Italian writers—there is no longer any doubt that Tiepolo was one of the greatest, most serious, and original artists of his day. The chapter devoted to him by Michael Levey as the culmination of his much-reprinted study of eighteenth-century Venetian painting is entitled "The Presiding Genius"[10]—which hardly seems an exaggeration. Anyone who climbs the great staircase of the Residenz at Würzburg and sees the universe created by Giambattista unfolding on the vault is fully aware of participating in one of the most exalting aesthetic experiences offered by European painting of any age (see frontis., p. 18; fig. 112).

Perhaps in the present cultural climate, in which interpretation based on ideologies no longer holds sway and the avant-garde no longer constitutes a determining criterion for value judgments about the painting of earlier eras, we are in a better position than in the recent past to appreciate Tiepolo. If he has appeared less innovative than some of his contemporaries, this is only because his imaginative daring has no point of comparison in his time but is more akin to that of Rubens and Bernini. More than the celebrated interpreter of the society and culture of the ancien régime, Tiepolo should be seen above all as one of the loftiest examples of the "pictorial intelligence":[11] as the creator of a wondrous world that has its raison d'être in its very visibility, that is, in its manifestation as a pure spectacle of painting. During his life the science of optics made great progress—Newton's experiments in refraction, revealing the composite nature of the colors of light, were enthusiastically received—and sight was considered among the greatest pleasures. In keeping with his age, Tiepolo created a formidable pictorial strategy for attracting and engaging sight, rewarding it with a feast of emotions for the eye.

At this juncture in our attempt to move closer to his art, a shortcut is offered by a reexamination of some of the judgments of a few of his contemporaries, who had keen eyes for appreciating his work and grasping its peculiarities. First in line are those of the well-known Venetian scholar and connoisseur Anton Maria Zanetti the Younger.

In 1771, the year following Tiepolo's death, Zanetti published the volume *Della pittura veneziana e delle opere pubbliche de' veneziani maestri*, a survey of five centuries of what could well

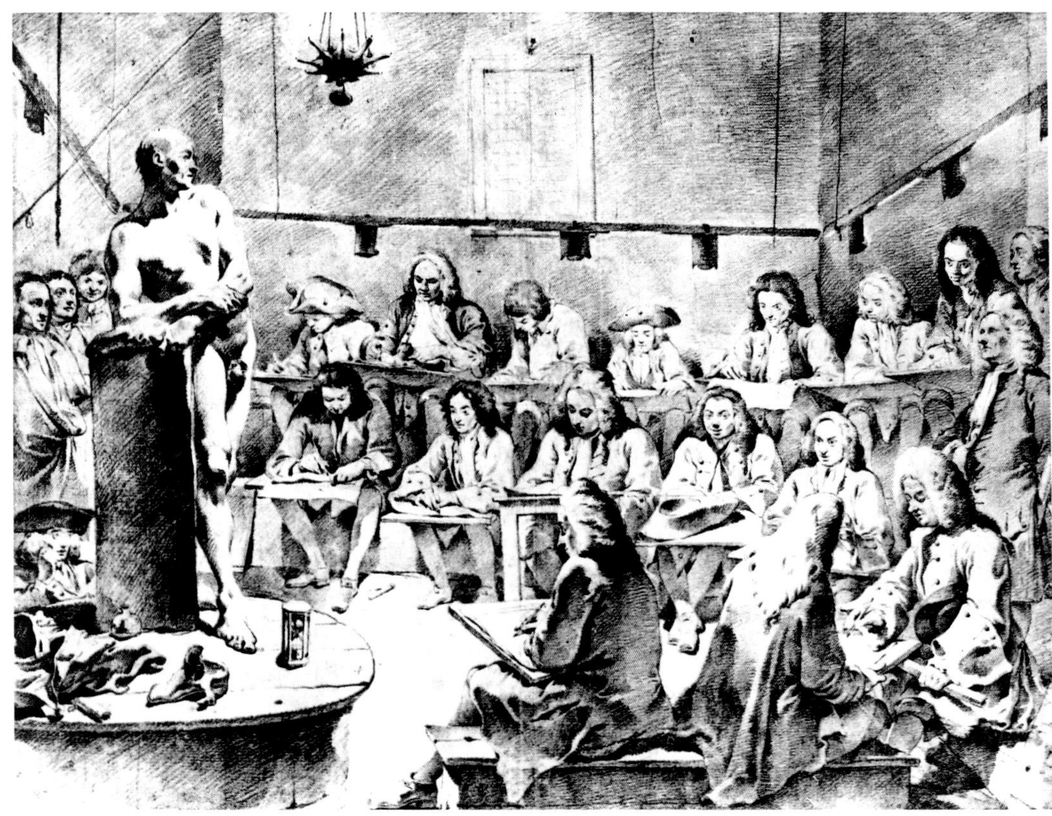

Fig. 1. *A Drawing Academy.* Black chalk. Private collection

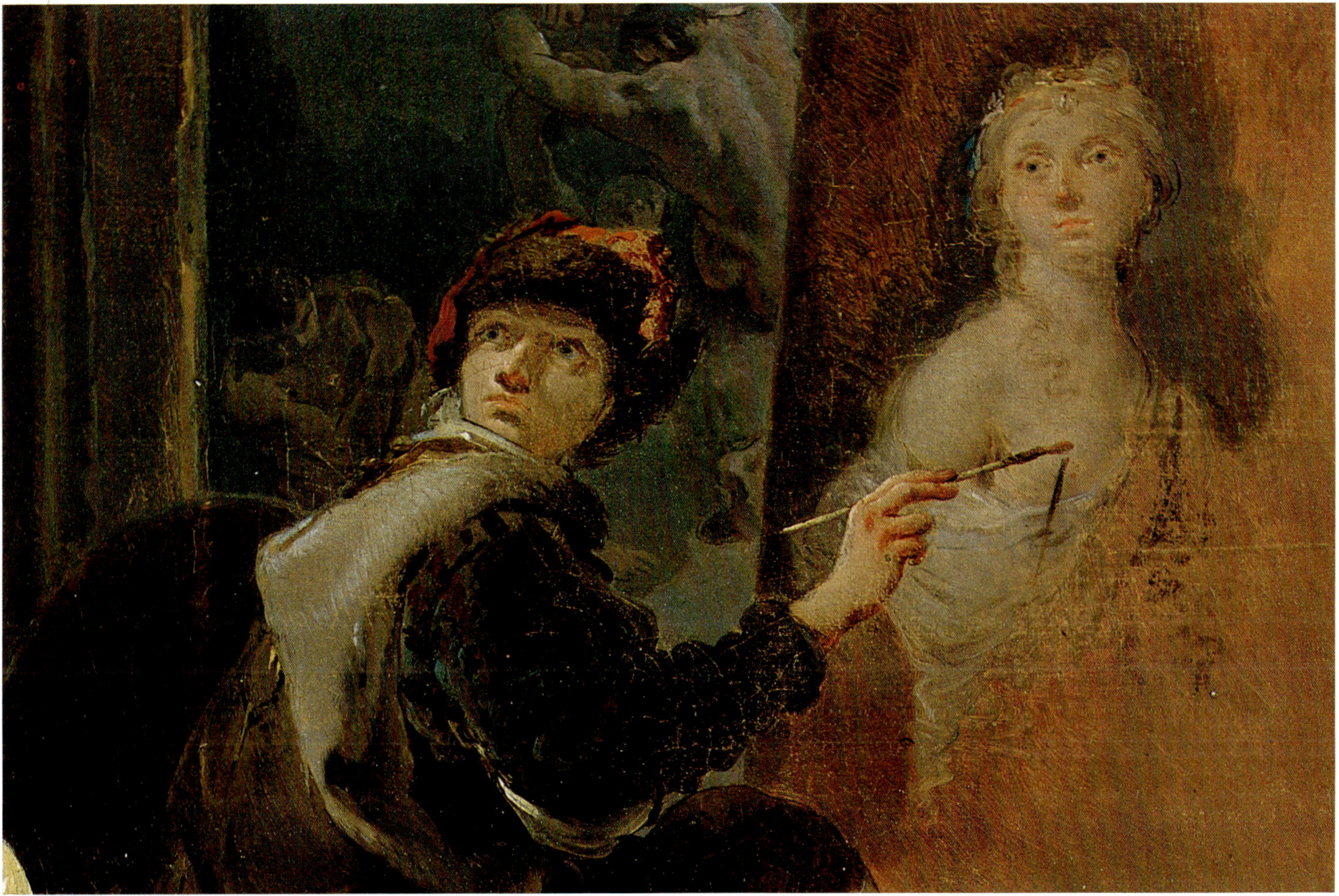

Fig. 2. Self-portrait (detail, *Apelles Painting Campaspe*, no. 11)

be considered the greatest and most venerable European school of painting. Book five discusses the painters of the eighteenth century whom Zanetti knew personally. Their works, characterized especially by "great and luxuriant beauty of color and imagery," seemed to him on the whole "a sweet dream, a purely sensual enchantment."[12] It is a suggestive, fitting appraisal, which would seem to have been inspired, above all, by Tiepolo's painting. Zanetti sketched a memorable critical profile of the recently deceased painter, capped by his observation that Tiepolo was able, "with marvelous art," to imbue his works with a "beauty and a sun that are perhaps without parallel."[13]

The word Zanetti uses here for "beauty" is *vaghezza,* which denotes a delicate, enchanting, artful beauty, one that does not look to some canon and the classical ideal: a beauty that has something indefinable about it and thus involves the subjective realm of taste and sensibility. Applied to painting in general, *vaghezza* also denotes, as one eighteenth-century text specifically states, "certain bright, luminous tones, broad strokes, good taste in the drawing, bands of light and shadow."[14] If *vaghezza* is a quality common to other "modern" painters, what is "perhaps without parallel" in Tiepolo's paintings is their sunny luminosity.

Tiepolo, then, is the painter of light, a term with the fullest possible resonance in a century that declared itself enlightened. Indeed, from the very start his painting revealed itself to be a glorification of light—of a light illuminating a virtually limitless space in which a passionate and boundless imagination celebrates its own magnificence. Apollo, god of the sun and the fine arts, is, in fact, a key figure in Tiepolo's Olympus: his appearances dot the continually ascending path of the painter's career, marking the stages in the conquest of an ever more intense and diffuse luminosity and an ever greater expansion of the creative imagination, until the final, triumphant culmination in the ceiling over the monumental staircase of the Residenz at Würzburg (see fig. 39). As Levey has written, "The god himself, beautiful, beneficent, radiant, indeed the essence of illumination and enlightenment in the world, became for Tiepolo more than a myth. It is as though in Apollo he sees the source of his power as an artist."[15]

Zanetti, however, in scrutinizing the splendor of this painting, especially the frescoes, noted that Giambattista had arrived at such stunning effect not by parading colors that were particularly beautiful and rare in themselves, as other painters did, but rather by juxtaposing "dark, dirty hues" with other "rather beautiful and clear" ones. In essence, the foundation of Tiepolo's painting lies in the artist's knowledge and skillful application of the "great art of opposites"—contrapposti.[16]

It is an observation that directly concerns the secrets of technique. Yet it may also be read as an exhortation to look deeper inside the Venetian master's art, to become more attuned to his complexity and the play of tensions underlying it, which the painter's formidable eye keeps under control after having stirred them up, so to speak, from within. A recurrent motif in his work that assumes emblematic prominence is that of the menacing old man standing next to or clinging to a young girl; they might be a river god and a nymph, Saturn and Venus, or, more frequently, scythe-bearing Father Time and naked Truth. Contrapposto here too. One is tempted to see this juxtaposition as an allegory of Tiepolo's artistic conception, a personification of that bold accord, given form in his painting, between the legacy of a civilization in decline and the novelty of a radiant beauty such as had never before been seen.

But there is still another contrapposto at work here. If Apollo presides over Tiepolo's universe, a mood that might be called saturnine—that "oddness of thought" noted by his contemporaries and which Lanzi surprisingly ascribed to the influence of Dürer's prints[17]—stokes his imagination and serves, like shadow, to reinforce the great spectacle unfolding in the light. It becomes explicitly manifest in the bewitching visions of the etchings, the only works, aside from the drawings, that Giambattista did not execute on commission. Yet this element of shadowy, troubled fantasy also spills over into the paintings, surfacing here and there in the arcane presence of certain Oriental figures of immemorial age, in the feverish intensity of certain eyes staring into the void, or, contrarily, in the dreamy or vacant expressions of faces that contrast with the frenzied animation of bodies. And one cannot help but notice that smiles are almost entirely absent from this apparently festive universe, whereas there is often a flicker of irony and at times even a hint of mockery and the grotesque.

The result is that sense of elusiveness this art transmits, making us feel as though a deeper meaning were being denied us even as everything seems to offer itself to view with the utmost clarity. Indeed, there is no painting that is so immediately enjoyable as Tiepolo's and that, at the same time, so tenaciously resists being caught in the web of historical-critical discourse: it presents itself each time anew, beyond all analysis and interpretation, with its enchantment and its enigma.

The difficulty of finding a proper perspective and a focus of interpretation for Tiepolo's art stems not only from its intrinsic elusiveness but also from the fact that it had no sequel (obviously the local imitators are of no historical importance, and the artist's son Giandomenico, when he finds his own voice, assumes positions different from those of his father). It is an art with no future, an art on which the vanguard movement that followed—Neoclassicism—turned its back; nor could it have sown seeds for later generations, since the historical and cultural topsoil that had made it possible was forever washed away. In this respect, Tiepolo's art soars through its age like the span of a bridge that remains suspended at its highest point, with no supporting pier on the other bank. Upon that span—to continue the metaphor—the entire past or, rather, the past of the preceding two centuries, with its beliefs, its fables, its forms, and its figures, comes together to make one final appearance, re-created in a supreme pictorial game and rendered perhaps more alive and appealing than ever before, so that each time it comes into view it provokes a sense of something that is at once wondrously complete and irretrievable.

For a more concrete approach, however, it may be useful to look to the artist's own words. Although his intelligence, like that of any true painter, lay entirely in his eye and hand, Tiepolo had an intellectual turn of mind. Above all, he loved to discuss art with connoisseurs. In a letter he sent to Francesco Algarotti from Montecchio Maggiore, where he was executing frescoes in Carlo Cordellina's villa (see fig. 40), he said he would have preferred, over all the amusements of villa life—which were, moreover, a hindrance to his work—the company of his learned friend and their discussions of painting.[18] We do not know what the painter said in such conversations, but his aesthetic credo is summarized in a kind of declaration he submitted to the press upon his departure for Spain in 1762: "Painters should aim to succeed in great works, the kind that can please noble, rich people, for it is they who determine the fortunes of the Masters, and not other people, who cannot buy paintings of great value. Therefore the mind of the painter must always be directed towards the Sublime, the Heroic, towards Perfection."[19]

It is worthy of note that the values Giambattista declared fundamental to a painter of merit correspond to those recognized as proper to genius by the man of letters Saverio Bettinelli in his essay "Dell'entusiasmo delle belle arti" of 1769: the soul of genius, in fact, "always strives for the beautiful, the sublime, perfection."[20] Bettinelli was a friend and great admirer of Tiepolo's and had composed a poem in praise of him some twenty years before he wrote the essay in question. Even though he does not name him explicitly in this text, it is very likely he was thinking of the Venetian master's painting when he was formulating his poetics of enthusiasm, which he

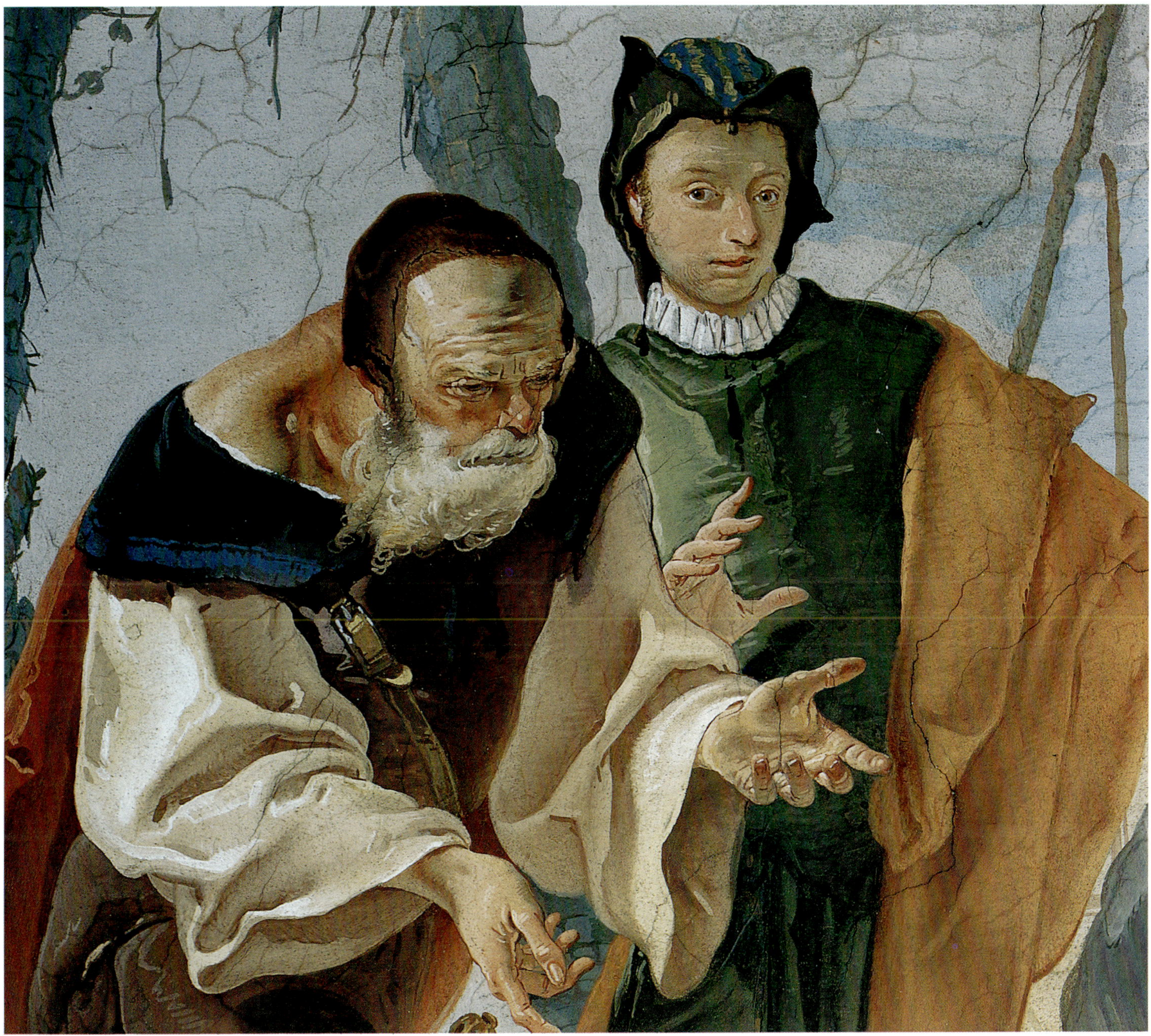

Fig. 3. Self-portrait (detail, *Rachel Hiding the Idols from Her Father, Laban*). Fresco. Arcivescovado (Patriarchal Palace), Udine

establishes as the foundation of the arts, counter to the dominant rationalism of his time. Enthusiasm, "that is, sensibility and imagination," he declares.[21] The typical attributes of enthusiasm, which one finds in a genius—"loftiness, vision, quickness, novelty, passion"[22]—also apply to Tiepolo. When Bettinelli wrote that "it is beneficial for poets and painters to enrich their minds with ideas, to wander in untrodden fields and on untraveled paths, gathering together the rarest and strangest things to be found in the sciences and arts, in nature and nations, and thereby to extend the boundaries of necessary invention,"[23] how can there be any doubt that he was thinking of Tiepolo's painterly endeavors, in which all these things were already manifest?

Then there are the "noble, rich people," that is, the high nobility, the powerful religious orders, and, at the summit, the princes and sovereigns. These are the patrons with whom Giambattista felt most in harmony, not so much, or not only, because of ideological agreement but because they were, thanks to the means at their disposal, in the privileged position of not placing limits on the grand scale of the artist's conception and operation. And, indeed, it was in the medium of the monumental fresco that Tiepolo most fully expressed himself, for here too he was the last exponent of an age-old and specifically Italian tradition. The spaces most congenial to him were the airy vaults of churches, galleries, and the most representative rooms of noble and royal palaces: the vaster the

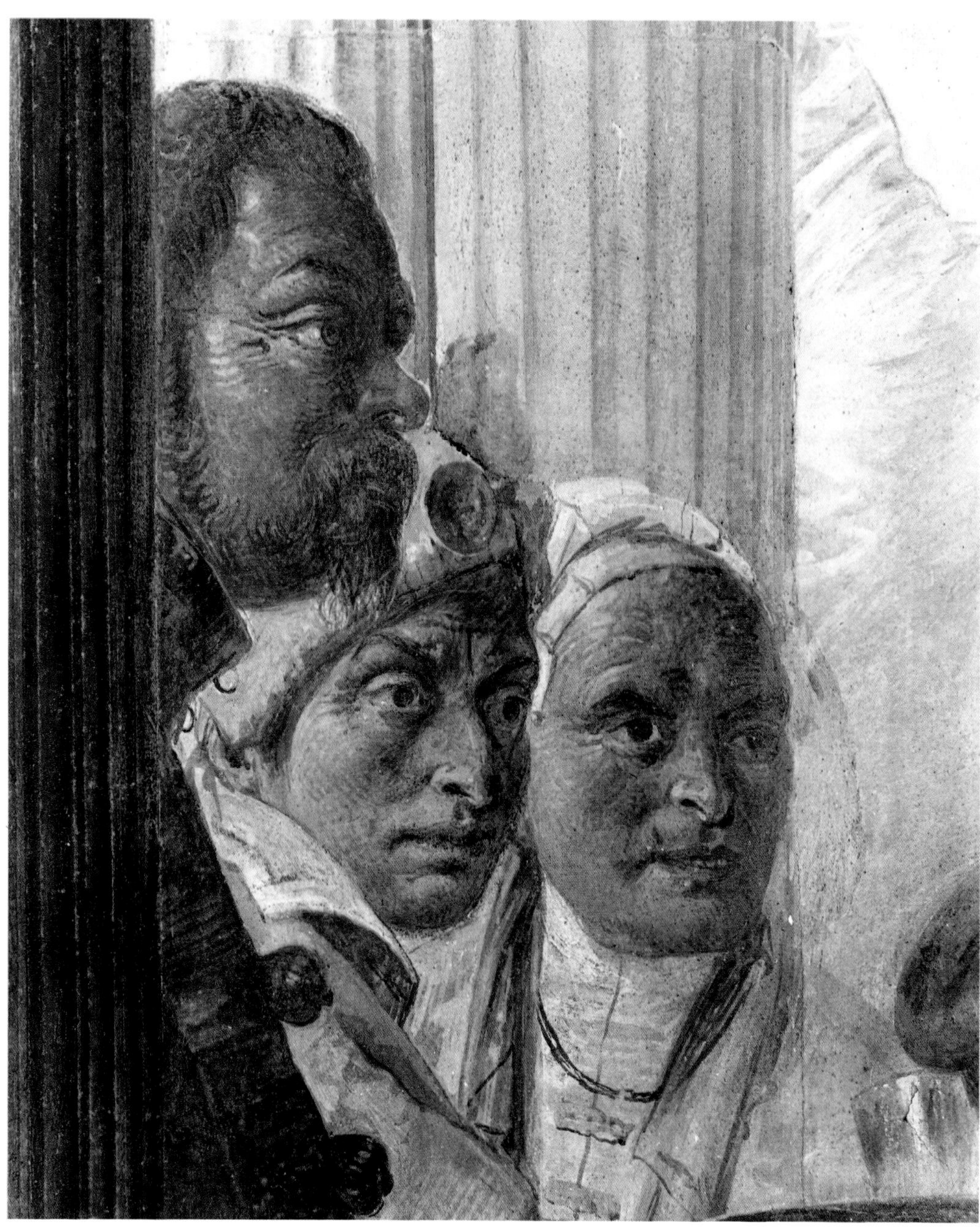

Fig. 4. Self-portrait with Girolamo Mengozzi Colonna (detail, *The Banquet of Cleopatra*). Fresco. Palazzo Labia, Venice

surface to be painted, the more his genius, free to roam, is stirred to exaltation. Tiepolo is first and foremost a painter of ceilings: his preferred stage is the mobile, open stage of the sky, where forms float freely and seem ceaselessly to break apart and recompose themselves (see nos. 25a, b, 48a, b, 49, 50a, 52, 53, 54a, b). His work, for the most part, demands to be seen with the head thrown back; but this is not the only reason, as someone has already observed,[24] that it gives us a slight feeling of vertigo. It is the figuration itself, seen from multiple points of view, that makes one dizzy: those deep rents of azure between clouds that appear to be moving, that heavenly drift of a multitude of creatures in another reality, caught in sudden foreshortenings.

In any case, Tiepolo's understanding with his patrons was always a perfect one, and he rewarded them with successes that exceeded their expectations in every instance. They were the first to recognize the rights of his imagination; indeed, precisely because of his gift, they demanded he give it free rein even when they proposed highly particularized subjects to him. When Algarotti commissioned a painting depicting "Timotheus or the effects of music," he provided specific iconographic instructions but was also well aware that "the decorations and expressions [would] spring readily from the fertile imagination [*fantasia*]" of the painter—who alone would receive credit if the work turned out to be a masterpiece.[25] Elsewhere the patriarch Dionisio Dolfin concluded, after showing Tiepolo how he wanted him to represent the glory of the two martyred Persian saints Abdon and Sennen, that only the painter would know how to invent what he, the patron, was not "capable of conceiving."[26]

Imagination, indeed, is one of the attributes of Tiepolo's genius that his contemporaries most frequently recognized in him. For them, as for us, it must have been cause for astonishment, and one of the real pleasures offered by his painting, to witness with what originality and magnificence of style he interpreted even the most traditional subjects—without, moreover, straying from the literary sources; in fact, keeping scrupulously close to them. As though casting a spell each time, Giambattista would transform old scripts into a new fable for the eyes. Thus, it should come as no surprise to read a contemporary's judgment: "Tiepolo can be called Painting's true magician, since his paintings are true magic and his inventions are outside of nature, and there is not a single thing expressed by this fine sensibility that does not bring with it novel figures and color."[27]

Like few other artists of his century, Tiepolo enjoyed international renown during his lifetime, even if his fame and commissions were limited primarily to Catholic countries. To visit the places where he executed or sent works, one travels through half of Europe. It is impossible, however, to overemphasize how important the protection given him by the Venetian aristocracy and clergy was to the expression of his talent, from the very start. In this respect, his case is fundamentally different from that of his celebrated older compatriots, masters of grand decorative painting in the "modern" style such as Ricci, Pellegrini, and Amigoni, who found commissions equal to their gifts and aspirations only outside of Venice. During a visit to Venice in 1761, Saint-Non noted that "a large number of palaces and churches are filled with the works of Tiepolo."[28] He could not have said the same thing about any of the other well-known painters of the period. In a way Giambattista is the official painter of eighteenth-century Venice: more than any other, he made his city aware that it was a capital of art, a privileged place where beauty was created, and that its prestige and strength lay in this very fact.

When he was beginning to gain prominence, about 1720, the Serene Republic had just emerged from what would prove to be its last war. With the Treaty of Passarowitz, signed in 1718, Venice closed in upon itself once and for all, finding isolation in neutrality. Yet in so doing it secured itself nearly a century of peace—exceptional in Europe at the time—during which, even as it was slipping off the stage of history, it was cultivating a projection of itself in the realm of myth. The allegory that Tiepolo painted in the Palazzo Ducale shortly after the middle of the century is emblematic in this regard: he depicts Venice as a very beautiful queen, a Cybele with her lion, to whom a vigorous and passionate Neptune is paying homage with the riches of the sea (no. 24).

And so the artists contributed to the creation of the myth: Tiepolo, of course, and, alongside him, Canaletto. This pairing of the painter generally considered the most conservative of his age with the most progressive should come as no surprise. Both established themselves in the Venetian milieu at more or less the same time; and in their artistic development they share the experience of an initial phase influenced by the dramatic, chiaroscuro style of Piazzetta. They also share the discovery of a light at once real and imaginary that permeates space and constitutes the precondition of all possible vision. If Canaletto celebrates the urban uniqueness of Venice, reflecting the city in the mirror of a painting in which one sees a "shining within the sunlight,"[29] Tiepolo turns Venice, its palaces, and its churches into a theater where the pagan Olympus and the Christian heaven, the characters of fable and the figures of allegory, and events remote in time and space all become visible, projected into the present. He expands, so to speak, the city's horizons, opening Venice up to a vaster, more meaningful dimension. Though we may call the works "visions" in the case of Tiepolo and "*vedute*," or "views," in the case of Canaletto, they are both distinguished by the same optical clarity.

Like some *vedutista* of fantasy pointing his camera obscura at the limitless spaces that the Baroque had opened up in the imagination, Tiepolo gives every form and figure a crystalline distinctness. He "invents" even as he "distinguishes";[30] and in this lucidity, this visual focusing of every detail, lies one aspect of his modernity.

There is, however, another reason why his contemporaries admired him: more than anyone else, he had succeeded, especially around midcareer, in reawakening "the sleeping, happy, exquisite ideas of Paolo Caliari."[31] For eighteenth-century connoisseurs, Caliari, known to posterity as Veronese, was the artist who had painted "with the most pleasing, delightful, and noble character [of all] . . . adding richness and charm to intelligence."[32] Tiepolo, too, sees and interprets Veronese this way, using him as a source of themes on which to compose new music. Yet for Tiepolo and his fellow Venetians, Veronese was also the painter of allegories, the one who had created, in his works in the Palazzo Ducale, the most spellbinding and noble personification of Venice ever conceived. Aligning himself with Veronese meant reuniting with a glorious past and at the same time conjuring up the mirage of a reborn golden age, at least on the level of art. It meant, in short, giving form to a dream in defiance of reality.

The icon of Venice triumphant created by Veronese separates into the two principal female figures in Tiepolo's theater: the Virgin Mary and Cleopatra. The glorification of the Virgin, traditional protector of the city of Venice, provides Giambattista with the starting point for his most inspired creations in the area of religious painting: the ceilings of the churches of the Gesuati (fig. 65), the Scalzi (no. 48a, b), the Pietà (no. 50a), and the Scuola Grande dei Carmini (fig. 66). Drawing from a visual culture nourished by two centuries of art, he opens up vast aerial spaces in which, amid shifting cloud structures shimmering with light, a consoling vision of the supernatural appears. After Correggio, Tiepolo is the most ingenious painter of angels, as well as the last: multipliers of beauty, his angels swarm around the Virgin, streaking across the heavens and revealing their eternally adolescent forms between flaps of wings and a rustle of silk gowns. In Tiepolo's conception the supernatural finds substance in a spellbinding beauty: the image in which it takes concrete form exalts the sensual realm, embracing and sublimating the yearnings of desire. This is why we feel attracted to it even while we take heed of its radical otherness. In any case, these sacred visions are Tiepolo's response to the glory painting of the Baroque, which had never before been quite at home in Venice.

The character of Cleopatra fascinated him no less deeply than the Virgin. Protagonist of the most spectacular fresco decoration of a Venetian interior, that of the Palazzo Labia (frontis., p. 28, fig. 38), Tiepolo's Cleopatra has been seen as one of the guises or masks of the eighteenth-century myth of Venice; and we may even consider her an incarnation of the *pouvoir des femmes* that marked mid-eighteenth-century European society. But the frescoes in Palazzo Labia are above all a demonstration of painting's powers of illusion, its ability to take us inside a play of appearances that attract us even more than they would if they were real forms.

Bergeret, during a visit to Venice with Fragonard in 1774, was struck by the grandiosity, nobility, and compositional richness of these frescoes. What fascinated him more than anything else, however, were the details, and he noted in his diary: "A thousand accessory dogs and dwarfs are admirable and in their proper places."[33] Actually, there are no more than three dogs, and there is only one dwarf (fig. 46); yet with that hyperbole the French art lover captured one of the characteristic aspects of Tiepolo's art: the multiplication and accumulation of details—people, animals, fabrics, jewels, crockery, banners—separated by airy spatial intervals. One's attention, continually aroused, begins to wander, trapped in a kind of delightful labyrinth of images. The model for this was, of course, Veronese. Tiepolo, however, by adding the bite of whimsy and the drug of exoticism and fantasy, attuned himself to the psychology of his contemporaries, who were forever in search of novelty and variety, perhaps to escape the malaise of boredom and emptiness. In regard to his painting, he might well have subscribed to what Montesquieu stated in his essay on taste: "The mind is forever searching for new things and is never satiated. Thus, we shall be forever certain of delighting the mind when we show it far more things than it had hoped to see."[34]

One of Tiepolo's favorite devices is to introduce characters drawn from everyday life into the world of legend and of sacred and profane ancient history. They are portraits of young women, children, and adolescents who are sometimes assigned parts in the stories; at other times they stare out at us with disturbing intensity, looking as if they were only there to demand our attention. Some of them have been taken to be members of the painter's family: his wife, Cecilia Guardi, and children. Yet he did not fail to insert himself in the world of his imagination as well, in roles that changed from time to time. Indeed, with this presence as guide, we can retrace certain significant steps in his artistic itinerary; and by closely studying his physiognomy, we may even gain insight into something of the secret of his personality.

We first encounter him in an early sketch of a drawing academy (fig. 1); like everyone else represented, he is engrossed in sketching the nude model from life, by the light of an oil lamp. The school is more likely that of Gregorio Lazzarini, Tiepolo's first teacher, than that of Piazzetta, as has also been supposed.[35] The style of the drawing, however, shows the young artist's adherence to Piazzetta's language, which was based on the "skillful contrast of lights,"[36] on a predilection for common subjects, and on the search for "truth and nature," to use the terminology of the age. In this drawing, which also bears witness to Tiepolo's early training, he so blends in with the other pupils that it is difficult to identify him with certainty.

However, in the painting *Apelles Painting Campaspe* (no. 11), executed a few years later, he promotes himself to the role of protagonist (fig. 2). We should dwell for a moment on this picture, which is the most programmatic of his early works, a veritable manifesto in paint. Fully aware of his gifts, he gives the most celebrated painter of antiquity his own features, assigning the role of Campaspe, Alexander's beautiful lover, to his wife, Cecilia Guardi, whom he had married several years earlier, in 1719. The two large canvases leaning against the wall in the background, in half-light, document compositions made by Giambattista himself in the Piazzetta-influenced style of his preceding period, and the young Moorish servant next to the easel, as well as the little Maltese dog, would seem to have come from his own domestic environment. Alexander and Campaspe, more than posing for Apelles, seem to have slipped into the studio from some other space, some other stage. The painter's studio—which is to say his mind—thus takes the form of a place in which past and present intersect, bringing both imagination and observation into the picture. Ancient history and family reality pass over into each other,

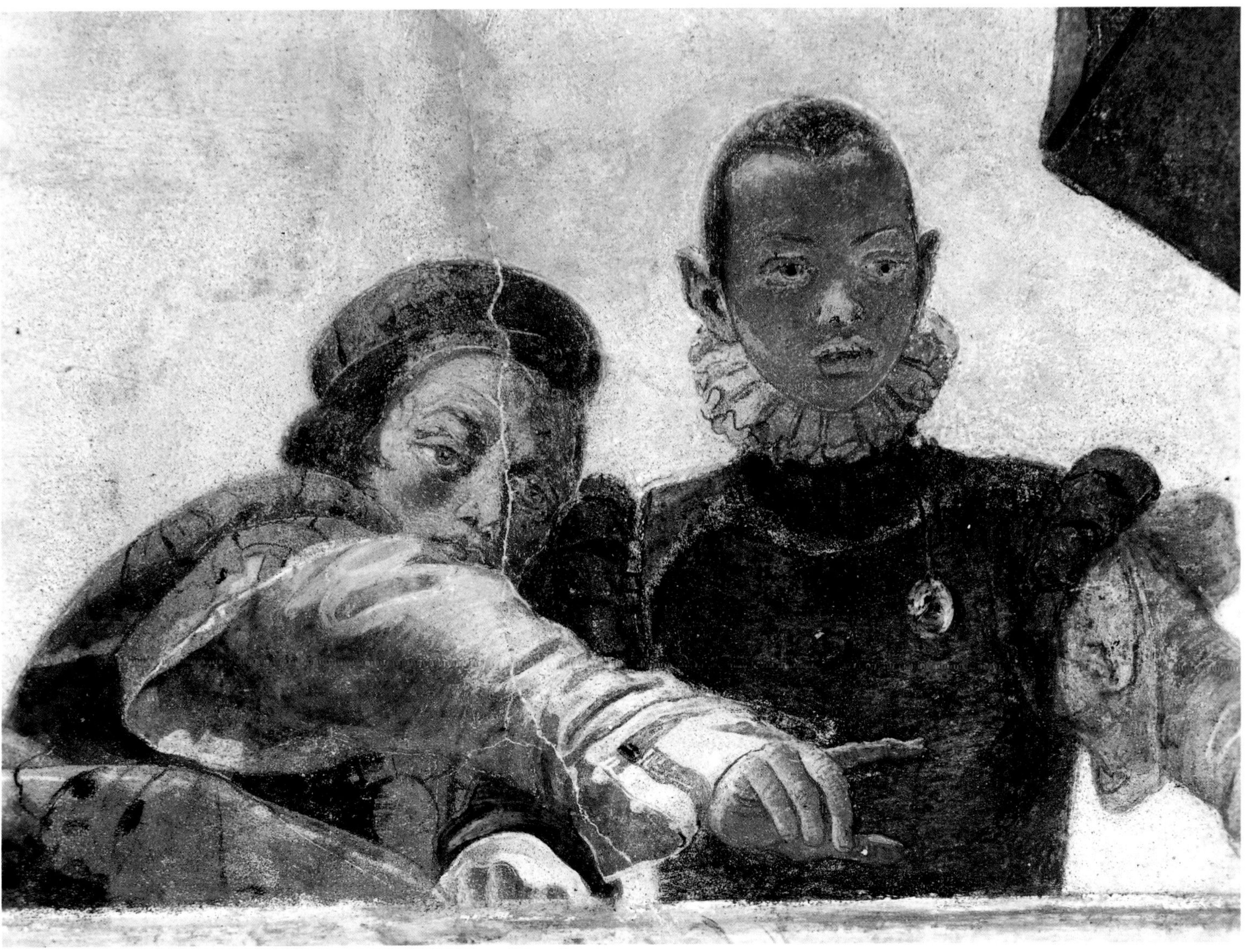

Fig. 5. Self-portrait with Giandomenico(?) (detail, *The Arrival of Henry III at the Villa Contarini*). Fresco. Musée Jacquemart-André Institut de France, Paris

just as the enthusiasm that gives wings to the imagination crossbreeds with a vein of irony arising from the juxtaposition of the heroic with the quotidian. Tiepolo-Apelles acts as a bridge between the two contiguous spaces: he keeps everything under the control of his circular gaze, turning his head like a periscope to include in his field of vision the group of characters behind him as well as the portrait that is taking shape on the canvas sitting on the easel. His dress, like this detail, reveals a touch of whimsy, being neither ancient nor contemporary. The fur busby that casts a mask of shadow over his eyes and the almost wild look in his eyes bring to mind some of Rembrandt's early self-portraits. Thus, while assuming the role of the ancient painter who infused his figures with grace and was the favorite of the powerful, and while paying homage to Veronese by borrowing from his paintings the motif of the luminous architectural backdrop, Tiepolo also hints at his attraction to the modern genius of Rembrandt—whose painterly nonchalance, lively scribbled style, and imaginative originality he must surely have admired. With so unconventional, even casual a treatment of the subject, Tiepolo is declaring his creative autonomy, his freedom of imagination, in regard to artistic tradition as well as to his patrons. And he would always remain faithful to this approach.

Giambattista's taste for disguise is deeply ingrained. It is part of the theatrical element of his vision, which plays at channeling reality into fiction and endowing fiction with the appearance of reality. We have already seen him in the role of Apelles. In the fresco showing Rachel hiding the idols from her father, Laban, in the gallery of the Arcivescovado (Patriarchal Palace) of Udine (fig. 25), he has assigned himself the part of the young Jacob (fig. 3). Dressed a bit like a sprite, wearing a double-brimmed cap, he places himself right in the middle of the scene; and while old Laban, beside him, is apparently asking his daughter where she has hidden the purloined idols, Jacob winks at the spectators, making them accomplices in Rachel's deception. The enchanting vein of humor that adds spice to the biblical stories in the gallery seems, in fact, to radiate

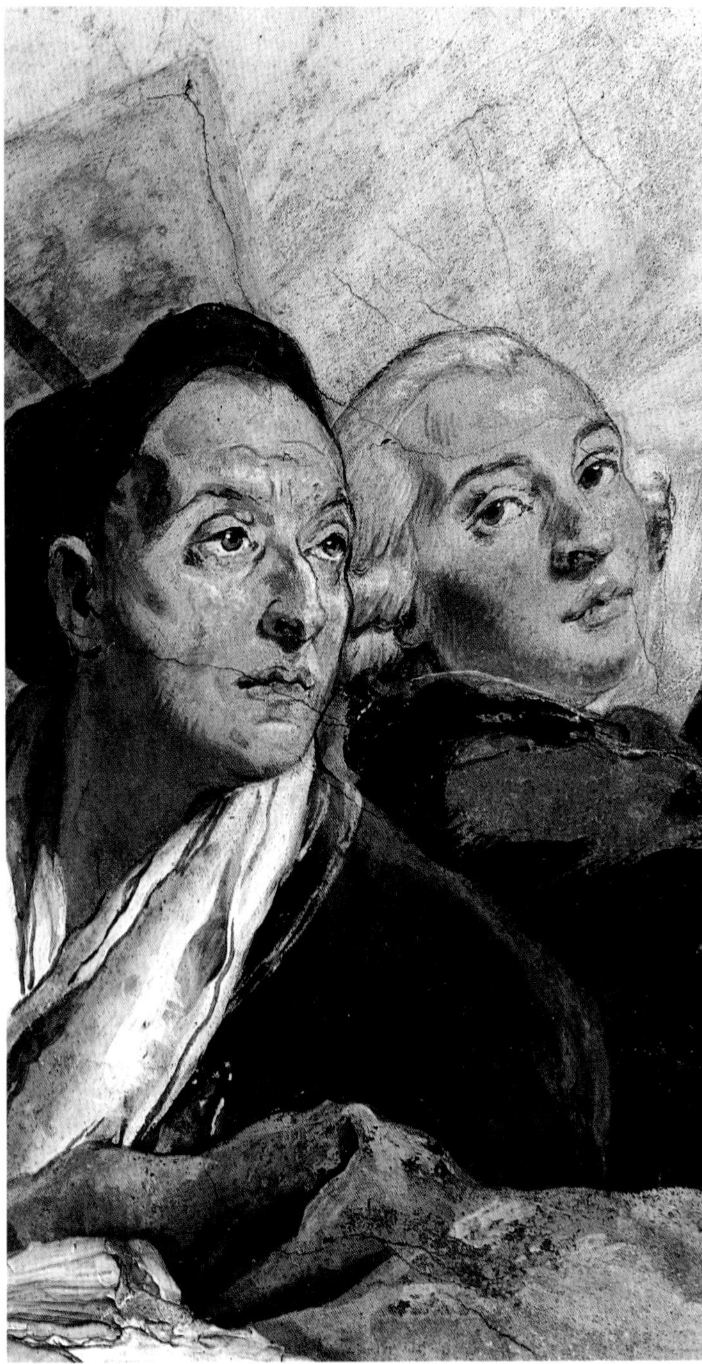

Fig. 6. Self-portrait with Giandomenico(?) (detail, *Apollo and the Four Continents*). Fresco. Residenz, Würzburg

from Tiepolo-Jacob's sly expression, as if this were its very emblem.

In his other great early undertaking for the Dolfin family, the series of episodes of Roman history he painted on canvas for the parlor of their Venetian palace (see no. 12a–g), Tiepolo again inserted a self-portrait: to the side, among the crowd making way for the triumphal procession of Marius, in the last painting in the series, executed in 1729 (no. 12e). A ray of glancing light calls attention to the artist's now-aquiline countenance, with its beaklike nose and bright eyes (frontis., p. 2). In keeping with the tradition of self-portraiture, he is looking outward, but with a brusque turn of the head, as if we had just called to him; this sudden movement betrays a touch of aggressiveness or arrogance. The physiognomy and expression are consistent with the new, resonant heroic style that Tiepolo created with this cycle of works.

Some twenty years later, in his other major enterprise for a Venetian palace—his frescoed room for the Labia family—the artist chose to place himself at Cleopatra's banquet, next to Girolamo Mengozzi Colonna, the painter of illusionistic architecture and set designs who collaborated with him on the magnificent spectacle (fig. 38). To camouflage himself in that milieu, which combines elements of the classical and the exotic, he dons a headdress that is vaguely Oriental in style; and like everyone else in the composition, his eyes are fixed on the priceless pearl that the queen is about to dissolve. Yet the tension furrowing his brow reveals his true role here: that of the director, who, looking on from the wings, controls how the climax of the plot will be realized onstage.

Tiepolo thus appears to be more and more taken in by his work, caught in his own painterly spell. In Villa Contarini-Pisani (whose fresco cycle, mentioned above, dates from about 1745) he appears at the balustrade that runs along the sides of the ceiling, in the company of his son Giandomenico, who has entered his father's profession (fig. 5). Both are wearing cinquecento clothing, like the rest of the spectators. With arm and index finger extended, Giambattista is pointing out to his son the reception of Henry III, depicted below on the front wall. It is the same gesture that appears in one of Tiepolo's *Scherzi di fantasia* (no. 60 s), where it is used by a magician to alert a young man to some obscure rite of pyromancy taking place: the burning of a skull, from which they perhaps expect an oracular response. Here, in Villa Contarini-Pisani, the magician is the painter who has performed the feat of bringing a moment of the past forever back to life.

Giambattista again portrays himself, this time next to a person who is probably his son Giandomenico, who in the meantime has become his finest assistant, in the work that marks the high point of his artistic career: the vast fresco on the vault over the monumental staircase at the Residenz in Würzburg, painted in 1753 (fig. 112). The apparent subject is the triumph of Apollo rising to shed light on the universe, the planetary deities in the heavens, and the four continents of the world, announcing the victory of civilization. But what really triumphs here is painting itself, in that it is painting that makes both created and imagined things visible, revealing them *sub specie coloris*—color being the substance of light.

Giambattista has put himself and his son somewhat to the side, behind the throne of Europe, protector of the fine arts (fig. 6). While Giandomenico is dressed according to the fashion of the time, with light blue jacket and powdered hair, and is looking out at the observer with mild, intelligent eyes (his face and gaze expressing a curiosity about what lies outside of the space of the fresco), Giambattista, renouncing all disguise, has portrayed himself in simple work clothes, with a scarf around his neck and a formless beret instead of a wig on his head. His lean face tense as though in deep concentration, he is looking toward the personification of Painting, who, close to Europe's side, is painting the terraqueous globe. This, as far as I know, is Tiepolo's last self-portrait, and it is certainly his most revealing.

To paint a world: this is, in fact, what he himself did. A world in which there was a place for mythology, allegory, and religion, the very things that were attacked by the dominant critical thought and rationalism of the age.[37] He availed himself of that now-worn-out repertory to assert, as if in defiance, the rights of the imagination and to celebrate the power of art, whose realm can embrace all that is about to be swept away by time and rejected by history. From the great stream of the Baroque, Tiepolo summoned the luminous vision of a space *retrouvé*, allowing us to contemplate the gods as if they still lived among us.

Notes

1. As exemplified by Charles Blanc (1868).
2. See Molmenti 1880.
3. Degas, letter to Rouart, 16 October 1883. As Francis Haskell (1967, p. 491) recalls in his important essay on Tiepolo's fortunes in the nineteenth century, the critic Paul Leroi wrote in 1876 (p. 298) that Palazzo Labia in Venice was "un lieu de pèlerinage pour tous les artistes, on trouve toujours quelques un entre eux occupés à copier ces magnifiques décorations."
4. Chennevières 1896.
5. Barrès 1889, p. 191: "Ses conceptions ont cette lassitude qui suit les grandes voluptés et que leur préfèrent des épicuriens délicats."
6. Da Canal 1732 (1809 ed.) p. XXXII: "tutto spirito e foco."
7. Of fundamental importance in this regard are the studies by Morassi, starting with his 1934 article in *Burlington Magazine*. Also worthy of mention here is the contribution of Mariuz and Pavanello 1985.
8. An innovative and fundamental study in this connection is Barcham 1989.
9. Longhi 1946.
10. Levey 1959.
11. See the acute essay by Alpers and Baxandall (1994).
12. Zanetti 1771, p. 396: "molta e lussureggiante vaghezza del colorito, e delle immaginazioni"; "un dolce sogno, un incanto puramente del senso."
13. Ibid., p. 465: "con arte meravigliosa"; "una vaghezza, un sole che non ha forse esempio."
14. Lacombe 1768, p. 392: "certi toni brillanti e luminosi, tocchi larghi, gran gusto nel disegno, strisciate di chiari et d'ombre."
15. Levey 1986, p. 60.
16. Zanetti 1771, p. 465: "tinte basse e sporche"; "belle alquanto e nette"; "grand'arte de' contrapposti."
17. Lanzi 1795–96, vol. 2, p. 168: "[Tiepolo] molto anche mirò nelle stampe di Alberto Durero, miniera de' copiosi compositori."
18. For the letter, dated 26 October 1743, see Fogolari 1942, pp. 34–35.
19. Tiepolo's declaration, to which attention was first drawn by Haskell (1963, p.253, n. 2), was published in the *Nuova veneta gazzetta* of 20 March 1762: "li Pittori devono procurare di riuscire nelle opere grandi, cioè in quelle che possono piacere alli Signori nobili, e ricchi, perchè questi fanno la fortuna de' Professori, e non già l'altra gente, la quale non può comprare Quadri di molto valore. Quindi è che la mente del Pittore deve sempre tendere al Sublime, all'Eroico, alla Perfezione."
20. Bettinelli 1769 (1969 ed., p. 824): "sempre tende al bello, al sublime, alla perfezione."
21. Ibid., p. 832: "cioè sensibilità e immaginazione."
22. Ibid., p. 829: "elevazione, visione, rapidità, novità, passione."
23. Ibid., p. 817: "giova ai poeti, ai pittori arricchirsi la mente d'idee, spaziare in campi e vie non battute, raccogliendo quanto v'ha di più raro e pellegrino nelle scienze, nell' arti, nella natura e nelle nazioni, onde stendere i confini della necessaria invenzione."
24. Bettini 1968–69, p. 67.
25. The subject of the painting, which was never executed, is described in a letter sent by Algarotti to Count Heinrich von Brühl in the summer of 1743. Cf. Algarotti 1764–65, vol. 8, pp. 379ff.: "gli ornamenti e le espressioni nasceranno agevolmente dalla feconda fantasia."
26. Dionisio Dolfin's letter of commission was sent to Tiepolo from Udine on 6 February 1760. This work, like the one ordered by Algarotti on the effects of music, was never executed. Cf. Bianco 1951–52: "capace di concepire."
27. The opinion was expressed by the little-known Bernardo Ziliotti; see Bortoluzzi 1994. Ziliotti was the author of the unpublished "Osservazioni sopra la pittura e sopra i più celebri pittori d'Italia," written between 1775 and 1779: "Il Tiepolo si può denominare il vero mago della Pittura, dappoiché le sue pitture sono una vera magia e i suoi ritrovati sono fuori di natura, né v'è cosa alcuna espressa da questo bell'umore che non porti seco novità di figure e di colorito."
28. See Rosenberg and Brejon de Lavergnée 1986, p. 206: "un grand nombre de Palais et d'Eglises sont remplis des ouvrages de Tiepolo." Saint-Non's judgment of the Venetian was, however, rather limiting. Tiepolo's works in his opinion are "tous avec un caractère et une manière à lui qui se fait aisément reconnoitre, mais toujours plutôt pour un homme de goût que pour un grand maître." On that occasion Fragonard executed some ten copies of Tiepolos.
29. The phrase is from a letter written by Alessandro Marchesini to Stefano Conti and sent from Venice on 14 July 1725. In this connection, see Haskell 1956, p. 297: "lucer entro il sole."
30. See Zanetti 1733, p. 62: "Suo distinto pregio è il pronto carattere d'inventare, e inventando distinguere e risolvere ad uno stesso tempo quantità di figure con novità di ritrovati, . . . unendo a ciò una esatta intelligenza di chiaroscuro, ed una lucidissima vaghezza."
31. Zanetti 1771, p. 464: "le sopite felici leggiadrissime idee di Paolo Caliari."
32. Zanetti 1733, p. 44: "con un carattere il più ameno, il più dilettevole, ed il più nobile . . . aggiungendo all'intelligenza, la ricchezza e la leggiadria."
33. Bergeret 1895, p. 388: "Mille accessoire de chiens, de nains sont admirables et bien à leur place."
34. Montesquieu 1757, p. 763: "l'âme cherche toujours des choses nouvelles, et ne se repose jamais. Ainsi on sera toujours sûr de plaire à l'âme, lorsqu'on lui fera voir beaucoup de choses ou plus qu'elle n'avait espéré voir."
35. According to Morassi (1971), the drawing represents Piazzetta's school; for Knox (1992, p. 211) it is Lazzarini's school.
36. Albrizzi 1760: "ingegnoso contrasto de' lumi."
37. Bettinelli 1769 (1969 ed., p. 836): "Il maraviglioso della mitologia diviene sospetto alle bell'arti de' tempi nostri, che son più severi per soda o per vana filosofia, credendo aprir gli occhi alla ragione, alla critica, alla verità, quasi uscendo dalla fanciullezza, onde non gustano più come prima i prodigi, gl'incanti e i quadri della fantasia."

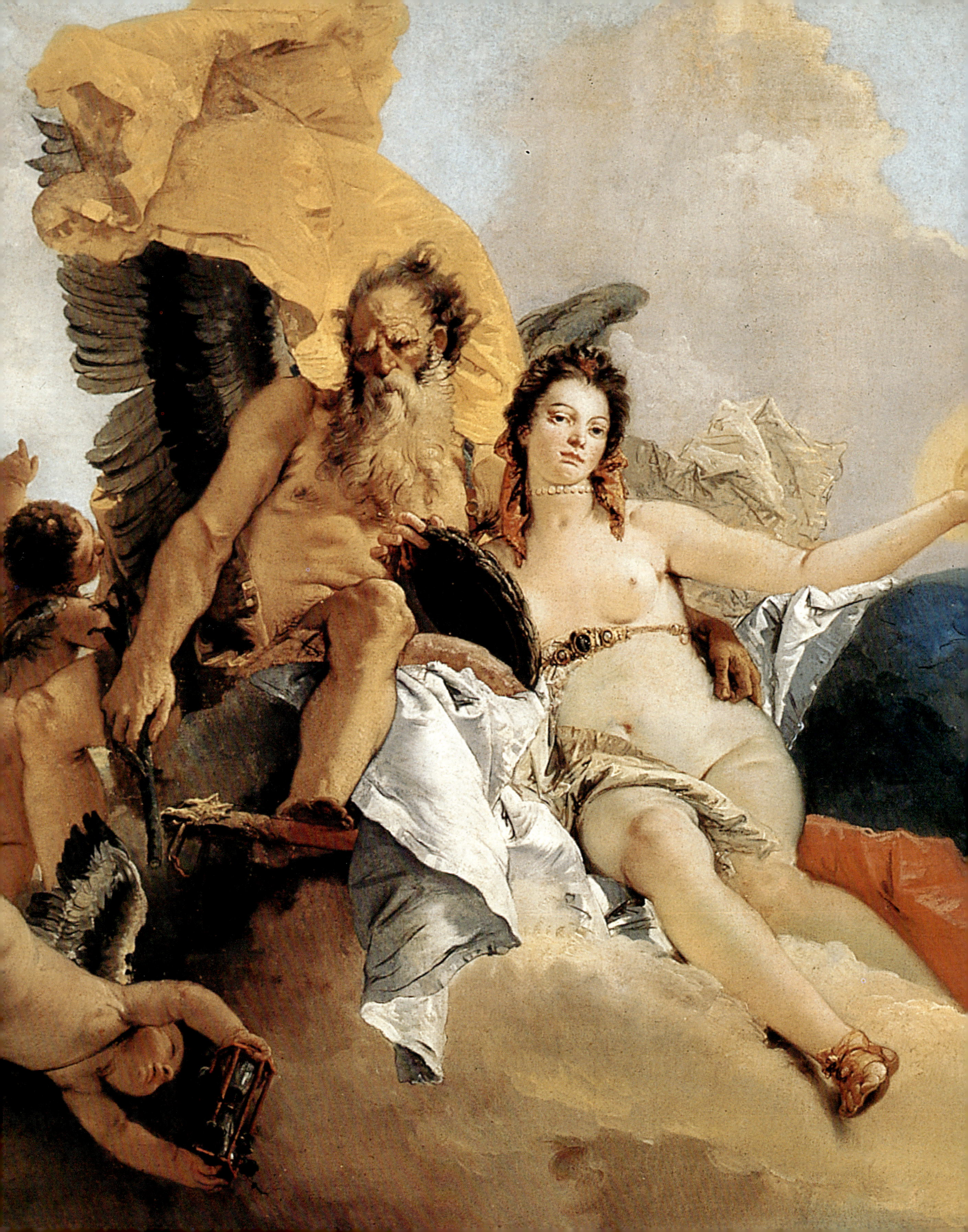

Giambattista Tiepolo: A Meditation on History, Time, and Death

GIANDOMENICO ROMANELLI

Wherever we go in Venice, we encounter the dense presence of Giambattista Tiepolo's paintings. They are distributed among the city's churches and palaces, its confraternities and public buildings; so much so that the inventions of this artist—by common consent the greatest and most representative eighteenth-century Venetian painter—create the impression of a fantastic analogue universe, populating both real architectural spaces and those implausible painted skies, various and contradictory, that belong to the final, triumphant, and precarious century of Venice, the Queen of the Adriatic.

Can we legitimately think of this presence as a unitary poem? That is, does an unbroken thread link his stories of Cleopatra, scenes of the Passion of Christ, views of Olympus and Parnassus—those holy warriors, heroes, muses, dreams, and inventions—as in a spiderweb? No poem, fable, or miracle depicted by Tiepolo can be confused with or assimilated into the products of any of the other artists who occupied the grand and varied stage of Venetian painting; this despite the fact that this stage was extraordinarily rich and fascinating. There were the dark shadows of the tenebrists, the realism reclaimed by Piazzetta, the transparent polychromy of Sebastiano Ricci, the levity of Pellegrini and Rosalba Carriera, the landscapes of the view painters, and the domestic interiors of Pietro Longhi. Alone among its participants, Tiepolo knew how to create an autonomous and unrepeatable trajectory whose character—indeed, whose very thematic wealth—was instantly recognized as unique and unsurpassable. The poetic course of Tiepolo's career has always seemed to possess the majestic certitude of a great river and the Apollonian equilibrium of a classical opera—limpid and solemn, spontaneous and natural.

In his canvases and frescoes, his easel paintings for private devotion, and his complex and abstruse cycles with historical or mythological subjects, Tiepolo progressively wove his own poem, his own history, his own discourse—one that was, nonetheless, tightly intermeshed with the very fabric of a collective history, a condition, and a sense of being distilled in the millenary vats of a world that had become separate and different. The visual universe that had settled into the collective consciousness of Venetian culture as well as into the fantasy of its artists fills Tiepolo's canvases, emerging like a lava flow barely restrained by the limitations of common experience and the rules of art. It was this universe that gave life to that poetic forest whose infinite paths we explore in search of a satisfactory interpretive key.

From the moment in about 1725 when he painted the ceiling in Palazzo Sandi, with its fresco the *Triumph of Eloquence* (fig. 22), to the time he produced his cycles of frescoes for the Rezzonico, Contarini, and Pisani families in Venice and its immediately surrounding territories (see no. 25a,b; fig. 108; no. 52)—thus, until his departure for Spain in 1762—Tiepolo created a sort of celebrative anthology that, as Michael Levey has noted, touched all chords and expressive keys and encompassed all genres: from the epic to the sublime, the sentimental to the pathetic, the sacred to the historical, the idyllic, encomastic, fantastical, realistic, devotional, folkloric, allegorical, and mythic. His narrative facility and the surprising fecundity of his figurative inventions helped Tiepolo to sustain the impression of fresh formal solutions—even when he was consciously recycling motifs—and of a style faithful to itself yet ever new: a style with unpredictable and surprising accents, embodied in his increasing preference for silvery, precious colors and in compositional solutions in which, as occasion and subject demanded, he isolated a single figure or staged a complex scene, to create spiraling forms or expand his paintings with majestic, symphonic cadences.

Tiepolo's themes do not differ significantly from those employed by late Baroque artists in Venice at the end of the seventeenth century and the beginning of the eighteenth.

Detail, *Time Uncovering Truth* (no. 18)

Allegories, myths, and the moral lexicon of symbols and emblems constitute the material he deployed in his scenographies, refashioned with his costumes, hoisted into those transparent skies, and pitted against the fantastical backgrounds of Veronesian inspiration. The exemplary historical episodes he treated recur in the iconographies of previous centuries: Alexander and Darius, Scipio, Marius, Sophonisba and Massinissa, Orlando, Achilles, Agamemnon, Iphigenia, Dido. . . . In his art, history and literature blend in a sort of grand theater of virtues, heroism, vices, passions, enthusiasms, and offenses, pastoral interludes and clamorous battles, betrayals, recognitions, meetings, desertions. Within this mass of work Tiepolo scattered the indices of his interior evolution, his insistent self-questioning, his querying of history and fable, the grandiose dreams and details of the everyday lives of men and women.

The vision of the world held by Tiepolo and exemplified in his art emerges in the trifling and even fleeting trace of a search conducted in competition with or perhaps despite the iconographic demands of patrons. It is a vision laden with anxiety and questions—far more than might be supposed by those convinced that the character of this sublime decorator is identifiable with that of the scenography and rhetoric of his costumed theater. The first theme Tiepolo took up when he was still a youth is the one he painted on a small copper oval—not much larger than a miniature—showing Death and Youth, *Memento Mori: Age and Death* (no. 1). Employing terms that cannot help but surprise us, the subject curiously anticipates scenes carried out years later: it is a meditation on death and on the passing of time, eloquently exemplified by the hourglass held by the skeleton emerging from a tomb. To this first, embryonic dark memento would be added others that fill out the psychological and poetic aspects of the artist's production, including works juxtaposing a young woman with an old man—an allusion to the frailty of beauty, its vanity, and the way it impedes or screens the revelation of a more profound, if crude truth.

The theme of Time Uncovering Truth was repeated throughout Tiepolo's long career (see no. 18); it was, of course, a common eulogistic theme—part of the rhetorical arsenal of Baroque imagery (usually accompanied by other symbols and emblems, such as Fame, Merit, and Glory). And yet the very insistence of this theme in Tiepolo's work is like a nightmare or a worm burrowing deeper and becoming more burdensome as the young, brilliant artist passed from maturity to old age, troubled by a question that never ceased to assail him. From the outset Tiepolo engaged in a protracted mental game about the meaning of the ineluctable flight of time. He asked and reasked the same question, destined to remain unanswered, advancing it with fretfulness or masking it with a sarcasm that could not assuage the discomfort of the inevitable human condition. He sought its incarnation in literature and mythology, and he transformed it into splendid decorative and poetic subjects, adapting it to the expectations of his patrons: the course of the chariot of the Sun; the theme of Virtue and Merit; the proclamation of Fame; personifications of Courage; Glory; Nobility; Eloquence. Presiding over these was Apollo, radiant, vivifying, and eternalizing the quest by raising it to the realm of poetry and art. Above all, Tiepolo made it the leitmotiv of his private production—his luminous and mysterious prints, the esoteric *Capricci* and *Scherzi* (nos. 59a–j; 60a–w).

With these indicators Tiepolo guides us into the felicitous contradictions around which he constructed his extraordinary world of poetry. The distress evoked by beauty that has passed its bloom becomes the equivalent of the consciousness that history too must end and that time will inevitably consume all life. He pauses on the threshold of a definitive yet impossible happiness to meditate on the destiny of himself and of the world. How many meetings and good-byes momentarily unite and then separate his heroes and heroines—Angelica and Medoro, Dido and Aeneas, Rinaldo and Armida, Apollo and Daphne, Antony and Cleopatra, Achilles and Iphigenia, Andromeda and Perseus, Orpheus and Eurydice? How many splendid maidens are juxtaposed with whitebeards? How many of Chronos's scythes stand out against the transient eternity of glories that are no more real than theater!

Time passes—a circle without beginning or end, a chain that cannot be broken, a limit beyond which even the fearless virtuosity of Tiepolo's art cannot advance. Time checkmates his fantasy and throws the artist into the pathetic shadow of melancholy. Even the episodes of Tasso's *Gerusalemme liberata* could assume the quality of a paradigm of that condition (see nos. 17a–g; 22a,b); and so too the drama of Iphigenia (fig. 98) or the reign of Flora (no. 13). Even the passion of Antony and Cleopatra in Palazzo Labia (see frontis., p. 28, fig. 38) seems to dissolve into the arena of the romantic and sentimental rather than the epic. The feathers and armor, halberds and plumed helmets are more credible as props for a costumed cantata than as parts of the setting for a Roman story.

However, beyond the romantic and pathetic keys, Tiepolo discovered another dimension—one that soothed his insatiable anxiety with fantasy and liberated him from the nightmare of the passage of time and the consumption of the pages of history. He immersed his world in a golden age that predated history and was without time or place—in the impossible and suggestive time and space of myth: of the old men, magicians, monkeys, skeletons, ephebes, and stray dogs of his *Capricci* and *Scherzi*. This epoch before history enabled Tiepolo to escape the servitude of Chronos's scythe. The exotic dimension of his work enabled him to create a world beyond common experience, with its own geography and psychology and thereby to postpone indefinitely the ironclad constructions of time through the incommensurability of an infinite and total space. The theme of the Four Continents of the World, already adumbrated on the ceiling of Palazzo Sandi, returned in various other cycles, finding its most felicitous and complete treatment on the ceiling of Palazzo Clerici in Milan and, above all, that over the staircase of the Residenz in Würzburg (see frontis., p. 18, no. 49). At the Residenz the great ebonized matron Africa atop her camel, the elephant and chinoiserie of Asia, the feathered headdresses of America, and the whole historical and literary burden of the civilization of Europe—extending from Greece and Rome to Emperor Frederick Barbarossa, to bishops, cardinals, and princes—are sustained by vivacious contrasts and a dazzling kaleidoscope of colors, figures, and details. Certainly all of Tiepolo's favorite themes are in evidence: the fierce physiognomy of wanton old men, a self-portrait (fig. 6), an idealized portrait of the patron (fig. 37), Chronos, Apollo, and the Muses (fig. 39). Yet the dominant tone is that of a rich pastoral fable, a game of fantasy and inventiveness played out with the most up-to-date and refined visual language, so virtuosic as to at once stupefy and dazzle the viewer. The work ensnares us in a web of the spectacular—fleeting and protean—impossible to encompass but yielding to a slow reading, in the course of which we become mute and rapt, drunk with the space evoked and with the figures, colors, and light envisioned. In this play of fantasy and invention, this manner of creating *ex novo* his own consistent poetic dimension, in the immense repertory of creatures and humans, of physiognomies and improbable assemblages, of virtuosity and irony, of Baroque grotesquerie, Rococo delights, and encyclopedic enlightenment, Tiepolo reanimated the fire of his creativity. He subdued the whole weight and geniality of his craft to take up the unbroken threads of a grand poem and set in motion the mechanism and fantastic automatons of his magical and infinite theater.

Tiepolo reserved his meditation on the meaning of history for the abstruse scenes of the *Scherzi*. If in Piranesi's etchings known as the *Grotteschi,* the dawn of history bursts forth from a complex of signs, as from the primeval material of the world, in Tiepolo's prints those same signs and ruins appear on the point of sinking into the quicksand of fable and myth, at once ineffable and unreal. Indecipherable stone slabs with mocking hieroglyphs—or no inscription at all (as in the frontispiece of the *Scherzi* showing a flock of owls [no. 60a]): a world that has lost the ability to speak and has been transformed through the processes of memory and history into an *other*; a myth both derisive and tragic but in any case illusory. Thus, the ruins, altars, capitals, marble slabs, pyramids and obelisks, the cornices, vases, and decorative heads lend an esoteric perfume to these ambiguous landscapes where altars are employed for sacrifices of serpents and alchemical experiments, providing even the alien setting for the discovery of Punchinello's tomb (is this perhaps a sarcastic allusion to the frenetic and senseless activity of archaeologists in their endeavor to retrieve a world that cannot be revived?).

Beyond any meditation or message there remains the art of Tiepolo in all its unrepeatable splendor: the avariciousness of a sign that cannot be duplicated; the uncontainable expansion of an immense white space in scenes always on the point of self-destruction; the exploration of the clear, dark nights of reason. In the etchings, as in the last, splendid frescoes at Ca' Rezzonico in Venice (rather than those in Villa Pisani at Strà), Tiepolo—prior to that final departure from Venice—definitively traced out his own thought and delineated an itinerary of his search, long-suffering and problematic yet possessing a luminous grandiosity (no. 25a, b). He left in the painted skies of his native city the hieroglyphs of his own cultural and pictorial legacy, replete with irony, self-quotation, stubbornly reproposing the basis of his lucid poetics—above all in the exaltation of that diffused light that is perhaps the greatest achievement of his art.

In the *Scherzi* the spirit of Tiepolo also wanders among the underground passages of history—among Roman altars and the blasphemed temples of seers and fortune-tellers, with hermaphrodites and satyrs, soldiers, old Orientals, skeletons, and serpents beneath skies bathed with a brilliant but sunless light in the dawn-streaked regions of a Promethean time. Here primeval forces and the mocking folly of Punchinellos find their place. Here this hybrid legion of creatures—monsters and demigods—in whom savagery and humanity are inextricably blended, seem to burden themselves yet again with the question that Tiepolo has formulated to no avail. In the *Memento Mori* the eternal question is posed to Death itself. Confronted with the seers evoked by the labyrinths of history, Death appears, consulting an enormous book that is none other than the Book of Life containing the destiny of each and everyone. The hieroglyphs on the pages of that book are fated to remain indecipherable, both to Tiepolo and to us.

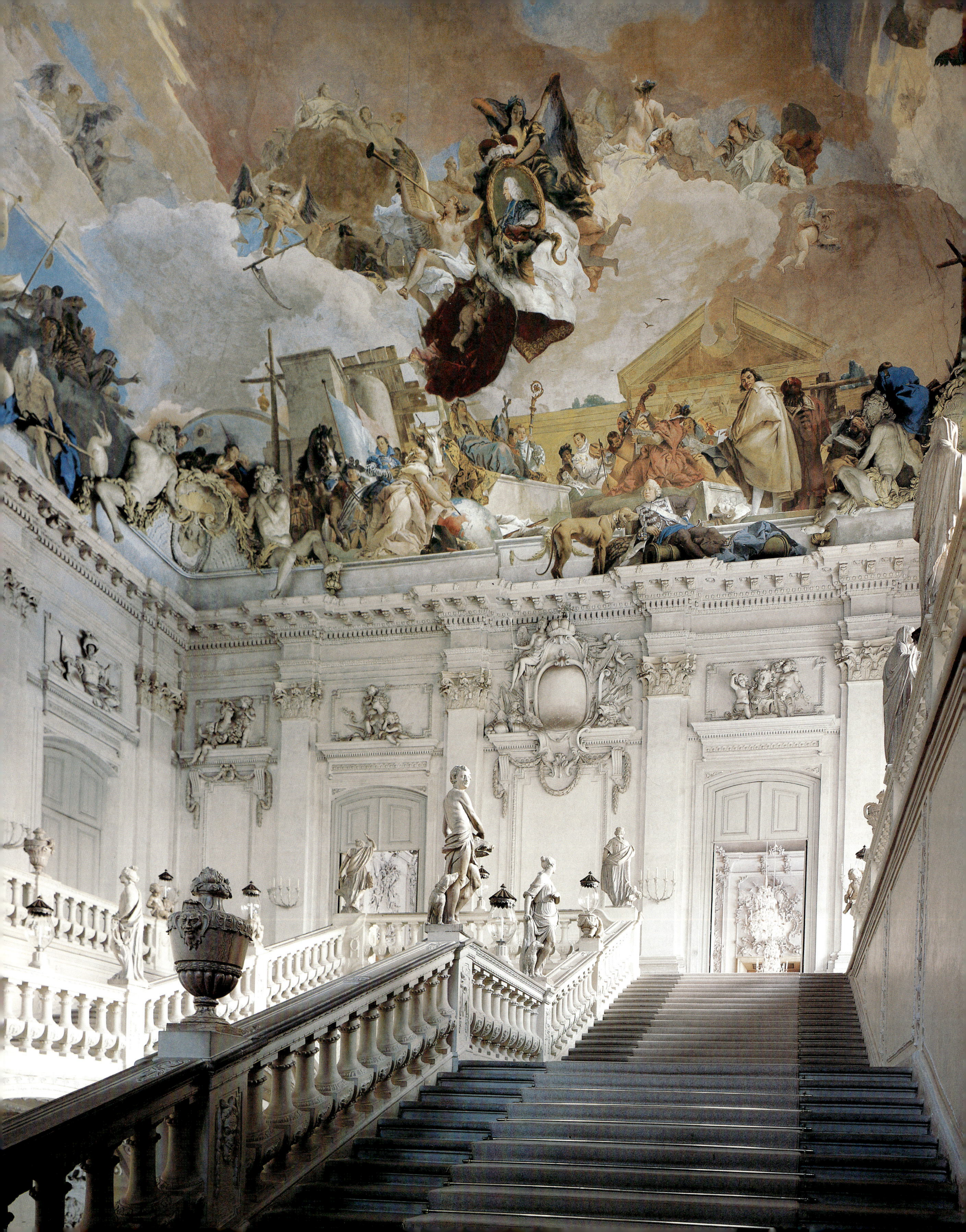

Tiepolo and the Artistic Culture of Eighteenth-Century Europe

DONALD POSNER

It may seem somewhat disconcerting to begin with a comparison of Tiepolo's fresco on the ceiling over the stairwell in the Residenz in Würzburg (frontis., opposite) and Antoine Watteau's canvas *Gersaint's Shop Sign* (fig. 7). The former decorates a vast area of plaster surface (19 by 30.5 meters) and is part of a permanent architectural complex; the latter, although the largest picture Watteau ever painted (in its present form 1.66 by 3.06 meters), could be framed, hung on the wall of a collector's gallery, and relocated when necessary. The artists were the outstanding geniuses in the history of eighteenth-century painting, and the Würzburg ceiling is arguably Tiepolo's greatest work, as the *Shop Sign* is Watteau's. Aside from their importance in the oeuvre of each man, however, the only thing they have in common is that they were painted in the eighteenth century in Western Europe. But that fact illuminates the extraordinary heterogeneousness of the artistic culture of the time and ultimately clarifies Tiepolo's place in it.

Watteau's picture was painted in Paris, along with London and Rome one of the urban crucibles in the making of the modern world. Its subject was chosen by the artist, and it was undertaken on his own initiative, not on commission. Made as a gift for an art dealer, Gersaint, the painting advertises his shop and celebrates the open market in the art trade. It employs what was a lowly pictorial type, the shop sign, to create a work of high art while transforming a scene of everyday reality into a poetic image of a society that thrives on beauty and culture.

Tiepolo's masterpiece was painted in the provincial environment of a petty principality in Franconia, where art and society looked for inspiration backward in time to the Versailles of Louis XIV. The fresco was commissioned by the prince-bishop, Carl Philipp von Greiffenclau, and was programmed to glorify his person and position and to advertise his pretensions.

Staircase with ceiling *Apollo and the Four Continents*. Fresco. Residenz, Würzburg

Its message and the pictorial form in which it is expressed—an otherworldly, allegorical vision of an Olympian heaven and of the four continents—are based on traditions that since the Renaissance had served the propagandistic needs of the ruling elites of Europe.

To us the Würzburg painting represents a world of the past, gone, not much lamented, and recuperable only by an act of the historical imagination. Watteau's *Shop Sign* signals the new, the beginnings of the modern world and of modern art as well. In all ways the picture still seems vital today. Watteau was twelve years older than Tiepolo, and ironically, his *Shop Sign* was painted, and he himself was dead, in 1721, thirty years before Tiepolo began work at Würzburg. Viewed from the perspective of the present, the Würzburg fresco, and, in fact, the greatest part of Tiepolo's production, devoted as it is to the ideals of the old aristocracy and of the Catholic Church triumphant, is likely to appear to us as an anachronism even in the eighteenth century. But the appearance is misleading.

It is true that Tiepolo worked mainly for marginalized and reactionary societies, and primarily in northern Italy, which he left only twice in his life. Venice itself, the site of his principal activity, lacked political and economic power in the eighteenth century and clung as best it could to the traditions of its glorious past. But neither Tiepolo's mode of artistic expression nor the ideology it supported was a real obstacle to his reception in most major European centers. He could easily have made distinguished and appropriate contributions to the ornamentation of churches and palaces in Rome, and, were it not for the presence in that city of such gifted decorators as Sebastiano Conca and Corrado Giaquinto, he might well have been sought out for major commissions there. He did, in fact, receive one commission from Rome late in his life (which he could not fulfill), but that was for S. Marco, the Venetian church in the city.[1]

Understandably, outside of Venice and its neighboring territories his services were solicited only where local artistic talent was unavailable or deemed inadequate: Würzburg, as

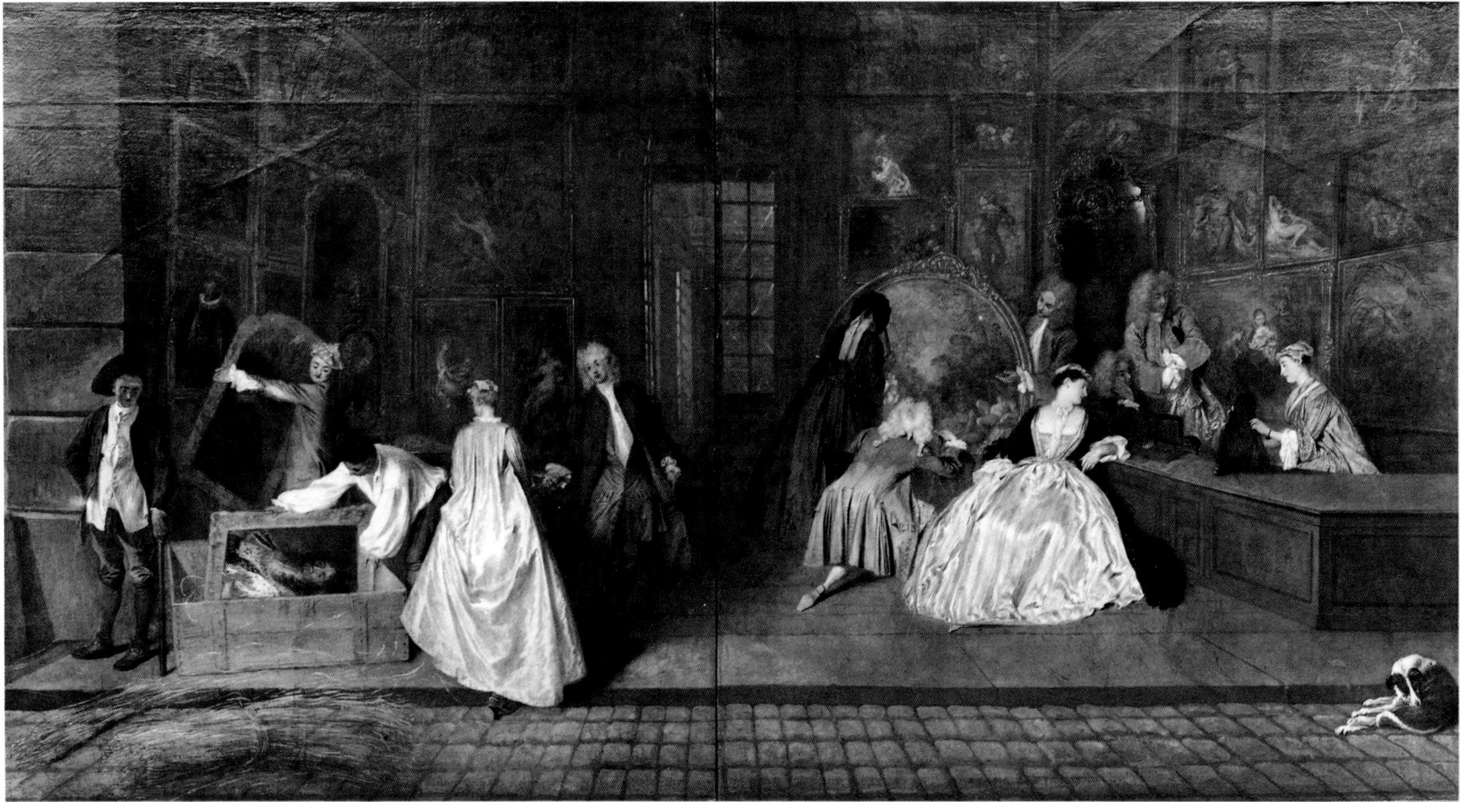

Fig. 7. Antoine Watteau. *Gersaint's Shop Sign*. Oil on canvas. Schloss Charlottenburg, Berlin

provincial artistically as it was politically; and Madrid, where it had become customary to import Italian artists for major decorative enterprises, and where, following Luca Giordano and Corrado Giaquinto, Tiepolo went in 1762 and worked for the last eight years of his life (see nos. 53–58). It can only have been an accident, not the result of antipathy to his art, that he was not invited to work for the Hapsburg rulers in Vienna, a city in which Venetian painters were much admired and patronized.[2] In 1736 he was considered for the commission to decorate the royal palace in Stockholm, but he was ultimately rejected as too expensive. The Russians procured his services, but by shipment only: in Saint Petersburg Prince Youssoupov and Count Vorontsov had houses ornamented with Tiepolo's works, and Empress Elizabeth Petrovna commissioned paintings from him, including some for the ceiling of the throne room in the Winter Palace.[3]

There was, to be sure, no demand for Tiepolo's personal services in the great cultural centers of Northwestern Europe, which we think of today as modern in ways that Venice and other places for which he worked were not. But modernity did not so rapidly eliminate the usefulness of the pictorial and iconographic forms that were Tiepolo's main stock-in-trade. In Amsterdam the painter Jacob de Wit could scarcely keep up with the commissions for ceiling paintings ordered by patrician families eager to ornament their houses with displays of their authority and privilege. The Dutch artist's sketch for a ceiling showing the *Apotheosis of Aeneas* (fig. 8)[4] (a subject Tiepolo painted later on a ceiling in the royal palace of Madrid) differs only in its Rubenesque accent from scenes of heavenly apotheosis designed by the Venetian such as the Metropolitan Museum's *Glorification of the Barbaro Family* (no. 21a).

Tiepolo's art would also not have seemed as foreign in England or France as we might imagine today. In fact, but for bad timing Tiepolo might have been a presence in the English art world of the eighteenth century. By Tiepolo's day England had long been an importer of artists, and early in the eighteenth century the two finest history painters active in the country were Venetians, Sebastiano Ricci and Gian'Antonio Pellegrini. The attraction of Venetian art in England owed much to the fact that an important segment of the English aristocracy of the time took on political and social characteristics that to some extent paralleled those of the Venetian oligarchy.[5] Lord Manchester, the duke of Marlborough, and other Whig noblemen must have sensed the connection, and they gave visual expression to their status and style of life by decorating their city and country houses after the manner of the palaces and villas of the noble families of Venice.

By about 1720, just when Tiepolo's career was beginning, however, a changing political and artistic environment greatly reduced the opportunities available to history painters in England, especially if they were foreigners. This new environment was characterized by a rising tide of nationalism that already had been responsible, in 1715, for Ricci's loss of the commission to paint the dome of Saint Paul's, which was awarded to the Englishman James Thornhill. Still, it was possible for a modestly endowed Venetian history painter, Jacopo Amigoni, to find employment in England for most of the decade of the 1730s. Of course, by then Tiepolo did not lack for patronage at home and had no need to seek work abroad. Indeed, on the two occasions he was induced to leave Italy, he was persuaded, in the case of Würzburg, by an exceptionally high fee and, in that of Madrid, by the intervention of the Venetian authorities on behalf of the Spanish king. But there is no reason to think that his style and much of his preferred subject matter would have been inappropriate in the England of the time. There would have been a place even for his religious paintings, for, as Ricci and other Italian artists proved with their productions for churches and chapels in England, Catholic and Anglican imagery had much in common. Tiepolo in England early in the eighteenth century is a fantasy; but if we fantasize, what could be more fitting to envision in the age when Alexander Pope translated Homer's epics than an English Palladian country house decorated by Tiepolo in the manner of the Villa Valmarana at Vicenza, with scenes from Homer's *Iliad* (fig. 9) and Virgil's *Aeneid*?

The Würzburg frescoes, with their autocratic political content, however, are scarcely imaginable in an English context. But they would not seem so anomalous in France. Today, when we think of eighteenth-century French painting, works like Watteau's *Gersaint's Shop Sign* come most readily to mind. But French art lovers of the middle of that century, if asked to name the finest, most important French painting of their time, were unlikely to have thought of pictures by our favorites, Watteau, Boucher, or Chardin. In an age when history painting was viewed as the most challenging and inherently significant of all pictorial genres, and when grandiosity was still admired, François Lemoyne's *Apotheosis of Hercules* in the palace of Versailles (fig. 10) would almost certainly have been the work chosen.

Lemoyne's great ceiling painting, completed in 1736 and much too little appreciated today, in many ways parallels Tiepolo's work at Würzburg. Although only about half the size of the ceiling over the stairwell, the Versailles decoration is nonetheless huge in scale and effect, opening the room to an unbroken vista of sky and scores of figures. Like the Tiepolo, it pictures an Olympian heaven and uses an arcane language of allegory to glorify and legitimize the ideals of absolutism by showing, as the artist himself explained, how "obstacles [to

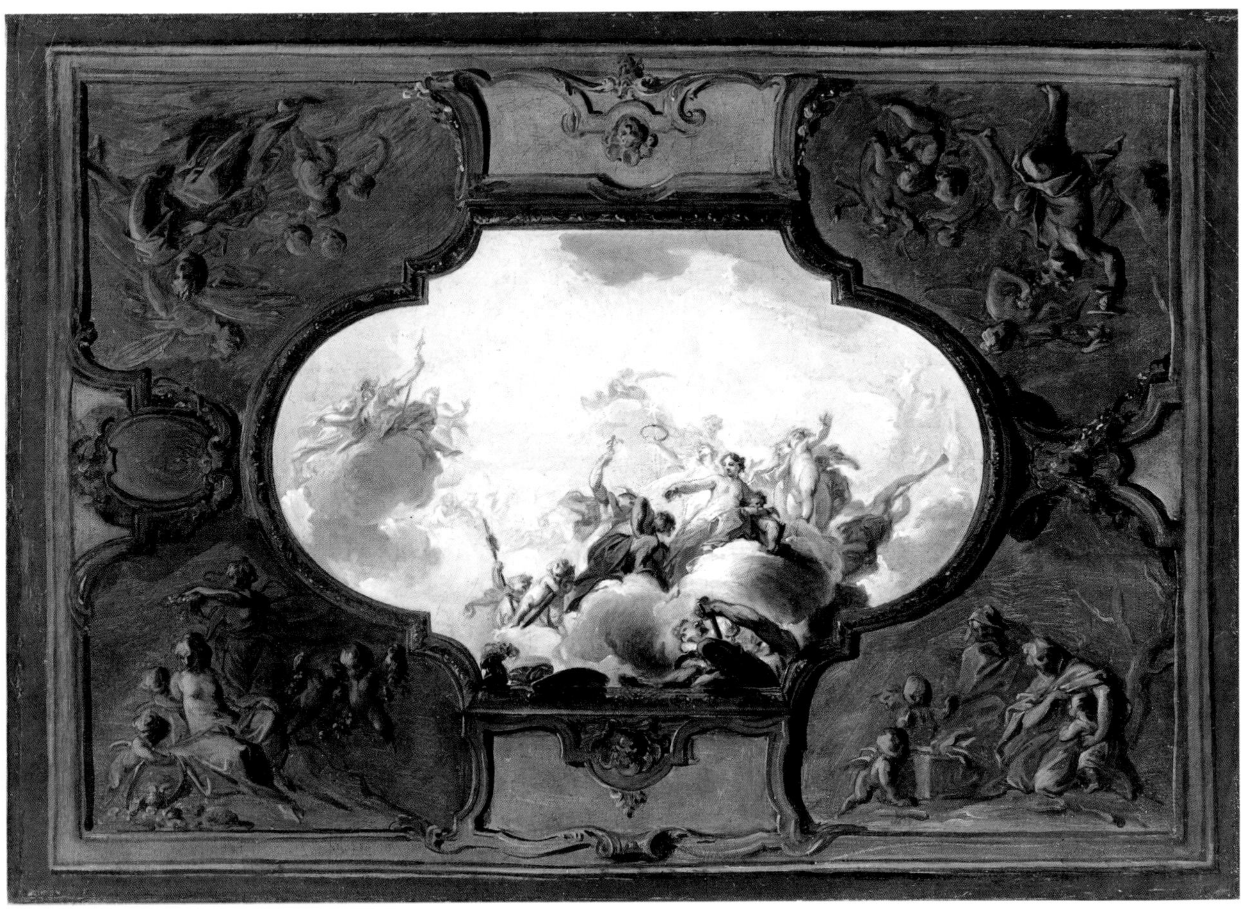

Fig. 8. Jacob de Wit. *The Apotheosis of Aeneas*. Oil on canvas. Rijksmuseum, Amsterdam

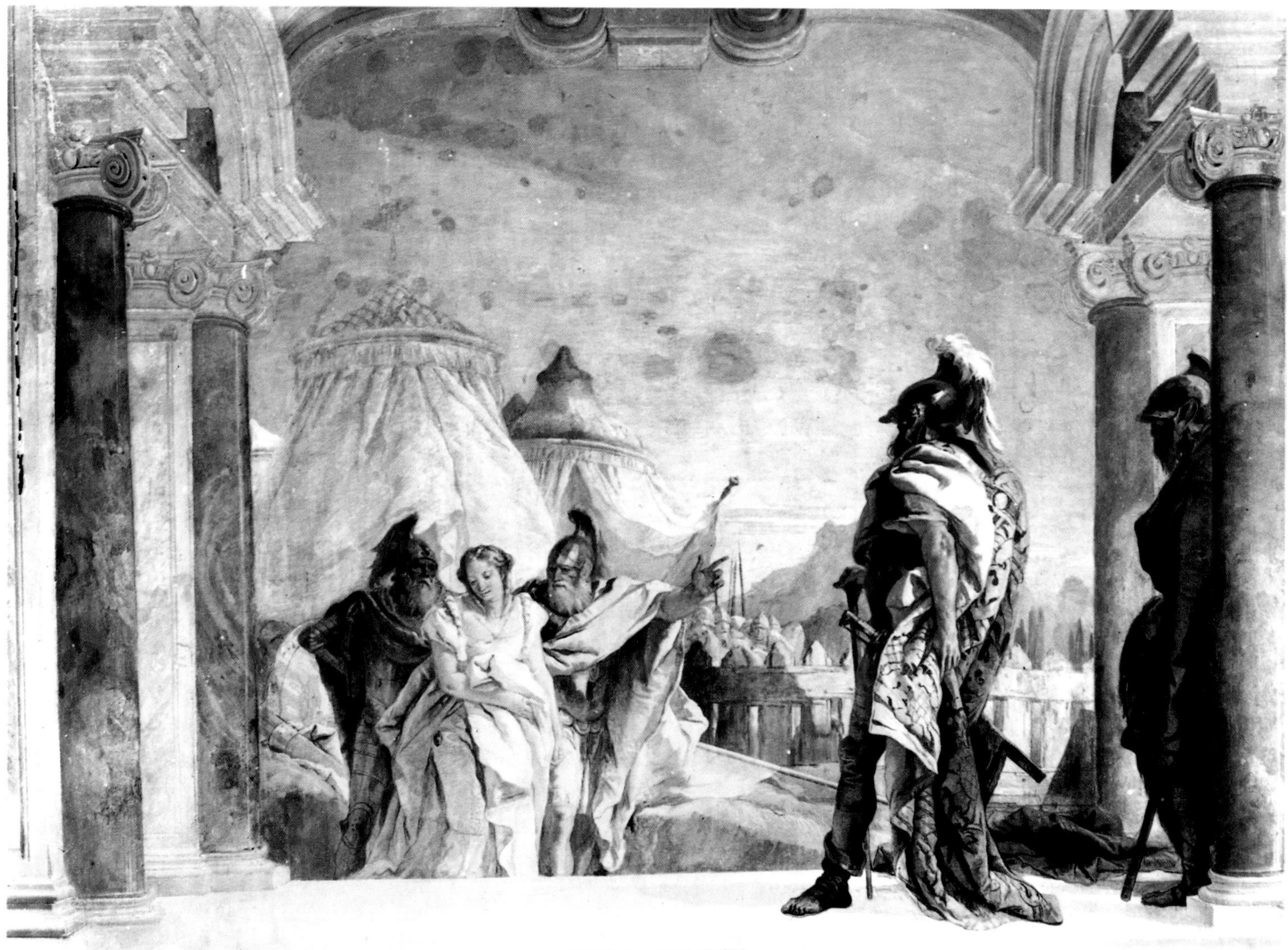

Fig. 9. *Briseis Brought to Agamemnon*. Fresco. Villa Valmarana, Vicenza

virtue] vanish at the sight of king and fatherland."[6] There is nothing, in short, about the subject matter or the character of the decorative enterprise that Tiepolo would have found unfamiliar.

Concerning this subject matter, it should be stressed that the apparent social and intellectual modernity of Enlightenment France sometimes tends to obscure that culture's continuing commitment to the ideals of the ancien régime. Despite his passion for political reform, Voltaire was an ardent admirer of those two great absolute monarchs of his own time, Frederick of Prussia and Catherine of Russia, as well as of the French king who dominated the previous century. In fact, in eighteenth-century France a very conscious effort was made, especially involving the arts about 1750, to revive the grandeur of the age of Louis XIV;[7] this suggests that the contemporaneous cultural ambitions of the prince-bishop of Würzburg were not a merely provincial and *retardataire* phenomenon. Except in England and Holland, the political ideology underlying Tiepolo's imagery still dominated the life and thought of Europe.

Tiepolo's Catholicism was no less universal, although many of his religious pictures reflect the specifically Venetian context that nourished his own beliefs and piety.[8] Altarpieces such as his *Last Communion of Saint Lucy* (no. 36a) could have served a French audience as well as the Venetian one for which it was made. Indeed, granting evident differences of style and—most notably—of quality, the *Last Communion* draws on much the same scenic repertory and traditional spiritual vocabulary as Carle van Loo's *Saint Peter Healing the Lame Man* (fig. 11), painted some six or seven years earlier for a Parisian church. Tiepolo's spectacular, illusionistic visions of the Christian heaven and of miraculous occurrences, such as the *Miracle of the Holy House of Loreto* (no. 48a, b), executed for the church of the Scalzi in Venice, also might not have seemed entirely out of place in the France of his time. In Paris, two years after Tiepolo completed the Scalzi painting, Charles-Joseph Natoire began the decoration of the Chapelle des Enfants Trouvées. Unfortunately destroyed in the nineteenth century, this remarkable orchestration of pictures illustrating the Adoration of the Infant

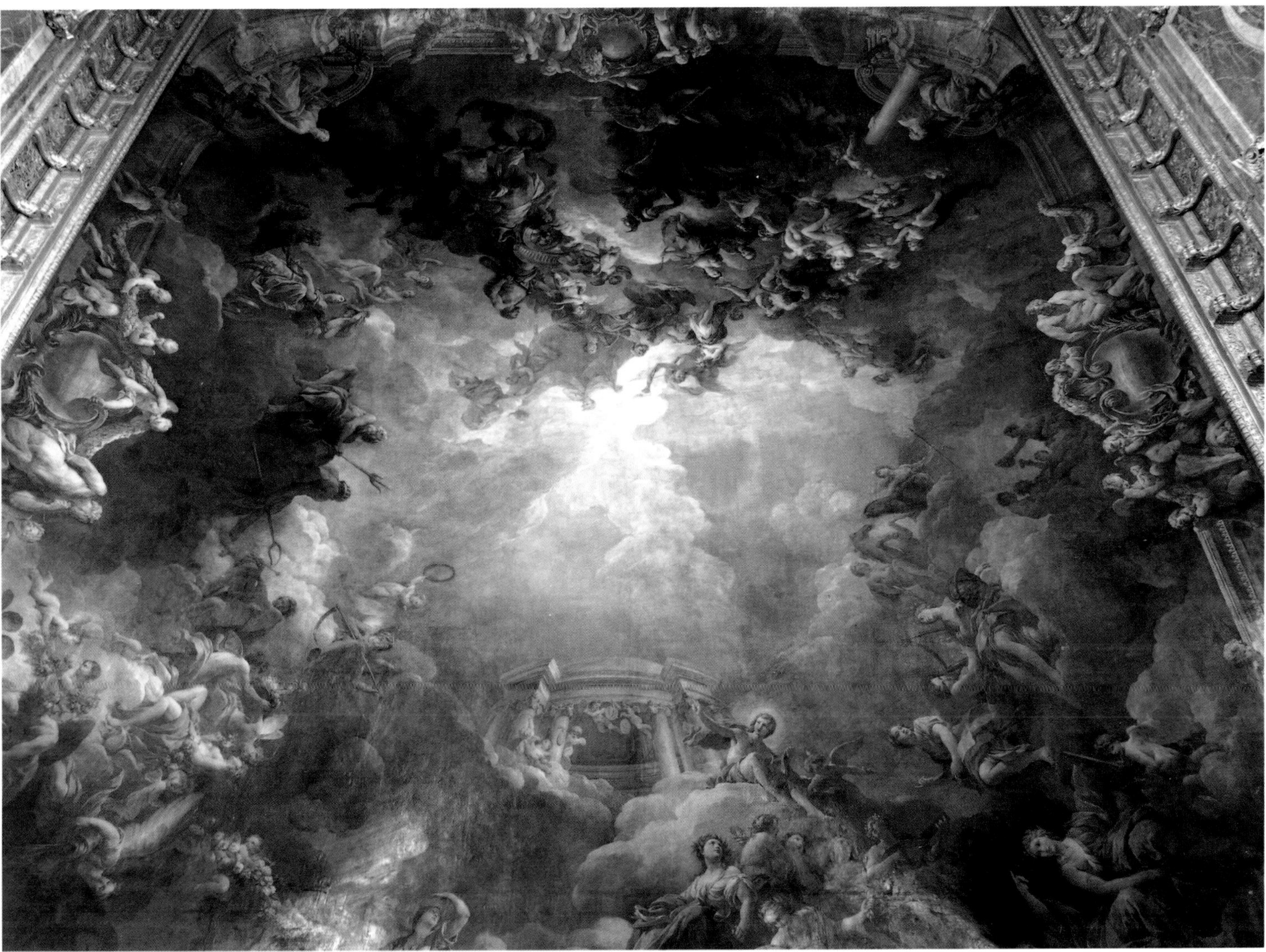

Fig. 10. François Lemoyne. *The Apotheosis of Hercules*. Fresco. Musée et Domaine National de Versailles, Château de Versailles

Christ, attended by a host of music-making angels, witnessed by a crowd of nuns and children, and covered by the feigned ruin of the vault, was as "theatrical" and illusionistic an expression of the Christian universe as anything painted by Tiepolo in Italy.

When the Chapelle des Enfants Trouvées was unveiled in 1751, the pious hope was voiced that French artists might find more opportunities to display their talents for such large-scale decoration.[9] For social and economic reasons, however, opportunities of this kind were relatively limited, and, as in England, foreign artists had little chance to capture them. Nationalist sentiment and the economic self-interest of native artists worked toward the exclusion of alien competition. The peripatetic Venetian painter Gian'Antonio Pellegrini had gone from England and Düsseldorf to Paris, where he was welcomed and, in 1720, painted the now-destroyed ceiling of the gallery in the Banque Royale. (His theme on this ceiling—peace and flourishing commerce as the products of a wise monarchy—incidentally, was one that Tiepolo was later to take up in the throne room of the royal palace of Madrid [no. 53].)[10] The choice of Pellegrini was opposed, very vigorously, by Lemoyne, who had himself aspired to the commission, and, indeed, after 1720 no major artistic enterprise in France was entrusted to a foreigner. Only when artists from abroad could provide something not readily available locally were they called upon. Hence, the Italian Gaetano Brunetti and his son, specialists in illusionistic architectural painting, were employed to assist Natoire at the Enfants Trouvées. Tiepolo's services, however appropriate they might have been, were neither needed nor wanted in France.

There were other obstacles to the appreciation of Tiepolo's art in France, obstacles that help to explain why virtually none of his easel pictures were acquired by French collectors of the time. Tiepolo's images are articulated with a distinctive eighteenth-century Venetian accent that seemed unnatural to French spectators, and they have a social and psychological inflection that must have sounded, or rather looked, dated to many of these viewers.

The French artist and critic Charles-Nicolas Cochin, after visiting Italy from 1749 to 1751, concluded that modern Venetian art, in its commitment to the seductive charms of an exaggerated colorism, was no longer following the dictates of Nature. Tiepolo, in particular, he criticized for what he considered an excessive luminosity of color, especially as seen in the painter's frescoed ceilings. Cochin's ideal was surely the colorism of Lemoyne, which is itself much dependent on the example of sixteenth-century Venetian art, but also of Rubens, and which has as its goal warmth, depth, and atmospheric unification. The dazzling, cool brilliance and chromatic richness and contrasts of Tiepolo's work, which tend to obliterate shadows, can only have appeared unnatural to Cochin and art lovers like him.[11]

We might imagine that Tiepolo's pictures would have appealed to an audience accustomed to the cosmetic colorism of François Boucher. But the paintings of Boucher, who never used fresco, do not confront the viewer with quite the same degree of luminous intensity as those of Tiepolo. Furthermore, Boucher himself, beginning about 1750, was severely criticized in Paris precisely for what many regarded as an excessively artificial style characterized by overly pretty color.

A comparison of the work and careers of Tiepolo and Boucher, who was only seven years younger than the Venetian, reveals fundamental disparities in the cultural foundations of their art.[12] Both were born decorators, fluent and inventive in approach; both were very successful history painters and wonderful storytellers who delighted in illustrating the myths of classical antiquity. But how different they were when telling the same story.

In the *Aeneid* Virgil describes Venus's visit to the forge of Vulcan to procure arms and armor for her son Aeneas. Tiepolo, in his picture on the theme (no. 26), imagined an architectural setting, with thick masonry walls, massive columns, and a barred window. Workmen tend the fiery furnace. Color and effects of light suggest the heavy heat and the noise of the place. It is the appropriate environment for an awesome event from distant, heroic times. Boucher, in a painting that is

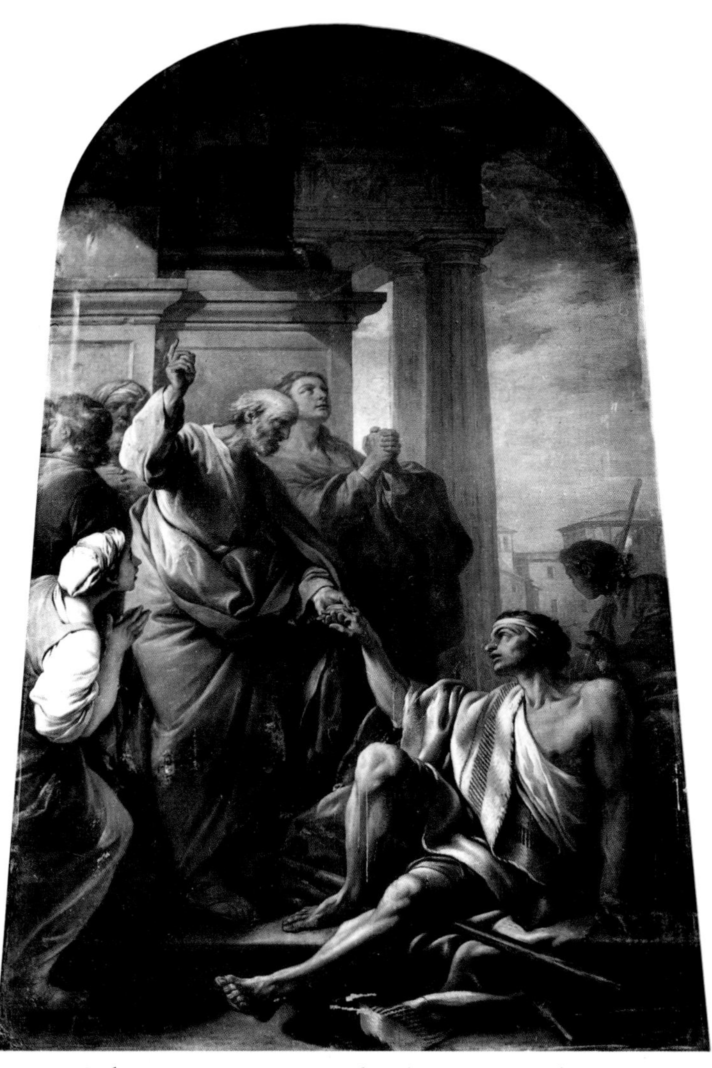

Fig. 11. Carle van Loo. *Saint Peter Healing the Lame Man*. Oil on canvas (?). Saint-Louis-en-l'Île, Paris

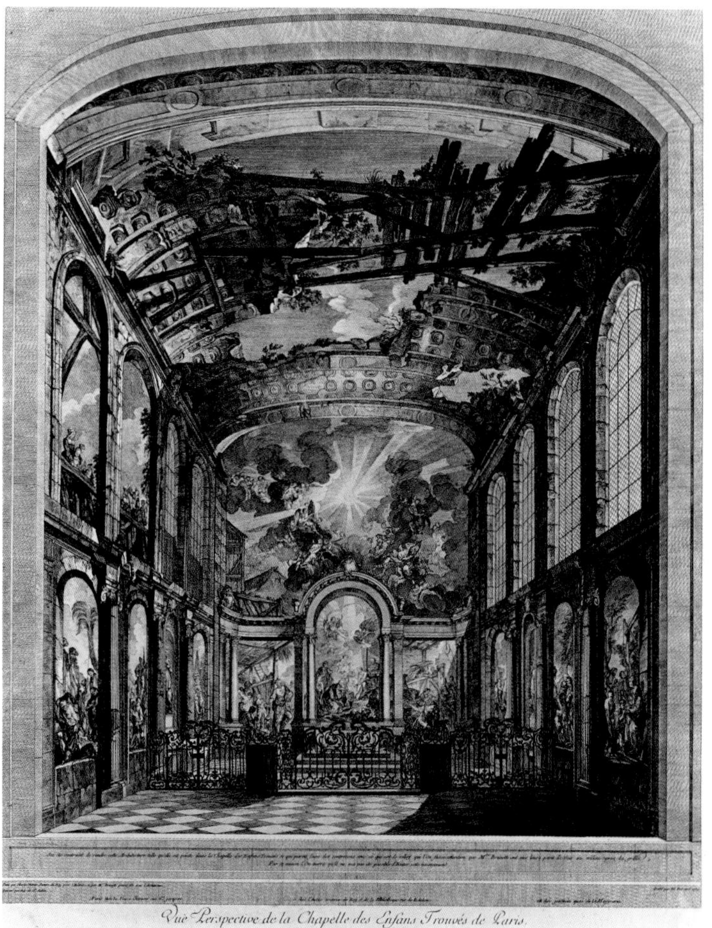

Fig. 12. E. Fessard after Charles-Jacques Natoire. *Chapelle des Enfants-Trouvés* (destroyed). Engraving. The Metropolitan Museum of Art, New York; The Elisha Whittelsey Collection, The Elisha Whittelsey Fund, 1959 (59.570.49)

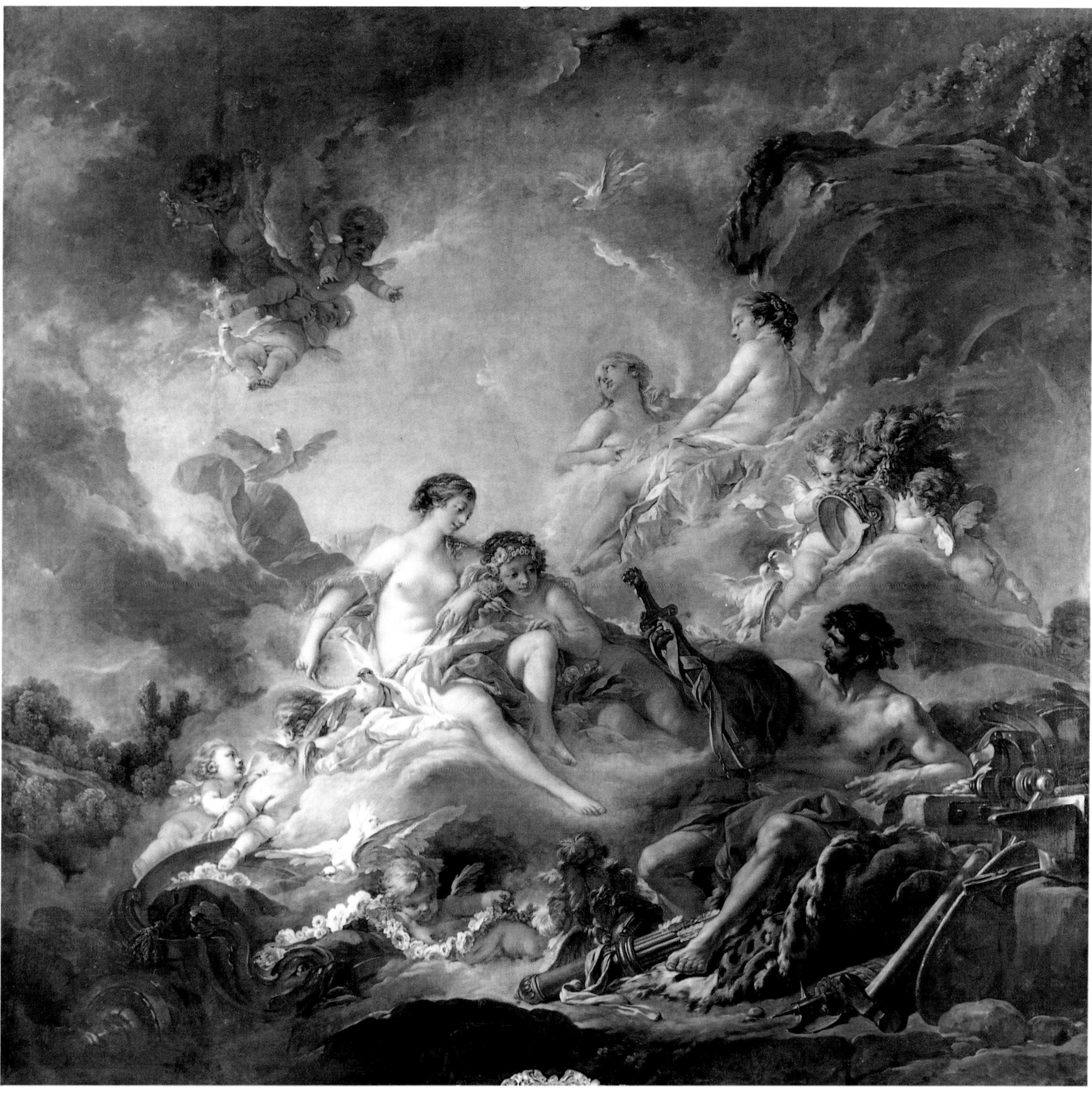

Fig. 13. François Boucher. *The Forge of Vulcan*. Oil on canvas. Musée du Louvre, Paris (2707 bis)

contemporary with Tiepolo's picture (fig. 13), placed the scene in a pretty landscape, enlivened by clouds and blue sky, by nymphs and flying putti and a cupid weaving a garland of roses. Only a glimpse of Vulcan's tools and the arms he has made suggests the presence, somewhere nearby, of a workshop. This is ancient story as picturesque fable, not to be taken very seriously in an enlightened, sophisticated modern world. Boucher's Venus is a plump, lovely young woman who (according to Virgil) has her way with Vulcan by virtue of her seductive wiles. Tiepolo's regal Venus, however, brilliantly lit and dominating the scene, head held high and gazing down imperiously at Vulcan, has come not to seduce but to command.

It is plain that Tiepolo's picture is informed by a nostalgia for an aristocratic culture that still had functional value in the eighteenth century in Venice and, surely, also in Germany and Spain. This sentiment was, of course, comprehensible in France too, and, in a rather pale way perhaps, it is reflected in the contemporary work of the French artist Jean Restout; but it could no longer be taken seriously in a society that was becoming ever more skeptical of authority and witnessing the gradual erosion of class distinctions. Distinctions there were, but reasonableness and good taste effectively tempered their ostentatious display. One would have been hard pressed, certainly, to find a patron in France—not to say England—for images of family glorification such as Tiepolo's *Apotheosis of Francesco Barbaro*. In Paris the very idea of such a picture would have been thought laughable.[13]

In France the market for history paintings in general, even those not primarily motivated by didactic or propagandistic aims, was slackening, despite the fact that theorists and critics continued to rank histories above all other subjects in art. It is telling in this connection that about 40 percent of Boucher's lifetime production was devoted to work in the "lesser" genres, such as pastorales, scenes of everyday life, and landscapes, pictorial types that are almost totally absent from Tiepolo's oeuvre.[14]

Tiepolo, based in Venice, worked principally on commission for the aristocracy and for the Church. Amply supported by such patronage, he was in no way dependent on the wide, public art market with its demands for novelty and variety in subjects and approach. In his time, however, everywhere in Europe the audience for art was growing rapidly and becoming more socially diverse; the modern world of the art trade, defined by buying and selling and the promotion of new talent and ideas, was growing and diversifying with it. Watteau's *Gersaint's Shop Sign* symbolizes that world for us today.

Watteau was, in fact, a talent discovered and encouraged by dealers. They found a market for his work among a relatively modest class of collector[15] that valued the brilliance of the artist's crayons and brushes in transcribing natural appearances, even if his pictures told no story and taught no lesson. Grasping the plain truth about nature through the activity of eye and hand had itself become a central task of the artist.[16]

A fascination with the "natural," combined with the art market's passion for variety, provided an especially strong stimulus for the development of the several genres that represented the world as it is (or was thought to be): portraiture; scenes of everyday life; landscapes and cityscapes; animal and still-life painting. These pictorial types, which in the seventeenth century still seemed clearly inferior and marginal to the main currents of European art, began to challenge the supremacy of history paintings.

The challenge was an international one, although naturally posed in different forms in different places. Scenes of everyday life, for instance, were pictured with satiric wit by Hogarth in London and Troost in Amsterdam, with idyllic elegance by Lancret in Paris, and with gentle irony by Pietro Longhi in Venice. But the commonality of these works, which show life as it is in the here and now, is apparent, and as types they represented alternatives for artists and art lovers to the imaginings of the history painters. In Tiepolo's own Venice, as elsewhere, taste was changing. In 1750 the poet Carlo Goldoni declared Longhi to be "a man who is looking for the truth." And it was not long before the Venetian critic Gasparo Gozzi, obviously thinking of works such as Tiepolo's, was to ridicule pictures of heavenly apparitions, with their exaggerated color and light effects and their figures in fanciful costumes; by contrast he praised Longhi for painting "what he sees with his own eyes."[17]

In England history painting languished for most of the eighteenth century, while portraiture and landscape and genre painting flourished. English art enthusiasts had virtually no interest in Tiepolo's work. Although the *Saint James of Compostella* (no. 37) went to London, it was commissioned for the chapel of the Spanish embassy there; another picture by Tiepolo, the *Finding of Moses* (no. 16a), was acquired by an English collector, but perhaps only because he mistakenly thought it was painted by one of the sons of the great Venetian Renaissance master Veronese.[18] The English were, however, avid collectors of the miraculously real depictions that Canaletto made of Venetian views, and they provided eager patronage when he went to work in England for a decade beginning in 1746.

In the more conservative culture of France, history painting persisted, but almost all its practitioners—including Lemoyne, Boucher, and Carle van Loo—felt the need to demonstrate their ability to capture the "real" face of nature. Their portraits, landscapes, and genre paintings represent some of their best work. Even in German-speaking lands the attraction of the new naturalism was taking hold. Tiepolo's stay in Würzburg, although glorious in outcome, was brief. After his departure analogues of his noble decorative style were produced by local artists, some of them, like Anton Franz Maulbertsch, of great talent. However, the Venetian painter whose art matured and flourished in Germany was Bernardo Bellotto, the nephew of Canaletto. Bellotto accepted an invitation to the court at Dresden in 1747, and from then until his death in 1780, working in Vienna and Warsaw as well as in Dresden, he devoted himself to the study of nature in a body of view paintings that stands among the finest accomplishments of eighteenth-century art.

Tiepolo was of course aware of developments in the lesser genres, which were successfully practiced in the Venice of his time, but he was rarely tempted to try his hand at them. He did not despise them, however, as is clear from works that issued from his studio, most notably the delightful genre scenes painted by his son Giandomenico. He himself produced a few portraits (see nos. 43, 46) and some pseudoportraits, for example his *Woman with a Mandolin* and other pictures that appear in the present exhibition (nos. 44, 45a, b). But they were for him only occasional exercises, the range and significance of which are discussed in "Tiepolo and the 'Art' of Portraiture" by Diane De Grazia in this publication.

Tiepolo's own experience suggested to him that only history paintings could command the kind of prices that were worthy of his efforts,[19] and his departure from the noble genre was therefore rare. On two occasions, however, Tiepolo was moved, and certainly not primarily for reasons of financial gain, to leave the high ground of ancient and biblical imagery in order to explore a lower genre other than portraiture. But the particular genre that interested him, in fact, stands above the depiction of ordinary, everyday life and occupies the realm of fantasy.

The desire to capture the image of nature in its entirety stimulated an interest in representing, in addition to the familiar, the strange, the bizarre, the imaginary and fantastical. The chinoiserie and *turquerie*, exotic images of alien people and places, created by such artists as Boucher and Guardi; the caprice views of a Venice topographically rearranged by Canaletto; the unbuildable prisons pictured by Piranesi; the fanciful ruins conjured up by Hubert Robert; and ultimately the dream visions of Fuseli and Goya, are different species of the same pictorial family. Tiepolo's contribution to this family, widely appreciated in eighteenth-century Europe and today frequently and justly compared to Goya's *Caprichos*, were his two suites of enigmatic, riveting etchings, the *Capricci* and the *Scherzi* (nos. 59, 60).

By virtue of their subjects and medium the prints are exceptions in Tiepolo's oeuvre, and they are his only works that truly can be described as modern in their own time. The painted expanse of pagan and Christian heavens, the domains of gods and saints, were the natural abodes of his artistic imagination. As I have stressed, these were territories still real and meaningful throughout Europe in the eighteenth century, and Tiepolo was not alone in depicting them. But hardly any of his contemporaries attempted tasks as numerous and complex as those he accepted eagerly, and certainly none rivaled him in the ease and power of visualization and execution with which he accomplished them.

If we should not fault Tiepolo for his lack of modernity, we also should not try to take his measure on the scale we use for Watteau or other "modern" artists, whose artistic and professional aims were different and, it seems fair to say, more modest than his. Tiepolo's view of his own mission was determined by traditions that date to the beginning of the Renaissance. He is reported to have explained, late in his life, that "painters should aim to succeed in great works, the kind that can please noble, rich people. . . . Therefore the mind of the painter must always be directed towards the Sublime, the Heroic, towards Perfection."[20] With his own mind so directed, he celebrated the ideals of the ancien régime in the most stupendous body of work produced by a painter in eighteenth-century Europe.

Notes

1. Morassi 1962, pp. 236–37.
2. London 1994, pp. 45–47.
3. Ibid., pp. 54–55.
4. London 1995, pp. 38–39.
5. Haskell 1963, pp. 278–81, 286–87.
6. Bordeaux 1974, p. 309.
7. Honour 1968, pp. 23–27.
8. See Barcham 1989.
9. Conisbee 1981, p. 46.
10. For a study of this painting, see Jones 1981.
11. Ivanoff [1972], pp. 51–52.
12. See Cailleux [1972].
13. Ibid., p. 97.
14. Ibid., p. 88.
15. See Posner 1984, pp. 121–28.
16. Levey 1966, chap. 4.
17. Quoted in Haskell 1963, pp. 323–25.
18. London 1994, p. 58.
19. See Haskell 1963, p. 253 n. 2, and Adriano Mariuz, "Giambattista Tiepolo: 'Painting's True Magician,'" n. 19, this publication.
20. Haskell 1963, p. 253 n. 2.

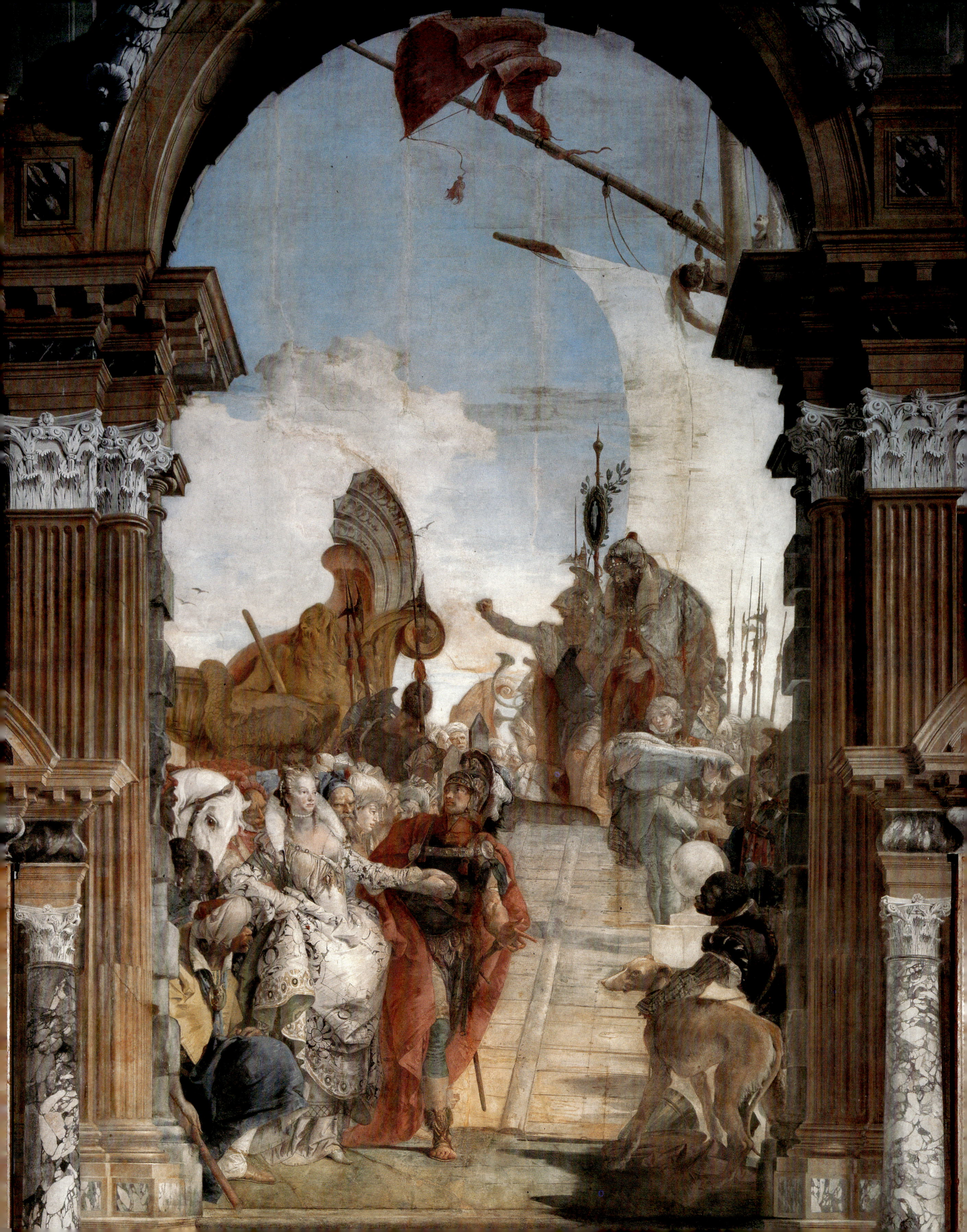

A Documented Chronology of Tiepolo's Life and Work

ANDREA BAYER

Unless otherwise indicated, churches, residences, and other buildings are in Venice.

1696
5 March Tiepolo is born in Venice, in *sestiere* (district) of Castello. Baptized on 16 April in church of S. Pietro di Castello (Urbani de Gheltof 1879, pp. 1–3).

1710
Probable year he enters workshop of Gregorio Lazzarini.

1715–16
Date assigned by da Canal (1732 [1809 ed., p. xxxii]) to Tiepolo's series of apostles in S. Maria dei Derelitti (the Ospedaletto) (see no. 2a, b).

1716
According to da Canal (1732 [1809 ed., p. xxxii]), Tiepolo, now age twenty, exhibits a painting, *Crossing of the Red Sea* (lost), at annual festival at Scuola Grande di S. Rocco.

Florentine collector Francesco Gabburri owns drawing by Tiepolo showing a saint's martyrdom (Campori 1870, p. 536).

Ca. 1716–19
Presumed date of *Assumption of the Virgin* (fig. 14) fresco in parish church, Biadene, which da Canal asserts is Tiepolo's "prima opera a fresco" (1732 [1809 ed., p. xxxii]; Mariuz and Pavanello 1985, p. 101).

1717
Tiepolo's name appears for first time in records of *Fraglia* (guild) of Venetian artists (Nicoletti 1890, p. 708).

Ca. 1717
Publication of Domenico Lovisa's *Il gran teatro delle pitture e prospettive di Venezia*, which includes four drawings by Tiepolo after other works of art. Second edition appears in 1720 (Moschini 1815, vol. 1, p. xxix, and Gorizia 1983, p. 230).

Detail, *Meeting of Cleopatra and Antony*, Palazzo Labia, Venice

1717 or 1719?
Date of *Abraham Banishing Hagar*(?) (no. 8) as read by Morassi (1937, p. 53) but no longer visible.

1718
Villa at Massanzago purchased by Giovanni Battista Baglioni. According to da Canal, frescoes in main hall (see fig. 15) are Tiepolo's (1732 [1809 ed., p. xxxii]; Mariuz and Pavanello 1985, p. 103).

1719
21 November marries Cecilia Guardi, sister of Gian Antonio and Francesco Guardi.

1721
Madonna of Mount Carmel (fig. 19) commissioned for Carmelite church of S. Aponal; it remains unfinished by 24 April 1727 (Moretti 1984–85, p. 379).

1722
Date of commission *of Martyrdom of Saint Bartholomew* (fig. 16) (Moretti 1973, pp. 318–19).

1722 or 1723
Date read on fresco *Saint Lucy in Glory* in parish church, Vascon, by Aikema (1987b, p. 443) and by Moretti (1984–85, pp. 379–80); the work is ascribed to the young Tiepolo by da Canal (1732).

1723
Competition held for ceiling decoration of chapel of S. Domenico in SS. Giovanni e Paolo; Tiepolo submits a *modello* (fig. 18) (Moretti 1984–85, p. 378).

Paintings *Saint Peter* and *Saint Paul* (lost) are given to Scuola di S. Teodoro (Moretti 1984–85, p. 380).

Ca. 1724
Scipione Maffei invites Tiepolo to make drawings of antiquities for Maffei's *Verona illustrata*, published 1731–32, with engravings by Andrea Zucchi (Franzoni 1978, p. 95).

1726
Confraternity of the Most Holy Sacrament of cathedral in Udine commissions Tiepolo to fresco its chapel (Joppi 1894, p. 43).

Daniele III Dolfin (1654–1729) states in his will that he wishes to have famous artists carry out the paintings for principal room of his palace (see no. 12a–g) (Conticelli 1996).

1727
Giandomenico Tiepolo is born.

1729
Patriarch Dionisio Dolfin (1663–1734) adds portraits to collection in Arcivescovado (Patriarchal Palace), Udine, and has others repainted by "a better hand." According to a local source, this work was carried out by Tiepolo (Biasutti 1958, pp. 22–23).

Date on *Triumph of Marius* (no. 12e), one of Tiepolo's ten canvases for *salone* of Ca' Dolfin.

1730
Receives commission for frescoes in Palazzo Archinto, Milan; completed spring–summer 1731 (destroyed World War II) (Sohm 1984, p. 70).

Publication of F. Mediobarbo's *Imperatorum Romanorum numismata*, with Tiepolo's engraving *Italy Offering the Manuscript to the Emperor Charles VI* as frontispiece.

1731
Tiepolo writes Count Gaspare Casati that he will begin frescoes for Palazzo Casati (now Dugnani), Milan, when his commitments in Palazzo Archinto are fulfilled (Calvi 1885, vol. 4, s.v. Casati, pl. 17).

1732
Adoration of the Christ Child (no. 28) executed for S. Giuliano (Zanetti 1733, p. 486).

Begins frescoes in Colleoni Chapel, Bergamo; completed autumn 1733 (Molmenti 1909, p. 128; see also Morassi 1962, p. 231).

Almost certainly date of fresco *Agony in the Garden* in S. Maria di Nazareth (the Scalzi) as well as of altarpiece the *Education of the Virgin* painted for S. Maria della Consolazione (Fava), as they are mentioned by Zanetti (1733), although not cited in da Canal (1732).

1733
Tiepolo is paid by Patriarch Dionisio Dolfin for altarpiece *Saint Francis of Sales* (Museo Civico, Udine) for S. Maria Maddalena dei Filippini, Udine (Molmenti 1909, p. 82 n. 4).

1734
Probable completion date of *Immaculate Conception* (Museo Civico, Vicenza) painted for church of the Aracoeli, Vicenza (Saccardo 1977, p. 12).

Finishes *Madonna in Glory with Apostles and Saints* for high altar of church of Ognissanti, Rovetta. The painting is put into its carved altar frame in 1736 (Frizzoni 1902, pp. 271, 274; see Morassi 1962, p. 46).

Tiepolo writes in a letter that he is hard at work on frescoes in villa of Count Nicolò Loschi (now Zileri Dal Verme), Biron di Monteviale, outside Vicenza (see fig. 42) (Fogolari 1942, pp. 33–34); inscription in *salone* confirms date.

Contract for *Martyrdom of Saint Agatha* for S. Antonio, Padua (fig. 81), installed in 1737 (Gonzati 1852–53, vol. 1, docs. CXXIII, CXXIV).

1735
Signed and dated *Madonna of the Rosary* (no. 30a).

1736
Lorenzo Tiepolo is born.

Count Carl Gustaf Tessin offers Tiepolo work at royal palace in Stockholm, but no agreement is reached. Tessin purchases *modello* of *Execution of Saint John the Baptist* (Nationalmuseum, Stockholm) from Colleoni Chapel, Bergamo, and *Danaë and Jupiter* (no. 15) and brings them to Stockholm (Sirèn 1902, pp. 107, 112).

1737
In June Tiepolo is paid for his *Guardian Angel* for S. Maria Maddalena dei Filippini, Udine (Museo Civico, Udine), and *Saints Ermagora and Fortunato* (cathedral, Udine), both commissioned by Patriarch Daniele Dolfin, patriarch of Aquileia (1685–1762) (Biasutti 1957, pp. 17, 19).

In May Tiepolo is commissioned to fresco ceiling of S. Maria del Rosario (the Gesuati [fig. 65]), which is completed October 1739 (Arslan 1932, p. 26, and Niero 1979, pp. 28–32).

1738

In June Tiepolo is paid for his *Trinity with Christ Crucified,* commissioned by Patriarch Daniele Dolfin for altar of Santissima Trinità, cathedral, Udine (Joppi 1894, p. 43, and Biasutti 1957, p. 19).

In July Tiepolo is paid for his altarpiece *Saints Agostino, Louis, John the Evangelist, and a Bishop Saint* (destroyed) for Cornaro chapel in S. Salvador (Mariacher 1959–60, p. 238).

With sculptor Antonio Gai, Tiepolo inventories sculpture collection of Sagredo family (Brunetti 1951, p. 158).

1739

Dedication date of chapel in convent church at Nymphenburg, for which Tiepolo paints *Vision of Saint Clement* (Alte Pinakothek, Munich), commissioned by Prince-Elector Clement Augustus of Cologne (Heine 1974, p. 149, and Würzburg 1996, vol. 1, p. 122).

Probable date of commission for altarpiece *Madonna and Child with Saints Catherine, Rose of Lima, and Agnes of Montepulciano* (no. 35) for the Gesuati. Recorded as under way by Albrizzi (1740), it is not installed until 1748 and is consecrated in 1749 (Arslan 1932, pp. 19–20).

Receives commission from Augustinians in Diessen, Bavaria, for *Martyrdom of Saint Sebastian* altarpiece (Molmenti 1909, pp. 159–60).

1739–40

December 1739, January 1740 Scuola Grande dei Carmini commissions Tiepolo to replace some of its ceiling paintings (fig. 66) (Urbani de Gheltof 1879, pp. 103–6, and Niero 1976–77, pp. 373–74).

1740

Executes frescoes in Palazzo Clerici, Milan, for Marchese Giorgio Antonio Clerici, in honor of his marriage to Fulvia Visconti in 1741 (Morassi 1962, p. 233, and Sohm 1984, p. 77 n. 2).

Commissioned by Foschi family to paint altarpiece *Vision of Saint Philip Neri* (no. 32) for S. Filippo Neri, Camerino (Venice 1969b, p. 372).

In January Tiepolo writes a letter concerning commissioning of *Gathering of the Manna* and *Sacrifice of Melchisedek* by Count Gian Francesco Gambara for parish church, Verolanuova (BS). According to a letter of 1742, they are to be installed within the year (Marini 1907, p. 145; Boselli 1971; Pagiaro 1983, p. 27).

1741

According to Morassi (1962, p. 60), the frescoes in Palazzo Papadopoli Arrivabene bear this date.

Date of the inscription on verso of *Beata Laduina* (no. 42).

1743

Along with Piazzetta, Tiepolo is asked to draw up inventory of paintings in Sagredo family collection (Brunetti 1951).

Starts frescoes in villa of Carlo Cordellina, Montecchio Maggiore, near Vicenza (fig. 40). Work here almost certainly continues through following spring (Fogolari 1942, pp. 34–35).

The eight lateral compartments, but not the central scene, of ceiling of Scuola Grande dei Carmini are put in place (Niero 1976–77, p. 382).

Begins frescoing *Apotheosis of the Admiral Vettor Pisani* in Palazzo Pisani Moretta. Work is completed by 1745 (Puppi [1972], pp. 131–33, and Chiappini di Sorio 1983, pp. 270–71).

Probable date of portrait *Antonio Riccobono* (no. 43) (Puppi [1972], pp. 131–33).

Praises a *Rape of Europa* by Veronese that Francesco Algarotti wishes to purchase for Dresden court and makes a copy of it at Algarotti's request (Posse 1931, pp. 41, 45, and Levey 1960, pp. 250–53).

Algarotti commissions a painting of Caesar with the Head of Pompey (now lost) for royal gallery of Dresden; it is delivered in 1746 (Posse 1931, p. 51).

Algarotti commissions two works from Tiepolo—*Maecenas Presenting the Arts to Augustus* (The Hermitage Museum, Saint Petersburg) and *Triumph of Flora* (Fine Arts Museums of San Francisco)—for Count Heinrich von Brühl, minister of Augustus III of Saxony and Poland. These are sent to Dresden in 1744 (Posse 1931, p. 49).

Commissioned by Carmelites of the Scalzi to paint *Miracle of the Holy House of Loreto* (destroyed; see no. 48a, b). Receives final payment for the work in 1745 (Fogolari 1931, pp. 30–32; Morassi 1962, p. 234; Barcham 1979, p. 430, no. 1).

Receives commission for altarpiece *Martyrdom of Saint John, Bishop of Bergamo* for cathedral, Bergamo, which is installed in 1745 (Pinetti 1931, p. 67, and Zava Boccazzi 1976, pp. 235, 237, 239).

1744
Banquet of Cleopatra (fig. 53), begun for another patron, is purchased by Algarotti for Brühl and sent to Dresden (Posse 1931, pp. 64–65) with *Maecenas Presenting the Arts to Augustus* and *Triumph of Flora*. *Modello* for *Banquet* (no. 19) belongs first to Joseph Smith and later to Algarotti, who gives it away before his death.

Probable date of monochrome frescoes for Sagredo chapel in S. Francesco della Vigna (Barcham 1983, p. 120).

Frescoes commissioned by Piero Barbarigo for Palazzo Barbarigo. Payments begin, and continue in 1745 (Lorenzetti and Planiscig 1934, p. 19).

1745
Probable date of frescoes for Villa Contarini-Pisani at Mira (then Pisani di S. Maria Zobenigo) (see fig. 108), as this is year of marriage of the patron, Vincenzo I Sebastiano Pisani, and Lucrezia Corner (Pavanello 1979, p. 57).

Terminus ante quem of altarpiece *Saints Maximus and Oswald* for SS. Massimo e Osvaldo, Padua, established by stone slab in chapel that gives this year as death date of the patron, priest Giuseppe Cogolo di Thiene.

1746
Members of Scuola Grande dei Carmini make inquiries concerning Tiepolo's intentions for central canvas of its ceiling (Niero 1976–77, p. 382).

1746–47
Terminus ante quem of frescoes in ballroom in Palazzo Labia (see frontis., p. 28, fig. 38), established by drawn copies by German artist Franz Martin Kuen (Würzburg 1992, pp. 111–18).

1747
Date on *Meeting of Antony and Cleopatra* (Museum, Arkangelskoye). In 1751 the *modelli* for this canvas and its pendant, the *Banquet of Cleopatra* (Museum, Arkangelskoye), are in Palazzo della Vecchia, Vicenza (Cochin 1758, p. 181).

1748
Probable date of ceiling canvas *Nobility and Virtue Combating Ignorance* (fig. 52) for Palazzo Dolfin Manin, as site was restructured this year on occasion of wedding of Ludovico Manin and Elisabetta Grimani (Succi 1992, pp. 16–17, 23).

1749
Date on central canvas of ceiling at Scuola Grande dei Carmini.

Commissioned by Ricardo Wall to paint altarpiece *Saint James of Compostella* (no. 37) for chapel of Spanish embassy, London. Painting arrives at embassy in August 1750 but is sent to Madrid in 1751 (Pérez-Sánchez 1977, p. 75).

Commissioned by Canon Antonio di Montegnacco of Udine to paint *Consilium in Arena* (Museo Civico, Udine), possibly carried out by Giandomenico (see Morassi 1962, p. 234, and Gemin and Pedrocco 1993, p. 511 n. 55).

1750
Probable date of ceiling painting for Palazzo Barbaro (no. 21a), as it is the year that the patron, Almoró Barbaro, is elevated to rank of procurator of S. Marco (Aikema 1987a, p. 148).

By May Tiepolo has decided to go to Würzburg to work in Residenz for Prince-Bishop Carl Philipp von Greiffenclau (Kossatz 1996, doc. 7; all documents for the period of Tiepolo's activity in Würzburg are brought together by Kossatz).

Description of Kaisersaal of Residenz, and program for its frescoes, sent to Tiepolo in Venice. This is followed in October by contract for the decoration (Kossatz 1996, docs. 9, 10, 12).

In December Giambattista, Giandomenico, and Lorenzo Tiepolo arrive in Würzburg (Kossatz 1996, doc. 13).

1751
Decoration of ceiling and walls of Kaisersaal begins. In May ceiling is gilded by Ignaz Roth; in July completed ceiling is unveiled (Kossatz 1996, docs. 17, 21, 22).

1752
Date on *Investiture of Bishop Harold as Duke of Franconia* in Kaisersaal.

In July work in Kaisersaal is completed (Kossatz 1996, doc. 24).

In April Tiepolo presents Greiffenclau with *modello* for *Apollo and the Four Continents* (no. 49) for vault over principal staircase of Residenz. In June commission is awarded (Kossatz 1996, doc. 27) and in July decoration begins; fresco is signed and dated 1753.

Tiepolo paints unidentified works for Greiffenclau's sister, Baroness Anna Sofia von Sickingen (Kossatz 1996, doc. 32).

Date on *Fall of the Rebel Angels* and *Assumption of the Virgin* for Hofkapelle of Residenz.

1753
Coriolanus before the Walls of Rome and *Mucius Scaevola before Porsenna* (Martin von Wagner-Museum, Würzburg) painted for Balthasar Neumann before his death in August.

Date on *Adoration of the Magi* executed for Benedictine monastery, Münsterschwarzbach.

In November Tiepolo and his sons leave Würzburg to return home to Venice (Freeden and Lamb 1956, p. 30).

1754
In May *Vision Appearing to Saint John Nepomuk* installed in S. Polo (Gradenigo 1942, p. 11).

In April commissioned to execute frescoes in S. Maria della Visitazione (the Pietà) (no. 50a, b). They are unveiled in August 1755 (Kaley 1980, pp. 20–21, and Howard 1986, pp. 27–28). Pietro Gradenigo follows progress of work in his diary (Gradenigo 1942, pp. 12, 17).

1755
A local chronicler writes that *Martyrdom of Saint Agatha* (no. 38) has "recently" been installed in its altar in S. Agata, Lendinara (Sgarbi 1990, p. 169).

Tiepolo is among painters chosen to compile rules of Academy of Painting and Sculpture, newly founded by Republic of Venice; he is made its first president in 1756 (Dall'Acqua-Giusti 1873, pp. 18, 20).

1756
Dated inscription on altar erected by Vincenzo da Thiene and his wife, Elisabetta Conti, with Tiepolo's *Saint Gaetano da Thiene in Glory* (no. 39) in parish church, Rampazzo.

1757
Dated fresco commissioned by Giustino Valmarana in Foresteria (guesthouse) of Villa Valmarana, outside Vicenza.

Commission for altarpiece *Saint Sylvester Baptizing the Emperor Constantine* for S. Silvestro, Folzano; painting is delivered in 1759 (Molmenti 1909, pp. 152–53).

Frescoes two ceilings in Ca' Rezzonico (no. 25a, b) in honor of marriage of Ludovico Rezzonico and Faustina Savorgnan (Frerichs 1971a, p. 241).

Lends governors of the Pietà six thousand ducats toward the cost of the church's decoration (Urbani de Gheltof 1879, p. 126).

1758
Probable date of frescoes in Palazzo Contarini.

Commission for altarpiece *Saint Thecla Praying for the Plague-Stricken* (see no. 51) for cathedral, Este; the painting is set into place before Christmas 1759 (Molmenti 1909, p. 111).

1759
Date on *Vision of Saint Anne* (Gemäldegalerie Alte Meister, Dresden) for S. Chiara, Cividale dei Friuli.

Frescoes and *Immaculate Conception* altarpiece commissioned by Patriarch Daniele Dolfin (cardinal from 1747) for Oratorio della Purità, Udine (Rizzi 1967, p. 44).

Commission for *Madonna and Child* (Museum of Fine Arts, Springfield, Massachusetts) to be used as model for processional standard for S. Maria Mater Domini (Pallucchini 1944, pp. 16–18).

Cardinal Daniele Dolfin commissions two paintings for S. Marco, Rome; correspondence about them continues through 1760 (see Morassi 1962, p. 236).

1760
Tiepolo presents a painting to King Louis XV of France and receives gifts in exchange (Molmenti 1909, p. 25).

Probable date of frescoes in Palazzo Porto, Vicenza, in honor of marriage of Count Orazio Porto and Lavinia di Lodovico Porto in January 1761 (Menegozzo 1990, p. 118).

Tiepolo's letters to Algarotti and others describe preparations for his frescoes in Villa Pisani, Strà (see no. 52); work there continues throughout 1761 (Fogolari 1942, pp. 36–37).

In December Tiepolo agrees to make a *modello* for frescoes in Palazzo Canossa, Verona; he is working there in September 1761, at time of marriage of Count Giovanni Battista d'Arco and Matilde di Canossa, in whose honor the frescoes were commissioned (Battisti 1960, pp. 78–79, and Gaetani di Canossa 1988, pp. 68–70).

1761

Commission for ceiling painting for audience chamber of Scuola di S. Giovanni Evangelista, a work carried out not by Tiepolo but by Giuseppe Angeli in 1761 (Urbani de Gheltof 1895, pp. 24–25, 62–63).

In a letter principally concerning work at Strà, Tiepolo mentions a ceiling for the court at Moscow (Fogolari 1942, pp. 36–37).

Paints copy (National Gallery of Ireland, Dublin) of Veronese's *Supper in the House of Simon* for Algarotti (Fogolari 1942, p. 37, and Wynne 1986, p. 123).

In September King Charles III charges his quartermaster general in Venice to come to terms with Tiepolo regarding his departure for Spain. In December Tiepolo writes in a letter that he is preparing to leave for Spain (Molmenti 1909, pp. 25–26).

1762

In March Tiepolo writes in a letter that he has finished the *modello* for *Wealth and Benefits of the Spanish Monarchy* (no. 53) for throne room of royal palace in Madrid (Molmenti 1909, pp. 26–27).

From 31 March to 4 June Tiepolo and his sons travel to Madrid (Urbani de Gheltof 1880, p. 171, and Molmenti 1909, p. 41 nn. 15, 29).

When Tiepolo arrives at court of Charles III, he is granted same salary as Corrado Giaquinto and Anton Raphael Mengs (Urbani de Gheltof 1880, p. 174).

1764

Date on fresco *Wealth and Benefits of the Spanish Monarchy* in throne room of royal palace, Madrid.

In August Tiepolo writes in a letter that he is at work on *modelli* for various ceilings, including *Apotheosis of Aeneas* in guardroom and *Apotheosis of the Spanish Monarchy* in queen's *saleta*, royal palace, Madrid. In November 1766 he reports that he is finished in guardroom (Urbani de Gheltof 1879, pp. 24–25, and Whistler 1984, p. 95 n. 69).

1767

Tiepolo offers to remain in Spain in the service of Charles III to paint seven altarpieces for S. Pascual Baylon, under construction at Aranjuez. Prepares *modelli* and begins canvases (see nos. 40a, b, 41a, b) in September. They are completed by August 1769 (Urbani de Gheltof 1880, pp. 177–79, and Whistler 1985a, pp. 323–24).

1769

In a letter Tiepolo voices fears that his Aranjuez paintings were not completely satisfactory; Charles III reassures him on this subject (Urbani de Gheltof 1880, p. 180, and Matilla Tascon 1960, doc. 191).

In September Tiepolo receives commission to execute frescoes for cupola of S. Iledefonso, La Granja (Muller 1977, p. 20), for which he completes a *modello* (National Gallery of Ireland, Dublin). After Tiepolo's death, Francisco Bayeu would be given the assignment.

Tiepolo proposes project for orangery of collegiate church, Aranjuez, and presents drawings showing his ideas; Charles III approves it (Urbani de Gheltof 1880, pp. 181–82).

1770

27 March Tiepolo dies in Madrid; he is buried in S. Martino. The news reaches Venice on 21 April.

When Charles III learns of Tiepolo's death, he has altarpieces prepared for S. Pascual Baylon brought to the church immediately. They are present in the new church for its benediction ceremony in May (Urbani de Gheltof 1880, pp. 182–83, and Whistler 1985a, pp. 324–25).

Charles III decides to replace Tiepolo's altarpieces in S. Pascual Baylon with others by Mengs, Bayeu, and Mariano Salvador de Maella. The substitutions are made in 1775 (Whistler 1985a, pp. 325–26).

CATALOGUE

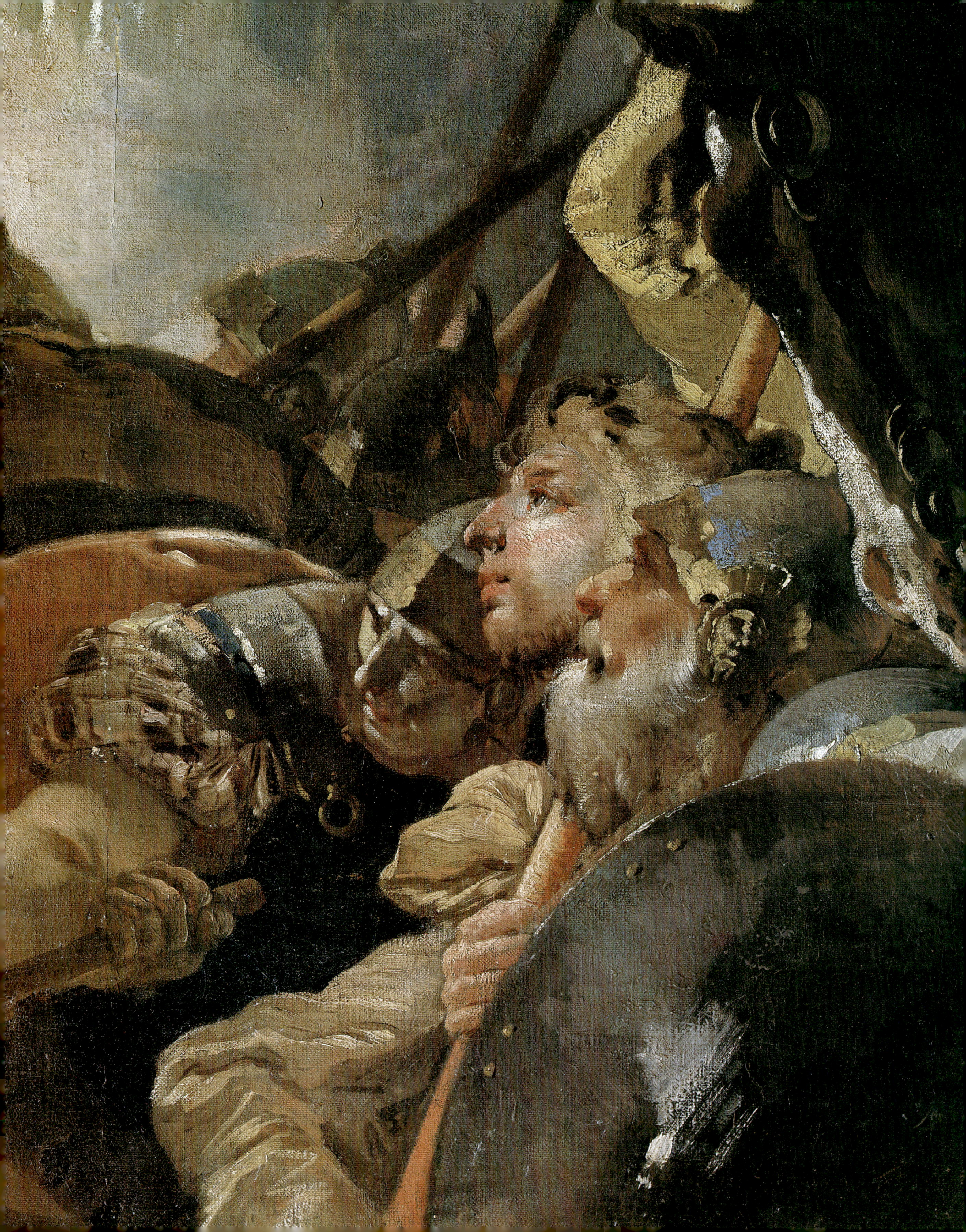

Becoming Tiepolo

FILIPPO PEDROCCO

Giambattista Tiepolo was born on 5 March 1696, in *corte* S. Domenico, located in the populous *sestiere* (ward) of Castello in Venice. Forty-two days later, on 16 April, he was baptized in the cathedral church of S. Pietro.[1] The artist's childhood—as a series of recently discovered documents bears out[2] —was deeply affected by his family's financial straits, which resulted from the sudden death in 1697 of his father, Domenico, a minor entrepreneur who had earned his livelihood in the maritime trade.

By 1710 the fourteen-year-old Giambattista had already been admitted into the workshop of Gregorio Lazzarini. Thanks chiefly to a network of relations established at home and abroad over the course of a fruitful and protracted career, Lazzarini was one of the most successful Venetian artists of the time. What relevance this affiliation with the older painter may have had for the young Giambattista has been much debated. Their association presumably lasted until 1717, when Tiepolo's name was first registered in the *Fraglia*, or guild, of Venetian painters. Antonio Morassi, followed by most other critics, tended to underestimate Lazzarini's lessons, maintaining that the master merely taught the young Tiepolo the "mechanics" of painting—drawing, perspective, and composition—as well as encouraged a somewhat exalted decorative taste, a penchant for luminous backgrounds, and above all "a facility in boldly shifting complex figural groups within vast pictorial compositions":[3] in short, a rather generic instruction that only marginally affected the style of his ingenious pupil.

By contrast, it seems to me that Lazzarini's lesson was far more incisive. Lazzarini was above all an eclectic artist whose career was marked by the most diverse experiences. Trained in the school of Francesco Rosa, who widely and effectively disseminated the dramatic idiom of the Genoese painter Giambattista Langetti, Lazzarini also appears to have been entirely conversant with the great tradition of the Venetian cinquecento, specifically with the examples of Tintoretto and Veronese. The most striking trait Lazzarini's production reveals is his capacity to employ different stylistic modes in accordance with the theme being treated. Such was the legacy the old teacher bequeathed to his pupil: the ability to observe, to assimilate cues and suggestions from the works of others, and to process and elaborate them through his own sensibility.

Certainly, to assert that Tiepolo was an eclectic painter, as the term is commonly understood, would be too simplistic. However, there is no denying that during the initial period of his career he studied with varying degrees of attention works of the most diverse artists in Venice: he looked at pictures by his major contemporaries—from Federico Bencovich to Giambattista Piazzetta, from Sebastiano Ricci to Louis Dorigny, Andrea Celesti, Antonio Bellucci, Antonio Molinari, Giovanni Segala, Nicolò Bambini, and the Lombard Paolo Pagani—as well as paintings by such seicento artists as Giulio Carpioni, Carl Loth, and Antonio Zanchi, and the production of the leading protagonists of the golden age of Venetian painting, most notably Jacopo Tintoretto and Paolo Veronese. In this way—not unlike Lazzarini before him—the young Tiepolo accumulated a prodigious visual heritage that, from the very beginning of his career, he reelaborated and adapted to his own expressive needs.

In reconstructing the career of the young Giambattista, our primary source of information is the thoroughly documented biography of Lazzarini written in 1732 by Vincenzo da Canal, a nobleman from Vicenza.[4] In his valuable little book da Canal devotes several pages to the most brilliant of Lazzarini's many pupils. Not only does he mention Tiepolo's principal production from 1715 to 1730, he also provides some useful insights into the question of the pupil's relationship to his teacher: "Of spirited and fiery temperament, he departed from his [master's] studied manner of painting and, all spirit and fire, embraced a quick and resolute style."[5] Da Canal's words have been variously interpreted and often appropriated to account for Tiepolo's abrupt turn from his teacher's measured, academic style toward the more intensely dramatic modes of Bencovich and Piazzetta. But da Canal more likely intended to emphasize the divergent psychological dispositions of the master and the pupil—almost a personality conflict—manifest in their adoption of distinct pictorial techniques.

This divergence is apparent in even the earliest of Tiepolo's surviving works: the spandrels with paired images of the apostles

Detail, *The Capture of Carthage*, no. 12f

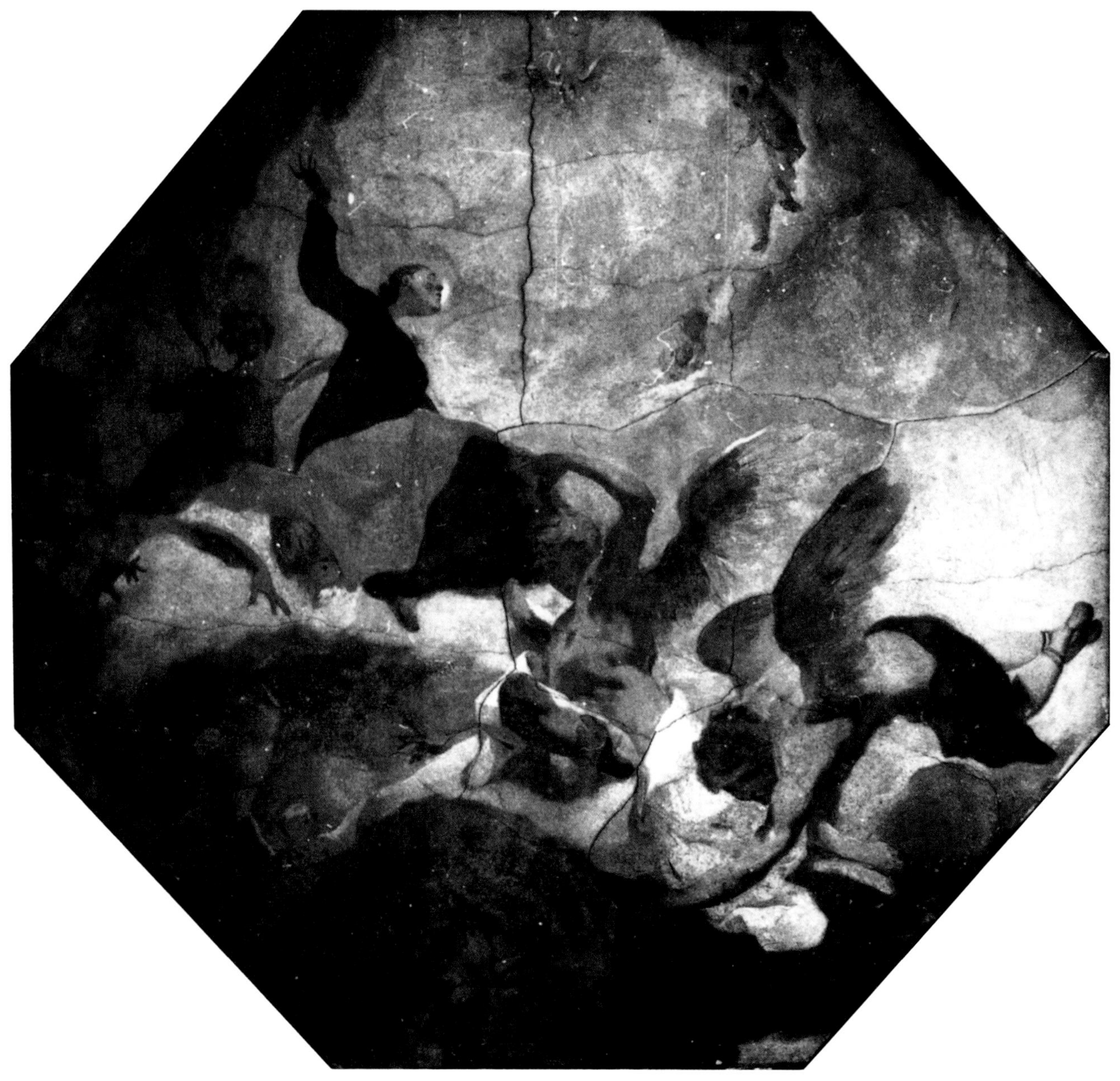

Fig. 14. *The Assumption of the Virgin* (ceiling). Fresco. Parish church, Biadene

(see no. 2a, b) painted between 1715 and 1716 for the Venetian church of the Ospedaletto[6] and the oil sketch of the *Crossing of the Red Sea*. This last work was exhibited on 16 August 1716 at the annual feast of Saint Roch, possibly—as Barcham suggests—on the occasion of a competition for the decoration with Old Testament subjects of the church of SS. Cosma e Damiano on Giudecca.[7] In addition to demonstrating the nervous draftsmanship and the swift and already confident manner of the twenty-year-old artist, these paintings, with their dark tonality and dramatic play of light, testify to his attention to the works of his fellow tenebrists, especially Bencovich and Piazzetta.

On the basis of stylistic affinities, to these paintings recorded by da Canal can be added others of exceptional interest. Among them are a small copper *Memento Mori* (no. 1), characterized by an expressive draftsmanship and a sharp tonality, the *Triumph of David* (Musée du Louvre, Paris), once wrongly ascribed to Giambattista Crosato,[8] as well as a *Soldier before a Sacerdote* (private collection) painted on canvas. This last picture should be considered Giambattista's debut as a history painter. It initiates a long series of works, in my view all datable before 1720 and marked by the presence of more or less elaborate architectural settings within which the painter has staged his characters with theatrical emphasis. These pictures include *Tullia Driving Her Chariot over the Body of Her Father* (formerly Simon collection, Berlin); *Scipio Freeing Massiva(?)* (private collection, Milan), an oil sketch for the large canvas now in The Walters Art Gallery, Baltimore (no. 4); as well as *Esther and Mordecai before Ahasuerus* (Mazoh collection, New York), close in date to the *Abraham Banishing Hagar(?)* (no. 8), which once bore a date transcribed as 1717 or 1719.

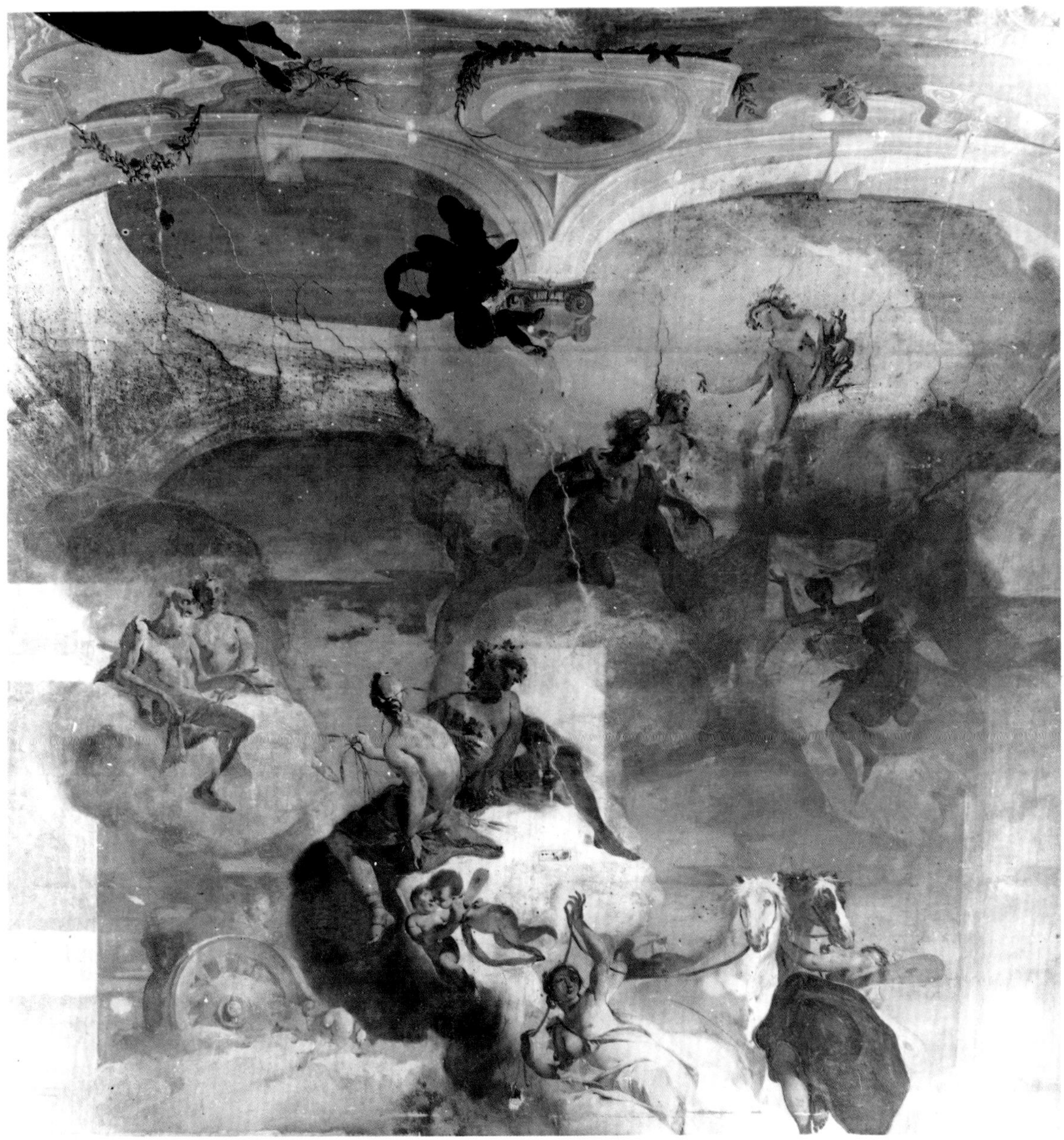

Fig. 15. Detail, *The Myth of Phaethon*. Fresco. Villa Baglioni, Massanzago

Da Canal records that at the time he produced the series of apostles for the Ospedaletto, Giambattista "was painter to Doge Corner at S. Polo in whose lavish residence he oversaw the hanging of paintings and also made many overdoors with portraits and fine pictures."[9] In the nineteenth century the Palazzo Corner in S. Polo was stripped of its furnishings, but two of the portraits mentioned by da Canal (no. 3a, b) were recently rediscovered by Martini.[10] These truly surprising works are warm in color, with light tones strongly reminiscent of the paintings of Ricci. The portraits, which depict Doge Giovanni II Corner (ca. 1647–1722) and an ancestor, Marco Corner (ca. 1286–1368), were clearly conceived as overdoors. Despite their lighter tonality, they display the same nervous draftsmanship and hard contours with the same rich brushwork typical of Tiepolo's other early works.

These portraits are datable to about 1716, and at this time Giambattista made his debut as a frescoist, with the decoration of the ceiling of the parish church of Biadene, near Treviso, in which he represented the Assumption of the Virgin (fig. 14).[11] It should be pointed out that Giambattista learned fresco painting from Lazzarini, who, as da Canal attests, was versed in this technique, having used it in the decoration of a room in Pietro Liberi's palace in Venice.[12]

Tiepolo's exceptional decorative instinct emerges clearly in the frescoes he executed about 1719–20 for Giambattista Baglioni, who had recently entered the ranks of the Venetian aristocracy. Giambattista painted the *Triumph of Aurora* on the ceiling and the *Myth of Phaethon* on the walls of the main hall of this wealthy publisher's villa in Massanzago, near Padua (fig. 15): his frescoes cover the room, illusionistically collapsing

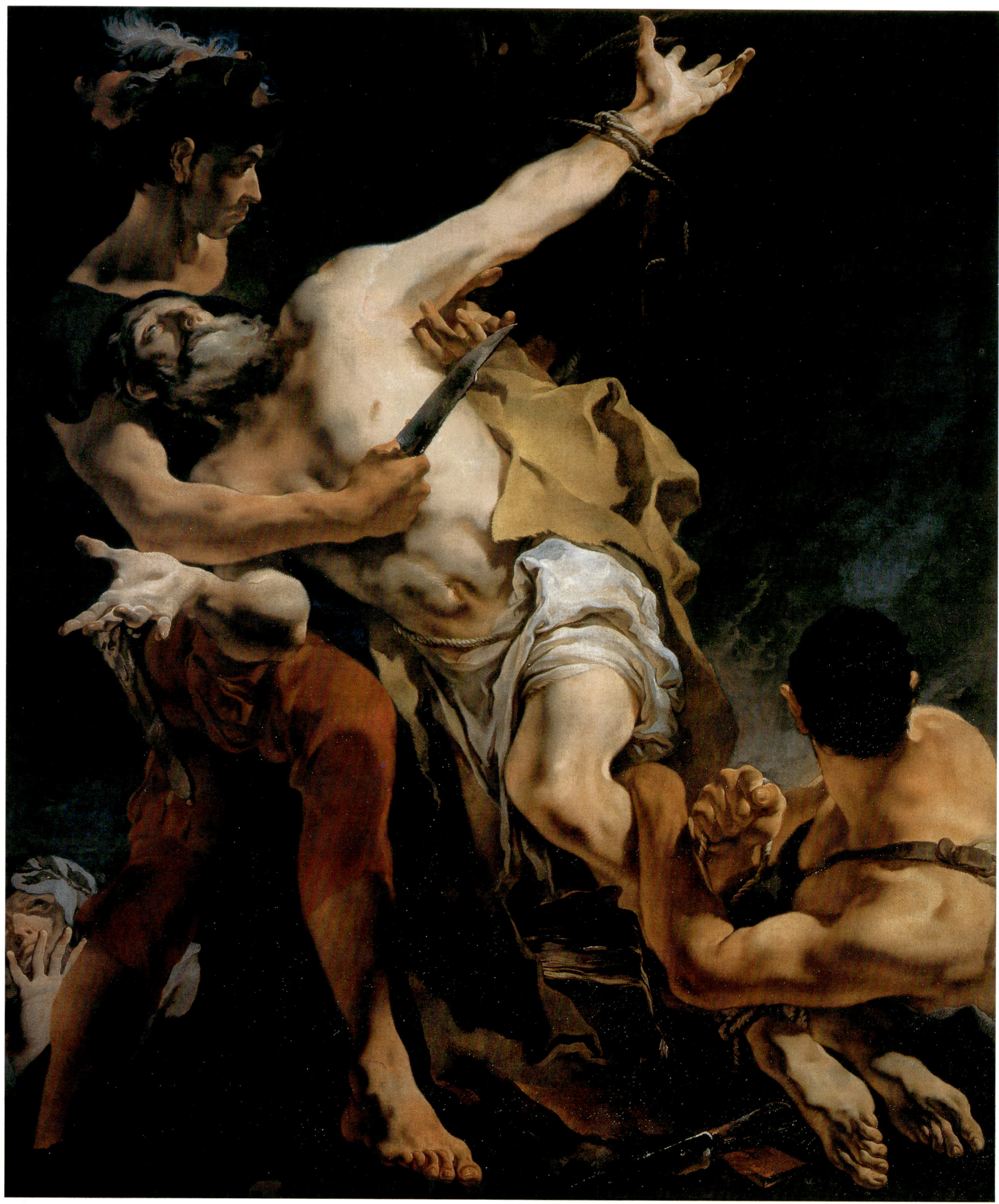

Fig. 16. *The Martyrdom of Saint Bartholomew*. Oil on canvas. S. Stae, Venice

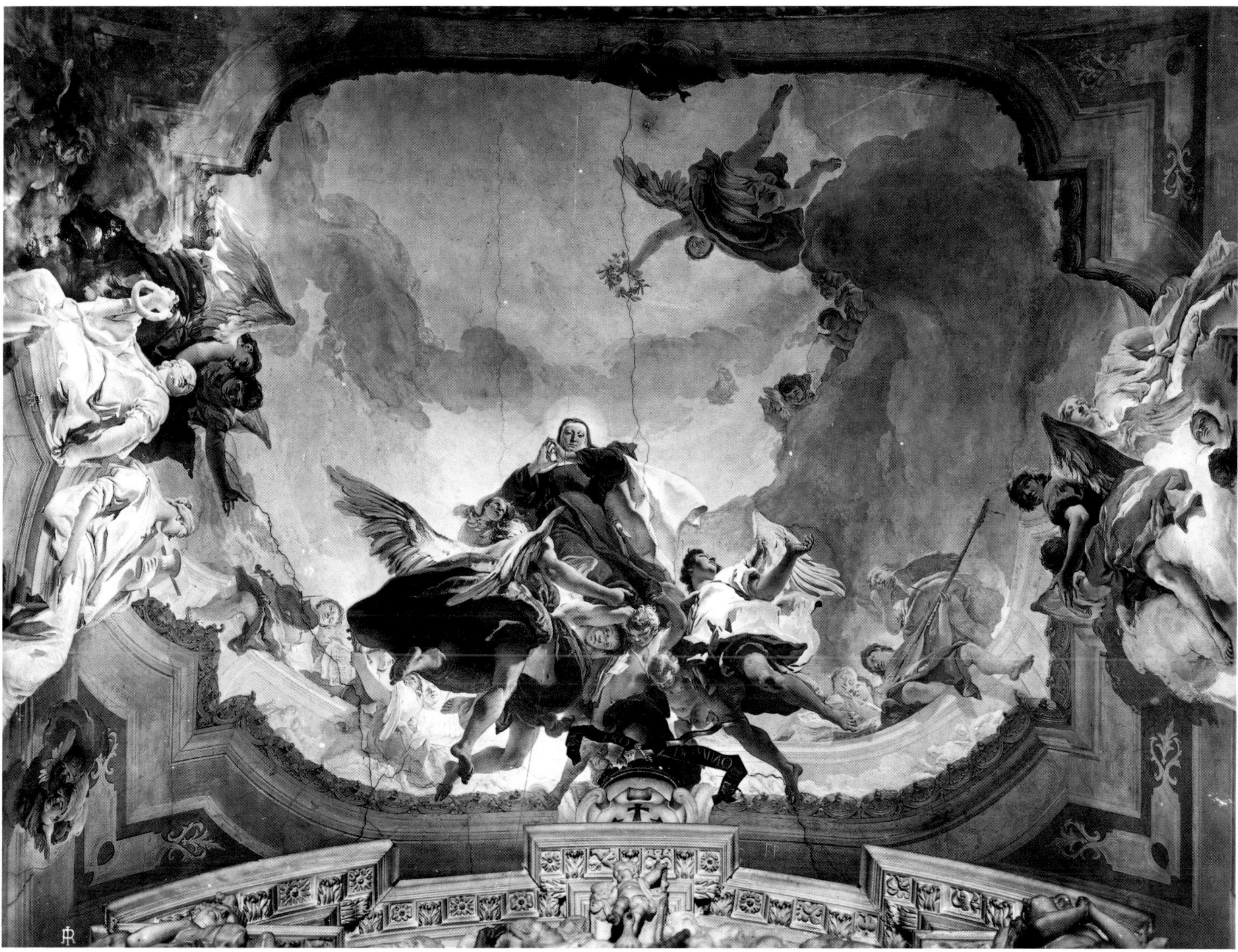

Fig. 17. *The Apotheosis of Saint Teresa* (ceiling). Fresco. S. Maria di Nazareth (the Scalzi), Venice

the ceiling and walls in a way that foreshadows a decorative mode that would recur throughout his long career and that his patrons found especially congenial. As Mariuz rightly maintains, "With the execution of this work Tiepolo fully realized his own talent and vocation as a peerless frescoist."[13] Thenceforth the artist would receive numerous commissions for decorative frescoes. To the years immediately following the Massanzago undertaking we can plausibly assign the *Saint Jerome with the Cross* (sacristy of S. Giovanni Crisostomo, Venice), recently published by Mariuz and Pavanello as a work of about 1721 by Giambattista,[14] as well as the *Apotheosis of Saint Teresa* at S. Maria degli Scalzi, Venice (fig. 17), to my way of thinking datable about 1722 (but see proposals in this catalogue for a date as late as about 1730). In both works the sculptural effect of the figures and the prominent use of chiaroscuro are strongly evocative of Piazzetta's formulations. Quite different, however, is the style that Tiepolo adopted for the much-damaged *Saint Lucy in Glory*, dated 1722 (parish church of Vascon), in which he looked, instead, to the example of Dorigny.[15] The suite of four mythological scenes in the Gallerie dell'Accademia, Venice (no. 6a, b, figs. 28, 29), dates from about 1720–22 and belongs to a group of works on mythological subjects that, while still strongly plastic, already reveals a noticeable chromatic lightening.

In 1722 Giambattista and eleven other artists, including Ricci, Piazzetta, Giovanni Antonio Pellegrini, Antonio Balestra, and Lazzarini, were summoned to provide a series of paintings on the lives of the apostles for the church of S. Stae, Venice, in accordance with the will of the patrician Andrea Stazio; although the canvases were to decorate the nave, they were ultimately transferred to the presbytery. Each man was charged with executing one painting in the sequence, and the picture assigned to the young Giambattista was the *Martyrdom of Saint Bartholomew* (fig. 16). Even on this occasion the youthful painter demonstrated his ravenous appetite for extracting figurative elements from the work of other artists: the thug

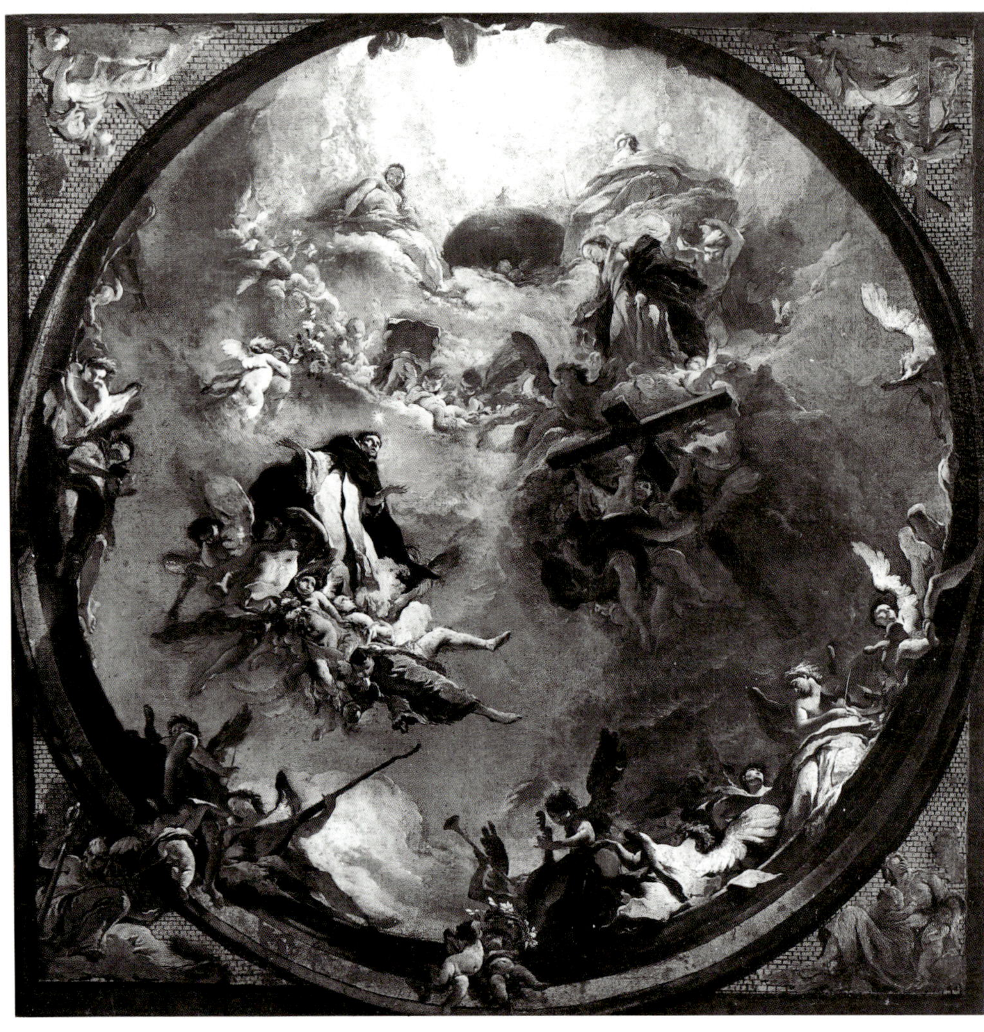

Fig. 18. *Saint Dominic in Glory*. Oil on canvas. Gallerie dell'Accademia, Venice

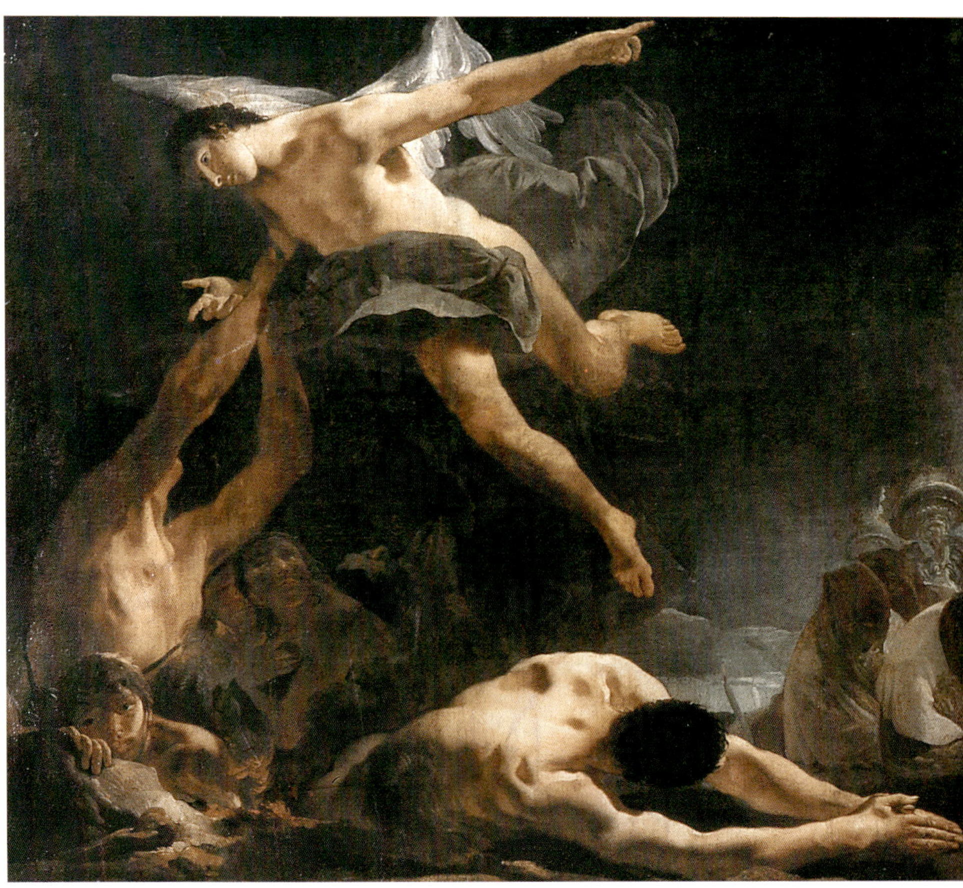

Fig. 19. *Madonna of Mount Carmel*. Oil on canvas. Pinacoteca di Brera, Milan

on the right of his picture is the reverse of the figure of the servant in Francesco Solimena's *Rebecca and Eleazer* (Gallerie dell'Accademia, Venice), which during the eighteenth century belonged to Giambattista Baglioni, the patron of Tiepolo's frescoes at Massanzago. Yet the expressive vigor, dramatic tension, and powerful chiaroscuro that distinguish the *Martyrdom of Saint Bartholomew*—where the figure of the saint, brilliantly lit, emerges forcefully from the murky background—signal that Giambattista had by now developed his own unmistakable style. Quite comparable to the S. Stae canvas is the small *Saint Dominic in Glory* (Gallerie dell'Accademia, Venice), painted before the end of March 1723 for a competition to decorate the ceiling of the chapel of Saint Dominic in the church of SS. Giovanni e Paolo—a competition won by Piazzetta.

Meanwhile Tiepolo must have completed the greater part of the vast *Madonna of Mount Carmel* (fig. 19), a canvas the pharmacist Giacomo Tonini had commissioned for one of the side chapels in the church of S. Aponal, Venice, in 1721, but which was not set in place until 1727. This grand painting, dismantled in 1810 and later transferred to the Pinacoteca di Brera, Milan, clearly displays the attributes of Tiepolo's style of the early 1720s. As Barcham suggests, Tiepolo probably began working on this painting as soon as it was commissioned, leaving only the right side incomplete.[16] This he finished five or six years later, with the execution of the figures of the prophet Elijah and some cherubs.

Another large painting that can be assigned to the same period was commissioned by yet another pharmacist—in this case one whose name is not known but whose portrait Tiepolo included in an oval frame in the lower left corner of the canvas: the *Crucifixion* for the church of S. Martino on the island of Burano, datable to 1722–25 (fig. 92). The Burano canvas is considerably brighter than the *Madonna of Mount Carmel* and in this way foreshadows the series of paintings that Giambattista executed for a room in the Ca' Zenobio, near the Carmini, and which da Canal cites as "one of his earliest undertakings."[17]

This cycle—centered on the life of Queen Zenobia—originally comprised four large paintings, which were taken down and sold after Alvise Zenobio's death in 1817. One canvas, *Queen Zenobia Addressing Her Soldiers* (fig. 20), is now at the National Gallery of Art, Washington, D.C.; another, *Queen Zenobia and Aurelius* (fig. 21), is at the Museo del Prado, Madrid; and the *Triumph of Aurelius* belongs to the Galleria Sabauda, Turin. Of the fourth, which probably depicted a hunting scene that included Zenobia and her husband, Odenato, there survive only two fragments: a *Hunter with a Deer* and a *Hunter on Horseback* (Crespi collection, Milan). The series—which Shapley and Knox have thoughtfully reconstructed[18]—represents a considerable advance in the evolution of Tiepolo's style toward an increasingly brighter palette.

The Ca' Zenobio undertaking coincided with the definitive establishment of Giambattista's reputation in Venice, as the

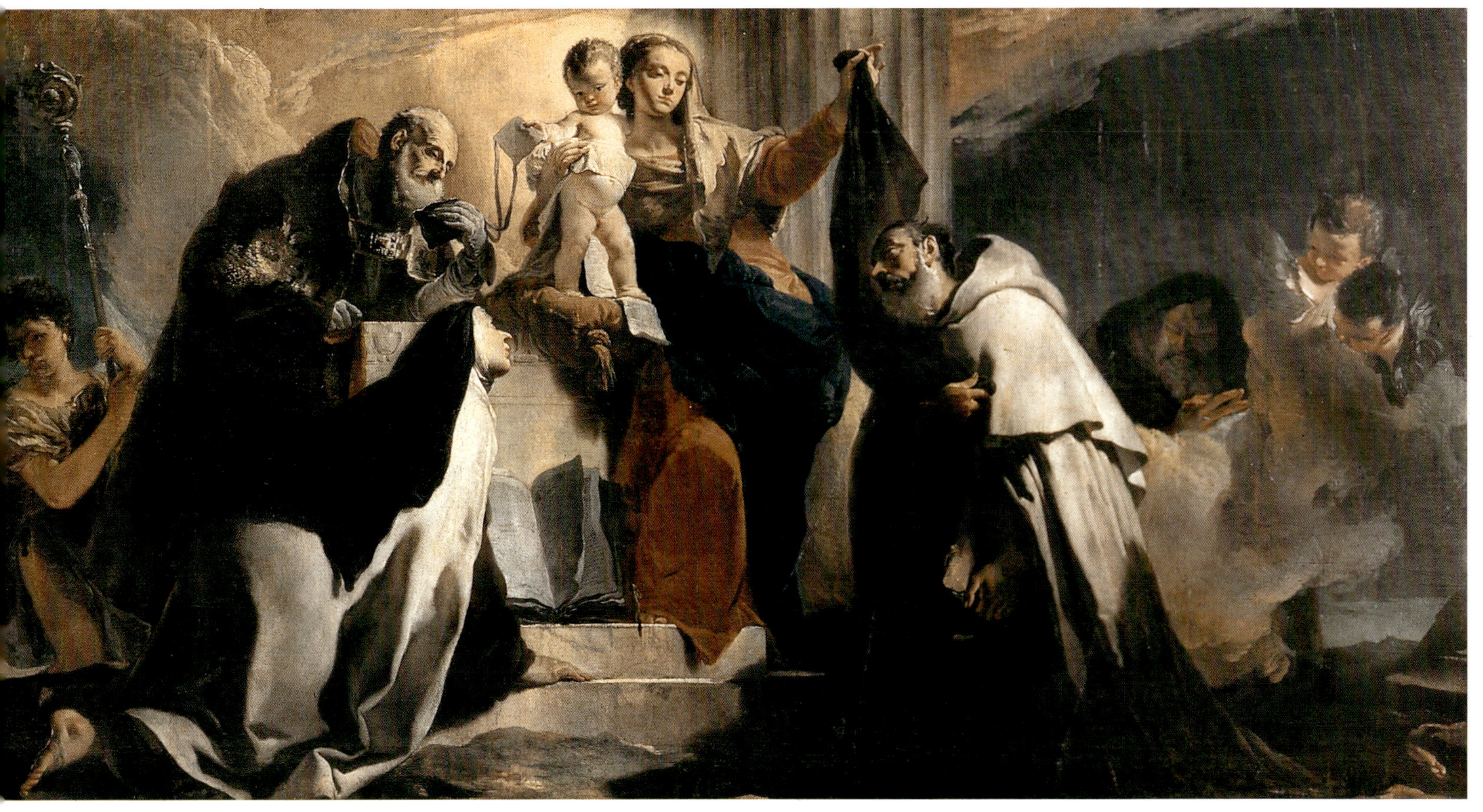

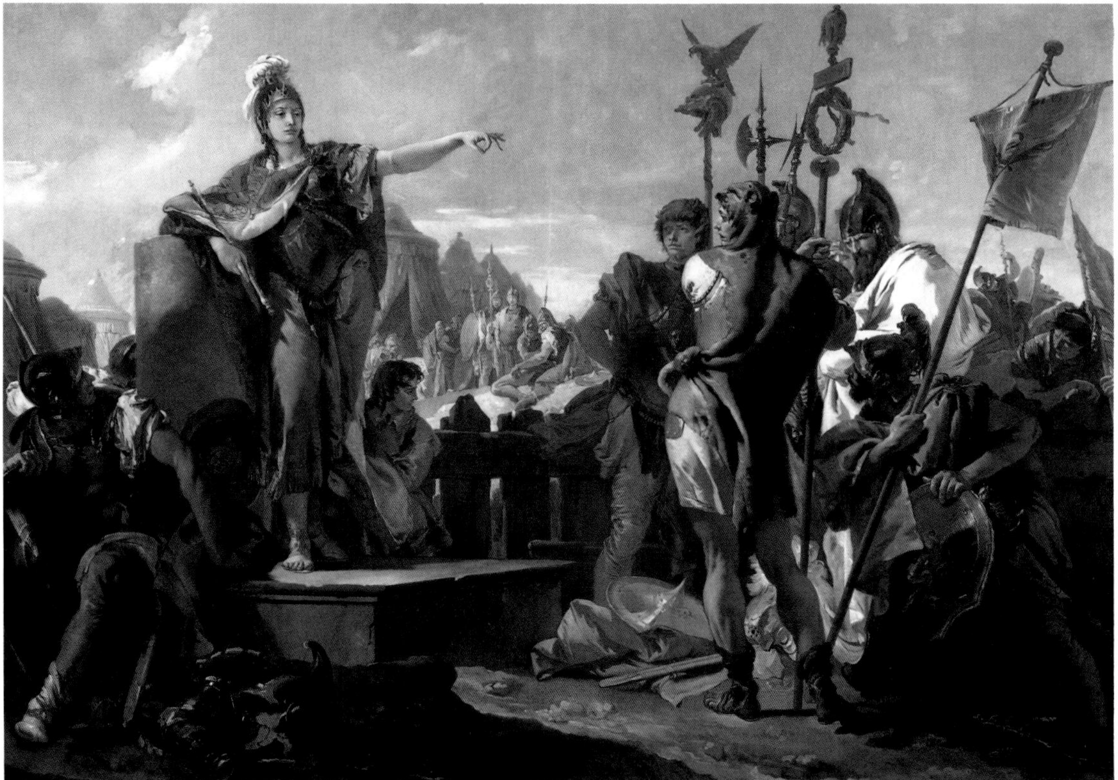

Fig. 20. *Queen Zenobia Addressing Her Soldiers*. Oil on canvas. National Gallery of Art, Washington, D.C., Samuel H. Kress Collection

large number of commissions that he subsequently received indicates. Perhaps in 1724, for example, he was called on to execute the last in the series of spandrels in the church of the Ospedaletto—where he had already worked from 1715 to 1716—and painted the *Sacrifice of Isaac* (no. 5). Although most critics, based on a misreading of da Canal's text, consider it an early work, the canvas seems more likely to have originated at this time:[19] not only is its style perfectly consistent with that of such paintings of the same period as the *Martyrdom of Saint Bartholomew* in S. Stae, which is dated 1722, but also its date can be linked to a document of 1724 published by Muraro.[20]

The execution of this second project at the Ospedaletto marks the beginning of Giambattista's collaboration with the Ticino-born architect Domenico Rossi (1657–1737), an association that would prove exceptionally fruitful. But beginning in 1724 their association became especially close: it was Rossi who conducted the renovation of the Palazzo Sandi in S. Angelo, Venice, on the ceiling of whose principal room Giambattista painted the *Triumph of Eloquence* about 1724–25 (fig. 22); the same architect worked in the cathedral of Udine, where Tiepolo painted the frescoes for the chapel of the Holy Sacrament in 1726 (fig. 23); and Rossi was also responsible for the restoration of the residence of the patriarchs of Aquileia, the Arcivescovado (prior to 1751 the Patriarchal Palace) in Udine, in which the painter completed the superb frescoes in the well of the grand staircase and in rooms on the *piano nobile* (figs. 24–26) between 1726 and 1729. Temanza—whose testimony appears to be entirely credible—attributes to Rossi as well the eighteenth-century renovation of the Ca' Dolfin in S. Pantalon, whose reception room accommodated the ten large canvases treating episodes of Roman history (no. 12a–g, figs. 33–35) that Giambattista painted concurrently with the frescoes of the Arcivescovado in Udine.[21]

Such were the major decorative projects that Giambattista undertook in the second half of the 1720s, a period in which the painter's style evolved significantly toward that mastery of light, that radiant luminosity that would definitively characterize his production of the 1730s. It is difficult to determine to what extent Tiepolo's association with Rossi influenced this stylistic development, since we know little about the architect except that he was an artist of solid Baroque culture who nevertheless was not unresponsive to the refinements of the Rococo.[22] Certainly, though, an interesting index to his taste is provided by the fact that the buildings he designed were often decorated by the Frenchman Dorigny, one of the artists in the Veneto who distanced himself furthest from the tenebrists, preferring a light palette with clear tones and a style of emphatic formal elegance. It is quite conceivable that in these years of close contact with Rossi, Giambattista's art developed at least partially in response to the architect's suggestions.

The decoration of the Palazzo Sandi was undertaken about 1724–25, that is to say, concurrently with the completion of

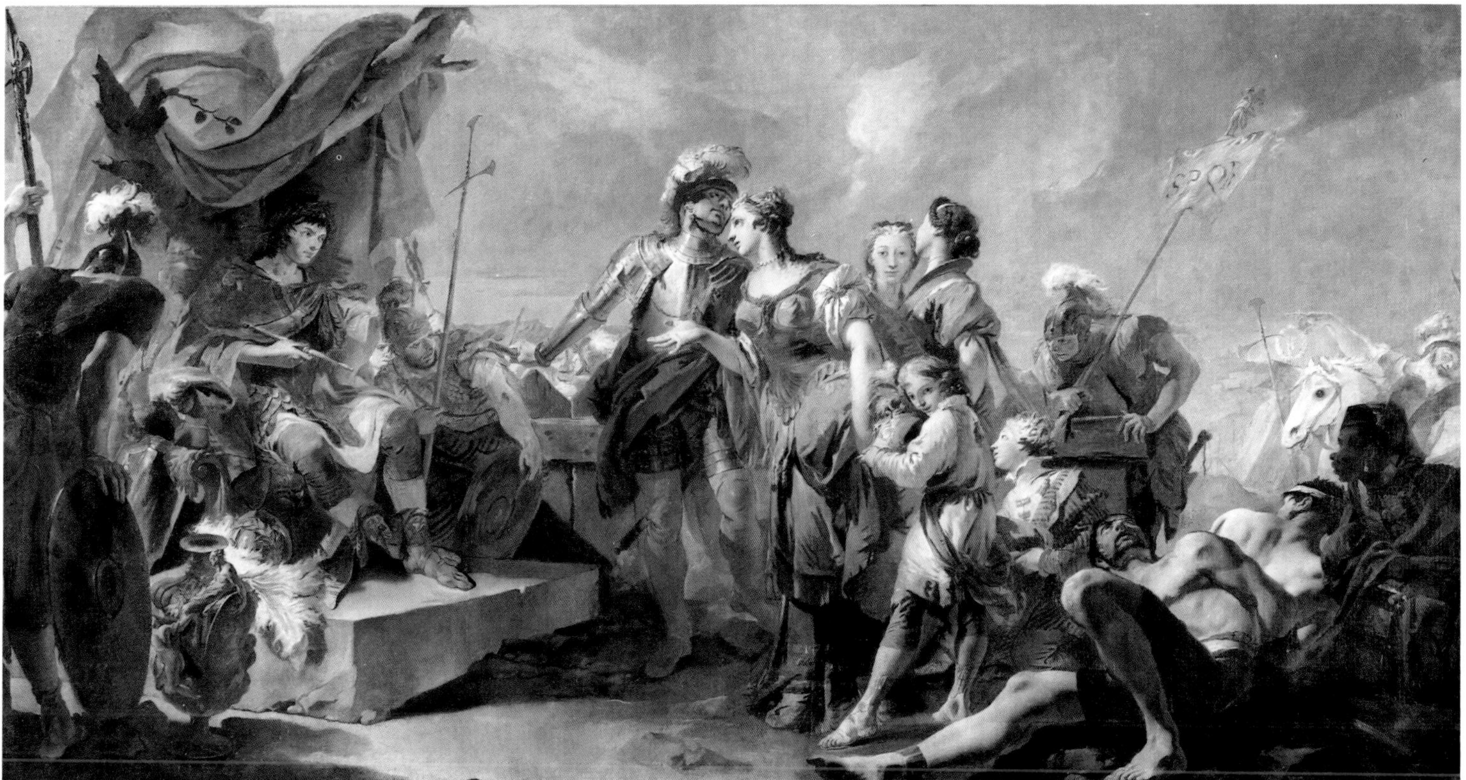

Fig. 21. *Queen Zenobia and Aurelius.* Oil on canvas. Museo del Prado, Madrid

Rossi's renovation of the building. Tiepolo's contribution—a fresco on the ceiling of the *salone* and three canvases with mythological subjects (no. 9a, b, fig. 30)—closely recalls some of the greatest decorations of the seventeenth century, particularly Luca Giordano's ceiling in the Palazzo Medici-Riccardi in Florence. When Tiepolo was engaged at the Palazzo Sandi, he had never traveled outside the borders of the Republic of Venice; however, it is possible that he had come to know of such works through Dorigny, who, in the course of his journeys to Italy's leading centers, had had the opportunity to study and appreciate firsthand the production of the foremost Baroque decorative painters. Tiepolo's rendering of the mythological episodes is intense and dramatic in its violent chiaroscural contrasts and "powerful areas of violently foreshortened figures wedged into their spaces by a strong backlighting," while the deities at the center are light in tonality and appear almost to be absorbed by the concentric circles of clouds.[23]

The typical compositional structure of Tiepolo's large decorative projects is defined by this fresco: subsequently, Giambattista would often resort to similar schemes, in which many figures are arrayed along the outer border of the scene, while the center is occupied by the vast blue expanse of the heavens, variously peopled by mythological deities, heroes, or sacred figures. The Palazzo Sandi ceiling is extremely important in another respect as well: as has recently been observed, this undertaking signals Tiepolo's definitive alignment with the tradition of Paolo Veronese.[24] This alignment is evident in the use of colored shadows, for example, in the face of the child who looks at the viewer in the scene showing Amphion. Veronese's lesson emerges even more clearly, however, in the canvas the *Discovery of Achilles* (fig. 30), in both compositional structure, with the main figures arranged in the foreground against a landscape, and in the artist's insistence on the coloristic and decorative effects of the costly silks and damasks, with their rich sheen. In fact, a specific Veronesian model for the *Ulysses* can be identified: the *Finding of Moses*, a large canvas that came to Dresden in 1747 from the Venetian residence of the Grimani.

Giambattista's ambitious undertaking in Udine began in 1726. In June of that year the administrators of the Confraternity of the Most Holy Sacrament assigned the fresco decoration of their newly refurbished chapel in the cathedral to the "renowned and illustrious painter" Tiepolo.[25] The artist faced a challenging task, for he had to work on a semioctagonal area of conspicuously vertical proportions. In order to compensate for the peculiarity of the architecture, he emphasized the monumentality of the figures and focused on the contrast between the monochromatic lower section, in which he painted the *Sacrifice of Isaac* and the *Dream of Abraham,* and the vault, where brightly colored angels with wings spread wide are disposed beneath a trompe-l'oeil oculus open to a blue sky (fig. 23).

Critics now agree that it was also in 1726 that Giambattista began painting the fresco above the stairwell and the rooms of

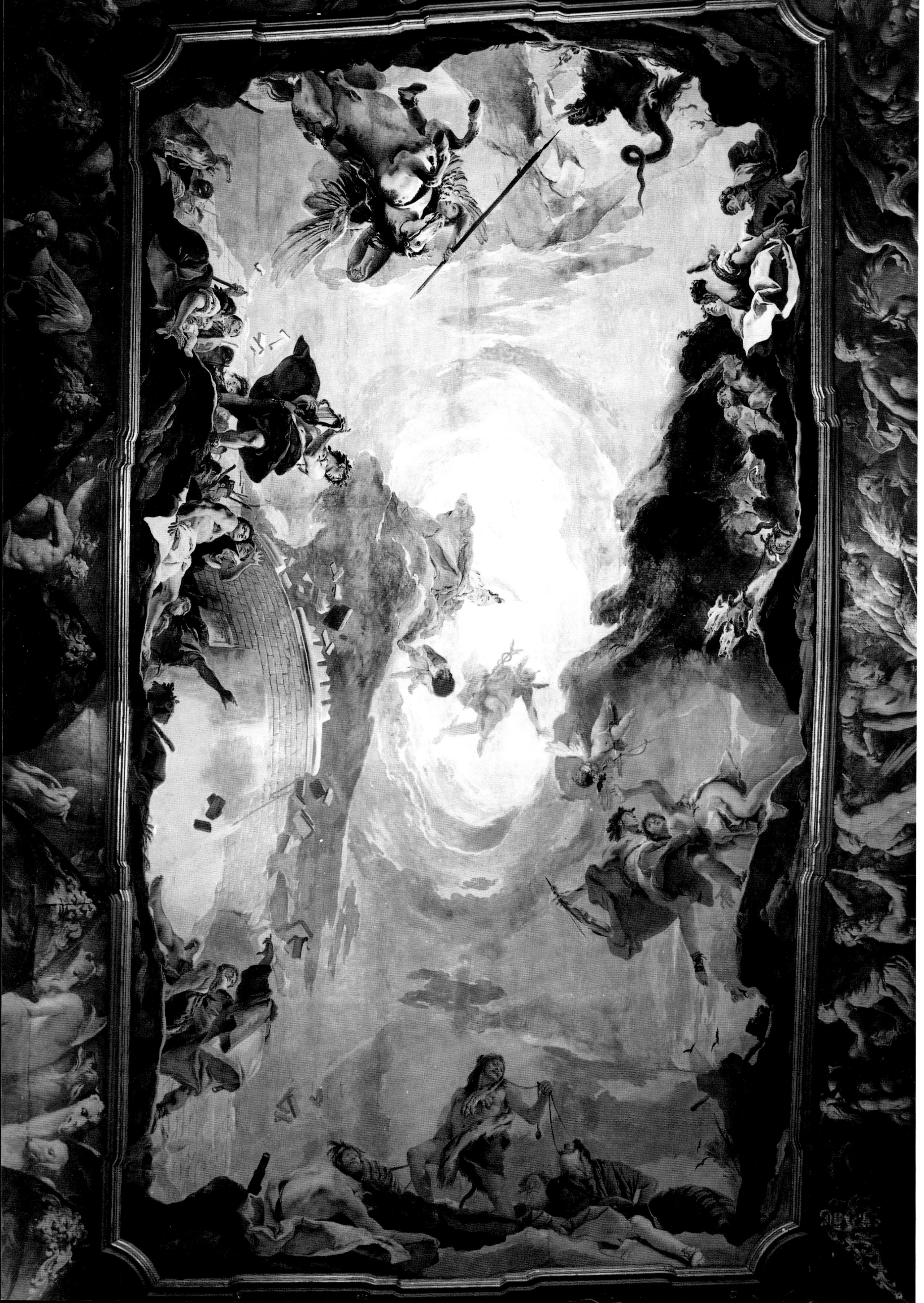

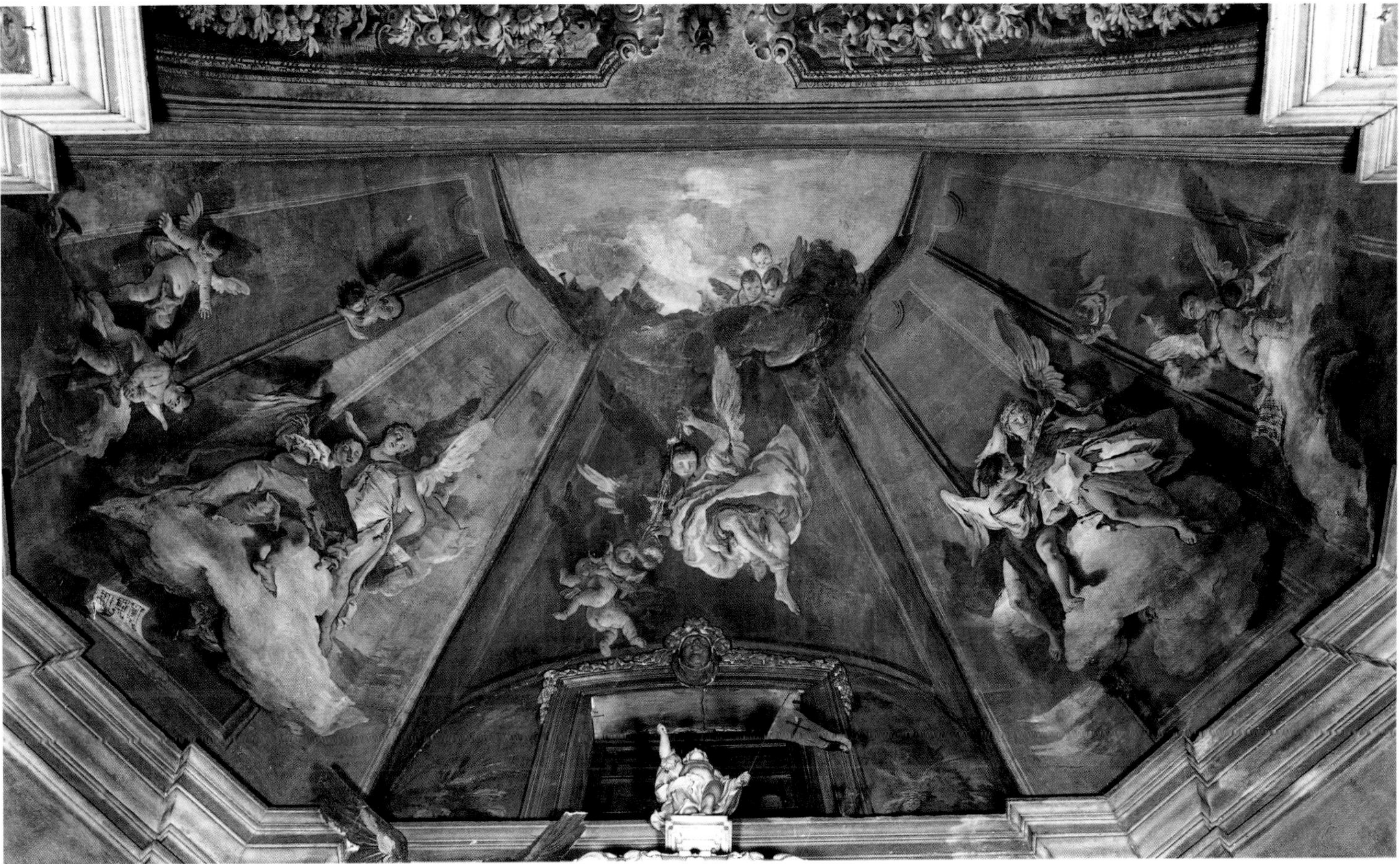

Fig. 23. Detail, *Music-Making Angels* (vault). Fresco. Chapel of the Holy Sacrament, cathedral, Udine

the *piano nobile* of the Arcivescovado in Udine. (Previously they had dated the Arcivescovado frescoes earlier.) This new project was commissioned by the reigning patriarch, the Venetian Dionisio Dolfin. Refurbishing of the cinquecento palace, initiated in 1708, had only recently been completed under the supervision of Rossi. As contemporary documents show, construction of the staircase began in 1725; thus it appears probable, since Giambattista was present in Udine in the summer of 1726 to paint the frescoes in the cathedral, that he worked on the ceiling over the staircase immediately thereafter.

He frescoed the *Fall of the Rebel Angels* in the central section of the latter decoration and a series of monochromatic scenes from the Book of Genesis in eight lateral divisions. In the central scene the archangel Michael hurls himself toward the rebels, who tumble down precipitously. From below, the fresco appears compressed by the monumental architecture; perhaps in order to improve this visual effect, the painter attempted to expand the pictorial space illusionistically by modeling parts of the falling angels in stucco over the heavy frame.

After completing the ceiling over the staircase, Tiepolo proceeded to fresco three rooms on the *piano nobile*: the gallery (figs. 24, 25), the Ecclesiastical Tribunal, or Sala Rossa (fig. 26), and the throne room. Contemporary documents and accounts indicate that Tiepolo must have worked in the gallery in 1727 and in the Sala Rossa in 1728, concluding his task the following year with the execution of a number of portraits of patriarchs in the throne room.

Fig. 22. *The Triumph of Eloquence* (ceiling). Fresco. Palazzo Sandi, Venice

In the gallery—a narrow corridor that receives light from five windows—Giambattista painted episodes from the lives of the ancient patriarchs, drawing inspiration from Genesis. The principal scenes, *Abraham Visited by Angels*, *Rachel Hiding the Idols from Her Father, Laban* (fig. 25) and the *Angel Appearing to Sarah*, are enclosed by lavish trompe-l'oeil frames and separated by monochromatic feigned statues of prophetesses in niches. The decoration of the ceiling is simpler: the central scene, the *Sacrifice of Isaac*, is framed by an irregularly shaped illusionistic molding and flanked by two oval frescoes representing Hagar in the Desert and the Dream of Jacob. The Ferrarese specialist in illusionistic architecture, or *quadratura*, Girolamo Mengozzi Colonna, played an important role in the realization of this magnificent ensemble. Mengozzi Colonna had probably collaborated with Tiepolo before they worked at Udine and would become his loyal associate in nearly all

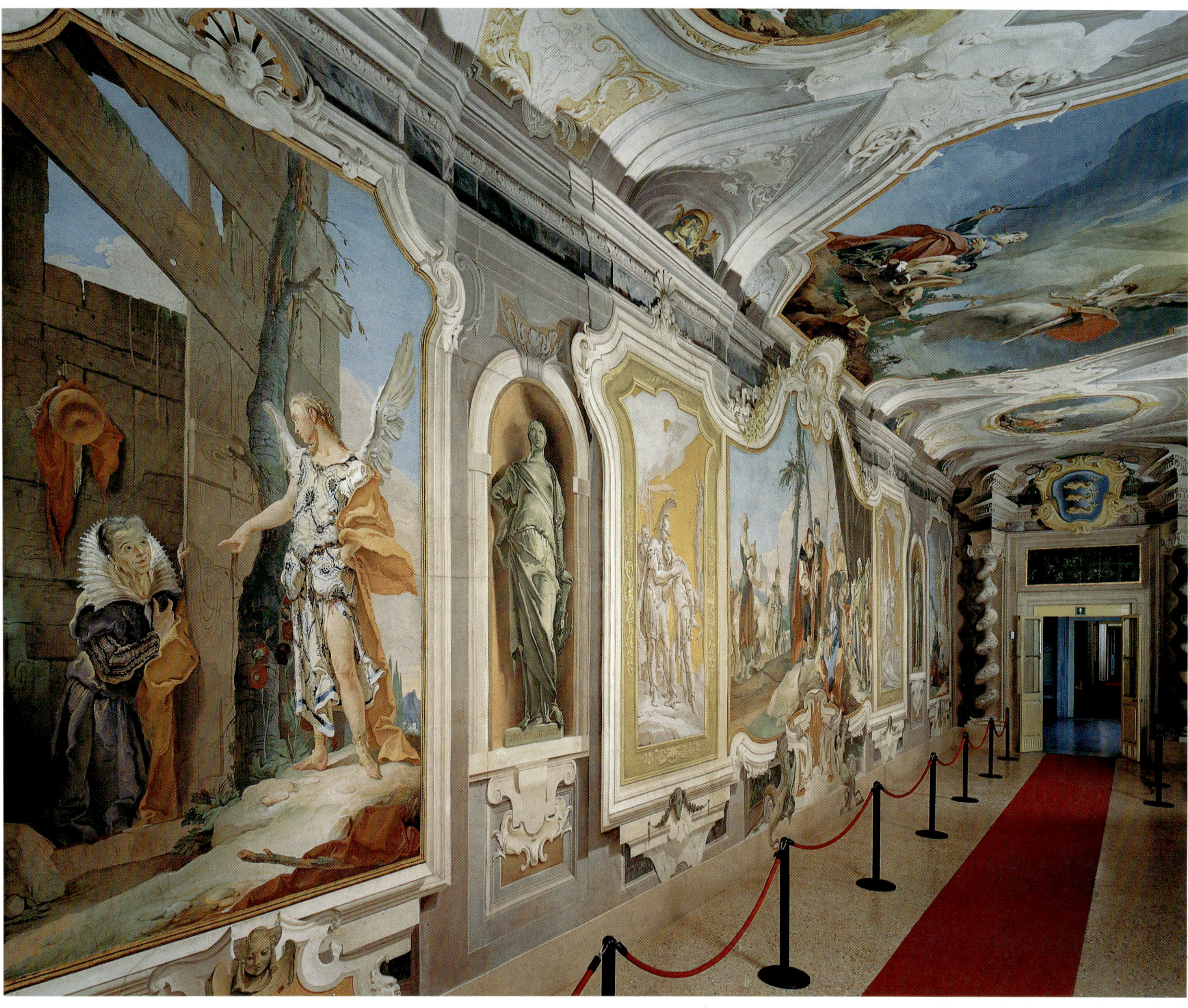

Fig. 24. View of gallery. Fresco. Arcivescovado (Patriarchal Palace), Udine.

the major decorative projects Tiepolo undertook in Venice and throughout the Veneto.

Tiepolo's definitive alignment with the art of Veronese is apparent in the Arcivescovado frescoes. It was an alignment that developed gradually and began with a general and occasional brightening of colors, then proceeded to the adoption of colored shadows—evident in the Palazzo Sandi decorations—and culminated, at Udine, with the use of pure complementary colors: in other words, with that interaction of light and color that, from a technical standpoint, constitutes the key attribute of Veronese's art. This progressive alignment with Veronese's style was certainly influenced by a number of Tiepolo's contemporaries, such as Dorigny, Ricci, and Pellegrini. Nonetheless, Tiepolo's capacity for assimilating his predecessors' lessons was such that he far surpassed his fellow artists in the renewal of the example of Veronese, so much so that, as his contemporaries recognized, he truly became a new Veronese—"Veronese redivivo."

The frescoes in the Arcivescovado gallery are not only dominated by a lush and luminous color; they also display a new, balanced approach to narrative distinguished by an unprecedented realism, notable especially in the superb landscape backgrounds; this too is indebted to the study of Veronese's work.

On the ceiling of the Sala Rossa, Tiepolo painted the *Judgment of Solomon* (fig. 26)—appropriate enough for a space used as a civil and ecclesiastical tribunal. The compositional scheme seems already to foreshadow such masterpieces as the *Investiture of Bishop Harold* in the Residenz at Würzburg. In the corners of the ceiling are framed compartments with the prophets Isaiah, Jeremiah, Ezekiel, and Daniel. Less interesting, partly on account of their poor state of conservation, are the portraits in the throne room, which certainly are not all by Giambattista.

Probably during the winter months of his involvement at Udine, Tiepolo painted the cycle of ten large canvases that, until 1872, were installed in the reception hall of the Ca' Dolfin in Venice. The series was commissioned by Patriarch Dionisio's brothers, Daniele III and Daniele IV, both of whom were actively involved in the civic affairs of the Republic of Venice, the former as an ambassador, the latter as a military leader who had valiantly fought the Turks at the side of Francesco Morosini in the Peloponnese. The cycle had a patently celebratory aim: to exemplify in episodes of Roman history drawn from Lucius Annaeus Florus's *Epitomae de Tito Livio bellorum* the Dolfin brothers' own patriotic fervor. Tiepolo's art attains full maturity in these canvases, embodied above all in an effect of diffuse luminosity, obtained by means of a masterly use of complementary colors. The only dated canvas in the series is the *Triumph of Marius* (no. 12e), in which the medallion hanging from one of the upraised staffs bears the inscription 1729. This date unmistakably refers to the year this important decorative undertaking was concluded and thus corroborates the hypothesis that the Dolfin cycle and the frescoes of the Arcivescovado in Udine were executed contemporaneously.

During the second half of the 1720s Giambattista also painted a conspicuous number of canvases, often of small format. Some are veritable jewels by virtue of their magnificent qualities of color and their refined compositional invention: for example, the *Temptation of Saint Anthony* (Pinacoteca di Brera, Milan), characterized by strikingly free and lively handling of paint; the ironic *Venus with a Mirror* (formerly Gerli collection, Milan), almost a reprise of Titianesque models; and the *Saint Luigi Gonzaga in Glory* (fig. 61), probably painted on the occasion of the saint's canonization in 1726.

Another masterpiece among Giambattista's small canvases is *Apelles Painting Campaspe* (no. 11). The subject of this picture is inspired by a passage from Pliny: Apelles portrays Campaspe, the mistress of Alexander the Great, in the famous leader's

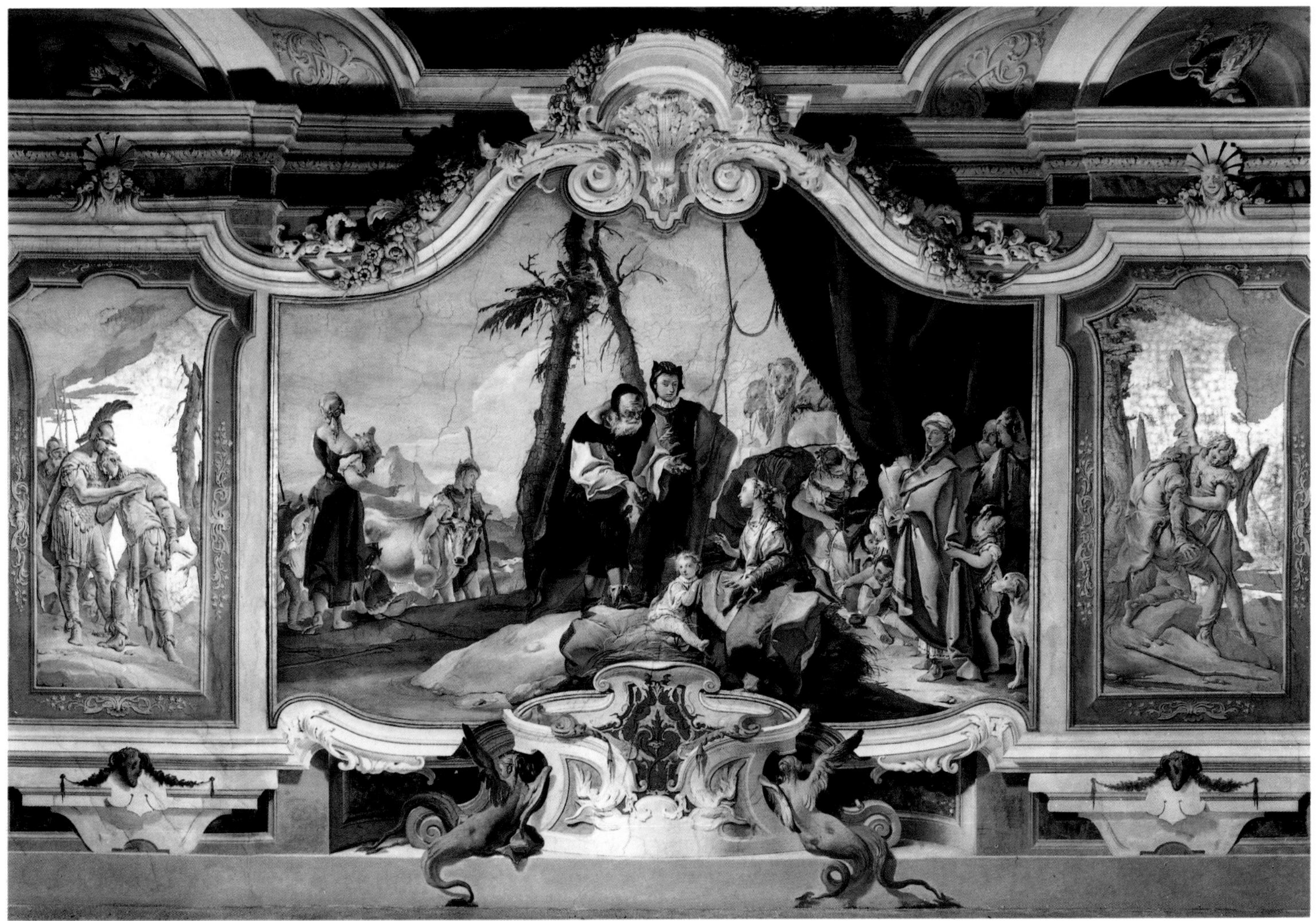

Fig. 25. *Rachel Hiding the Idols from Her Father, Laban*. Fresco. Arcivescovado (Patriarchal Palace), Udine

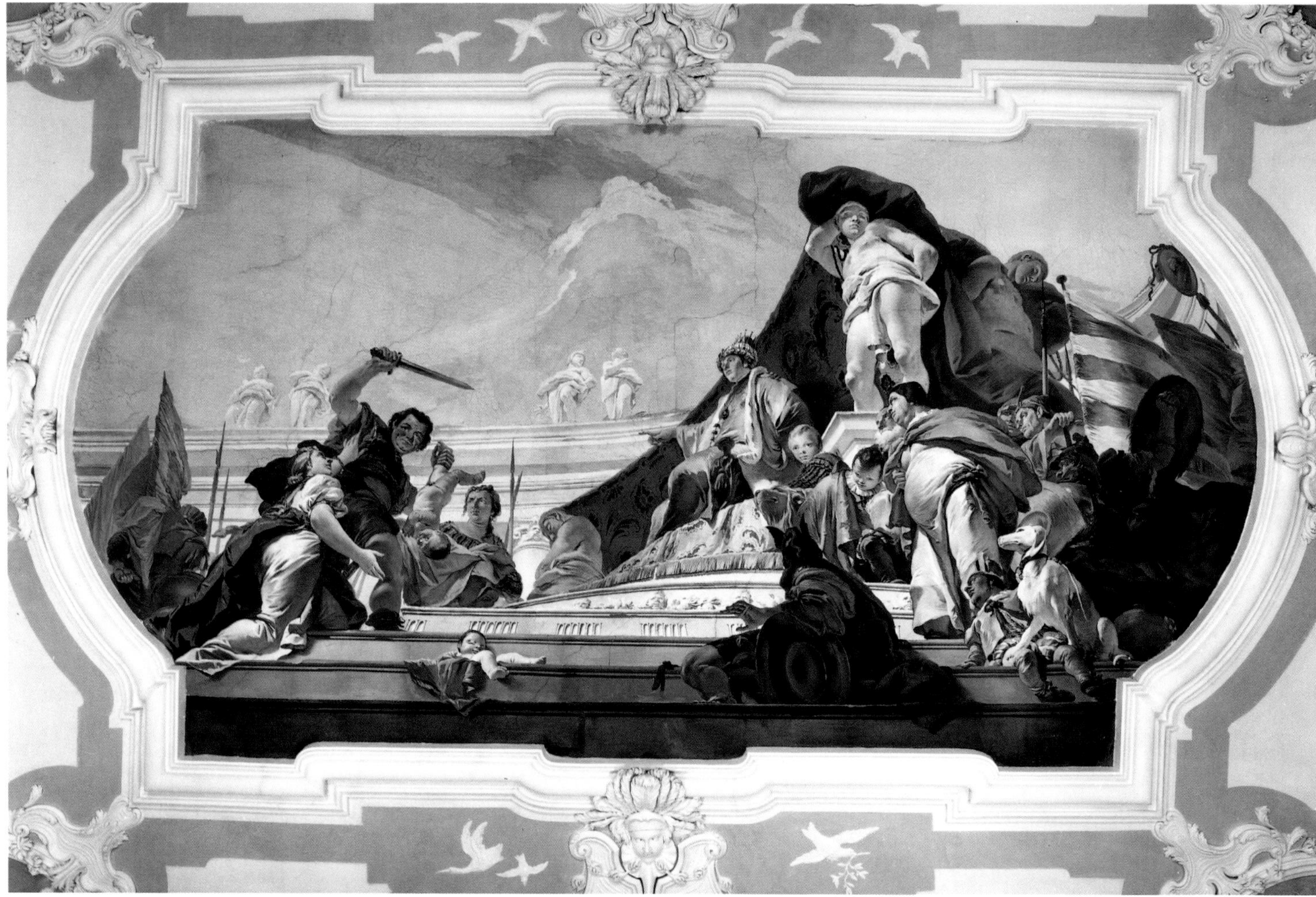

Fig. 26. *The Judgment of Solomon* (ceiling). Fresco. Arcivescovado (Patriarchal Palace), Udine

presence; while depicting Campaspe, Apelles falls in love with her, and Alexander magnanimously gives her to the painter. As Pignatti correctly surmises, Tiepolo conferred on Apelles his own features and on Campaspe those of his wife, Cecilia Guardi, whom he married in 1719—without publishing the banns, for fear that objections to the union would be raised on account of her family's poverty.[26] The painting is thus invested with exceptional autobiographical value: as Giambattista's tribute to his young wife's beauty and as the painter's proud statement of awareness of his own talent, which was such that he portrayed himself as the most celebrated painter of antiquity. This awareness was indisputably well motivated: having emerged from a complex formative period, Giambattista had finally attained full expressive maturity with a highly personal style that would characterize the remainder of his extraordinary career.

NOTES

1. The fact that the Venetian aristocrat Giovanni Donà attended Giambattista's baptism, and indeed served as his godfather, has frequently been interpreted as evidence of the presumed kinship of the Tiepolos of *corte* S. Domenico with the house of Tiepolo, on which a noble Venetian title had long ago been bestowed. Nonetheless, Giambattista's father, Domenico Tiepolo, was variously mentioned in contemporary documents as "capitano da mar" (sea captain), "percenevolo di vascello" (coproprietor of a number of commercial vessels), or "mercante" (tradesman). There are, therefore, no grounds to assume that he may have belonged to a branch of the aristocratic family whose name he bore. In fact, his own name never appears in any of the numerous patrician genealogies that were drawn up during the seventeenth and eighteenth centuries. Moreover, as was recently established by Montecuccoli degli Erri (n.d.), Domenico's wife, Orsetta, was a Marangon, a family of clearly and firmly rooted plebeian and craftsmanly origins (*marangon* being Venetian for "carpenter"). This fact provides important evidence in support of those who believe that Giambattista's family was entirely unrelated to the noble line of Venetian Tiepolos.
2. Montecuccoli degli Erri n.d.
3. Morassi 1955a, p. 6. For a similar point of view, see Pallucchini 1995, p. 314.
4. Da Canal 1732 (1809 ed., pp. XXXI–XXXV). It was thanks to the efforts of the Venetian scholar Giovanni Antonio Moschini that the volume was first published in 1809.
5. Ibid., p. XXXII: "Quantunque si dipartisse dalla di lui maniera diligente, giacchè tutto spirito e foco ne abbracciò una spedita e risoluta."
6. The attribution of the five spandrels is disputed by Pilo; compare Aikema 1982 and Gemin and Pedrocco 1993, pp. 216–18, with Pilo [1985].
7. Barcham 1989, pp. 14–27.
8. Griseri 1993, p. 150.
9. Da Canal 1732 (1809 ed., p. XXXII): "fu pittore del doge Cornaro a S. Polo, nella cui ricca abitazione . . . presiedeva alla distribuzione delle cose pittoriche, oltre all'avervi fatto più sovra-porto con ritratti e quadri di buon gusto."

10. Martini 1974.
11. See Mariuz and Pavanello 1985.
12. Da Canal 1732 (1809 ed., p. XLVI).
13. Mariuz 1995, p. 219: "realizzando quest'opera, Tiepolo ha preso piena coscienza delle sue risorse e della sua vocazione di incomparabile frescante." The fresco at Massanzago, formerly attributed to Guarana, Crosato, and Pittoni, has correctly been assigned to Tiepolo by Mariuz and Pavanello (1985).
14. Mariuz and Pavanello 1995.
15. The Vascon fresco was rediscovered and published by Moretti (1984–85) and Aikema (1987b, pp. 441–44).
16. Barcham 1989, pp. 34–39.
17. Da Canal 1732 (1809 ed., p. XLVI): "una delle sue prime fatture."
18. See Shapley 1974 and Knox 1979. See also De Grazia (1993), who has argued that the canvases were carried out over an extended period of time.
19. On the disputed issue of this painting's date, see Gemin and Pedrocco 1993, pp. 40–44.
20. Muraro [1976]. I cannot agree with the analysis of Pilo, who dissociates the spandrel from the document (see entry for no. 5).
21. Temanza 1963, p. 203.
22. On Domenico Rossi, see Bassi 1962, pp. 207–32.
23. Pallucchini 1994, p. 334: "poderose quinte costituite dai personaggi violentemente scorciati ed incuneati nello spazio a forza di controluce."
24. Gemin and Pedrocco 1993, p. 60.
25. Joppi 1894, p. 43: "pittore celebre e chiaro."
26. Pignatti 1951, p. 31. For the marriage, see Pedrocco and Montecuccoli degli Erri 1992, p. 25.

1. Memento Mori: Age and Death

1. Memento Mori: Age and Death
Ca. 1715
Oil on copper, 11.5 × 9 cm (4⅝ × 3⅝ in.)
Gallerie dell'Accademia, Venice

This remains, to date, Giambattista Tiepolo's smallest known work. The subject is quite unusual for a painting and perhaps was inspired by an engraving—as Morassi suggested when he brought the work to light and published it in 1941–42 under the title *Allegory of Old Age*. Morassi called attention to the thematic affinity between this little painting on copper and a lost drawing by Tiepolo documented by a watercolor made by Francesco Zucchi[1] for use as an illustration for the 1742 Tumermani edition of Milton's *Paradise Lost*. The two works are, however, related in a very limited way and only in terms of their themes.

Morassi's characterization of the painting as an early work by Tiepolo was rejected by Levey in 1963 but promptly reconfirmed by Martini and fully argued by Rizzi on the occasion of the Tiepolo exhibition held in 1971, on the two hundredth anniversary of the master's death. However, the painting was subsequently treated with doubt and a bit of arrogance by González-Palacios ("a delightful snuffbox copper miniature," he called it). Sarcasm aside, the hypothesis that the tiny painting, because of its size, format, and subject, might have originally served as a snuffbox lid is not so easily dismissed; and if this was the case, the identity of the patron who commissioned the work or, better yet, that of the person for whom it was destined becomes a subject of livelier interest.

The theme of this fascinating painting is imbued with moral overtones that receive a weight appropriate to its esoteric component. An appreciation of the esoteric was no doubt part of Tiepolo's rich and varied cultural baggage, which would find even more effective expression in the *Scherzi* (no. 60 a–w).[2] In the gloomy setting over which there hangs a stormy sky illuminated by lightning—this blue is a constant feature in the palette of the young Tiepolo—a cold, spectral light highlights the figures and objects: the squared stones of the open tomb, the *imago mortis* emerging from it, the hourglass the skeleton is brandishing in the face of a man who stumbles as he clutches his crutches, barely supported by the young man behind him. The young person's head is ringed with a pad for bearing weights and a crown of plants. These plants, after a recent, cautious cleaning, reveal themselves to be laurel, the Apollonian shrub believed to offer protection from lightning and a symbol (because it remains forever green) of immortality: an immortality attained through victory—victory, evidently, over death. As far as the unity of the symbolism is concerned, the apparent contradiction resolves itself by understanding the concept of death as an ineluctable as well as a necessary passage toward the transcendence of death itself through the spiritual conditions that this implies: wisdom and heroism.

The young Tiepolo seems to have rendered such thematic density with means equal to it in power and expressive intensity. Morassi saw a possible influence of Magnasco;[3] however, he was hampered in his pursuit of the matter when he dismissed, or rather froze, the problematic issue of Tiepolo's participation in the painting of the works above the arches in the Ospedaletto in Venice, attributing to him only the *Sacrifice of Isaac* (no. 5)—an attribution seconded by Rizzi. Restoring to the young Tiepolo a more extensive role in that rich and varied cycle enables us to recognize the source of his language not in the work of Magnasco but in the charged expressiveness of the Dalmatian Federico Bencovich, whom Tiepolo studied with particular attention at this time—as Moschini pointed out long ago[4] and as the works themselves declare openly. The present work—together with the paintings in the Ospedaletto—reveals Tiepolo manipulating this language: one heightened by bright flashes and a powerful combination of color and light; formal tautness effected in fits and starts with a restless brush bearing unheard-of potential.

To take just one example, the old man's profile, created by the triangular form of the fully illuminated cheek, strongly underscored diagonally by the shadow of the jawbone, recurs in the *Saint John* of about 1715 in the Ospedaletto (no. 2b) and reappears in the Biadene *Assumption*, probably from the same time (fig. 14); in the Massanzago *Myth of Phaethon* (fig. 15); and, to keep to the same scale as the present work, in the *modello* for a *Madonna and Child Venerated by Four Franciscan Saints*.[5]

The most prominent aspects of this fascinating little work also display close affinities with well-known and confirmed early pictures by Tiepolo: the Ospedaletto

PROVENANCE:
Private collection (before 1942); Antonio Morassi, Venice (until 1968)

REFERENCES:
Morassi 1941–42, pp. 89–90; Morassi 1943, p. 13; Morassi 1962, p. 28; Levey 1963, pp. 294–95; Martini 1964, p. 60; Pallucchini 1968, p. 86; Moschini Marconi 1970, p. 240; Pallucchini 1971, p. 305; Udine 1971, p. 23; González-Palacios 1972, p. 86; Martini 1982, p. 509; Pallucchini 1984, pp. 367–68; Nepi Scirè and Valcanover 1985, p. 273; Pilo [1985], p. 138; Aikema 1987b, p. 444; Gemin and Pedrocco 1993, p. 215, no. 1; Pallucchini 1995, p. 318

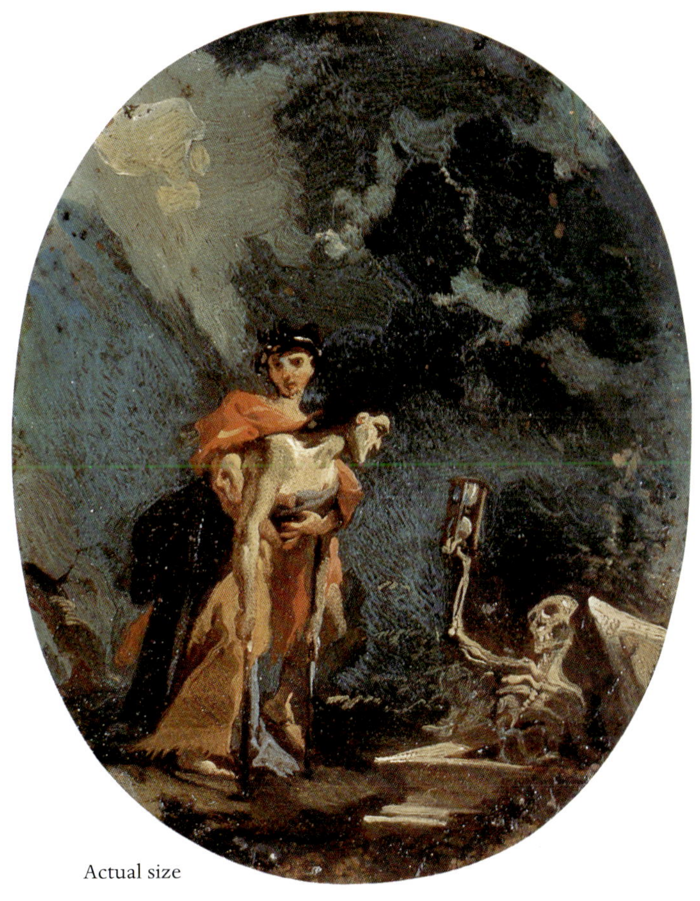

Actual size

paintings of the apostles Saint Thomas and Saint John (no. 2a, b) and the *modello* for the *Crossing of the Red Sea*, certifiably from 1716.[6] The particular accents and incandescent frankness of these other early paintings lead us to conclude that the *Memento Mori* preceded them slightly and probably dates from about 1715, or even before. It is, clearly, the effort of a beginner, in keeping with its private character and destination.

GMP

Notes

1. Pedrocco 1985, p. 74.
2. Pilo 1983, pp. 20–24.
3. Morassi 1941–42, pp. 89–90, and Morassi 1962, p. 28.
4. Moschini 1806–8, vol. 3, pp. 74–75.
5. The *Madonna and Child* was once attributed to Giuseppe Petrini by Suida (1930, p. 269) and to Bencovich by Pallucchini (1935–36, p. 205) but was restored to Tiepolo by Martini (1982, p. 509), who emphasized the strong relationship between Giambattista and the Dalmatian painter.
6. Da Canal 1732 (1809 ed., p. xxxii).

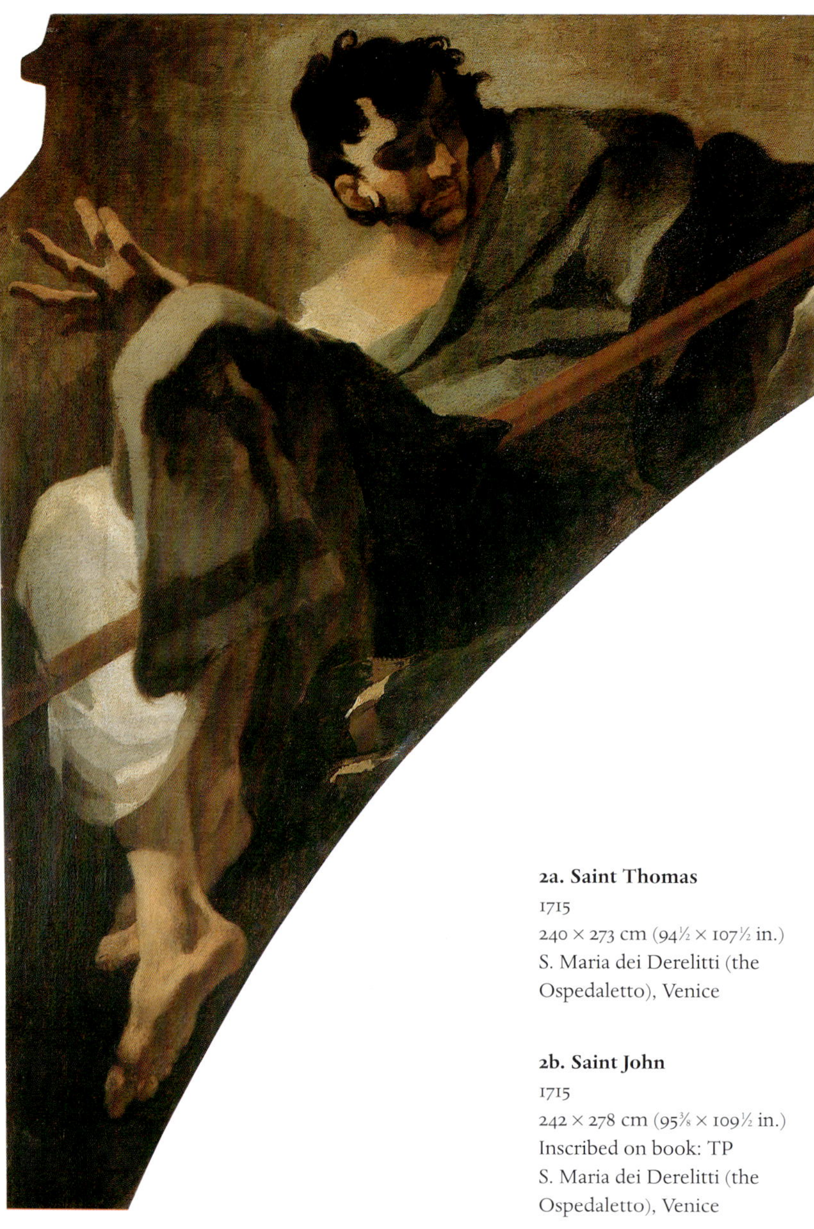

THE APOSTLES FOR THE OSPEDALETTO

2a. Saint Thomas
2b. Saint John

2a. Saint Thomas
1715
240 × 273 cm (94½ × 107½ in.)
S. Maria dei Derelitti (the Ospedaletto), Venice

2b. Saint John
1715
242 × 278 cm (95⅜ × 109½ in.)
Inscribed on book: TP
S. Maria dei Derelitti (the Ospedaletto), Venice

These two triangular canvases with apostles decorate the spandrels above the first of a series of arches on the left wall of the nave of the Ospedaletto. Saint Thomas is identified by the spear by which he was martyred in India. Saint John holds the cup of poison (symbolized by snakes) he was given by a pagan priest.

In his biography of 1732, da Canal attests that Tiepolo, a former pupil of Gregorio Lazzarini's, departed "from his [master's] studied manner of painting and, all spirit and fire, embraced a quick and resolute style. This is seen in the apostles that, at the age of nineteen, he painted above the niches of the church of the Ospedaletto." In the absence of firm documentation or a clear indication in other, later sources, the identification of these works carried out by the nineteen-year-old artist has proven extremely problematic for twentieth-century scholars (there are five pairs of apostles in the church). Yet, supported by the interpretation of the initials *TP* on Saint John's book as an abbreviation of *Tiepolo pinxit*, Zava Boccazzi and the present writer, independently of each other, have been able to recognize this pair of canvases as Tiepolo's. This view has been almost universally accepted, since the paintings manifest the young artist's unmistakable traits. His intellectual powers and exceptionally original inventive capacities are here expressed by means of a technique of richly colored brushwork that at once constructs the figures and, with but a few strokes, describes their form and volume; this is even more evident when the paintings are viewed in raking

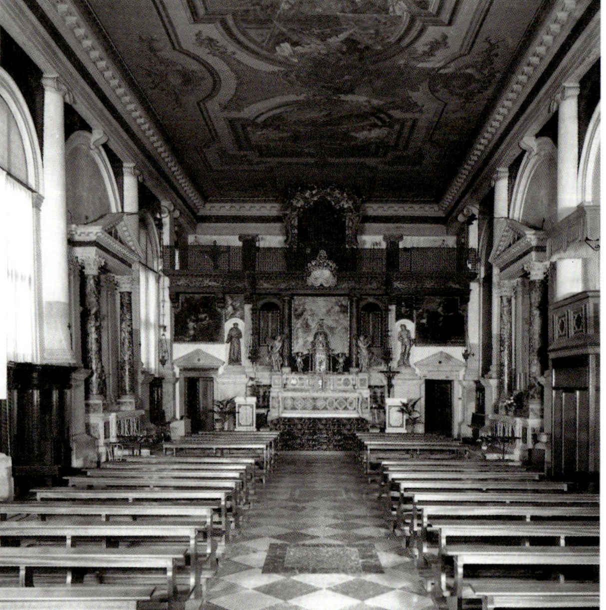

Fig. 27. Interior, S. Maria dei Derelitti (the Ospedaletto), Venice

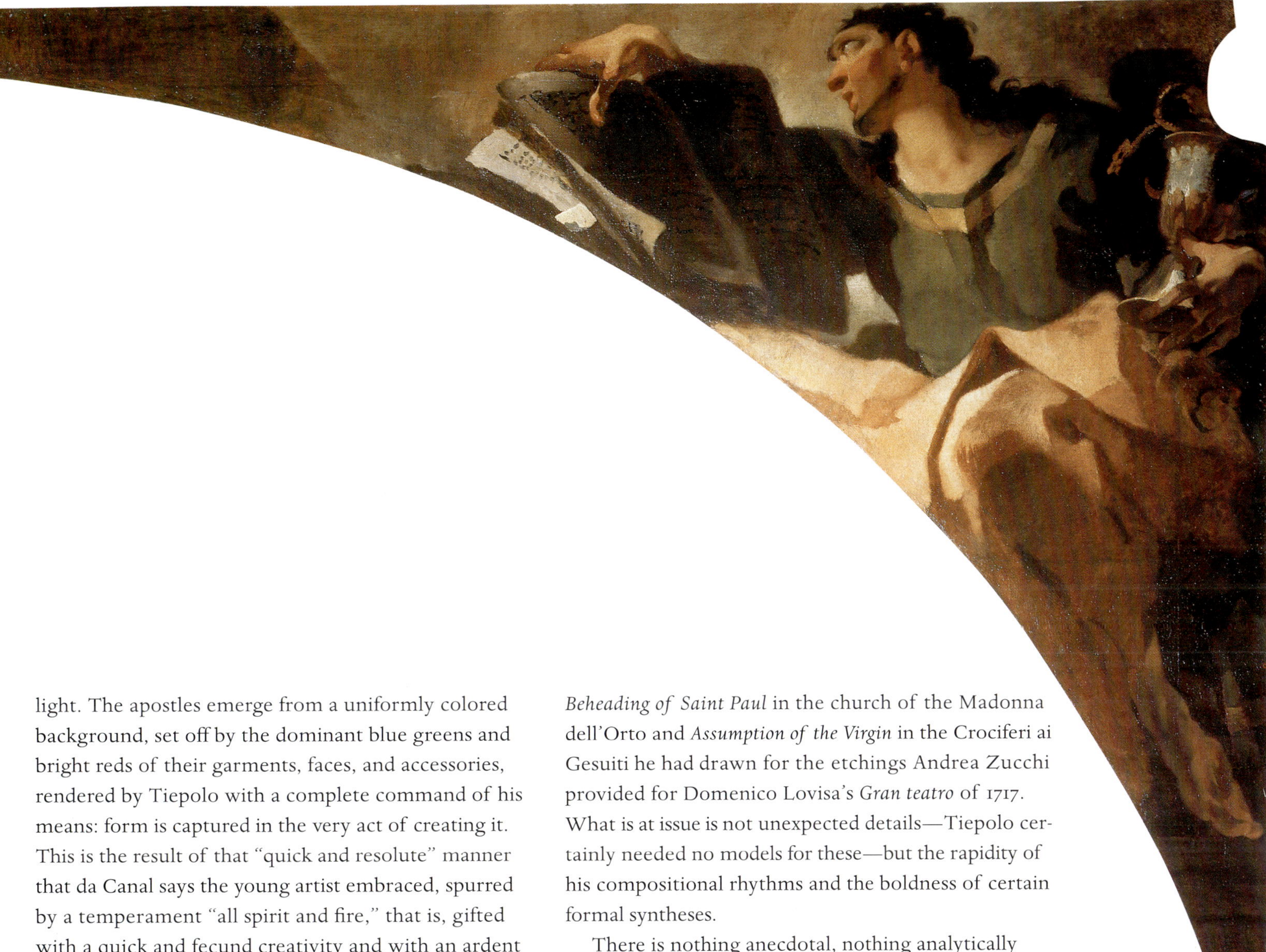

light. The apostles emerge from a uniformly colored background, set off by the dominant blue greens and bright reds of their garments, faces, and accessories, rendered by Tiepolo with a complete command of his means: form is captured in the very act of creating it. This is the result of that "quick and resolute" manner that da Canal says the young artist embraced, spurred by a temperament "all spirit and fire," that is, gifted with a quick and fecund creativity and with an ardent disposition.

There is little in these first, astonishing examples of his genius that can be ascribed to the influence of those artists cited by early sources. We find nothing of the "strong shadowing" of Piazzetta,[1] which was accompanied by a slow, halting construction of form and of which there are echoes in Tiepolo's later works—for example, his *Martyrdom of Saint Bartholomew* (fig. 16), which, like Piazzetta's contemporary *Saint James Led to Martyrdom*, was painted for S. Stae in Venice and is documented as dating to 1722–23. There is something of what da Canal called the "caricatural manner of Bencovich." But here too the real signs of influence seem to appear a few years later, as though the artist came to realize the need to review his achievements and bring them into line with congenial, contemporary models—the *Sacrifice of Isaac* (no. 5) is an example.

It is not unlikely that Tiepolo's creative fantasy was stimulated by his study of the great works of the past rather than by those of his contemporaries: not so much the art of Veronese as that of Tintoretto, whose *Beheading of Saint Paul* in the church of the Madonna dell'Orto and *Assumption of the Virgin* in the Crociferi ai Gesuiti he had drawn for the etchings Andrea Zucchi provided for Domenico Lovisa's *Gran teatro* of 1717. What is at issue is not unexpected details—Tiepolo certainly needed no models for these—but the rapidity of his compositional rhythms and the boldness of certain formal syntheses.

There is nothing anecdotal, nothing analytically descriptive, in Tiepolo's apostles. No concession is made to the "narrative" decoration of anatomical and chromatic details: Tiepolo abstracted all that with great power, creating absolute forms. Note the potent stereometry of the volumes of the figure of Saint Thomas, of his limbs and the clothes he wears, blocked out in terms of light. Or see the prominent swirls of Saint John's cloak. The same treatment, the same extraordinary density, is found in the faces: the faceted planes of the face and neck of Saint John, constructed by light and set in relief by a long shadow underscoring the cavity of the jaw, provide a virtual paradigm of the young Tiepolo's visual language. This is an absolute motif that marks, like an indelible seal, more or less all the works of those fervent years: the *Memento Mori* (no. 1), a *modello* for a Franciscan altarpiece (Castello Sforzesco, Milan), the fresco of the Assumption in the parish church at Biadene (fig. 14), the *Myth of Phaethon* in the Villa Baglioni at Massanzago (fig. 15), and the *Triumph of David* (Musée du Louvre, Paris). Thanks to the critical recovery of the Ospedaletto apostles, the attribution of

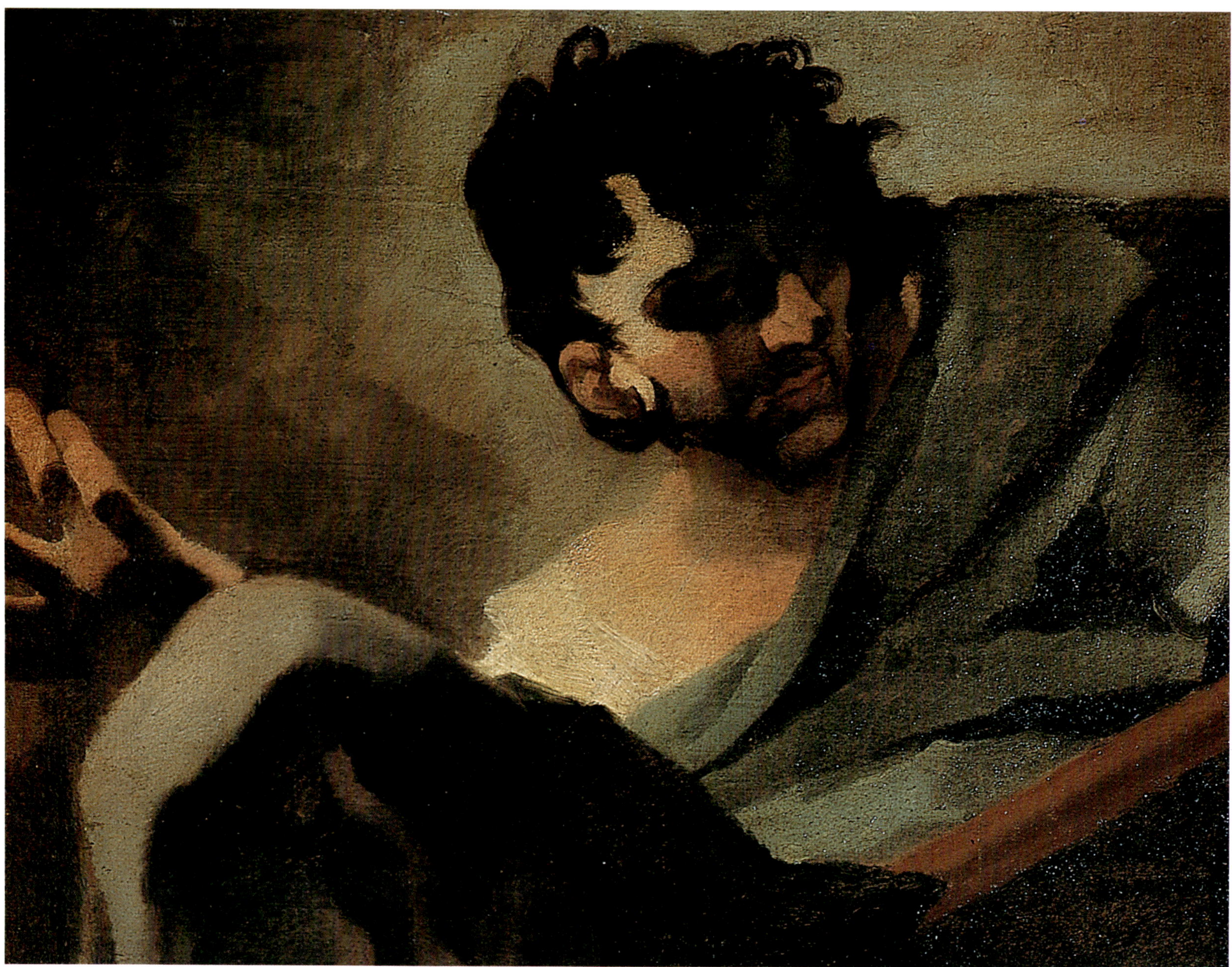

Detail, no. 2a

PROVENANCE:
S. Maria dei Derelitti, Venice

REFERENCES:
Da Canal 1732 (1809 ed., pp. XXXI–XXXII); De Vito Battaglia 1931, p. 196; Modigliani 1933, p. 147; Pallucchini 1934a, p. 338; Arslan 1935–36, p. 187; Martini 1974, p. 33; Zava Boccazzi 1979, p. 170; Aikema 1982, p. 360; Martini 1982, pp. 508–9; Pilo 1982, pp. 153–54; Moretti 1984–85, p. 378; Mariuz and Pavanello 1985, p. 109; Pilo [1985], pp. 130–31, 154; Sponza 1986, pp. 46–54; Sponza 1986–87, pp. 218–24; Gemin and Pedrocco 1993, p. 218, no. 6; Pallucchini 1995, pp. 319–21

these works to Tiepolo has acquired greater certainty and their chronology has been clarified.[2]

Tiepolo owes his fame to the greatness and splendor of his decorative commissions, but the essence of his poetics is already present in these incunabula. When we take into account the fact that da Canal, here as elsewhere, noted the artist's age at the completion of each work—thus he assigned the *Crossing of the Red Sea* to 1716 and, through a slip of the pen, gave Tiepolo's birth date as 1697 instead of 1696—his debut at the Ospedaletto can be dated to 1715. Additionally, it seems reasonable to suppose that not all the many canvases that constitute the series of apostles in the Ospedaletto were completed contemporaneously—even leaving aside those in the presbytery, which undoubtedly were painted earlier, and the *Sacrifice of Isaac*, which is later. The date 1716 inscribed on the volume held by the apostle Saint Paul in a nearby canvas, which to my mind is attributable to Nicola Grassi, may be taken as an indication of this fact—whether or not this work marks the beginning or the conclusion of Grassi's work in the Ospedaletto.[3] The directors of the Ospedaletto customarily awarded even significant commissions to young artists, probably as a part of sound administrative practice, in the course of which they made some fortunate and successful choices.[4]

GMP

NOTES

1. "Forte ombreggiamento": the terminology is Moschini's (1815, vol. 1, p. 184).
2. On the relationship between these works and Tiepolo's first essays in the Ospedaletto, see Pilo 1985, p. 131.
3. For contrasting views on this question, see Pilo 1981, pp. 67–83, and Pallucchini 1995, pp. 551–53.
4. On this practice, see Pilo [1985], p. xi.

THE CA' CORNER PORTRAITS

3a. Portrait of Giovanni Corner II (1647–1722)
3b. Portrait of Marco Corner (ca. 1286–1368)

3a. Portrait of Giovanni Corner II (1647–1722)
Ca. 1716
271 × 182 cm (106¾ × 71¾ in.)
Private collection

3b. Portrait of Marco Corner (ca. 1286–1368)
Ca. 1716
271 × 182 cm (106¾ × 71¾ in.)
Private collection

The sitters can be identified by other, documented portraits: an engraving by Francesco Zocchi of Giovanni Corner II, the tomb effigy of Marco Corner in S. Giovanni e Paolo, Venice, and a sixteenth-century posthumous portrait of Marco in the Palazzo Ducale, Venice, by Domenico Tintoretto. The Cornaro were among the most illustrious families of Venice and provided a number of doges. The branch in question had its residence in the splendid Palazzo Corner-Mocenigo in Campo S. Polo, designed by Michele Sanmicheli, where there was a rich collection of works of art that included two celebrated paintings in grisaille by Mantegna and Bellini (still cited in Moschini's guide of 1815). The palace is now the Comando della Guardia di Finanza. In 1711 the annual revenues of the Cornaro surpassed 14,400 ducats. Giovanni Corner II held a number of political offices before he was elected doge in 1719.

In his biography of Gregorio Lazzarini of 1732, da Canal wrote of the young Tiepolo—"now of great fame"—that he departed from the studied manner of his teacher and "embraced a quick and resolute style. This is seen in the apostles that, at the age of nineteen, he painted above the niches of the church of the Ospedaletto. He was painter to Doge Cornaro at S. Polo, in whose lavish residence he oversaw the hanging of paintings and also made many overdoors with portraits and fine pictures. At age twenty, in competition with other painters, he carried out the canvas showing the Crossing of the Red Sea, a work that was praised when exhibited on the feast day of Saint Roche."

All trace of the pictures Tiepolo painted for the Cornaro palace was lost until two—those of Marco Corner and Giovanni Corner II—were identified by the present writer, thereby opening a new chapter in our understanding of the young Tiepolo.[1] The portrait of Marco Corner was obviously an ideal likeness, while that of Giovanni II was certainly taken from life. Both had to be painted before 1722, prior to Giovanni's death. To date them more precisely, it is worth paying close attention to the chronology implied in the passage from da Canal quoted above. He noted first that Tiepolo was nineteen when he painted the apostles of the Ospedaletto (see no. 2a,b); second that he was Doge Cornaro's personal painter; and third that at age twenty he exhibited the *Crossing of the Red Sea*. If this chronology can be taken as an accurate indication of the real situation, then the young Tiepolo must have painted the Cornaro portraits when he was nineteen or twenty—that is, about 1716.

If the portraits were painted at that time or, as I am inclined to believe, slightly later, we find ourselves with documents of a new, surprising aspect of the artist and of the multifaceted experiments of the first years of his career. Until not long ago it was thought that during that period Tiepolo painted only dark, agitated works, in the style of Federico Bencovich and Giambattista Piazzetta. But the Cornaro portraits present a bright, sunny manner inspired by Sebastiano Ricci and, to an even greater degree, by Giovanni Pellegrini. What is more, they reveal a formal coherence that is stupefying. Yet in these paintings Tiepolo also betrayed idiosyncratic traits and links with his contemporary works in the description of the doges' hands, which in construction and in the nervous play of light are identical to the hands of his apostles in the Ospedaletto. The portraits demonstrate that even at this young age Tiepolo possessed a mastery of the figure matched by few—even among his elders. But in addition to giving evidence of an uncommon capacity and facility in various pictorial modes, the portraits reveal a concerted attempt on Tiepolo's part to find his own personal path, one that would open up not too long hence, in particular in the prodigious frescoes of the Arcivescovado (Patriarchal Palace) at Udine. It is interesting to note how similar the compositional schemes of the Cornaro portraits are to that of the figure of Solomon in the ceiling fresco of the Sala Rossa of the Arcivescovado (fig. 26). Even the pose of the two doges—especially that of Giovanni II—is analogous to Solomon's: monumental, conceived with a robust modulation of contour that will be found in many of his subsequent works—such as the Roman histories of Ca' Dolfin (no. 12a–g, figs. 33–35).

EM

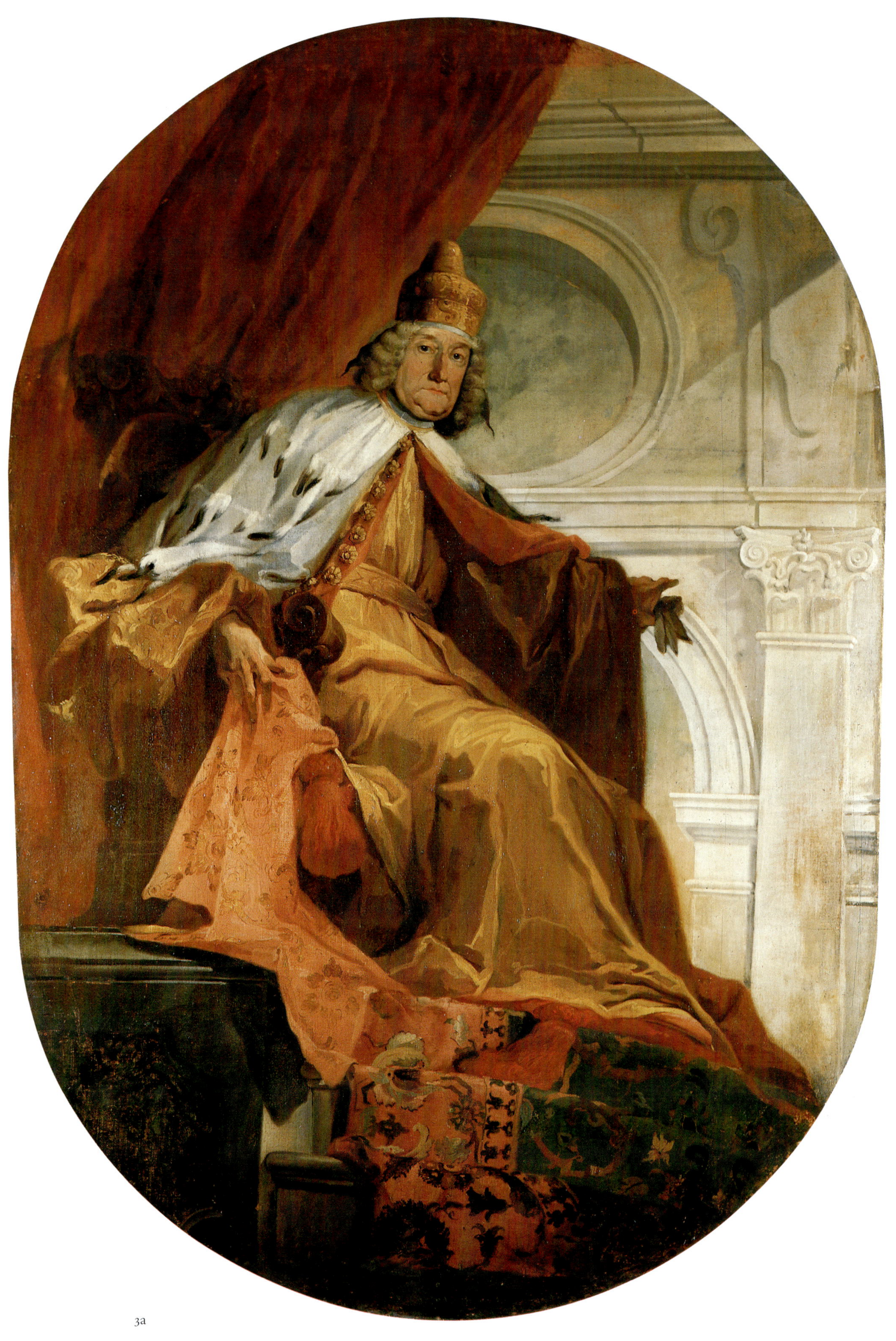

3a

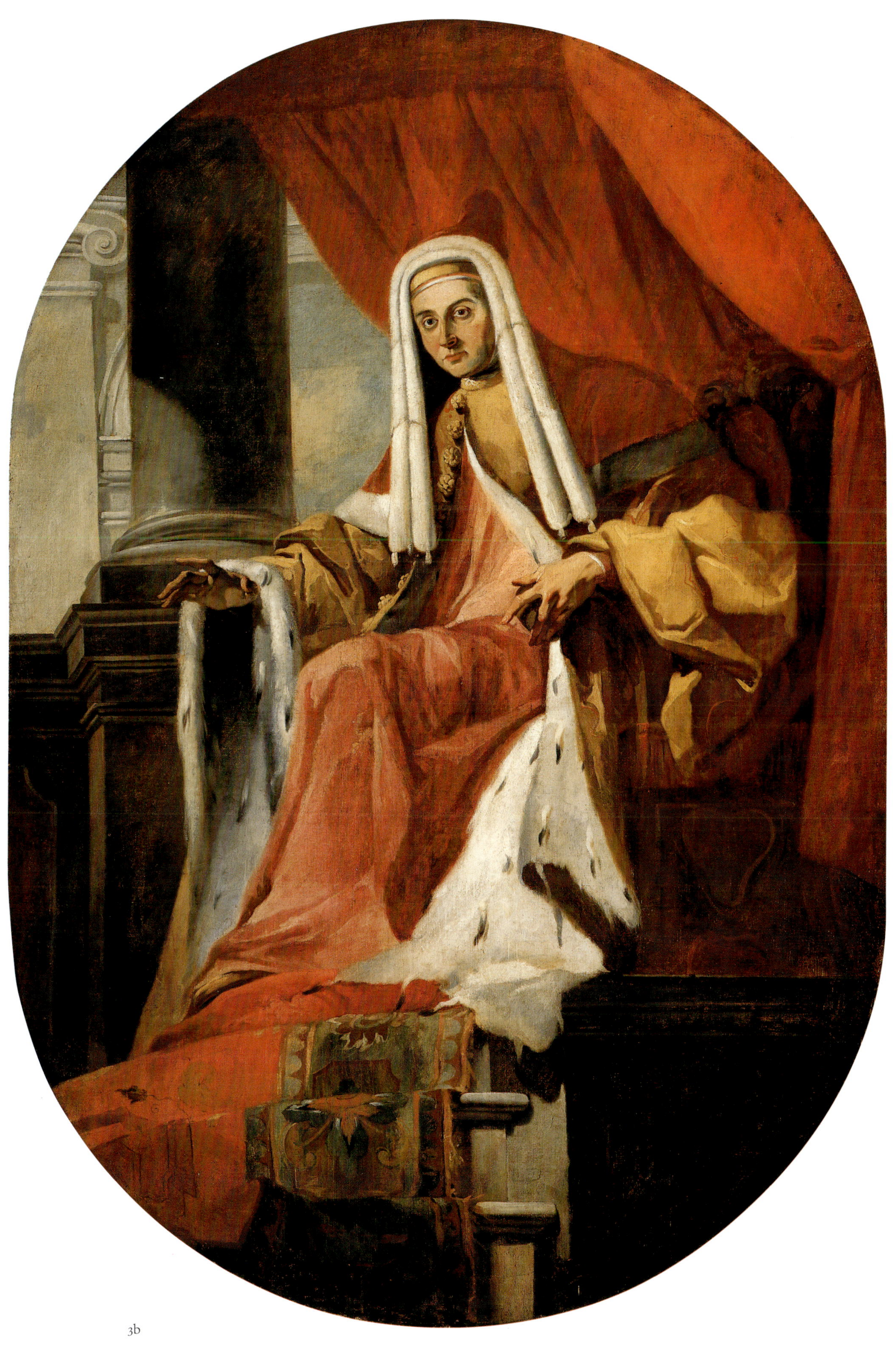

3b

PROVENANCE:
Palazzo Corner, Venice (until after 1847); art market, Venice (1974); private collection (from 1974)

REFERENCES:
Da Canal 1732 (1809 ed.), p. xxxii; Martini 1974; Knox 1979, p. 417; Knox 1980a, p. 36 n. 1; Martini 1982, p. 51; Levey 1986, pp. 10, 291 n. 9; Martini 1992, p. 324; Gemin and Pedrocco 1993, pp. 40, 220, nos. 11, 12; Pallucchini 1995, vol. 1, p. 317

Marco Corner was the fifty-ninth doge of Venice and held office from 21 July 1365 to 13 January 1368. His name is linked not so much to any significant historical event as to the realization of one of the greatest early masterpieces in the Palazzo Ducale in Venice: Guariento's vast fresco showing the Coronation of the Virgin on the wall behind the doge's throne in the Sala del Maggior Consiglio (which was almost entirely destroyed in the fire of 1577).

For the likeness of Giovanni II, Tiepolo could rely on the living sitter, who was probably his first important patron. However, for the effigy of Marco Corner he was constrained to refer to earlier images, particularly the posthumous portrait by Tintoretto in the Palazzo Ducale, which displays the same physiognomic features and dress as Tiepolo's canvas. This recourse to an early prototype at least partly explains the less appealing, more generic treatment of Marco's head as compared with the head in the pendant portrait of Giovanni II. But these differences certainly do not provide a sufficient basis for doubting Tiepolo's authorship of the former picture. The application of the paint in the two works is absolutely consistent, as is the character of the rich, light-saturated pigment, and the nervous manner of describing the contours of the costume and of the hands. The play of light is also identical.

For these two canvases Tiepolo evidently referred to earlier Baroque models, and it is interesting that thirty years after painting them he returned to the same sources for his portrait of Daniele IV Dolfin (no. 46). There too, the figure, dressed in red with the symbolic stole of his office, is silhouetted against an architectural backdrop painted in silver gray tones that suggests a notable depth with its arches and columns.

FP

NOTE

1. With these appeared two additional portraits of other Cornaro doges, Giovanni I and Francesco. They are by two different hands. The set of portraits may have numbered eight, inasmuch as there are eight doors in the main room of the Palazzo Corner. See Martini 1974, p. 35.

4. *Scipio Freeing Massiva(?)*

†4. Scipio Freeing Massiva(?)
Ca. 1719–21
279 × 488 cm (110 × 192 in.)
The Walters Art Gallery, Baltimore (37.657)

This badly damaged but marvelously animated and light-filled composition, recently transformed by a painstaking cleaning and restoration, is a neglected but pivotal work in Tiepolo's early career.[1] Together with the large *Rape of the Sabines* (The Hermitage Museum, Saint Petersburg) and the so-called Ca' Zenobio cycle of pictures carried out for Alvise Zenobio's palace on the Rio dei Carmini, Venice, between about 1718 and 1730 (Museo del Prado, Madrid [fig. 21]; Galleria Sabauda, Turin; National Gallery of Art, Washington, D.C. [fig. 20]), it is among the most ambitious essays in history painting Tiepolo produced prior to the commission for the canvases for Ca' Dolfin, Venice (see no. 12a–g). Its importance for understanding the sources and development of his early career can scarcely be exaggerated.

The event depicted has been variously identified: most frequently as the Numidian king Jugurtha brought before Sulla (104 B.C.), as recounted in Valerius Maximus's *Factorum et dictorum memorabilium* (6.9);[2] or as the captive Numidian king Syphax brought before Scipio (203 B.C.), as described by Livy (30.13), Appian, and Petrarch;[3] and, most recently, as Massiva, the young nephew of the greatest Numidian king, Massinissa, released by Scipio (209 B.C.), also as told by Livy (27.19).[4] The last two subjects are episodes in the history of the Punic Wars. Although neither has much prior visual history, a depiction of Syphax before Scipio was included in a cycle of paintings realized by various artists in the first decade of the eighteenth century for the Ca' Corner at S. Polo, Venice.[5] Given Tiepolo's close connection with the Cornaro family, for whom he painted two portraits (no. 3a, b), and the fact that his master, Gregorio Lazzarini, contributed to the Ca' Corner commission, he surely knew this cycle. Tiepolo treated the same or a closely related subject again in his frescoes of 1731–32

Opposite: Detail, no. 4

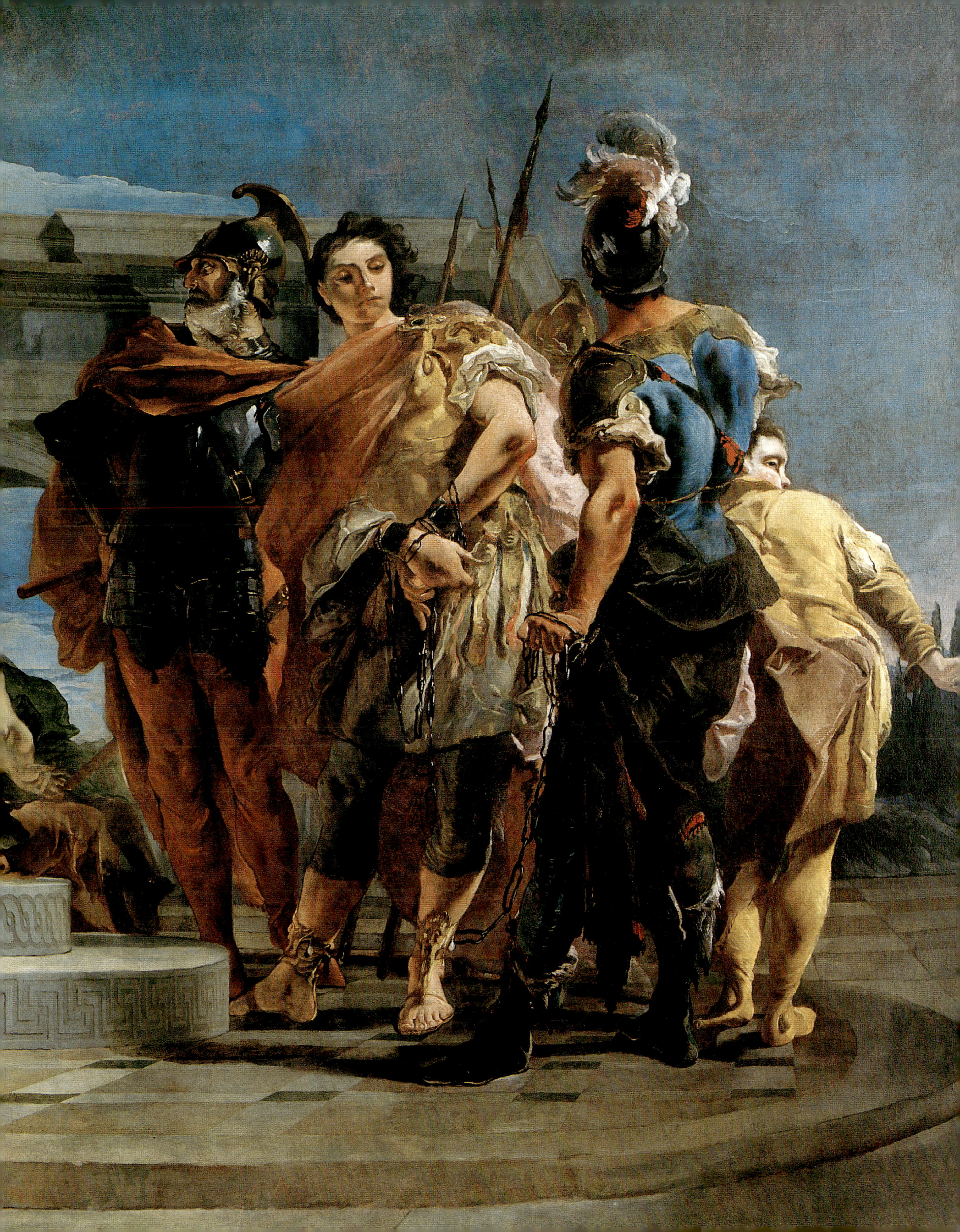

for Palazzo Dugnani, Milan. That scene has evaded firm identification, but in the event that the cycle was devoted to Scipio, the subject of Jugurtha before Sulla can be eliminated as a possibility.[6] One of the frescoes in Palazzo Dugnani shows Sophonisba, the wife of Syphax, taking poison, and this might support an identification of the related scene as Syphax before Scipio. However, the continence of Scipio is also included in the sequence of scenes. This is a subject complementary to the theme of Scipio freeing Massiva—a deed that persuaded Massinissa to become Scipio's ally, helping assure Scipio's later victories in Africa. At the time he released Massiva, Scipio was extremely young, as is the prisoner in both the Milan fresco and the Baltimore painting; moreover, in the Milan fresco a soldier appears to be removing the captive's chains. These details seem to indicate that the Massiva story is represented, yet, given the similarity of narrative elements in the two subjects, this identification of the theme of the Baltimore painting cannot be considered definitive, and there are circumstantial reasons, discussed below, for accepting it as a depiction of Syphax brought before Scipio.

During the first decade of his career Tiepolo experimented with a variety of styles. He was encouraged to do so by his training under the eclectic Lazzarini. Whose work Tiepolo looked to in a particular instance was partly determined by the kind of commission he had in hand and partly by predisposition. Like many young painters across the centuries, his curiosity extended not only to the dominant figures of the day and the giants of the past but also to lesser contemporaries. Because the range of his interest in other artists was so broad, a certain degree of latitude must be allowed in assigning dates to his earliest paintings, since at any given moment different manners coexist, and his development is not one of a clear succession of styles. Paradoxically, the one artist who might, at first, seem to have left the least trace on Tiepolo's work is Lazzarini himself. This was implicitly acknowledged by da Canal, who in 1732 noted how far Tiepolo had departed from the "studied manner" of his teacher. Yet when Tiepolo was faced with this commission for a large-scale history painting involving numerous figures enacting a drama in a complex architectural setting, Lazzarini's accomplished machines offered a far better example than the dark, reductive, exclusively figural works of Federico Bencovich and Piazzetta. A picture such as Lazzarini's enormous *Charity of Saint Lorenzo Giustiniani*, located in S. Pietro di Castello, in the heart of Tiepolo's native parish, could provide not only a model of academic practice, with its figures in a commensurable space conveying the sense of an action through gesture and expression; it afforded as well a clear indication of the importance of the works of Veronese and Tintoretto for a genuinely Venetian approach to history painting. Tiepolo was the one artist who truly understood this aspect of Lazzarini's teaching.

In the Baltimore canvas the curved architectural backdrop with the raised podium flanked by massive columns is unquestionably and probably indirectly based on Veronese's large painting of Christ among the Doctors (Museo del Prado, Madrid), and it is to this same source that the general disposition of the figures at the left is owed.[7] This is perhaps the earliest example in Tiepolo's oeuvre of the direct appropriation of a compositional invention from Veronese's work, and, although the results are only partly successful, his ambition to recover the glory of cinquecento painting is clear. Figures and space are not yet convincingly integrated, and the effect is of a choreographed narrative rather than a composed one, but the painting is nonetheless impressive. Not surprisingly, here Tiepolo saw Veronese through the eyes of his elders—especially Lazzarini, whose emphasis on gesture and the *affetti* reveals a close dependence on the tradition of Bolognese painting (a fact intimated by da Canal in his biography of Lazzarini). To be sure, the aspect of Veronese's art that proved of most significance was not composition but color. It is the Veronesian light-suffused color that gives this composition its open-air quality and visual magnificence and marks a new chapter in Tiepolo's development: one characterized not simply by a tendency toward decorative prettiness—that had already been achieved in the frescoes at Villa Baglioni at Massanzago (see fig. 15)—but also by a color that is at once splendid and natural seeming.

The other presiding influence in this canvas is that of Tintoretto (whose "intelligence of movement" had been singled out by da Canal). The elegantly postured boy viewed from the back at the extreme right, the commander seen in profile behind Massiva, and the soldier at the extreme left are shown in balletic attitudes reminiscent of figures in the work of Tintoretto, which Tiepolo studied from an early age. By contrast, the standard-bearer, shown advancing rapidly with his right arm raised, repeats the pose of the Magdalen in Titian's late Pietà (Gallerie dell'Accademia, Venice). In drawing on these many sources, Tiepolo had found his way back to the very foundation of modern painting in Venice and set the stage for a complete renewal of art—one combining a study of the old masters with reference to nature. That achievement still lay in the future, but its beginnings are already perceptible in this work. Just as Tintoretto is reported by Vasari to have

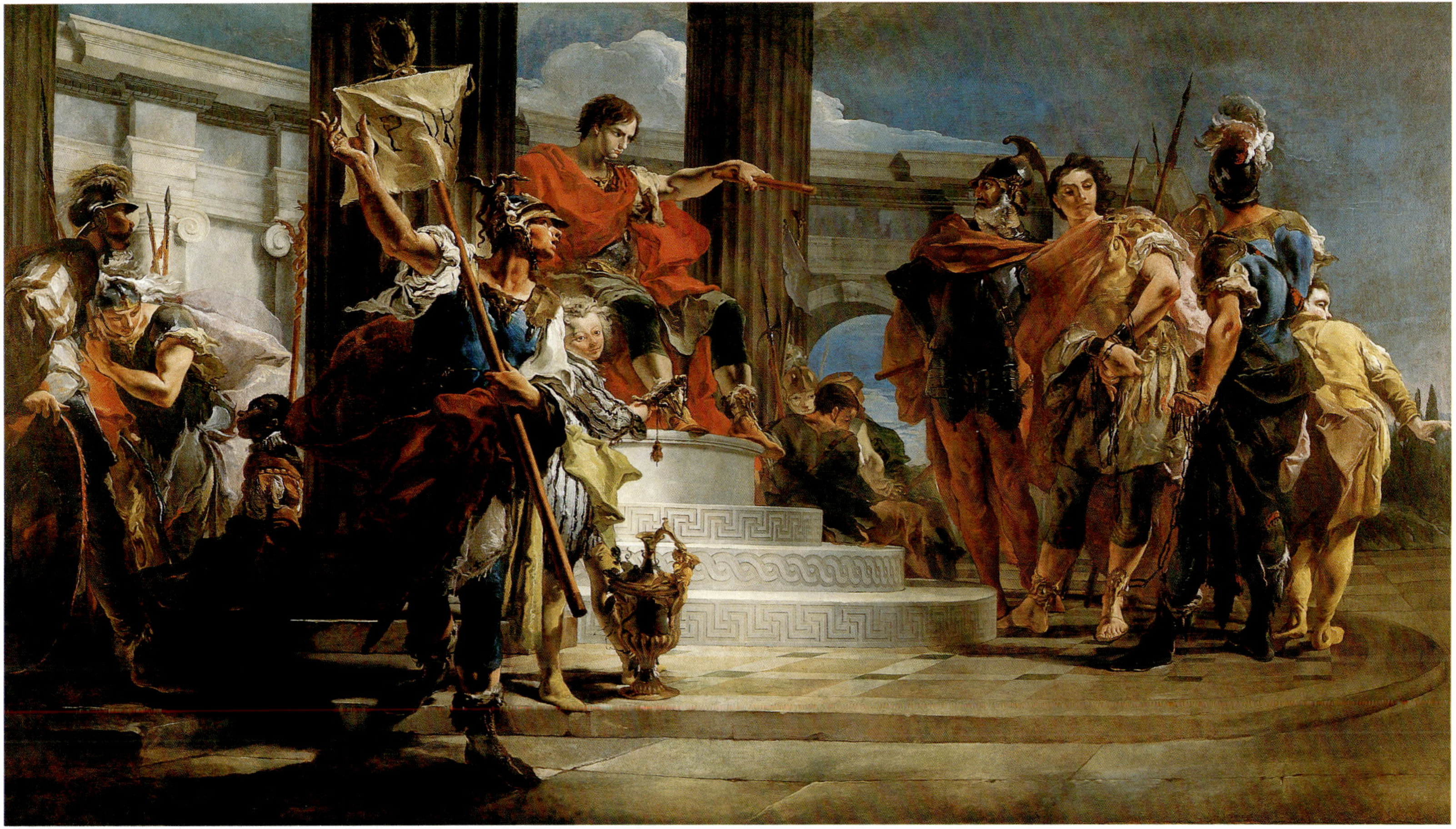

4

affixed to his workshop wall the motto "the drawing of Michelangelo and the color of Titian,"[8] so in this picture Tiepolo declared a double debt to the drawing of Tintoretto and the color of Veronese.

Inevitably, it was the limpid colors, broken brushwork, and handsome humanity of Veronese's art that proved the most important for Tiepolo. The Veronese-inspired page in a white-and-black-striped costume with a lime green sash in the Baltimore picture is the first in a long line of arrestingly lifelike figures turning from the depicted action to address the viewer. We next see him at the feet of Arion on the ceiling of Palazzo Sandi, Venice (fig. 22), and at Rebecca's knee in the gallery of the Arcivescovado (Patriarchal Palace) at Udine (fig. 25). In both of those frescoes, dating from the mid- to late 1720s, there is a far more developed narrative technique than in the *Scipio*—gesture is used with greater restraint and purpose, less to animate the composition than to underscore the mute dialogue between figures—and the poses of the protagonists are now fully integrated with the setting and action. The inclusion in the Baltimore canvas of the seated Moor—certainly Tiepolo's young servant Ali—announces that practice of weaving the appearances of his family and friends into the fabric of his art.

Because of the various styles Tiepolo explored in the picture, its date is not easy to establish. The animated contours of the figures and the use of bold modeling, with white highlights laid on in short, parallel strokes, are characteristic of his paintings presumed to date from the late teens and early 1720s; however, a preference for the reddish flesh tones seen here is not exclusive to his earliest efforts and is found in the *Sacrifice of Isaac* (no. 5), which shows extremely close similarities in the handling of the paint. The bright palette and such dazzling details as the vase with its figural decoration point the way to the great achievements of Tiepolo's early maturity—the frescoed ceiling and canvases of Palazzo Sandi (see no. 9a, b) and the Roman histories of Ca' Dolfin (see no. 12a–g).

The work closest in style to the Baltimore canvas is the painting for the Ca' Zenobio cycle, referred to above, showing the Triumph of Aurelian (Galleria Sabauda, Turin): it includes a figure viewed from the back that is very like the boy at the far right in the Baltimore *Scipio,* and the action in both pictures is similarly overstated. The Turin picture cannot be precisely dated, but da Canal considered the Ca' Zenobio cycle one of Tiepolo's earliest commissions. He was not literally correct, for it is more advanced in style than the frescoes in the parish

PROVENANCE:
Don Marcello Masarenti, Palazzo Accoramboni, Rome (before 1897–1902; Palazzo Accoramboni catalogue 1897, no. 404); William T. Walters, Baltimore (1902–31)

REFERENCES:
Morassi 1941–42, p. 89; Morassi 1955a, p. 10; Morassi 1962, pp. 2, 20, 22, 27; Garas 1965, p. 301 n. 26; Pallucchini 1968, p. 89, no. 30; Zeri 1976, vol. 2, pp. 559–60, no. 449; Knox 1979, p. 417; Gemin and Pedrocco 1993, pp. 19, 227, no. 28; Knox 1996

church at Biadene (fig. 14) and in Villa Baglioni (fig. 15), and the paintings in the sequence are from different moments—indeed, the Washington canvas must have been executed about 1730; yet the Turin painting is probably quite early and may well date to about 1718–20.[9] This would also be an appropriate date for the *modello* for the Baltimore *Scipio* (Marinotti collection, Milan), which still shows all the hallmarks of what Moschini described in 1806 as the "agitated style" of Bencovich.[10] X rays of the Baltimore canvas have revealed that its composition was originally closer to that of the *modello* and that in the finished picture Tiepolo increased the emphasis on gesture as a means of communicating action. He also moved his palette toward a brighter range. It is worth noting that Morassi thought the earliest Ca' Zenobio picture—that now in the Prado (misidentified and not yet associated with the Ca' Zenobio cycle at the time he wrote)—was a pendant to the Baltimore painting. In any event, 1719 to 1721 seems a reasonable time frame for the latter picture. In the *Scipio* Tiepolo redirected the raw, expressive vigor of his earliest, predominantly figural compositions toward the Venetian cinquecento ideal of a history painting that combines dramatic effect with decorative appeal. The next step in his stylistic evolution would seem to be represented by the great *Crucifixion* on Burano (fig. 92), in which the tension between Tintorettesque action and Veronesian splendor finds a calmer, more balanced, and more affective solution.

Nothing firm is known about the provenance of the Baltimore picture. Garas has made the tantalizing suggestion that it may be one of the paintings seen by Giambattista Carboni in the Palazzo Gaifami, Brescia, in 1760.[11] That work showed Syphax before Scipio and had a pendant by Nicolò Bambini, who also provided companions to Tiepolo's canvases in the Palazzo Sandi. Even more speculative is Knox's proposal that it is one of the unspecified paintings that da Canal reports Tiepolo carried out for Giovanni Corner. Knox has emphasized that the Corner/Cornaro family traced its ancestry to the *gens Cornelia*, to which Scipio belonged. Whoever the Baltimore picture was painted for, the composition has a pronounced right-to-left diagonal axis not evident in the *modello*.[12] The finished picture is strangely unresolved at the right and closed at the left, suggesting that the *modello* may have been revised with a view to the placement of the final canvas in a large room or hall with a lateral approach.

KC

Notes

1. As long ago as 1941 Morassi noted that a careful restoration of the picture was necessary if its qualities were to be properly evaluated. Restoration was undertaken in 1938 and again in 1944, but the retouching was so liberal as to constitute a repainting of large sections. The recent cleaning and restoration was carried out by the conservation staff at The Walters Art Gallery between 1994 and 1996. A primary problem is irreversible flattening and deformation of the surface caused by a transfer effected before 1902. There are myriad losses—the most important are in the face of the page wearing a striped outfit (now largely reconstructed on the basis of a related drawing), in the banner, and in the left proper eye of Scipio. The foreground pavement and the sky are badly abraded, and the darks have sunk. I would like to thank Eric Gordon for allowing me to follow the restoration in its later stages.
2. On this identification, see Zeri (1976, vol. 2, pp. 559–60), who explains that the subject exemplified the changes of fortune and behavior. Sulla had the reputation of a scoundrel but behaved as a hero when serving in the Roman army against King Jugurtha.
3. See Garas 1965, p. 301 n. 26.
4. For this identification, see Knox 1996.
5. On these paintings, see Knox 1992, pp. 33–38. The main pictures are at The Elms, Newport, Rhode Island. Knox ascribes the *Syphax before Scipio* to Piazzetta.
6. Gemin and Pedrocco (1993, p. 108) call the scene *Scipio Freeing Massinissa*, but Knox (1996) notes that this event is unknown to history.
7. The Prado picture was described by Ridolfi in 1648 (p. 304), when it was in the Contarini collection in Padua; it had already been sold to Spain in Tiepolo's lifetime, and he would have known the composition through a copy.
8. Vasari 1906, vol. 6, p. 588 n. 1.
9. See the analysis of De Grazia 1993, pp. 5–7. The commission may have been linked to the wedding celebrations of Alvise Zenobio and Alba Grimani in 1718. As De Grazia argues, the Prado canvas is the earliest in the series, and the Turin picture immediately succeeded it.
10. Moschini 1806, vol. 3, pp. 74–75: "Ma [Tiepolo] no fu pago di tener dietro alle sole tracce del maestro [Lazzarini]; ed avido d'imitare quanti godeano ai suoi giorni di reputazione ora emulò la maniera caricata del Bencovich ora il forte ombreggiamento del Piazzetta."
11. Carboni 1760, p. 151: "Nella Sala . . . Due gran quadri eguali nelle pareti, cioè Scipione Affricano davati al quale si mira Siface incatenato, dipinto da Giov. Batista Tiepolo, e il Trionfo di Giulio Cesare in Roma, di Mano del Bambini."
12. Another, related composition (formerly Clifford Smith, London) has sometimes been confused with the *modello*. It shows a Hebrew priest seated on a throne, and the flanking columns are Solomonic rather than fluted. The style appears to be very early indeed. The reappearance of the scheme in the *Scipio modello* and final canvas is an instance of Tiepolo's adaptation of a compositional formula created for one subject to the exigencies of another—a method of recycling he was to make peculiarly his own.

5. *The Sacrifice of Isaac*

This canvas now decorates the area above the arch between the second and third altars on the right side of the nave of the Ospedaletto (fig. 27). It was probably moved there at the beginning of this century, during extensive restorations of the church. In 1733 Anton Maria Zanetti recorded its original location in the space between the first and second altars on the same wall, above Gregorio Lazzarini's large *Pool of Bethesda*. Subsequently it was mentioned by Moschini and Soravia, who noted the replacement of Lazzarini's canvas by the *Assumption of the Virgin* by Giovanni Peruzzini, previously displayed in the presbytery. Other works in the cycle of decorations must also have been moved—although there are no documents that allow us to say which and where—and these changes are relevant to the putative genesis of the *Sacrifice of Isaac* and to its date. Unlike other pictures in the cycle of spandrel decorations in the church such as *Saint Thomas* and *Saint John* (no. 2a, b), the *Isaac* has never been doubted as a work by Tiepolo, to whom it is ascribed by old sources. Its date, however, has been and continues to be debated.

There is no doubt that the picture was painted several years after the *Saint Thomas* and the *Saint John* of about 1715. When the early Tiepolo—indeed, Tiepolo *tout court*—was rediscovered in the first decades of this century, it seemed natural to associate the *Sacrifice of Isaac* with the date of 1715 that da Canal gave the "Apostles" (that is, the *Saint Thomas* and the *Saint John*); there were, after all, no firm reference points in the cycle, and the dramatic accents of the picture seemed to reveal echoes of the poetry of Piazzetta's work, which were taken as a signature of Tiepolo's work following his apprenticeship with Lazzarini. This was the opinion of Modern, Molmenti, Sack, and even of Fogolari, who adopted a more nuanced critical view. De Vito Battaglia emphasized the "superior level of artistic realization" in the *Isaac*, noting the discrepancy in expressive quality between it and the other paintings in the cycle, the majority of which she attempted to ascribe to Tiepolo. In fact, her observation would seem to undermine her position, but from it she derived the proposal that the *Isaac* was later in date—which is true, notwithstanding her incongruous premise.

The strong dramatic accent in this work—the boldness of the invention and foreshortenings, the cold light playing on dryly modeled volumes, at once spare and harsh—points to Tiepolo's inspiration at this defining moment by the example of Federico Bencovich, and in particular the latter's *Sacrifice of Iphigenia* (Schönborn Collection, Pommersfelden). Arslan was the first to point this out, followed by Pallucchini, who confirmed the necessity of dating the *Sacrifice of Isaac* later than the *Saint Thomas* and the *Saint John*; Martini agreed.

Among Tiepolo's works of these years, the *Sacrifice of Isaac* is closest in style to the so-called *Abraham Banishing Hagar(?)* (no. 8), which, when first published by Morassi,[1] bore a signature and the damaged date 17[. . .]—read by the author as 1717 or, more convincingly, 1719 (for another interpretation, see entry for no. 8). This date would seem appropriate for the *Isaac* as well, given the strong blocking in of the forms, highlighted by a cold light, and especially the resulting appearance of the old man in each work.

Thus, a dating of the painting to 1724 or later, as some have proposed, does not seem possible. According to a document published by Muraro in 1975, in 1724 the architect Domenico Rossi advised the deputies of the Ospedaletto on the space above which the *Isaac* was located. Two superimposed choir lofts projected from the columns, and Rossi counseled removing them, since they violated the symmetry of the church. They were to be replaced by an arrangement similar to that in the area near the girls' choir, which was the first space near the presbytery. This would have involved putting in place "a large painting below, and above, in the arch, a half-moon window or grille."[2] Muraro thought that the "large painting" could be identified as the *Sacrifice of Isaac*, and he deduced from this the 1724 date as a terminus post quem. He has been followed in his opinion by Aikema and others.

In reality, the large painting proposed by Rossi was Lazzarini's *Pool of Bethesda*. This assumption is supported both by the size of Lazzarini's canvas and its pairing with Peruzzini's *Assumption of the Virgin*, then in the space near the high altar and the choir. And, in fact, above Peruzzini's painting there was a half-moon window—the grille referred to in Rossi's document. This was reproduced above Lazzarini's canvas: both windows are now obliterated but are visible in photographs of the interior dating from early in this century. There can, I think, be no doubt that had the *Sacrifice of Isaac* not already been

5. The Sacrifice of Isaac
Ca. 1719–24
244 × 378 cm (96⅛ × 149 in.)
S. Maria dei Derelitti (the Ospedaletto), Venice

PROVENANCE:
S. Maria dei Derelitti, Venice

REFERENCES:
Zanetti 1733, p. 255; Moschini 1815, vol. 1, p. 184; Soravia 1822, p. 215; Bianchini 1897, p. 17; Modern 1902, p. 22; Kiriaki 1907, p. 9; Molmenti 1909, pp. 46–50; Sack 1910, p. 156; Fogolari 1923, p. 61; Fiocco 1926, p. 16; Lorenzetti 1926 (1956 ed., p. 376); De Vito Battaglia 1934, p. 481; Pallucchini 1934a, p. 77; Pallucchini 1934b, p. 485; Morassi 1935, p. 144; Arslan 1935–36, pp. 184–87; Goering 1939, p. 146; Porcella 1941, p. 176; Morassi 1943, p. 13; Pallucchini 1944, p. 4; Venice 1951, pp. 5, 6; Pallucchini 1960, pp. 66–67; Morassi 1962, pp. 56–57; Martini 1964, pp. 60, 202; Pallucchini 1968, p. 86; Udine 1971, pp. 7, 23, no. 2; Martini 1974, p. 34; Zava Boccazzi 1974, pp. 179–83; Muraro [1976] pp. 62–65; Zava Boccazzi 1979, pp. 168–69; Aikema 1982, p. 372; Martini 1982, p. 508, n. 188; Pilo 1982, pp. 151–54; Pilo [1985], pp. 128–32, 158–59; Levey 1986, p. 11; Sponza 1986, p. 53; Sponza 1986–87, pp. 220–21; Barcham 1989, p. 53; Gemin and Pedrocco 1993, pp. 36, 40, 41, 43, 243, no. 62; Pallucchini 1995, pp. 319–21

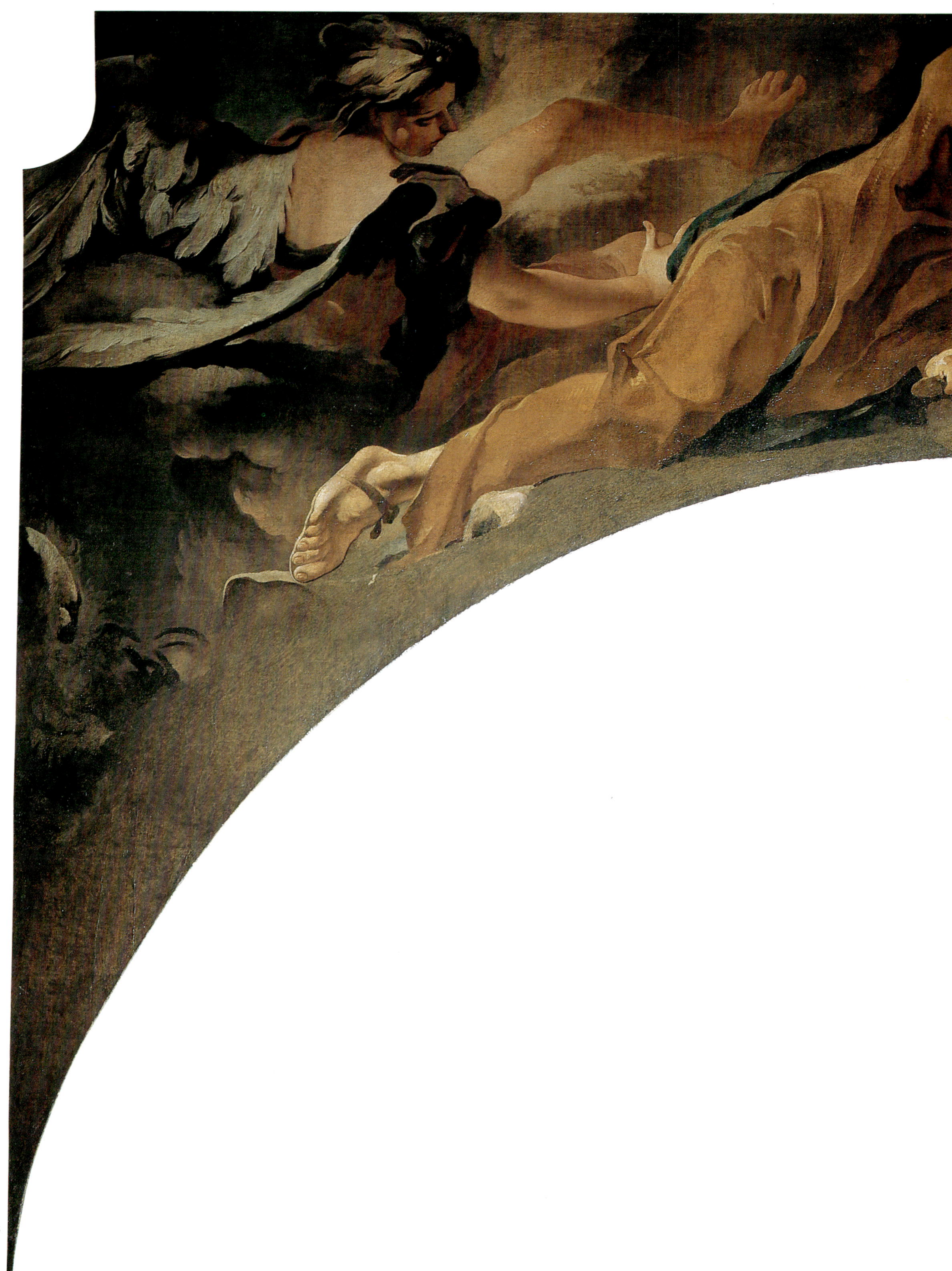

5

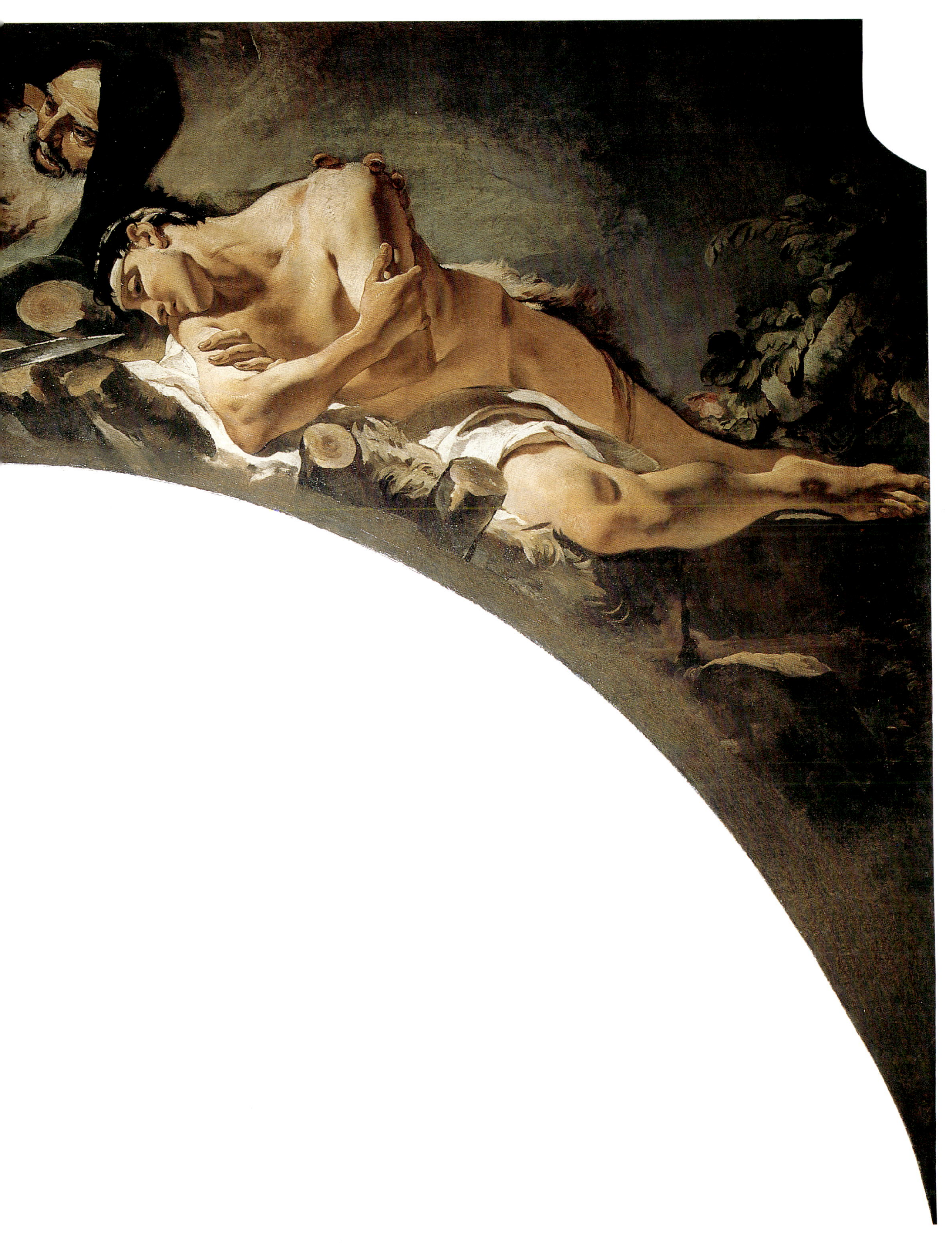

in place, Rossi—who was careful to note all the particulars of his project and was so sensitive to matters of symmetry—would have mentioned it explicitly. He did not, and the date of 1724 can therefore be taken not as a terminus post quem but as a terminus ante quem—the date before which the picture must have been painted: the circumstantial evidence of Rossi's proposal corresponds to the evidence of style.

To this writer, as to Fogolari and Arslan, the *Sacrifice of Isaac* is marked by forms that have the character of cast metal or molten copper and that speak of a slower, more measured tempo than do the fervid, aggressive rhythms that underlie the *Saint Thomas* and *Saint John*. Tiepolo here achieved a degree of formal beauty of a neo-Attic, neo-Aeginetan sort, a rare and compact equilibrium that we might almost call classical.

GMP

Notes

1. Morassi 1937.
2. Muraro 1975, p. 66: "un quadro grande di sotto a pittura, e di sopra nel volto la sua meza luna a finestra o sia gelosia."

THE ACCADEMIA MYTHOLOGIES

6a. Diana and Actaeon
6b. The Rape of Europa

6a. Diana and Actaeon
Ca. 1720–22
100 × 135 cm (39⅜ × 53¼ in.)
Gallerie dell'Accademia, Venice

6b. The Rape of Europa
Ca. 1720–22
100 × 135 cm (39⅜ × 53¼ in.)
Gallerie dell'Accademia, Venice

When these two pictures were acquired from the collection of Count Francesco Agosti of Belluno in 1898, they bore an attribution to Sebastiano Ricci. The same is true of their two companions, which are also based on Ovid's *Metamorphoses*: *Apollo and Marsyas* (fig. 28), and *Diana and Callisto* (fig. 29), acquired from Countess Capponi of Belluno for the Gallerie dell'Accademia, Venice, in 1907. It is likely that all four paintings originally decorated a palace in Belluno, as their dimensions and complementary subjects suggest. Their provenance from Belluno is probably responsible for the attribution to the Bellunese Ricci, to whose work they bear an undeniable affinity in terms of theme and in their development of the courtly style that inaugurates the Rococo. The *Diana and Callisto*—perhaps the most fascinating canvas in the series for the exquisite, tender preciosity of the female nudes—seems an overt homage to Ricci's mythological paintings of about 1703–4 formerly in the Palazzo Fulcis–de Bertoldi (Museo Civico, Belluno). Evidence of Tiepolo's authorship did not escape the eye of Julius von Schlosser, who brought them to the attention of Sack. Derschau expunged them from Ricci's oeuvre. They were nevertheless exhibited under Ricci's name in the 1922 exhibition of Italian paintings of the seicento and settecento held at Palazzo Pitti, Florence. There Voss recognized them as unmistakably by Tiepolo, although their exceptional character continued to give rise to hypotheses linking them to a Riccian milieu (a tentative attribution to the Belluno painter Gasparo Diziani was made, and Fiocco proposed Ricci's student Francesco Fontebasso).

We have here extremely suggestive, paradigmatic examples of Tiepolo's style at a moment of delicate and felicitous transition: that moment in the early 1720s when he had completely assimilated the caricatural and dramatic style associated especially with Federico Bencovich and was moving beyond it, spurred by his insatiable curiosity and the wealth and fecundity of his creative fantasy. Elements of recent, incandescent experiments are still present: for example, Diana's face is structured in the same manner as the face of the apostle in the *Saint John* at the Ospedaletto, Venice (no. 2b). And we find the same traits in a more developed form in the *Diana and Callisto*, the *Apollo and Marsyas*, the *modello* for the *Saint Dominic in Glory* of 1723 (Gallerie dell'Accademia, Venice), and in the ceiling fresco of about 1724–25 in Palazzo Sandi, Venice (fig. 22)—especially the scene of Amphion in the last decoration and its related *modello* (Courtauld Institute Galleries, London). These features now become part of the expressive language of the painter.

In 1716 Ricci had returned to Venice after a long sojourn in England and a passage through Paris, bringing with

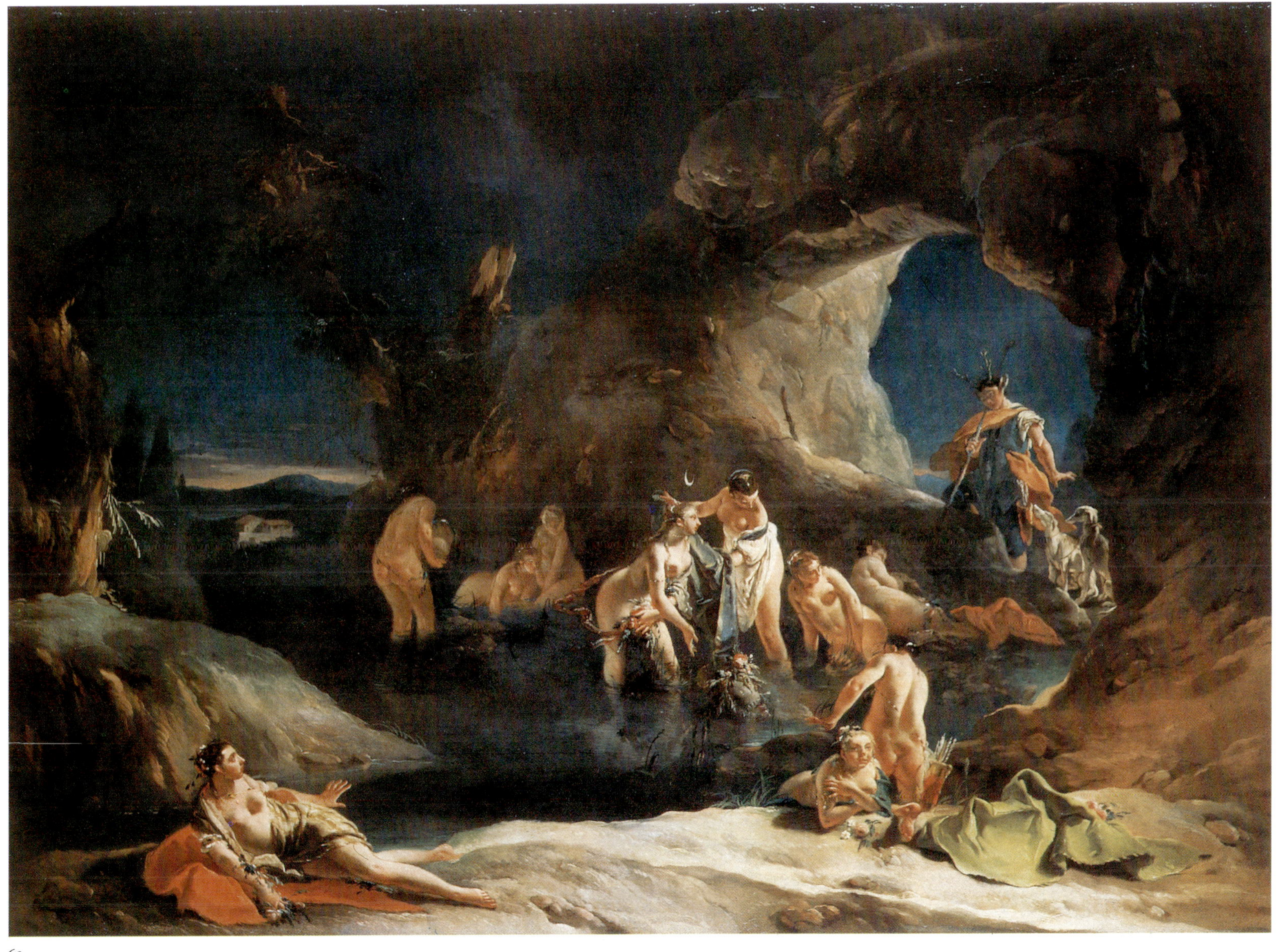

6a

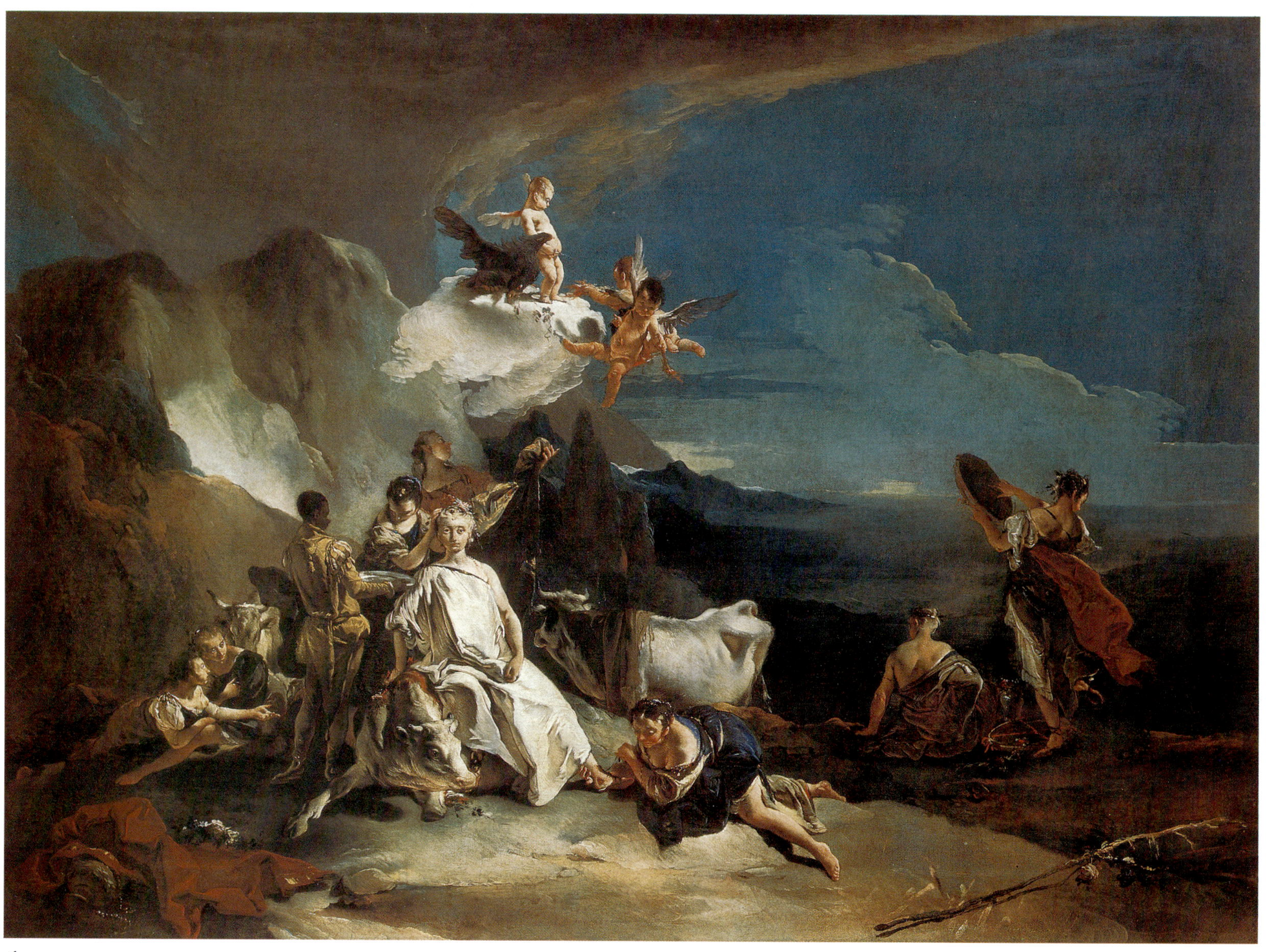

6b

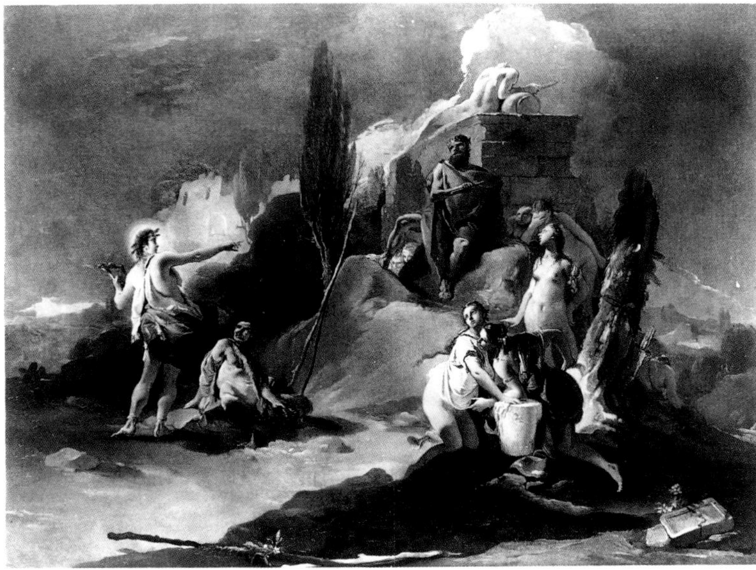

Fig. 28. *Apollo and Marsyas*. Oil on canvas. Gallerie dell'Accademia, Venice

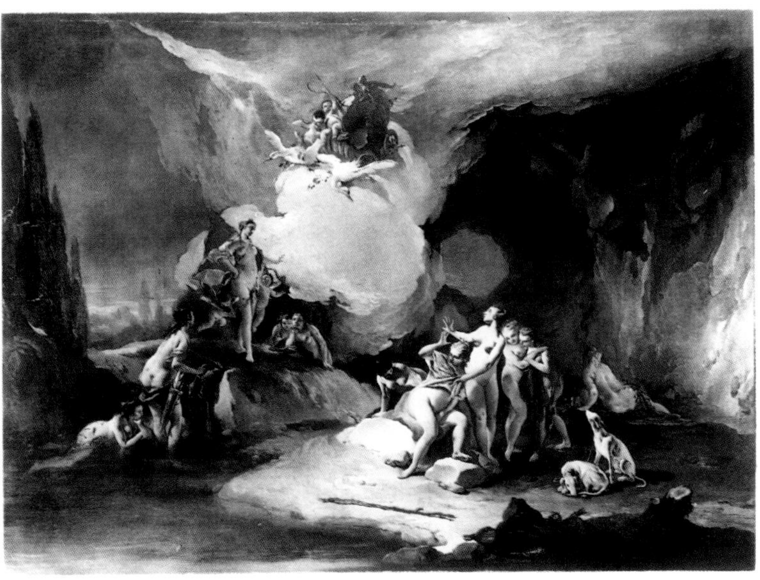

Fig. 29. *Diana and Callisto*. Oil on canvas. Gallerie dell'Accademia, Venice

him a luminous but sculptural manner of painting that may have had a positive effect on Tiepolo's interpretation of the Ovidian spirit of these refined mythologies. The *Diana and Actaeon* tells the story of the young hunter who, having surprised Diana at her bath, was transformed by the goddess into a stag and torn to pieces by his own dogs (*Metamorphoses* 3.99–252). The subject demanded a notable deployment of figural and scenic abilities: in particular because, as Levey noted in 1960, Tiepolo wished—perhaps more in this picture than in the others of the series—to be faithful to the narrative of the ancient poet. The fablelike atmosphere—the deep recess of the Gargaphia valley, with its shady grotto circumscribed by a natural arch of pumice and tufa, and the clear spring of silvery water ringed by a spacious grassy bank seen in a surreal light created by that extraordinary stage director Tiepolo—is populated by statuesque forms, figures of extreme elegance at once forcefully constructed and strong in visual effect. In the group of nymphs gathered around the goddess in the water and those relaxing on the grassy banks, as well as in the figure of the unfortunate hunter, glimpsed through the arch, surrounded by his dogs, his limbs showing signs of his tragic transformation, there is an exquisite beauty, as destructive as it is sustaining. Tiepolo employed a thick and firm medium laid on with compact, decisive brushstrokes to create forms that are poised between an ideal tension of a purity tending toward perfection—such as the myth demanded—and the enchanting reality of earthy carnality.

The theme of the *Rape of Europa* (*Metamorphoses* 2.836–75) was among the best-loved and most frequently treated subjects of the Venetian cinquecento. Paolo Veronese left a memorable interpretation of the story that, through Bertucci Contarini's 1713 bequest, had become part of the public patrimony of Venice in the Palazzo Ducale. Yet the degree to which Veronese's painting spurred Tiepolo's imagination is unclear. He was certainly familiar with Ovid's text: the proof of it is in his own picture, in which effective motifs drawn from Ovid are interpreted poetically. Above all, he revealed an innate propensity for the harmony of the philosophical wisdom and the lyrical detachment of Ovid's tale. This allowed Tiepolo to visualize important passages of the narrative with great subtlety and wit: Zeus, transformed into a bull, mingling with the maidens; his white coat; his apparent gentleness, so great that he wears a fine dewlap around his neck and takes flowers from the hands of the object of his desire; his prone position on the tawny-colored sand of the shore, offering himself to the virginal caresses of the girl, who, innocently, has climbed onto his back. At the same time Tiepolo invented an enchanting setting: a magical landscape (perhaps the first of his career) comprising the little beach wedged between crags sloping down into a dark blue sea illuminated, like the nocturnal blue of the sky, by distant flashes; the characters and salient motifs seen in full light—perhaps lunar, perhaps artificial, as though the artist, with his captivating, precocious abilities as a stage director, possessed floodlights. Into his creation Tiepolo infused elements of his personal temperament, taking the opportunity to develop for his own gratification motifs as bold as they are amusing.

In 1717 the widow of Domenico Guardi, Claudia Picler, succeeded in having her fifteen-year-old daughter, Cecilia, accepted into the Ospedaletto, despite rules

PROVENANCE:
Count Francesco Agosti, Belluno (until 1898); Gallerie dell'Accademia, Venice (from 1898)

REFERENCES:
Rassegna bibliografica dell'arte italiana, vol. 2 (1899), pp. 101ff.; Cantalamessa 1902, pp. 30–31.; Sack 1910, p. 163; Serra 1914, p. 208; Derschau 1916, pp. 165–66; Derschau 1922, p. 160; Florence 1922, pp. 83, 115; Voss 1922, pp. 426ff.; Fogolari 1923, pp. 54ff.; Nugent 1925, p. 221; Fiocco 1929a, p. 544; Fiocco 1929b, pp. 65, 80; Arslan 1935–36, pp. 247, 250; Fiocco 1938, p. 152; Goering 1939, p. 146; Morassi 1941–42, p. 96; Morassi 1943, p. 14; Venice 1951, pp. 17–20; Morassi 1952, p. 91; Morassi 1955a, p. 10; Morassi 1962, pp. 53–54; Pallucchini 1968, p. 87; Rizzi in Venice 1969b, p. 346; Moschini Marconi 1970, pp. 107–8; Nepi Scirè and Valcanover 1985, pp. 173–74; Levey 1986, pp. 16–18; Nepi Scirè 1991, pp. 242–43; Gemin and Pedrocco 1993, pp. 52, 228, nos. 29, 30; London 1994, pp. 174, 494; Magrini in Venice 1995a, p. 232; Pallucchini 1995, p. 333

to the contrary.[1] It was here that Tiepolo and the girl probably first met—furtively, we must assume. Two years later, in 1719, the two married. The circumstances were not propitious, for Tiepolo requested permission to dispense with posting the banns and registration of the marriage to avoid the disapproval of his family.[2] In light of this situation, it seems plausible that Tiepolo gave Agenor's proud daughter, the beautiful Phoenician princess kidnapped by Zeus, the features of his young wife.[3] He followed the same impulse a few years later, in a painting portraying Cecilia in the guise of Campaspe, the mistress of Alexander the Great, and himself as Apelles, the prince of painters in the ancient world (no. 11).

In the *Rape of Europa* Tiepolo identified himself not with the most famous painter of antiquity but, audaciously, with the ruler of the gods. If we accept the conceptual metaphor of the picture, the artist himself is the bull who will abduct Europa-Cecilia, a domestic model who has become part of his repertory of images—in the most conspicuous role of all, and one that admits no intruders. In fact, to make matters absolutely clear, above Europa is a small cloud on which an eagle, the symbol of Zeus, presses the point home with spread wings. Next to him is a cupid who, with an action both eloquent and brazen, wards off his companions who are attempting to approach: "Be gone!"

Tiepolo as Zeus. . . . To the artist's well-founded confidence in his abilities and in his superiority—intellectual and rational more than emotional—was joined a capacity for self-criticism. This capacity reveals itself in an attitude of subtle self-mockery that presides over the courtly, sumptuous representation. Hyperbole finds an elegant resolution through a rare balance of various potentialities. This equilibrium is among the most notable of the components of Tiepolo's rich personality; and from this same trait derives the mildly playful unfolding of the composition, which surely is not at odds with the formal elegance that creates the visual effect of the image but rather integrates it in a felicitous fashion. Therein lies the power of Tiepolo's sublime Arcadia.

GMP

Notes

1. See Ellero 1995.
2. See Bortolan 1973, pp. 51–52.
3. Levey 1986, p. 18.

7. Susanna and the Elders

7. Susanna and the Elders
Ca. 1720–22
56.2 × 43.4 cm (22⅛ × 17⅛ in.)
The Wadsworth Atheneum, Hartford, Gift of Mr. and Mrs. Arthur L. Erlanger (1954.196)

PROVENANCE:
Böhler and Steinmeier, Munich; Albert Keller, New York; Schaeffer Galleries, New York (until 1946); Mr. and Mrs. Arthur L. Erlanger, New York (1946–54)

REFERENCES:
Morassi 1949, pp. 75–76; Buckley 1955; Morassi 1962, pp. 13–14; Pallucchini 1968, p. 88, no. 26; Mariuz and Pavanello 1985, p. 109; Barcham 1989, pp. 39, 42; Cadogan 1991, pp. 234–36; Gemin and Pedrocco 1993, p. 239, no. 56

The subject is from the Old Testament Apocrypha. While bathing in her garden, Susanna was set upon by two aged judges who had hidden themselves in the shrubbery in order to watch her. They threatened to falsely accuse her of having an illicit relationship with a young man if she did not submit to their desires. Susanna chose to be slandered; she was initially condemned but eventually vindicated by Daniel, who revealed the old men's testimony to be untrue.

On the model of Piazzetta, Tiepolo set the scene with a minimum of props and a notable lack of interest in space. The basin and fountain, with its Berninesque statue and fanciful silver urn filled with flowers, establish the foreground stage for the dramatic confrontation, theatrically closed off at the back by a raised curtain and a distant landscape view. One judge hovers menacingly above his victim, lasciviously fingering her body, while the other excitedly tempts her with a material reward. Susanna, her head turned back and the undulating form of her naked body set off by a swath of red drapery, attempts to gather up her shift with one hand as she raises the other in a gesture of helpless alarm. The same contraction of space, diagonal orientation, and use of dramatic gesture to convey a story are found in Tiepolo's *Martyrdom of Saint Bartholomew* (fig. 16), which also offers an analogy for the sharp color contrasts of the *Susanna*. The *Saint Bartholomew* was commissioned in 1722, and this provides a terminus ante quem for the smaller, brighter, and airier *Susanna*. (Morassi's dating of the canvas was premised in part on a comparison of it to the *Sacrifice of Isaac* [no. 5], which he incorrectly believed was painted in 1715.) We may note that the pose of Susanna was taken up again by Tiepolo on the ceiling of Palazzo Sandi in Venice, where, reversed, it was used to express Eurydice's surprise.

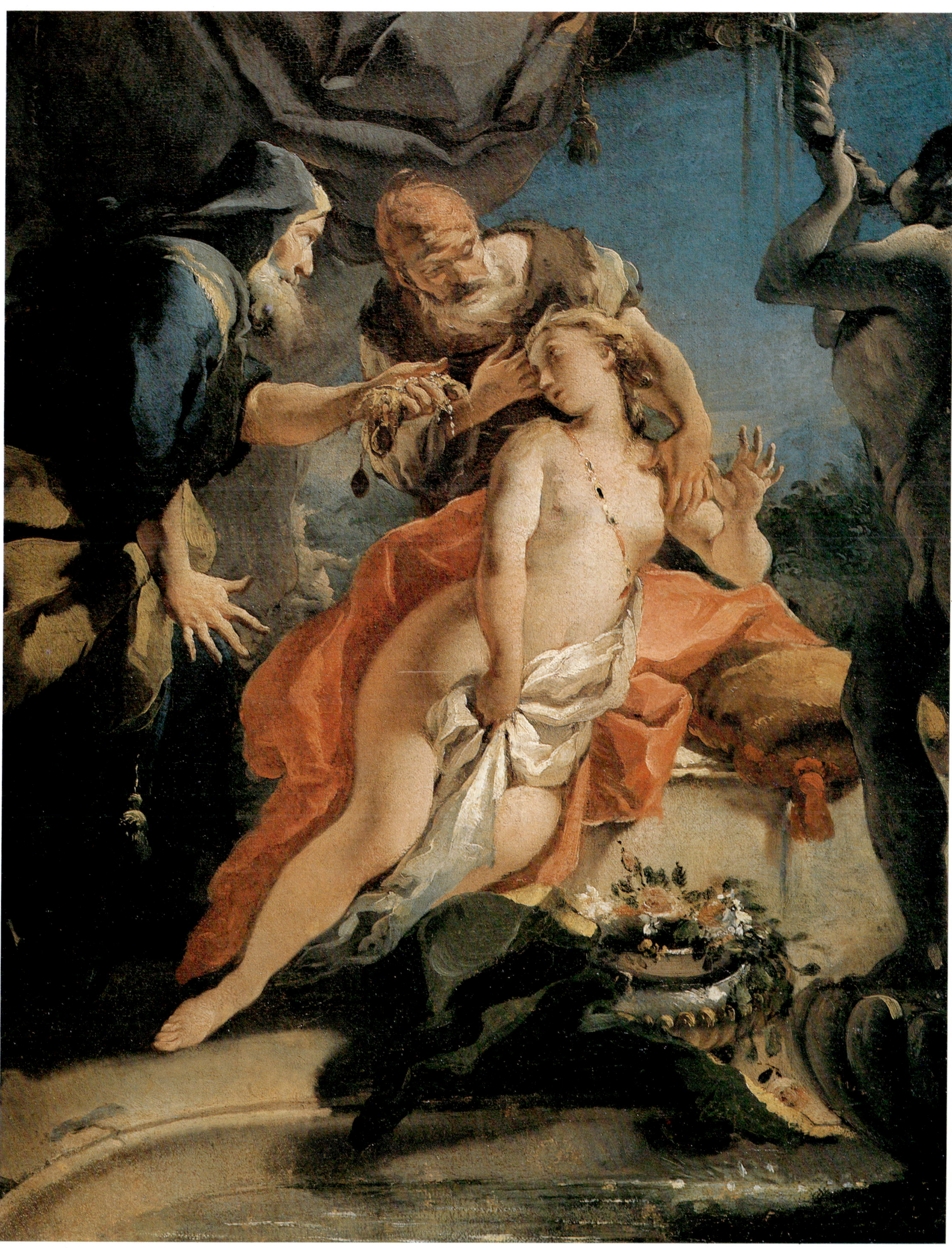

The Piazzettesque moment of Tiepolo's art is defined by an interest in dramatic contrasts of light and dark, spatial and compositional compression, and emphatic gesture—so contrary to the academic training he received in Lazzarini's studio but completely in keeping with his admiration for Tintoretto; its climax is marked by the six-and-a-half-meter-wide *Madonna of Mount Carmel* (fig. 19), commissioned in 1721 but delivered only in 1727. *Susanna and the Elders* does not exhibit the fluency and elegance of Tiepolo's mature treatment of mythology and legend—it is, after all, a work of modest dimensions that did not pose great demands. But in it he accommodates key elements of the work of his most illustrious living compatriot to his own more witty and fanciful imagination. And the informal character of the picture allowed him to use his brush with a wonderful liveliness, or *prontezza*, as well as to show off his innate abilities as a storyteller.

KC

8. Abraham Banishing Hagar(?)

8. Abraham Banishing Hagar (?)
Ca. 1722–24(?)
96 × 136 cm (37⅞ × 53⅝ in.)
Private collection

The subject of this arresting and enigmatic picture—recognized as a keystone of Tiepolo's early career since it was first published in 1937—has never been convincingly established. It is usually described as Abraham banishing Hagar, as told in Genesis 18.6. To obtain an heir, Abraham's wife, Sarah, charged her maidservant, Hagar, to sleep with Abraham. But when Hagar conceived, she lorded it over Sarah, who demanded that Hagar be banished. Tiepolo's painting shows a figure in priestly vestments apparently ordering a pleading woman into a templelike structure, while two figures look on in astonishment. The action ill accords with the Genesis story, and the identification is almost certainly wrong.[1] No more convincing is the recent attempt to associate the subject with another Old Testament story, Esther 1.11–22, recounting how the Persian king Ahasuerus punished his queen, Vashti, for refusing his summons:[2] the event shown finds no precise point of reference in the biblical narrative, and moreover, the story itself is merely a footnote to the history of Esther. Alternatively, and equally unsatisfactorily, the classical story of the sacrifice of Polyxena has been proposed as the theme.[3] As told by Ovid in the *Metamorphoses*, the ghost of Achilles appeared to Agamemnon and his men, demanding the sacrifice of Priam's daughter, Polyxena, on a pyre before his tomb. This rite was performed by a priest, who was reduced to tears by the maiden's courage and noble words. That the story is represented here is unlikely, for the subject was often painted—several times by Tiepolo's contemporary Giambattista Pittoni—but never in a fashion remotely similar to that employed in this picture. Tiepolo's approach to narration could be discursive but not abstruse or tentative (he is, arguably, one of the great storytellers of Western art); we can, therefore, be confident that the difficulties encountered in identifying the subject of this canvas have to do with its recondite source rather than with Tiepolo's treatment, which reveals his habitual attention to dramatic moment, gesture, and expression.

According to Morassi, the picture was signed and indistinctly dated 1717 or 1719 on the firebrand next to the incense brazier. However, no trace of an inscription is now visible, and the accuracy of Morassi's reading cannot be confirmed. Since the picture is frequently treated as one of Tiepolo's few dated works, and since its style is so difficult to reconcile with a date in the teens, it is worth recording the statement Morassi made when he first published the picture. "The two last figures are barely legible," he wrote, "and the upper portions are almost obliterated. Nevertheless, it is clear that the third figure is a 1, while the last might be a 7 or a 9."[4] What is unclear is how predisposed Morassi was to read an indistinct date as in the teens because of the presumed chronology of the works to which he related its style. Interestingly, those works are now quite firmly assigned to the 1720s, not the teens. They include the *Heliodorus and the High Priest Onias* (no. 10), the *Madonna of Mount Carmel* (fig. 19), the four mythologies in the Gallerie dell'Accademia, Venice (see no. 6a, b), and the frescoes in the Arcivescovado (Patriarchal Palace), Udine (fig. 24). Morassi also insisted that the *Sacrifice of Isaac* (no. 5)—now detached from a putative date of about 1716 and placed more credibly about 1719–20—

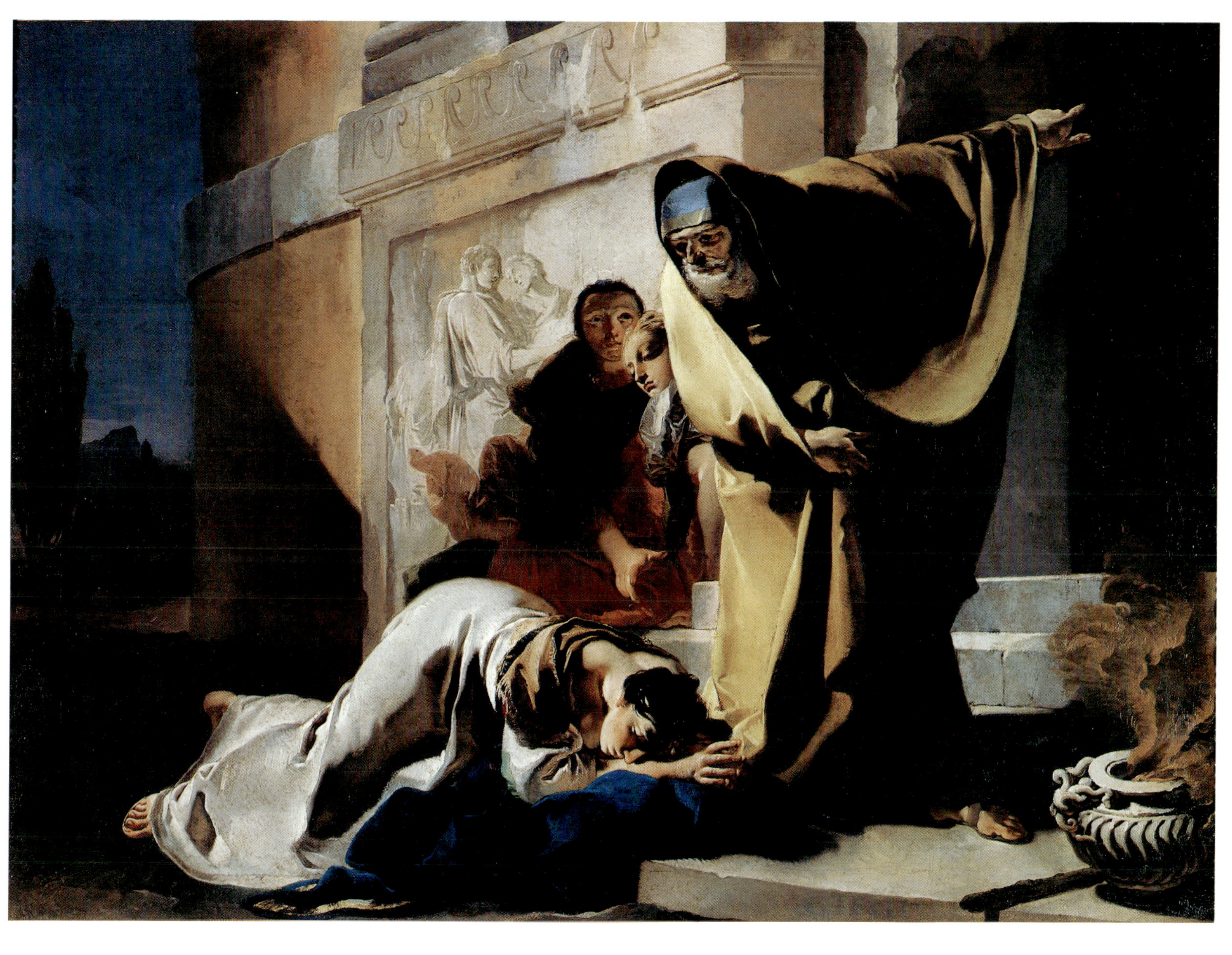

PROVENANCE:
Count Giovanni Rasini, Milan (by 1937)

REFERENCES:
Morassi 1937, pp. 53–54; Morassi 1943, p. 13; Venice 1951, p. 7, no. 2; Bordeaux 1956, p. 22, no. 47; Morassi 1962, p. 28; Pallucchini 1968, p. 87, no. 13; Knox 1979, p. 417; Aikema 1982, p. 361; Levey 1986, p. 14; Aikema 1987b, pp. 450–52; Barcham 1989, pp. 39–43; Gemin and Pedrocco 1993, p. 56 n. 101, p. 225, no. 22

was unquestionably earlier than the *Hagar*. What we now know of Tiepolo's early career does not recommend a date for the *Hagar* much before about 1722—the year he began work on the intensely Piazzettesque *Martyrdom of Saint Bartholomew* (fig. 16).

Tiepolo's youthful productions show an exceptional variety of style and modes reflecting his restless experimentation, and it is dangerous to be dogmatic about precise dates. This picture is certainly among his most striking early narratives. Yet there is no trace in it of either the haunting, chimerical vision of Federico Bencovich or the decorative instinct of Louis Dorigny—the two poles to which he was so strongly attracted in the teens. Nor has the dark, dramatically charged, chiaroscural world of Piazzetta played a significant part in shaping the narrative. Rather, the painting looks ahead both to the *Madonna of Mount Carmel* and the light-filled, frescoed ceiling of Palazzo Sandi in Venice (fig. 22). In the frescoes we find the same striking use of emphatic gesture coupled with figures placed obliquely one to the other, the same modeling in broad planes of light, a similar range of colors (allowing for the paler tonality of the frescoes), and the same fluency in execution. Nothing could be further from the angular contours of the figures in Tiepolo's first works, with their raw vigor, abrupt shifts in modeling, and disjointed disposition. Far from marking the climax of Tiepolo's earliest, tenebrist style, the picture testifies to an integration of space and figural action that will mark all of his subsequent production. (The demonstrative gesture of the male figure might even be said to look ahead to some of the *Scherzi*.)

The somewhat heretical date suggested here would eliminate the possibility that this was one of the many pictures that da Canal asserted had been painted by the very young Tiepolo for Doge Giovanni II Corner.[5] It would also clear the way for positing a more coherent development in Tiepolo's first ten years as an artist.[6]

KC

NOTES

1. Barcham (1989, p. 42 n. 68) has pointed out some analogies with Pietro da Cortona's painting of Hagar returning to Abraham (Kunsthistorisches Museum, Vienna), but in that picture there is no temple and no prostrate woman, and instead of two astonished bystanders, the figure of Sarah is shown.
2. Gemin and Pedrocco 1993, p. 56 n. 101.
3. See Aikema 1987b, p. 452.
4. Morassi 1937.
5. Aikema 1987b, p. 452.
6. A related drawing was sold at Bascher, Paris, on 1 April 1993.

THE DECORATIONS FOR PALAZZO SANDI

9a. Hercules and Antaeus
9b. Apollo and Marsyas

9a. Hercules and Antaeus
Ca. 1725–26
270 × 125 cm (106⅜ × 49¼ in.)
Private collection, Vicenza

9b. Apollo and Marsyas
Ca. 1725–26
270 × 125 cm (106¼ × 49¼ in.)
Private collection, Vicenza

Together with a large, horizontal canvas showing Ulysses discovering Achilles disguised as a maiden among the daughters of King Lycomedes, these two pictures constitute part of the decorations Tiepolo carried out with his older compatriot Nicolò Bambini for the main room, or *salone*, of Palazzo Sandi in Venice. Located in the parish of S. Angelo on the Corte dell'Albero, the palace was designed by Domenico Rossi and built for Tommaso Sandi (1674–1743), reportedly between 1721 and 1725.[1] Tiepolo's contribution to the decorative ensemble comprised a ceiling fresco (fig. 22)—his earliest surviving work of this kind in Venice—and the three canvases, the largest of which, the *Discovery of Achilles* (fig. 30), filled the space of a lateral wall; the two vertical ones, exhibited here, were hung as a pair to one side of the entrance door. Around the frescoed ceiling, Bambini painted a frieze executed in oil on canvas and showing battling animals, satyrs, and

Opposite: Detail, no. 9a

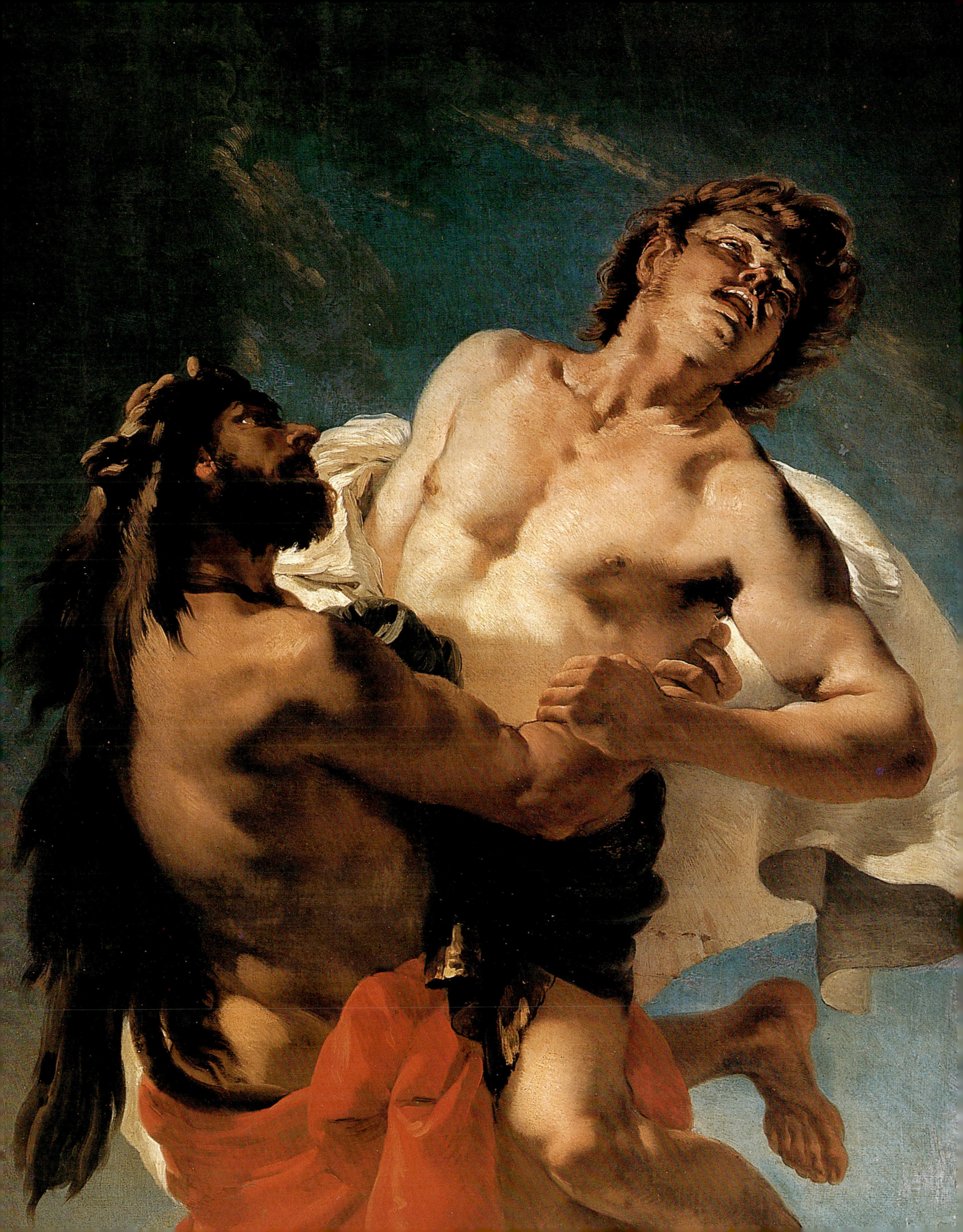

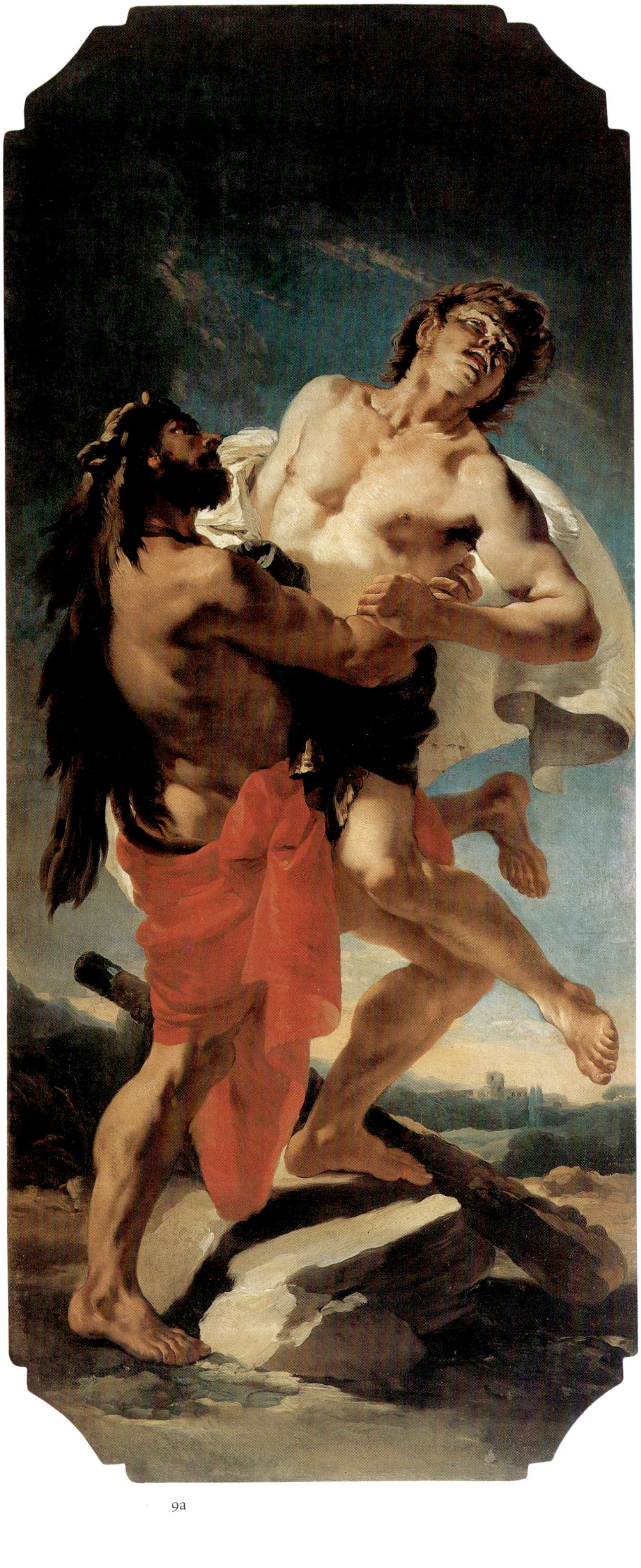

9a

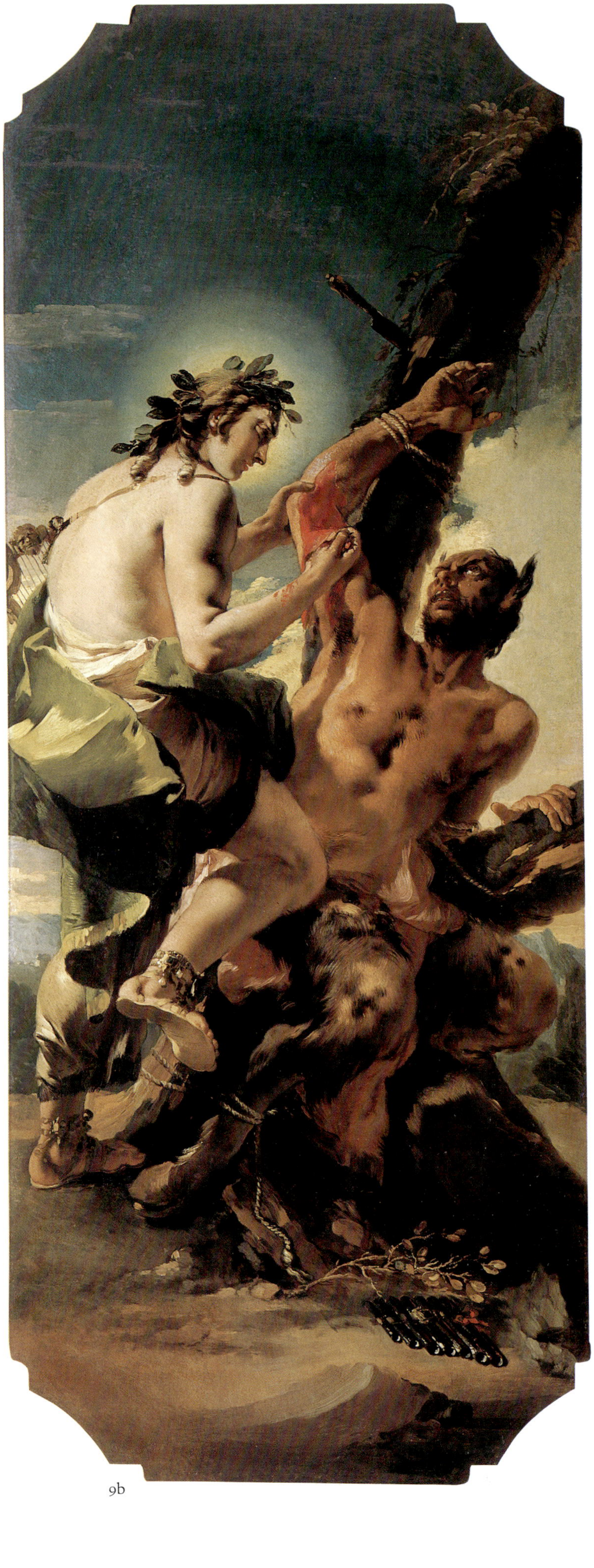

9b

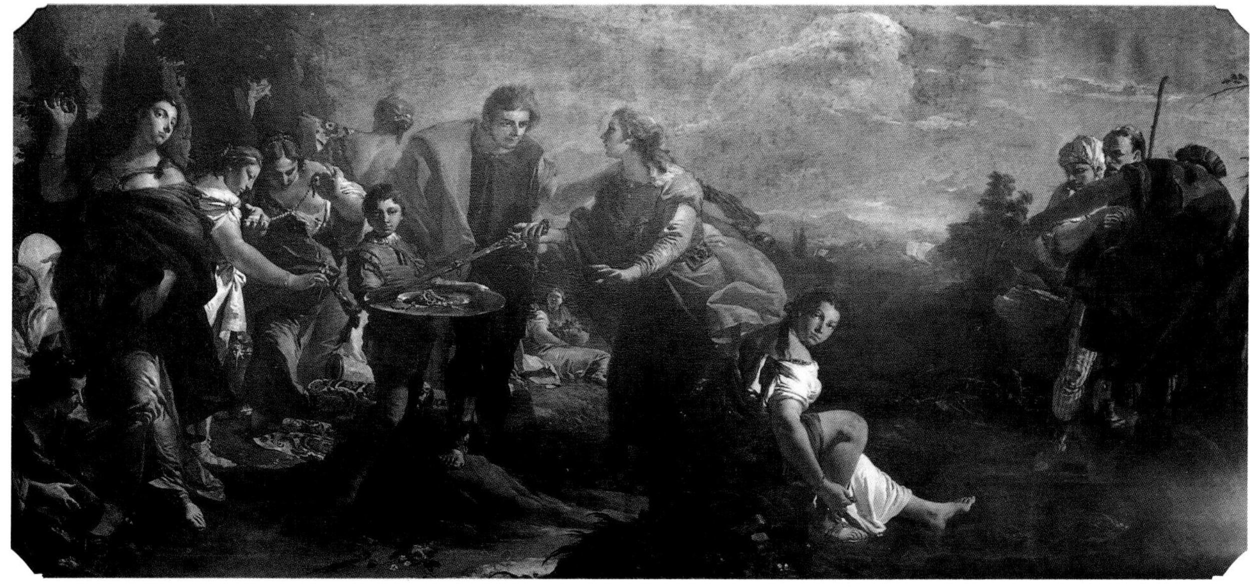

Fig. 30. *The Discovery of Achilles*. Oil on canvas. Conti da Schio, Castelgomberto

men, a horizontal canvas representing Veturia pleading with her son Coriolanus to spare Rome—a pendant to Tiepolo's large picture on the opposite wall—and, for the other side of the entrance, a vertical canvas portraying the Three Graces.[2] The combination of frescoes and oil paintings may strike us as peculiar, but it was quite common in early-settecento Venice; the same formula was adopted in Ca' Dolfin as well, where Bambini frescoed the ceiling and Tiepolo painted canvases to be set into the wall (see no. 12a–g). The *salone* in Palazzo Sandi is modest in size—10.6 by 6.65 by 5.1 meters—and the combined effect of the fresco and the canvases must have been overpowering.

In 1732 da Canal described the theme of the ceiling as the power of eloquence, and, in fact, the scenes all relate to examples of eloquence found in those standard Baroque manuals of iconography, Vincenzo Cartari's *Imagini degli dei* and Cesare Ripa's *Iconologia*.[3] Mercury, the god of eloquence, and Minerva, goddess of prudence, preside at the center of the ceiling, while around the periphery of the composition are shown Orpheus leading Eurydice out of Hades, having procured her release through the power of his music; Bellerophon on Pegasus slaying the Chimera, thereby civilizing his habitat; Amphion causing the walls of Thebes to build themselves to the sound of his lyre; and the Celtic Hercules holding his listeners enthralled, symbolized by a chain stretching from his tongue to his captives. The canvas portraying Apollo and Marsyas relates to the theme of musical eloquence represented on the ceiling by the stories of Orpheus and Amphion: Marsyas had challenged Apollo to a musical contest and lost and, as punishment for his audacity, was flayed alive by the god. The story of Hercules vanquishing the giant Antaeus, whose strength derived from contact with the earth, by lifting him in the air and crushing him, was clearly chosen to complement the depiction of Hercules on the ceiling and, like it, symbolizes the triumph of civilization over the bestial.

Tiepolo had rarely treated subjects of such concentrated physical violence—each composition involves just two figures confronting each other—and he seems to have sought inspiration in seventeenth-century painting. Morassi was reminded of the dark, muscular work of the Venetianized German Carl Loth, and the paintings of the Neapolitan Francesco Solimena have also been cited. Tiepolo's interest in Solimena's work, with its blend of classical idealism and tenebrist drama, is well

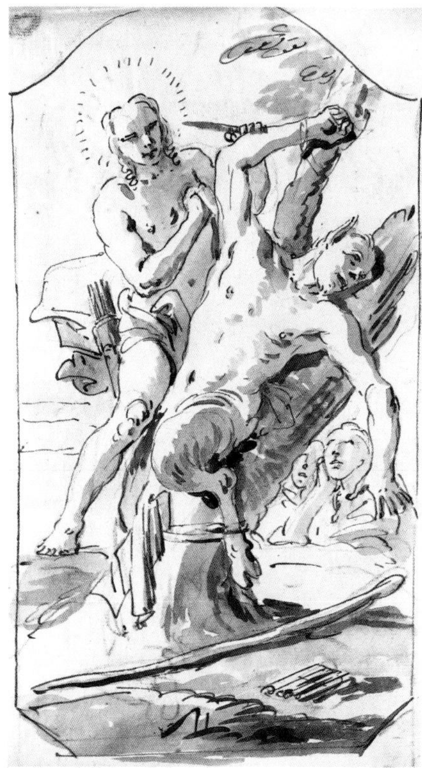

Fig. 31. *Apollo and Marsyas*. Pen and ink and wash over traces of graphite. Victoria and Albert Museum, London (D.1825.195–1885)

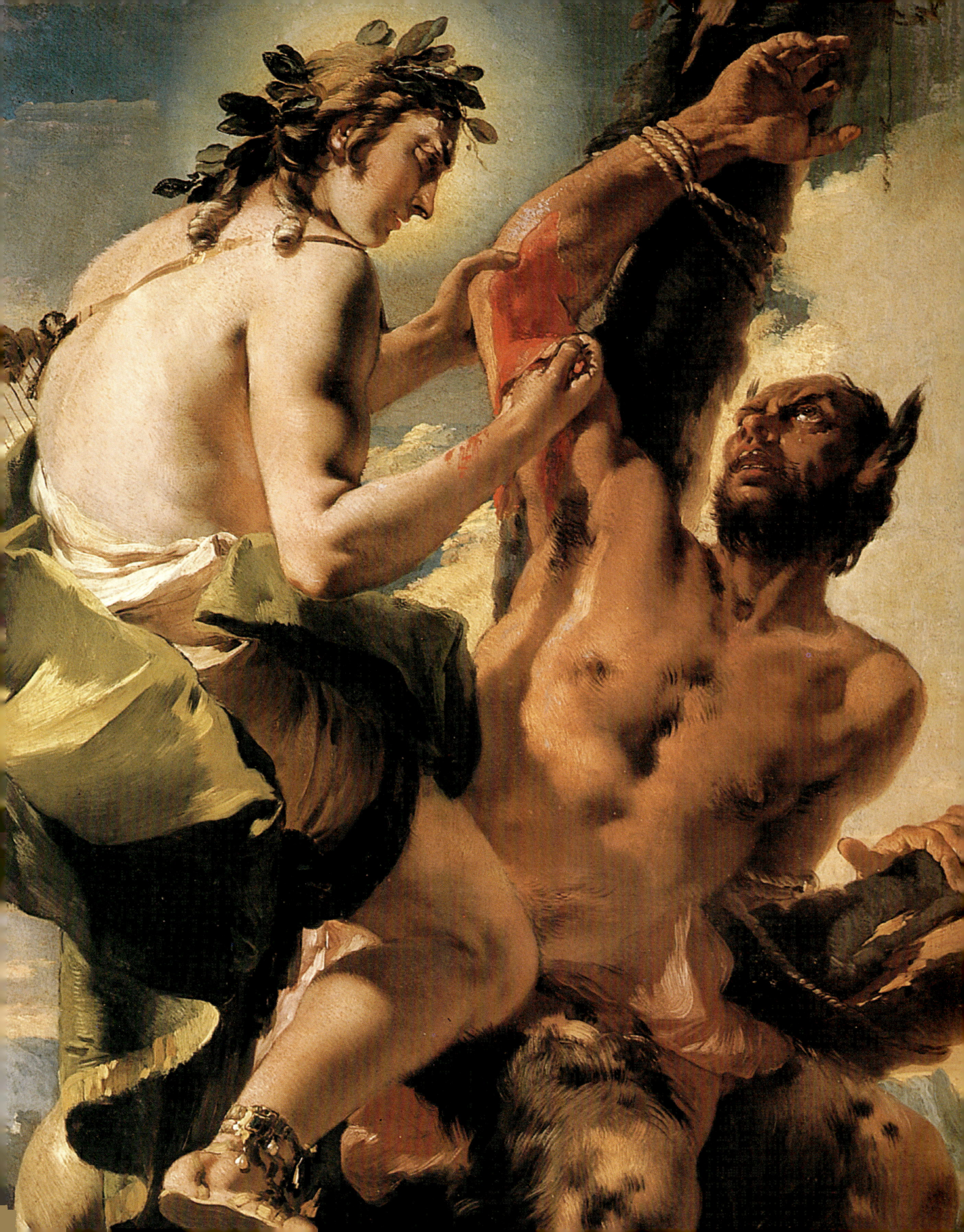

known. One of the executioners in his *Martyrdom of Saint Bartholomew* (fig. 16), painted for the church of S. Stae in Venice in 1722–23, derives from a figure in Solimena's *Rebecca and the Servant of Abraham* (Gallerie dell'Accademia, Venice), then in the collection of the Baglioni, who were early patrons of Tiepolo's; the pose of the Virgin in Tiepolo's *Madonna of Mount Carmel* (fig. 19) loosely derives from the same picture. However, especially in the open-mouthed expression of the *Antaeus* and the coarse realism of the *Marsyas*, Tiepolo seems to have looked beyond Solimena's brand of tenebrist classicism to Luca Giordano's svelte synthesis of Neapolitan realism with Venetian color. Giordano worked in Venice in the 1650s and 1660s and left a number of altarpieces in its churches as well as a vast quantity of pictures in private collections. In the Baglioni collection Tiepolo could have studied the artist's *Hercules and Iole*, and a 1749 inventory of Palazzo Labia lists over eight paintings by Giordano.[4] Whether he also turned to Giordano's primary source of inspiration, Ribera, is difficult to say, but the expression of Antaeus recalls the latter's well-known etching of noses and mouths. Moreover, in the *Apollo and Marsyas* Tiepolo seized on the same grisly motif Ribera had used in his treatment of the theme: a knife stuck into the bark of the tree to free the god's hands so that he can peel back his victim's skin unhindered. And how Ribera would have appreciated the detail of the drops of blood coursing down Apollo's arm—bitingly contrasted to the effeminate golden locks of hair on his shoulders.

In the *Martyrdom of Saint Bartholomew* Tiepolo employed a dramatic use of light and dark and ecstatic gesturing characteristic of the work of Piazzetta. A preparatory drawing for the *Apollo and Marsyas* (fig. 31) demonstrates that initially he thought along these same lines for the Palazzo Sandi canvas.[5] Emphasis in the drawing is on the bound Marsyas with outflung arms, while Apollo is placed behind the tree, facing the viewer. The heads of two spectators peer from behind a hillock, echoing a hooded woman in the *Saint Bartholomew*. In the finished painting Apollo is viewed from the back—as is Hercules in the pendant picture—and the composition is at once less demonstrative and more highly focused. The figures have the compactness of free-standing pieces of sculpture set against a light-filled pastoral landscape. Tiepolo has moved beyond that moment da Canal characterized as "tutto spirito e foco" to achieve a more sober and, in the end, more subtly varied interpretation of subject. This is accomplished also in the large horizontal companion canvas showing Achilles among the daughters of Lycomedes, for which his primary source of inspiration was the work of Veronese. In these paintings Tiepolo's youthful, seemingly inexhaustible experimentation in different styles has become the basis of modal variation effected to accord with the nature of the subject treated.

The Palazzo Sandi decorations announce Tiepolo's coming of age. In the frescoed ceiling he abandoned once and for all the raw vigor of his early style—those angular contours, abrupt shifts in modeling, and that love of attenuated forms so conspicuous on the ceiling of the parish church at Biadene (fig. 14) or the lunettes in the Ospedaletto in Venice (see no. 2a, b). Gone too is the more purely decorative idiom, heavily indebted to the facile style of Louis Dorigny, characteristic of his work in the Villa Baglioni at Massanzago (see fig. 15). We find, instead, a sunny naturalism, pleasing in its developed sense of feminine beauty, yet at the same time robust and expressive. Unquestionably, Tiepolo's primary model for his renovation of Venetian art was Veronese, but his achievement depended less on the superficial imitation of the work of his great forebear—or that of any other single artist—than on a personal reformulation of the basis of Veronesian style. (It was the combination of an elevated ideal of beauty and an ingratiating naturalism in Veronese's art that so impressed eighteenth-century critics, and these were the primary features on which Tiepolo built.) In the two vertical canvases Tiepolo shifted the balance from the airiness and grace of the ceiling to density and physical power, carried through with a realistic bent he was rarely to attempt in succeeding years. The paint is thick, and the coarse bristles of the brush lend the surface a textural quality found also in the Ca' Dolfin paintings, but never again to this degree. In such observed details as the sun-tanned neck of Antaeus contrasted with the whiteness of his torso we have clear evidence of Tiepolo's continued devotion to life studies. To no less a degree than the frescoed ceiling, but in a different way, the *Apollo and Marsyas* and *Hercules and Antaeus* constitute a manifesto of his art at the moment it assumed its defining traits.

The dating of the decorations in Palazzo Sandi enjoys a rare consensus of opinion. They are almost universally placed between 1725, when the palace was completed, and 1726, the first documented instance of Tiepolo's activity at Udine. It should, nonetheless, be remembered that in these years Tiepolo had numerous commissions, and while he probably quickly set about painting the ceiling, he may have taken up the canvases sporadically, as time permitted. They are, in any event, closely related to the earliest of the Ca' Dolfin canvases, which were begun in late 1726 and were worked on until 1729.

KC

PROVENANCE:
Tommaso Sandi, Palazzo Sandi, Venice (ca. 1725–43); by descent, Palazzo Sandi, Venice (1743–ca. 1925/29); Conte Giovanni da Schio, Villa Piovene–Da Schio, Castelgomberto (Vicenza) (from ca. 1925–29); by descent

REFERENCES:
Modern 1902, p. 23; Sack 1910, p. 153, nos. 41–42; Morassi 1941–42, p. 92; Venice 1951, pp. 21–23, nos. 14–15; Morassi 1962, p. 8; Pallucchini 1968, p. 89, no. 33a, c; Udine 1971, vol. 1, p. 32, vol. 2, p. 16; Knox 1975a, p. 37; Aikema 1986, pp. 167–70; Levey 1986, p. 28; Vicenza 1990, pp. 32–34; Barcham 1992, p. 50; Gemin and Pedrocco 1993, p. 246, nos. 67–68; Knox 1993, pp. 135–41; Venice 1995a, p. 234, nos. 50–51

Opposite: Detail, 9b

Notes

1. Lawyers by profession, the Sandi were parvenus; it was Tommaso's father who purchased a hereditary title in 1685. Aikema (1986, p. 167) suggests that Tiepolo's commission might have been related to the marriage of Tommaso's son Vettor to Elisabetta Donato in 1724. The marriage, however, took place in 1734, not 1724 (see Vicenza 1990, p. 32). The dates of construction of the palace are given by Moschini (1815, p. 603), and Sack (1910, p. 153).
2. Although it is universally accepted that the canvases were placed in the *salone*, neither da Canal (1732) nor Moschini (1815) specifies how they were arranged or where they were located. Of the canvases, da Canal mentions only the *Achilles*, which he qualifies as "assi bella per le graziose idee di quelle femmine, e per la disposizione della storia."
3. The program is fully treated by Knox 1993, pp. 135–41.
4. For lists of Giordano's paintings in eighteenth-century Venice, see Ferrari 1966, vol. 2, pp. 388–90.
5. See Knox 1975a, p. 37. The drawing indicates that the intended picture field had cut corners at the bottom and an arched top; thus, the final shape had not been settled on when the sketch was made. There seems to me no compelling reason for disassociating the drawing from the canvas, as has sometimes been done.

10. *Heliodorus and the High Priest Onias*

10. Heliodorus and the High Priest Onias
Ca. 1726–27
195 × 231 cm (76⅞ × 91 in.)
Museo di Castelvecchio, Verona (666)

According to the Book of Maccabees from the Old Testament Apocrypha, upon learning of the wealth of the Jewish Temple, Antiochus the Great charged Heliodorus to confiscate the money in the care of the high priest Onias. Despite Onias's objections and the supplications of the populace, Heliodorus proceeded with his mission until he was attacked by a divine apparition, which left him unconscious and near death. Onias later prayed for the recovery of Heliodorus, who offered sacrifice in thanksgiving for being spared.

This picture, with its striking *di sotto-in-sù* viewpoint, is from a cycle of canvases by various artists illustrating the deeds of Judas Maccabeus, commissioned to decorate the church of S. Sebastiano in Verona. Early sources mention that they were displayed above monochromatic scenes of the lives of Saints Stanislas and Louis by Louis Dorigny, whose frescoes had a notable impact on Tiepolo. Tiepolo was the only Venetian to participate in the series, and his is the only surviving canvas (the others were either seriously damaged or completely destroyed during World War II).

Tiepolo's painting has always been identified by twentieth-century critics as showing Heliodorus receiving the treasure of the Temple, but it departs significantly from the way the subject is usually presented. Maccabees describes the high priest as deeply pained by having to give over the Temple treasure, "for his face and the change in his color disclosed the anguish of his soul." Heliodorus never entered the treasury but was beaten back by a mounted rider and two angelic men: it is this episode that is invariably illustrated in works ranging from Raphael's celebrated fresco in the Vatican to paintings by the Veronese Giulio Carpioni and the Venetian Gasparo Diziani. Tiepolo's canvas shows Onias officiating at the altar and Heliodorus kneeling, his eyes upturned, holding a salver of gold coins. Might the scene actually represent Heliodorus's sacrifice and vows made before the high priest after he recovered?

Although a canvas, the picture responds to the same concerns with location and point of view that Tiepolo typically expressed in his fresco paintings. The viewer seems to look up a steep flight of stairs, beyond a projecting still life of a metal tray and an elaborate censer, toward the commanding figure of Onias, who is dressed in the vestments of a rabbi and places one hand on an open book. Heliodorus, his body compressed as much by foreshortening as by his submissive posture, has inadvertently let his salver go askew, and Tiepolo has used this slip as an opportunity to make a tour-de-force display of the falling coins—captured in midair much as he had earlier arrested the movement of the bricks sailing through the space of the ceiling of Palazzo Sandi in Venice. Behind Heliodorus and the helmeted soldier who furtively steals a coin for himself is a Jewish youth, his hands raised in prayer. The gesture was exploited by Tiepolo again and again as a leitmotiv of supplication, in efforts as various as the ceiling frescoes of the Gesuati and Scalzi in Venice and the depiction of Asia in the Residenz at Würzburg. The steeply angled view, no less than the splendid arch filling the background, strongly recalls the work of Veronese, and there can be

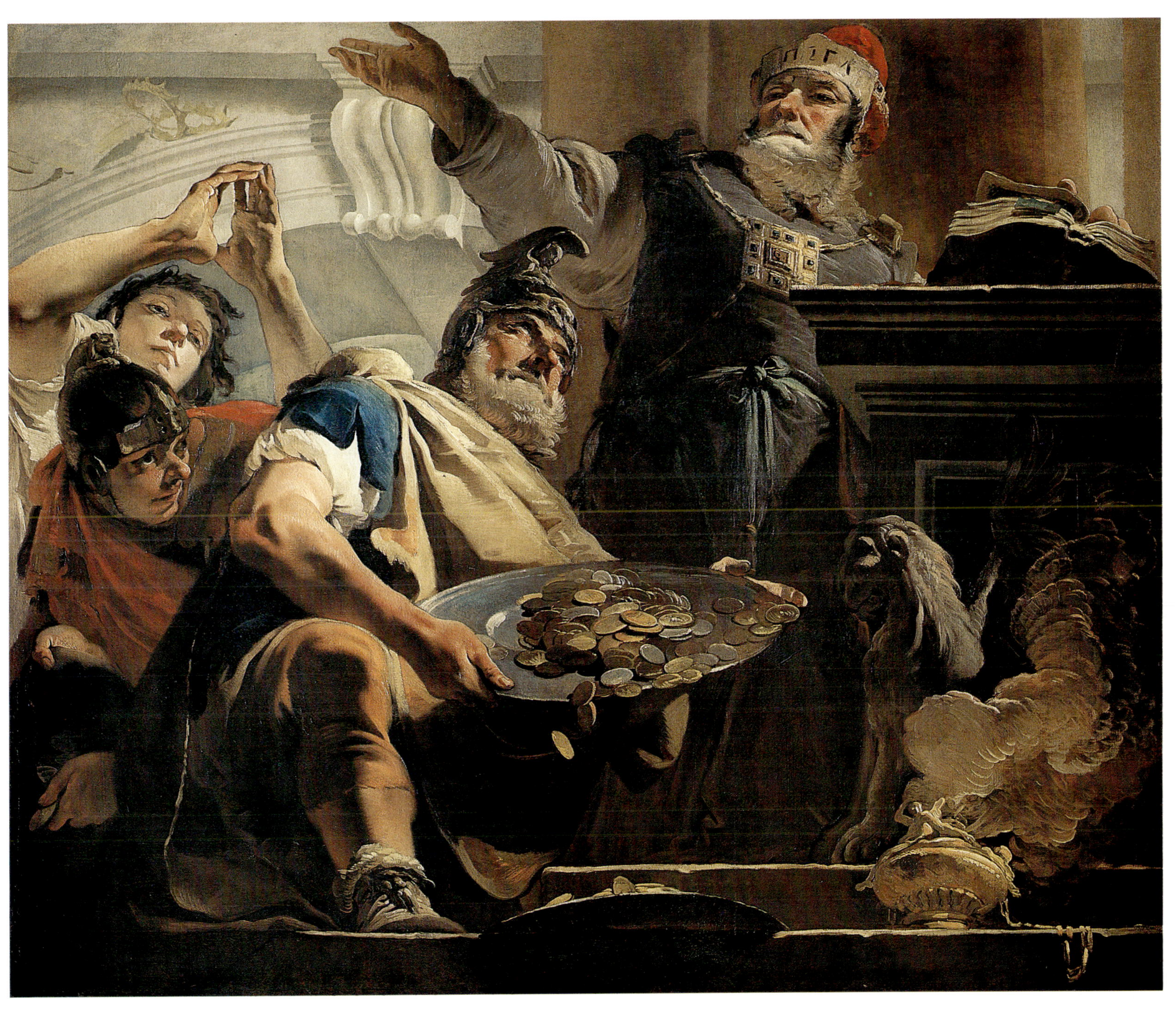

PROVENANCE:
Church of S. Sebastiano, Verona (until 1897)

REFERENCES:
Lanceni 1733, p. 16; Biancolini and Bragadino 1749, p. 702; da Persico 1820, p. 207; Bennassuti 1831, p. 58; Molmenti 1909, pp. 113–15; Avena 1937, p. 6; Venice 1951, p. 26; Morassi 1962, p. 63; Pallucchini 1968, p. 93, no. 51; Marinelli 1978, pp. 217–21; Marinelli 1983, p. 120; Gemin and Pedrocco 1993, p. 244, no. 64

little doubt that with this picture Tiepolo intended to lay claim to his position as Veronese's heir in that artist's native city.

Marinelli has noted that in 1724 Tiepolo was called to Verona to make drawings after ancient statues as illustrations for Scipione Maffei's *Verona illustrata*, and it may have been at this time that the Jesuits of the church of S. Sebastiano established contact with him. However, even allowing the possibility that their commission for the *Heliodorus* dates from this time, he is unlikely to have painted it much before 1726–27, when he may already have been engaged with the cycle of Roman histories for Ca' Dolfin in Venice (see no. 12 a–g). It is with those works as well as with the fresco showing the Judgment of Solomon on the ceiling of one of the rooms of the Arcivescovado (Patriarchal Palace) at Udine (fig. 26)—another Dolfin commission of the years about 1726 to 1729—that the *Heliodorus* can be best compared. The fact that other decorations in the church of S. Sebastiano were completed in 1727 suggests that Tiepolo must have finished the present picture by that date. Like the Ca' Dolfin paintings, the Verona canvas announces Tiepolo's coming of age. Under the aegis of Veronese, he had moved beyond his experiments in the more decorative style of Dorigny and the personal, darkly expressive modes of Bencovich and Piazzetta to create an idiom at once grand and dramatic, decorative and human.

KC

11. *Apelles Painting Campaspe*

11. Apelles Painting Campaspe
Ca. 1726–27
57.4 × 84.2 cm (22⅝ × 33⅛ in.)
Montreal Museum of Fine Arts, Adaline Van Horne Bequest (1945.929)

PROVENANCE:
O. Zaeslin, Basel (before 1902); Sigmaringen Museum, Germany (1902); Eugene Schweitzer, Berlin (by 1909); P. and D. Colnaghi, London (1911); Sir William Van Horne, Montreal (from 1911); Adaline Van Horne, Montreal (until 1945)

REFERENCES:
Molmenti 1909, pp. 272–73; Sack 1910, p. 193, no. 352; Morassi 1943, p. 17; Pignatti 1951, p. 31; Venice 1951, p. 33, no. 23; Bordeaux 1956, p. 24, no. 52; Morassi 1962, pp. 29–30; Pallucchini 1968, p. 90, no. 42; Udine 1971, p. 37, no. 17; Levey 1986, pp. 18–19; Barcham 1989, pp. 81–86; Gemin and Pedrocco 1993, p. 264, no. 97; Alpers and Baxandall 1994, pp. 10–11; London 1994, p. 494, no. 92; Venice 1995a, p. 236, no. 52

In the *Natural History* (35.10), Pliny tells the story of Apelles painting Campaspe, the mistress of Alexander the Great, as an example of the nobility of painting and the generosity of a prince. While painting the beautiful woman, Apelles fell in love with her. Alexander, who frequently visited the artist in his studio, realized this and granted Campaspe to him. By the eighteenth century the story had assumed the character of a topos: it was the conventional frame of reference for praising an artist's work. Significantly, Tiepolo painted two versions of the theme within a few years.[1] Both present the same cast of characters and a similar setting. The artist is shown at his easel working on a bust-length portrait of Campaspe, who is posed next to Alexander on a raised dais. Large canvases with finished compositions are propped against the walls, and there is a view past a columned opening into a vast courtyard decorated with a monumental statue of Hercules (based on the famous ancient sculpture in the Farnese collection, one of the most widely admired works of art of antiquity and an exemplum of virility).

Although some have maintained that in both pictures Apelles is a self-portrait of Tiepolo, only in the Montreal painting is this identification certain. There can, in fact, be little doubt that, in tongue-in-cheek fashion, Tiepolo has recast the ancient story in self-referential terms, showing himself at work at his easel painting his young wife, Cecilia Guardi (for Campaspe has her features), while a young Moor who appears in other early works—probably Tiepolo's servant Ali—looks on admiringly.[2] In this masquerade the viewer assumes the position of a voyeur, standing behind Campaspe and Alexander, with the canvas in full view. A small, rather ridiculous-looking dog gazing attentively out of the canvas offers the only acknowledgment of the viewer's presence (in the other picture as well as in the Montreal version). With his customary wit Tiepolo has shown himself in a fur hat, studying his model not to better render some facial feature or a prize jewel but to position her nipple on his painting. No less amusingly, he depicted Campaspe—her face visible to the viewer, it should be noted, only via his craft, on the canvas he is painting—as a winsome but slightly homely woman, quite different from the more conventionally lovely person in the other, earlier work.

The two canvases propped against the wall are religious compositions. One represents the Israelites and the brazen serpent; the other has been identified as portraying Saint Cecilia, her betrothed, Valerian, and an angel.[3] According to da Canal, Tiepolo painted a picture of Saint Cecilia for the church of S. Martino in

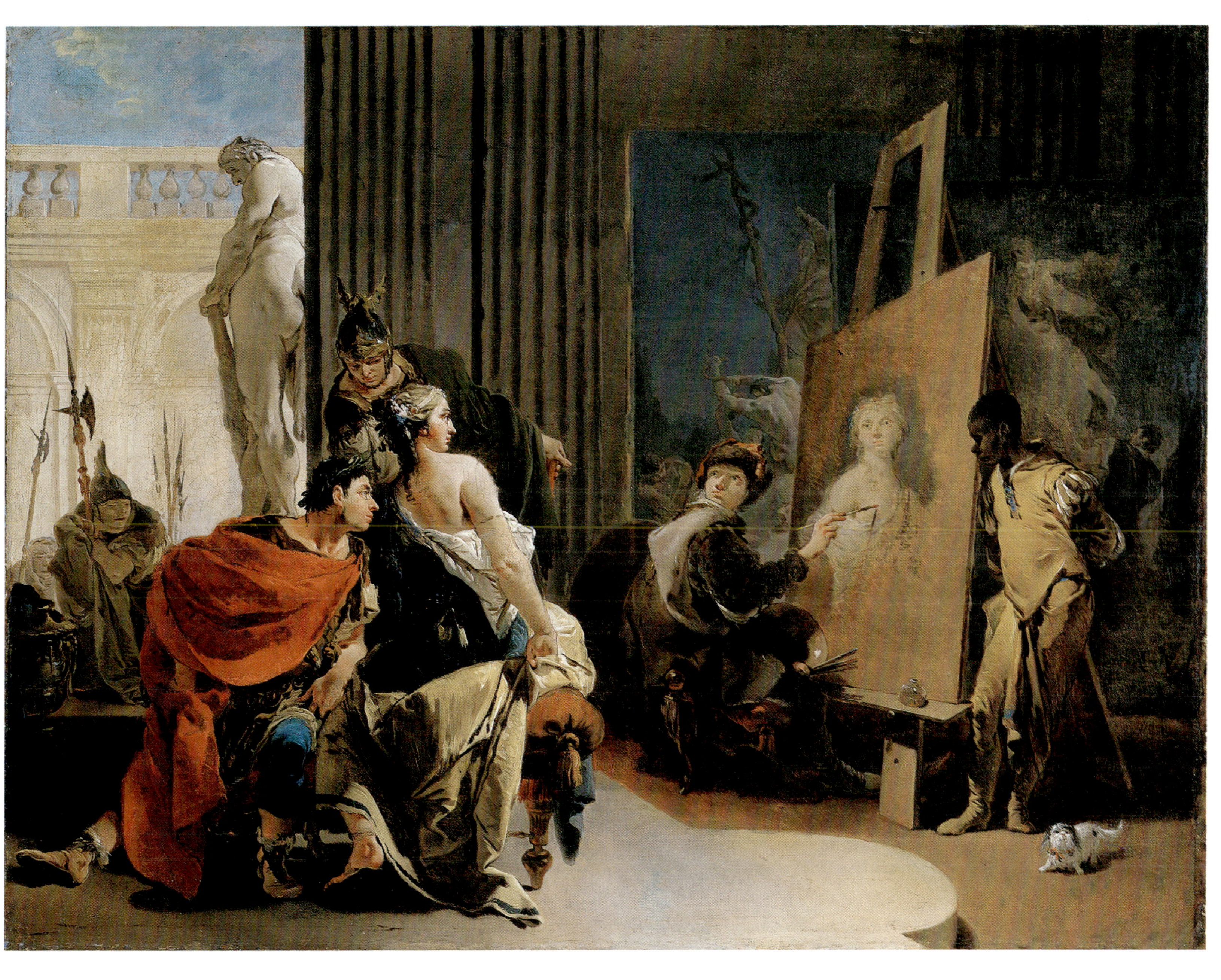

Venice, and it is possible that the artist has, in these pictures within a picture, shown actual works he painted. Given the self-referential quality of this sparkling canvas, there is a strong probability that Tiepolo painted it for himself or for a close acquaintance who could appreciate its lighthearted humor. The picture is universally assigned to the mid- to late 1720s; a date about 1726–27—when Tiepolo was beginning his work at Udine and in Ca' Dolfin, Venice—seems reasonable. The artist appears younger than in his self-portrait in the *Triumph of Marius* of 1729 from the Ca' Dolfin series (fig. 12e) and about the same age as in the fresco in the Arcivescovado (Patriarchal Palace), Udine, showing Rachel hiding the idols from Laban (fig. 25).

KC

NOTES

1. The second picture, in a private collection, was published by Morassi 1964. A third, later treatment of the theme is in the Musée du Louvre, Paris.
2. Long before Pignatti (1951, p. 31) studied the identifications, Molmenti made note of the tradition that Apelles is a self-portrait. Although he doubted the identification, the features of the painter are undeniably those of Tiepolo.
3. See Barcham 1989, p. 83.

THE DECORATIONS FOR CA' DOLFIN

12a. Mucius Scaevola before Porsenna
12b. Veturia Pleading with Coriolanus
12c. Fabius Maximus before the Roman Senate
12d. Cincinnatus Offered the Dictatorship
12e. The Triumph of Marius
12f. The Capture of Carthage
12g. The Battle of Vercellae

12a. Mucius Scaevola before Porsenna
Ca. 1726–28
387 × 227 cm (152⅜ × 89⅜ in.)
Inscribed on banderole (barely visible): . . . TAMQVAM MANVS REGIS ARDERET
The Hermitage Museum, Saint Petersburg

12b. Veturia Pleading with Coriolanus
Ca. 1726–28
387 × 224 cm (152⅜ × 88¼ in.)
Inscribed at top: . . . FILIV[M] / MATER VITVRIA EXARMAVIT
The Hermitage Museum, Saint Petersburg

12c. Fabius Maximus before the Roman Senate
Ca. 1726–29
387 × 224 cm (152⅜ × 88¼ in.)
The Hermitage Museum, Saint Petersburg

Tiepolo's early career culminated in two spectacular commissions from the patrician Dolfin family. For Dionisio Dolfin (1663–1734), the patriarch of Aquileia, he frescoed the luxurious, newly completed Patriarchal Palace at Udine, the Arcivescovado, with two cycles of Old Testament stories (figs. 24–26). And for Dionisio's brother, Daniele III (Giovanni) (1654–1729), who held public offices and served as an ambassador, and Daniele IV (Gerolamo) Dolfin (1656–1729), whose fame derived from the leading role he had played in the last, great naval victories of the Republic of Venice over the Turks under Francesco Morosini, Tiepolo provided ten monumental canvases with scenes from Roman history. These were installed in the grand reception room of the family palace on the Rio di Ca' Foscari, just off the Grand Canal, in the parish of S. Pantalon. Seven of these paintings are reassembled here for the first time since their removal from Ca' Dolfin in 1872. (Five are now in The Hermitage Museum, Saint Petersburg; three in The Metropolitan Museum of Art, New York; and two in the Kunsthistorisches Museum, Vienna.)

The two commissions consolidated Tiepolo's emerging reputation as the greatest living Venetian painter. Although his subsequent career was marked by spectacular achievements, he never surpassed the playful inventiveness and lyrical freshness of the Arcivescovado frescoes or the drumroll pomp and brassy drama of the Ca' Dolfin Roman histories. In 1732 da Canal described the ten canvases as "among [Tiepolo's] most singular works," a judgment echoed almost thirty years later, when the Abbé de Saint-Non, during a visit to the palace in May or June 1761 with his traveling companion, Fragonard, declared the paintings "one of the most beautiful things [Tiepolo] has done in Venice"; Fragonard himself made drawings of portions of five of the compositions (see fig. 32), which were later published as etchings by Saint-Non.[1] Giandomenico Tiepolo continued to mine the histories for ideas as late as 1755, when he adapted motifs from the battle pictures for his own *Siege of Brescia* in the church of S. Faustino, Brescia. And about the same time Francesco Guardi took inspiration from the composition in the series showing Mucius Scaevola for his own treatment of the theme.[2]

Opposite: Detail, no. 12b

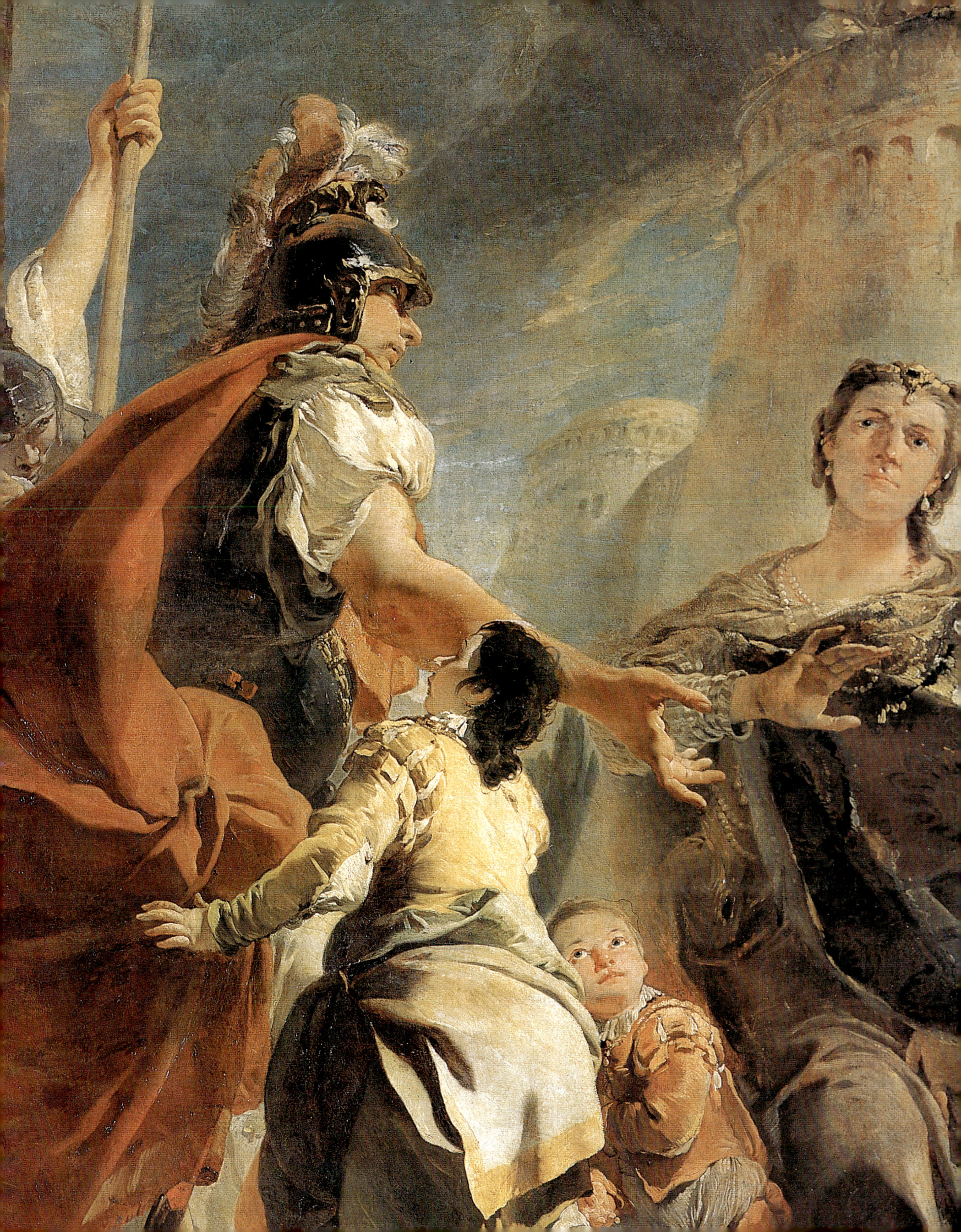

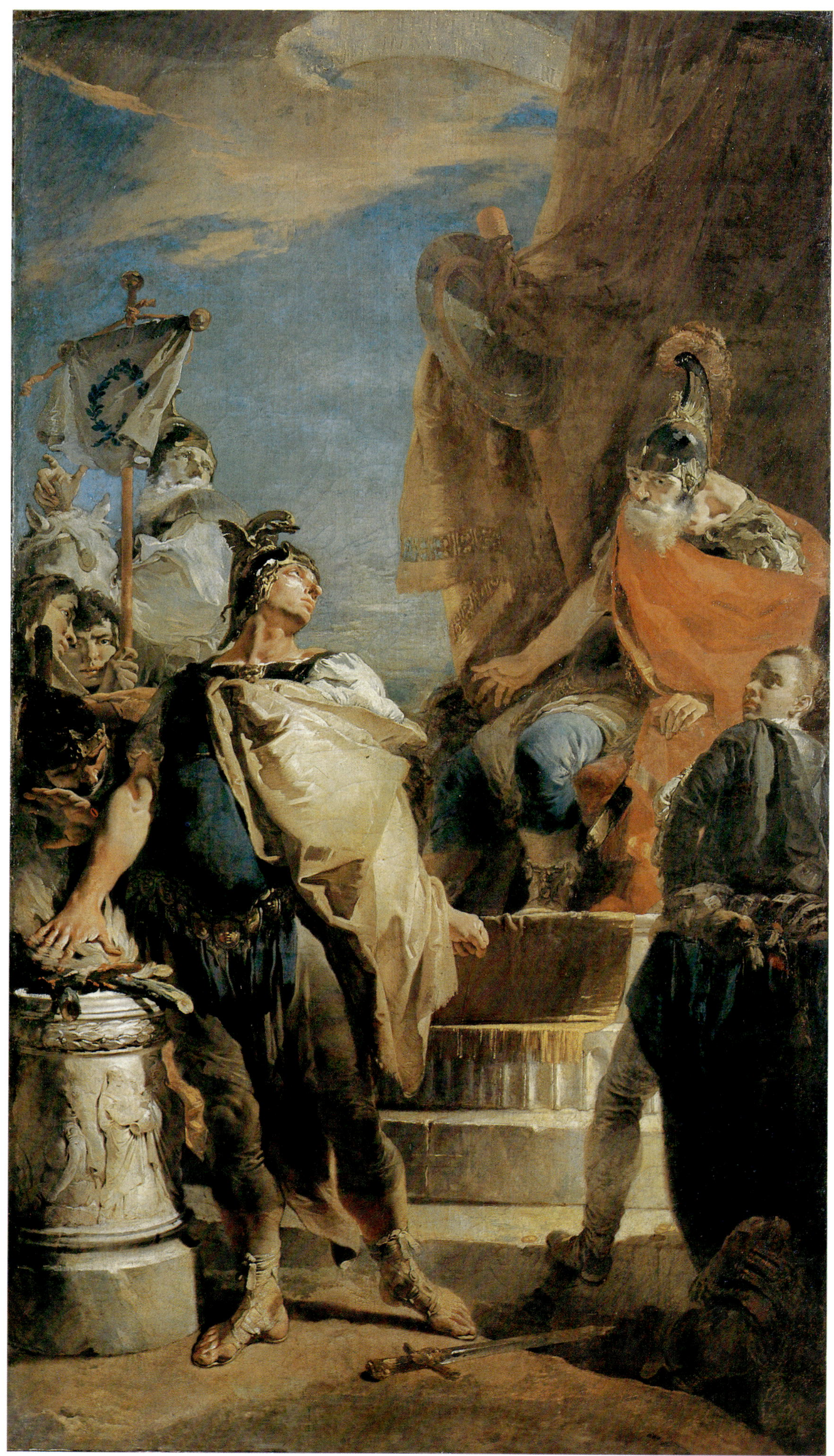

12a

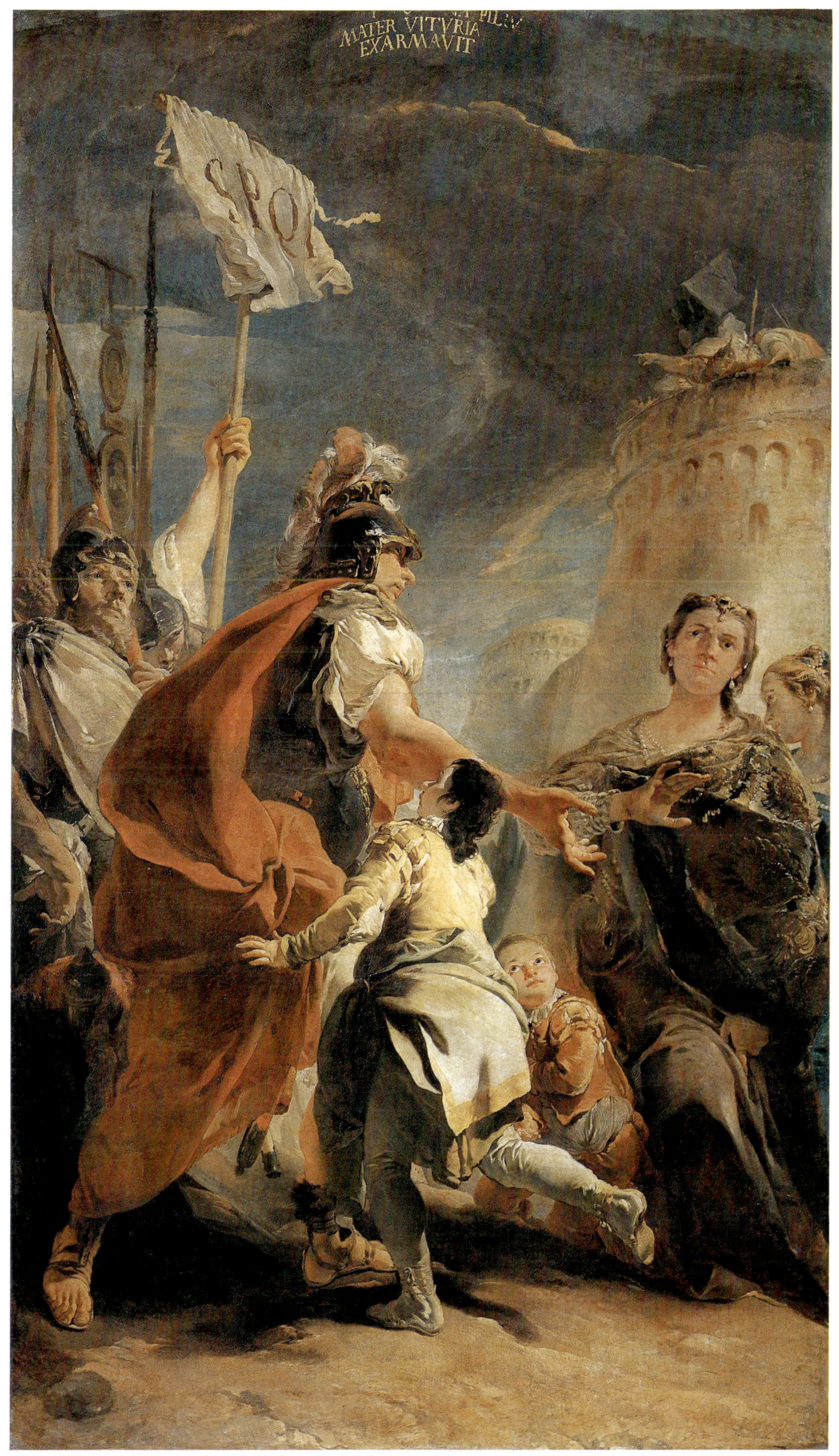

12b

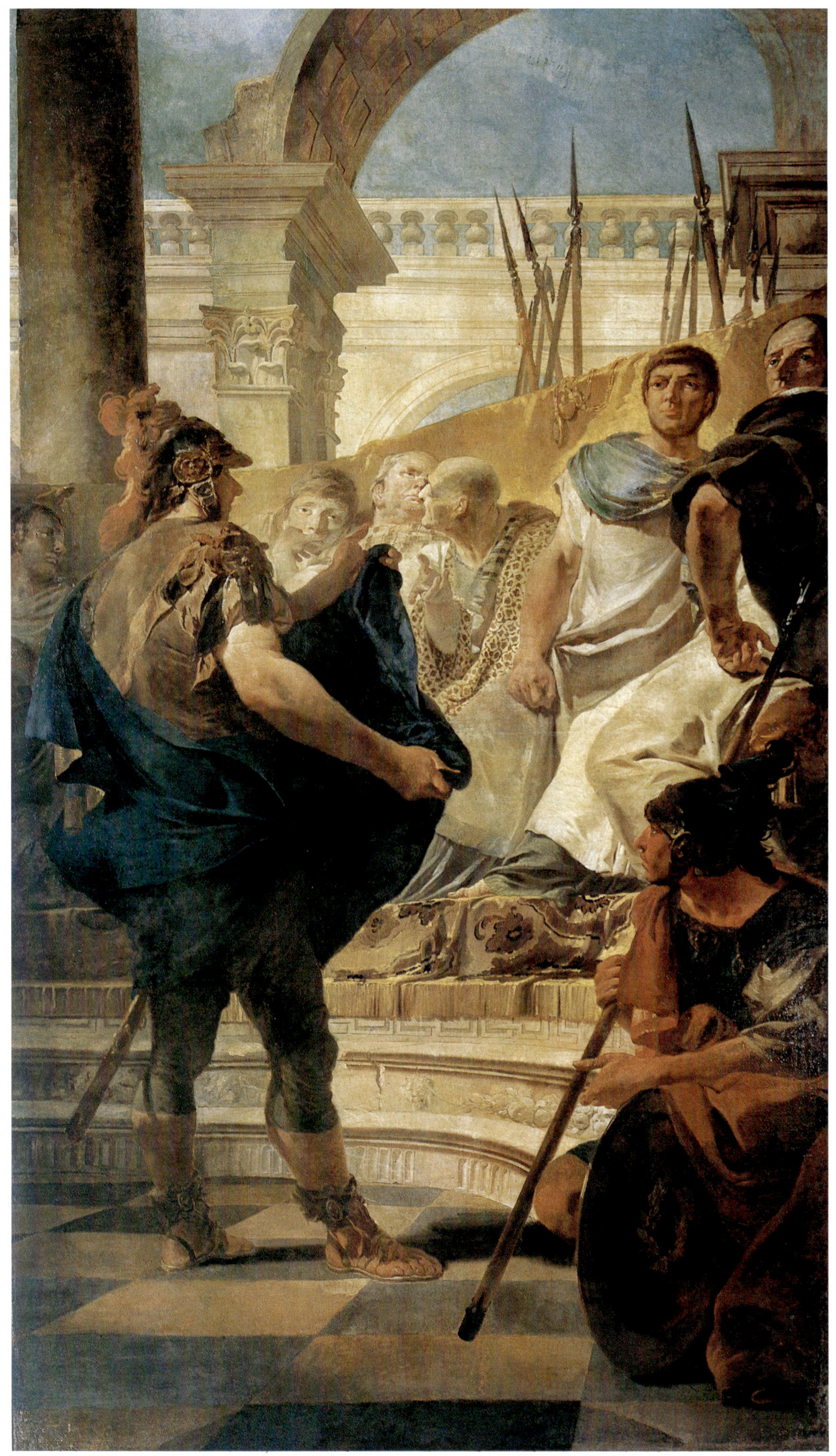

12c

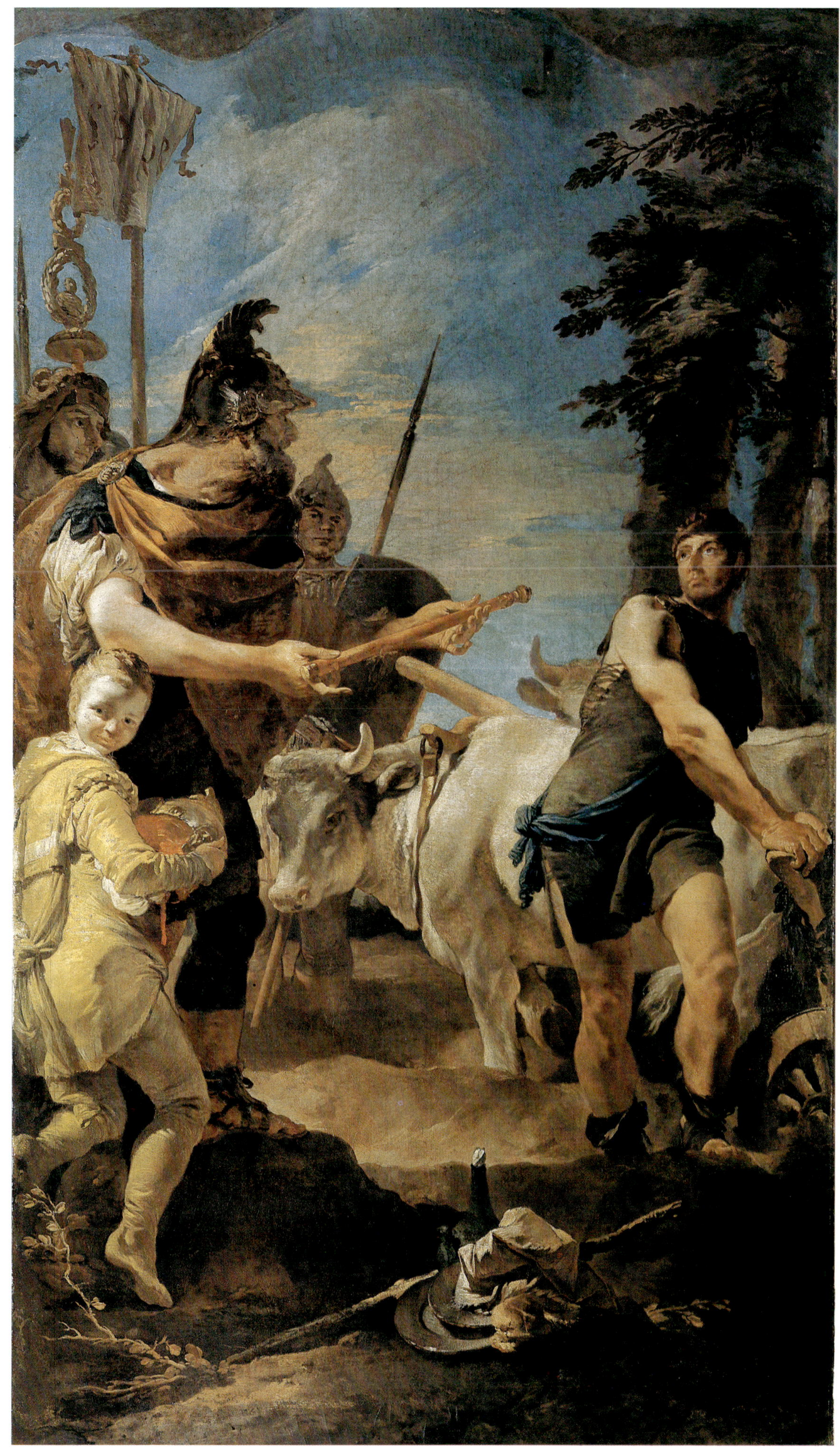

12d

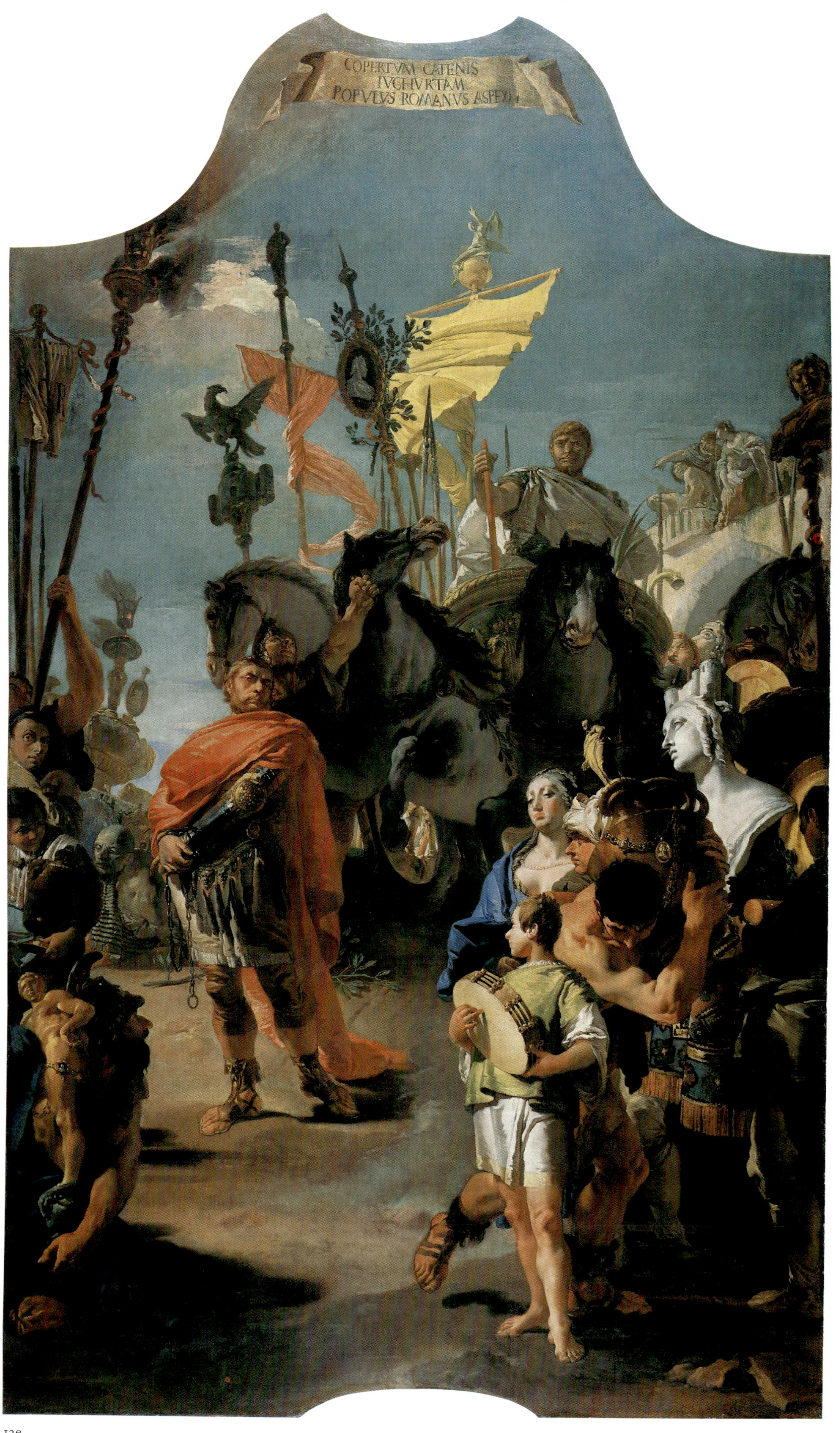

12e

Opposite: Detail, no. 12e

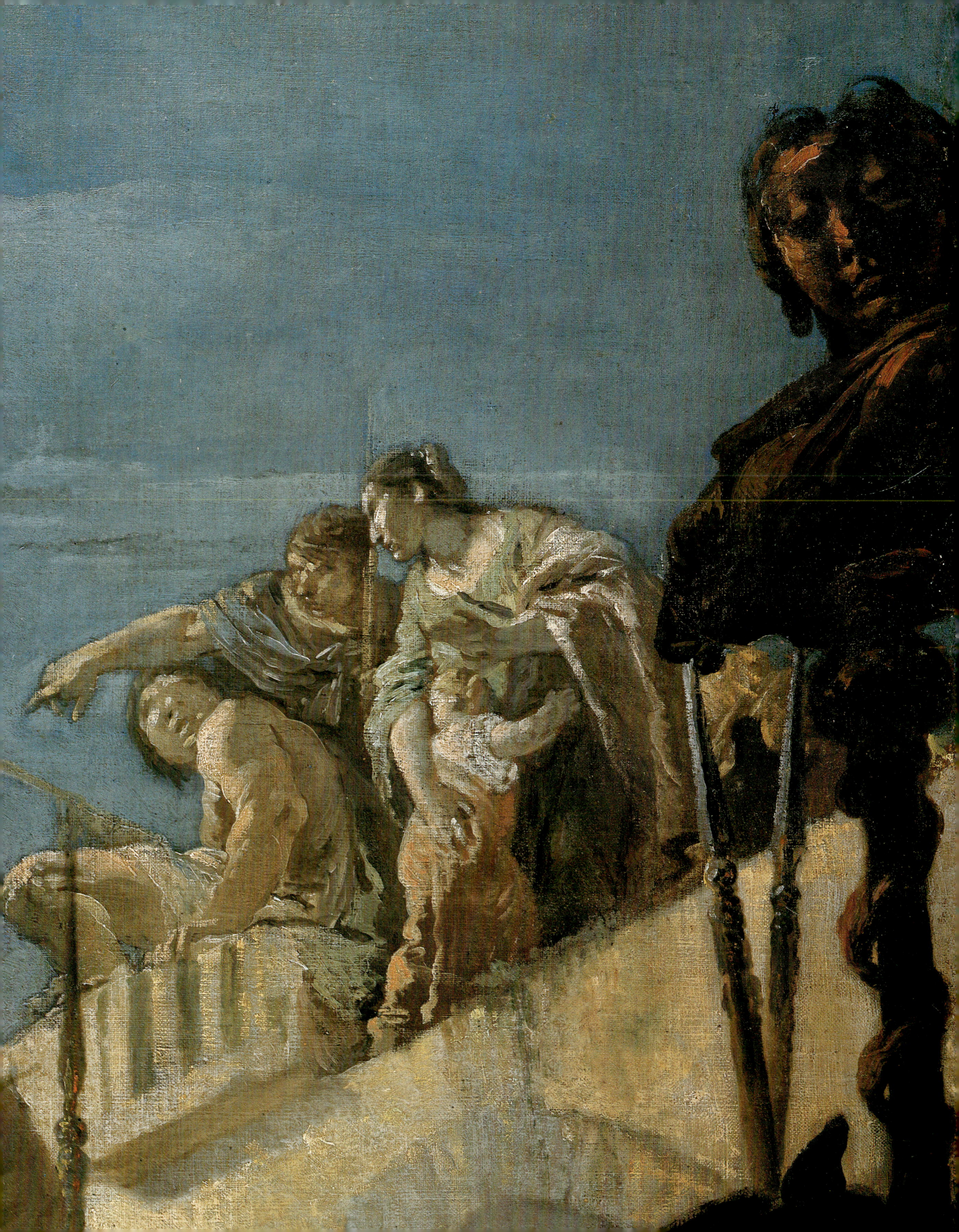

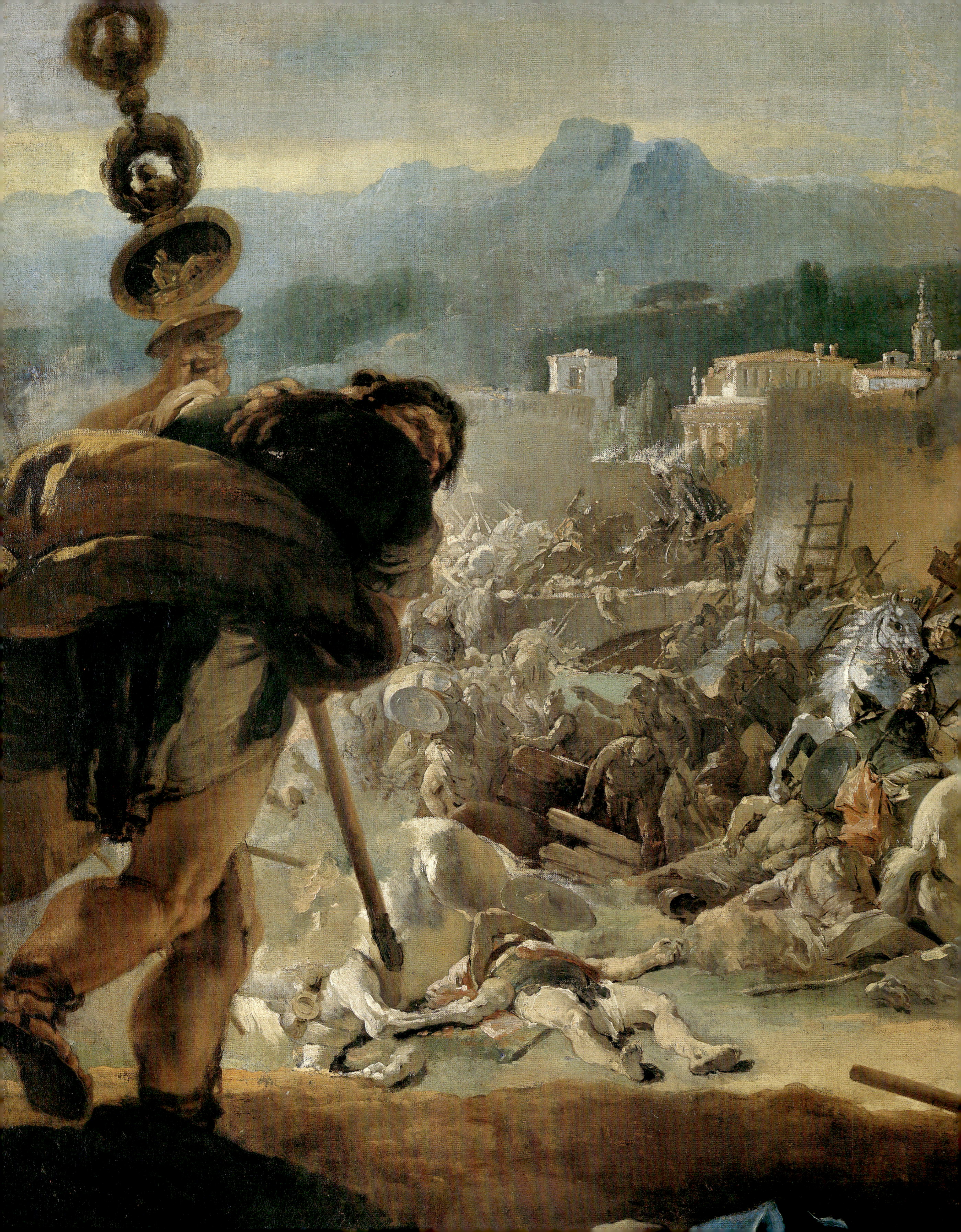

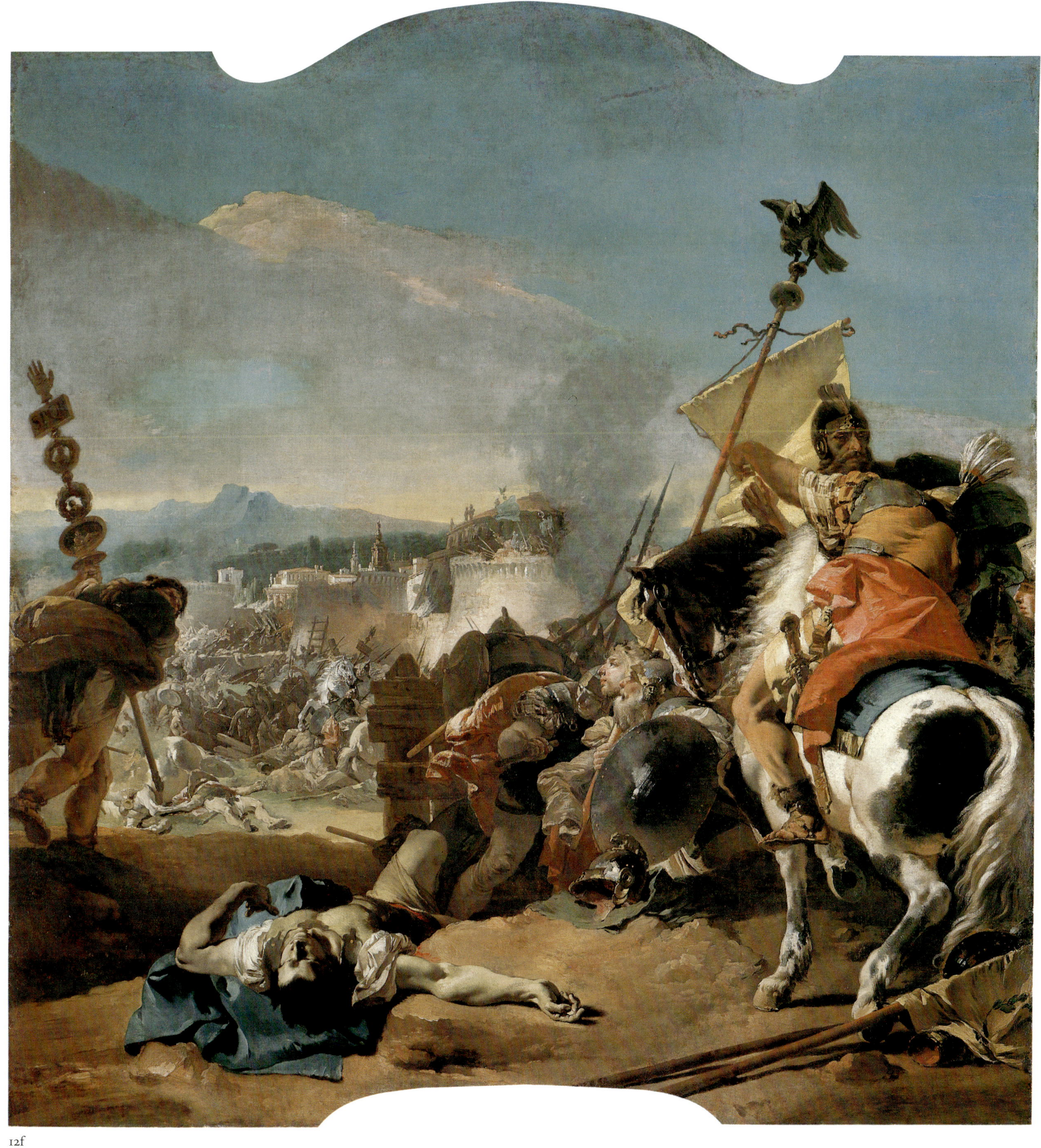

12f

Opposite: Detail, no. 12f

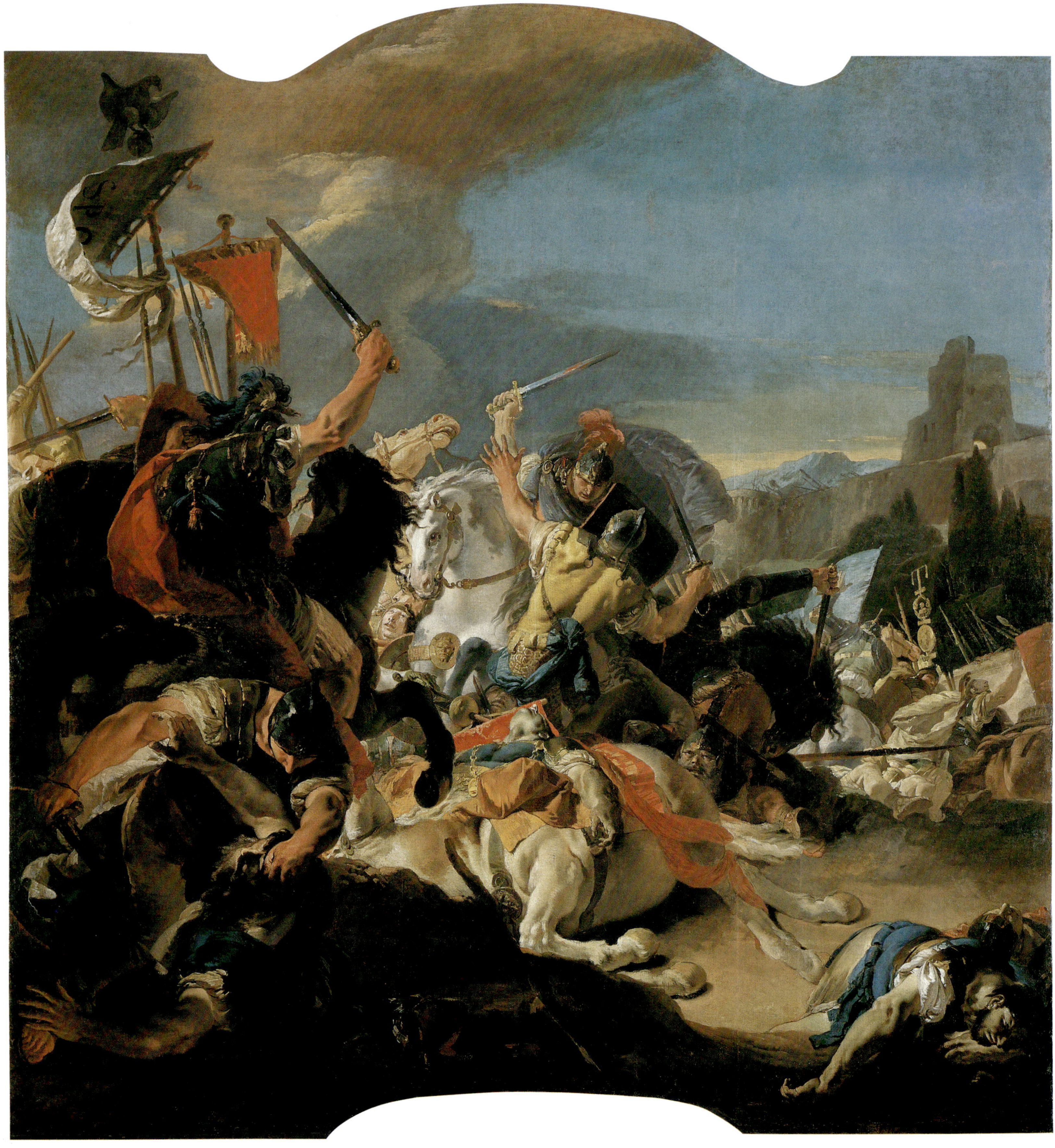

12g

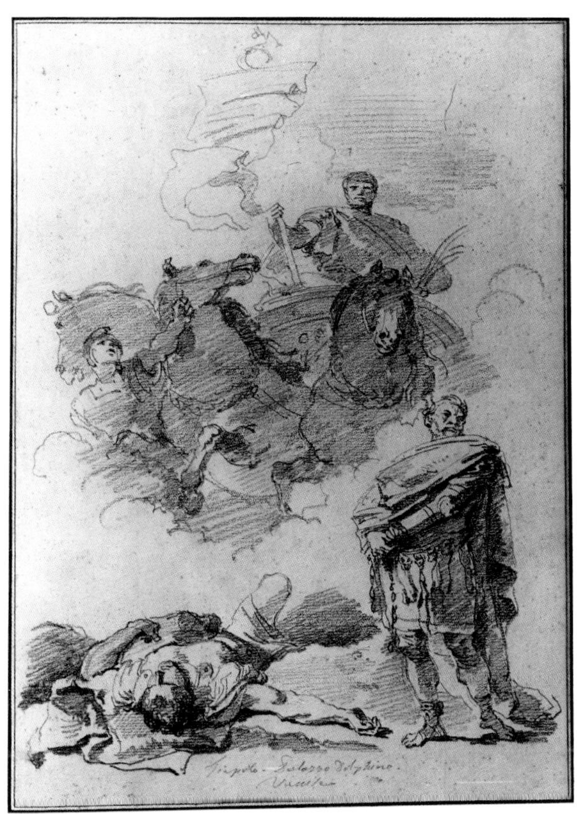

Fig. 32. Jean-Honoré Fragonard. Studies of *The Triumph of Marius* and *The Capture of Carthage* after Tiepolo. Chalk. Norton Simon Museum of Art, Pasadena

On 30 April 1726, prior to assuming a post as Venetian representative in Constantinople, Daniele III made his will. According to a notice discovered by Valentine Conticelli, he expressed to his notary the intention that "God willing, I will have the canvases in the room [of the palace] painted by the most famous painters."[3] As it turned out, Daniele III did not return to Venice but died in Constantinople. It fell to his younger brother, Daniele IV, to carry out the project, which was entrusted not to an *équipe* of artists but to Tiepolo alone. When the commission was awarded cannot be said with precision, but it cannot have been long after Daniele III's departure; the latest canvas in the cycle is dated 1729. In June 1726 Tiepolo was in Udine, where he had been hired to decorate a chapel in the cathedral (fig. 23) and was probably also at work on the frescoes in the Arcivescovado.[4] Fresco painting is a seasonal task, and in Udine Tiepolo would have worked on the frescoes in the spring and summer months and in Venice on the canvases in the winter ones, but he had to find time for other commissions while engaged with these prestigious and extensive enterprises.[5] In Udine, Tiepolo was able to determine the overall design of the frescoes and collaborated with his preferred specialist in architectural painting, the *quadraturista* Girolamo Mengozzi Colonna. The result was a brilliant union of illusionistic architecture and framing devices with dazzling figurative compositions. By contrast, in Ca' Dolfin he had to accommodate his ideas to a somewhat heavy-handed and awkward preexisting scheme. Perhaps on the occasion of the festivities sponsored by Daniele IV Dolfin in honor of King Frederick IV of Denmark in February 1709, Nicolò Bambini and the Ferrarese *quadraturista* Antonio Felice Ferrari had frescoed the ample *salone* measuring 11 by 17 meters; they supplied, respectively, an apotheosis of the Dolfin family on the ceiling and an illusionistic architectural framework around ten recesses in the walls intended to receive paintings on canvas.[6] For whatever reason, the canvases were not painted until Tiepolo was commissioned to provide martial scenes from Roman history.

The irregular profiles of the canvases, dictated by the recesses into which they were set, were altered when the pictures were removed from the palace in 1872 (the canvases in Vienna and New York have been restored more or less to their original formats).[7] However, the recesses survive, filled with mirrors, making a definitive reconstruction of the arrangement of the cycle possible. The room has a main entrance on one long wall and, on the opposite side, five windows overlooking a canal; these provide the only source of light for the space, and Tiepolo took this fact into consideration in his pictures. On each end wall were three canvases, forming a sort of triptych with an immense vertical picture of a Roman triumphal procession at the center: on the west wall (and lit from the left) the so-called *Triumph of Marius* (12e) with *Fabius Maximus before the Roman Senate* (12c) on one side and *Cincinnatus Offered the Dictatorship* (12d) on the other; opposite (and lit from the right) the *Tarentine Triumph*[8] (fig. 33) flanked by *Mucius Scaevola before Porsenna* (12a) and *Veturia Pleading with Coriolanus* (12b). To either side of the main doorway were the two, squarish, battle scenes (12f, g), while facing them, in spaces to either side of the center window, were two narrow canvases, the *Death of Lucius Junius Brutus* (fig. 34) and *Hannibal Contemplating the Head of Hasdrubal* (fig. 35).

Da Canal described the cycle as showing the battles and triumphs of Coriolanus and other Roman histories, but in this he seems to have been mistaken. With the exception of the two battle scenes, the compositions bear—or once bore—banderoles with identifying inscriptions from Lucius Annaeus Florus's *Epitomae de Tito Livio bellorum . . . Libri II* (although painted out in the nineteenth century, some of these were uncovered in restoration; those that remain are damaged).[9] Only one canvas (12b) certainly illustrates an episode from the life of Coriolanus, the patrician Roman general of the fifth century B.C., and in it he appears not as a hero but as a traitor to his country and an ally of the Volsci,

12d. Cincinnatus Offered the Dictatorship
Ca. 1726–29
387 × 224 cm (152⅜ × 88¼ in.)
Inscribed on banderole: [SIGNA] FILIV[M] MATER VITVRIA EXARMAVIT
The Hermitage Museum, Saint Petersburg

†12e. The Triumph of Marius
Dated 1729
559 × 327 cm (220⅛ × 120¾ in.)
Dated on oval medallion, upper center: 1729; inscribed on banderole: COPERTVM CATENIS / IVGHVRTAM / POPVLVS ROMANVS / ASPEXIT
The Metropolitan Museum of Art, New York; Rogers Fund, 1965 (65.183.1)

†12f. The Capture of Carthage
Ca. 1728–29
412 × 377 cm (162 × 148⅛ in.)
The Metropolitan Museum of Art, New York; Rogers Fund, 1965 (65.183.2)

†12g. The Battle of Vercellae
Ca. 1728–29
412 × 377 cm (162 × 148⅜ in.)
The Metropolitan Museum of Art, New York; Rogers Fund, 1965 (65.183.3)

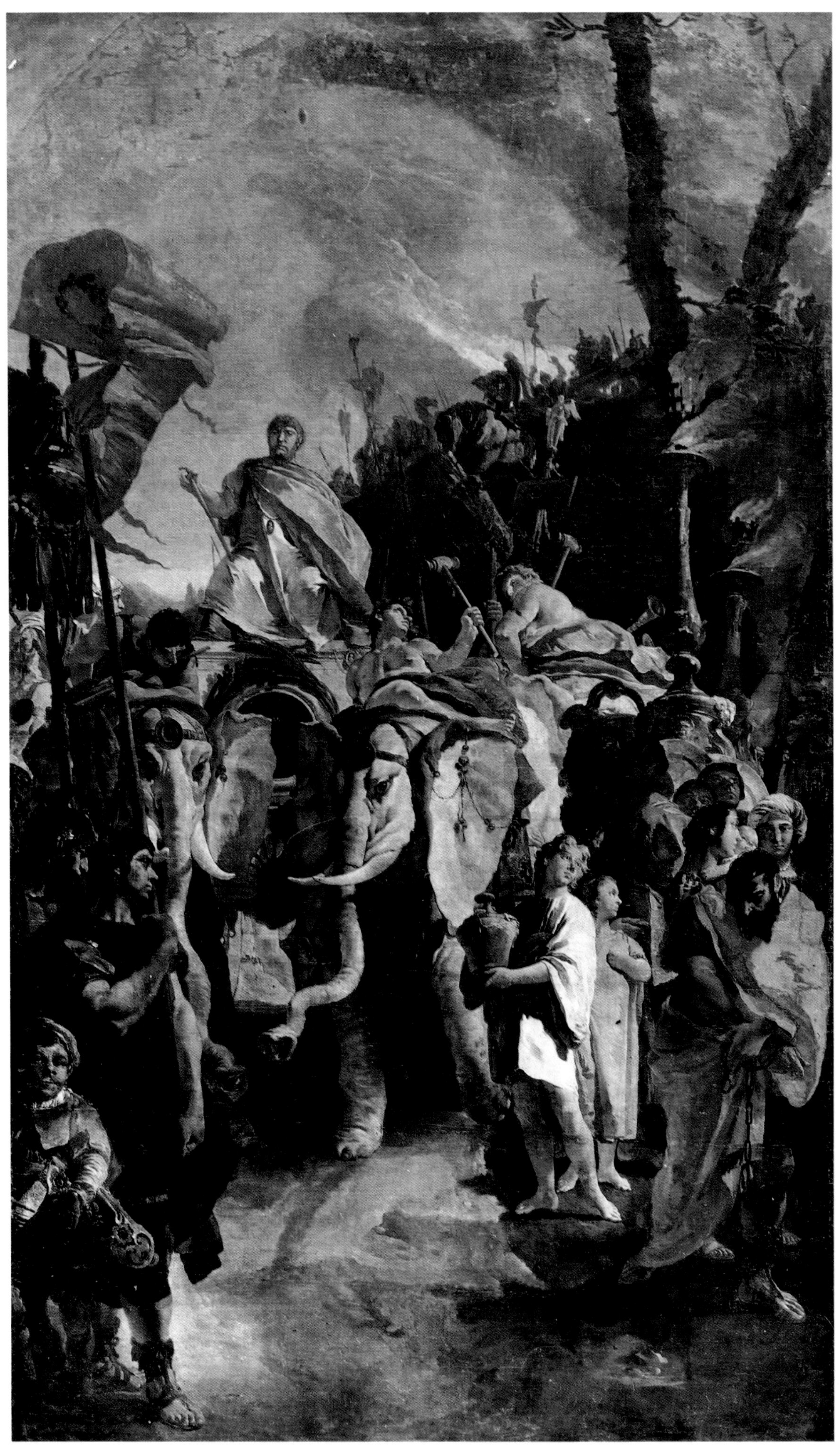

Fig. 33. *The Tarantine Triumph (?)*. Oil on canvas. The Hermitage Museum, Saint Petersburg

dissuaded from attacking Rome by the entreaties of his wife, Volumnia, and his mother, Veturia; it is Veturia rather than Coriolanus who is the protagonist of this composition.[10] Taken as a whole, the series offers a synoptic account of the expansion and defense of Rome from the time of its founding to the period of its domination of all of Italy, and it is based on both Florus and Livy. Pride of place naturally fell to famous triumphs and examples of patriotic fervor, as these were most appropriate for a patrician Venetian family and the Dolfin in particular. The earliest event (actually a legend) illustrated, in *Mucius Scaevola before Porsenna* (12a), concerns Rome's struggles with neighboring tribes: Mucius Scaevola is shown defiantly placing his hand in a blazing flame to demonstrate Roman resolve against the Etruscan king Porsenna, a supporter of the Tarquins. The inscription underscores the dramatic moment Tiepolo portrays.[11] One of the two canvases in Vienna (fig. 34) depicts the Roman Brutus, mounted on his horse, and the Tarquin Arruns simultaneously killed by each other's spears (509 B.C.).[12] In the *Coriolanus* Veturia halts the Volscian enemy by her entreaties (487 B.C.). The *Cincinnatus* (12d) shows this upright Roman noble tilling his fields when he is called from his self-imposed exile to assume the dictatorship and lead the army to victory over the Latin Aequi and Volsci (458 B.C.).[13] Next would come the triumph celebrated after the victory over the Tarantines (275 B.C.), who dominated the south of Italy and were supported by Carthage and by Pyrrhus. Canvases representing episodes of the Punic Wars followed. Fabius Maximus (12c) is shown before the Senate at Carthage, brazenly threatening war if Hannibal is not surrendered (217 B.C.),[14] while the second painting in Vienna (fig. 35) depicts Hannibal, appalled by the sight of his brother's severed head, which had been thrown into his camp. Hannibal correctly took this as an omen of his own impending defeat by Scipio.[15] The *Triumph of Marius* (12e) shows the victorious general Gaius Marius leading the African barbarian Jugurtha through Rome in chains (104 B.C.).[16]

There remain the two large paintings of battles (12f, g), which have no inscriptions. These are usually identified as showing the bloody capture of Carthage by Publius Cornelius Scipio (146 B.C.)[17] and Marius's victory over the invading Cimbrian Gauls at Vercellae, in Lombardy (101 B.C.).[18] Alternatively, it has been proposed that, in accordance with da Canal's report, two victories of Coriolanus were intended: his battle against the Volsci and the fall of Corioli.[19] There is no way to satisfactorily determine which battles are portrayed, for the paintings include no features that might clearly distinguish them. Nonetheless, the setting in the so-called *Capture of Carthage*

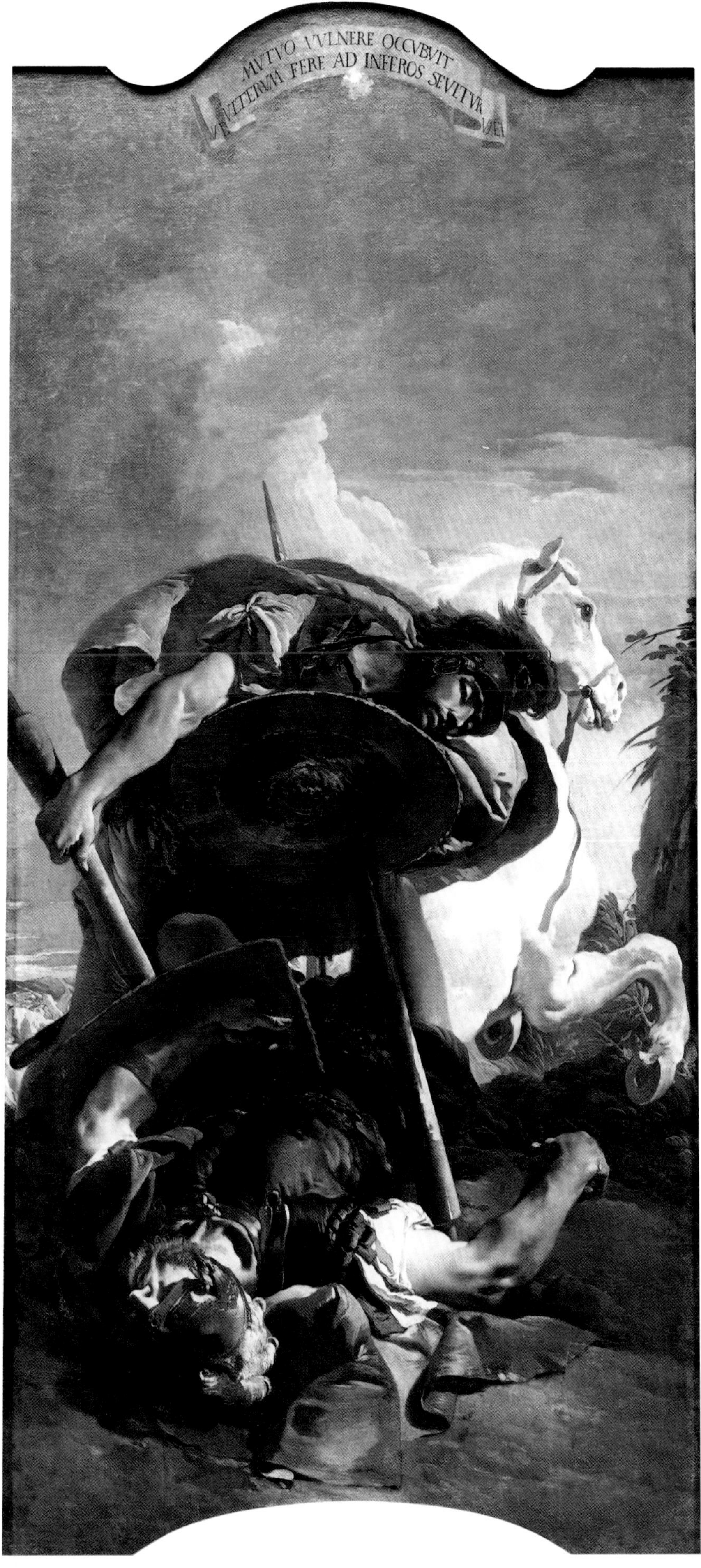

Fig. 34. *The Death of Lucius Junius Brutus*. Oil on canvas. Kunsthistorisches Museum, Vienna

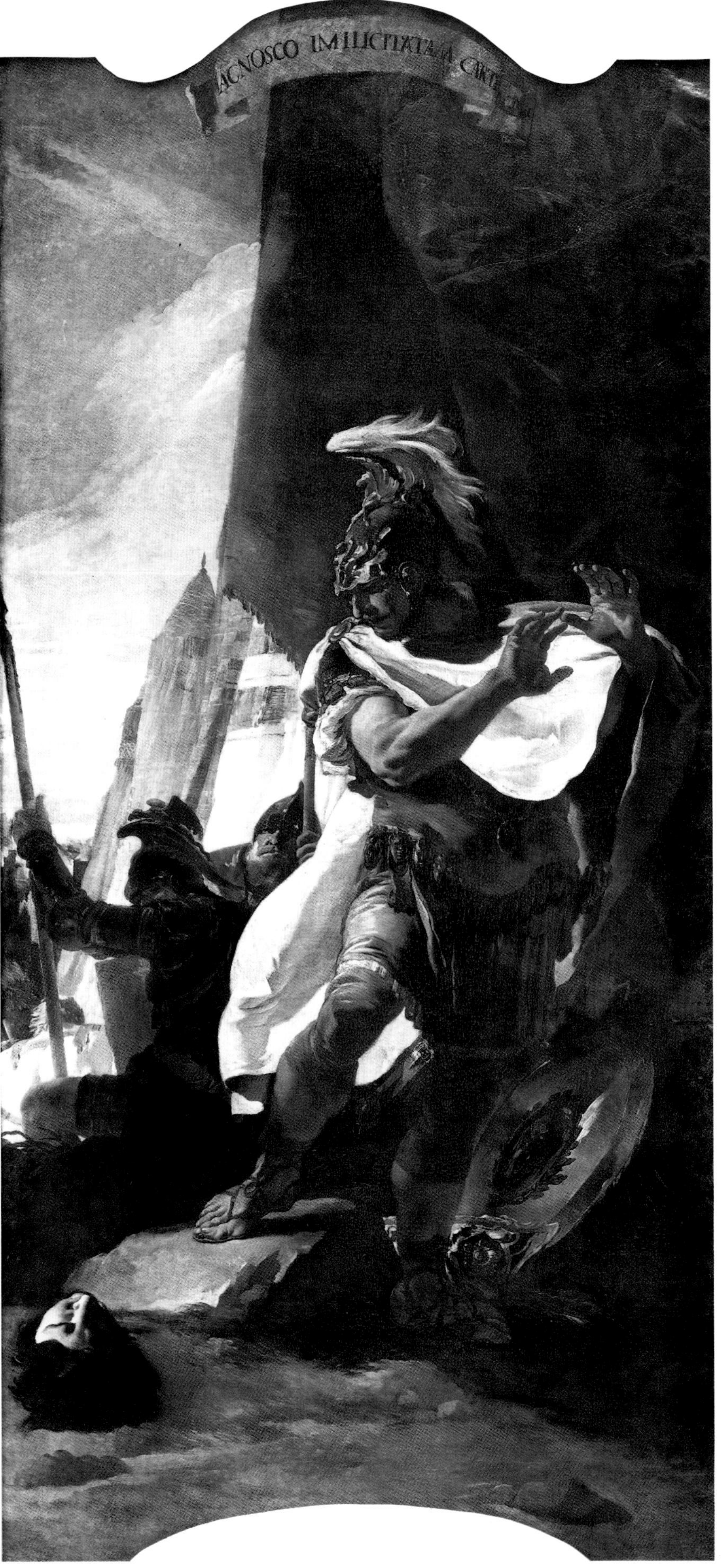

Fig. 35. *Hannibal Contemplating the Head of Hasdrubal*. Oil on canvas. Kunsthistorisches Museum, Vienna

is a great metropolis, with a citadel, temples, and statues, such as would be appropriate for the great city of Dido described by Virgil. The carnage depicted in the background also conforms to accounts of the battle. As one of the pivotal events in Roman history, the defeat of Carthage would not likely have been omitted from a series such as the Dolfin cycle. Ideally, the battle scenes should relate to the triumphs, and if it could be demonstrated that the *Tarantine Triumph* actually showed the triumph of Scipio, the matter of their identification would be closer to resolution.

In this alternation of battles, triumphs, and valorous acts, it is difficult to discern any didactic program, except in the most general sense. Levey has written, "The state and its demands on the individual form the theme. Rome conquers—especially its traditional enemy Carthage (for which might be read Venice versus the Ottoman Empire)."[20] It may have been in this allusive fashion that the Dolfin viewed the pictures, for it is not difficult to imagine them finding in the military conquests and territorial expansion of republican Rome a flattering analogy with the history of Venice and in some of the heroes a reflection of their own patriotic commitment to the Venetian state. Certainly the effect of the lines from Florus inscribed on each canvas is to transform historical events into axioms of conduct and action. Daniele IV may not have put his hand in a fire, but he did lose four fingers of his left hand in battle against the Turks in 1690.

What makes these pictures so compelling as works of art is the manner in which Roman history is treated as staged theater rather than archaeological fact. To a degree, this approach was typically Venetian, but Tiepolo stands apart from his contemporaries in his insistence on narrative clarity and dramatic focus: at no point does he sacrifice intensity of expression to decorative concerns. Exceptionally, in the *Fabius Maximus* he created an antique-seeming setting and, in the figures huddled in discussion, a suggestion of ancient statesmen that the Roman Sacchi of the previous century might have envied. By contrast, in the *Triumph of Marius* the arch through which the procession passes resembles a Gothic bridge, and the fortifications shown in the remaining paintings of the series are, again, more Gothic than Roman in appearance. (Is there a veiled allusion in these details to the medieval fortifications in the Veneto?) Similarly, save for the marble bust of Cybele in the *Triumph of Marius*, the vases, standards, and other props show none of the learned, archaeological instinct of Mantegna or Rubens; instead they are allusively and evocatively *all'antica* (even the altar into whose flames Mucius Scaevola thrusts his hand is almost Piranesian in its free use of classical models). We are reminded that

Tiepolo's drawings after the antiquities of Verona—carried out for Scipione Maffei's *Verona illustrata* about 1724—are distinguished for the life and animation conferred on ancient statues, fragments, and busts, which give them the quality of still lifes rather than archaeological record. With this in mind, we should not be surprised that in the *Coriolanus* the eager sons who have darted out from behind their stern grandmother to greet the general of the Volsci are dressed in sixteenth-century finery. The procession in the *Tarantine Triumph* is headed by a court dwarf, on the left, and two picturesque Gypsies, on the right. This is the sort of local color that Tiepolo was to bring to all of his subsequent history paintings. Time and again we are captivated by a figure or face obviously based on a specific living model: the wide-eyed youth who stares in disbelief at Mucius Scaevola is but one example. Tiepolo even found a place for himself among the colorful bystanders in the *Triumph of Marius* (frontis., p. 2).

The greatest challenge Tiepolo faced in the Ca' Dolfin canvases was the need to adapt visually complex stories to restrictive vertical picture fields. In Venice horizontal rather than vertical canvases had been the usual vehicle for narrative paintings of this sort. Tiepolo's problem was especially acute in the two triumphs—previously triumphs had always been shown as processions across the picture surface. But he managed to turn this limitation to advantage, rotating each procession ninety degrees, so that it moves from the background into the foreground, threatening to spill out of the picture plane into the real space of the spectator. He must have derived inspiration for this solution from Veronese's splendid *Triumph of Mordecai* on the ceiling of S. Sebastiano in Venice, but that work, viewed decisively *di sotto-in-sù*, could serve only as a point of departure. In the two triumphs we have the first intimation of the brilliant, illusionistic scheme Tiepolo was to invent a decade and a half later for Palazzo Labia in Venice, where Cleopatra proceeds from her barge toward fictive stairs leading into the actual hall of the residence (frontis., p. 28). To no less a degree, in Ca' Dolfin the viewer is made to participate in the scenes depicted (it is, indeed, the viewer that Jugurtha fixes with his proud gaze).

Clearly the pictures took a number of years to complete, and Tiepolo's increasing mastery of spatial problems is fully demonstrated by a comparison of the *Tarantine Triumph* with the *Triumph of Marius*. In the former the space is ambivalent and the arrangement of the figures casual. The placement of the victorious general atop his curious cart is awkward, and the billowing banner on the left and the descending diagonal of spectators on the right confuse rather than articulate the composition. Its brilliant effect derives less from

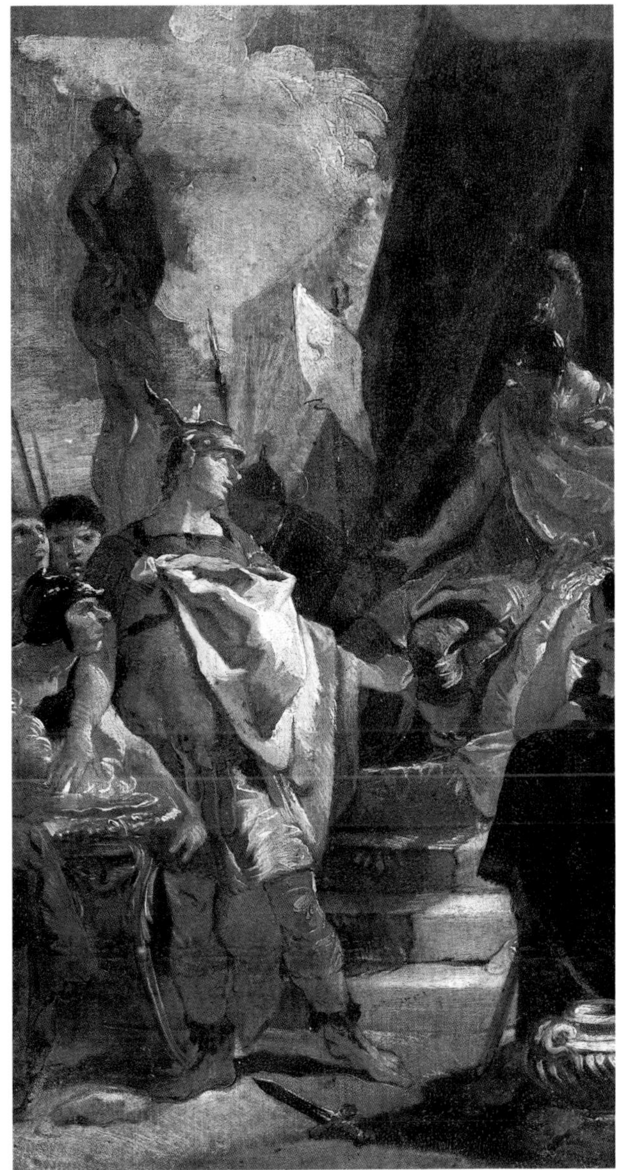

Fig. 36. *Mucius Scaevola before Porsenna*. Oil on canvas. Musée Magnin, Dijon

the composition as a whole than from individual details and figures viewed against the intensely colored sky. By contrast, in the *Triumph of Marius* Tiepolo organized the composition around a simple arc, accented by the measured placement of the figures of the boy with a tambourine in the foreground, Jugurtha in the middle ground, and Marius at the crest of a hill, his torso set off by the receding wall of the distant arch. The spears and ensigns create a vertical grid, while the yellow standard, crisply fluttering above Marius, falls on the vertical axis, anchoring the scheme. No less notable is the powerful construction and ponderous, forward-moving gait of the protagonists, so different from the tentative description of the figures in the *Tarantine Triumph*. The shift from the sharply lit, brilliant colors of the *Tarantine Triumph* to the more

PROVENANCE, 12a–d:
Daniele IV Dolfin, Ca' Dolfin, Venice (until 1729); Dolfin family, Ca' Dolfin (1729–98); by descent, Gasparo Lippomano, Ca' Dolfin, Venice (until 1854); Count Giovanni Querini Stampalia, Ca' Dolfin (1854–68); Michelangelo Guggenheim, Venice (1870–72); Baron Miller von Aichholz, Vienna (1872–76; sale, Hôtel Drouot, Paris, 15 April 1876, lots 5–8); Polovzeff, Saint Petersburg (1876–86); Stieglitz Central School of Technical Drawing, Saint Petersburg (1886–1934); The Hermitage Museum (from 1934)

PROVENANCE, 12e–g:
Daniele IV Dolfin, Ca' Dolfin, Venice (1729); Dolfin family Ca' Dolfin (1729–98); by descent, Gasparo Lippomano, Ca' Dolfin (until 1854); Count Giovanni Querini Stampalia, Ca' Dolfin (1854–68); Michelangelo Guggenheim, Venice (1870–72); Baron Miller von Aichholz, Vienna (1872–1919 [installed in baron's new residence, 1886]; sale, Hôtel Drouot, Paris, 15 April 1876, lots 1, 2, 4 [bought in]); Camillo Castiglioni, Palast Aichholz, Vienna (1919–34); Stefan Mendl, Zurich and Saranac Lake, New York (1934–55); his estate (1955–65)

REFERENCES:
Da Canal 1732 (1809 ed.) p. xxxiv; Florio [1747], p. 39; Saint-Non (1760) in Rosenberg and Brejon de Lavergnée 1986, p. 202; Moschini 1806, vol. 3, p. 75; Chennevières 1898, p. 18; Modern 1902, pp. 22–23, 53; Molmenti 1909, pp. 276–77; Saint Petersburg 1910, p. 38; Sack 1910, pp. 33–35, 151, 203; Dolfin 1924, p. 187; Fiocco 1931, pp. 173–74; Scherbachova 1941; Morassi 1941–42, pp. 92, 259–64; Morassi 1955a, pp. 11–12; Morassi 1962, pp. 15, 34, 66; Pallucchini 1968, pp. 91–92, no. 48; Stuttgart 1970, p. 127; Cailleux [1972], pp. 96, 100 n. 29; Zeri and Gardner 1973, pp. 60–63; Pradella 1979–80; Brejon de Lavergnée 1980, pp. 107–9; Knox 1980a, pp. 60–64; Levey 1986, pp. 52–53; Knox 1991; Fort Worth 1993, pp. 157–60; Gemin and Pedrocco 1993, pp. 61–63, 258–62, nos. 87–89, 91–94

subtle modulations in the *Triumph of Marius* is equally remarkable.

The *Triumph of Marius* is unquestionably the latest picture in the cycle (this is, quite obviously, why it is dated and why Tiepolo included his portrait in it), and the *Tarantine Triumph* must be among the earliest. The *Tarantine Triumph* could have been painted as early as about 1726—that is, possibly before Tiepolo had completed the canvases in Palazzo Sandi in Venice (there are affinities with the *Discovery of Achilles* [fig. 30]). Having begun the Ca' Dolfin cycle with the *Tarantine Triumph*, Tiepolo seems to have turned—perhaps in the early months of 1727—to its two companions and then to the remaining compositions, including the battle scenes.[21] Each stage of his progress on the cycle was accompanied by greater mastery of his pictorial means. In the battle scenes and in the *Triumph of Marius* the brush is manipulated to suggest a range of textures: the weave of cloth, the pelt of a horse, the rough skin of a soldier. Highlights are scumbled with consummate control, almost as though Tiepolo were drawing with colored light. The background scene in the *Capture of Carthage* (frontis., p. 36) and the impressive Moorish prisoner in the *Triumph of Marius* are carried out in near-monochrome tones of gray, blue, and buff with a loose, broken brushwork that looks ahead to Goya and Delacroix: rarely again did Tiepolo achieve such a tactile effect in his work. Although it is frequently stated that fresco was Tiepolo's natural medium, the latest of the Ca' Dolfin paintings reveal him as an unsurpassed master of oil. One might almost reverse the judgment and say that what makes his frescoes so remarkable is the degree to which he managed to simulate the textural effects of the Ca' Dolfin pictures in a medium that is, by nature, transparent and smooth. In the Ca' Dolfin canvases Tiepolo appears as a Piazzetta who has discovered color, realized the potential of light as an animating as well as a dramatic force, and harnessed his overt emotionalism to the dictates of narrative drama.

Tiepolo's art was to undergo profound changes: the airy, decorative style of the Chicago Tasso paintings (no. 17a–d) exemplifies the very different direction—really more of a Rococo detour—Tiepolo's art was to take a decade or so later. Yet behind his finest subsequent achievements—the cinematic richness of the two gigantic canvases with Old Testament stories in the parish church of Verolanuova, the dignified narrative idiom of the Roman stories at Montecchio Maggiore (see fig. 40), the resonant pathos of the *Martyrdom of Saint Agatha* (no. 38), and the elevated realism of the genrelike details in the ceiling over the staircase of the Residenz in Würzburg (see fig. 95)—there is the echo of these extraordinary pictures carried out for Ca' Dolfin at the threshold of his maturity.

Three oil sketches have been associated with the cycle, but only one of them—the very beautiful *modello* for the *Mucius Scaevola* (fig. 36)—is certainly autograph.[22]

KC

NOTES

1. Of the paintings, Saint-Non wrote, "Une des meilleure choses qu'il ait fait à Venise sont de grandes fresques [*sic*], dans un grand salon, au Palais Delphino di San Pantaleone, morceau de la plus belle couleur, de la composition et de l'Effet le plus séduisant." See Rosenberg and Brejon de Lavergnée 1986, pp. 202–6. Four of the five drawings by Fragonard are in the Norton Simon Museum of Art, Pasadena; the fifth is in a private collection, Paris.
2. See Morassi 1973, pp. 93–95, 110, 325 no. 93, 326 nos. 95–100. Interestingly, Guardi's rendition seems to be based less on the final composition than on the *modello* in Dijon (for which, see text below), which shows the same tripod brazier and the same vase in its foreground included by Guardi. This is of significance as evidence that Tiepolo's *modelli* were available to other artists.
3. "Se Dio me darà vita farò dipingere dalli più celebri pitori li quadri che sono nella sala." I wish to thank Valentina Conticelli for allowing me to cite her important discovery prior to her presentation at the Tiepolo symposium in Italy in October 1996. At face value it would seem that bare canvases had already been prepared for the commission when Daniele III left for Constantinople.
4. Whether the commission from the Confraternity of the Most Holy Sacrament to decorate a chapel in the cathedral of Udine was in some way connected with his work for Dionisio Dolfin in the Arcivescovado cannot be said; however, in the documents the artist was referred to as "the celebrated painter," and it seems probable that the means by which his reputation was established in Udine was the Dolfin commission. Tiepolo's fresco showing the Fall of the Rebel Angels on the vault above the staircase of the Arcivescovado is usually accepted as his earliest work in the palace; the staircase was completed in 1726. To my eye, Tiepolo's first frescoes in the Arcivescovado are those on the vault of the gallery, for they consciously refer to the style of Dorigny, whose work in the cathedral of Udine established the standard for decorative painting in the city. The frescoes on the Arcivescovado vault could date as early as 1725. Tiepolo worked in the city's castello as well as in the Arcivescovado and the cathedral between 1726 and 1729: obviously he made the most of his stays in the Friuli.
5. In addition to the paintings at Udine mentioned in note 4 above, he was working on the *Madonna of Mount Carmel* (fig. 19), commissioned in 1722 but finished only in 1727. On the basis of viewing this picture after its recent cleaning, I believe it was begun on the right side about 1723–24 and completed on the left side—which bears strong affinities with the Ca' Dolfin canvases—about 1727. Work on the cycle of Roman histories for Ca' Zenobio, Venice, seems to have been suspended during this period. The ceiling of the chapel of Saint Teresa in the Scalzi may well date from this moment, and there also were numerous lesser commissions.
6. The authorship of the ceiling is established by a note in the traveling journal of Edward Wright. See Mariuz 1981, p. 184. Wright was in Venice in 1720–21 and was shown the palace by Bambini, who declared that he had carried out the frescoes in fifteen days. The Ferrarese author Girolamo Baruffaldi records Ferrari's participation. Bambini also frescoed the library of the Arcivescovado in Udine not long before 1711.

addition of pieces of canvas to the tops and bottoms. This was most likely done by the dealer Guggenheim, who sold them to Baron Aichholz. The two canvases at Vienna (figs. 34, 35) were partly returned to their original shapes before 1909, when they were reproduced by Molmenti; a full restoration was undertaken upon their acquisition by the Kunsthistorisches Museum. In 1995 the Metropolitan Museum canvases were restretched in an effort to re-create their initial formats. Unfortunately, only an approximation could be attempted. Although the technical evidence of the canvases was not clear enough to establish definitively the profiles of the bottom and top edges, it did conflict with the profiles of the recesses, which must have been modified to receive mirrors when the much-damaged room they are in was restored by the purchaser of the palace, the Milanese architect G. B. Brusa.

8. The identification of this triumph has long been disputed and still poses a puzzle. It has been thought to show the triumph of one of the Scipios or of Aurelian. The triumphs of Scipio Africanus in 201 B.C.and of Scipio Aemilianus in 146 B.C., following their respective defeats of Carthage, would seem obvious choices for a cycle of this sort. However, the fragmentary inscription on the badly damaged banderole reads MISSIS CUM PYRRHO ELEPHANTIS . . . ROMA GRATULATUR. Although the source of this quote has not been traced, the reference to Pyrrhus's elephants indicates that the triumph must be the one celebrated after the defeat of Pyrrhus and his Tarantine allies by Rome in 279 B.C., in which elephants were featured (see Knox 1980a, p. 65 n. 5). Yet even this identification is not entirely satisfactory, since it does not account for the prominent prisoner in the foreground or the general riding a cart—anomalies for the Tarantine celebrations. These details would better accord with the triumph of Scipio Africanus, at which the Numidian king Syphax is said to have appeared as a prisoner.
9. For the restoration and inscriptions, see Scherbachova 1941.
10. Florus 1929, I.xvii.3–4: "Nec minus ille ferociter iniuriam armis vindicasset, nisi quod iam inferentem signa filium mater Veturia lacrimis suis exarmavit" (And he would have avenged his wrongs by force of arms with even greater severity if his mother, Veturia, had not disarmed him by her tears when he was already advancing).
11. Ibid., I.iv.6–7: "'En, ut scias,' inquit, 'quem virum effugeris' . . . hic interritus, ille trepidaret, tamquam manus regis arderet" ("Behold," he said, "and know from what sort of a man you have escaped" . . . Mucius was unafraid, but the King was startled as though his own hand were burning).
12. Ibid., I.iv.8: "donex Arruntem filium regis manu sua Brutus occidit superque ipsum mutuo volnere expiravit, plane quasi adulterum ad inferos usque sequeretur" (Brutus with his own hand killed Arruns, the king's son, and fell dead on his body from a wound dealt him by his foe, as though he would pursue the adulterer even to the infernal regions).
13. Ibid., I.v.13: "Medium erat tempus forte sementis, cum patricium virum innixum aratro suo lictor in ipso opere deprehendit" (It happened to be the middle of the season of sowing, when the lictor found the patrician actually at work bending over his plough).
14. Ibid., I.xxii.7: "Et excusso in media curia togae gremio non sine horrore, quasi plane sinu bellum ferret, effudit" (He spread out his toga with a gesture which did not fail to produce the alarm which might have been expected had he really carried war in its folds).
15. Ibid., I.xxii.45: "'Agnosco' inquit 'infelicitatem Carthaginis'" ("I recognize," he said, "the ill luck of the Carthaginians").
16. Ibid., I.xxxvi.17: "Opertum catenis Iugurtham in triumpho populus Romanus aspexit" (The Roman people saw Jugurtha led in triumph loaded with chains).
17. Ibid., I.xxi.
18. Ibid., I.xxxviii.11–18. Florus recounts that the tribes were weakened by their stay in the Veneto: "The very mildness of the country and of the air sapped their vigour." This sort of topical detail could well have recommended the subject to the Dolfin.
19. That the two battle pictures might show victories of Coriolanus is tentatively suggested by Zeri (Zeri and Gardner 1973, p. 62) and is argued more extensively by Knox (1991, p. 309).
20. Levey 1986, p. 52.
21. Since 1975 Knox has maintained that the battles were painted in the mid-1750s, after Tiepolo's return home from Würzburg. The primary evidence supporting this hypothesis is three chalk drawings in a style like that of Tiepolo's work of the 1750s that are related to the pictures (for which, see Knox 1980a, p. 226, no. M135, 262, no. M419, 288 no. M673). He considers them preliminary drawings by Tiepolo; I believe them to be by Giandomenico and extraneous to any dating of the paintings. Quite apart from any proof the drawings may or may not offer, however, there are the simple facts that da Canal clearly states that the room contained ten pictures and that the battle scenes and the other paintings are entirely consistent stylistically.
22. The oil sketch at Montecarlo showing Fabius Maximus before the Senate of Carthage (Fort Worth 1993, pp. 157–60, no. 6, and Gemin and Pedrocco 1993, p. 261, no. 93a) can be little more than a weak workshop replica, as Whistler (1993, pp. 857–58) has recognized. That depicting Cincinnatus (Gemin and Pedrocco 1993, p. 262, no. 94a), now in the Mainfränkisches Museum, Würzburg (Lg. 49796), is also a poor copy—but of a *modello* for another composition known through a feeble picture in the Art Museum of Notre Dame University, South Bend, Indiana, for which see Urbana 1962, no. 32. A very poor replica of the Mainfränkisches picture is in the museum at Kiev. The Notre Dame canvas is a prime example of the kind of recycled compositions Tiepolo and his workshop began to produce, already at the time of the Dolfin commission, to meet an inexhaustible demand for his work. The *modelli*-like copies establish that the early call for Tiepolo's drawings reported by da Canal was quickly transferred to oil sketches, which were sometimes counterfeited to meet the market. A number of drawings—all in pen and ink with wash and showing soldiers—have also been associated with the series. None bear close enough affinities with the final works to indicate with certainty that they are preparatory to the canvases. See Cambridge 1970, no. 8; Knox 1975a, p. 38, no. 6; and Grigorieva [1976].

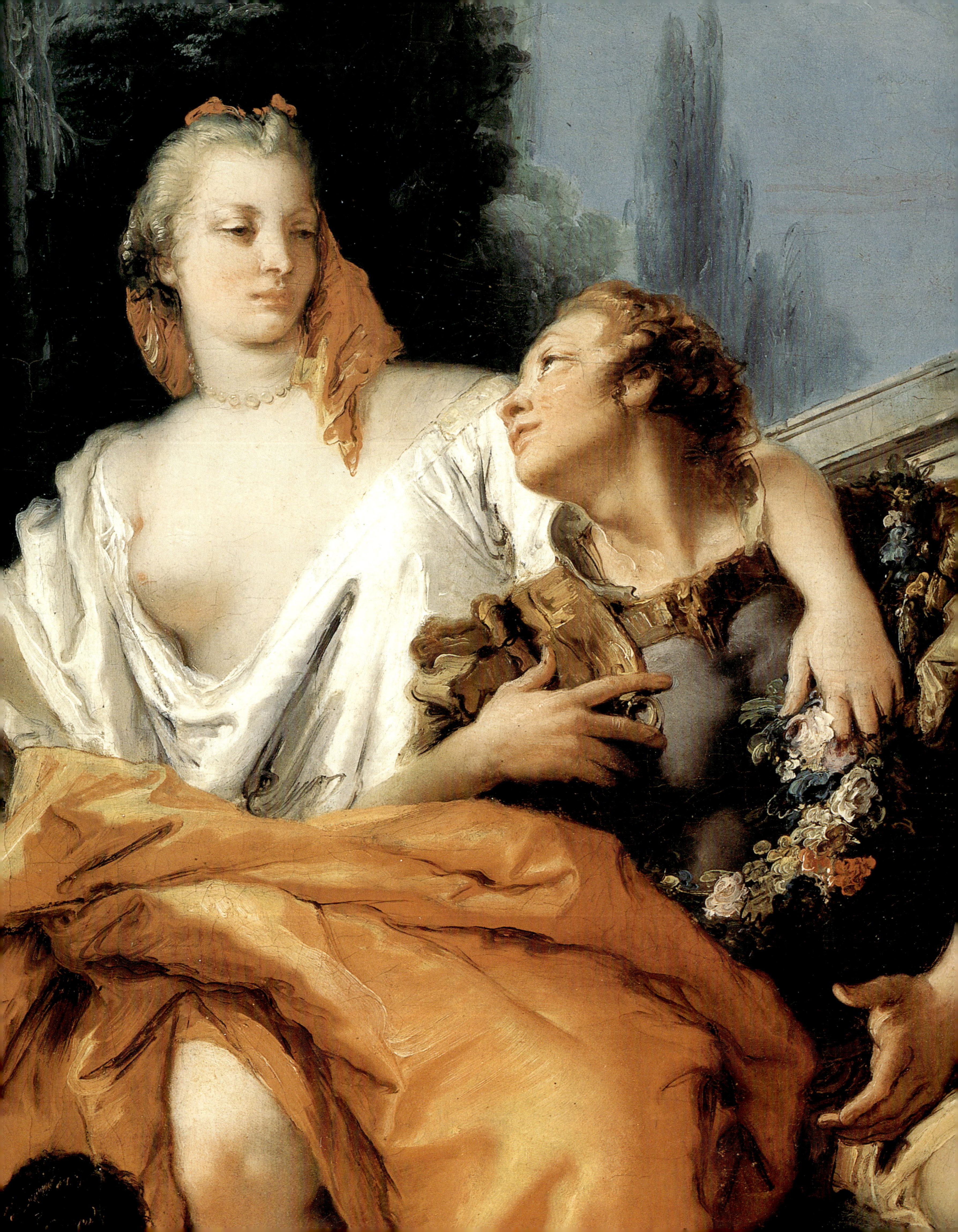

Tiepolo as a Painter of History and Mythology and as a Decorator

WILLIAM L. BARCHAM

Throughout the span of his more than fifty-year-long, peripatetic career, Tiepolo covered canvases, walls, and ceilings with religious and secular subjects. The cloud-filled vaults of the Kaisersaal and stairwell of the Residenz in Würzburg (frontis., p. 18) and the amorous rendezvous of Antony and Cleopatra in the *salone* of the Palazzo Labia in Venice (frontis., p. 28, fig. 38) enchant modern viewers and fill them with unbounded admiration for the painter's genius. With their allegories, mythologies, and histories, these and other fresco cycles, far more than his many altarpieces and devotional paintings, have come to define Tiepolo's place in European art. The reason for this lies not only in the sheer attractiveness of his protagonists—the flawless beauty of his beguiling heroines and the virile strength of his heroes—but also in the variety and range of the subjects in them. In the annals of European painting no one can compete with him for the brilliance of his histories and mythologies: their heroic scope, the grandeur of their conception, and above all their spirited impact on the viewer. Those who have experienced his fresco cycles firsthand know how much their success is due to the uncanny partnership the spectator and the paintings share in space. Tiepolo predicated the conception of his frescoes on the peculiarities of their architectural sites, and he responded sensitively to the changing light that fills them. He shrewdly understood the dramatic potential in the relationships between one surface or segment of a decorative complex and another, and he took into account the distances affecting and the optical stimuli operating on the perambulating viewer. Like his own brilliantly sunlit figure of Apollo, whose muscular body arches above the center of the Würzburg stairwell (fig. 39), Tiepolo reigns supreme in the realm of allegory, history, and mythology, his art radiating its luminous power over the beholder.

Although we still admire the beauty of Tiepolo's secular works, their sometimes recondite associations often escape spectators nowadays. There are even viewers who believe that a serious knowledge of his subjects is superfluous to an appreciation of the pictures; that Tiepolo's rapturous color, for example, affords satisfaction enough. For these observers subject matter becomes irrelevant, perhaps even bothersome, and the search for its elucidation can hinder the spontaneous response his work seems to require. But for anyone trying to understand the impetus behind Tiepolo's secular paintings, the relevance, for example, of *Queen Zenobia Addressing Her Soldiers* (fig. 20) to the Zenobio family's anxious need to establish its ancestry is hardly an incidental fact. On the contrary, this need is a fundamental consideration, for it inspired the act of patronage that engendered Tiepolo's monumental composition and the lofty conception of character he realized in the work. Desirous to please his royal, ecclesiastical, and patrician patrons, and concerned that the interiors of their palaces and villas mirror the estimable ideals they publicly espoused, he filled numerous *saloni* and halls with narratives and allegories that reflected his employers' political ambitions, their cultural aspirations, and personal dreams. Middle-class society now finds such themes pretentious, but in the eighteenth century they were still accepted as part of Western Europe's long and meaningful heritage. Our modern alienation from this tradition is a loss, sad in itself; it also hampers our appreciation of an ennobling art such as Tiepolo's.

What moral values, cultural attitudes, and intellectual assumptions distinguish Tiepolo's secular frescoes and canvases? At least three principal themes interested him: virtue and honor leading to victory; steadfast resolve and intrepid action betrayed by defeat; and stories of love and passion. Sometimes these themes are paired, combined, and intermingled to enhance one another. Victorious virtue and honor, comprising valor, excellence, and merit, ranked highest among the themes as the most noble values in the hierarchy of his society's moral achievements. As Tiepolo perceived them, virtue and honor could lodge naturally within a hero's soul, but they could also result from personal choice or a heroic deed. Alternatively, they could be a ruler's birthright or simply hover as abstract ideals.

Detail, *Rinaldo and Armida in the Garden*, no. 22a

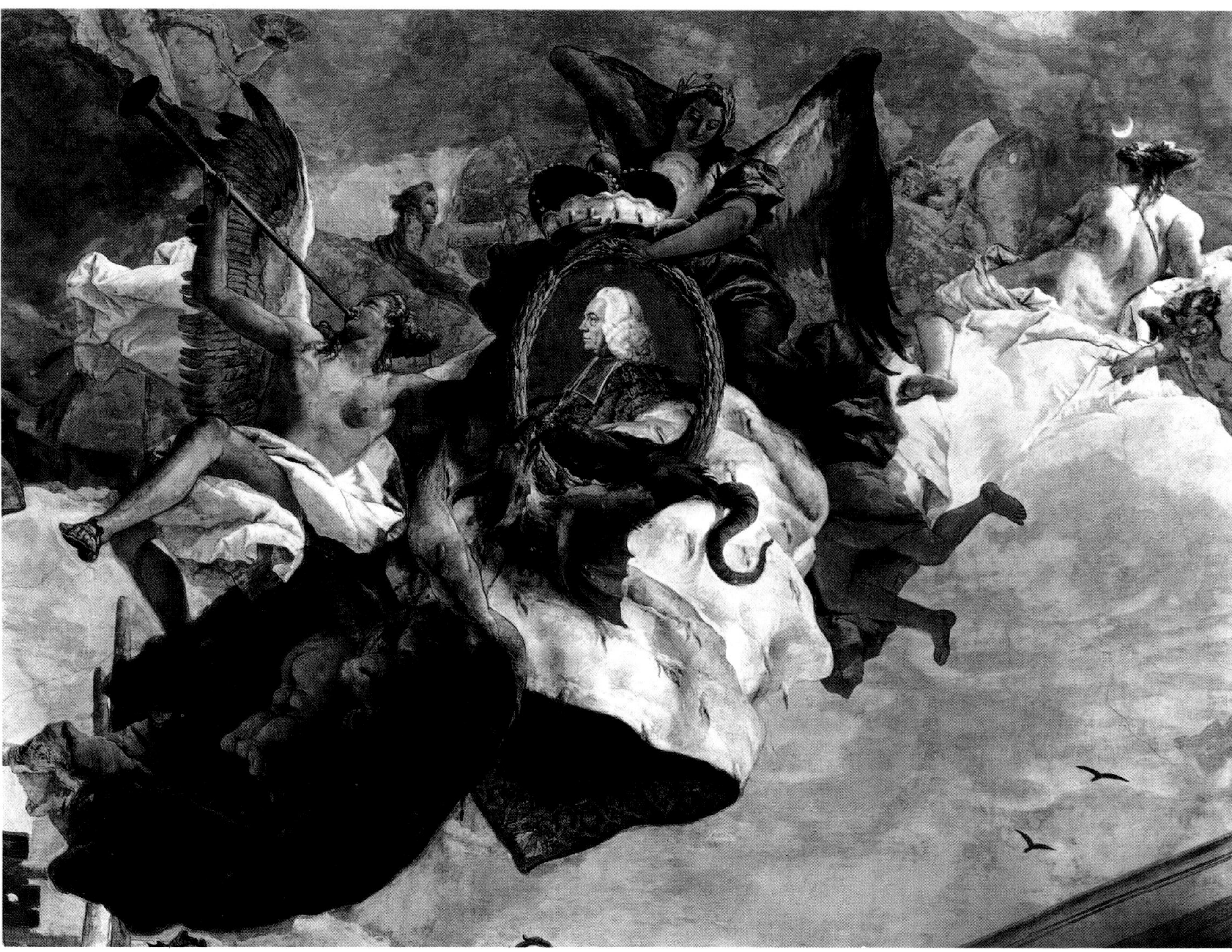

Fig. 37. *Allegory of Europe: Apollo and the Four Continents, Portrait of Carl Philipp von Greiffenclau.* Fresco. Residenz, Würzburg

Among Tiepolo's early secular cycles are three canvases he painted about 1725 for the *salone* of Tommaso Sandi's palace at S. Angelo near the Grand Canal. The two smaller works are *Hercules and Antaeus* and *Apollo and Marsyas* (no. 9a, b), each exemplifying virtue overcoming arrogance and presumptuousness. The group centered around the large *Discovery of Achilles* (fig. 30), which recounts an episode in Achilles' early life. Here the youthful Achilles, unable to restrain his innate military valor despite his enforced disguise as a maiden, is shown impulsively reaching for a sword hidden amid the jewels Ulysses had brought to the king of Scyros's court. In praising the spontaneity of the legendary hero's courage, Tiepolo's painting indirectly lauds the valor of the Sandi, for, as newly inscribed members in the Venetian patriciate, they had assumed a ready part in the state's defenses against the Turks; like Achilles, the family willingly accepted public responsibility and played a meritorious role in society.[1]

Only a few brief years after he completed the Sandi cycle, Tiepolo painted another group of canvases depicting stories from the ancient world, again for a patrician Venetian family. But this time the series was monumental in size and consisted of histories, and the patrons belonged to the old aristocracy, not to a circle of newcomers. In his ten immense paintings for Ca' Dolfin near S. Pantalon (no. 12a–g, figs. 33–35) Tiepolo portrayed great Roman heroes, drawing parallels between them and the Dolfin, loyal and bold defenders of the Most Serene Republic. That the family chose historical events rather than myths as the subjects of their pictures is consistent with their documented involvement in state affairs, ecclesiastical history, and real battles. Among their ancestors the Dolfin counted a doge, fourteen procurators of the republic, and six cardinals, and they could trace the family's

Opposite: Fig. 38. *The Banquet of Cleopatra.* Fresco. Palazzo Labia, Venice

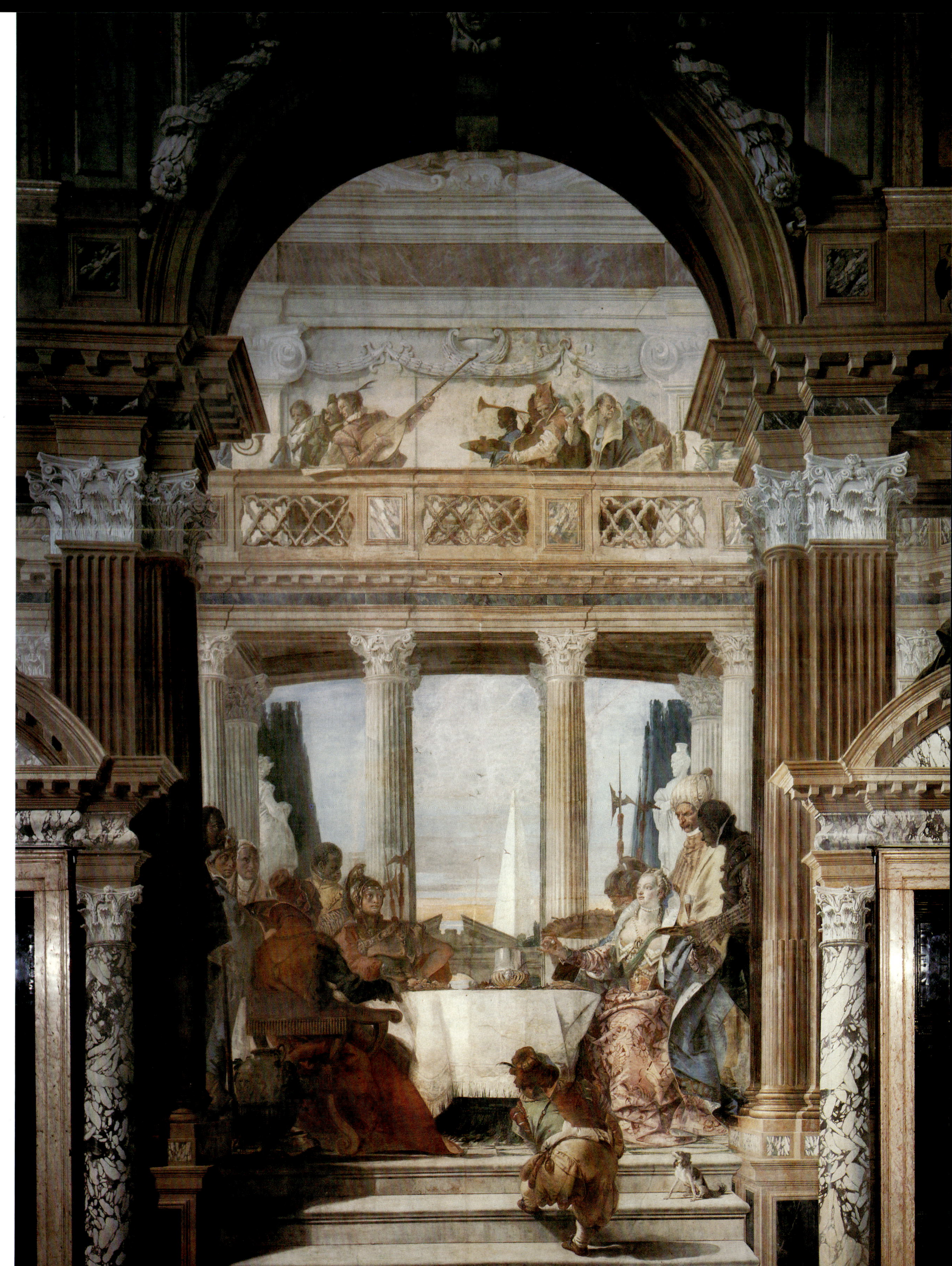

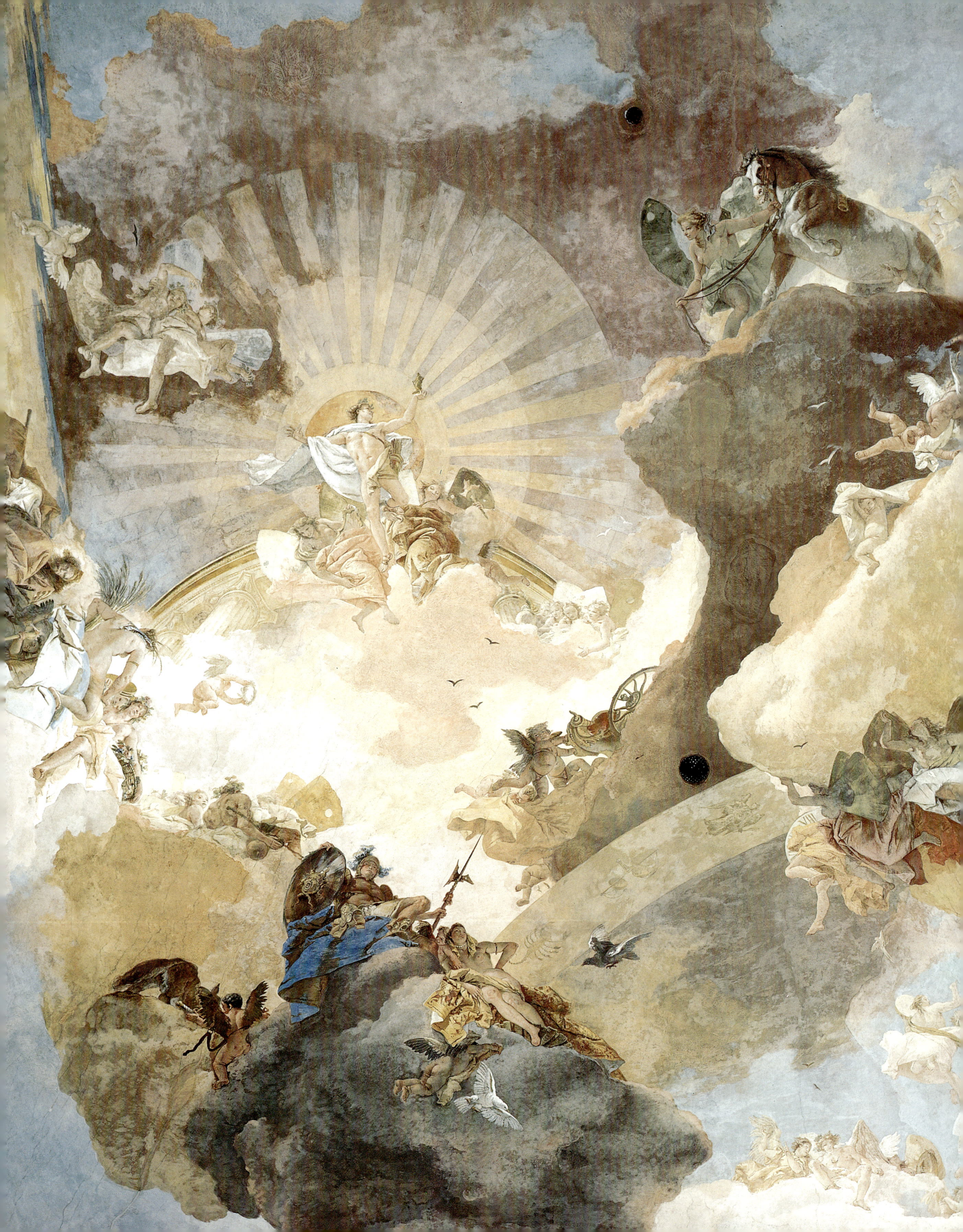

public history back for centuries, unlike the Sandi, whose participation in Venetian matters had only recently begun.

While eight of the Dolfin paintings narrate acts of heroism, the two largest isolate the triumphal processions of, respectively, Gaius Marius (no. 12e) and, less certainly, Publius Cornelius Scipio (fig. 33). Hieratically posed and majestically drawn toward the viewer's space—Marius in a quadriga and Scipio in a chariot pulled by two tusked pachyderms—the heroes hold martial batons and parade among flapping banners, military lances, plaques, and trophies. Each hero's head is frontal and manifestly a copy of a Roman portrait bust. The intention is unmistakable: Tiepolo sought to glorify the virtue of patriotism. Enjoying pride of place in the *salone* of Ca' Dolfin through their remarkable size and central positioning on the two principal walls, the pair of triumphs shifts the narrative mode of the series into encomium, transforming historical fact into an apotheosis of civic virtue.[2]

The Sandi and Dolfin paintings are large historical cycles painted on canvas, a mode of pictorial ornamentation unknown in Venice during the Renaissance but newly fashionable in Venetian palaces at the end of the seventeenth century.[3] Covering the walls of the largest reception rooms in the homes of wealthy patricians, such series offered exemplars of heroic deeds and laudatory behavior; patrons who wanted a classical lineage especially favored them because they provided a desirable genealogical pedigree. Tiepolo satisfied such clients as the Sandi and the Dolfin better and more often than any of his Venetian colleagues, and by the time he left Venice definitively in 1762, he had single-handedly executed about two dozen cycles of the kind in both oils and fresco, in Venice itself and in nearby cities and villas on the mainland.

Apart from glorifying nation and state in the Sandi and Dolfin paintings, Tiepolo represented stories that focus on the more private virtues of generosity and compassion, often expressing emotions that touch us deeply. For example, in 1731 he frescoed scenes in the *salone* of Palazzo Dugnani, Milan, portraying the magnanimous Scipio Africanus, and in 1744 he depicted one of those episodes again, when he decorated the *salone* of the villa of Carlo Cordellina, at Montecchio Maggiore near Vicenza, with the *Continence of Scipio*.[4] As the companion fresco to the picture in Villa Cordellina, Tiepolo produced the *Family of Darius before Alexander* (fig. 40), one of his most affecting works. With a sensitivity perhaps inspired by the story's theme of princely generosity, Tiepolo contrasted the openhearted Alexander, whose magnificent military tent embodies his warm munificence and liberality, with the pleading figure of Darius's mother, her deep cobalt blue gown giving visual expression to her woeful lament on imprisonment.

Opposite: Fig. 39. Detail, *Apollo and the Four Continents*. Fresco. Residenz, Würzburg

Tiepolo's composition in the Alexander fresco is indebted to Paolo Veronese's version of the same story, once in Palazzo Pisani, Venice (fig. 41). Transcribing both the loggia in the distance and the sympathetic horse on one side of his famous sixteenth-century predecessor's scene, Tiepolo also used many of the same human characters—for example, the page on the right and the elderly, bearded man in the center. Most significantly, Tiepolo re-created here, as well as elsewhere (see nos. 16a, 19), Veronese's ornamental splendor and rhetorical language, building a reputation both at home and throughout Western Europe as a follower of the great Paolo.[5] By linking himself with one of his city's Renaissance geniuses, Tiepolo purposefully recalled Venice's past artistic greatness. His neo-Veronese style struck just the right note, in particular because its rich coloration and opulent material display evoke the political and economic distinction of the republic in its halcyon days.

Tiepolo used not only myth and history to commend nobility of character but also traditional personifications culled from emblem books. First published with illustrations in 1603 and enjoying later editions as well, Cesare Ripa's *Iconologia* was one of the painter's favorite iconographic manuals. The Cordellina *salone* boasts several Virtues taken from Ripa, and the Villa Loschi, near Vicenza, whose stairwell and *salone* the artist had decorated a decade before he worked at Montecchio Maggiore, contains more than a dozen such figures, all richly colored and large in scale. Serious in demeanor and posing like ancient statuary, Innocence, Liberality, Honor (fig. 42), and Truth at Loschi convey the rigor and solemnity needed to attain the very noble ends they personify.[6] These figures are colder and more ceremonious than Tiepolo's usual embodiments of Virtue, such as the pair of beautiful damsels, clothed in white brocades and embellished with pale rose and green draperies, who enact the *Triumph of Virtue and Nobility over Ignorance* as they fly high above the Cordellina *salone*. Here and at numerous other sites, Tiepolo located his Virtues in ceiling paintings, for they were especially effective in extolling moral rectitude because of their physical elevation overhead and their celestial connotations, traditional in Italian decoration, implying immortality.

To laud valor and merit on a ceiling or vault, Tiepolo often employed the pantheon of classical deities in addition to personifications. His greatest painting with such an array, frescoed on the vault over the stairwell of the Residenz in Würzburg in 1753, praises Carl Philipp von Greiffenclau, prince-bishop of that small German city (fig. 37). Tiepolo showed Greiffenclau's likeness within a medallion-shaped portrait borne triumphantly

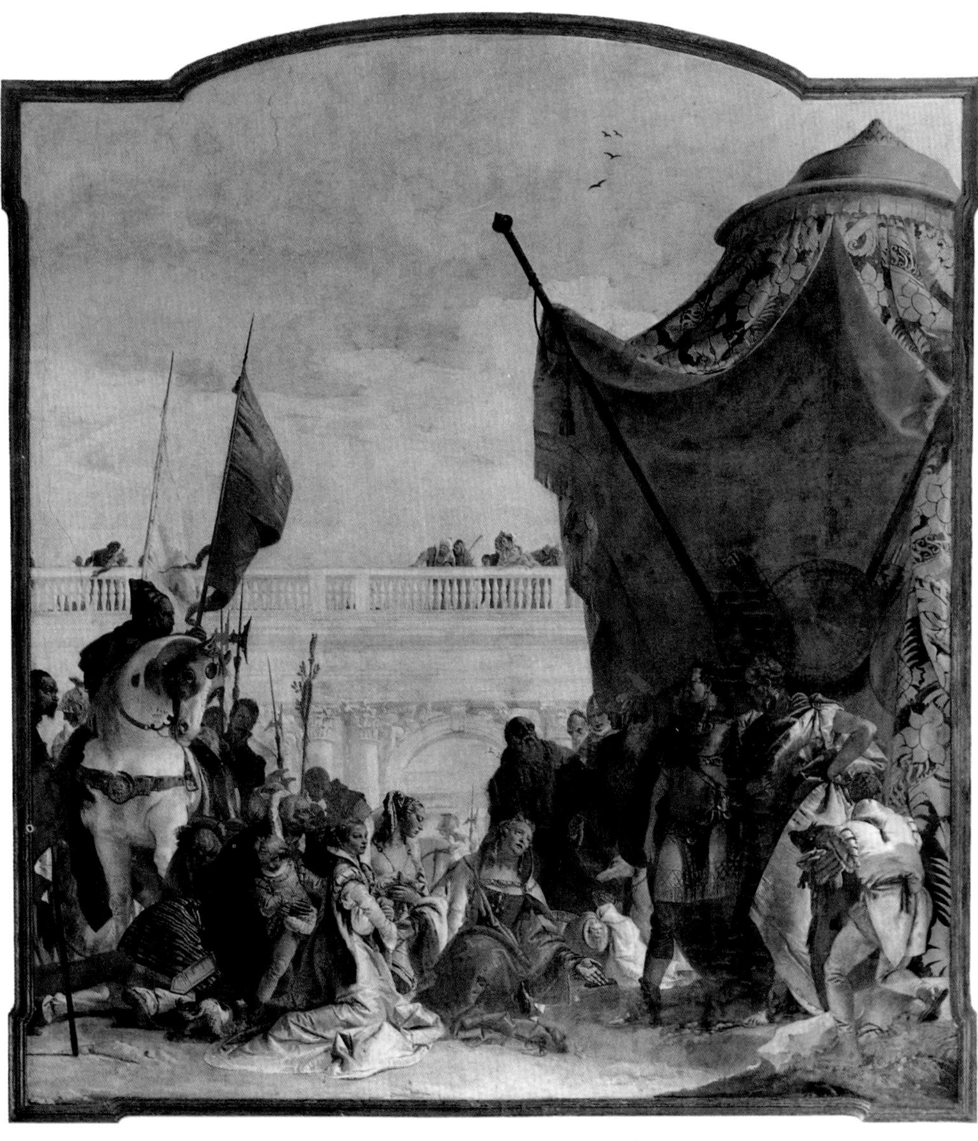

Fig. 40. *The Family of Darius before Alexander*. Fresco. Villa Cordellina, Montecchio Maggiore

into the heavenly realm of gods and goddesses. Crowned by Truth, accompanied by the winged and trumpeting figure of Fame, and heralded by the soaring Mercury, the bishop's portrait will shortly ascend past Jupiter, Saturn, Diana, Venus, and Minerva toward the brilliantly radiant Apollo, majestically posed before the Temple of Wisdom, the summit of human endeavor. Personifications and allegorical figural groupings of the Four Continents (fig. 95) decorate the cornice below and pay tribute to the sun god and, by association, to Bishop Greiffenclau, a prince with only one truly historic distinction: that of having hired Balthasar Neumann to design his residence and Tiepolo to decorate it. It must have been Greiffenclau, keen to promote himself within Würzburg's illustrious episcopal and aristocratic lineage, who directed that his portrait be shown rising ceremoniously over the monumental stairwell of the Residenz, for the artist had omitted his patron's image from the preliminary oil sketch (no. 49). Never before or again did Tiepolo glorify an individual with like pomposity. Despite this bit of princely vanity and historical foolishness, the stairwell fresco is breathtaking and the experience of approaching it overwhelming. With this unforgettable paean to sovereign splendor, Tiepolo achieved his own apotheosis in the firmament of European art.[7]

Less fortunate in Tiepolo's art than the divinely endowed Achilles, the magnanimous Scipio, and the noble Greiffenclau are the heroes and heroines who suffer pain and humiliating defeat. Although denied the summit of Olympus, these unhappy individuals are nonetheless honored for their resolve and bravery. The young artist portrayed one such figure, the widowed but courageous queen of Palmyra, in *Queen Zenobia Addressing Her Soldiers* (fig. 20), in which she urges her troops to victory before their battle with the Romans, and subsequently he depicted her disgrace at the hands of the emperor Aurelius in two related paintings now in the Museo del Prado, Madrid (fig. 21), and the Galleria Sabauda, Turin.[8] The contemporary Dolfin commission likewise retells stories of the sacrifices of

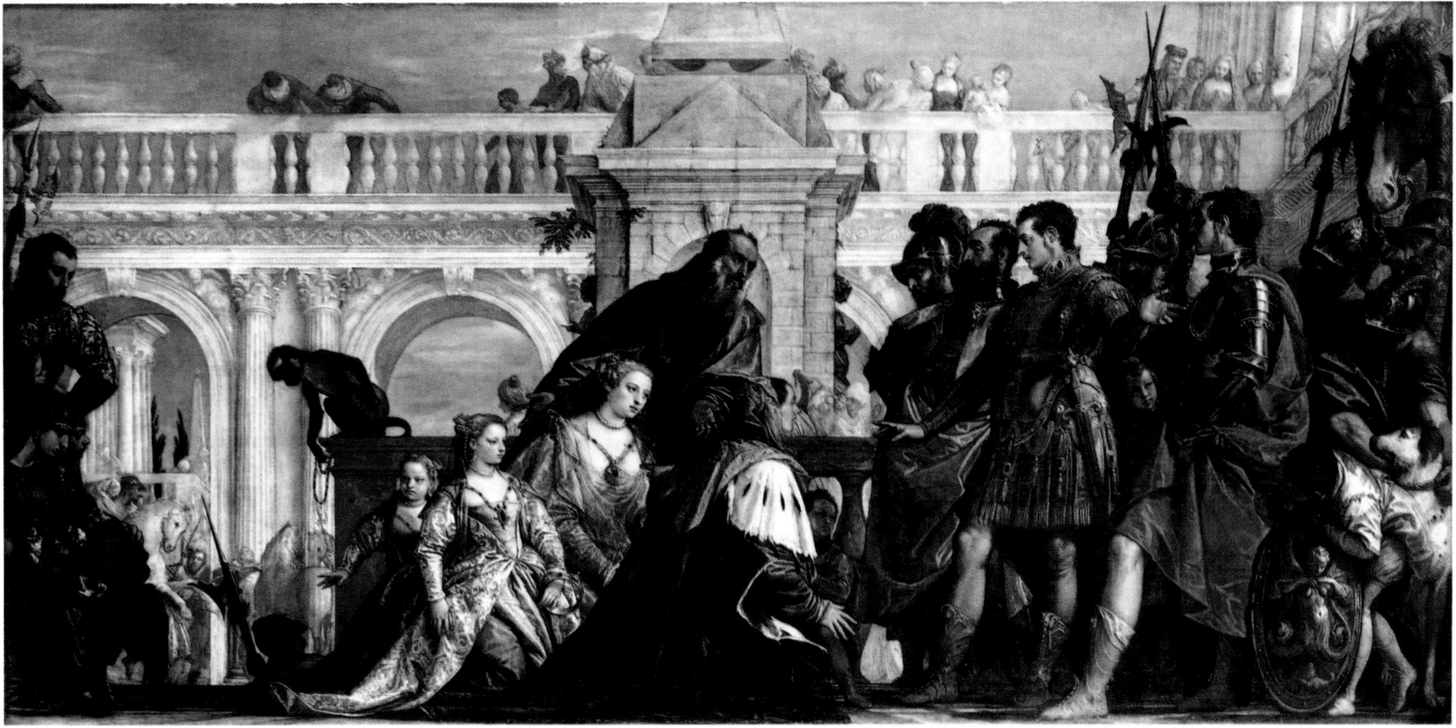

Fig. 41. Paolo Veronese. *The Family of Darius before Alexander.* Oil on canvas. The Trustees of the National Gallery, London

conquered leaders, in this instance, Coriolanus and Cincinnatus (no. 12b, d). In the same series Gaius Mucius Scaevola bravely displays indifference to physical pain by holding his hand in the fire before Porsenna, an Etruscan chieftain (no. 12a). In the Dugnani and Cordellina series and in his later cycles, Tiepolo crowned such heroic acts with glorifying ceiling paintings that apotheosize the virtuous protagonists shown on the walls below. Unlike the early pair of commissions, however, the second type pays honor to loss and self-sacrifice, as exemplified in Tiepolo's decorations for Palazzo Barbaro, Venice (no. 21a–d), for heroines unjustly suffer death in two of its canvases.[9]

Although they fall outside the context of this essay on secular imagery, Tiepolo's many scenes of Christian martyrdom cannot be omitted here because they too laud resolve and heroic self-sacrifice. Such portrayals filled the length of his career and range from the youthful *Martyrdom of Saint Bartholomew* (fig. 16), carried out in 1722 as part of a cycle of twelve paintings of apostles by twelve artists for the church of S. Stae, Venice, to his moving and final canvases of about 1769 showing Christ's death and burial (no. 58a, b), painted in Spain. He produced, however, only four sets of religious works that can be called decorative schemes. These are the frescoes of 1732–33 representing the martyrdoms of Saints Bartholomew and John the Baptist in the Colleoni Chapel, Bergamo; the frescoes of 1737 illustrating the deaths of Saints Victor and Satyrus in the S. Vittore chapel in S. Ambrogio, Milan; the

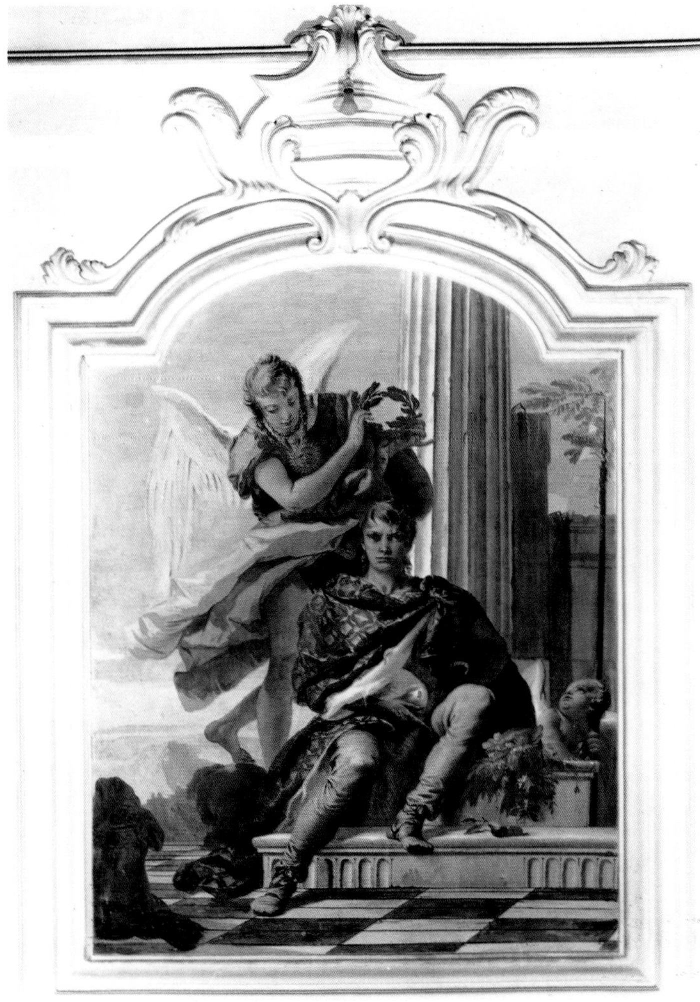

Fig. 42. *Virtue Crowned by Honor.* Fresco. Villa Loschi, Biron

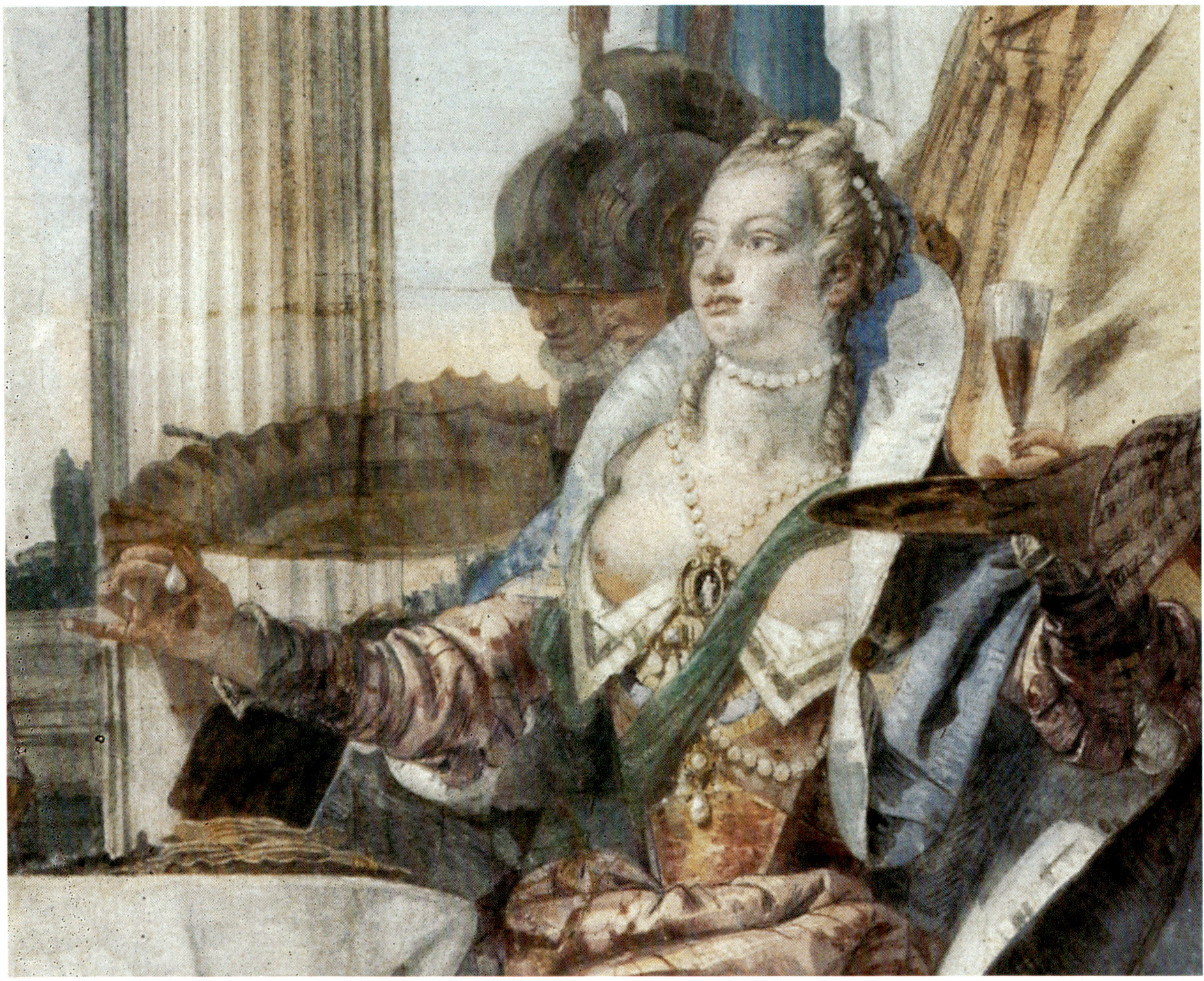

Fig. 43. Detail, *The Banquet of Cleopatra*. Fresco. Palazzo Labia, Venice

magnificent triptych of about 1738–40 on the Passion of Christ in S. Alvise, Venice (no. 31, figs. 69, 70); and a group of canvases done in collaboration with his son Giandomenico and depicting Christ's Passion and Resurrection (see no. 33, figs. 71, 72).[10]

Through noble virtue and honor, and steely resolve and daring action, Tiepolo's heroes and heroines exemplify moral values, offering us a glimpse into a superior world. Such, alas, is rarely the case with his lovers, who enchant us in a way that their more reputable counterparts do not. These couples, painted during the 1740s and 1750s, while the mature and still very active artist was enjoying his large family, prosperity, and exalted reputation, constitute some of the most ravishing images of deeply felt love and sensual desire his century produced. The most romantically charged are those showing amorous exploits in the so-called Tasso Room, painted for a Venetian palace in the early 1740s (no. 17a–d); in Palazzo Labia, Venice, in the mid-1740s (fig. 43); and in Villa Valmarana, Vicenza, in 1757 (figs. 44, 45).[11]

The Tasso paintings of Rinaldo and Armida are the most magical of the three cycles, Tiepolo responding in them to the sorcery in the epic narrative *Gerusalemme liberata* of the Renaissance poet Torquato Tasso. The luminous atmosphere and the space, nearly without reference to architecture, display an enchanting range of colors. Set within pale, mossy green landscapes and against a cerulean blue sky are the rich ochers and yellow cadmiums that lend color to Armida's fruity-hued draperies—apricots, melons, and peaches that appear nowhere else in his oil paintings—and the Prussian blues and red cadmiums that bejewel Rinaldo's robes. Here Tiepolo captivates viewers with a chromatic wizardry that visually approximates the glamorous witchcraft of Armida's own spell over Rinaldo. Enjoying the eleven paintings within their original site must

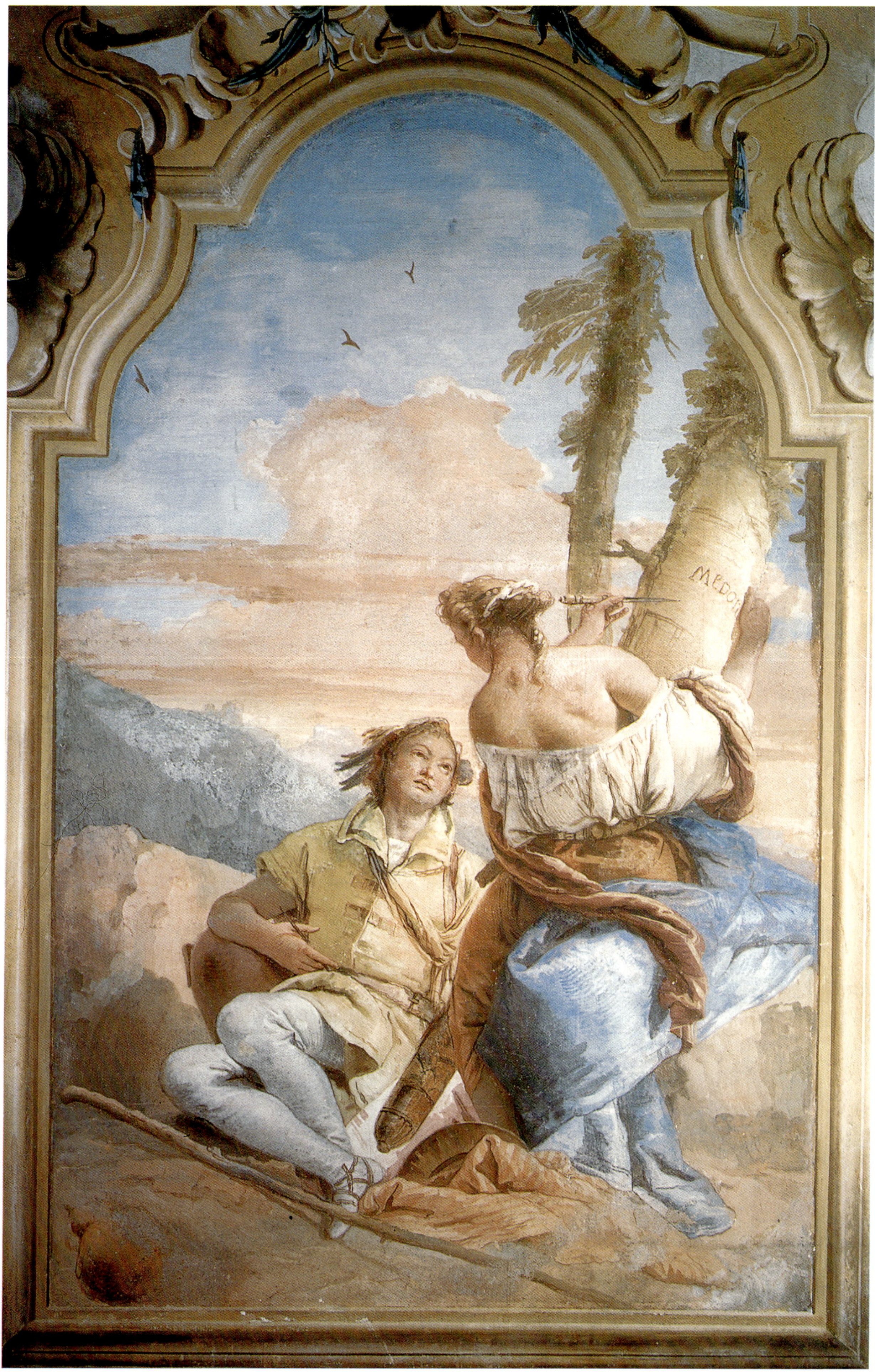

Fig. 44. *Angelica Carving Medoro's Name*. Fresco. Villa Valmarana, Vicenza

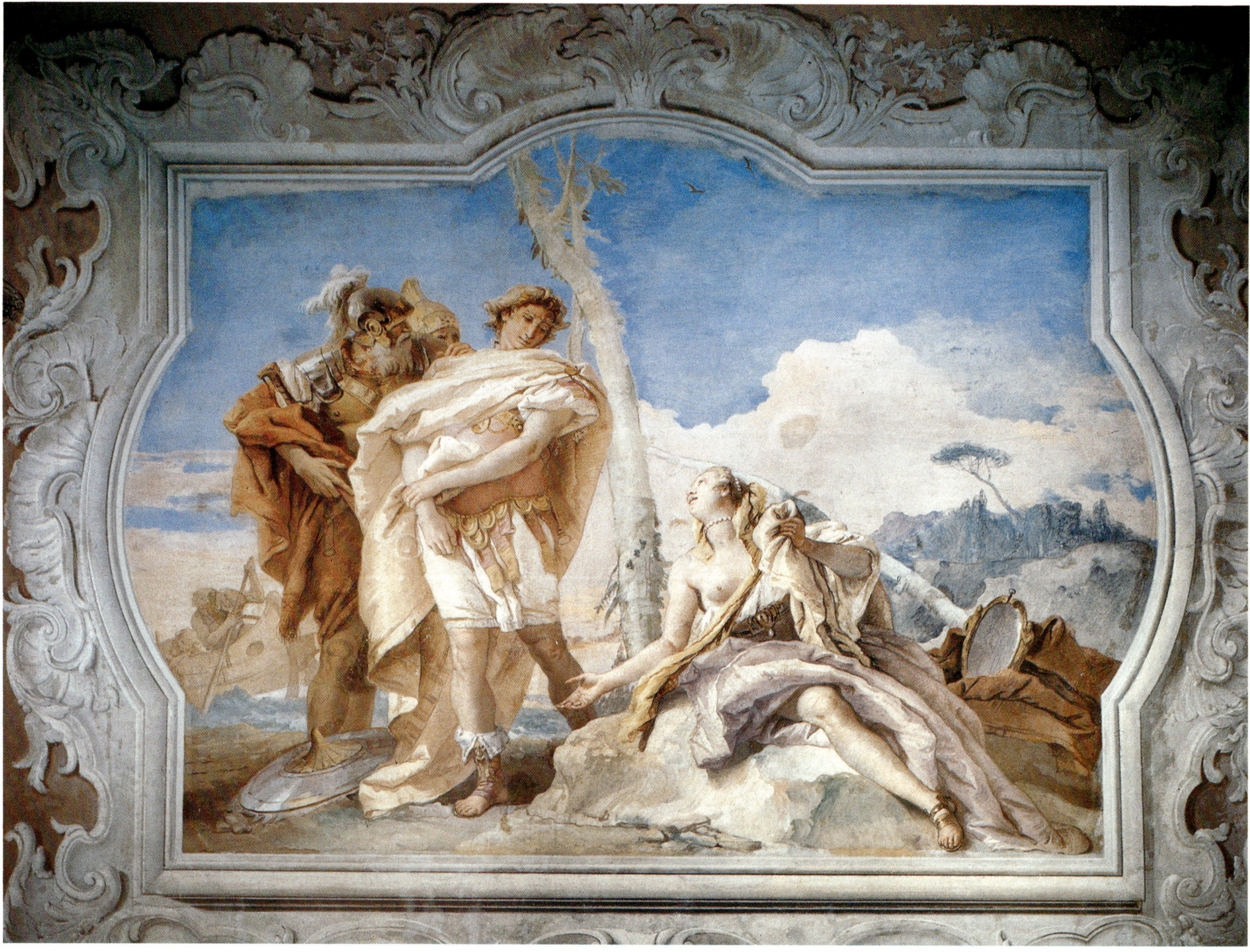

Fig. 45. *Rinaldo Abandoning Armida*. Fresco. Villa Valmarana, Vicenza

have been as intoxicating an experience as reading Tasso's amorous fairy tale.

Only a short time after he completed the Rinaldo and Armida cycle, Tiepolo painted a different pair of lovers for another Venetian palace, the Palazzo Labia, replacing the sorcery of Tasso's *Gerusalemme liberata* with the spectacle of Antony and Cleopatra in frescoed scenes suggested by the *Natural History* of Pliny the Elder and by other ancient histories (see entry for no. 19). Assisting him in the task was Girolamo Mengozzi Colonna, an Emilian architectural painter with whom he had collaborated on earlier commissions. In the Labia *salone* Mengozzi Colonna produced an entirely fictive architectural framework, creating extravagantly illusionary spaces that appear to be in front of and beyond the walls. Within this scenographic stage two events take place before our eyes: in one the lovers advance toward four steps as though to descend into our space; in the other a dwarf leads our ascent up steps as though we are participants in the banquet in his space (fig. 46). Wagering that she could entertain Antony with the most costly feast in history, Cleopatra is about to execute her coup de théâtre by dissolving a precious pearl in a glass of vinegar. Tiepolo's scenic tension is masterly. Two helmeted soldiers, a turbaned Asian, and an African servant stand for the queen's military, scholarly, and faithful court. A brilliant sun brightens Cleopatra's rose-colored gown and warms her voluptuously exposed breasts; in one hand, set before a brightly lit column, she ostentatiously dangles the pearl, while with the other she takes the goblet of vinegar from a tray proffered by the servant. Antony and the guests look on raptly. Like the pearl, the climactic moment is held in calculated suspense. But is it all a lighthearted joke, merely a good story? For the tiny pup and misshapen dwarf on the steps inject a note of wry humor and folly into the tense drama coupling this most beautiful of heroines with her hero. Yet Tiepolo himself, inserted at the far left, dressed in a blue robe that echoes the color of Cleopatra's cloak, watches with complete seriousness

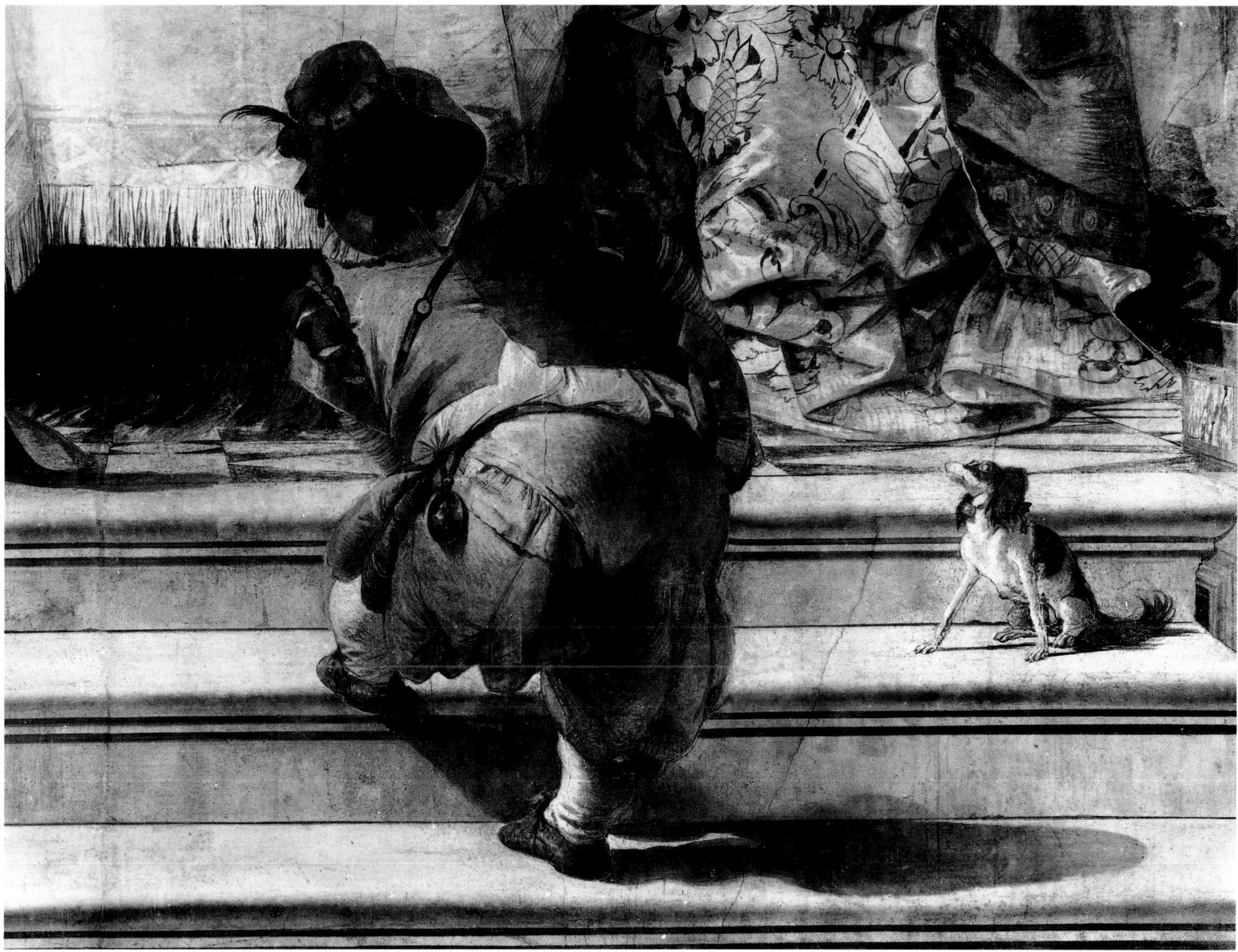

Fig. 46. Detail, *The Banquet of Cleopatra*. Fresco. Palazzo Labia, Venice

the scene he has conjured up. For a brief moment we are asked to believe that the powerful Roman general will dissolve in the arms of the queen of Egypt after the pearl liquifies.

When Tiepolo frescoed the five principal rooms on the ground floor of Giustino Valmarana's Vicentine villa some dozen years after he decorated the Palazzo Labia, he chose to interpret stories from Greek, Latin, and Italian epic poetry. The painter captured the contrasting states of reciprocal love and spurned love in *Angelica Carving Medoro's Name* (fig. 44) from Ludovico Ariosto's *Orlando furioso* and *Rinaldo Abandoning Armida* (fig. 45) from Tasso's *Gerusalemme liberata*, showing "passionate ardour" suffusing Medoro's face and Armida's "despairing expostulation" in scenes that sit diagonally across from each other on opposite corners of the villa.[12] And Tiepolo represented an impressive array of loving relationships throughout the rooms: Agamemnon's feeling for his daughter Iphigenia in the *Sacrifice of Iphigenia* in the villa's vestibule (fig. 98); Thetis's for her son Achilles in the Room of the Iliad; Dido and Aeneas's politically resonant dalliance in the Room of the Aeneid; and the mutual infatuation of Rinaldo and Armida in the Room of the *Gerusalemme liberata*.[13] Why Valmarana proposed such subjects can only be surmised; that the more than sixty-year-old Tiepolo brilliantly caught the devotion, sadness, and rapture of love, however, is as apparent to his audience today as it must have been to his patron when he first saw them.

The literary sources for Tiepolo's secular subject matter range across the standard ancient and modern works that Italian artists of the seventeenth and eighteenth centuries usually read or consulted. The Hebrew Bible was one of the richest volumes available to painters, and Tiepolo used it frequently, especially in his early career, not just for prefigurations of Christian revelation but also because Hebraic Scriptures offered stories whose political connotations closely paralleled the contemporary Venetian experience.[14] Greek and Latin literature, above all, contained narratives concerning heroic individuals, and the epics of Homer, Virgil, and Ovid, Philostratus's *Imagines*, and the histories of Livy, Pliny the Elder, and Plutarch sustained Tiepolo's creativity throughout his lifetime. Dense, many layered, and hallowed as these sources were, however, they were not the only wellsprings of inspiration from which he drew. Italy's two epic poems of chivalry composed by Ariosto and Tasso in the sixteenth century fired the painter's imagination as he conceived canvases and frescoes. Vincenzo Cartari's *Immagine degli Dei degli antichi,* Ripa's *Iconologia,* and, to a lesser extent, Andrea Alciati's *Emblematum liber* are emblem manuals whose many sixteenth- and seventeenth-century editions served Tiepolo time and again, from the beginning of his career to its end. Finally, the new genre of guidebooks and vade mecums was fundamental to his formulation of the Four Continents in the Residenz in Würzburg, just as contemporary political tracts influenced his *Wealth and Benefits of the Spanish Monarchy* in the royal palace in Madrid (no. 53).[15]

Of course, Tiepolo needed more than the written word to prepare a painting. And however facile it may be to reduce to a few sentences the complex issue of his pictorial sources, particularly without identifying precise points of correspondence, it is vital to mention at least the artists to whom Tiepolo most often turned. Beyond Paolo Veronese, the entire Venetian artistic tradition nourished him.[16] Other Italian schools counted for little, and Raphael alone emerges from them as a figure to whom he sometimes looked for figural motifs. Among foreign painters of the previous century, Nicolas Poussin and Peter Paul Rubens contributed to his repertory of ideas. One of Tiepolo's favorite sources was antique sculpture, his familiarity with Roman statuary originating in his youth and his subsequent adaptation of it extending through his frescoes in Würzburg and Spain.

Tiepolo knew a large number of the literary and pictorial sources that informed his painting from his own reading and looking. But others surely were brought to his attention by the many different men who employed him and with whom he worked. Such patrons as Sandi, the two Dolfin brothers, Nicolò Loschi, and Giustino Valmarana had solid grounding in the classics and must have provided essential suggestions and counsel. There were also *illuministi*, men of the Enlightenment, with whom Tiepolo occasionally formed what might be called working partnerships: Scipione Maffei, a Veronese antiquarian whose *Verona illustrata* of 1731–32 contains prints after the artist's drawings of Roman busts; Giovanni Poleni, a professor of science at the university in Padua for whose five-volume compendium of antiquities of 1737 Tiepolo helped prepare the frontispieces; and most notably Francesco Algarotti, a classically trained Venetian who traveled widely and who not only commissioned paintings from Tiepolo for Augustus III of Saxony and his minister Count Heinrich von Brühl in the 1740s but also befriended the painter and himself bought a few of his works (see entry for no. 19).

Tiepolo enjoyed a sure knowledge of the grand literary and pictorial traditions, and his colorful allegories, mythologies, and histories are suffused with the wisdom and grace of moral edification and the vivid sentiment of amorous passion. To be sure, his paintings will never be confused with Poussin's elegiac, sometimes ponderous, and certainly more learned images. Lacking subtlety and shorn of rigorous attention to archaeological detail, Tiepolo's secular art is more extravagant than finely spun, melodramatic in tone rather than austerely dramatic. By no means, however, do its visual splendor and epic sweep gainsay its erudition. But because that erudition—which was so profound in his society and so deeply embedded in it—is not shared by our own world, even today's well-educated public may find that Tiepolo's references stand on the other side of a broad cultural canyon. His century encompassed events and saw the emergence of ideas that irrevocably divorce his political and artistic civilization from ours. To wit: Tiepolo was born in a thousand-year-old republic that died shortly after he did, and the Rome that witnessed the successful papacy of Clement XI at the opening of the settecento saw Pius VI flee the city when foreign troops invaded in 1798. Slightly farther afield from Venice, the old Louis XIV still reigned securely in France in 1700, but the monarchy was overturned four generations later. Little more than a hundred years after Emperor Leopold I struggled in the 1690s to retake parts of the Hapsburg realm lost to the Turks, Metternich unilaterally imposed his will on Central Europe. William III of the House of Stuart sat on the English throne in 1700, but a century later William Pitt led Parliament as the Hanoverian George III suffered periodic bouts of insanity. And, finally, far across the Atlantic Ocean, the United States for the first time inaugurated a president in the new city of Washington in 1801, a hundred years after American settlements had first received charters as British colonies. Precisely because Tiepolo's breathtakingly beautiful paintings of classical and poetic subject matter speak a language of a lost culture but originate in a time so close to ours, they offer the modern world a unique gateway to the past.

Notes

1. For the Sandi cycle, which includes a ceiling fresco by Tiepolo and oils by Nicolò Bambini, see Aikema 1986; Gemin and Pedrocco 1993, p. 246; Knox 1993; and a forthcoming essay by Barcham.
2. For the Dolfin paintings, see Zeri and Gardner 1973, pp. 60–63, and Gemin and Pedrocco 1993, pp. 258–62.
3. Knox 1992, pp. 16–25.

4. See Gemin and Pedrocco 1993, pp. 270–71 (for Palazzo Dugnani), 348–51 (for Villa Cordellina).
5. Count Carl Gustaf Tessin wrote to the Swedish court in 1736 that Tiepolo "est sectataire de Paul Véronèse" (Sirèn 1902, p. 108, quoted in Sohm 1990, p. 90).
6. See Menegozzo 1990, pp. 7–40; Barcham 1992, p. 17; Gemin and Pedrocco 1993, pp. 298–301.
7. For Würzburg, see Levey 1986, pp. 167–212; and Gemin and Pedrocco 1993, pp. 422–27; and Alpers and Baxandall 1994, chap. 3; all with earlier bibliography.
8. Knox 1979 no. 8, and Gemin and Pedrocco 1993, pp. 236–37.
9. Aikema 1987a; Gemin and Pedrocco 1993, pp. 408–9; De Grazia and Garberson 1996.
10. On these, see entry for no. 33 by Catherine Whistler.
11. For the Tasso Room, see Knox 1978 and Gemin and Pedrocco 1993, pp. 356–60; for the Labia commission, see Levey 1986, pp. 143–66, and Gemin and Pedrocco 1993, pp. 394–97; for the Villa Valmarana, see Levey 1957 and Gemin and Pedrocco 1993, pp. 438–47.
12. Quoted from Levey 1986, pp. 236, 238.
13. Another love Tiepolo celebrated during his artistic maturity is Apollo's for Hyacinth, which he depicted in the *Death of Hyacinth* (no. 23).
14. Barcham 1989, pp. 14–99.
15. See Ashton 1978 (for Würzburg) and Jones 1981 (for Madrid).
16. See especially Barcham 1989, pp. 27–55.

13. The Triumph of Zephyr and Flora

13. The Triumph of Zephyr and Flora
Ca. 1731–32
395 × 225 cm (155¼ × 88⅝ in.)
Museo del Settecento Veneziano, Ca' Rezzonico, Venice (2248)

Painted about 1731–32 as a ceiling for a room on the *piano nobile* in Ca' Pesaro in Venice, *Zephyr and Flora* provides a valuable glimpse of the kind of large decorative masterpieces Tiepolo executed in churches, palaces, and country villas and demonstrates his extraordinary ability to project flying and hovering figures onto ceilings and vaults and high upon walls. This talent was first apparent in the *Assumption of the Virgin* (fig. 14) and the *Myth of Phaethon* (fig. 15), two frescoes painted on the mainland between about 1718 and 1720. In Venice in the 1720s, he frescoed the impressive *Apotheosis of Saint Teresa* on the vault of the Saint Teresa chapel in the church of the Scalzi (fig. 17) and the spectacular *Triumph of Eloquence* on the ceiling of the *salone* in Palazzo Sandi (fig. 22). His most accomplished ceiling frescoes of the decade, however, are in the Arcivescovado (Patriarchal Palace) in Udine (fig. 26).[1] Time and again in these early works, the young artist gave proof that his draftsmanship was virtually infallible—despite the dizzying foreshortening he had to effect to launch his figures in complicated positions in space. The connoisseur Anton Maria Zanetti the Elder, one of Tiepolo's first critics, noted that the artist painted "a quantity of figures, implementing them with a multiplicity and [an] excellent disposition of innovative ideas."[2] Zanetti's comment, made about 1732, is exactly contemporary with the Pesaro ceiling. The style of the painting and the typology of the figures both argue for a dating in the first years of the century's fourth decade, as do events in the Pesaro family. On 8 December 1731 a nuptial contract was drawn up between Caterina Sagredo and Antonio Pesaro, who were to be married in 1732.[3] Tiepolo probably painted his ceiling to commemorate that marriage, which linked two old patrician families, each boasting a recent doge.

The epithalamic nature of the *Triumph of Zephyr and Flora* is shared by other commissions that fell to Tiepolo during his long career. His numerous ceiling paintings celebrating a patron's marriage include the frescoed *Course of the Sun* of 1740 in Palazzo Clerici in Milan and *Wedding Allegory* of the Rezzonico and Savorgnan families of 1757 in Ca' Rezzonico in Venice (no. 25a).[4] *Zephyr and Flora* precedes these two in date, but it was by no means Tiepolo's first effort in the genre. It followed by just a year or two his grandest epithalamic commission, the five ceilings frescoed in Palazzo Archinto in Milan in 1730–31 and unfortunately destroyed by bombs during World War II.[5] The Pesaro canvas is, of course, much smaller in scope than the Archinto project was. It is nonetheless more pointed in intent, for the union of Zephyr and Flora—he one of the Four Winds in pagan mythology, and she the goddess of flowers—refers specifically to earthly renewal, springtime, and fecundity.[6] The marriage of Caterina Sagredo and Antonio Pesaro was clearly meant to produce heirs. But luck quickly ran out: poor Antonio died shortly after the marriage, leaving Caterina a childless widow.[7]

Notwithstanding the painting's ineffectiveness as a talisman, the Pesaro mandate to Tiepolo confirmed his ongoing success among Venetian patricians, for this new commission followed others he had fulfilled for the Cornaro, Dolfin, and Zenobio families. *Zephyr* joined as well the handful of notable works of art financed by Pesaro money: Giovanni Bellini's splendid triptych the *Virgin and Child with Saints* of 1488, Titian's renowned altarpiece the *Madonna and Child with Saints and Members of the Pesaro Family* of 1519–26, and Baldassare Longhena's massive tomb for Doge Giovanni Pesaro (d. 1659). All decorate the interior of the church of the Frari and proclaim the clan's social standing and cultural visibility from the Renaissance through the Baroque period. But the boldest statement of Pesaro power and wealth is the enormous family palace on the Grand Canal that was designed by Longhena just before 1630. It was for this building, whose imposing mass and bizarre decorative sculpture still overwhelm the boaters who pass it, that Tiepolo painted his *Triumph of Zephyr and Flora*. Despite the painting's anticipation of a flowering future and the hope it embodies for dynastic longevity, the family that commissioned the image beheld the death not just of Antonio Pesaro but also of its very class. In 1797 one Francesco Pesaro had the distasteful task of negotiating with Napoleon the peace that led to the French occupation of Venice, the end of the city's political independence, and the dissolution of the patriciate. The same branch of the Pesaro whose expectations for the future engendered Tiepolo's marriage allegory stood, paradoxically, as godparents to the demise of the Republic of Venice.

Many eighteenth-century painters in addition to Tiepolo depicted Zephyr and Flora, for the subject was

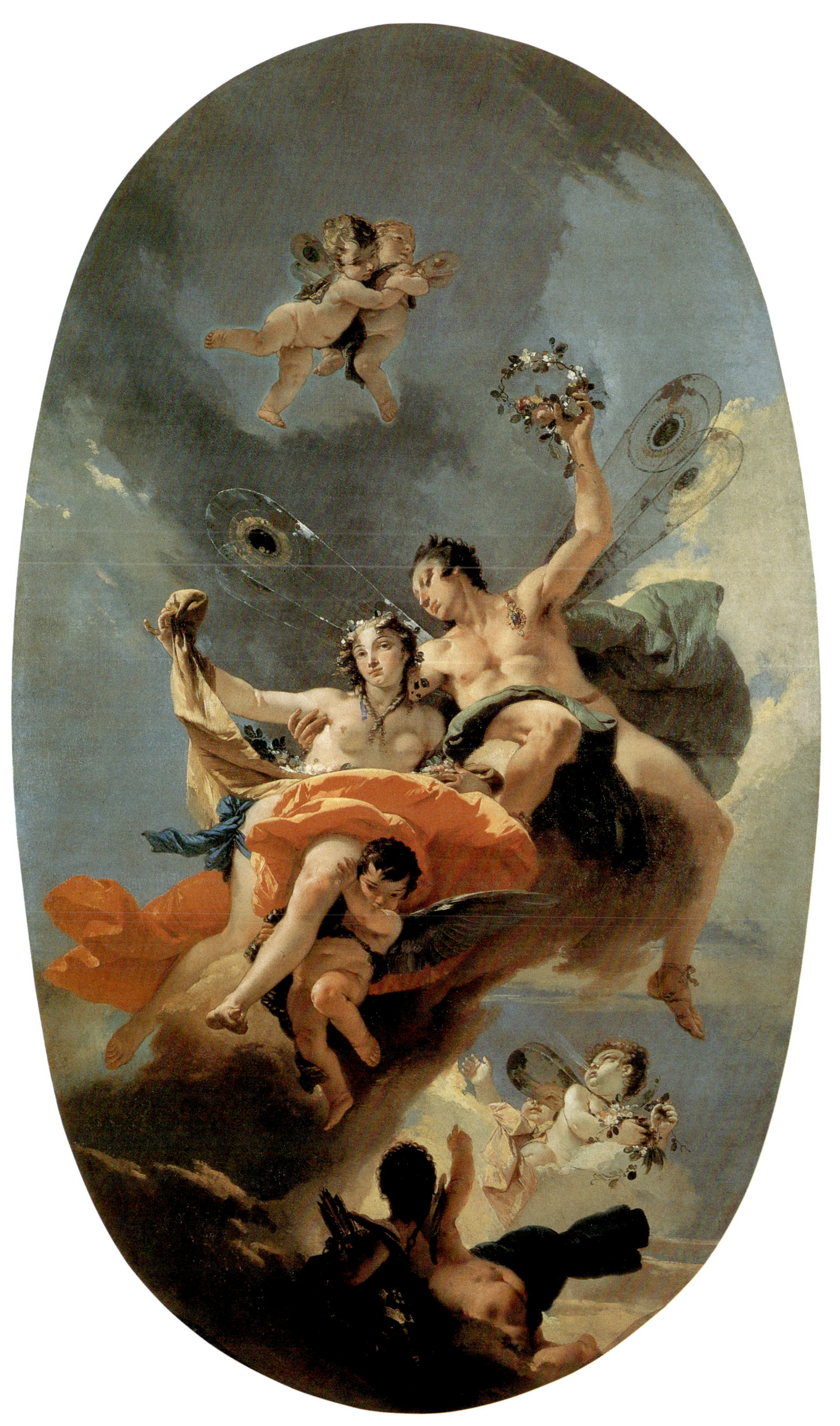

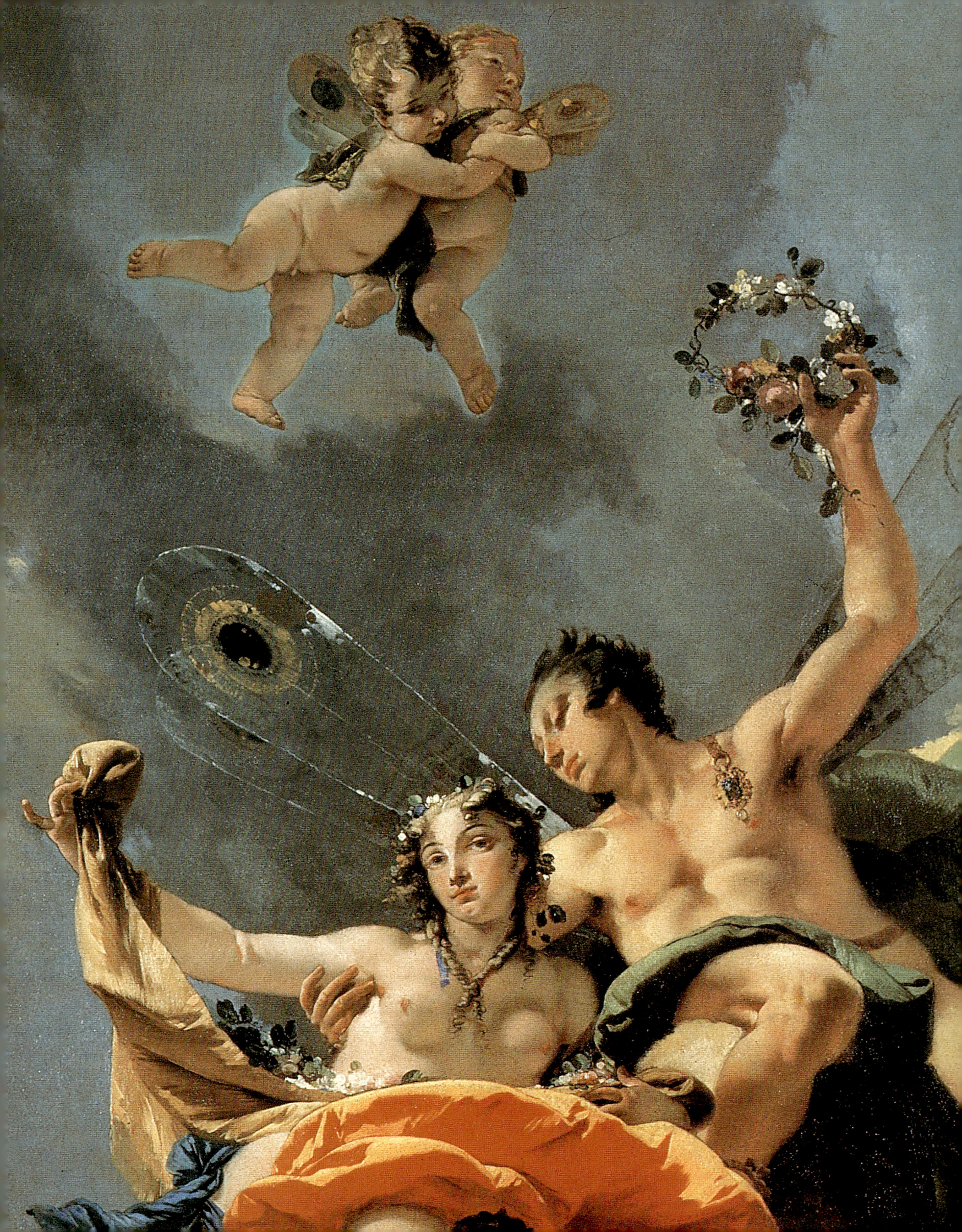

especially popular in French and Italian art of the period.[8] Antoine Watteau, for example, painted a version about 1715 (formerly private collection, England) as part of a cycle of four canvases representing the seasons, and Jacopo Amigoni depicted the theme (The Metropolitan Museum of Art, New York) at approximately the same time Tiepolo did.[9] Although their paintings are in other respects most unlike, both Watteau and Amigoni interpreted the couple in terms of human love; in each picture the two deities are entirely absorbed in each other. Tiepolo imagined a very different encounter, one in which the magnificent mythological creatures—Zephyr's muscular chest contrasting with the goddess's perfectly spherical breasts—proudly display themselves to the world. Theirs is not a union of tender affection but a symbolic triumph of regenerative nature. To exalt this theme, Tiepolo devised a figural grouping that is propelled centripetally across outstretched limbs and wings to unfurling draperies and dense cloud formations. The tilt of the winged putti hints at impending movement, as does the rhomboidal arrangement of the two protagonists. Tiepolo's delight in painting the superb pair must have been matched by his pleasure in depicting many of the details: the brilliant red-orange drapery anchoring the goddess in space; the jeweled pendant on Zephyr's shoulder and the two long curls crisscrossing between Flora's breasts; his massive and her delicate fingers; and the tiny spring buds. But most impressive of all, indeed magical in their painterly reality, are the transparent gossamer wings attached to Zephyr's powerful back. Modeled on the wings of a dragonfly, they sparkle vivaciously and, as a flickering iridescence on their upper left manages to catch our glance momentarily, flutter tremulously in space.

WLB

NOTES

1. For these early frescoes, see Gemin and Pedrocco 1993, nos. 15, 25, 46, 65, 81–83.
2. Zanetti 1733, p. 62.
3. I am grateful to Giandomenico Romanelli for confirming this information for me from documents in the library of the Museo Correr, Venice. Antonio and his father, Lunardo (Leonardo), were from the family branch whose residence was Ca' Pesaro at S. Stae. Caterina was the daughter of one of contemporary Venice's most famous art collectors, Gerardo Sagredo. The Pesaro and Sagredo palaces are near each other but on opposite sides of the Grand Canal.
4. Gemin and Pedrocco 1993, nos. 237, 459, and Sohm 1983.
5. Gemin and Pedrocco 1993, nos. 101–6, and Sohm 1984.
6. Ovid recounts the story in his *Fasti* (5. 200–206).
7. Her second marriage, to Gregorio Barbarigo, took place in June 1739 and produced two daughters. Caterina and her daughters, her sister and her sister's son, and their mother all sat for a portrait by Pietro Longhi about 1750 (Fondazione Scientifica Querini Stampalia, Venice). For the painting, see Venice 1993, no. 78.
8. Pigler 1974, vol. 2, pp. 272–73. Tiepolo himself painted another *Zephyr and Flora*, on the ceiling of the Sala degli Specchi in Palazzo Labia, Venice (Gemin and Pedrocco 1993, no. 377).
9. For Watteau's painting, see Washington, D.C., 1984, p. 326, fig. 5, and Posner 1984, p. 97, pl. 15. For Amigoni's, see Venice 1995a, no. 138.

PROVENANCE:
Ca' Pesaro, Venice (until 1936); Ca' Rezzonico, Venice

REFERENCES:
Fiocco 1925, p. 24; Lorenzetti 1936, p. 50; Venice 1951, pp. 50–51; Pignatti 1960, p. 330; Morassi 1962, p. 55; Pallucchini 1968, no. 95; Romanelli and Pedrocco 1986, p. 84; Museo del Prado 1990, pp. 202–3; Gemin and Pedrocco 1993, p. 304, no. 179; Venice 1995a, no. 55

Opposite: Detail, no. 13

14. Joseph Receiving Pharaoh's Ring

14. Joseph Receiving Pharaoh's Ring
Ca. mid-1730s
106.1 × 178 cm (41¾ × 70⅛ in.)
Dulwich Picture Gallery, London (158)

Here Tiepolo has depicted the moment described in Genesis 41 when Pharaoh gives his ring to Joseph in token of his new standing in the kingdom of Egypt, granted for interpreting the ruler's dream. It is not known who commissioned this unusual Old Testament scene; Levey has suggested that it may have been purchased in 1790 by John Strange, British Resident in Venice, whose correspondence mentions a "Giuseppe" by Tiepolo.[1] This would account for its presence in England and its inclusion in the great Bourgeois bequest of 1811 to the Dulwich Picture Gallery, London. The attribution was questioned by Richter, who found it "more elaborate than the authentic works of this master" and believed it to be an important work by Giandomenico. Such was the authority of Richter's 1880 catalogue of the Dulwich collection, and of its subsequent editions, that his judgment was not questioned until Morassi correctly reattributed the painting to Giambattista in 1955.[2]

Morassi also convincingly dated the picture to the middle years of the 1730s, on the basis of its similarities to Tiepolo's *Brazen Serpent* (Gallerie dell'Accademia, Venice) painted about 1733–34 for the church of SS. Cosma e Damiano on the Giudecca and his frescoes of 1734 in the Villa Loschi al Biron, near Vicenza. Many of the pictorial effects closely resemble those of the *Brazen Serpent*: sharp, even dissonant color harmonies; figures cropped and pressed forward toward the picture plane; and a beautifully observed fall of light that contributes to the drama of the narrative. In addition, as Levey notes, the standard-bearer's helmet, with its distinctive dragon crest, is identical to the helmet worn by Valor in one of the frescoes of the Villa Loschi.

A drawing included in the large group of studies from the Bossi-Beyerlen collection sold in Stuttgart in 1882 can be connected to the Dulwich *Joseph*. In black chalk on blue paper, it is a study of three heads that appear in the painting: the helmeted man, the small boy at the far right, and one of the trumpeters (which Levey has suggested is a self-portrait of the artist). Knox, who attributes the drawing to Giambattista, considers the sheet to relate stylistically to others of about 1744 and dates the painting to the same moment. However, given the arrangement of the heads on the page, which is not comparable to their order in the painting, and the rather generic quality of the trumpeter's facial features, it is questionable whether the sheet functioned as a preparatory study. It may instead be a record of details of the painting, perhaps made by Giandomenico.

Joseph Receiving Pharaoh's Ring may have been inspired by an engraving of an Old Testament subject from the Rembrandt school, a source that is suggested especially by the richness of Pharaoh's costume and the horizontal format that emphasizes the relationship between the protagonists. This format, in which sacred drama is enacted by half-length figures, is more typical of seventeenth-century Bolognese paintings (Guercino's *Christ and the Adulteress*, in the Dulwich Picture Gallery, London, is an example) than of Venetian pictures and is exceptional in Tiepolo's work. It may be that Tiepolo produced the *Joseph* for a collector—such as Strange—who would have displayed it alongside similar works. He enlivened the scene by painting it with brilliant colors and setting it among massive columns, announcing Joseph's rise to power with the sharp noise of the trumpeters.

AB

PROVENANCE:
Sir Peter Francis Bourgeois, London (by 1811)

REFERENCES:
Richter and Sparkes 1880, no. 158; Morassi 1955b, p. 11; Morassi 1962, p. 17; Pallucchini 1968, p. 101, no. 107; Knox 1980a, vol. 1, p. 238, no. M222; Murray 1980, p. 129; Levey in Washington, D.C., 1985, pp. 108–10, no. 30; Gemin and Pedrocco 1993, p. 312, no. 206

NOTES

1. Haskell 1960, p. 268 n. 55; Levey in Washington, D.C., 1985, p. 110. None of the numerous auction catalogues listing works from Strange's collection refers specifically to this picture; however, a Tiepolo owned by Strange and sold at Christie's on 15 March 1800 and described only as "a subject, historical" could be the *Joseph*.
2. However, see Murray (1980, p. 129), who leaves the attribution open.

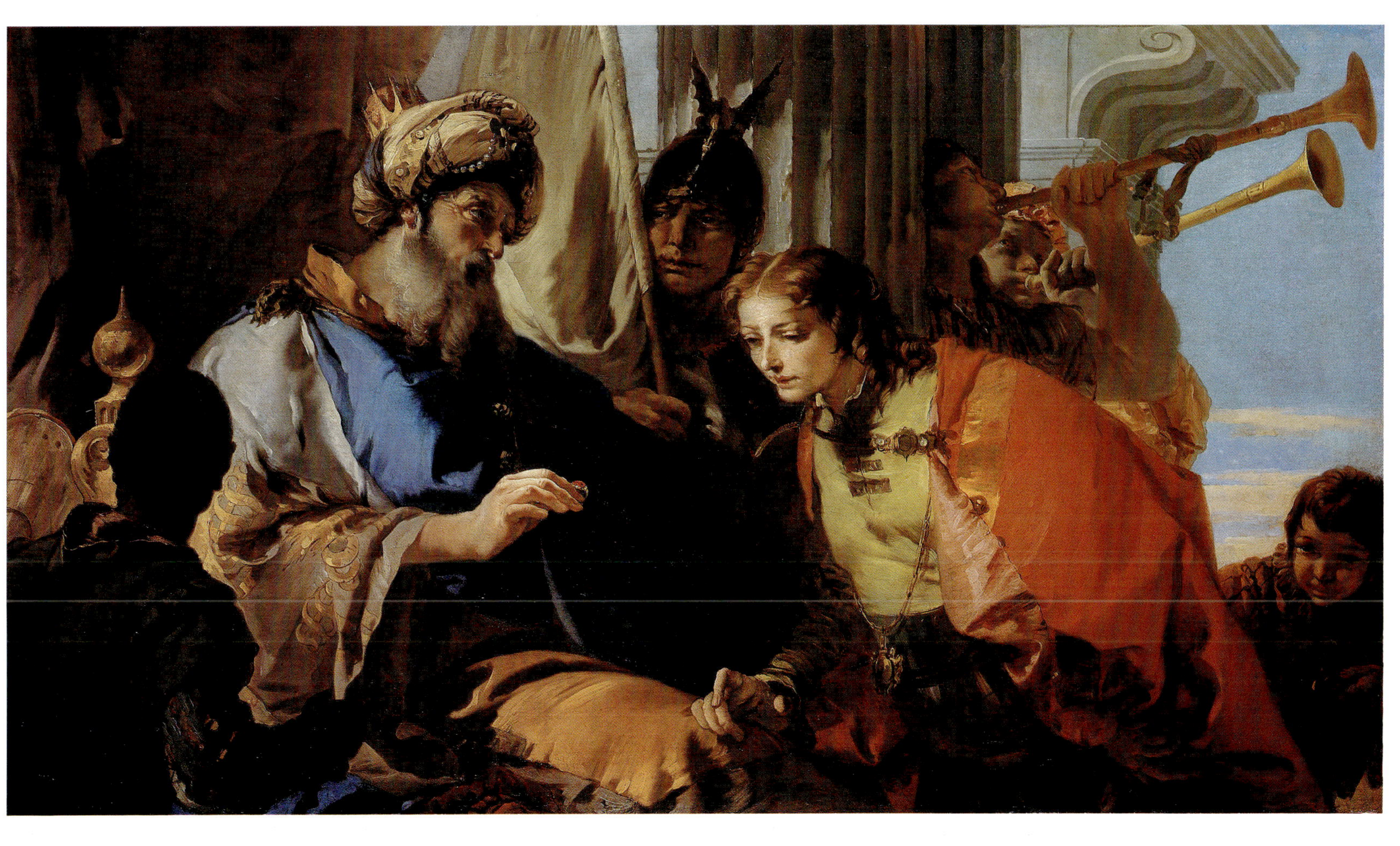

15. Danaë and Jupiter

15. Danaë and Jupiter
1734–36
41 × 53 cm (16⅛ × 20⅞ in.)
The Stockholm University Art Collection

This painting, unique in Tiepolo's career, marked his entry into the contemporary ranks of internationally known artists. In 1736 Count Carl Gustaf Tessin, son of the architect Nicodemus Tessin the Younger, arrived in Venice charged to hire Tiepolo to paint a ceiling in the Swedish royal palace. Because the fee he offered fell below the artist's surprisingly high demands, Tessin was forced to disappoint his patrons in Stockholm, but he satisfied his own taste for Tiepolo's paintings by buying two of his small works: the oil sketch (Nationalmuseum, Stockholm, Staatens Kunstmuseer) for the *Beheading of Saint John the Baptist* frescoed in the Colleoni Chapel, Bergamo, in 1733 and the present canvas, a wry interpretation of Danaë's amorous encounter with Jupiter. The tale derives from ancient mythology, but Tiepolo probably knew it from Boccaccio's *De genealogia deorum gentilium*, begun about 1350. According to the story, Acrisius, a minor Egyptian king, was told by an oracle that his grandson would eventually kill him and so imprisoned Danaë, his only child, in a tower. Heavy locked doors secured the building, and savage dogs guarded it. Not one to be shut out by mortals when impelled by lust, Jupiter mystically entered the tower as a shower of gold. He impregnated Danaë, and from their union issued Perseus. Years later the young Perseus fulfilled the oracle's terrible prophecy by accidentally killing his grandfather with a discus he threw in a contest.

Tessin's purchase of *Danaë and Jupiter* in 1736 establishes its latest possible date of completion. At the time of its acquisition the canvas must have rather recently come from Tiepolo's easel, for its bright tonality punctuated with areas of localized shadow situates it close in time to other pictures that, like it, were executed in oil paint.[1] Among these related works are the *Immaculate Conception* of 1733–34 (Museo Civico, Vicenza) and the *Virgin in Glory with Apostles and Saints* of 1734 (parish church, Rovetta, Bergamo), Tiepolo's first ambitious altar painting and a brightly sunlit scene that represents a decisive turn away from the generally murky hues of his earlier altarpieces. Thus, Tiepolo had been a working artist for about twenty years when he finished *Danaë and Jupiter*, but never before had he been such a master of his talents. The radiance and rich color of *Danaë*, its shrewd use of ideas from sixteenth-century Venetian painting, and its humorous fusion of the divine and mortal on a tiny stage make plain that the forty-year-old Tiepolo was on the cusp of a new phase in his career when he produced it. Indeed, after he finished this small painting, he began *Saint Clement Adoring the Trinity*, whose pictorial effect results from a perfect unification of the visionary and the tangible worlds.[2] And in 1738 he completed an altarpiece, later destroyed by fire, whose surviving *modello* reveals a masterly organization of figures in a small space, as well as a sophisticated use of architectural formulas familiar from the Venetian pictorial tradition.[3]

A good part of the painterly attraction of *Danaë and Jupiter* rests on Tiepolo's pictorial contrasts, drawn, for example, between the warm reds and golds of the draperies and the silvery and pearl-like brightness of the background loggia and Danaë's flesh. Tiepolo likewise juxtaposed the princess's pudgy, voluptuous body with her servingwoman's tautly stretched skin, and he set the earthbound, boyish page on the left across from the airborne, flaccid king of the gods. Although the drama is enacted in a minimum of foreground space, the platform, columns, and arcade hint at a vast palace courtyard. Jupiter's whirling haze wafts amid richly described and tangibly felt goods: an ornately decorated bed covered with disheveled linens and draperies, a lavishly sculpted marble urn, objects of gleaming gold, and coins cascading through the air. Age plays against youth, ugliness against beauty, architectural solidity against vapor, and a tiny terrier yelps threateningly but absurdly at a screeching eagle. Such polarities typify Tiepolo's paintings of the mid-1730s. For example, the Rovetta *Virgin in Glory* confirms the ethereal nature of the floating Mary by contrasting her with the sculptural, intensely real saints on earth; *Saint Clement Adoring the Trinity* juxtaposes a splendid young Christ and angels with a tottering old God the Father (played by the same man who acted the role of Jupiter!) and enunciates a vision of the Trinity so physically tangible that architectural reality is belittled by comparison; and the sketch of the *Beheading of Saint John the Baptist* that Tessin bought along with *Danaë*, horrifically pairs the elegantly gowned Salome with the bleeding trophy of John's head.

The charm of the small *Danaë and Jupiter* lies, too, in its clever use of Paolo Veronese's scenic devices to

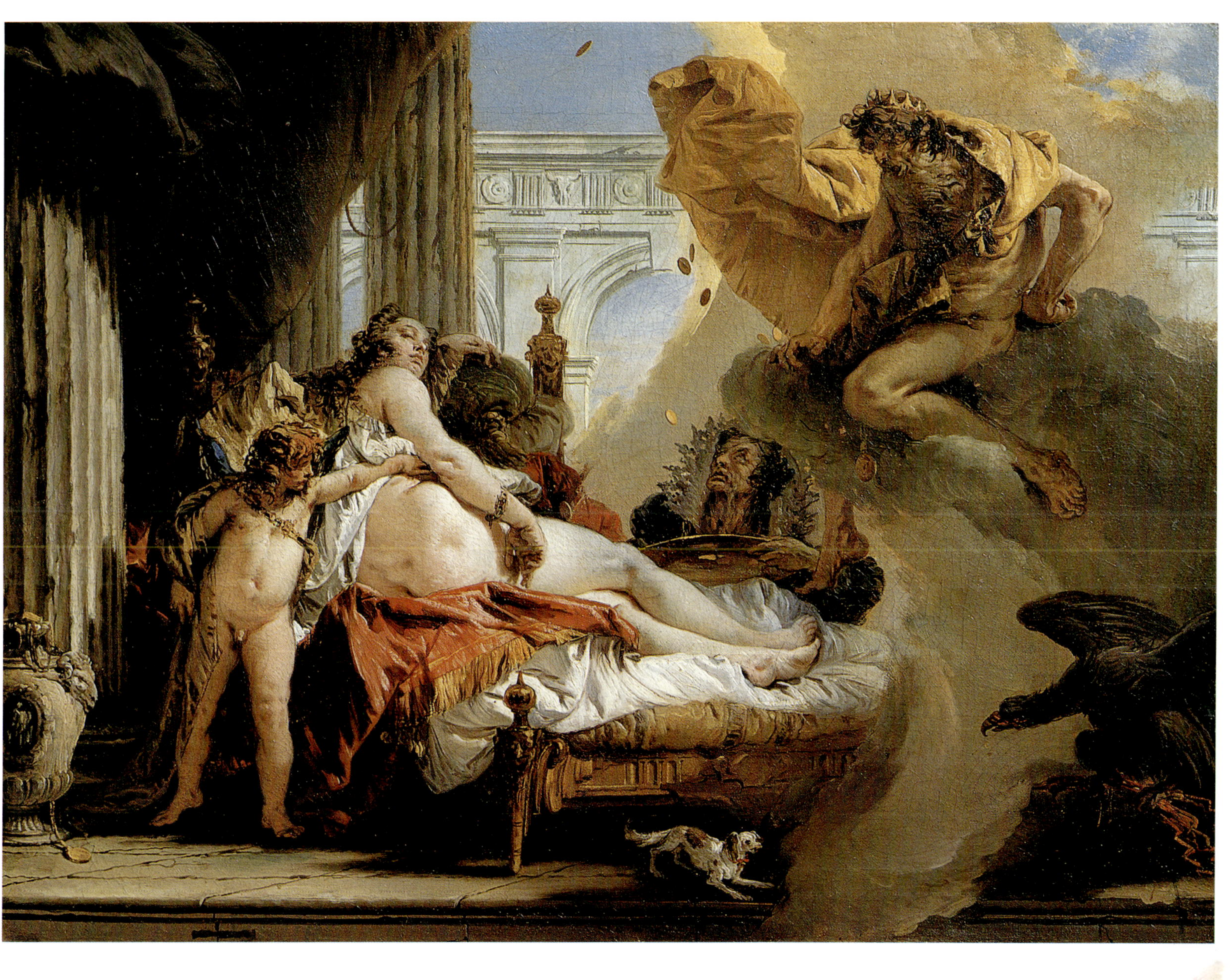

PROVENANCE:
Count Carl Gustaf Tessin, Stockholm (1736–49); Crown Princess Lovisa Ulrika of Sweden (1749–77); Gustav III of Sweden (1777–92); Hertig Fredrich Adof, duke of Ostergötland (1792–1805); Princess Sophia Albertina (1805–29); probably Lolotte Stenboch (1829); Segersten collection; Pier Swartz, Norrköping (1901); Stockholm University (1915)

REFERENCES:
Sirèn 1902, pp. 109–12; Sack 1910, p. 205; Morassi 1955a, pp. 16, 154; Morassi 1962, p. 49; Pallucchini 1968, no. 111; Karling 1978, pp. 233–35; Levey 1986, pp. 70–73; Barcham 1992, pp. 68–69; Gemin and Pedrocco 1993, p. 313, no. 209; London 1994, no. 103

suggest the landscape of classical mythology. The Veronesian details here were among Tiepolo's earliest such references but were far from his last (see entry for no. 16a). Probably inspired not only by the architectural setting of the *Danaë* but also by the rich brocades and elegant finery of the earlier *Execution*, Tessin himself recognized Tiepolo's link to Veronese, calling him a votary, or follower, of the great Paolo.[4] But in fact Tiepolo's dependence on Veronese, at least in the two paintings he sold to Tessin, is more apparent than real. Although the draped columns in *Danaë*, the raised foreground platform, the little dog, and the abbreviated architecture in the distance all recall similar elements in such works by Veronese as *Susanna and the Elders* (private collection, Genoa)—also a story of male lust—nothing in Tiepolo's little painting repeats specific motifs used by Veronese. But in employing a Veronesian style to narrate the myth, Tiepolo associated Venice's golden century of painting, Paolo's age, with the golden age of antiquity. By the end of the first quarter of the eighteenth century, the Renaissance was a fabled past in Venice, and Tiepolo and his contemporaries realized that their republic mattered little on the international stage; they knew it was so weak militarily that it had to resort to political neutrality, and they surely understood that its economy was barely viable. However, the sixteenth century had been Venice's halcyon era; what better place to anchor myth than in that legendary past?

Yet Tiepolo conceived his pagan tale irreverently, honoring neither the serious interpretation of myth and allegory that prevailed during the Renaissance nor the authority that ancient culture traditionally enjoyed. His small canvas tickles the funny bone. Unlike his many larger paintings that treat classical myth and history, the *Danaë* has no intention of teaching a moral lesson. His very setting provokes laughter. No guarded tower or fierce dogs for him; an open loggia fills the stage, and a leaping pup and raucous eagle set it astir. Jupiter's appearance in the princess's cell is not divine manifestation but the breathless presence of a hoary old man clumsily riding a cloud, his legs vulgarly spread wide. Danaë does not receive the king of the gods in the hushed, accepting manner of an innocent and youthful maiden; instead she languorously rolls over, unable to open her eyes and hardly stirring before her awesome guest. One can only wonder what impulse moved Tiepolo to deviate so radically from the time-honored image of a luminous shower of golden light coupling with an eager but subdued young princess explored in earlier interpretations of the subject by Correggio (Galleria Borghese, Rome), Titian (Museo e Gallerie Nazionale di Capodimonte, Naples), and Rembrandt (The Hermitage Museum, Saint Petersburg). Happily married to the woman he loved, Tiepolo may have seen the May-December romance of Danaë and Jupiter, the two united in a business merger of golden coins, as inherently funny.[5]

It is also possible that Tiepolo drew inspiration for both his comic interpretation and his small, stagelike setting from intermezzi, a minor manifestation of contemporary opera practice, although it is hardly imaginable that either Danaë or Jupiter would have sung in the buff. Early in the eighteenth century comic intermezzi began to achieve independence as a literary genre and were published separately from the librettos of the opere serie with which they often shared evenings. By the time Tiepolo painted *Danaë and Jupiter*, these intermezzi were mounted on their own, rather than as entr'actes sandwiched in during performances of tragic opera.[6] Tiepolo's small cast of characters indeed supports a connection with the opere buffe of his day; their casts of soprano soubrette, elderly bass, valet or page, and old nurse or servingwoman were identical in size and kind to his own. Finally, the airy luminosity of *Danaë and Jupiter* and the perception that the loggia in the background is not three-dimensional and that the bed is but a piece of furniture to be pushed on or off the stage encourage one's sense that the story is only make-believe. In painting the myth as a ridiculous stage comedy, almost a farce, Tiepolo burlesques the classical world and implies—as he rarely did elsewhere in his art—that the old gods were both salacious and corrupt.[7]

WLB

NOTES

1. Gemin and Pedrocco 1993, nos. 175, 180, and Barcham 1992, pp. 64–67.
2. Gemin and Pedrocco 1993, no. 224, and Barcham 1992, p. 70. The painting was placed on its altar in 1739.
3. Gemin and Pedrocco 1993, no. 232.
4. See Sirèn 1902, p. 108, quoted in Sohm 1990, p. 90, for Tessin's letter of 16 June 1736 to Carl Hårleman, the architect of the royal palace in Stockholm, in which he remarked: "Il est sectataire de Paul Véronèse."
5. Bortolan (1973) published the story of Giambattista's marriage to Cecilia Guardi in 1719 and of his wish to protect her from the inconvenience of published marriage banns.
6. Bellina and Brizi 1985, pp. 359–69. The example of the type best remembered today is *La serva padrona,* written by Giovanni Battista Pergolesi in Naples during the 1730s.
7. Rembrandt had also satirized mythology in his *Rape of Europa* (J. Paul Getty Museum, Malibu) and *Rape of Ganymede* (Gemäldegalerie, Dresden), and Tiepolo himself made a wry comment on Jupiter's activities in his early *Rape of Europa* (Gallerie dell'Accademia, Venice).

THE FINDING OF MOSES

16a. The Finding of Moses
16b. A Halberdier in a Landscape

***16a. The Finding of Moses**
Ca. 1736–38
202 × 342 cm (79⅝ × 134⅝ in.)
The National Gallery of Scotland, Edinburgh (92)

***16b. A Halberdier in a Landscape**
Ca. 1736–38
205 × 132 cm (80¾ × 52 in.)
Private collection

Among the most singular commissions Tiepolo received in the 1730s was one for a large horizontal canvas treating the Old Testament story of the infant Moses rescued from the bulrushes by Pharaoh's daughter, who had gone to the river with her maids to bathe (Exodus 2.3–10). The picture was conceived à la Veronese, and in 1769—within Tiepolo's lifetime—it actually passed as a work by Veronese's assistant and brother, Benedetto Caliari.[1] Today it is divided between The National Gallery of Scotland, Edinburgh, and a private collection, having been cut into two pieces of unequal size to create a more centralized narrative section (16a) and an attractive if highly unconventional genre-landscape (16b).[2] The intact composition can be reconstructed from a photograph taken when the two pieces were temporarily juxtaposed (fig. 47) and from a smaller and slightly distorted copy (Staatsgalerie Stuttgart) sometimes ascribed to Giandomenico Tiepolo.[3] Thanks to the research of Douglas Lewis, it is now possible to identify the patron of the picture as Andrea Antonio Giuseppe Corner (1672–1742), a member of the great patrician Cornaro family.[4] In 1717 Andrea was elected to the high office of *procuratore di San Marco di supra*. He seems to have been a person of intellectual as well as political standing and had his Palladian villa at Piombino decorated with a cycle of frescoes relating to Freemasonic imagery.[5] The *Finding of Moses* was painted for his Venetian palace, the neo-Palladian Palazzo Corner della Regina, designed by Domenico Rossi in 1725 and located on the Grand Canal between S. Stae and the Palazzo Pesaro.[6] It is not clear from the 1744 inventory drawn up by the painter Pietro Cardinali where Tiepolo's painting, valued at three hundred ducats, hung in the residence, but its exceptionally oblong proportions—when intact it would have measured approximately 205 by 475 centimeters—would have made it a suitable decoration for the long *salone* on the *piano nobile*, with the windows overlooking the Grand Canal on the right. The asymmetrical composition, with the action on one side and a landscape on the other, is not unusual in Venetian paintings of this format and, like its other elements, derives from Veronese.

Tiepolo's association with the various branches of the Cornaro family was of long standing and particularly intense in the 1730s. Andrea Corner's cousin Doge Giovanni Corner had been one of Tiepolo's first patrons, commissioning two oval portraits and a number of other paintings for his palace (see no. 3a, b). Another member of the family, Alvise Corner, donated Tiepolo's three magnificent canvases of about 1738–40 portraying the Passion of Christ to the church of S. Alvise (no. 31, figs. 69, 70); and it was to Alvise Corner that Giandomenico would dedicate his etchings on the Passion of Christ in 1749. In 1737–38 Tiepolo was paid for an altarpiece for the church of S. Salvatore in Venice undertaken for "the most excellent Cornaro family"—a work destroyed by fire in the eighteenth century,[7] and a decade later he painted the *Last Communion of Saint Lucy* for the Cornaro chapel in SS. Apostoli in Venice (no. 36a). His ruined frescoes in the Villa Cornaro at Merlengo seem to date from about 1748 to 1750.[8] Splendid though these works are, none of them brings us so close to Tiepolo's notion of originality and creativity as the *Finding of Moses*. This is so because none posited such a direct relationship with a work by the artist Tiepolo most admired, Paolo Veronese.

In order to appreciate fully the special character of this painting—for it is far from typical of either Tiepolo's religious or mythological works—a number of factors must be borne in mind: the artist's reputation as a follower of Veronese; the high repute Veronese's paintings enjoyed throughout Europe in the eighteenth century; the already established tradition of and market for pictures painted in imitation or emulation of Veronese's work; and the notion of a pictorial caprice—a *capriccio* or *scherzo*.

As it happens, the earliest testimony to Tiepolo as an artist who revived Veronese's style also links him with the Cornaro family.[9] In 1736 the Swedish minister, Count Carl Gustaf Tessin, came to Venice to find a painter to decorate the royal palace in Stockholm (see entry for

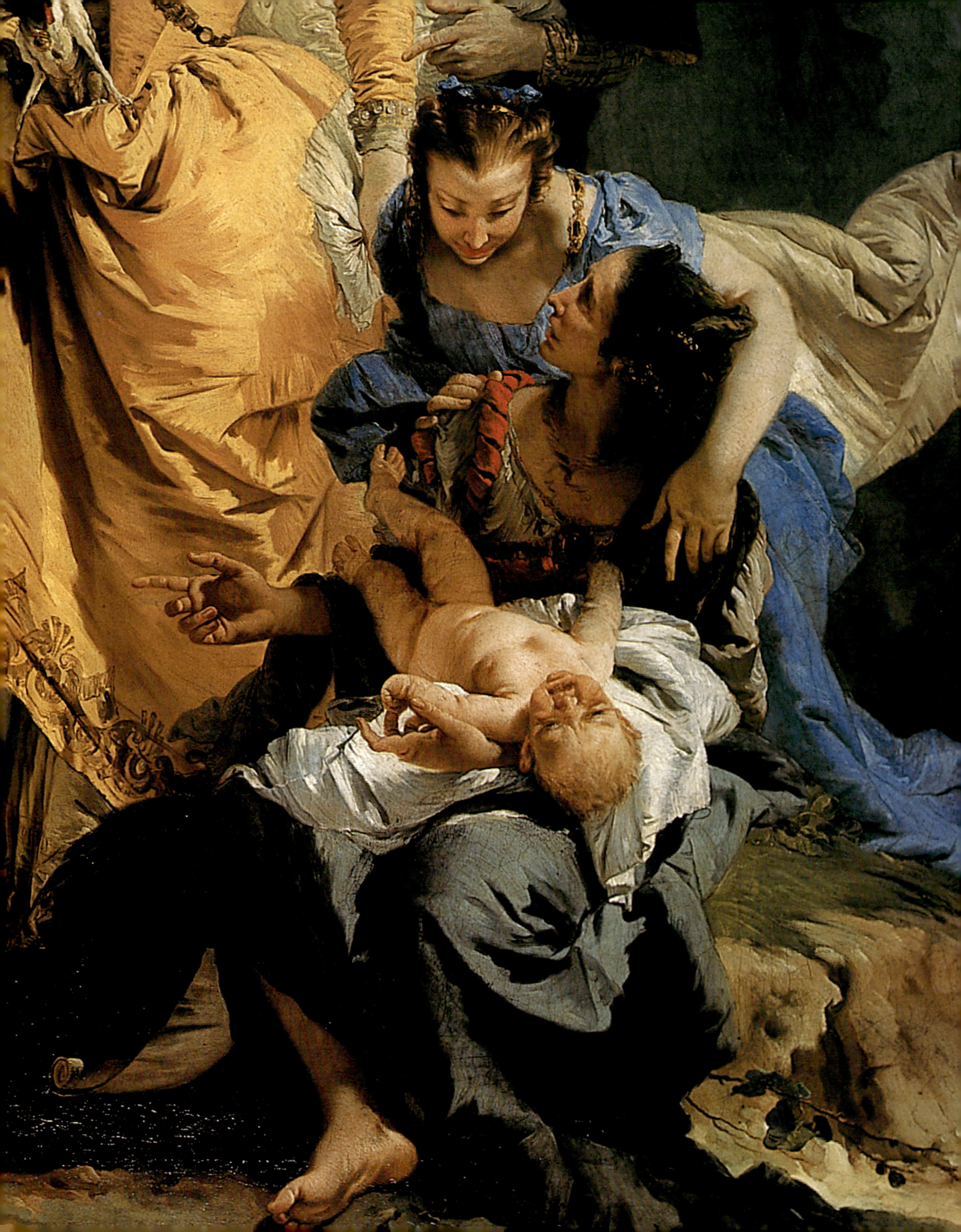

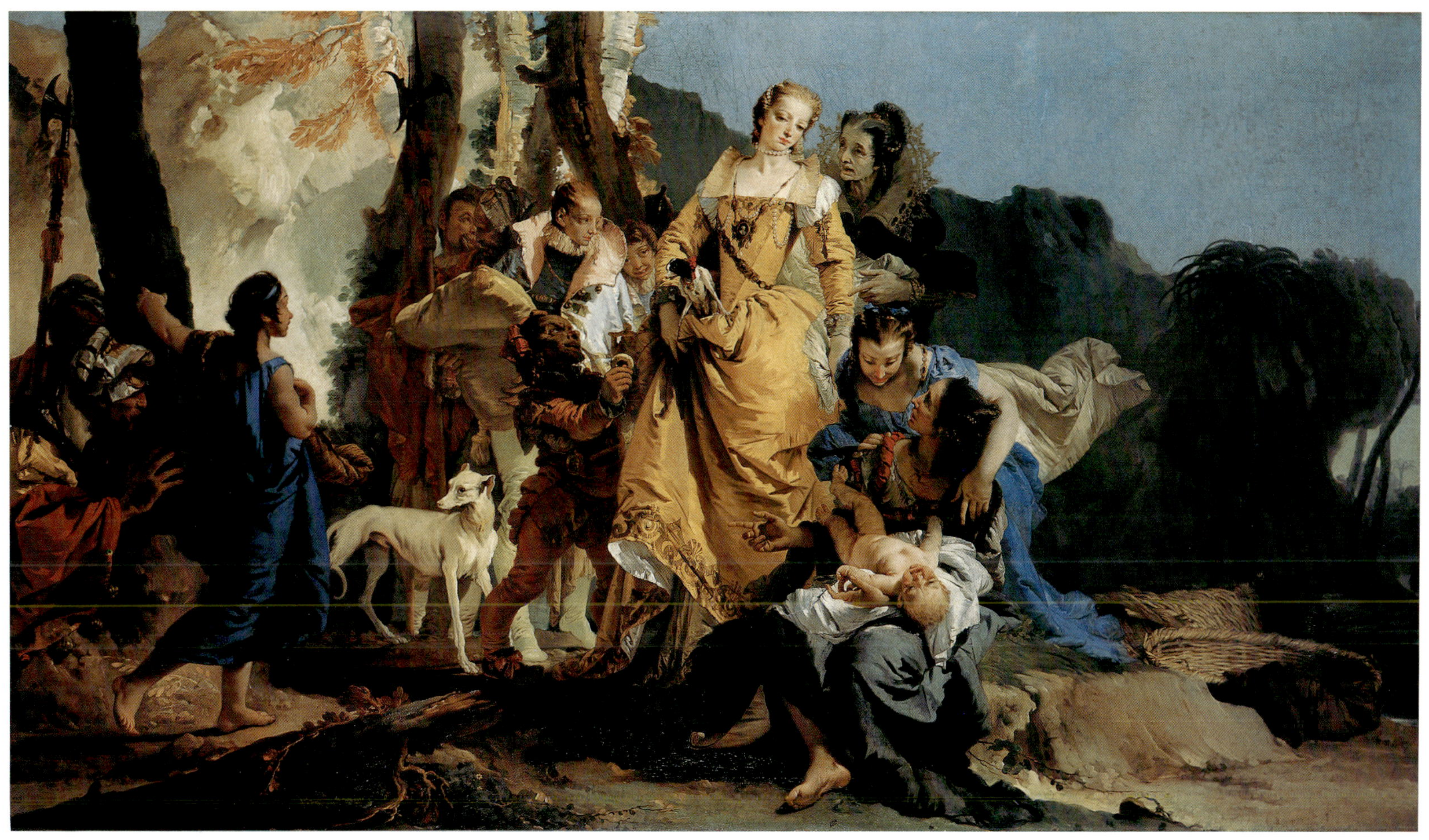

16a

Opposite: Detail, no. 16a

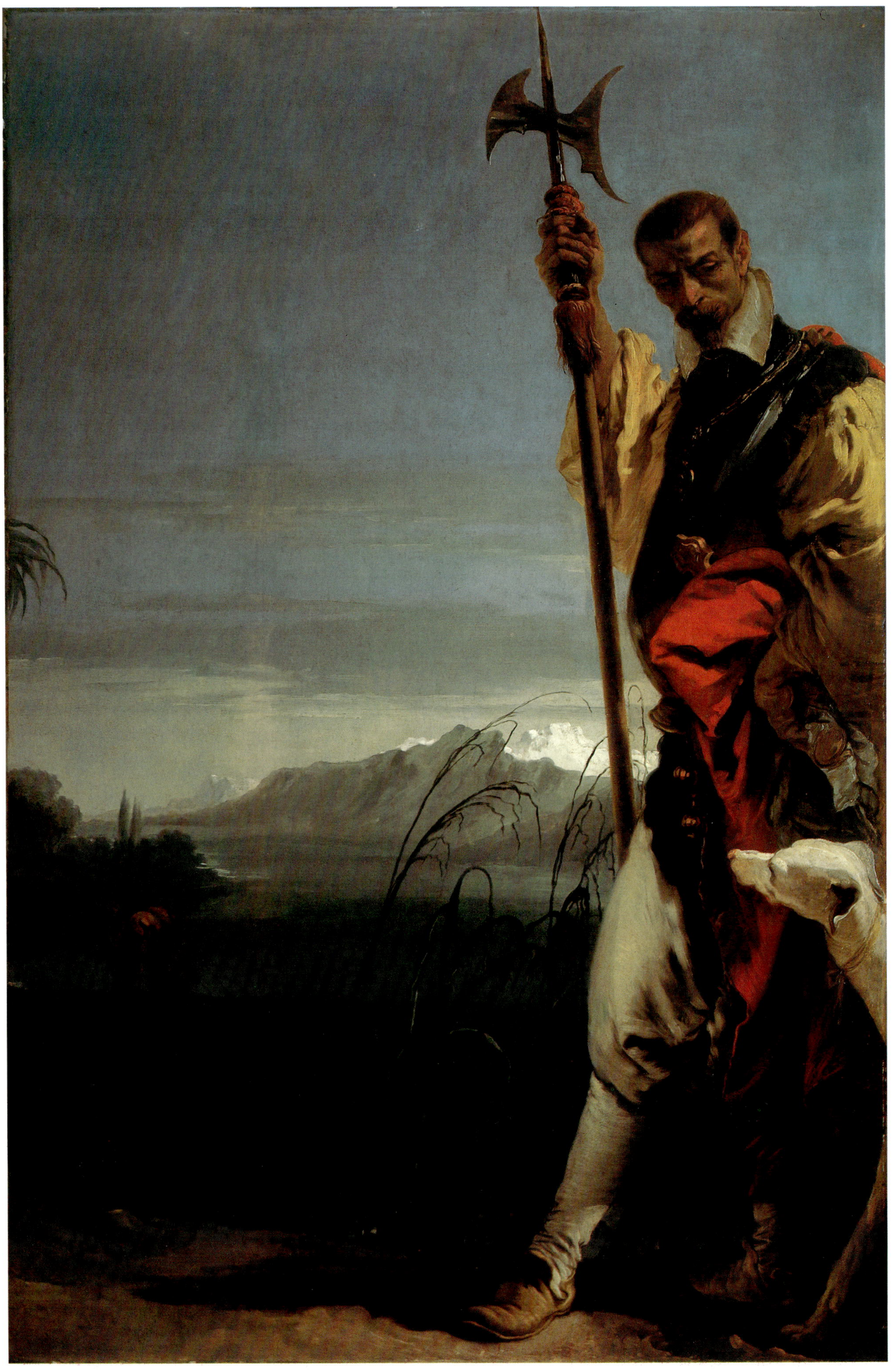

16b

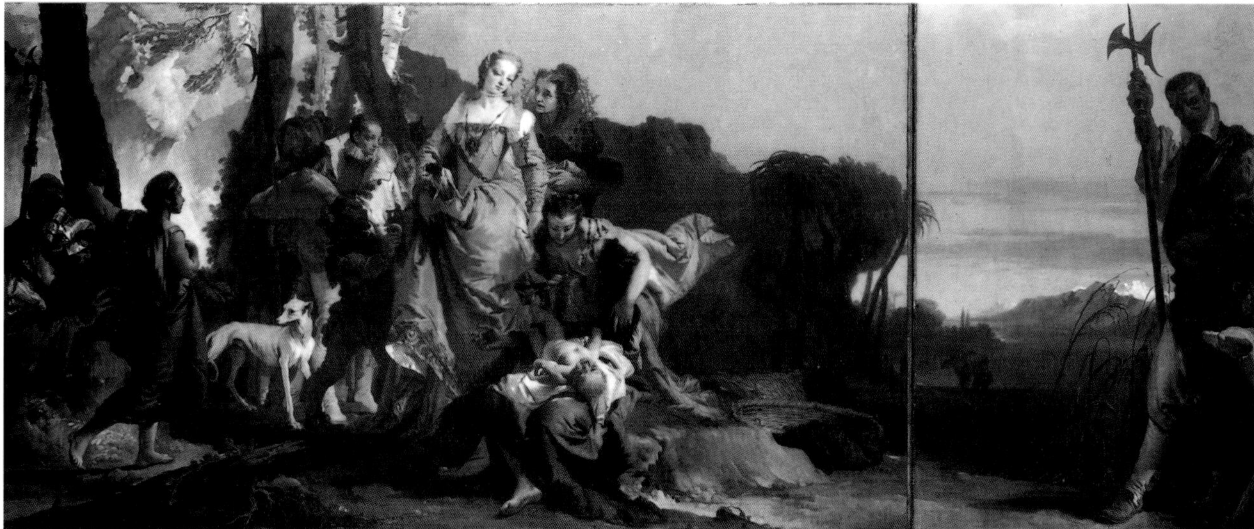

Fig. 47. Installation view, *The Finding of Moses* and *A Halberdier*, National Gallery of Scotland, Edinburgh

no. 15). His choice fell on Tiepolo, whom he described in a letter as "a follower of Paolo Veronese." Tessin continued, "Everyone in his pictures is richly dressed, even the beggars, etc. But isn't this the fashion? Besides, he is full of wit, as compliant as Taraval [a French painter in the employ of the king of Sweden], with boundless inspiration, a dazzling sense of color, and works with astonishing rapidity. . . . As he is currently employed by the noble Cornaro for five or six months, I was unable to obtain a positive response from him."[10] The work for the Cornaro mentioned by Tessin has often been identified with the S. Alvise paintings or with the frescoes at Merlengo, but it is perhaps more likely related to the *Finding of Moses*, which incarnates virtually every quality he noted and which it is reasonable to assume would have taken five or six months to execute. Several years later, in 1743, Francesco Algarotti arrived in Venice to buy pictures for his patron, Augustus III, king of Poland and elector of Saxony. Among the works he was most keen to procure was a *Rape of Europa* ascribed to Veronese.[11] In recommending it, he noted that "all the painters of Venice are in love with it. Tiepoletto, who, among others, has always studied the works of Paolo Veronese, told me that he regards this *Europa* as much finer than the one in the Palazzo Ducale, and that he wanted to pay more than two hundred gold ducats so that he could put it in his atelier to have it always before his eyes as a lesson and a continuous example."[12] Over the next four years no fewer than ten additional paintings attributed to Veronese were sent to Dresden—some on the recommendation of Algarotti, some on the advice of other agents. One of these, a *Finding of Moses* from the Grimani collection in Venice, seems to have provided the point of departure for Tiepolo's canvas.[13]

The widespread demand for Veronese's work, well illustrated by the purchases of the Dresden court, naturally encouraged imitations, copies, and outright fakes, and some of these have a direct bearing on Tiepolo's picture.[14] Sebastiano Ricci's activity in this area was notoriously successful and is said to have elicited the acerbic comment of the French painter Charles de la Fosse: "Believe me, sir, make only works by Paolo Veronese and none by Sebastiano Ricci."[15] A number of Ricci's paintings after Veronese were acquired for the collection of George III of England, including studies of individual heads from Veronese's celebrated *Feast in the House of Levi* (Gallerie dell'Accademia, Venice) and copies of entire compositions, such as the *Magdalen Anointing Christ's Feet* (Galleria Sabauda, Turin). Additionally, a painting by Ricci that is either a pastiche or a copy of a lost Veronese *Finding of Moses* was sold to King George III by the collector-dealer Consul Joseph Smith as a work by Veronese; the deception was quite obviously perpetrated by Smith to secure a high price.[16]

Tiepolo is also known to have made direct copies of Veronese's compositions on occasion. For example, Algarotti's inventory lists a copy by Tiepolo of Veronese's *Magdalen Anointing Christ's Feet*—the same painting Ricci had copied. And before he sent the Veronese *Rape of Europa* to Dresden, Algarotti evidently asked Tiepolo to make a copy for his personal collection. Moreover, in 1760 Algarotti negotiated with Tiepolo about touching up a work by an anonymous painter so that it would appear to be a *modello* by Veronese; Tiepolo was unable or unwilling to oblige.[17] Only in the last instance does there seem to have been an attempt to deceive, and even this was in the way of a sophisticated joke. The deception involved in the 1769 sale of Tiepolo's *Finding of Moses* as a work by Veronese's brother, like Consul Smith's misrepresentation

PROVENANCE, 16a:
Andrea Corner, Palazzo Corner della Regina, Venice (until 1742); by descent, Cecilia Mocenigo (1742–45/46; inv. 1744);[22] John, third earl of Bute, Luton Park, Bedfordshire (1769–92); by descent, John, second marquess of Bute, Luton Park (1792–1822; cat. 1799, no. 43, as Carletto Caliari or Teniers; cat. 1822, no. 28, as Paolo Veronese; sale, Christie's, London, 7 June 1822, lot 50, as by Tiepolo in the manner of Veronese); Emerson (1822); Thomas Hamlet, Denham Court, Buckinghamshire (until 1841; sale, Christie's, London, 22 May 1841, bought by Heilbron); Robert Clouston, Edinburgh (1841–45); by whom given to Royal Institution, Edinburgh

REFERENCES:
Waagen 1854, vol. 3, p. 271; Molmenti 1909, p. 263; Sack 1910, p. 128; Hénard 1914; Morassi 1943, p. 35; Robertson 1949; Morassi 1962, p. 11; Levey 1963, p. 294; Pallucchini 1968, p. 105, no. 131; Brigstocke 1978, pp. 142–45; Levey 1986, pp. 77–80; Brigstocke 1993, pp. 159–62; Gemin and Pedrocco 1993, p. 314, no. 212; Alpers and Baxandall 1994, pp. 1–3, 8–10; London 1994, p. 496, no. 104

PROVENANCE, 16b:
Detached from 16a about 1822–30, after which its history is:[23] Charles Stuart, twelfth Lord Blantyre, Erskine House, Rewbrewshire (until 1900; estate sale, Christie's, London, 19 April 1912, lot 60); Galerie Charles Brunner, Paris (1912); A. Fauchier Magnan, Paris (by 1930); private collection (until 1936; sale, Sotheby's, London, 9 December 1936, lot 56); Ronald Tree, Ditchley (by 1949); private collection, Turin (by 1962)

REFERENCES:
Uhde-Bernays 1913; Willis 1913; Hénard 1914; Robertson 1949; Morassi 1962, p. 20; Levey 1963, p. 294; Pallucchini 1968, p. 105, no. 131; Brigstocke 1978, pp. 142–45; Levey 1986, pp. 77–80; Brigstocke 1993, pp. 159–62; Gemin and Pedrocco 1993, p. 314, no. 213; Alpers and Baxandall 1994, pp. 1–3, 8–10

of Ricci's canvas, reflects not the artist's intentions in painting the picture but the owner's in selling it. Tiepolo's *Finding of Moses*, like most of his works in a Veronesian style, was inspired by rather than copied from a work by his great predecessor. In this it is similar, for example, to the fresco portraying the family of Darius before Alexander the Great (fig. 40) in the Villa Cordellina, Montecchio Maggiore, which derives from a celebrated painting by Veronese originally in the Palazzo Pisani-Moretta, Venice (fig. 41). (Algarotti, who owned a copy of Tiepolo's *modello* for the fresco, had hoped to obtain a copy of Veronese's work as well.) In contradistinction to the grandiloquent style of that monumental fresco, the *Finding of Moses* has been painted with an ironic, semicomedic intent, at once embracing and lightly mocking Veronese's grand manner.

The character of the picture depends for its effect on artificiality and contrivance rather than on opulent naturalness. The princess and her retinue are shown as though on an organized outing, protected by the castle guards and accompanied by the requisite dwarf and the usual page, who holds a cushion for his mistress to sit on (while she bathes?). Veronese's courtly figures have become aristocratic thoroughbreds, as overrefined as their pet dogs, and figure scale is so arbitrary that were the turbaned man at the left, peering around a tree trunk, to stand, he could not be contained within the height of the canvas. The extravagant costumes are reminiscent of garments of the seventeenth, not sixteenth, century: this is especially true of the ridiculously high-collared coat worn by the page and the starched lace collar of the governess—an old crone identical to the servant attending Danaë in the picture Tessin purchased in 1736 (no. 15). Although the landscape at the right side contains a distant vista, we would be at a loss to describe the position of the rocky forms on the left and their relationship to the main figure group; the effect is of a painted backdrop, not an open-air setting. The narrative moment itself has shifted from the traditional finding of Moses—the basket lies discarded on the riverbank—to the comic situation of dealing with an unhappy, hungry baby. This newly introduced theme is actually based on a close reading of the biblical text, which states that when the basket containing the child was opened, "behold, the babe wept." The effect could not help but be humorous, and Tiepolo has played it to the hilt. The princess looks on with an air of genteel detachment, while her governess whispers into her ear. The dwarf is too busy teasing the princess's dog to help. Moses' barefoot sister, Miriam—looking perhaps less like an Israelite than a Gypsy child—runs forward to suggest her mother as the wet nurse. We need only compare the howling Moses, whose head is shown upside down, with the placid babies in Veronese's paintings in Dresden and Madrid—in the latter the infant is also viewed head-on—to appreciate the wit and irony Tiepolo has interjected into Veronese's courtly ceremony.[18] At work here is the same irreverent spirit to which he was to give free rein in the *Capricci* (no. 59a–j) and *Scherzi* (no. 60a–w), and, indeed, the picture might properly be called a *capriccio sopra un'idea di Veronese*.

The notion of a picture as a caprice or lighthearted joke should hardly surprise. It derives from a long and illustrious tradition in literature and music and was perfectly suited to the sophisticated tastes of eighteenth-century collectors. In the seventeenth century Guido Reni had painted at least one such work based on the ancient tale of Bacchus and Ariadne.[19] Few comparisons could better demonstrate Tiepolo's versatility and sense of decorum than one that contrasts this wonderfully ironic, playful picture—religious in the biblical source of its theme but in all important respects a secular work for a private residence—with his approximately contemporary ecclesiastical paintings for S. Alvise, with their emphasis on drama and pathos.

The picture has been dated variously. Morassi placed it, implausibly, in the 1750s, but Levey recognized that it could not be much later than about 1740. Brigstocke has argued for a date in the early 1730s. Because of the unique character of the picture, a precise date is difficult to suggest. However, there are affinities of style with the *Joseph Receiving Pharaoh's Ring* (no. 14) as well as with the series of altarpieces Tiepolo carried out for Daniele Dolfin for the cathedral of Udine between 1736 and 1738.[20] According to the documents discovered by Lewis, in the early summer of 1742 a Girolamo Fabri was hired to hang new pictures in the Palazzo Corner della Regina, some of which were large enough to require reinforced wire cords.[21] This might be taken as the terminus ante quem for the date of the painting.

KC

NOTES

1. The purchase of the picture as a Benedetto Caliari in 1769 by Sir James Wright for the third earl of Bute was discovered by Francis Russell. Wright's letter to the earl is cited by Brigstocke (1993, p. 162 n. 22) but deserves to be quoted here: "The Great Benedetto Caliari of yours I have had much difficulty of packing, being painted in varnish, it would not bear rolling, I therefore had it plac'd on a cimi cir[cl]e of board, to which it was nailed and then the circle cased up by this Meens I hope it will come safe."
2. The mutilation took place between about 1822 and 1830. The *Halberdier* was subsequently reduced on its left side by turning back the canvas and enlarged on its right side by an addition, to make a completely independent composition. When the picture was first published in 1913, it was assumed to be a rare portrait

by Tiepolo. Hénard (1914) recognized it as a fragment of the Edinburgh picture and published the results of its restoration.

3. For the ascription to Giandomenico, see Morassi 1962, p. 50. The Stuttgart copy further exaggerates the elongated proportions of the figures and stretches out the landscape laterally. This is of some importance in weighing the comments in Alpers and Baxandall (1994), which are largely based on an analysis of the copy.
4. I would like to thank Douglas Lewis for generously making his unpublished material available to me.
5. See Lewis 1988.
6. For the building history of the palace, see Olivato 1973.
7. The picture was begun in 1737; on 6 June 1738 Tiepolo received 660 lira "per fatura di una palla di altar di raggione delle Ecc.me Casse Cornero." Quoted in Morassi 1962, p. 232.
8. Brown (in Fort Worth 1993, pp. 264–67) summarizes the arguments for the dating of the fresco cycle, perhaps commissioned in anticipation of the marriage of Andrea Corner and Maria Foscarini in 1751, by which time Tiepolo was already in Würzburg. Alternatively, a date in the 1730s has been proposed on the basis of the passage in Tessin's letter cited below.
9. For a review of Tiepolo's reputation as a new Veronese, see Sohm 1990.
10. Quoted in Morassi 1962, p. 232: "Il est sectataire de Paul Véronèse;—Ainsi comme vous le dites fort bien: Tout est dans ces Tableaux richement vétu jusqu'au gueux etc. Mais n'est-ce pas la grande mode? Au reste, il est plein d'esprit, accomodant comme un Taraval, un feu infini, un coloris éclatant, et d'une vitesse surprenante. . . . Comme il est actuellement occupé chez le Noble Cornaro pour 5 à 6 mois: ainsi je n'ai jamais pû obtenir une Reponse positive."
11. It is now usually given to the workshop. See Pignatti 1976, p. 178, no. A68.
12. Quoted in Posse 1931, p. 41: "Tous les Peintres de Venise en sont amoreux. Tiepoletto entr'autres, qui a etudié toujours d'apres Paul Veroneze m'a dit lui meme, qu'il regarde cette Europe comme bien au dessus de celle, qui est dans le Palais du Doge, et qu'il vouloit lui meme en donner au dessus de 200 ducats d'or pour la mettre dans la Chambre ou il peint affin de l'avoir toujours devant les yeux comme une leçon et une etude continuelle." In another letter (ibid., p. 45) Tiepolo appears in an equivocal role, offering to provide a certificate for the work.
13. It should, however, be noted that Andrea Corner owned two pictures ascribed in the 1699 and 1744 inventories of his collection to Carletto (Veronese's son): a Presentation in the Temple and a Rest on the Flight into Egypt. If the latter resembled the painting of the same subject now in the National Gallery of Canada, Ottawa, its appearance would be relevant for Tiepolo's *Moses*. See Pignatti 1976, no. 322. The 1699 inventory is published in Olivato 1973, p. 49.
14. On copies and fake Veroneses in the eighteenth century, see Garas 1990.
15. Lépicié 1752, quoted in Garas 1990, pp. 67–68.
16. There is a related woodcut of 1741 by J. B. Jackson that names Veronese as the author of the painting. Jackson's woodcut either copies the lost Veronese or mistakenly attributes Ricci's picture; the latter is a bit difficult to credit. See Coutts 1982. Smith clearly knew what he was doing when he sold the king a work by Ricci with an attribution to Veronese, and the evidence suggests that this practice was far from uncommon.
17. On these paintings, see Levey 1960c. Tiepolo's copy of the *Magdalen Anointing Christ's Feet* is in the National Gallery, Dublin. Despite the notice in the inventory of Algarotti's collection, Levey considers Giandomenico, not Giambattista, to be its author. To my eyes, the architecture appears to be by one hand—possibly that of Antonio Visentini, who is known to have painted the architecture in the picture Algarotti submitted to Tiepolo in 1760—while the rest of the work seems to have been done by another; Tiepolo may well have touched up certain areas. We may wonder whether the composition necessarily was laid in by either Giambattista or Giandomenico, for Algarotti owned a painting of Diana and Actaeon (Bührle collection, Zurich) that is listed in his inventory as a Tiepolo but is patently by someone else, Tiepolo having merely added some touches to the foliage and still-life details in the lower corners. Morassi (1962, p. 23) published another *Finding of Moses* (National Gallery of Victoria, Melbourne) as a pastiche by Tiepolo; the attribution is difficult to sustain when the picture is compared to the Edinburgh example.
18. For the picture in the Museo del Prado, Madrid, see Pignatti 1976, p. 146, no. 240. Pignatti (figs. 563–69) illustrates a number of other treatments of the theme from Veronese's workshop.
19. See Pepper 1983.
20. For these altarpieces, see Gemin and Pedrocco 1993, pp. 320–21, nos. 220–22. The landscape backgrounds and the attenuated proportions and morphology of the figures in the altarpieces are remarkably close to the analogous features in the *Finding of Moses*. When making this comparison, one must make allowance for the fact that of the altarpieces only the *Trinity* is fully autograph.
21. Information kindly furnished by Lewis.
22. See Brigstocke (1993, pp. 161, 162 n. 21), who quotes from the unpublished findings of Douglas Lewis. Lewis notes that in 1747 Cecilia Mocenigo was reprimanded by her sons for having sold paintings from Andrea's palace.
23. See ibid., p. 161 n. 1. When and if the picture was owned by W. A. Baird, as stated in the Sotheby's 1936 sale catalogue, cannot be confirmed.

THE TASSO CYCLE

17a. Rinaldo Enchanted by Armida
17b. Rinaldo and Armida in the Garden
17c. Rinaldo Abandoning Armida
17d. Rinaldo and the Magician of Ascalona
17e. Satyr
17f. Satyress with Two Putti and a Tambourine
17g. Satyress with a Putto

17a. Rinaldo Enchanted by Armida
Ca. 1742–45
186.9 × 214.7 cm (73½ × 84½ in.)
The Art Institute of Chicago, Gift of James Deering (25.699)

17b. Rinaldo and Armida in the Garden
Ca. 1742–45
186.8 × 259.9 cm (73 × 102⅛ in.)
The Art Institute of Chicago, Gift of James Deering (25.700)

17c. Rinaldo Abandoning Armida
Ca. 1742–45
186.8 × 259.9 cm (73 × 102⅛ in.)
The Art Institute of Chicago, Gift of James Deering (25.701)

17d. Rinaldo and the Magician of Ascalona
Ca. 1742–45
186.9 × 214.7 cm (73½ × 84½ in.)
The Art Institute of Chicago, Gift of James Deering (25.702)

17e. Satyr
Ca. 1742–45
60 × 96 cm (25⅝ × 37¾ in.)
Galleria Nazionale d'Arte Antica, Rome

According to a thesis convincingly argued by Knox almost twenty years ago, these paintings are the main narrative components and decorative oval overdoors of a captivating pictorial setting that once decorated the room of a patrician palace in Venice.[1] The other elements can be identified as four upright canvases now in London (figs. 48–51)—narrative interludes, so to speak, to the Chicago paintings (indeed, only two have a demonstrative narrative connection with the story)—and, more problematically, a magnificent allegorical ceiling (fig. 52). Tiepolo may have produced the entire series of twelve works for the Palazzo Dolfin Manin, facing the Grand Canal near the Rialto Bridge, but only the ceiling appears in an inventory of December 1799 listing and evaluating paintings in that palace.[2] Thus, either the eleven wall canvases that constituted the ensemble were sold before the inventory was compiled or they never belonged to the Manin family. In that second case, any connection between them and the ceiling is mistaken, and the question of which palace originally housed the fascinating group of paintings shown here still awaits an answer.

The Chicago and London canvases depict episodes or figures from Torquato Tasso's *Gerusalemme liberata*, or *Jerusalem Delivered*, one of the poetic masterpieces of Italian literature, while the three ovals divided between Rome and Pasadena function as pictorial metaphors of the cycle. First published in 1581, the *Gerusalemme liberata* is an epic poem that treats the theme of righteousness and morality battling evil and vice. Using history, legend, and poetic invention, Tasso wrought a tale about the chivalric Crusades fought by Christian armies to liberate Jerusalem from the Saracens in 1099; his wide-ranging narrative also tells the love story of the knight Rinaldo and the pagan enchantress Armida. Three of the works in Chicago portray specific episodes involving Rinaldo and Armida, and the fourth represents a later and related moment. The quartet constitutes the nucleus of a large and ambitious pictorial program whose elements apparently were meant to hang in a preordained arrangement. Sequential groupings of paintings for the embellishment of noble interiors were not new in north Italian art of the eighteenth century; their history can be traced back to the Renaissance. But the commissioning of grand pictorial series for private palaces in Venice began only toward 1700.[3] Such sets usually responded to the desires of patrons to glorify their status, ambitions, and accomplishments, and the works often depicted heroic subject matter exalting extraordinary deeds, exceptional virtues, and high-minded self-denial.[4] Themes and aims of this kind are mirrored in Tiepolo's Palazzo Sandi and Ca' Dolfin cycles (no. 9a, b, fig. 30, no. 12a–g, figs. 33–35), painted during the 1720s, the first for a new patrician family and the second for members of the old nobility. The Tasso sequence, which marks a departure from this thematic tradition, was produced in the early 1740s, a date based not only on stylistic evidence but also on the existence of etchings made by Tiepolo's sons prior to 1750 of one of the Chicago compositions and three of those in London.[5]

While Tiepolo's Tasso series follows upon a long list of painted cycles drawn from the *Gerusalemme liberata*, such cycles appear to have been restricted to palaces in the geographic areas in and around Genoa and Paris.

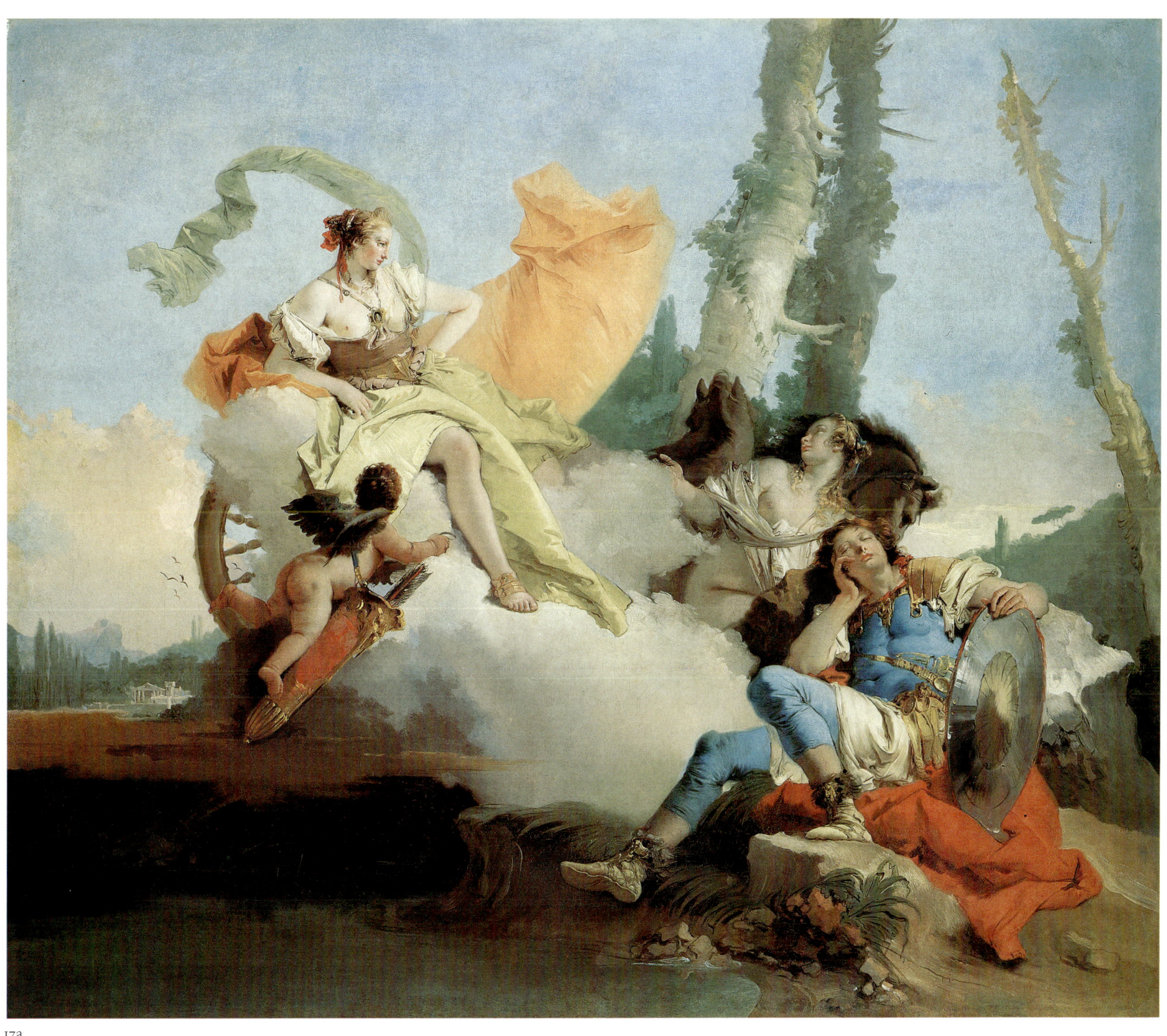

17a

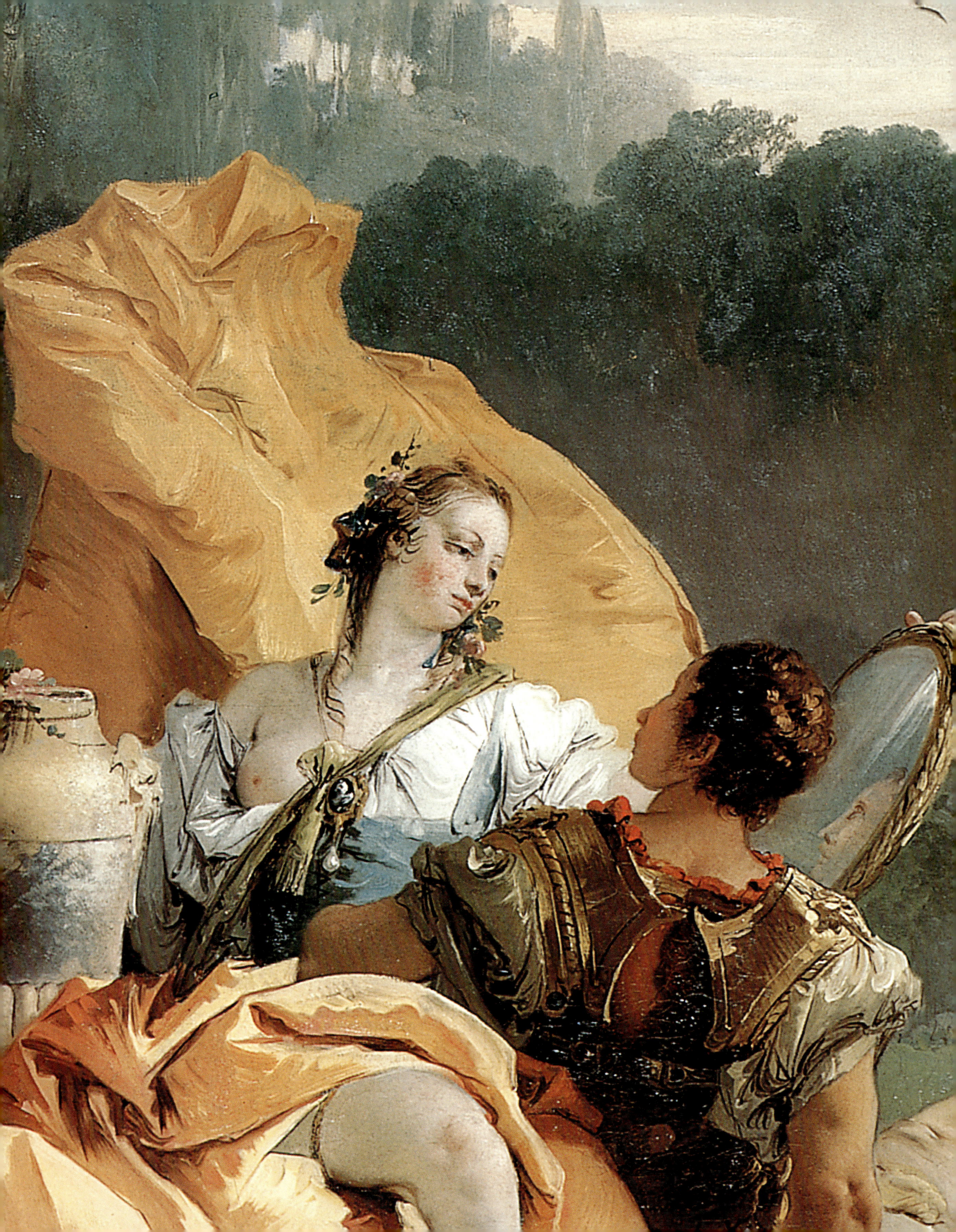

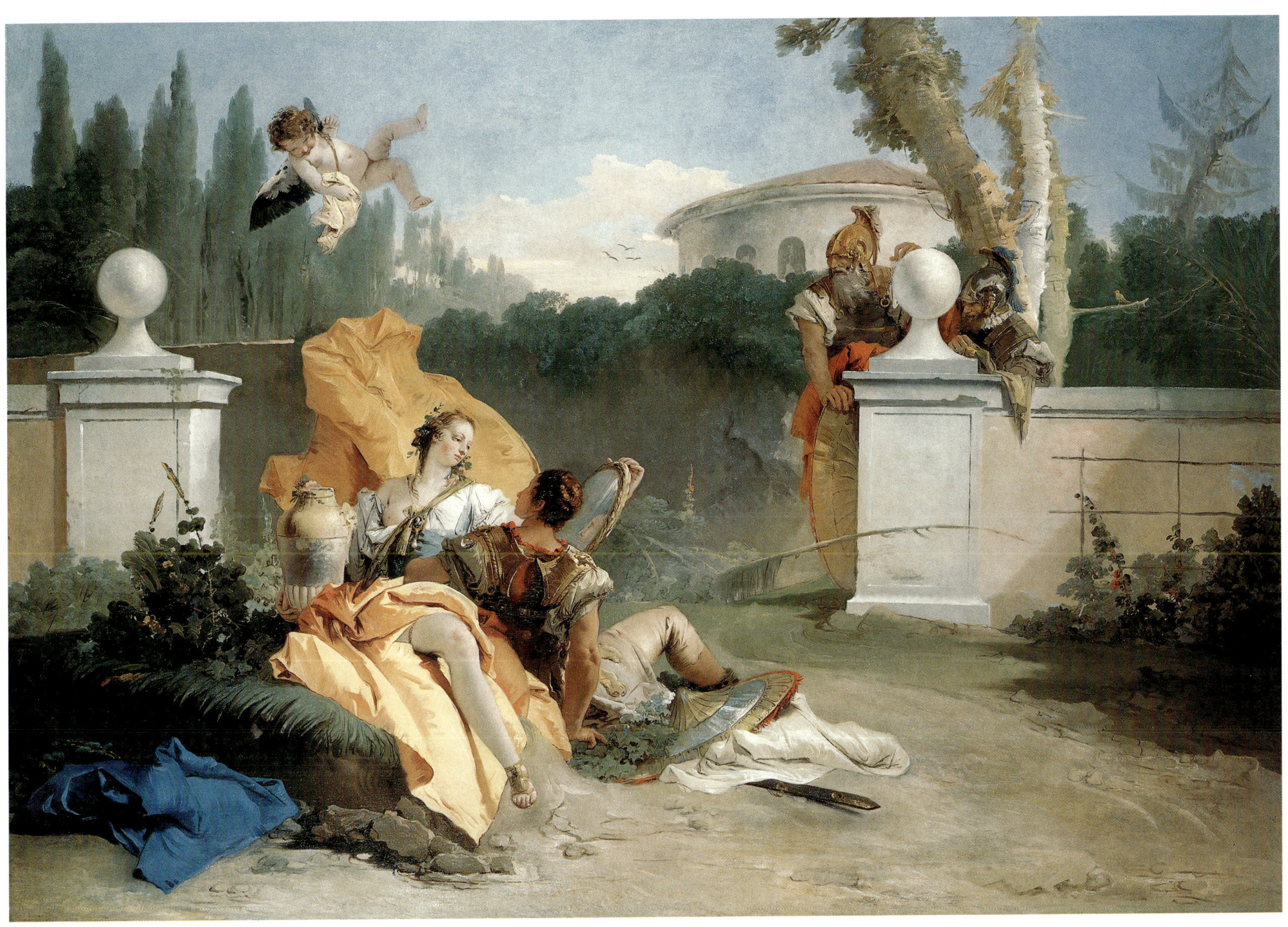

17b

Opposite: Detail, no. 17b

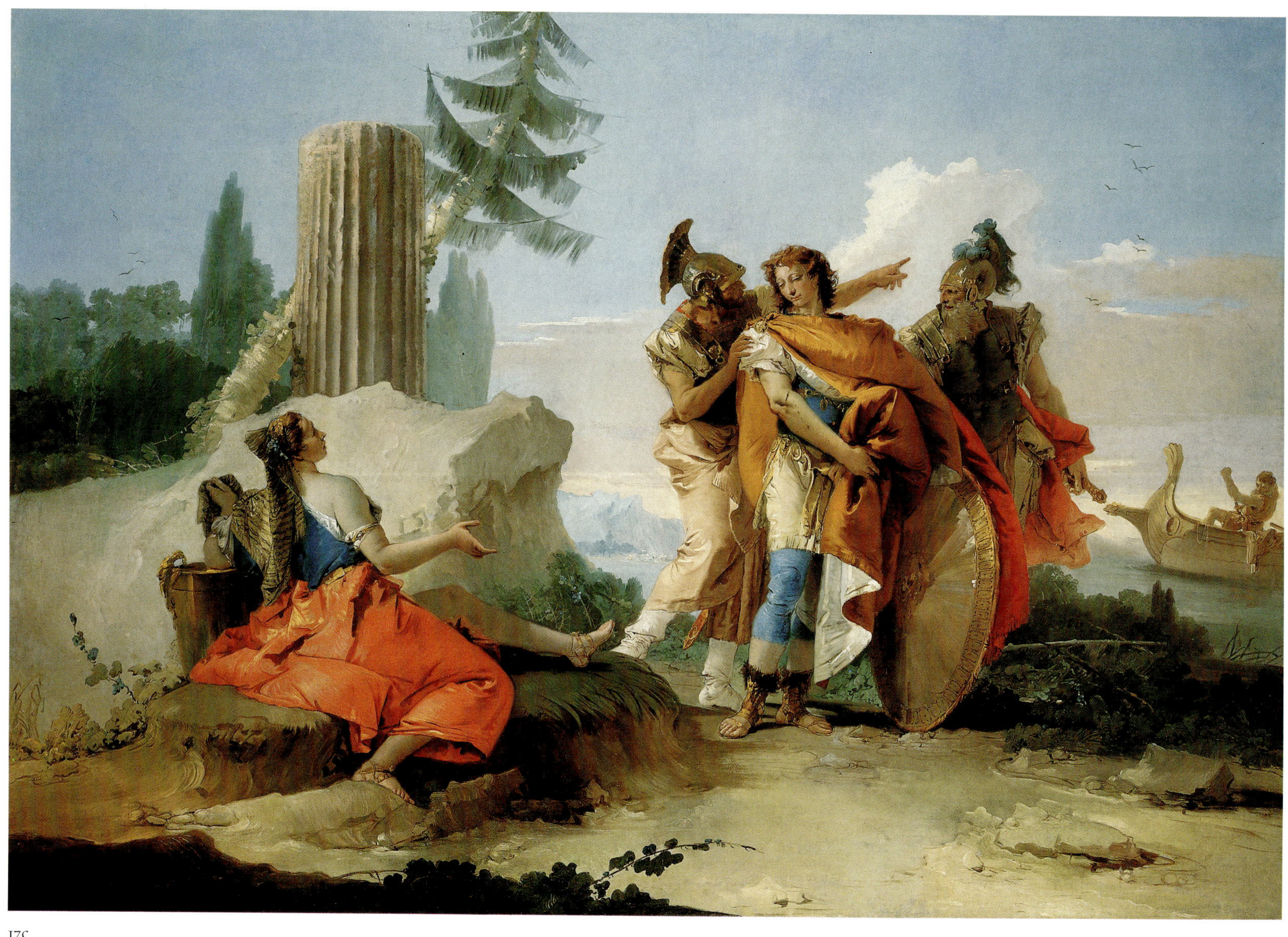

17c

Opposite: Detail, no. 17c

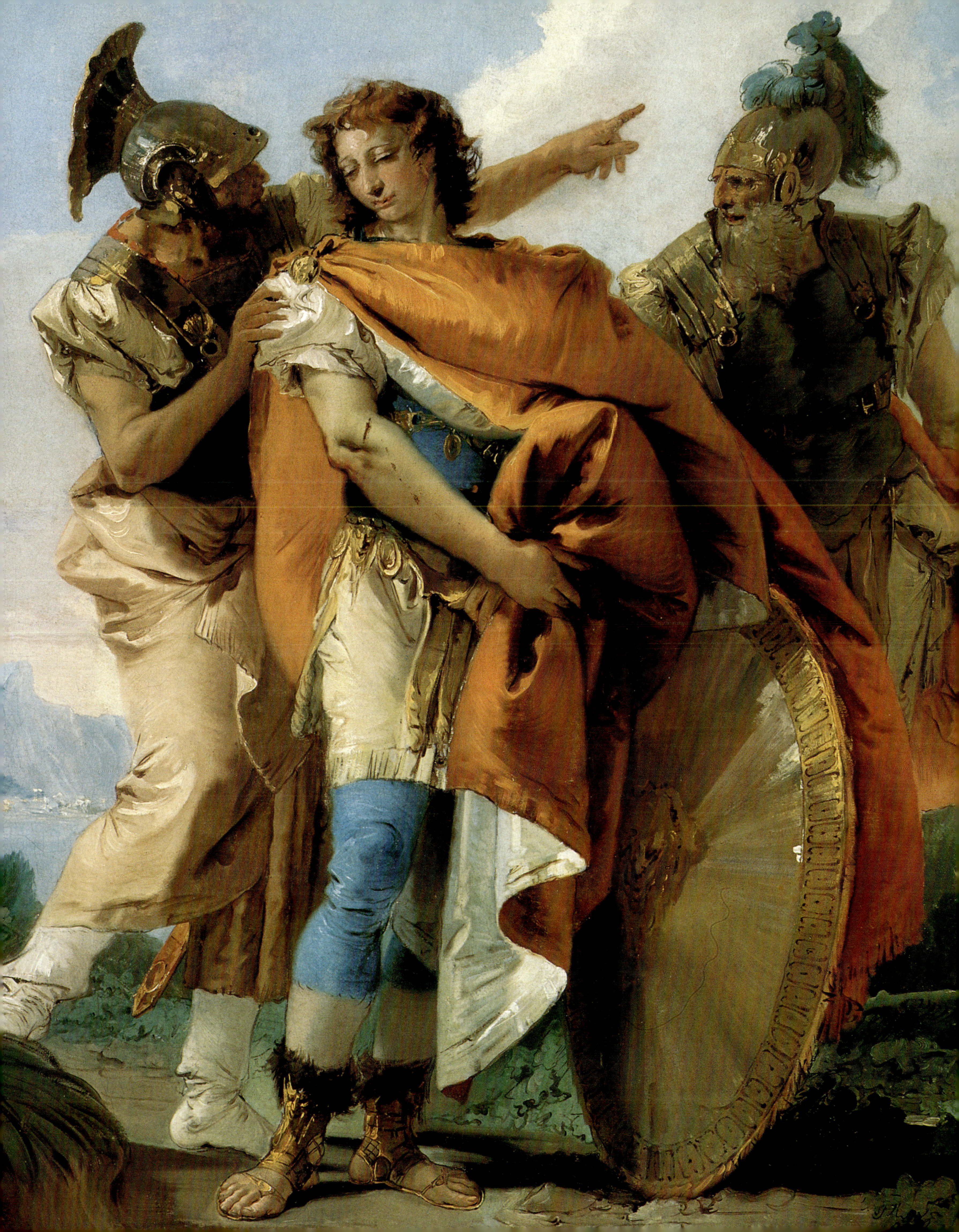

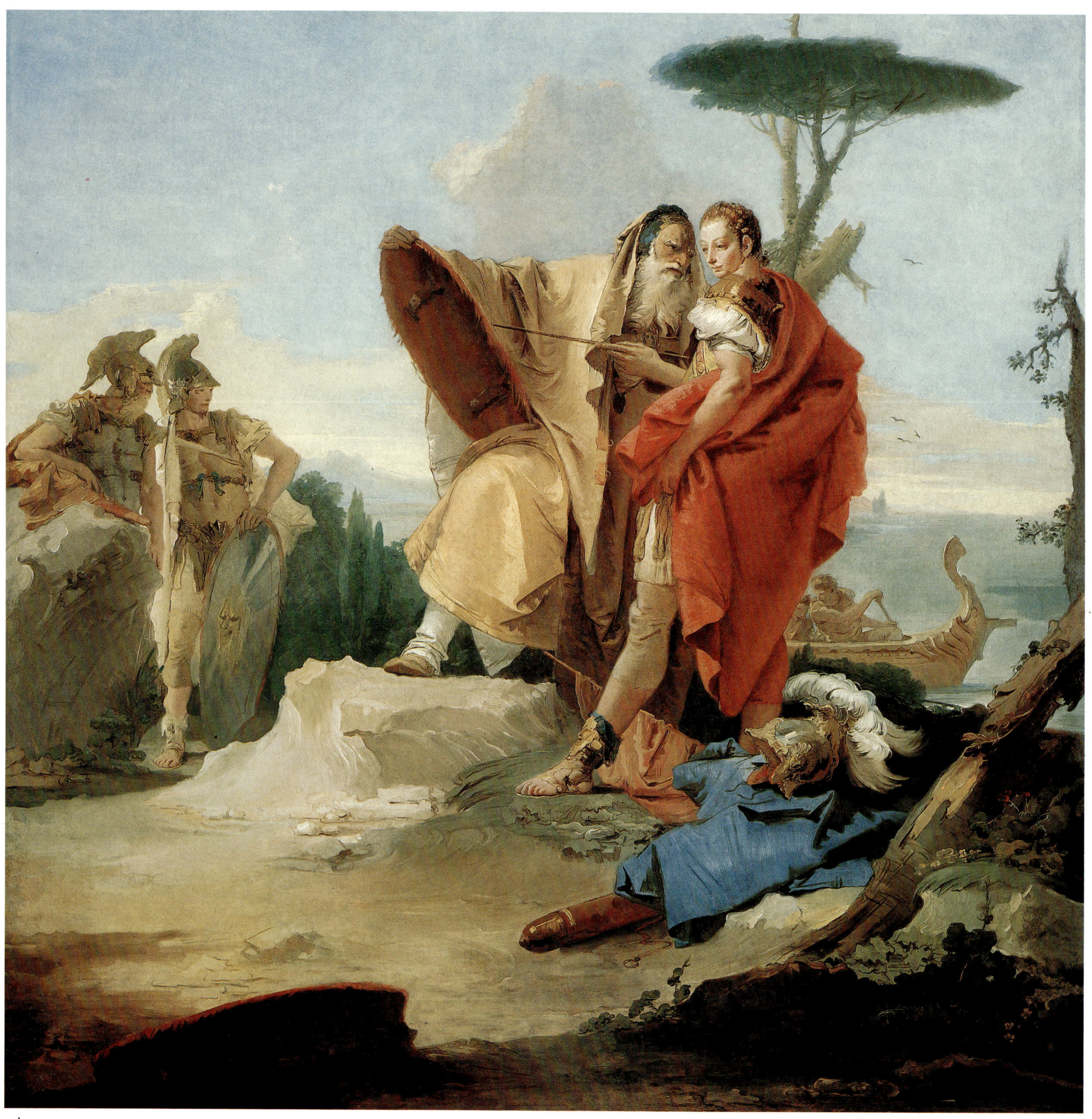

17d

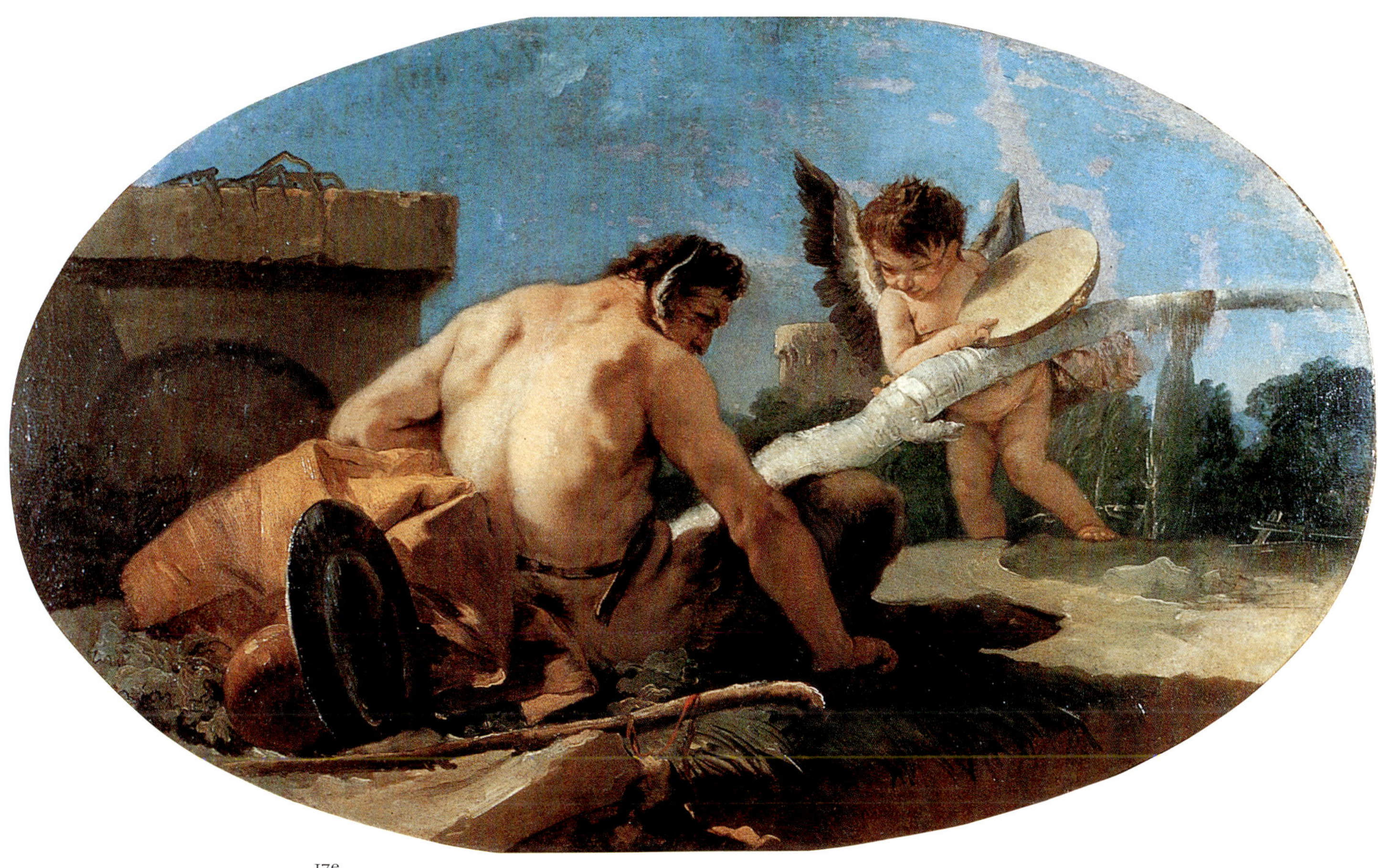

17e

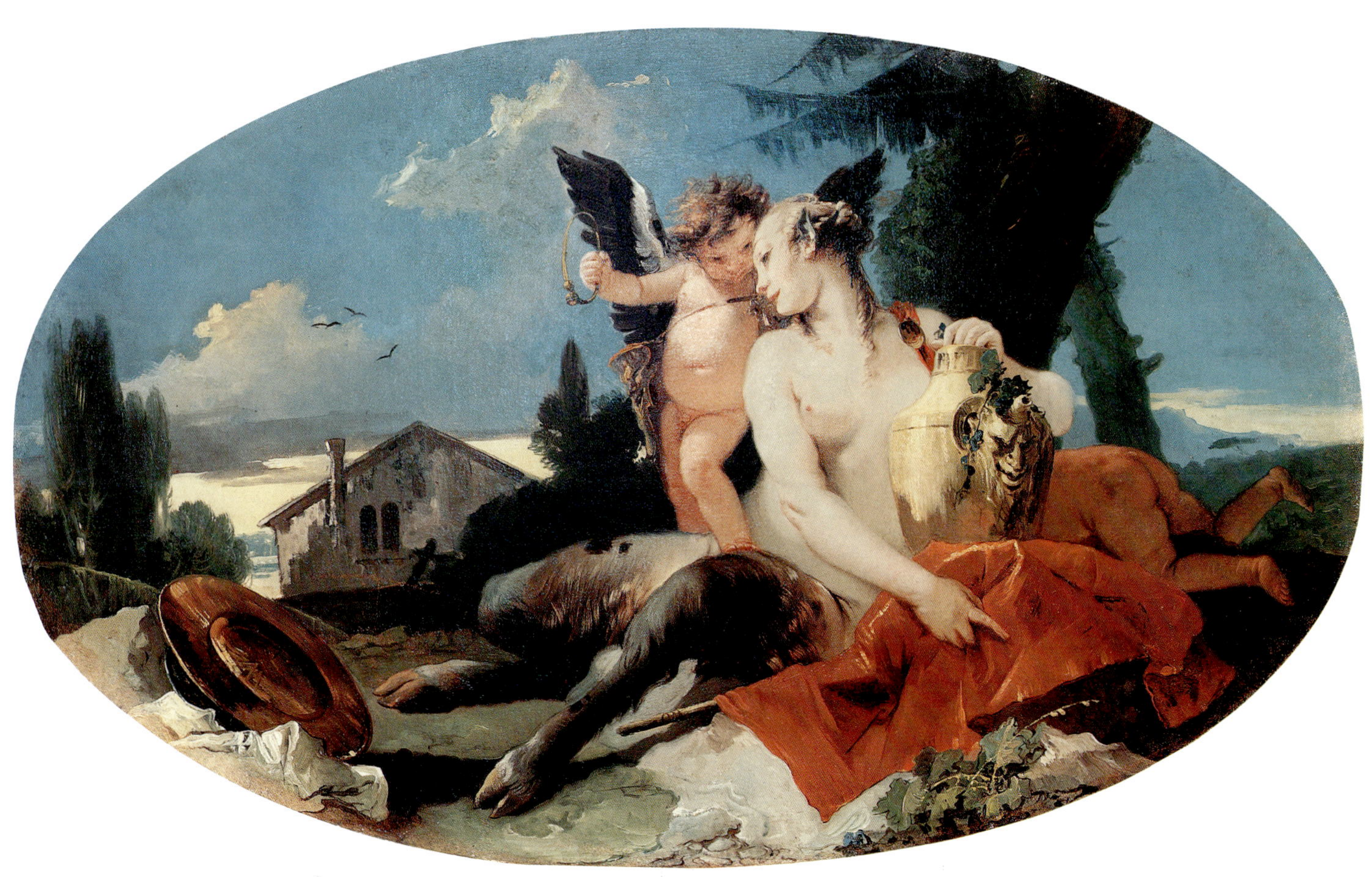

17f

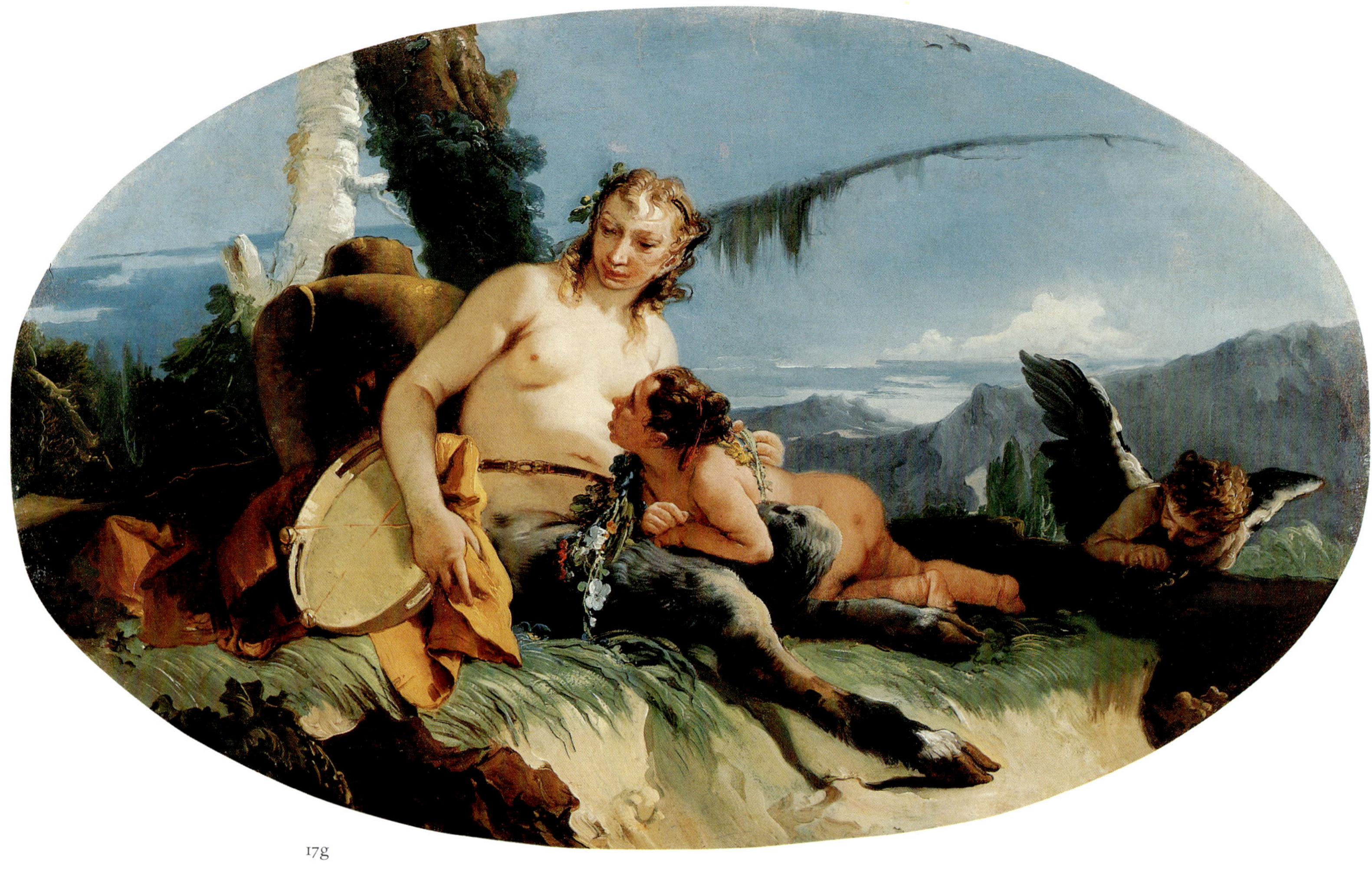

17g

17f. Satyress with Two Putti and a Tambourine
Ca. 1742–45
60 × 95.9 cm (23⅝ × 37¾ in.)
Norton Simon Art Foundation, Pasadena

17g. Satyress with a Putto
Ca. 1742–45
60 × 95.9 cm (23⅝ × 37¾ in.)
Norton Simon Art Foundation, Pasadena

For reasons not readily apparent, nobles in and near those two cities found Tasso's tales especially attractive as source material for the sumptuous settings of their residences.[6] The taste for decorations based on the *Gerusalemme liberata* accelerated in Paris in the early eighteenth century, bringing forth cartoons by Charles-Antoine Coypel and François Boucher for the weaving of tapestries. Tasso-inspired decorations then emerged in the Veneto, first in Tiepolo's series of the early 1740s, later in a cycle of eight canvases by Gian Antonio Guardi of about 1750, and, finally, in the four scenes Tiepolo frescoed in Villa Valmarana in Vicenza in 1757.[7]

The only way to appreciate fully Tiepolo's achievement in the Tasso cycle is to envision the canvases installed in their original setting, which was probably a *salone*, or reception hall: for the primary focus of most decorative enterprises in Venice was the *salone*, the site of receptions, balls, and small concerts. As often as not, this was a rectangular room with a long wall with windows extending from ceiling to floor and facing onto a canal or public square. Knox arranged the Chicago paintings into symmetrical groups on three walls of such an interior: the two smaller ones each flanked by a pair of the narrow canvases now in London, were divided between the facing walls and the two larger canvases hung as pendants on the wall opposite the windows; the ovals, presumably, were placed over the doors.[8] This scheme is problematic, however, in that the narrative sequence is not strictly observed. Moreover, the fictive light sources in the London works and the three ovals are not coordinated when they are arranged in this manner: three of the upright canvases are lit from the right and one is lit from the left, while the light falls from the right in two of the ovals and from the left in the other. Perhaps the Tasso Room had two fenestrated walls, and perhaps the four London canvases did not flank the smaller Chicago pictures: a pair of the London canvases might, for example, have decorated spaces between windows.

The cycle begins with *Rinaldo Enchanted by Armida* (17a). In canto 14 of the *Gerusalemme liberata*, Tasso recounts through the person of the Magician of Ascalona how Armida happens upon the sleeping Rinaldo. Amazed by the knight's beauty, she contemplates him as he dozes, unaware of her presence (14, st. 66). Armida plucks flowers from the adjacent riverbanks and weaves delicate but tenaciously strong chains with which she binds Rinaldo's neck, arms, and feet; she then abducts him

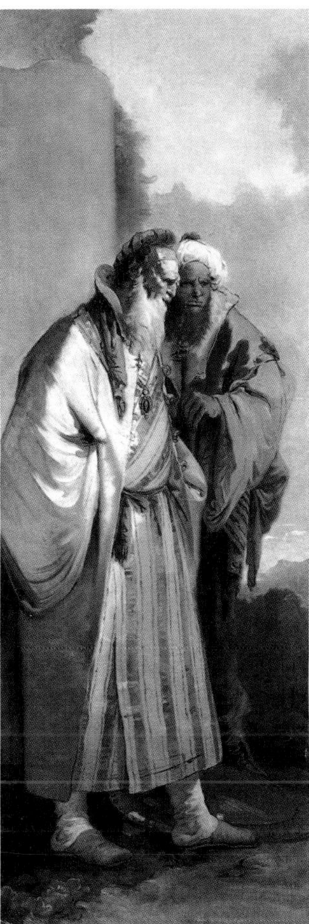
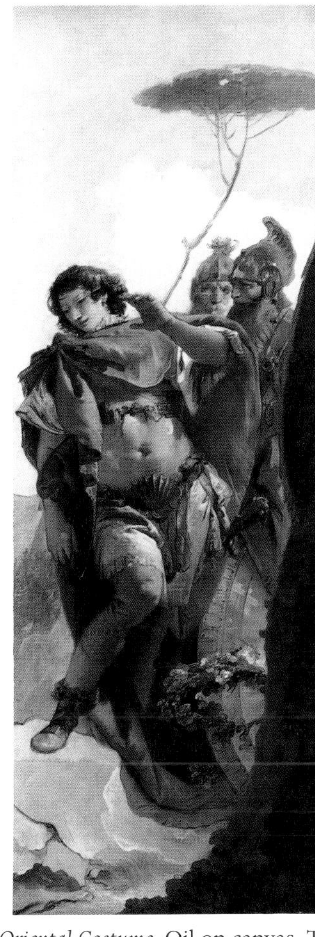
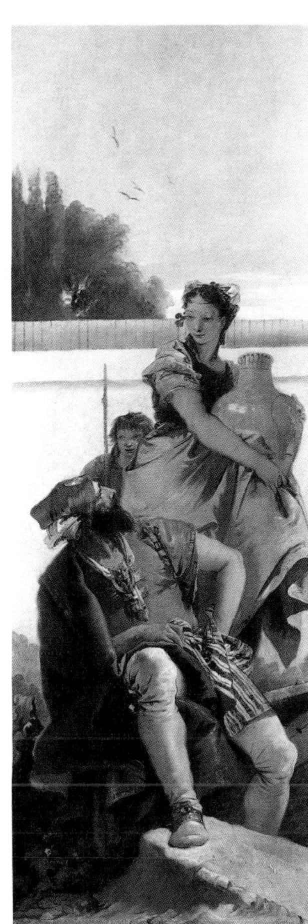
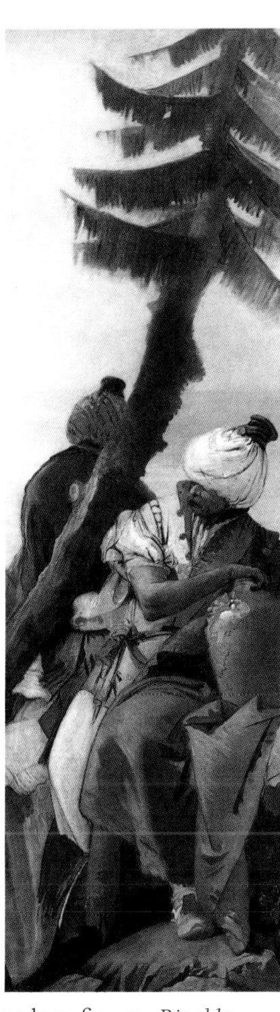

Left to right: fig. 48. *Two Men in Oriental Costume*. Oil on canvas. The Trustees of the National Gallery, London; fig. 49. *Rinaldo Turning in Shame from the Magic Shield*. Oil on canvas. The Trustees of the National Gallery, London; fig. 50. *A Seated Man, a Woman with a Jar, and a Boy*. Oil on canvas. The Trustees of the National Gallery, London; fig. 51. *Two Orientals Seated under a Tree*. Oil on canvas. The Trustees of the National Gallery, London

while he slumbers, her chariot carrying the pair across the skies to the enchantress's magical garden (14, st. 68). Depicting Armida's first glimpse of the knight, Tiepolo encircled her flying vehicle with clouds settling downward, the horses reduced to two heads whose abbreviated shapes in part repeat the forms of a single wheel to the left, Rinaldo's shield to the right, and the curving draperies cascading over as well as billowing up behind the temptress. He painted the shimmering, silken fabrics of Armida's costume the colors of summer fruits, thereby enhancing the tones of the seductress's ivory white skin and intensifying its contrast to the deep, jewel-like hues of Rinaldo's armor and cape. The two protagonists themselves are ideally beautiful: Armida a classical goddess in her perfection and Rinaldo a hero of noble physical proportions and youthful comeliness. The earth beneath them, however, is almost featureless, and the landscape beyond is reduced to a distant and flattened screen of mountains and trees. Having partially suspended gravity, dimension, and time, Tiepolo depicts the moment of Armida's rapt encounter in terms of pure fable.

Next in the sequence would have been *Rinaldo and Armida in the Garden* (17b) and *Rinaldo Abandoning Armida* (17c), the largest of the Chicago paintings, together with the narrow canvas showing Rinaldo's ultimate release from Armida's enchantment (fig. 49). Based on episodes in canto 16, this triad portrays first the passion the knight and sorceress briefly enjoyed in her magical bower beyond Egypt and then their subsequent and painful parting. Tasso relates that Carlo and Ubaldo, Rinaldo's two comrades-in-arms, arrive on the scene and search for their abducted friend in the witch's palace and gardens; he also tells of the soldiers' discovery of the voluptuous couple, "he in the lady's lap, and she [lying] on the ground" (16, st. 17).[9] Carlo and Ubaldo watch while the lovers, as if enchanted, marvel at their own reflections, Armida looking into her magical mirror and he into his partner's captivating eyes (16, st. 20). This is the moment Tiepolo seized upon in *Rinaldo and Armida in the Garden*. Although Tasso supplies an exquisite description of Armida's garden, the painter reduced the setting to essentials, as he had in the initial scene of the series. He partially hid Carlo and Ubaldo from view,

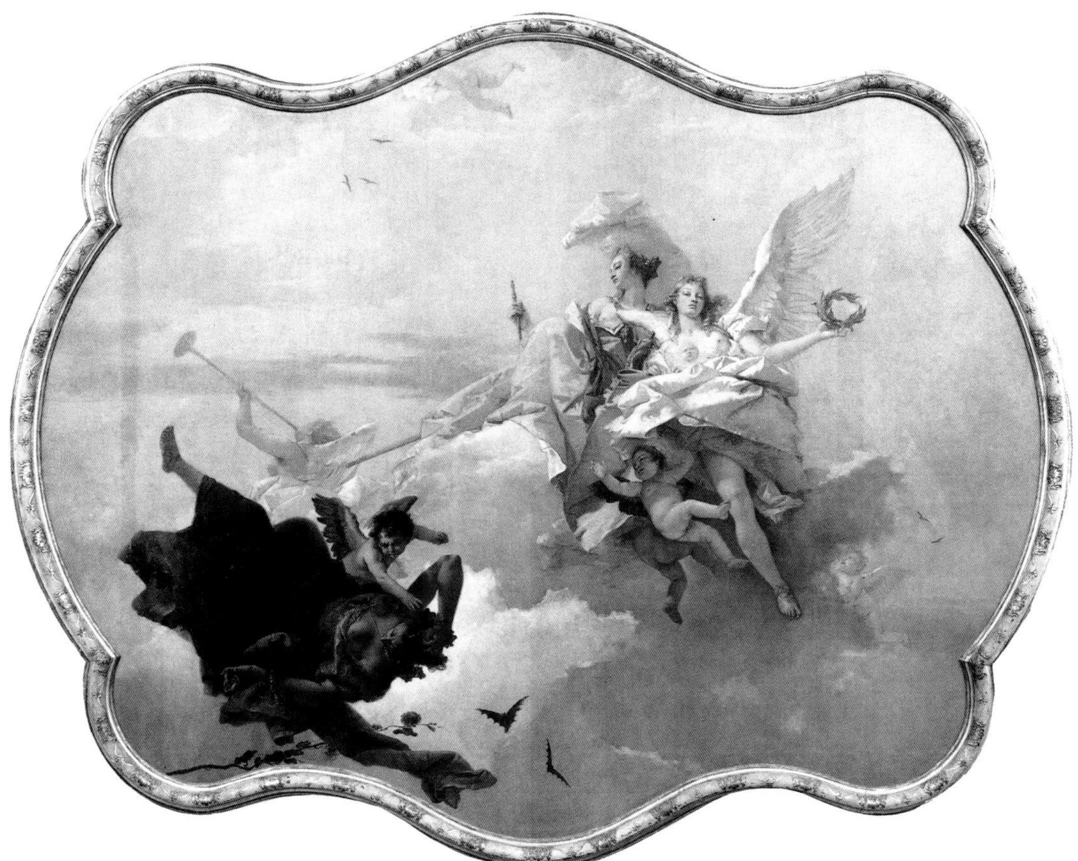

Fig. 52. *Nobility and Virtue Combating Ignorance*. Oil on canvas. The Norton Simon Foundation, Pasadena

but with trees that arch behind them and call attention to their presence, he underscored their tense surveillance of the lovers. The same amor who helped guide Armida to Rinaldo in Tiepolo's initial canvas reappears, shorn of his quiver and arrows, catapulting through the air. Still immobile but no longer asleep, Rinaldo is transfixed, his attention riveted upon Armida, just as hers had been fastened upon him when she first saw him on the ground. Her golden drapery flutters behind her like a cloth of majesty, and her white blouse, open wide in the other picture, now exposes only one breast, suggesting a new and surprising modesty on her part. The most dramatic change Tiepolo introduced is in Armida's expression: proud and aloof in the first scene, it is vulnerable here. Having bewitched Rinaldo, she is herself captivated by him and has unexpectedly fallen in love.

Rinaldo Abandoning Armida and *Rinaldo and Armida in the Garden* form a pair of disparate scenes in which the same four protagonists enact contrasting moments of rapture and despair. In Tasso's narrative, after Armida leaves Rinaldo alone in her garden, Carlo and Ubaldo reveal themselves to him. They hold up his reflective shield so that he can see how Armida has weakened and unmanned him—the incident pictured in one of the London canvases (fig. 49). The two soldiers remind him of Europe's war against Asia and urge him to take up arms against the enemy (16, st. 27–34). Tasso then recounts how Rinaldo is persuaded by his friends and is espied by his paramour as he escapes from the meandering labyrinths of her garden. She calls after the knight and pleads with him; his companions press him to ignore her supplications. Like Aeneas in Virgil's ancient epic, Rinaldo is torn between love and duty. Armida responds pitifully with yet more entreaties; in doing so, she is transformed into a tender lover who moves the reader deeply. Tiepolo also redefined his heroine in depicting this moment in the *Rinaldo Abandoning Armida*: he showed her with both arms raised in a plaintive gesture and head turned upward, beseeching the knight, and he painted her golden robe a darker and more burnished hue than it was in the first two canvases. Rinaldo, too, is altered: he is now standing rather than recumbent and has donned his armor and bronze-colored mantle (its white lining visible to the viewer, the cloak lies beneath the shield in the garden scene). The major difference between this scene and the earlier episodes is one of narrative focus, for here Tiepolo obliges the viewer to scrutinize Rinaldo and heed his momentous decision rather than delight in Armida and fall under her enchantments. The knight's choice is a difficult one. Tiepolo conveys Rinaldo's momentary vacillation through his pose and gesture but hints at the eventual outcome and the hero's impending departure with the fir tree angled to the right and his friend's arm pointing in the same direction, toward a boat that awaits the trio of soldiers.

Rinaldo and the Magician of Ascalona (17d), the final narrative work from Chicago, follows the London canvas that portrays Armida colluding with the Indian prince Adrastes after she has fled to the Asian camp to seek vengeance upon her former lover (fig. 50).[10] Tasso relates this episode (17, st. 43) and immediately thereafter tells that Rinaldo and his two companions arrive in Palestine, where, under a tree hung with weapons, they find the old man, or magician, of Ascalona (17, st. 58). The wizard shows the knight a shield, urging him to fix his gaze upon it, for he will see the feats of his ancestors reflected therein (17, st. 64–65). Instructed by the noble examples so revealed, Rinaldo feels impelled to battle the pagan enemy, thus serving the Christian cause and fulfilling his destiny. Tiepolo compressed narrative time in this final large painting. The soldiers appear to have disembarked in the Holy Land only moments before Rinaldo's meeting with the magician, as Carlo and Ubaldo look seaward to their boat, the same sort of vessel that had awaited them offshore in the previous painting. Rinaldo is again lost in thought, but unlike Hercules at the crossroads, he does not face a choice between vice and virtue. Rather, he ponders his military duties, Tiepolo clarifying the knight's new responsibilities by prominently displaying a large quiver and a plumed helmet in the foreground. To describe Rinaldo's resolve, for the first time in the series the painter portrayed him as animated and dynamic. He also presented the hero and the magician as monumental figures, larger and more imposing than any others in the quartet of paintings. Respectively authoritative and well proportioned, the old man and the young champion are pictorially assertive, concluding the cycle forcefully as if sounding insistent chords.

The shift from the amorous fable of a beautiful heroine and her lover shown in the first elements of the narrative sequence to the moralizing oration of teacher to student represented in the last is sudden and unexpected and has been criticized as ending "the story on a downbeat."[11] But that judgment overlooks the key reason for the commissioning of this episode, which, when taken into account, suggests that the unanticipated redirection of the plot constitutes a sharpening of focus on the part of both patron and painter. Even without knowing the identity of Tiepolo's patrician client and the precise nature of his tastes and aspirations, the modern viewer may well conjecture that this pictorial program was shaped by more than merely aesthetic or decorative considerations. That moral precepts lie behind its choice may at first seem questionable, if not actually doubtful. Tiepolo's perfumed romance of Armida and Rinaldo, his use of dazzling colored robes and draperies, his emphasis on magic, love, and exoticism, and his lack of concern for specifics of time and place all contribute to the impression that the cycle is frivolous in plan and only precariously related to reality: a tale of enchantment and adventure meant, at the very most, to delight a cultivated audience. But there is every reason to suspect that the owner of the Tasso series was motivated by goals as earnest as those that governed the patrons of almost all other large-scale ensembles of secular paintings in Venice during the first half of the eighteenth century.[12] These aims rested on time-honored assumptions that virtue and honor were the bedrock of noble and principled conduct. The *Gerusalemme liberata* is a Christian epic, and the ethical precepts it espouses are expressed throughout the narrative. All well-schooled Venetian patricians of the settecento were familiar with the work and its objectives. Moreover, Tiepolo insinuated that the protagonists of his series are exemplars of good or evil behavior as well as beautiful to behold. Viewers who follow his unfolding story on the superficial level of simple anecdote without recognizing that the dramatic changes the enchantress and the knight undergo express their moral education are as uncomprehending as those who misconstrue the majesty of Tiepolo's representations of the Virgin Mary as an indication of arrogance and aloofness rather than a sign of celestial prerogative.

Tiepolo introduced Armida, in *Rinaldo Enchanted by Armida*, as a glorious apparition; profiled against the skies, she is deified by her association with a magical flying chariot. Although enfolded in a golden drapery when she is next shown, in *Rinaldo and Armida in the Garden*, the alluring enchantress is somewhat less exalted, for Tiepolo has moved her to the ground, as Tasso required. In her final appearance, in *Rinaldo Abandoning Armida*, she is utterly earthbound and vanquished. In addition to these alterations in Armida's position, Tiepolo's patron would have noticed that the artist structured the sorceress's arms, legs, and head differently in each work, to indicate developments in the drama and shifts in her emotional state. He would also have seen that changes in the configurations of Rinaldo's head, arms, and legs in the various episodes redefined the hero's character and his role in the story. Thus, Rinaldo's condition improves from canvas to canvas, at the same time that Armida's physical state and moral standing deteriorate. The knight's progression through the stages of the narrative is, in effect, a journey from infancy to maturity. First slumbering like a babe, Rinaldo next becomes an awestruck lad; he personifies youthful hesitancy when he abandons Armida, and finally, at the end, he has evolved into an upright and responsible warrior.

In sum, we are persuaded that Rinaldo has not merely renounced Armida to follow his historical destiny in the way Aeneas deserted Dido to found Rome; for, in Tiepolo's cycle as in Tasso's poem, the knight has increased his spiritual worth through his transformation into a virtuous soldier ready to battle evil. Indeed, a more appropriate comparison than the one traditionally drawn between Rinaldo and Virgil's stalwart Trojan can be made with a figure created in the same century as Tiepolo's Tasso Room, that is, Mozart and Emanuel Schikaneder's Tamino, hero of *The Magic Flute*. The similarities between Rinaldo and Tamino are remarkable: each is recognized for his beauty as he sleeps in the opening scene of his respective love story; soon thereafter both become infatuated with the women they desire; the two then undergo trials that test their moral purpose, overcome their doubts, and effect the necessary renunciations; finally, after instruction from a wise and all-seeing mentor, they attain fulfillment.[13] In response to objections that Tiepolo's paintings are no more than a seductively rendered romantic fable, we can counter that this is true only if the canvases are considered as discrete entities. *The Magic Flute* can also be enjoyed merely as a sequence of individually enchanting elements—in this case arias, duets, and trios—but its true greatness becomes clear only when it is appreciated as a musical totality. Significantly, just as Mozart's opera culminates in a triumph over human travail achieved through Sarastro's enlightening wisdom, Tiepolo's pictorial cycle concludes with a scene in which Rinaldo heeds the magician's moral precepts that urge him toward spiritual renewal. The salient point here is that Tiepolo's delightful sequence, like Mozart's sublime opera, captivates its audience at the same time that it asserts an ethical imperative.

That Tiepolo and his patron indeed saw virtue and moral regeneration as the theme of the Rinaldo cycle is substantiated by the three nonnarrative works now in Rome and Pasadena that were once united with the eight paintings in Chicago and London. Presumably these ovals, which show male and female satyrs, decorated the Tasso Room as overdoors. Tiepolo's use of satyrs in relation to the Rinaldo-Armida romance may perplex modern viewers, for such creatures are absent from the *Gerusalemme liberata*. The artist's contemporaries, however, would have understood their meaning. But rather than identifying the half-goat, half-human figures with the poem's "constant preoccupation with sorcery, with good and bad magicians, and with benign and malevolent sorceresses," as a modern writer has done,[14] they more likely would have seen them as references to the bestial in nature. According to classical mythology, satyrs roamed wild in the landscape of legendary antiquity, always seeking gratification for their passions and cravings. In this sense they express the immoral and self-indulgent love Armida and Rinaldo delighted in, an ardor that dissipates as the hero reforms. However, Tiepolo depicted the satyrs not in the pursuit of physical pleasure but quietly seated on the ground and accompanied by putti, draperies, and a motley of objects. Accommodating the disposition of these elements to the standard horizontal format of overdoors, he conceived the satyrs as weary counterparts to the indolent figures of Armida and Rinaldo that appear in three of the Chicago canvases. Lassitude mirrors languor, on the level of parable rather than storytelling. Drawn from the tradition of classical poetry, the satyrs must be read as moral emblems defining the narrative canvases that hung below them at the same time they contravened the noble allegories that almost surely were represented on the ceiling above.[15]

It is highly probable but not certain that the Tasso Room was indeed crowned with a ceiling painting, as were most of Tiepolo's secular decorations of the 1740s.[16] Knox proposed the beautiful *Nobility and Virtue Combating Ignorance* (fig. 52) from the Palazzo Dolfin Manin as the most likely candidate for this ceiling, which would have represented the pictorial culmination of the sequence.[17] Although his theory is problematic, it is worth considering the effect that this, or a similar ceiling canvas, would have had on the meaning of the cycle. The personifications in the Dolfin Manin canvas would lend both explicit and implicit thematic relationships with Tasso's narrative. Rinaldo's mastery over himself and his denial of the temptress could be seen as manifestations of the allegorical triumph of Nobility and Virtue. At the same time the overthrow of Ignorance could readily refer, in grander and less personal terms than those of the Rinaldo and Armida story, to Christianity's ascendancy over Islam: a struggle not only at the core of the *Gerusalemme liberata* but also at the center of Venice's foreign policy since 1453, when the Ottoman Turks began to rival the Venetians in the eastern Mediterranean. We might even imagine details such as the conspicuous red blooms hurtling down beneath Ignorance as an allusion to Armida and her magical use of flowers to enchain Rinaldo and enchant him in her garden.[18]

When Tiepolo returned to Venice in 1740–41 after frescoing the vault of the *salone* of the Palazzo Clerici in Milan and undertook the Tasso cycle, he embarked on the most remarkable decade of his professional life. Although he later painted unique pictorial complexes in and around Venice, and in Würzburg and Madrid, no other period of his career boasts an array of brilliant achievements comparable to those of the 1740s. The monumental canvases for the parish church of Verolanuova, the nine ceiling paintings of the Scuola

Grande dei Carmini (see fig. 66), and the immense fresco on the vault of the church of the Scalzi (no. 48a, b) express the conviction of a deeply pious man committed to exalting his faith through his art. Similarly, the fresco decorations in the *saloni* of Villa Cordellina (fig. 40) and Palazzo Labia (frontis., p. 28, fig. 43) bring to life the secular splendor, triumphs, and royal prerogatives of history's leaders. Although part of that impressive succession of paintings, the Tasso Room also stands distinct from it. Concerned neither to inculcate religious belief nor to re-create the noble past, in this cycle Tiepolo sought instead to envision a moment of intoxicating but enfeebling love. That Tiepolo and Tasso before him considered such infatuation perfidious may at first be obscured by the visual and poetic beguilements they offer. But Tiepolo's lofty conception of character and moral sense are among the foundations of his art, and never more significantly than in his beautiful essay on Rinaldo's growth from slavish admirer to independent hero.[19]

WLB

NOTES

1. Knox 1978, pp. 53–72.
2. Biblioteca del Seminario Patriarcale, Venice, Busta 788, f. 13.
3. Knox 1992, pp. 4–25.
4. See, for example, Knox [1976].
5. Thomas (1969) was the first to propose that the paintings in Chicago were executed in the 1740s. Levey (1971, pp. 226–27) has suggested, however, that the four canvases in London date to about 1757.
6. Ferrara 1985, pp. 214–23, 234–45, 286–89. Late sixteenth and early seventeenth-century Genoese fresco programs based on Tasso's story include Lazzaro Tavarone's sequence in Palazzo Grimaldi and Bernardo Castello's in Palazzo De Franchi and Palazzo Imperiale di Campetto; Castello also executed one in Villa Imperiale Scassi in nearby Sampierdarena. The first aristocratic French interiors with decorations inspired by Tasso's poem were royal apartments: Ambroise Dubois worked on a cycle of canvases for the apartments of Marie de Médicis at Fontainebleau and subsequently collaborated with other artists to create a Tasso room for the queen in the Palais du Louvre in Paris. Among other French examples of Tasso-inspired decorations are sixteen paintings on the Rinaldo and Armida episode painted for a Parisian *hôtel* by Simon Vouet during the 1630s.
7. For the eighteenth-century French examples and for Guardi's paintings, see Knox 1978, pp. 49–53, 89–95. See Pallucchini 1968, nos. 238–39, for a pair of Italian decorative panels depicting Rinaldo and Armida. Formerly in the Wrightsman Collection, these two paintings were sold in Milan in November 1988 (*Giornale dell'arte*, February 1989) but appeared on the market again in November 1991, in the annual exhibition in Palazzo Strozzi, Florence.
8. Knox (1978, pp. 53–72) readily admits that no such hall can be found in Palazzo Dolfin Manin. Nor could the ensemble have been organized according to Knox's scheme in any of the existing rooms on the palace's *piano nobile*: because of the location of the windows, it would have been necessary to hang three of the canvases Knox presumed formed a triptych as separate entities. For Tiepolo's earlier triptychlike arrangements, see his central frescoes in the gallery of the Arcivescovado (Patriarchal Palace), Udine (Gemin and Pedrocco 1993, no. 82; for a photograph of the ensemble, see Barcham 1992, p. 55), and the three scenes of Christ's Passion in the church of S. Alvise, Venice (no. 31, figs, 69, 70). Six of the canvases in Palazzo Dolfin at S. Pantalon, Venice (no. 12a, b, fig. 33; no. 12c–e), were hung in two groups of three but are not, strictly speaking, triptychs, nor is the series of three pictures Tiepolo painted for Palazzo Sandi, Venice, because the two canvases (no. 9a, b) that complement the larger *Discovery of Achilles* (fig. 30) did not hang on the same wall as that work.
9. Tasso 1581 (1973 ed.), 16, st. 17: "egli è in grembo a la donna, essa a l'erbetta."
10. Knox (1978, p. 62) notes that the London canvas *Two Orientals Seated under a Tree* (fig. 51) seems unrelated to any moment in the *Gerusalemme liberata*; Levey (1971, p. 227) even questions the authorship of this painting.
11. Knox 1978, p. 62.
12. The most glaring example of a commission that was not impelled by such high-minded principles is Tiepolo's own cycle in the Palazzo Labia, Venice.
13. It is clear at the beginning of *The Magic Flute* that the Three Ladies have chosen Tamino to reclaim Pamina because he is "ein holder Jüngling"; Tamino's first passion for the princess, inspired by only a small portrait, is, like Rinaldo's infatuation with Armida, superficial. The three trials that Sarastro imposes on the prince and princess bring them to mutual understanding and the Temple of Isis.
14. Knox 1978, p. 65.
15. The themes of the wall and ceiling decorations carried out by Tiepolo and Nicolò Bambini for the *salone* in Palazzo Sandi (see no. 9a, b) show a similar relationship. On the Palazzo Sandi decorations, see Aikema 1986; Knox 1993; and this author's discussion in a forthcoming Italian publication devoted to eighteenth-century Venetian painting.
16. Villa Cordellina, Montecchio Maggiore, Vicenza, on the ceiling of whose *salone* Tiepolo frescoed another *Triumph of Virtue and Nobility over Ignorance* (Gemin and Pedrocco 1993, nos. 262–74); Palazzo Barbarigo, Venice (ibid., nos. 329–43); Villa Contarini-Pisani, Mira (ibid., nos. 360–63); Palazzo Labia, Venice (ibid., nos. 370–77); Villa Cornaro, Merlengo (ibid., nos. 398–402).
17. Knox 1978, pp. 65–68. Succi (in Milan 1992) has contested Knox's point, citing the lack of documentary evidence linking the Dolfin Manin ceiling to the Tasso Room (see text above). He charges, furthermore, that because it presumably celebrated the Manin-Grimaldi marriage of 1748 and coincided with contemporary structural work in the palace, the painting from Palazzo Dolfin Manin must date to 1748 and so cannot be part of a commission of about 1742. But despite the association between the ceiling and those events, which is itself only hypothetical, there is no evidence that the ceiling was actually executed in 1748. Moreover, should documents eventually prove that the canvas was indeed painted then or slightly earlier, in 1746–47, it is still possible that it was executed as the conclusion to the Tasso series and was either a belated addition to the cycle or a work delivered late by the artist. The most famous example of Tiepolo's tardy completion of a large-scale decorative ensemble, in fact, dates to this very period. He delivered the lateral canvases for the ceiling of the Scuola Grande dei Carmini, Venice, in 1743 but did not finish the central canvas until 1749; see Niero 1976–77. Gemin and Pedrocco (1993, no. 381) support Succi.
18. As was his usual practice, Tiepolo drew his personifications from Cesare Ripa's *Iconologia*. See Ripa 1603 (1992 ed., pp. 180 [Ignorance], 314–15 [Nobility], 471–72 [Virtue]). Ripa calls for poppies to circle the head of Ignorance as a garland (p. 180): "in capo haverà una ghirlanda di Papavero." For the association between Armida and flowers in Tiepolo's *Triumph of Flora* (Gemin and Pedrocco 1993, no. 307), see Barcham 1993, p. 77 n. 18.
19. For Tiepolo's drawings for the Tasso paintings, see Knox 1978, pp. 72–84.

PROVENANCE, 17a–d:
Purportedly Count Serbelloni, Palazzo Pisani a S. Stefano, Venice; Giulio Cartier, Genoa (before 1908); Galerie Sedelmeyer, Paris (by 1913); Charles Deering, Chicago (until 1925)

REFERENCES:
Molmenti 1909, pp. 145–46; Sack 1910, p. 236; Morassi 1943, p. 35; Morassi 1955a, pp. 150–51; Art Institute 1961, pp. 448–49; Morassi 1962, p. 8; Levey 1963, p. 294; Pallucchini 1968, nos. 221A–D; Thomas 1969; Rizzi 1971, nos. 146, 225; Udine 1971, no. 63; Knox 1978; Levey 1986, p. 238; Gemin and Pedrocco 1993, pp. 358–59, nos. 288–91; London 1994, no. 90; Knorn 1995, pp. 102–7; Venice 1995b, nos. 270, 272

PROVENANCE, 17e:
Julius Böhler, Munich (until 1911); Galleria Nazionale d'Arte Antica, Rome (from 1911)

REFERENCES:
Hermanin 1912, p. 369; Venice 1929, p. 61; Morassi 1962, p. 45; Pallucchini 1968, no. 133; Knox 1978, pp. 64–65; Gemin and Pedrocco 1993, p. 360, no. 292

PROVENANCE, 17f, g:
Galerie Cailleux, Paris (until 1980); Norton Simon, Pasadena (from 1980)

REFERENCES:
Knox 1966, p. 584; Paris 1971, nos. 235–36; Paris 1974, nos. 4, 5; Knox 1978, pp. 64–65; Gemin and Pedrocco 1993, p. 360, nos. 293–94

18. *Time Uncovering Truth*

18. Time Uncovering Truth
Ca. 1743
254 × 340 cm (100 × 133⅞ in.)
Museo Civico, Vicenza (A.341)

PROVENANCE:
Carlo Cordellina, Vicenza or Venice (ca. 1743–94); Ludovico Cordellina, Vicenza (1794–1800); by descent, Niccolò Bissari, Vicenza (1800–1829); by descent, Collegio Convitto Cordellina, Palazzo Cordellina, Vicenza (1829–1934)

REFERENCES:
Arslan 1934, p. 10; Fasolo 1940, p. 112, no. 341; Venice 1946, p. 199, no. 326; Valcanover 1958, p. 257; Barbieri 1962, pp. 238–39; Pallucchini 1968, p. 108, no. 148; Puppi 1968a, pp. 212–14; Ballarin 1982, p. 169; Schiavo in Vicenza 1990, pp. 334, 337; Gemin and Pedrocco 1993, p. 363, no. 300

This luminous oval ceiling canvas, in which the elderly Time has uncovered youthful Truth while casting out Lies, was painted for Tiepolo's great patron in Vicenza, the lawyer Carlo Cordellina (1703–1794). It came to the museum in Vicenza from the grandiose palace that Cordellina built late in his life on the Contra' Riale in Vicenza. However, as Fasolo first noted, it could not have been painted for that location, as the construction of the palace did not begin until 1776, some years after the artist died. He suggested that it was commissioned instead for the Villa Cordellina at Montecchio Maggiore, the main *salone* of which was decorated by Tiepolo (fig. 40).

A well-known letter to Algarotti shows that Tiepolo was at work on the frescoed ceiling of the principal room at Montecchio Maggiore in October 1743, and it is generally agreed that the *Time Uncovering Truth* dates to about the same time. In addition, its subject continues the allegorical celebration of virtue found in the frescoed ceiling, in which Virtue and Nobility triumph over Ignorance. Therefore, it may well be that the canvas was installed in the villa, perhaps inserted directly into the stuccowork of one of the rooms. If this indeed was the case, it might explain why *Time Uncovering Truth* was not listed in an 1829 inventory drawn up by the family's heir, Niccolò Bissari: the picture would have seemed part of the decorations of the villa rather than movable property.[1]

Cordellina may, however, have intended the painting for a different residence, for he bought and renovated two other homes in the 1740s. Much of his time was spent in Venice, where he had his legal practice, and in 1743 he acquired a palace on the Campo S. Maurizio from the Molin family. This too was a possible destination for the canvas: he lived here for many years, adding a building to the original property in 1766.[2] The combined houses were sold to Gabriele Stae in 1792, when the ceiling could have been moved to Vicenza.[3] In Vicenza, Cordellina owned a house on the Contra' de Piancoli, and in 1740 he reported to the authorities that he had acquired three small adjacent houses and intended to renovate the whole complex. A letter from one of his sons to the architect Ottone Calderari and a possible project drawing by Calderari suggest that a major rebuilding of this palace was considered as late as 1770.[4] Tiepolo's ceiling could easily have been meant for the enlarged Contra' de Piancoli house, for only about 1774 did Cordellina shift his focus to the new site on the Contra' Riale.

Nor is the iconography of the scene necessarily tied to the scheme at Montecchio Maggiore; rather, it reflects the patron's values in general. The attributes of the figures are taken from traditional sources such as Cesare Ripa's *Iconologia*: Truth with the sun in one hand, a palm wreath in the other, and the globe at her feet; Time as a winged old man holding a scythe, with a serpent underfoot and an hourglass. Truth is nude, literally unveiled by Time, and she has been brought into the light, symbolized by the sun. The meaning of the allegory underscored the reputation for virtue that Cordellina strove to attain, mirroring the description of him in the rather eulogistic biography written by his friend G. B. Fontanella in 1801. In extolling Cordellina's qualities as a lawyer, to those of eloquence and intelligence Fontanella added "honesty without equal and a complete absence of venality," as well as powers used "not to deceive, but to persuade correctly."[5] It is likely that Tiepolo's allegorical frescoes in the villa at Montecchio Maggiore allude to Cordellina's virtues and that works with similar significance were placed in the patron's other residences. This appears especially probable because Cordellina seems to have been much more interested in commissioning meaningful and unified decoration for the spaces in which he worked and entertained than in amassing a heterogeneous collection of paintings.

Tiepolo painted ceilings on the subject of Time Uncovering Truth for the Villa Loschi al Biron, near Vicenza, in 1734 and the Palazzo Barbarigo in Venice in 1744–45 (see no. 20). The Cordellina canvas and the Barbarigo ceiling share many similar elements, but in the latter work Time is shown in the act of unveiling Truth. Recent restorations of the Palazzo dei Conti Valle in Vicenza have revealed another ceiling by Tiepolo on this same theme, close in conception to that of the Palazzo Barbarigo and also probably dating from the mid-1740s.[6] The Cordellina painting stands out for the care with which the composition has been structured and for the brilliance of its brushwork, apparent in the head and torso of Time and other details. It shares with the best works of these years—such as the Tasso series

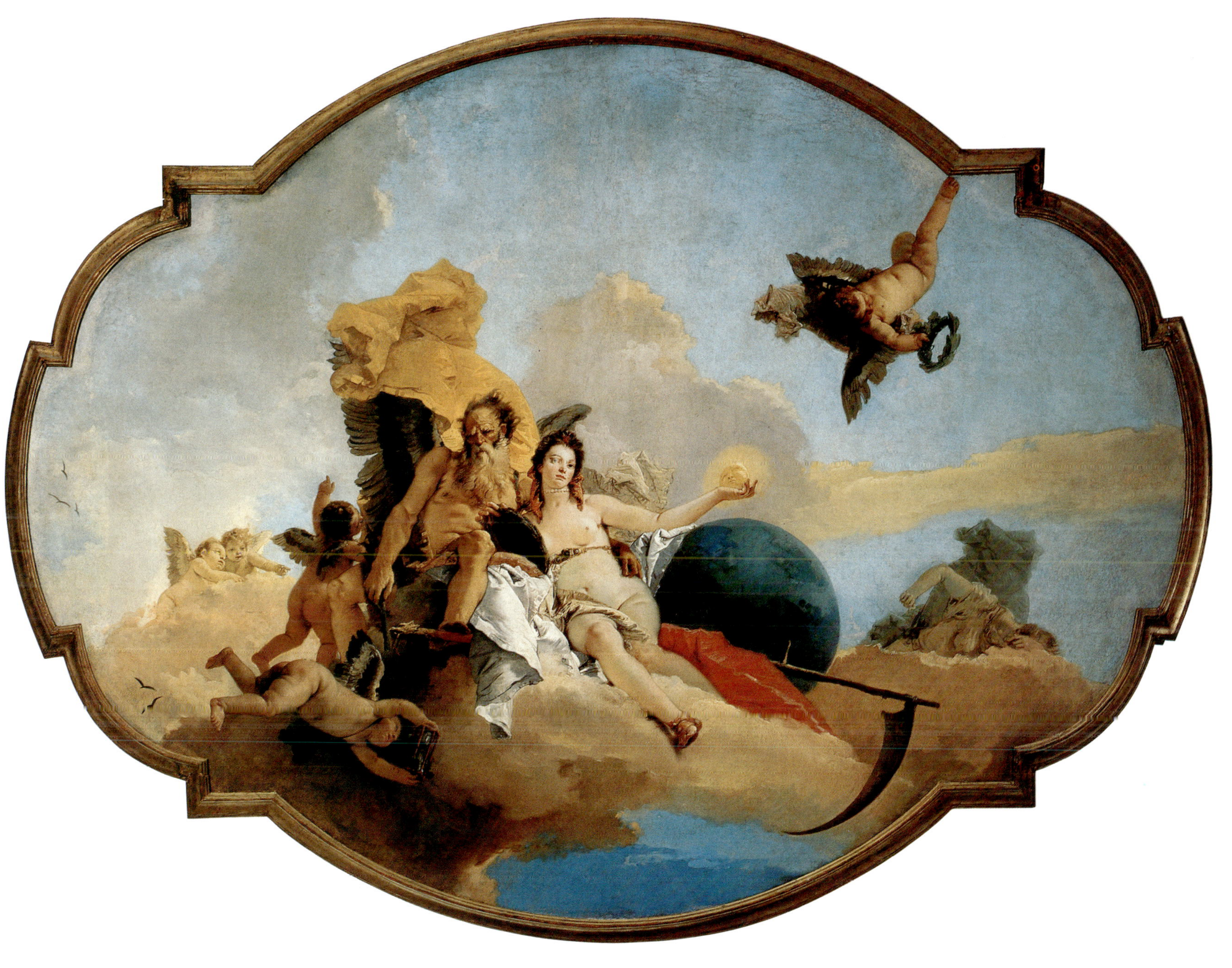

now in Chicago (no. 17a–d)—a wonderful decorative bravura, embodied in the drapery that flies up behind Time, and a lighthearted quality, epitomized in the darting putti. Although the picture was in a fragile state when it entered the Museo Civico, Vicenza, in 1934, a restoration of the 1950s revealed its high quality, which was widely recognized upon its inclusion in an exhibition of 1958 in Munich devoted to the European Rococo.

AB

Notes

1. Schiavo in Vicenza 1990, pp. 334, 337.
2. Battilotti in Vicenza 1990, p. 303.
3. See Puppi (1968a, pp. 213–14), who implies erroneously that it is a detached fresco.
4. Ibid., p. 213, and Barbieri 1987, p. 159.
5. See Menegozzo 1990, p. 45.
6. Sgarbi, Veller, and Cova 1986, fig. 33.

19. *The Banquet of Cleopatra*

19. The Banquet of Cleopatra
Ca. 1742–43
50.5 × 69 cm (19⅞ × 12¼ in.)
Musée Cognacq-Jay, Paris

Behind this small gem of a work extends the shadow of a man central in Tiepolo's art during the 1740s: Francesco Algarotti. In May 1743 Algarotti, a cultivated Venetian in the service of Augustus III, king of Poland and elector of Saxony, returned from Germany to his native Venice to buy paintings by old and modern masters for the royal collections in Dresden. Tiepolo was among the several "moderns" Algarotti commissioned. The collaboration between the two Venetians could not have taken place at a more felicitous moment for either man. The thirty-one-year-old Algarotti, handsome and charming, and steeped in the tradition of Italian humanism, possessed the prestige and dignity of a foreign diplomat; he spoke several languages and had traveled in France, England, Germany, and Russia. The forty-seven-year-old Tiepolo was, like Algarotti, at the summit of his career and profession. Working in both fresco and oils, he had completed monumental paintings treating stories from Christian and biblical history and scenes of classical mythology and allegory; throughout northern Italy he enjoyed public acclaim as an artist without peer. Tiepolo and Algarotti's business partnership developed quickly into a relationship characterized by warm rapport, mutual respect, and shared interests. This small *Banquet of Cleopatra*, which Algarotti owned and kept until his death, commemorates their friendship.

On the last day of January 1744, Algarotti wrote Count Heinrich von Brühl, his patron in Dresden and chief minister of the Saxon government, that he had seen an unfinished painting in Tiepolo's studio that the artist had begun for "others" but was willing to complete for Augustus. That picture is the large *Banquet of Cleopatra* now in the National Gallery of Victoria, Melbourne (fig. 53); the Paris *Banquet of Cleopatra* served as the *modello* for it. In the event that the larger painting was still unfinished in January 1744, the Paris picture was likely conceived and executed earlier in the decade, soon after Tiepolo returned in 1740 from Milan, where he had frescoed a ceiling in the Palazzo Clerici.[1] The Paris *Banquet* was thus the very first of almost a dozen large and small paintings by Tiepolo dealing with the romance of the queen of Egypt and Mark Antony. In about 1745–46, after he executed the Paris painting and the Melbourne version, he frescoed the *Banquet* along with the *Meeting of Antony and Cleopatra* in the *salone* of Palazzo Labia, Venice (frontis., p. 28; fig. 38); and a year or so later he designed pictures of the same subjects (one dated 1747) for an unknown Russian client (Museum, Archangelskoye). A *modello* exists for each

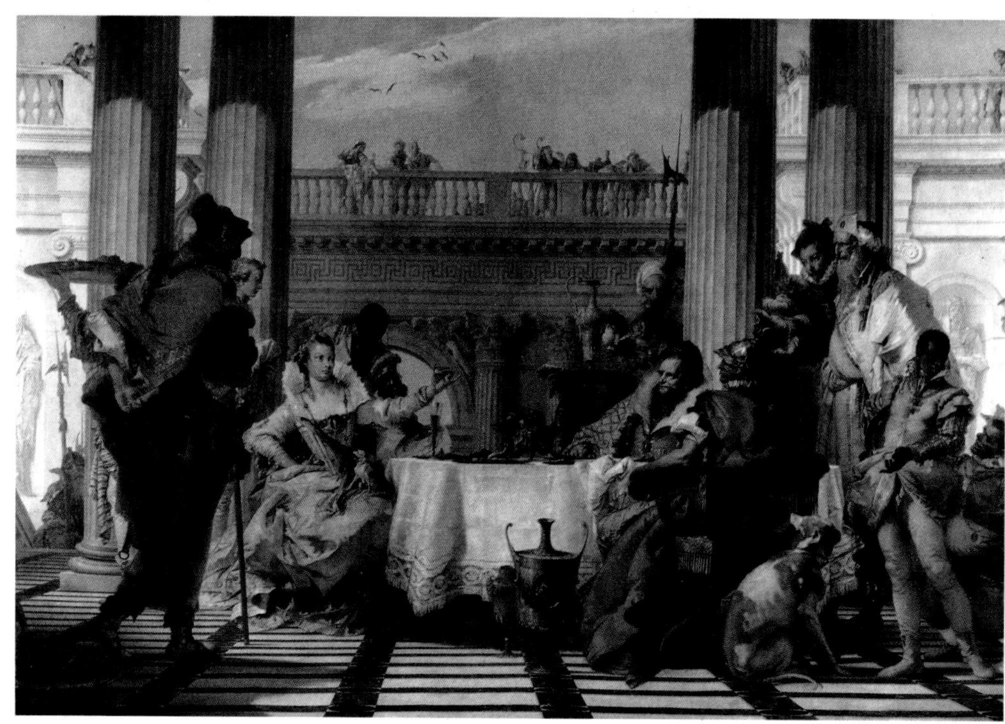

Fig. 53. *The Banquet of Cleopatra*. Oil on canvas. National Gallery of Victoria, Melbourne, Felton Bequest, 1932

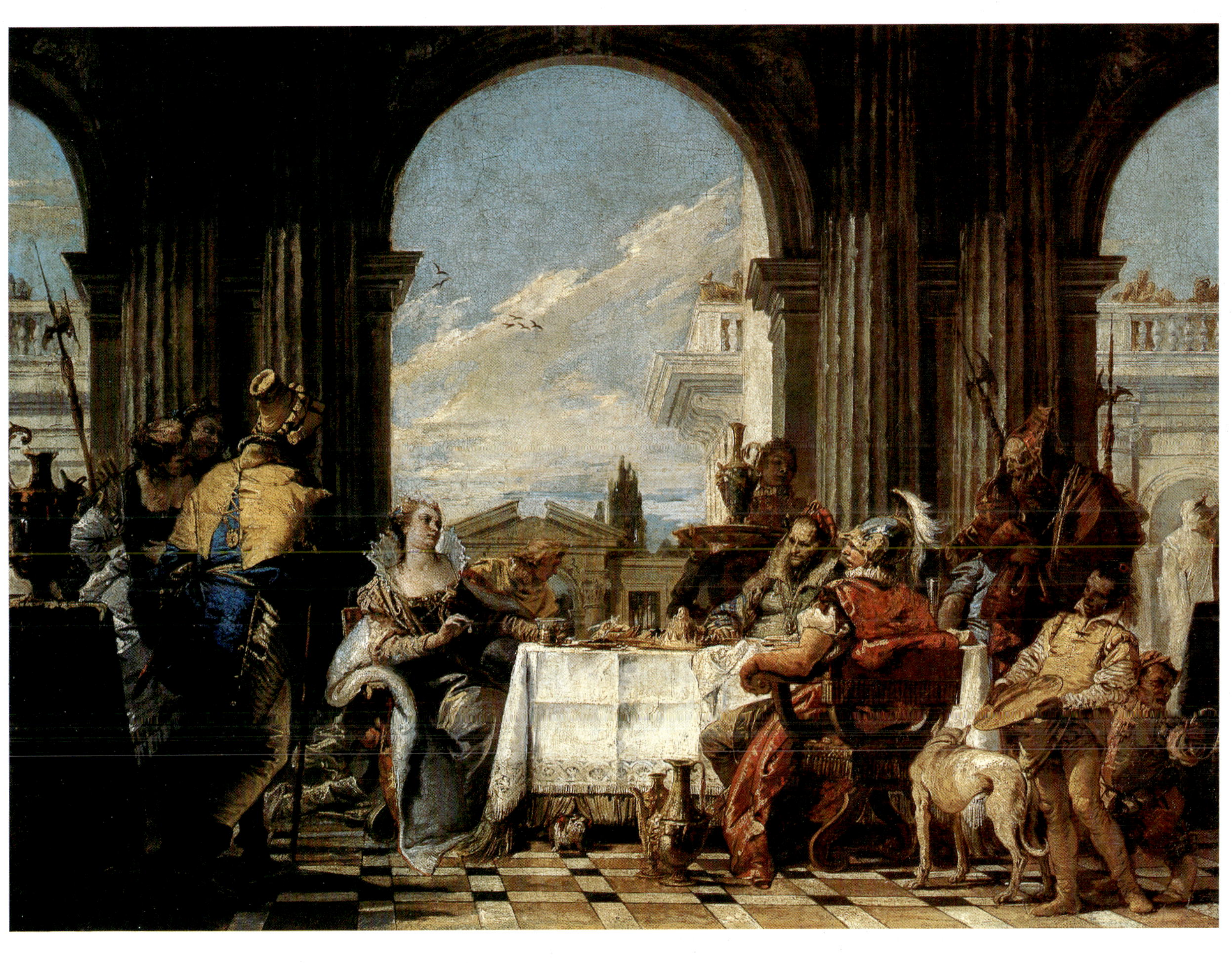

PROVENANCE:
Joseph Smith, Venice (before 1744); Francesco Algarotti, Venice (1744–64); Cosimo Mari, Venice (from 1764); Princess Mathilde Bonaparte, Paris (until 1904; sale, Galerie Georges Petit, Paris, 17 May 1904, lot 68); Ernest Cognacq, Paris (1904–28)

REFERENCES:
Sack 1910, p. 82; Molmenti 1911, p. 199; Fry 1933, p. 132; Levey 1955; Haskell 1958; Morassi 1962, p. 39; Knox 1965; Levey 1965; Pallucchini 1968, no. 155; Knox 1974; Burollet 1980, pp. 192–96; Haskell 1980, pp. 352–53; Knox 1980b; Levey 1986, pp. 130–32; Gemin and Pedrocco 1993, p. 368, no. 308a

of these four very grand paintings, but none is executed with the delicacy and finish of the Paris picture, which is less like a sketch than a finished work.[2]

Tiepolo drew the story of Cleopatra's love affair with the Roman general from three ancient sources: Pliny the Elder's *Natural History*, Plutarch's *Lives*, and Cassius Dio Cocceianus's *History of Rome*. Cleopatra and Antony met in Cilicia about 40 B.C.; during a feast they wagered about which one could offer a more expensive banquet. Losing no time and taking no chances, the wily Cleopatra dissolved one of her matchless pearls by dropping it into vinegar in the course of her banquet. Antony's coconsul, Lucius Plancus, immediately judged her the winner of the bet. She had, however, lost a pearl; yet in recompense she gained a Roman lover, who—we must imagine—dissolved in her arms as the precious gem had liquefied in her goblet. The Paris *Banquet* captures the extravagant melodrama enacted by the two lovers, Cleopatra holding the vinegar while her guests and the court watch incredulously. In the painting later sent to Dresden, Tiepolo altered a number of elements, the most important of which are Cleopatra's gestures and the surrounding architecture. The queen is now poised, ready to let the pearl drop into the vinegar, and the moment is more pregnant with suspense. The architectural setting, however, is more imposing in the *modello* than it is in the final version. But the real beauty of the Paris *Banquet* lies in its jewel-like surface, for the quickness of the brushwork and the near-liquid application of paint create a sparkling brilliance.

The Paris *Banquet* is distinguished not only by its aesthetic appeal; it is also the most historically significant of the entire group of Cleopatra paintings, for it is the first to illustrate Tiepolo's reliance on the art of Paolo Veronese. Although many modern critics have condemned Tiepolo's use of motifs and stylistic quotations from his great sixteenth-century Venetian predecessor, his contemporaries praised such artistic practice because it preserved pictorial tradition, in which they firmly believed.[3] The earliest relevant surviving comment is one made in 1736 by a foreign visitor to Venice, Count Carl Gustaf Tessin. Recommending the forty-year-old painter to the Swedish court as a possible decorator for a ceiling in the royal palace in Stockholm, Tessin wrote that "Tiepolo is a follower [votary] of Paul Veronese"; his paintings are opulent and "richly dressed," he maintained, and wondered if this is not "la grande mode."[4] Depending for their general composition as well as their architectural setting on such works by Veronese as the *Feast in the House of Levi* (Gallerie dell'Accademia, Venice) and the *Marriage at Cana* (Musée du Louvre, Paris), both of which Tiepolo must have known firsthand, the Dresden/Melbourne and Paris versions of the *Banquet of Cleopatra* confirm Tessin's remark. That Tiepolo turned to Veronese's luxuriously furnished banqueting scenes to suggest Egyptian-Roman majesty should not be surprising to modern viewers, given the firm anchoring of his art in the Venetian past. Nor is it unexpected that the style that attracted Tessin should captivate Algarotti; both were agents for northern courts seeking a modern Venetian painter capable of reviving, as the Swede so aptly put it, "la grande mode." Tessin and Algarotti, moreover, were not the only men seduced by Tiepolo's Veronesian taste for pictorial opulence. So too, of course, was the original patron of the Dresden/Melbourne *Banquet*, the man who forfeited the painting to Augustus III and for whose commission Tiepolo had evidently executed the Paris *modello*. Probably he was Joseph Smith, a longtime English resident in Venice who was named consul to the republic in 1744 and whose collection of paintings, including many by Veronese, filled his palace on the Grand Canal, near the Rialto Bridge.[5] Like Tessin and the repatriated Algarotti, Smith came from the North, and he probably conceived of the local pictorial tradition largely in terms of Veronese, the only artist whose painting simulates the architecture of Venice and breathes its light and color. Tiepolo's modern interpretation of Veronese's scenic extravagance must have entranced Smith for the same reasons it did Tessin and Algarotti.[6]

Algarotti's particular fascination with the *Banquet of Cleopatra* derived from more than the work's dependence on Veronese's painterly banquets. His admiration was founded as well on his belief in Tiepolo's unique status in the Venetian artistic tradition, which he expressed in a letter to Brühl. Algarotti recognized that the lavish costumes and magnificent settings of the *Banquet* were debts Tiepolo owed to Veronese. But to his mind Tiepolo had corrected his famous predecessor, normalizing his "bizzarria," as it were, so that Veronese's "belle Mascherate," or beautiful masquerades, were happily absent from the *Banquet*. Furthermore, Algarotti made a case for the nobility and classical balance of the ancient architecture Tiepolo represented in the work and for the historically apt inclusion of the statues of Isis and Serapis in the background of the *modello* and of the small sphinx in the lower left-hand corner of the version sold to Augustus. According to Algarotti, these elements demonstrated that Tiepolo was not a typical local artist but one of "pittoresca erudizione," pictorial erudition or sophistication, which he associated with the Roman school of painting but found lacking in the Venetian.[7] Algarotti concluded that his friend Tiepolo transcended the Venetian tradition and ranked alongside the classical artist Nicolas Poussin, whose own paintings boasted *pittoresca erudizione* a century before Tiepolo's did. Confused and mistaken as this assessment may seem today, Algarotti's basic tenet that Tiepolo's art conformed to tradition cannot be faulted.

Algarotti and Tiepolo enjoyed a friendship that extended even to sharing exercises in drawing and printmaking. Together they produced several etchings of heads and decorative motifs, some of which are clearly linked to details in both the Dresden / Melbourne and Paris *Banquet* pictures.[8] On his own, Algarotti also composed works showing groups of archaeologically correct ancient vases, and he may be responsible for the antique-looking urn so conspicuously present in the Dresden / Melbourne painting (and very different from the less obtrusive version in the Paris canvas). But most of the time he spent with Tiepolo was more likely devoted to talking about art rather than to creating it. Tiepolo himself informs us of that in a letter he wrote to Algarotti on 26 October 1743, from the elegant Villa Cordellina, near Vicenza, where he was executing frescoes: "I swear I enjoy spending one day in your company and talking about painting more than I do the delights of this villa, which—believe me—are far from few."[9] For both Venetians, time-honored tradition was the bedrock from which greatness developed. The Paris *Banquet* is testimony to that belief in pictorial tradition, to the friendship the two men shared during the 1740s, and to Algarotti's love for Tiepolo's great art.

WLB

NOTES

1. Gemin and Pedrocco 1993, no. 237, and Sohm 1984.
2. For the paintings in Venice and Archangelskoye, see Gemin and Pedrocco 1993, nos. 375–76, 379–80, and for a version of the *Banquet* in a private collection, Milan, see ibid., no. 309.
3. Sohm 1990 and Lenz 1996.
4. Sirèn 1902, p. 108, quoted in Sohm 1990, p. 90, for Tessin's letter of 16 June 1736 to Carl Hårleman, the architect of the royal palace in Stockholm: "Il est sectataire de Paul Véronèse."
5. Vivian 1971. In 1743 Pietro Monaco published a collection of fifty-five prints after paintings with sacred stories; the series included Tiepolo's *Banquet of Cleopatra*, which masqueraded, without the famous pearl, as the *Banquet of Nabal* (1 Samuel 25.36). Monaco's print identifies the painting's owner as Joseph Smith.
6. Why then did Smith cede the work to Augustus III? One can only speculate whether, in his new role as consul from the Court of Saint James's, Smith was under official pressure to do so or, perhaps, that the very able and diplomatic Algarotti persuaded him through flattery, by associating the Englishman's taste and discrimination with that of the royal court in Dresden. Algarotti also might well have offered a very grand sum of money to Smith, who was well known as the "merchant of Venice."
7. Algarotti n.d.
8. Succi in Gorizia 1985, nos. 62–63.
9. Quoted in Menegozzo 1990, p. 50.

20. *Virtue and Nobility Triumphing over Ignorance*

***20. Virtue and Nobility Triumphing over Ignorance**
1744–45
280 x 420 cm (110¼ x 165⅜ in.)
Museo del Settecento Veneziano, Ca' Rezzonico, Venice

This ceiling was painted for the Palazzo Barbarigo at S. Maria del Giglio in Venice and was acquired by the Musei Civici Veneziani from the counts Donà dalle Rose in 1935; since that time it has been installed in the Ca' Rezzonico.

According to documents published by Lorenzetti and Planiscig, Tiepolo worked in the Barbarigo palace in 1744–45 together with his trusted associate, the *quadraturista* Girolamo Mengozzi Colonna, who designed pavements in two of the rooms.[1] Only the frescoes in one of the two rooms decorated by Tiepolo on the main floor are still in situ. These include a ceiling showing Time uncovering Truth and two overdoors with female allegorical figures. The ceiling of the other room, painted in oil on canvas, was originally framed by eight monochrome frescoes: four of them circular with allegorical depictions of the liberal arts—History, Astronomy, Geography, and Astrology—and four others, irregular in shape, representing the arts—Painting, Sculpture, Music, and Poetry. The ceiling canvas was transferred to Ca' Rezzonico, and in the 1950s the frescoes were detached and removed to the Palazzo Luccheschi in Venice; since 1961 they have been in a private collection in Milan.

Tiepolo's patron was the nobleman Pietro Barbarigo (1711–1801), known as lo Zoppo. One of the republic's most rigid conservatives, he was famous for his profound religiosity and intransigent habits as well as for his hard-fought victories in the Venetian senate over the innovative proposals of his former friend and ally Andrea Tron

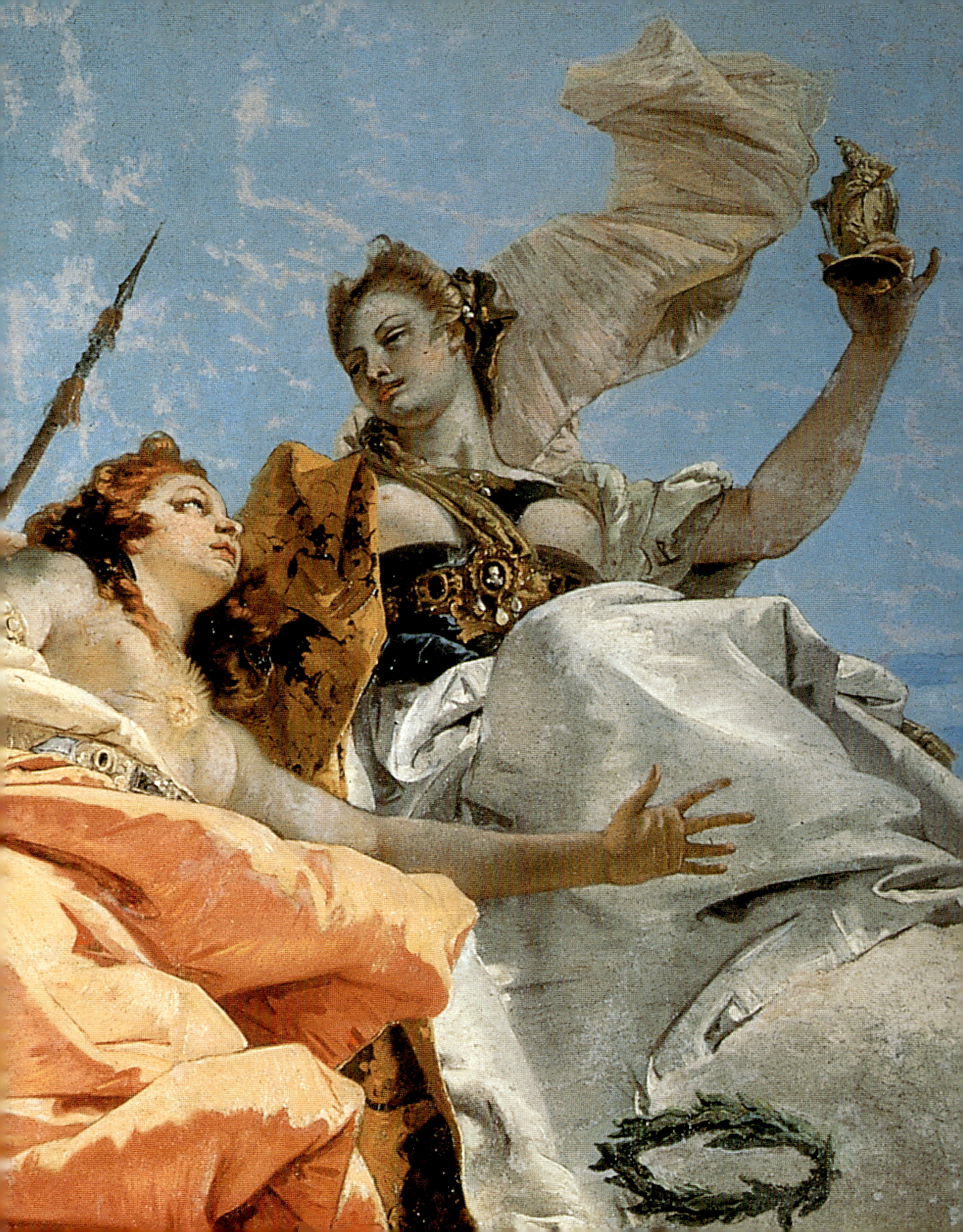

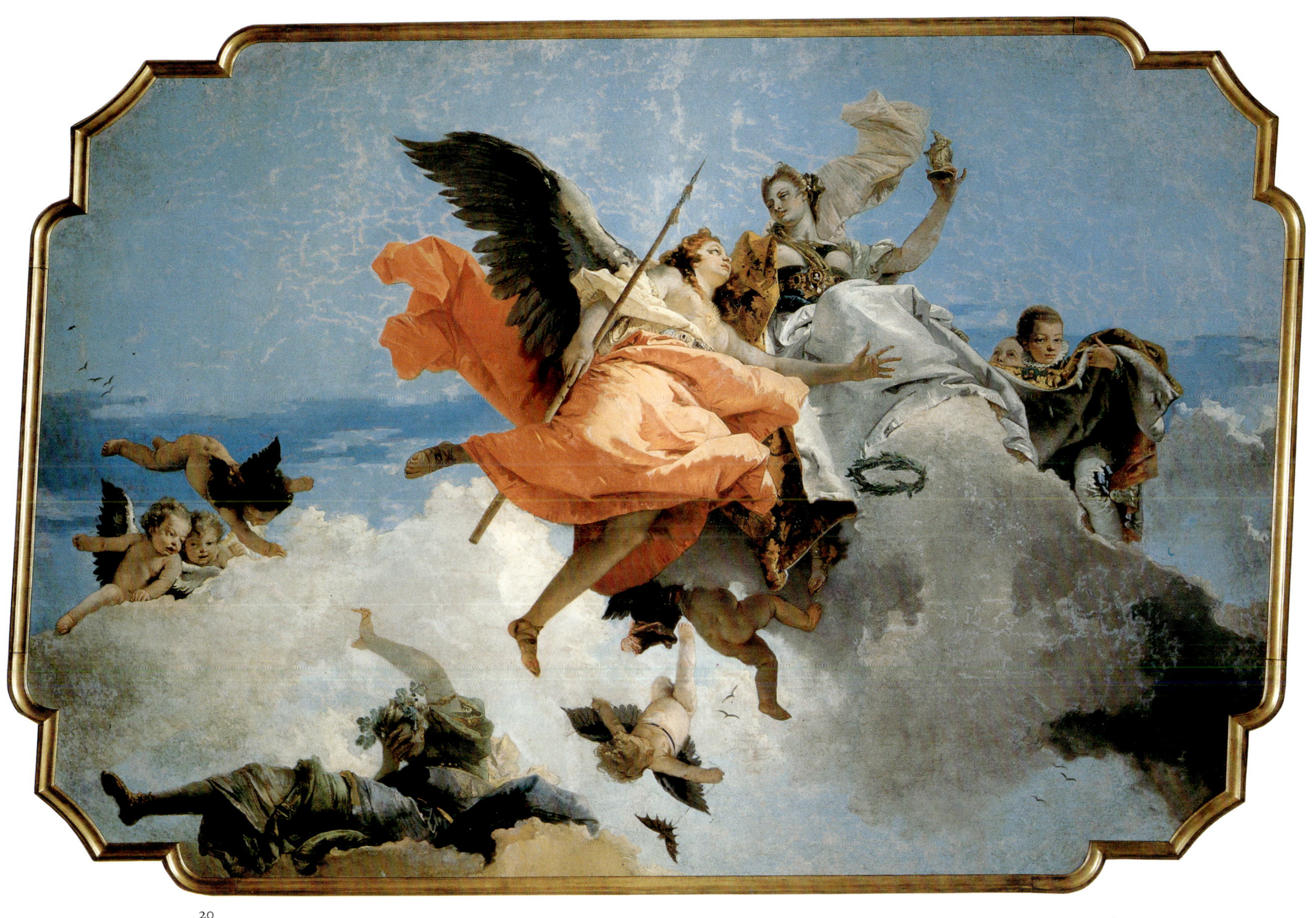

20

Opposite: Detail, no. 20

PROVENANCE:
Pietro Barbarigo, Palazzo Barbarigo, Venice (1744/45–1801); Contarina Barbarigo, Palazzo Barbarigo (from 1801–4); by descent, Marcantonio Michiel, Palazzo Barbarigo (1804–34); by descent, Leopardo Martinengo, Palazzo Barbarigo (1834–84); Giustina Martinengo, Palazzo Barbarigo (1884–96); by descent, Count Antonio Donà dalle Rose, Palazzo Barbarigo(?) (1896–1935; cat. 1934, no. 73); Ca' Rezzonico, Venice (from 1935)

REFERENCES:
Molmenti 1909, p. 65; Sack 1910, p. 149; Lorenzetti and Planiscig 1934, p. 19; Lorenzetti 1936, p. 28; Muraro 1960, pp. 24–25; Pignatti 1960, p. 331; Morassi 1962, p. 62; Pallucchini 1968, p. 110, no. 160; Romanelli and Pedrocco 1986, p. 37; Gemin and Pedrocco 1993, pp. 375–77, no. 332; Venice 1995a, p. 500

regarding the regulation of ecclesiastical institutions and religious affairs. His name is also linked with a minor but significant incident in the cultural life of Venice of the last quarter of the eighteenth century: he was one of five *correttori*, or overseers of public life, who in 1774 promulgated the law that closed the Ridotto of Palazzo Dandolo at S. Moisè—which since 1638 had been designated a gambling casino by the senate. His comrade in this initiative was Lodovico Flangini, the future patriarch of Venice under the Austrian government.

Caterina Sagredo, who became the second wife of Pietro's brother, Gregorio, probably introduced Tiepolo to Barbarigo in 1739. Tiepolo was closely associated with Caterina's father, Gerardo Sagredo, as well as with Marina Sagredo, the wife of Almorò Alvise II (Andrea) Pisani—the man who commissioned Tiepolo's great fresco at Strà (see no. 52). The connection of Tiepolo with the Sagredo-Barbarigo is confirmed by his painting of the coats of arms of these two families supported by angels (formerly Crespi Collection, Milan; present whereabouts unknown).

The Ca' Rezzonico ceiling is often mistakenly cited in the literature as showing Fortitude and Wisdom triumphing over Falsehood. However, reference to Cesare Ripa's *Iconologia*, Tiepolo's customary iconographic source, makes clear that it in fact represents Virtue and Nobility triumphing over Ignorance, who in the wake of her fall drags a bat, her symbol, which is tethered to a winged cherub. The theme carried flattering allusions for patrons and was repeated by Tiepolo throughout his career. It first occurred in his work about 1740, in a ceiling for the Palazzo Gallarati Scotti in Milan. He took up the subject again for the ceiling of Villa Cordellina at Montecchio Maggiore in 1743 and in a contemporary ceiling canvas now in the Museo Civico at Udine.[2] The composition of the Udine ceiling is closely related to the Barbarigo canvas but lacks the magnificent page holding the train of Nobility. Muraro has tentatively suggested that this figure and his companion might be nephews of Barbarigo's, but the model was probably Tiepolo's son Giuseppe Maria, who, unlike his brothers Giandomenico and Lorenzo, became a priest rather than a painter, entering the religious order of the Somaschi. The identification of the page finds support in the similarity he bears to a youth Giandomenico inserted in his painting of the eighth station of the cross—one of a series of fourteen canvases he carried out in 1748–49 for the Venetian Oratorio del Crocefisso, adjoining S. Polo.[3] We have here another example of Tiepolo's recourse to his family for models. The page's companion can tentatively be identified as a self-portrait of Tiepolo.

In the refined elegance of the composition, which recalls the art of Veronese, and in the calculated color harmonies, all in a light range but made intense through their juxtaposition, the ceiling typifies Tiepolo's mature style. A brilliant, Apollonian light dominates, bringing out the rich effects of the shot fabrics worn by the principal figures, while it leaves Ignorance in shadow. A similar note is struck in a later interpretation of the same subject, the ceiling Tiepolo evidently painted in 1748 on the occasion of the wedding of Ludovico Manin and Elisabetta Grimani (Norton Simon Museum of Art, Pasadena).

FP

NOTES

1. See Domenichini 1983–84.
2. Contrary to what is usually stated, the ceiling at Udine was not painted for Palazzo Caiselli, where it can be traced only in the nineteenth century.
3. See Knox 1980a, p. 33.

THE DECORATIONS FOR CA' BARBARO

21a. *The Glorification of the Barbaro Family*
21b. *Scene from Ancient History*
21c. *The Betrothal of Alexander and Roxanne* or *Latino Offering His Daughter Lavinia to Aeneas in Matrimony*
21d. *Tarquin and Lucretia*

Tiepolo contributed paintings to two of the sumptuous interiors of the Palazzo Barbaro a S. Vidal in Venice. Renovations of the quattrocento palace had been undertaken by Alvise Barbaro (1636–1698), who was especially concerned with the design of the large *salone*, or *cameron*, overlooking the Grand Canal, for which he commissioned a famous group of pictures by Antonio Zanchi, Sebastiano Ricci, and Giambattista Piazzetta. Four oval overdoors by Tiepolo (21b–d, fig. 54) were in all probability installed in this room and must have been commissioned by Alvise's son, Almorò (1681–1754). One of Tiepolo's greatest ceiling canvases (21a), an allegory extolling the virtues of the Barbaro, was also painted for Almorò and hung in another *salone*, which faced the courtyard behind the palace.[1]

This ceiling painting was long thought to represent the glorification of an illustrious fifteenth-century member of the family, Francesco Barbaro (1398–1454). Soldier, statesman, and humanist, Francesco wrote an important treatise on marriage, the *De re uxoria*. Zanchi's paintings on the ceiling of the *cameron* represent famous women from antiquity and may allude to the treatise.[2] Because Tiepolo's overdoors depict similar subjects and were mistakenly thought to have hung in the room with his ceiling canvas, critics concluded that Francesco was portrayed in the ceiling amid symbols of his military and literary success.[3]

It now appears clear that the ceiling refers not to a single Barbaro but rather to the entire family. As Garas and later Aikema have pointed out, this can be deduced first from the evidence of Giandomenico's etching after the painting, which is titled *Valore, fama, prudenza e nobiltà*, implying that the meaning is allegorical and that the central figure is Valor.[4] Moreover, since the ceiling canvas did not hang with the overdoors, it need not be strictly associated with the subjects of Francesco's writings. As Aikema has argued convincingly, if a specific person is celebrated in this allegory, it is the patron himself, Almorò Barbaro. The generally accepted date of the painting, 1750, coincides exactly with Almorò's elevation to the rank of procurator; the work may indeed commemorate this event, but within a broad context that lauds the virtues of generations of Barbaro.

The allegorical figures closely follow the descriptions provided by Cesare Ripa in his *Iconologia*. Valor dominates the picture, seated off-center, in military garb, wearing a laurel wreath and holding a scepter in one hand, while caressing a lion with the other. He is surrounded by Fame, who blows her trumpet and grasps a branch, and Virtue, also holding a laurel garland and with an image of the sun emblazoned on her chest. The two majestic female figures at the lower left are Nobility, who holds a statue of Minerva, and Prudence, seen from the rear, with two faces and a serpent wrapped around her arm. Of Tiepolo's several ceilings that treat similar elements, this canvas is among the most successful. The virile nature of the allegory is clearly legible in the very weightiness of the composition. And there is a remarkable variety in the density of the brushwork, with details, such as the branch held by Fame, made up of separate touches that appear almost transparent against the background. That Tiepolo was fully involved in the production of this brilliantly executed commission seems evident.

Several oil sketches have been related to the Barbaro ceiling because they share certain compositional similarities with it, but these are now generally associated with a commission for the Morosini family and may represent the *Apotheosis of Doge Francesco Morosini*.[5]

21a. The Glorification of the Barbaro Family
Ca. 1750
243.8 × 466.7 cm (96 × 183¾ in.)
The Metropolitan Museum of Art, New York; Anonymous Gift, in memory of Oliver H. Payne, 1923 (23.128)

21b. Scene from Ancient History
Ca. 1750
140.3 × 109.3 cm (55¼ × 43 in.)
Samuel H. Kress Collection, National Gallery of Art, Washington, D.C. (1939.1.365)

21c. The Betrothal of Alexander and Roxanne or **Latino Offering His Daughter Lavinia to Aeneas in Matrimony**
Ca. 1750
140.5 × 109.5 cm (55¼ × 43⅛ in.)
Statens Museum for Kunst, Copenhagen (4201)

21d. Tarquin and Lucretia
Ca. 1750
140 × 103 cm (55⅛ × 40½ in.)
Staatsgalerie am Shaezler-Palais, Städtische Kunstsammlungen Augsburg (12582)

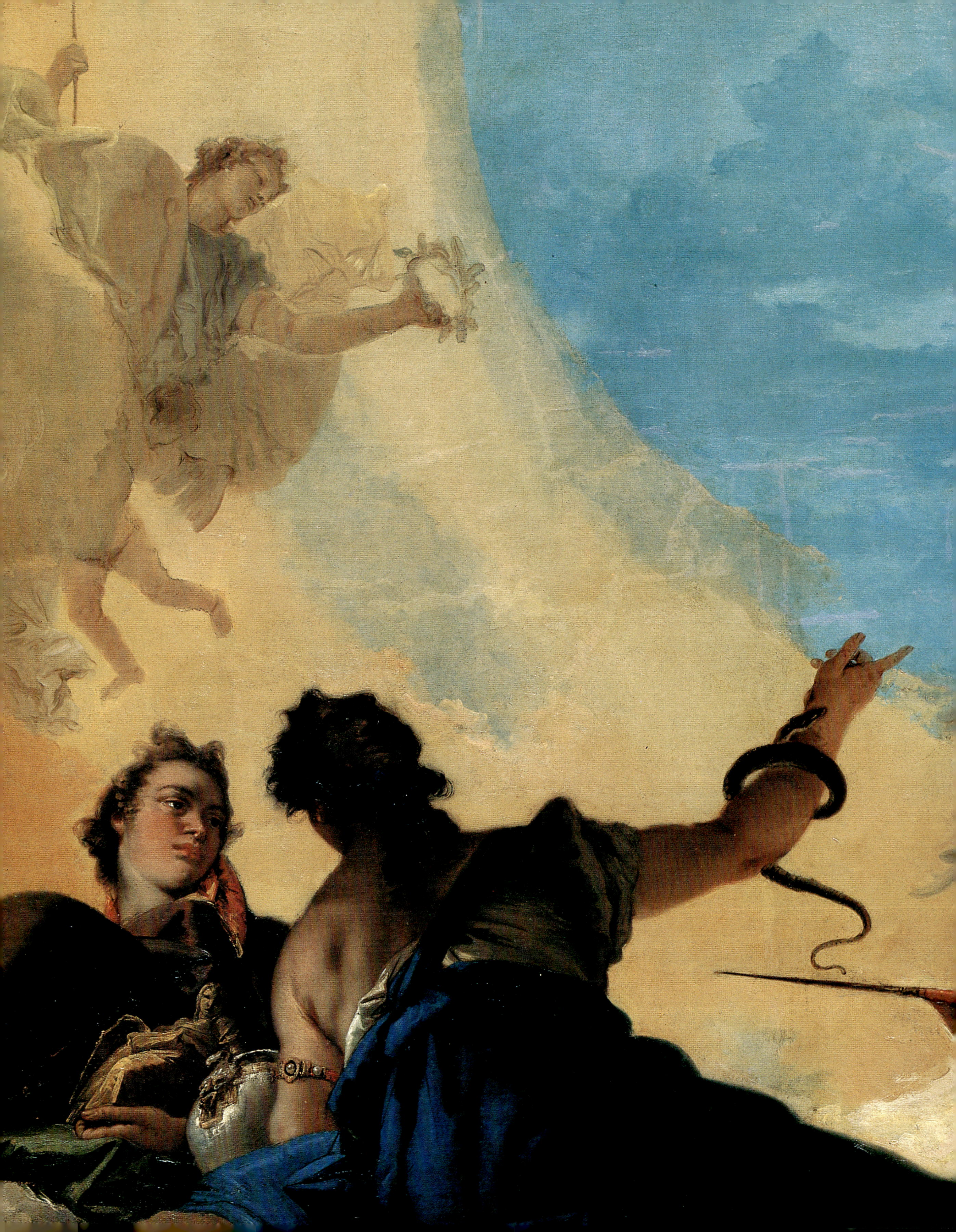

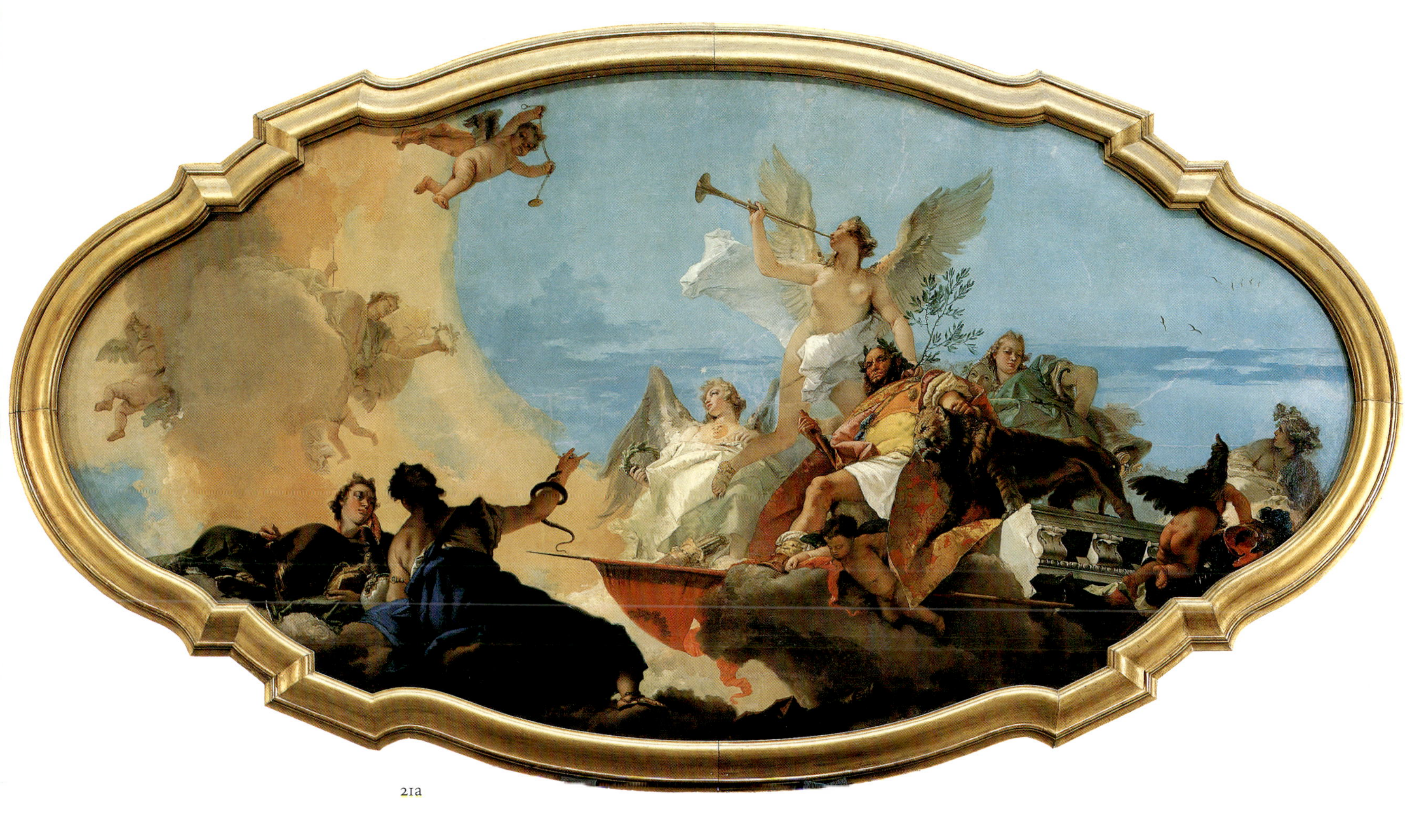

21a

Opposite: Detail, 21a

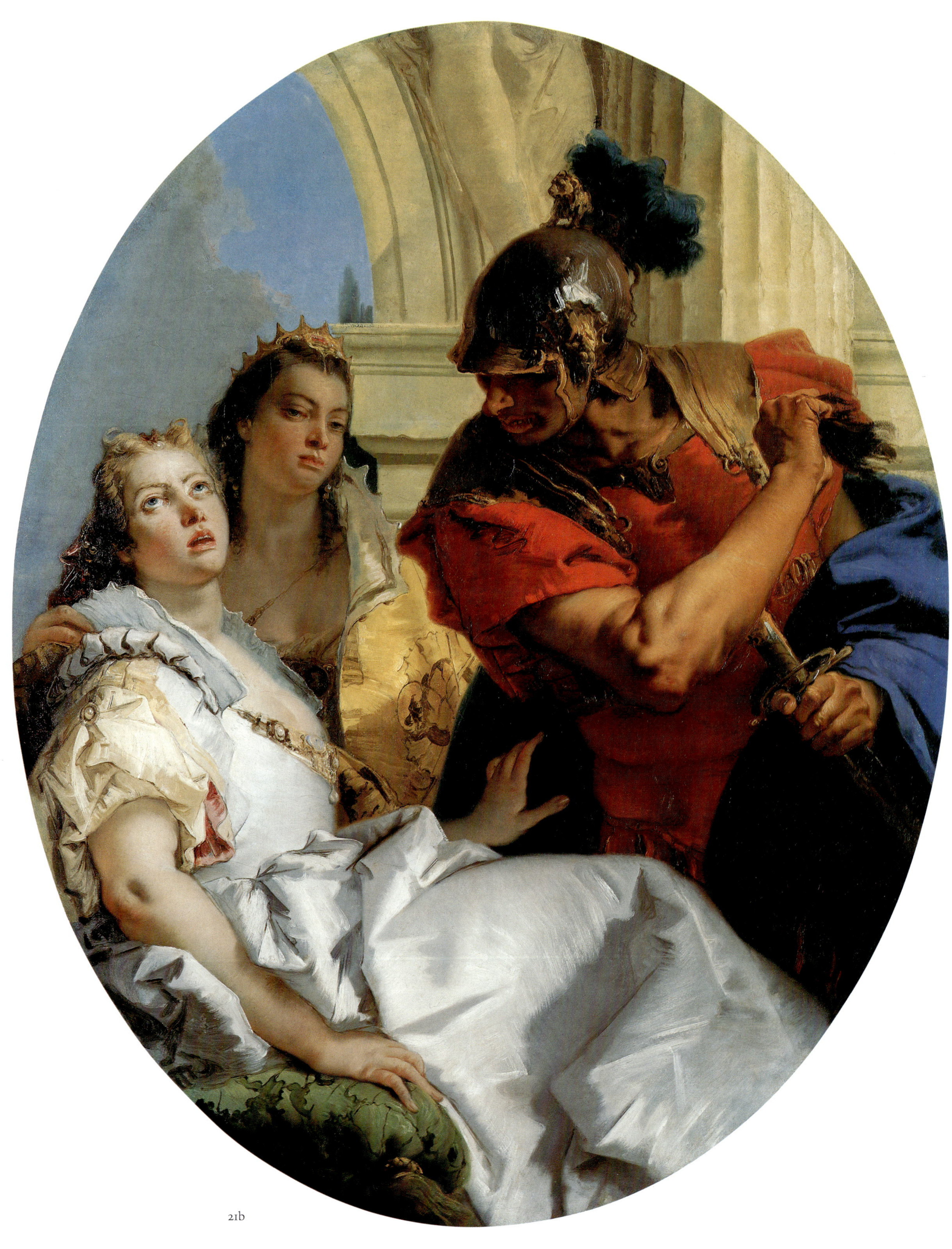

21b

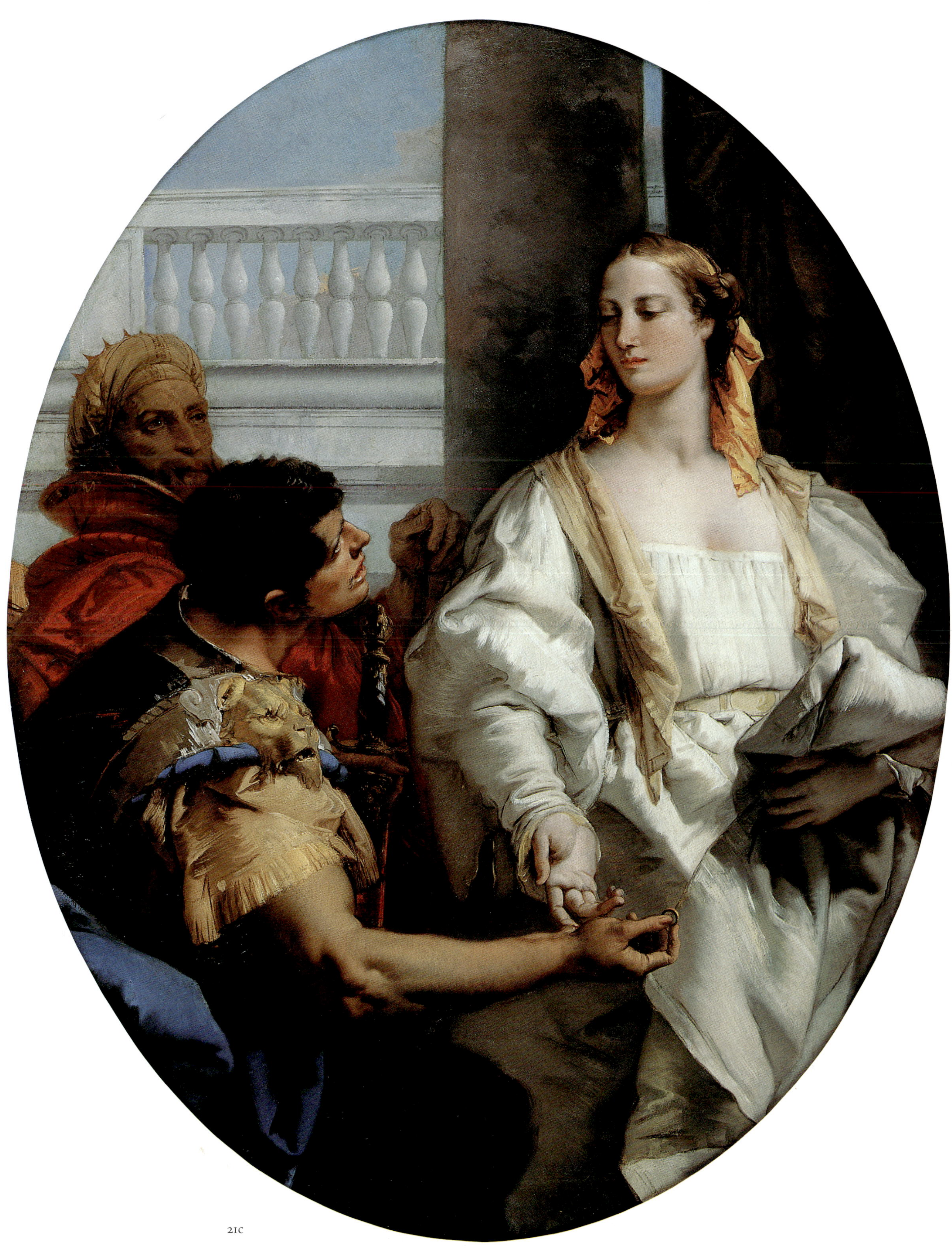

21C

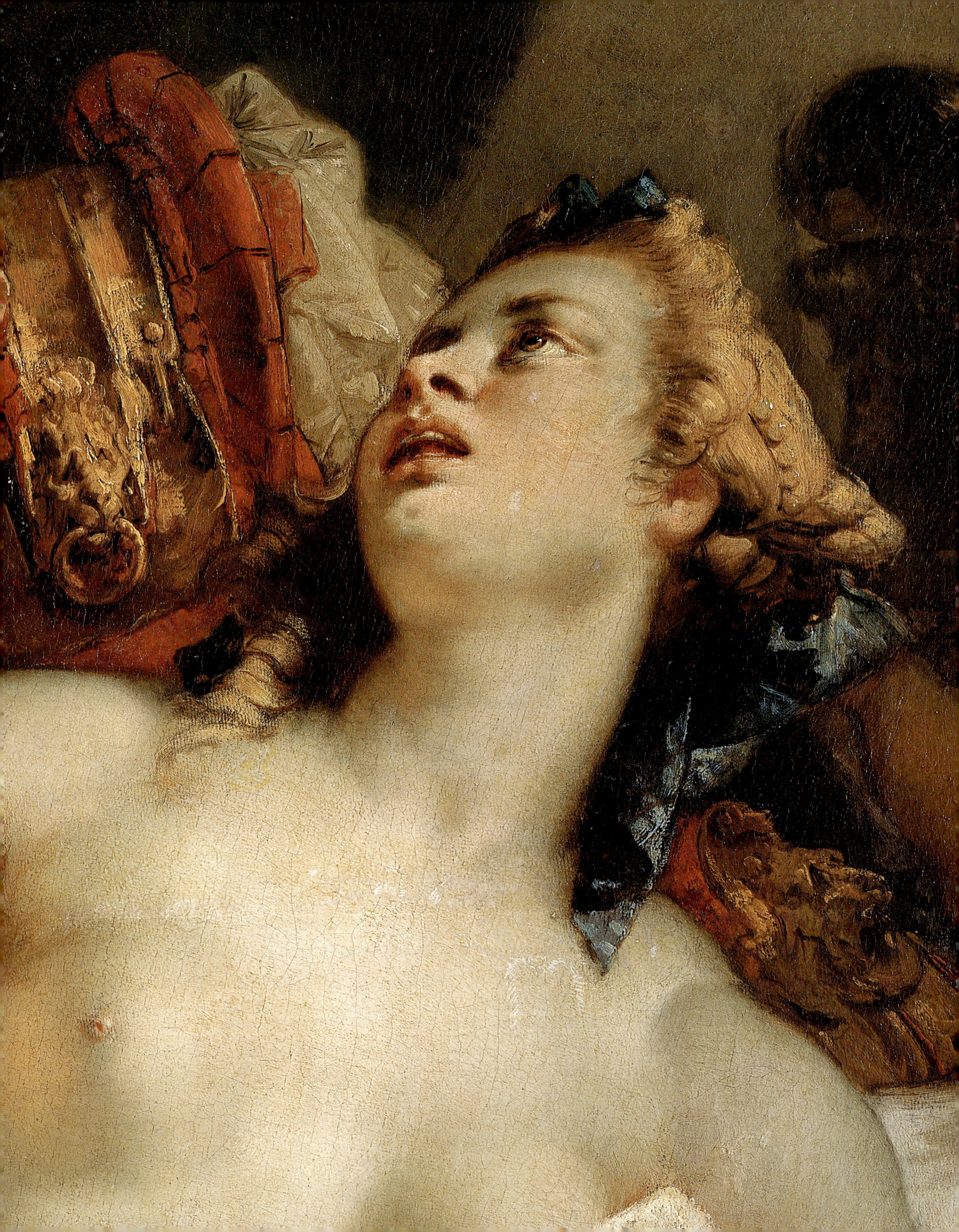

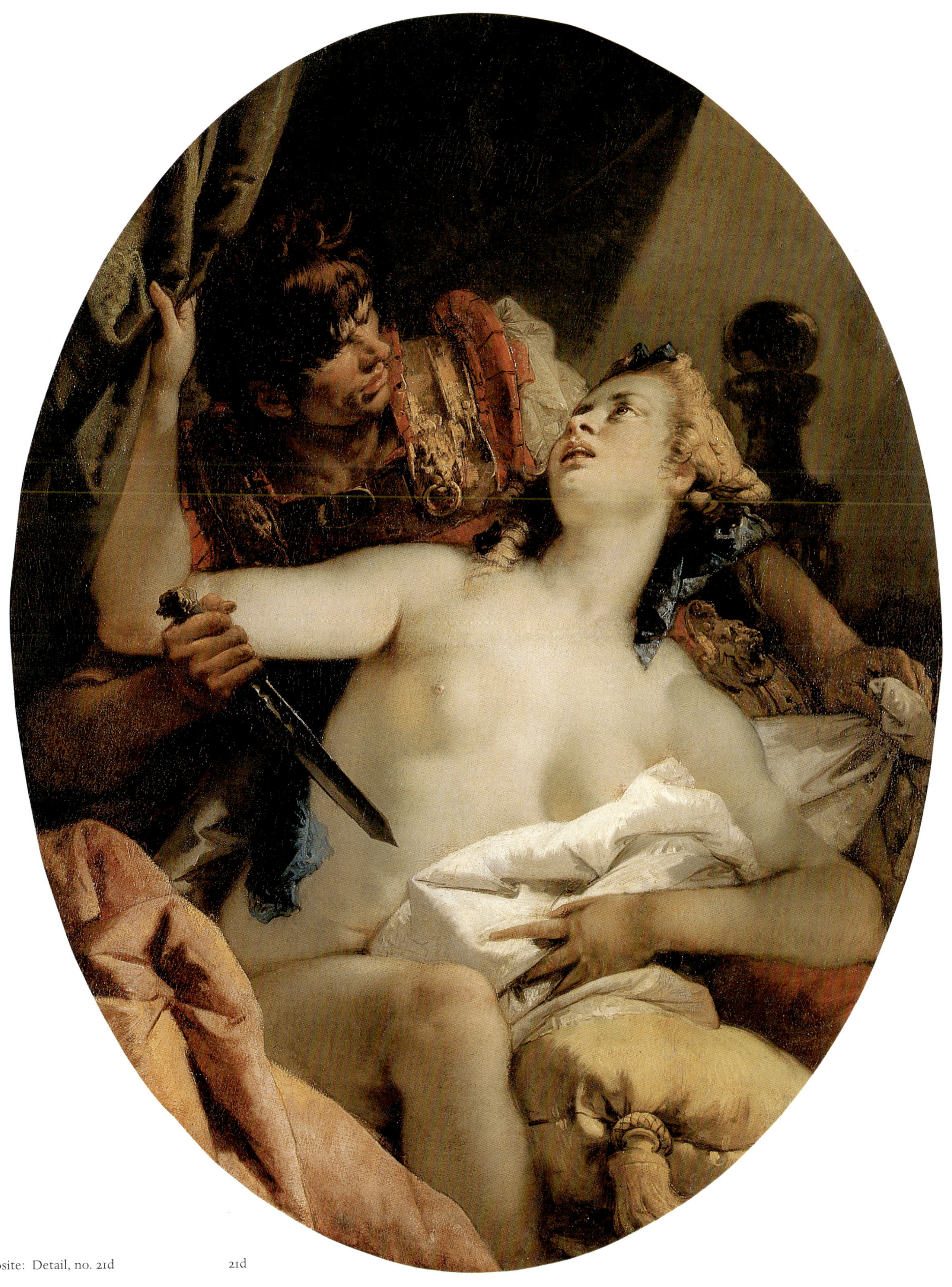

Opposite: Detail, no. 21d

21d

PROVENANCE, 21a:
Almorò Barbaro, Palazzo Barbaro, Venice (ca. 1750–54); Barbaro family; Marcantonio Barbaro, Palazzo Barbaro (until 1860); by descent, Elissa Bassi, Palazzo Barbaro (1860–66); Vincenzo Favenza, Venice (1866); private collection, France (sale, Hôtel Drouot, Paris, 9 February 1874); Count Isaac de Camondo, Paris (1874–93; sale, Galerie Georges Petit, Paris, 1 February 1893); Camille Groult, Paris(?); Manuel de Yturbe, Paris(?); Heilbronner, Paris(?); Stanford White, New York (before 1906);[18] Colonel Oliver H. Payne, New York; Mrs. H. O. Havemeyer, New York (until 1923)

REFERENCES:
Chennevières 1898, p. 118; Molmenti 1909, pp. 83, 258; Sack 1910, pp. 113, 150; Burroughs 1924; McComb 1934, pp. 102, 127; New York 1938, no. 14; Wehle 1940, pp. 282–83; Lorenzetti 1942, p. XXVI; Morassi 1955a, p. 22; Morassi 1962, p. 33; Garas 1965, p. 294; Pallucchini 1968, p. 114, no. 192; New York 1970, p. 285, no. 324; Zeri and Gardner 1973, pp. 56–57; Aikema 1987a, pp. 148–51; Gemin and Pedrocco 1993, pp. 408–9, no. 388; New York 1993, pp. 280, 379

PROVENANCE, 21b:
Almorò Barbaro, Palazzo Barbaro, Venice (ca. 1750–54); Barbaro family; Marcantonio Barbaro, Palazzo Barbaro (until 1860); by descent, Elissa Bassi, Palazzo Barbaro (1860–66); Vincenzo Favenza, Venice (1866); private collection, France (sale, Hôtel Drouot, Paris, 9 February 1874); Count Isaac de Camondo, Paris (1874–93; sale, Galerie Georges Petit, Paris, 1 February 1893); Eugène Féral (possibly as agent for Baron Adolphe de Rothschild); Baron Adolphe de Rothschild, Paris; by descent, Baroness and Baron von Springer, Vienna; Dr. Joseph Kranz, Vienna (by 1902); Palais Roth, Vienna (by 1911); Stefan von Auspitz, Vienna (by 1931); K. W. Bachstitz, The Hague (by 1935); Samuel H. Kress Foundation, New York (1937)

Although Valor is featured as the principal figure in these sketches, he is presented beside an allegory of Faith and above putti playing with a doge's cap, which neither appear in nor are appropriate to the Barbaro ceiling.

Nineteenth-century sources make clear that at least two, and probably all four, of Tiepolo's oval canvases were overdoors that hung in the *cameron* beneath Zanchi's ceiling and alongside the works by Ricci and Piazzetta.[6] They were installed as elements in a renovation of the room undertaken by Almorò, probably in the 1740s. Almorò substituted elaborate stuccowork, which included surrounds for six new overdoors, for the gilded leather that had covered the walls of the room when it was completed about 1700.[7] Two nineteenth-century watercolors depicting the *cameron* show five of them before they were sold and replaced with portraits. At least two of Tiepolo's ovals must have been replaced before 1874, when they were sold at auction in Paris together with his ceiling.[8]

Only two of the five overdoors shown in the watercolors are recognizable as works by Tiepolo: the *Scene from Ancient History* now in Washington (21b) and the *Betrothal of Alexander and Roxanne* or *Latino Offering His Daughter Lavinia to Aeneas in Matrimony* now in Copenhagen (21c). These are the two ovals that were sold with the ceiling in Paris in 1874. The two others, the *Tarquin and Lucretia* in Augsburg (21d) and the *Matronalia Offering Gifts to Juno Regina* in Atlanta (fig. 54), first reappeared in the Thedy collection in Vienna about the turn of the twentieth century. The dimensions of the paintings in Washington and Copenhagen are identical, while the canvases in Augsburg and Atlanta are slightly different. Nonetheless, it seems highly likely that all four originally hung in the *cameron*. The precision of the watercolors is open to doubt, for the ovals are sketchily drawn and two of them closely resemble the picture now in Copenhagen. Moreover, Giandomenico, who also etched his father's Barbaro ceiling, made chalk drawings of the Augsburg and Atlanta paintings and then etchings.[9]

To be sure, the themes of the four ovals, each of which features a female protagonist, constitute the strongest evidence linking them to the room's decorative program. There has been much debate about the precise subjects of the scenes, and only two can be identified with confidence. These are the works that are recorded under brief titles in Giandomenico's list of etchings: *Tarquin and Lucretia* and *Matronalia Offering Gifts to Juno Regina*. The *Tarquin and Lucretia*, which Giandomenico called *Lugrezia Romana*, has its principal source in Livy (*Annals*, book 1). It depicts Lucretia, who would take her own life to escape the dishonor that followed Tarquin's attack, represented here. The second, listed by Giandomenico as *Romane e vergini vestali*, also shows a subject from Livy (book 27, chap. 37).[10] Here Livy tells how during the Second Punic War the temple of Juno Regina (symbolized in Tiepolo's painting by Juno's bird, the peacock) was struck by lightning. He recounts that in response to this terrible portent soothsayers recommended that the matrons of Rome, or *matronalia*, make contributions from their dowries. From this metal was cast a golden vessel that was presented to the temple, quite clearly the event pictured by Tiepolo. In each of these tales women's virtues are extolled.

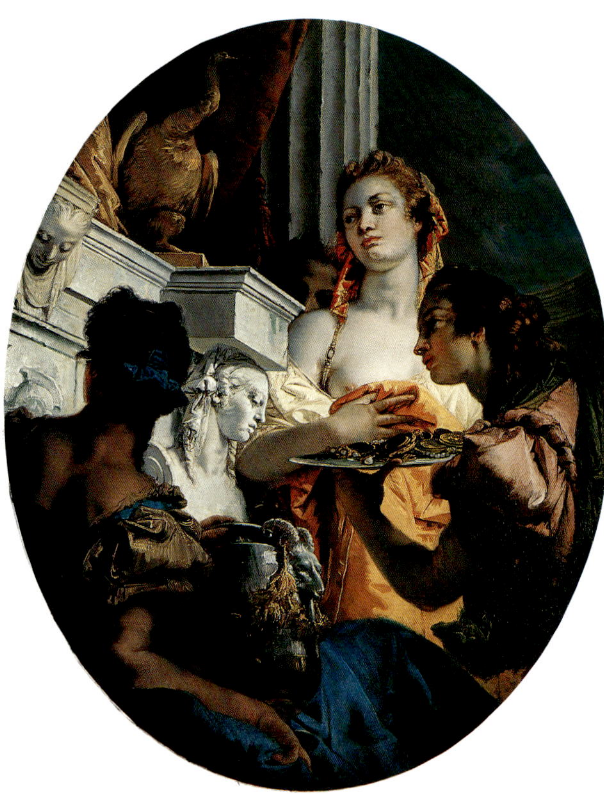
Fig. 54. *Matronalia Offering Gifts to Juno Regina*. Oil on canvas. High Museum of Art, Atlanta, Gift of the Samuel H. Kress Foundation (32.6)

It is less easy to explain the narratives of the paintings in Copenhagen and Washington. In the former a man offers a ring to a majestic woman, while another, crowned man looks on. Although the subject portrayed has sometimes been described simply as the Betrothal or the Rejected Proposal, two specific themes drawn from antique sources have, with some plausibility, been suggested recently. One, the Betrothal of Alexander and Roxanne, would shift the scene from Rome to Greece.[11] The picture would center on the story in which, as told by Plutarch (*Lives*, chap. 47) and Arrian (*Anabasis of Alexander*, book 4), Alexander won peace between the Macedonians and the Bactrians by proposing marriage to Roxanne, the daughter of the Bactrian leader, Oxyartes. Conceivably it is Oxyartes who is shown behind the two principal figures, presumably Alexander and Roxanne, and approvingly observes his daughter's demonstration of filial obedience and acceptance of her role. The second possibility suggested involves a Roman setting, in which Latino, king of Lazio, offers his daughter Lavinia to Aeneas in marriage.[12] One of the key episodes in the second half of the *Aeneid*, and related as well in Boccaccio's *De claris mulieribus*, the subject is infrequently portrayed in painting. However, it would have been well known in Venice as the theme of two operas: *Le nozze d'Enea con Lavinia*, by Monteverdi, and *Sponsali d'Enea*, probably by Bartolomeo Cordans, first performed there in 1641 and 1731, respectively. Another, earlier hypothesis regarding the picture's subject bears repeating, although it is less convincing. According to this theory, the story of King Candaules, his wife, and Gyges is represented.[13] It is hard to connect the version recounted by Herodotus with the painting, but an interesting passage in Plato's *Republic* (Book 2) featuring a magical gold ring could be relevant. Plato writes that the shepherd Gyges gained extraordinary powers from a ring he found and tells us tersely, "He seduced the king's wife and with her aid set upon the king and slew him and possessed his kingdom."[14] Although the ring is a prominent element in the narrative and in Tiepolo's canvas, the tale focuses not on a virtuous woman but on the ways in which power leads to license and is therefore difficult to imagine within the context of the decoration of the Barbaro *salone*.

The painting now in Washington has proven to be the most enigmatic of the group. Here a helmeted soldier holding a sword and a lock of hair threatens a woman, behind whom stands a second, crowned woman. The subject has traditionally been described as an episode in the tale of Timoclea and the Thracian commander as told by Plutarch in his *Life of Alexander* (chap. 12) and in the volume on the Bravery of Women in his *Moralia* (chap. 14). However, nothing in this story of a woman who takes revenge on a marauding Thracian soldier by casting him into a well seems to be reflected in Tiepolo's picture. Recently it has been suggested that the Death of Arsinoe, as ordered by her sister Cleopatra, is portrayed.[15] The presence of two noble ladies, one crowned, the other menaced, accords well with this narrative, but a crucial detail—the hank of hair brandished by the soldier—does not figure in any version of the story. Moreover, the tale of Arsinoe, who was not known for her high principles, like the story of Gyges and his ring, cannot be reconciled with the emphasis on virtuous women in Barbaro's treatise and the presumed themes in the other decorations of the room. Therefore, the subject remains unidentified for the present but may ultimately be found in one of the various sources, by an author such as Valerius Maximus or Plutarch, that inspired the other images in the sequence.

Morassi once noted that these paintings represent the classical moment in Tiepolo's art.[16] This is indeed an apt characterization of scenes in which statuesque women are set against massive columns and entablatures; where the protagonists exhibit the gravitas of the saints in the roughly contemporary Gesuati altarpiece (no. 35); and the compositions display a noteworthy equilibrium, perhaps inspired by sixteenth-century examples. Painted with broad strokes, especially in the draperies, the canvases have a strong and immediate impact, as befits overdoors seen from some distance. Yet great attention has been paid to the details, in particular the fanciful animal heads that decorate metallic surfaces, such as the handle of the great vessel offered to Juno by the *matronalia*.

There are no known variants of the Washington and Copenhagen paintings, but several replicas exist of the *Tarquin and Lucretia* and *Matronalia Offering Gifts*, and these add to the confusion surrounding the history of these works and their dispersal. It now seems clear that the paintings in Augsburg and Atlanta are the originals by Tiepolo. They were shown together in an exhibition at Würzburg in 1896, appeared in the collection of Max Thedy in 1902, and were sold in New York in 1920 by a collector who probably bought them directly from Thedy.[17]

AB

NOTES

1. A letter of 1924 from Ralph Latimer to Bryson Burroughs of the Metropolian Museum (Department of European Paintings files) describes a second, smaller ceiling by Tiepolo. He notes that it was sold in the 1870s to Grand Duchess Marie of Russia, who took it to her villa outside Florence, and that after her death it was removed to Saint Petersburg, where it was lost to view. This is probably the ceiling by Giandomenico listed in Mariette's index to Giandomenico's prints as "Il merita che corona la virtù" (see Frerichs 1971b, p. 219, and Aikema 1987a, p. 151).
2. An edition of the text appears in Gnesotto 1915–16; King (1976, pp. 31–35) outlines the underlying themes of the treatise, which was written in 1415–16 as a defense of the nobility of marriage. Hannegan (1983) identifies the scenes in Zanchi's ceiling paintings based on a description in *La Galleria di Minerva* of 1697. Some of the protagonists in both Zanchi's ceiling canvases and in Tiepolo's overdoors are discussed in the treatise, while others are not mentioned.
3. Zeri and Gardner 1973, p. 56.
4. See Garas 1965, pp. 294, 301, no. 24, and Aikema 1987a, p. 148. The print is no. 37 in the catalogue Giandomenico compiled in Madrid after Giambattista's death.
5. See Fort Worth 1993, no. 33.
6. Fontana, original publication, date unknown, mid-nineteenth century; reprint 1967, p. 172 (as Domenico and Lorenzo Tiepolo); followed in this century by Lorenzetti 1942, p. xxvi.

REFERENCES:

Modern 1902, pp. 36, 52; Molmenti 1909, pp. 274–75; Sack 1910, pp. 114, 150; Molmenti 1911, pl. 227; Borenius 1932; Fröhlich-Bume 1932, p. 399; Chicago 1938, p. 26, no. 23; New York 1938, no. 15; Morassi 1962, p. 67; Pallucchini 1968, p. 114, no. 190D; Shapley 1973, pp. 145–47; Shapley 1979, pp. 443–45; Aikema 1987a, pp. 150–51; Bell 1987; Gemin and Pedrocco 1993, pp. 408–9, no. 392; De Grazia and Garberson 1996, pp. 264–72

PROVENANCE, 21C:

Almorò Barbaro, Palazzo Barbaro, Venice (ca. 1750–54); Barbaro family; Marcantonio Barbaro, Palazzo Barbaro (until 1860); by descent, Elissa Bassi, Palazzo Barbaro (1860–66); Vincenzo Favenza, Venice (1866); private collection, France (sale, Hôtel Drouot, Paris, 9 February 1874); Count Isaac de Camondo, Paris (1874–93; sale, Galerie Georges Petit, Paris, 1 February 1893); Eugène Féral (possibly as agent for Baron Adolphe de Rothschild); Baron Adolphe de Rothschild, Paris; by descent, Baroness and Baron von Springer, Vienna; Dr. Joseph Kranz, Vienna (by 1902); Palais Roth, Vienna (by 1911); Stefan von Auspitz, Vienna (by 1931); K. W. Bachstitz, The Hague (by 1935–38)

REFERENCES:

Modern 1902, pp. 36, 52, 114; Molmenti 1909, pp. 274–75; Sack 1910, p. 150; Molmenti 1911, pl. 227; Borenius 1932; Fröhlich-Bume 1932; Chicago 1938, p. 26, no. 24; Statens Museum for Kunst 1946, p. 300; Statens Museum for Kunst 1951, pp. 309–10, no. 698; Olsen 1961, p. 92; Morassi 1962, pp. 9–10; Pallucchini 1968, p. 114, no. 190C; Shapley 1973, pp. 145–47; Shapley 1979, pp. 443–45; Zafran 1984, p. 67; Aikema 1987a, pp. 150–51; Bell 1987; Gemin and Pedrocco 1993, pp. 408–9, no. 391; De Grazia and Garberson 1996, pp. 264–72

PROVENANCE, 21d:
Almorò Barbaro, Palazzo Barbaro, Venice (ca. 1750–54); Barbaro family; Marcantonio Barbaro, Palazzo Barbaro (until 1860); by descent, Elissa Bassi, Palazzo Barbaro (1860–66); private collection, Austria (probably from 1874); Max Thedy, Weimar (by 1902); C. F. Dieterich, New York (by 1911–20 sale, Anderson Galleries, New York, 8–9 April 1920, lot 109); Dr. Muller; Karl Haberstock, Munich (until 1936); Karl and Magdalene Haberstock Foundation, Munich (until 1983)

REFERENCES:
Modern 1902, p. 36; Molmenti 1909, pp. 242–43, 271, 275; Sack 1910, pp. 114, 150, 336; Molmenti 1911, pl. 213; Venice 1951, pp. 85–86, no. 63; Pallucchini 1961, p. 92; Morassi 1962, p. 2; Pallucchini 1968, p. 114, no. 190E; Shapley 1973, pp. 145–47; Levey 1978; Zafran 1984, p. 67; Aikema 1987a, p. 150; Augsburg 1991, pp. 60–63, no. 17; Gemin and Pedrocco 1993, pp. 408–9, no. 389

7. Aikema 1987a, p. 150.
8. Aikema (ibid., p. 151) hypothesized that the unaccounted-for ovals showed Barbaro family emblems, but the watercolors of the interior of the room, published by De Grazia (in De Grazia and Garberson 1996, pp. 264–72), reveal that at least five were paintings with narrative scenes. De Grazia discusses the implications of the watercolors and suggests that the ovals that were not by Tiepolo may have been painted by Giambattista Pittoni. Photographs of the watercolors (Patricia Curtis Vigano collection) were made available to me by the Department of Paintings, National Gallery of Art, Washington, D.C.
9. Stuttgart 1970, nos. 66, 67.
10. Levey 1978, pp. 418–19. Levey's interpretation of the subject supersedes earlier explanations.
11. Bell 1987, pp. 159–62.
12. Aikema 1987a, pp. 150–51.
13. Statens Museum for Kunst 1951, p. 310.
14. Plato 1930–35, vol. 1, book 2, p. 119.
15. Aikema 1987a, pp. 150–51. De Grazia (1996) has pointed out that the subject of the Venetian libretto to which Aikema refers, Giacomo Castoreo's *Arsinoe* (Venice, 1655), is not Cleopatra's sister but the daughter of the king of Armenia.
16. Morassi 1943, p. 26.
17. The painting now in Atlanta is illustrated in the *Catalogue of the Valuable Paintings . . . Collected by Mr. C. F. Dieterich*, Anderson Galleries, New York, 8–9 April 1920, lot 108. Before it went to Atlanta it was in the Contini Bonacossi and Kress collections. It differs from a painting formerly in the Necchi collection, Pavia, and now in a private collection which is often considered the original, in the full depiction of the console with the mask of a female head in the architecture of the temple at the left and in the suggestion of additional architecture in the background at the right. The ex-Necchi picture is certainly not the prime version.
18. The exact whereabouts of the painting in the late nineteenth and the early twentieth century is by no means clear. According to Chennevières (1898, p. 118), it was purchased from the Camondo collection by Manuel de Yturbe, Paris, in 1893, while Sack (1910, p. 150) says that in 1893 it was sold to Camille Groult in Paris. The caption for Sack's illustration (p. 113) places it in the collection of Manuel de Yturbe, but this is impossible because it was in New York by 1910. In 1924 Ralph Latimer, nephew of Mrs. Daniel Curtis, who owned Palazzo Barbaro until she died in 1919, wrote in the letter to Bryson Burroughs cited in note 1 above that "when Camondo failed in the Panama affair, the ceiling was again sold at Hotel Drouot [*sic*] and bought by a Monsieur Groult, marchand des [*sic*] pâte alimentaire." We do not know when or from whom Stanford White bought the canvas, but it seems to have been sold to Oliver Payne during White's lifetime. (It is not listed in the catalogues of White's extensive belongings that were auctioned by the American Art Association after his death in 1906.)

THE TASSO PICTURES FOR WÜRZBURG

22a. Rinaldo and Armida in the Garden
22b. Rinaldo Abandoning Armida

22a. Rinaldo and Armida in the Garden
Ca. 1752
105 × 140 cm (41⅜ × 55⅛ in.)
Signed lower left: B. Tiepolo
Residenz, Würzburg, Filialgalerie der Bayerische Staatsgemäldesammlungen in der Residenz, on loan from Bayerische Verwaltung der Staatlichen Schlösser, Gärten und Seen, Munich (Wü. Res. G159)

During the almost two years he executed frescoes in the prince-bishop's Residenz in Würzburg, Tiepolo also produced several oil paintings. Among them was this pair of canvases on the theme of Rinaldo and Armida, completed at about the same time as the *Death of Hyacinth* (no. 23) but about a decade after he painted his series showing the same lovers from Tasso's *Gerusalemme liberata* in Venice (for the story, see entry for no. 17a–g). Smaller in size than their Venetian counterparts, the two German works may have functioned originally as overdoors: the small strips of canvas stitched around their perimeters argue for their possible insertion into stuccoed frames; moreover, the compositions seem well adapted to read clearly from a low vantage point—especially the *Rinaldo and Armida in the Garden*, in which Armida's lap seems curiously disconnected when viewed straight on.[1]

Despite their differences in date and function, the two sets of Rinaldo and Armida paintings readily invite comparison, for the contrasts between them cast light on the innovative nature of Tiepolo's later interpretation of the subject and say much about his growth as an artist in the ten years separating the commissions. Perhaps the most obvious distinction between the

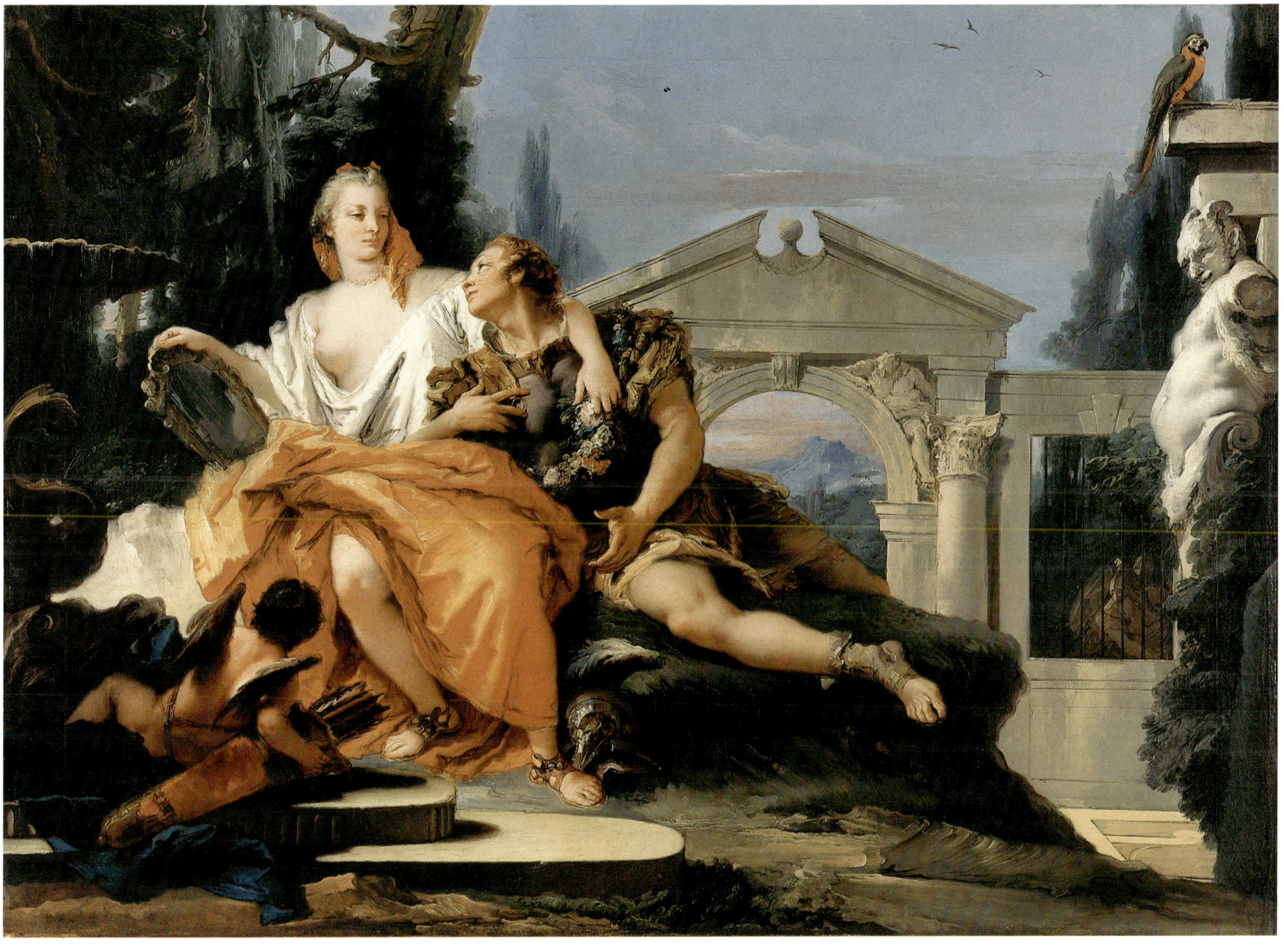

22a

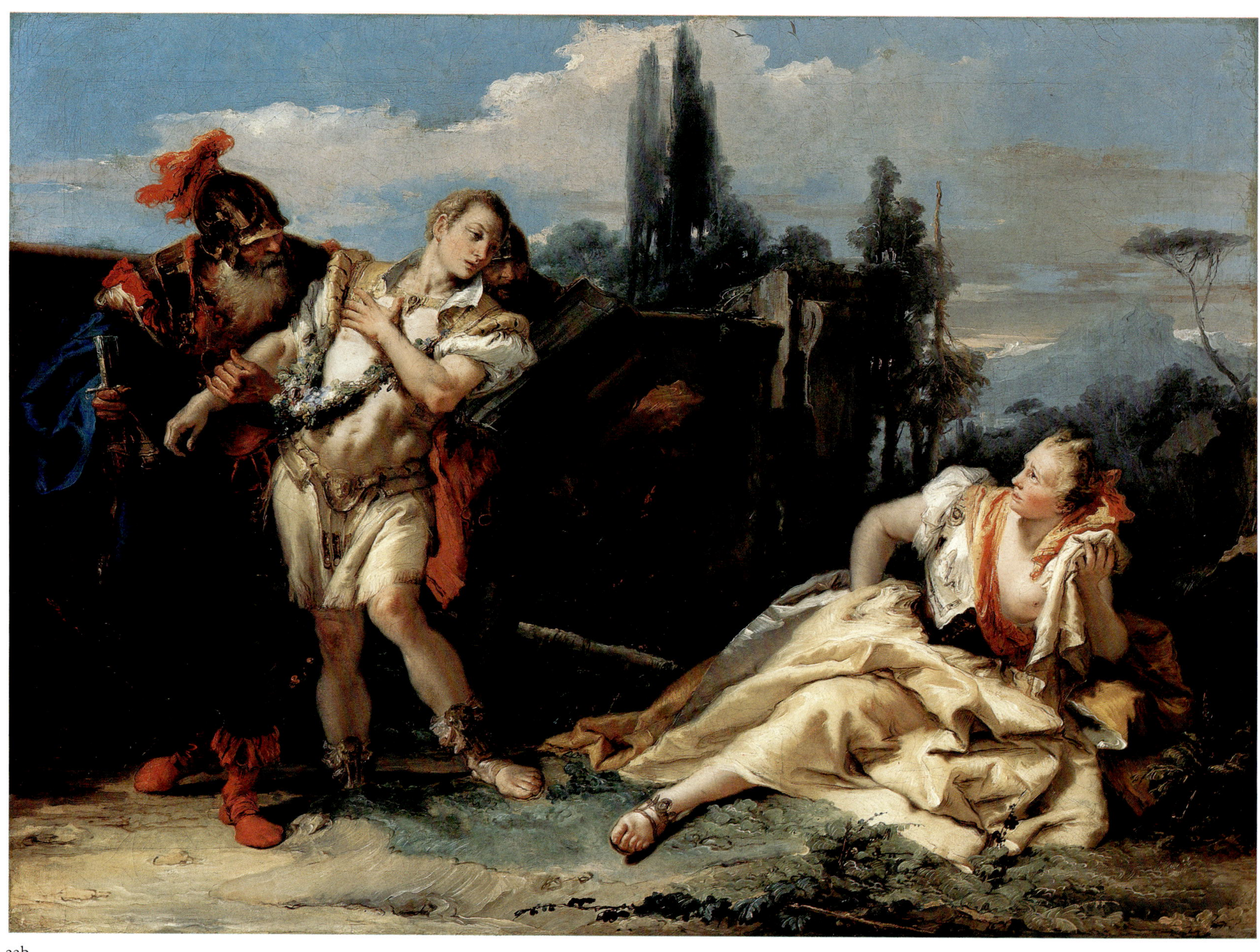

22b

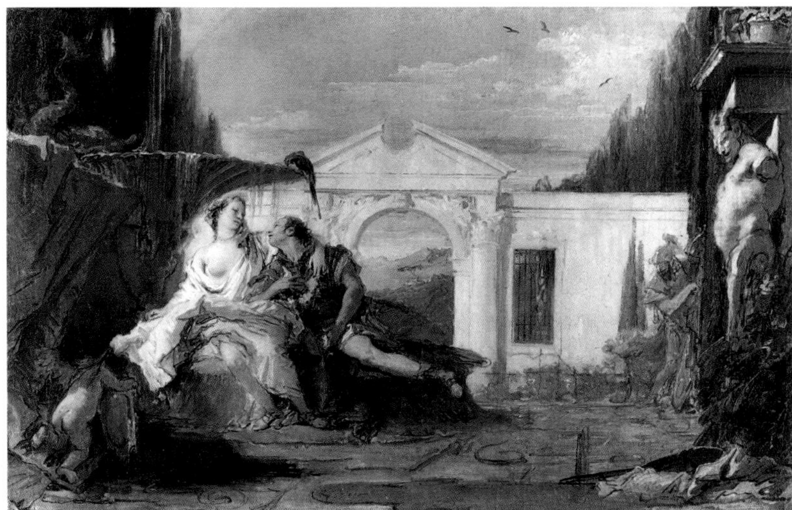

Fig. 55. *Rinaldo and Armida in the Garden*. Oil on canvas. Gemäldegalerie, Staatliche Museen zu Berlin, Preussischer Kulturbesitz (459D)

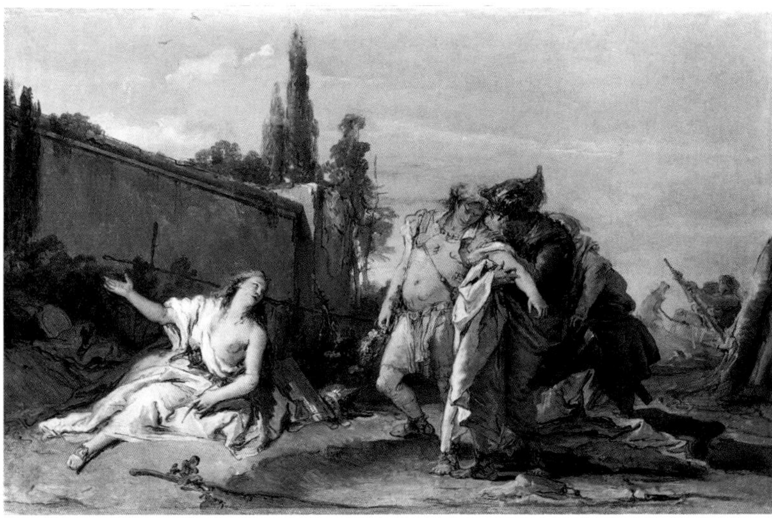

Fig. 56. *Rinaldo Abandoning Armida*. Oil on canvas. Gemäldegalerie, Staatliche Museen zu Berlin, Preussischer Kulturbesitz 3(/79)

groups lies in the realm of color. The earlier works, now in Chicago, are lighter in tonality; shadows are more transparent and fewer in number, the sky is a brighter blue, and draperies are generally blonder. The mood, by and large, is arcadian. The German canvases, on the other hand, are decidedly passionate in spirit, both in the dark vibrancy of their shadows and in the emotional intensity that is in part expressed by their more vivid hues. The changes Tiepolo effected in the narratives make clear his desire to accentuate the drama of each scene, to deepen the aura of spellbinding passion the lovers share in *Rinaldo and Armida in the Garden* and to heighten the sense of the loss they suffer in *Rinaldo Abandoning Armida*. Significantly, he compressed space. In the first painting he introduced a massive garden wall with an imposing gateway at the rear, a raised fountain with sculpture in the left foreground, and an architectural fragment decorated with a Pan figure on the right that close off the picture space and frame the two protagonists, locking them into the center of the scene. He surrounded Armida's garden with tall, thick trees and placed a mountain range in the far distance to cut it off even further from the outside world. A wall similarly isolates the quartet of players in the second work, and several cypresses in the center of the canvas effectively divide the composition in half, hinting at the division of the lovers that will follow Rinaldo's imminent desertion of the pagan sorceress. By means of these devices and through his positioning of the knight and the temptress at the front of the sealed space in each work, Tiepolo made his compositions tighter and denser than the related scenes he had painted in Venice.

The most important innovations that Tiepolo realized in the Würzburg versions concern Rinaldo and Armida themselves. The protagonists in the Chicago series are lyrical actors; their gestures are few, and their expressions are quiet. Their German equivalents behave a great deal more theatrically. In the Würzburg garden scene Rinaldo vigorously declares his love, avowing devotion to the enchantress with both hands as well as with the turn of his head, its upward inclination emphasized by the straining tendon in his neck (frontis., p. 104). Less yielding than in the earlier scene, Armida pulls the knight toward her, actively entrapping him as she lures him toward the sin of voluptuousness. The gaping mouth of the serpent or dragon figure that decorates the fountain at the far left of the painting, just beyond the witch's magical mirror, is hardly an incidental element but rather adds a powerful dramatic accent. In the second Würzburg canvas, as in the first, Rinaldo raises an arm to his breast, but here his gesture expresses his commitment to Christianity (16, st. 53–56). Armida, too, performs a variation on her appearance in the garden scene. Again she draws off to one side, but instead of remaining nearly vertical, she has sunk toward a horizontal position. The impact of the two Armidas, presumably projected from pendant overdoors across the space of a bright Rococo interior, must have been grand indeed. In playing one against the other, Tiepolo dramatized the sorceress's plight. Enthroned and upright at the far left of the first composition, voluptuously wrapped in a robe of flaming orange, she is a powerful figure. Then, on the far right of the second picture, shorn of her magical talisman

22b. Rinaldo Abandoning Armida
Ca. 1752
105 × 140 cm (41⅜ × 55⅛ in.)
Signed lower left: B. Tiepolo
Residenz, Würzburg, Filialgalerie der Bayerische Staatsgemäldesammlungen in der Residenz, on loan from Bayerische Verwaltung der Staatlichen Schlösser, Gärten und Seen, Munich (Wü. Res. G160)

PROVENANCE:
Residenz, Würzburg (by 1778–1919; inv. 1778);[4] Alte Pinakothek, Munich (1919–74); Residenz, Würzburg (from 1974)

REFERENCES:
Sack 1910, p. 197; Molmenti 1911, pl. 189; Morassi 1962, pp. 30–31; Pallucchini 1968, nos. 203–4; Knox 1978, pp. 87–88; Andersson 1984, pp. 84, 128–50; Ferrara 1985, pp. 91, 115; Gemin and Pedrocco 1993, p. 430, nos. 419–20; Aurnhammer 1994, pp. 91–93; Aurnhammer 1995, pp. 582–83; Knorn 1995; Renner 1995; Würzburg 1996, vol. 1, nos. 88–89, vol. 2, pp. 77–78, 179 doc. 47, 180 doc. 53

and holding a handkerchief identical in color to her pale-hued gown, she has fallen to the ground, a rejected woman whose face reflects her deep sorrow.

Working in a manner very different from the mode he had adopted for the Venetian Tasso pictures, Tiepolo here employed rhetorical gesture to express the tensions and conflicts of his protagonists. In its dependence on dramatic formalities, his new approach is similar to that of Nicolas Poussin and Rubens. Like his seventeenth-century predecessors, Tiepolo understood that heroic figures depicted in large paintings and seen across noble spaces needed to recite grandiloquently. Two *modelli* for the pictures (figs. 55, 56) and a preparatory drawing (Victoria and Albert Museum, London, D. 1825.63–1885) demonstrate that he did not arrive at the final formulation instinctively but worked toward it through a series of self-critical stages (in much the same way that he developed the formal gestures in the *Hyacinth* [no. 23]).[2] One wonders if his emphasis here reflects the influence of his friend, the dilettante and international figure Francesco Algarotti, who had discussed his appreciation of the use of gesture to express the *affetti*, or passions, with Tiepolo in the 1740s. Algarotti published his theories on the *affetti* years later, joining Tiepolo's name with those of Rubens, Poussin, and even Charles Le Brun in his consideration of the subject.[3]

However close to Neoclassical interpretations the Würzburg Tasso paintings may be in their use of highly charged gesture, they nonetheless display a typically late Baroque handling of paint: a bravura manipulation of the brushwork to describe texture and shadow, especially apparent in the brilliant depiction of Armida and her rich costume.

WLB

NOTES

1. I am grateful to Bettina Schwabe of the Bayerische Verwaltung der Staatlichen Schlösser, Gärten und Seen, Munich, for discussing the two paintings with me and for suggesting that they might be overdoors. It should be noted that the inventory of 1778 describes them simply as framed pictures: the current frames may be the "geschnittenem verguldeten Rahmen" mentioned.
2. Whether the pair of small canvases now in Berlin were painted as *modelli* or whether Tiepolo produced them independently, later in the same decade, has been disputed. See Knorn 1995, p. 95, and Würzburg 1996, vol. 1, pp. 156–57, nos. 90–91. Supporting a connection with the Würzburg pictures are similarities of format and composition, the recurrence of several pictorial details, and a like interest in expressive content. Yet the different positions of both the fountain and the parrot in the garden scenes, as well as the dissimilar placement of Carlo and Ubaldo and the total reversal of the positions of the hero and heroine in the two versions of the *Rinaldo Abandoning Armida*, might argue against the association. The red-chalk drawing, which is preparatory to the *Rinaldo and Armida in the Garden*, is crucial to the discussion and encourages the hypothesis that the Berlin canvases were, indeed, done as *modelli* for the Würzburg pictures, for its recto and verso reveal Tiepolo experimenting with alternatives that link the two sets of paintings. The recto shows that Tiepolo designed Armida's head twice: once inclining slightly to the right and again in a more upright position. These are exactly the two variations seen in the two painted versions. The verso seems more plausibly related to the Berlin solution, for although the cupid is turned toward the viewer (he turns away in the Würzburg version), rounded shapes identifiable as the heads of Carlo and Ubaldo occupy the positions they do in the Berlin canvas (in the Würzburg painting they have been evicted from the enclosed garden). There are, of course, independent departures, but inventions of this kind were intrinsic to Tiepolo's usual creative process, as the rich number of surviving studies for the *Hyacinth* eloquently testify. The London drawing suggests that Tiepolo produced ideas that he worked out in the *modelli* and then changed and refined in the larger paintings. One such change is the alteration made in the position of the parrot that is mentioned in canto 16 of the *Geru-salemme liberata*. It is as though, between the time the *modello* was completed and the final painting begun, the bird had taken flight and moved from the fountain to the cornice above the statue of the leering Pan—the very same perch it chose in the contemporary *Hyacinth*.
3. See Algarotti 1763b (1963 ed.), in particular the section entitled "Della espressione degli affetti." Roettgen (1996) has recently proposed that the portrait Giambattista painted alongside his own on the ceiling over the stairwell of the Residenz represents not his son Giandomenico but rather Algarotti; the implication is that the painter elevated his friend to the eminently visible position of collaborator because he relied on him so heavily. The suggestion is certainly tantalizing, but there is no visual evidence of Algarotti's appearance in the 1750s to support it.
4. It has been suggested that the paintings were commissioned by Baron Adam Friedrich von Seinsheim and acquired from him for the Residenz in 1754. See Würzburg 1996, vol. 1, p. 153.

23. The Death of Hyacinth

Tiepolo represented Apollo the sun god in almost two dozen works, ranging from the youthful *Myth of Phaethon* of about 1720 in the Villa Baglioni, Massanzago, to the *Wealth and Benefits of the Spanish Monarchy* of 1764 in the royal palace in Madrid (fig. 117). But none is as startling as this large canvas depicting an episode from Ovid's *Metamorphoses* (10.162 ff.). According to this Latin poem, which explores change and transformation in the natural world, Apollo and his beloved, the Spartan prince Hyacinth, paused one day in their wanderings over hill and dale to try their skill at discus throwing; the sun god hurled his discus so high into the heavens that it fell to earth with immense force, accidentally striking Hyacinth, who was trying to retrieve it. Mortally wounded, Hyacinth dropped to the ground; where his blood seeped into the soil a small flower sprouted—"but it was purple in color, where lilies are white."[1] Apollo lamented his dead lover and bemoaned his own guilt.

The famous Benvenuto Cellini and Rubens, as well as other artists, had already united Apollo and Hyacinth in their work before Tiepolo pictured them.[2] But Tiepolo's large and imposing painting is singular, for it transforms Ovid's discus contest into a modern game of tennis. Catching viewers off guard with three balls and a racket lying in the foreground and a slack net drooping in the background, Tiepolo has proposed that death came to Hyacinth because a tennis ball went awry! Given Hyacinth's stalwart physique, the accident strains credulity. Yet Tiepolo was in fact following the text—not of Ovid's poem in its original Latin but of Giovanni Andrea dell'Anguillara's 1561 Italian translation, which substitutes the fashionable *jeu de paume*, or game of the palm, today known as tennis, for discus throwing.[3] The new sport was popular among Renaissance nobility, enjoying a special vogue in England during the reigns of Henry VIII (1509–47), himself a very good player, and his daughter Elizabeth I (1558–1603), who attended organized tennis matches during her tours of the country. Anguillara's *Metamorphoses* was contemporary with Elizabeth's rule and was first published in Venice, where it saw further printings during the seventeenth century, one of which Tiepolo must have had in hand.[4]

Two of Tiepolo's ideas for the *Death of Hyacinth* are noted on drawings that also show motifs for the frescoes he executed in the Residenz in Würzburg between 1751 and fall 1753,[5] and several other sketches for the canvas evidence the Würzburg style. Thus, it seems probable that Tiepolo painted this impressive canvas while engaged on the vast frescoes commissioned by Prince-Bishop Carl Philipp von Greiffenclau, his patron in Würzburg. Assisted by his two sons Giandomenico and Lorenzo, during this intense period he also painted the *Fall of the Rebel Angels* and the *Assumption of the Virgin* for the Residenz Chapel; the pendants *Rinaldo and Armida in the Garden* and *Rinaldo Abandoning Armida* (no. 22a,b), based on Tasso's *Gerusalemme liberata*; the pair of ancient history pictures the *Family of Darius before Alexander* and the *Mucius Scaevola before Porsenna*; and the grand *Adoration of the Magi*.[6] Father and sons moved tirelessly from one commission to another, alternating time spent on the scaffolding in the Kaisersaal and the stairwell of the Residenz with hours in their studio before the easel or their drafting boards. The surviving drawings for *Hyacinth* imply that Tiepolo's creative imagination was especially challenged by this Ovidian story. Despite the wide variety of themes he had painted during his previous thirty-five-year career, no subject had ever before required that he represent a pair of beautiful male lovers bound beyond death in lament. How was he to express their last moments together?[7]

He began, so it would seem on the evidence of one drawing (fig. 57), picturing Hyacinth lying with his legs extended to the right, not to the left, as in the painting; Apollo is shown both standing and kneeling, and in each case he effortlessly supports the prince's lifeless body, thanks to his own superhuman strength.[8] The sun god reaches affectingly toward his lover, exactly as he does on the recto and verso of a drawing in Trieste, where the same compositional alternatives, with slight variations, are sketched.[9] Tiepolo subsequently reversed the couple in another drawing (fig. 58), placing Hyacinth's body in almost the same position as in the painting, but retained Apollo's simple and direct gestures.[10] The first bystanders appear here, a zigzagging brushstroke delineating a broad shadow sweeping down on one of them. Then, in the painting Tiepolo slightly repositioned the prince in space so that his head turns sweetly toward Apollo, while his body epitomizes the ideal of classical beauty instead of expressing human frailty; and he radically altered the scene by transforming the sun god's tender gestures into grand rhetoric. What in the drawing

23. The Death of Hyacinth
Ca. 1752–53
287 × 232 cm (113 × 91⅜ in.)
Fundación Colección Thyssen-Bornemisza, Madrid (1934.29)

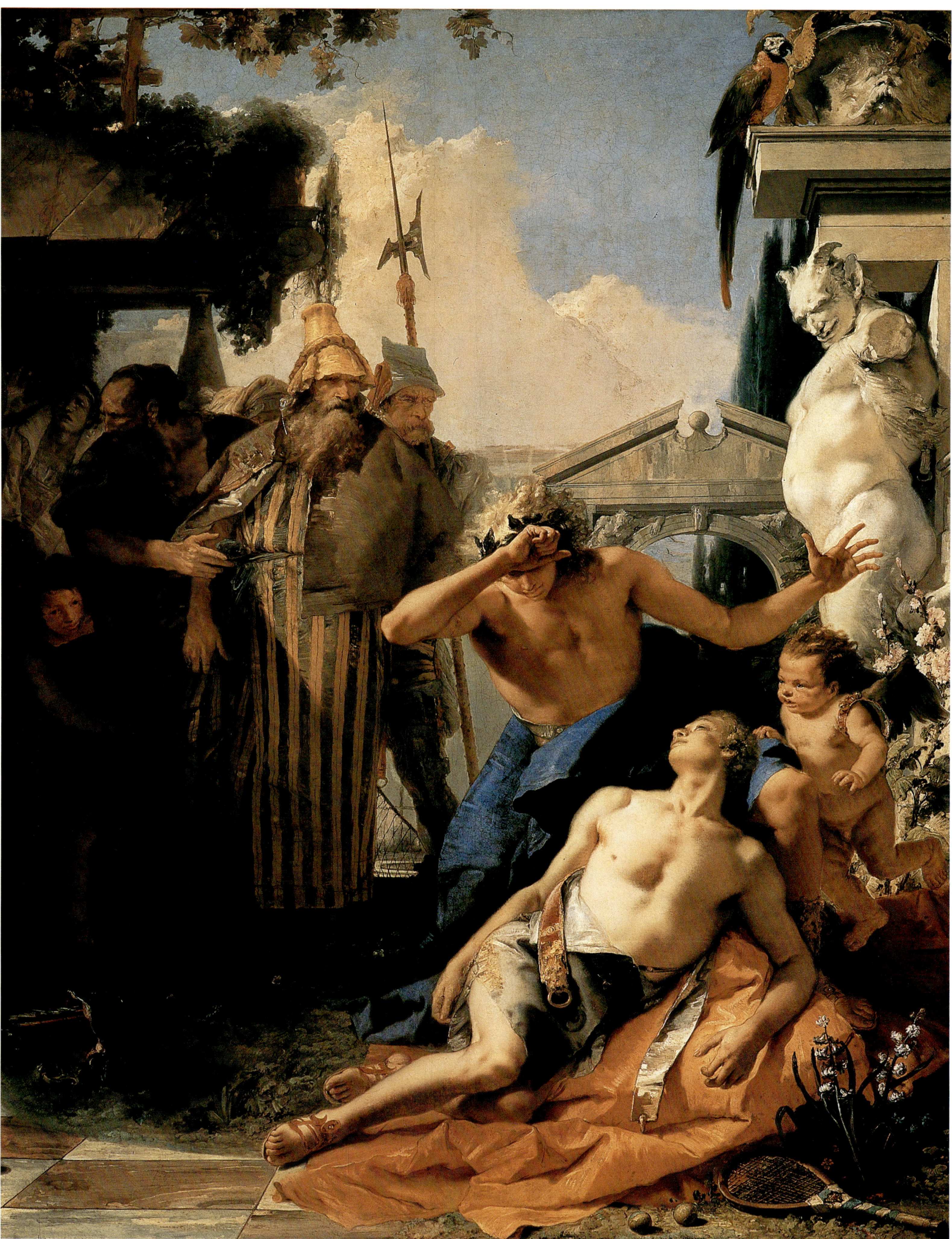

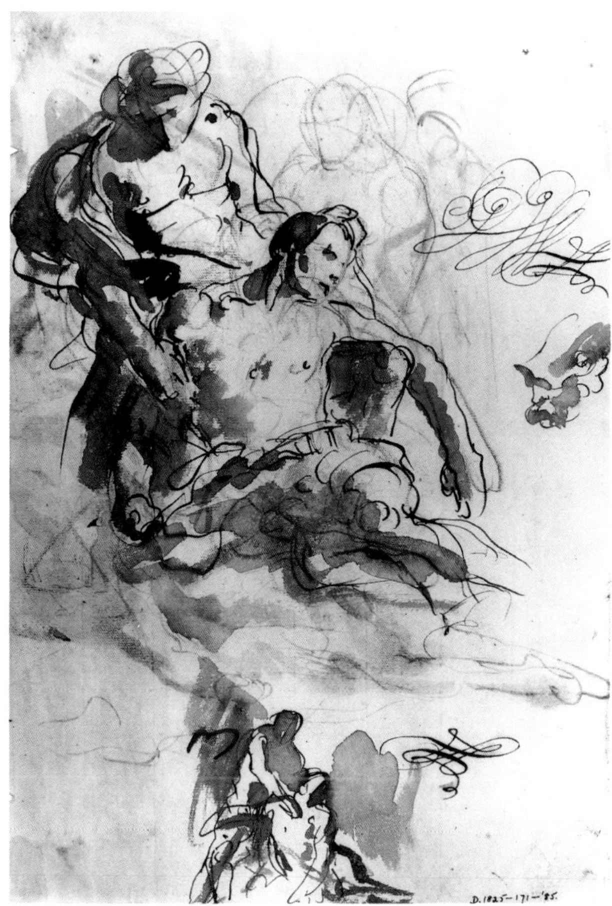

Fig. 57. *Compositional Study for "The Death of Hyacinth,"* recto. Pen and ink and wash over red chalk. Victoria and Albert Museum, London (D.1825.171-1885)

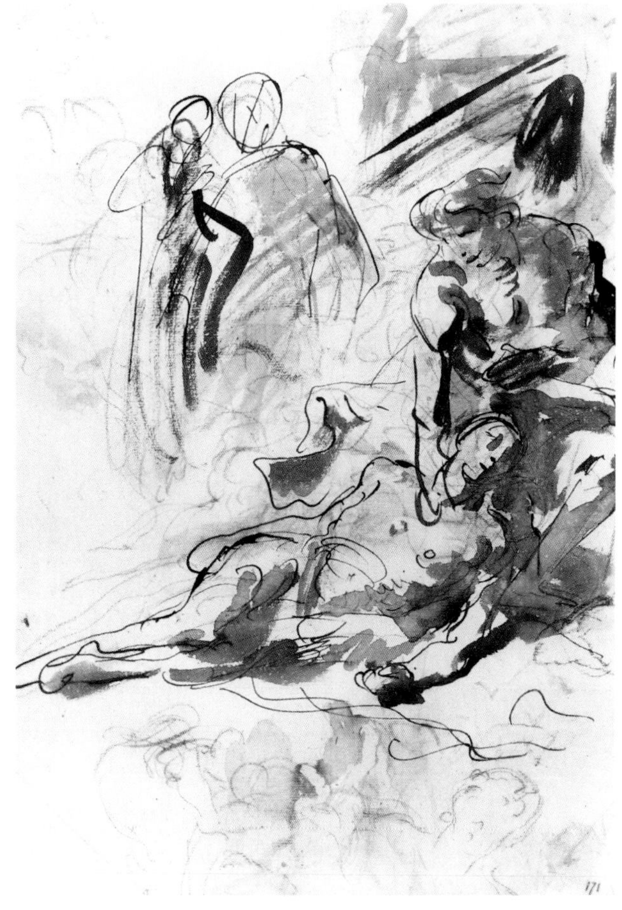

Fig. 58. *Compositional Study for "The Death of Hyacinth,"* verso. Pen and ink and wash over red chalk. Victoria and Albert Museum, London (D.1825.171-1885)

had been an intimate moment of quiet grief is now a public display of eloquent oratory and stately heroism.

Tiepolo's Apollo was conceived contemporaneously with his other splendid sun god, who reigns at the summit of Olympus on the ceiling over the stairwell in the Residenz and whose stance reiterates that of the *Apollo Belvedere*, the renowned ancient sculpture in Rome. Like his frescoed twin, Apollo here has a massive chest, a laurel wreath ornamenting his curly blond hair, and a bent left knee (albeit less flexed), and he extends one arm exactly as his counterpart on the ceiling does. But that arm is now unencumbered (in the fresco it is draped), and the hand is tellingly silhouetted against the private parts of a Pan-like caryatid that leers at the dead Hyacinth. This grinning creature, whose face is the most expressive in the painting, establishes the startling tone of the scene by commenting sardonically on the events taking place; in this he performs the same function as two similar figures, one in Tiepolo's own

Opposite: no. 23
Overleaf, left: Detail, no. 23
Overleaf, right: Detail, no. 23

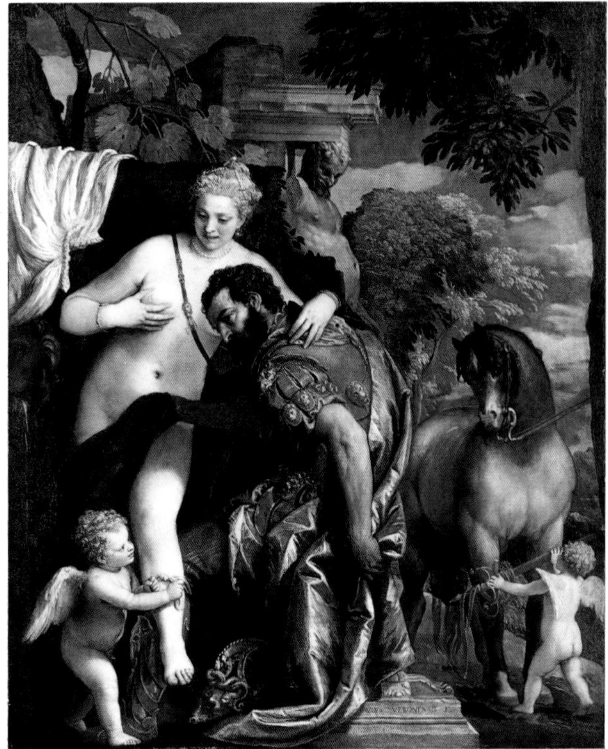

Fig. 59. Paolo Veronese. *Mars and Venus United by Love*. Oil on canvas. The Metropolitan Museum of Art, New York; John Stewart Kennedy Fund, 1910 (10.189)

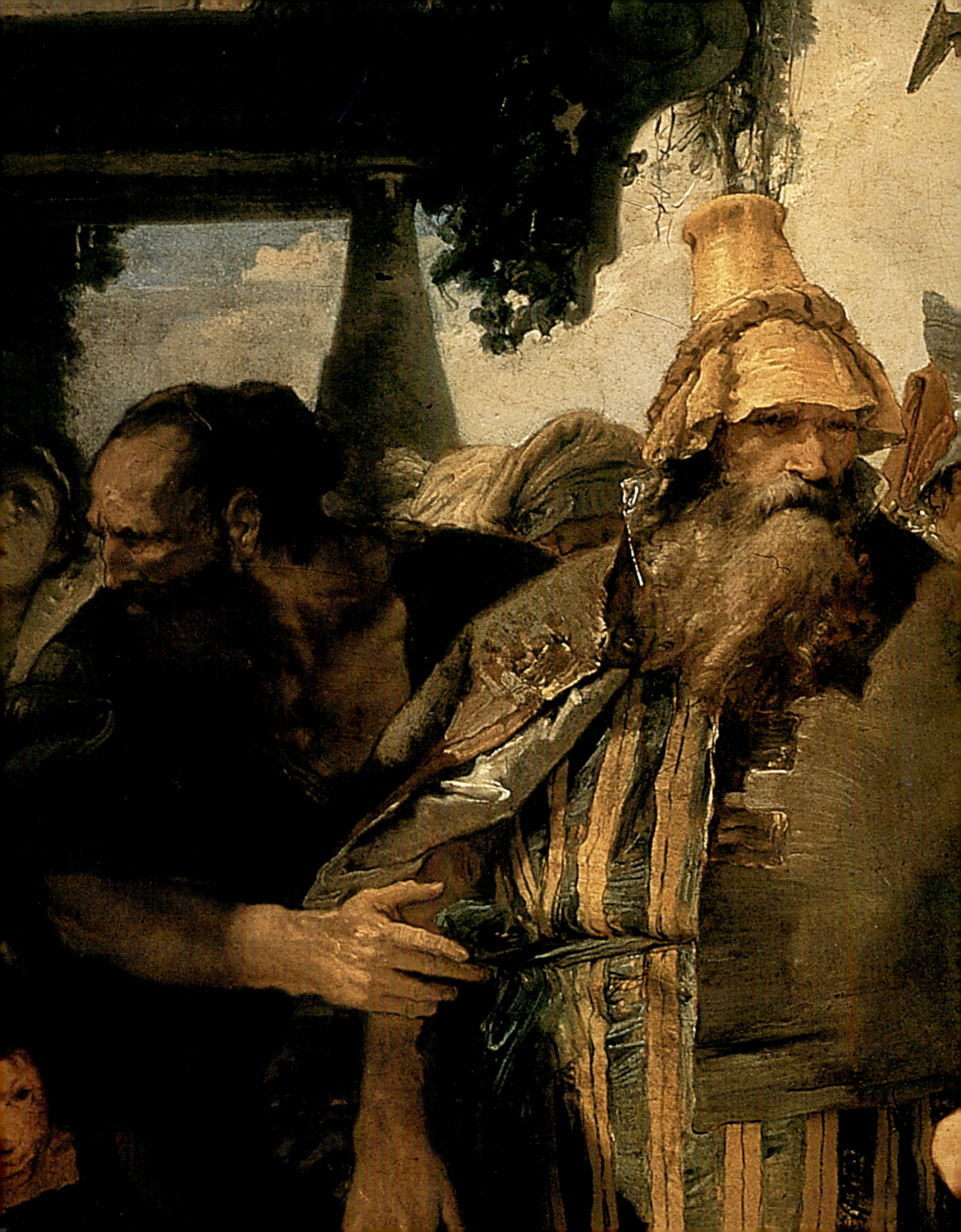

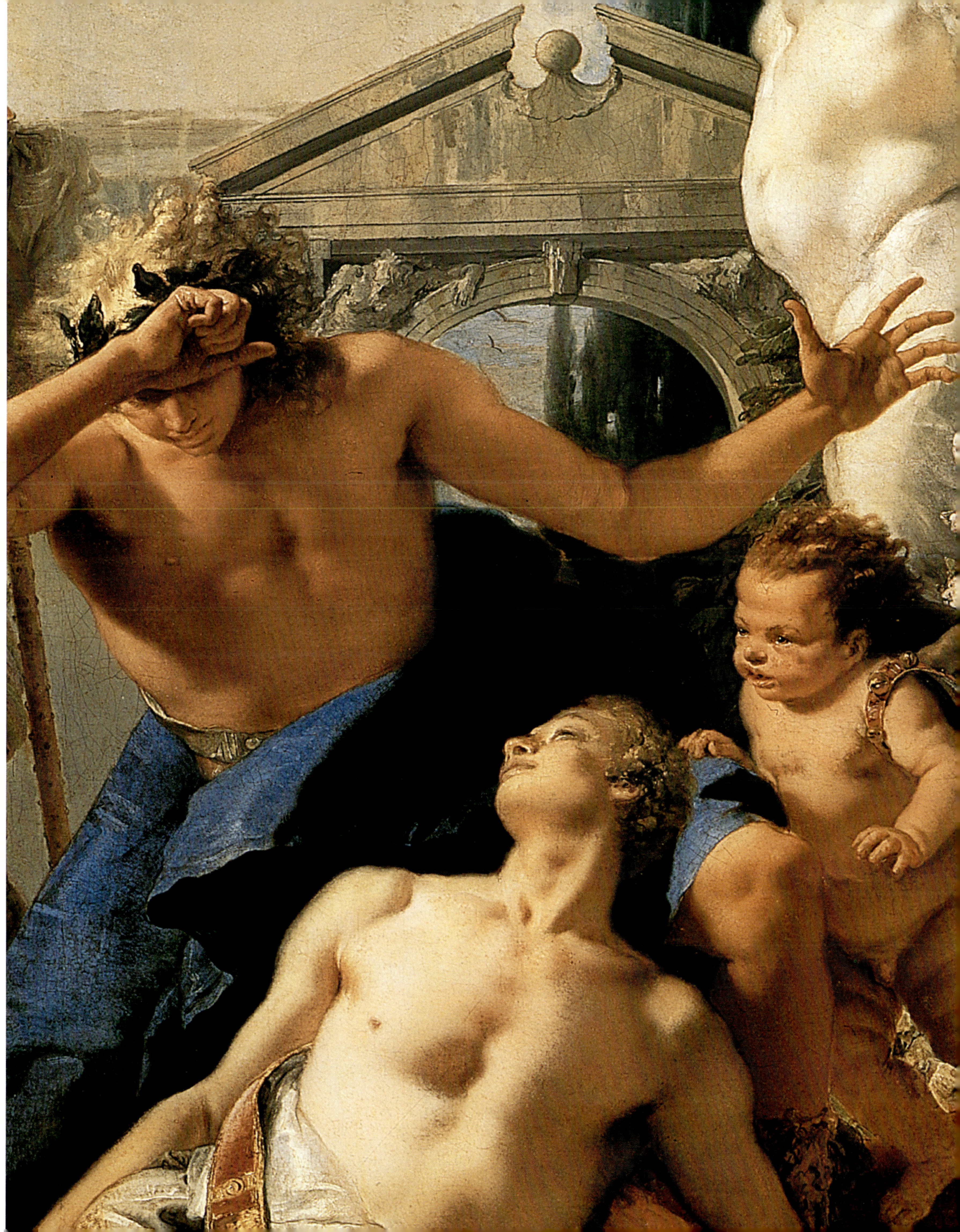

PROVENANCE:
Graf Wilhelm Friedrich Schaumburg-Lippe Bückeburg, Niedersächsen (1752/53–77);[16] by descent, Fürsten von Schaumburg-Lippe, Bückeburg (until 1934); Baron Heinrich Thyssen-Bornemisza, Schloss Rohoncz, Lugano, and Villa Favorita, Castagnola (Lugano) (1934–88)

REFERENCES:
Sack 1910, pp. 109–11; Heinemann 1937, p. 149; Morassi 1955a, p. 29; Knox (1960) 1975a, nos. 185–86; London 1961, no. 105; Morassi 1962, p. 20; Heinemann 1971, no. 301; Heckscher 1974; Fehl 1979; Knox 1980a, vol. 1, p. 330; Hagen and Hagen 1985; Barcham 1989, pp. 110–11; Fehl 1992, pp. 339–40; Gemin and Pedrocco 1993, p. 432, no. 423; Würzburg 1996, vol. 1, pp. 138–48, vol. 2, pp. 91–92

Rinaldo and Armida in the Garden and the other in Veronese's *Mars and Venus United by Love* (fig. 59), both paintings concerned, like the *Hyacinth*, with forbidden love. To help make his point in the *Hyacinth*, Tiepolo added a supertitle, as it were, in the form of a luxuriously plumaged parrot, a symbol here, as in other paintings of the period, of both self-indulgence and licentiousness.[11] Pan and parrot are jarringly paired with a cupid rushing forward in distress and with distant cypresses, a traditional emblem of mourning. A ball ornament in the pediment above the main figure group leads our glance directly downward to Hyacinth's lifeless eye and hand, the fingers of which remain curved to cup the fateful ball the prince was attempting to retrieve. The spare balls lying near the racket at the bottom of the painting are a kind of footnote to the composition's uneasy balance of discordant elements.

Several figures on the left view the tragedy before them, but they stand separated from it by a quiver on the ground arranged parallel to the legs of the Spartan prince. Two elderly men in the group gaze almost passively at Hyacinth's body and observe Apollo's heroic grief over his lover's untimely death, as if their dispassion is meant to neutralize the disturbing emotional tensions played out under the bright sun to our right. Do the bystanders pronounce silently on the scene while Pan lewdly grimaces over the lovers and the tennis racket nullifies Ovid's mythic past? Tiepolo perhaps offered the wise graybeards and the sharply silhouetted military halberd as a moralizing counterweight to the carnal pleasures and fun-filled games of Apollo and his lover. Do the wide-eyed innocence of the boy in shadow and the rusticity of the overhanging architecture behind the crowd counteract the squawking parrot and the highly refined sculpture and architecture of its perch? Has Tiepolo insinuated, in fact, that Apollo has forsaken his divine obligations? As god of philosophy, he must inculcate morality and religion in society, but has he not instead gone astray, in the words of the *Metamorphoses*, "per scherzo, e per amore"?[12] As god of archery, he is duty bound to undertake virile pursuits, but he has surely neglected such responsibilities; why else does the manly quiver of arrows lie abandoned in shadow while the elegantly rendered tennis racket bathes in the warmth of the sun? Finally, is a moral lesson to be learned here, as there is from the contemporary *Rinaldo and Armida*, where another Pan and parrot hold sway while an enchantress unmans a hero?

Tiepolo's talent for fashioning revisionist interpretations of classical myth had produced a comical *Danaë and Jupiter* (no. 15) in the 1730s; in that painting he had also skillfully employed dissonant realities, but to amusing rather than enigmatic effect. The kind of artistry that distinguishes the *Death of Hyacinth* Tiepolo most frequently made use of in his two sets of etchings, the *Capricci* and the *Scherzi* (see nos. 59, 60). Indeed, a number of specific elements that enliven the prints appear as well in the *Hyacinth:* the aged and strangely garbed philosophers, the laughing faun, and the haunting confrontation of timeless beauty and irrevocable death.[13] *Hyacinth* again resembles the enigmatic prints in that it too refuses to yield answers to the questions it poses. But the presumed circumstances surrounding the origin of the painting may explain its subject and mood. Wilhelm Friedrich Schaumburg-Lippe Bückeburg, the supposed patron of *Hyacinth*, was twenty-eight years old when the work was commissioned, by which time, according to his letters, he had had a passionate affair with a young Hungarian man. He had subsequently met a Spanish musician with whom he briefly lived in Venice and whom the baron's father referred to in a letter as "your friend Apollo." The Spaniard died in 1751,[14] that is, just before the *Hyacinth* was commissioned. If not only the provenance of the painting but also its genesis can indeed be securely linked with Bückeburg, the questions of why the canvas is so large, what impulses fueled the choice of story, and how the depth of sorrow represented can be explained all find easy solutions.

Nonetheless, there are still no clues regarding Tiepolo's motive for injecting bitter humor into his depiction of intense grief. But his son Giandomenico understood and adopted that humor when he modulated and paraphrased elements from the painting in his own art. He restated the dead prince in reverse in the clothed figure of a deformed, sleeping clown, shown with a tennis racket lying nearby, in the fresco *Punchinello in the Countryside*, which he painted in his small villa on the mainland. And in at least two drawings for his series on the life of Punchinello entitled *Divertimenti per li regazzi*, Giandomenico again quoted from his father's *Hyacinth*: in one work two clowns more or less reenact Apollo's mourning over the prince as Giambattista first imagined it in one of his preparatory studies for the canvas; in another an Oriental type dressed in a turban and a striped robe stands quietly watching a collapsed clown who lifts his arm to his forehead in a gesture reminiscent of that of the grieving Apollo.[15] Giandomenico appreciated and to an extent retained the pictorial power of his father's deeply expressive figures, as well as the capacity of some of them to invite personal interpretation from the audience. What the son could not translate, however, was the unsettling irony that Giambattista created when he corrupted transcendent beauty with whispers of wanton sexuality.

WLB

Notes

1. Ovid 1967, p. 230.
2. For Cellini's work, see Barbaglia 1981, p. 93, no. 46, and Pope-Hennessy 1985, pp. 230–31, fig. 131; for Rubens's, see Alpers 1971, pp. 222–23, no. 32a, fig. 123, and Held 1980, vol. 1, p. 282.
3. Fehl 1979 and Fehl 1992.
4. A copy dated 1669 is in the library of the Museo Correr, Venice.
5. Stuttgart 1970, nos. 82, 84.
6. Gemin and Pedrocco 1993, nos. 418–22.
7. It seems more likely that this was Tiepolo's problem, rather than his concern with what Alpers and Baxandall (1994, p. 60) express as "wash patterns . . . [that he] himself found bad."
8. Knox 1975a, no. 186. For a discussion of other drawings by Tiepolo and his workshop, both for and after *Hyacinth*, see Würzburg 1996, vol. 1, nos. 72–81, vol. 2, pp. 91–92.
9. Rizzi 1990, no. 67, r, v.
10. Knox 1975a, no. 185 r.
11. Parrots began to play an important role in European visual art and literature after the discovery of new animal species in the Americas; one of the most famous of the birds introduced at this time is John Locke's speaking parrot in his *Essay Concerning Human Understanding* (1689). For the parrot's appearance in visual art, see Jongh 1968–69.
12. Anguillara 1669, p. 324.
13. Succi in Gorizia 1985, nos. 55 (*Family of the Happy Satyr*), 59 (*Six Figures Watching a Snake*).
14. This intriguing information and the assertion that Schaumburg-Lippe was an avid tennis player appear in Hagen and Hagen 1985 but with only a brief general reference to the baron's writings and with no documentary evidence.
15. Bloomington 1979, nos. 9, 16.
16. According to an inventory cited by Sack (1910), the picture was acquired directly from Tiepolo in Venice for two hundred zecchini. Given the fact that drawings related to this work contain motifs derived from the fresco over the main stairwell at Würzburg, the date of the picture and the place it was painted are not in doubt. However, the inventory has never been checked. Neither Dr. Roswitha Sommer at the Schaumburg-Lippischer Heimatverein, Bückeburg, nor Dr. Böhme at the Niedersächsisches Staatsarchive was able to confirm the information. The former has kindly noted in a letter that the collection includes a large number of Italian paintings and especially works by Tiepolo.

24. *Neptune Offering Gifts to Venice*

24. Neptune Offering Gifts to Venice
Ca. 1756–58
135 × 275 cm (53¼ × 108¼ in.)
Palazzo Ducale, Venice (328)

Neptune Offering Gifts to Venice is an allegory of state; unique in Tiepolo's career, it represents a form rare in eighteenth-century Venetian art in general. The genre had flourished in Venice during the late Gothic period and the Renaissance, and by the end of the third quarter of the cinquecento, most of the great artists who had worked in the city—Guariento, Gentile da Fabriano, the brothers Gentile and Giovanni Bellini, and Titian, to name just the most outstanding—had covered the walls of the Palazzo Ducale with such paintings glorifying the republic. Those works perished, however, in the devastating fires of 1574 and 1577 and were replaced in the late sixteenth and early seventeenth centuries with paintings by Paolo Veronese, Jacopo Tintoretto, Jacopo Bassano, and Palma il Giovane, among others. But some of those later works, particularly the frescoes, eventually deteriorated, and only a very few new ones were commissioned to replace them during the late seicento and the settecento. Tiepolo's *Neptune*, his only canvas in the Palazzo Ducale, was one of those few.

Tiepolo painted *Neptune Offering Gifts to Venice* to decorate the Sala delle Quattro Porte, or Room of the Four Doors, a large rectangular hall. Although no governmental body deliberated there, the significance of the *sala* as a public space was beyond question. Not only is it the first large hall awaiting all who ascend the monumental Scala d'Oro, or Golden Staircase; it also stands as a central passageway connecting the four chambers in which Venice's most powerful governmental organs met: the Collegio; the Senate; the much-feared Council of Ten; and the Three Heads, or Capi, of the Council of Ten. Every influential patrician serving in those bodies walked through the Sala delle Quattro Porte on an almost daily basis, every foreign diplomat waited there before he was summoned for his official meetings with representatives of the government, and every royal visitor to the republic passed through the room in a formal ceremony. The late-sixteenth-century sculptural and pictorial decoration of the *sala* reflected its pivotal position. Statues, slightly smaller than lifesize, stand on the cornices over each of the four doorways, and large canvases fill the two long walls. On the richly ornamented vault designed by Palladio, Tintoretto frescoed eleven scenes apotheosizing Venice's terrestrial power and unique virtues.[1] He also painted two lunettes

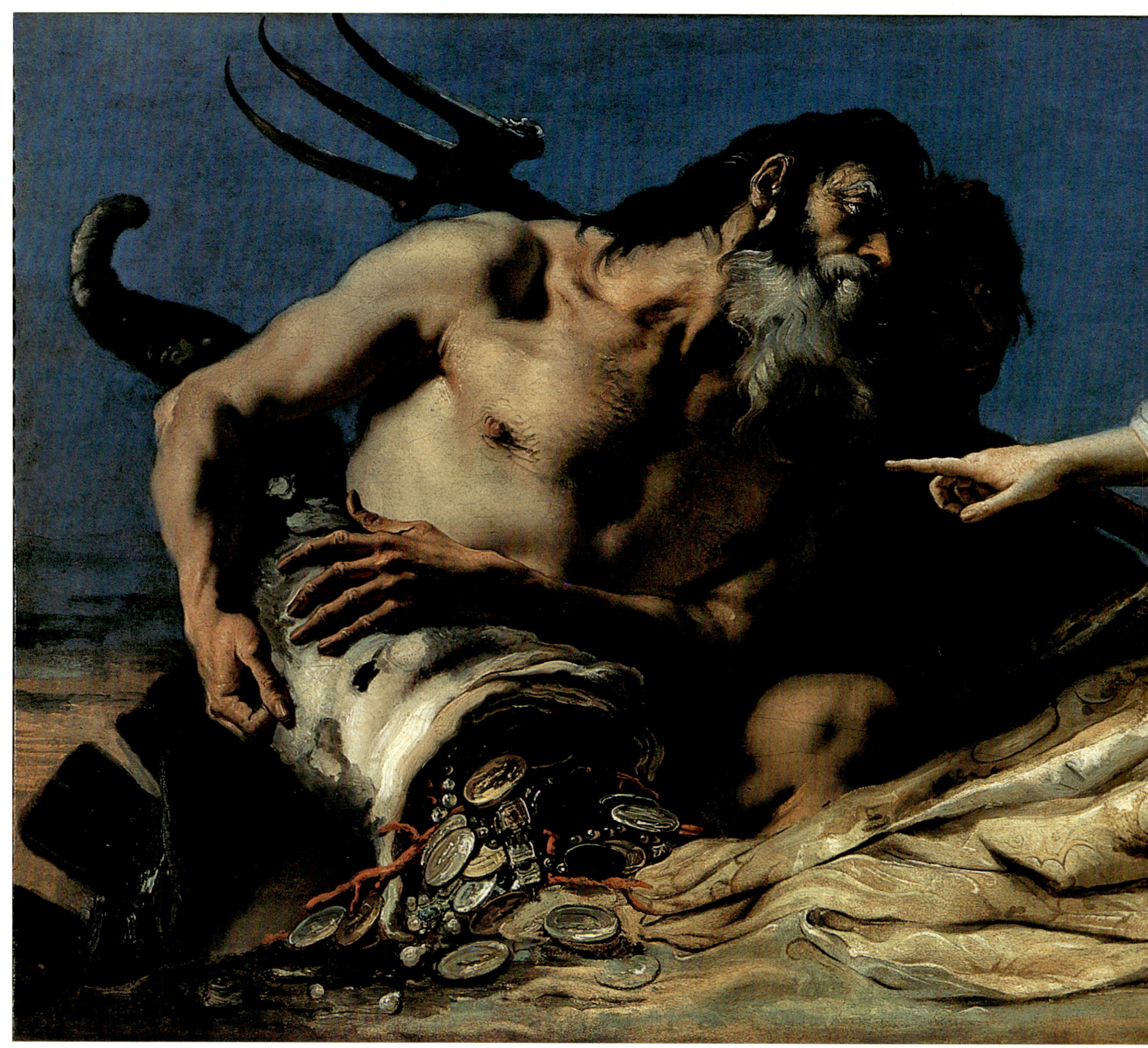

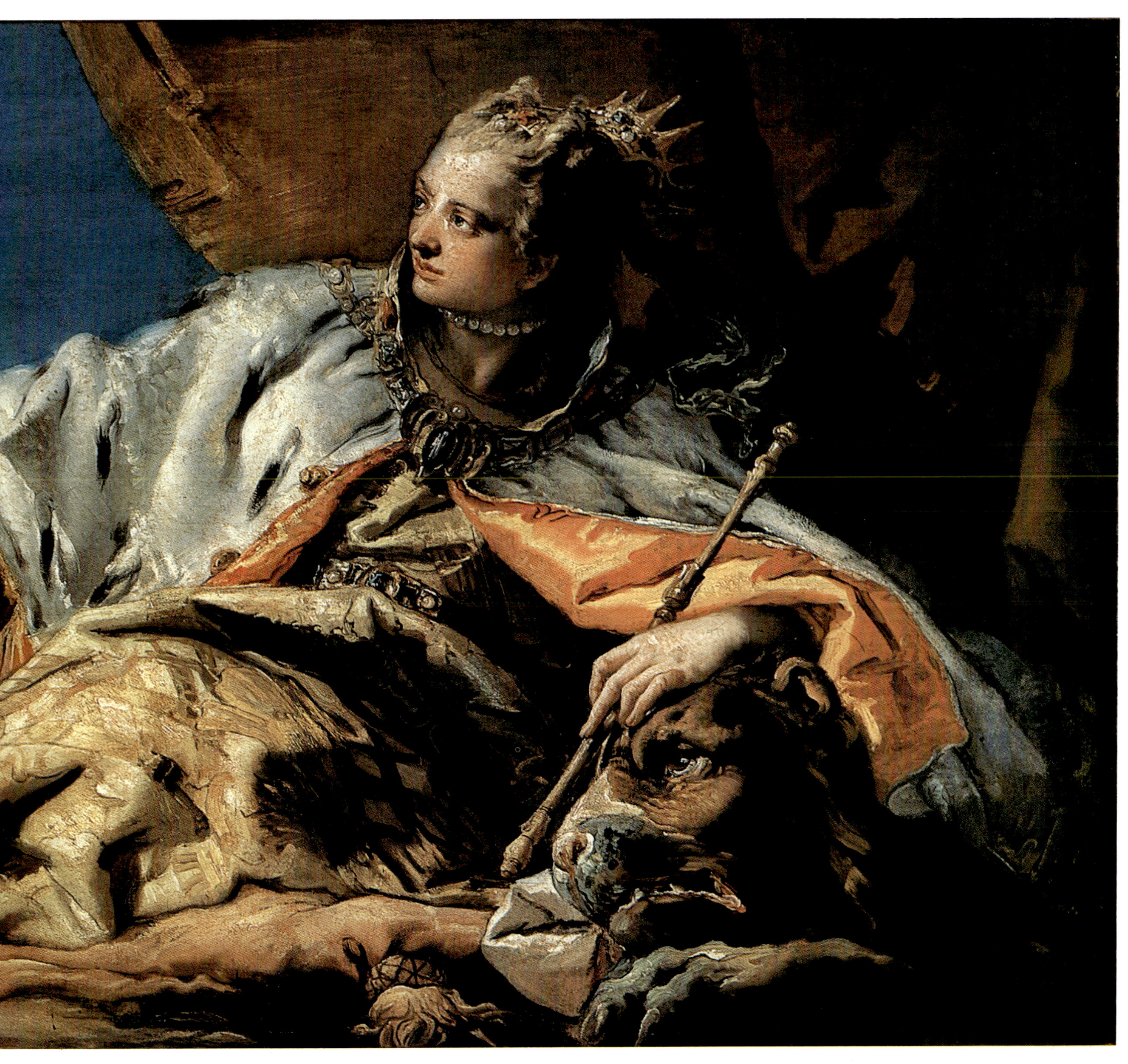

PROVENANCE:
Palazzo Ducale, Venice

REFERENCES:
Zanetti 1771, p. 468; Molmenti 1909, p. 51; Pignatti 1951, pp. 102–10; Morassi 1962, p. 58; Pallucchini 1968, no. 189; Frerichs 1971a; Frerichs 1971b, p. 224; Pignatti in Franzoni, Pignatti, and Wolters 1990, p. 306; Gemin and Pedrocco 1993, p. 458, no. 470; Venice 1995a, no. 60

below the vault, one on each of the room's two short walls.

By 1733 Nicolò Bambini, one of Venice's most appreciated and seasoned painters of the period, had restored all of Tintoretto's damaged frescoes except the completely ruined lunette with *Venice Resting on a Globe*; this he replaced with his own frescoed version of the subject that today still sits on the wall facing the palace's courtyard.[2] Bambini's restoration of Tintoretto's other lunette, on the opposite wall, with *Venice's Marriage with Neptune*, must not have lasted, however, for about twenty-five years after it was completed Tiepolo executed his *Neptune Offering Gifts to Venice* on canvas as its substitute. No documentation has been found to establish the precise date of Tiepolo's *Neptune*, but on various counts it can reasonably be placed between 1756 and 1758.[3] First, Giandomenico, Tiepolo's son, had already made an engraving after *Neptune* by 1758, for he sent an invoice for it dated June 1758 to Pierre-Jean Mariette, the French connoisseur.[4] Second, the facial and body types of both Neptune and the personification of Venice are almost identical to those of figures populating Tiepolo's works dating to the years between 1756 and 1758 (the frescoes of 1757 in the Villa Valmarana, Vicenza; the two ceiling frescoes of 1757–58 in Ca' Rezzonico, Venice [no. 25a,b]; the canvas *Venus Giving a Babe to Father Time*, painted for a contemporary ceiling in Villa Contarini-Pisani, Mira; and the great altar painting *Saint Thecla Praying for the Plague-Stricken,* unveiled in the cathedral of Este in 1759 [no. 51]).[5] Finally, Tiepolo's brushwork in the *Neptune*, especially in the brilliant jewels and the resplendent draperies worn by Venice, matches exactly the painterly handling of his oils known to date to the mid- to late 1750s. Thus, it is clear that when he made his engraving, Giandomenico was reproducing one of his father's most recent works, one contemporary with a small number of other commissions in the Palazzo Ducale.

Although they were portrayed only forty years before the demise of the Republic of Venice, Tiepolo's protagonists proclaim the source of the city's wealth in the sea and exalt its saintly dedication to the evangelist Mark. Neptune, the lion of Saint Mark, and the personification of Venice appear in many different combinations and configurations throughout the sculptural and pictorial decoration of the Palazzo Ducale. Indeed, Tiepolo's image sums up much of the Gothic and Renaissance iconography of Venetian political allegory, echoing elements of such varied paintings as Donato Veneziano's *Marcian Lion* and Vittore Carpaccio's *Lion of Saint Mark*, on the one hand, and Veronese's *Mars and Neptune* and *Venice with Justice and Peace*, two panels in the ceiling of the nearby Sala del Collegio, on the other.[6] But Tiepolo diverged from pictorial tradition in representing both Neptune and Saint Mark's lion as tired and beleaguered. Although large-boned and muscular, the hoary-bearded Neptune seems to be merely a worn-out indentured servant, and even if the lion has massive claws and grimaces fiercely, he is so tame that Venice can rest her arm on him. In order to accommodate his long horizontal format, Tiepolo forced his figures into supine positions that diminish the pictorial power of Neptune and the lion but emphasize the royal prerogative historically claimed by Venice.

In fact, Venice is the shining star of the painting. Her ample but severely foreshortened form dominates the work; she is crowned, bejeweled, dressed in the ducal robes of state, and belted with heavy gold, and she holds the baton of military power. Her trappings include as well the ermine or lynx cape worn by the doge in appropriate weather on the most august occasions and which appears in innumerable paintings throughout the Palazzo Ducale. Venice is coiffed like a patrician woman of the late sixteenth or early seventeenth century, and the pearls around her neck, like the coral and gold that spill from Neptune's cornucopia, confirm the source of the wealth that the Most Serene Republic had historically enjoyed.[7] It was a celebrated fact that the state had built its power through its domination of the Adriatic Sea, although that domination was no longer assured by the middle of the eighteenth century. The historic link between the republic and the sea is made clear by the placement of Tiepolo's canvas in the Sala delle Quattro Porte: for just as Bambini's *Venice Resting on a Globe* sits on the room's western wall, toward the mainland, thereby sustaining Venice's claim to an empire on terra firma, so *Neptune Offering Gifts to Venice* asserted the republic's traditional source of power by decorating the east wall, facing the Rio di Palazzo and the Adriatic Sea, or, in the Venetians' time-honored phrase, "il golfo nostro."

WLB

NOTES

1. Wolters 1987, pp. 59–66.
2. Zanetti 1733, p. 102.
3. The first notice of its execution was made by Zanetti (1771, p. 468): Tiepolo "dipinse sopra i finestroni le figure di Venezia e di Nettuno, per rimettere una vecchia pittura consumata dal tempo."
4. Frerichs 1971a and Frerichs 1971b.
5. For these paintings, see Gemin and Pedrocco 1993, nos. 432–55, 459–60, 472, 486. The facial and figure types and the brushwork of *Neptune* are even closer to those in *Time Revealing Truth* (The Museum of Fine Arts, Boston; ibid., no. 471), which, although undated, is clearly also a work of the same period.

6. Relevant too is Veronese's *Allegory of Venice*, a canvas formerly on the ceiling of the Audience Room in the Granai di Terranova, Venice; the Szépmüvészeti Múzeum, Budapest, holds a work it claims to be the original but judged a copy by some. See Minneapolis 1995, pp. 200–201, and Schulz 1968, p. 139, no. 88.
7. The cornucopia spilling forth gold is also associated with the personification of Liberality by Cesare Ripa in his *Iconologia*.

THE DECORATIONS FOR CA' REZZONICO

25a. Wedding Allegory
25b. Nobility and Virtue Accompany Merit to the Temple of Glory

These two frescoed ceilings at Ca' Rezzonico were executed by Giambattista with the collaboration of his eldest son, Giandomenico, and the *quadraturista* Girolamo Mengozzi Colonna during the winter of 1757.[1] The first is in the Sala dell'Allegoria Nuziale and the second is in the Sala del Trono, between the Rio di San Barnaba and the Grand Canal. The occasion for the decorations was the marriage of Ludovico, son of Giambattista Rezzonico, to Faustina Savorgnan, celebrated on 16 January 1758; Gaspare Diziani and Jacopo Guarana painted frescoes in the same wing, in the Sala del Pastelli and the Sala degli Arazzi, respectively.

In the *Wedding Allegory* Giambattista returned to the theme of Apollo's chariot with its team of four fiery horses, which he had previously used at the Residenz in Würzburg. Here the wedding couple is placed in the chariot, while the sun god stands behind them. All around is the ritual array of allegorical figures: Fame blowing her trumpet, the Three Graces sitting on a cloud just below the chariot, Wisdom and Merit (the old man crowned with laurel and holding a banner bearing the coupled coats of arms of the newlyweds' two families). Over the whole a bright sunlight and a crystalline clarity of color dominate, both revived by a restoration in 1990 that involved the removal of dirt and of numerous old repaints in oil that had obscured the fresco's original chromatic orchestration, making it scarcely legible.

The central section, which is framed by Mengozzi Colonna's *quadratura*, was executed in its entirety by Tiepolo in just twelve days of work. Although it does not seem possible to verify Giandomenico's likely collaboration, the four couples of satyrs and satyresses on the cornice at the bottom of the fresco can almost certainly be attributed to the hand of Giambattista's son.

A small canvas in the Museo di Castelvecchio, Verona, was published by Trecca in 1912 as a preparatory sketch for the Ca' Rezzonico ceiling; it must instead be the work of an anonymous assistant in Tiepolo's studio and a derivation from the fresco.

The subject of the fresco in the Sala del Trono was formerly thought to be the Triumph of the Poet Quintilian Rezzonico. It was Lorenzetti[2] who correctly identified its iconography, thanks to the discovery of a poem celebrating the Rezzonico-Savorgnan wedding, composed by the Paduan abbot Giuseppe Gennari. In the poem the fresco's theme is described as follows: "Merit is he /who directs his steps to the temple of Glory / whence Nobility and Virtue /see him and lead him to the immortal abode."

Sánchez Cantón proposed that a small painting he found in an unidentified private collection in Madrid represented a stage in the evolution of the fresco's

***25a. Wedding Allegory**
1757
Fresco, 630 × 1,030 cm
(248 × 405½ in.)
Museo del Settecento Veneziano, Ca' Rezzonico, Venice

***25b. Nobility and Virtue Accompany Merit to the Temple of Glory**
1757
Fresco, 600 × 1,000 cm
(236¼ × 393¾ in.)
Museo del Settecento Veneziano, Ca' Rezzonico, Venice

PROVENANCE, 25a:
Ca' Rezzonico, Venice

REFERENCES:
Molmenti 1909, p. 69; Sack 1910, p. 153; Trecca 1912, p. 138; Lorenzetti 1936, p. 31; Lorenzetti in Venice 1951, pp. 112–14; Mazzariol and Pignatti 1951, p. 74; Morassi 1962, p. 63; Pallucchini 1968, no. 245; Frerichs 1971a, p. 241; Romanelli and Pedrocco 1986, pp. 18–22; Levey 1986, p. 228; Gemin and Pedrocco 1993, p. 451, no. 459; Pedrocco in Venice 1995a, p. 490

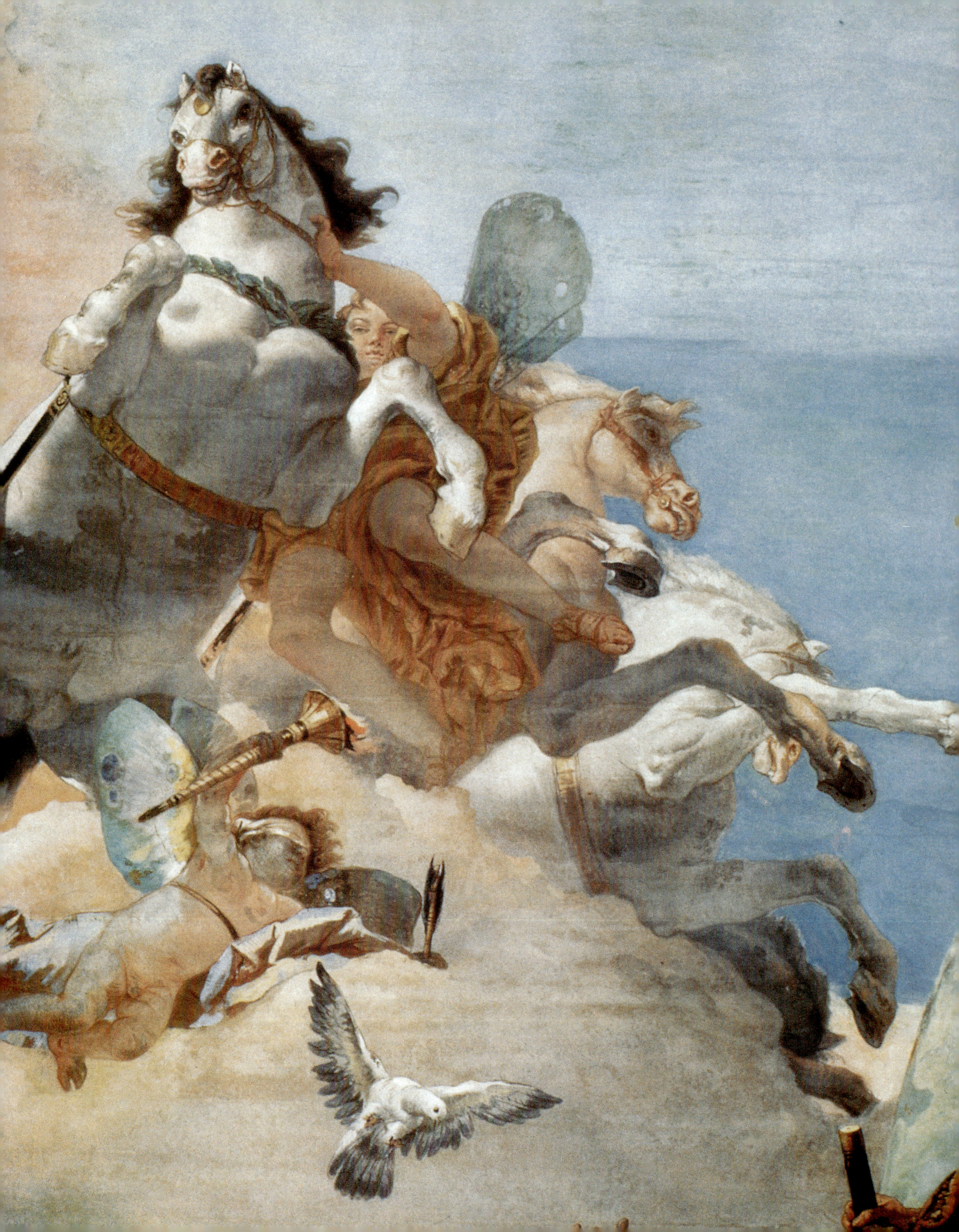

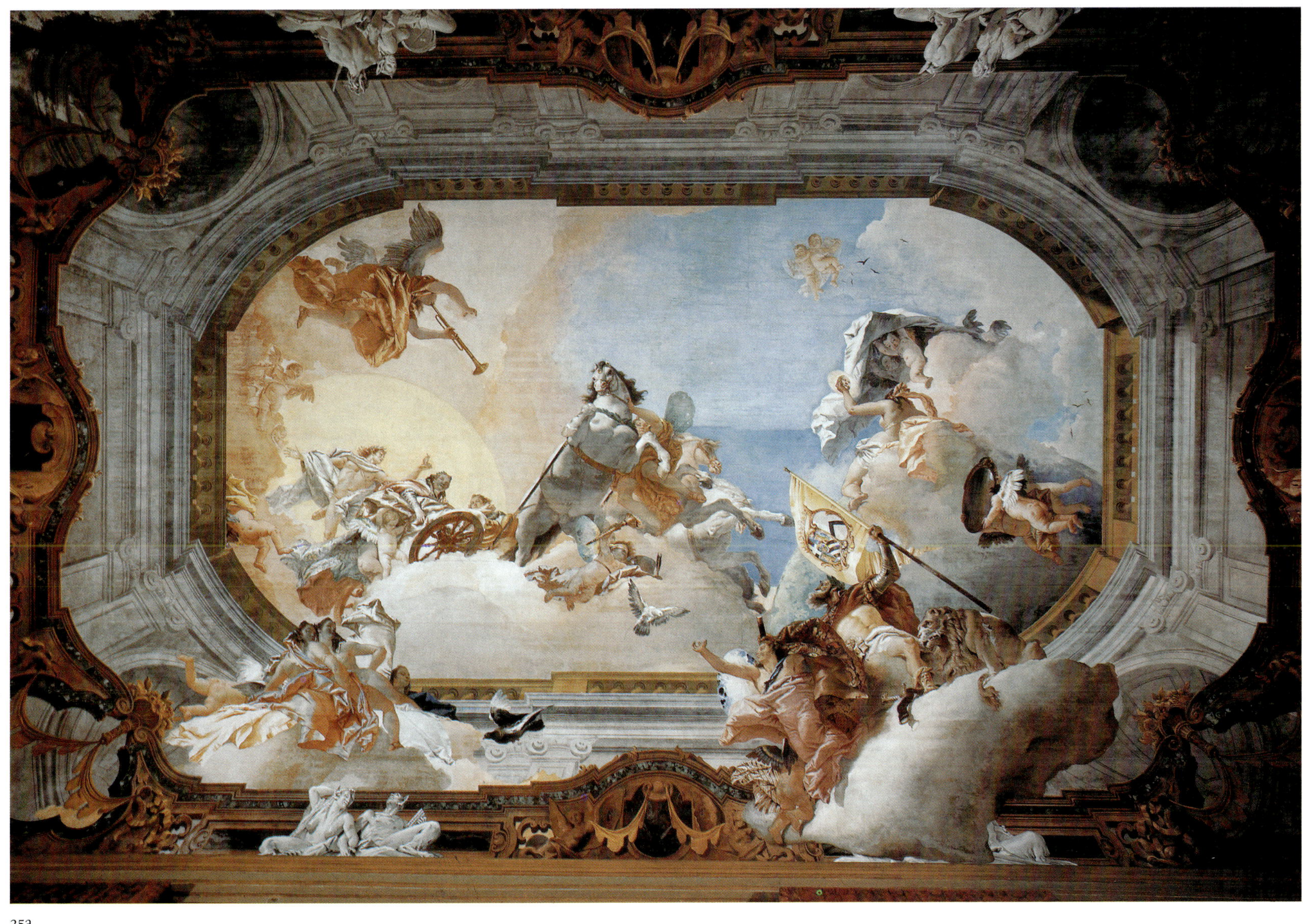

25a

Opposite: Detail, no. 25a

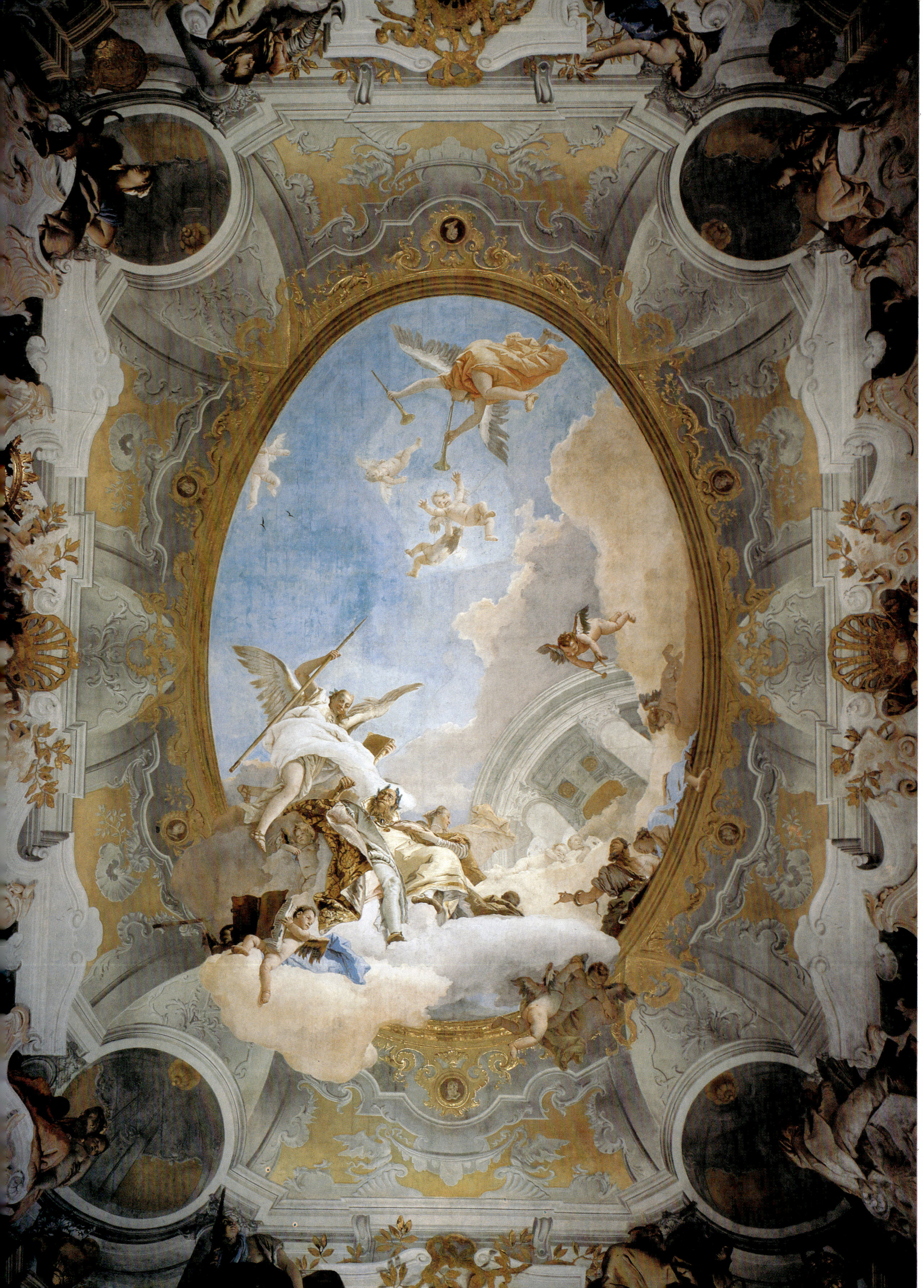

25b

conception. The attribution of the painting to Giambattista was accepted by Morassi but refuted by Pallucchini. To judge from a photograph of it, the attribution to Tiepolo seems plausible. In any case, the painting's differences with respect to the larger work suggest that it is a first idea modified substantially—perhaps at the behest of the patrons—during the execution of the fresco.

In the realization of this fresco, as well as of the Sala dell'Allegoria Nuziale ceiling, Giambattista displayed his habitual lightning-quick speed of execution: indeed, to complete the central section required only eleven days of work. Of note, in this case, is the use—exceptional for Tiepolo—of *a secco* painting for part of the sky: he may have been forced to choose this method by faulty drying of the plaster, caused by adverse winter conditions (fresco, of course, is usually executed during the warm months). The collaboration of Giandomenico, whose hand Mariuz saw in the "two female figures corresponding to the Temple of Glory," cannot be confirmed with certainty.

The fresco and the contemporary *Wedding Allegory* stand as the last decorative cycle undertaken by Tiepolo in Venice before his conclusive move to Madrid in 1762. The Ca' Rezzonico decorations have not always been judged in a positive light by critics, and even recently Levey, underscoring their borrowings from other, earlier works, has written that they lack "poetry and *élan*." Following their restoration, however, this criticism appears ungenerous. Indeed, it now seems legitimate to consider the two frescoes among the highest achievements of Tiepolo's last period, particularly for the luminosity of the colors and the superb pictorial rendering visible even in such minor details as the allegorical figures on the cornice.

FP

NOTES

1. Frerichs 1971a, p. 241.
2. Lorenzetti in Venice 1951, pp. 112–14.

PROVENANCE, 25b:
Ca' Rezzonico, Venice

REFERENCES:
Molmenti 1909, p. 69; Sack 1910, p. 153; Lorenzetti 1936, p. 26; Lorenzetti in Venice 1951, pp. 112–14; Mazzariol and Pignatti 1951, p. 74; Sánchez Cantón 1953, pp. 25, 36; Morassi 1962, p. 63; Pallucchini 1968, p. 136, no. 245; Frerichs 1971a, p. 241; Mariuz 1971, p. 62; Romanelli and Pedrocco 1986, pp. 34–35; Levey 1986, p. 228; Gemin and Pedrocco 1993, p. 451, no. 460; Pedrocco in Venice 1995a, p. 496

26. *Venus and Vulcan*

Venus, seated on a cloud, has descended into the smithy of her husband, Vulcan. Their colloquy concerns the armor that Venus has asked Vulcan to make for Aeneas (*Aeneid* 8. 416–54, 609–731) and which is shown, in pieces, scattered throughout the painting: the sword held by one of the goddess's handmaidens, the suit of armor behind Vulcan, and the helmet and shield resting on a rocky base below the cloud. The scene is set in a marvelously imagined space, part prison (one of Venus's doves gazes out through the barred window), part forge with rough-timbered roof and tiled floor—to which the two great fluted columns nevertheless lend a hint of Olympus.

The original destination of this painting is unknown, and both its date and function are open to debate. In a sale catalogue of 1872, it was listed as a pendant to the *Apollo Pursuing Daphne* (fig. 60),[1] and the two paintings have been linked in most of the subsequent literature. The connection is supported by their very similar sizes (the *Apollo* measures 68.8 by 87.2 centimeters) as well as by their mirrorlike compositional arrangement—especially since Tiepolo balanced the compositions of a number of known pendants in much the same way (see no. 22a, b). Moreover, the contrast between exterior and interior settings and between the distress of the unlucky lover Apollo and the complacency of the successful Venus would make their juxtaposition interesting.[2] Both paintings were hung as overdoors when they were in the Gsell collection, during the nineteenth century.[3] However, details in the *Venus and Vulcan*, such as the tools hanging on the back wall above the open fire, have been rendered with great care, making it unlikely that at least this picture was meant to be seen at a distance.

Because the figure of Venus is similar to a depiction of Iphigenia in the frescoes at the Villa Valmarana, Vicenza (fig. 98), the painting is now usually dated about 1758–60, like the fresco cycle.[4] Nonetheless, a suggestion made in 1913 by Berenson that the *Venus and Vulcan* was painted some years later in Spain seems more convincing than recent proposals. Berenson believed the work might be a sketch for the lower

26. Venus and Vulcan
Ca. 1765
69.2 × 87.3 cm (27¼ × 34⅜ in.)
The John G. Johnson Collection, Philadelphia Museum of Art (287)

PROVENANCE:
Friedrich Jakob Gsell, Vienna (until 1871; sale, Künstlerhaus, Vienna, 14 March 1872); Baron de Beurnonville, Paris (until 1881; sale, Paris, May 1881); Spiridon, Paris; John G. Johnson, Philadelphia (by 1902)

REFERENCES:
Perkins 1905, p. 132; Sack 1910, p. 233, nos. 607–8; Berenson 1913, p. 190, no. 287; Venturi 1933, pl. 593; Chicago 1938, no. 10; Morassi 1962, p. 44; Sweeny 1966, p. 75, no. 287; Pallucchini 1968, p. 127, no. 254; Shapley 1979, pp. 449–50; Gemin and Pedrocco 1993, p. 462, no. 478; De Grazia and Garberson 1996, pp. 296–97

section of the fresco in the Sala de los Alabarderos, now called the Sala de Guardias, in the royal palace of Madrid: Tiepolo's *Apotheosis of Aeneas* painted about 1765, which includes a scene of Venus delivering newly forged armor to Aeneas. Berenson's thesis is not strictly accurate, as the *Venus and Vulcan* is an independent work rather than a sketch. However, comparison to the two undisputed oil sketches for the ceiling (Museum of Fine Arts, Boston, and Fogg Art Museum, Cambridge, Massachusetts) reveals persuasive parallels and is instructive about the correct dating of the *Venus and Vulcan*. In both oil sketches Vulcan's forge is shown in a lower corner, but in the more evolved Cambridge work and in the finished ceiling, Vulcan has been moved to the foreground and is seen from the rear, leaning on his cane and supervising his workers, just as in the painting in Philadelphia. It seems unlikely that Tiepolo would have invented this figure and grouping earlier, dropped it in the first of the sketches, and then revived it for the second.[5] The Venuses in all three works are also comparable, and other elements of the Philadelphia picture recall Tiepolo's paintings of the 1760s. The beautifully rendered domestic details of tiled floor and beamed ceiling also appear in the *Annunciation* (no. 56), painted during the last years of the artist's life, and the delicate intimacy of the scene is characteristic of many of his pictures of this time. Throughout this period Tiepolo produced numerous small-scale, independent easel paintings such as the present canvas (see nos. 56–58) alongside his major commissions. They are among his most astonishingly beautiful works, and no less a connoisseur than Mason Perkins considered the *Venus and Vulcan* one of the artist's finest achievements of this kind.

AB

NOTES

1. Catalogue of the sale of works belonging to Friedrich Jakob Gsell at the Künstlerhaus, Vienna, 14 March 1872, p. 110, lot 506a, b. In the introduction to the catalogue Georg Plach states that Gsell began forming his collection in 1849.
2. Technical analysis has shown that the pigments used in the grounds of the two works differ somewhat, although this does not exclude the possibility that they were conceived as pendants. See De Grazia in De Grazia and Garberson 1996, p. 297, no. 20. Earlier doubts that the paintings in Washington, D.C., and Philadelphia were both painted on canvas can be laid to rest here. The original support of the *Venus and Vulcan* has been difficult to determine with precision, as the picture was transferred, and traces of paper are visible beneath the painted surface. Recent examination has shown that the presence of paper must be a result of the transfer process and that the work was done in oil on canvas, the original weave of which is seen in the paint layers. I would like to thank Joseph Rishel, Curator of European Paintings and Sculpture, and the members of the conservation staff of the Philadelphia Museum of Art for examining the painting and reevaluating the evidence.
3. Gsell sale catalogue, p. 110, and Sack 1910, p. 233, nos. 607–8.
4. See, for example, Gemin and Pedrocco 1993, p. 462, no. 478. Similarly, Giacometti (in London 1994, p. 499, no. 114) has likened the figures in the *Apollo Pursuing Daphne* to those in the *Apollo and Diana* in Tiepolo's frescoes in the Foresteria of the Villa Valmarana, Vicenza, which are dated 1757, and De Grazia (in De Grazia and Garberson 1996, p. 296) has posited a date for the painting in the second half of the 1750s.
5. For the *Apotheosis of Aeneas*, the two oil sketches, and the order of their genesis, see Fort Worth 1993, pp. 313–17, nos. 57–58. For the suggestion that Tiepolo may have come back to this figure for the Spanish ceiling years after he first painted it, see Chicago 1938, no. 10.

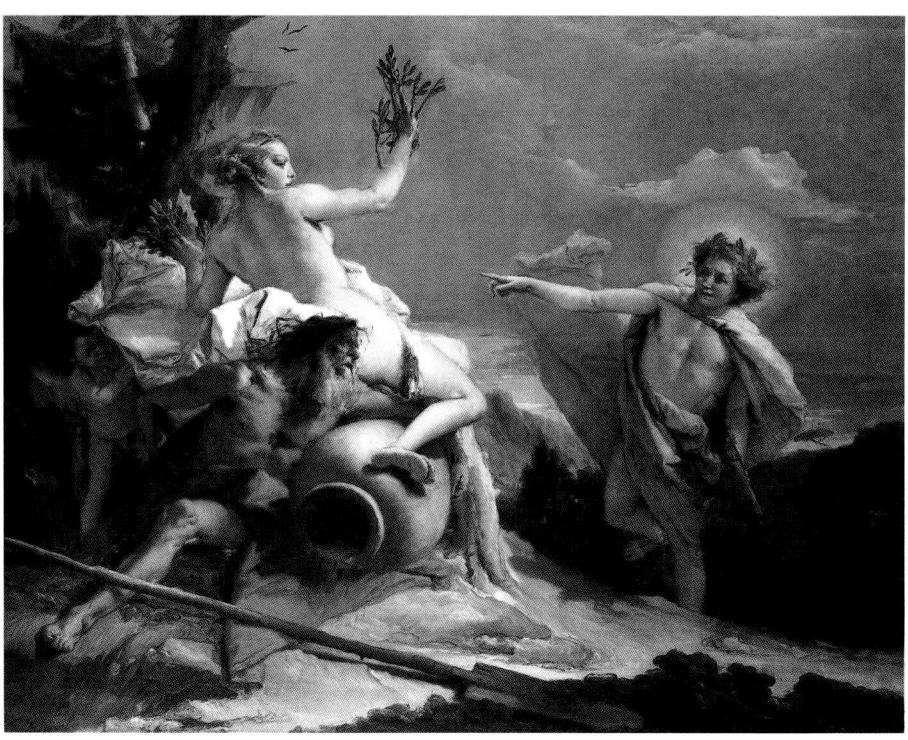

Fig. 60. *Apollo Pursuing Daphne*. Oil on canvas. National Gallery of Art, Washington, D.C. (1157)

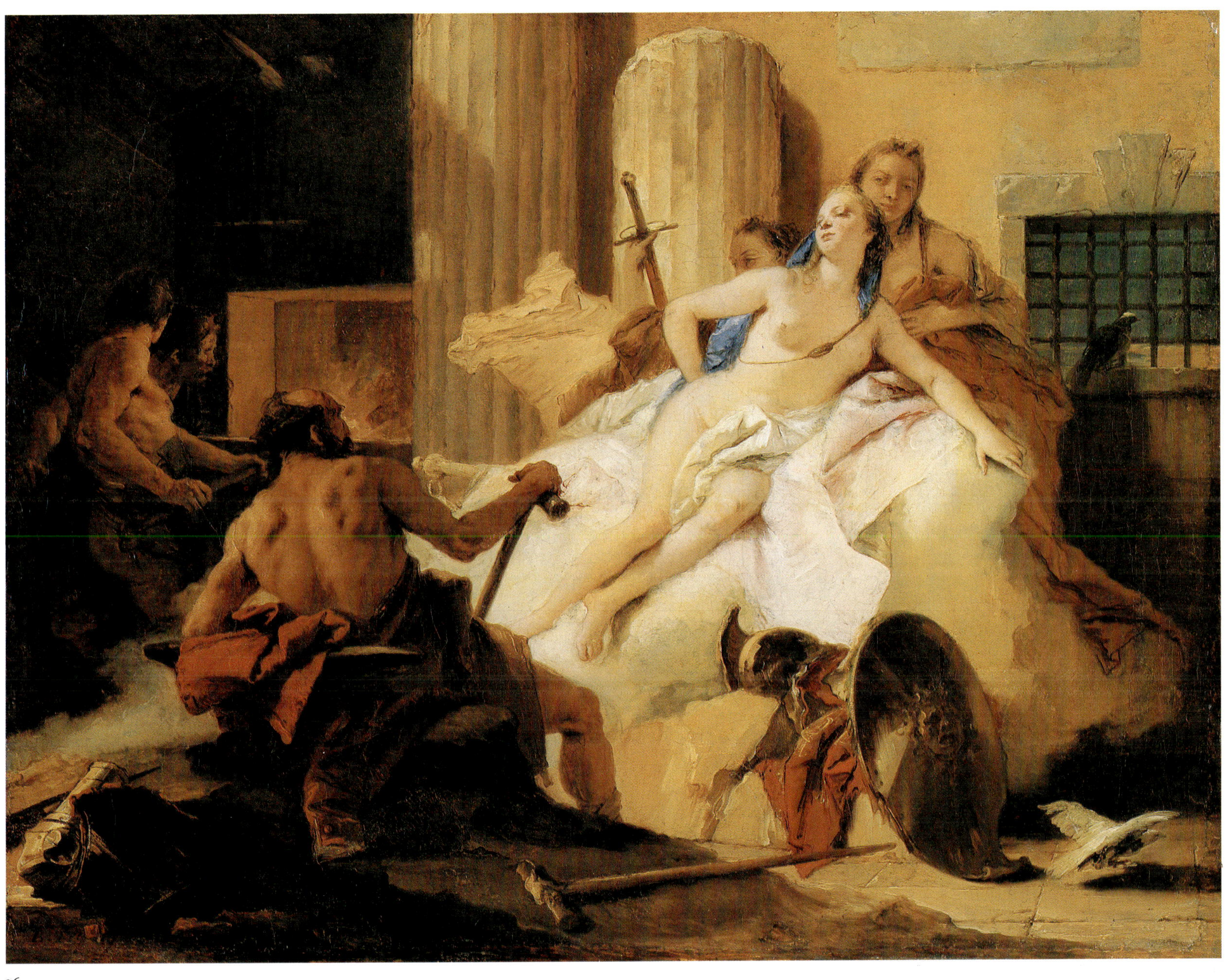

26

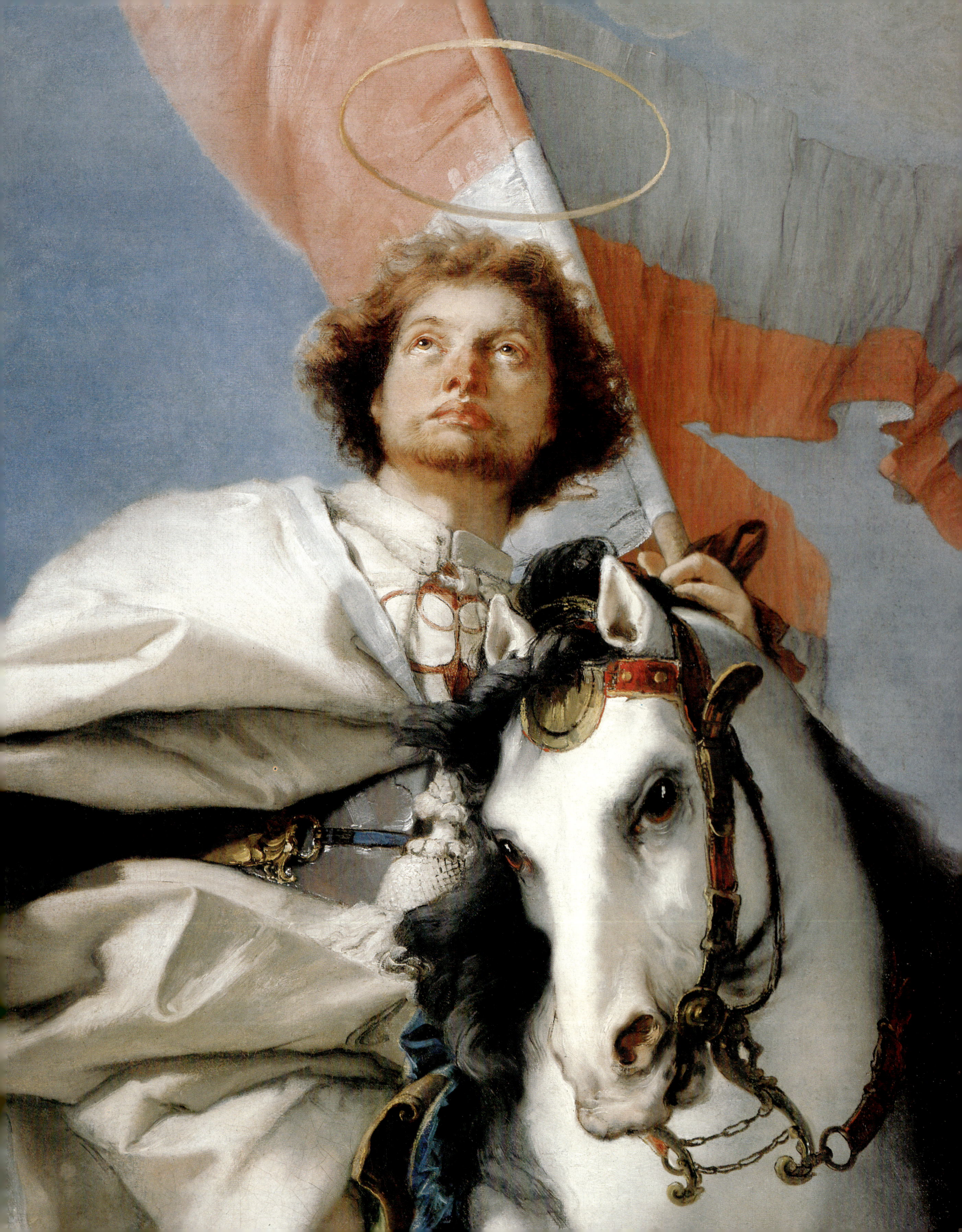

Tiepolo as a Religious Artist

CATHERINE WHISTLER

"In my view, a religious artist is a kind of preacher who is clearer, more striking, more easily understood, and closer to the ordinary people than the curate and the parish priest."[1] When Diderot wrote these words in 1765, he may have incorporated a sideswipe at the inadequacies of the clergy, but he also summed up the challenges facing the painter of religious subjects in the mid-eighteenth century. Perhaps the most essential quality in a religious painting (particularly from the Counter-Reformation onward) is intelligibility, since the picture will illustrate an important sacred event or instruct the faithful in more abstract points of doctrine or provide a suitable theme for spiritual contemplation. Whatever the subject, the religious painting commissioned for a place of worship will also have to fulfill the aim of exhorting the faithful to a life of piety within the fold of the Catholic Church. These demands of clarity and orthodoxy seem rather restricting, in that they apparently confine the artist to working within safely established pictorial conventions on a limited range of themes. Yet religious art in eighteenth-century Venice is especially interesting because a surprising amount of innovation and, indeed, individual expression seems to have been possible, even in this highly conservative and traditionally Catholic society.

These accomplishments were possible, in part, because of the complex nature of religious images and the different strands of religious experience to which they relate. For instance, while an image can be a stepping-stone on a spiritual pilgrimage toward the worship of God, it is also to some extent the fruit of contemplation of a sacred theme and possibly a stage in the artist's own spiritual voyage that allows him or her a certain license. Thus, in 1739, when Tiepolo was commissioned to paint the ceiling of the Scuola Grande dei Carmini (fig. 66) chapter room, he questioned the confraternity's proposals (which it subsequently changed), and members noted that the artist "lived in devotion" to the Madonna of Mount Carmel; apparently his ideas were to be taken seriously because of his own attachment to this cult.[2] Variety and innovation could also be attained because the Catholic Church in eighteenth-century Venice was not a static or monolithic body. Apart from theological debates and some internal conflicts in the Church as a whole (which were followed with interest in Venice), different religious orders promoted certain kinds of spirituality or encouraged new devotional cults, which we find reflected in their commissions. The beatification of exemplary figures and the canonization of new saints also provided fresh subject matter in art. Saint John Nepomuk, canonized in 1729, for instance, was especially revered in Venice and was depicted by various artists, including Giambattista Piazzetta, Tiepolo, and Giambattista Pittoni; and Saint Gerolamo Emiliani, beatified in 1747 and canonized in 1767, was popular with the Tiepolo family—in 1759 Giandomenico decorated the chapel of the Tiepolo villa at Zianigo with frescoes celebrating his life and works, and Giuseppe Maria Tiepolo was a priest in the Sommaschi order, which the saint had founded.

Tiepolo often had to paint new or unfamiliar subjects for different kinds of patrons. He executed an oil sketch showing the Glory of Saint Luigi Gonzaga (fig. 61) shortly before 1726, the year the saint was canonized: with its free, sketchy handling, this may have been a *modello* for a small altarpiece.[3] Tiepolo visualized the twenty-three-year-old Jesuit saint as a fervent, boyish figure, transported into a luminous sacred zone in which an allegorical statue of Faith appears. Here he is granted a vision of the Eucharist; the angels who accompany him themselves embody a kind of idealized youthful beauty. For a recent representation of Saint Luigi, Tiepolo could look to an altarpiece by Antonio Balestra in the Jesuit church in Venice, but when he was asked to paint the Blessed Paola Gambara in the early 1730s, he had to invent an appropriate image (fig. 62).[4] Renowned for her beauty, chastity, and piety, Paola Gambara (1464–1515) had been a member of the Third Order of Franciscans. Although her cult was particularly strong in Brescia, it had not yet been formally approved by the Church at the time of the commission. Tiepolo's roundel depicting her may have had a public function in promoting this cult, as is suggested by the lengthy identifying inscription, which includes a reference to miracles.[5] When Tiepolo was commissioned in the mid-1740s to paint an altarpiece showing Saint Patrick for the Lateran Canons at S. Giovanni in Verdara in

Detail, *Saint James of Campostella*, no. 37

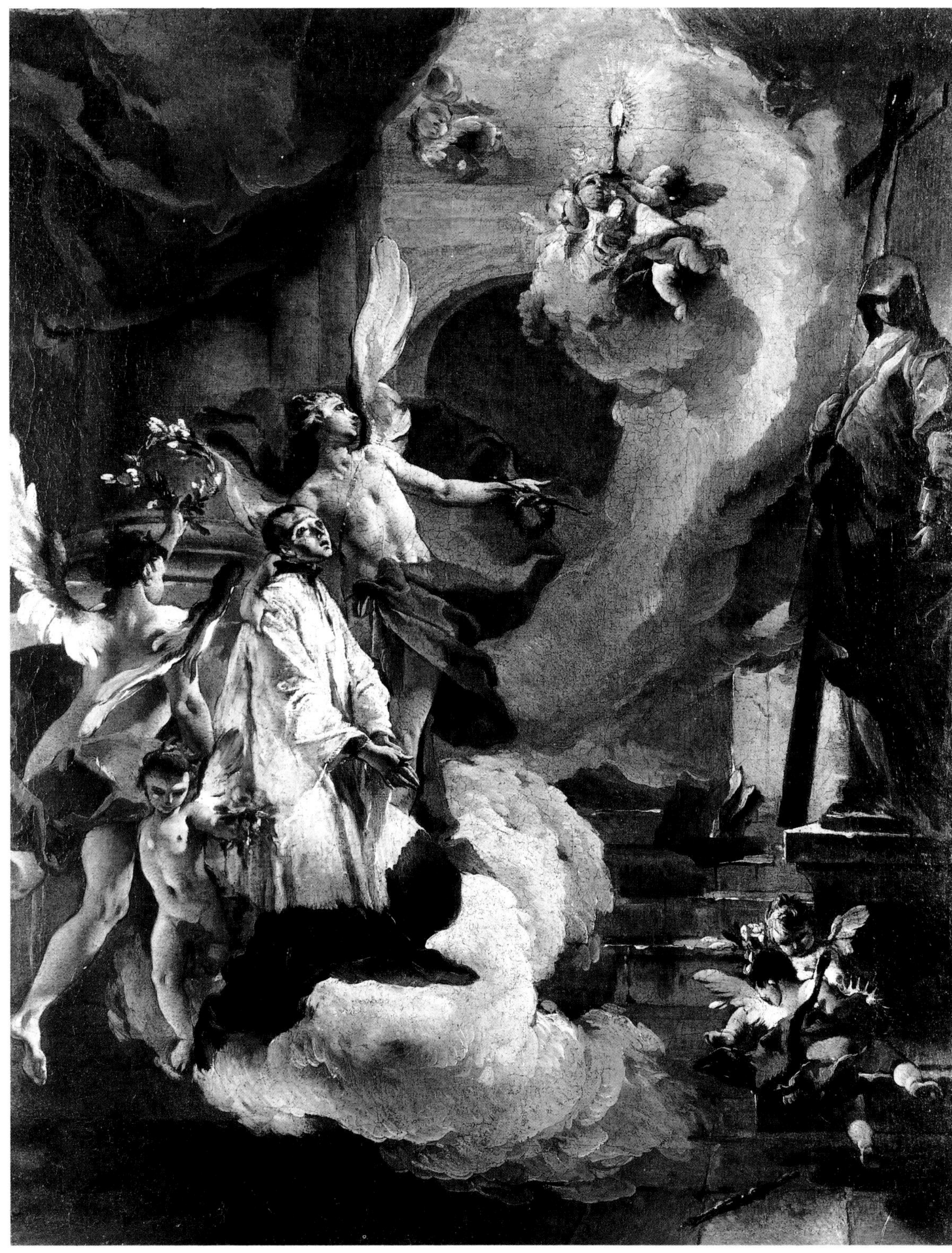

Fig. 61. *Saint Luigi Gonzaga in Glory*. Oil on canvas. Courtauld Institute Galleries, London, Seilern bequest, 1978

Padua, who revered the saint as a member of their own order, it was not immediately obvious to him how to convey the holy qualities of this rarely represented figure.[6] In a large group of pen-and-ink drawings, Tiepolo experimented with possible compositions showing the saint healing a young boy or preaching or exorcising a demon, before inventing a splendid, compact image that incorporates all of these ideas (fig. 63).

Tiepolo's skill in painting unusual religious subjects had been tested early in his career, with an important commission of late 1721 to paint the *Madonna of Mount Carmel* (fig. 19) for the left wall of the Carmine chapel at S. Aponal in Venice.[7] Here a Carmelite confraternity prayed for the souls of the dead and for their liberation from the torments of purgatory through the intercession of the Madonna. While the cult of the Madonna of Mount Carmel was not a new one, it saw a new upsurge of devotion in the late seventeenth and early eighteenth centuries, which culminated in the formal institution of her feast by Benedict XIII in 1726. Benedict's sermons evoked the power of Mary, Queen of Heaven, whose domain extended to purgatory.[8] The wide rectangular shape of

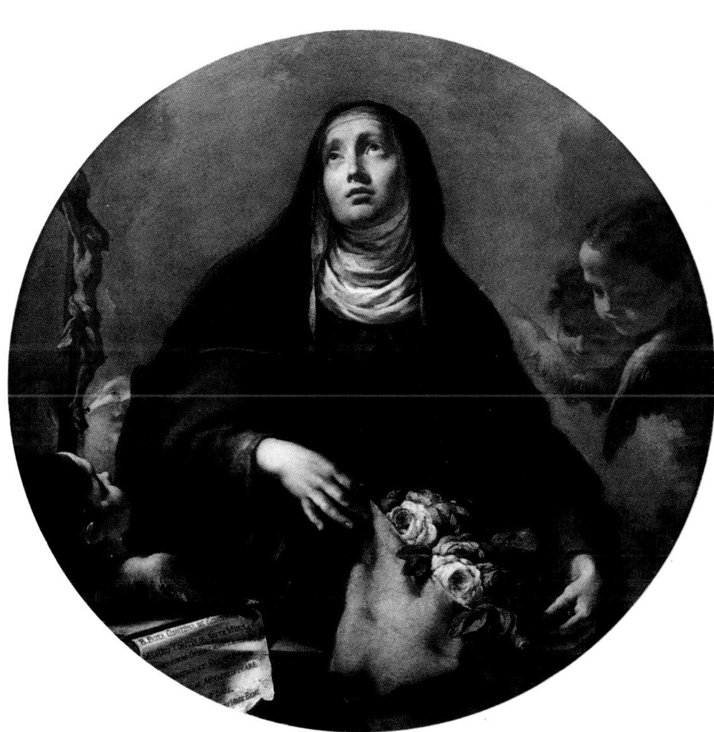

Fig. 62. *The Blessed Paola Gambara*. Oil on canvas. Castello di Zoppola dal Rizzi, Udine

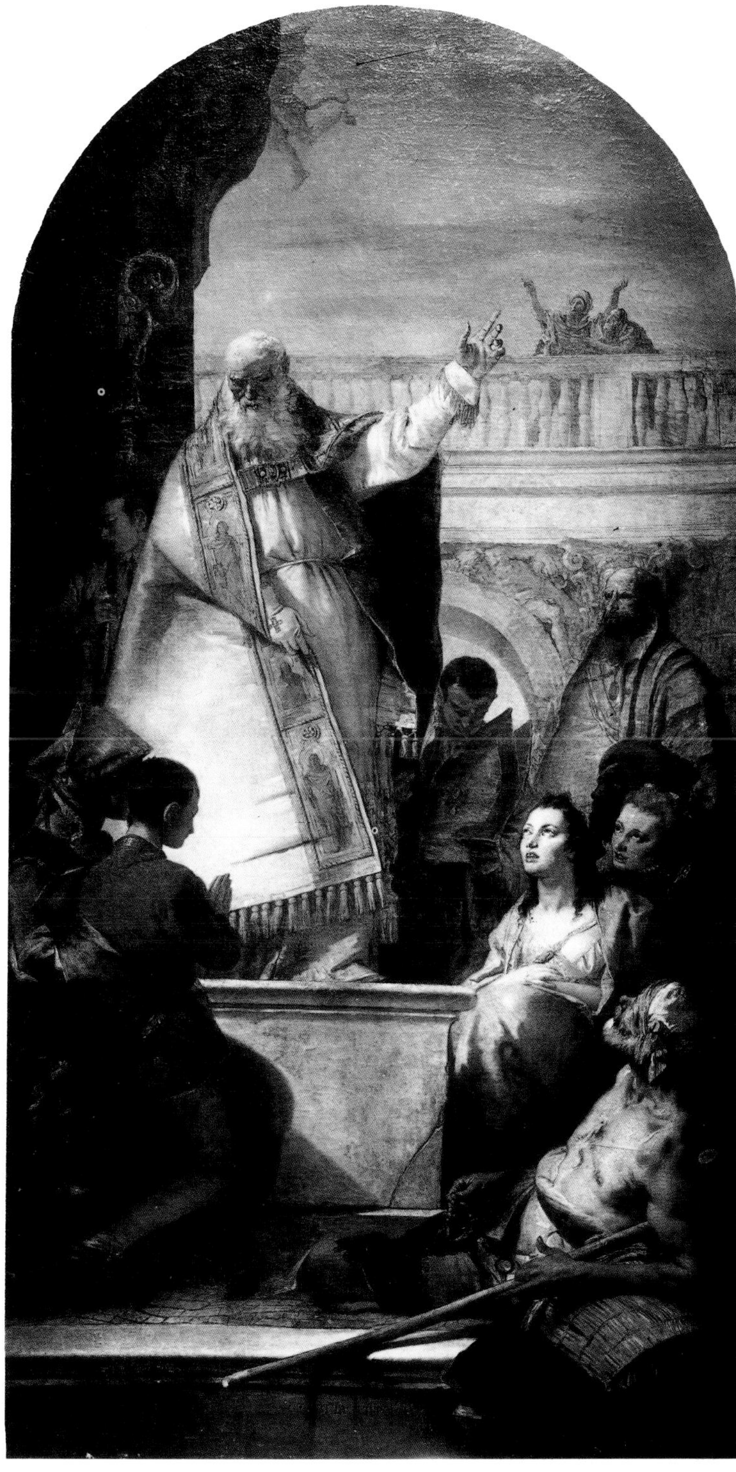

Fig. 63. *Miracle of Saint Patrick of Ireland*. Oil on canvas. Museo Civico, Padua

Tiepolo's canvas is a traditional one for narrative pictures associated with Venetian confraternities, and the artist incorporated a strong narrative element in this essentially devotional painting. The dramatically lit area on the left balances striking images of despair and deliverance, with one of the half-hidden, isolated figures of the souls in purgatory electrified by the dynamic, liberating gesture of the angel. In the center the more disciplined line of human devotees, wearing the scapular, or robe, of their Carmelite confraternity, is led by an angel toward the brightly lit, architecturally defined area of divine aid and heavenly order. Here, in the part of the painting closest to the chapel's altar, the Virgin and Child each present the scapular (as a robe and as two small pieces of cloth to be worn around the neck, respectively) to a group of Carmelite saints. The Virgin has all the solemnity and assurance of a Madonna by Veronese, while the strong figure of Saint Teresa, leaning heavily, almost clumsily, forward, adds a touch of homely realism. By combining a *sacra conversazione*, or gathering of saints around the Virgin and Child, with an angel releasing a soul from purgatory (a reference to another cult, that of the guardian

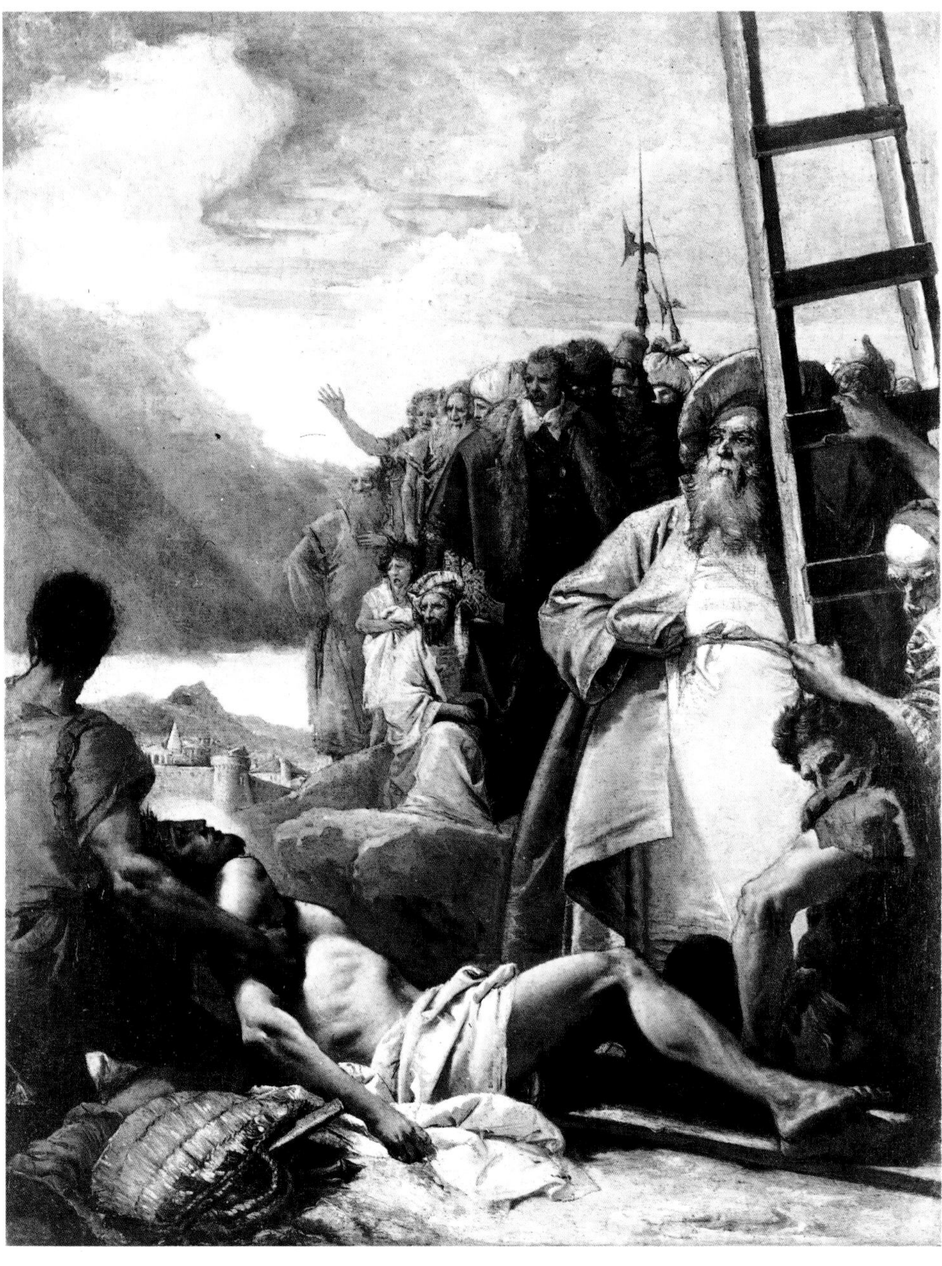

Fig. 64. Giandomenico Tiepolo. *Via Crucis, Station XI: Jesus Is Nailed to the Cross*. Oil on canvas. S. Polo, Venice

angel, which recently had been the subject of paintings by Piazzetta and by Sebastiano Ricci)[9] and including confraternity members in the scene, Tiepolo created an extraordinarily rich religious image.

A new cult that became immensely popular by the mid-eighteenth century was the *Via Crucis*, or Way of the Cross, which had been promoted by the Franciscan order: the zealous Leonardo da Porto Maurizio (1676–1751), later to be canonized, obtained the cult's formal sanction from Clement XII in 1731. The *Via Crucis* was a measured and rigorously controlled spiritual exercise in fourteen set pieces, with a combination of images and prescribed meditation. The aim of the *Via Crucis* was to inspire a deep awareness of personal sinfulness by encouraging the devotee to identify step-by-step with the sufferings of Christ during the Passion and to relate them metaphorically to his or her own life. For instance, in studying the scene of the nailing of Christ to the cross, the spectator is invited to consider sins as nails agonizingly planted in Christ's body; the empathetic pain felt on contemplating this image will in turn "nail down" those uncontrolled emotions that are at the root of all sin.[10] Giandomenico Tiepolo's *Via Crucis* of 1747–49 for the Oratorio del Crocefisso at S. Polo, Venice (fig. 64), is an early and highly original painted representation that epitomizes the nature of this cult.

Tiepolo's three Passion scenes for the church of S. Alvise, Venice (no. 31, figs. 69, 70), are not a *Via Crucis* as such, but they are related to this contemporary mode of devotion in which attention is focused on raw violence and tangible pain, on a mood of pathos and distress. The *Flagellation*, the *Crowning with Thorns*, and the large, magnificent *Way to Calvary* that make up this triptych were painted in the mid- or late 1730s.[11] There is nothing comparable in terms of scale and emotional pitch in the work of Tiepolo's older contemporaries, such as Ricci and Piazzetta. Tiepolo surely studied Tintoretto's great Passion scenes in the Scuola Grande di S. Rocco, Venice, as part of his preparation and undoubtedly was influenced by Titian's *Crowning with Thorns*, with its moving expression of grief and pain, which he probably had seen in S. Maria delle Grazie, Milan.[12] Christ's suffering is the principal theme of the triptych. This is presented in strongly realistic terms—his face, for example, is turned to the spectator in each painting—with the implicit message that humankind bears the responsibility for his pain. The monumental central scene of the *Way to Calvary*, set in a cool-toned landscape, incorporates a number of episodes: Christ, in the foreground, now falling under the weight of the cross, has already met his mother, who stands farther back with Mary Magdalen, symbolically in the shadow of Calvary, and, on the right, Veronica, who has just wiped the face of Christ with her veil, contemplates this precious relic in her hands.

Here Tiepolo painted with the *franchezza pittorica*, or fresh, vibrant handling of the medium, for which Vincenzo da Canal had earlier praised him.[13] Hence the pictures have a sense of immediacy and authenticity that is striking (and even disconcerting to such later viewers as John Ruskin, who found them reprehensibly modern).[14] Very different in effect are the smaller *Crowning with Thorns* (fig. 71) and an *Agony in the Garden* (no. 33) that were made for a private client. These pictures do not have the public function and strongly charged message of the S. Alvise triptych but share a more intimate tone, with the emphasis on pathos and quiet dignity rather than on brutality and suffering. Giandomenico surely took his cue from his father's S. Alvise triptych when he began work on his own *Via Crucis*. He displayed a predilection for forceful images in a high emotional key in his own religious art, while Giambattista, by contrast, retained a sense of decorum and balance. Even at his most painfully realistic, as in the S. Alvise pictures, the elder Tiepolo instinctively avoided the strident and the melodramatic.

By the end of the 1730s, Tiepolo's experience of large-scale work in fresco in northern Italy and the Venetian mainland gave him the edge over Piazzetta, Pittoni, and other artists whose religious pictures were sought after but who rarely, if ever, painted in fresco. The clarity and lucidity of Tiepolo's religious art, together with his speed of execution, must have recommended him to those patrons planning grand-scale church decoration. Two commissions for important ceiling frescoes, made within five years of each other, show Tiepolo's carefully considered responses to the demands of different religious orders in Venice. These projects were the ceiling of the nave of the Dominican S. Maria del Rosario (fig. 65), decorated between 1737 and 1739, and that of the Discalced Carmelite S. Maria di Nazareth, realized between 1743 and 1745 (see no. 48a, b). In each case Tiepolo collaborated, as he had done before, with Girolamo Mengozzi Colonna, a specialist in providing illusionistic architectural and decorative settings in large-scale frescoes. Both ceilings were to show visionary scenes on the theme of the Virgin Mary as protector and benefactor of humanity. However, no paintings could be less alike in the kinds of impact they were intended to make on the spectator.

Tiepolo's task in the ceiling fresco at S. Maria del Rosario, known as the Gesuati, was to celebrate Saint Dominic, founder of the Dominican order, and the Madonna of the Rosary, a cult that was particularly popular in the eighteenth century. The central fresco compartments are surrounded by monochrome medallions showing the fifteen Mysteries of the Rosary (events from the life of Mary and the Passion of Christ for the faithful to meditate on while reciting the ritual number of prayers). The subject of the principal fresco is the Institution of the Rosary (fig. 65): Saint Dominic has received the rosary from the Virgin Mary, and he distributes it to a grateful Venetian crowd, several members of which are already telling their beads in prayer, while vices are banished thanks to the efficacy of the rosary. Tiepolo made play with the dynamic conditions of illumination within the church, where the three high windows on either side of the nave throw their light upward onto the vault, so that the fresco is bathed in a reflected light,[15] and the cool, silvery blues and grays of the overall tonality evoke the quality of light and atmosphere in Venice itself.

The air of clarity and actuality that results is to an extent part of the message of the fresco: what Tiepolo emphasized is the nature of the community that will benefit from the rosary. Thus, the crowds are disposed in an ample architectural setting that is distinctly Venetian and local, since it recalls the type of Palladio-inspired architectural settings seen in paintings by Veronese, while the neo-Palladian Gesuati church faces a group of churches by Palladio on the opposite side of the Giudecca Canal. Visible are monks and nuns, a bishop, a doge, and richly clad personages; especially prominent are the elderly woman and young girl on the right, the standing mother and child on the left, and the bareheaded character who prostrates himself in worship beside them. The spectator below in the church, rich or poor, could identify with these figures and in a sense could gain access to this scene of devotion and gratitude, since the stone steps depicted descend downward, as it were, into the space of the church itself. Tiepolo's conservative Dominican patrons undoubtedly wished to stress the importance of the communal prayer of the rosary (which is recited aloud) as opposed to the suspect, unorthodox types of individual spiritual flights sought by adherents of the movement known as Quietism.[16] Furthermore, the emphasis in the fresco on the possibility of salvation through the fervent repetition of prayer was a timely assertion of Dominican theology in the face of current disputes within the Church on the nature of grace and salvation.[17]

The ceiling fresco at the Carmelite church of S. Maria di Nazareth, known as the Scalzi, was largely destroyed in World War I but is known through photographs (fig. 111), and Tiepolo's two oil sketches also illuminate his response to this commission for the *Miracle of the Holy House of Loreto* (no. 48a, b).[18] The subject is the miraculous rescue by angels in the thirteenth century of the house in which the Virgin Mary had lived at Nazareth and its transportation to Italy, where it was enshrined at Loreto under Carmelite protection. The underlying theme, however, is the exaltation of the Virgin as an authoritative figure with a commanding role in the heavens. As the mother of the Christ Child, whom she holds, Mary is endowed with extraordinary divine graces. The elaborately constructed illusionistic vault is a reminder of the distance between her and ordinary mortals. Old Testament kings and prophets, placed as painted witnesses at the springing of the vaults, testify by their presence to her authority and to her unique powers, while closer to the heavenly scene, Old Testament prefigurations of the miraculous event are found in two fictive bas-reliefs. Humankind plays a far more limited role in the celebratory event shown here than in the Gesuati fresco; everyday figures appear only around the margin of the heavenly scene as foreshortened heads and shoulders reacting in wonder and awe to the marvelous vision far above, and in the distant corners of the painted vault as stiffly costumed groups looking up in rapturous prayer. Similar is the spectator's role below in the church, since the main scene is presented as intangible and inaccessible in time and space, for it is a dynamic and glorious miracle that must inspire profound veneration of the Virgin Mary.

The design of Tiepolo's altarpieces is equally informed by a consciousness of his audience's possible responses. For example, the high viewpoint of the Gesuati altarpiece (no. 35) actively distances the spectator from the privileged mystical communion with Christ enjoyed by the three Dominican saints depicted there. By contrast, in the *Saint Patrick* altarpiece the contemporary spectator is invited to participate in venerating the saint practically at the same level as that of the painted crowd. Tiepolo's symbolic use of architecture to denote sacred spaces, and to mark the different relationships between humans and saints, in both the altarpieces and the frescoes, is a key element in his mature religious painting. A strong vein of realism is another, but this is securely balanced by his inclusion of exotic or decorative motifs and above all by his poetic fantasy. Thus, Tiepolo consistently focused on angels as subjects for creative exploration, as exemplified in his strong, liberating angel in the *Madonna of Mount Carmel* of 1722–27, his gorgeously clad messenger in the *Angel Appearing to Sarah* of about 1725 in the Arcivescovado (Patriarchal Palace) at Udine,[19] and the protective figure glowing with a sensuous benevolence in his *Hagar and Ishmael* (no. 27). Later his angels become distinctively noble, compassionate creatures with a more chiseled beauty, as demonstrated in the ceiling of the Scuola Grande dei Carmini of 1748 (fig. 66) and the Saint Thecla altarpiece of 1759 in the cathedral at Este (fig. 115).[20] Tiepolo's essentially poetic response to this subject is perfectly in harmony with contemporary piety, as expressed, for instance, in the meditation of Saint Luigi Gonzaga on angels, which was popular in the eighteenth century: "Now, my soul, contemplate the beauty of these heavenly Citizens, who in the guise of many morning stars and brightest Suns, shine in the City of God, and in them, as in the clearest mirrors, glitters the Divine perfection, the infinite power, the eternal wisdom, the ineffable goodness and most ardent charity of the Creator. O how graceful, how pure, how beloved are these blessed spirits!"[21]

Tiepolo's interest in the character of saintly individuals and in the nature of their spiritual experience, seen, for example, in his treatment of the female saints in the Gesuati altarpiece, is evident throughout his religious art. This interest stimulated other kinds of explorations, although Tiepolo never strayed beyond the bounds of theological correctness. For example, the *Adoration of the Christ Child* (no. 28) is a highly unusual image because of the important expressive role Saint Joseph is given within this familiar subject, since it is he rather than the Virgin who cradles and contemplates the newborn Child. And Tiepolo's deepening consideration of the psychology of Saint Francis and the nature of his stigmatization is revealed in the way the figure of the saint evolves from the *modello* to the final altarpiece he produced for S. Pascual Baylon at Aranjuez (no. 41a,b). He certainly knew Piazzetta's *Saint Francis* altarpiece of about 1729 for the church of the Aracoeli at Vicenza (fig. 67), an awe-inspiring exploration of a well-known subject. Here Piazzetta chose to draw out to the full the supernatural implications of the saint's mystical state in the moment after receiving the stigmata. This decision was presumably in keeping with the wishes of his Franciscan patrons, although the final painting verges on the unorthodox.[22] The ecstatic saint is not only depicted in a state of almost total abandonment, his eyes closed and the color drained from his flesh; he is also shown half suspended in midair with blood flowing freely from his wounds, which are tended by an angel. It is principally

Opposite: Fig. 65. *Institution of the Rosary*. Fresco. S. Maria del Rosario (the Gesuati), Venice

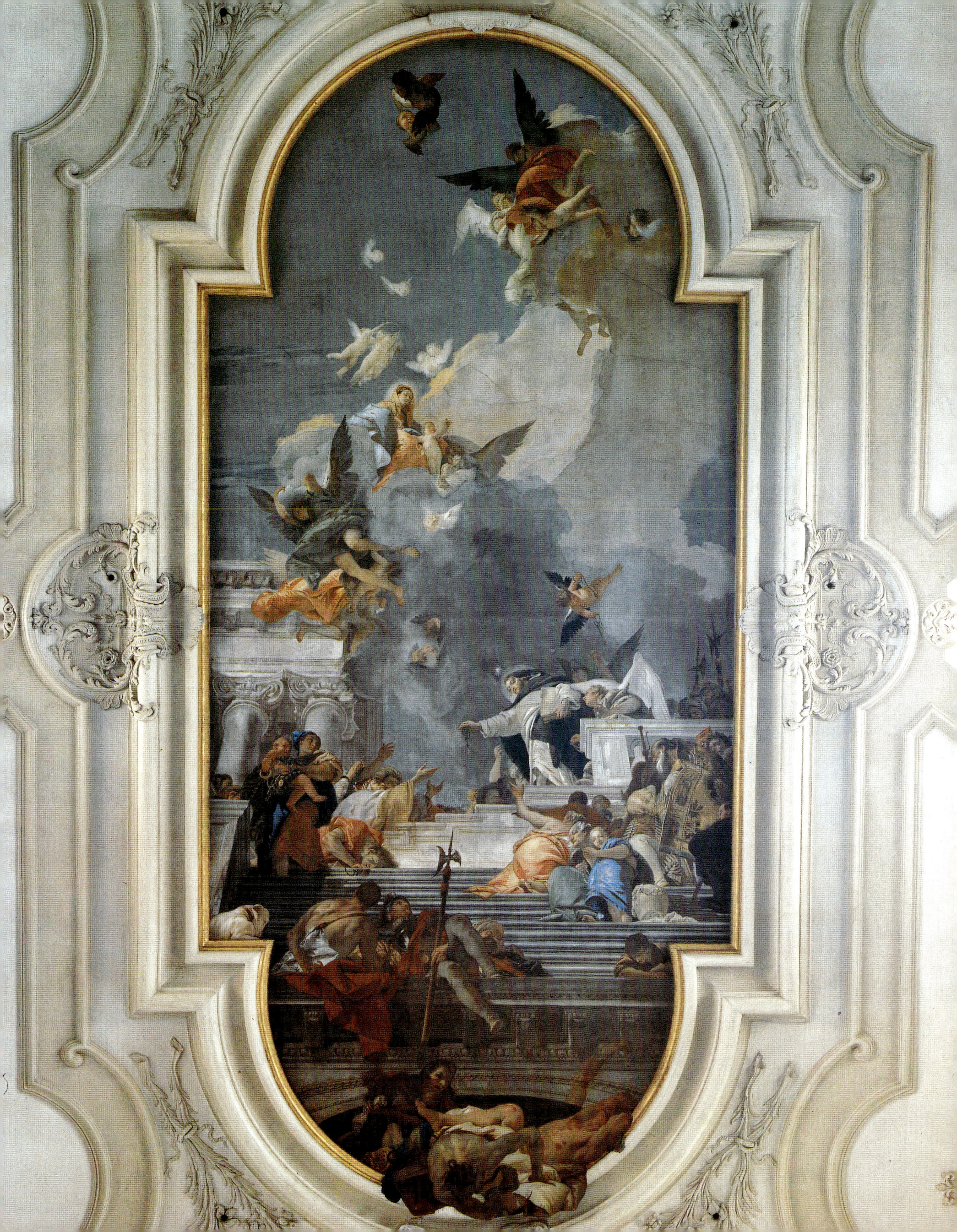

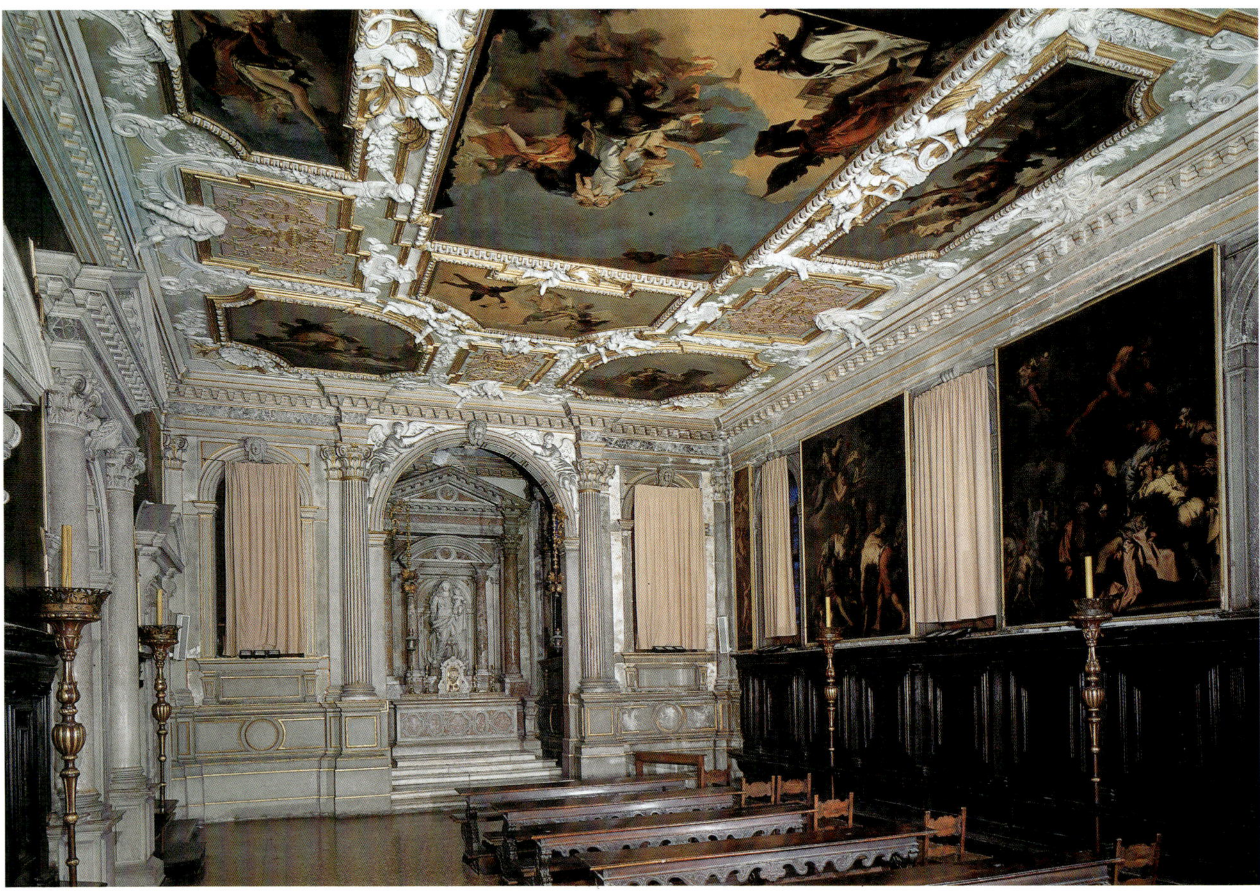

Fig. 66. Scuola Grande dei Carmini, with ceiling paintings by Tiepolo

Piazzetta's use of tone and color that conveys the physical and emotional extremity of this spiritual experience: hot hues burn together in a painfully narrow range of color between deep turquoise and orange ocher, against brownish and reddish shades.

Piazzetta's religious art often evokes a kind of fervor and a burning asceticism, whereas Tiepolo's approach to sacred themes takes away their mystery and impenetrability. His *Saint Francis Receiving the Stigmata* altarpiece is in some ways a more realistic and humane depiction than Piazzetta's, stressing the historical reality of the event and playing down its rapture and torment. In the *modello* Tiepolo had shown the saint with downcast eyes and bowed head, as though overcome by pain, but in the altarpiece his presentation of the theme is more profound. The significance of the stigmatization lies not in the pain of the wounds but rather in their cause, which is inexpressible divine love, and in their subject, the saint who burns with love for Christ.[23] Therefore, Tiepolo presented the saint as alert and wide awake, in accordance with orthodox theology. The conventional six-winged seraph, missing from Piazzetta's altarpiece, is shown in order to emphasize divine intervention, since the saint's state is not loosely defined or even self-willed, but one determined by God.

Tiepolo's individuality emerges in his exploration of the relationship between the saint and the supporting angel (which is, in any case, an unusual element, since angels generally are depicted consoling the saint after the stigmatization, as in Piazzetta's painting, not during it). The intensely human angel radiates tenderness and pity, so that the spectator identifies with the feeling of compassion conveyed. However, the figure of the saint demands not pity but awe, for his expression indicates his communion with the divine. Furthermore, the angel plays a didactic role in explicitly pointing to the wounds of the stigmata: Saint Francis is supported in this way as a reference to traditional images of angels holding the dead Christ, whose wounds signify his love for humanity. The sense of actuality and of the saint's genuine suffering, deriving from the unidealized depiction of this weak and poorly clad figure and from the sharp tones, pale colors, and graphic delineation of the foreground area, exists side by side with its counterpart, the presentation of the saint as an emblematic image.

The seven images Tiepolo painted between 1767 and 1769 for the royal church of S. Pascual Baylon (see no. 40a, b) at Aranjuez are intricately related in theme and in composition, and the final altarpieces represent a distillation of his lifetime's experience of religious art. Their tone is deliberately one of

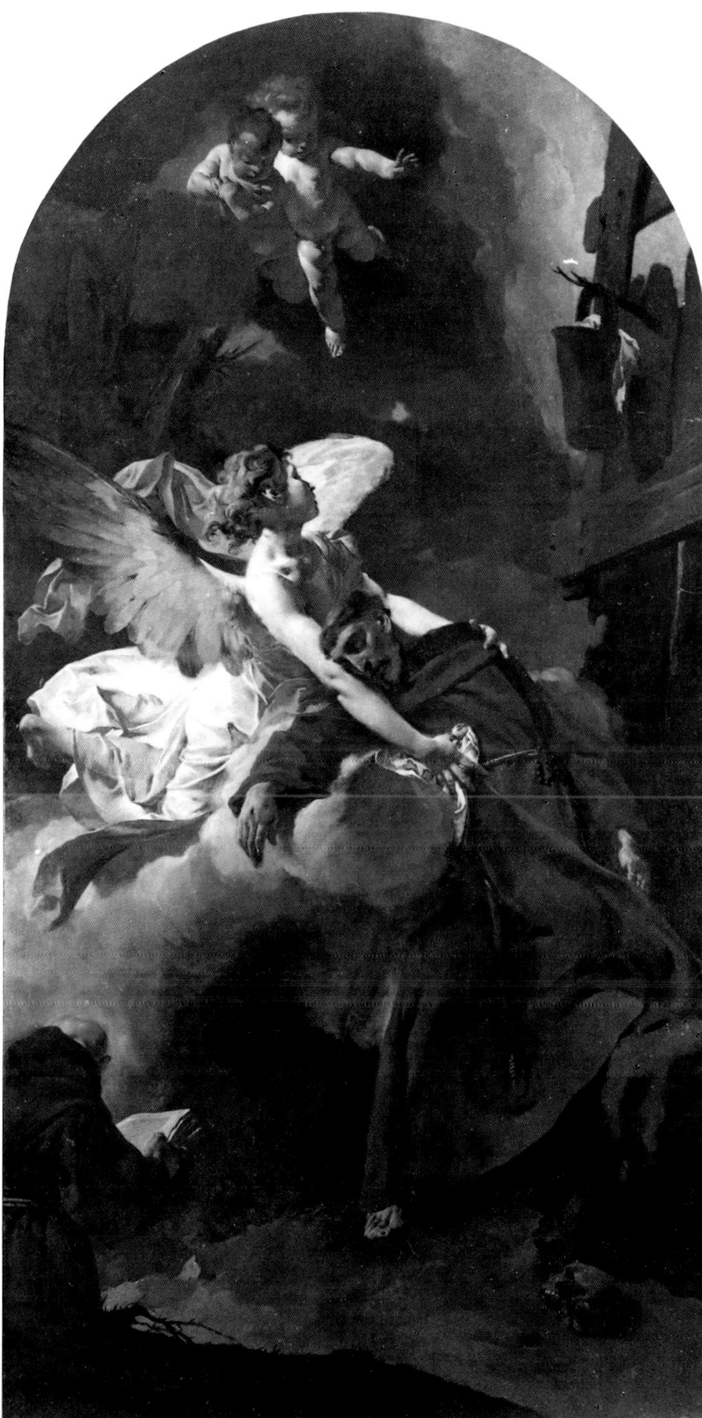

Fig. 67. Giambattista Piazzetta. *Saint Francis as a Man of Sorrows*. Oil on canvas. Museo Civico, Vicenza

humility and simplicity, since they were intended for the complete pictorial decoration of a church of the Alcantarine Franciscan order, whose ethos was one of poverty and austerity. At the same time the altarpieces include decorative and beautiful elements, for the monastery was supposed to display magnificently the king's piety and generosity.[24] Nevertheless, Tiepolo's fundamentally humanist approach to sacred art, his lucidity and modernity, combined with his fresh, picturesque handling of paint, in the end was found inappropriate to the public image and the conservative religious sentiment of Charles III of Spain. In his native Republic of Venice, Tiepolo's deeply considered religious art had been fully in tune with the mainstream of spirituality there. At the Spanish court the revived Bolognese classicism promoted by Anton Raphael Mengs, with its hallowed forms and polished finish, was in favor in official circles. Ultimately, Tiepolo's serious and searching late altarpieces and his tremulously painted, moving small-scale religious images (nos. 55–58) found their true resonance in the mature religious art of Francisco Goya.

Notes

1. Diderot 1765 (1793 ed., p. 302): "A mon sens, un peintre d'église est une espêce de prédicateur plus clair, plus frappant, plus intelligible, plus à portée du commun des hommes que le curé et son vicaire."
2. Barcham 1989, p. 144, and Brown in Fort Worth 1993, p. 256.
3. Gemin and Pedrocco 1993, p. 249, no. 74.
4. For the Balestra altarpiece, the *Virgin and Child with Saint Luigi Gonzaga, Saint Stanislas Kostka, and Saint Francisco Borgia* of 1704, see Polazzo 1990, p. 61, fig. 7.
5. Gemin and Pedrocco 1993, p. 305, no. 181. The inscription has never been transcribed. See *Bibliotheca Sanctorum* 1961–69, vol. 6, cols. 27–29.
6. Gemin and Pedrocco 1993, p. 392, no. 368. On the iconography, see Whistler 1985c.
7. Gemin and Pedrocco 1993, p. 241, no. 59. For a detailed discussion of the iconography and devotional context, see Barcham 1989, pp. 34–39, 146.
8. Benedict XIII 1728.
9. Piazzetta treated the theme of the Guardian Angel Protecting the Soul from Purgatory in an altarpiece for the Scuola dell'Angelo Custode, Venice, in 1717–18, and as a substitute for this work Ricci painted another in 1720. See Knox 1992, pp. 74–83.
10. Leonardo da Porto Maurizio 1759, p. 238.
11. Gemin and Pedrocco 1993, pp. 330–31, nos. 234–36, with additional references.
12. Wethey 1969–75, vol. 1, no. 26, now in the Musée du Louvre, Paris.
13. Da Canal 1810, pp. 15, 20.
14. Ruskin (1884, p. 112) refers to them as "pieces of plausible modern sentiment," comparing their qualities unfavorably with the quaintness and simplicity of Carpaccio.
15. See Alpers and Baxandall 1994, pp. 84–93.
16. For the history of Quietism, see Knox 1950, chap. 11, and Niero 1982.
17. See Barcham 1989, pp. 130–35.
18. Gemin and Pedrocco 1993, pp. 379–81, nos. 346–53. For a detailed account of the iconography, see Barcham 1979.
19. Gemin and Pedrocco 1993, p. 255, no. 82.
20. Ibid., p. 467, no. 486.
21. Cacciaguerra 1740, pp. 304–5: "Ora, anima mia, contempla la bellezza di questi celesti Cittadini, i quali, a guisa di tante stelle mattutine, e chiarissimi Soli, risplendono nella Città dei Dio, e in essi, come in specchi limpidissimi, rilucono le divine perfezioni, l'infinità potenza, l'eterna sapienza, l'ineffabil bontà, e ardentissima carita del Creatore. O quanto sono graziosi, quanto puri, e quanto amabili questi beati spiriti!"
22. The spirituality of the Franciscans and of the Jesuits, including their encouragement of mysticism, was viewed with deep suspicion by many Catholic reformers in the eighteenth century. See Vecchi 1967, chap. 2, especially pp. 196–98.
23. See Askew 1969; see also the corrections to Askew by Treffers 1988.
24. On the commission, see Whistler 1985a.

27. Hagar and Ishmael

†27. Hagar and Ishmael
Ca. 1732
133 × 112 cm (52⅜ × 44⅛ in.)
Scuola Grande
Arciconfraternita di
S. Rocco, Venice

A companion piece to this painting is the *Abraham and the Angels*, also in the Scuola Grande di S. Rocco, Venice (fig. 68). Both pictures were acquired by the Scuola—one of Venice's wealthiest lay confraternities—in 1785, and nothing is known of their provenance. They could have been made as independent works for a collector, since they are relatively small in size. Tiepolo's rich handling of paint and attention to fine decorative detail suggest that the paintings were intended for close-up viewing, perhaps in a private picture gallery. However, the subjects were also appropriate for the decoration of the public apartments of a convent or monastery, for spaces such as the guest rooms or the refectory. Whatever the original setting of the pictures, the charitable activities of the Scuola Grande di S. Rocco made it a suitable destination for them.

Abraham and the Angels incorporates the theme of hospitality to strangers in an Old Testament narrative in which God's messengers tell Abraham that his barren wife, Sarah, will bear him a son (Genesis 18.1–15). *Hagar and Ishmael* illustrates a later episode relating to Abraham that also includes the apparition of an angel and the theme of hospitality, here symbolized by the offering of food for the weary (Genesis 21.14–20). After the birth of Isaac, his son and heir, Abraham cast out, at Sarah's behest, his illegitimate son, Ishmael, and Hagar, Ishmael's Egyptian mother. Hagar and Ishmael wandered in the wilderness. When their food and water were gone, Hagar despaired, but God sent an angel to guide her to a well and to comfort her with the promise that Ishmael would be the father of a great nation.

In both paintings Tiepolo placed the human protagonists at the very forefront of the composition, silhouetted against the heavenly apparitions, who in turn almost fill the remaining picture space, so that there is little room for the depiction of landscape backgrounds. Thus, the emphasis is on gesture and expression and on the gravity of the interchange between the sacred and the mortal. While in *Abraham and the Angels* this sense

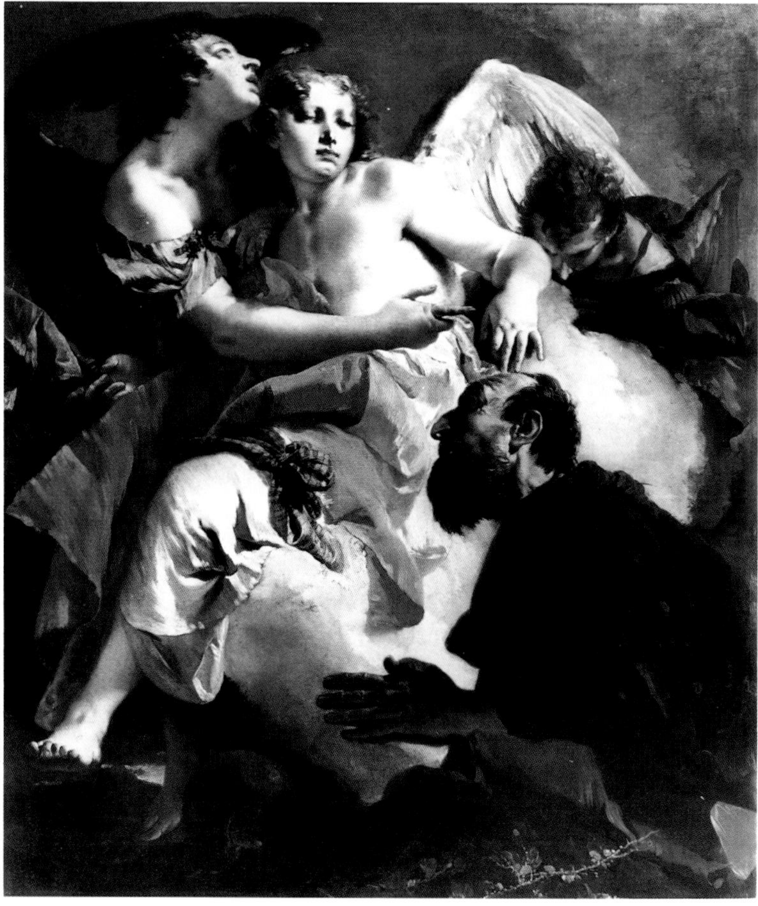

Fig. 68. *Abraham and the Angels*. Oil on canvas. Scuola Grande di S. Rocco, Venice

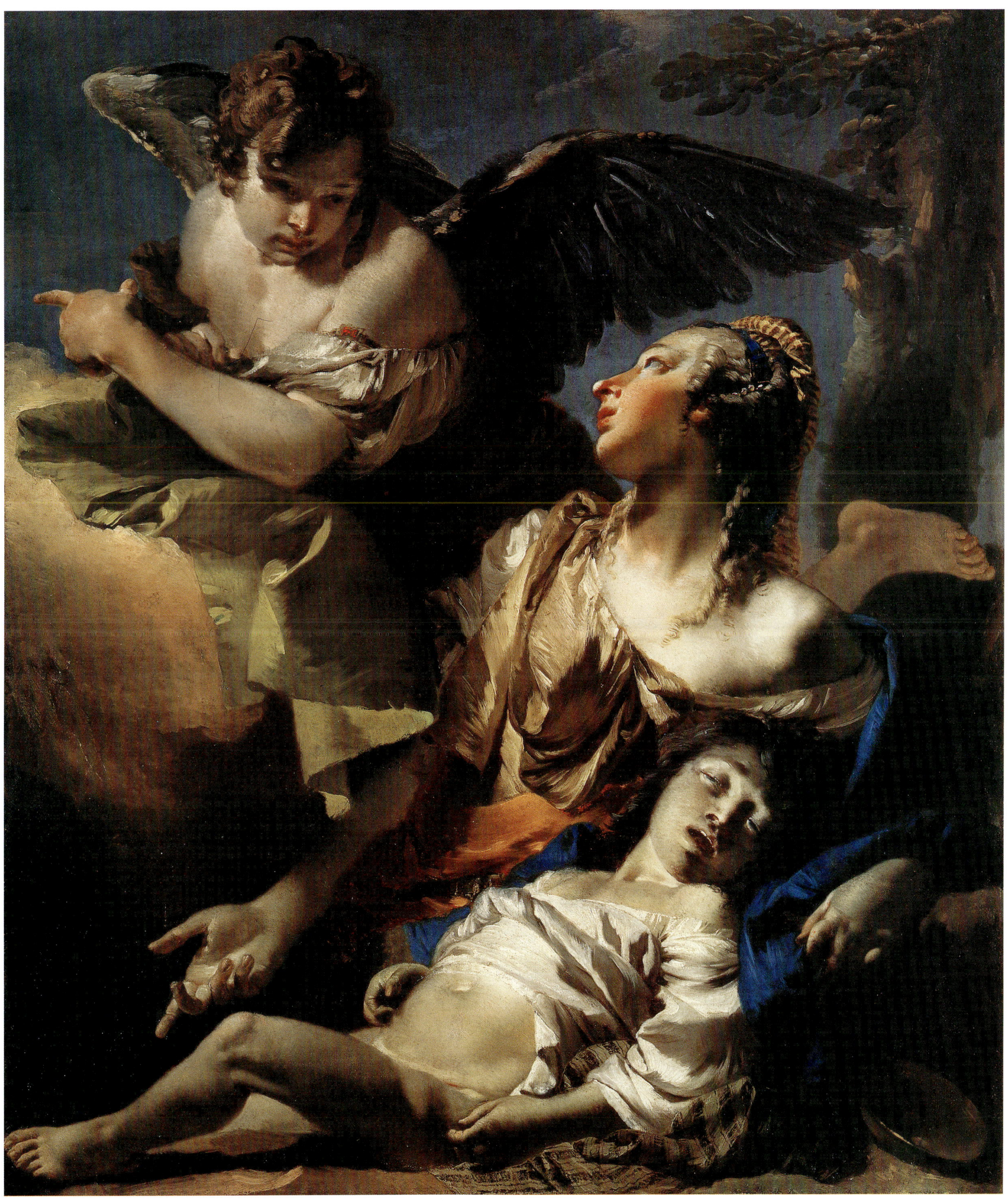

PROVENANCE:
Scuola Grande di S. Rocco, Venice (from 1785)

REFERENCES:
Molmenti 1909, p. 326; Sack 1910, pp. 38, 158; Arslan 1935–36, p. 248; Venice 1951, p. 41, no. 30; Morassi 1955a, p. 144; Morassi 1962, p. 58; Barcham 1989, p. 182; Gemin and Pedrocco 1993, pp. 74, 279, no. 121; Venice 1995a, p. 238, no. 53

of gravity arises from the momentous annunciation by the angels of God's plan for Abraham and his seed, in *Hagar and Ishmael* it stems from the merciful alleviation of human woe. The exhausted, hungry child appeals directly to the spectator; he is enclosed by his mother's protective form, but her gesture indicates her helplessness. Hagar has turned in the direction of the angel, and her face is suffused with color, as though to imply the return to health her pallid son will soon enjoy. The angel leans forward, his head turned to one side, and he looks directly at Ishmael, while his drapery brushes against Hagar as a tangible assurance of divine aid. Heavenly light from the upper left of the picture illuminates the child's chest and stomach, throws the features of both mother and son into focus, and picks out Hagar's pearls and decorative headdress. The same device casts most of the angel's face into shadow; his features are more softly painted than those of the humans, accentuating his expression of benevolence and compassion.

The two paintings are likely to date from about 1732, when Tiepolo was looking closely at Giambattista Piazzetta's solemn, tenebrist religious art. He clearly was impressed by the sense of monumental presence and the resonant chiaroscuro so characteristic of Piazzetta's devotional works. However, Tiepolo's fluid brushwork, luminous effects, and singing colors (especially the warm blue and golden orange of Hagar's drapery, repeated in her headdress) set his paintings apart from Piazzetta's more austere pictures.

Tiepolo had painted both subjects in fresco at the Arcivescovado (Patriarchal Palace) at Udine, between about 1725 and 1727, as part of a larger sequence of Old Testament themes. In the late 1720s and early 1730s he made a series of highly worked drawings of religious subjects, apparently for private collectors, including an *Abraham and the Three Angels* that was later owned by the engraver and publisher Pietro Monaco.[1] This independent drawing is close in composition to the S. Rocco painting, but one can only conjecture as to which work of art was produced first. *Hagar and Ishmael* would have been a likely subject for the drawings series, as a complement to the depictions it included of male hermit saints in landscape settings.

CW

NOTE

1. Now in the Museo Civico, Bassano. Monaco, who went to Venice in 1732, published an engraving of the drawing in his *Raccolta di cinquantacinque storie sacre incise in altrettanti rame* of 1743. Knox (1965) suggests that the engravings in this volume may date as early as 1739.

28. *The Adoration of the Christ Child*

28. The Adoration of the Christ Child
Doc. late 1732
228 × 160 cm (89¾ × 63 in.)
Sacristy of the Canons, Basilica of S. Marco, Venice

Painted for the church of S. Giuliano (Zulian in local usage), Venice, the picture was recorded by Anton Maria Zanetti, in a final note to his *Descrizione di tutte le pubbliche pitture della città di Venezia,* published in 1733, as ready to be put in place "in questi giorni," that is, at the very end of 1732, on the "colonna diritta dell'Altar Maggiore," the column to the right of the High Altar.

The subject is the familiar one of the adoration of the newborn Christ Child, but it is a most unusual image. The Child is taken in the lap of Saint Joseph, rather than that of the Virgin, who is placed in the foreground, her back turned to the assembled group. The rolls of bandage in the straw and carried by the cherub hovering above the protagonists, and the tender attention of the two angels to the half-seated Virgin, suggest that the Child has just been born. Mary's upturned face and eyes may indicate her adoration of the divine nature of the Christ Child, while Joseph's gentle concentration on the babe whom he is about to cover signifies his fatherly care for the Redeemer's humanity. Devotional pictures of Joseph with the Child, or of the Holy Family with Joseph holding the Child, were quite common by the eighteenth century, but this motif very rarely occurs in representations of the Nativity.[1]

Tiepolo presented Joseph here as a strong, meditative figure, which is exactly the perception of the saint conveyed in contemporary sermons and devotional literature. These lay stress on the saint's true fatherhood, a condition that stemmed from his love for Christ and

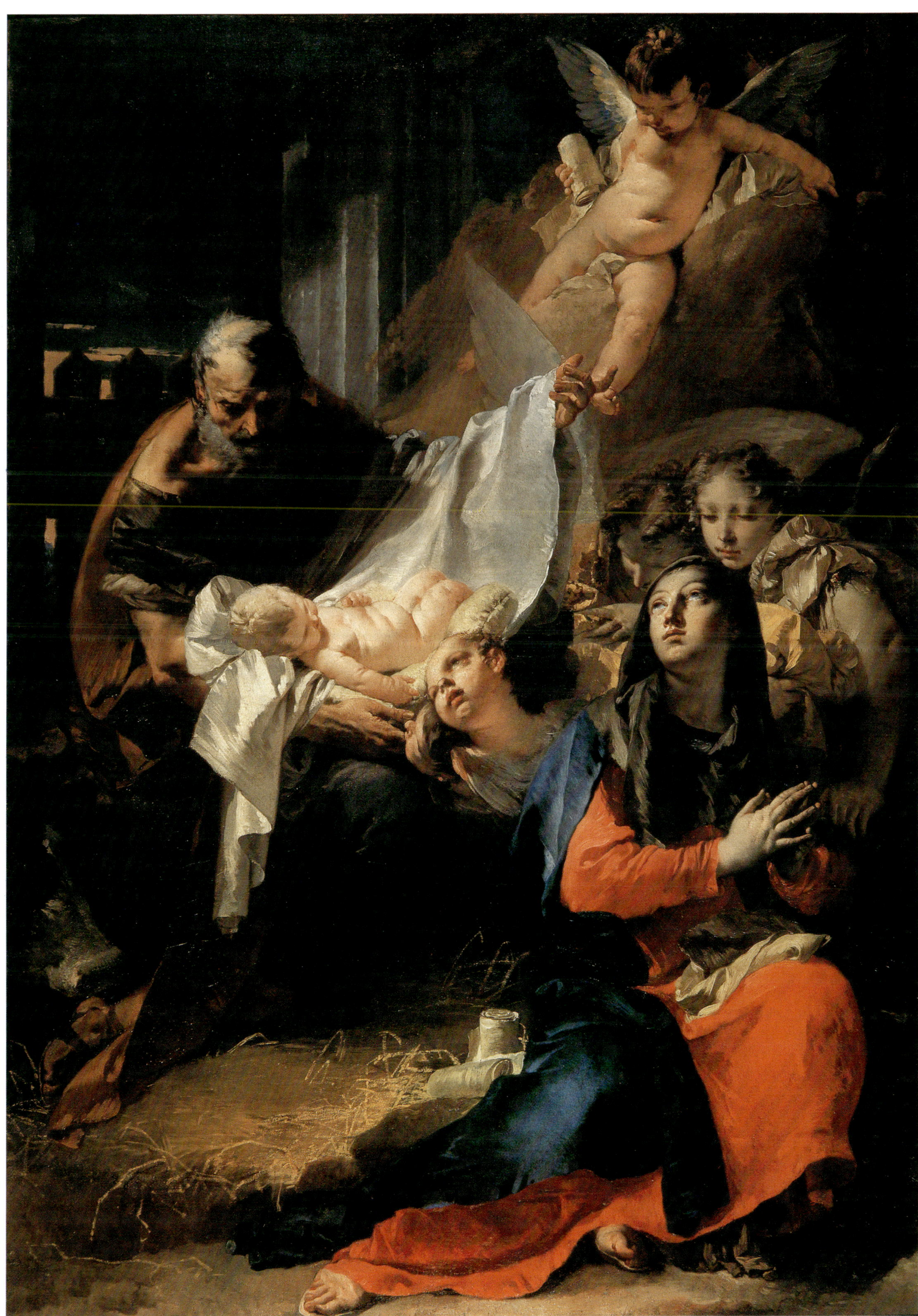

PROVENANCE:
Church of S. Giuliano, Venice; Basilica of S. Marco, Venice

REFERENCES:
Zanetti 1733, p. 486; Zucchini 1784, vol. 2, p. 376; Molmenti 1909, p. 50; Arslan 1935–36, p. 248; Venice 1951, p. 39; Morassi 1955a, p. 15; Pallucchini 1960, p. 72; Morassi 1962, p. 56; Venice 1969b, p. 352; Udine 1971, no. 19; Barcham 1989, p. 179; Gemin and Pedrocco 1993, p. 279, no. 123

his role as protector and provider for his adopted son.[2] Joseph's face in the painting is half shadowed, giving him a troubled air. This is in keeping with the dignified status and complexity of emotion allowed the saint in devotional writings, which describe feelings that include his sorrow and joy at the thought of the Passion: sorrow because of the pain Christ would suffer and joy at the prospect of Redemption.[3] Saint Teresa of Avila had been particularly devoted to Saint Joseph, and thanks to her authoritative writings his cult gained great momentum from the later seventeenth century; indeed, in 1729 Benedict XIII inserted his name in the Litany of Saints. Although there is no documentary evidence for the S. Giuliano commission, Zanetti's recording of a painting of the Death of Saint Joseph by Angelo Trevisani on the base of the column to the left of the high altar perhaps allows the conjecture that Tiepolo's *Adoration* was made as a pendant.[4]

If Joseph is a focus for human emotion, then Mary, supported by angels, expresses the mystery and exaltation of the momentous sacred event that is portrayed. Her face is sculpted by heavenly light into an image of rapturous communication with the divine. The restricted palette, strong chiaroscuro, and the sheer concentration of expression in the figures in this small devotional painting show Tiepolo at home with an idiom developed by Giambattista Piazzetta. Tiepolo's magnificent altarpiece the *Education of the Virgin* in the church of S. Maria della Fava in Venice (no. 29) was painted at about the same time as the *Adoration*, and similar attendant angels, with crisp ringlets and silken draperies, are found in both pictures. In what may be a deliberate reference to the older master, Tiepolo was adapting the type of angel Piazzetta had depicted in his *Guardian Angel* altarpiece of 1727–30 at S. Vidal, Venice. He may also have been attempting to rival his great contemporary, for the Fava altarpiece is cooler in tone and more splendid in its coloring and polished finish than Piazzetta's sonorous *Saint Philip Neri* altarpiece of late 1726 in the same church. When he painted the *Adoration* and the *Education of the Virgin* after a successful period of fresco decoration in Milan and Bergamo in the summer seasons of 1731 and 1732, Tiepolo was reminding his Venetian audience of his many-faceted talents.

CW

NOTES

1. The *Holy Family with God the Father* altarpiece by Carl Loth in the church of S. Silvestro, Venice, shows a standing Saint Joseph holding the Child while Mary kneels: this is a Holy Family and not a Nativity, however. It was painted in 1681 for the confraternity of Saint Joseph. See Ewald 1965, no. 312. Tiepolo's painting may have been a source for Giambattista Pittoni in his altarpiece dedicated to Saint Joseph at S. Giacomo, Como. See Zava Bocazzi 1979, no. 47, fig. 436.
2. See, for example, Patrignani 1709. The theme reappears in another altarpiece by Tiepolo of much the same period, the *Saints Joseph, Anne, and Francis of Paola* for S. Prosdocimo in Padua, now in the Gallerie dell'Accademia, Venice, where a vigorous, expressive Saint Joseph, holding the Child, is the focus.
3. See Deluca 1760 or the meditations on the seven sorrows and seven joys of Saint Joseph in the *Officium Beatae Mariae Virginis* 1772, pp. 315–17.
4. That there was a tradition of devotion to Saint Joseph at S. Giuliano is attested by the existence there, recorded by Coronelli (1724, p. 140), of a Soffragio della Buona Morte (a confraternity that met to pray for the privilege of a good death), of which Joseph would have been the patron saint.

29. *The Education of the Virgin*

***29. The Education of the Virgin**
1732
362 × 200 cm (142½ × 78¾ in.)
S. Maria della Consolazione (della Fava), Venice

No documents survive relating to Tiepolo's altarpiece for the Oratorian church of S. Maria della Consolazione, popularly called della Fava after the nearby canal of that name. Nonetheless, there is universal agreement that this important painting must date to 1732, since it is not mentioned in the Vicentine nobleman Vincenzo da Canal's brief biography of Tiepolo dating from that year but is described in Anton Maria Zanetti's 1733 guide to the public paintings of Venice. In all likelihood the painting was completed only at the end of 1732. This notion is supported by the similarities of style it shares with a work with a documented date of 1732, the *Adoration of the Christ Child* (no. 28), painted for the Venetian church of S. Zulian and then transferred to the basilica of S. Marco.

Opposite: Detail, no. 29

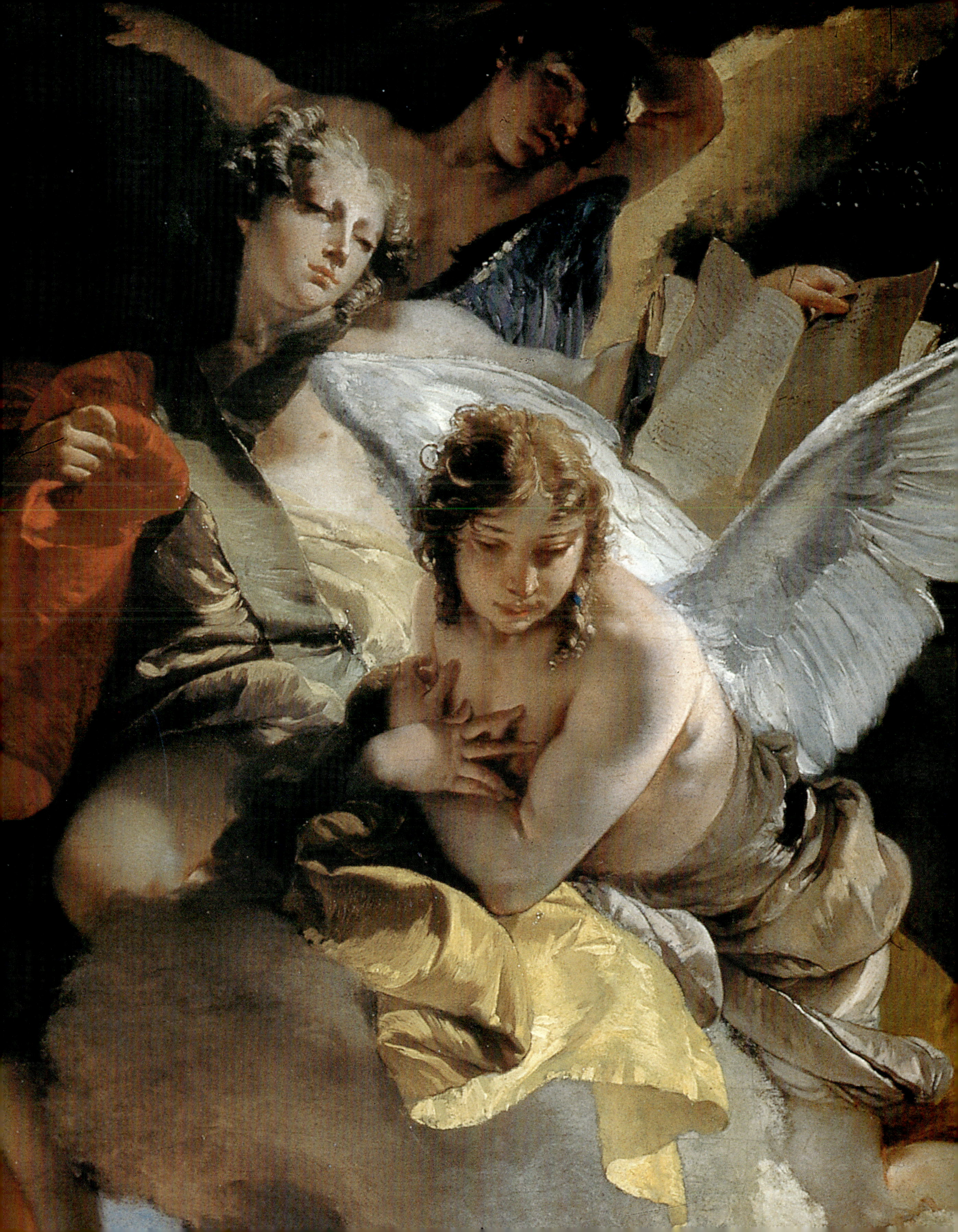

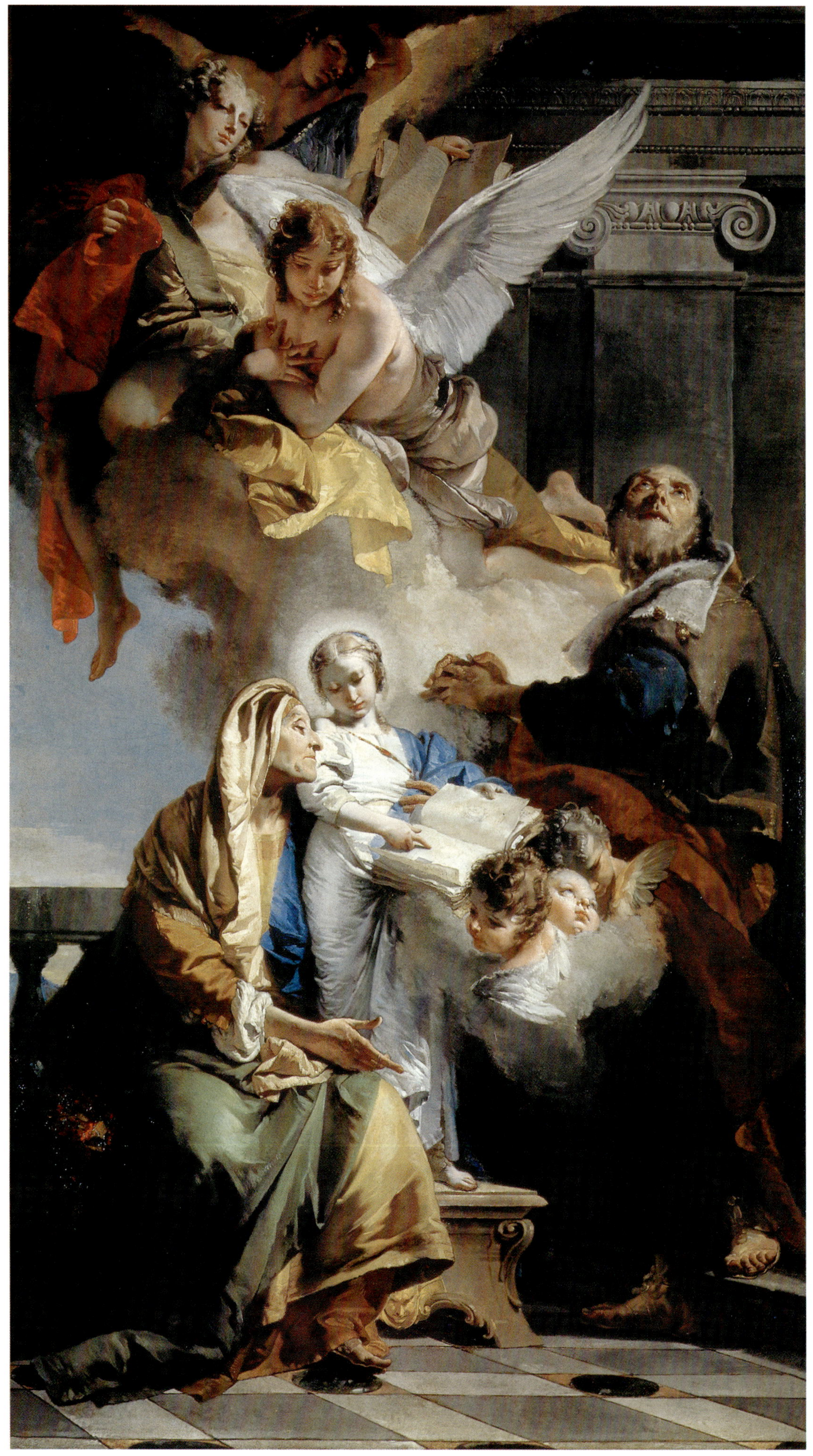

29

Tiepolo's Fava altarpiece can be seen as the culmination of a long process of elaboration on the theme of the Education of the Virgin that began in the 1720s. An oval picture now in the Musée du Louvre, Paris, is perhaps his earliest treatment of the subject, and the next step is represented by a small picture in the Musée des Beaux-Arts, Dijon, in which the composition is radically altered in ways that anticipate the Fava canvas. However, it was only after he completed the Dijon picture that Tiepolo had occasion to take up the theme again, in a painting now in the Cini collection, Venice. He may already have had the Fava commission in hand when he painted the Cini picture—which of the related works comes closest to the Oratorian altarpiece in composition and quality. Despite these similarities and their close proximity in date, the two nonetheless show marked differences in the arrangement of their figures and, to no less a degree, in their architectural settings.

The axis of the Fava composition is the figure of the child Mary, enveloped in an incandescent light. To her left appears Saint Anne, whose advanced age is indicated by the almost crudely realistic features of her face, and to the right, standing, is Saint Joseph. The large angels above, in their physiognomy and poses, are reminiscent of those depicted in Tiepolo's contemporary canvases of Old Testament subjects in the Scuola Grande di S. Rocco (see no. 27).

Of notable effect is the orchestration of colors, which centers on the contrast between the refulgent blue of the Virgin's cloak and the less strong tones of the costumes of the other figures. The chiaroscural play of darks and lights—however subdued—has been interpreted by critics as Giambattista's response to elements in Piazzetta's art: a response motivated by the desires of his patrons, who would have wanted Tiepolo's canvas to harmonize with the most important altarpiece in the Fava—Piazzetta's *Apparition of the Virgin to Saint Philip Neri*, delivered in 1726. It should, however, be noted that in the *Education of the Virgin* the connection to Piazzetta's style is more apparent than real. It is limited to the physiognomy of some of the figures and to the already mentioned chiaroscural play in the upper part of the altarpiece. By contrast, the intense and almost physical luminosity that pervades the scene (enhanced by the recent cleaning), the masterly relating of the figures one to another through the dynamics of gesture and gaze, and the Apollonian beauty of the faces of the angels are all elements that belong entirely to the poetics of Tiepolo.

FP

PROVENANCE:
Church of S. Maria della Consolazione (della Fava), Venice

REFERENCES:
Zanetti 1733, p. 190; Albrizzi 1740, p. 95; Moschini 1815, vol. 1, p. 216; Paoletti 1839, p. 277; Molmenti 1909, p. 51; Sack 1910, pp. 49, 157; Lorenzetti 1926, p. 313; Arslan 1935–36, p. 248; Santangelo 1935–36, p. 48; Hegemann 1940, p. 47; Morassi 1943, p. 19; Mazzariol and Pignatti 1951, p. 46; Pignatti 1951, p. 43; Venice 1951, pp. 43–44; Morassi 1955a, pp. 144–45; Pallucchini 1960, p. 72; Morassi 1962, p. 56; Pallucchini 1968, p. 96, no. 70; Zampetti in Venice 1969b, p. 354; Levey 1986, pp. 64–66; Barcham 1989, pp. 174–76; Barcham 1992, p. 60; Fort Worth 1993, pp. 152–56; Gemin and Pedrocco 1993, p. 281, no. 128; Manno and Sponza 1995, pp. 545–50; Pallucchini 1995, p. 362

THE MADONNA OF THE ROSARY

30a, b. The Madonna of the Rosary

It seems that Tiepolo adapted an earlier idea when he came to paint this impressive, modestly scaled altarpiece for an unknown patron in 1735. In the oil sketch of about 1727 to 1729 he had portrayed a statuesque Madonna of the Rosary, set against a golden niche that recalls similar motifs in Venetian painting of the early sixteenth century.[1] At the time he produced this oil sketch, Tiepolo was working for the patriarch of Aquileia, Dionisio Dolfin, at Udine, and the picture may therefore represent an unrealized or delayed commission. Given the renewed promotion of the prayer of the rosary under the Dominican pope Benedict XIII (r. 1724–30), the sketch may equally have been painted for sale or for display to potential patrons.

In 1735, perhaps by chance, Tiepolo returned to the same subject and rearranged the elements of his earlier design. (To judge by the dangling tassel and the absence of stretch marks along the upper edge of the canvas, the picture has been cropped at the top; although the cropping may be minimal, it is possible that, like the oil sketch, the altarpiece was arched.) He retained the sonorous red of the Madonna's robe, but the composition is recast in a more splendid setting, with the patterned gold damask on the wall now providing a

30a. The Madonna of the Rosary
Doc. 1735
246 × 156 cm (96⅞ × 62½ in.)
Signed and dated at bottom: Joa. Batta. Tiepolous. F/1735
Private collection

30b. The Madonna of the Rosary
Ca. 1727–29
44.2 × 23.9 cm (17½ × 9½ in.)
Courtauld Institute Galleries, London, Princes Gate Collection (P.G. 341)

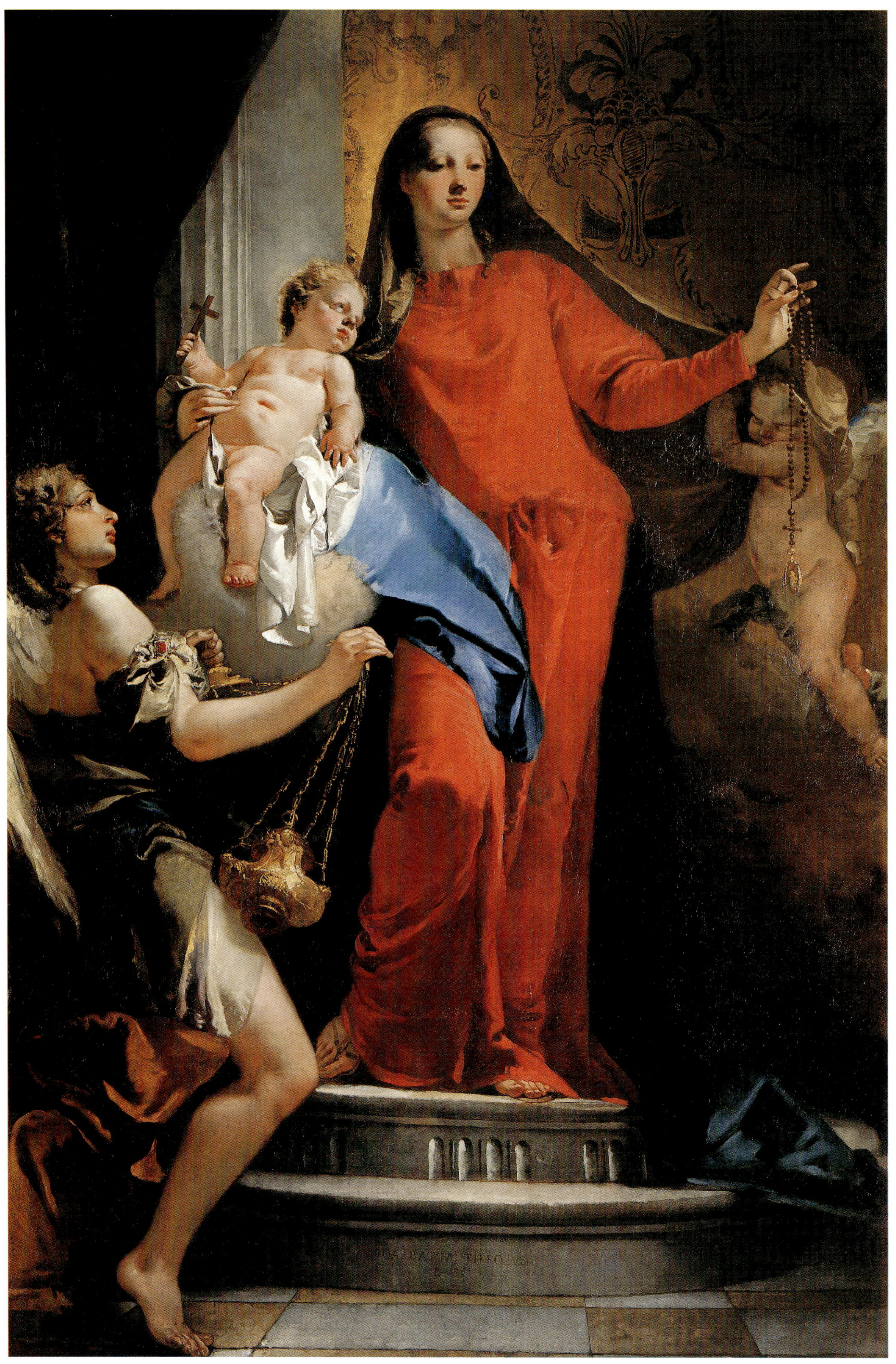

30a

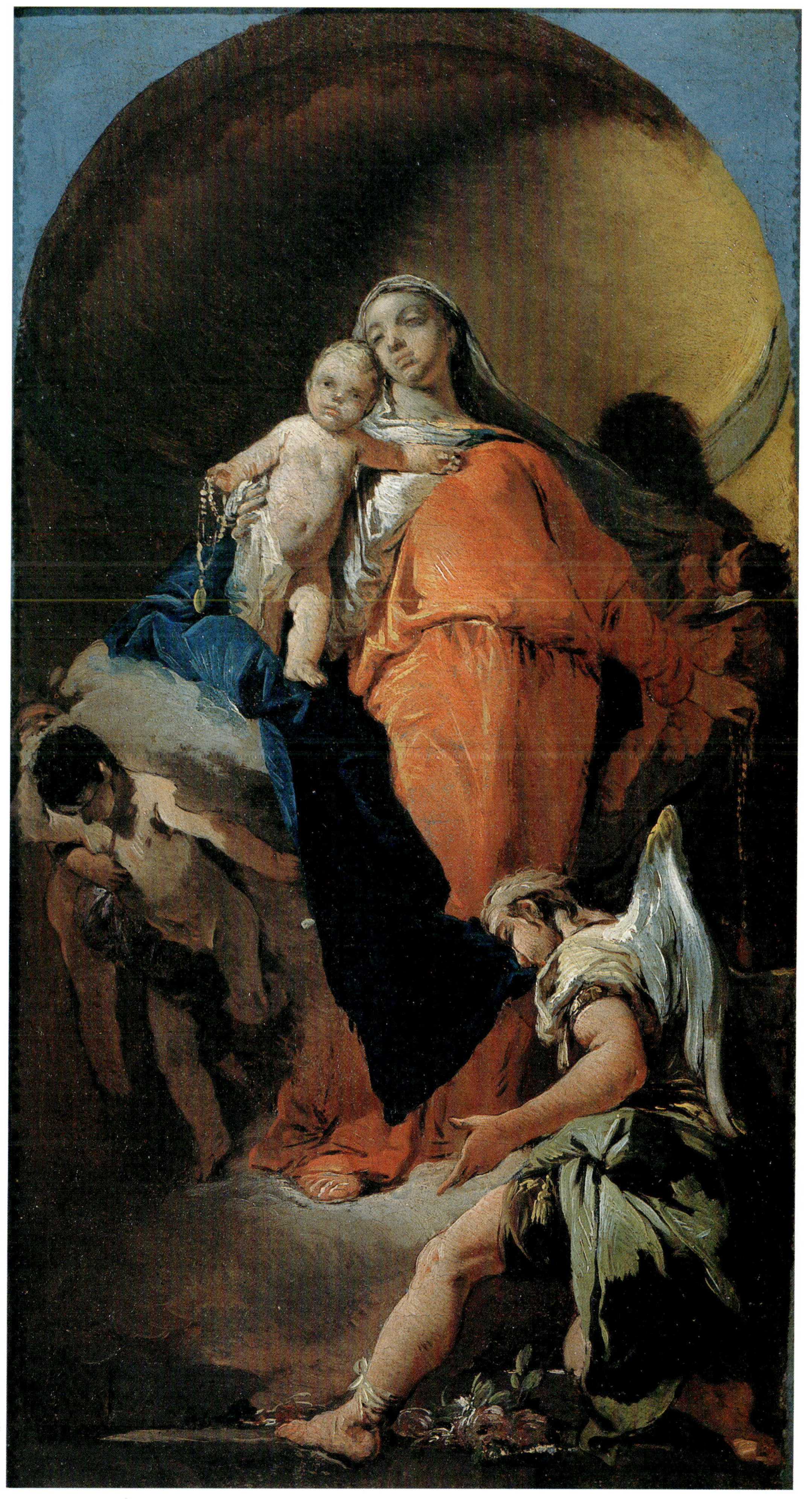

30b

PROVENANCE, 30a:
Probably John Webb, London (before 1824; sale, Stanley's, London, 31 March 1824, lot 6); Peacock collection, London (sale, Foster's, London, 28–29 February 1844, lot 29); Hugh A. Munro, Novar, Scotland (before 1865); his estate (1865–78; sale, Christie's, London, 1 June 1878, lot 116); Galerie Sedelmeyer, Paris (1878–98); Sir Joseph Robinson, Dudley House, London (1898–1929; sale, Christie's, London, 6 July 1923, lot 45 [bought in]); by descent (sale, Sotheby's, London, 5 July 1989, lot 73)

REFERENCES:
Molmenti 1909, p. 260; Sack 1910, p. 219, no. 497; Molmenti 1911, p. 198; Frölich-Bume 1958, pp. 4–5; Scharf 1958, pp. 300, 303, n. 15; Shipp 1958, p. 41; Reitlinger 1961, p. 461; Morassi 1962, pp. 4, 19, 43; Pallucchini 1968, pp. 83, 90, 101, no. 106; Seilern 1969, p. 28, no. 341; Braham 1981, p. 73, no. 107; Gemin and Pedrocco 1993, pp. 86, 249, 312, no. 207

PROVENANCE, 30b:
Jaffé, Berlin; private collection, Bergamo (by 1962–64); Count Antoine Seilern, Princes Gate, London (1964–78)

REFERENCES:
Goering 1939, p. 147; Morassi 1962, pp. 4, 19; Pallucchini 1968, no. 41; Seilern 1969, p. 28; Braham 1981, p. 73; Barcham 1989, pp. 164–68; Gemin and Pedrocco 1993, p. 249, no. 73

reference to earlier Venetian paintings by such artists as Giovanni Bellini. The position of the elegant attendant angel in the altarpiece recalls similarly placed figures in the art of Correggio and Parmigianino.[2] This angel is now given a more active, sacerdotal role than in the early oil sketch. He swings a thurible in which incense burns, thus carrying out part of the ritual of veneration of the Eucharist fulfilled by the priest at Mass and Benediction; moreover, the angel, like the spectator, is placed in front of a curtain that has been pulled back to reveal the Madonna and Christ Child. In a mildly playful touch, the vaporous cloud upon which the Child sits is located directly above the puffs of smoke from the thurible. This beautifully crafted piece of goldsmiths' work adds an air of luxury to the painting that is counterbalanced by the more austere garb of the Madonna. (Shortly after he completed the present work, Tiepolo used a similar but larger thurible in his *Saint Clement Adoring the Trinity* altarpiece of 1737–38 for Schloss Nymphenburg.) The Madonna is a splendidly sculptural figure: her assertive, expansive stance, with her arm outstretched to present the rosary, emphasizes both her womanly form and her protective role as the Mother of God. The monumentality of the Madonna is accentuated by the curved stone steps that describe the rounded space she occupies. In his frescoes at the Villa Loschi, near Vicenza, painted during the summer before he executed the altarpiece, Tiepolo had created similarly imposing, lucid allegorical figures. However, the sharp definition with which he painted these frescoes does not characterize his oil paintings in this period. Working in oil, and above all on religious subjects, Tiepolo was still conscious of the strengths of Piazzetta; thus in his own altarpieces he favored warm tones, rich contrasts of color, and chiaroscuro effects similar to those seen in that master's religious canvases.

Tiepolo's references to sixteenth-century precedents in his altarpieces and small devotional paintings of the 1730s are varied.[3] The expressiveness of certain religious paintings by Titian and Tintoretto, and the sense of grandeur conveyed in the religious art of Veronese, proved highly stimulating to him in this period. Moreover, particular ecclesiastical patrons may have actively encouraged recognizable references to past great masters. A canvas that may respond to a client of this kind is the *Saints Ermagora and Fortunato* in the cathedral at Udine, which Tiepolo painted as one of a group of altarpieces for Daniele Dolfin, nephew of Dionisio, in early 1737 and which recalls early-sixteenth-century compositions by such artists as Cima da Conegliano.[4] The *Madonna of the Rosary*, a sophisticated and polished painting, may also have been tailored to suit the taste of an individual patron. Since the cult of the rosary was especially promoted by the Dominican order, and since Tiepolo had been working in Vicenza in 1734, it is possible that this altarpiece was made for a Dominican church there.

CW

NOTES

1. For precise references to precedents in the work of Giovanni Bellini and Sebastiano del Piombo, see Barcham 1989, p. 168.
2. For instance, the figure of Saint John the Baptist in Correggio's *Madonna of Saint George*, (Gemäldegalerie, Dresden), or the angel at the left in the *Madonna del Collo Lungo* by Parmigianino (Palazzo Pitti, Florence).
3. See Barcham 1989, pp. 168–69, and Brown in Fort Worth 1993, pp. 185–86.
4. Gemin and Pedrocco 1993, p. 321, no. 221. Cima da Conegliano's *Constantine and Helena* of 1501–3 in S. Giovanni in Bragora, Venice, is a possible precedent.

31. The Crowning with Thorns

†31. The Crowning with Thorns
Ca. 1738–40
450 × 135 cm (161½ × 53¼ in.)
S. Alvise, Venice

Toward the end of the 1730s Tiepolo painted this tall, narrow canvas as the left wing of a large triptych, with the *Way to Calvary* in the center (fig. 70) and the *Flagellation* (fig. 69) on the right. The three pictures apparently were donated to the church of S. Alvise (Saint Louis of Toulouse) in Venice by Alvise Corner. Members of the Cornaro family were long-standing patrons of the artist's (see entries for nos. 3a, b, 16a, b, 36a, b): early in his career, Tiepolo had been employed by Doge Giovanni Corner, Alvise's father.[1] It seems likely that Alvise Corner had a special devotion to the Passion of Christ, since Giandomenico

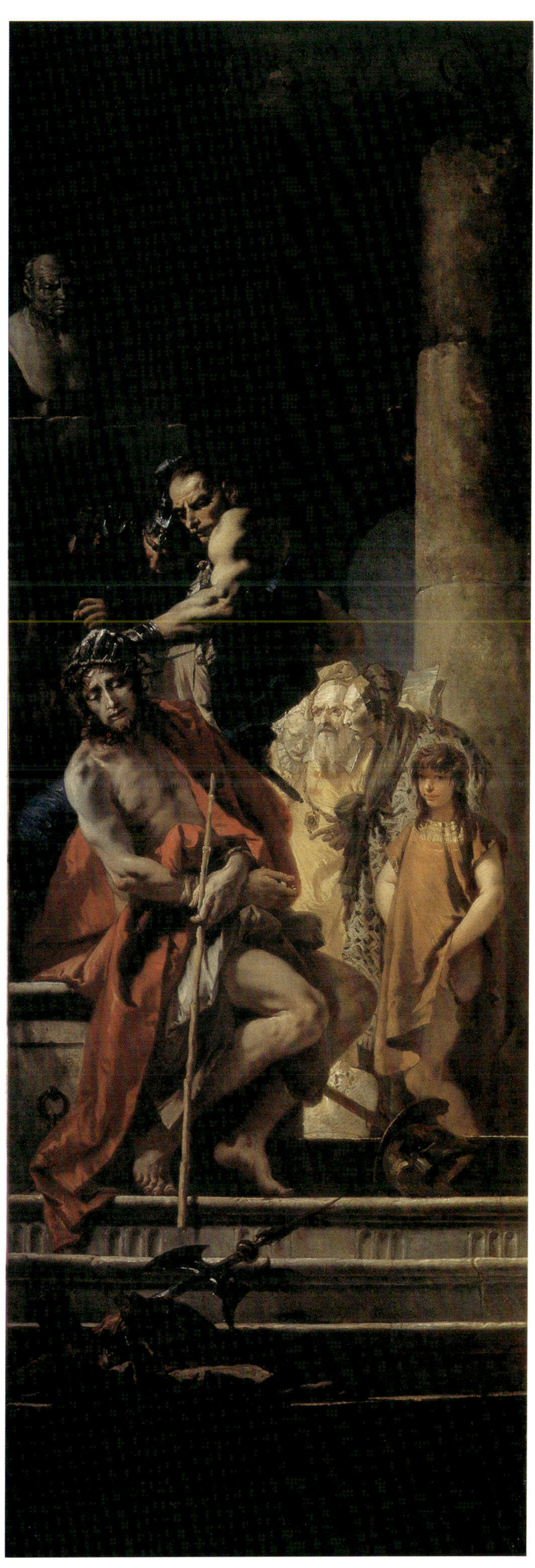

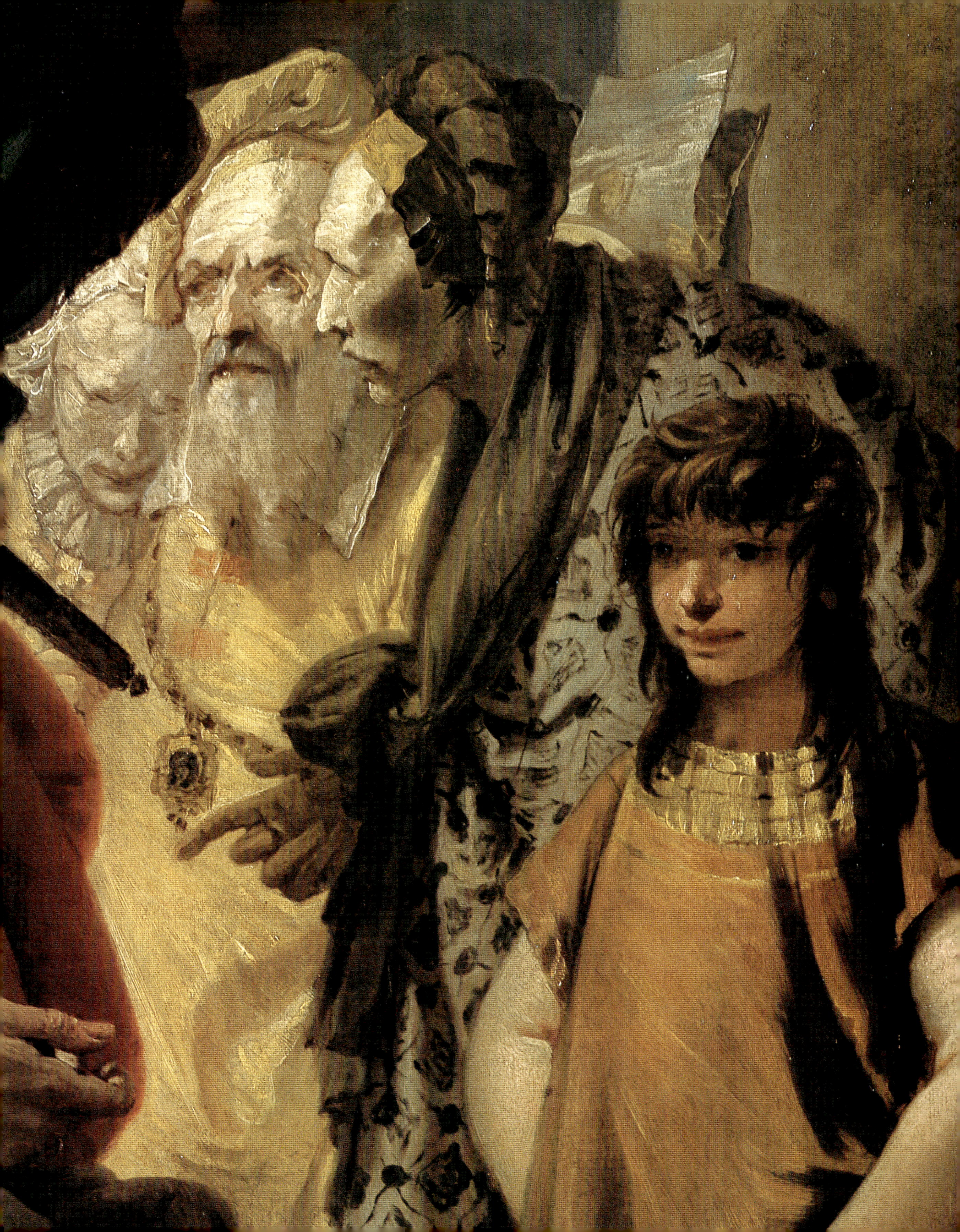

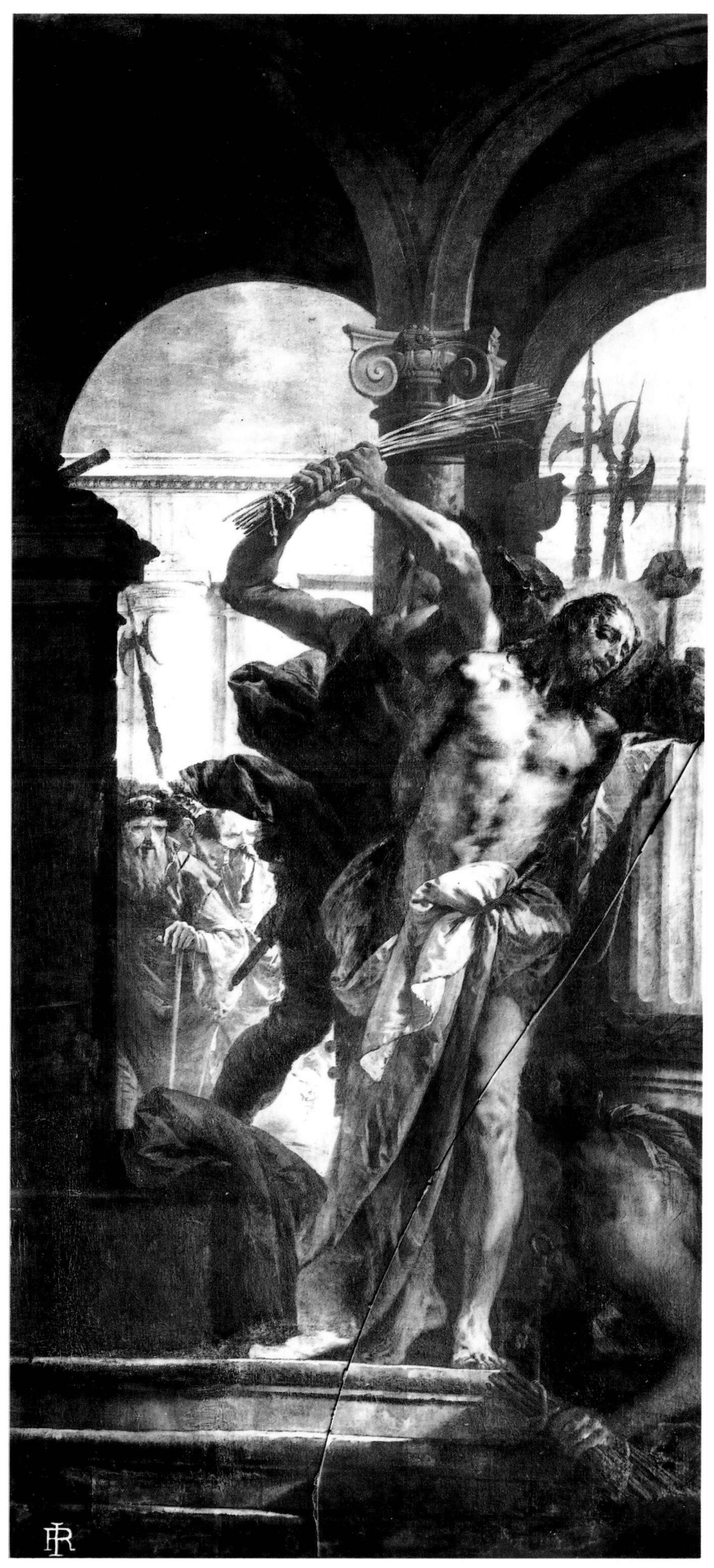

Fig. 69. *The Flagellation of Christ*. Oil on canvas. S. Alvise, Venice

Opposite: Detail, no. 31

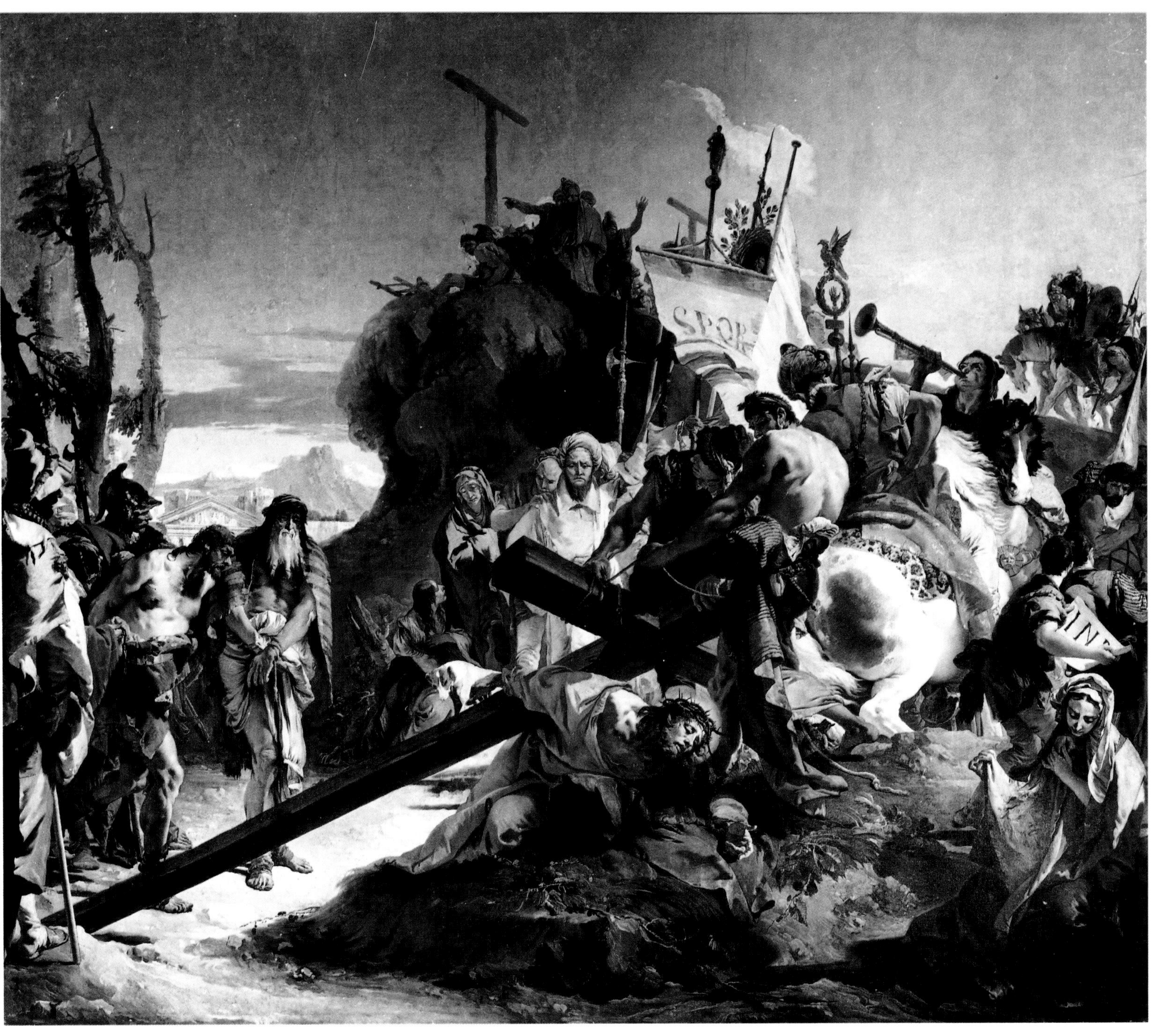

Fig. 70. *Way to Calvary*. Oil on canvas. S. Alvise, Venice

Tiepolo dedicated his set of etchings after his *Via Crucis* in S. Polo, Venice, to him in 1749. It was particularly appropriate that Alvise should donate the triptych to the church of S. Alvise, because one of the most precious and revered objects there was a relic of the crown of thorns on which traces of the Savior's blood could be seen.[2]

Tiepolo had treated themes of violence and bloodshed in his religious art of the 1730s, notably in the fresco the *Martyrdom of Saint John the Baptist* of 1733, high up on the walls of the Colleoni Chapel in Bergamo, and in the *Martyrdom of Saint Agatha* of 1736 for the basilica of S. Antonio in Padua (fig. 81). The S. Alvise triptych was on a far grander scale than those paintings and presented a different kind of challenge, with its format of two narrow scenes, each depicting a single episode of raw suffering and humiliation, flanking one enormous scene in which several moments of the Passion are narrated in an open-air setting (see "Tiepolo as a Religious Artist," above). Although Tiepolo looked increasingly to Veronese in this period when he painted meditative or visionary themes, here his sources were the spiritually charged Passion scenes of Titian and Tintoretto and, as Levey suggests, the robust religious art of Rubens.[3] For the impressive *Way to Calvary* Tiepolo was stimulated by Tintoretto's powerful orchestration of religious drama dating to 1566–67 in the Sala dell'Albergo of the Scuola Grande di S. Rocco, Venice. In the largest of his paintings there, Tintoretto encircled the still, central event of the Crucifixion with groups engaged in vigorous activity and with depictions of other moments in the story, such as the gambling for Christ's garments. For his *Way to Calvary* Tiepolo adapted Tintoretto's idea of an expressive, affecting fulcrum in a composition imbued with rhythmic and narrative momentum. By contrast, he chose a very different model for the *Crowning with Thorns*, perhaps encouraged by Alvise Corner. This was Titian's celebrated depiction of the subject, painted about 1541 for the Confraternity of the Santa Corona, or Holy Crown, at S. Maria delle Grazie, Milan.[4] When he was in Milan, Tiepolo had certainly studied the picture, and the eager brutality of the torturers that Titian showed, as well as the anguished expression on the face of Christ, must have made a memorable impression. Tiepolo made specific reference to this masterpiece in his choice of architectural setting and in the motif of the bust of Tiberius presiding over the scene.

Although modern viewers have sometimes found the S. Alvise paintings to be overwrought and melodramatic, their tone is utterly in keeping with contemporary devotional sensibilities, which laid much emphasis on the reality of Christ's suffering for mankind. Nor, it seems, did eighteenth-century viewers who visited S. Alvise for aesthetic rather than religious reasons find fault with the triptych: Bergeret de Grancourt, for instance, was struck by the apt expression of emotion in the *Way to Calvary*.[5]

In each of the tall, narrow compositions, Tiepolo constructed an architectural setting appropriate to the subject; in each, as well, the viewpoint is a low one, with steps leading up to the figure of Christ in the forefront. In the *Crowning with Thorns* the weighty, oppressive architecture adds to the emotional energy of the scene: thus, the rough blocks of the unfinished column echo the crude strength of the tormentor who clamps the crown of thorns heavily on Christ's head. Yet the high-pitched drama of this central group is undercut by the utter detachment of the Oriental figures gathered behind the protagonists. Tiepolo had adapted, and paid homage to, Titian's painting, where a single image of pathos and aggression makes an extraordinary impact. However, Giambattista needed to sustain both a level of emotional engagement and a sequence of narrative across three separate canvases—hence his replacement of some of Titian's torturers with contemporary spectators. These observers provide a linking thread with the other two canvases; more important, the Oriental figures in the *Crowning with Thorns*, who are markedly unresponsive witnesses to the Passion, may represent another kind of brutality, that of total indifference. The *Flagellation* is less intense in tone: again, the emphasis is on a realistic portrayal of the pain inflicted on Christ, but the lighter forms of the architecture, and the sense of space and open air behind the main scene, gently diminish its forceful impact. It is not clear from contemporary guidebooks whether the three paintings ever hung as a triptych in S. Alvise.[6] However, Tiepolo surely intended them to be viewed together, with the *Crowning with Thorns* and *Flagellation* presenting two solemn, harsh moments for contemplation on either side of the vivid and dynamic sequence of events shown in the central scene.

CW

NOTES

1. Although the name Alvise is a common one in the family, it is clear that this Alvise was the doge's son: Giandomenico Tiepolo's dedication refers to the fact that Alvise Corner was a Knight of Malta; Doge Giovanni's son, born in 1677, was a member of the Council of Ten and a Knight of Malta (Coronelli 1741, p. 40).
2. Corner 1749, vol. 1, p. 308. According to a document of 1456 recorded by Corner (ibid., p. 313), the church had also housed a piece of the column to which Christ was tied during the Flagellation.
3. Levey 1986, p. 90.
4. Like the church of S. Alvise, the Milanese confraternity treasured a relic of the crown of thorns.
5. Quoted in Tornézy 1895, p. 388: "On ne peut rien de mieux composé, de mieux groupé; l'expression est juste partout."
6. In 1740 Albrizzi mentioned Tiepolo among those who contributed to the church's decoration, but the first person to list the three works was Zanetti, who did so in 1771. By that time the two lateral paintings were displayed together on a side wall and the *Way to Calvary* occupied the choir. A contemporary commentator on Zanetti's text, Domineco Farsetti, noted that this arrangement was made when a new organ was installed, in 1760. See Gallo 1939.

PROVENANCE:
Church of S. Alvise, Venice

REFERENCES:
Albrizzi 1740, p. 171; Zanetti 1771, p. 468; Molmenti 1909, p. 66; Sack 1910, pp. 79–80, 157, no. 98; Fogolari 1913, p. 22; Gallo 1937, pp. 253–54; Morassi 1943, p. 23; Venice 1951, p. 64, no. 49; Morassi 1955a, pp. 16–17; Morassi 1962, p. 55; Pallucchini 1968, p. 104, no. 128a; Udine 1971, p. 59, no. 30; Brunel 1991, pp. 117–19; Barcham 1992, p. 76; Gemin and Pedrocco 1993, p. 330, no. 234

32. The Vision of Saint Philip Neri

32. The Vision of Saint Philip Neri
Doc. 1740
360 × 182 cm (141¾ × 71¾ in.)
Museo Diocesano, Camerino

PROVENANCE:
Church of S. Filippo Neri, Camerino

REFERENCES:
Zampetti 1964; Pallucchini 1968, no. 129; Venice 1969b, pp. 374–75; Pallucchini 1983, pp. 261, 263; Gemin and Pedrocco 1993, p. 335, no. 238; Rome 1995, no. 142

While Tiepolo's fame as a religious artist was growing in the 1730s, in general his commissions came from the Veneto, from the north of Italy, and from beyond the Alps. It seems surprising that an altarpiece should have been commissioned from him for the small city of Camerino, in the Marches, in 1740. Yet trading routes through the Adriatic, with Venice as the principal commercial focus, ensured that the Serenissima was still a major point of reference for the nobility along the eastern seaboard at this time. Thus it was probably not unusual that Antonio Foschi of Camerino should have looked for a Venetian artist to paint an altarpiece for the Foschi family altar in the newly built Oratorian church of S. Filippo Neri there. The altarpiece was first documented when it was put in place on 25 May 1740, the eve of the saint's feast day.

Saint Philip Neri (1515–1595) was a humble yet extremely influential figure in the Counter-Reformation church, being a counselor to popes, a spiritual adviser to Carlo and Federico Borromeo, and a close friend of Ignatius Loyola's. He was the founder of the Oratorian congregation, famous for its music, which brought together laypeople and members of religious congregations from all walks of life to participate in new kinds of devotions.[1] Tiepolo was presumably requested to provide an image of the Madonna and Child appearing to the saint while he kneels in prayer, and his first response to the commission is seen in his *modello* (private collection). He changed this idea for the composition once he discovered that the altarpiece would hang in a very high position in the right transept of the church.

The figure of Philip Neri in the oil sketch is directly modeled on the famous image of the saint by Guido Reni, painted in 1615 for Philip Neri's own church of S. Maria in Vallicella in Rome, which Tiepolo would have known through an engraving. The saint's likeness was familiar from contemporary portraits by Cristofano Roncalli, Federico Zuccaro, and others, and Reni's depiction of him kneeling before a vision of the Madonna and Child had become the standard representation by Tiepolo's day. Because it was so difficult to view the altarpiece, Tiepolo brought the saint's figure forward in his composition and set him in profile before the Madonna and Child, who in turn occupy a higher and more ample position in the picture space. The strongly silhouetted head of Philip Neri, with his Roman nose and jutting chin, and the fall of his vestments to some extent recall Piazzetta's representation of the saint in his altarpiece of 1726 for S. Maria della Fava, the Oratorian church in Venice. However, Tiepolo's image has little else in common with the searing, ecstatic vision presented by Piazzetta. While the delicate, heavy-lidded Madonna is a refined version of the more statuesque type Tiepolo had earlier developed in response to the older master's work, the appealing Christ Child and the charming Correggio-like angel directly below him lend the altarpiece an air of sentiment and sophistication that is appropriate to its Oratorian subject.

Another notable change in the altarpiece is the introduction of a more elaborate architectural setting, again an alteration that probably arose from details Tiepolo received from his patron regarding the context in which the painting would hang. The new Oratorian church had been built by Pietro Loni and Domenico Cipriani in a light, modern Baroque mode, and the Foschi chapel was decorated with stucco reliefs with scenes from the life of Saint Philip Neri. Tiepolo therefore designed a cool, elegant setting of white stucco and polished green marble, and he added a prominent piece of sculpture in the background, identifiable as a representation of Saint Paul, who was especially revered by Philip Neri. The fine, elaborate candelabra in the left foreground, present in a variant form in the *modello*, is typical of the ornate bronze pieces, often with fantastic embellishment, found from the sixteenth century in Venetian churches and may have been intended as a deliberate reference to Tiepolo's native city.

CW

NOTE

1. See Gasbarri 1964.

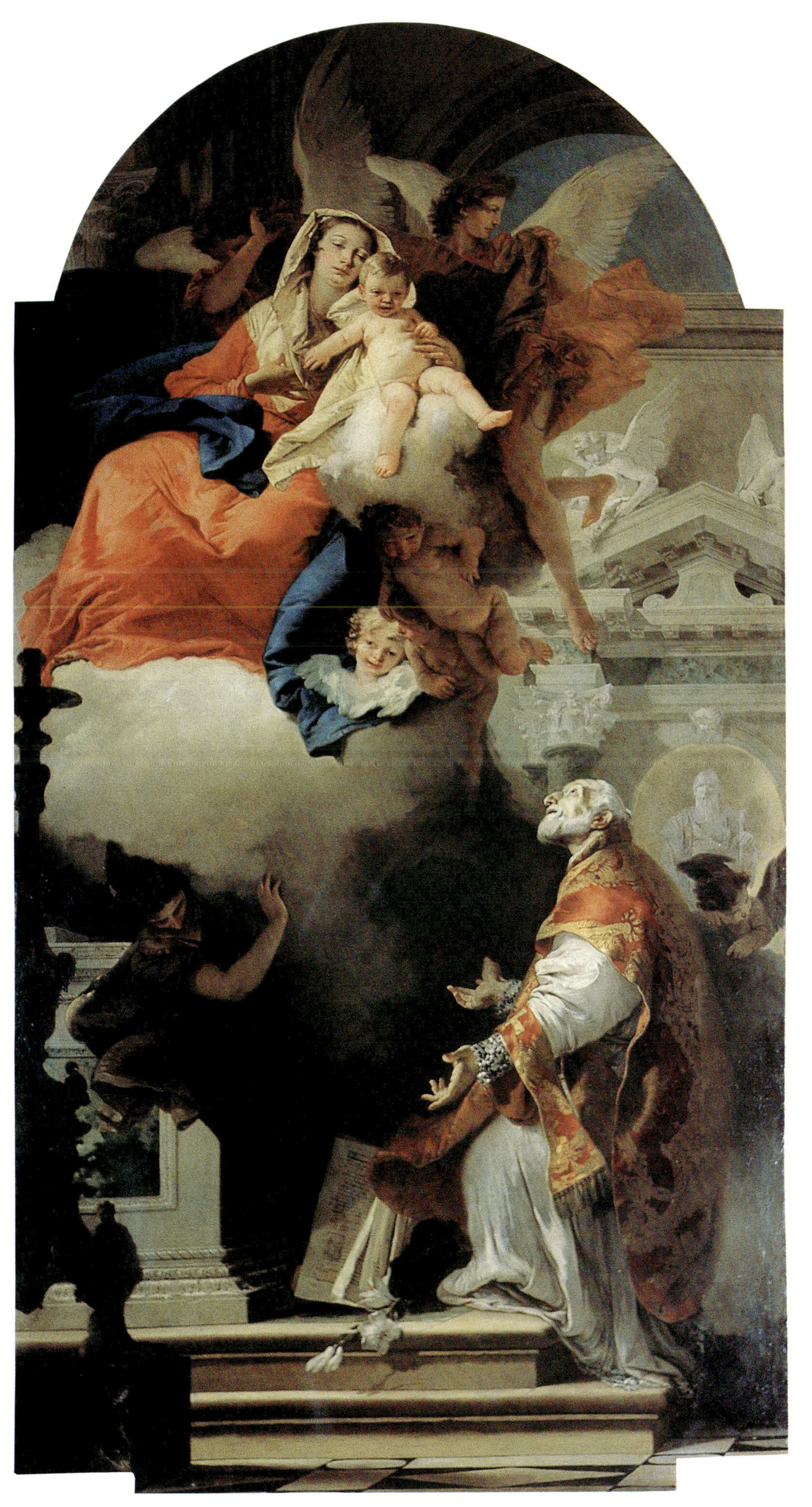

33. The Agony in the Garden

***33. The Agony in the Garden**
Ca. 1747
79 × 90 cm (31⅛ × 35½ in.)
Kunsthalle, Hamburg (643)

According to the engraved reproduction of the canvas Pietro Monaco published in 1763, the *Agony in the Garden* belonged to Giacomo Concolo at S. Polo in Venice.[1] A *Crowning with Thorns* (fig. 71), also in the Kunsthalle, Hamburg, and with the same provenance, is very likely to have been a companion piece. The *Agony in the Garden,* in its nocturnal landscape setting, makes a fine contrast to the *Crowning with Thorns*, with its massive architecture and flooding sunlight. In each picture Christ is presented high in the middle ground, more or less encircled by other figures. Furthermore, the intense mental agony Christ suffers in one scene is counterbalanced by the physical pain and humiliation inflicted on him in the other.

These two pictures have often been associated with other paintings of Passion scenes of similar dimensions, including the *Last Supper* (Musée du Louvre, Paris), *Crucifixion* (Saint Louis Art Museum), *Crucifixion* (Museum Boymans-van Beuningen, Rotterdam), *Deposition* (National Gallery, London), and *Ascension* (Virginia Museum of Fine Arts, Richmond). Opinion has differed in regard to the dating and the authorship of the entire group: most scholars agree that the majority of the paintings were made between about 1745 and 1750. It has been strongly argued that the Saint Louis and Rotterdam *Crucifixion* pictures are by Giandomenico Tiepolo and that the Richmond *Ascension* is also by his hand and was executed about 1750.[2] One painting quite clearly does not belong to the series: the National Gallery *Deposition*, which, although surely by Giandomenico, seems very likely to date from between 1750 and 1760.[3]

Two interesting questions are raised by this group of canvases: to what extent are they a collaborative effort, and do they, in fact, constitute a single commission, as has been supposed? Barcham, among others, has suggested that the *Agony in the Garden* is a work of collaboration.[4] Giambattista was greatly in demand in the mid-1740s, so much so that some important commissions were subjected to long delays. Moreover, in this period at least three enthusiastic students, Giandomenico Tiepolo, Francesco Lorenzi, and the German Franz Martin Kuen, were busy absorbing his style by copying drawings and paintings in the studio.[5] *Ricordi*, or replicas, of small oil sketches were produced for collectors,[6] and students took pride in emulating the master's handling:

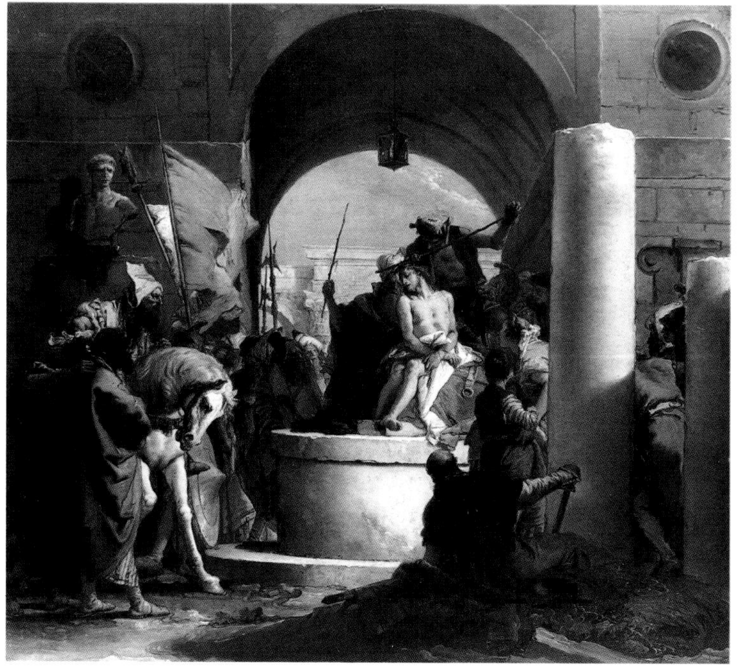

Fig. 71. *Crowning with Thorns*. Oil on canvas. Kunsthalle, Hamburg

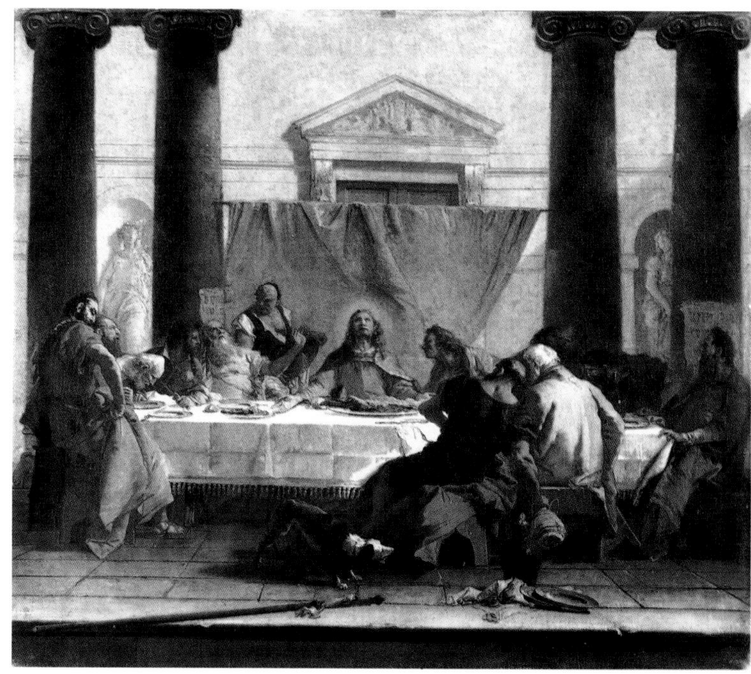

Fig. 72. *The Last Supper*. Oil on canvas. Musée du Louvre, Paris

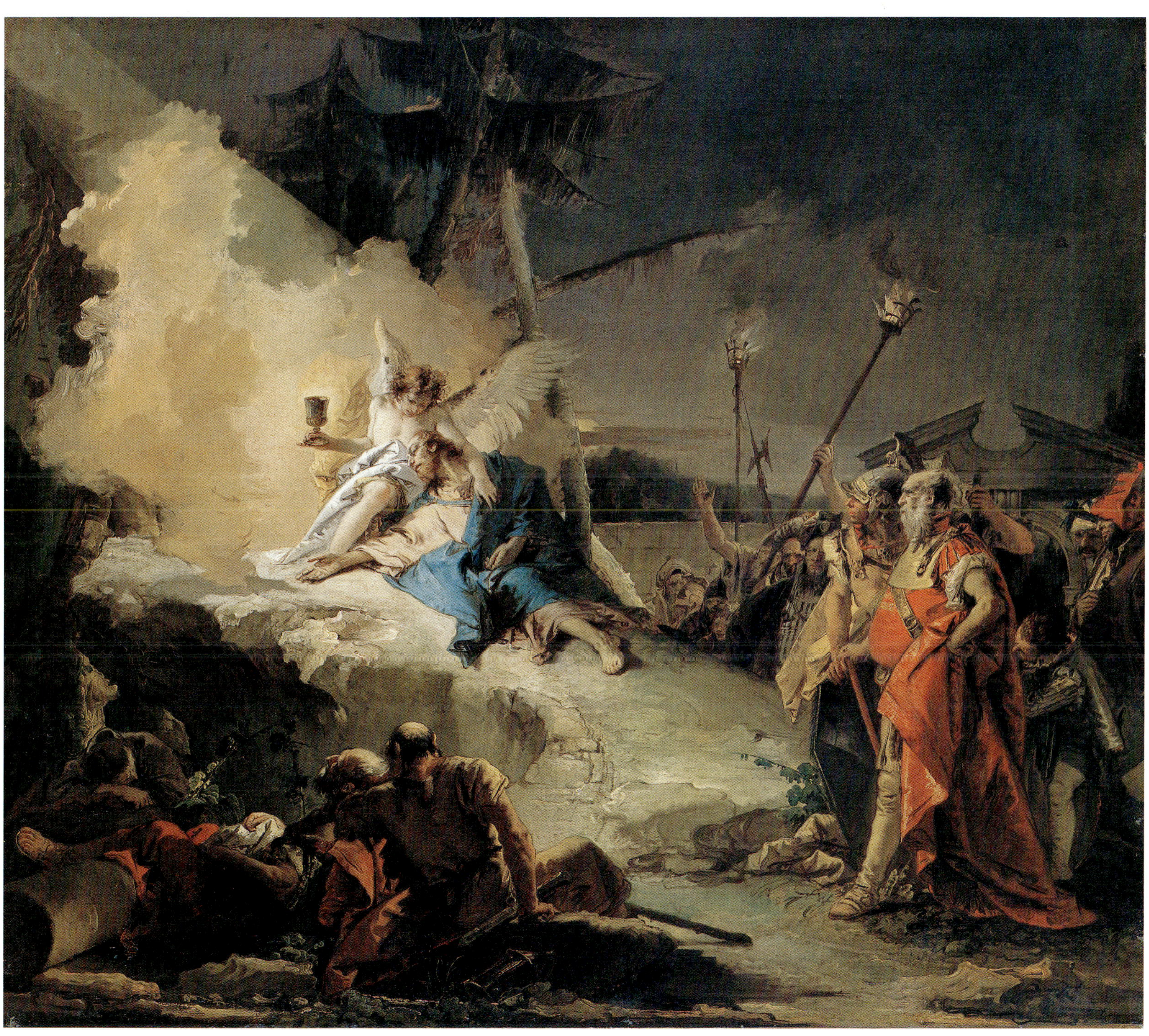

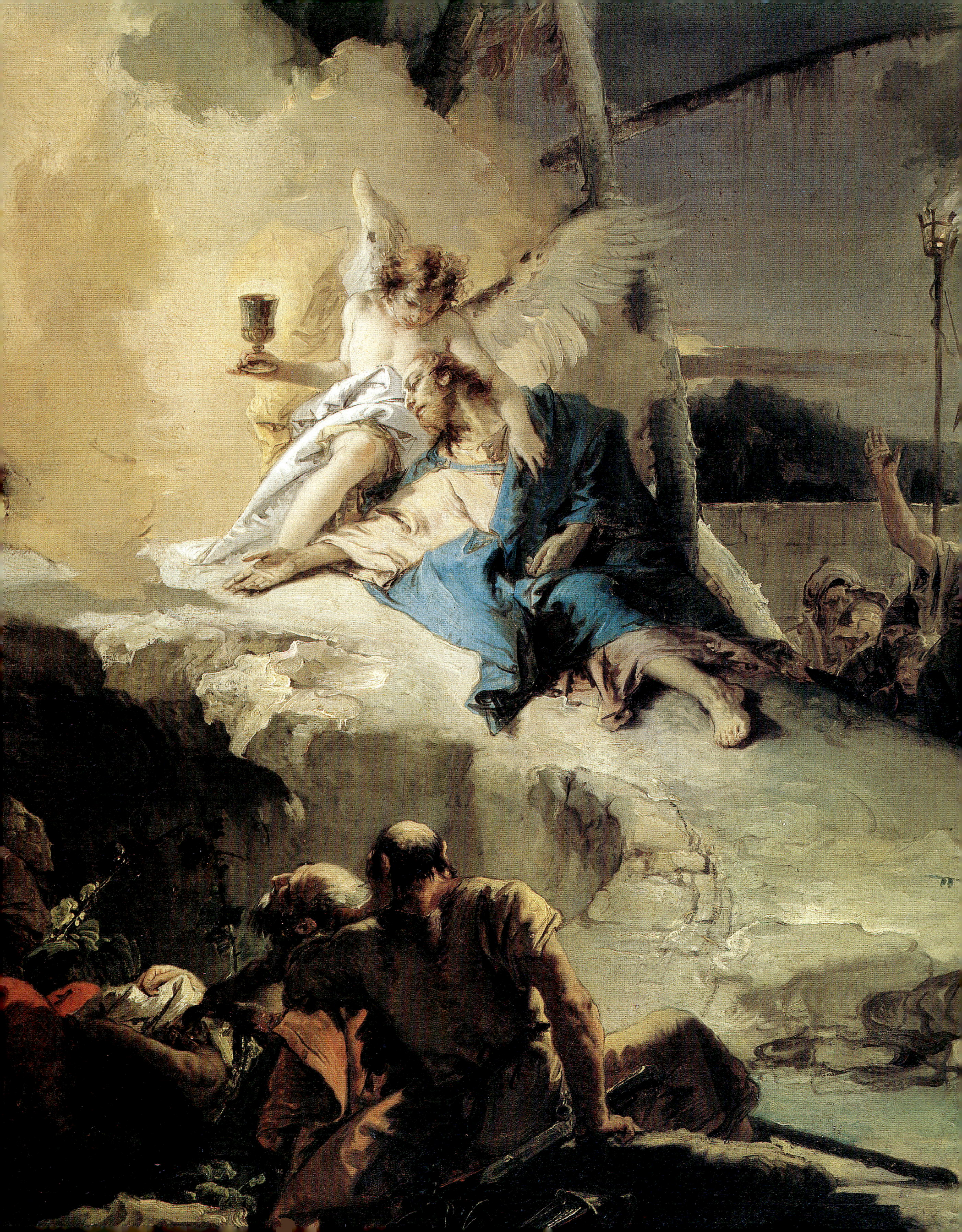

Lorenzi, for instance, is said to have made a copy of an *Agony in the Garden* by Tiepolo that was so close to the original that even the master could not tell the two apart.[7] Most important in this context, Giandomenico Tiepolo was being trained to work as his father's principal assistant at the time these small Passion scenes were produced. It is likely that the execution of some of them was delegated to Giandomenico, probably in 1746–47. He would have worked from his father's designs, imitating his manner as closely as possible; but the source of the invention was Giambattista, who would have picked up the brush every so often to make corrections or to enliven his son's handling of paint. In the *Agony in the Garden* the hunched figure of the angel, whose arm is awkwardly bent outward so that the chalice he holds is seen in silhouette, and the seated apostle in the foreground, with his small head and hulking shoulders, reveal Giandomenico's angular, sometimes gauche manner rather than his father's easy assurance. Giambattista must have intervened, however, to ensure that his design was faithfully reproduced and that the finished picture would display his characteristic verve, since the handling of paint is very fine. Apart from providing intensive lessons in collaboration, these Passion scenes would have constituted an ideal preparation for Giandomenico's first independent commission, the *Via Crucis* paintings of 1747 for S. Polo, Venice.[8]

The *Last Supper* (fig. 72) is intriguing because of the prominence given to Saint James, who is recognizable by his attribute of a pilgrim's shell. He sits beside Saint Peter, who, together with Saint John, is traditionally placed close to Christ in representations of the subject, and the fact that Saint James is so carefully distinguished here suggests that the patron's name may have been Giacomo. Possibly Giacomo Concolo commissioned three devotional subjects from Tiepolo as a small triptych with the *Last Supper* at the center.[9] It may be significant that one or more early painted copies exist of the *Agony in the Garden*, *Crowning with Thorns*, and *Last Supper*, but not of the other pictures listed above as part of the group to which they belong.[10] Thus if the Hamburg and Paris pictures were made as a single commission, with Giandomenico's collaboration, his fellow students might have worked simultaneously on their own versions. Tiepolo could have encouraged this as a useful artistic exercise, with praise from the master and possible sales to collectors in view; hence the anecdote picked up by Lorenzo's biographer to the effect that his copy was indistinguishable from the original.

Two of the pictures generally associated with the group as listed above, the *Crucifixion* in Rotterdam and the *Ascension* in Richmond, were, apparently, made for an entirely different purpose. It has not previously been noticed that major sections of the fresco decoration of the Order Chapel in Schloss Ludwigsburg, near Stuttgart, are based on Tiepolo's designs, although the frescoes were painted by the court artist Livio Retti in 1747.[11] The ceiling above the elliptical nave shows the *Last Judgment* and derives directly from the large composition by Tiepolo today at the Cassa di Risparmio, Venice, which until now was thought to be an oil sketch for a lost ceiling fresco of the early 1730s.[12] Above the left transept is the *Crucifixion*, facing the *Ascension* above the right transept, whose adaptation from the Rotterdam and Richmond paintings is clear.[13] The close correspondence in color as well as in composition suggests that these canvases, rather than annotated drawings, provided the models for the chapel decoration;[14] it is not known how they came to be used for this purpose, however. The connection with the Ludwigsburg decoration at least clarifies the dating of the three pictures, which must have been painted by the spring of 1747, since Retti's frescoes were executed during the succeeding summer.[15]

CW

Opposite: Detail, no. 33

PROVENANCE:
Probably Giacomo Concolo, Venice (by 1763); H. O. Miethke, Vienna; Seeger, Berlin (by 1910–25); Kunsthalle, Hamburg (from 1925)

REFERENCES:
Sack 1910, pp. 121, 184, no. 303; Hegemann 1940, pp. 36, 38; Venice 1951, pp. 58–59; Morassi 1955a, pp. 21–22, 145, nos. 30–33; Hentzer 1956, p. 153, no. 643; Morassi 1962, p. 13; Hentzer 1966, pp. 159–60, no. 643; Pallucchini 1968, p. 112, no. 182; Udine 1971, p. 68, no. 35; Barcham 1992, p. 98, no. 27; Gemin and Pedrocco 1993, p. 411, no. 394

NOTES

1. Monaco 1763, no. 71.
2. Knox 1980a, p. 299, under P.69.
3. Levey 1971, pp. 240–41.
4. See Barcham 1992, p. 98, and Knox 1980a, p. 299; but Gemin and Pedrocco (1993, no. 394) assert Giambattista's authorship. Haskell and Levey (1958, p. 423) identify the *Agony in the Garden* and the *Crowning with Thorns* as painted by Giandomenico.
5. For a further discussion, see Whistler 1993.
6. For a discussion of workshop copies and versions, see Brown in Fort Worth 1993, under nos. 31, 32, 41.
7. Biadego 1891, p. 427.
8. Pedrocco (1989–90, p. 110) suggests that this commission was first offered to Giambattista, who could not accept it owing to pressures of other work.
9. That Count d'Angiviller (1730–1809) may have owned the *Last Supper* does not exclude the possibility that the picture originally belonged to Giacomo Concolo.
10. A replica of the *Last Supper* (77 × 87 cm) is in the Muzeum Narodowe, Warsaw, and another was recorded by Molmenti (1911, p. 194) as in Duino. Replicas of the *Agony in the Garden* (79 × 87 cm, 77 × 87 cm) are, respectively, in the National Gallery, Alexandros Soutzos Museum, Athens, and formerly at Sotheby's, London (sale. 10 July 1968, lot 54). A replica of the *Crowning with Thorns* (80 × 95 cm) is in the Museo Civico, Vicenza. Knox records these and other variants (1980a, under P.206, P.69, P.70, respectively).
11. This discovery will be fully discussed at the Convegno Internazionale di Studi sul Tiepolo, Venice, 1996. The chapel is documented as having been decorated in 1746–48 for Duchess Elisabeth, who had married Duke Carl Eugen shortly after his accession in 1744. The subjects to be depicted are mentioned in a document of 12 May 1747, and the frescoes were painted in the summer of 1747.

12. Gemin and Pedrocco 1993, p. 275, no. 117.
13. The *Pentecost*, above the altar, and the *Nativity*, above the entrance, may be based on lost designs by Tiepolo. The other frescoes in the chapel have no connection with Tiepolo, or with any Venetian painting, and are Livio Retti's own inventions.
14. Although Tiepolo's *Crucifixion* and *Ascension* are both rectangular compositions, each was modified in the fresco, without significant changes, to the form of a lunette. Interestingly, the *Last Judgment* oil sketch includes indications of a curiously shaped frame. The final fresco, in fact, is surrounded by festive stuccowork that breaks into the ceiling in an asymmetrical and elaborate pattern. The original design, like that of many of Tiepolo's ceiling *modelli*, needed to be expanded to fit the field to be painted, and Retti would have made these additions.
15. Kunze (in Würzburg 1992, pp. 85–87) published a drawing by Kuen after a detail of the *Last Judgment*, thereby showing that the picture was painted before Kuen left Venice in mid-1747.

34. *Saint Catherine of Siena*

34. Saint Catherine of Siena
1746
70 × 52 cm (27⅝ × 20½ in.)
Signed and dated on arm of cross: G.B. [. . .]6
Kunsthistorisches Museum, Vienna

PROVENANCE:
Church of the Gesuiti, Padua(?); Imperial Collection, Vienna (by 1765); Archduchess Maria Anna, Prague; Kunsthistorisches Museum, Vienna (by 1822)

REFERENCES:
Rossetti 1765, p. 177; Modern 1902, p. 31; Molmenti 1909, p. 274; Sack 1910, pp. 202–3; Glück 1931, pp. xxiv, 59, 203; Venice 1951, pp. 91–92; Morassi 1962, p. 66; Pallucchini 1968, no. 174; Ferino-Pagden, Prohaska, and Schutz 1991, p. 121, pl. 247; Gemin and Pedrocco 1993, p. 393, no. 369

Saint Catherine of Siena (1347–1380) was famous as a mystic and visionary; she worked with the sick and plague-stricken and lived a life of severe self-punishment. In one of her visions Catherine was directed to take on a more active, apostolic role in the Church, and she became highly influential through her writings and travels, notably in advocating the return of the papacy to Rome from Avignon.[1]

Tiepolo's image lays stress on the harshness of Catherine's life as well as on her beauty. The saint is shown in anguished prayer, her thin, almost skeletal face and supplicant eyes conveying her asceticism and her fervid desire for spiritual union with God. The marks of the stigmata identify Catherine as a sanctified being who has attained this mystical union, but here they are not primarily signs of suffering. Instead the crown of thorns, the saint's traditional attribute, is carefully rendered as an instrument of torture, its points pricking the delicate flesh of her forehead. This haunting image of a tormented yet privileged spirituality is profoundly divergent from Tiepolo's depiction of Saint Catherine in the Gesuati altarpiece executed a year or two later (no. 35). Although the saint is shown there with the same attributes, she is presented as a statuesque and serene figure. The strikingly different effect of the *Saint Catherine of Siena* undoubtedly reflects Tiepolo's response to the requirements of his patron.

This oval painting was clearly admired, since it was engraved by both Marco Pitteri and Pietro Monaco. Pitteri made something of a specialty of highly worked prints after Piazzetta's rapt male saints, engraving fifteen heads and half-lengths of this type in 1742; he also reproduced a lost *Saint Teresa of Àvila* by Piazzetta. Tiepolo's *Saint Catherine* is an expressive religious image in a very similar devotional mode, and Pitteri dedicated his print to the Jesuit-trained Pope Clement XIII Rezzonico (r. 1758–69). Although the inscription on Monaco's print states that the *Saint Catherine* was in the church of S. Giustina in Padua, this may have been an error, because contemporary sources do not record any paintings by Tiepolo in this famous Benedictine church.[2] However, G. B. Rossetti's authoritative guidebook to Padua describes "an oval painting, Saint Catherine of Siena, half-length, a beautiful work by Giovambattista Tiepoletto, engraved on copper by the celebrated Venetian Marco Pitteri" on the altar to the left of the high altar in the Gesuiti church.[3] This church was demolished after the Jesuit order was suppressed in 1773, and the Ospedale Civile built on its site.[4] In the early 1740s Tiepolo had worked on commissions for patrons in Padua, including three altarpieces, completed by 1745 for the church of SS. Massimo e Osvaldo, and another painted in 1746 for S. Giovanni di Verdara. The remains of a date decipherable on the *Saint Catherine* suggest that this altarpiece was also painted in 1746. If, as seems probable, the *Saint Catherine* was ordered for the Jesuit church, this no doubt accounts for the painting's intense, emotional character as well as its lucidity: Tiepolo would have known that such qualities were central to the type of religious art that had been promoted by the Jesuit order since the mid-seventeenth century.

CW

NOTES

1. See Oddasso 1963.
2. The collection of paintings there is well documented; see the extensive literature in Pozzi 1903. The anonymous *Descrizione della Chiesa di S. Giustina di Padova* (Padua, 1759) does not mention any work by Tiepolo in the church.
3. Rossetti 1765, p. 177: "Su questo altare v'è un quadro ovale, S. Catterina da Siena, in mezza figura, opera bellissima, di Giovambattista Tiepoletto, intagliata in rame dal celebre Marco Pitteri veneziano."
4. Toffanin 1988, p. 85.

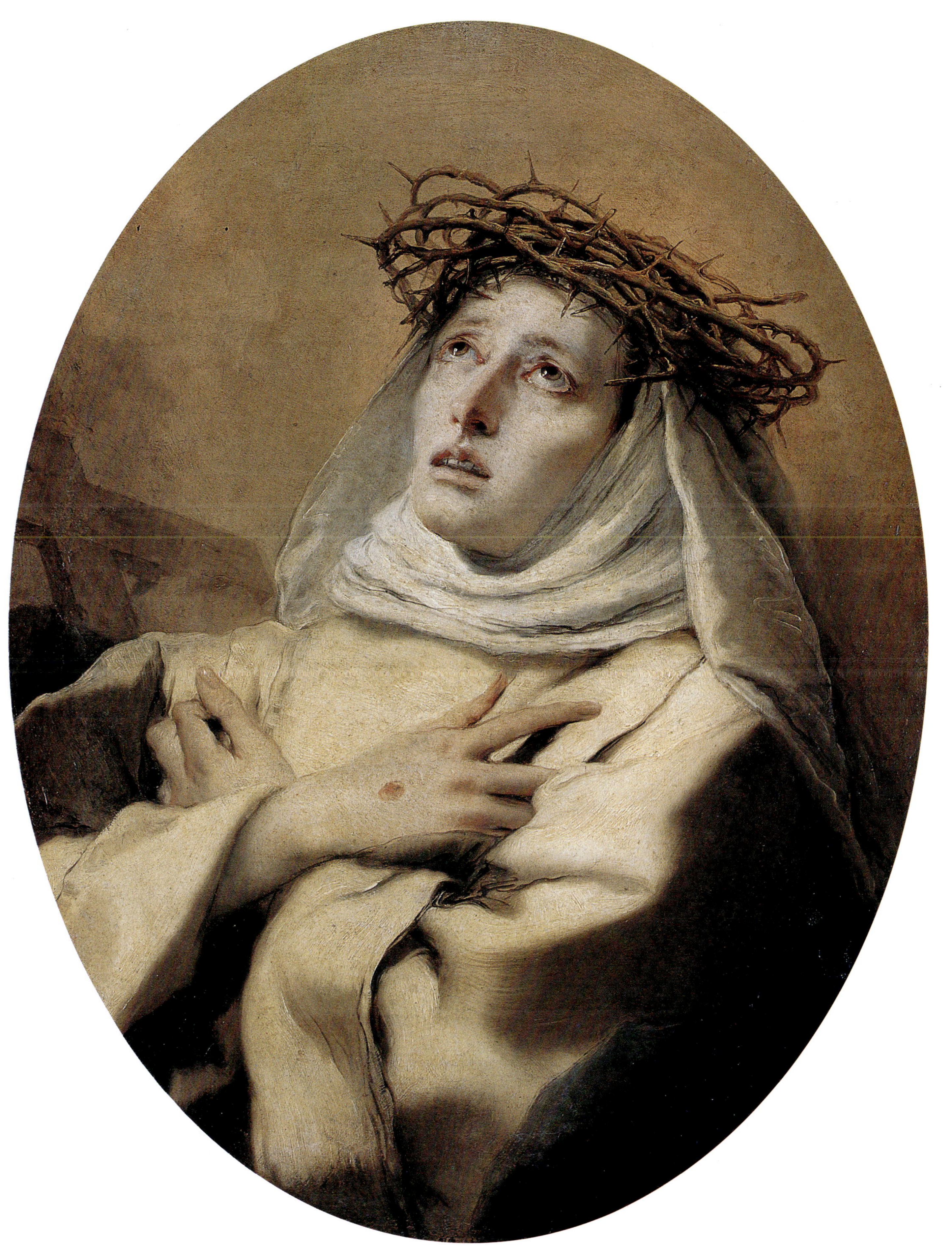

35. The Madonna and Child with Saints Catherine of Siena, Rose of Lima, and Agnes of Montepulciano

†35. The Madonna and Child with Saints Catherine of Siena, Rose of Lima, and Agnes of Montepulciano
Doc. 1748
340 × 168 cm (133⅞ × 66⅛ in.)
S. Maria del Rosario (the Gesuati), Venice

Although this altarpiece was commissioned soon after Tiepolo completed the fresco decoration of the ceiling of the Dominican church of S. Maria del Rosario, Venice (fig. 65), in October 1739, he did not have time to work on it in the very busy years that immediately followed, and it was not put in place until April 1748. The newly built church celebrated the Virgin Mary, Saint Dominic, and the cult of the rosary in its ceiling decoration (see "Tiepolo as a Religious Artist" above) and recently canonized Dominican saints as well as the more familiar members of the order in its altarpieces. Tiepolo was charged with painting the three female Dominican saints who had held the Child Jesus in their arms in their visions. His altarpiece was destined for the first altar on the right of the entrance to the church. Rose of Lima (1586–1617), the first person from the Americas to be canonized, was made a saint in 1671; she lived a life of extreme austerity and penitence, blessed by heavenly visions. Her model was Saint Catherine of Siena (1347–1380), the great mystic whose reputation for self-mortification was equaled by the fame of her charitable and apostolic activities. Saint Agnes of Montepulciano (1274–1317), canonized in 1726, was renowned for her sanctity from childhood and for the prodigies that occurred in her presence. She was venerated by Saint Catherine of Siena.

In the church Tiepolo's picture faces Sebastiano Ricci's *Saint Pius V with Saint Thomas Aquinas and Saint Peter Martyr* of 1731–32 on the first altar on the left; on the third altar on the right is Giambattista Piazzetta's *Saint Louis Bertrand, Saint Vincent Ferrer, and Saint Hyacinth* of about 1736–37. Tiepolo took account of both works in designing his altarpiece, ensuring that his would at once complement the other two and remain highly distinctive.

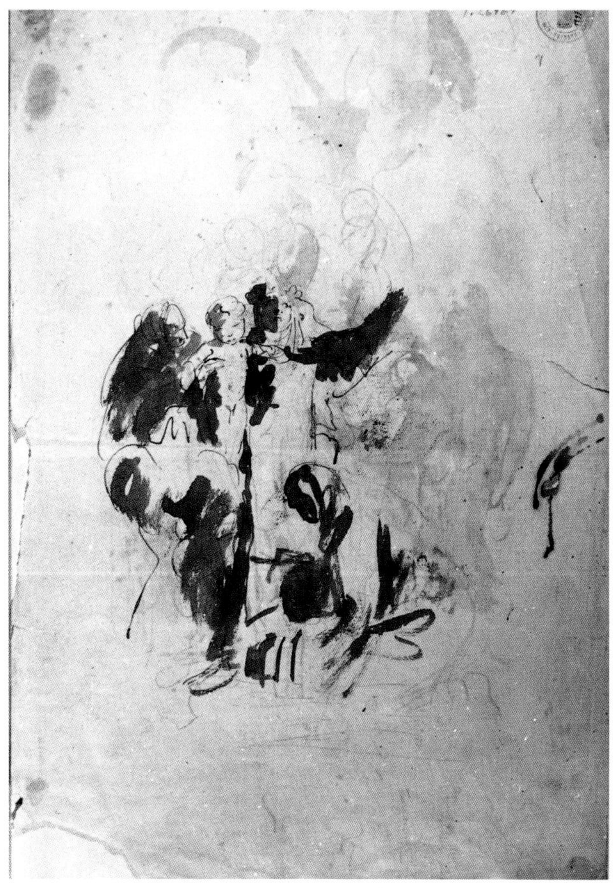

Fig. 73. *Saints Rosa, Catherine, and Agnes.* Pen and wash. Civici Musei di Storia e Arte, Trieste (1997a)

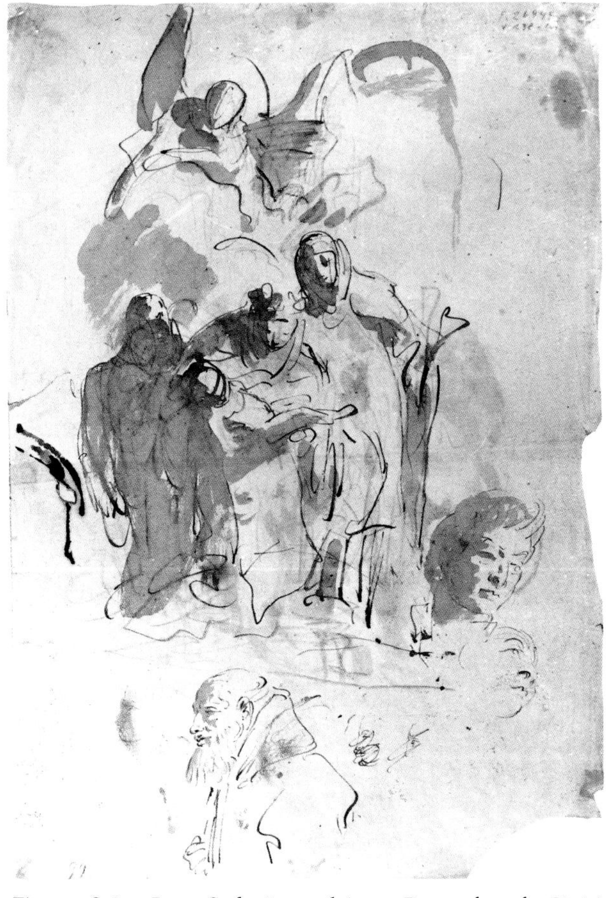

Fig. 74. *Saints Rosa, Catherine, and Agnes.* Pen and wash. Civici Musei di Storia e Arte, Trieste (1997b)

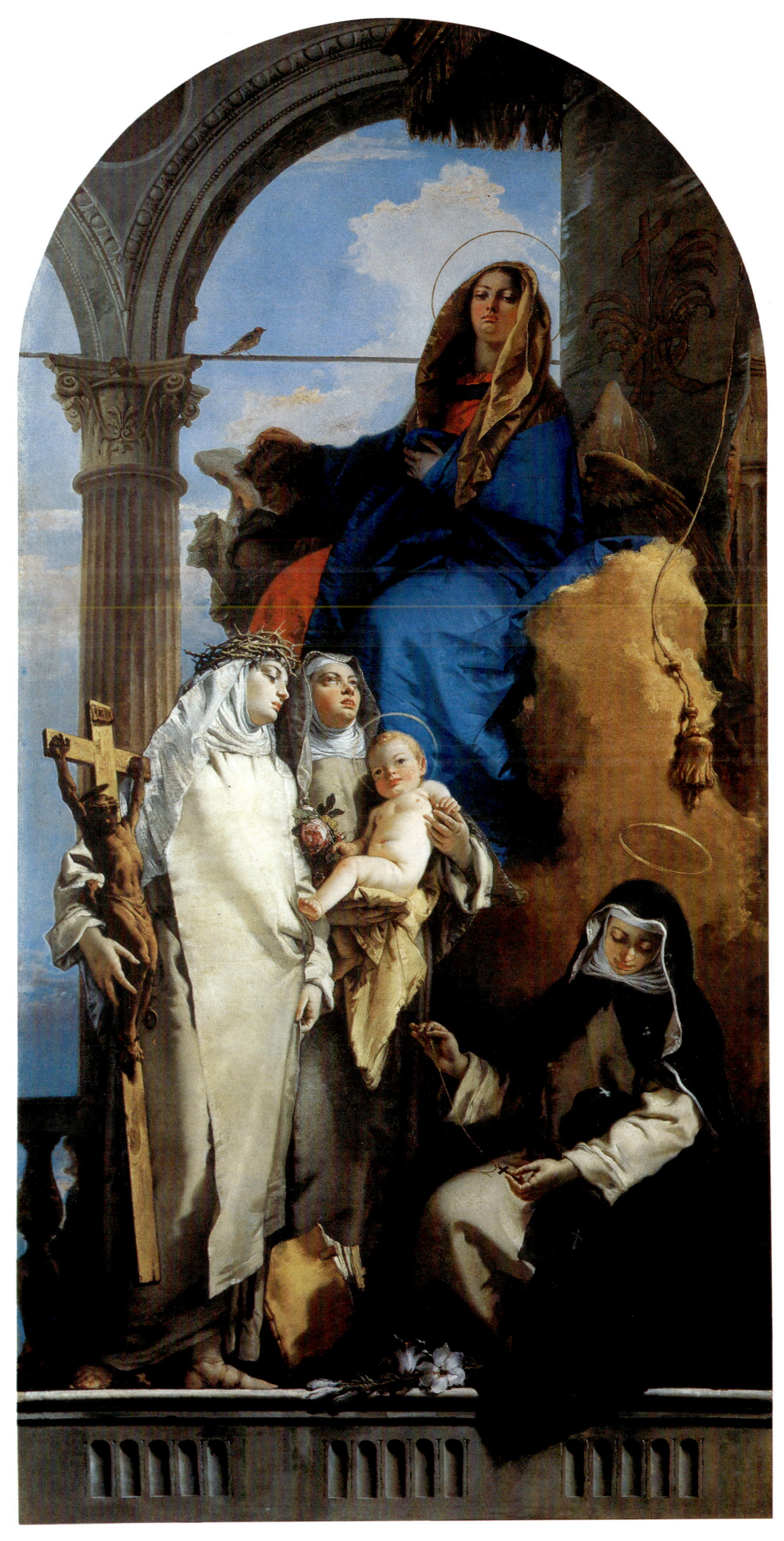

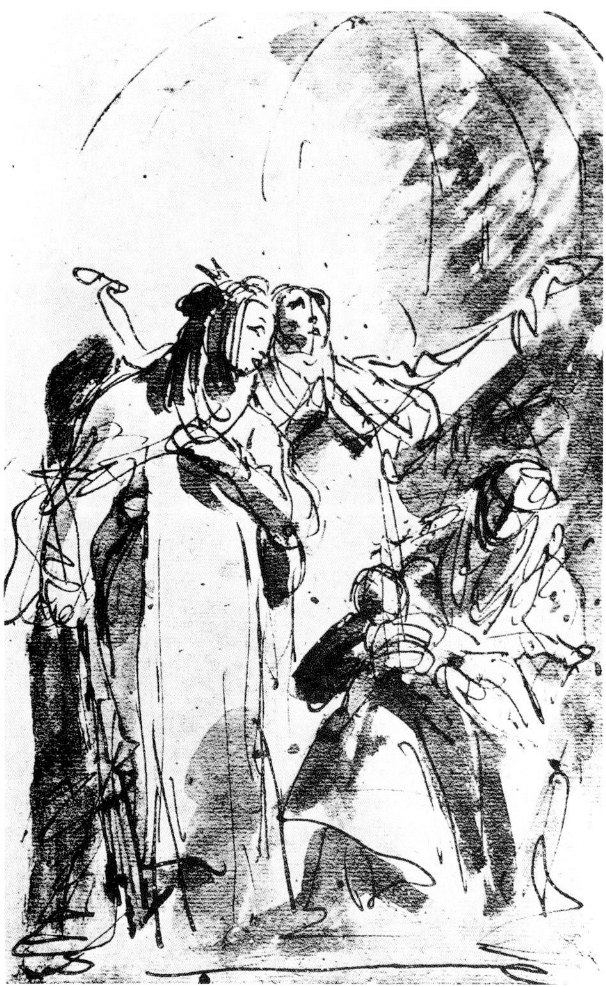

Fig. 75. *Madonna with Two Female Saints.* Pen and wash. Formerly Orloff collection, Paris.

He chose splendid accents of red, blue, and orange gold to lend a warmth and richness to his painting, and in his treatment of the group of female saints in the lower half of the picture, he composed a symphony of subtle contrasts and delicate transitions from white through pale pink and yellow to brown and black. By comparison, Ricci had painted with an elegant but muted palette of dark green, crimson, and black with shades of cream and white, and Piazzetta had achieved an electrifying effect by placing his strongly contrasted figures against a background of icy turquoise. Tiepolo paid tribute to Ricci's canvas in his Renaissance architectural setting and pyramidal figure group, and the tranquil concentration of the female saints in the presence of a majestic Madonna in his altarpiece provided an appropriate response to the intense asceticism and dramatic impact of Piazzetta's image.

No oil sketch has survived for Tiepolo's altarpiece, but his early ideas can be seen in some pen-and-ink drawings, in which he experimented with the relationship of the three saints and with the position of the Christ Child (figs. 73–75).[1] Such studies would have preceded a painted *modello*. Tiepolo apparently began by contemplating a composition closer to that of Piazzetta's altarpiece; in his early drawings the three saints were shown alone with the Child Jesus and, in one drawing, with an angel on a cloud above. Presumably these ideas arose from the initial demands of his Dominican patrons. However, Catherine, Rose, and Agnes are united by their adoration of the Christ Child and had to be depicted together as an intent group, unlike the separate male saints in Piazzetta's painting. Tiepolo quickly considered the problem of the empty space left in the upper part of the composition as he first conceived it: either one of the female figures could be shown with an arm upraised or an angel could be placed above the main group. Clearly, neither of these solutions was satisfactory. Tiepolo's introduction of a new element in the composition, the enthroned Madonna, presumably made with the approval of his patrons, involved a radical alteration to the initial design of the altarpiece and resulted in an enhancement and deepening of its meaning.

In the final work the three Dominican saints are depicted as participating in a mystical state wherein each has experienced a vision of the Madonna and the Child Jesus. Tiepolo's contemporaries, familiar with the lives of the saints, would follow the unfolding narrative in the scene and would enjoy details such as the nightingale perched high in the background, a reference to the bird that sang during Saint Rose of Lima's Lenten fasts. Thus too, Agnes, who has just held Jesus and has been given the little crucifix that she raptly contemplates, wears her identifying attribute, a habit embroidered with small white crosses that allude to this gift. Rose, who carries the Christ Child in her arms, will be presented with her attribute, the rose that is now in his hands. And Catherine, who in one of her visions received a ring from the Christ Child as a symbol of their mystical marriage, has lovingly turned toward him as his foot touches her habit. The relaxed posture of the three saints, their stillness, and the pallor of their hands and feet—Catherine's flesh is the color of ivory—are all signs of the passing from contemplation into ecstasy as characterized by Saint Teresa of Ávila, who described precisely the growing coldness and numbness and the loosening hold of the senses that accompany this mystical state.[2] The heightening ecstasy of the three saints is blessed by the majestic, authoritative figure of the Madonna.

The type of spirituality presented in this altarpiece is neither anguished, like that shown in Tiepolo's *Saint Catherine of Siena* (no. 34), nor languorously withdrawn. Rather Tiepolo evoked a serene and tender world in which contemplation has been actively focused on the

Child Jesus by these holy women, who are rewarded by a mystical communion with him. However, the viewpoint in the picture is high: this is a privileged space, literally above the heads of mortals, and fully occupied by the blessed few. The elegant setting of Lombardo-style colored marble, the refined carving of soffit and capital, the silken tasseled hanging with its Dominican emblem, and the orange-gold puffs of cloud forming a throne for the Madonna all confirm the impression of a distant, inaccessible world that the faithful must revere from afar, without any aspiration toward participation. The Dominican order was resolute in its opposition to the more extreme varieties of mysticism and viewed with suspicion their encouragement by the Jesuit and Franciscan orders.[3] Tiepolo would certainly have realized that his altarpiece was not intended to celebrate the torments and delights of mysticism; he knew that it was instead meant to provide an affirmation of the beauty and dignity of these three famous Dominican saints at their profoundest moment of union with the divine, under the protection of the Madonna.

The beauty and nobility of the Virgin and saints in this altarpiece have led some modern critics to characterize Tiepolo as an artist unsuited to religious subjects: according to this view, these female figures intrinsically belong to a purely secular world, which, depending on the observer's standpoint, is one of sensuous languor or of ancien-régime decadence. This mid-twentieth-century view stems from a generalized antipathy toward late Baroque religious art—often perceived from this perspective as overblown or frivolous—and from the consideration of Tiepolo's picture in isolation from its immediate context. Thus, if the intricate relationship of the painting with the altarpieces by Ricci and Piazzetta is overlooked, and if no weight is given to the particular kind of spirituality Tiepolo was celebrating here, a whole range of significance is lost, and both the tone and the effect he created can be misinterpreted.

The critics who consider Tiepolo's religious art shallow or even cynical would probably find sincerity or decorum in the sacred pictures of Giovanni Bellini or Cima da Conegliano. Yet just as the devotional ethos of Tiepolo's paintings is embedded in the piety and traditional practices of Venetian Catholicism, so too the character of his religious art is organically linked with that of his great predecessors in Venice. The quality of aristocratic haughtiness that some authors have detected in Tiepolo's Madonnas, for instance, can be perceived instead as a supreme sense of dignity. This characteristic of Tiepolo's Virgin is a long-standing feature of Venetian religious art, originating with hieratic Byzantine images, blossoming in the gravity of Bellini's full-faced Madonnas, and continuing in the dignified, assured Madonna type painted by Veronese. The stately Virgin of the Gesuati picture undoubtedly belongs to this native tradition. The distinctive late quattrocento architectural setting of Tiepolo's canvas, its pellucid blue sky, and its precise rendition of detail call forth a *sacra conversazione*, a timeless, sacred world in which the saints are utterly absorbed in contemplation. Tiepolo looked to this Renaissance theme, so often encountered in the work of Bellini, Cima, and their contemporaries, as an appropriate model for the atmosphere of gentle but concentrated meditation he wished to represent. Indeed, the orthodox message of the altarpiece, with its measured evocation of a mystical state, gains further authority through Tiepolo's reference to Venetian Renaissance art.

CW

Notes

1. Two compositional ideas are recorded on the recto and verso of the sheet in the Museo Civico, Trieste (Vigni 1972, no. 152), and a third study, which was formerly in the Orloff collection (Hadeln 1928, no. 38), is more elaborate.
2. See Teresa d'Ávila 1755, vol. 2, *Castello interiore*, Sixth Mansion, chaps. 4, 5, on these phenomena, and also vol. 3, letters, p. 60. The saint's writings were popular in Venice, where a number of editions were published by Baglioni and by Zerletti between 1707 and 1758.
3. For a more detailed discussion of the iconography of the picture and the context of theological debate in Venice, see Niero 1979.

PROVENANCE:
Church of S. Maria del Rosario (the Gesuati), Venice

REFERENCES:
Albrizzi 1740, pp. 262–63; Moschini 1815, vol. 2, p. 320; Urbani de Gheltof 1879, p. 118; Molmenti 1909, pp. 65–66; Sack 1910, p. 155; Fogolari 1913, p. 25; Arslan 1932, pp. 19–25; Longhi 1946, p. 41; Knox 1960, p. 19; Morassi 1962, p. 56; Pallucchini 1968, no. 130; Frerichs 1971a, p. 235; Udine 1971, p. 31, no. 37; Levey 1986, pp. 87–88, pl. 90; Barcham 1989, pp. 164, 202; Knox 1992, p. 145; Gemin and Pedrocco 1993, p. 402, no. 383

THE LAST COMMUNION OF SAINT LUCY

36a, b. The Last Communion of Saint Lucy

36a. The Last Communion of Saint Lucy
Ca. 1748–49
222 × 101 cm (87½ × 39¾ in.)
SS. Apostoli, Venice

36b. The Last Communion of Saint Lucy
Ca. 1748
40 × 23.5 cm (21¾ × 13⅞ in.)
Pinacoteca del Castello Sforzesco, Milan

Members of the Cornaro, or Corner, family were among Tiepolo's earliest and staunchest patrons in Venice, and the care the artist lavished on this small altarpiece during an extremely busy period speaks of his respect for the noble family, who ordered it for their chapel in SS. Apostoli. The date of the commission is not known, but Barcham has convincingly argued that the altarpiece was completed before Tiepolo's departure from Venice for Würzburg in November of 1750 and is likely to date from 1748–49.[1] If this dating is correct, the commission would have coincided with some renovation work in SS. Apostoli: the roof of the church was in poor condition by 1748, and the new parish priest, Angelo Maria Ropelli, ordered repairs to be carried out. The new ceiling fresco by Fabio Canal, unveiled in 1753, depicted the Communion of the Apostles.

An early Christian martyr, Saint Lucy was put to death by the sword for her beliefs; her cult was particularly strong in Venice, since her body was preserved in the church of S. Lucia there.[2] Perhaps because her name is associated with light (*luce*), Saint Lucy was said to have been blinded and miraculously cured. Some versions of her story relate that she tore her own eyes out because a suitor admired them so much. Saint Lucy is traditionally painted with the identifying attribute of a plate bearing her eyes. Tiepolo referred to this tradition in the altarpiece by including the plate in the foreground, although this detail does not appear in the oil sketch.

Saint Lucy was one of the titular saints of the church of SS. Apostoli and was especially venerated by the Cornaro family. Her final Communion, received just before her death, was an appropriate subject both for the church and for the Cornaro funerary chapel there. Tiepolo's painting was commissioned to replace an altarpiece by Benedetto Diana that apparently showed Lucy with two other saints.[3] The chapel includes richly colored marble in its fine Renaissance decoration, and although Tiepolo did not precisely repeat its decorative motifs in his painting, the colors of the marble in his altarpiece are the same as those in the chapel itself. Similarly, the plain Corinthian columns of the altar appear in the picture, albeit in a more splendid, colorful form. The chapel is rather dimly lit by elegant roundels high in the lunettes and by two arched windows on either side of the altar. With his use of singing tones of orange, blue, and yellow and shades of white and cream, Tiepolo countered both the relatively low lighting in the chapel and the shadows cast on the painting by the altar's architectural decoration.

The oil sketch, of about 1748, shows Tiepolo's first response to the commission, and it seems that he began by considering two important earlier compositions. The first was Veronese's *Martyrdom and Last Communion of Saint Lucy* of 1582–83 (fig. 76); this hung in the church of S. Croce, Belluno, and had been the inspiration for a larger representation of the same subject by Sebastiano Ricci, painted in 1730 for the church of S. Lucia in Parma, which Tiepolo may well have known. Tiepolo's passion for Veronese was at its height in the 1740s, and he sought to achieve in his own religious art the same balance between seriousness of approach and beauty of painting attained in the devotional works of his great predecessor. Perhaps his Cornaro patrons suggested that Tiepolo lay emphasis on the exemplary courage of Saint Lucy, who had been mortally wounded yet insisted on receiving Communion before dying. In the *modello* he showed the saint with a dagger at her throat, but this rapidly sketched idea was discarded in the final work, perhaps because it would have lacked decorum in a larger-scale painting. In the altarpiece a bloodstained sword in the foreground remains as a prominent reminder of the saint's suffering, together with a barely visible wound to her neck.

Tiepolo's second source for study, as Brown has pointed out,[4] was Domenichino's *Last Communion of Saint Jerome* of 1614 (Musei Vaticani, Rome), which he would have known through an engraving. His incorporation in the oil sketch of a landscape passage with classical buildings reflects the same motif in the painting by Domenichino, although Tiepolo's buildings, which include a prominent Palladian-style church, could belong to the Veneto. Tiepolo's decision to place the foreshortened sword in the foreground of

Opposite: Detail, no. 36a

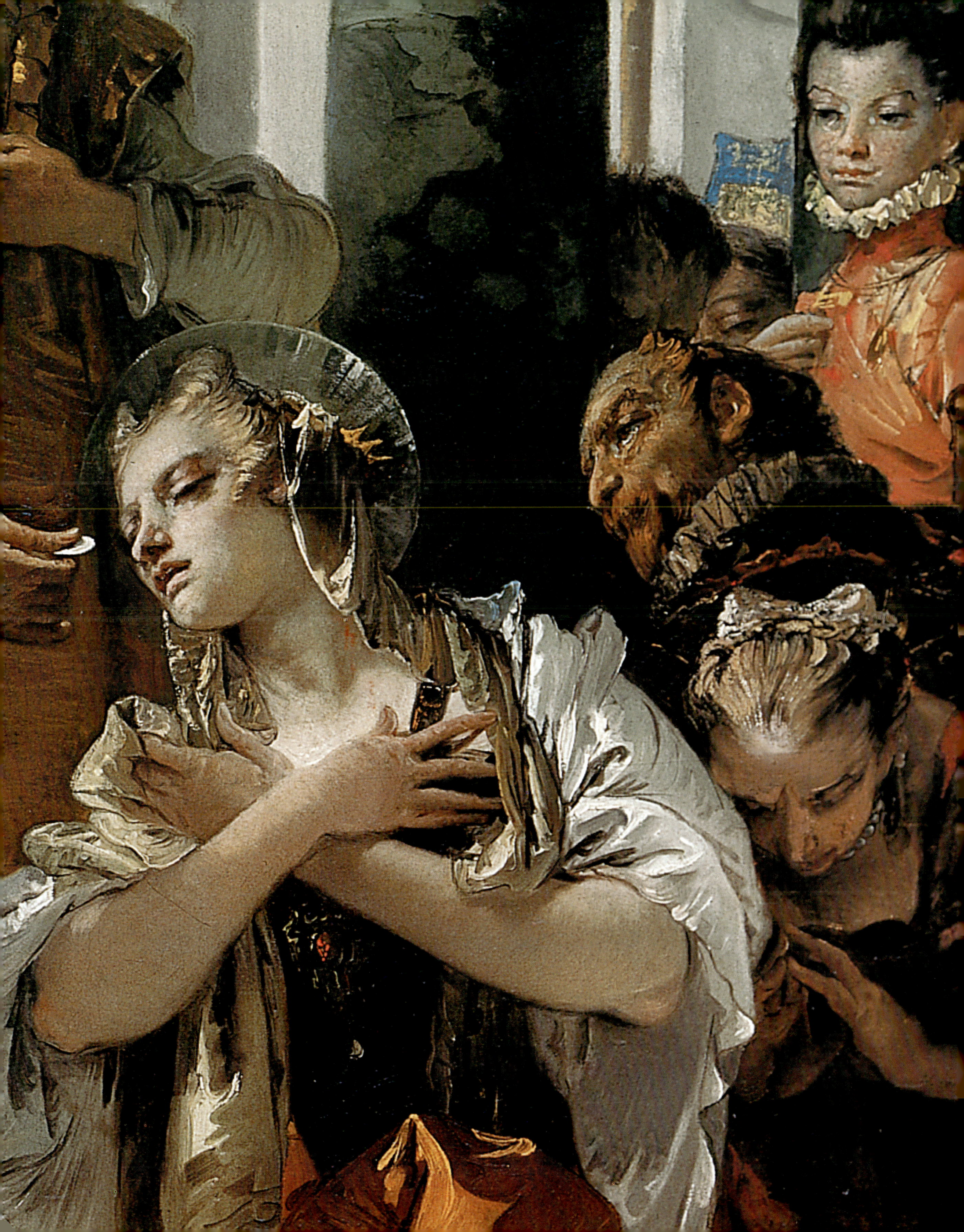

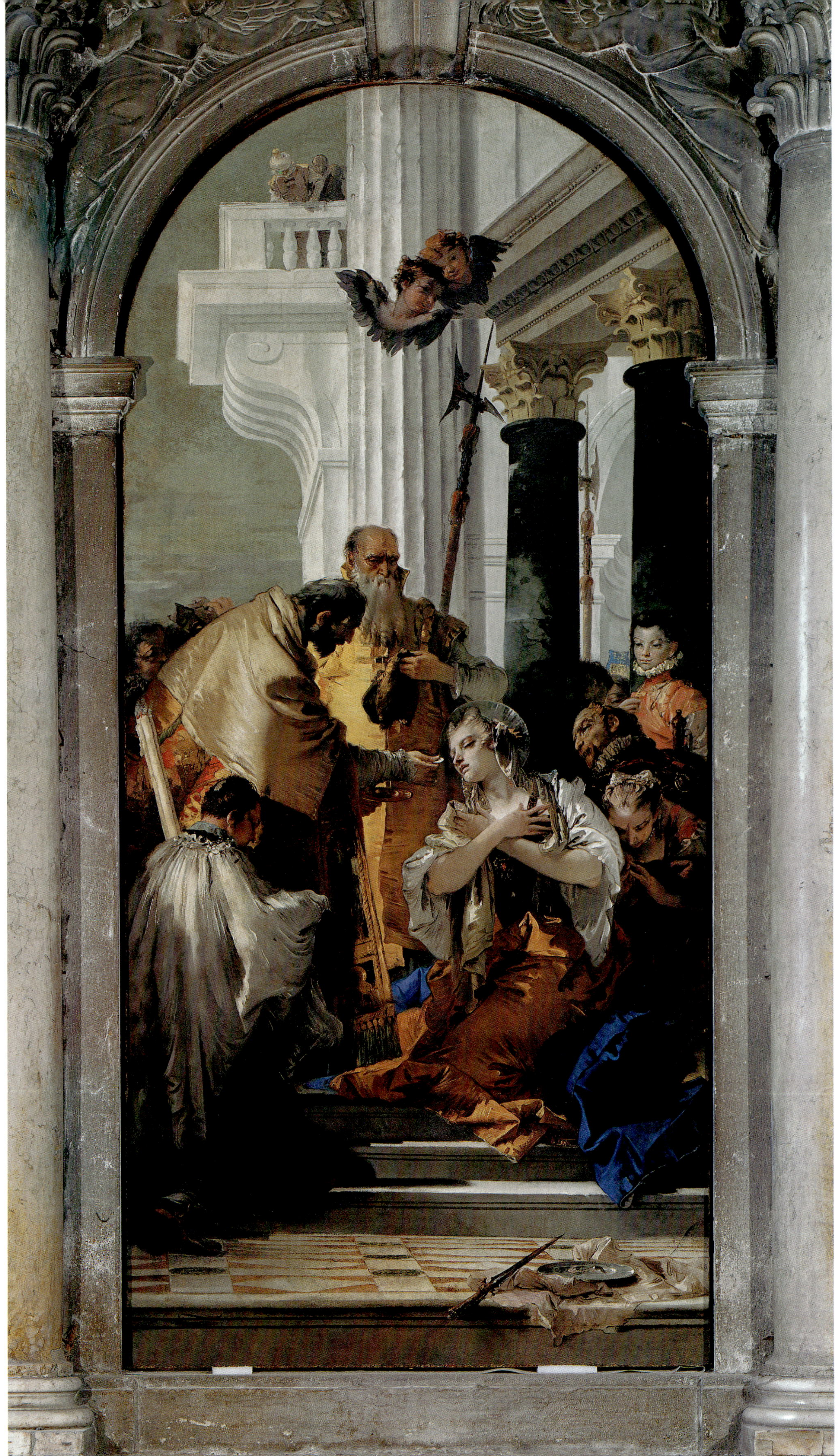

36a

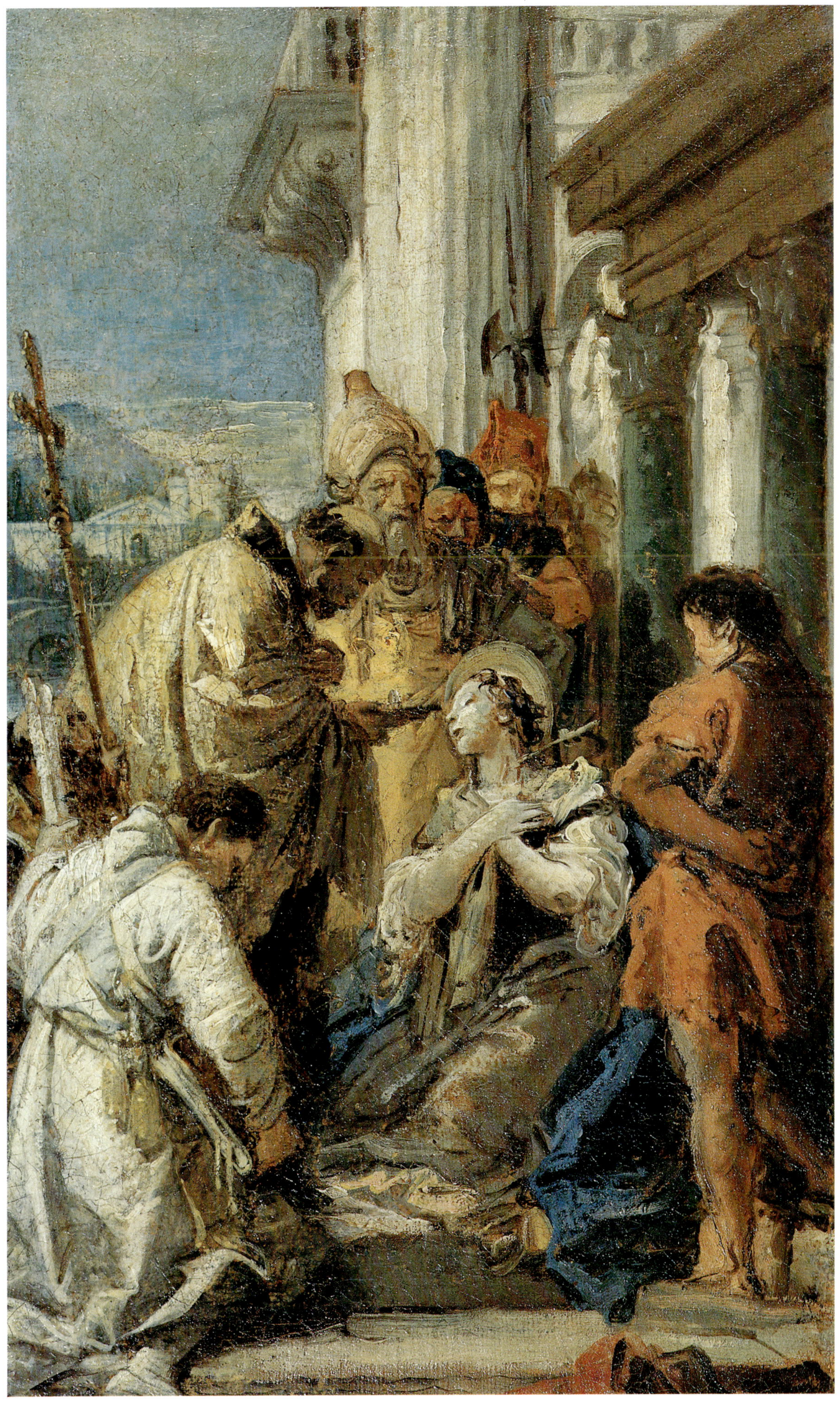

36b

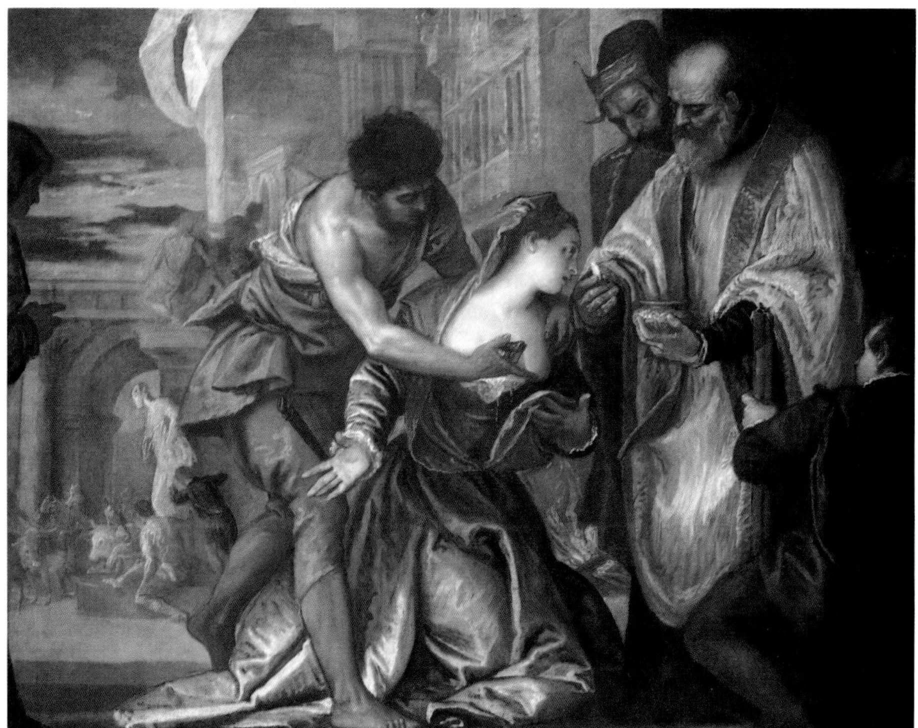

Fig. 76. Paolo Veronese. *The Martyrdom and Last Communion of Saint Lucy*. Oil on canvas. National Gallery of Art, Washington, D.C., Gift of the Morris and Gwendolyn Cafritz Foundation and Ailsa Mellon Bruce Fund

PROVENANCE, 36a:
Cornaro family chapel, SS. Apostoli, Venice

REFERENCES:
Zanetti 1771, p. 604; Albrizzi 1772, p. 197; Moschini 1815, vol. 1, p. 665; Zanotto 1837, p. 376; Zanotto 1856, p. 365; Molmenti 1909, p. 66, Sack 1910, pp. 92, 157; Moschini 1931, p. 44; Venice 1951, pp. 93–95; Morassi 1962, pp. 24, 55; Udine 1971, no. 55; Barcham 1989, pp. 202–6; Barcham 1992, p. 100, no. 28; Gemin and Pedrocco 1993, p. 134, no. 385; Vicenza 1993, pp. 84–88; London 1994 no. 118

PROVENANCE, 36b:
Bequest of Antonio Guasconi, 1863

REFERENCES:
Molmenti 1909, p. 149; Sack 1910, pp. 157, 171; Molmenti 1911, p. 114; Morassi 1962, pp. 24, 55; Undine 1971, p. 102; Florio and Garberi 1987, pp. 39, 138; Brown 1988, p. 68, n. 19; Barcham 1989, pp. 205–8; Barcham 1992, p. 100; Fort Worth 1993, no. 39; Gemin and Pedrocco 1993, p. 405, no. 385a

the altarpiece necessitated the addition of a broad step here, and the raising and distancing of the figures. This slightly higher viewpoint left less space for a passage of landscape, and thus the buildings are absent from the work. An undoubted derivation from Domenichino's composition, however, is the motif of the Greek vestments worn by the priest and the acolyte in the oil sketch. These were appropriate in Domenichino's altarpiece, which was made for the church of S. Girolamo della Carità in Rome, where the Greek rite was observed. As Brown argues, Tiepolo, perhaps on the advice of the ecclesiastical historian Flaminio Cornaro, changed the vestments in his altarpiece to those used in the Roman Catholic rite, specifically in the administration of the sacrament of Extreme Unction or last Communion to the dying.

One of the most obvious differences between the oil sketch and the altarpiece is seen in the placement of the secondary figures. Perhaps because of the taller, narrower shape of the altarpiece, Tiepolo removed from the front of the composition the red-clad character (the executioner?) on the right of the oil sketch, possibly to avoid crowding the foreground in the final composition and to ensure that the saint would remain the principal focus. Instead of retaining this individual behind Saint Lucy, Tiepolo incorporated two expressive kneeling figures, a man and a woman, as well as a young boy who self-consciously stands beside the Cornaro family coat of arms. Although it has been suggested that all three figures added to the altarpiece are portraits of members of the Cornaro family, it is probable that only the boy is a likeness:[5] the man and woman are more or less stock types in Tiepolo's compositions of this period, and, as Barcham proposes, the woman may be intended to represent the saint's mother, Eutichia.[6] The turbaned Oriental in the oil sketch, reminiscent of the severe, exotically dressed figure who stands directly behind the priest in Veronese's painting, has been slightly altered in the final picture. Still a strong, austere presence, he has removed his fur-lined hat in veneration of the Eucharist and gazes with reverence at the enactment of the sacrament. This change is in keeping with the final emphasis in the altarpiece on the last Communion rather than on the martyrdom of Saint Lucy. As Barcham proposes, this shift in focus may be linked to the iconography introduced in the decoration of the church of SS. Apostoli by the new ceiling fresco, whose central theme is the Communion of the Apostles.[7]

CW

NOTES

1. Barcham 1989, pp. 202–6. Knox (1980a, p. 36 n. 1) provides useful information on the Cornaro family's patronage of Tiepolo.
2. When this church was demolished in 1860 to make way for a railway station, Saint Lucy's relics were transferred to the church of S. Geremia, also in Venice.
3. Boschini 1674, p. 21: "Nella Cappella di Casa Cornara, la Tavola con S. Lucia, e due altri Santi." Diana's painting was still in situ in 1740. See Albrizzi 1740, p. 160.
4. Brown in Fort Worth 1993, p. 261.
5. Brown (ibid., p. 262) also suggests that the standing Oriental figure may be a portrait of Flaminio Cornaro. Merkel (in Vicenza 1993, pp. 84–88) argues that the altarpiece dates from 1745–46 and identifies the kneeling man as Nicolò Cornaro, *procuratore di supra*, and the boy as his fifteen-year-old son, Giulio. If the generally accepted dating of 1748–49 for the altarpiece is correct, the latter identification is unlikely because the boy looks younger than eighteen.
6. Barcham 1989, p. 207.
7. Ibid., p. 206.

37. Saint James of Compostella

The apostle Saint James is the patron saint of Spain: according to a tradition going back to the seventh century, he preached the gospel there and is buried at Compostella. The saint miraculously appeared at the battle of Clavijo in 844 in order to assist the Spaniards in their fight against the Moorish invaders.

The Spanish ambassador in London, Ricardo Wall, commissioned this magnificent altarpiece from Tiepolo in August 1749 for the chapel in his government's embassy.[1] After it was displayed at S. Marco in Venice, where it was admired by Doge Pietro Grimani, the painting was sent to London, arriving in September 1750. Wall's letters show him to have been impulsive and even careless regarding the commission to "the famous artist Tiepolo of Venice":[2] almost immediately after ordering the painting, he wondered if he should not have used the services of a Spanish artist, and incorrect measurements were supplied, so that the picture proved too large for the chapel's altar.

Tiepolo had provided a dashing image of Spain's patron saint, suitable for an ambassadorial residence. He presented the apostle less as a saintly figure to be venerated than as a ringing metaphor for Spain itself—a proud, victorious warrior mounted on a magnificent steed, emerging unscathed and unstained from the heat of battle (frontis., p. 188). A gorgeously clad Moor kneels before Saint James, who touches him with his sword in a gesture redolent of chivalry: the Moor will arise a Christian. This submissive and exotic figure was presumably intended to evoke in the minds of English viewers the riches of Spain's far-flung subject states.

By the eighteenth century altarpieces showing Saint James on horseback and in battle had long been popular in Spain, and some dynamic images had been painted by Baroque artists there.[3] However, it is unlikely that Tiepolo had direct knowledge of earlier Spanish representations of the theme. Yet he rose superbly to the challenge of this foreign commission to depict the apostle who was as important to Spaniards as the apostle Mark was to Venetians. Although Wall seems to have appreciated his efforts,[4] the chaplains at the embassy were quick to point out that the appearance in an altarpiece of a horse as prominent as Tiepolo's might shock the Protestant English and provoke unwanted criticism of the Spanish Catholic cult of religious images. Consequently, by December 1750 Wall had decided to send the painting to Madrid, and he suggested that a traditional subject, such as the Crucifixion, might be more suitable in England. In fact, Francisco Preciado de la Vega, who had long studied and worked in Rome,[5] was commissioned to paint a substitute altarpiece showing the more acceptable image of a pilgrim Saint James.

The painting's destination in Madrid is unknown. It was probably added to the royal collection, although it is not identifiable in any inventories. The Tiepolos presumably saw it in Madrid in the 1760s: just before he went to Spain, Giandomenico Tiepolo listed his etching of the *Saint James* as reproducing a painting in London, and after his trip he recorded the work's location as Madrid.[6] Giambattista's preparatory study in chalk for the head of the Moor was reused by Giandomenico as a model for an etching of an expressive head.[7] Another chalk drawing showing the head of Saint James was made by Giandomenico probably in preparation for his etching after the altarpiece (fig. 77).[8]

CW

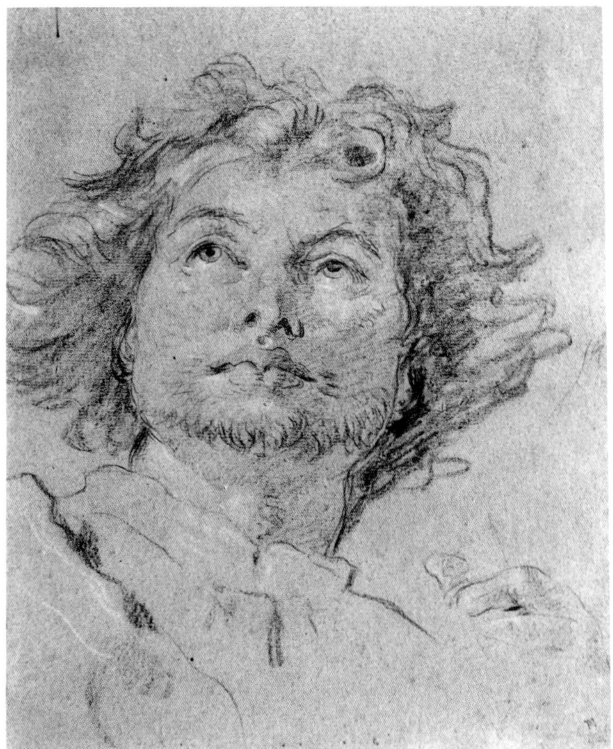

Fig. 77. Giandomenico Tiepolo. *Study for the Head of Saint James*. Black chalk. Szépművészeti Múzeum, Budapest

37. Saint James of Compostella
Doc. 1749
317 × 163 cm (124⅞ × 64¼ in.)
Signed on sword: G. TIEPOLO F.
Szépművészeti Múzeum, Budapest (649)

PROVENANCE:
Count Edmund Bourke, Madrid and London (by 1811–21; sale, London, by private contract with William Buchanan,[9] June 1816, lot 49 [bought in]; sale, London, European Museum, March 1819, lot 590 [bought in]; his estate (1821); Prince Paul Esterhazy, Vienna and Budapest (1821–66; inv. 1821, no. 1082); Szépművészeti Muzeum, Budapest (from 1870)

REFERENCES:
Molmenti 1909, p. 282; Sack 1910, p. 200; Precerutti Garberi 1958, pp. 118–19; Morassi 1962, p. 7; Garas 1968, p. 17, no. 15, pls. 15, 16; Pérez Sánchez 1977; Levey 1986, pp. 167–70; Gemin and Pedrocco 1993, p. 417, no. 403; London 1994, no. 113; Minneapolis 1995, no. 25

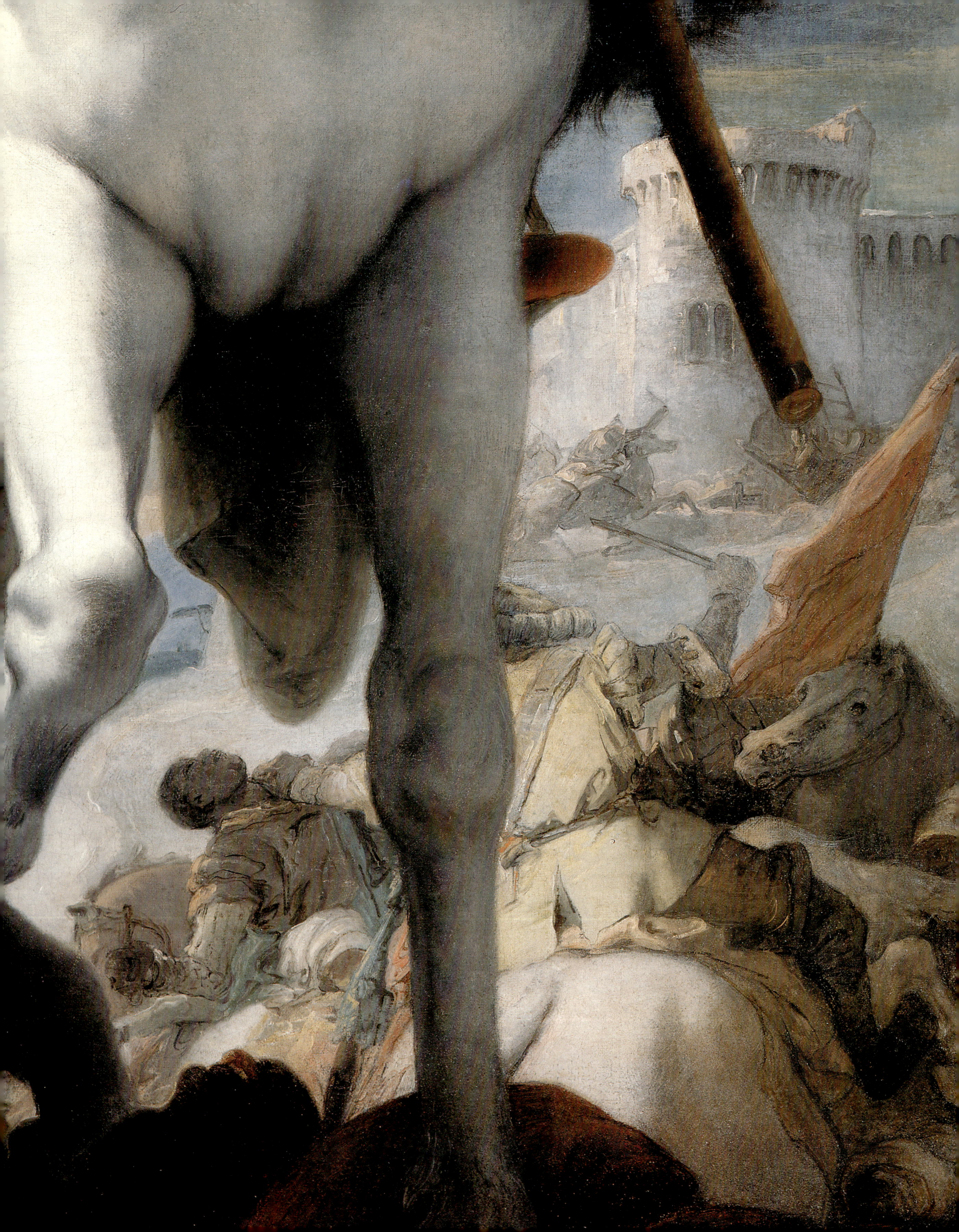

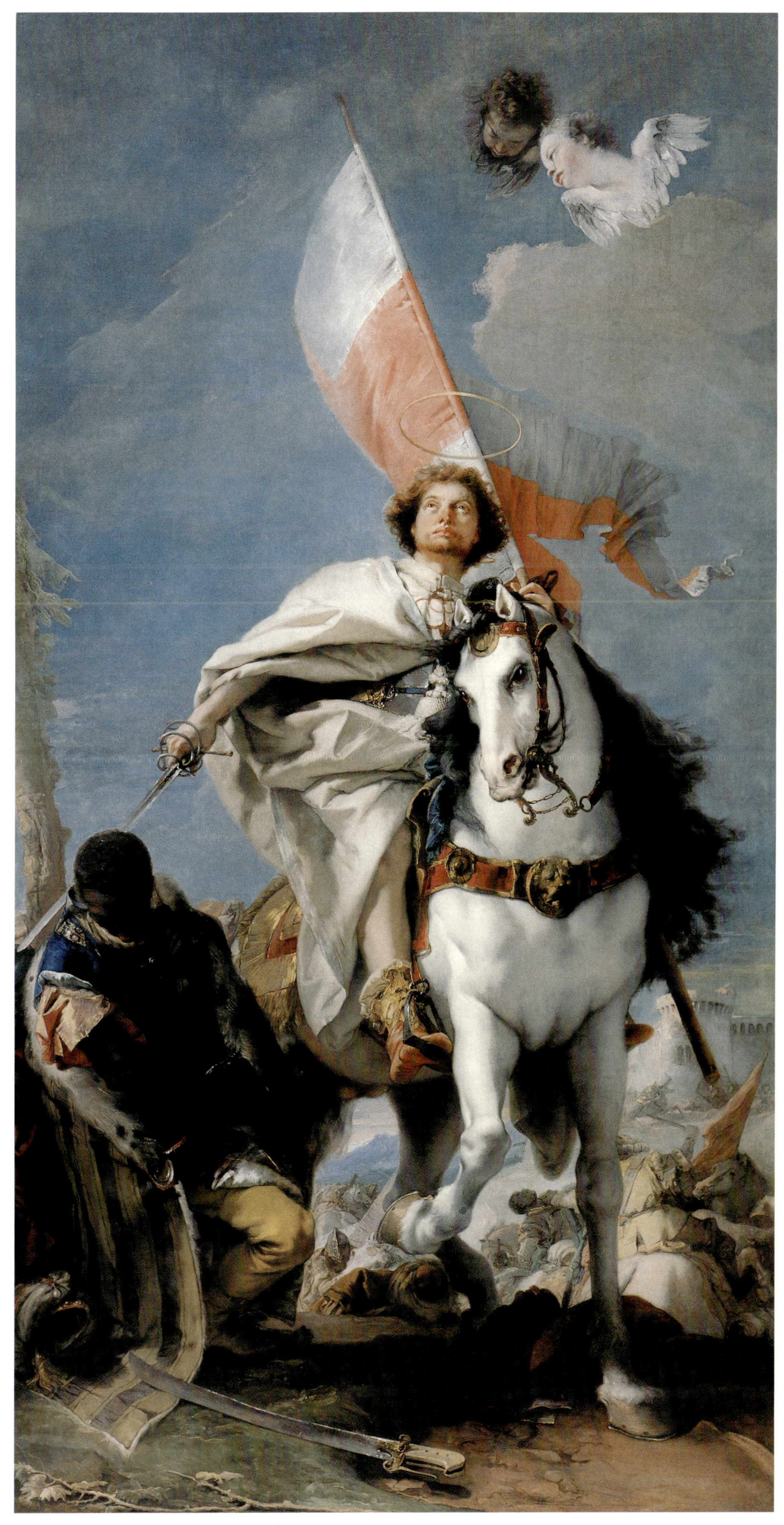

Opposite:
Detail, no. 37

37

Notes

1. Pérez Sánchez 1977.
2. Letter of 6 September 1750, in Pérez Sanchez 1977, p. 75.
3. An extreme version is Juan de Roelas's altarpiece for the cathedral in Seville in 1609, showing the saint on a rearing horse, sword wildly flailing; reproduced in Camon Aznar 1977, fig. 146.
4. See Wall's letter of 3 December 1750 (Pérez Sánchez 1977, p. 76), in which he wrote that although he was no expert, he agreed with the general view that it was a good painting.
5. For his biography, see Rome 1989, p. 144.
6. Frerichs 1971a, p. 238, and Mirano 1988, p. 172, no. 73, where the painting is incorrectly dated.
7. Knox 1980a. no. M.451, formerly in the duc de Talleyrand collection and with Hazlitt, Gooden and Fox, London, in 1991: the model for the etching in Giandomenico's *Raccolta di teste* (1.20).
8. Ibid., no. M.116, also in the Szépmüvészeti Múzeum, Budapest (1929-2164).
9. See Minneapolis 1995, no. 25, for the provenance. Bourke was Danish ambassador to Madrid from 1801 to 1811 and to London from 1814 to 1819.

38. *The Martyrdom of Saint Agatha*

38. The Martyrdom of Saint Agatha
Ca. 1755
184 × 131 cm (72½ × 51⅝ in.)
Gemäldegalerie, Staatliche Museen Preussischer Kulturbesitz, Berlin

Originally painted for the high altar of the eponymous church belonging to the Benedictine nuns at Lendinara, near Rovigo, this altarpiece once had an arched top, as the reproductive etching by Giandomenico Tiepolo (fig. 78) indicates. Although the precise date of the commission is unknown, the painting was certainly executed soon after Tiepolo's return to Venice from Germany, since it was recorded by Girolamo Silvestri in 1755 as a recent work, made as a substitute for a picture of the same subject by Palma il Vecchio. In the mid- and late 1750s, Tiepolo worked extensively for patrons on the mainland, and this Benedictine altarpiece may have led to further commissions: in 1758 he painted a major altarpiece for the cathedral at Este (see no. 51), not far from Lendinara, and in 1759 he signed and dated an altarpiece for the church of the Benedictine nuns at Cividale.

Saint Agatha was an early Christian martyr from Catania, whose cult is documented since the fourth century. On the orders of the Roman consul Quintilian, she was subjected to torture on the rack, by fire, and by mutilation, and she died in prison. In the winter of 1736, Tiepolo had painted a Martyrdom of Saint Agatha for the basilica of S. Antonio in Padua (fig. 81). There, as in the near-contemporary S. Alvise triptych (see no. 31), Tiepolo confronted themes of pathos and brutality without resorting to crudeness or melodrama (see "Tiepolo as a Religious Artist" above). Contemporary spectators were supposed to flinch at the violence involved in Christ's Passion and in Agatha's martyrdom, while venerating the supreme sacrifice made by their Savior and the saintly qualities of the martyr. Tiepolo's realistic yet decorous approach to these subjects was greatly admired in the eighteenth century.

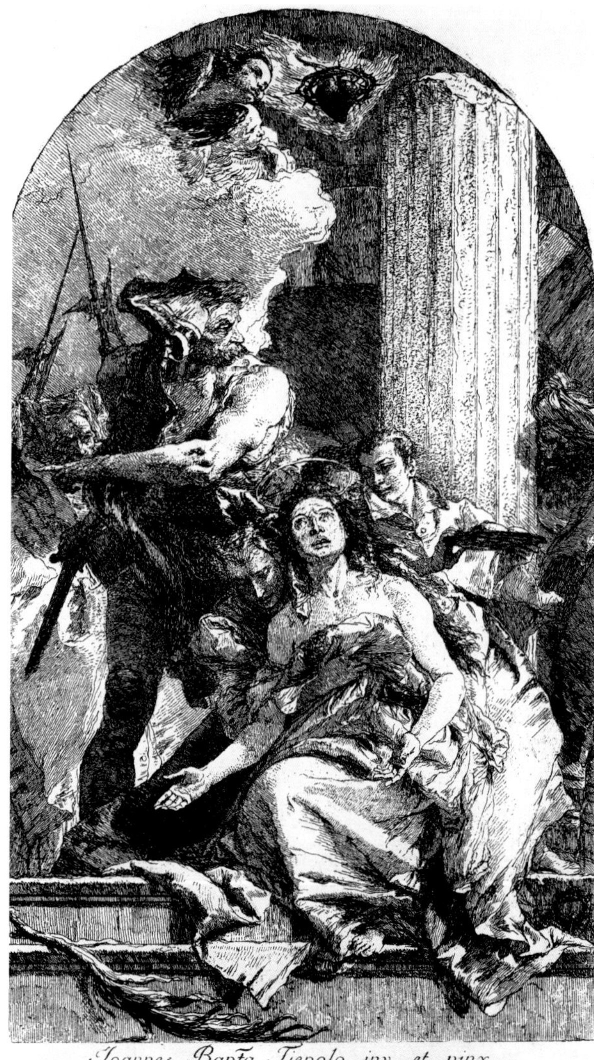

Fig. 78. Giandomenico Tiepolo. *The Martyrdom of Saint Agatha, after G. B. Tiepolo*. Etching. The Metropolitan Museum of Art, New York; Rogers Fund, 1922 (22.81.39)

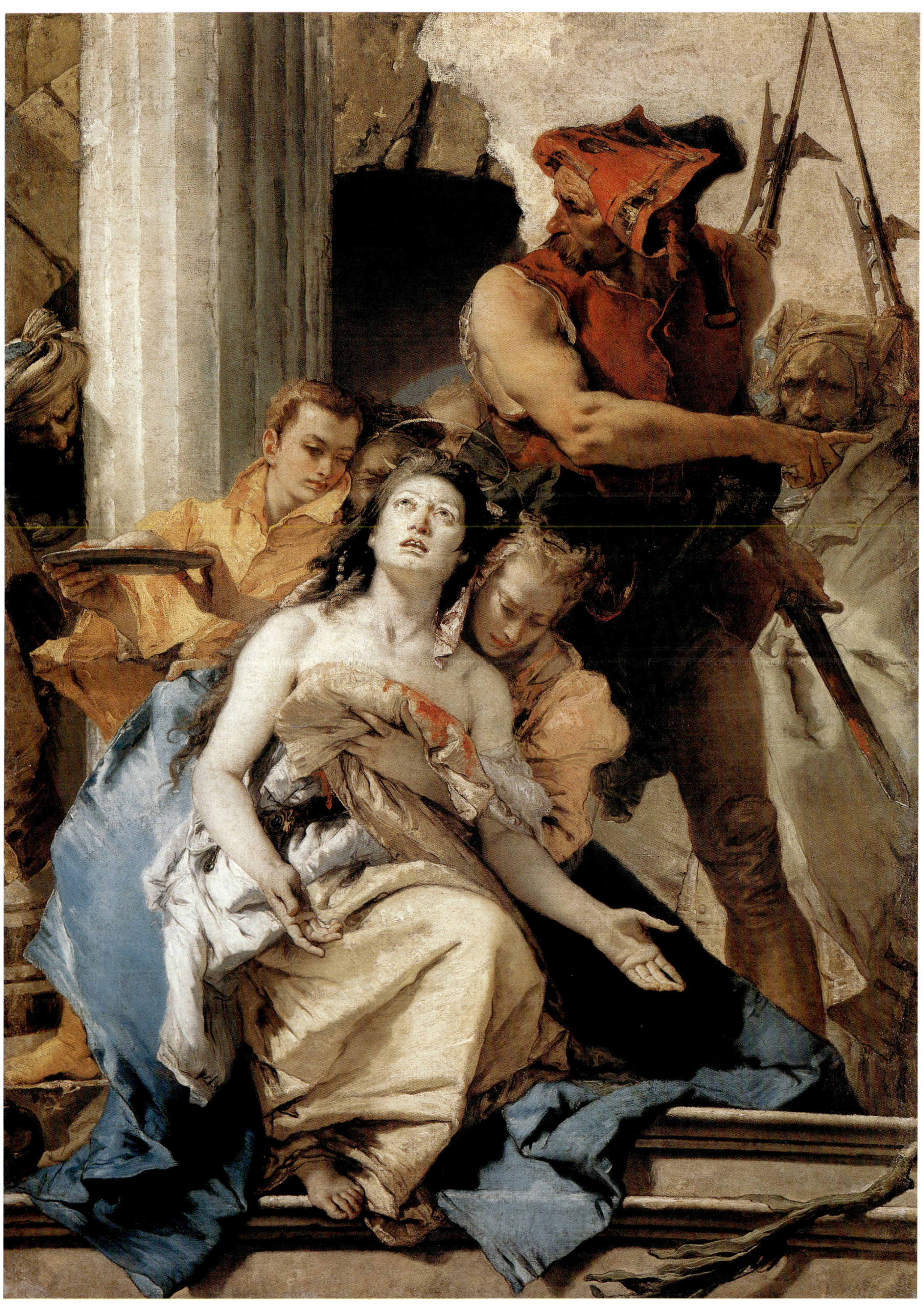

Overleaf, left: Detail, no. 38
Overleaf, right: Detail, no. 38

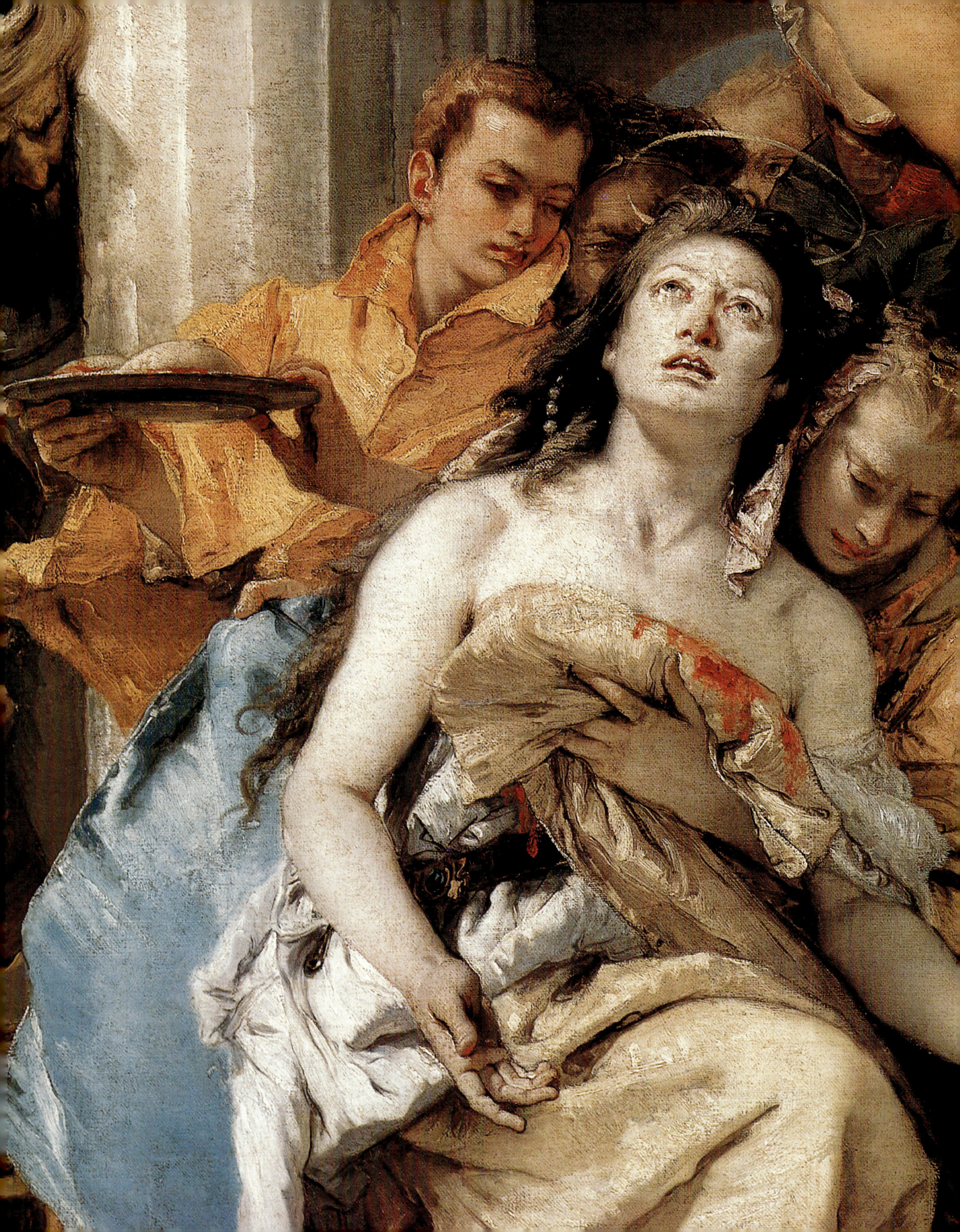

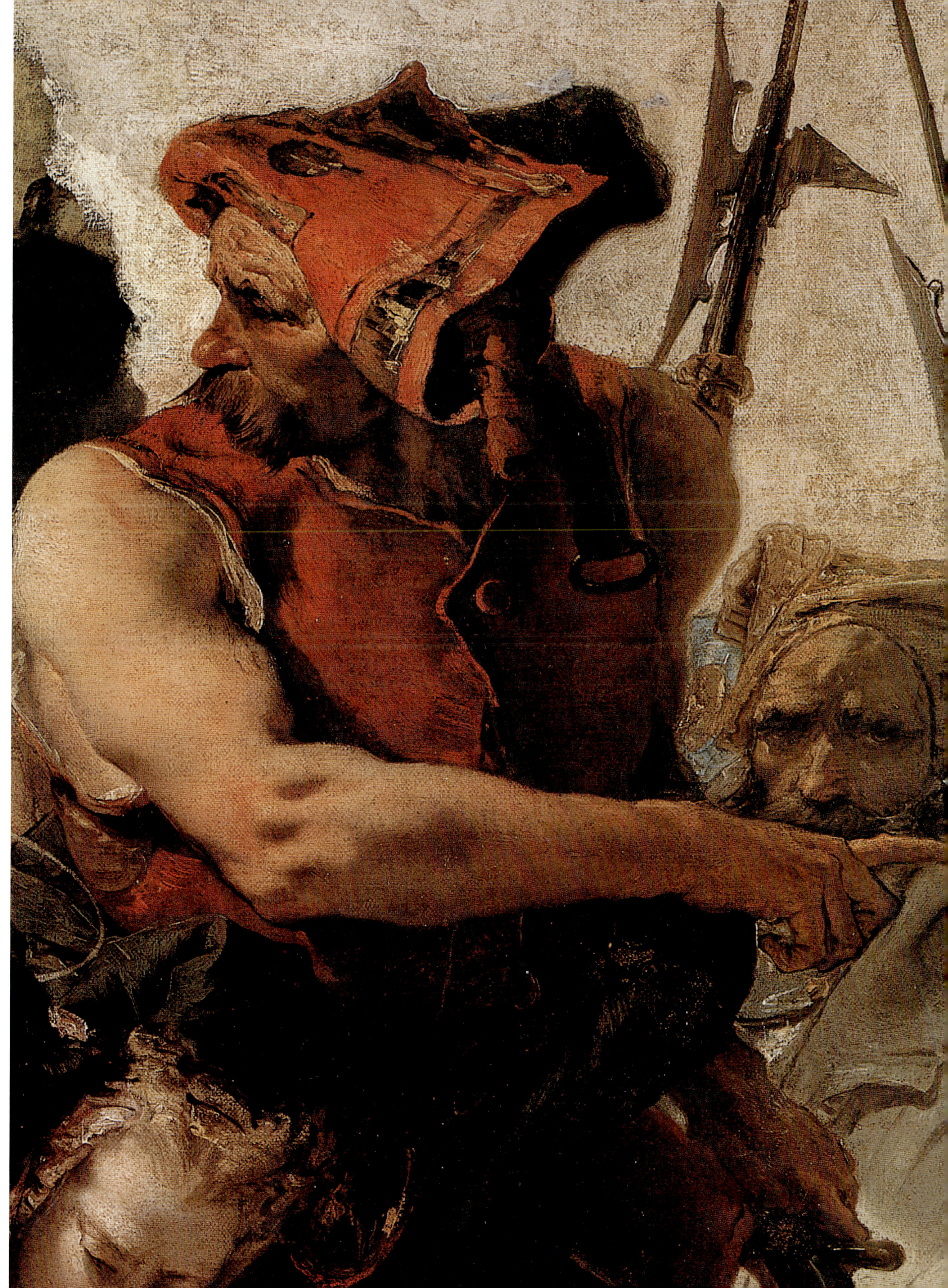

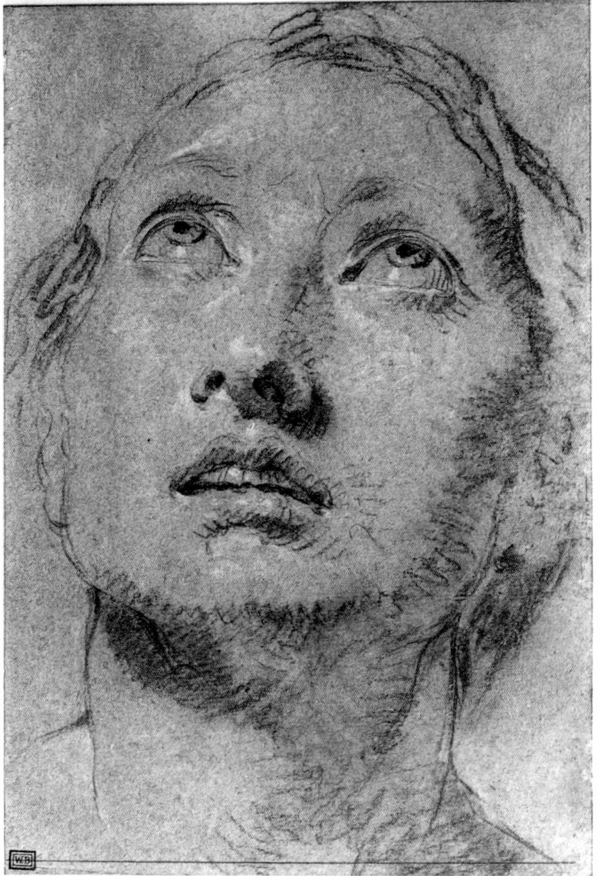

Fig. 79. *Study for "The Martyrdom of Saint Agatha."* Red and white chalk on blue paper. Kupferstichkabinett, Staatliche Museen, Preussischer Kulturbesitz, Berlin

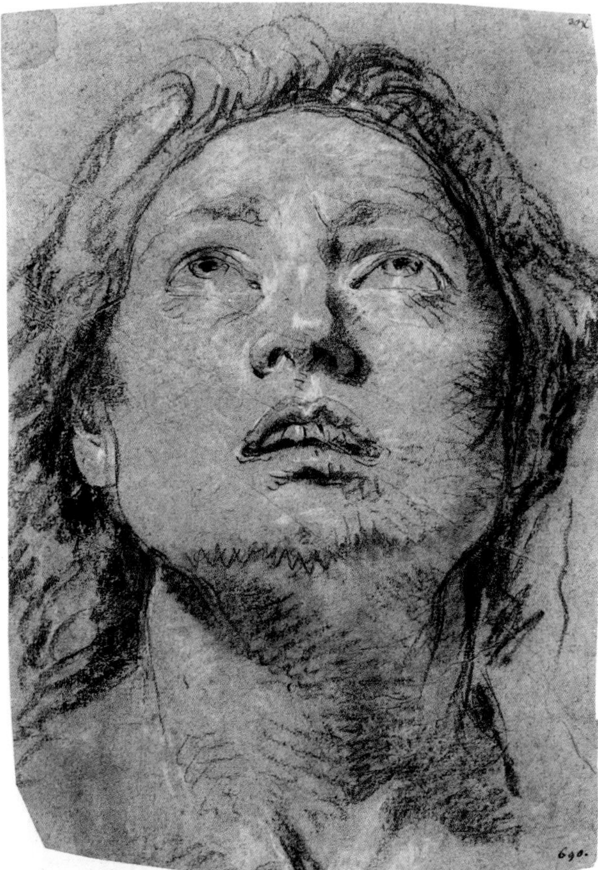

Fig. 80. *Study for "The Martyrdom of Saint Agatha."* Red and white chalk on blue paper. Kupferstichkabinett, Staatliche Museen, Preussischer Kulturbesitz, Berlin

PROVENANCE:
Church of S. Agata, Lendinara (suppressed 1810; altarpiece sold by 1832–35); Hugh A. Munro, London (before 1865; Munro 1865, p. 15, no. 236); his estate (1865–78; sale, Christie's, London, 1 June 1878, lot 115); Galerie Sedelmeyer, Paris (1878); Gemäldegalerie, Berlin (from 1878)

REFERENCES:
Silvestri (1755) cited in Sgarbi 1990, p. 169; Brandolese 1795a, pp. xxiii–xxxiv; Molmenti 1909, p. 264; Sack 1910, p. 183, no. 288; Kunze 1931, no. 459B; Morassi 1943, p. 32; Venice 1951, pp. 114–15; Morassi 1955a, pp. 24, 151; Morassi 1962, p. 4; Pallucchini 1968, p. 115, no. 198; Frerichs 1971a, p. 237; Sgarbi 1990, pp. 49–50, 169–73; Gemin and Pedrocco 1993, p. 437, no. 431; London 1994, p. 500, no. 117

Francesco Algarotti wrote of the Paduan *Martyrdom of Saint Agatha* that "in the saint's face . . . one may clearly read the pain of the wound inflicted by the executioner intermingled with [the saint's] pleasure at seeing, with this act, Paradise opening."[1] Charles Nicolas Cochin praised Tiepolo's taste and truthfulness in this painting; at the same time he admired the expressiveness of the saint's head.[2] No travelers' comments on the more remote Lendinara altarpiece are recorded, although local historian Pietro Brandolese had high praise for its beauty and realism: Saint Agatha, he wrote, "wonderfully displays resignation to her inexpressible torments, combined with a sincere longing to be united with the Lord."[3]

The *Martyrdom of Saint Agatha* is undoubtedly a masterpiece of religious art, in which Tiepolo responded to the pathos and the spiritual intensity of the subject with an expressiveness that recalls Bernini's sculpture and a frankness that anticipates the religious paintings of Goya. Tiepolo's increasing interest in the humanity of saintly figures and his sensitivity to the layers of significance in this particular theme of martyrdom make the Lendinara painting a beautifully orchestrated, moving image. Giambattista here achieved a greater dramatic intensity and a more profound meditation on the saint's ordeal than he had in the earlier picture, where Agatha is shown as a piteous, girlish figure. Although there are close similarities in the casts of characters and in the settings of both works, in the later altarpiece the saint is depicted as a mature woman, and she becomes a more powerful figure in the composition. Tiepolo deliberately used elements of architecture in his altarpieces to denote the relationship between the viewer and the sacred image or event. Hence in both paintings the viewpoint is a low one and steps lead into the picture space; but only in the Lendinara altarpiece is Saint Agatha placed at the very edge of the steps. She is seen frontally, with heavy, spreading draperies extending her presence across the foreground, and the young boy and woman behind her both lean forward, accentuating the impression that Agatha's outstretched hands reach into the viewer's own space. Thus, the saint's figure is intended to make an immediate, striking impact; moreover, her stark pallor and ravaged face contrast strongly with the golden tonality and melting beauty of the two flanking characters. Tiepolo studied Saint Agatha's face with intense care, making two detailed chalk drawings, the first perhaps drawn from the life (fig. 79), and the second worked up as a more expressive ideal (fig. 80).[4] The muscular, Rubenesque executioner also swings toward the very front of the painting. His forceful movement and the warm reds of his costume and flesh evoke a sense of the violence that has just occurred. Saint Agatha alone is aware of the heavenly vision above: none of the surrounding figures follows her upward gaze, although one Oriental man does look arrestingly out at the viewer.

In the altarpiece at Padua, Tiepolo had painted Saint Agatha's vision of Saint Peter, whose appearance, according to legend, was followed by the miraculous healing of her wounds. The heavenly vision in the upper part of the altarpiece at Lendinara is of the Sacred Heart. The cult of the Sacred Heart was strongly promoted by the Jesuit order from the late seventeenth century, and it became more popular and more formalized about the mid-eighteenth century, receiving full papal approval in 1765. However, devotion to the Sacred Heart, which focused on the memorable and compact image of a burning heart surrounded by thorns, symbolizing the love of Christ for humanity and the suffering he endured, had originated with the Benedictines, the patrons of the Lendinara *Saint Agatha*.[5] Thus, in contrast to his treatment in the Padua altarpiece, where the presence of Saint Peter promises relief from pain, Tiepolo's emphasis in this more complex and affecting image is on Saint Agatha's courageous and Christ-like qualities.

CW

Notes

1. Algarotti 1763b (1963 ed., pp. 123–24): "E nel volto di una santa . . . pare che si legga chiaramente il dolore della ferita fattagli dal manigoldo misto col piacere dal vedersi con ciò aperto il Paradiso."
2. Cochin 1758, p. 384.
3. Brandolese 1795a, p. xxiii: "[S. Agata] mostra a meraviglia la rassegnazione nell'inesprimabile tormento, unitamente al vivo desiderio d'unirsi al suo Signore."
4. Kupferstichkabinett, Staatliche Museen, Preussischer Kulturbesitz, Berlin, 13650, 24626; Knox 1980a, nos. M.22, M.41.
5. See Hanon 1953.

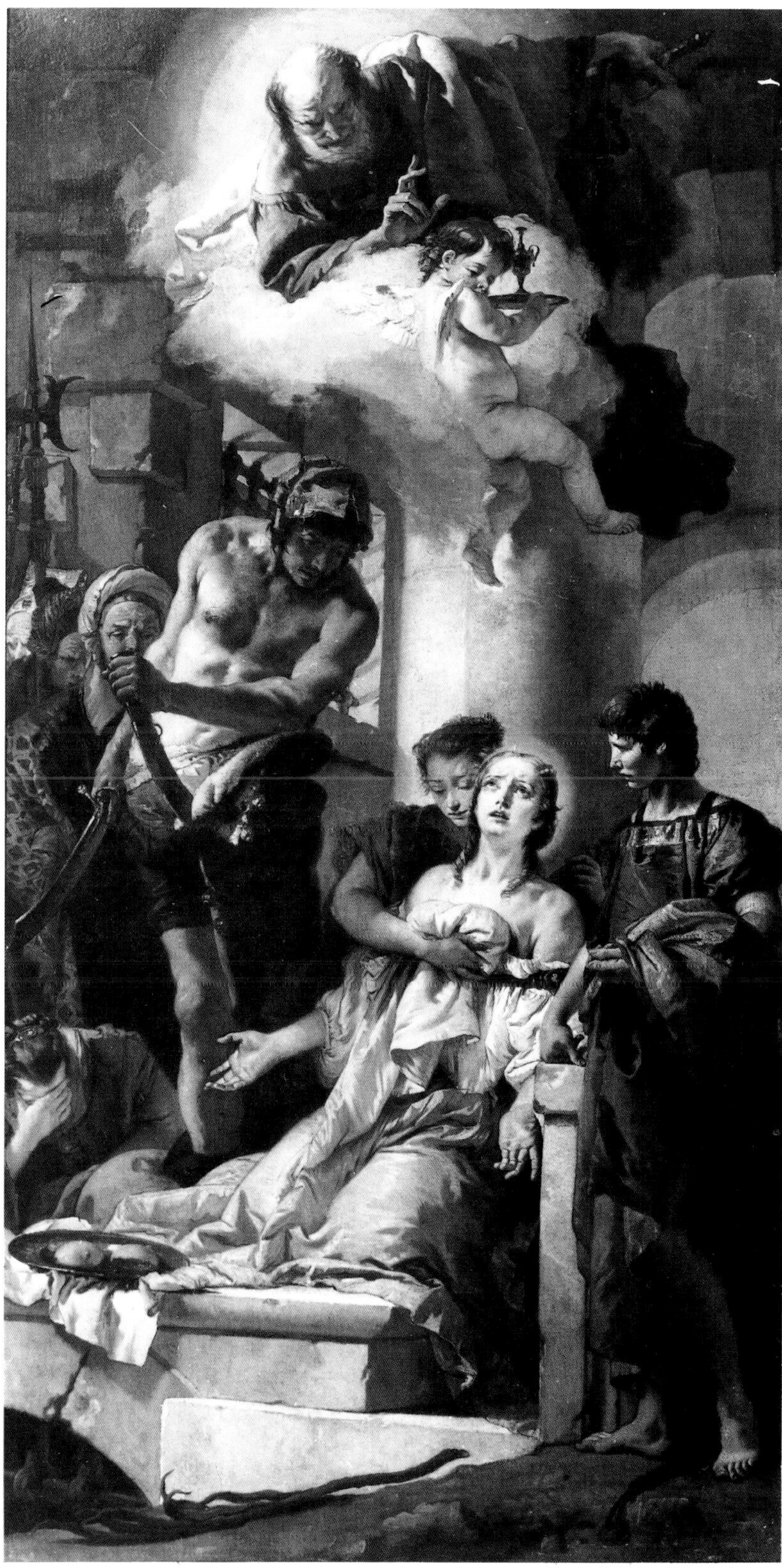

Fig. 81. *The Martyrdom of Saint Agatha*. Oil on canvas. S. Antonio, Padua

39. *Saint Gaetano da Thiene in Glory*

39. Saint Gaetano da Thiene in Glory
Ca. 1756
210 × 119 cm. (82¾ × 46⅞ in.)
S. Maria Maddalena, Rampazzo

Saint Gaetano da Thiene (1480–1547), the founder of the Theatine order, is shown holding a book, to signify his erudition, and a lily branch, referring to his purity and chastity, is nonchalantly placed nearby. He looks resolutely heavenward and indicates with his right hand the bustle and activity below him as a new church nears completion.

The altarpiece is imbued with local references. The church depicted is S. Maria Maddalena in Rampazzo, where Tiepolo's painting normally hangs. Originally erected in 1505 by Gaetano and his brother Battista, members of the noble Thiene family, the church was the first of many that Gaetano was to found in a lifetime dedicated to preaching and to the care of the sick and the poor. Two hundred years later the brothers Michele and Giacomo da Thiene paid for its rebuilding, finished in 1706, in the form of the elegant church seen under construction in Tiepolo's painting. In 1756 Count Vincenzo da Thiene and his wife, Elisabetta Conti, had an altar erected there in honor of Saint Gaetano, and the altarpiece was doubtless commissioned at the same time from Tiepolo. The artist worked on a number of commissions for the Vicentine nobility in the 1750s, including the frescoes at the Villa Valmarana, near Vicenza, completed in 1757.[1]

Tiepolo had certainly looked at Francesco Solimena's altarpiece of about 1723 in the church of S. Gaetano in Vicenza (fig. 82), for he made deliberate reference to it: reference that was appropriate, as Solimena's work was another Thiene family commission.[2] Thus, Tiepolo's saint wears the same clerical garb, brown shoes, and golden stole as Solimena's, and the strong accent of orange-red drapery lit with yellow appears in both pictures. Tiepolo's Saint Gaetano is recognizably similar to the saint in the earlier altarpiece, although his features also recall the heroic male type in the *Saint James of Compostella* of 1749–50 (no. 37). But unlike Solimena's composition, where a purely heavenly space is evoked, the Rampazzo altarpiece is firmly grounded in local imagery with which the viewer can identify. With his gesture and upward gaze, Tiepolo's Saint Gaetano is depicted as a patron and protector of the church and its congregation. His firm features and alert posture, his plain clerical garb and brightly polished shoes testify to his determination and practicality—this is no bland, idealized vision of holiness, but a convincing image of a vigorous, active Christianity. In the lower left the saint himself is shown as a protagonist in an earthly drama. His right arm is raised in blessing over a prostrate figure before him, and the vivid vignette they constitute may refer to a miraculous event that took place during the building of the sixteenth-century church.[3]

Tiepolo's preparatory oil sketch was in the collection of Baron Schwiter in Paris in 1886, when it was identified as a *Saint Anthony*.[4] Its present location is unknown.

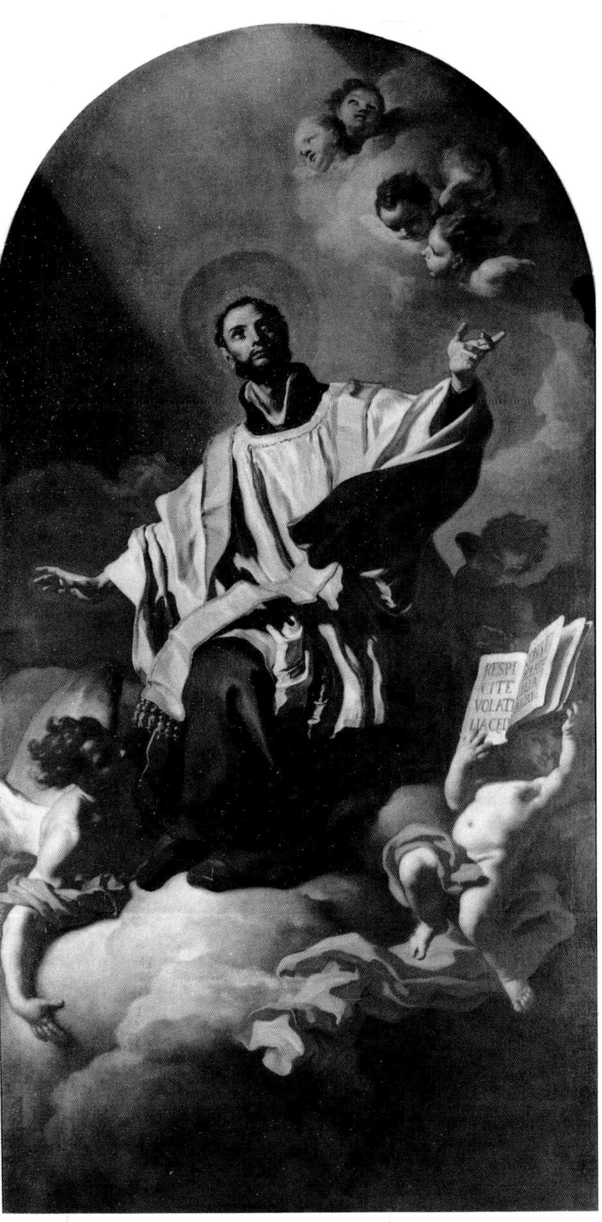

Fig. 82. Francesco Solimena. *Saint Gaetano da Thiene*. Oil on canvas. S. Gaetano, Vicenza

PROVENANCE:
Church of S. Maria Maddalena, Rampazzo

REFERENCES:
Chennevières 1898, pp. 93, 109; Pallucchini 1945, p. 129; Mariacher 1950, p. 153; Pignatti 1951, p. 130; Venice 1951, p. 117; Morassi 1962, pp. 43, 45; Udine 1971, no. 64; Barcham 1989, p. 222; Vicenza 1990, pp. 37–38; Gemin and Pedrocco 1993, p. 450, no. 458

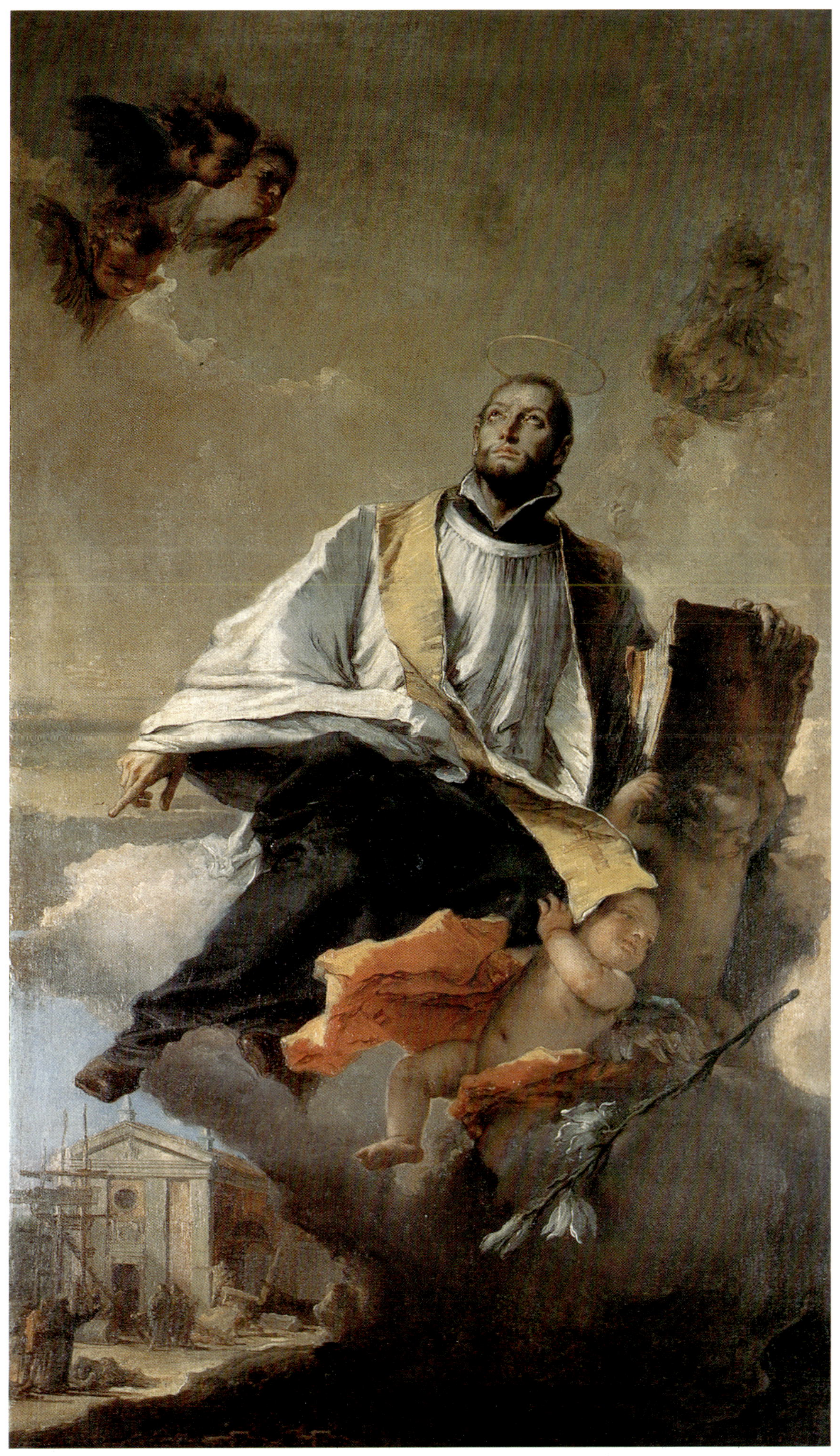

39

This oil sketch shows a rapidly executed first idea, in which a small passage of landscape is envisaged: the historical and local references in the final work were later additions, perhaps made at the patrons' suggestion and surely after Tiepolo had seen the church at Rampazzo. Giandomenico Tiepolo reproduced the altarpiece in an etching.[5]

CW

NOTES

1. Both the Marchesini and the Vecchia families, for which Tiepolo worked in Vicenza in the 1750s, were related by marriage to the Thiene family. See Menegozzo 1990.
2. For this altarpiece, see Vicenza 1993, pp. 79–80, no. 2.4.
3. Mariuz (in Vicenza 1990, p. 38) makes this interesting suggestion.
4. Chennevières 1898, pp. 93, 109.
5. Mirano 1988, p. 200, no. 93.

SAN PASCUAL BAYLON: THE IMMACULATE CONCEPTION

40a, b. The Immaculate Conception

40a. The Immaculate Conception
Doc. 1767
63.7 × 38.9 cm (25⅛ × 15⅜ in.)
Courtauld Institute Galleries, London, Princes Gate Collection (P.G. 342)

40b. The Immaculate Conception
Doc. 1767–69
279 × 152 cm (110 × 59⅞ in.)
Museo del Prado, Madrid

The *Immaculate Conception* at the Prado and its related *modello* in the Courtauld mark the climax of Tiepolo's long career as a painter of religious subjects. The picture now in Madrid was commissioned by Charles III of Spain in March 1767 as one of seven altarpieces for the new convent church of S. Pascual Baylon at Aranjuez, a royal retreat on the river Tagus famed for its pleasure gardens.[1] This was the king's first major religious foundation, and it was occupied by reformed Franciscans of the order of Saint Peter of Alcantara, of which Charles's confessor, Joaquín de Eleta, was a member. Eleta was in charge of the building project and would have drawn up the subjects of the altarpieces in consultation with the king. On the high altar was the *Vision of Saint Paschal Baylon* (fragmentary state, Museo del Prado, Madrid); on the altars to the left and right, respectively, were the *Immaculate Conception* and the *Saint Francis Receiving the Stigmata* (no. 41b). There were two altars on either side of the nave: the *Saint Joseph with the Christ Child* (Detroit Institute of Arts; fragments, Museo del Prado, Madrid, and Courtauld Institute Galleries, London), on the left, was to face the *Saint Charles Borromeo Venerating the Crucifix* (Cincinnati Art Museum), and the *Saint Peter of Alcantara*, also on the left, was opposite the *Saint Anthony with the Christ Child* (Museo del Prado, Madrid). No oil sketches for the last two paintings, which are oval, have come down to us. The altarpieces depicted Franciscan saints or patrons (Saint Charles Borromeo was the cardinal protector of the Franciscan order) and cults strongly promoted by that order: fervent belief in the Immaculate Conception was a long-standing tenet of the Franciscans, and Saint Joseph had been particularly venerated by Saint Peter of Alcantara.

The project marks the first time Tiepolo was charged with the entire pictorial decoration of a new church in seven distinct paintings, and this presented a challenge different from that of fresco decoration. Moreover, Giambattista would have found the Aranjuez commission unusual in its emphasis on ascetic male saints in meditation or states of ecstasy, although he had often painted images of individual male saints. Tiepolo brought an appropriate sense of restraint and austerity to this Franciscan cycle, whose subjects by their nature did not permit him to portray the variety of character and emotion he could develop in a scene of miracles or martyrdom. The differences between his *modelli* (all Courtauld Institute Galleries, London) and the final paintings testify to changes that are as much the result of Tiepolo's concentrated reflection on the subjects and on the interlocking themes of the altarpieces as of possible alterations ordered by Eleta. Furthermore, the church was still under construction when Tiepolo painted his oil sketches, so that at that stage he would

Opposite: Detail, no. 40b

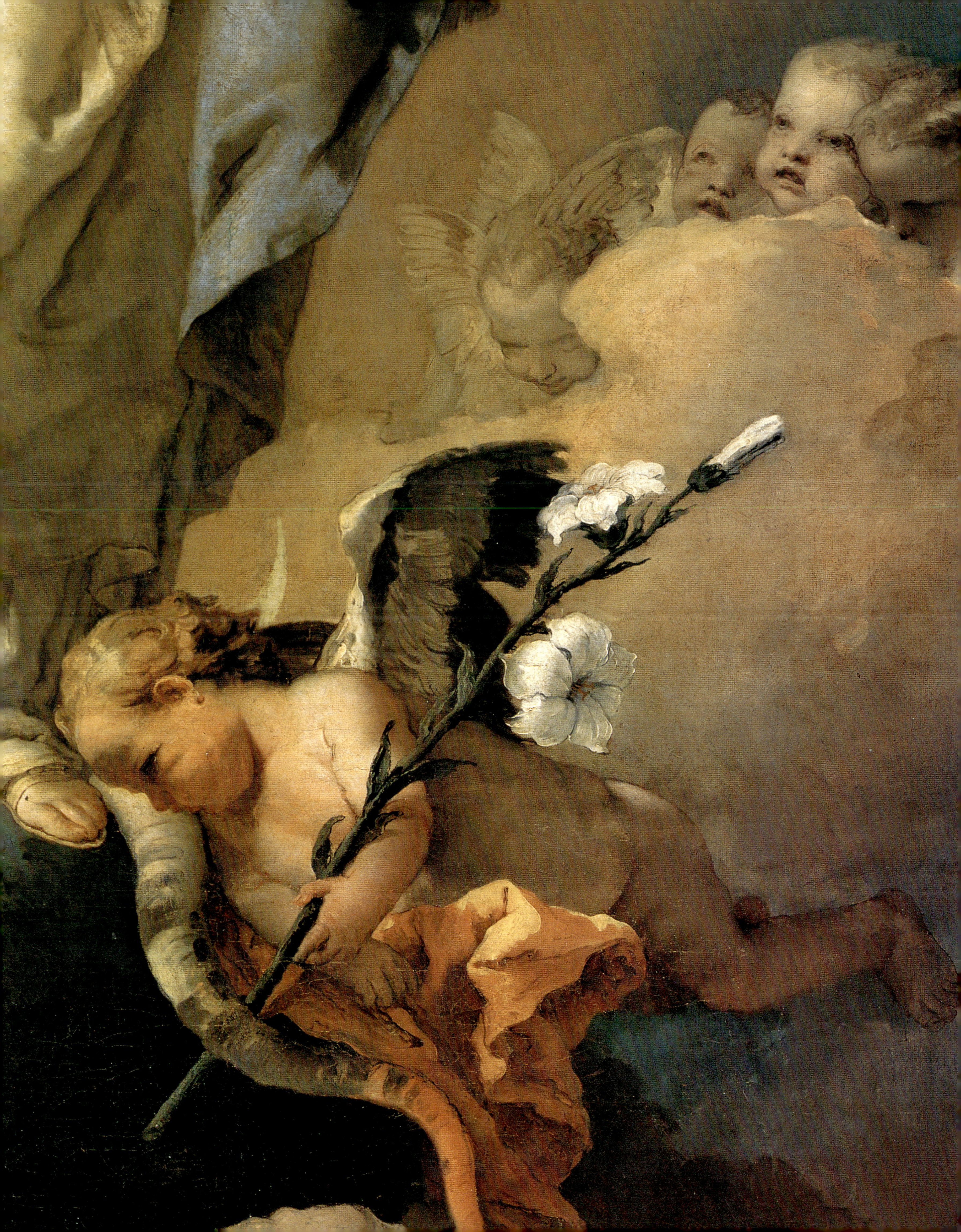

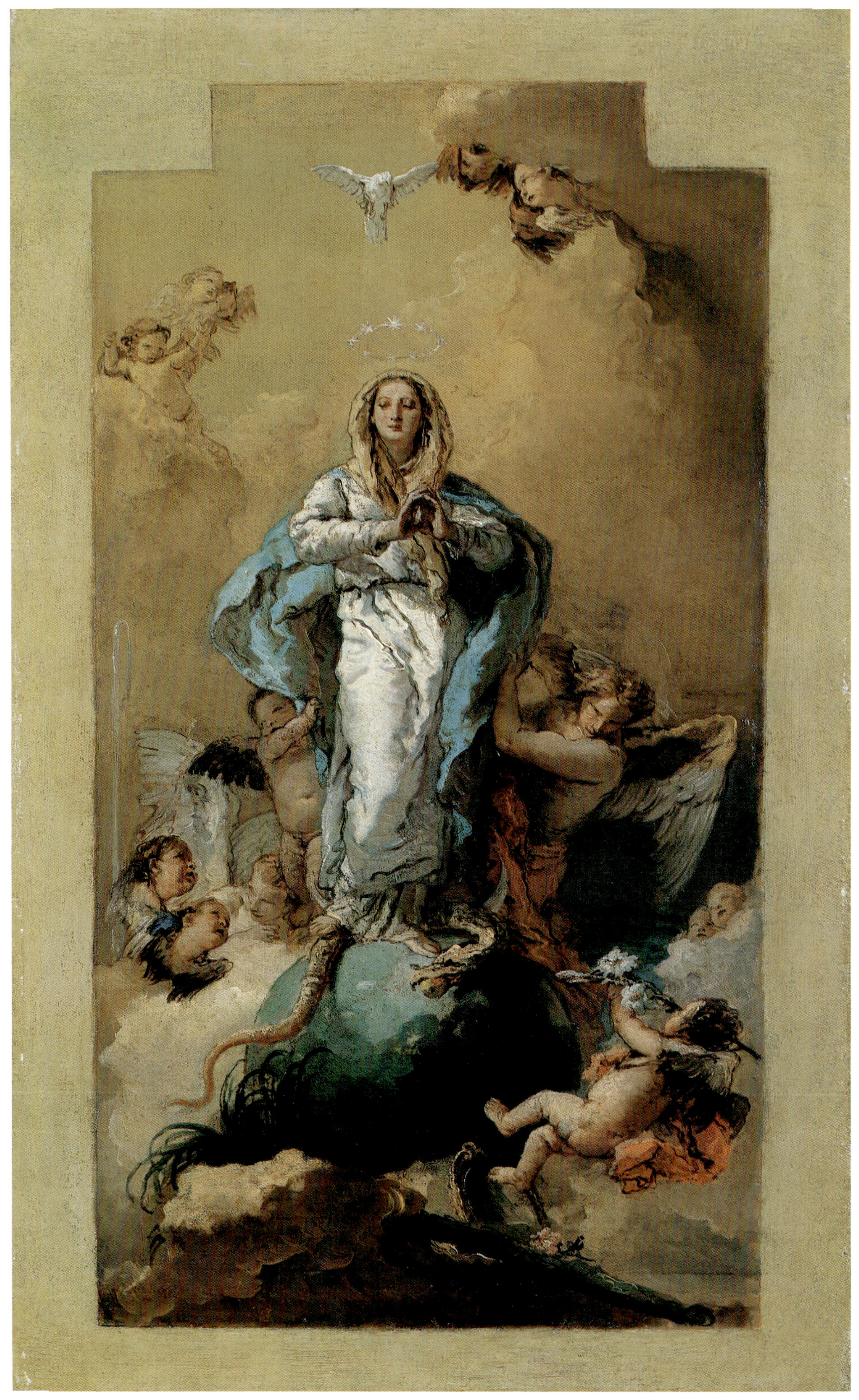

40a

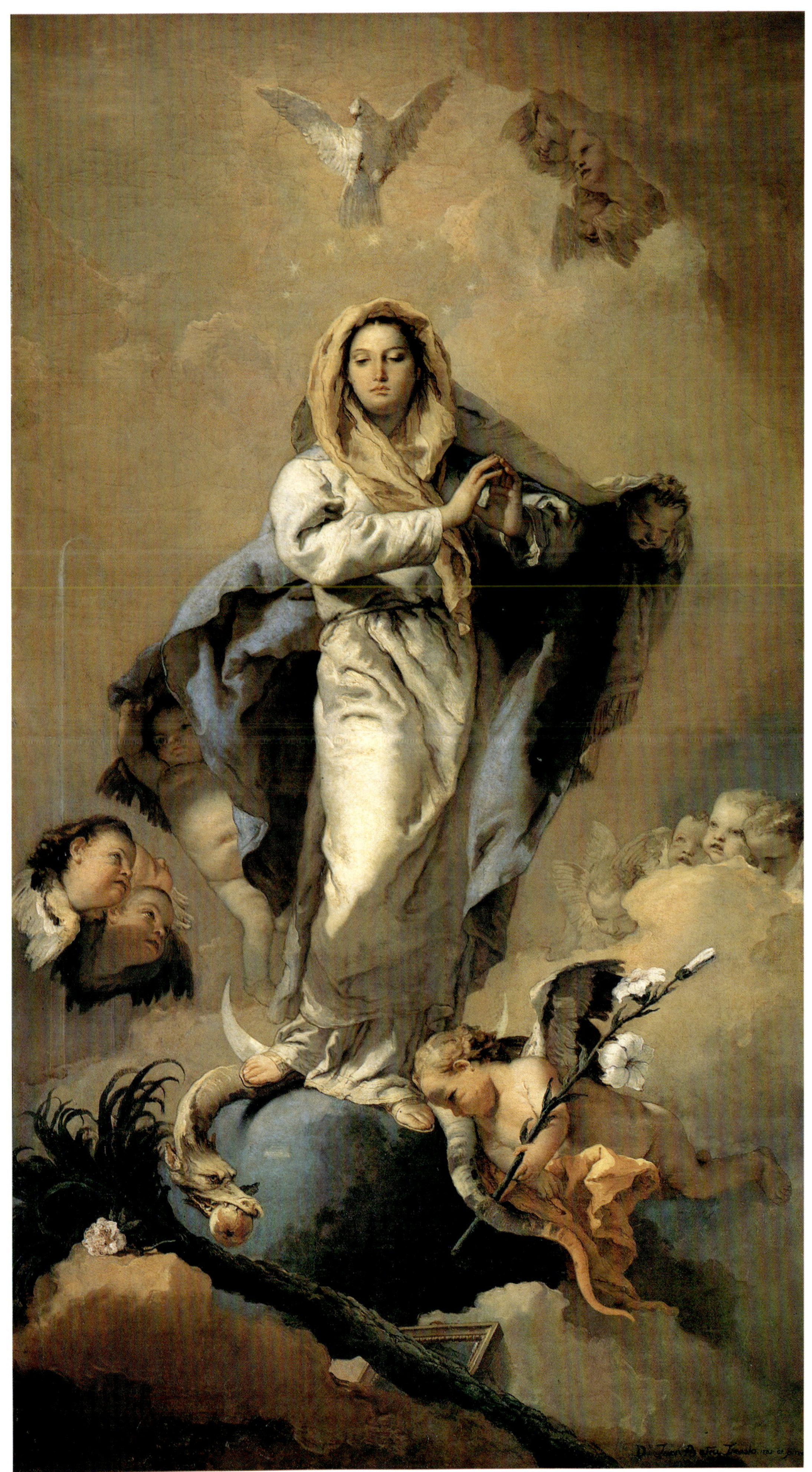

40b

PROVENANCE, 40a:
Francisco Bayeu (by 1771–95; inv. no. 135); Leonardo Chopinot, Madrid (from 1795);[12] George William Fox, ninth Baron Kinnaird, Rossie Priory, Perthshire (by 1826–78); by descent, Kenneth Fitzgerald, twelfth Baron Kinnaird (1923–67); Count Antoine Seilern, Princes Gate, London (1967–78)

REFERENCES:
Molmenti 1909, p. 193; Sack 1910, p. 226, no. 551; Morassi 1955, p. 37; Morassi 1962, p. 19; Braham 1981, pp. 75, 77; Whistler 1985a, p. 323; Levey 1986, pp. 274–76, 279; Farr 1987, p. 64; Barcham 1992, p. 46; Gemin and Pedrocco 1993, p. 492, no. 520a

PROVENANCE, 40b:
Church of S. Pascual Baylon, Aranjuez (1770–75); Convent of S. Pascual Baylon, Aranjuez (1775–1827); Museo del Prado, Madrid (from 1827)

REFERENCES:
Chennevières 1898, p. 102; Molmenti 1909, p. 192; Sack 1910, pp. 142–44, 209, no. 438; Sánchez Cantón 1927, pp. 5–6; Sánchez Cantón 1942, p. 643; Morassi 1943, pp. 37–39; Morassi 1955a, p. 37; Sánchez Cantón 1963, p. 27; Braham 1981, p. 75; Whistler 1985a, pp. 323, 326; Levey 1986, pp. 274–76, 279; Gemin and Pedrocco 1993, p. 492, no. 520

not have had full details of the lighting conditions and of the decorative elements inside the building.[2] Thus, the fact that the angel in the *Saint Paschal* altarpiece is more splendid and richly clad than the corresponding figure in the *modello* may reflect Tiepolo's new awareness that the high altar would be extremely ornate in comparison with the other altars, and that his final painting would in effect have a frame of colored marble.[3] The other altarpieces, by contrast, were placed in relatively plain settings with gilded stucco surrounds. By the same token, Tiepolo may have altered the design of the *Saint Joseph* once he realized that the rather young saint shown with a seated, upright Child was perhaps too similar to the young Saint Anthony and the seated Child of his vision in the altarpiece diagonally across the church.

The *modelli* are all highly finished and were made for approval by the king, who saw them in late August 1767. Tiepolo then began the altarpieces, continuing to work on them until the summer of 1769. We know from a letter the artist wrote on 29 August 1769 that he was acutely anxious lest Eleta find fault with the finished paintings; however, on 2 September he received assurances of the king's satisfaction with his efforts and was awarded an additional religious commission.[4] The church of S. Pascual was not ready to receive the altarpieces until mid-May 1770, so that they were still in Tiepolo's studio at his death. The *Saint Charles Borromeo* was not installed in the church as planned;[5] instead the altar to Saint Charles, for which it was intended, was rededicated at a late stage to the crucified Christ, and an imposing crucifix was placed there. With its bold coloring and magnificent architectural setting, the *Saint Charles* is the most opulent of the cycle of altarpieces, and its absence undoubtedly upset the balance Tiepolo had clearly sought to achieve. The ceremonial blessing of the church and its paintings, sculpture, and liturgical ornament took place on 16 May 1770, the eve of the feast of Saint Paschal. By early November, however, a decision had been made to have Tiepolo's altarpieces replaced with works by Anton Raphael Mengs and his Spanish pupils, Francisco Bayeu and Mariano Salvador Maella, showing exactly the same subjects. The new images were to be painted in a manner more pleasing to the king and his confessor: that is, in the eclectic, polished style based on seventeenth-century Bolognese classicism that Mengs was promoting as a radical alternative to contemporary art.

Charles III was familiar with Mengs's religious paintings, since his bedroom was hung with four scenes from the Passion painted by Mengs between 1765 and 1768, which recall the art of Correggio, Domenichino, and Carlo Maratta; also in his private apartments was a *Noli me tangere* executed by Mengs in the late 1760s, in a punctilious re-creation of Annibale Carracci's mature classical style. The king and his advisers apparently found the academic idealism and the perfect finish of Mengs's religious art well attuned to the public image of an authoritative Catholic sovereign that they wished to promote in the turbulent years between 1766 and 1770. By comparison, Tiepolo's freshly handled paintings did not evoke the sanctity of tradition but explored sacred and mystical themes in a lucid and humane manner: their rhetoric was appropriate to a modern Franciscan church but not, in the end, to His Most Catholic Majesty's new foundation. Tiepolo's altarpieces were transferred in mid-1775 to the convent adjoining S. Pascual Baylon, where the *Saint Peter of Alcantara* hung in the entrance hall, the *Saint Paschal Baylon* on the staircase, and the four other paintings in the upper cloister. About 1827 the *Immaculate Conception* was selected for display in the new Museo del Prado in Madrid, and perhaps the *Saint Joseph*, *Saint Francis*, and *Saint Paschal* were removed at the same time, for when the convent was suppressed in 1836, only the two oval altarpieces were recorded there.[6]

Although theologians were still defining and defending belief in the Immaculate Conception of the Virgin Mary in the mid-eighteenth century, images representing this abstract idea were by that time conventional and familiar. Theologians argued that the particular qualities bestowed on Mary in order to allow her to become the Mother of Christ, and thus an instrument of salvation, must have included the unique grace of immaculacy, or freedom from original sin.[7] A concentrated, almost hieroglyphic visual image expressing these concepts, including references to purity and strength, had become solidly established by the seventeenth century. Portrayals by Guido Reni and by Murillo were particularly influential, showing the Virgin as a beautiful girl clothed in blue and white, with long, flowing hair and the attributes of a crown of twelve stars, a crescent moon, and flowers. In keeping with this seventeenth-century tradition, Tiepolo had painted an altarpiece on the theme of the Immaculate Conception for the Franciscan church of the Aracoeli at Vicenza in 1734, depicting Mary as a young, coolly severe yet graceful woman.[8]

Tiepolo's *modello* for the Aranjuez altarpiece shows the Virgin supported by angels on either side, as an almost iconlike figure held aloft for admiration and veneration. The final altarpiece, however, becomes a statement of the undisputed triumph and sweeping confidence of the spotless Virgin. The proportions have changed, so that Mary commands more space than in the *modello*. Her femininity and humanity are played down—indeed, her plain, heavy clothing does much to disguise her female form—and a majestic and solemn presence is evoked. The figure of the Virgin is in fact as beautiful and remote as that of the angel bearing the Eucharist in the *Vision of Saint Paschal Baylon* on the high altar, and this affinity is appropriate, if not deliberate, since the Immaculate Virgin was, in effect, the first tabernacle for Christ, present in the Eucharist.

The symbols in the *modello*, retained with variations in the altarpiece, refer to the role and the qualities of the Immaculate Conception.[9] The Virgin vindicates the original weakness of Eve by trampling on the serpent whose evil coils are spread over the globe at her feet. The palm tree symbolizes her victory and exaltation, the mirror her freedom from all stain and the concept that she is the mirror of all virtues. The crescent moon and twelve stars recall the Apocalyptic Woman of Revelations 12. 1–10, while in itself the crescent is an ancient symbol of chastity. At the same time its light derives from the sun, just as the special grace of Mary derives from the merits of Christ, her Son.[10] The shimmering profile of an obelisk in the background is a further reference to traditional symbols linked to the Immaculate Conception: the Tower of David and the Tower of Ivory, with their associations of impregnability, purity, and virginity.

An obvious difference between the oil sketch and the altarpiece is that the prominent, muscular angel who holds up the Virgin and gazes toward the serpent in the *modello* has disappeared from the final version: this character could have been intended as a reference to the archangel Michael, whose defeat of Lucifer prefigures the role of Mary as an instrument of salvation.[11] The change of emphasis in the altarpiece, wherein the feminine Virgin of the *modello* is transformed into a hieratic and powerful figure, could have been suggested by Eleta. Or Tiepolo may have decided that the motif of the angel supporting Mary might echo, inappropriately, the same motif in his *Saint Francis Receiving the Stigmata* in the opposite transept. In either case, the typology of the full-faced, mature, and remote Virgin of the final painting is one that Tiepolo had already developed in Venice, for example in the beautiful *Madonna and Child* of 1759 (Museum of Fine Arts, Springfield, Massachusetts).

CW

Notes

1. For the building and decoration of this church, and the fate of Tiepolo's altarpieces, see Whistler 1985a.
2. For instance, a decision was taken on 29 September 1767 to insert a large window in the upper part of the church for the better illumination of the friars' gallery (Archivo General del Palacio Real, *Obras del Palacio*, legajo 391).
3. Levey (1960a, p. 123) suggests that the change in costume was ordered by Eleta on theological grounds, since the humeral veil shown on the angel in the *modello* is inappropriate for him. (This veil is worn by the priest during Benediction when he holds the monstrance with the Eucharist.) However, the angel in the altarpiece by Anton Raphael Mengs that was substituted for Tiepolo's painting wears a humeral veil, indicating that the alteration to Tiepolo's design may have been made for aesthetic reasons.
4. See Whistler 1986 and Levey 1986, pp. 271–72.
5. This altarpiece is now in the Cincinnati Art Museum. Perhaps it is the same picture referred to in a memo of December 1778 (Archivo General del Palacio Real, *Aranjuez*, legajo 43). Here it is noted that an unframed painting of Saint Charles Borromeo presently kept in the king's apartments at Aranjuez would be transferred to the altar of the mortuary chapel of the new Hospital of Saint Charles Borromeo. Completed in 1776 by Manuel Serrano, the hospital stands opposite the church of S. Pascual.
6. The court artist Vicente López y Portaña recorded in 1836 that the *Saint Peter of Alcantara* was in the convent and the *Saint Anthony* was on the altar in the sacristy of the church. In 1826 Ferdinand VII ordered the court painter José Antonio Rivera and Luis Eusebi, the director of the Prado, to survey the royal possessions and to select pictures for display in the new museum. Since six paintings were presented by the king to the convent of S. Pascual in 1827, it is likely that they replaced others that had been removed. In any case, the *Saint Paschal* seems to have belonged to the Prado from its opening, and the *Saint Francis* was inventoried there in 1859.
7. For a summary of contemporary views, see Alfonso de' Liguori 1750, vol. 2, p. 7, and Aguirre 1725, p. 17.
8. Gemin and Pedrocco 1993, p. 302, no. 175. In a second altarpiece of 1759, for the Oratorio della Purità at Udine, Tiepolo presented the Immaculate Conception as a painted statue set on a pedestal within a gilded niche, complementing the painted grisaille relief panels on the surrounding walls (ibid., p. 470, no. 492).
9. For a history of the iconography, see Levi D'Ancona 1957.
10. Godinez (1738, chap. 12) elaborates on the mystery of the Immaculate Conception, using metaphors of the sun and moon.
11. Tiepolo reused this idea in a later oil sketch now in the National Gallery of Ireland, Dublin (Gemin and Pedrocco 1993, p. 500, no. 538).
12. It is possible that the *Immaculate Conception* was among the "cinco borrones de barias obra de Tiepolo" acquired by Don Manuel Godoy from the widow of Chopinot, jeweler of the queen and a dealer (see Salas 1968–69, p. 31). Bayeu owned nine works by Tiepolo, including six *modelli* for the altarpieces at S. Pascual Baylon, but some of these he had sold before his death.

S. PASCUAL BAYLON: SAINT FRANCIS RECEIVING THE STIGMATA

41a, b. Saint Francis Receiving the Stigmata

41a. Saint Francis Receiving the Stigmata
Doc. 1767
63.5 × 38.9 cm (25 × 15⅜ in.)
Courtauld Institute Galleries, London, Princes Gate Collection (P.G. 173)

41b. Saint Francis Receiving the Stigmata
Doc. 1767–69
278 × 153 cm (109½ × 60¼ in.)
Museo del Prado, Madrid

Saint Francis's stigmatization took place just before dawn on 17 September 1224, the feast of the exaltation of the Holy Cross, on the desolate mountain of Alvernia, where he had gone with three other friars to pray and fast for forty days. Although Francis asked his companions to leave him, Brother Leo remained to witness the mystical event. Thomas of Celano's *Vita prima*, written in 1228–29, recorded that Saint Francis received the stigmata from a six-winged seraph, whereas Saint Bonaventura recounted in his *Legenda maior* of 1261–62 that they emanated from the figure of a six-winged crucified Christ. The Christ-like qualities of Francis are emphasized in these early sources, with the moment of stigmatization symbolizing the saint's complete possession by the divine, at the climax of his spiritual journey.

Years before he executed this work, one of the seven altarpieces commissioned in 1767 for the royal foundation at S. Pascual Baylon, Aranjuez, Tiepolo had represented the subject in a painting that is now lost and in an independent drawing of the late 1720s, known through an engraving by Pietro Monaco.[1] In the drawing he showed the stigmatization as a dramatic event, with the startled Saint Francis transfixed by a stream of heavenly light and the modest figure of Brother Leo watching the scene from behind a bank of clouds. Brother Leo, prostrate in prayer, a familiar element in depictions of the subject, is included in the *modello* for the Aranjuez altarpiece, but he is absent from the final painting. As I have argued (in "Tiepolo as a Religious Artist" above), the changes in composition and in expression effected in the altarpiece after the oil sketch was completed make for a more profound and, in a sense, truer representation of this mystical theme. Furthermore, the paring down of the composition to essentials is in keeping with the relative position of the altarpiece in the church. The viewer, emerging from the darkened nave, with its low ceiling, faced the high altar, where the patron saint, Paschal Baylon, was shown in rapture before a vision of an angel bearing the Eucharist; directly on the left was the powerful single image of the Immaculate Virgin in a heavenly setting; and directly on the right could be seen Saint Francis, supported by an angel, in mystical communion with God. The four remaining altarpieces similarly depict single figures with visionary or divine elements. And of all six other paintings only the *Saint Anthony with the Christ Child* includes a human witness to the saint's tranquil, ecstatic state—which may have prompted Tiepolo to dispense with the figure of Leo in the *Saint Francis*.

While the surviving Aranjuez *modelli* have rightly been viewed as among the most moving and beautiful of Tiepolo's paintings, critical opinion has been less enthusiastic regarding the altarpieces, which have been judged to be largely by the hand of Giandomenico Tiepolo. The taste for the rapid, agitated handling of paint in the oil sketches and the delight in sensing the artist's immediate response to the subject (seen, for instance, in the touching depiction of Saint Francis in pain in the present *modello*) have prevailed over the appreciation of the large-scale, lucid images made for public devotion. Moreover, the condition of some of the altarpieces is problematic. The *Saint Francis* has been heavily restored on the left side: a photograph taken soon after its discovery in the Prado storerooms in 1914 shows extensive damage to that area, which includes the landscape passage and part of the angel's wing.[2]

Although Tiepolo had plenty of time to paint the seven Aranjuez altarpieces, he probably made use of Giandomenico's services as a long-standing collaborator. It is quite apparent, however, that Giandomenico was not given a free hand but rather that the two artists worked very closely together, with Giambattista's taste and preferences predominating.[3] No one was more aware than he of his son's talents and limitations, and Tiepolo would have ensured that every detail of this important commission was executed as he himself wished. Giandomenico's own manner of handling paint can be seen in the Passion series he made for the church of S. Felipe Neri in Madrid between 1770 and 1772.[4]

PROVENANCE, 41a:
Francisco Bayeu (by 1771–95; inv. no. 138); Leonardo Chopinot, Madrid (from 1795); Anatole-Auguste Hulot, Paris (until 1891; sale, Galerie Georges Petit, Paris, 10 May 1892, lot 141);[6] private collection, Brazil; private collection, Milan (before 1937); Count Antoine Seilern, Princes Gate, London (1937–78)

REFERENCES:
Molmenti 1909, p. 193; Mayer 1935, p. 300; Morassi 1943, p. 38; Venice 1951, p. 140, no. 99; Sánchez Cantón 1953, pp. 19–20; Morassi 1955a, p. 38; Morassi 1962, p. 20; Braham 1981, pp. 75, 78; Whistler 1985a, p. 323; Levey 1986, p. 280; Gemin and Pedrocco 1993, p. 492, no. 521a

Opposite: Detail, no. 41a

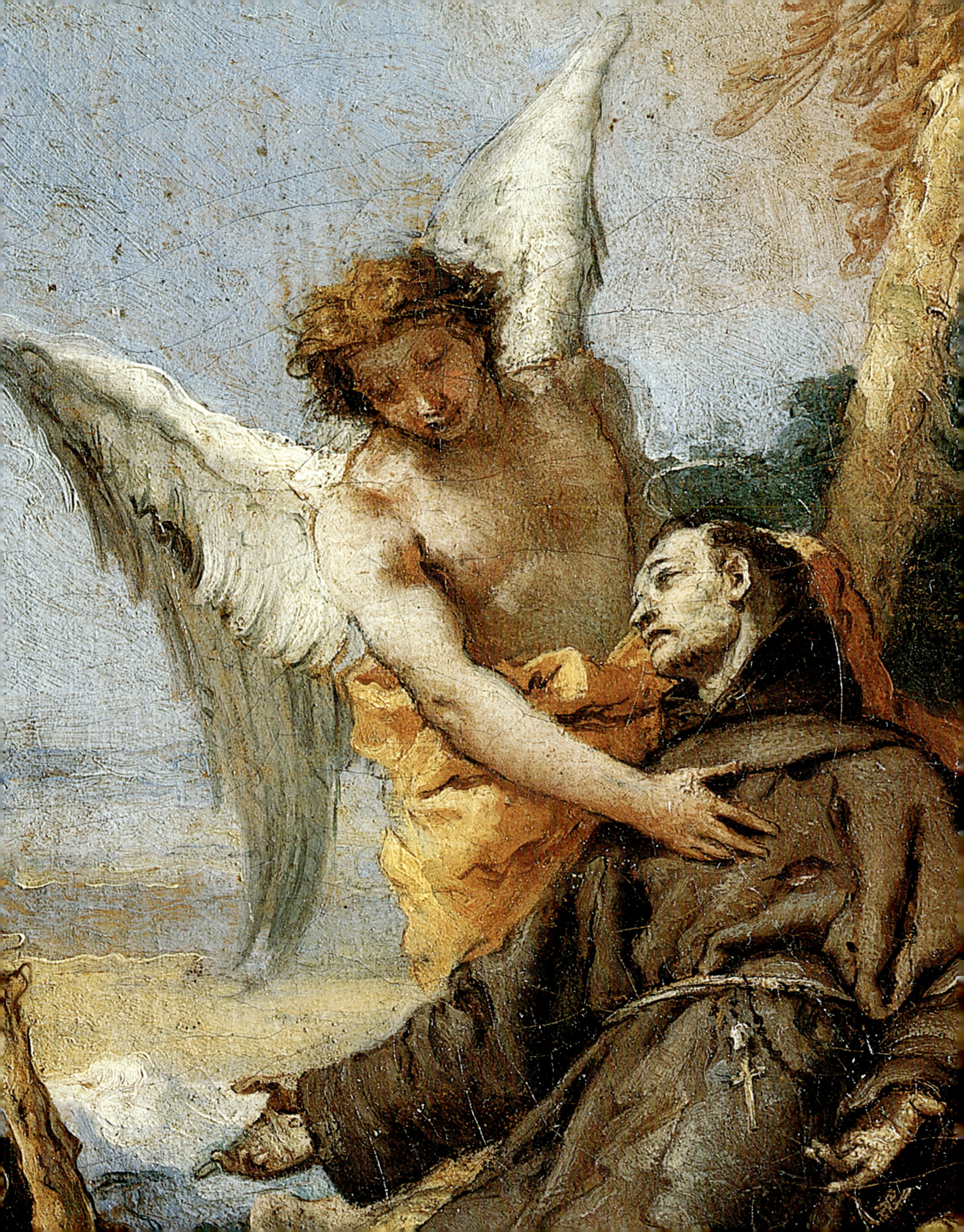

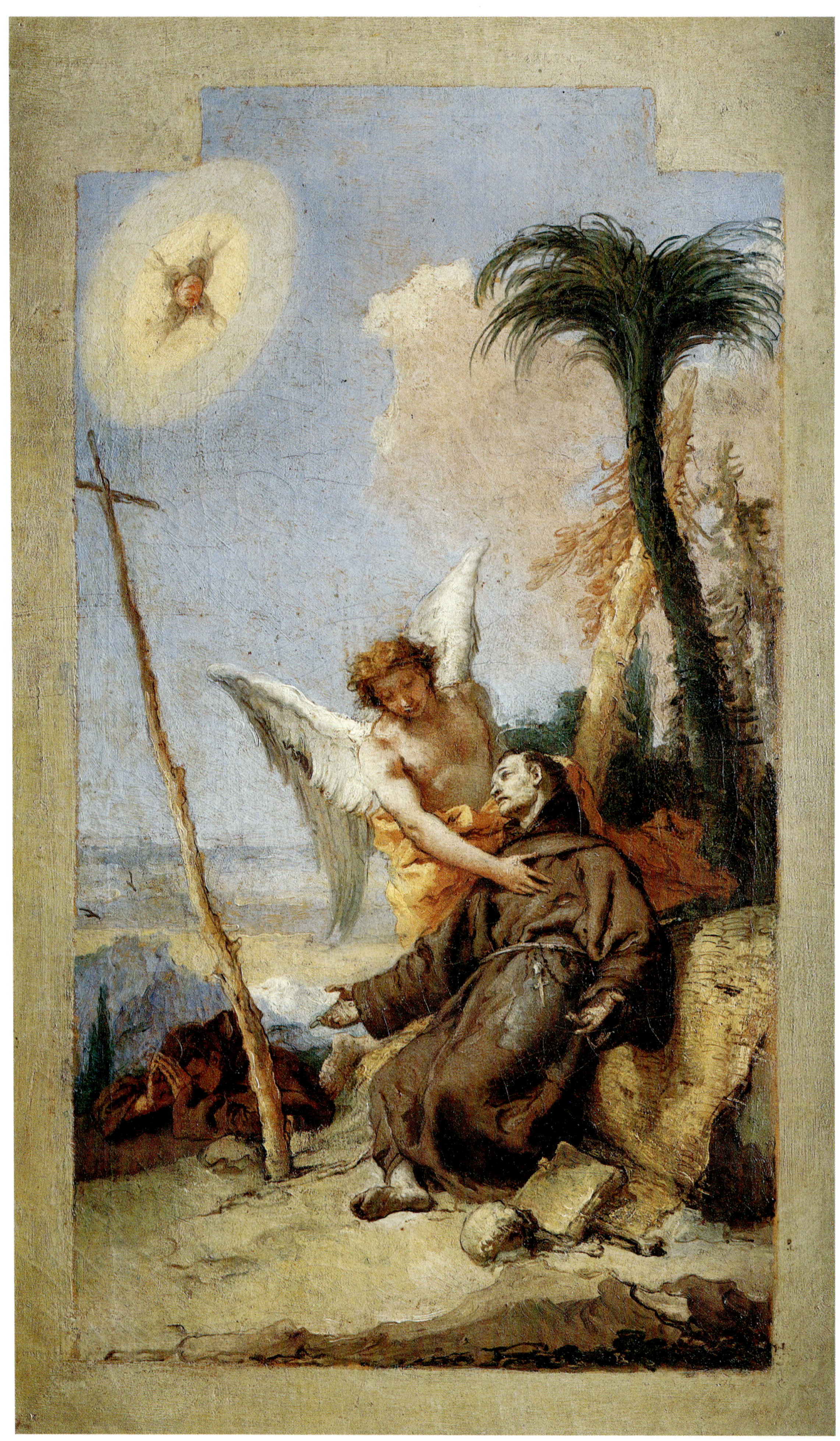

41a

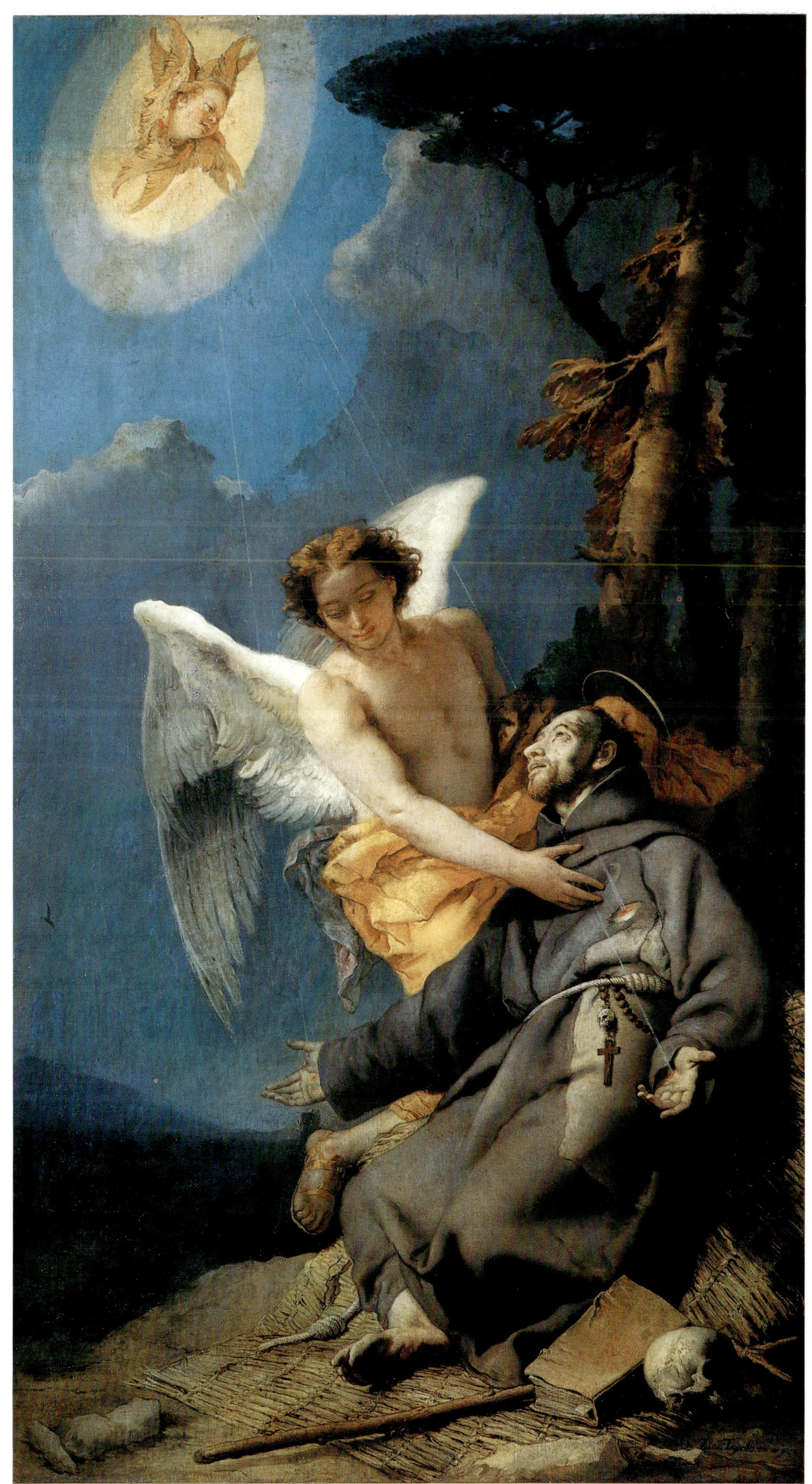

41b

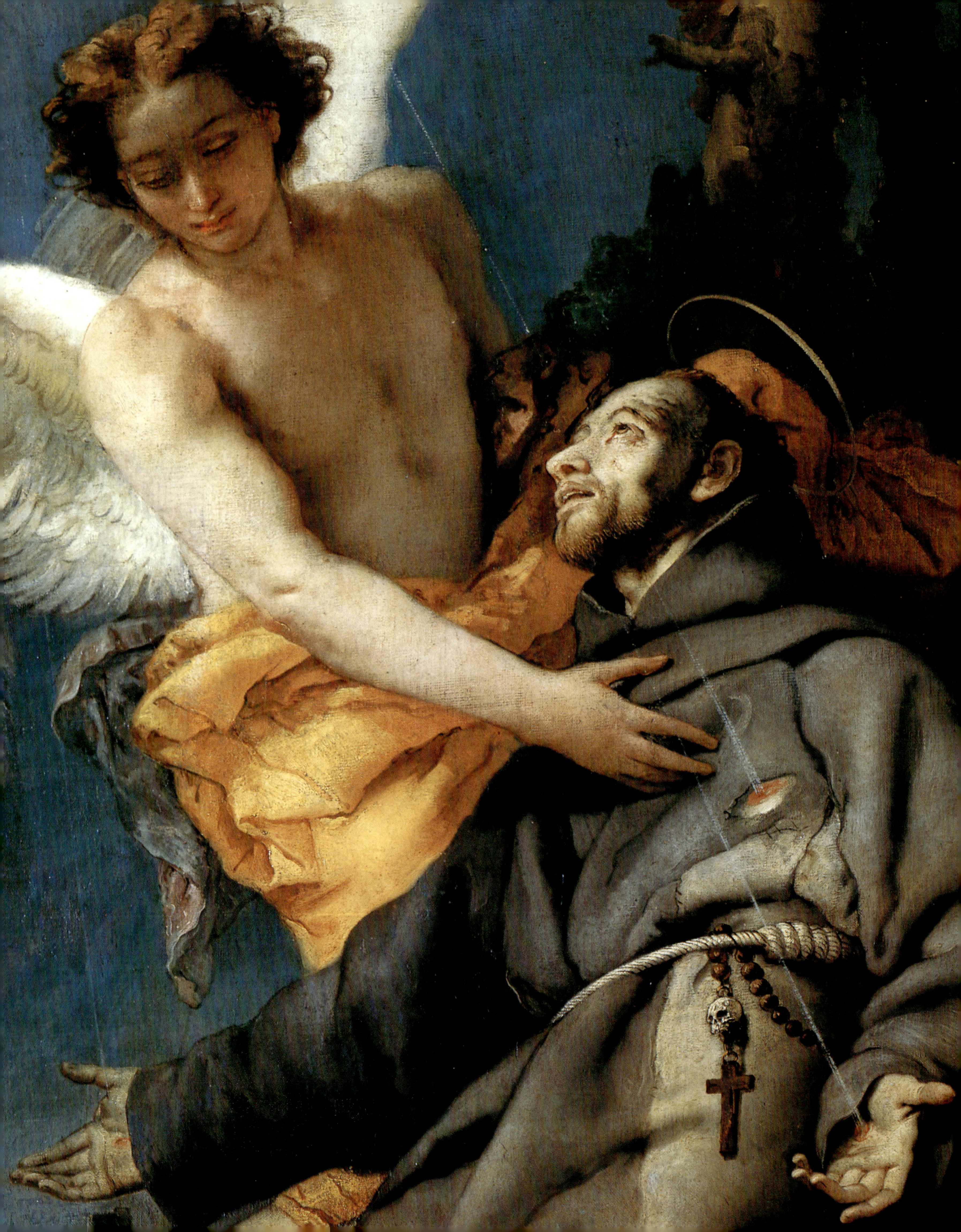

He favored predominantly chalky colors with occasional stronger accents, laid on a reddish priming, and used thin, flickering gray and pinkish gray graphic annotations to suggest shadowed areas on flesh. Among the Aranjuez altarpieces only in the *Saint Anthony* is Giandomenico's contribution absolutely clear: Giambattista had probably decided that this subject above all the others in the cycle was suited to his son's temperament, yet, even so, Giandomenico would have been painting under his direction. The young saint's ecstatic state is expressed in the light, pinkish tonality of the picture and in the matte, lifeless treatment of his rosy flesh, in keeping with descriptions of ecstasy in which the senses are gently and sweetly numbed and the soul melts like wax before the flame of divine love.[5] The splendid *Immaculate Conception* (no. 40b), Tiepolo's mature vision of a humbly clad but utterly majestic figure, seems to be entirely by Giambattista: even the yellow ocher background shows a complex variegation of hue and tone that evokes a deep, shimmering area of heavenly light. In the *Saint Francis* it is hard to see what contribution Domenico could have offered, apart from blocking in the area of sky and landscape details. It was certainly Tiepolo who chose to contrast the chill tones of gray and washed-out yellow of the saint's habit and the foreground details, recalling the cold atmosphere of dawn, with the golden orange accents of the angel's drapery. These warm tones are picked up in the angel's shadowed flesh and hair, emphasizing his radiant and sympathetic presence. The highly expressive group of the stiff, enraptured saint and the reverent yet tender angel is surely by Tiepolo's own hand.

CW

NOTES

1. Zanetti (1771, p. 467) mentions a *Saint Francis* in the church of S. Ternità, Venice. Monaco's engraving is reproduced by Knox (1965, fig. 1).
2. Sánchez Cantón 1916, facing p. 63.
3. A clear example of an altarpiece painted entirely by Giandomenico in a Tiepolesque manner, based on his father's *modello* and preparatory drawings, is the *Miracle of Saint Anthony* (Gemin and Pedrocco 1993, p. 473, no. 496) made for the parish church of Mirano about 1759. The disconcerting changes in the architectural setting, the very dry handling of paint, and the relatively dull use of color are characteristic of Giandomenico's work.
4. Mariuz 1971, pls. 232–39; the paintings are now in the Museo del Prado, Madrid.
5. Scaramelli 1754, pp. 249–50.
6. According to the sale catalogue, Hulot (1811–1891) specialized in medals and the production of stamps. He was a friend of Delacroix, Géricault, Decamps, and Troyon. His collections included prints, paintings, pastels, and bronzes. He would appear to be one of a number of French artist-collectors of the mid-nineteenth century who prized the work of Tiepolo.
7. Sánchez Cantón (1927, p. 10) states that the painting was inventoried that year.

PROVENANCE, 41b:
Church of S. Pascual Baylon, Aranjuez (1770–75); Convent of S. Pascual Baylon, Aranjuez (1775–1827?); Museo del Prado, Madrid (from 1827?; first recorded 1859)[7]

REFERENCES:
Chennevières 1898, p. 102; Molmenti 1909, p. 192; Sack 1910, pp. 142, 145, 209, no. 442; Sánchez Cantón 1927, pp. 5–6; Morassi 1943, pp. 37–38; Sánchez Cantón 1952, p. 644; Morassi 1955a, p. 37; Braham 1981, p. 75; Whistler 1985a, pp. 323–24; Levey 1986, pp. 279–81; Barcham 1989, p. 229; Gemin and Pedrocco 1993, p. 492, no. 521

Opposite: Detail, no. 41b

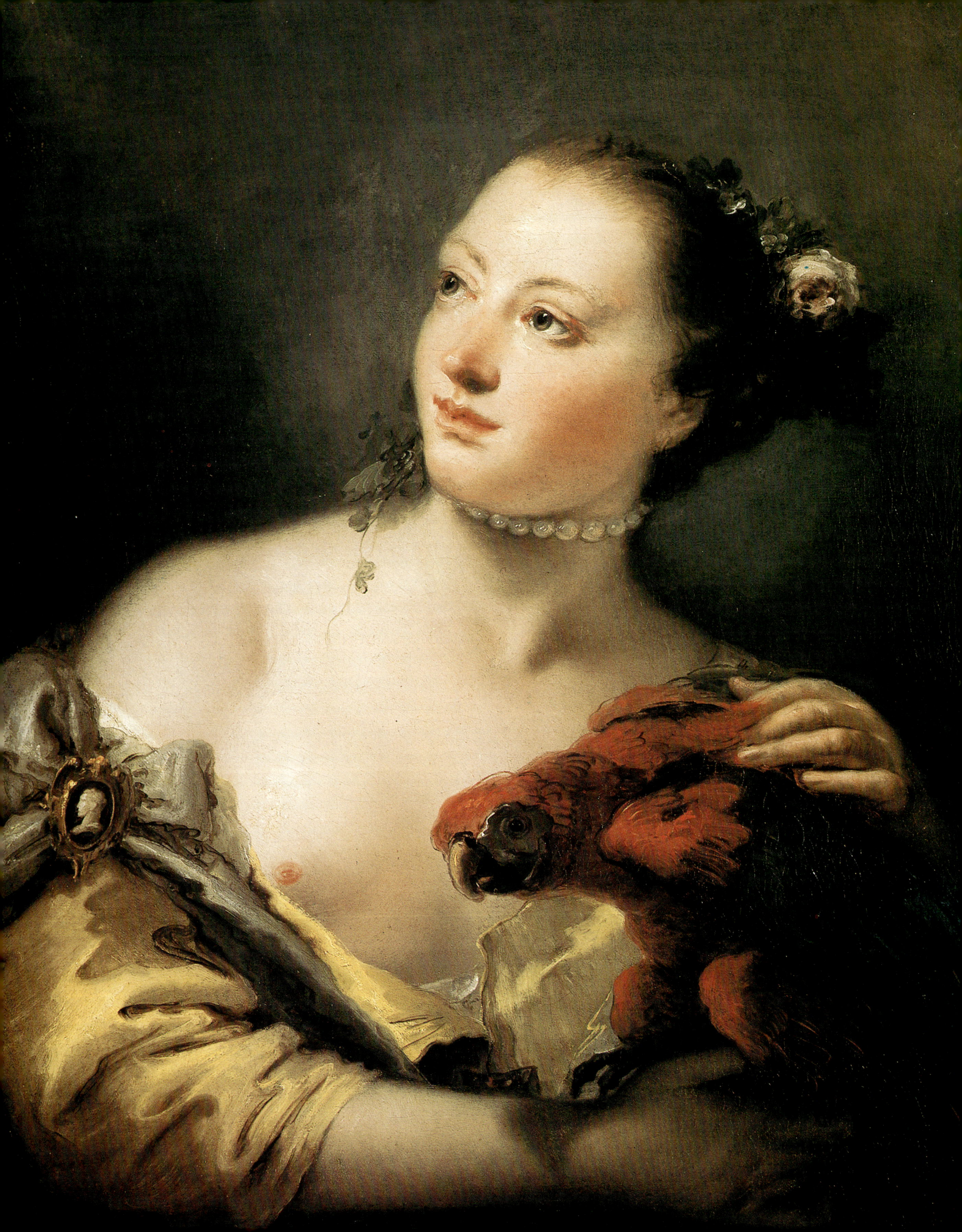

Tiepolo and the "Art" of Portraiture

DIANE DE GRAZIA

Tiepolo's rare excursions into portraiture, his depictions of figures in exotic and fanciful dress, and his bust-length saints and philosophers make up less than 1 percent of his total output, but their historical interest significantly outweighs their numbers. Giandomenico produced two books of etchings after his father's studies of heads (the *Raccolta di teste*, begun about 1757), and he and his brother Lorenzo painted copies and variants after the philosopher heads to meet what must have been an extensive market (a production within the Tiepolo workshop that has, understandably, created considerable problems in attribution). Tiepolo's bust-length pictures of beautiful women in elaborate dress were no less popular and remain among his most appealing works.

Tiepolo was not known as a portraitist in his lifetime, and we may well ask ourselves whether he ever painted portraits in the conventional sense. There are, of course, numerous individualized personages in his religious, historical, and mythological scenes (sometimes identified as members of his family masquerading as supernumeraries), and occasionally even an intentional portrait and self-portrait are included (frontis., p. 2, see figs. 3–6), but there is no mistaking that Tiepolo's attitude toward portraiture was ambivalent. For this reason a consideration of the types he employed for his various characters is more interesting than an attempt to identify his models.

Only a handful of independent portraits can, with any plausibility, be ascribed to Tiepolo, and some of these are known by most critics only from photographs: *Portrait of Giovanni Corner II* and the pendant *Portrait of Marco Corner* (no. 3a,b), *Antonio Riccobono* (no. 43), the *Portrait of a Procurator* (*Daniele IV Dolfin*) (no. 46), a *Self-Portrait* of about 1730 (whereabouts unknown), and the much-repainted posthumous portraits of patriarchs in the Sala dei Ritratti, Biblioteca Arcivescovile, Udine, of 1729.[1] Letters suggest that other portraits once existed, but they cannot have been numerous. For example, in 1761 Tiepolo wrote to Count Francesco Algarotti concerning a portrait that was either of Algarotti or of Frederick the Great.[2] More ambiguous is the mention of a request by Elena Barozzi di Pietro for Tiepolo to paint her dogs.[3] What is striking about the surviving portraits is that almost all are posthumous likenesses despite their highly individualized appearance. In one of these Doge Marco Corner (ca. 1286–1368) stares down at us from a high throne (consistent with the painting's original placement above a door) with wide eyes in a handsome, believable face. In another, Antonio Riccobono (1541–1599), distinguished by his receding hairline, furrowed brow, and piercing eyes, glares at the intruder who interrupts his reading. In Tiepolo's portrait of a procurator, credibly identified as his early patron Daniele IV Dolfin (1656–1729) but painted as much as twenty years after the sitter's death, the figure watches us intently, his face marked by high cheekbones, a prominent long nose, and a cleft chin. Through these vivid characterizations we are seduced into believing that we are looking at authentic images of living men, whereas what in fact confront us are eloquent examples of Tiepolo's fertile imagination and deceitful genius. This becomes evident when we compare a sixteenth-century engraved likeness of Riccobono (fig. 89)[4]—our only clue to the actual appearance of any of these subjects, all long deceased by the time they were painted—to Tiepolo's rendering of the man. Only the fur-trimmed coat, receding hairline, and ridged brow are similar. The hooked nose has been made more aquiline, the cheekbones raised, and the hair color changed, so that the sitter has become more conventionally handsome. Tiepolo's portrait presents us not with the "real" Riccobono (that is, an image faithful to the sixteenth-century engraving) but with the artist's idea of an orator and philosopher of the sixteenth century: Tiepolo chose a particular type to express a certain point.

Tiepolo's portrait of Riccobono was one of several commissioned by the canon Ludovico Campo to adorn the Accademia dei Concordi, Rovigo, with painted images of the most prominent men of the region.[5] As such, it belongs to a long tradition of posthumous as well as contemporary portraits of famous men (*uomini famosi*). These portraits formed series that decorated princely residences, city halls, libraries, academies, and other buildings. The earliest known examples in Italian art date to the fourteenth century and have as their written equivalent Petrarch's *De viris illustribus*.[6] The practice of representing virtuous rulers and thinkers, however, had its

Woman with a Parrot. Oil on canvas. Ashmolean Museum, Oxford origin in the writings of the ancients and can be traced back at least to Cicero and possibly to the Greeks.[7] The purpose of these portrait collections, whether written or visual, was to provide exemplars to the reader or viewer as an inducement to lead a life as virtuous as those of the individuals depicted. The idealization of the features of each hero was meant to encourage the viewer in this pursuit. Tiepolo went a step beyond this kind of idealization by endowing the figure with an active pose and an intellectual fervor that suggest the fire of the philosophic mind at work. Thus, it is of little consequence whether the physical features presented in Riccobono's picture or in Tiepolo's other posthumous portraits conform to the physical reality of the person shown, because it is the characterization of the figure that was the artist's chief goal.

Important collectors of pictures of famous men and women abounded in the sixteenth century. Paolo Giovio had a group of portraits of political and military leaders, popes, artists, poets, philosophers, and women of high status. Inspired by Giovio, Giorgio Vasari acquired portraits of artists with which to illustrate his biographies. The Counter-Reformation writer Cardinal Gabriele Paleotti believed in the value of portraits of virtuous men to instruct and encourage morality. Throughout the seventeenth and eighteenth centuries the practice of assembling these portrait collections continued, but their original intent sometimes became obscured. Libraries and academies such as the Accademia dei Concordi maintained the tradition of honoring virtuous thinkers by commissioning images of them, and series dedicated to the Twelve Apostles, the Church Fathers, and other religious figures, as well as ancestor portraits, remained popular. Private collectors, however, became fascinated with other, less morally uplifting series devoted to beautiful women, figures in exotic dress, and depictions of ancient philosophers.

Indeed, by the eighteenth century the moral justification for collections was no longer considered important.[8] Portraits of the sort popular at this time might commemorate an ideal of beauty or character as much as the physical qualities of the person portrayed. Augustus III of Saxony devised a room to house his collection of pastels of various women by Rosalba Carriera, and Empress Elizabeth of Russia had rooms for her extensive holdings of paintings of beautiful women by Pietro Rotari. It is within this convention that Tiepolo's depictions of women in fancy dress belong.

There are three extant paintings of women in fancy dress that have been widely accepted as autograph works by Tiepolo:[9] the *Woman with a Parrot* (frontis., p. 254),[10] the *Woman with a Mandolin*, and the *Young Lady in a Tricorn Hat* (no. 45a,b). Another painting, now lost but generally considered autograph, of a young woman wearing a fur, is known through photographs and a copy in pastel by Lorenzo Tiepolo (fig. 83).[11] Because Lorenzo also made a pastel copy of the *Woman with a Parrot* and because the dimensions of that picture and of the lost *Woman with a Fur* are almost identical, scholars have rightly considered the two a pair. Stylistically, the *Woman with a Mandolin* and the *Young Lady in a Tricorn Hat* date to Tiepolo's last years in Venice and were probably among "some half-length figures of women done *a capriccio* for the empress of Moscow" mentioned in a letter of 1760.[12] Whether these two works belonged to a larger set illustrating the senses or the seasons is unknown, but the fact that only two pastels by Lorenzo exist suggests that they constituted a set of only two, with no expanded allegorical meaning. The dimensions of the *Woman with a Mandolin* and the *Young Lady in a Tricorn Hat* do not match and they differ from those of the *Woman with a Parrot* and the *Woman with a Fur*, indicating that they were probably independent commissions. Other fancy-dress paintings, now reattributed to Giandomenico (see fig. 84), Lorenzo, or various followers, suggest that prototypes by Giambattista may have existed and, at the very least, confirm the popularity of Tiepolo's handling of the genre.[13]

Like Tiepolo's posthumous portraits, the fancy-dress pictures stem from a long-standing pictorial and literary tradition, in this case a tradition that originated in sixteenth-century Italy—and one that enjoyed special popularity in Venice.[14] Paintings by Raphael, Parmigianino, Titian, Veronese, and others portray idealized women whose beauty represented a fusion of the charms of various individuals or arose from the wellspring of the artist's imagination. As he did for his historical and mythological compositions, as well as for his posthumous portraits, so for these images of beautiful women Tiepolo looked to the cinquecento for inspiration. He was obviously also aware of contemporary portraits and allegorical half-length representations by Rosalba, whose pastels were collected throughout Europe. The hair of the subject of the *Woman with a Parrot* and the hazy contours of her head and the fluid brushwork of the flowers in her coiffure replicate in oil Rosalba's pastel technique. Although many of Rosalba's pastels of women were made in sets of the senses or the seasons, they were really only veiled excuses for the portrayal of feminine charm.[15]

It is the dishabille of Tiepolo's women, two of whom reveal their breasts, that seems to make reference to another Venetian cinquecento tradition, that involving the depiction of feminine beauty in the guise of a courtesan.[16] Whether these women were meant to be perceived by the viewer as courtesans is unknown, but it is clear that the physical aspects of their beauty are emphasized over the spiritual component, which was assumed by literary critics to be impossible to

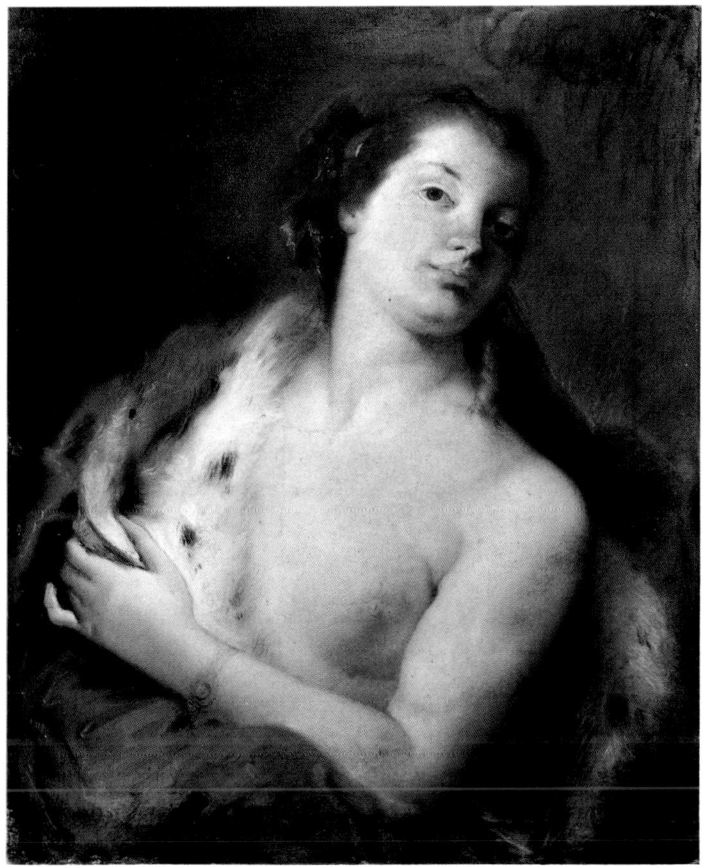

Fig. 83. Lorenzo Tiepolo. *Allegory of Winter (after Tiepolo)*. Pastel. El Paso Museum of Art

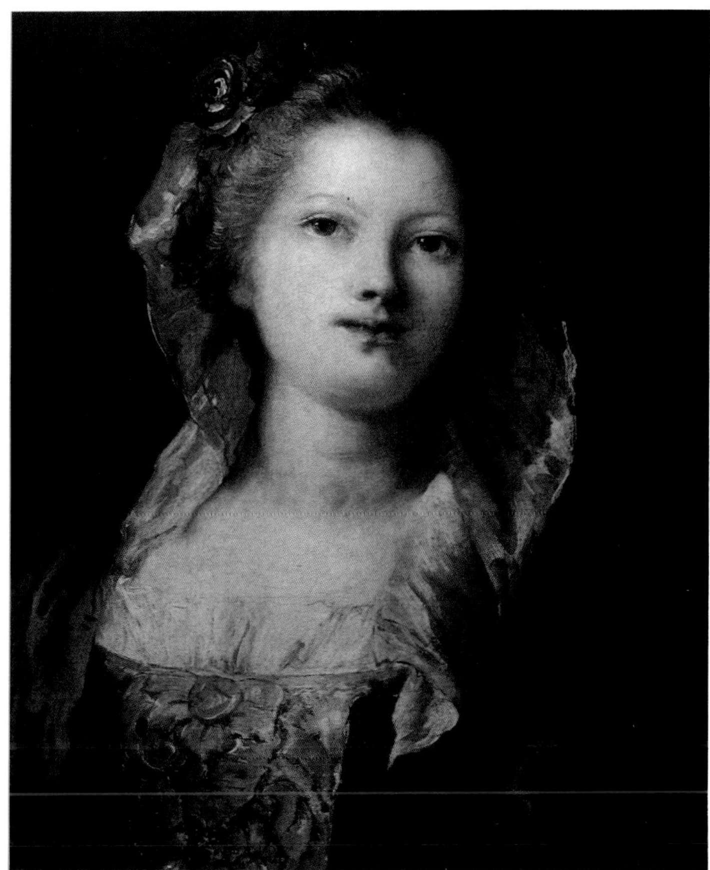

Fig. 84. Giandomenico Tiepolo. *Portrait of a Woman*. Oil on canvas. The Cleveland Museum of Art

convey.[17] The attributes of a Venetian courtesan are evident in the roses, yellow dress, costly pearls, uncovered breast, and the parrot—a symbol of luxury—in Tiepolo's *Woman with a Parrot*.[18] The model in the *Woman with a Mandolin*, like her counterpart with a parrot, is expensively coiffed and attired and dressed in yellow with a breast exposed; her hair is also tied up and it is bejeweled. Moreover, she tunes an instrument, whose notes were widely interpreted as messengers of love. In a sense, these women can be read as contemporary Venuses. Although the mysterious and coy subject of the *Young Lady in a Tricorn Hat* is fully dressed and may be perfectly respectable, her expression seems to betray something more piquant, which perhaps can be interpreted in the same light as the two more provocatively costumed subjects. We know that in 1760 some women promenaded in the Piazza San Marco during carnival dressed as nuns and priests, often with their breasts exposed.[19] Prostitution was rampant in Venice in the eighteenth century, and courtesans enjoyed a certain prestige in the city—so much so that the authorities sometimes had to initiate severe measures to curb the practice.[20]

It would be misguided to attempt to identify the "sitters" in these depictions by Tiepolo: his intention was not to commemorate the features of particular courtesans, let alone of his wife or a daughter or his fictitious lover Cristina (awarded him only in the nineteenth century),[21] but to assert an ideal of feminine beauty within the context of the legacy of Venetian images of beautiful women and the contemporary culture of courtesans. As noted in the letter of 1760 to the empress of Russia cited above, these or similar paintings were made *a capriccio*. *A capriccio* had the same meaning in eighteenth-century Venice as it did in the seventeenth century for the Florentine Filippo Baldinucci, who defined it in his dictionary of art terms as: "one's own idea or invention: thus, done *a capriccio* or *di fantasia;* that is, of one's own idea or invention."[22] Tiepolo was less interested in the beauty of a particular individual than in his personal notion of an ideal beauty.

Another category of heads, which Tiepolo began to produce in the 1740s, are bust-length pictures that can be divided into three classes: saints, young boys, and bearded old men, or philosopher types. Compositionally, these heads derive from seventeenth-century, mostly Bolognese, sources. Bolognese models of studies of saints and young boys were most likely filtered to Tiepolo through the work of Giambattista Piazzetta. Depictions of heads of saints made as small devotional images for private patrons by Guido Reni and other painters had gained wide popularity in the seventeenth century,[23] and the Bolognese artists Guercino and Giuseppe Maria Crespi produced small works of this kind as a profitable sideline. During his stay in Bologna, Piazzetta came under the influence of both Guercino and Crespi, and he brought their vision of the small religious picture with him on his return to Venice. What Piazzetta transmitted was not merely an image of the saint with eyes upraised to the heavens, familiar from the many versions of Reni's saints, but also a heightened psychological drama that took advantage of the powerful effects of chiaroscuro contrasts of light and shade seen in the paintings of Guercino and Crespi. For precedents for his own saints, Tiepolo probably looked no further back than Piazzetta's images. His painting *Beata Laduina* (no. 42), for example, is comparable in intensity of religious feeling to Piazzetta's *Saint Teresa in Ecstasy* (fig. 88).[24] Attributes are eliminated, and without external documentation there is no way of knowing whether a saint is, in fact, represented. In the *Beata Laduina*, as in the later *Saint Catherine of Siena* (no. 34), Tiepolo emphasized the psychological state of religious ecstasy by concentrating on the head, which in the former picture is contained and accentuated by the circular brushstrokes of the scarf and the windswept hood.

In its treatment the *Beata Laduina* is more like a character study than a saintly devotional image (which is the reason it is included in this section of the book); similarly, the *Boy with a Book* (no. 44) is closer to a character study than a simple portrait of Tiepolo's son Lorenzo, the probable sitter for the work. Like the *Beata Laduina*, the *Boy with a Book* is directly dependent on Piazzetta's work—in this case, especially his popular drawings of bust-length figures turning toward or away from the viewer to convey an impression of immediacy and spontaneous action interrupted.[25] (Many of Piazzetta's heads of this kind and some of Tiepolo's represent members of their own families.) In one extant painting, the *Astronomer*,[26] Tiepolo—or Giandomenico working from his father's design—intensified the sense of action in Piazzetta's single figures to create a narrative context. The *Astronomer*, which depicts two youths (students?) intently watching an astronomer who holds a book and points to a chart with his compass, also depends on Piazzetta's drawings of two and three figures shown together.[27] Whereas Piazzetta's drawings portray figures in pensive contemplation and involve little overt motion, Tiepolo revealed his astronomer as an active personality captured in a momentary action or movement.

Perhaps as early as the mid-1740s, along with his bust-length saints, Tiepolo began producing heads of bearded old men (see fig. 85), some of which were commemorated in Giandomenico's etched *Raccolta di teste* . It is difficult to discuss these works as a group or as a specific commission because the attributions of many are questioned, most are known to critics only in photographs, and few have been seen together for purposes of comparison of style and assigning of dates (indeed, none are

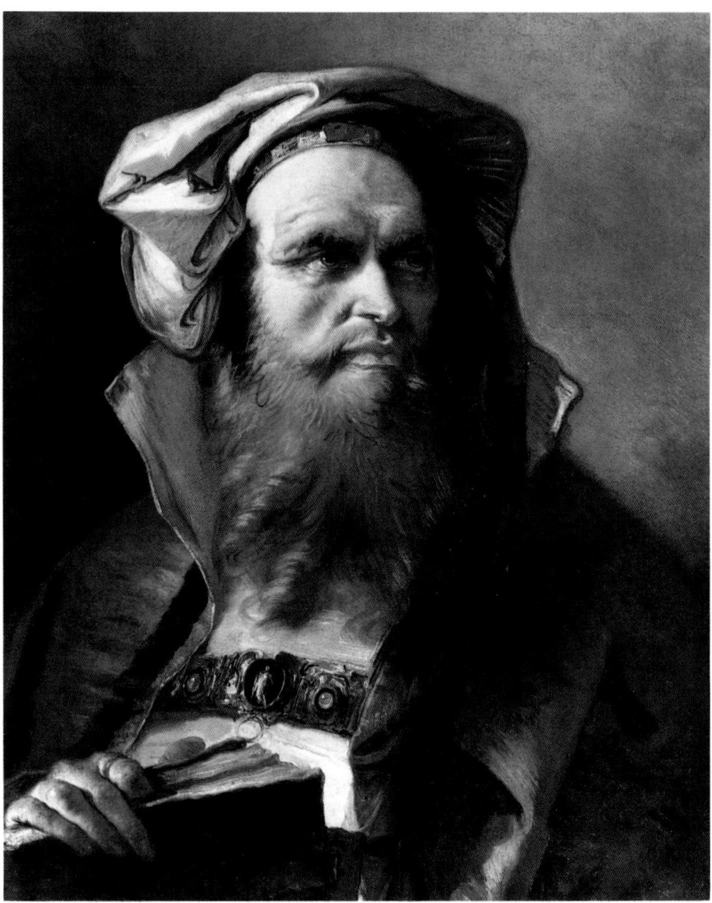

Fig. 85. Attributed to Tiepolo. *Philosopher*. Oil on canvas. Bob Jones University Gallery of Sacred Art and Bible Lands Museum, Greenville, South Carolina

exhibited here). Nevertheless, Knox's conclusion that these heads formed a series, based on their similar dimensions and compositions, is plausible.[28] Tiepolo launched a new career in etching in the mid-1740s, producing the *Capricci* and the *Scherzi di fantasia* series (nos. 59, 60),[29] which depict enigmatic subjects and include philosopher types in various kinds of exotic dress. Although the artist had always been interested in figures exotically garbed in antique and Orientalizing clothing—well documented in these drawings—his penchant for such subjects increased dramatically during this period and was probably encouraged by his friendship with Algarotti, who had returned from abroad to his native Venice in 1743.[30] Critics agree that Algarotti encouraged Tiepolo to paint classical subjects, but some have argued that under his influence the works became less energetic and spirited. He may, however, have had a stimulating impact on Tiepolo's imagination, about which he wrote enthusiastically. In his *Saggio sopra l'accademia di Francia che è in Roma* of 1763 Algarotti praised Tiepolo for his depth of imagination: "Tiepolo, who is still alive, is a universal painter endowed with one of the most fecund imaginations. He has known how to unite Paolo Veronese's manner of painting with that of Castiglione, Salvator Rosa, and the most bizarre painters, carrying out everything with harmonious colors and an inexpressible facility of brushwork."[31] One of the longest chapters in the *Saggio sopra la pittura* is on invention, which Algarotti defined as the discovery of true things adapted to the subject being represented and of that which is most proper to excite the admiration of spectators and please them at the same time.[32] That Algarotti was impressed by Tiepolo's *Capricci* and classical and Orientalizing heads is evidenced by the Tiepolo-inspired print he himself produced showing various bearded and unbearded, hatted and bared heads in profile.[33]

Tiepolo's so-called philosopher portraits may have been based loosely on posed models, but, like the *Riccobono*, they more likely arose from the artist's imagination. These bust-length figures carry cryptic attributes—a book, baton, sword, or compass—that do little to identify them as particular ancient philosophers, warriors, saints, or poets. How unimportant these attributes were to the popularity and to the audience's understanding of the portraits is proved by the fact that Giandomenico eliminated them from the prints in the *Raccolta* and from his painted copies. In respect to the function of these objects, these portraits differ radically from the well-known series of apostles or philosophers by Jusepe de Ribera and Luca Giordano,[34] in which attributes are used to identify the subjects. Rather than as representations of specific individuals, then, Tiepolo's philosophers should be seen as character studies.

When he painted these heads, Tiepolo certainly looked at Rembrandt's prints of bearded old men in Oriental garb: the capes, hats, and gilt chains around the chests of some of his figures recall like details in several of the Dutch master's etchings,[35] and, in particular, Tiepolo consciously reinterpreted Rembrandt's etching of a bearded man wearing a cap with a jewel clasp (fig. 86). But in contrast to Rembrandt's philosophers, who are shown in repose and retain the specific characteristics of the models who posed for them, Tiepolo's bearded men turn, glare, or otherwise actively engage the viewer and, instead of projecting a sense of portraitlike particularity, evoke an emotional state appropriate to the philosopher theme through attitude and configuration of generalized facial features. Tiepolo also turned to Castiglione's prints for inspiration for his philosophers, just as he had for his *Capricci*,[36] and he certainly knew the works of his Venetian predecessor Pietro della Vecchia and his contemporary Giuseppe Nogari, both of whom were influenced by Castiglione's etchings. (Algarotti purchased a number of Nogari's philosopher-like heads for Augustus of Saxony.) A connection between Castiglione's work and Tiepolo's is clear and documented by Algarotti's mention in a letter that he had a print of a head of an old man by Castiglione that Tiepolo had given him.[37] Nevertheless, Castiglione's heads, although more menacing than those of Rembrandt (whose etchings inspired them), seldom engage the viewer directly.[38]

Tiepolo's philosophers, together with his posthumous portraits and bust-length women and saints, deserve to be considered not only in the context of the precedents to which they seem most obviously to relate but also in terms of the tradition of *têtes expressives*, or expressive heads. The expressive heads are studies meant to convey the interior states, the emotions, through the description of the features of the face. They have their basis in the "science" of physiognomy, which claimed to gain an understanding of the human mind by exploring the conformation of the human head and to achieve insight into the passions of man through analysis of facial expressions and gestures. Physiognomy dates to ancient times and became popular in the sixteenth century, with the appearance of Leonardo da Vinci's studies of grotesque heads and the publication of Giacomo della Porta's *De humana physiognomia*. Later artists such as Annibale Carracci believed that the passions could be expressed through certain *affetti*, or outward gestures and expressions. Rubens made drawings of antique statues and animals whose features he compared with those of men. Most influential of all for artists, however, was Charles Le Brun's presentation to the French Academy in 1668 of a series of lectures on the delineation of the various passions and the

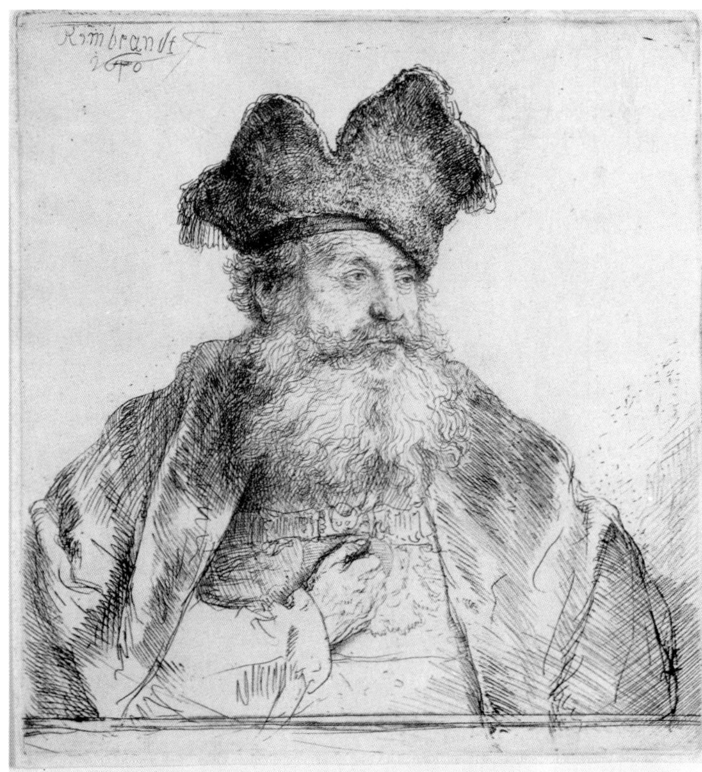

Fig. 86. Rembrandt van Rijn. *Old Man with a Divided Fur Cap*. Etching and drypoint. First state of two. The Metropolitan Museum of Art, New York; Gift of Douglas Dillon, 1983 (1983.1140.3)

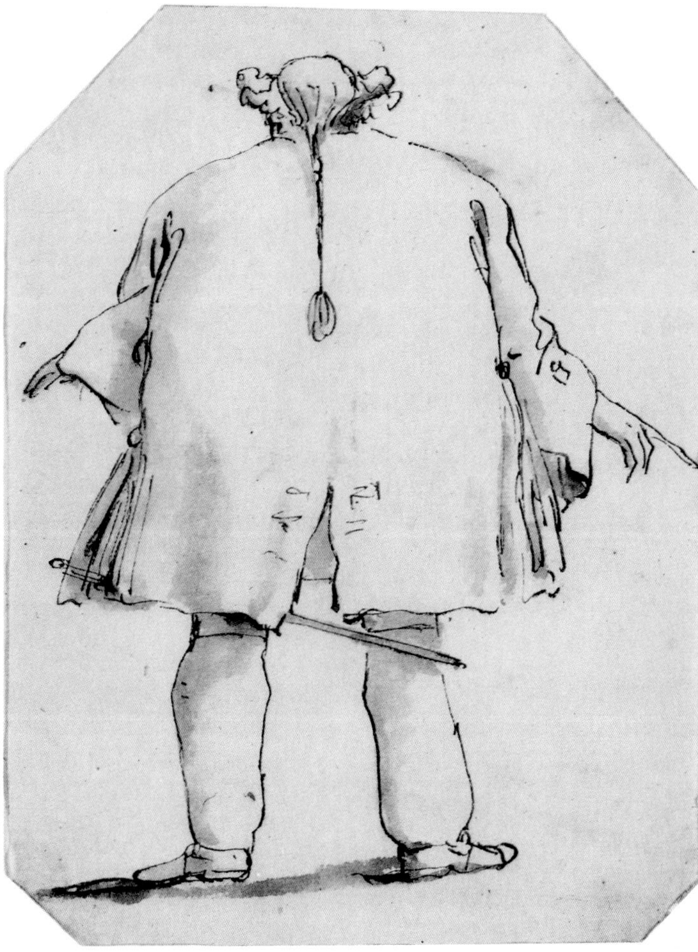

Fig. 87. *Caricature of a Man Seen from the Back*. Pen and ink and wash over pencil. The Metropolitan Museum of Art, New York; Robert Lehman Collection, 1975 (1975.1.495)

subsequent publications of prints after his drawings of heads expressing these passions.[39] In the eighteenth and nineteenth centuries the interest in physiognomy continued, as the Dutchman Pieter Camper, the Swiss Johann Kaspar Lavater, and the German Franz Joseph Gall each produced well-received pseudoscientific illustrated lectures and publications.[40] Tiepolo must have known prints after Le Brun's drawings, and it is possible that he subscribed to the widely held contemporary theory that the different types of human character were visible in the outward appearance of man and that the passions were expressed in the facial features. His friend Algarotti, who insisted that the artist convey the thoughts and feelings of his subjects through their facial expressions,[41] certainly agreed with this view.

Tiepolo's belief that human type and human emotion could be categorized is attested to by the fact that he generalized the faces in his posthumous portraits, half-length philosophers, saints, and beautiful women, as well as those of the protagonists in his historical and religious paintings, to emphasize character. For example, he chose a certain conformation of the head and a particular facial expression for his male saints: a high forehead and cheekbones and a narrow chin and an emotionless demeanor that confer an ascetic appearance. Throughout his career he used this type not only for portrayals of such saints as Roch, Gaetano, and Norbert but also for Saint Carlo Borromeo and Saint Philip Neri, whose features were known from contemporary portraits, prints, and death masks, to make them look more austere. Roman emperors are strong, handsome youths with broad cheekbones and eyes widely placed to convey a sense of benevolent power, while his mythological heroes have wavy dark hair and round, full features that allude to their romantic natures. The oval faces, slim noses, and pouty lips of his heroines and beautiful women in fancy dress demonstrate an ideal of feminine beauty, whereas the furrowed brows, squinting eyes, and heads turned to one side of the philosophers and poets express the interior state of active minds. Even Tiepolo's caricatures reveal the artist's tendency to typecast. The art of caricature in Italy before and after Tiepolo depended on the exaggeration of features of certain identifiable individuals, but not one of Tiepolo's caricatures has been associated with a known contemporary of the artist's. Tiepolo showed his figures from the back, elongated, or distorted, not to poke fun at friends or enemies but to reveal character types or certain attitudes expressed through physical appearance (see fig. 87). It may be that an early drawing of an unspecified academy where the same figure is repeated to represent many of the students (fig. 1) is meant as a portrayal of an ideal academy and can be classified as a caricature (which in Tiepolo's hands becomes an exercise in the *capriccio* form).

Tiepolo thus seems to have painted no conventional portraits—pictures whose primary function is to record the features of an individual—and instead made only representations of the human face in its various aspects. If Tiepolo did not invent new forms but worked within existing traditions, he nonetheless enlarged on those traditions and took them to the limits of his imagination. Anton Maria Zanetti was prophetic when he wrote in 1733 that Tiepolo had a ready *invenzione* and that each figure he painted was new and different, for he was describing qualities of mind and work that would remain in force throughout the artist's lifetime.[42] Tiepolo's character heads and fancy-dress portraits of the 1740s and 1750s may have been made to take advantage of a ready market established by Rosalba Carriera and Piazzetta for modest, intimate paintings for the smaller rooms of households. They may have been a response to Pietro Longhi's mundane representations of the Venetian world or to Jean-Étienne Liotard's realistic portraits.[43] Or, conversely, they may have been painted in an attempt to extend Tiepolo's inquiry into the variety of human types. Tiepolo himself asserted in an interview that the painter must always aspire to the sublime, to the heroic, and to perfection.[44] By changing the purpose of portraiture, his genius and *invenzione* achieved this goal. Rather than attempting to reproduce the ordinary by strictly adhering to nature, Tiepolo sought to represent the ideal and universal through the generalization of character type.

Notes

1. See Gemin and Pedrocco 1993, p. 282, no. 129 (for the self-portrait), p. 257, no. 84 (for the Sala dei Ritratti).
2. Levey 1986, p. 246.
3. Urbani de Gheltof 1879, p. 84.
4. Accademia dei Concordi, Rovigo, inv. no. 291. The photograph was kindly supplied by Antonio Romagnolo of the Accademia dei Concordi. Dazzi (1925, p. 73) first suggested that Tiepolo relied on the engraving for his portrait.
5. Puppi [1972], p. 131. See also no. 43.
6. On the origins of the *uomini famosi*, see Donato 1985. The author is grateful to Eric Garberson for discussing his ideas on the *uomini famosi*.
7. See Joost-Gaugier 1982.
8. For the justification of portraiture in the sixteenth century, see Campbell 1990, p. 195.
9. For dissenting opinions, see entry for no. 45a, b.
10. Gemin and Pedrocco 1993, p. 478, no. 502.
11. Ibid., p. 479, no. 503.
12. F. M. Tassi to Count Carrara, 15 December 1760: "alcune mezze figure di donne a capriccio per l'imperatrice de Moscovia." See Udine 1971, p. 138.
13. For paintings attributed to Giandomenico, see Mariuz 1971, pls. 221–31.
14. For paintings of beautiful women in the sixteenth century and their meaning, see Cropper 1976 and Cropper 1986.
15. For works of this kind by Rosalba, see, for example, Sani 1988, pls. 87–90.
16. On the iconography of courtesans in Venetian art, see Pedrocco 1990.
17. See Cropper 1986, pp. 181–83.
18. Venice 1990, p. 90.
19. Ravoux-Rallo 1984, p. 39, and Gambier 1990, p. 37.
20. Ravoux-Rallo 1984, p. 14, and Gambier 1990, p. 38.
21. By Urbani de Gheltof 1879, pp. 90–91, and often accepted as fact since. Most recently, Gemin and Pedrocco (1993, p. 479, no. 503) identified the subject in the *Woman with a Mandolin* as one of Tiepolo's daughters.
22. Baldinucci 1681, p. 28: "Proprio pensiero e invenzione. Quindi, fatto a capriccio o di fantasia, cioè di proprio pensiero e invenzione."
23. Half-length images of the Madonna and Child are not considered here because their iconic representation by Tiepolo is based on a centuries-old unchanging tradition.
24. Mariuz 1982, pl. 28.
25. See Washington, D.C., 1983, nos. 26, 28, 32.
26. Gemin and Pedrocco 1993, p. 344, no. 255.
27. See, for example, Washington, D.C., 1983, nos. 45–51.
28. Knox 1975b, p. 148.
29. See Gorizia 1985, pp. 111–73, nos. 41–80.
30. On Algarotti's friendship with Tiepolo, see Levey 1986, pp. 125–41.
31. Algarotti 1763a (1963 ed., p. 22): "il Tiepolo che vive tuttavia, pittore universale e di fecondissima immaginativa, che col fare paolesco ha saputo unire quello del Castiglione, di Salvator Rosa e de' più bizzarri pittori: ogni cosa condito con un'amenità di tinte e con una disinvoltura di pennello indicibile."
32. Algarotti 1763b (1963 ed., p. 105).
33. For a reproduction of this print, see Gorizia 1985, p. 32.
34. In 1636 the prince of Liechtenstein commissioned Ribera to execute a series of twelve philosophers. See New York 1992, nos. 35–40. For philosopher portraits by Giordano, see Ferrari and Scavizzi 1992, vol. 2, pp. 471–78, figs. 85–103.
35. See, for instance, *Old Man with a Divided Fur Cap* and *Bearded Man Wearing Velvet Cap with Jewel Clasp*, reproduced in White and Boon 1970, p. 208, no. 265, p. 264, no. 313.
36. On the influence of Rembrandt and Castiglione on Tiepolo's philosophers, see Knox 1970.
37. Algarotti 1764–65, vol. 6, p. 63.
38. See Philadelphia 1971, nos. E15, E19, M12.
39. See, for example, L. Simonneau's prints after Le Brun in *Livre de portraiture* (before 1727). For the context of Le Brun's lectures and their influence, see Montagu 1994.
40. For a short history of physiognomy in art, see Baltrušaitis 1957, pp. 8–46.
41. Algarotti 1762 (1972 ed. p. 201).
42. Zanetti 1733, quoted in London 1994, p. 180.
43. Liotard was not admitted to the French Academy in the 1740s because his style was considered too close to the truth. See Loche and Roethlisberger 1978, p. 83.
44. *Nuova veneta gazzetta*, 20 March 1762, quoted in Haskell 1963, p. 253 n. 2. See also Adriano Mariuz, "Giambattista Tiepolo: 'Painting's True Magician,'" n. 19, this publication.

42. The Blessed Laduina (Beata Laduina)

42. The Blessed Laduina
(*Beata Laduina*)
Doc. 1741
65 × 48 cm (25¾ × 19 in.)
Inscribed on reverse of canvas: 1741 Fu fatta dal Sig . . . Batta Tiepolli Insigne Pittore Veneziano, La Beata Laduina
Stanley Moss and Company, Inc.

The *Beata Laduina* represents the Blessed Lydwina of Schiedam (1380–1433), a Dutch woman whose faith had already generated a cult following in her lifetime.[1] At sixteen the holy Laduina suffered an accident while ice-skating. Her slight injury worsened, and she spent the rest of her life in agony, which she bore without complaint. After her death her body, distorted as the result of years of sickness, was miraculously restored to its former beauty.

Tiepolo represented Laduina in the double guise of a young girl wrapped in winter clothing, possibly as she appeared before her accident, and as the faithful sufferer at peace with herself. There are no attributes to associate her with Laduina, who was rarely portrayed in Italian art, and we would assume that she is a contemporary Venetian beauty were it not for the inscription that identifies her. Rather than portray her with the sores of her affliction, Tiepolo represented a contemporary young woman whose spirituality is embodied in her beauty. Unlike Tiepolo's somewhat more loosely painted ideal beauties from the 1750s, the *Beata Laduina* exhibits the tighter brushwork typical of his work of the 1740s. No documents exist to identify the patron for this picture. The subject of Laduina is esoteric, but the depiction of a saintly person accepting the example of the suffering of Christ reflects a survival of Counter-Reformation subject matter. In fact, Tiepolo's half-length figure is reminiscent of seventeenth-century paintings of suffering saints. Such traditional representations persisted into the eighteenth century and were made popular in Venice by Tiepolo's older contemporary Giambattista Piazzetta.

DDG

Note

1. Her cult was officially recognized by the Catholic Church in 1890. On Lydwina, see *Butler's Lives of the Saints* 1956, vol. 2, pp. 95–98. Biographies of her were written by John Brugman and Thomas à Kempis. See *Acta Sanctorum*, April, vol. ii.

PROVENANCE:
Collection Cristoforo Benigno Crespi, Milan (by 1900–1914; sale, Galerie Georges Petit, Paris, 4 June 1914, lot 86); F. Kleinberger and Co., New York (1914–18; sale, American Art Association, New York, 23 January 1918, lot 37); Collection François Ralston Welsh, Nirvana, Devon, Pennsylvania (1918–38; sale, Parke-Bernet, New York, 25–27 May 1938, lot 256); William J. Calhoun, New York (1938–44; sale, Parke-Bernet, New York, 17 February 1944, lot 73); private collection (sale, Christie's, London, 24 February 1967, lot 124); private collection, New York (sale, Christie's, London, 27 November 1970, lot 23); private collection, Stamford, Connecticut (1973–80)

REFERENCES:
Venturi 1900, pp. 185–86; Sack 1910, pp. 99, 172, no. 187; Molmenti 1911, p. 113; Margel 1914, p. 103; Morassi 1962, p. 27, fig. 427; Pallucchini 1968, p. 106, no. 141; Gemin and Pedrocco 1993, p. 340, no. 250

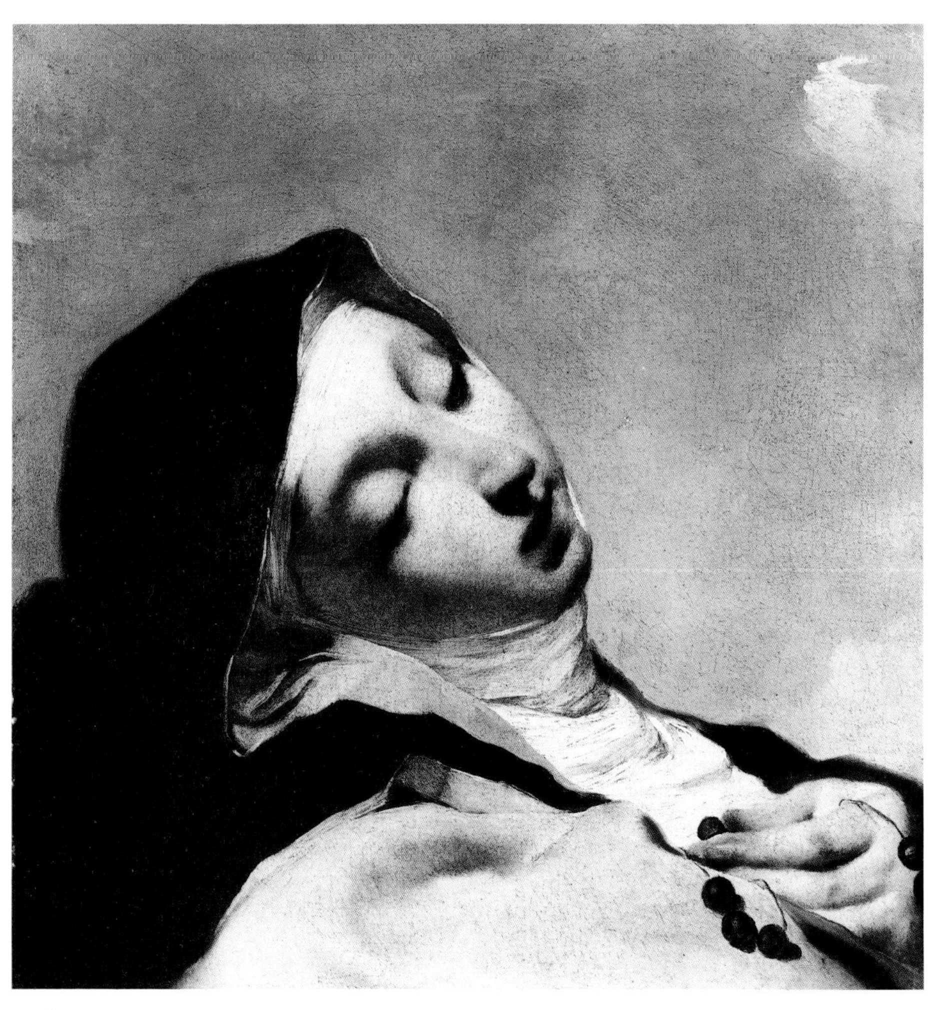

Fig. 88. Detail, Giambattista Piazzetta. *Saint Teresa in Ecstasy*. Oil on canvas. Nationalmuseum, Statens Konstmuseer, Stockhom

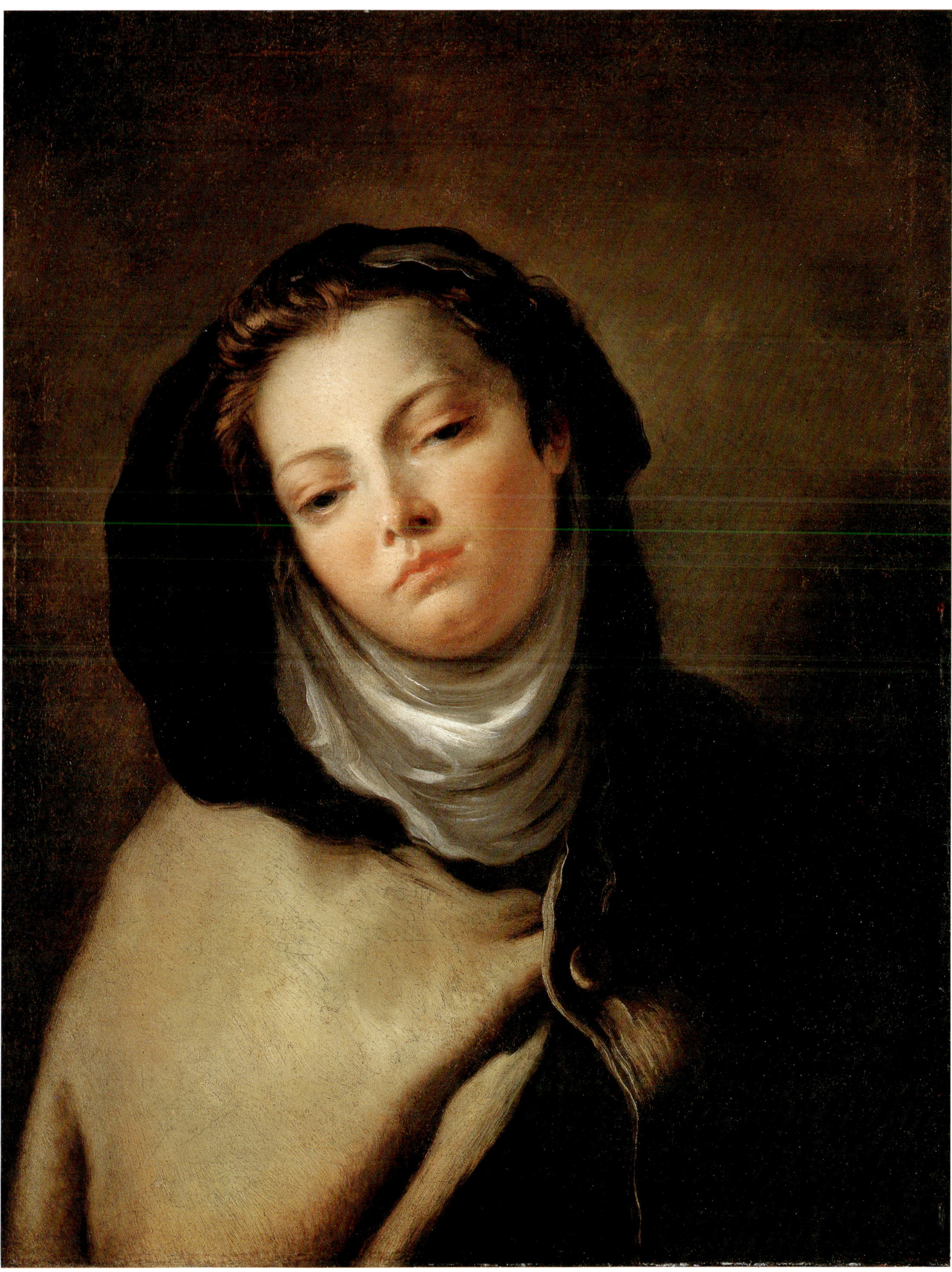

43. *Antonio Riccobono*

43. Antonio Riccobono
Ca. 1743
102 × 89 cm (40¼ × 35⅛ in.)
Pinacoteca dell'Accademia dei Concordi, Rovigo

Antonio Riccobono (1541–1599) was a distinguished professor from Rovigo who held the chair in Eloquence at the University of Padua. His posthumous portrait belongs to a series of pictures commissioned from various Venetian artists, including Giambattista Piazzetta, Giambattista Pittoni, and Tiepolo, that commemorate celebrated members of the Accademia dei Concordi in Rovigo.[1] The canon Ludovico Campo negotiated the transactions for the commissions, which began in 1740. On the evidence of a letter mentioning the lateness of its delivery, Tiepolo's painting was probably finished in 1743.[2] This date accords with the style of the picture, whose vibrant color and brushwork typify Tiepolo's production during the 1740s. Riccobono is shown at his desk, turning toward the viewer, who seems to have interrupted his reading. Although the sitter's appearance was known from a sixteenth-century engraving (fig. 89), Tiepolo appropriated from that work only the beard, the receding hairline, and the fur-trimmed robe characteristically worn by scholars. In other respects the portrayal is conceived as a contemporary likeness, informed by a deep understanding of portrait traditions. From local sixteenth-century precedents—especially the paintings of Titian—Tiepolo took over the use of the three-quarter-length figure turned toward the viewer, and he obviously emulated Veronese's lively brushwork and color. The convention of the scholar portrayed in the act of reading or writing at his desk remained fashionable throughout the seventeenth century, examples by van Dyck and Rembrandt being especially pertinent here (Tiepolo was an avid student of Rembrandt's prints). Tiepolo's dependence on earlier practice was a liberating factor, for he did not merely imitate his models but reinterpreted them. His depiction of Riccobono in an active contrapposto pose, for example, animates a traditional formula, lends it originality, and brings it up-to-date.

DDG

Notes

1. On the commission and other portraits, see Puppi [1972].
2. Ibid.

PROVENANCE:
Ludovico Campo, Rovigo (until 1765); Accademia dei Concordi, Rovigo

REFERENCES:
Bartoli 1793, p. 14; Urbani de Gheltof 1833, p. 187; Biscaccia 1846, p. 64; Fogolari 1908, p. 115; Molmenti 1909, pp. 107–8; Sack 1910, p. 99; Fogolari 1913, p. 19; Tarchiani in Florence 1922, p. 179; Ojetti 1927, p. 226; Morassi 1943, p. 27; Venice 1946, p. 200; Venice 1951, pp. 77–78; Morassi 1955a, pp. 146–47; Valcanover 1956, p. 242; Morassi 1962, p. 47; Valcanover 1962, pp. 9–10, pl. 28; Pallucchini 1968, no. 169; Venice 1969b, p. 282; Pallucchini 1971, p. 336; Udine 1971, no. 51; Puppi [1972]; Ruggeri 1972, pp. 95–96, no. 69; Saint Petersburg 1973, pp. 42–43; Romagnolo 1975, p. 1; Zava Boccazzi 1979, p. 158; Romagnolo 1981, pp. 192–94; Paris 1982, no. 45; Fantelli and Lucco 1985, p. 94; Levey 1986, p. 18; Gemin and Pedrocco 1993, p. 343, no. 254

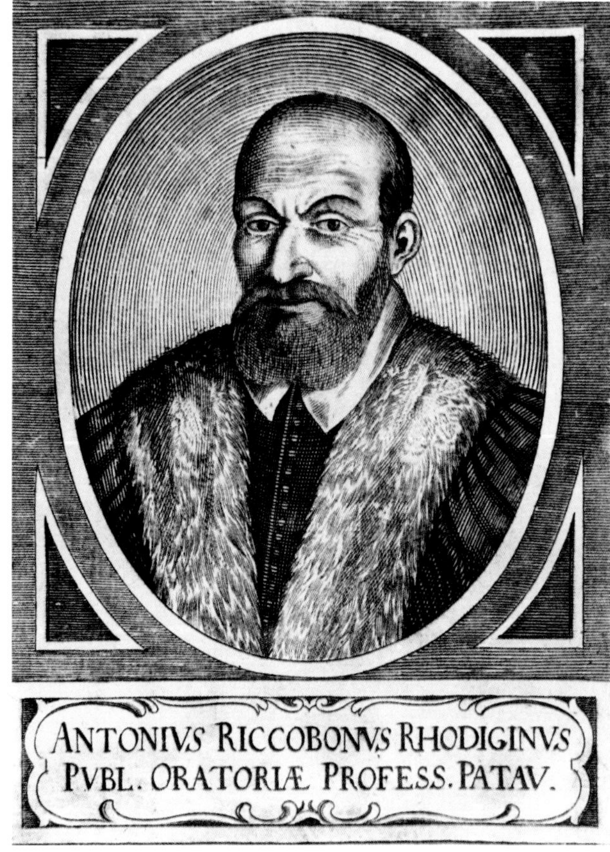

Fig. 89. Anonymous. *Portrait of Antonio Riccobono*. Engraving. Pinacoteca dell'Accademia dei Concordi, Rovigo

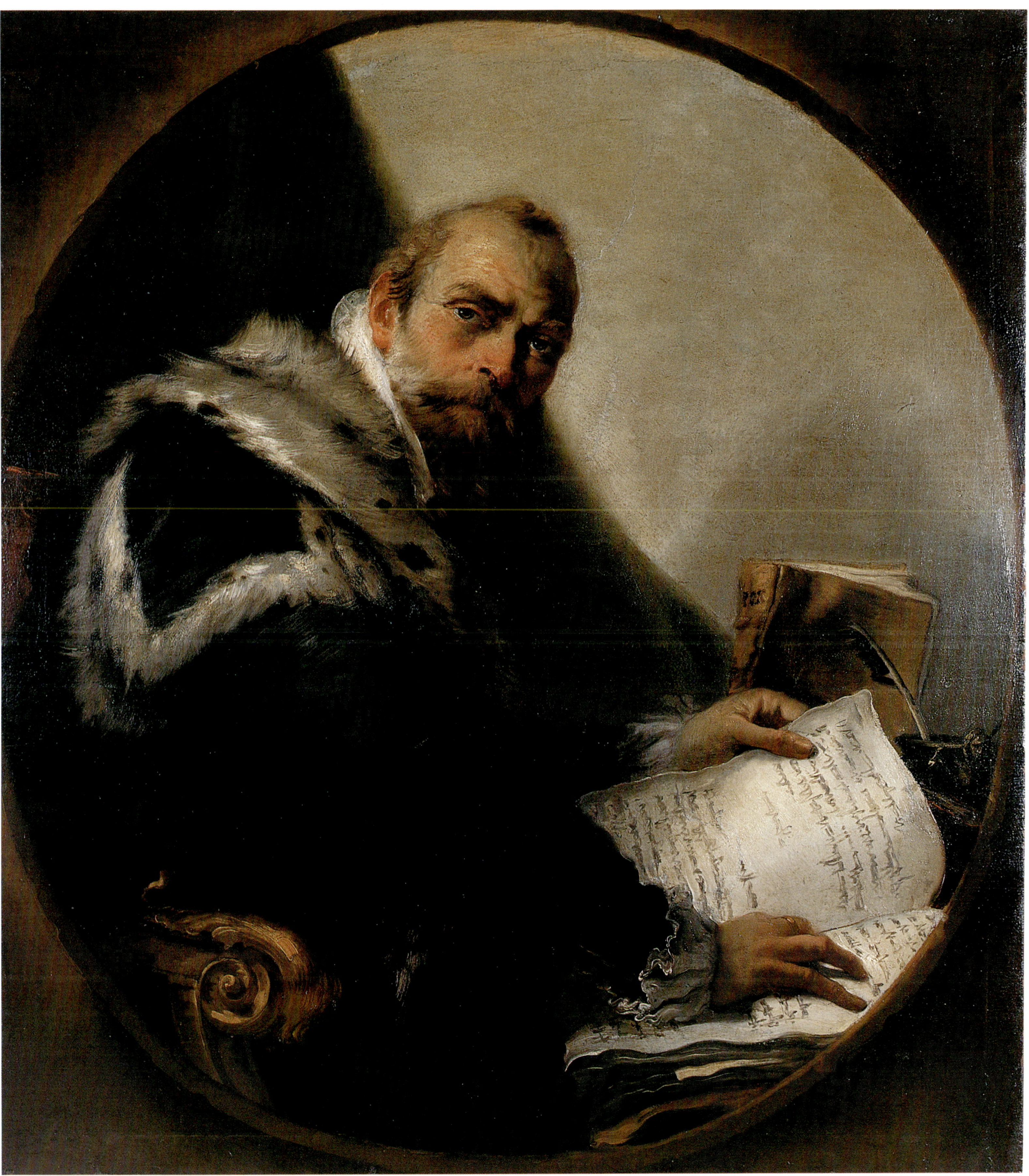

44. Boy with a Book (Portrait of Lorenzo Tiepolo)

44. Boy with a Book (Portrait of Lorenzo Tiepolo)
Ca. 1743
48.3 × 39.1 cm (19 × 15⅜ in.)
New Orleans Museum of Art (61.87)

PROVENANCE:
Duke Visconti di Modrone, Milan; Count Alessandro Contini-Bonacossi, Florence (until 1932); Samuel H. Kress Foundation, New York (1932–53); Isaac Delgado Museum of Art, New Orleans (1953–61)

REFERENCES:
National Gallery of Art 1941, p. 195, no. 221; Kress Collection 1953, pp. 60–61; Morassi 1962, p. 33; Pallucchini 1968, p. 111, no. 173; Puppi [1972], pp. 131–33; Shapley 1973, vol. 3, pp. 142–43; Gemin and Pedrocco 1993, p. 344, no. 256; Raleigh 1994, pp. 245–47, no. 47

This character study represents Tiepolo's son Lorenzo (1736–1777), whose distinctive protruding ears and prominent widow's peak are known from paintings and drawings by his father.[1] The age of the sitter appears to be about seven or eight, which places the painting in the early to mid-1740s. The clear, sharp colors and controlled brushwork are characteristic of Tiepolo's paintings of this period and can be seen in his contemporary head studies and such portraits as the *Beata Laduina* (no. 42) and the *Antonio Riccobono* (no. 43). Like Riccobono, the boy turns toward the viewer as if interrupted while reading, holding the book open with his fingers. The laughing satyr represented on the clasp of the child's garment may constitute a lighthearted jest directed at the tradition of the serious philosopher portrait. Philosophers, including those painted by Tiepolo, were often depicted wearing furs and commemorative gold chains and staring at the viewer with open books before them. Lorenzo's devilish widow's peak and pointed ears lend to the air of mischievousness. On the other hand, the *Boy with a Book* may simply follow a tradition of casual representations of the Venetian artisan class at leisure. It is much like the drawings of single and paired half-length figures by Giambattista Piazzetta, who also used his family as models.[2]

The *Boy with a Book* proved popular in Tiepolo's time and inspired several inferior copies.[3]

DDG

NOTES

1. For reproductions of accepted portraits of Lorenzo, see Thiem 1993, figs. 1–7. Another version of the painting, published by Cailleux (in Paris 1952, no. 53), was identified as a portrait of Lorenzo.
2. See Washington, D.C., 1983, nos. 26, 28, 32.
3. A painting in a French private collection was published by Fiocco 1932, pp. 474–75. Another was published by Cailleux in 1952 (see note 1 above). A painting formerly in the Los Angeles County Museum of Art was published by Goering 1936, p. 31, pl. 33.

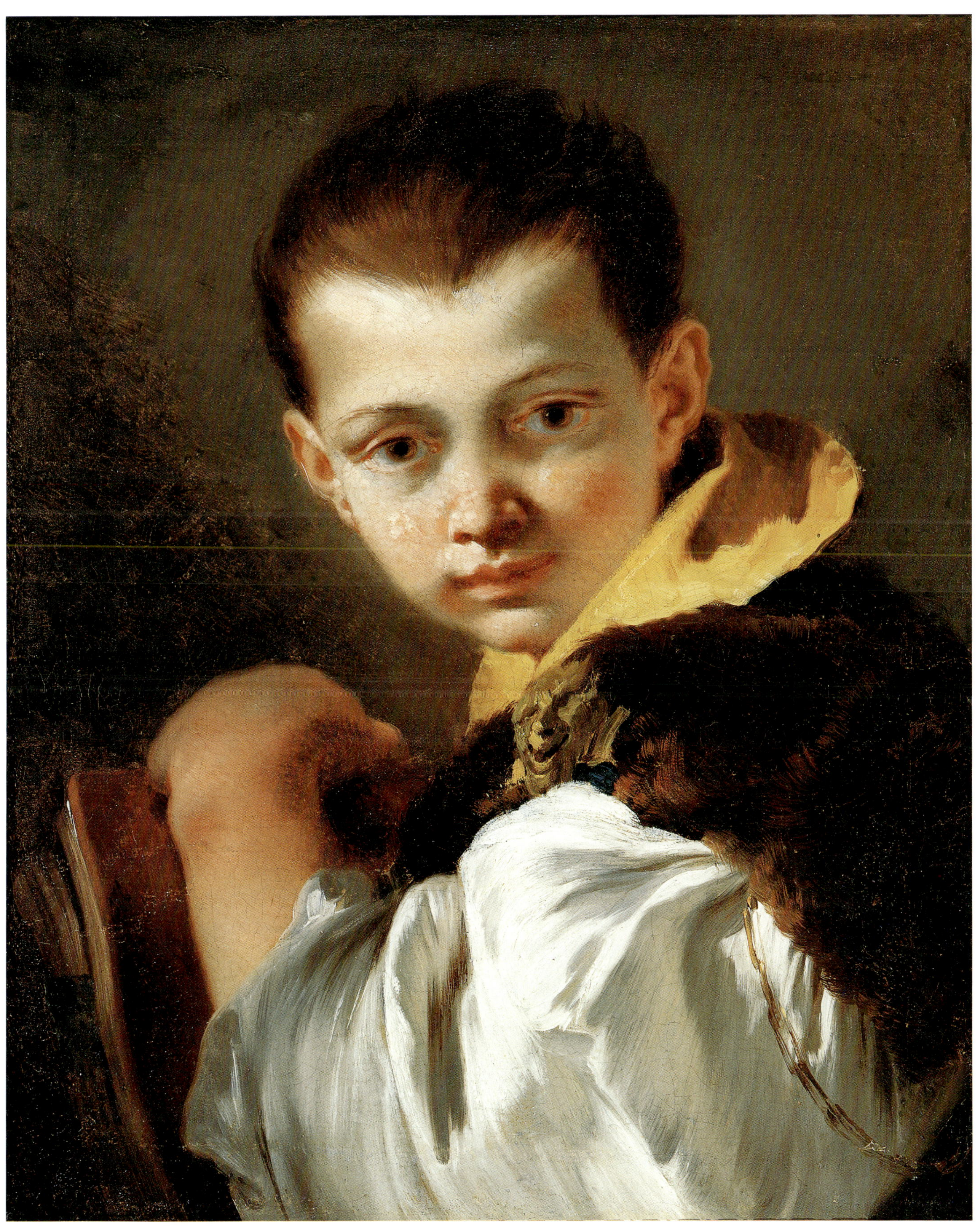

WOMEN IN FANCY DRESS

45a. Woman with a Mandolin
45b. Young Lady in a Tricorn Hat

45a. Woman with a Mandolin
Ca. 1755–60
92.1 × 74.9 cm (36¼ × 29½ in.)
The Detroit Institute of Arts, Gift of Mr. and Mrs. Henry Ford II (57.180)

45b. Young Lady in a Tricorn Hat
Ca. 1755–60
62 × 49 cm (24⅜ × 19⅜ in.)
Samuel H. Kress Collection, National Gallery of Art, Washington, D.C. (1952.5.77)

PROVENANCE, 45a:
Maurice de Talleyrand-Périgord, Duke de Dino, Paris (until 1937); Duchess de Talleyrand-Périgord, Paris and New York (from 1937); Henry Ford, New York (until 1957)

REFERENCES:
Richardson 1957–58; Morassi 1958, pp. 177–79; Morassi 1962, p. 10; Precerutti Garberi 1964, p. 257; Pignatti [1966], p. 211; Pallucchini 1968, p. 127, no. 251; Udine 1971, p. 140, no. 71; Levey 1986, p. 246; Gemin and Pedrocco 1993, p. 479, no. 504

PROVENANCE, 45b:
Pisa collection, Florence (their sale, 1938); Italico Brass, Venice (from 1938); Schaeffer Gallery, New York; Samuel H. Kress Collection (1948); National Gallery of Art, Washington, D.C. (1952)

REFERENCES:
Goering 1939, p. 154; Rome 1941, p. 43; Morassi 1943, p. 28; Morassi 1958, pp. 180, 185; Pallucchini 1960, p. 93; Morassi 1962, p. 67 (as Giandomenico); Pallucchini 1968, no. 252; Shapley 1979, vol. 1, pp. 440–41 (as Giandomenico); Paris 1982, no. 47; Barcham 1992, p. 118; Gemin and Pedrocco 1993, p. 479, no. 505; De Grazia and Garberson 1996, pp. 289–93

The *Woman with a Mandolin* and the *Young Lady in a Tricorn Hat* are among a small group of fancy-dress portraits of women attributable to Tiepolo and datable toward the end of the 1750s. They may have been destined for the collection of Empress Elizabeth of Russia.[1] It is unlikely that they formed a suite with two pendant paintings: the *Woman with a Parrot* in the Ashmolean Museum, Oxford (frontis., p. 254), and a lost composition of a woman in a fur that is known from a pastel copy by Lorenzo Tiepolo (fig. 83). In terms of their dimensions, compositions, and subject matter the *Woman with a Mandolin* and the *Young Lady in a Tricorn Hat* do not relate closely to the pendants, and the facture of each differs notably from that of the Ashmolean painting. In the *Woman with a Mandolin* sharply defined contours and carefully controlled brushwork replace the hazy contours and bravura execution of the Ashmolean picture. Although the *Young Lady in a Tricorn Hat* retains the nervous, rapid brushwork and indistinct contours that characterize the Ashmolean painting, it is set apart from the latter work by its subdued and subtle palette of various blacks and use of the back of the brush dragged across the surface to differentiate texture and color.

The variations in style between the *Woman with a Parrot*, whose autograph status has never been questioned, and the *Woman with a Mandolin* and *Young Lady in a Tricorn Hat* have led a number of critics to question the attribution of the Washington picture and one to doubt the Detroit painting. Although the popularity of Tiepolo's fancy-dress images of women encouraged his sons to make copies and versions of his paintings in this genre, the high quality of the Detroit and Washington pictures argues for Giambattista's authorship of both. Moreover, the same rapidly executed and skillful handling of the brushwork found in the *Young Lady in a Tricorn Hat* is seen in the incontestably autograph *Portrait of a Procurator (Daniele IV Dolfin)* (no. 46), and the model for the *Woman with a Mandolin* appears in other compositions of the 1750s by Tiepolo, most notably the frescoes of about 1757 at Villa Valmarana, near Vicenza (see figs. 44, 45).[2]

These pictures are not meant to be portraits in the conventional sense of likenesses of real people but are instead fanciful interpretations, or *capricci,* and specifically *capricci* in the well-established Venetian tradition of depictions of beautiful women, including courtesans. The woman playing her mandolin may be emblematic of Love, whose methods of seduction include using the power of music to enchant its victims. Her breast is bare and she is dressed in yellow, a color associated with courtesans. The young subject in a tricorn hat is dressed in carnival costume; she stares directly at the viewer with her fan held against her chin in what has been construed as a flirtatious gesture. Both women may be prostitutes or may simply be models posed as allegorical representations. Tiepolo's fanciful portraits deliberately defy interpretation precisely because they were painted *a capriccio*. Tiepolo chose to represent the theme of a beautiful woman loosely related to a pictorial tradition that engaged his imagination, and in his hands that subject became a means of displaying his painterly skill: in these works done *a capriccio* it is not the individual depicted but the convention, the composition, and the bravura brushwork that constitute the true subject.

DDG

NOTES

1. See Diane De Grazia, "Tiepolo and the 'Art' of Portraiture," above.
2. Gemin and Pedrocco 1993, pp. 438–41.

Detail, no. 45a

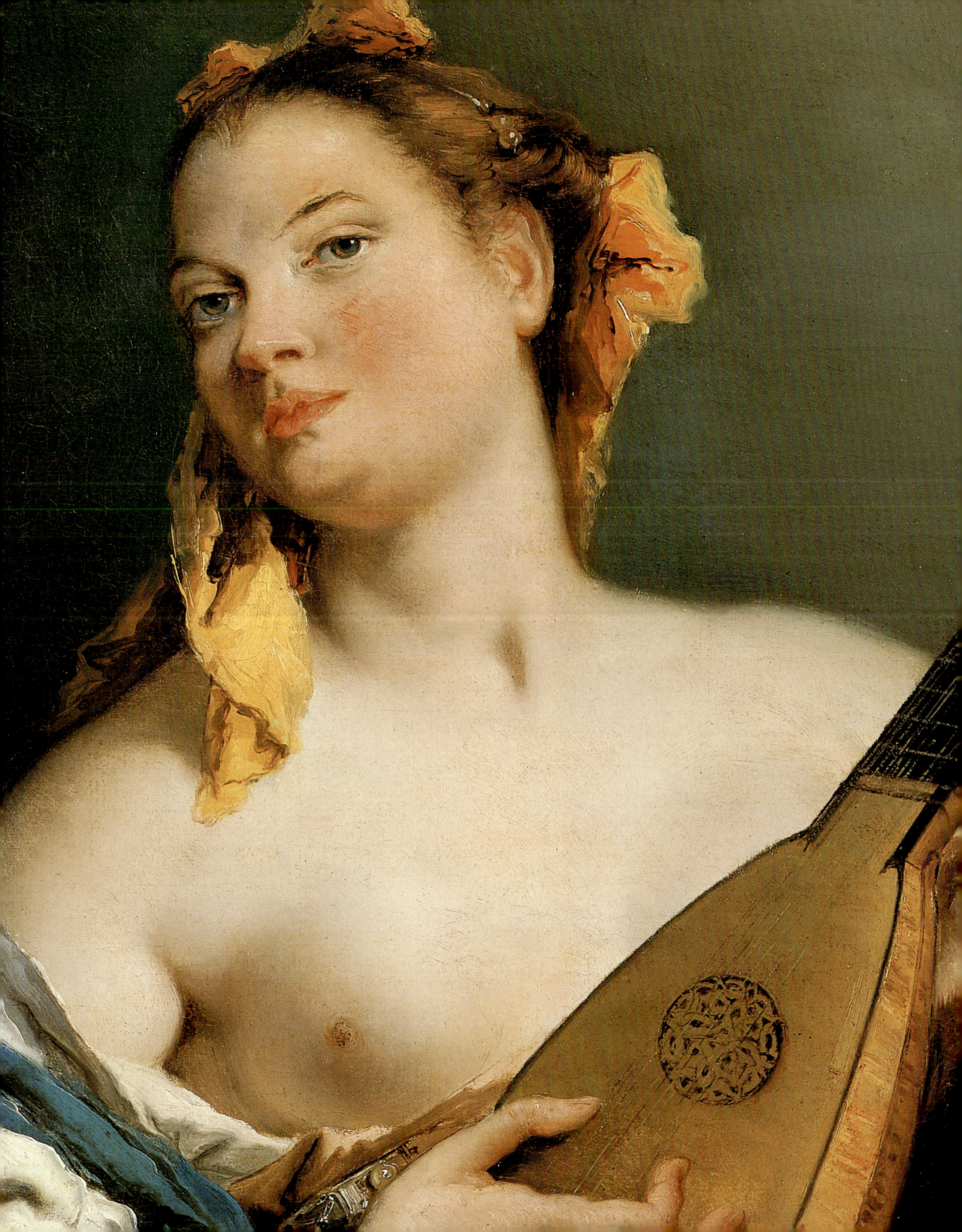

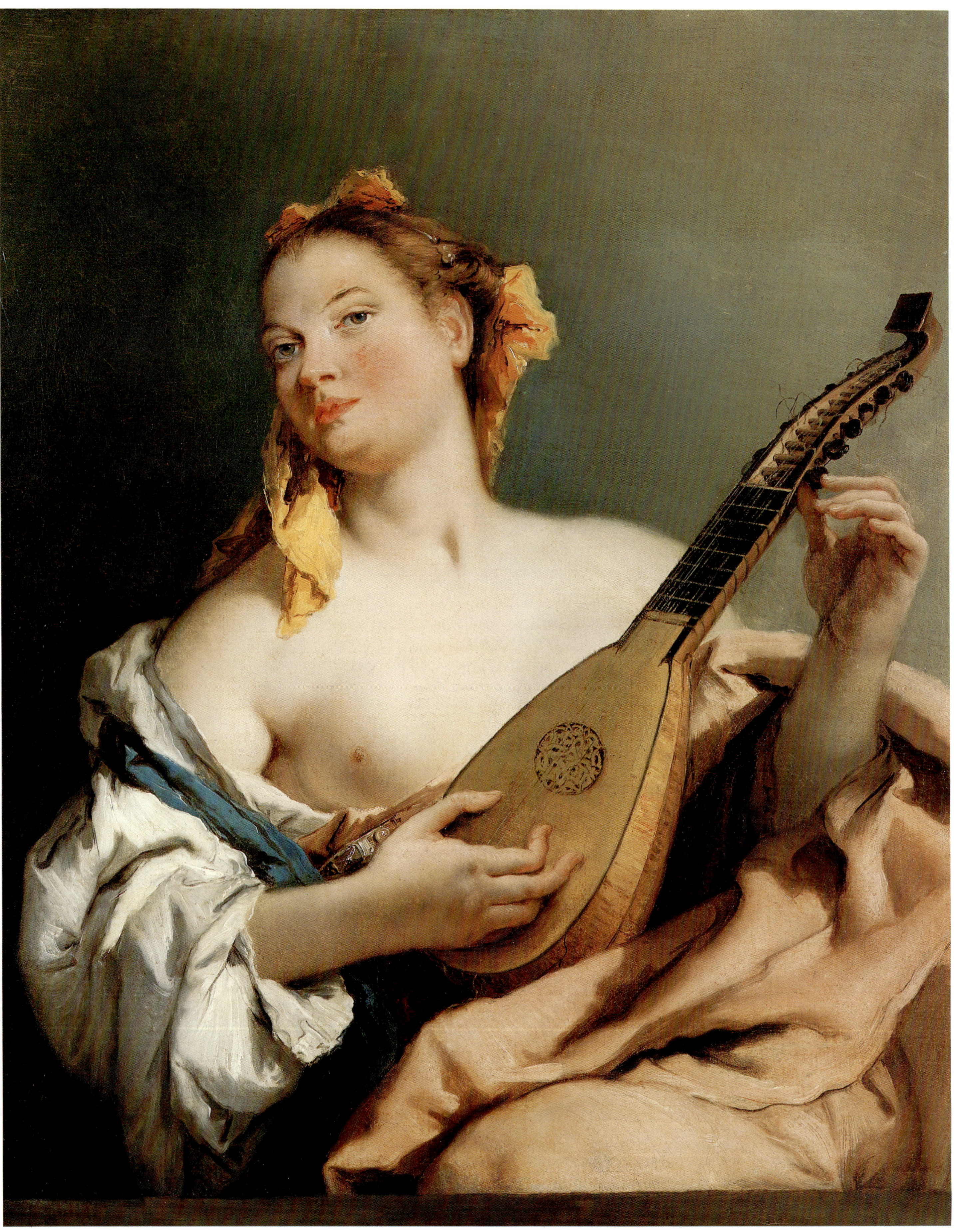

45a

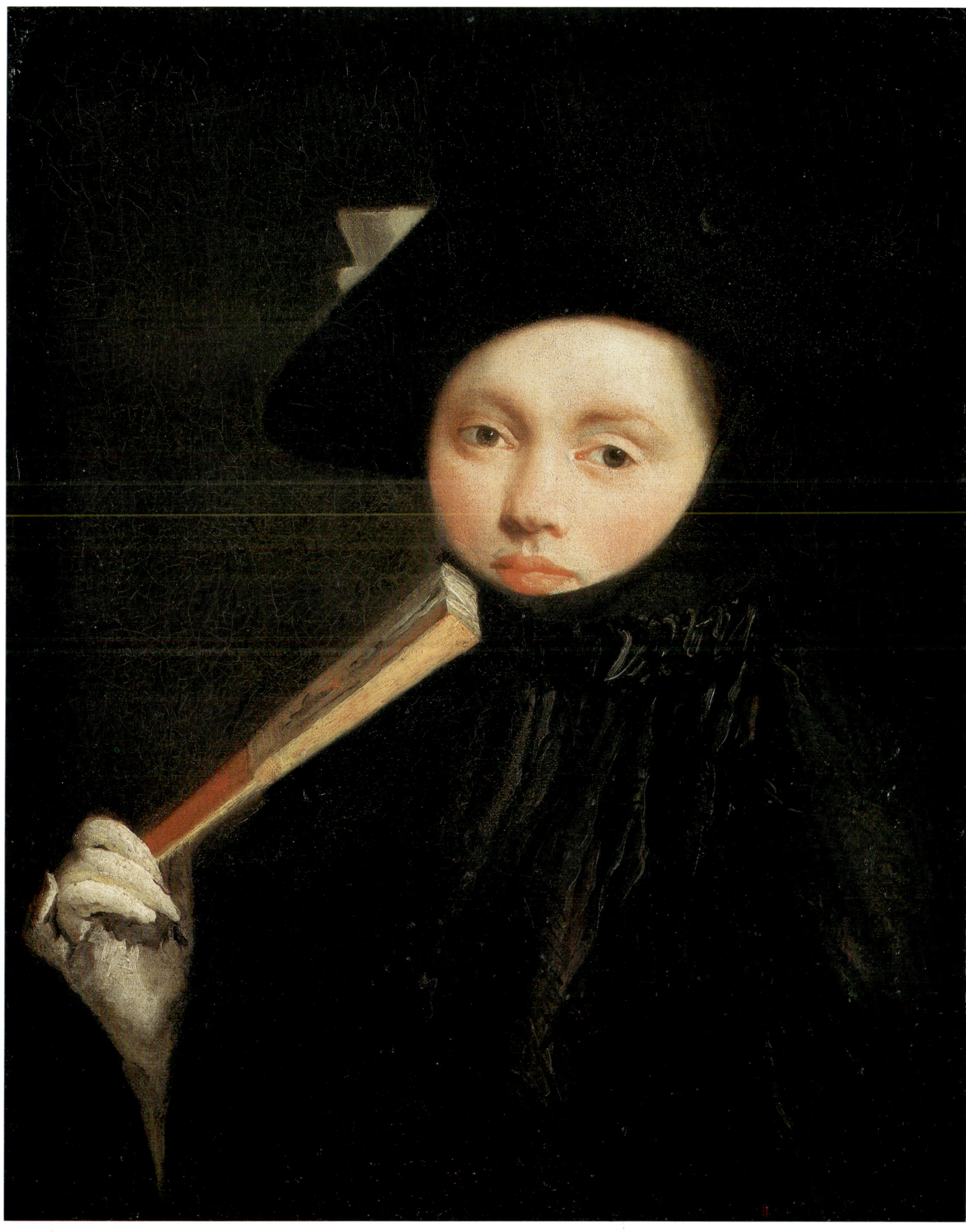

45b

46. Portrait of a Procurator (Daniele IV Dolfin)

***46. Portrait of a Procurator (Daniele IV Dolfin)**
Mid- to late 1750s
235 × 158 cm (92½ × 62¼ in.)
Pinacoteca della Fondazione Scientifica Querini Stampalia, Venice

PROVENANCE:
Cardinal Daniele Dolfin? (d. 1762), Ca' Dolfin, Venice; by descent, Ca' Dolfin (1762–98); by descent, Gasparo Lippomano, Ca' Dolfin (until 1854); by descent, Count Giovanni Querini Stampalia, Palazzo Querini Stampalia, Venice (1854–68)

REFERENCES:
Molmenti 1909, p. 77; Sack 1910, pp. 98–99; Morassi 1943, p. 27; Pallucchini 1947, p. 50, no. 95, pls. 57–58; Pignatti 1950, p. 218; Dazzi 1951; Morassi 1955a, pp. 145–46; Pallucchini 1960, pp. 43, 92; Levey 1961, pp. 140–41; Morassi 1962, p. 55; Pallucchini 1968, p. 114, no. 193; Udine 1971, p. 106; Dazzi and Merkel 1979, pp. 22, 86–87, no. 175; Gemin and Pedrocco 1993, pp. 134, 136, 406, no. 387; Mariuz in London 1994, p. 178; Venice 1995a, pp. 248–49, no. 58

The identity of Tiepolo's sitter has only recently become certain. Because the painting is part of the Querini Stampalia collection, he was once thought to be Giovanni Querini, a captain of the Venetian fleet and procurator of S. Marco. However, Pignatti proved that the features of Querini were not the same as those portrayed in this picture.[1] Later Dazzi and Merkel showed that the painting, along with the Ca' Dolfin at S. Pantalon, was inherited by Giovanni Querini Stampalia in 1854 from a collateral branch of the Dolfin family. This suggested that the sitter was a member of the Dolfin family, for which Tiepolo worked in the 1720s, painting his series of Roman history subjects (see no. 12a–g) and decorating the Arcivescovado (Patriarchal Palace) in Udine. As first proposed by Dazzi and Merkel and supported by Mariuz,[2] he must be Daniele IV Dolfin (1656–1729), called Girolamo, one of the most distinguished heroes of the Venetian *armata*. As head of the Venetian fleet, Dolfin defeated the Turks in numerous battles, including those at Athens (1687), Albania (1692), and Corfu (1701).[3] He was an ambassador for the Republic of Venice (to Germany in 1700 and to Poland in 1717), was elected senator in 1711, and became head of the Venetian navy and procurator of S. Marco in 1714. When he defeated the Turks at the battle of Metilino in 1690, he lost four fingers of his left hand.

Although posthumous, the likeness must be fairly trustworthy. Mariuz proposed convincingly that Tiepolo emphasized Dolfin's mutilated hand by placing it, gloved, at the very front of the composition on the plane closest to the viewer. Unlike Francesco Zugno, who depicted a complacent, puffy-faced Dolfin and identified him by a deformed left hand holding a letter and by a battleship in the background,[4] Tiepolo monumentalized and idealized the war hero, referring to his naval career with a captain's hat and a baton on the table to his left. Tiepolo accentuated the dignity, magnificence, and power of the man by placing him on a step that is almost like a pedestal, far above the spectator's viewpoint. Dressed magnificently in the procurator's red brocade and fur, with the hair of his wig flowing across his robe, Dolfin gazes down with authority. The bright red of the robe is emphasized by the neutral colors of the background, thrusting him forcefully into our space. The excited handling of the brush on the right sleeve, hair, and glove add an immediacy to the presentation, marking the *Procurator* as Tiepolo's masterpiece of portraiture.

The *Procurator* has been accepted as autograph by all authorities except Levey, who attributes the painting to Giandomenico Tiepolo. Some scholars have placed the picture in the late 1740s, prior to Giambattista's trip to Würzburg, but it probably dates to the mid- to late 1750s. The looseness of brushwork and the large areas of paint juxtaposed with forms broadly delineated by means of black strokes accord with the technique of other works of this period, especially Tiepolo's depictions of women in fancy dress (no. 45a, b). In 1759 Tiepolo was again working for the Dolfin in Udine, where together with Giandomenico he decorated the Oratorio della Purità for Cardinal Daniele Dolfin, who may have asked the artist to memorialize his illustrious ancestor.[5]

Memorial portraits were not unusual in eighteenth-century Venice. During his early career Tiepolo painted a group of them for the Cornaro family (see no. 3a, b) and one of Antonio Riccobono (no. 43). Many artists were required to paint commemorative portraits, but Tiepolo alone among his contemporaries could make these posthumous likenesses come alive.

DDG

NOTES

1. Pignatti 1950, p. 218.
2. Mariuz in Venice 1995a, p. 248.
3. On the extraordinary life of Daniele IV Dolfin, see Dolfin 1924, pp. 171–75.
4. Pignatti 1950, p. 216, fig. 1 (as Giovanni Raggi). The painting was once given to Nogari and also to Pietro Longhi and was attributed by Dazzi and Merkel (1979, p. 87, no. 176) to Zugno.
5. Gemin and Pedrocco 1993, pp. 470–71, nos. 490–92.

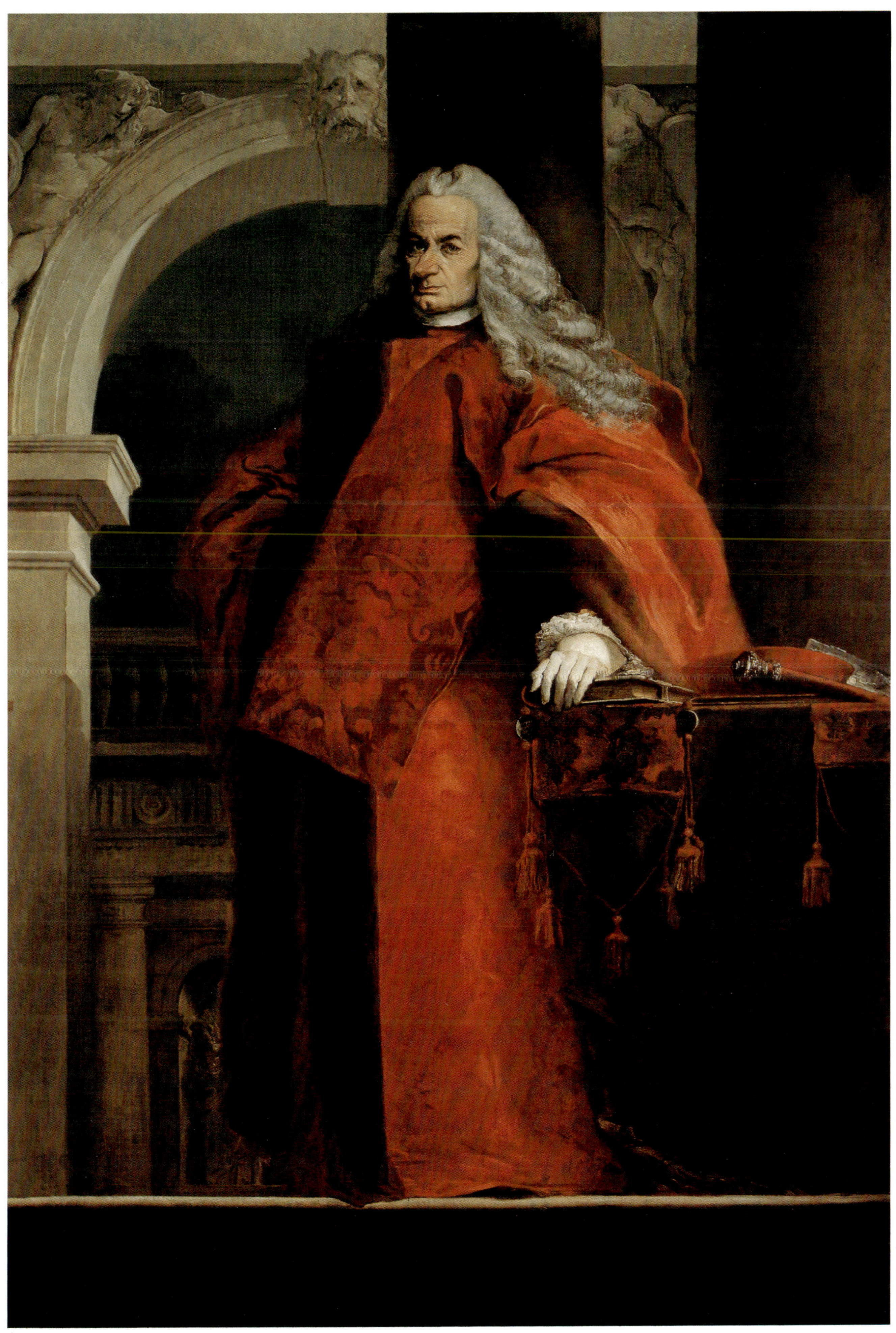

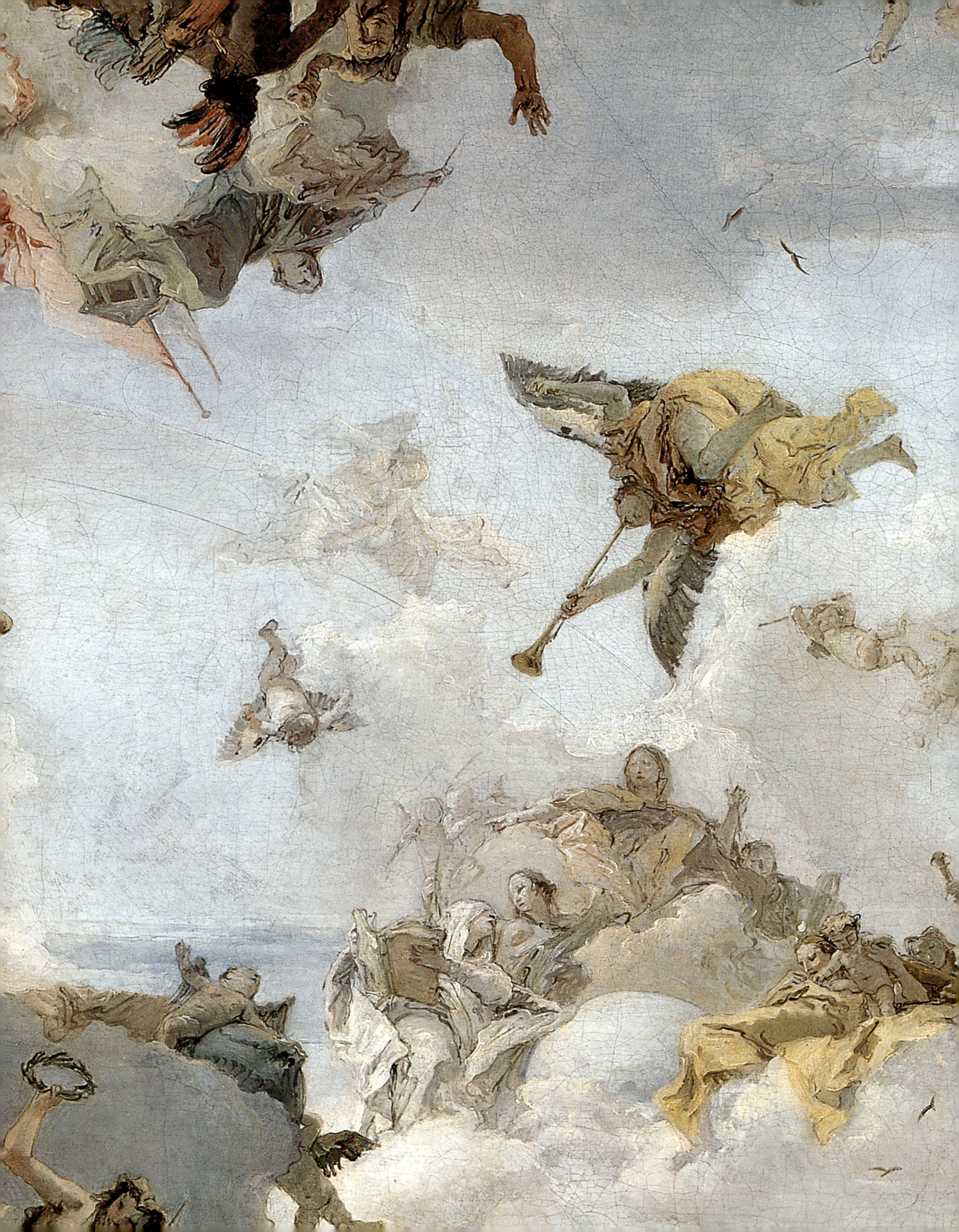

The Fiery Poetic Fantasy of Giambattista Tiepolo

KEITH CHRISTIANSEN

"There is but one way for the moderns to become great, and perhaps unequalled; I mean, by imitating the ancients." With these words from his polemical tract written in Dresden in 1755, Johann Winckelmann signaled the advent of a new age and a new art, whose traits of "noble simplicity and calm grandeur" were inspired by the example of ancient Greece.[1] The prophet of this new style, which was to culminate thirty years later in Jacques Louis David's austere masterpiece the *Oath of the Horatii*, was Winckelmann's friend and compatriot Anton Raphael Mengs. In 1761 Mengs painted on the vault of Cardinal Albani's villa outside Rome a *Parnassus* with impeccable lineage: the pose of the fleshy, effeminate Apollo was conspicuously patterned on that of the *Apollo Belvedere*—a work that sent Winckelmann into paroxysms of admiration—and the rosy-cheeked, brightly clad Muses were, with no less artistic ostentation, appropriated from Raphael's celebrated fresco in the Vatican. To modern eyes the *Parnassus* is, at best, an equivocal performance, but to the minds of Mengs's contemporaries its clarity and restraint announced the death of those flights of the imagination epitomized by Tiepolo's illusionistic ceilings and fancifully staged mythological scenes. Mengs's biographer, Giuseppe d'Azara, pointedly praised the *Parnassus* for its rejection of strong foreshortening and of *di sotto-in-sù* viewpoint. Winckelmann declared as a sort of epitaph that Tiepolo's work, once seen, is forgotten, while that of Mengs remains forever.[2]

As fate would have it, the very year Mengs completed his *Parnassus*, Tiepolo was putting the last touches on the vast ceiling in the Villa Pisani at Strà (fig. 116), a work that, in its depiction of figures hurtling vertiginously through a silvery empyrean, is the antithesis of Mengs's art. Once these projects were finished, both men transferred their seats of activity to Spain, where they were employed by Charles III to decorate the royal palace. Tiepolo's reputation was then at its peak, but the current of fashion was running with the nascent Neoclassical movement, and after he died in 1770, Mengs was called on to help replace the altarpieces Tiepolo had carried out for the royal foundation at S. Pascual Baylon (nos. 40, 41).

Detail, *Apotheosis of the Pisani Family*, no. 52

It is difficult not to see in this posthumous rejection of the most successful and productive career since those of Bernini and Rubens a foretaste of Tiepolo's critical fate: to be judged by standards that have little to do with his art.[3] Echoes of Winckelmann's verdict can still be heard today among those who find Tiepolo's work superficial, facile, and, in its emulation of the paintings of Paolo Veronese, derivative. Such judgments should carry no weight, for they overlook the real animating forces of his art, which were concerned less with a sense of high moral purpose or truth to nature than with the artist's powers of invention and the exaltation of the imagination. From start to finish Tiepolo's painting is an affirmation of what the seventeenth-century apologist of Venetian art Carlo Ridolfi summed up in the term *pittoresco*, and if we are to do the work justice, we must begin by attempting to understand the sources of its inspiration and to explore the prominence it gives to imagination and fantasy. And then we must trace the manner in which these elements shape the appearance and very facture of his paintings.

Tiepolo's imagination was nourished by a close familiarity with art of the recent past rather than of Greek or Roman antiquity. He was brought up on Venetian painting—above all that of Tintoretto and Veronese—but he was also an avid student and collector of prints, notably those of Stefano della Bella, Salvator Rosa, Castiglione, and Rembrandt.[4] This interest in prints was greatly facilitated by his friendship with the internationally connected publisher, engraver, and print dealer Anton Maria Zanetti the Elder, who promoted Tiepolo's etchings, publishing his *Capricci* in 1743 and 1749.[5] Acknowledgment of the importance of these artists to Tiepolo recurs like a litany in modern discussions of his graphic work, but it is necessary to insist on the fact that past art, whether local or foreign (and in Venice, all non-Venetian art was viewed as foreign), was a liberating rather than a constraining force: something to be varied and played upon with a freedom and detachment that is alternatively serious or piquantly irreverent.

This is true even in the case of Veronese's work—the lens through which Tiepolo's achievement was seen. In a picture such as the sumptuous *Finding of Moses* (no. 16a) the fantastically attired and no less fantastically attenuated figures—as

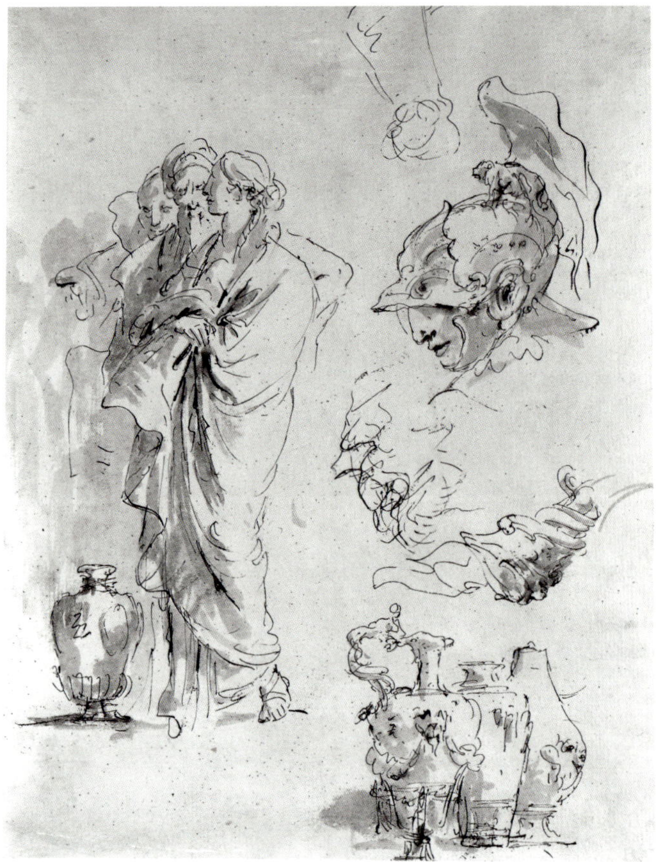

Fig. 90. *Studies of Figures and Vases*. Pen and ink and wash. Victoria and Albert Museum, London (D.1825.68-1885)

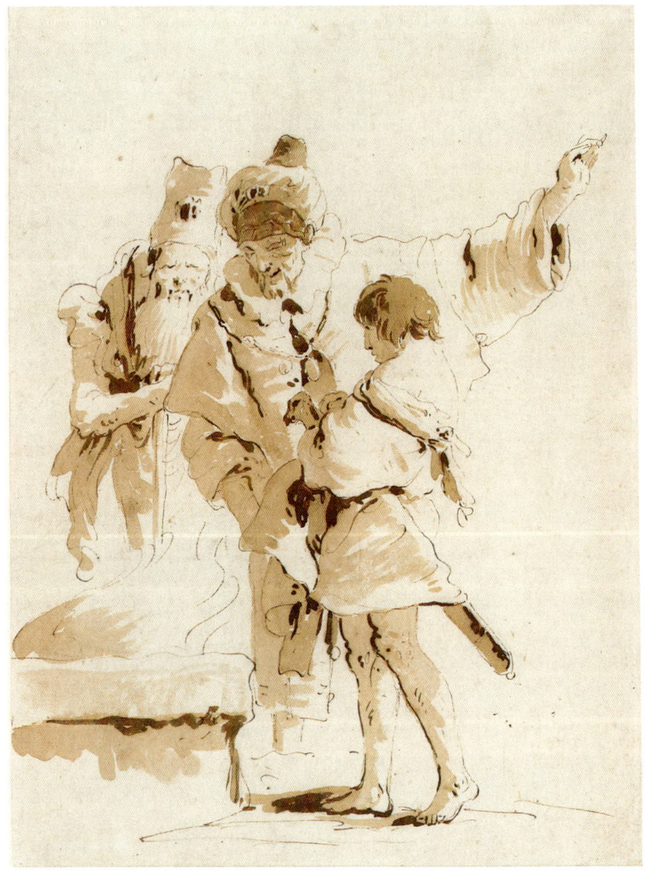

Fig. 91. *Scherzo di Fantasia: Two Standing Orientals and a Standing Youth*. Pen and ink and wash over black chalk. The Metropolitan Museum of Art, New York; Rogers Fund, 1937 (37.165.13)

overbred as their pet dogs—constitute a sophisticated parody of Veronesian opulence and refinement (see fig. 41), while the sixteenth-century artist's ceremonial approach to subject matter is wittily lampooned by the insertion of an all-too-actual infant Moses, his upside-down face contorted into an inconsolable howl.[6] The picture at once asserts its mastery of a past idiom and makes elegant jest of the eighteenth-century fashion for Veronese's work[7] and Tiepolo's own emerging reputation as the new Veronese—Veronese redivivus.[8] Tiepolo's patron, Andrea Corner, must have appreciated this grand and brilliantly executed, but nonetheless double-edged, "homage" to one of the protagonists of Venetian painting precisely along these lines. We are reminded that one of Tiepolo's most devoted friends and admirers, the dilettantish but worldly wise and highly regarded Francesco Algarotti, was not beyond proposing that the artist touch up a cheap copy of a work by Veronese he had managed to procure so that it would appear to be an autograph sketch or a *modello*.[9] The intent was to create a joke, or *scherzo*, of a kind later played out in Rome, in a different guise and a different, Neoclassical context, when Mengs deceived Winckelmann with a fake Roman fresco whose subject, Jupiter and Ganymede, was calculated to appeal to his friend's sexual inclinations.

Tiepolo's extraordinarily critical detachment—for wit derives its power from critical detachment as much as from a fertile imagination and insight into the foibles of its subject—came fully into its own in his drawn caricatures (see fig. 87) and his prints, the *Capricci* (no. 59a–j) and the *Scherzi* (no. 60a–w), the first series issued in 1743, the latter completed by 1757. The *Capricci* seem to have begun as personal variations on the prints of Castiglione (see fig. 122) and Rosa (see fig. 123), authors of perhaps the most remarkable graphic legacies of the seventeenth century. For Tiepolo, Castiglione's and Rosa's prints provided motifs and themes—soldiers and shepherds, philosophers and seers—that could be isolated and reconfigured to achieve novel visual effects, in most cases suggestive of no precise subject. (Tiepolo had already made a first step in this direction in some of his drawings for incidental portions of his large compositions [see fig. 90], subsequently developed in independent pen-and-ink wash studies gathered into albums [see fig. 91].) In the *Scherzi* his rumination on a vast, accumulated storehouse of artistic ideas produced independent fantasies on a spectrum of themes ranging from secularized Holy Families seemingly marooned during their flight into Egypt, lone satyr families indolently sitting among the fragments of a past civilization, a stray Punchinello expostulating to an assortment of mesmerized spectators, and, most prominently, groups of enigmatic figures in exotic dress involved in acts of magic and necromancy in the midst of animal bones, discarded weapons, and an array of Roman and Egyptian

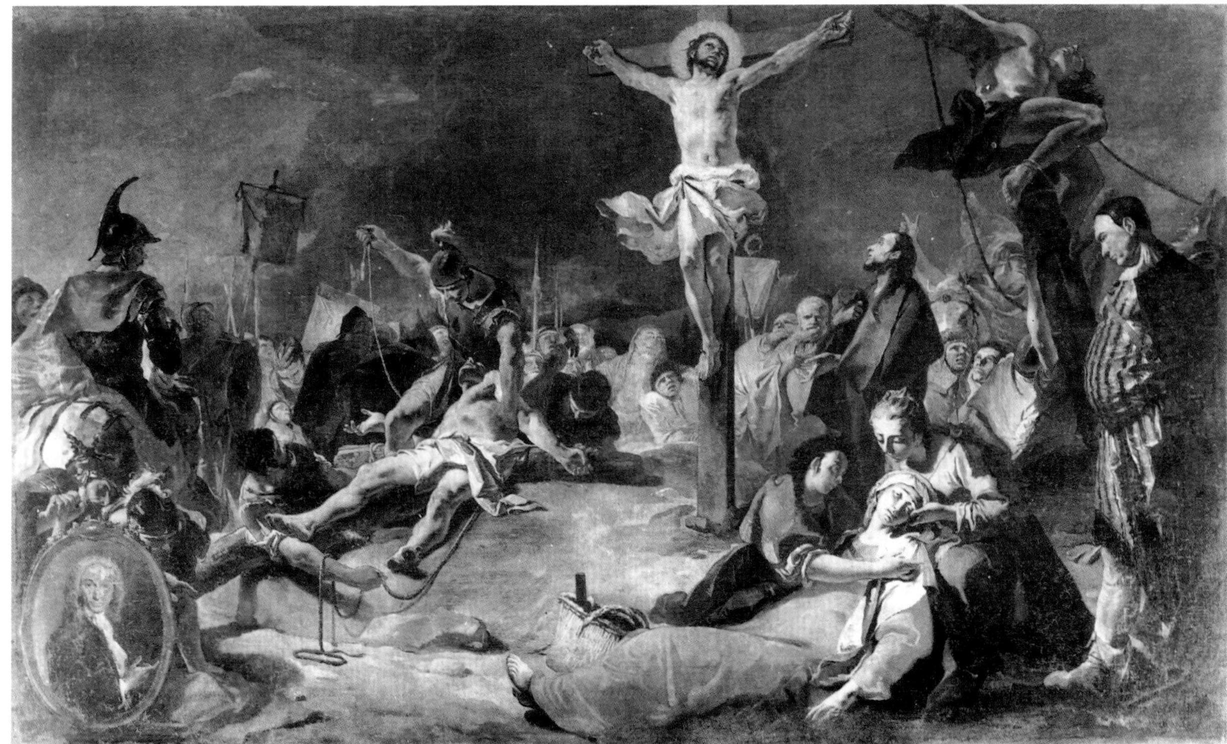

Fig. 92. *The Crucifixion*. Oil on canvas. S. Martino, Burano

ruins. (It is these last examples that most forcibly call to mind the *Caprichos* of Goya, who unquestionably knew and perhaps owned a set of Tiepolo's etchings.) Far from having a didactic intent, they are exercises in ambiguity, marvelously underscored by the disconnected and careworn stares of figures attending some illicit act of conjuring or sacrifice.

On one level the *Capricci* and *Scherzi* can be seen as the culminating expressions of Tiepolo's enduring fascination with the act of observing—embodied in bystanders whose presence in his religious and mythological paintings can sound a note of actuality or exoticism and who not infrequently create a mood of disconcerting ambivalence. These figures constitute one of the most modern and haunting aspects of Tiepolo's work and mark the point at which his eighteenth-century vision intersects with the pre-Romantic creations of Goya, reminding us of those clustered spectators in the *Disasters of War* who observe with vacant stares the most horrific crimes of violence. By the early 1720s we find the approach fully adumbrated in the remarkable *Crucifixion* at Burano (fig. 92). The composition is patently inspired by Tintoretto's dramatically charged canvas in the Scuola Grande di S. Rocco in Venice, but, unlike his predecessor, Tiepolo created a sense of malaise by including a complement of emotionless witnesses: in the background spectral figures who observe the action with detached fascination; in the foreground a potbellied Roman dressed in an absurd striped costume utterly incongruous with the first century A.D.—he is one of those darkly comic figures who appear consistently in Tiepolo's work—staring impassively at the holy women tending the inconsolable Virgin,

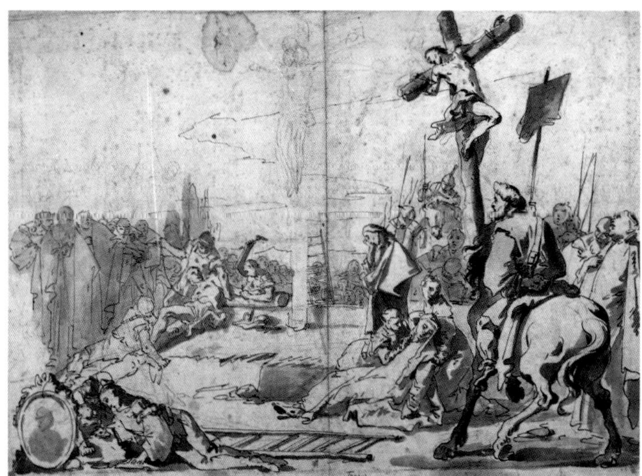

Fig. 93. *Study for the Crucifixion*. Pen and ink and wash with pencil. Graphische Sammlungen, Tiroler Landesmuseum Ferdinandeum, Innsbruck (I 541)

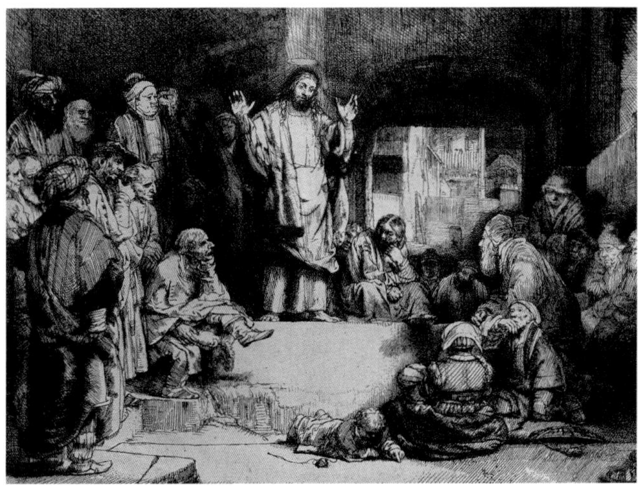

Fig. 94. Rembrandt van Rijn. *Christ Preaching ("Petite Tombe")*. Etching, burin, and drypoint. The Metropolitan Museum of Art, New York; The H. O. Havemeyer Collection, Bequest of Mrs. H. O. Havemeyer, 1929 (29.107.18)

whose grief-stricken face is turned toward the viewer. Emphasis on what might be thought a secondary element of the composition is even greater in the preliminary drawing (fig. 93). It may be that Tiepolo drew inspiration for this discursive approach from Rembrandt's etching *Christ Preaching* (fig. 94), in which he would also have discovered an interest in exotic costumes kindred to his own and a motif that recurs throughout his work—the oblivious child absorbed in some game or action.

The group of quizzical spectators Tiepolo introduced into the background of the S. Alvise *Crowning with Thorns* (no. 31) adds an unsettling note to the tragic drama of the picture that inspired his work, Titian's canvas for S. Maria delle Grazie in Milan (Musée du Louvre, Paris). And in the *Death of Hyacinth* (no. 23), Apollo's demonstrative gesture of lament over his dead companion is set off in disturbing fashion by a marble statue of a leering faun and an unexpected and disruptive group of exotic figures who seem to have wandered off a sheet of one of the *Scherzi*. Their presence effectively destroys any conceit of a mythic past and makes of Ovid's story a staged event—a fiction that calls attention not to some level of reality but to a process of artistic re-creation based on a profoundly ironic sensibility. The effectiveness of the allegories of the continents frescoed above the cornice of the stairwell at Würzburg (see no. 49) depends in no small degree on the sometimes disquieting, sometimes witty disjunction between primary and secondary figures, and between passive bystanders and areas of activity. Perhaps the most memorable example occurs in the depiction of America (fig. 95), in which a macabre assemblage of severed heads (one with an arrow piercing its cranium) is piled, unobserved, beneath a ridiculous-looking crocodile and behind a man in European dress—evidently an itinerant artist recording the customs of the New World; posed on the cornice, with a fashionably pointed shoe dangling over the edge and a drawing board in hand, this character (who is not present in the *modello*) is transfixed by the spectacle of a cannibalistic barbecue.[10]

As the above remarks suggest, a love of exotic costume—whether used to introduce an element of festivity or strangeness (what contemporaries referred to as *bizzarria*) or simply to add another dimension to the story—is an intrinsic part of Tiepolo's imagination: one well documented in his numerous

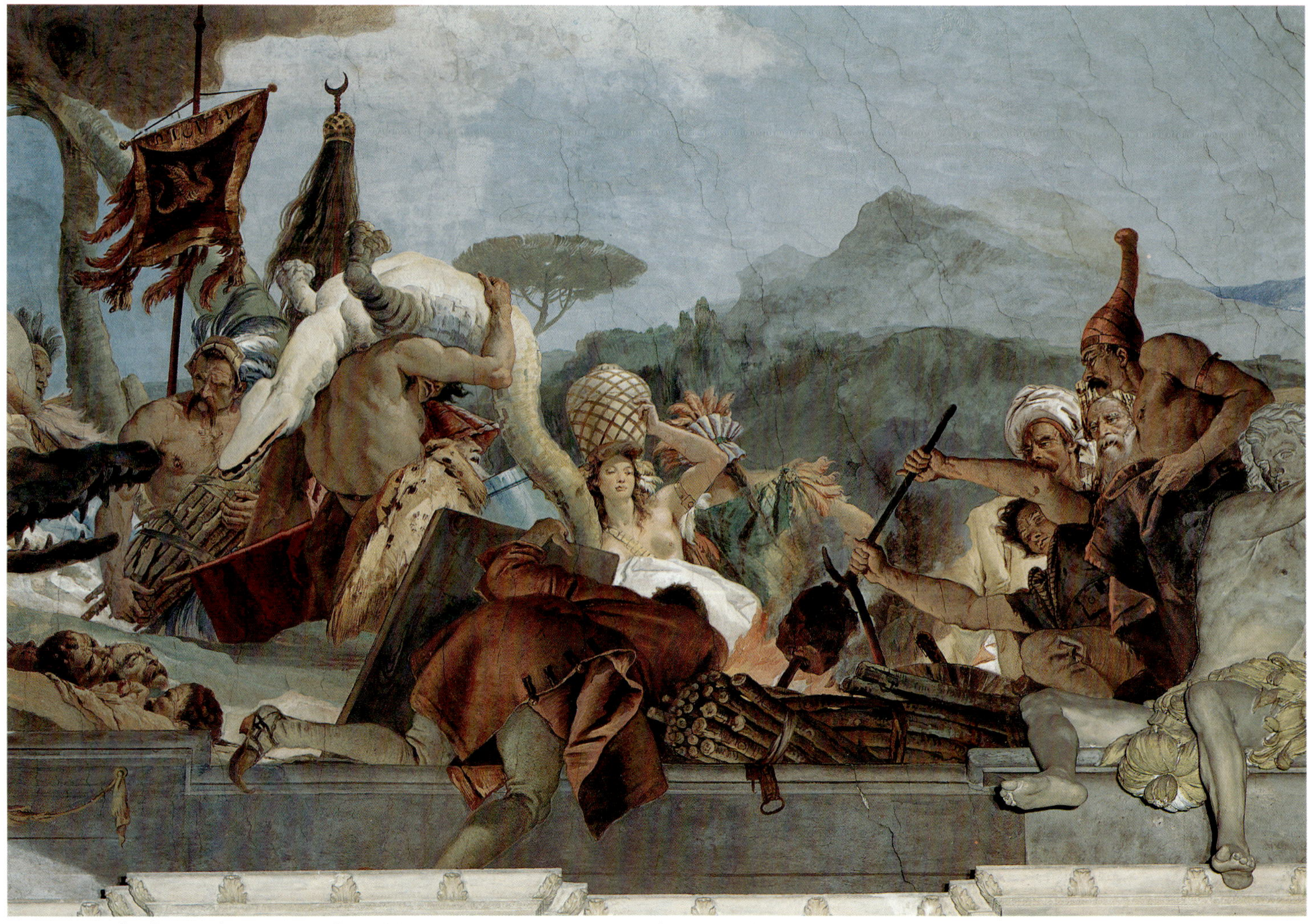

Fig. 95. Detail, *Allegory of America: Apollo and the Four Continents*. Fresco. Residenz, Würzburg

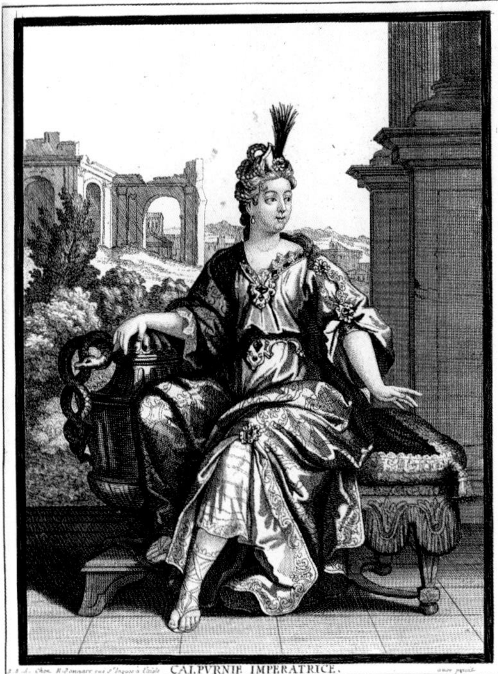

Fig. 96. N. Bonnart. *The Empress Calpurnia, Plate 126 from an Album of 146 Costume Plates, Dated 1683–1695*. Engraving. The Metropolitan Museum of Art, New York; The Elisha Whittelsey Collection, The Elisha Whittelsey Fund, 1957 (57.559.5)

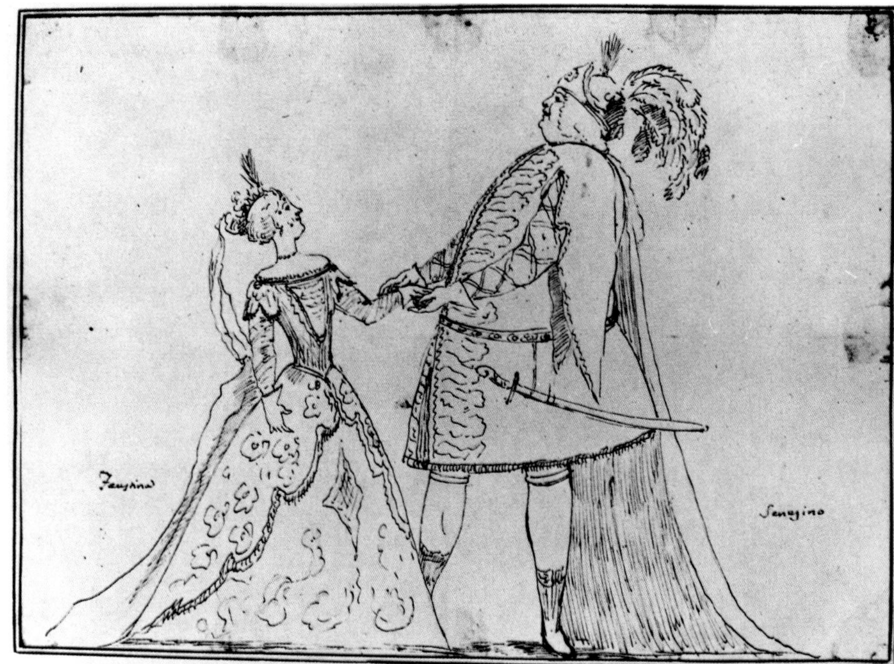

Fig. 97. Anton Maria Zanetti. *Caricature of Faustina Bordoni and the Castrato Francesco Bernardi, Called Senesino*. Pen and ink. Fondazione Cini, Venice

drawings of individual figures and heads (see fig. 102). It is frequently asserted that the costumes in Tiepolo's work are integral to his Veronesian style, and to a degree this is true. Certainly, Veronese's handling of costume and drapery was much admired by eighteenth-century critics—not least Algarotti.[11] Yet the situation is more complex than this analysis might indicate. It is clear, for example, that for his costumes Tiepolo drew as much inspiration from Rembrandt as from Veronese. The prominent role he accorded Oriental garb in his work depended not only on a long line of precedents in Venetian painting, stretching back beyond Carpaccio to Altichiero, but also very much on an eighteenth-century taste for anything foreign. In the 1845 catalogue of the sale of prints, drawings, and books that belonged to Giandomenico Tiepolo (and, presumably, also to his father) is listed that touchstone of sixteenth-century dress, the 1590 edition of Cesare Vecellio's *Degli abiti antichi et moderni*, with its illustrations of European and foreign dress. Additionally, there is found an album of costumes from the reign of Louis XIV (see fig. 96).[12] This obvious fascination with elaborate, often fantastic dress is closely allied with contemporary theater practice, wherein characters from ancient history and mythology—whether Caesar, Dido, or Apollo—were more likely to be extravagantly costumed à la Louis XIV than in anything remotely reminiscent of ancient Greece or Rome. Even in Paris, which set the standard for theatrical conventions, historicizing costumes gained acceptance on the stage only after about 1760, in part due to the influence of such critics as Diderot, who lamented the prevailing taste for patterned silks, plumage, and powdered coiffures and demanded greater attention to historical accuracy. When the celebrated tragedienne Marie-Françoise Dumesnil appeared at the Comédie Française in Racine's *Athalie*, she wore a lavish costume almost interchangeable with those Tiepolo gave to his Cleopatras, and the singers in a 1737 staging of Rameau's *Castor and Pollux* were every bit as elaborately dressed.[13] In Venice the costuming was, if anything, even more opulent, as is readily demonstrated by Zanetti's humorous caricatures of leading singers, such as one showing the celebrated soprano Faustina Bordoni lifting her head admiringly toward the massive bulk of the castrato Senesino (fig. 97).[14] The costumes in Tiepolo's work are restrained by comparison, but they are just as effective in transporting the event depicted from its proper historic period to the mythic time of the stage—in converting history into a poetic fiction. Once again, the emphasis is on art and the imagination rather than on some notion of truth and historicity.

Tiepolo's paintings have frequently been called theatrical and operatic (usually with an implied criticism), but the only serious investigation of the matter is a brilliant and suggestive article by Levey on the cycle of frescoes at Villa Valmarana in Vicenza illustrating stories from Homer, Virgil, Ariosto, and Tasso.[15] These were the very authors to whom writers of librettos turned for material, and it is surely of interest that the patron of the frescoes, Giustino Valmarana, was interested in theater[16] and that Tiepolo's friend and admirer Algarotti

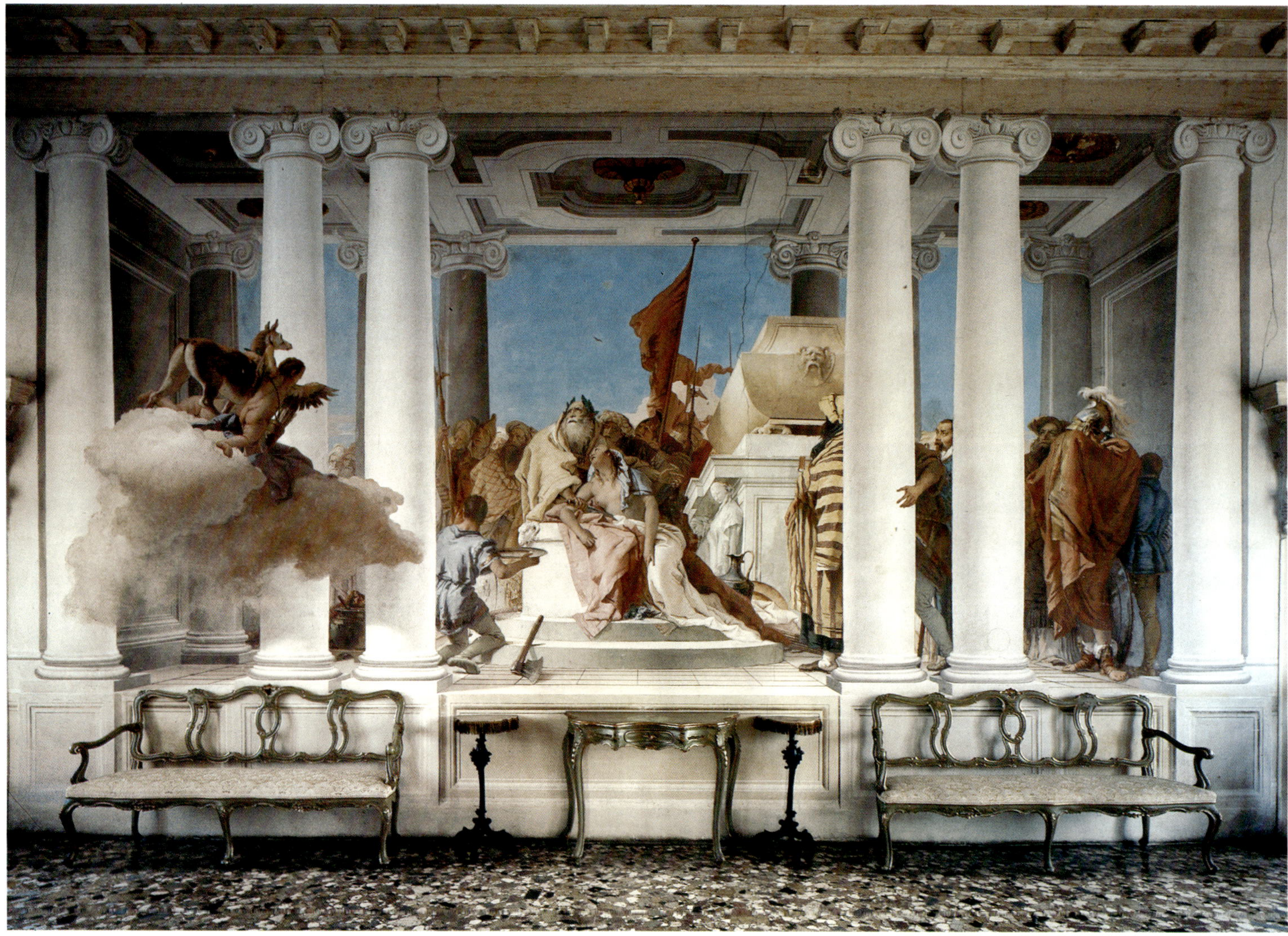

Fig. 98. *Sacrifice of Iphigenia*. Fresco. Villa Valmarana, Vicenza

explicitly endorsed the same literary sources in his treatise on opera, the *Saggio sopra l'opera in musica*. Yet too much importance should not be attached to this concurrence, which, after all, reflects a common literary heritage. Rather, the meaningful connections are to be sought in those areas in which Tiepolo's pictorial means demonstrate an apparent affinity with the practices of contemporary theater and opera: his use of fanciful costume, his exploitation of choruslike groups of spectators that set off the action of the protagonists, his remarkable mastery of facial expression and gesture, and his felicitous staging in so many works. These aspects gain further resonance in light of Tiepolo's close association with Algarotti, whose ideas about theater and opera were, in turn, informed by a love of painting—above all that of Veronese.[17]

In order to understand the possible nature of the relationship between the two art forms, it is important to recall that Algarotti was an advocate of reform in opera, which he hoped would reclaim its presumed roots in Greek classical drama.[18] To this end he emphasized the importance of the librettist's contribution over virtuoso singing or musical novelty: it was enough for music to be based on beautiful poetry, to be executed without affectation, and animated with decorous and noble gestures.[19] He urged a greater sobriety in set designs and a more sparing use of theatrical machinery, which in the highly competitive world of Venetian opera had become a prime attraction. Yet, despite the strictures he would impose, Algarotti insisted on a certain license and fully appreciated the vivifying power of settings and situations informed by fantasy and a feeling for the picturesque. Indeed, the principal reason he rejected purely historical subjects for operatic themes was that they did not offer the poet enough latitude and ran the risk of becoming ridiculous: "The trills of an aria do not seem to sit as well in the mouth of Julius Caesar or Cato as they would in the mouth of Apollo or Venus."[20] Unlike tales drawn from history, the writings of Homer, Virgil, Ariosto, and Tasso furnished not only familiar themes that centered on the passions but also stories involving magic, thus providing occasion for those special effects that even Algarotti expected. For Algarotti the goal of opera was verisimilitude (*il verisimile*), by which he meant that an opera should create a compelling poetic fiction rather than imitate reality (*il vero*). (A distinction between *verisimile* and *vero* is common among eighteenth-century writers.) Far more than the conventional observations he makes in his treatise on painting, the ideas he expresses in the *Saggio sopra l'opera* illuminate his appreciation of Tiepolo's work.[21]

We are able to compare Tiepolo's frescoed treatment of one subject—the sacrifice of Iphigenia depicted in the main hall of Villa Valmarana (fig. 98) (coincidentally, the subject illustrated on the frontispiece of Winckelmann's 1756 *Gedanken über die Nachahmung der griechischen Werke*)—with Algarotti's specifications for its realization onstage, and in all essentials the two friends made the same choices.[22] Nevertheless, it would be wrong to exaggerate the apparent relation of Tiepolo's paintings to theater and opera or the possible influence of Algarotti on his work. It is true that, to a degree unmatched by any of his Venetian contemporaries or, for that matter, by Veronese, Tiepolo insisted on facial expression and gesture—whether employed dramatically to articulate the narrative, demonstratively to signify an emotional state or underscore a symbolic meaning, or heraldically to embellish a pose or action. But this emphasis need not imply a source in theater. Rather, it was part of his inheritance from seventeenth-century academic practice—a lesson doubtless inculcated in the studio of Lazzarini but never developed in an academic vein.[23]

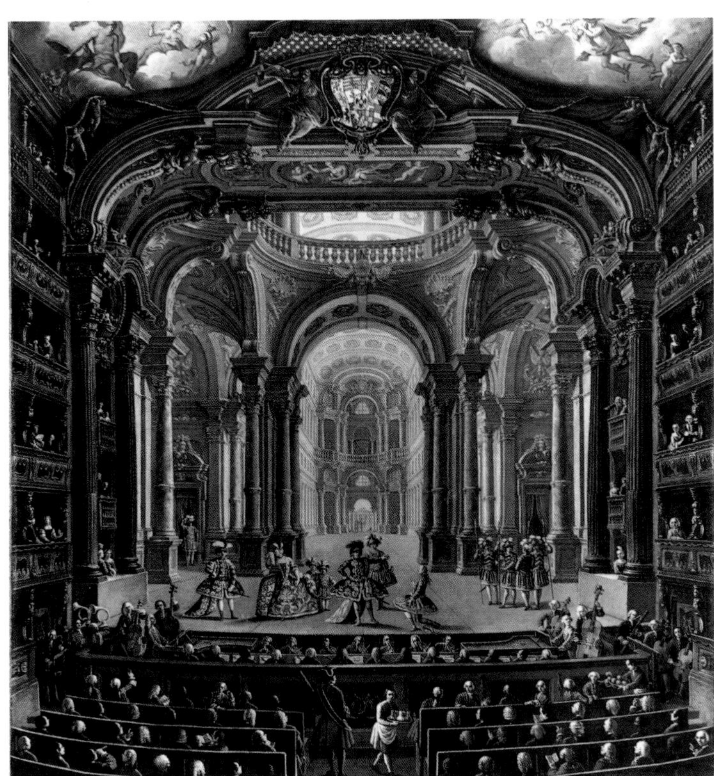

Fig. 99. Pietro Domenico Olivero. *The Teatro Regio, Turin, with Bibbiena's Set for Francesco Feo's Opera "Arsace" (Libretto by Metastasio)*. Oil on canvas. Museo Civico d'Arte Antica, Turin (420)

Ultimately, the tradition of ancient rhetoric, as represented by Cicero and Quintilian, provided a common source for painting and theater.[24] Similarly, the perspectival settings of Tiepolo's work, which Algarotti on one occasion suggestively characterized as "questa pittoresco erudizione,"[25] bear only a generic resemblance to stage design. Tiepolo conspicuously avoided the sorts of elaborate diagonal recessions introduced into theater practice by the Bibbiena (see fig. 99) and instead drew on a native, north Italian pictorial tradition stretching back through Veronese and Battista Zelotti to Andrea Mantegna. This heritage is particularly obvious in his decoration of Villa Contarini-Pisani at Mira (Musée Jacquemart-André, Paris), which shows a historical event taking place on a raised podium and, overhead, an open-air balcony with figures gesturing toward the viewer (fig. 108)—a scheme reminiscent of Mantegna's formulation in the Camera degli Sposi in Mantua as well as of Veronese's at Villa Maser.[26] Where the resemblance to contemporary stage practice seems incontrovertible, in the stupendously elaborate architectural framework of the Cleopatra scenes in Palazzo Labia in Venice (figs. 100, 101), there is reason to suspect that the impetus came from Tiepolo's collaborator, Girolamo Mengozzi Colonna, who also worked as a set designer. In the two surviving *modelli* for the Labia decoration Tiepolo followed his invariable approach, treating the main action with no reference to the elaborate feigned architecture, and in the frescoes he necessarily modified their design to adapt them to Mengozzi Colonna's tripartite "proscenium."[27] Yet a simple comparison of Tiepolo's treatment of the theme with that of his contemporary Mattia Bortoloni at Villa Raimondi reminds us how distant Tiepolo was from the exuberance of contemporary stage practice—the obvious source for Bortoloni's work.

If it is not possible to assert with any certainty the direct influence of settecento opera on Tiepolo's art, an affinity nonetheless remains.[28] Of all his contemporaries, whether painters, poets, or musicians, it is Handel that Tiepolo calls most to mind. He had a like facility and inventive fecundity; was similarly endowed with an innate sense of rhythmic structure; was able to manipulate his unmistakable style to suit the various emotional and dramatic demands of the occasion; felt equally at ease with operatic scale and sonata-like intimacy; and had the same shameless, practical attitude toward recycling the successful bits of a composition. We may well feel that the most eloquent exposition of Tiepolo's poetic aspirations is provided not by a contemporary critic of painting but by the poet Pietro Metastasio (1698–1782), whose universally admired librettos were singled out by Algarotti and were employed by generations of composers, ranging from Vinci and Pergolesi to Vivaldi, Handel, Paisiello, Gluck, Mozart, and Meyerbeer.[29]

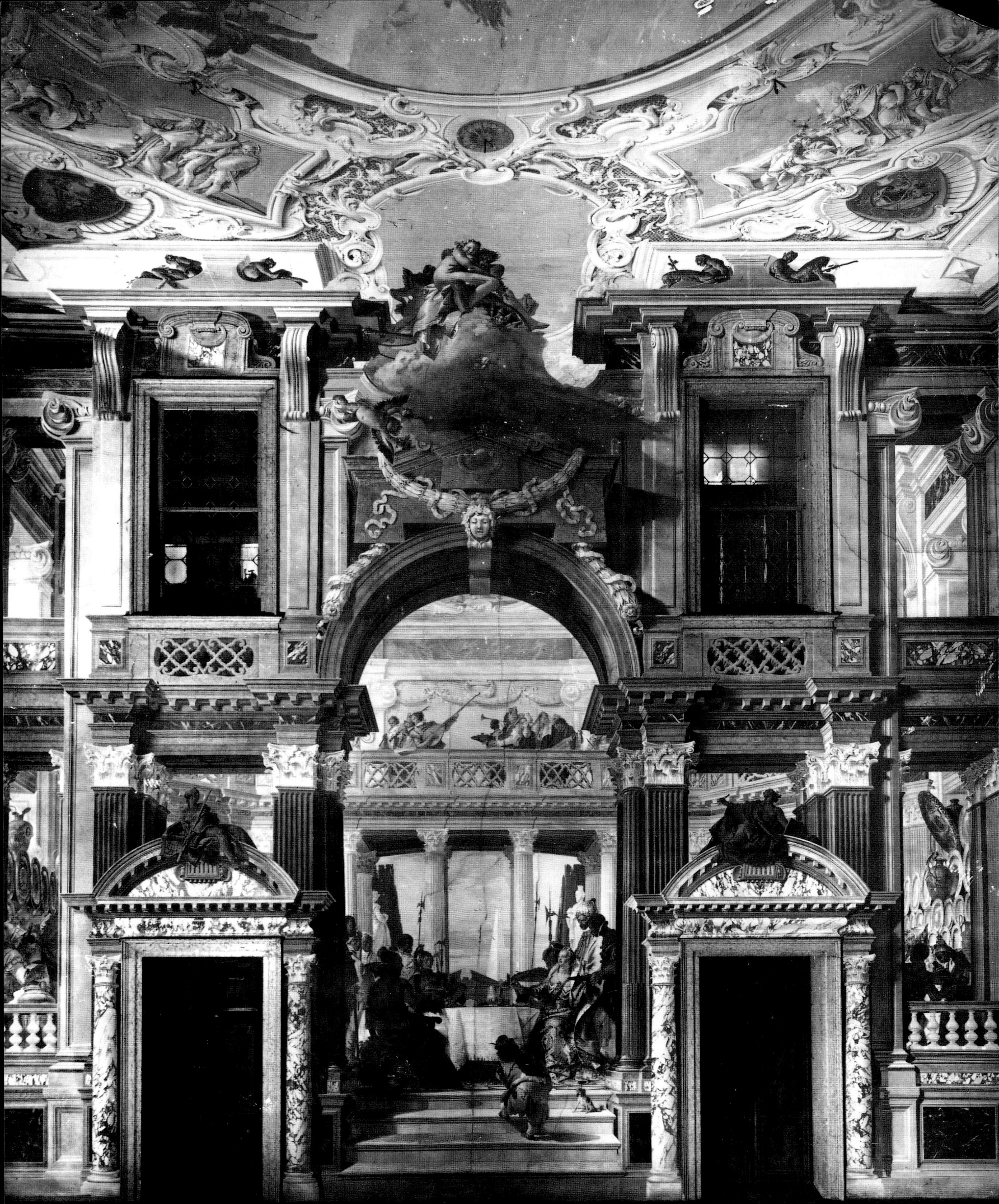

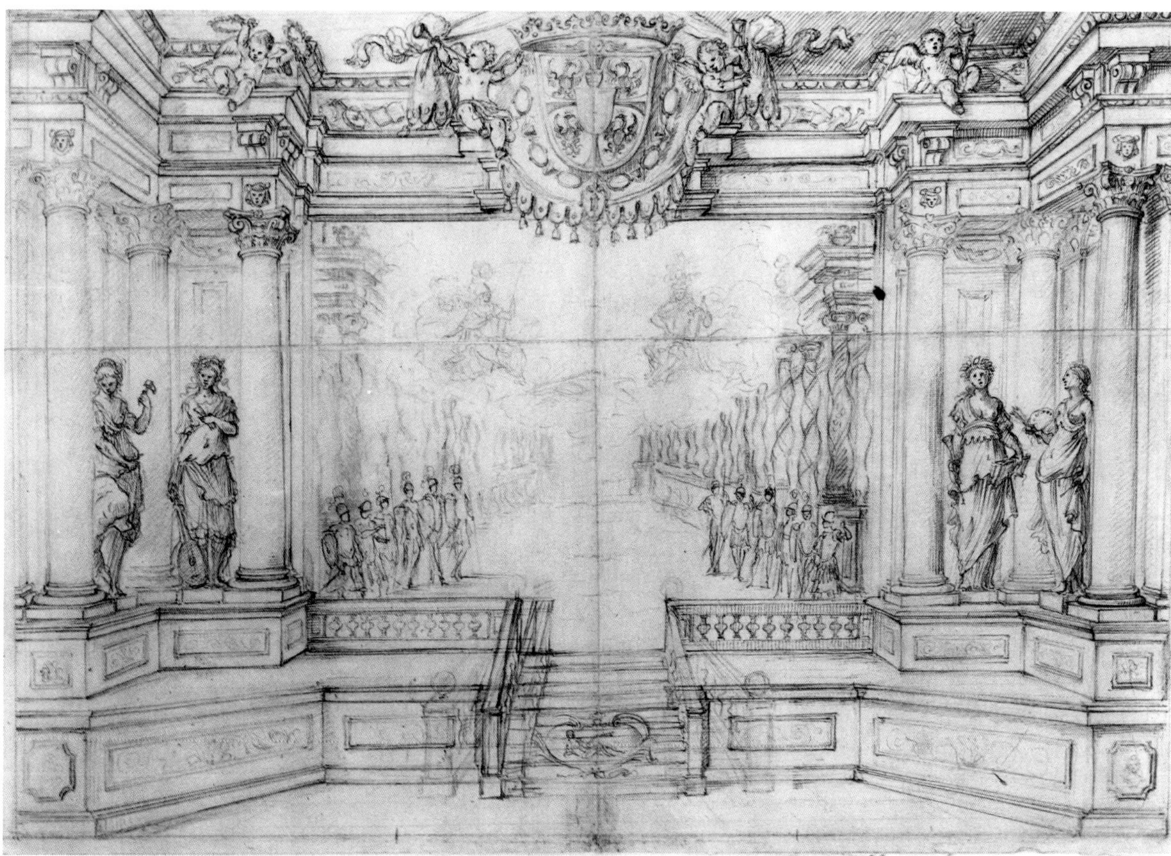

Fig. 101. Attributed to Giuseppe Maria Mitelli. *Design for a Proscenium and Stage Set for an Opera in Mantua: Courtyard with Athena and Apollo in Clouds and Soldiers Below.* Pen and ink and black and red chalk. Cooper-Hewitt Museum, Smithsonian Institution National Museum of Design, New York (1938.88.114)

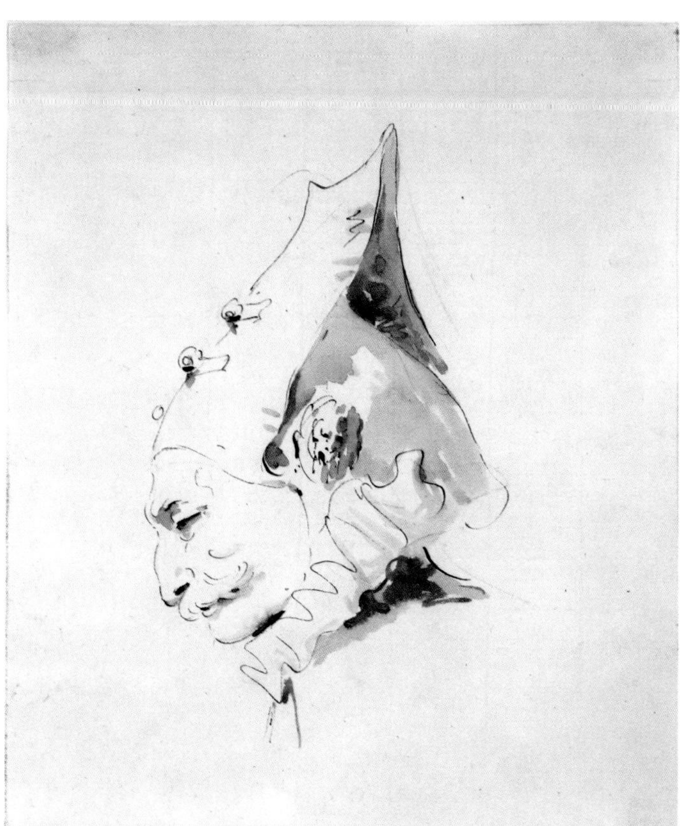

Fig. 102. *Head of a Man in Exotic Costume.* Pen and ink and wash over graphite. The Metropolitan Museum of Art, New York; Robert Lehman Collection, 1975 (1975.1.435)

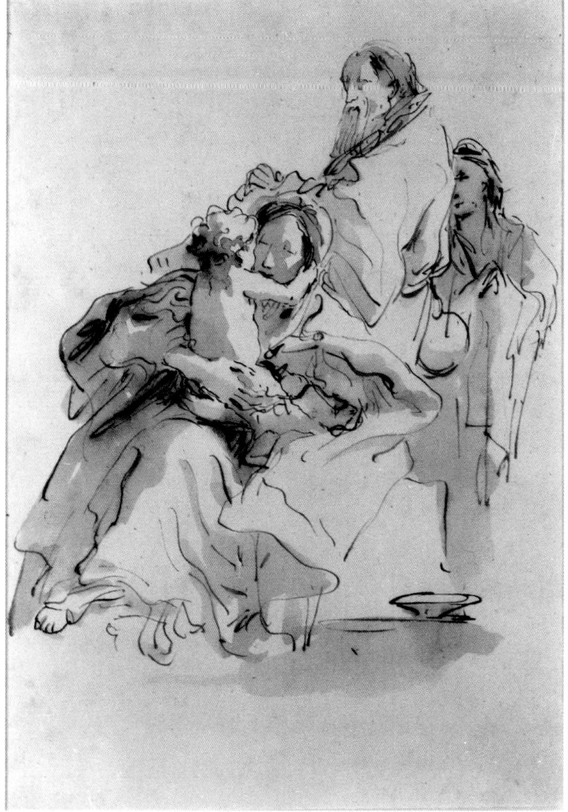

Fig. 103. *The Holy Family with Saint John.* Pen and ink and wash. The Metropolitan Museum of Art, New York; Robert Lehman Collection, 1975 (1975.1.441)

Opposite: Fig. 100. *The Banquet of Cleopatra.* Fresco. Palazzo Labia, Venice

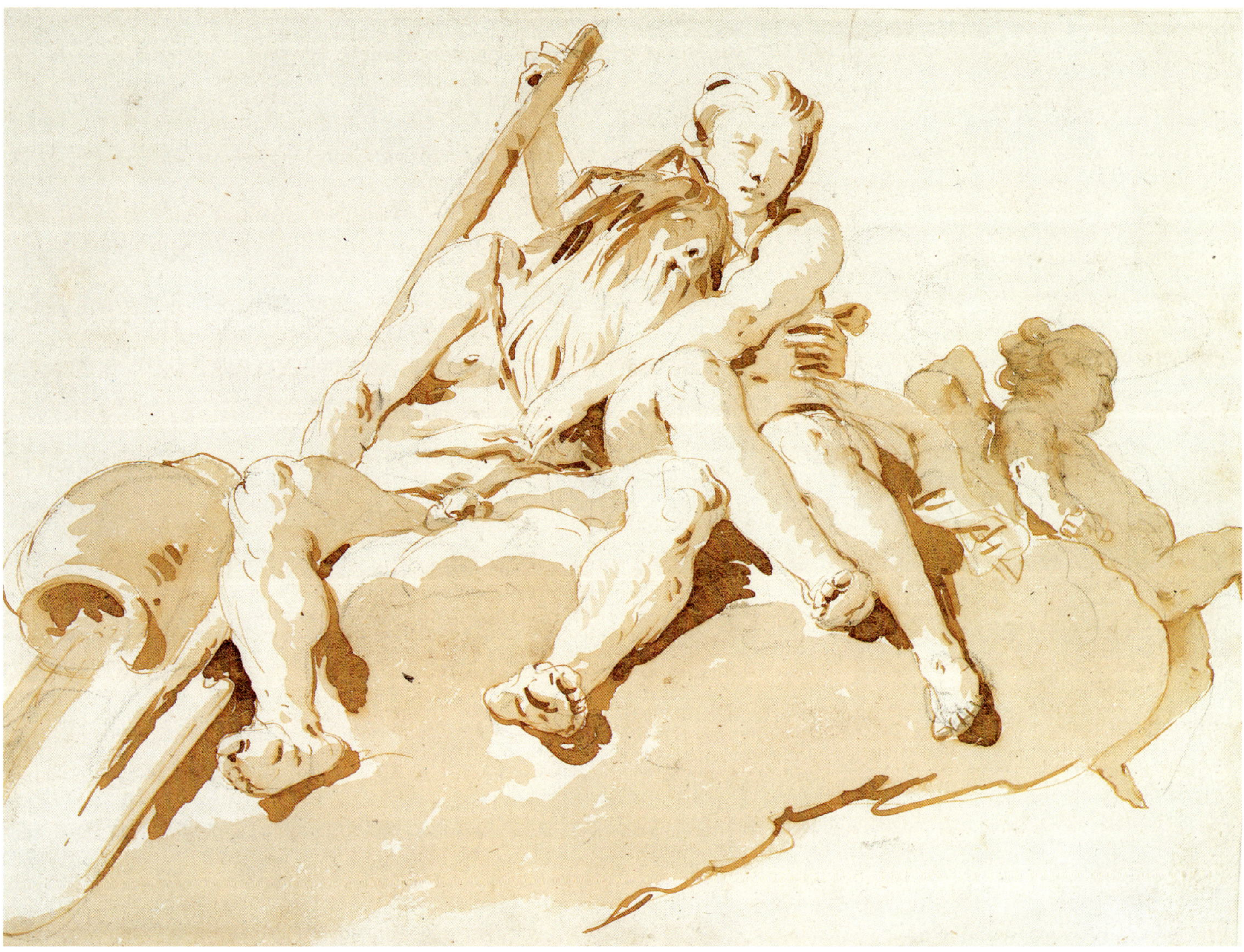

Fig. 104. *Seated River God, Nymph with an Oar, and Putto* (study for the ceiling in Palazzo Clerici, Milan). Pen and ink and wash over black chalk. The Metropolitan Museum of Art, New York; Rogers Fund, 1937 (37.165.32)

> *Dreams and fables I fashion; and even while I sketch and elaborate fables and dreams upon paper, fond as I am, I so enter into them that I weep and am offended at ills I invented. But am I wiser when art does not deceive me? Is my disturbed mind perhaps calmer then? Or does love and scorn perhaps spring from firmer cause?*
>
> *Ah, not only what I sing and write are fables; but what I fear and hope for, all is falsehood, and I live in a feverishness. The whole course of my life has been dream. O Lord, let me find rest in the bosom of truth, when finally I come to wake.*[30]

The words are Metastasio's and refer to the writing of his celebrated libretto the *Olimpiade*, but they could as easily have been Tiepolo's.

Tiepolo's creative energies are most fully realized in his frescoes, but it is in his drawings, oil sketches, and etchings, and in his late, small-scale canvases treating conventional themes in a novel, indeed unprecedented, manner, that we come in most intimate contact with the workings of his imagination: what the artist's earliest biographer, Vincenzo da Canal, referred to as that spirit and fire ("tutto spirito e foco")[31] and Michelessi called a fiery poetic fantasy ("infiamata poetica fantasia").[32] Long after the tide of changing taste had swept away serious consideration of Tiepolo's illusionistic ceilings, secular fresco cycles, and opulent altarpieces, the demand for his drawings and oil sketches remained undiminished. The seven altarpieces he completed shortly before his death for the royal foundation at S. Pascual Baylon may have been removed within months of their installation, but the *modelli* for them (nos. 40a, 41a) were acquired by Francisco Bayeu, who, like Mengs, was hired to paint their replacements. (Bayeu's brother-in-law, Goya, must have been as familiar with the *modelli* as he was with Tiepolo's etchings.) Mengs himself was reputed to be an avid collector of Tiepolo's oil sketches.[33] In 1804 the greatest Neoclassical sculptor, Antonio Canova, wrote from Rome to the inspector-general of the Venetian public collections,

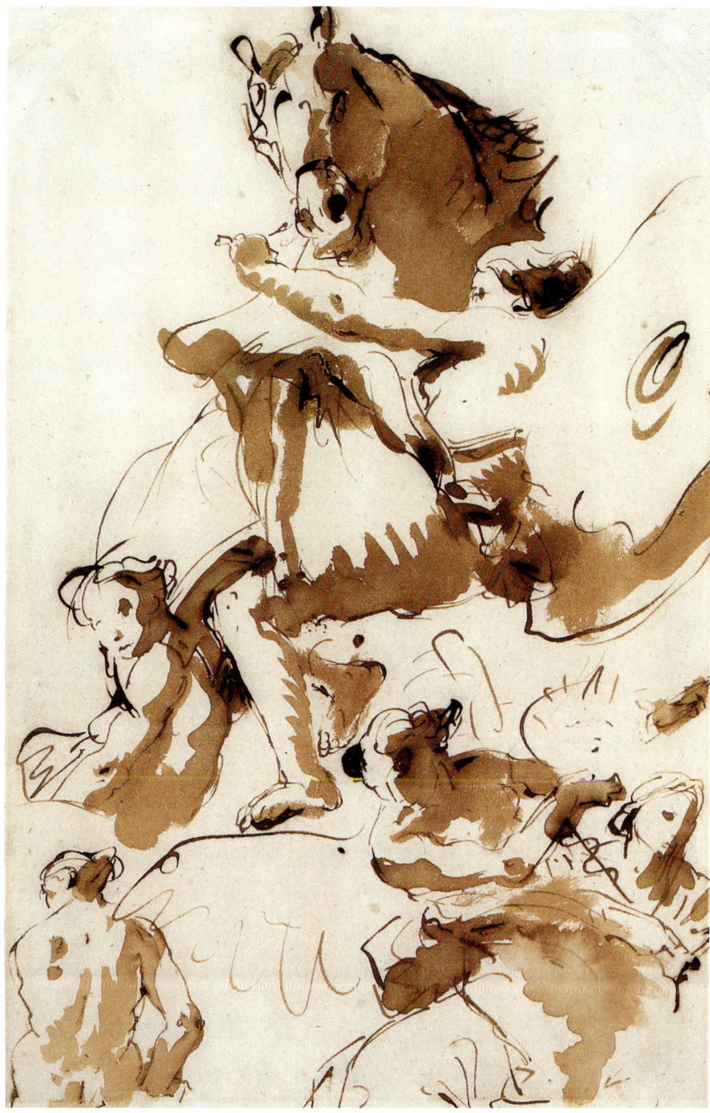

Fig. 105. *One of the Hours Holding the Bridle of a Horse of the Sun and Other Figures* (possibly a study for the ceiling over the staircase in the Residenz, Würzburg). Pen and ink and wash. The Metropolitan Museum of Art, New York; Robert Lehman Collection, 1975 (1975.1.445)

Pietro Edwards, in an effort to obtain an oil sketch by Tiepolo.[34] (Interestingly, Canova later owned an album of drawings containing more than sixty-seven studies on the theme of the Holy Family and over ninety studies of heads: see figs. 102, 103.)[35] He was told that this was no simple task, since Tiepolo's best oil sketches had all been snapped up by dealers, who charged exorbitant prices. Still, Edwards was able to offer Canova a *modello* of an Immaculate Conception—a work he considered not of Tiepolo's most energetic period and unfortunately surcharged with small cherub heads added, he thought, by Giandomenico, but nonetheless notable for its elevated, Dantesque conception ("ottimo per una certa elevatezza di pensiere dantesco"). It has been proposed that the picture in question is a sketch for an unexecuted mural in the church of S. Ildefonso at La Granja, now in the National Gallery of Ireland, Dublin.[36]

The continued popularity of Tiepolo's oil sketches may be ascribed, in part, to a notion that they transmitted his inventive capacities more directly than a finished painting. This was by no means a novel idea.[37] On at least one occasion Sebastiano Ricci asserted that his completed altarpiece would be but a copy of the *modello*, in which the initial idea, or *pensiero*, was worked out.[38] Looseness of handling was no impediment to appreciation: at the close of the seventeenth century, Roger de Piles had already argued the virtues of the sketch, noting, "Imagination supplies all the features which are missing or which have not been finished, and each person who sees the sketch fills them in according to his taste."[39] The comment was worthy of an admirer of Rubens, who painted the only corpus of oil sketches that vie with Tiepolo's for their combination of inventiveness and quickness of hand. In the eighteenth century oil sketches were collected as self-sufficient works of art. Prior to their meeting in 1743, Tiepolo was known to Algarotti as a *pittore di macchia* (the term had no fixed meaning and may allude either to Tiepolo's reputation for facility or to his production of oil sketches). Although Algarotti recommended Tiepolo's large-scale canvases to his patron, Augustus III, king of Poland and elector of Saxony, he acquired the artist's oil sketches and small-scale paintings for himself—a choice surely only partly motivated by financial restrictions. Edwards's comment to Canova takes us beyond this general context. His recommendation pointed less to a quality of immediacy than to the poetic frame of mind Tiepolo's *modello* seemed to him to exemplify. We may find his term of comparison surprising—did he mean simply to allude to a quality of the sublime imagination associated with Homer, Virgil, Dante, and Shakespeare, or was he referring to something more specific, such as Dante's great hymn to the Virgin that concludes the *Paradiso* (canto 33)?

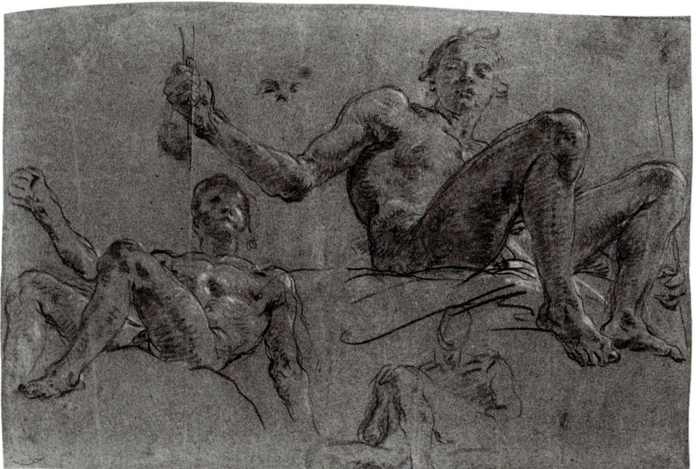

Fig. 106. *Two Studies of Nudes* (studies from life for the figure of Mars on the ceiling over the staircase in the Residenz, Würzburg). Red and white chalk on blue paper. Kupferstichkabinett, Staatliche Museen zu Berlin, Preussischer Kulturbesitz

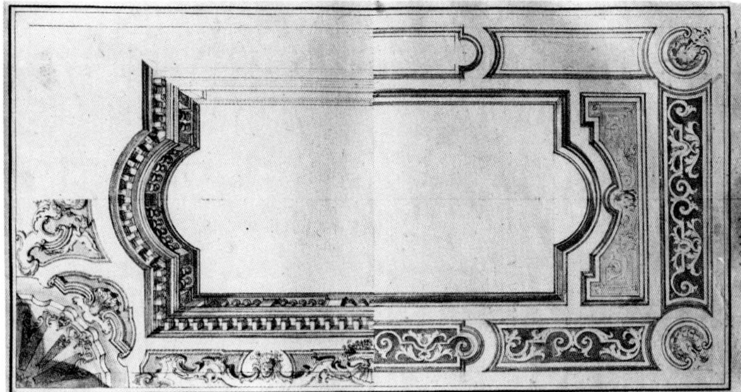

Fig. 107. Girolamo Mengozzi Colonna. *Study for the Ceiling of the Villa Contarini-Pisani at Mira*. Pen and ink and wash. Museo Correr, Venice

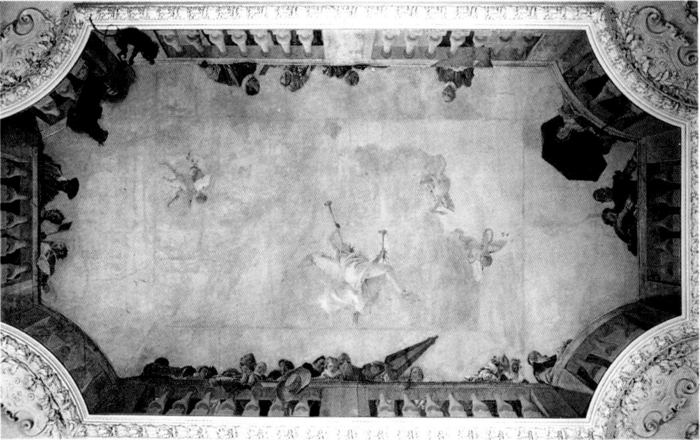

Fig. 108. *Ceiling of the Villa Contarini-Pisani at Mira*. Fresco. Musée Jacquemart-André Institut de France, Paris

Whatever his intent, in recognizing the fundamentally poetic quality of Tiepolo's invention, he hit on the central feature of Tiepolo's creative genius.

The term "oil sketch," employed as a synonym for *modello*, *bozzetto*, or *macchia*, has only an approximative meaning when applied to Tiepolo's work.[40] According to Algarotti, the small *Banquet of Cleopatra* he owned (no. 19) served as a *modello* for the large picture he hoped Augustus of Saxony would acquire, but its exquisite finish fits no conventional notion of an oil sketch. Vice versa, the fluid handling of the series of paintings based on the life of the Virgin (nos. 56, 57)—unquestionably conceived as independent works—differs scarcely at all from that of the *modelli* for the altarpieces of S. Pascual Baylon. Tiepolo responded strongly to the medium in which he was working and to the size of the sheet of paper or canvas before him, and his *modelli*, whether quickly sketched in or more carefully executed, are characterized by a seemingly innate balance of invention, technical finish, and scale. It was this balance rather than details of design that Tiepolo strove to maintain as he progressed through the various stages of his creative process: from his rapid, preliminary drawings in pen and ink with wash studying figures and figure groups—some exploring poses in steep foreshortening, others actions or relations between figures (see figs. 104, 105)[41]—to the *modelli* and then to additional, detail drawings—sometimes in chalk on blue paper (see fig. 106)—and, in the case of frescoes, full-scale cartoons that led up to the finished work.[42]

Tiepolo was hardly alone in treating his *modelli* as though they were independent exercises of artistic expression and in endowing them with that quality of resolution associated with self-sufficient works of art, but the fact that he could simultaneously conceive of alternative, equally authoritative solutions for the same theme remains astonishing (see no. 54a, b). Nowhere is the inherent independence of the *modelli* more evident than in the sketches for the vast ceiling projects, in which the figures are invariably larger in scale than in the final work. Had he not adopted this approach to relative scale, the sketches would have read mostly as empty space rather than as unified compositions articulated by their figurative component. Clearly, many patrons must have been won over to proposals for large, decorative projects precisely because of the resolution, legibility, and brilliance of handling that characterize the *modelli*. In turn, these very qualities created a market demand for sketchlike replicas that must have kept Tiepolo's workshop busy.[43]

Modelli served not only a promotional end as a means of winning approval for a proposal. They also allowed patrons to judge key iconographic elements. This would have been especially important when the work in question was for a particular religious order or a demanding client. The difference in dramatic presentation between the *modello* for the *Last Communion of Saint Lucy* and the finished altarpiece (no. 36a, b) may reflect a requested change. However, Tiepolo was celebrated for his "genio vigoroso," to use Zanetti's expression,[44] and the evidence suggests that he reserved the prerogative to alter those incidental details that conferred vivacity and character on a design. Thus, in assessing the disparity between the sketch for the vast ceiling over the stairwell in the Residenz at Würzburg and the fresco itself, we would probably be correct to ascribe the transposition of Europe and America and the inclusion in the final work of a portrait of the prince-bishop to the demands of the patron; but the manner in which the main figural groups of the *modello* (no. 49) were elaborated to fill out the area above the cornice, and the transformation of the spiraling sky of the *modello* into the four-cornered empyrean of the ceiling, can only be Tiepolo's response to the physical space of the stairwell and the multiple points of view offered by the continuous balcony. The result was a fresco that necessarily sacrificed the discrete compositional unity of the *modello*, which was meant to be taken in by the patron at a glance, to the realities of complex, on-site viewing. This versatility and

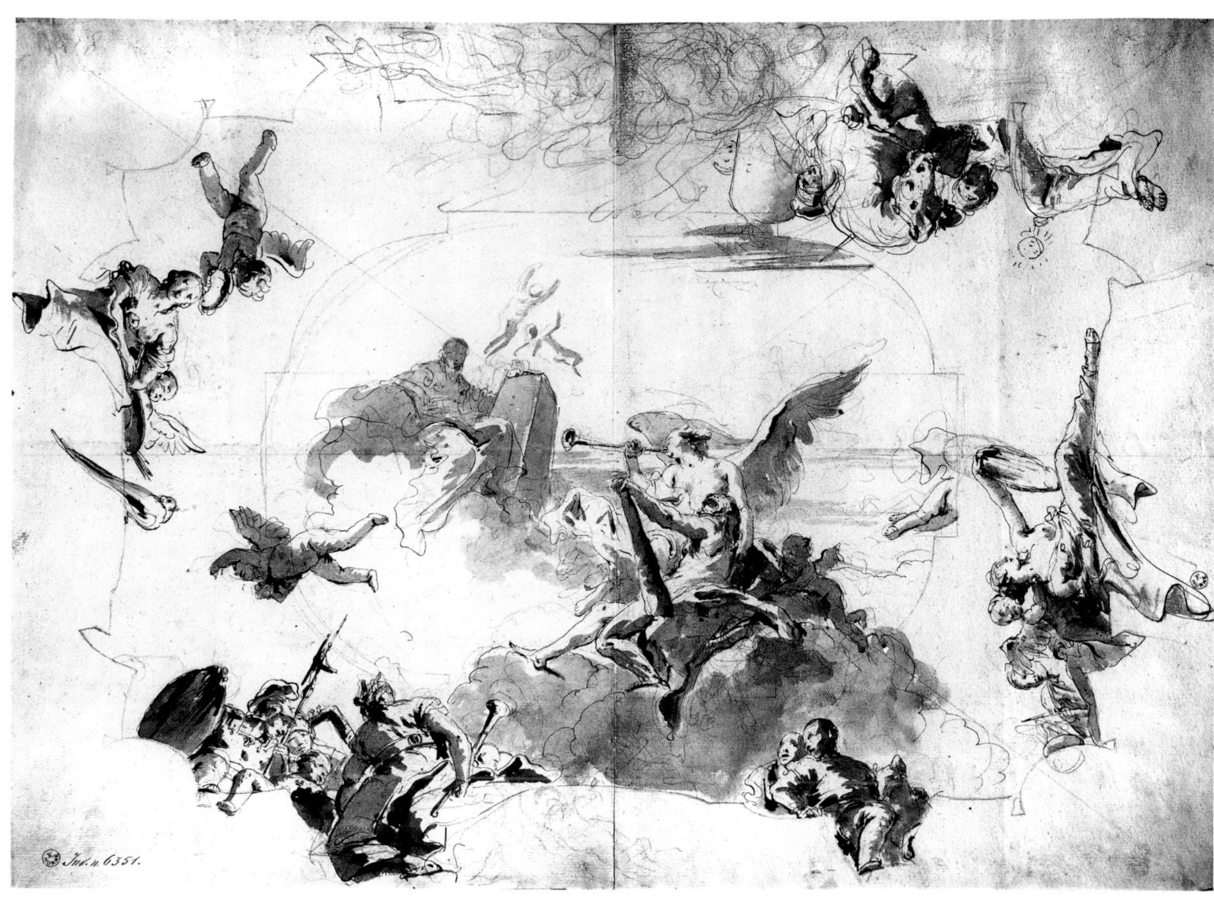

Fig. 109. *Study for a Ceiling: The Triumph of Hercules*. Pen and ink and wash over red chalk. Museo Horne, Fondazione Horne, Florence

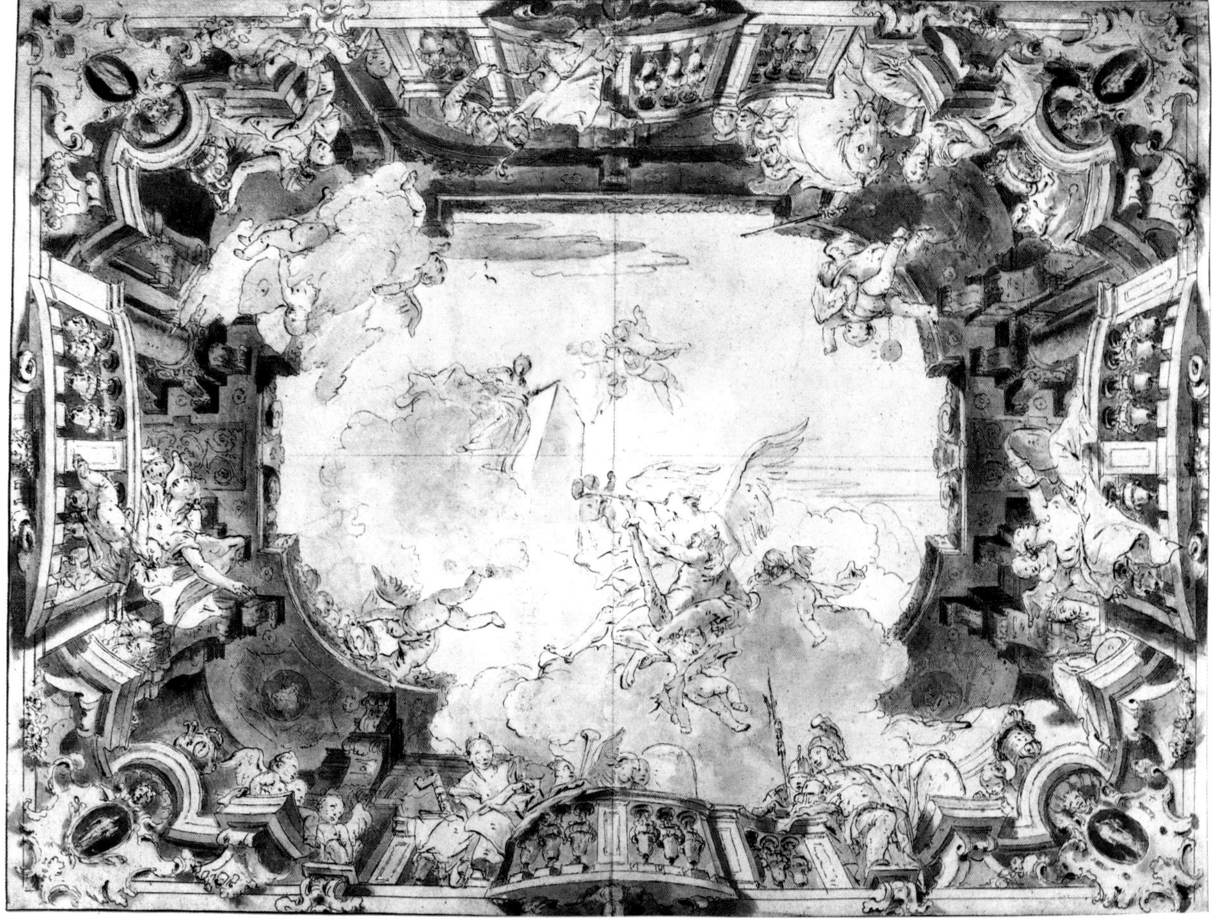

Fig. 110. *Design for a Ceiling: The Triumph of Hercules*. Pen and ink and wash over black chalk. The Pierpont Morgan Library, New York (1968.8)

accommodation of means to end is also part of Tiepolo's "fecondissima immaginativa."[45]

In the *modello* for the ceiling of the throne room in the royal palace in Madrid (no. 53), it was the foreshortening of the figures around the periphery that had to be adjusted to make allowance for the depressingly low height of the actual ceiling. How Tiepolo's heart must have sunk when confronted with the hall for which he had prepared his brilliant *modello* before leaving for Spain! The diminished effect of the final decoration—commented on by every modern critic—reminds us of something that should be obvious: the success of Tiepolo's frescoes was in no small part dependent on the real architecture that housed them and on the feigned architecture that frequently surrounded them. The light-filled churches, palaces, and villas of the great neo-Palladian architect Giorgio Massari were ideally suited to Tiepolo's work. (Indeed, to a degree, Tiepolo's revival of Veronese's style was a response to the neo-Palladian reform in architecture that constituted the Venetian prelude to Neoclassicism.) But if the imaginative *quadraturista* settings of Mengozzi Colonna greatly enhanced Tiepolo's airy frescoes, the heavy, gilt ceiling at the Villa Pisani in Strà, which was the work of the Milanese *quadraturista* Pietro Visconti, demonstrates how easy it was to throttle the scheme of a dazzling *modello* (no. 52). As Algarotti noted in a letter written following a visit to the Villa Contarini at Mira, where the frescoes by Tiepolo and Mengozzi Colonna functioned together to impressive effect (see figs. 107, 108), "You know how rarely it happens that the figurative artist and the *quadraturista* who collaborate on a fresco also harmonize. The one usually wants to shine at the expense of the other, [whereas] the *quadraturista* should be the bass to the figurative painter's soprano."[46]

Ideally, Tiepolo would be put in charge of the whole decorative project at a given site, as he was in the Carmelite church of the Scalzi in Venice. There he planned his fresco before turning to Girolamo Mengozzi Colonna for the architectural surround. He then adjusted the design he had already worked out (and presumably submitted to the monks) in two *modelli* to suit the picture field shaped by Mengozzi Colonna's framework (see no. 48a, b).[47] Sometimes Tiepolo must have effected this kind of revision in the form of a drawing rather than an oil sketch, and in one unique instance two drawings allow us to observe the procedure he followed in making changes to accommodate the perspectival setting of an undocumented project (figs. 109, 110).[48] Occasionally, account is taken in the oil sketches of stuccowork and sculptural decoration. At the Residenz in Würzburg these elements must have been devised in collaboration with the stuccoist Antonio Bossi and were realized with completely felicitous results. (It has been shown that Tiepolo similarly had a hand in the design of the garden sculpture at Villa Cordellina, near Vicenza.)

Throughout the various stages of his work, Tiepolo maintained a complete fluidity and freshness of approach, which remind us of Guercino's response when the illustrious collector Don Antonio Ruffo asked the artist to provide a drawn *modello* showing the appearance of a commissioned work: "As I already wrote, it is not my habit to make drawings for anyone because I cannot and do not wish to tie down my freedom of action. Nevertheless, to condescend to please your illustrious personage I will make one so that you will, in a certain sense, be able to see the direction of my idea [*pensiero*] without, however, obligating myself to the design, since I wish to be able to change [the composition] as need arises for its improvement."[49] Tiepolo had no objections to providing his clients with *modelli*—examples of his *pensieri*—but he too refused to be bound by their details.

This freedom of invention, combined with an inexpressibly effortless handling of the brush ("una disinvoltura di pennello indicibile"),[50] reached a memorable climax in the marvelous series of pictures on the theme of the life of the Virgin that Tiepolo carried out during his last years in Madrid. We know virtually nothing about the circumstances of their creation, but, like the *Capricci* and *Scherzi*, they give us privileged access to the inner workings of Tiepolo's imagination; and it is typical of him that their utterly conventional subjects—as old as Venetian art itself—should have provided the material for deeply personal ruminations. Whether we care to characterize the creative impulse that lies behind these exquisite and haunting religious *capricci* as Dantesque or Metastasian is, in the end, irrelevant to the heightened poetic genius to which they testify.

Notes

1. Winckelmann 1756, p. 3: "Der einzige Weg für uns, groß, ja, wenn es müglich ist, unnachahmilich zu werden, ist die Nachahmung der Alten." The English translation is from Eitner 1970, vol. 1, p. 6.
2. Winckelmann 1763, p. 27: "Thiepolo macht mehr in einem Tage, als Mengs in einer Woche: aber jenes ist gesehen und vergessen; dieses bleibt ewig."
3. Even during Tiepolo's lifetime his art was criticized, especially by French observers prone to consider it from a pedantically academic position. Typical is Mariette's (1858–59) verdict: "il est pourtant vrai que cette trop grande facilité a fait tort à la correction, et qu'on peut luy reprocher d'avoir négligé cette partie en se livrant trop à la fougue de son imagination. Il n'a pas été plus curieux de la vérité de ses teintes. Son coloris est faux, quelque séduisant qu'il soit. Il ne sçut jamais faire des têtes gracieuses. Voilà ses défauts, qui sont relevés par tous les avantages d'un génie riche et fertile et par tout ce qui produit l'illusion sur des yeux qui aiment à estre séduits." See also the observations cited by Levey 1960b and Cochin's grudging remarks in his *Voyage d'Italie* (1758).
4. The astonishing breadth of Tiepolo's interest in prints is best demonstrated by consulting the catalogue of the sale held in Paris in 1845 of works owned by Giandomenico Tiepolo, most of which presumably were inherited from Giambattista (see Lugt 1953, vol. 2, no. 17909; I consulted the copy in the

Frick Art Reference Library, New York). In addition to prints by the artists noted above, the catalogue cites graphic works by Dürer, Lucas van Leyden, Marcantonio Raimondi, Mantegna, Goltzius, van Dyck, and Callot—virtually an anthology of outstanding printmakers north and south of the Alps.

5. In 1759 Zanetti engraved twelve drawings by Castiglione. Tiepolo had access to many of the great private collections of prints and drawings in Venice. In 1743 he assisted Piazzetta in compiling an inventory of the collection of Zaccaria Sagredo. Sagredo, a friend of Zanetti's, owned, among much else, two paintings by Salvator Rosa and was one of the earliest collectors of Castiglione's drawings and prints; his taste for Castiglione's work was later shared by Algarotti. See Haskell 1980, pp. 266–67.
6. Tiepolo's painting evidently combines elements of two of Veronese's works on the same theme: the large horizontal painting at Dresden and an upright composition, lost but documented by a preparatory drawing and by a painting by Sebastiano Ricci in Hampton Court. (On the lost putative Veronese, see, most recently, Coutts 1982.) From the former he took over general features of the elongated composition—a typical Venetian format—and the prominent halberdier (now detached from the picture; no. 16b); from the latter he adapted the foreshortened figure of the infant Moses. The quality of humor Tiepolo brought to the subject is typified by the new activity he gave the dwarf-jester, who no longer restrains hunting dogs, as he did in Veronese's pictures, but instead teases the princess's diminutive pet with a Venetian biscuit.
7. There was a considerable trade in fake Veroneses as well as in contemporary copies of his work. On this phenomenon, see Garas 1990.
8. The praising of later artists as reincarnated Veroneses is discussed, most recently, by Sohm (1990). Sohm notes that the earliest reference to Tiepolo as a disciple of Veronese dates from 1736, when Count Carl Gustaf Tessin referred to the artist, then being courted to work in Stockholm, as a "sectataire de Paul Véronèse"(ibid., p. 90). Curiously, Sohm maintains that Tiepolo realized the fullest expression of his Veronesian style only after he met Francesco Algarotti in 1743, a notion arrived at by giving too much weight to textual sources.
9. The picture was a copy after Veronese's celebrated *Christ in the House of Simon* (Musée du Louvre, Paris). Antonio Visentini enhanced the architecture, but Tiepolo departed for Spain in March 1762 and was unable to oblige Algarotti. See Morassi 1962, p. 238.
10. On the imagery of the ceiling, which derives from a number of popular sourcebooks, such as Cesare Ripa's *Iconologia*, and travel literature, see the brilliant article by Ashton (1978). Ashton has perfectly characterized Tiepolo's witty approach.
11. See Algarotti's comments on drapery in his *Saggio sopra la pittura* (1763b [1963 ed., p. 89]).
12. See note 4 above. The entry for lot 22 reads: "Personnages et costumes du regne de Louis XIV, dit Messieurs et Mesdames à la mode. Soixante-neuf pièces publiées par les Bonnart, Mariette, et autres." It is impossible to say which of the costume prints of Bonnart and Mariette were included, but worth pointing out that the album could have contained Bonnart's illustrations of eminent women of antiquity, all wearing elaborate seventeenth-century court costume, and those by Mariette showing foreign figures in national dress.
13. See, for example, the comments and illustrations in Blum 1928, pp. 133–36; Nagler 1959, pp. 325–28; and Lesure 1972, pl. 60. Barcham (1984, pp. 153–66) discusses opera costumes and includes sagacious remarks on their relation to Tiepolo's work.
14. See Venice 1969a. Algarotti owned a similar group of caricatures, for which see Toronto 1980.
15. Levey 1957. See also Barcham 1984 regarding staging.
16. See Puppi 1968b. Puppi argues convincingly that the celebrated garden statues of dwarfs at Villa Valmarana relate to the commedia dell'arte and were very likely designed by Giambattista or Giandomenico Tiepolo.
17. See Algarotti 1762c (1963 ed., p. 181), where Veronese's work is cited as a reference point for stage sets. That Algarotti made this connection is not surprising, given Veronese's use of Sebastiano Serlio's architectural treatise.
18. For useful introductions to the subject of Algarotti's position in the movement to reform opera, see Lippman 1992, pp. 137–53, and Kimbell 1994, pp. 229–37. It should be emphasized that Algarotti genuinely loved opera and displays none of the censorious attitude that so decidedly marks the writings of the influential Lodovico Antonio Muratori, whose treatise he had, of course, read and many of whose criticisms he adopted in a milder form. (Muratori's *Della perfetta poesia italiana* was first published in 1706. His comments on opera are in book 3, chaps. 4–5.)
19. Algarotti 1762c (1963 ed., p. 172): "E se una melodia espressiva accompagnata da strumenti convenevoli avesse per base una bella poesia, e fosse dal cantore eseguita senza affettazione e animata con un gesto decente e nobile, la musica avria potere di accendere a voglia sua e di calmare le passioni."
20. Ibid., p. 154: "non pare che i trilli di un'arietta stiano così bene in bocca di Giulio Cesare o di Catone, che in bocca si starebbono di Apollo o di Venere."
21. The disparity between Algarotti's professed ideas about painting and his taste for Venetian art is well known; but such incongruity is by no means unique to him and arose because the language of criticism was forged in Florence and Rome, not Venice. Throughout his treatise there are echoes of Alberti, Leonardo da Vinci, and Bellori. Nonetheless, in discussing invention in painting, Algarotti declares that the painter "finge con la fantasia." In this context, we might note, parenthetically, that in his eleventh discourse Sir Joshua Reynolds remarks on some inapposite comments on Titian in Algarotti's treatise (which he had read thoroughly): "but connoisseurs will always find in pictures what they think they ought to find." It is worth recalling that Algarotti's own, quite amateurish prints show a direct dependence on Tiepolo's work as well as a preference for the imaginative over the classical. For a general discussion of Algarotti's ideas, see Gabbrielli 1938. The most recent addition to our knowledge of Algarotti's work as a draftsman and printmaker is Aikema 1994.
22. Algarotti's treatment is in the libretto he appended to the *Saggio sopra l'opera*. His stated sources are Euripides and Racine, but the scenes in question depend on Euripides alone. Algarotti describes the stage set as showing on one side Diana's grove and her temple, and on the other the Greek camp and the port of Aulis with the Greek fleet. Tiepolo divides his scenes between facing walls, with the port on one wall and the interior of the temple—interpreted as the proscenium—on the other. Algarotti has a chorus announce the sacrifice of Iphigenia and implore Diana to take her victim and release the winds for the Greek fleet. Tiepolo shows the winds on the ceiling, their cheeks puffed out. To one side of the ceiling Agamemnon buries his head in his cloak—a motif the ancient painter Timanthes had included in his celebrated rendition of the subject and which Algarotti also retained. At the entrance of Algarotti's goddess, both the chorus and the priest Calchas sing "Ah prodige!" and as Diana appears in the heavens on Tiepolo's ceiling, sending in a sacrificial hind, astonishment registers on the spectators' faces. In Algarotti's libretto the animal, "toute ensanglanté," miraculously materializes on the altar; Tiepolo's solution is actually more in accord with theatrical practice, since it involves a miraculous appearance on clouds. Levey (1957, pp. 308–9) describes the scene on the ceiling as "conceived operatically rather than dramatically," but we may well question the distinction, for his interpretation is, in general, curiously unsympathetic to the emotional tenor of the work. See also Guerrini in Ferrara 1985, pp. 345–48.
23. Tiepolo's masterly use of gesture seems to me one of the least recognized components of his art. Yet anyone who has visited Udine will have been impressed by the way the dialogue between Rachel and Laban that he depicted there is underscored by meaningful gesture: his fresco has, indeed, an almost Carraccesque emphasis on narrative clarity via the *affetti*. This aspect of Tiepolo's work reached a climax in the decade 1743 to 1753. Certainly, Tiepolo did not subscribe to Charles Le Brun's academic approach to expression; yet even a casual comparison of his fresco at Montecchio Maggiore portraying the family of Darius before Alexander with Veronese's painting of the same subject in the National Gallery, London, will reveal how Tiepolo restructured the scene to emphasize narrative and expressive

clarity—without, however, diminishing the Veronesian effect of opulence and ceremony. No less indicative of Tiepolo's approach are the preparatory drawings for the *Hyacinth* (no. 23, figs. 57, 58), which show that Tiepolo began by conceiving the gestures in less formal, less rhetorical terms. The same is true of the *modelli* for the two paintings of Rinaldo and Armida in Würzburg (no. 22a, b, figs. 55, 56). It is in the sense of this kind of clarity that Algarotti's comparison of Tiepolo to Raphael and Poussin becomes understandable—however wide of the mark we may think it. In his *Saggio sopra la pittura* (1763b [1963 ed., p. 114]) Algarotti notes how few Venetian paintings show a concern for expression, alluding to a work of Tiepolo's as exceptional. He makes the same point in a draft of a letter to Count Brühl, perceptively analyzed by Haskell 1958. Recently Aikema (1995, p. 50) has emphasized that Lazzarini was a conduit to Tiepolo for Bolognese ideas, but the possible importance of Carracci-Bolognese traditions for Tiepolo's use of gesture has yet to be examined.

24. For an idea of the gestures used onstage in the eighteenth century, see the treatise of Riccoboni (1728). Siddons (1822) refers actors to Cicero's precepts in the *De oratore*, and especially to book 3, chapter 59. Ebert-Schifferer (1992) has extremely acute comments on the relationship of the *stile recitativo* in early opera to classical oratory and rhetoric and, in turn, to gesture in painting. Algarotti makes reference to such early practitioners of opera as Jacopo Peri. It is especially pertinent to cite the example of Guercino in the context of a discussion of gesture, since he is not normally associated with academic theory. His progression from the use of a highly charged, chiaroscural style to a more formal one employing gesture for demonstrative rather than dramatic effect is not without a parallel in Tiepolo's development and points up the need for investigating further the impetus behind the Veronesian revival in Venetian painting and the specific direction in which Tiepolo took it.
25. See Algarotti's letter concerning the *Banquet of Cleopatra* now in the National Gallery of Victoria, Melbourne (Haskell 1958, p. 213).
26. Obviously, both painting and stage design depend on the same traditions of perspective. Here, again, it is worth citing Algarotti's *Saggio sopra la pittura* (1763b [1963 ed., p. 70]), in which he writes that "la prospettiva . . . non si rimase già confinata ne' teatri, ma nelle scuole trapassò della pittura, come un'arte non meno necessaria a' quadri, di quello che si fosse a' teatri medesimi." In the *Saggio sopra l'opera* (1763c [1963 ed., pp. 177–78]) Algarotti calls Bibbiena "il Paolo Veronese del Teatro" and, in the same context, stresses that painting reached its apogee in the cinquecento. This surely illuminates one aspect of Tiepolo's Veronese revival. It should be stressed that, contrary to what Levey (1957, pp. 310–13) suggests, the stagelike settings of the Room of the Iliad decorations at Villa Valmarana are less like those of contemporary theater practice, which were far more complicated, than those of sixteenth-century frescoes.
27. The collaboration between Tiepolo and Mengozzi Colonna can be described as one of carefully coordinated and complementary independence. Tiepolo's figurative component—even when it is merely a figure reclining on a feigned entablature or pediment (as occurs in Palazzo Labia, Venice, and in Ca' Rezzonico, Venice)—is invariably contained on its own *giornata* and carried out with the artist's habitual sensitivity to light and is clearly distinguishable from the contribution of Mengozzi Colonna. For further comments on the collaboration, see below in text and notes 47, 48.
28. For incisive comments on this affinity, see the entries by Mariuz in Pallucchini 1978, vol. 1, especially pp. 261–63.
29. For a list of the composers and the places of the first performances of operas based on Metastasio's librettos, see the entry in *New Grove Dictionary of Music* 1980, vol. 12, pp. 216–17. On 18 October 1743 Algarotti wrote Metastasio, who was then in Vienna, that he hoped the poet would write a treatise on poetics. "[S]arà il legere il Trattato di pittura del Vinci, le memorie del Montecuccoli," he declared (Algarotti 1784, pp. 22–25).
30. See "Sonnetto 4," composed in Vienna in 1753 while Metastasio was writing the *Olimpiade*. Metastasio 1857, p. 781: "Sogni e favole io fingo; e pure in carte / mentre favole e sogni orno e disegno, / in lor, folle ch'io son, prendo tal parte, / che del mal che inventai piango e mi sdegno. / Ma forse, allor che non m'inganna l'arte, / più saggio sono? E l'agitato ingegno / forse allor più tranquillo? O forse parte / da più salda cagion l'amor, lo sdegno? / Ah! che non sol quelle ch'io canto o scrivo / favole son; ma quanto temo e spero, / tutto è menzogna, e delirando io vivo. / Sogno della mia vita è il corso intero. / Deh tu, Signor, quando a destarmi arrivo, / fa' ch'io trovi riposo in sen del vero." The English translation is from Kay 1965, pp. 232–33.
31. Da Canal 1732 (1809 ed., p. XXXII).
32. Michelessi 1770, p. XCII. Michelessi thought Algarotti had had a beneficial, tempering effect on Tiepolo's imagination.
33. Mengs's reputed appreciation for Tiepolo is asserted in an entry (pp. 19–20) in a catalogue of a sale of 10 December 1789 in London. The picture in question was a painting by Tiepolo of Esther before Ahasuerus, described as "a rich and capital work of this great modern master of the Venetian school; of whom the late celebrated Chev. Mengs used to say, 'that he was born a painter'; and indeed, he cultivated every part of the art, instinctively, in a manner with true genius. Mengs, who worked with him at Madrid, both in the service of the king of Spain, collected with avidity, at his death, every stroke of his brush, or pencil, that he could possibly meet with; as it is mentioned, somewhere, in the life of Mengs, lately printed in Italy."
34. The letter was first published by Haskell (1960, p. 276).
35. The album appears to have passed through Tiepolo's son Giuseppe, a priest at S. Maria della Salute, Venice, to its convent's library and thence to Leopoldo Cicognara, who gave it in exchange to Canova. See Knox 1975a, pp. 5–7, and Knox and Byam Shaw 1987, p. 104.
36. The suggestion that the Dublin picture is a *modello* for a mural destined for the church of S. Ildefonso was made by Whistler (1985b). The painting is discussed in detail by Brown in Fort Worth 1993, pp. 326–28, no. 63.
37. For a convenient summary survey of the history of oil sketches and an introduction to those of Tiepolo, see the essays in Fort Worth 1993.
38. The work in question was a *modello* for an altarpiece commissioned by Count Giacomo Tassis in Bergamo. It is discussed in correspondence between Ricci and his patron (first published by Bottari and Ticozzi 1822–25, vol. 4, pp. 90–98) that is directly relevant to Tiepolo. Upon receiving the commission, Ricci asked for specifications. Once he obtained these, he submitted a description of his idea for comment and only then proceeded to paint what he referred to as a "modello ben terminato" that Tassis could add to his collection. Evidently, to execute such a *modello* was outside Ricci's usual practice, and he maintained that it had required as much work as the altarpiece itself, which could, indeed, be considered only a copy of the *modello*. See the analysis of Daniels 1976, pp. 10–11. Quite apart from Ricci's obvious desire to enhance the appeal of the object that his patron would possess, the letters demonstrate the circumstances under which a *modello* exceeded the definition of an oil sketch, or *macchia*, and could be considered an independent work of art. They also reveal the close connection in Ricci's mind between the *pensiero* and the *modello*; a *pensiero* that the altarpiece could develop or copy but on which it would nonetheless be dependent.
39. Piles 1715, pp. 69–70.
40. The meaning of the three terms in the eighteenth century is discussed by Brown in Fort Worth 1993, p. 17. Alpers and Baxandall (1994, p. 64) make some pertinent observations on the subject. When Algarotti described Tiepolo as a "pittore di macchia," he probably was referring to his facile manner of working, but in a letter of May 1756 to Giampiero Zanotti in Bologna he noted that he owned a *macchia* of Tiepolo's fresco in Villa Contarini at Mira, using the word interchangeably with *modello*.
41. Surely the most remarkable aspect of this prolific activity is the series of albums that gathered together types of drawings under such titles as *Vari studi e pensieri*, *Sole figure vestite*, and *Sole figure per soffitti*. It is now quite firmly established that these albums, nine of which were owned by Edward Cheney and sold after his death in 1884, were assembled in Tiepolo's workshop sometime before his departure for Spain. See especially Stuttgart 1970, pp. xiv–xvi, and Knox 1975a, pp. 3–9. These drawings must have served as a repertory to which Tiepolo (and his sons) could refer for inspiration, and

they certainly account for the recurrence of various gestures and motifs in his work. It is worth recording a few of the most signal instances of Tiepolo's adaptation of motifs invented for one commission to another. In developing his treatment of a ceiling for the Chiesa delle Cappuccine a Castello, Venice, Tiepolo exchanged the narrative interpretation of the story of Saint Helena discovering the true cross of the *modello* for the expository approach of the actual ceiling (both Gallerie dell'Accademia, Venice). He substituted the dramatic back view of the saint in the preliminary oil sketch for a saint whose statuesque pose was appropriated from the allegorical figure of Faith on the ceiling of the Scuola Grande dei Carmini, Venice. In the ceiling of the Kaisersaal in the Residenz, Würzburg, the figures of the river god and nymph repeat, with minor variations, two similar figures on the ceiling of the Palazzo Clerici, Milan, for which a pen-and-ink and wash study exists in the Metropolitan Museum (fig. 104); this is from an album from the Biron collection; see Bean and Griswold 1990, no. 199). The horse-drawn chariot of the Kaisersaal was recycled for a ceiling in Ca' Rezzonico, Venice, by simply reversing the design (or perhaps the cartoon). It was then further adapted for Palazzo Canossa, Verona, where the foreshortening was readjusted and the head of the most prominent horse turned in a different direction. See also the entry for no. 25a, b.

42. Because of the truly specious conjectures that have been advanced about Tiepolo's working procedure and fresco technique—represented in their most extreme form by Alpers and Baxandall (1994, pp. 74–78)—it is necessary to emphasize that his fresco practice was in all respects conventional. The physical evidence of the frescoes leaves no doubt that he used full-scale, detailed cartoons, the designs of which were transferred to the damp plaster by tracing with a stylus (see Staschull in Würzburg 1996, vol. 2, pp. 128–47). On the ceiling over the stairwell in the Residenz, Würzburg, for example, it is clear where the stylus occasionally punched through the cartoon and gouged the wall. Most work was done *a fresco*, with *a secco* reserved for specific pigments, details, and adjustments. This enabled Tiepolo to proceed with extraordinary rapidity—as the relatively small number of *giornate* well attest—and to use assistants in an efficacious and almost indiscernible fashion. A technical analysis of the ceiling at Würzburg has demonstrated that there is no validity to Knox's notion that a group of drawings of disputed and dubious attribution was used by Tiepolo as substitutes for cartoons and is related to the divisions of the wall into *giornate*. The attribution of these drawings rests on their real qualities rather than on a putative function. It was Knox who first postulated an unconventional fresco technique based on assumptions about the function of the various drawings he ascribes to Tiepolo and about the lack of any extant cartoons. See, for example, Knox (1960) 1975a, pp. 17, 24–25; Stuttgart 1970, pp. 9–10; and Knox 1980a, pp. 14–18, 45–48. The cartoons may not have survived, but we have several notices relating to their use. Thus, in April 1751 Tiepolo is recorded as beginning his work at the Residenz with tracing ("durchbauschen"). In 1764 the artist wrote a previous patron in an attempt to procure a cartoon that he wanted to recycle for a commission in Madrid. And in 1784 Giandomenico, whose technique must have mirrored that of his father, noted in a letter that in Genoa he had been assigned space in a convent where he could begin work on cartoons for his ceiling. See Urbani de Gheltof 1879, pp. 24–25, 34. I would like to thank Ottorino Nonfarmale for taking the time to discuss the Ca' Rezzonico frescoes with me, and Werner Rescher and Ingrid Stümmer for guiding me through their investigation of the Würzburg ceiling from the vantage point of the scaffolding.

43. Perhaps the most obvious example of this activity is provided by the numerous replicas of a composition with three figures of saints and an acolyte that derive from Tiepolo's altarpiece of Saints Maximus and Oswald in the church of S. Massimo, Padua. It cannot be said whether these *modelli* relate to another, lost altarpiece or represent an attempt to meet the market demand created by the local veneration of the saints in the Padua commission. Brown (in Fort Worth 1993, pp. 235–41) discusses the problem at length. It should, however, be noted that one of the two pictures exhibited at Fort Worth (no. 32) was certainly a workshop replica. The finest version is that in the National Gallery, London. See Keith 1994.

44. Zanetti 1771, p. 464.

45. See Algarotti 1763a (1963 ed., p. 22).

46. The letter, which dates from 1756, is cited by Pavanello 1979, p. 53. It could apply, with equal justice, to the cycle at Valmarana and underscores, again, the degree to which parallels between opera and painting pepper Algarotti's writings.

47. This practice is documented visually by Mengozzi Colonna's drawing in the Museo Correr, Venice, for the ceiling of the Villa Contarini at Mira. He concerned himself exclusively with the feigned balcony, and it must have been with this drawing in hand that Tiepolo worked out the poses of the figures who were to be shown leaning over it. See ibid., pp. 52–57. Just how closely the two artists were allied is demonstrated by a second drawing by Mengozzi Colonna, for an independent project that was, according to an inscription on the verso, evaluated by Tiepolo and a professional scenographer, Romualdo Mauri. See Moschini 1963.

48. The drawing in the Pierpont Morgan Library, New York, shows an elaborate balcony populated with figures and a ceiling with an irregularly shaped opening. The related drawing in the Museo Horne, Florence, includes only the outlines of the architecture, traced as an aide-mémoire in working out the figural portion. It is not possible to state with certainty which was made first, but it is reasonable to suppose that a drawing of the architecture had initially been executed—possibly by Mengozzi Colonna—and was then copied onto two separate sheets of paper, only one of which was worked up in detail by Tiepolo. Were a painted *modello* to survive, we would expect it to relate only to the composition of the ceiling opening. For the Morgan drawing, see New York 1971, p. 44, no. 69.

49. For the letter, dated 23 November 1661, see Ruffo 1917, vol. 1, p. 59: "io (come già scrissi) non uso far disegni ad alcuno perche non mi posso, nè voglio legar l'arbitrio nel opera, tutta volta però per condescendere al piacere di V. S. Ill.ma faronne uno acciò in certo modo vedino ove penderà il pensiero senza però intendermi obligarmi al detto perchè voglio poter cangiare conforme il bisogno per meglioramento del opera."

50. Algarotti 1763a (1963 ed., p. 22).

THE MYTH OF PHAETHON

47a. Phaethon and Apollo
47b. Phaethon and Apollo

47a. Phaethon and Apollo
Ca. 1733–36
67.8 × 52.5 cm (26¾ × 20¾ in.)
Gemäldegalerie der Akademie der Bildenden Künste, Vienna (484)

47b. Phaethon and Apollo
Ca. 1733–36
91 × 73.6 cm (35⅞ × 29 in.)
The Bowes Museum, Barnard Castle, County Durham, England (51)

PROVENANCE, 47a:
A. Lamberg-Sprinzenstein bequest (1822)

REFERENCES:
Molmenti 1909, p. 274; Sack 1910, pp. 169, 203; Dodgson 1917; Morassi 1941–42, p. 265; Lorenzetti in Venice 1951, p. 35, no. 24; Morassi 1955a, p. 34; Benesch 1957, pp. 218–19; Morassi 1962, pp. 3, 66; Pallucchini 1968, pp. 94–95, no. 61b; Rizzi in Udine 1971, pp. 51, no. 18; G. Knox 1975a, p. 12; Martini 1982, p. 510 n. 194; Giltay in Rotterdam 1983, pp. 170–73, no. 49; Levey 1986, pp. 60–61; Barcham 1989, p. 175, n. 29; Fort Worth 1993, pp. 161–68, no. 7; Gemin and Pedrocco 1993, p. 314, no. 211

PROVENANCE, 47b:
John and Josephine Bowes, Barnard Castle, County Durham, England (before 1874)

REFERENCES:
Morassi 1941–42, p. 265; Lorenzetti in Venice 1951, p. 35; Morassi 1962, pp. 3, 66; Pallucchini 1968, pp. 94–95, no. 61b; Knox 1975a, p. 12; Martini 1982, p. 510 n. 194; Giltay in Rotterdam 1983, p. 172; Levey 1986, pp. 60–61; Fort Worth 1993, pp. 165–66; Gemin and Pedrocco 1993, p. 314, no. 210

Ovid (*Metamorphoses*, 2.35 ff.) tells the story of how Phaethon, son of Apollo and the mortal Clymene, sought out his father in the god's luminous, columned palace and, as proof of his paternity, foolheartedly demanded permission to drive the chariot of the sun across the heavens; granted this privilege, he perished in the process of his ride. Tiepolo followed Ovid in including, on banks of clouds, the four seasons: a garlanded, Bacchus-like Autumn standing next to Winter, "with white and shaggy locks,"[1] and the two female beauties, Spring and Summer. Putti prepare the golden chariot forged by Vulcan, while the Hours yoke the team of eager horses. In the Vienna picture the sinister figure of Time hovers, vulturelike, above Phaethon, who is shown rapt before his radiant father. In the Barnard Castle version Time hurries the youth to his doom, interrupting a poignant farewell between father and son. In the latter painting a nocturnal bat flees the rays of dawn above a sleepy couple. In the former a star-spangled morning sky serves as the backdrop, together with the arc of the zodiac (Scorpio, who frightens Phaethon so that he drops the reins and loses control of the horses, plays a prominent role); Lucifer, the morning star, extinguishes his torch with a jug of water at the approaching dawn, and a winged figure lies slumped over in the foreground.

The subject had been treated memorably by Poussin in the previous century (Gemäldegalerie, Staatliche Museen zu Berlin; engraved by Nicolas Perelle, ca. 1666). Prior to 1720 Tiepolo had frescoed the theme on the walls of Palazzo Baglioni, Massanzago, near Padua (fig. 15), and between 1730 and late spring or early summer 1731 he decorated one of five ceilings in Palazzo Archinto, Milan (destroyed, World War II), with the story. Tiepolo may have used Giovanni Andrea dell'Anguillara's 1561 translation of the *Metamorphoses*, as Poussin did (he referred to the same edition for the *Hyacinth* [no. 23]).

Despite the view expressed by Morassi in 1942 that the Vienna and Barnard Castle pictures are independent works, they are usually associated with the Palazzo Archinto ceiling, painted to celebrate the wedding of Filippo Archinto and Giulia Borromeo.[2] The Vienna picture shares a number of features with the ceiling, for which there is a related *modello* (Los Angeles County Museum of Art), but its closest affinities are with an exceptionally large and detailed drawing in pen and ink with brown wash (British Museum, London),[3] in which Time, the Hour riding the horse, and the sleeping winged figure are very much alike. Despite these similarities, the drawing—surely a preliminary study for the ceiling, although it develops the composition horizontally rather than vertically—is viewed *di sotto-in-sù* rather than head-on and shows an expansive sky with the individual figure groups arranged in a sort of counterpoint instead of the densely packed figural composition of the easel painting. By comparison with the Los Angeles *modello*,[4] the two pictures catalogued here, especially the Barnard Castle painting, are blonder in tonality and freer in execution, with little of the tight, scumbling brushwork or deep colors that are characteristic of Tiepolo's oil sketches of the years about 1730 and, in particular, of those directly related to the Palazzo Archinto ceilings.[5] Rather, the Vienna and Barnard Castle oil sketches relate to Tiepolo's work from after about 1733, and it is perhaps worth noting that the same loosening of execution, with broader, more diaphanous areas of shadow, appears in the ink-wash drawings associated with his frescoes of 1734 for Villa Loschi at Monteviale, near Vicenza. Brown has singled out the style of the Barnard Castle oil sketch, notably its bluish ground, as atypical for Tiepolo; without accepting her radical conclusion that this exceptionally beautiful work is a mid-nineteenth-century pastiche—her argument does not make sufficient allowance for Tiepolo's constant experimentation (the color of his grounds is rarely as consistent as some would claim)—we may take her observations as supporting the notion that the two oil sketches are not necessarily contemporary. Interestingly, Levey describes the Barnard Castle picture as "of around 1731, possibly a little later," but then analyzes that work and the Vienna painting as though they represent sequential stages in the creation of the Palazzo Archinto ceiling.

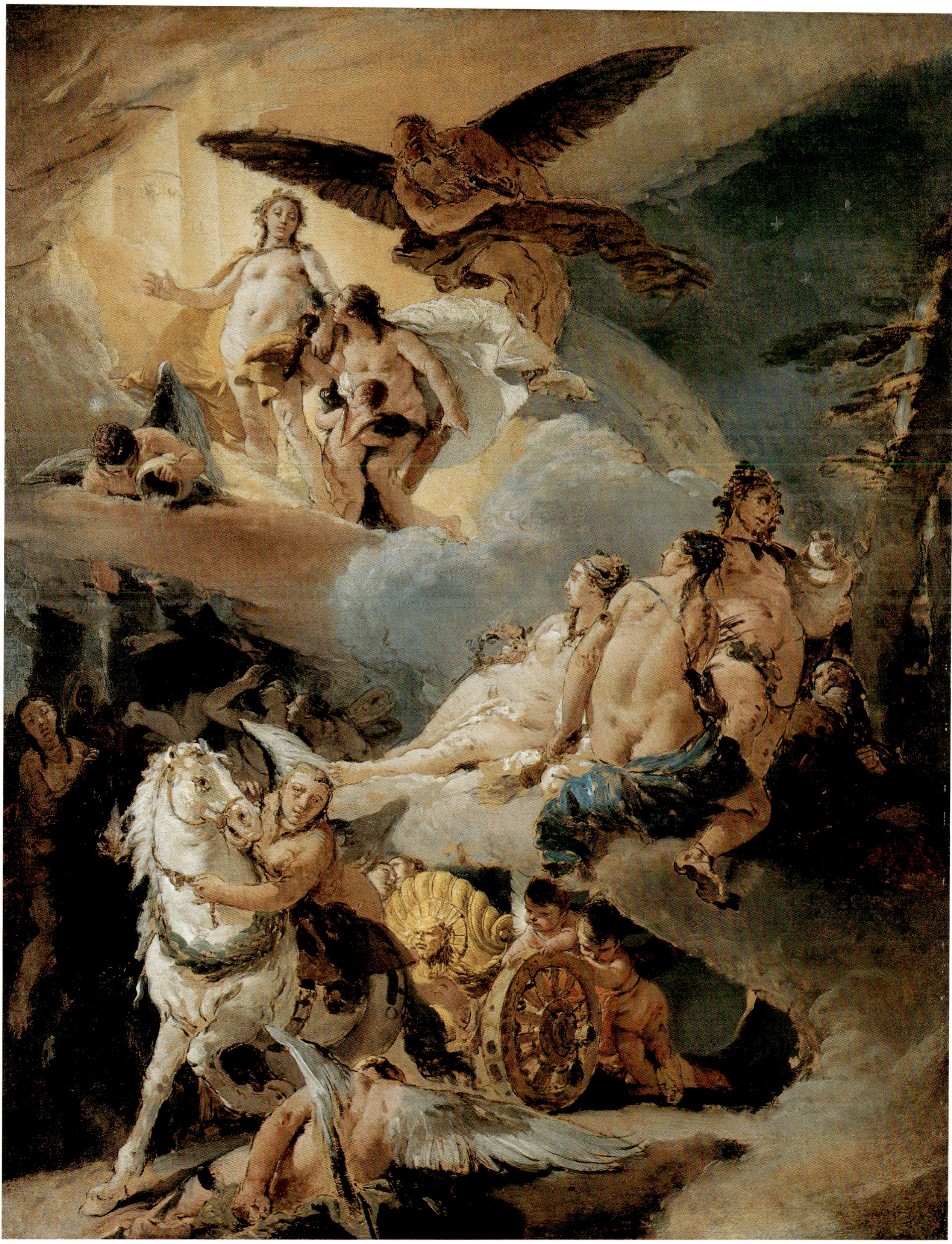

47a

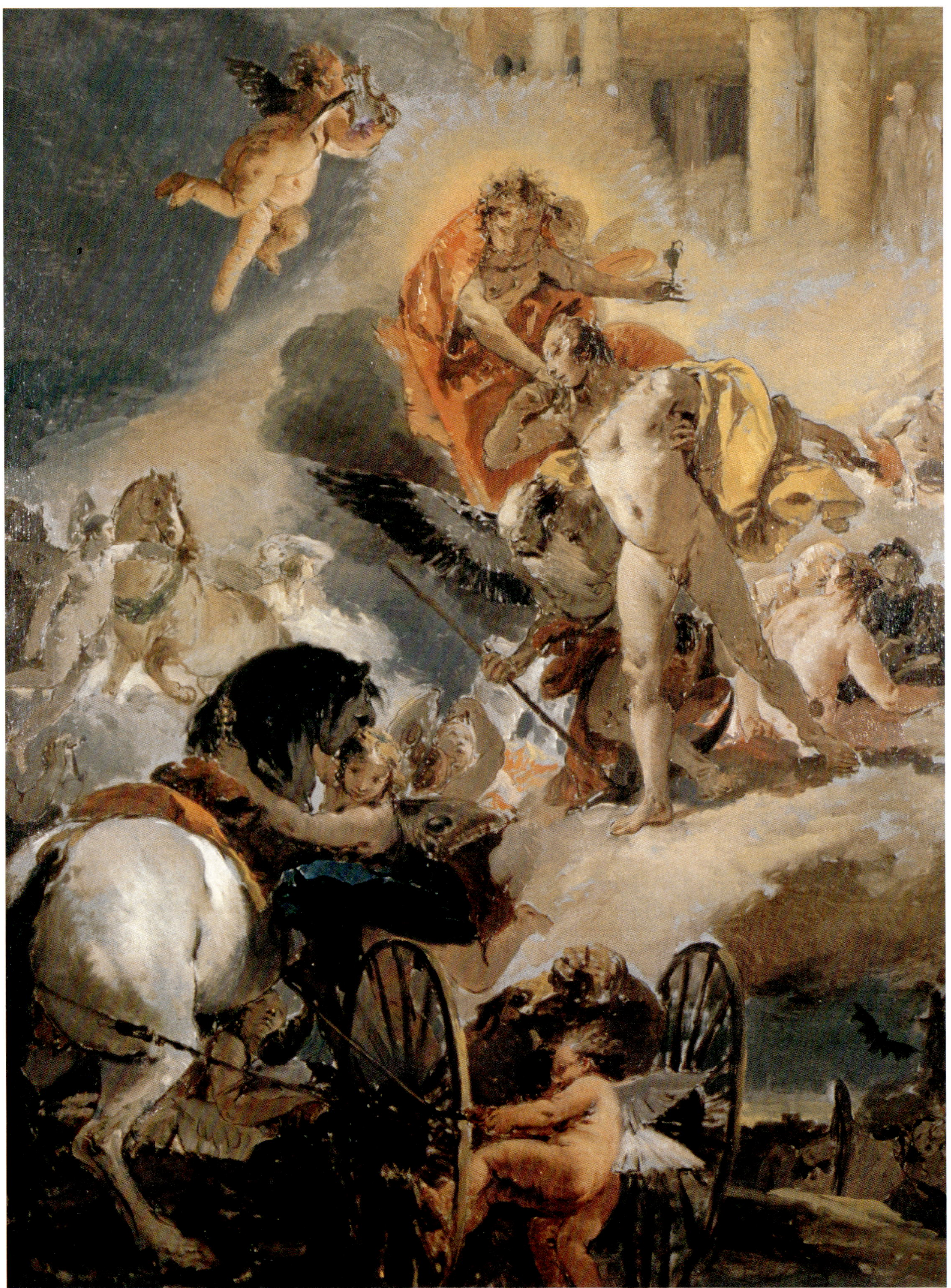

47b

What we seem to have here is an instance of Tiepolo reworking a theme treated earlier and for another context by, in the Vienna painting, varying and rearranging the motifs and, in the other, radically reconsidering the entire composition toward new expressive ends. It cannot be said whether the two pictures are independent exercises or alternative proposals for one or more larger, undocumented commissions: the Barnard Castle canvas, although summarily painted, is unusually large for a *modello*, while the Vienna painting is finished with a care that would make it suitable for a collector. In analyzing the merits of the individual compositions and their relation to each other, it is important to recall that Tiepolo is one of those artists who developed his ideas less through a process of self-editing and increasing concision than through one of variation. When he reworked a composition, it was generally not in the interest of obtaining a tighter structure or bringing a narrative exposition into sharper focus but of giving it a different tone, a new emphasis, or more animation. Thus, in the Vienna picture there is a contrast between the voluptuous Hour advancing on horseback toward the viewer, her lounging companions, and the brilliance of Apollo's realm, whereas in the Barnard Castle painting the focus is on Phaethon bidding his father farewell, given a tragic dimension by the action of Time.

KC

Notes

1. Ovid 1967, p. 50.
2. See Sohm 1984, pp. 71–74.
3. See Dodgson 1917 and Knox 1975a, p. 12.
4. Brown (in Fort Worth 1993, p. 167), calls the Los Angeles picture a *ricordo* rather than a *modello*. This is really no more than a conjecture, and one that I cannot accept inasmuch as the work seems to me completely uniform in style and character with the other known *modelli* (which include an example at the Frick Collection, New York, that also has a carefully shaped picture field).
5. See Martini 1982, p. 510, n. 194, and Gemin and Pedrocco 1993, p. 314, nos. 210–11.

THE SCALZI CEILING

48a. Miracle of the Holy House of Loreto
48b. Miracle of the Holy House of Loreto

48a. Miracle of the Holy House of Loreto
1743
124 × 85 cm (48⅞ × 33½ in.)
Gallerie dell'Accademia, Venice

48b. Miracle of the Holy House of Loreto
1743
123 × 77 cm (48½ × 30⅜ in.)
J. Paul Getty Museum, Malibu
(94.PA.20)

These brilliantly painted canvases—dazzling in their free, draftsmanlike brushwork—are alternative *modelli* for the vast ceiling of the seventeenth-century Venetian church of the Discalced Carmelites, S. Maria di Nazareth (or degli Scalzi) (fig. 111). Destroyed by an Austrian bomb on 28 October 1915, the ceiling was perhaps Tiepolo's most stunning ecclesiastical decoration, incorporating a tour de force of illusionistic architecture painted by Girolamo Mengozzi Colonna. The visionary central scene was shown as though viewed through a balustraded opening in the vault, the squinches of which contained feigned balconies with spectators gazing raptly at the miracle, while the pendentives were decorated with niches containing Old Testament prophets and the undersides of the large, triangular groins displayed feigned reliefs with Old Testament stories relating to the Virgin.[1] The squinches and pendentive sections survive, detached, in the Gallerie dell'Accademia, Venice. For reasons quite apart from the quality of illusionistic invention elicited—abundantly apparent in these two *modelli* and in a number of preparatory drawings[2]—the commission is of special interest: both for the subject, never before treated in such compelling terms and on such a monumental scale, and for a remarkable series of associated documents that enables us to follow in considerable detail the stages by which a collaborative scheme of enormous complexity was created.[3]

According to legend, in 1291 the Virgin's simple house in Nazareth was miraculously transported through the air by angels to protect it from the advancing Muslim armies. Landing first at Tersatz, on the Adriatic coast,

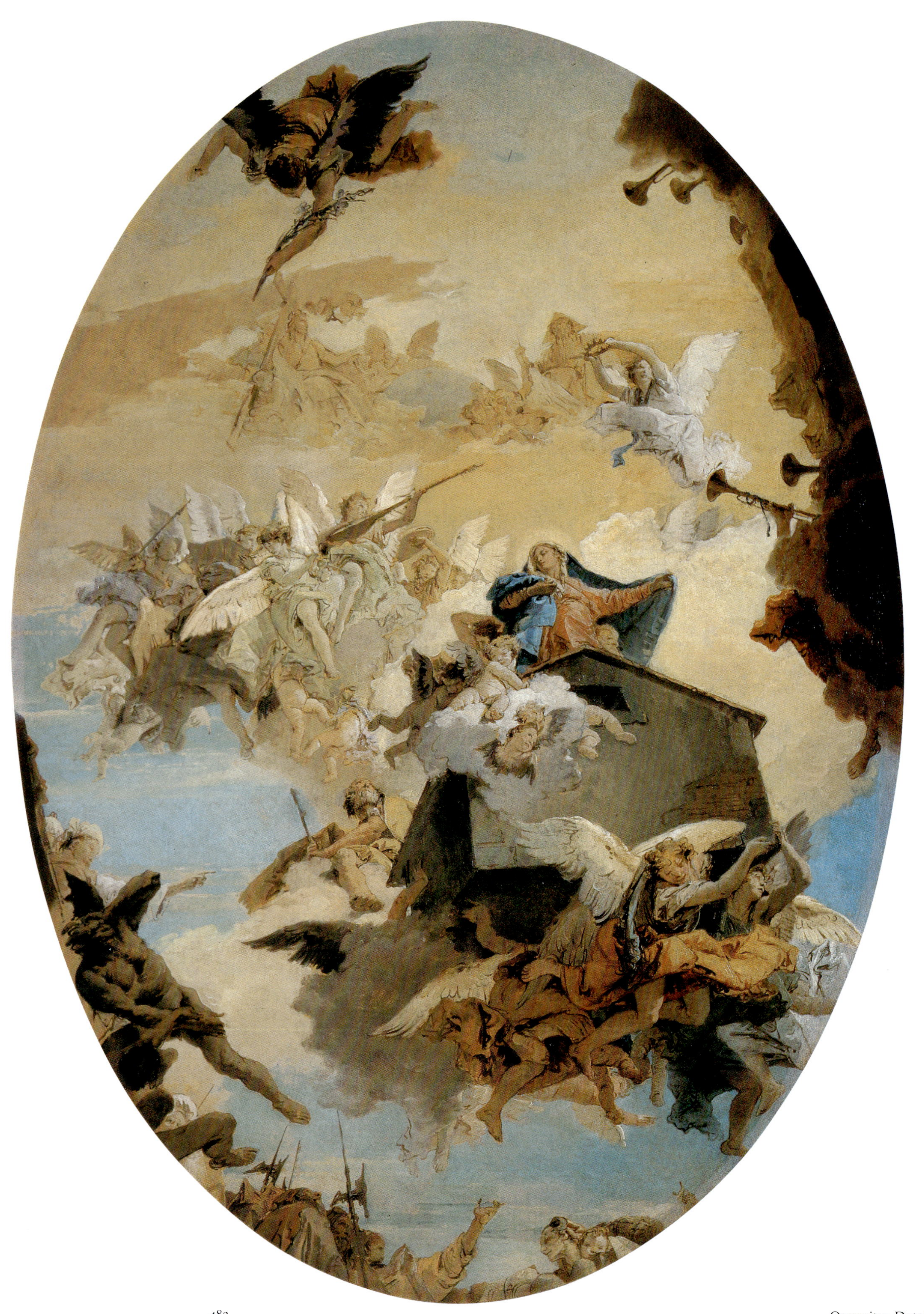

48a

Opposite: Detail, no. 48a

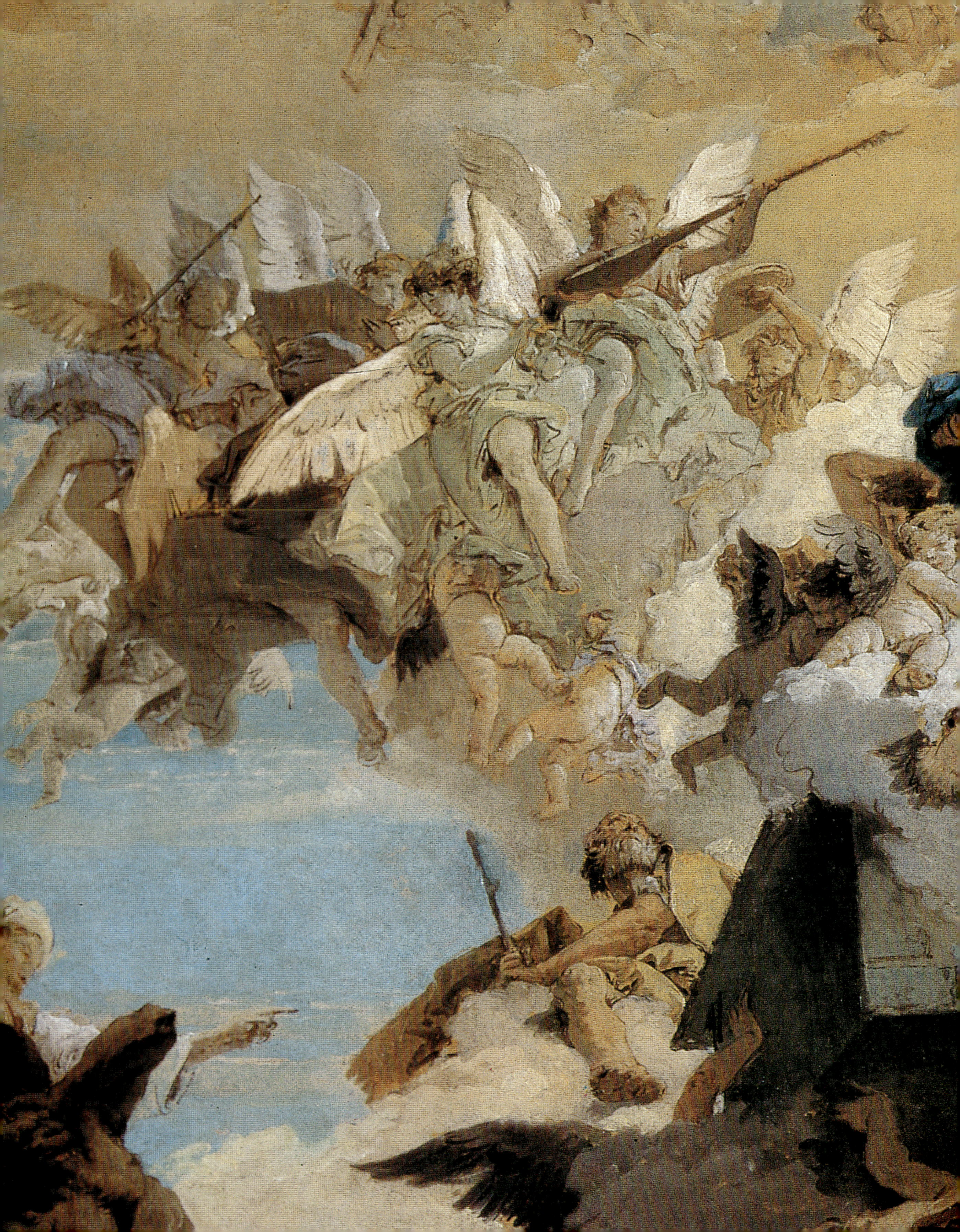

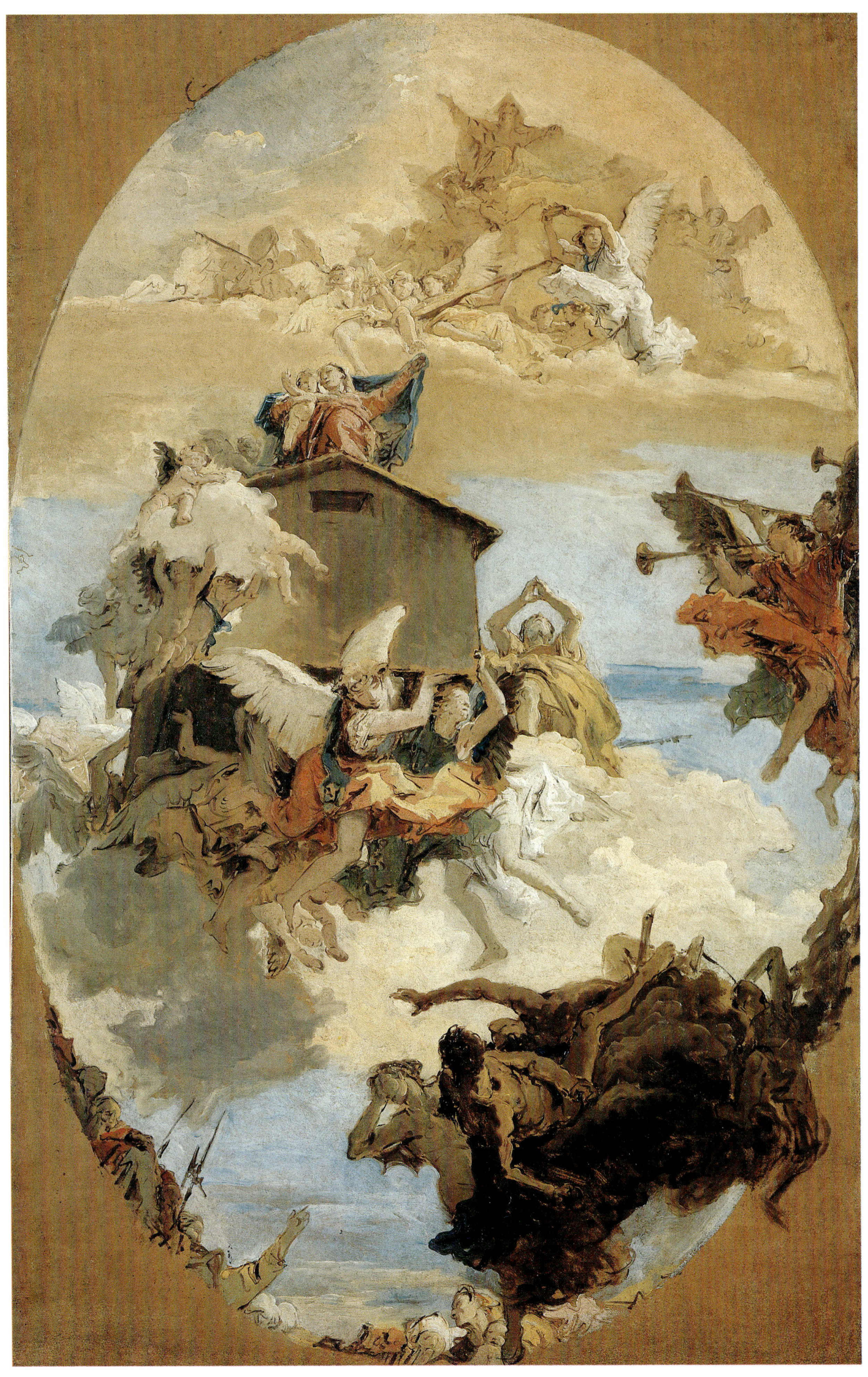

48b

Opposite: Fig. 111. *Miracle of the Holy House of Loreto* (ceiling, destroyed). Fresco. S. Maria di Nazareth (the Scalzi), Venice

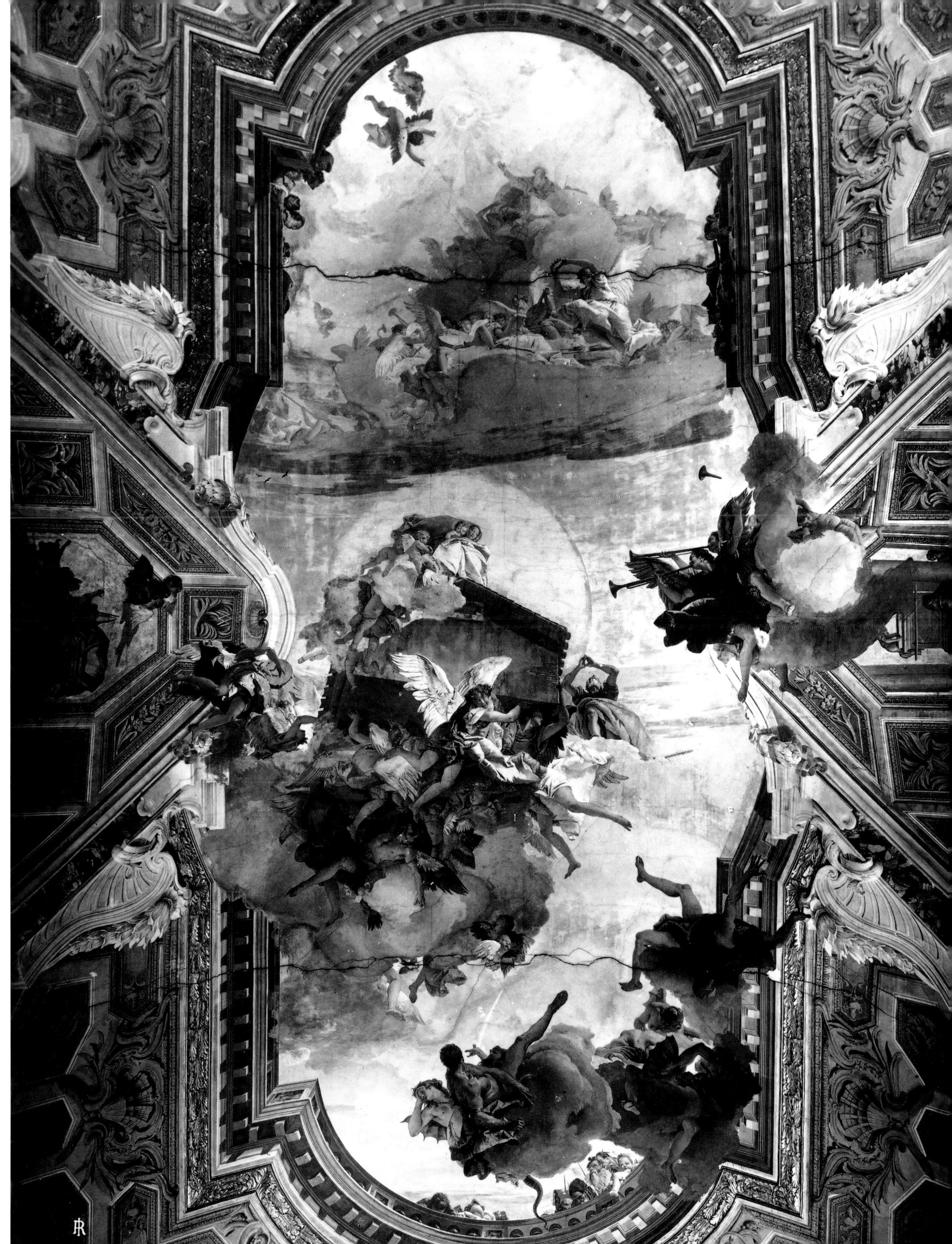

PROVENANCE, 48a:
Private oratory, Crespano (until ca. 1890); Antonio dal Zotto, Venice (ca. 1890–1918); his heirs (1918–30); acquired for Gallerie dell'Accademia, Venice (1930)

REFERENCES:
Modern 1902, p. 30; Molmenti 1909, p. 65; Sack 1910, pp. 85, 154; Moschetti 1928, p. 50; Fogolari 1931, pp. 18, 24, 28–29; Morassi 1943, p. 25; Lorenzetti in Venice 1951, pp. 67–69, no. 50; Mras 1956, pp. 41–44; Morassi 1962, pp. 19, 54, 57; Rossacher in Darmstadt 1965, p. 166; Knox 1968, p. 397; Pallucchini 1968, pp. 108–9, no. 151; Zampetti in Venice 1969b, p. 378, no. 175; Rizzi in Udine 1971, p. 92, no. 45; Barcham 1979, pp. 430, n. 1, 438; Levey 1986, pp. 112–15; Barcham 1989, p. 137; Nepi Scirè 1991, p. 247; Barcham 1992, p. 88; Fort Worth 1993, pp. 228–31; Gemin and Pedrocco 1993, pp. 123, 379–81, no. 346a; Alpers and Baxandall 1994, pp. 66, 148

PROVENANCE, 48b:
Possibly Tiepolo's widow, Cecilia Guardi, Venice; Edward Cheney, London and Badger Hall, Shropshire (until 1885; sale, Christie's, London, 29 April 1885, lot 160); Archibald Philip, fifth earl of Rosebery, Mentmore (1929–74); Eva, countess of Rosebery (sale, Sotheby's, London, 11 December 1974, lot 15); British Rail Pension Fund (1974–94)

REFERENCES:
Waagen 1857, p. 173; Lorenzetti in Venice 1951, pp. 67–69, no. 51; Watson 1952, p. 44; Mras 1956, pp. 41–44; Morassi 1962, pp. 19, 54, 57; Rossacher in Darmstadt 1965, p. 166; Knox 1968, p. 397; Pallucchini 1968, pp. 108–9, no. 151; Rizzi in Udine 1971, p. 92; Barcham 1979, pp. 430 n. 1, 438; Levey 1986, pp. 112–15; Barcham 1989, p. 137; Barcham 1992, p. 88; Fort Worth 1993, pp. 228–31, no. 29; Gemin and Pedrocco 1993, pp. 123, 379–81, no. 346b; Alpers and Baxandall 1994, pp. 66, 148

in 1294 the house removed itself to Italy, where it eventually settled at Loreto. By the end of the fifteenth century Loreto had become a major pilgrimage site, and two centuries later there were numerous Loreto shrines throughout Europe. The Carmelites, who originated in Palestine and traced their roots to the Old Testament prophet Elijah, had claimed guardianship of the house when it was still in Nazareth, and in 1489 they were granted custody of the shrine in Loreto. The church of the Discalced Carmelites in Venice was dedicated on the Feast of the Translation of the Holy House in 1650[4] and had as its high altarpiece a fifteenth-century image of the Virgin of Nazareth. That the miracle of the holy house of Loreto should be the subject given to Tiepolo is, therefore, no more surprising than the fact that his composition includes secondary references to the Immaculate Conception—a doctrine the Carmelites vigorously supported.[5]

The choice of Tiepolo to carry out the commission was almost inevitable. In the Scalzi itself he had already frescoed the vaults of the chapels of Saint Teresa (between about 1727 and 1730, although the decorations are often dated earlier; see fig. 17) and the Crucifix (about 1732–33). Additionally, for the Carmelite church of S. Aponal, Venice, he had painted a large canvas showing the Virgin of Mount Carmel (documented 1722–27; fig. 19). And in 1740 he undertook to decorate the ceiling of the Scuola Grande dei Carmini, Venice, with eight canvases (the ceiling was unveiled, without the central canvas, three months before the contract with the Scalzi was signed; fig. 66).

The contract for the new decorations at the Scalzi dates from 13 September 1743 and bound Tiepolo to complete the work within two years for 4,500 ducats. He was to supervise all aspects of the project, but Mengozzi Colonna—who had executed the *quadratura* for the chapels of Saint Teresa and the Crucifix—was to collaborate by painting a fictive architectural setting that would "correspond with good harmony with the rest of the church." Tiepolo was also to see to hiring a plasterer to prepare the ceiling. On 15 September a Master Alvise de Preti was employed to put up the scaffolding, described as the "armatura per dipingere il soffitto," and to provide protective covering for the three main chapels and the organ. A further agreement, of 1 October, obliged Mengozzi Colonna "to make a drawing that would also be in keeping with the conception of Sig. Giovanni Battista Tiepolo" and stipulated that his portion of the total salary would be 1,500 ducats. Mengozzi Colonna's work was interrupted on 14 November, when Alvise de Preti was brought in again to modify ("accomodare") the vault by removing the central part and restructuring it with a system of wood slats and plaster like that typically used in Venetian frescoed ceilings. This was to be done to the satisfaction of Mengozzi Colonna, who received payments from December 1743 through October 1745. After obtaining 100 zecchini from the prior on 13 September 1743, Tiepolo was not paid again until 14 April 1745. The vault was completed on 18 November 1745, and Tiepolo received his final payment on 23 November. Thus, frescoing apparently began with the execution of Mengozzi Colonna's *quadratura*, and the central scene seems to have been painted last. While Mengozzi Colonna was painting his frescoes, Tiepolo is known to have undertaken other commissions (he was producing altarpieces and working concurrently with Mengozzi Colonna on a ceiling decoration for the Capuchins). During this period he also had to prepare the cartoons for the Scalzi's central scene as well as for the figurative sections of Mengozzi Colonna's fictive architecture.

Although the documents establish that Tiepolo had complete control of the project, Mengozzi Colonna obviously played a crucial role. It was, for example, evidently on Mengozzi Colonna's advice that the vault was restructured, and it was certainly his architectural setting that gave Tiepolo's central scene its final shape and illusionistic élan. Nonetheless, the primary features of that scene (as opposed to the figurative portions of his collaborator's painted architecture) were worked out early on—probably shortly after 13 September 1743—and independent of their architectural surround. It is for this reason that both *modelli* have the same oval format, rather than the elongated quatrefoil format of the ceiling. This seemingly obvious point needs to be emphasized, since it has become common to explain the unusual existence of two, alternative *modelli* as a consequence of Tiepolo's response to the structural work done on the vault and to the modified picture field—despite the fact that this presumed modification is not taken into account in the second *modello*.[6] The changes made in the second *modello* are in fact best understood as Tiepolo's response to the demands of his Carmelite patrons.

In the earlier *modello* (no. 48a) Tiepolo gave the Virgin the aspect of the Annunciate and included a lily-bearing angel acrobatically descending toward her—a motif borrowed from a contemporary altarpiece portraying the Martyrdom of Saint John, bishop of Bergamo (cathedral, Bergamo).[7] This narrative interpolation—meant as a gloss on some of the Old Testament scenes Tiepolo would place in the architectural surround—was suppressed in the second *modello*, in which the Virgin was provided with the fully visible Child common to most depictions of the translation of the holy house. Christ was removed from the heavens of this later *modello,* leaving them occupied solely by God the Father, the dove of the Holy Spirit, and a choir of angels. The house was moved higher in the picture field, sacrificing the powerful suggestion of movement that prevails in the first version but giving it greater prominence. Here the house is set in meaningful contraposition to a welter of diminutively winged figures plummeting through space and emblematic of falsehood and heresy, an obvious reference to the long-standing controversies surrounding the Virgin's immaculacy. In the finished fresco the Virgin, shown against an immense silver moon—her most enduring apocalyptic attribute—looks down at the falling figures. (Two sheets with pen-and-ink drawings document Tiepolo's concern with the attitude of the Virgin at the various stages of planning.)[8] Saint Joseph, who has nothing to do with the conventional iconography of the miracle of the holy house, was given a central place in the second *modello* (devotion to him was popularized by the great Discalced Carmelite Saint Teresa, and in 1729 his name was inserted into the Litany of the Saints by Benedict XIII).[9] His initially generic posture—interchangeable with any number of Tiepolo's seated figures viewed *di sotto-in-sù*—was replaced with one of ecstatic adoration borrowed from a contemporary ceiling design for the apotheosis of Saint Roch.[10] These alterations all relate to the essential meaning of the fresco, and they must have been worked out with the Carmelites or an adviser, as were the Old Testament scenes of Mengozzi Colonna's architectural surround. Significantly, except for the addition of the sphere of the moon, the compositional adjustments realized subsequent to the execution of the second *modello* were purely formal, made to accommodate the scene to Mengozzi Colonna's architectural framework and to enhance the illusionistic effect.

Because many writers have insisted that modifications to the structure of the vault impelled the changes seen in the later *modello*, it is worth pointing out that the one constant in all phases of Tiepolo's design is the triangular group of trumpeting angels on the right. These angels occur at precisely the point where the groin vault of a side chapel impinged on the nave vault, and they were Tiepolo's means of masking this structural intrusion. His placement of the Virgin's house in the picture field was no less mindful of this element, which even Mengozzi Colonna's feigned architecture was not able to disguise in a completely satisfactory way. There are few better examples of the way Tiepolo's inventive genius responded to practical issues. At the same time, a comparison of the initial conventional oval Tiepolo chose for the ceiling with the final quatrefoil shows how much the project profited from Mengozzi Colonna's architectural imagination. Interestingly, the balustraded opening, populated by the gesticulating infidels Tiepolo indicated in his two *modelli*, is closely related to the scheme Mengozzi Colonna devised for Tiepolo's frescoes at Villa Contarini-Pisani at Mira (fig. 108). Taken together, then, these two oil sketches demonstrate the ways Tiepolo's *modelli* sometimes functioned as tentative proposals rather than as fixed schemes and reveal as well how his own imagination responded to the dictates of site and patron and benefited from his collaboration with a brilliant *quadraturista.*

A smaller, highly improbable candidate for the third oil sketch by Tiepolo, which records—or rather copies—the final scheme, is known, as is a copy by Mariano Fortuny.[11]

KC

Notes

1. For the program of frescoes, see Knox 1968, pp. 394–97, and, especially, Barcham 1979, pp. 432–33, 440–42.
2. On the drawings, see Knox 1968.
3. For the documents, see Fogolari 1931, pp. 30–32, and Barcham 1979, p. 430 n. 1.
4. This church was subsequently replaced by the present church, which was designed by Baldassare Longhena in 1654. See Fogolari 1931, pp. 18–20, and Franzoi and Di Stefano 1976, pp. 98–99.
5. Barcham (1979, pp. 434–36, 444–45) gives the background for this.
6. Fogolari (1931, p. 19) was the first to advance the unfounded idea that prior to Alvise de Preti's work the nave vault presented a continuous surface, reflected in the design of Tiepolo's *modello*. In fact, the work undertaken with the approval of Mengozzi Colonna must have been an attempt to reduce the interference of the prominent groin vault. See Lewis 1979, p. 64.
7. See Gemin and Pedrocco 1993, pp. 382–83, no. 354.
8. On these, see Mras 1956.
9. Barcham (1979, pp. 442–43) discusses the devotion to Saint Joseph.
10. On the Saint Roch and the project with which it might be connected, see especially Brown in Fort Worth 1993, p. 208.
11. These two works are discussed by Rossacher (in Darmstadt 1965); Barcham (1979, p. 433; nn. 5, 6); Brown (in Fort Worth 1993, p. 231 n. 10).

49. Apollo and the Four Continents

†49. Apollo and the Four Continents
Doc. 1752
185.4 × 139.4 cm (73 × 54⅞ in.)
Inscribed at sides: EVROPA / AFRICAE / AMERICA / ASIA
The Metropolitan Museum of Art, New York; Gift of Mr. and Mrs. Charles Wrightsman, 1977 (1977.1.3)

From December 1750 to November 1753, Tiepolo was employed in Würzburg by Prince-Bishop Carl Philipp von Greiffenclau to decorate his magnificent palace, the Residenz, designed by Balthasar Neumann. The first commission was undertaken in the octagonal banqueting room, the Kaisersaal, where Tiepolo frescoed the vaults with an illusionistic ceiling and two large scenes relating to the life of the twelfth-century emperor Frederick Barbarossa and also produced allegories painted in monochrome and over-lifesize figures shown as though cavorting on the actual cornice of the room. A highly detailed program had been sent to the artist in Venice before he departed for Würzburg, and after it was translated into Italian, he seems to have set about preparing *modelli* to show his new patron.[1] (This was the same procedure adopted later for the commission for the royal palace in Madrid [see no. 53].) His collaborators in the brilliant undertaking at Würzburg were his son Giandomenico and the fabulously gifted Swiss-born stuccoist Antonio Bossi, who had been active in Franconia since 1733 and had already carried out projects in the Residenz. By July 1751 work in the Kaisersaal had progressed far enough for Greiffenclau to show it off to guests. However, the room was still incomplete on 21 April 1752,[2] when Greiffenclau and his sister, Baroness Sickingen, visited Tiepolo in his apartments in the Residenz to view a *modello* for a second, even grander project: the decoration of the vast ceiling over Neumann's staircase leading from the ground-floor entrance to the main floor—an area measuring over nineteen by thirty meters (see frontis., p. 18). The formal commission followed that July. All trace of the *modello* was lost until it was identified in 1954 by a diner at the Hendon Hall Hotel, outside London, where it was installed in the ceiling of a corridor;[3] it is now in The Metropolitan Museum of Art and shows the proposed fresco as well as the eight sculpted figures on the cornice realized in stucco by Bossi.

An initial program for the decoration of the palace, including the ceiling over the stairwell, had been drawn up in 1735 for the then prince-bishop, Philipp Franz von Schönborn—well before the staircase was completed. It provided for the division of the vault into five picture fields, each treating a historical subject. (Some of these themes were subsequently depicted in the Kaisersaal.) Revisions followed, together with proposals by a succession of artists. There is an oil sketch of about 1739–40 by Johann-Evangelist Holzer (Germanisches Nationalmuseum, Nuremberg) showing the requisite historical scenes viewed through an elaborate *quadratura* framework—a de rigueur element in German decorations at this time—and drawings exist as well by the local painter Anton Clemens Lünenschloss (Martin von Wagner-Museum, Würzburg), one of which is dated 1749, that also employ a five-part division. It may have been the lack of truly outstanding talent that prompted Neumann, in an architectural drawing with a cross-section view of the staircase, to consider an alternative project with stucco decoration of the type Bossi produced on the ceiling of the adjacent Weisser Saal, or White Room.[4]

A new impetus was given the project with the succession of Greiffenclau as prince-bishop in 1749 and his decision to engage Tiepolo to decorate the Residenz. There emerged another revised program, of which no written record exists, that abandoned local history in favor of a more conventional allegory lauding the prince-bishop as Apollo, the god of light and patron of the arts, illuminating—both literally and figuratively—the four corners of the earth. A point of inspiration may have been the much earlier ceiling Johann-Rudolf Byss painted over the staircase of the nearby castle of Pommersfelden. Initially, court portraiture and direct dynastic reference were to be restricted to a wall at the top of the staircase, where Greiffenclau was to be shown with his retinue on a feigned balcony. (A drawing documenting this scheme, formerly in the Mainfränkisches Museum, Würzburg, was destroyed during World War II.)[5]

Tiepolo's composition centers on the radiant figure of Apollo as he issues from his temple (the curved cornice of which is barely visible in the *modello*) and prepares to make his daily journey across the heavens.[6] Striking a pose adapted from the *Apollo Belvedere*, he holds in his left hand a statue that, through reference to the completed fresco, is identifiable as Fortune.[7] In front of and below him butterfly-winged Hours (Horae) present

Overleaf, left: Detail, no. 49
Overleaf, right: Fig. 112. *Apollo and the Four Continents* (ceiling over staircase). Fresco. Residenz, Würzburg

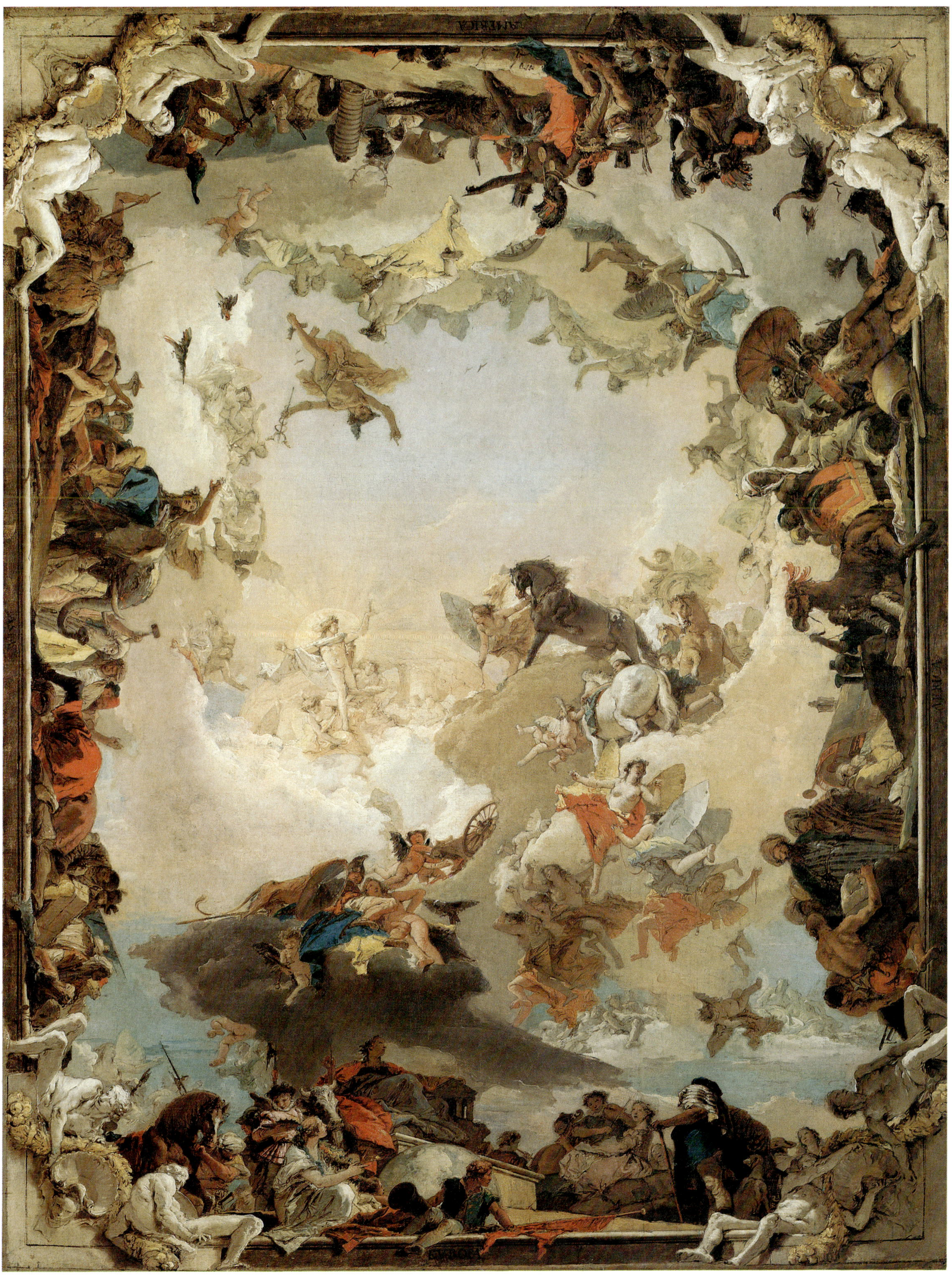

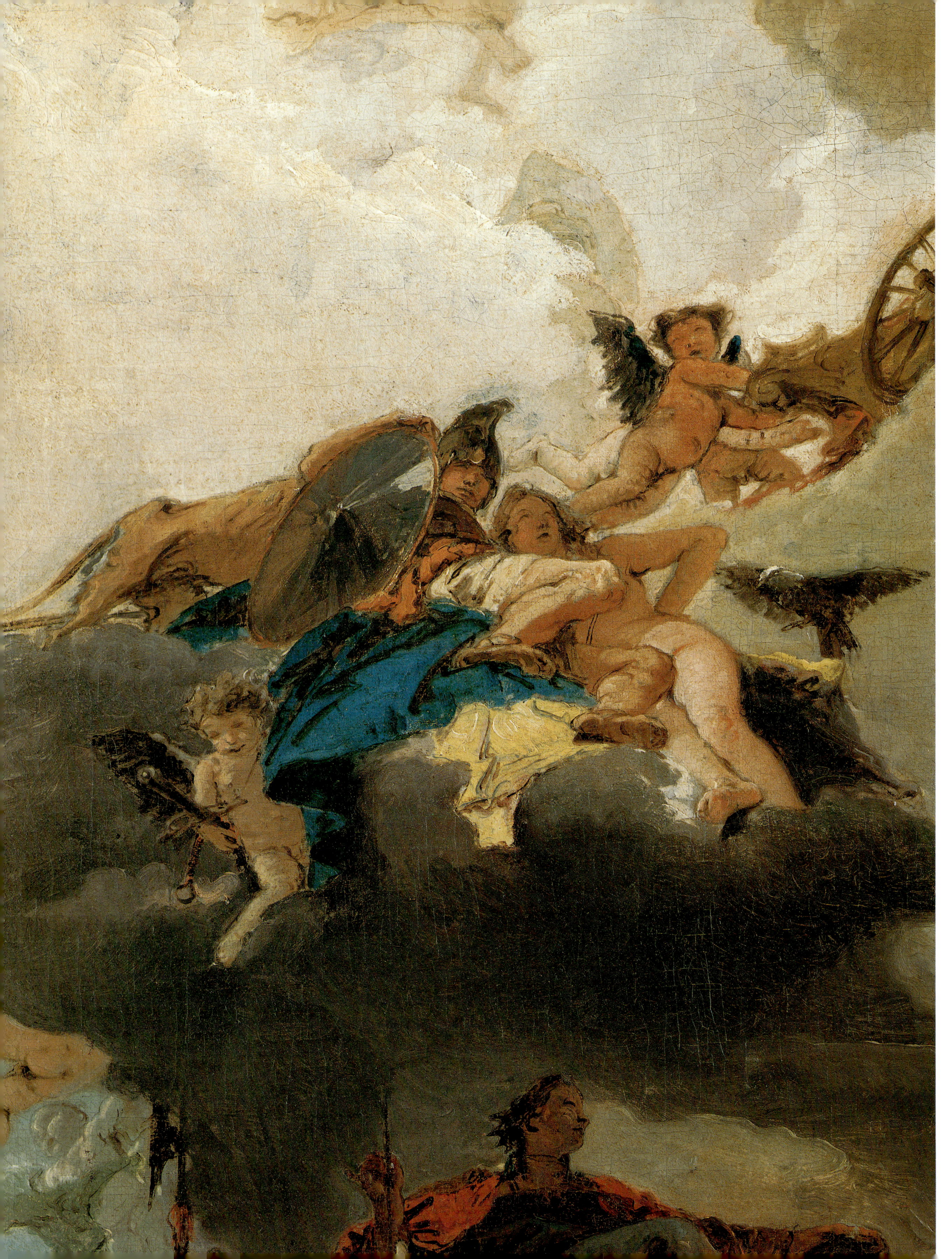

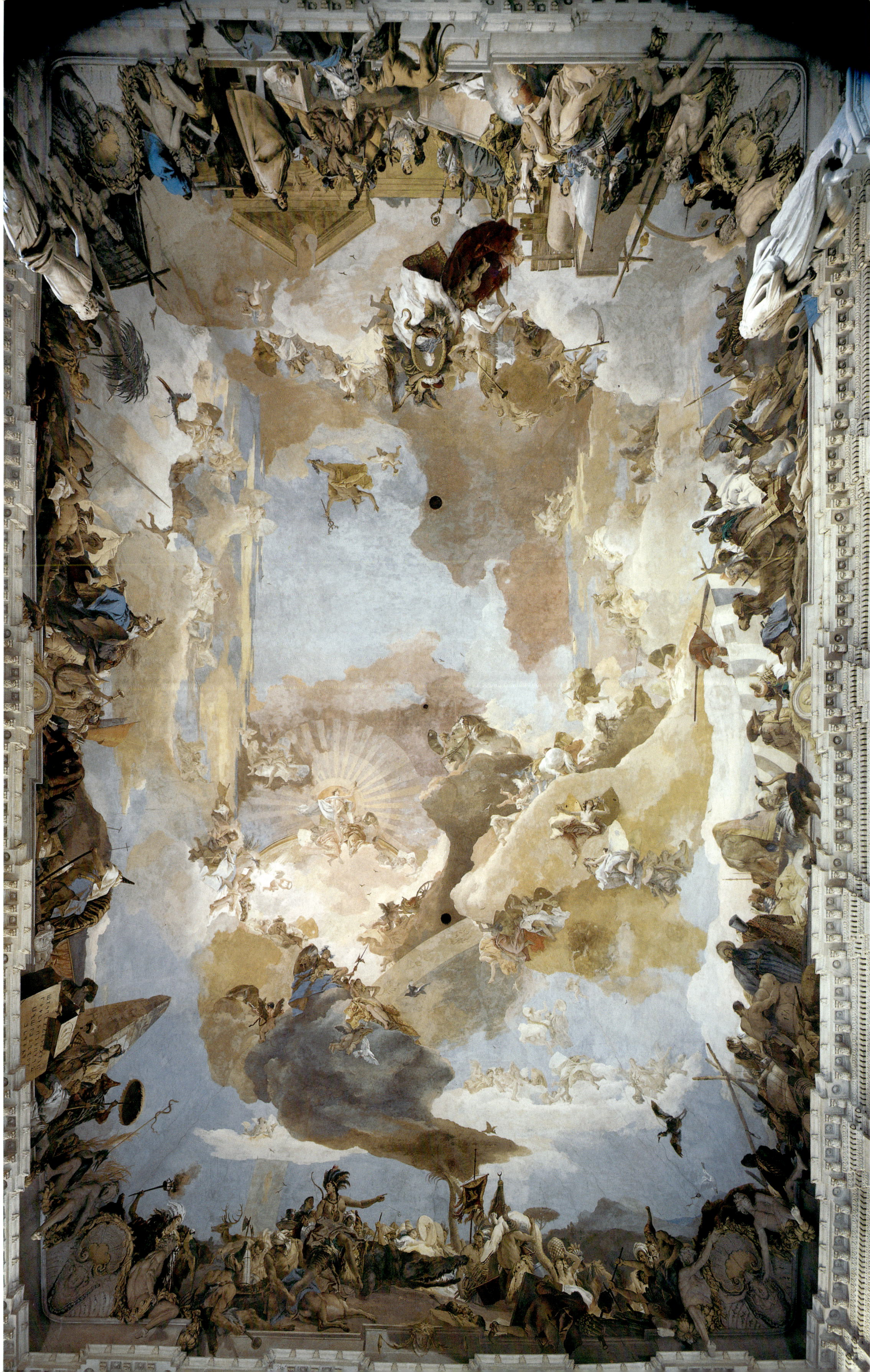

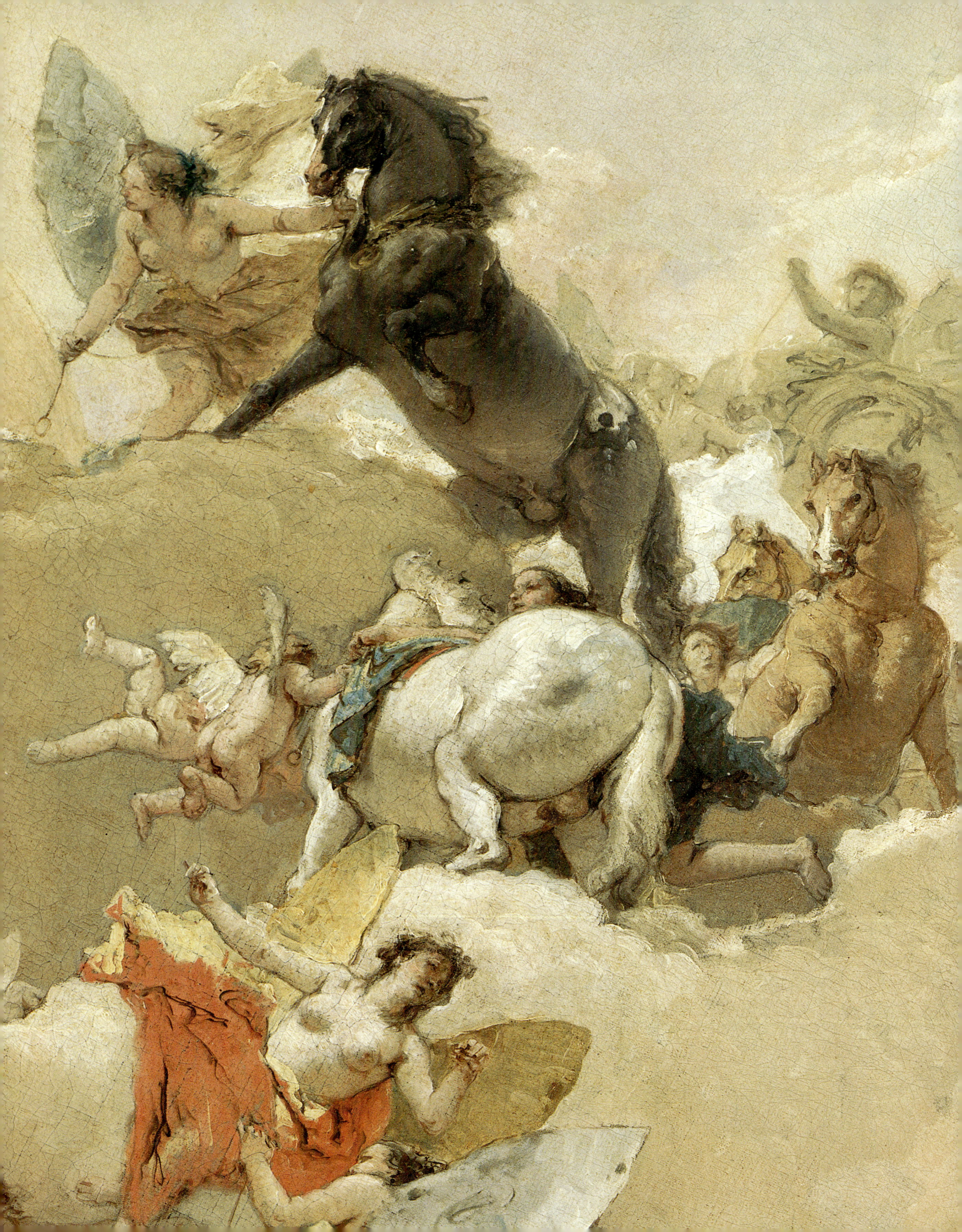

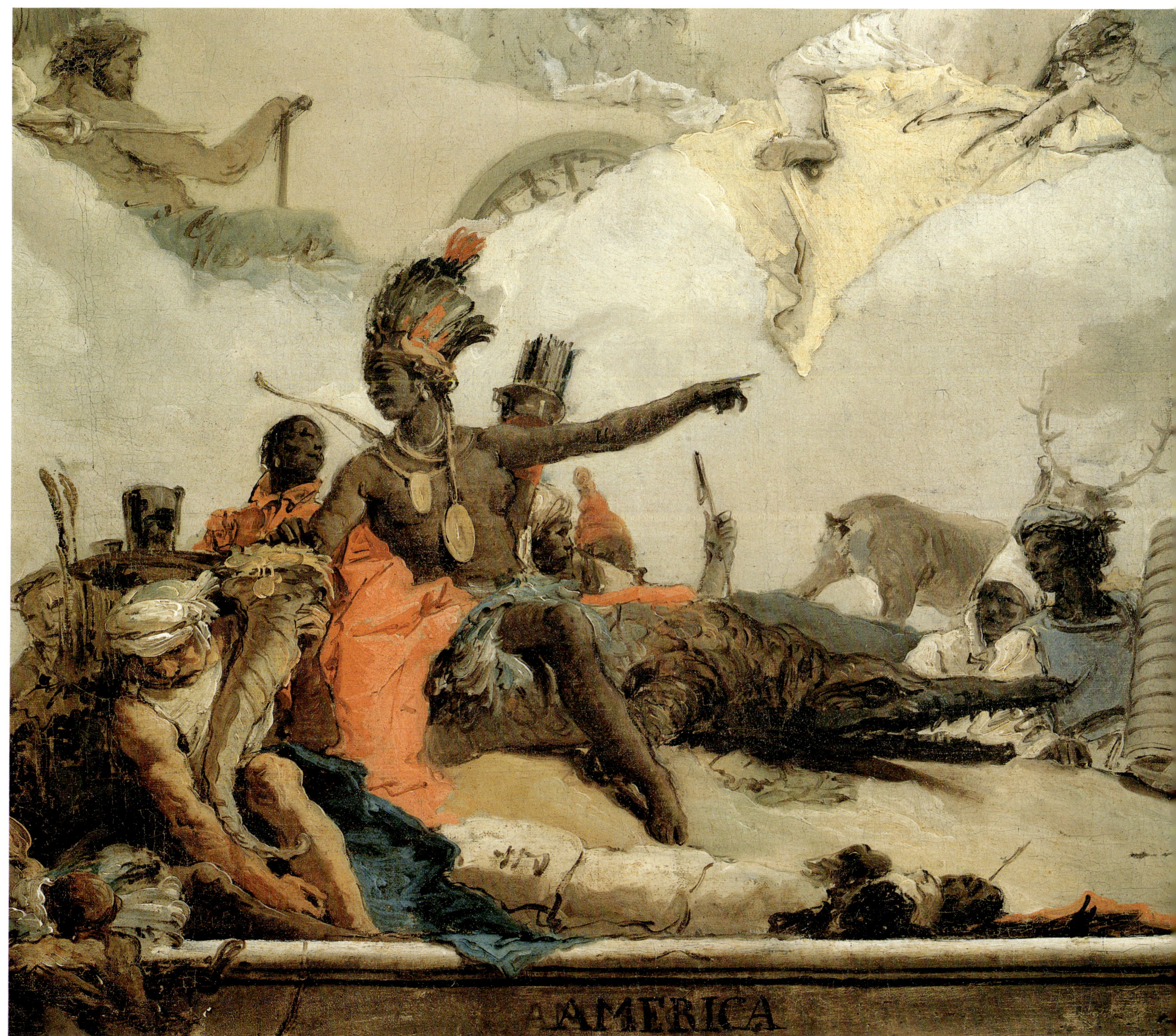

Opposite and above: Details, no. 49

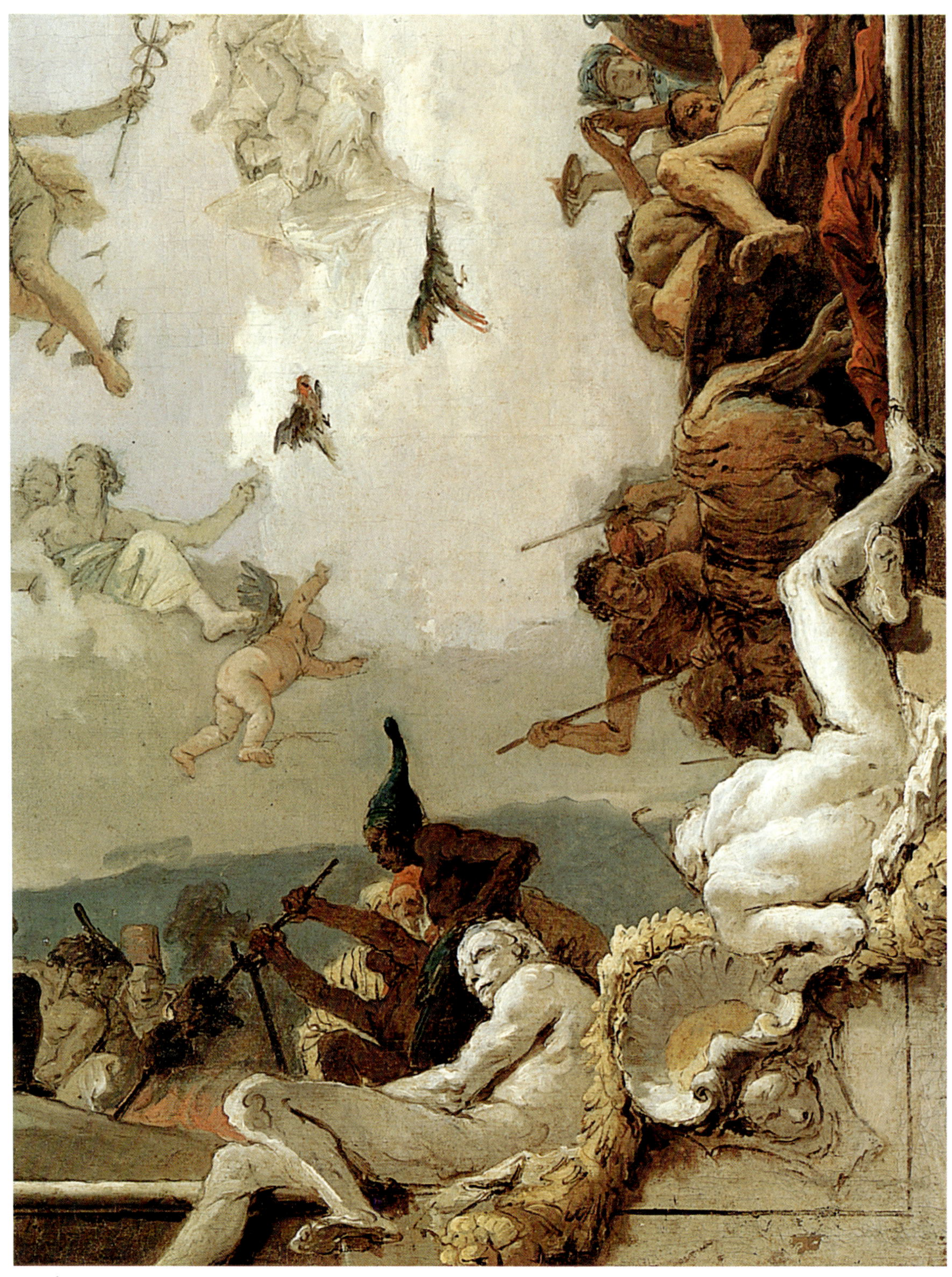

Detail, no. 49

his horses and reins, and putti push his heavy gold chariot up a bank of clouds. Around him are grouped the Olympian gods who govern the planets. Most prominent are Venus and Mars, who repose on a dark cloud. (Behind Mars is a lion, which in the fresco becomes Mars's proper symbol, the wolf.) Rotating 180 degrees, we have Mercury, his right hand pointing toward Apollo's horses as he announces the beginning of another day to Jupiter (shown with his cupbearer Ganymede); Saturn; a seated figure with a staff usually identified as Vulcan; and the more conspicuous Diana (goddess of the moon). Above Saturn are two maidens who bring out one of the bulls from Apollo's herd of 350 (symbolizing the number of days in the year).

Around the cornice are grouped depictions of the four continents and Bossi's stucco figures, painted in monochrome. Each continent is dominated by a female personification, whose costumes and attributes ultimately derive from Cesare Ripa's popular sourcebook, the *Iconologia,* but incorporate significant changes and interpolations inspired, as Ashton has shown, by popular travel books. The personifications are linked by gesture and glance and placed amid figures involved in a variety of activities. Europe, shown enthroned and holding a scepter, directs her gaze toward Africa. She is surrounded, and serenaded, by the Arts. The globe, diminutive temple, and bull accompanying her are her traditional symbols; the boy with a standard and a cannon barrel who sits on the cornice in front of her, and the horse on the extreme left signify her superiority in arms. Opposite Europe—and separated from her by the vast expanse of the heavens—is America. In conformity with reports of native costumes, America is portrayed crowned with feathers and adorned with hanging medallions, sitting on the back of a crocodile—or, in the words of Ripa, "a lizard more or less resembling a crocodile"; a pile of severed heads rests on the cornice near her. To the right cannibals roast meat (this too a motif that derives from Ripa's comments in the *Iconologia*). In a striking departure from Ripa, Asia sits on the back of an elephant instead of a camel and wears a turban instead of garlands. Two male subjects bow before her, and the elephant drags a pleading captive bound at the wrists. To the extreme right a European oversees the packing of goods for shipment to Europe, while at the extreme left a tiger hunt takes place. For Africa, Tiepolo evoked the commercial riches of Alexandria and Cairo, placing her on the back of a caravan camel and dispensing with the elephant hat prescribed for her by Ripa in favor of a loose turban. A maguslike figure presents an offering of smoking incense, observed by a white-bearded river god symbolizing the Nile. At the left Turkish merchants supervise the loading of goods onto a boat. An ostrich adds yet another exotic touch.

Tiepolo's *modello* surely appealed to Greiffenclau as much for its bold approach to the vast ceiling as a single, unified picture field, without any *quadratura* framework, as for its richly exotic detail. No less important would have been his discursive narrative treatment of the preparations in heaven for Apollo's trip and of the various activities on earth. But even more impressive must have been the way Tiepolo worked out the composition to respond to the different points of view experienced by a visitor to the palace: the initial, channeled prospect of the ceiling high overhead afforded from the first flight of stairs (this determined the course of the vertical crescendo proceeding from Europe through Mars and Venus to the figures of Apollo and the Hours with his horses); the wide vista of the opposite side of the composition that opens up after the spectator turns 180 degrees to mount one of the two return flights of stairs (here the scene is dominated by the lithe figure of Mercury pointing upward and by America gesturing toward Asia); and the close-up view of the continents encouraged by the wide, brightly lit balcony surrounding the stairwell.[8] The most important difference between the *modello* and the ceiling—the transposition of the continents of Europe and America—represents a change demonstrably made to fine-tune this aspect of Tiepolo's invention.[9] Rather than initiating the visitor's experience as she does in the *modello*, in the fresco Europe became its climax, heightened by the addition of an oval portrait of Greiffenclau swathed in an ermine-lined cloak, held aloft by Fame and Glory (or Virtue) and wittily embraced by an armorial griffin envisaged as an actual beast (fig. 37).

This modification and the many and various additional changes effected in the ceiling elucidate the function of the *modello* as a presentation piece and provide insights into the ways Tiepolo's initial concept developed even after he had formed the basic scheme for a large decoration. The first point that should be made here is that in the *modello* the light source is imagined as emanating from Apollo rather than from the various windows in the stairwell; even the stucco figures are shown, quite impossibly, as though lit from this notional source.[10] This choice alone makes it clear that to a degree Tiepolo viewed the *modello* as an independent work. Equally indicative of this attitude is the fact that he made no attempt to create a scaled depiction in the *modello*: its shape is squarer than the ceiling, and its figures are considerably larger in relation to the surrounding space—obviously to make the composition more effective as a presentation piece. From the outset he must have realized that narrative details could be dealt with best in the full-size cartoons he worked up for transfer to the wall.[11] What he needed to devise in the *modello* were the anchors of each compositional part, and he in fact changed little in the positions and configurations of the principal figure groups in the final decoration.

On the ceiling Apollo's foreshortened pose was modified, and the two female figures at his feet acquired his attributes, a lyre and a torch. Below him the signs of the zodiac were incorporated to create an arc across the heavens, and around one of the flying Hours was appended the Roman numeral VII, an allusion to the day of the month sacred to Apollo. The Seasons were added, as was a flying putto holding a crown of laurel leaves, and throughout the poses of the figures and their spatial relationship to one another were refined (note, for example, Mars and Venus). More significant changes occurred in the depictions of the continents. The anecdotal element increased as the composition

PROVENANCE:
Samuel Ware, Hendon Hall, London (by 1850–60); Charles Nathaniel Cumberlege-Ware, Hendon Hall (by 1860–ca. 1870); C. F. Hancock, Hendon Hall (by 1890); Hendon Hall Hotel (by 1923–54); art market, London (1954–56); Rosenberg and Stiebel, New York, and Fritz and Peter Nathan, Zurich (1956); Mr. and Mrs. Charles Wrightsman, New York (1956–77)

REFERENCES:
Morassi 1955a, p. 25; Watson 1955, p. 215; Freeden and Lamb 1956, pp. 29, 53–61, 77; Knox 1957; Morassi 1962, pp. 37, 68; Bott 1963, pp. 141–43; Watson 1963, pp. 247–48; Pallucchini 1968, p. 116, no. 199; Rizzi in Udine 1971, p. 108; Simon 1971, pp. 484–86, 494; Fahy and Watson 1973, pp. 232–47; Ashton 1978, p. 121; Büttner 1979, pp. 161–64 and passim; Büttner 1980, p. 94; Knox 1980a, p. 44; Levey 1986, pp. 191–95; Gemin and Pedrocco 1993, p. 426, no. 415a; Alpers and Baxandall 1994, pp. 74, 129–42, 153; Würzburg 1996, vol. 1, p. 98, vol. 2, p. 132

was extended laterally and the scale of the figures was reduced in relation to the field, and greater latitude was given to a play between the real and the fictive space. In America a large area was opened up between the personification of the continent on her crocodile and the group of men roasting meat on a spit. This was filled with a colorful native procession and a witty aside in the form of an itinerant European artist who, drawing board in hand, seems to dangle precariously over the real edge of the cornice for a view of the natives. (Europeans are conspicuous in all of the frescoed continents, either as observers or merchants.) Similarly, in the depiction of Europe, the diminutive temple of the *modello* became an architectural backdrop, a bishop and two acolytes were introduced, the musicians gained a prominent female singer, and heretofore conventional faces acquired portraitlike features. Balthasar Neumann and his dog replaced the boy with a cannon, and his position was altered so that he appears to be reclining on the real rather than the painted cornice. A sculptor (probably Bossi) stands in for the strongly foreshortened, faceless figure at the right of the *modello*, and a character who looks like a real court groom has been substituted for the anonymous turbaned figure restraining the horse. For all of these figures numerous drawings were carried out from life, and the frescoes gained enormously in their impact. Tiepolo, Giandomenico, and a third individual make an appearance, surveying their handiwork over the shoulder of one of Bossi's stucco figures. Above Europe, Fame and Truth display a commemorative portrait of Greiffenclau (fig. 37). This last element was a late interpolation, introduced after cartoons had been prepared and at least partly transferred, for examination of the ceiling reveals that the winged figure shown below Ganymede in the *modello* was traced onto the plaster in the area of the portrait but not painted. There can be little doubt that this change was occasioned by the decision to forgo painting Greiffenclau and his retinue on the wall below.

The ceiling has 218 *giornate*. Work began with Apollo and proceeded outward. There are a number of *a secco* revisions. Some of these involve such straightforward matters as the modification of a contour, the addition of a detail, or the change in emphasis of shadows and highlights. Others were more substantial. The drapery of the figure of Painting was gone over, the marble block to the right of Neumann was added (there are no incisions for its placement), and the sky was darkened in the right corner of the continent of Europe (the original pale blue can be made out along various contours). In the continent of America, the massive, dark cloud was extended downward, diagonally, covering palm fronds, and this necessitated the addition of others to replace them. In Europe there are two sets of tracings for the neck of the viola da gamba played by Music. These many changes underscore the nature of Tiepolo's restless genius and illuminate the fact that even a *modello* of this size and complexity documents only a stage in a constantly evolving process: a process that took place within the established limits of traditional fresco practice and balanced artistic license with iconographic models. Clearly, the *modello* had a dual function. If, on the one hand, it proposed an iconographic scheme, on the other, it served as an independent demonstration of Tiepolo's fantasy and artistic brilliance.[12]

KC

NOTES

1. The status of the various surviving *modelli* for the Kaisersaal has been the subject of debate. The brilliant oil sketch for the ceiling (Staatsgalerie Stuttgart) employs a picture field closely related in shape and proportion to the actual one in the Residenz, although its profile is a simple oval. (A painting in the Mainfränkisches Museum, Würzburg, sometimes also considered a *modello*, is clearly by a contemporary German artist.) By contrast, those for the two lateral frescoes (The Metropolitan Museum of Art, New York; Isabella Stewart Gardner Museum, Boston; National Gallery, London) employ fields notably different from the final one. Largely on this basis it has been proposed that they are variant derivations of the frescoes done by Tiepolo or in his workshop. Without entering into the complicated arguments involved in this issue, it is worth noting that the Metropolitan sketch—by common consent the finest and certainly a fully autograph work—is in crucial respects closer to the program sent to Tiepolo than is the final fresco and on this account deserves consideration as a proposal executed in Venice. For example, it shows the scene in an interior space, as specified, rather than the airy exterior setting of the fresco. It is repeatedly stated that the oil sketch is inappropriate for the anticipated picture field, which is a wide triangle. This argument overlooks the fact that Tiepolo employed a standard vertical canvas, which he used to study the center portion of the final composition; the quickly sketched-in curtains do no more than make casual reference to the elements that were carried out in stucco. (Contrary to Brown's contention [in Fort Worth 1993, p. 27], they were not painted as a second thought, over the architecture: there are points where architecture and curtains overlap; others where the architectural details stop short; and others where the ground color is visible between the architecture and the curtains.) The matter is of interest not only in terms of the Kaisersaal project but also for an understanding of the sorts of variations sometimes encountered between a *modello* and a fresco and the pitfalls associated with adopting an overly dogmatic position with respect to Tiepolo's practices. For some of the same reasons the Gardner and National Gallery sketches can only be understood as documenting progressive stages in the planning of the fresco. At the recent exhibition in Würzburg (1996), I was able to view all three together. Neither the Gardner nor the National Gallery sketch attains the quality of that in the Metropolitan. Nonetheless, the Gardner *modello*, which is badly damaged, has the same tonality as the Metropolitan painting and, like it, was probably painted in Venice. That in the National Gallery, of unquestionably inferior quality, is bluer—as

is the fresco—and—again like the fresco—reorients the composition to be read from right to left instead of left to right. Thus, although the matter of the authorship of the Gardner and National Gallery pictures remains problematic—are they replicas of lost *modelli*?—their importance for understanding the genesis of the frescoes seems clear.

2. Büttner (1979, p. 161) corrects the date of 20 April, which is usually given.
3. The diner was an architect, Jack Gold. The history of the picture prior to 1850, when it is described in a manuscript catalogue of the Ware collection at Hendon Hall, is not known. It has been suggested that it was purchased in Venice by David Garrick in 1756—three years after Tiepolo returned from Würzburg—but this seems unlikely: although Garrick owned Hendon Hall, he did not use it as his residence and therefore certainly would not have left a picture of this importance there. The matter is thoroughly discussed by Fahy and Watson 1973, pp. 239–40.
4. On these successive phases, see Freeden and Lamb 1956, pp. 18–23.
5. See ibid., p. 55, and Büttner 1979, pp. 163–64.
6. In the main, I have followed the identifications of Freeden and Lamb 1956, pp. 80–82; Büttner 1980, pp. 100–106; and Büttner in Würzburg 1996, vol. 2, pp. 57–60.
7. According to such manuals as Cartari's *Imagini degli dei*, Apollo should hold a statue of the Three Graces. Freeden and Lamb believe the statue symbolizes Art. For Bott (1963, p. 146) it is a Victory, while for Simon (1971, pp. 484–86, 494) it is Veritas, who should, however, be shown naked rather than clothed. Büttner (1979) argues convincingly that it is Fortune.
8. See the excellent analysis by Krückmann in Würzburg 1996, vol. 1, pp. 34–36.
9. Büttner (1979, p. 164) believes that Europe was always intended for the position she assumes in the fresco; he maintains that it was the heavens that were rotated and the continents of Asia and Africa that were transposed.
10. As always, Tiepolo strove for effects of poetic verisimilitude—what we might call artistic coherence or consistency. In the fresco he certainly took into consideration the quality and character of the light in the stairwell and made numerous and subtle adjustments—dictated partly by the fact that he now showed Europe and America under different cloud formations, but no less by the necessity of introducing greater variety and contrast to the immense space covered. Alpers and Baxandall (1994, pp. 107–27) give an enthusiastic but misleadingly elaborate analysis of Tiepolo's handling of light.
11. That Tiepolo made cartoons has, without any basis, been questioned. The matter is not open to speculation. See my essay in this volume, "The Fiery Poetic Fantasy of Giambattista Tiepolo," n. 42, and Würzburg 1996, pp. 128–47. Also worth mentioning here is the interpretation of a conspicuous number of red-chalk drawings at Stuttgart related to the frescoes. I believe most of these to be copies by Giandomenico after the frescoes; the idea that they are in some way substitute cartoons, as argued by Knox (1980a, pp. 39–50), is demonstrably wrong, as is his attribution to Giambattista of a group of incredibly weak and ungainly line drawings. See the relevant entries in Würzburg 1996.
12. It is this aspect of Tiepolo's *modelli* that misled both Watson (1963) and Knox (1957) in their evaluations of the Metropolitan painting. Watson believes the picture to be a record of the ceiling by Giandomenico. Knox reluctantly accepts it as the *modello* but suggests that it must have been painted by Giandomenico.

THE PIETÀ DECORATIONS

50a. The Coronation of the Virgin
50b. Fortitude and Peace

50a. The Coronation of the Virgin
Doc. 1754
102.6 × 77.3 cm (40⅜ × 30⅜ in.)
The Kimbell Art Museum, Fort Worth (AP 1984.10)

50b. Fortitude and Peace
1754
37.5 × 46 cm (14¾ × 18⅛ in.)
Private collection

Tiepolo left Würzburg on 8 November 1753, and just five months later, on 15 April 1754, he was engaged on what proved to be his last extensive ecclesiastical decoration in Venice. This was the project to fresco the ceilings of the nave (fig. 113) and chancel of the newly constructed church of S. Maria della Visitazione (also known as the Pietà), on the Riva degli Schiavoni. The church, built on an oval plan notable for its restrained elegance and luminosity, was designed in 1736 by the great neo-Palladian architect Giorgio Massari, who had also been responsible for the church of the Gesuati in Venice, which Tiepolo had decorated fifteen years earlier. One of Massari's key concerns at S. Maria della Visitazione was the acoustics, since the church was annexed to a foundling hospital (whence the name Pietà) with a celebrated music school (Vivaldi had worked there between 1704 and 1740). And, indeed, the musical activities of the church were fundamental to Tiepolo's decorations. In January 1751, following completion of the roof, a search was undertaken for an artist to fresco the ceiling; in addition to Tiepolo, Gasparo Diziani and Francesco Fontebasso were invited to take part in a competition, which did not take place until three years later. We may suspect that the delay was planned to enable Tiepolo, Venice's greatest artist, to participate.

Tiepolo, of course, won, and he completed the *al fresco* painting in an astonishing eighty days (there are, in fact, just thirty-five *giornate* in the ceiling).[1] Work began on 13 June 1754, and the final installment of the fee of 1,800 ducats was made on 8 October. However, the fresco was not unveiled for another ten months,

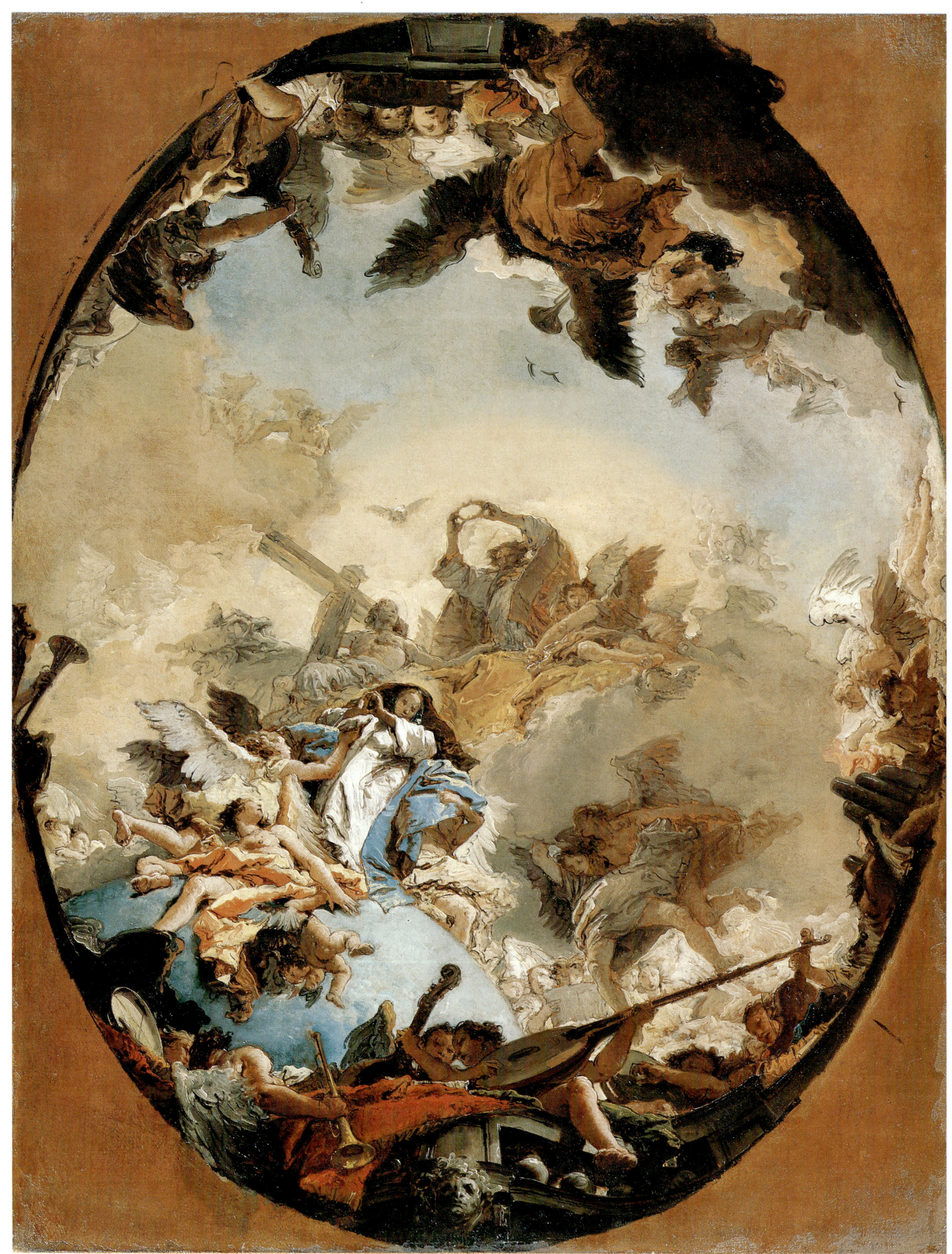

50a

Opposite: Detail, no. 50a

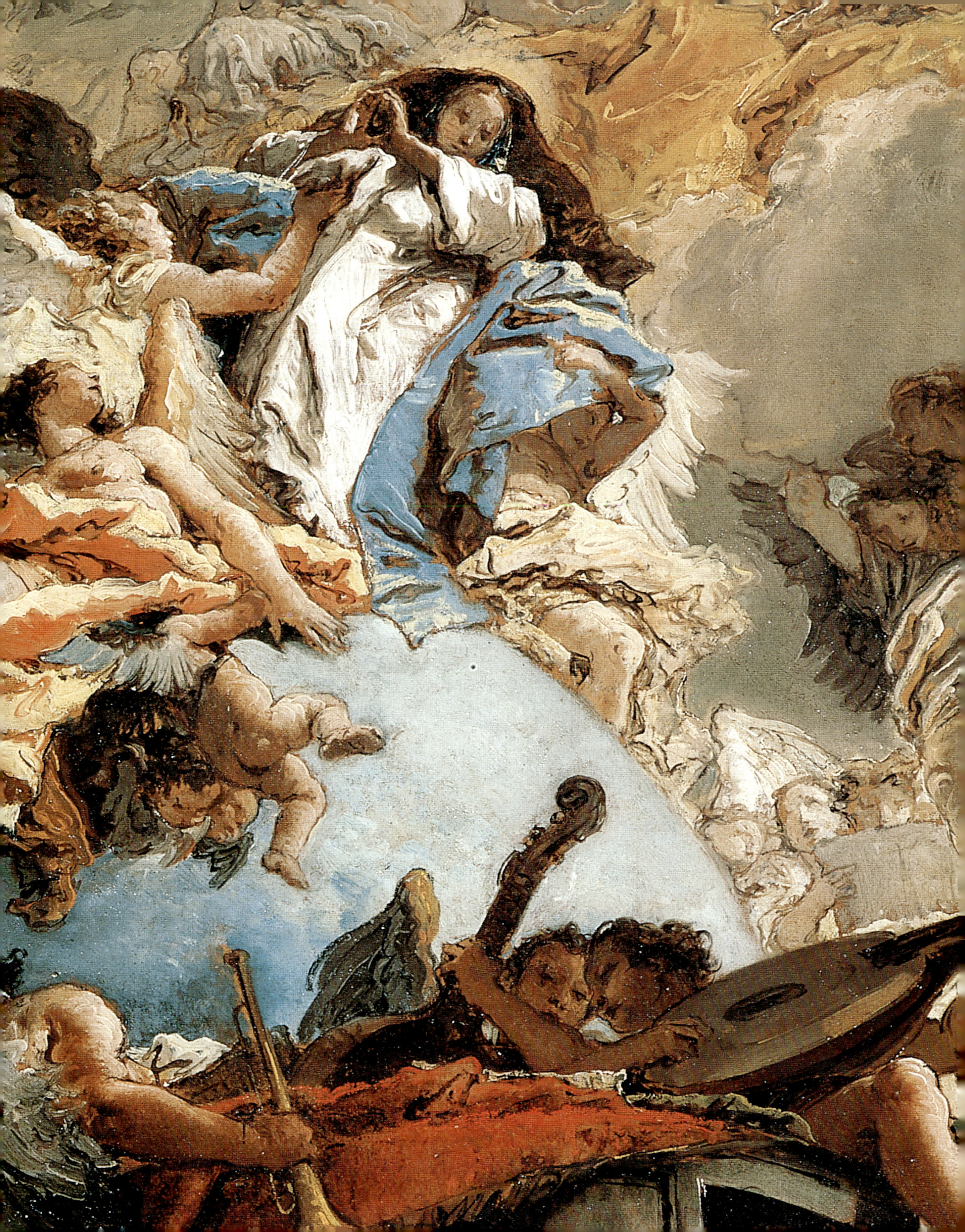

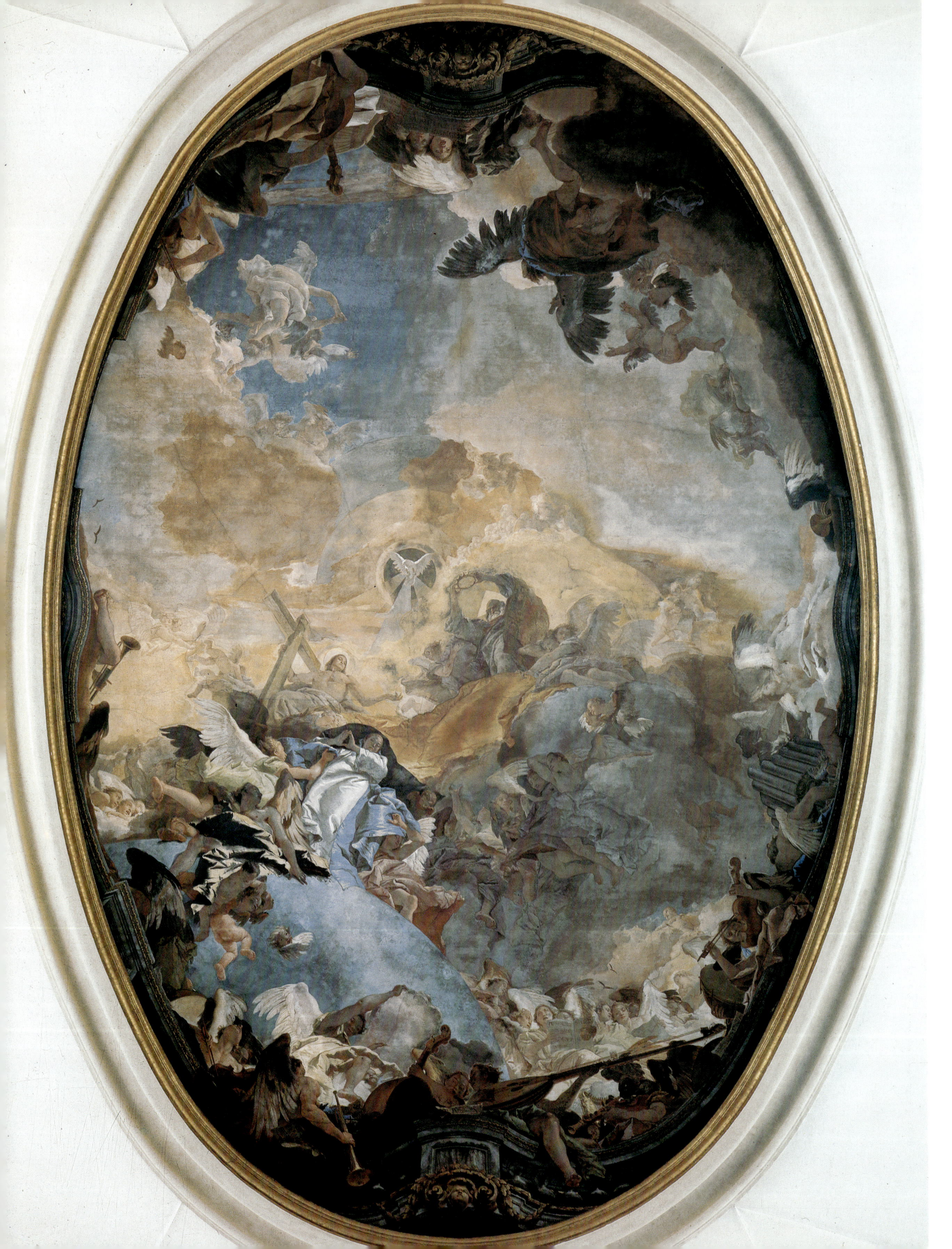

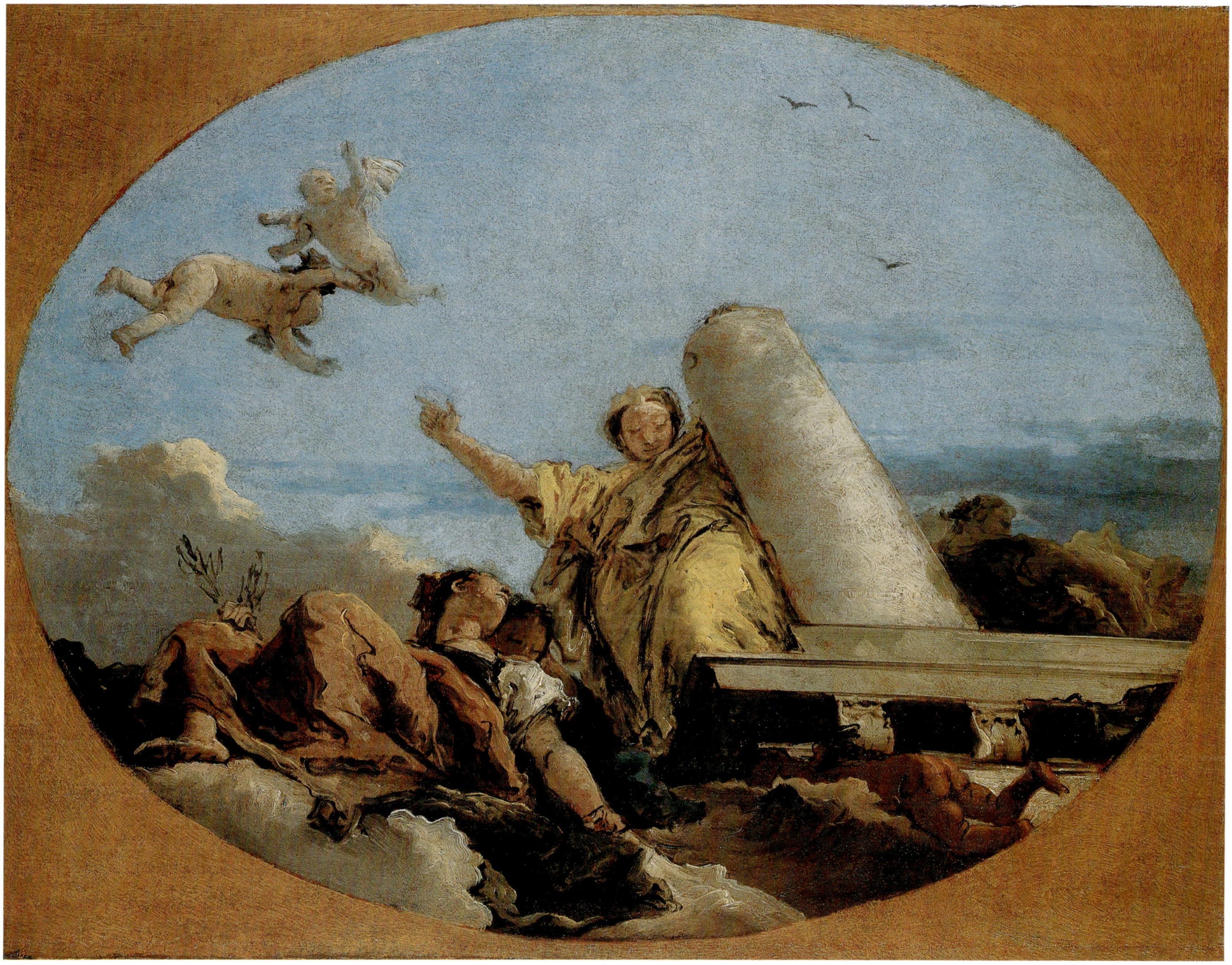

50b

on 2 August 1755, following an additional ten days spent doing *a secco* retouches.[2] The *modello*, among the most vibrant Tiepolo painted, must have been undertaken almost immediately upon the awarding of the commission. The surviving documents do not refer to the subject, but in the normal course of events the iconographic scheme would have been worked out by the Church governors and the artist. On the evidence of the procedure followed at the Scalzi (see entry for no. 48), it can be deduced that it was Tiepolo who enlisted Francesco Zanchi as his *quadraturista*.[3] Zanchi's role was a limited

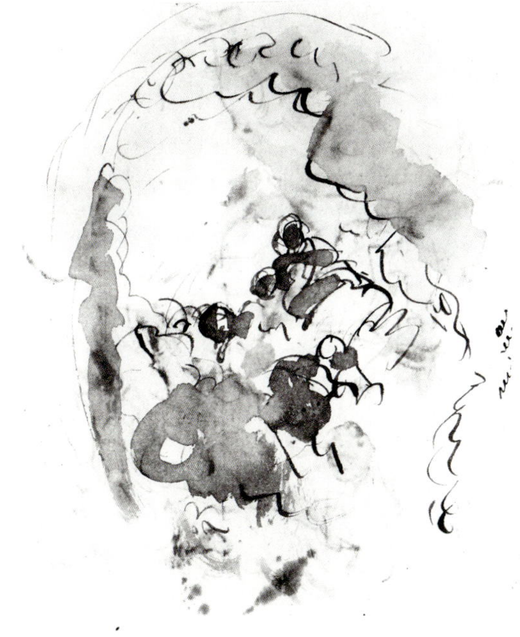

Opposite: Fig. 113. *The Coronation of the Virgin* (ceiling). Fresco. S. Maria della Visitazione (the Pietà), Venice

Right: Fig. 114. *Study for an Oval Ceiling*, recto. Pen and ink and wash. The Pierpont Morgan Library, New York (IV, 98D)

PROVENANCE, 50a:
Possibly Tiepolo's widow, Cecilia Guardi (from 1770);[10] Edward Cheney, London and Badger Hall, Shropshire (ca. 1842/52–84; sale, Christie's, London, 29 April 1885, lot 161); Archibald Philip, fifth earl of Rosebery (from 1885); by descent, Eva, countess of Rosebery (sale, Sotheby's, London, 24 March 1976, lot 11); private collection (sale, Sotheby's, London, 8 April 1981, lot 111 [bought in]); Newhouse Galleries, New York (until 1984)

REFERENCES:
Venice 1951, p. 111, no. 80*bis;* Watson 1952, p. 44; Morassi 1955a, p. 30; Morassi 1962, pp. 20, 57; Watson 1963, p. 244; Pallucchini 1968, p. 120, no. 216a; Knox 1980a, vol. 1, pp. 59–60; Howard 1986, pp. 14–16, 25 n. 54; Levey 1986, p. 220; Aikema and Meijers 1989, p. 206; Fort Worth 1993, pp. 274–77, no. 43; Gemin and Pedrocco 1993, p. 435, no. 426a; London 1994, p. 502, no. 125; Venice 1995a, p. 250, no. 59

PROVENANCE, 50b:
David P. Sellar, London (until 1889; sale, Galerie Georges Petit, Paris, 6 June 1889, lot 81);[11] Julius Böhler, Munich (until 1915); Dr. Anschütz-Kaempe, Munich (before 1962)

REFERENCES:
Sack 1910, pp. 117, 233, no. 605; Morassi 1962, p. 31; Pallucchini 1968, p. 118, no. 211; Howard 1986, pp. 14–15; Gemin and Pedrocco 1993, p. 436, no. 429a; Würzburg 1996, vol. 1, p. 161, no. 96

one, since the main fresco was to be contained by an architectural molding and required no elaborate surround of feigned architecture. The contract provided not only for the nave fresco but also for a small ceiling in the chancel with allegorical figures of Faith, Hope, and Charity and for a monochrome roundel on the wall depicting an angel appearing to King David. Not mentioned, but certainly part of the scheme, was another fresco in the atrium showing Fortitude and Peace, possibly destroyed when the present facade of the church was erected in 1904–5.[4] The composition of the atrium decoration, like that of the chancel fresco, was etched by Giandomenico, and its *modello* is exhibited here.[5]

In the oval space of the nave, Tiepolo depicted a glorification of the Virgin, clad in white and standing on a massive globe, received into paradise by the figures of the Trinity: Christ (holding his cross), the dove of the Holy Spirit, and God the Father (with a crown for the Virgin in his outstretched hands). Surrounding—indeed, dominating—the composition is a glory of music-making angels, obviously a reference to the activities that made the Church famous. The angels are shown behind an undulating balcony viewed in steep foreshortening, and it was this architectural feature that Zanchi was hired to paint.

A good deal of attention has focused on the choice of scenes and the precise identification of the subject presented on the nave ceiling. Moschini, writing in 1815, called it "a celestial Glory with various symbolic representations."[6] This is an apt description, for it is obvious from the stance of the Virgin, her placement on the globe, and the depiction of the Trinity that this is not simply a Coronation of the Virgin but also a glorification of her as protector of the foundlings and an assertion of her position as mediator with the Trinity.[7]

As is usually the case with Tiepolo's painting, the final composition and the *modello*, which has all the marks of a work done in the heat of inspiration, diverge in numerous respects. In the completed ceiling the dazzling angel viewed *di sotto-in-sù* with spread legs was discarded (did one of the governors perhaps find the pose indecent?), and space was found beneath the Virgin for the addition of an angel waving a sheet of music. Typically, the major change—and it is a significant one that underscores the semi-independent status *modelli* had for Tiepolo—consisted in profoundly altering the relative scale of the figures and the oval of the field: the Virgin is approximately one-sixth the full height of the *modello* and one-ninth the height of the fresco. This means that the *modello* was conceived essentially as a figurative composition, detailing the major components of the iconographic program. The fresco gives far greater prominence to the light-filled sky. The paler tonality of the fresco was determined by this fundamental change in balance between figures and space no less than by the fact that the *modello* was painted on a warm, reddish ground that gives the colors a rich, saturated quality.[8]

What is truly remarkable is the degree to which the *modello* suggests the illusionistic effect offered viewers as they pass through the atrium and glance upward to the nave ceiling, where their eyes are met by the projecting balcony over which an angel has casually slung his leg, and the way Tiepolo has used his dynamic brushwork in the canvas to generate a feeling of excitement and moment. The abstract basis of this composition is perhaps best appreciated by referring to a rapidly executed drawing in pen-and-ink wash (fig. 114) that is often associated with the Scalzi ceiling (no. 48a, b).[9] Whatever project it is connected with, the drawing is extraordinarily revealing of the manner in which Tiepolo went about mapping his compositional ideas. Tiepolo's primary concern was with spatial effects obtained through dynamic contrasts of light and shade and with undulating forms that hug the perimeter of the field. In the Pietà ceiling such abstract shapes acquire the allure of active figures and shifting, luminous clouds.

KC

NOTES

1. See Kaley (1980, pp. 45–52), who gives a report on the cleaning of the ceiling. It is necessary here to correct, once again (see entry for no. 49), the notion that this speedy execution was possible because Tiepolo used chalk drawings instead of cartoons. This idea, promoted by Knox (1980a, pp. 49–60) and repeated by Howard (1986, p. 15) and Brown (in Fort Worth 1993, p. 274) is, quite simply, wrong. In fact, it was the use of cartoons that enabled Tiepolo to employ his son, his *quadraturista*, Francesco Zanchi, and other assistants in an efficient and expeditious manner. The chalk drawings discussed by Knox (1980a,, pp. 59, nos. M.115, 247, 422–426, 616) are, in my view, by Giandomenico and are copies after the frescoes.
2. For the documents, see Howard 1986, pp. 27–28.
3. Zanchi was paid sixty-four ducats on 12 September "p[er] il ovado." See Aikema and Meijers 1989, p. 206.
4. The fresco is recorded by Sack 1910, p. 117. See also Howard 1986, p. 14, and Aikema and Meijers 1989, p. 206.
5. It is worth considering whether the ten days of additional work in July 1755, "per aver ritocato il soffito nella nova Chiesa," did not also provide the occasion for the atrium fresco. See references under 1754 in "A Documented Chronology of Tiepolo's Life and Work," by Andrea Bayer, this publication.
6. Moschini 1815, vol. 1, p. 101.
7. For more elaborate interpretations, see Howard 1986, pp. 17–20. Howard wrongly identifies the flying angel as a plummeting Satan and implausibly argues that the Virgin is intended as a reference to Venice. Brown (in Fort Worth 1993, pp. 276–77) perhaps errs also but takes the argument in the opposite direction, by insisting that the image is a simple Coronation of the Virgin, with no direct relation to the Immaculate Conception.

8. The color of this ground has led certain scholars, such as Watson, to doubt the ascription to Tiepolo, and indeed for many years a shadow of critical misgiving hung over the picture. It is difficult to take seriously a dogmatic position that denies Tiepolo the authorship of this brilliant oil sketch and of the *modello* for the ceiling over the Residenz stairwell (see entry for no. 49). Perhaps Watson's view can serve to emphasize the dangers of trying to fit Tiepolo's working habits into a tidy, formulaic pattern. The ascription of the Pietà *modello* is also doubted by Lorenzetti (in Venice 1951).
9. For the drawing, see Knox 1968, p. 394. The drawing has on the verso a study of angels in poses not seen in either the Scalzi or the Pietà ceiling.
10. In the *Journal des Goncourt* 6 (1892), p. 281, is recounted the story that Tiepolo's wife, an inveterate gambler, one night used as stakes her collection of *modelli* by her husband, as well as her villa and lost all. Chennevières (1898 p. 105) elaborates that on his return to Venice from Spain, Giandomenico was able to recoup some of her losses but had to give up a number of oil sketches. These are presumed to have passed to Count Corniani degli Algarotti, from whom Edward Cheney made significant purchases. See Knox 1975a, pp. 6–9.
11. Sellar owned a total of six oil sketches by Tiepolo, including two for the Gesuati ceiling (Gemin and Pedrocco 1993, nos. 230a, 232a, 500).

51. *Saint Thecla Praying for the Plague-Stricken*

According to the apocryphal Acts of Saint Paul, Saint Thecla was converted to Christianity by Saint Paul at Iconium and martyred in Seleucia. Famed for her powers of healing, she is the patron saint of Este (thirty kilometers south of Padua) and the titular saint of its cathedral. She was the object of prayers during the plague that devastated the Veneto in 1630. On 29 June 1758—almost 130 years after the event—the commune of Este provided for an altarpiece to celebrate her as the protector of the town and to serve as a fitting decoration for its new cathedral, designed early in the century by the Venetian architect Antonio Gaspari and dedicated in 1748 by Cardinal Carlo Rezzonico, bishop of Padua.[1] This beautiful and deeply affective oil sketch, transported by Tiepolo to Spain and sold after his death to the Spanish painter Francisco Bayeu (Goya's brother-in-law), is the *modello* for the altarpiece (fig. 115).[2] It shows Saint Thecla praying to God for deliverance from the plague, personified by a female figure expulsed by angels in a darkened sky that contrasts with the sunlit, topographical view of Este in the background. The altarpiece, which was installed in the cathedral in the artist's presence on Christmas Eve 1759,[3] is among the largest canvases painted by Tiepolo—it measures 675 by 390 centimeters—and can on a number of counts be considered his religious masterpiece. It is marked by a gravity and descriptive restraint that could scarcely be anticipated from the evidence of Tiepolo's earlier work: there is nothing of the demonstrative emotionalism of, for example, the S. Alvise *Way to Calvary* (fig. 70) of two decades earlier or the dramatic pathos of the more nearly contemporary *Martyrdom of Saint Agatha* (no. 38). Whether the qualities of the *Saint Thecla* can be ascribed to his awareness of the current artistic climate in Rome or, as seems more likely, to renewed contact with his friend and admirer of long standing Francesco Algarotti is difficult to say. (Algarotti, who had been abroad, was again in Venice between 1754 and 1757.) That there was a conscious effort on Tiepolo's part to move his art in a fresh direction is indicated by the differences between the *modello* and the finished altarpiece.

In the event that the altarpiece was to fill the curved space between two enormous pilasters in the apse of the church, Tiepolo first conceived the work in terms of a fresco. From his decorations on the ceiling over the stairwell in the Residenz at Würzburg, he borrowed the illusionistic ledge decorated by a female head, behind which is projected the raised street or bridge on which Saint Thecla kneels. The ledge is one of those stock devices Tiepolo employed to relate the fictive world conjured up by his brush with the real space of the viewer, but it worked against the serious tone of the subject, and in the altarpiece it was dropped, together with the no less conventional and emotionally anomalous pair of angel's feet dangling from the cloud below God the Father. In the altarpiece the cloth-covered wheelbarrow, used to pick up the dead, is shown sandwiched between the stone street and the gilt molding. It has frequently been pointed out that in his moving depiction of the dead woman and her hungry child, Tiepolo made pointed reference to two celebrated sources: Marcantonio Raimondi's engraving after a design by Raphael, the *Plague in Phrygia*, and Poussin's celebrated canvas the *Plague of Ashdod*, which Tiepolo would have known from a print. In a powerfully descriptive passage Bellori had discussed Poussin's picture, pointing out its own debt to Marcantonio's print and

51. Saint Thecla Praying for the Plague-Stricken
Doc. 1758
81.3 × 44.8 cm (32 × 17⅝ in.)
The Metropolitan Museum of Art, New York; Rogers Fund, 1937 (37.165.2)

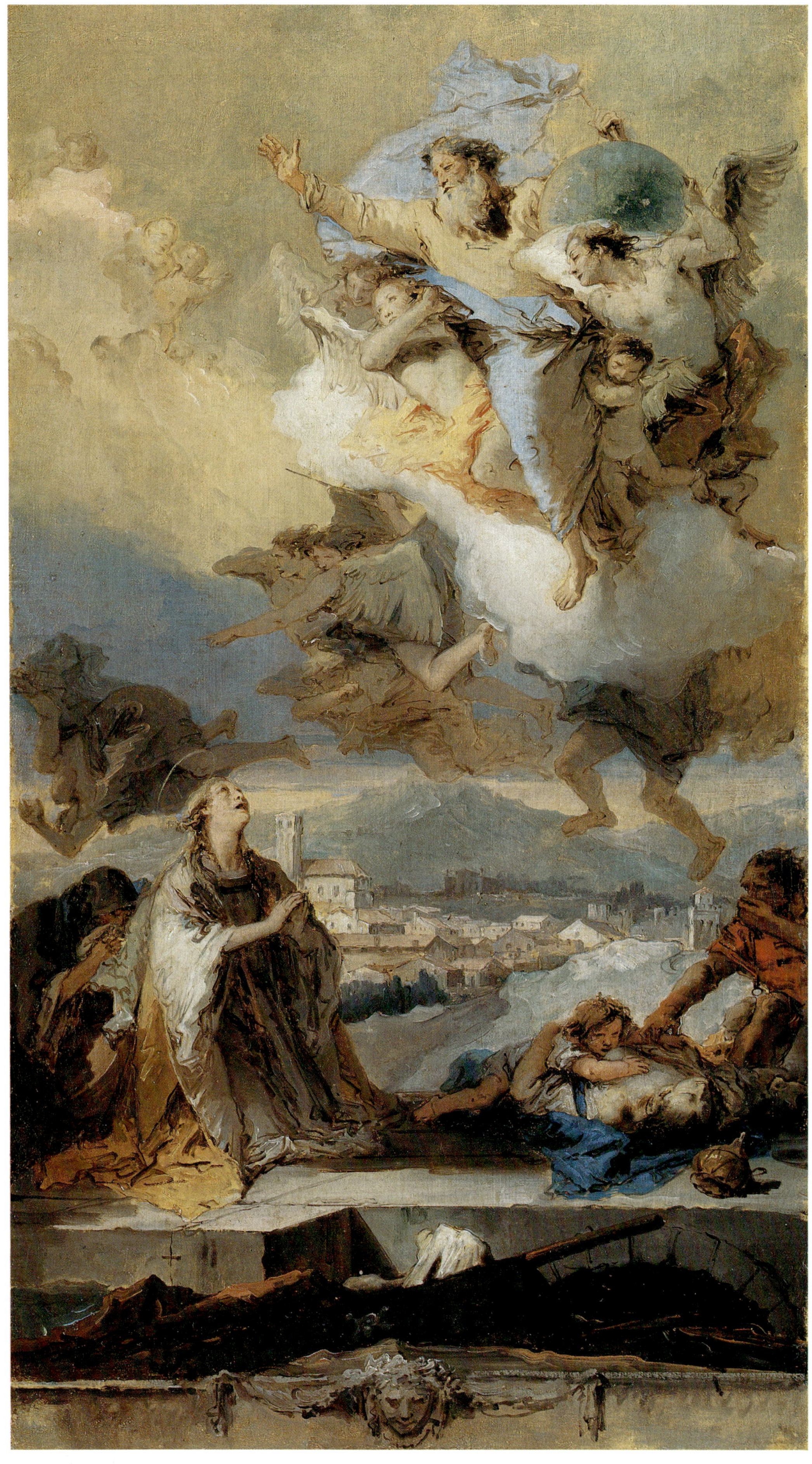

51

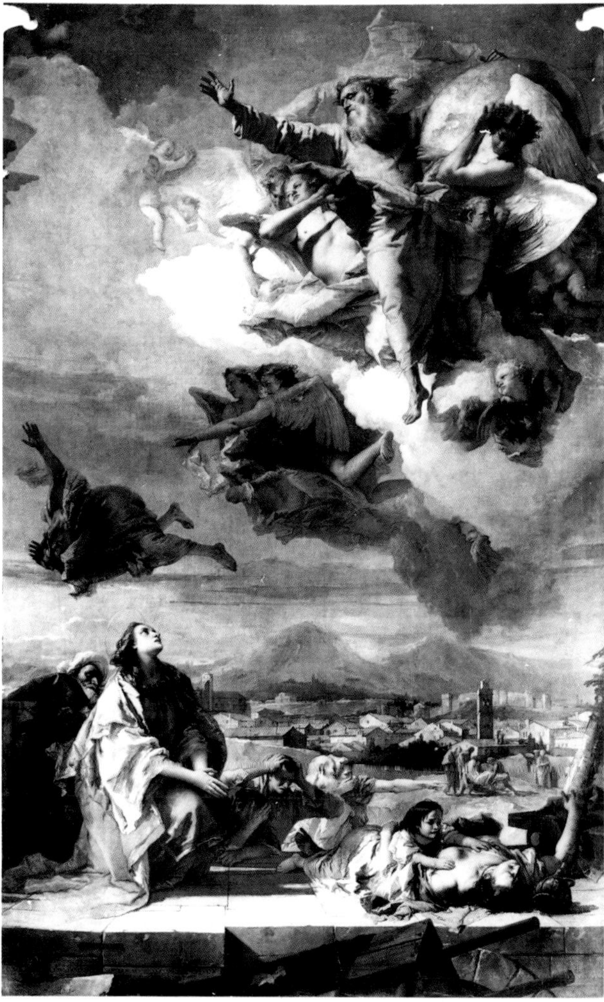

Fig. 115. *Saint Thecla Praying for the Plague-Stricken*. Oil on canvas. Cathedral, Este

commending its emphasis on the expressions and actions of the figures.[4] There can be little doubt that the woman shown prostrate in a foreshortened position on a squared pavement in both Tiepolo's *modello* and his final altarpiece constitutes a conscious reference to Poussin's painting. Both Marcantonio's print and Poussin's work include the detail of a male figure covering his nose with one hand while with the other he pulls away the child trying to suckle at its mother's breast. The male figure appears in the *modello* but was suppressed in the altarpiece, where two men lamenting the awful sight were added at the foot of the woman and another detail from Poussin's painting was included: the figures carrying a shrouded victim to burial. As though to further emphasize the relation to Poussin's canvas, in the altarpiece Tiepolo gave stronger emphasis to the perspective grid of the pavement and the play of cast shadows on it. The expressions and gestures of the additional figures in the middle ground—one resting on the pavement with his hand covering his face, the other inconsolably raising both hands to his head—were obviously conceived with a view to academic notions of the *affetti*, while the increased contrast between the beautiful, imploring face of the early Christian virgin and the grandiloquent God the Father relates to ideas of decorum. (The pose of the figure of God the Father—not without reminiscences of the Saint Michael in the *Fall of the Rebel Angels* Tiepolo had painted at Würzburg—is studied in a pen-and-ink-wash drawing that was once part of the Orloff album).[5] In a letter of 1743, Algarotti had recommended Tiepolo to Count Brühl as a modern Raphael or Poussin, but only at this stage of Tiepolo's career does the characterization seem applicable.

It is not only in the various motifs and gestures of the Saint Thecla compositions that Tiepolo revealed a new artistic direction. In the altarpiece Tiepolo restrained his hallmark vibrato brushwork, which plays such an important part in creating the sense of fervent urgency in the *modello*, emphasizing instead smooth, more polished surfaces. He enlivened the uniformly low-key color scheme with almost strident accents in the final painting—particularly in Saint Thecla's vermilion cloak, which replaces the ocher one she wears in the *modello*. And in place of the warm, hazy, and diffuse light of the sketch, he chose a cold, directed one that casts sharp shadows and highlights details. In no earlier commission do we encounter such a marked difference in the technical means and artistic ambition of the *modello* and the finished work. These features are sometimes interpreted as signaling a decline in Tiepolo's creative powers or an increased reliance on Giandomenico to carry his projects through to completion. They should, instead, alert us to his remarkable ability to respond to new cultural stimuli.

KC

PROVENANCE:
Francisco Bayeu (by 1771–95; inv. no. 134); Infanta Maria Amalia de Borbón, Naples (before 1860); Infante Don Sebastián Gabriel de Borbón y Braganza (before 1860–75); Prince Pedro de Borbón, duke of Durcal, Paris (1875–90; sale, American Art Galleries, New York, 10–13 April 1889, lot 60 [bought in]; sale, Hôtel Drouot, Paris, 3 February 1890, lot 47); Schiff, Paris (1890–ca. 1910); Marquis de Biron, Paris and Geneva (after 1910–37)

REFERENCES:
Chennevières 1898, p. 113; Sack 1910, pp. 132, 167, 216; Venice 1951, pp. 129–30, no. 92; Saltillo 1952, p. 75; Sánchez Cantón 1953, pp. 25–26; Morassi 1955a, pp. 33, 151, 155; Morassi 1962, p. 33; Gaya Nuño 1964, p. 90; Pallucchini 1968, p. 126, no. 248a; Byam Shaw 1970, p. 238; Rizzi in Udine 1971, p. 135; Zeri and Gardner 1973, p. 58; Levey 1986, pp. 222–25; Barcham 1989, p. 228; Barcham 1992, p. 116; Fort Worth 1993, pp. 281–83, no. 45; Gemin and Pedrocco 1993, p. 467, no. 486a

NOTES

1. For the letter of 1758 commissioning the altarpiece, see Molmenti 1909, p. 119 n. 35.
2. A copy of the *modello*, formerly in the collection of Felix Boix, Madrid, was published as an autograph work by Sánchez Cantón (1929, pp. 137–38). See Zeri and Gardner 1973, p. 58.
3. See Molmenti 1909, p. 119 n. 35. Barcham (1992, p. 116) has suggested that Cardinal Carlo Rezzonico had a hand in the selection of Tiepolo. Apart from the fact that Rezzonico consecrated the church of Saint Thecla in 1748, in 1758 Tiepolo was engaged to fresco the ceilings of two rooms of the Rezzonico palace to celebrate the marriage of the cardinal's nephew (see no. 25a,b). In 1758 Carlo Rezzonico was elected pope as Clement XIII.
4. Bellori 1672, pp. 415–16. By the eighteenth century Marcantonio's print was a topos, and Tiepolo's painting is indebted to the motif rather than the formal arrangement, which is much closer to Poussin's treatment.
5. See Hadeln 1928, pl. 100. The drawing shows God the Father with angels more or less as he appears in the *modello*. The sheet also contains a study for the fleeing figure of the Plague, shown in reverse.

52. *Apotheosis of the Pisani Family*

52. Apotheosis of the Pisani Family
Doc 1760
140 × 96 cm (55⅛ × 37⅞ in.)
Musée des Beaux-Arts, Angers

The composition, with its seemingly limitless depths defined by billowing clouds and a silvery sky, is divided into contrasting halves bound together by the fluttering figure of Fame blowing her trumpet. Below her, enthroned in clouds above a sphere, Divine Wisdom presides over a harmonious realm. At her feet are the Virtues: Faith (veiled, holding a book), Justice, Charity (with a baby), Hope (with an anchor), and, almost hidden behind her mistress, Fortitude. A vigorous figure of Italy, viewed from the back, wearing a turreted crown, and astride a globe, gestures to a group of celebrating nymphs and advances toward a personification usually understood as Venice, who looks across the ceiling to the allegorical figure of Europe opposite her; thus, Venice mediates between Italy and Europe, who complete the crucial political triad of the allegory. In the care of Venice and her companion, Truth (shown nude), are four children of Ermolao III Alvise Pisani, procurator of S. Marco, and his wife, Paolina Gambara: Alvise (b. 1754), Carlo (b. 1756), Elena (b. 1755), and Elisabetta (b. 1758). Below Italy are the Arts: Astronomy (winged, holding a telescope in one hand and resting the other on a globe), Music (with two horns), Sculpture (leaning on a block of marble, with her right hand on an unfinished bust), and Painting (holding a brush or stylus). At the left Peace (holding fronds) sinks back into the clouds, while Abundance (holding a wreath) seems, literally, to stride through the air above an umbrella pine, below which music-making peasants take their rest. In contrast to this idyllic world, on the opposite side of the composition is shown a majestic Europe (holding a scepter, with her attribute, a temple, at her side) presiding over the three other continents: Asia (wearing a fantastical elephant headdress), who bows her head in submission to Europe's dominion, America (with feathered headdress and crocodile), and Africa. Below them, along the periphery, are visible the groveling forms of two men in long cloaks—most likely Turks—surrendering to attacking Europeans, while, farther along, two half-naked women and a winged dragon, possibly symbolizing Discord or Heresy, flee, glancing back over their shoulders toward Divine Wisdom. Located opposite them are two emaciated figures that probably refer to the effects of pestilence and war, and above them a group of figures cower together. In some details, such as the banners next to Europe, there are doubtless allusions to the victories won against the Turks in 1717 by Andrea Pisani, uncle of Ermolao III Alvise.

Mariuz has noted that the presence of the Pisani children transforms the allegory from a mere celebration of past glories into a paean on the promise of a new generation. We might add that by embedding the children in the general scheme rather than separating them out, the composition links them with the political future of the Venetian state. The Enlightenment slant is summarized by Mariuz: "Civilization, the light emanated by wisdom, is founded on the exercise of the virtues and the progress of the arts, while Peace (symbolized by the dancing girl holding olive branches) is the fundamental condition of its triumph." This quite accurately conveys the illusory vision held by members of the Venetian oligarchy at a time when their city's real powers had all but vanished and its military glory was a thing of the past.

Tiepolo's ceiling in the ballroom of the grandiose Villa Pisani at Strà, on the Brenta Canal, was the most important project he had undertaken before leaving Venice for Madrid (fig. 116). It involved the central, sky-filled apotheosis of the Pisani family, for which this ravishing picture is the *modello*, set into a heavy architectural framework painted by the Milanese *quadraturista* specialist Pietro Visconti, and, on the walls above a balcony, feigned classicizing reliefs of mythological-allegorical subjects painted by Giandomenico. The room is large, 23 by 13.85 meters, with Tiepolo's center scene measuring 12.7 by 7.7 meters, and in a letter addressed to Francesco Algarotti on 10 May 1760, the artist estimated that it would take him three to four years to accomplish the task. He was obviously making allowance for numerous other competing projects, for when put under pressure to finish his Italian commissions and depart for Spain, he completed the work at Strà in somewhat more than a year and a half.

The project got off to a slow start. In May 1760 the sixty-four-year-old Tiepolo was, uncharacteristically, bedridden with gout, and in his letter of that month to Algarotti he expressed fear that he would have to abandon a previous commitment in Milan, since his first responsibility was to paint the Villa Pisani *modello*.

Detail, no. 52

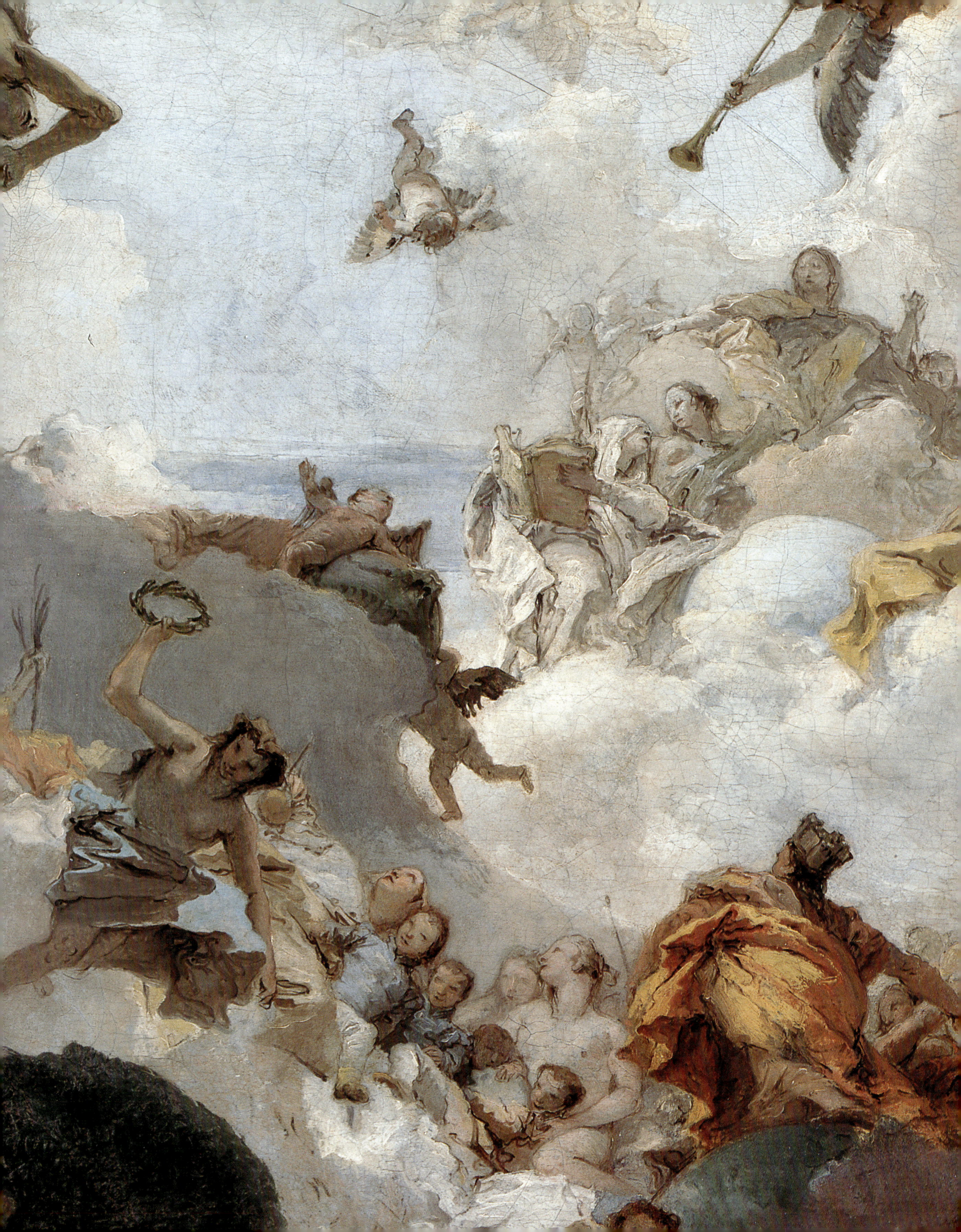

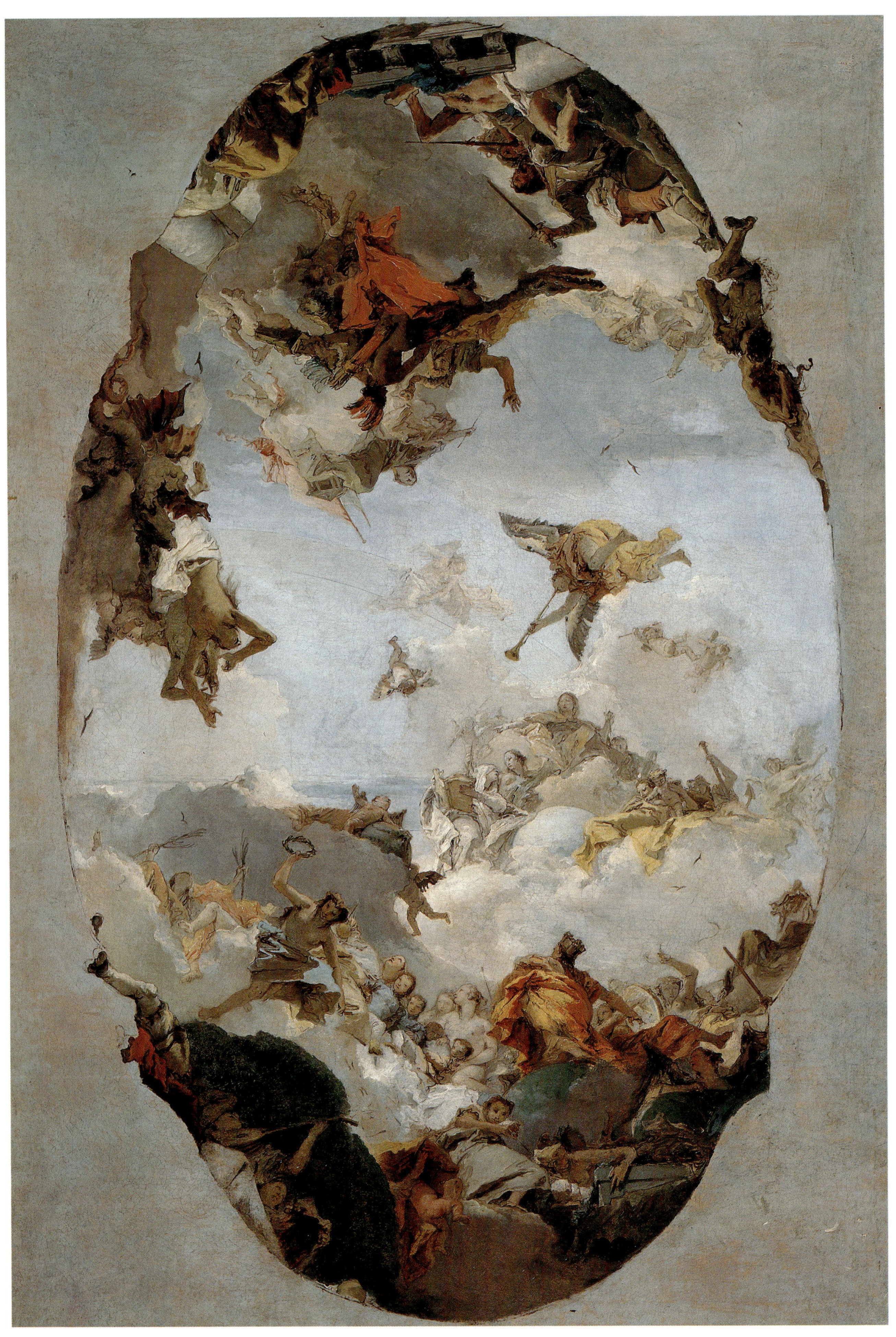

Opposite: Fig. 116. *The Apotheosis of the Pisani Family* (ceiling).
Fresco. Villa Pisani, Strà

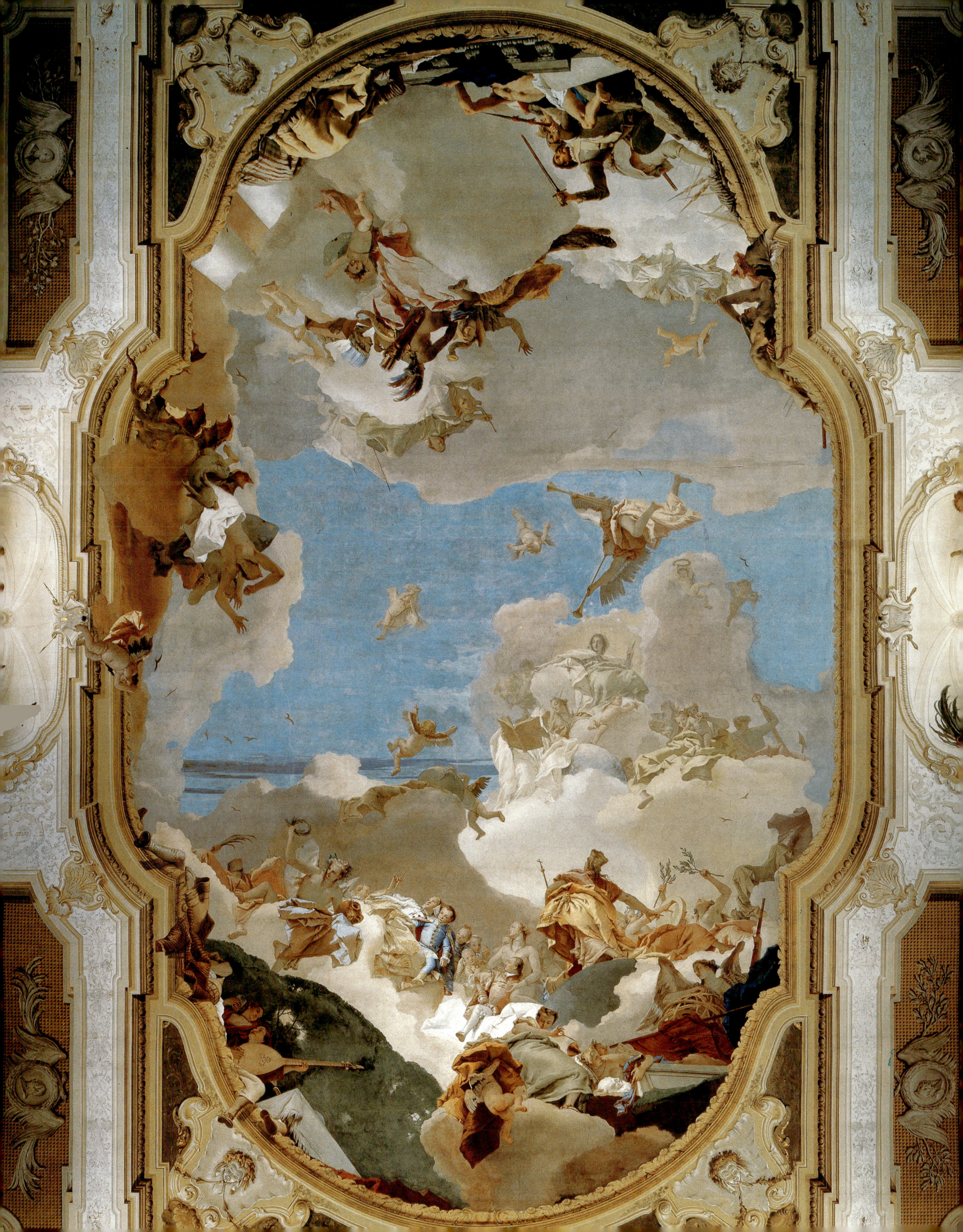

PROVENANCE:
Jean Robin de Chalonnes, by whom bequeathed to Musée des Beaux-Arts, Angers (1864)

REFERENCES:
Jouin 1881, p. 85, no. 273; Molmenti 1909, p. 40; Sack 1910, p. 212, no. 456; Gallo 1945, p. 72 n. 2; Lorenzetti in Venice 1951, p. 131, no. 93; Morassi 1962, pp. 1–2; Pallucchini 1968, p. 129, no. 277a; Precerutti Garberi 1968, p. 153; Paris 1971, p. 160, no. 243; Knox 1975a, p. 28; Mariuz in Pallucchini 1978, p. 247; Levey 1986, p. 249; Tiozzo 1986, p. 55; Gemin and Pedrocco 1993, pp. 186, 483, no. 511a; Alpers and Baxandall 1994, p. 66

The carefully contoured shape and the scrupulously articulated program of the *modello* indicate that the overall scheme of the decoration, including Visconti's feigned architectural surround, had been worked out before this date. Once the *modello* was finished, Tiepolo must have proceeded to the cartoons, but when he actually began painting is uncertain: on 16 March 1761 he wrote Algarotti that his greatest obligation remained the ceiling at Villa Pisani (among other projects, he was also engaged to paint two altarpieces to be sent to Rome; a large ceiling on canvas for the court of Moscow; and a frescoed ceiling, again in collaboration with Visconti, for the Canossa family in Verona). In April he was juggling his commitments at both Villa Pisani and Palazzo Canossa, and when Fragonard and Saint-Non stopped at the villa at Strà that June, the room was inaccessible because of ongoing work.[1] Tiepolo completed the ceiling at Palazzo Canossa that fall, and on 22 December 1761 he announced in a letter that he would finish at Strà by February; he left for Madrid at the end of March, having already prepared the *modello* for his work there. The organization and speed of execution this extraordinary sequence of events presupposes is borne out by a reckoning of the *giornate* on the ceiling: thirty-two for the center section; twelve for Tiepolo's figures in the *quadratura*; thirty-two for Visconti's architectural surround and ornamentation—representing, in all, less than three months of actual painting time.[2]

Not surprisingly, this is one case in which there are only relatively minor, albeit numerous, compositional differences between Tiepolo's *modello* and final work: even the relative figure scale is notably consistent. The Pisani portraits were redone from life to update the appearance and ages of the sitters, and another child, Marina (b. 7 August 1759), was included in the fresco. (The children are readily identifiable in Alessandro Longhi's contemporary portrait of the Pisani family in the Bentivoglio d'Aragona collection, Venice.) The other alterations range from the addition of a putto who, in the ceiling, flies out over the frame in front of the fleeing women, to a change in the action of Abundance (now given a different attribute in the form of a large vase) and a regrouping of the peasants below her (in the fresco one dangles his leg over the edge, while another indulges in some hidden escapade under the draped table). In the ceiling the winged figure to the right of the Virtues was suppressed (although its silhouette as shown in the *modello* determined the shape of a cloud in the fresco); Hope turns her back to the viewer; one of the putti on a cloud below Faith takes flight; Peace has shifted from the left to the right side of the Arts, while Music has gained a score, Fame a second trumpet, and Europe her bull. However, the major difference is one of visual emphasis: in the ceiling there is an evident contrast, absent in the *modello*, between the virile armed men (standard in Tiepolo's practice) and the refined, delicate allegorical figures opposite them; but most notable is the shift in tonality. For once, the fresco—however blond and airy—does not attain the cool silvery tone of the *modello*, as it substitutes subtle pinks and greens for puces and grays. Still, in its suggestion of a vast, open space and of diaphanous figures inhabiting its depths, the ceiling, like the *modello*, marks a new phase in Tiepolo's work that climaxes, on a completely different scale and in a different vein, in the late religious *capricci* on the life of the Virgin (no. 57a–d). A crucial, but ultimately unanswerable, question is whether Giandomenico played a role in encouraging this *ultima maniera*, for in the decade preceding his departure for Spain, the aging master seems to have responded to a youthful, rejuvenating force. Certainly, Tiepolo must have depended increasingly on his son's assistance and could not have helped being impressed by Giandomenico's more intimate, colloquial style. In the Angers *modello* Tiepolo conjures a universe too vast to be conquered by the physical prowess of its inhabitants, and this lends the work a special, almost fragile, quality. The pity—to appropriate Algarotti's analogy of collaboration between painters to musical practice—is that this exquisite ceiling, scored for violins, did not receive the sympathetic *quadratura* basso accompaniment it deserved, and that in the villa the feigned architecture sounds a heavy, discordant note.

There exist a number of drawings related to the seated fauns and satyrs Tiepolo painted on Visconti's architecture.[3] Of interest for the history of the collecting of Tiepolo oil sketches is the fact that Jean Robin, who at some unspecified time before 1864 purchased the Angers *modello*, was a pupil of Guérin and Gros and became a collector after inheriting a fortune from his uncle.

KC

NOTES

1. See Rosenberg and Brejon de Lavergnée 1986, p. 215.
2. On the technique and probable sequence of work at Strà, see Tiozzo 1986.
3. For these, see Knox in Stuttgart 1970, p. 142.

53. *The Wealth and Benefits of the Spanish Monarchy*

†53. The Wealth and Benefits of the Spanish Monarchy
Doc. 1762
181 × 104.5 cm (71¼ × 41⅛ in.)
National Gallery of Art, Washington, D.C., Samuel H. Kress Collection (1943.4.39)

On 13 March 1762 Tiepolo wrote a correspondent—probably his friend of twenty years, the learned Francesco Algarotti: "At present I am finishing the *Modello* of the Great Work that is so vast it is enough to reflect that it is one hundred feet; all the same, I would like to think that the completed idea will be well adapted and suited to that Great Monarchy—certainly a heavy task, but for such a Work one needs courage."[1] The task in question was the commission to fresco the ceiling of the throne room of the royal palace in Madrid for King Charles III of Spain (fig. 117); the *modello* is the picture exhibited here, painted by Tiepolo in Venice and transported with him to Madrid, where he arrived on 4 June after an arduous two-month journey via Genoa and Barcelona.

Tiepolo was first approached for this prestigious commission—one that put a royal stamp on his reputation as Europe's greatest decorator—in the summer of 1761, while he was still engaged on the ceilings in Palazzo Canossa, Verona, and Villa Pisani, Strà (see no. 52). Pressure was put on him through official channels to curtail his work on other projects (he, in fact, dropped a commission for two altarpieces destined for Rome and left the lower portion of the ballroom at Strà for Jacopo Guarana to paint). Tiepolo had started to plan his Würzburg decorations before leaving Venice, and he did not wait for his departure to begin formulating his ideas for Madrid. Measured plans were sent to him, he explained, "so that, in anticipation, I can make a start with my studies and *modelli*."[2] Clearly, he wished to impress the king with his proposal, for, save only the *modello* for the ceiling over the stairwell of the Residenz in Würzburg (no. 49), this is the largest and most elaborate of Tiepolo's oil sketches. The size was partly a function of the importance of the commission, partly a response to the size of the room, and partly a matter of accommodating the dense iconographic program, which, in the words of Francisco José Fabre, author of the earliest detailed explication, concerns "the majesty of the Spanish Monarchy, exalted by poetic beings, attended by virtues, and surrounded by its diverse states."[3] No written record of the scheme and its organizing ideas survives, but guidelines must certainly have been given to Tiepolo.[4]

The principal portion of the composition is in the lower area of the canvas, where the figures rise into the sky like a monumental pyramid whose base is on the short side of the ceiling over the wall obviously intended for the throne.[5] Positioned on a globe, and thus dominating the world—between statues of Hercules (strength) and Apollo (wisdom) and trumpeted by Fame (in a pose that repeats one Tiepolo used on the ceiling of Villa Loschi, outside Vicenza, some thirty years earlier)—is the personification of the Spanish Monarchy.[6] The configuration constitutes an allusion to depictions of Divine Wisdom, and in the fresco Tiepolo underscored this analogy by replacing Hercules with Minerva, patron of knowledge and science. The appearance of the throne derives from Tiepolo's fresco of the investiture of Bishop Harold in the Kaisersaal at Würzburg, and indeed throughout the design of the ceiling, recollections of the Würzburg frescoes—which were recorded in albums of detailed drawings by Giandomenico—shaped the imagery.

Below the Monarchy are the attributes that guide and sustain it. Immediately at her feet is Justice (a sword in one hand and barely visible scales in the other). Three women identifiable as Clemency, Abundance (holding a cornucopia), and Moderation, together with a laurel-crowned male figure signifying Merit or Counsel (eliminated from the fresco, where Mercury hovers instead), are gathered beneath the statue of Hercules. Abundance—the result of enlightened government—turns toward the Spanish Monarchy. Farther down are shown Princely Glory (the female figure with the pyramid, which in the fresco is inscribed with Charles III's name),[7] Generosity (with a lion), Affability (holding a ring), and what appears to be Hope (only the ringed top of her anchor is visible, and in the fresco she gains the globe proper to Intelligence). A putto holds out a wreath of lilies symbolizing the Bourbon dynasty over the head of a winged figure. Beneath the statue of Apollo is the winged female figure of Virtue, accompanied by other, unidentifiable, females, and below her are Faith (holding a chalice and cross and standing in a pose reminiscent of that of her much earlier counterpart on the ceiling of the Scuola Grande dei Carmini, Venice), Fortitude (pictured here with what appears to be a diagonally oriented column and transformed into Hope holding her anchor in the fresco), Prudence (with a snake wrapped around one arm, a mirror in the other, and assuming a pose that

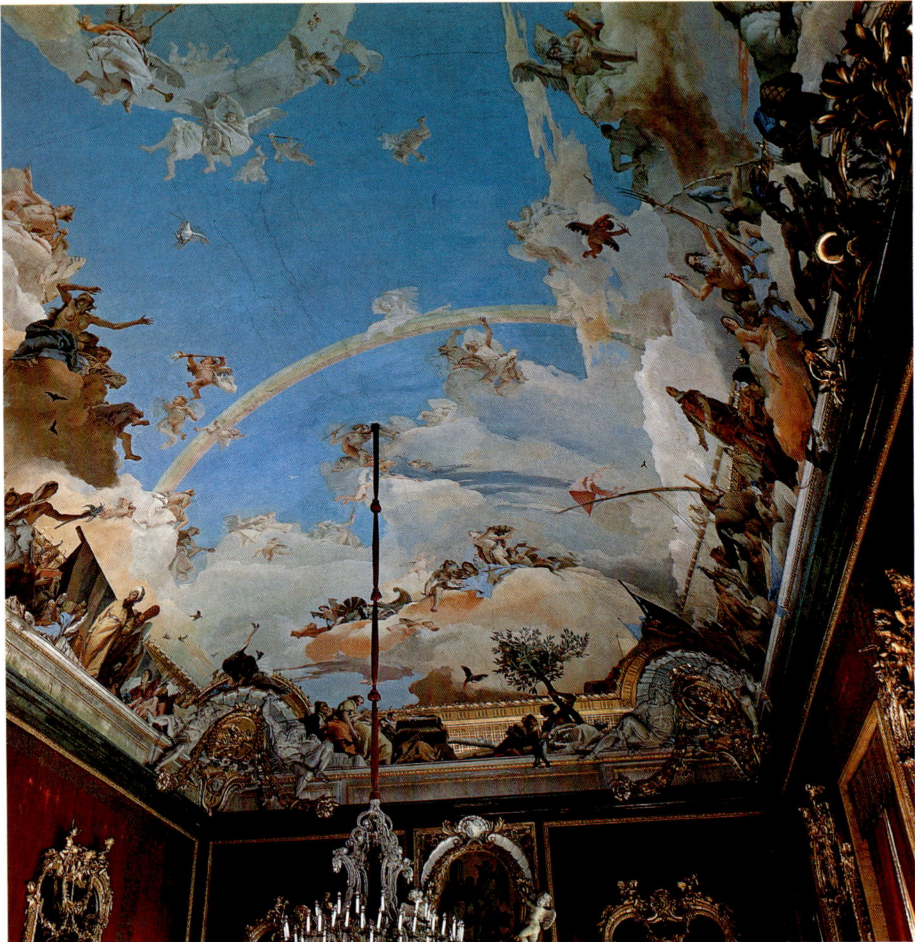

Fig. 117. *The Wealth and Benefits of the Spanish Monarchy* (ceiling of throne room). Fresco. Palacio Real, Madrid

repeats, in reverse, that of her counterpart in the Scuola Grande dei Carmini), and a winged figure with a palm signifying Victory. On the cornice are figures representing some of Spain's conquered territories: a groom leading the celebrated Arabian horses, two Andeans offering tribute, and a female whom Fabre thought stood for Seville.

On one long side Crime, Terror, and Fury are banished by torch-bearing putti (the light of reason) above a depiction of the commercial and agricultural products of Spain together with the wealth of Asia ("India Oriental")[8]—where Spain's primary possession was the Philippines. The kingdom of Castile may be alluded to by the figures in European dress. The main characters on the cornice here are quite obviously reconfigurations of those on the Würzburg ceiling (see frontis., p. 18), while the falling man recalls a similar individual in the Scalzi ceiling (see fig. 111). On the opposite side Neptune guides a treasure-laden galleon from America ("India Occidental"), symbolized by natives with feather headdresses. (In the fresco the prominent figure on the ship gains an apposite sixteenth-century costume—an allusion to Columbus and sixteenth-century Spanish expansion into the New World.) Farther along are three women evidently meant to personify Geography, Navigation, and Industry (with a bolt of red fabric). (In the fresco this group is considerably altered and includes more figures.) On the remaining short side Thetis (holding her shell and signifying "la inmensidad de las aguas")[9] guides a chariot with Mars and Vulcan (see catalogue frontis.). (In the fresco Thetis is accompanied by her husband, Oceanus.) On the cornice below are shown women with a variety of attributes (tree trunks, a citrus tree), possibly intended to represent the kingdom of Aragon. In the corner, at the border of Spain proper, are the Pillars of Hercules, standing for Gibraltar (suppressed in the fresco in favor of an ostrich like the one Tiepolo had used at Würzburg to represent the continent of Africa). To their left are shown Hercules (seated in the clouds with his club) and Ceres or Ariadne, and above are the figures of Jupiter and Minerva. As at Würzburg, Tiepolo anticipated stucco figures in the corners; here, however, they have the traits of ancient river gods and hold gilt reliefs and shelter beneath giant shells to elaborate on the idea of Spanish dominion over the seas. Above one of these is a depiction of Painting and Poetry.

The scheme is a less unified, less poetic one than that conceived for the stairwell fresco at Würzburg: static panegyric replaces narrative fantasy. The individual elements are more diverse, and the overall composition substitutes grandiose effect for unfolding, visionary splendor. Instead of the dynamic zigzag configuration of the Würzburg ceiling, which reveals itself only gradually as the viewer moves up the staircase, there is a series of concentric circles that anchor the composition, lead back into space, and emphasize the centrality of the Spanish Monarchy. As indicated above, many of the motifs derive from earlier projects; indeed Tiepolo seems to have used his albums of drawings as pattern books. Nevertheless, and typically for Tiepolo, the effect is new and exactly suited to the formal setting of a throne room, where the narrative action, abundant picturesque exotica, and lighthearted wit of the Würzburg ceiling would have been as indecorous as the bucolic details of Villa Pisani.

At Würzburg the *modello* determined the overall configuration of the composition, and the figures added after the sketch was completed embellished the scheme with local color without altering the fundamental meaning. This was not entirely the case at Madrid, where parts of the program underwent substantial revision and a wide variety of elements evidently detailing the Spanish provinces, not provided for in the *modello*, was introduced. Jones has explained that these modifications and additions were made in response to a changed political

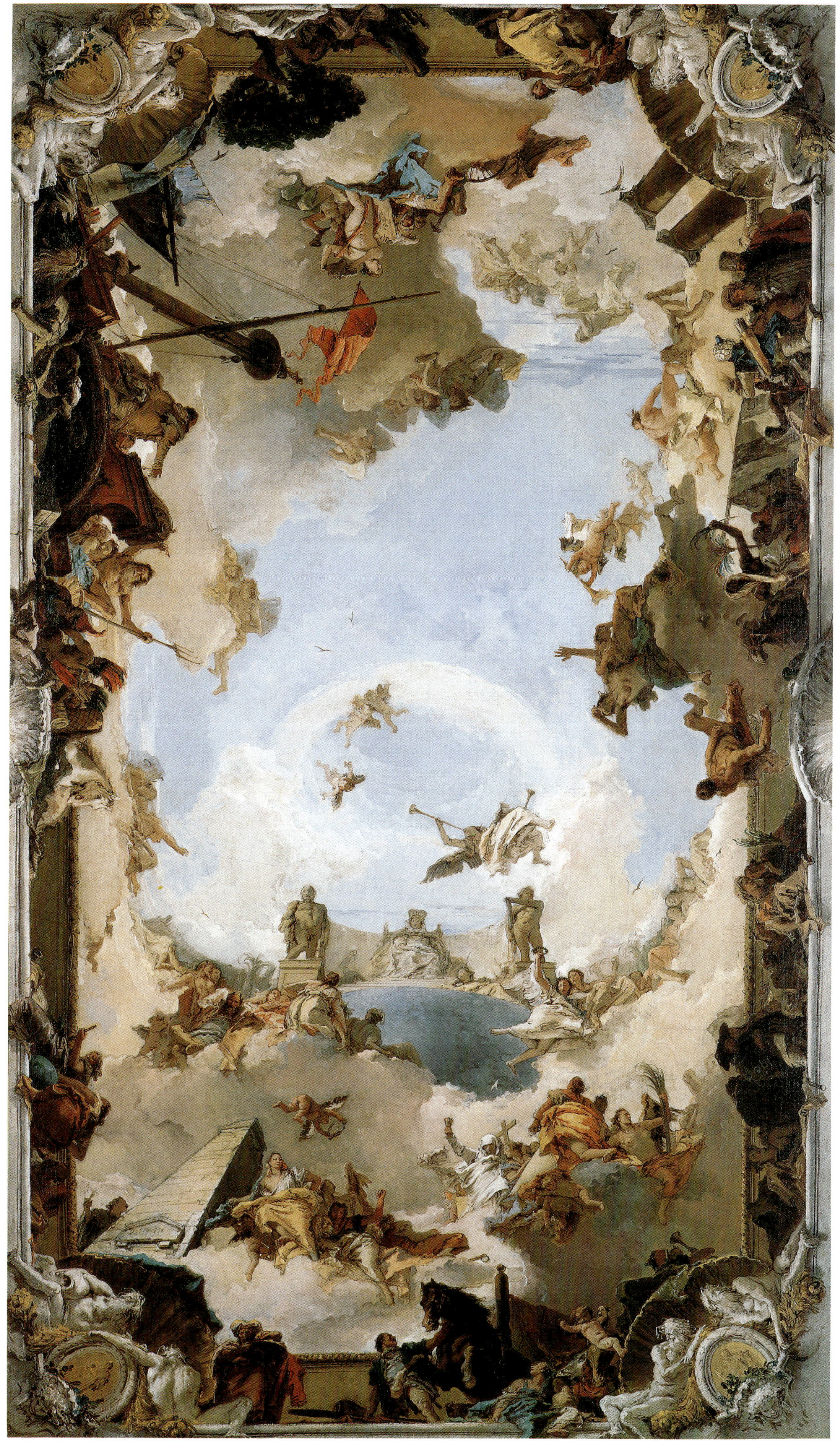

53

PROVENANCE:

Possibly Pagliano, Venice;[12] possibly Edward Cheney, London and Badger Hall, Shropshire (1842–52); possibly Col. Alfred Capel Cure, Badger Hall (1884–96); Francis Capel Cure (1896?–after 1910); Count Alessandro Contini Bonacossi, Florence (before 1935); Samuel H. Kress, New York (1935–43)

REFERENCES:

Sack 1910, pp. 139, 223; Gerstenberg 1952, pp. 152–53; Morassi 1955a, p. 35; Morassi 1962, pp. 21, 67, 238; Watson 1963, p. 247; Gaya Nuño 1964, p. 92; Knox 1964, p. 25; Pallucchini 1968, p. 132, no. 279a; Udine 1971, p. 143; Shapley 1973, pp. 150–52; Knox 1975a, p. 96; Shapley 1979, pp. 445–48; Knox 1980a, p. 75, n. 1; Jones 1981, pp. 226–27; Levey 1986, pp. 254–63; Barcham 1992, p. 45; Fort Worth 1993, pp. 304–9, no. 55; Gemin and Pedrocco 1993, p. 486, no. 516a; London 1994, pp. 213, 503, no. 128; Venice 1995a, p. 256, no. 62; De Grazia and Garberson 1996, pp. 272–84

situation—Spain signed a humiliating peace treaty with England in 1763—and a desire to deemphasize martial themes.[10] The ceiling, completed in 1764, was made to include more pointed references to the Bourbon rule. But beyond these considerations, the alterations probably also reflect a simple fact of court life: that meddling advisers have their say; it can hardly be coincidental that two alternative *modelli* survive for each of the other ceilings Tiepolo painted in the royal palace (see no. 54a, b).

Apart from the changes in iconography, the most significant alterations introduced into the fresco for the throne room were the use of heavy gilding on the feigned wall above the cornice and the modified foreshortening of the figures who stand in front of it. Not only is the room dimly lit and lacking in architectural character, but the ceiling is also oppressively low, and the steep foreshortening Tiepolo anticipated in the *modello* proved to be inappropriate for the viewing conditions at the actual site. There is in addition the matter of a dramatic shift in style: in the fresco the painterly vigor of the sketch gives way to a slightly banal descriptive treatment fundamentally at odds with Tiepolo's earlier work. The figure of Neptune, for example, perhaps too closely resembles a real naked man to sustain the fiction of the fresco as a whole. It can be argued that this descriptiveness was a response by Tiepolo to the two ceilings Anton Raphael Mengs was carrying out in the palace in his habitual laborious fashion, achieving a remarkable if slightly uneasy blend of elegance and academicism. There can be no doubt that both Giandomenico and Lorenzo played leading roles in the painting of the throne-room ceiling, and we may suspect that Giambattista employed them in particular in the areas in which they could give free reign to their innate feeling for genre and portraiture. All these factors help explain why the completed ceiling—however impressive when judged on its own terms—does not fulfill the promise of the *modello*.[11]

KC

NOTES

1. Molmenti 1909, pp. 26–27: "Al presente sono al fine del Modello della Gran Opera, che tanto è vasta, basta solo riflettere, ch'è di cento piedi; tuttavia voglio sperare che l'idea compita sarà molto ben accomodata et adattata a quella Gran Monarchia, fatica grande, certamente ma per tal Opera ci vuol coraggio." Whether the correspondent was Algarotti, as the tone of the letter and its contents suggest, or the patrician Tomaso Farsetti, for whom Tiepolo was carrying out some work, is uncertain.
2. Letter of 28 September 1761 sent by Tiepolo, then in Verona, to the Spanish ambassador at Venice (Battisti 1960, p. 79).
3. Fabre 1829, p. 107.
4. It has been suggested that the program was the brainchild of the Benedictine friar Martin Sarmiento, who had conceived the iconography for the sculptural decoration of the palace in the 1740s. See Brown in Fort Worth 1993, p. 306; Jones 1981, p. 221, with previous bibliography; and the cautionary comments of De Grazia and Garberson 1996, p. 280.
5. Beginning with Knox (1980a, p. 75 n. 1), authors have commented that the present location of the throne on one of the long walls cannot be what Tiepolo envisaged and must represent a change made after he completed the ceiling.
6. For the identifications proposed I have relied heavily on the detailed texts of Fabre 1829, pp. 106–31; Jones 1981; and especially De Grazia (in De Grazia and Garberson 1996), who has made a fundamentally new interpretation. As De Grazia notes, many of Fabre's interpretations are conjectural, since there was no fixed iconography for the depiction of the Spanish provinces.
7. According to Cesare Ripa's *Iconologia*, the woman signifies the magnanimous thoughts of princes, and the pyramid manifests their glory.
8. The attributes are the same ones Tiepolo used for Africa at Würzburg, but Fabre (1829, pp. 120–22) did not hesitate to identify the figure as "India Oriental," and Ripa, in his *Iconologia*, has Asia on a camel and Africa on an elephant. De Grazia calls this group the East Indies.
9. Fabre 1829, p. 110.
10. See Jones 1981, pp. 225–27. It should, however, be noted that Jones is inaccurate about some of the changes he perceives: the figure of Abundance and her direct gaze at the Spanish Monarchy were not added to the fresco but were already present in the *modello*, and the very prominent depiction below the Spanish Monarchy is more martial in the ceiling, not less. Brown (in Fort Worth 1993, p. 308) has noted that X rays of the *modello* reveal that beneath the Spanish Monarchy Tiepolo originally painted a rainbow, which reappears in the fresco at the opposite end of the ceiling. On these issues, see De Grazia and Garberson 1996, p. 275.
11. The sometimes banal handling of details in the fresco is well characterized by Levey (1986, p. 262).
12. The early provenance of the picture is uncertain and depends on a notice in Sack 1910 (p. 223), to the effect that the work, in the collection of Francis Capel Cure when Sack was published, was bought from the husband of a granddaughter of Tiepolo's and was part of an inheritance of oil sketches and unfinished work from Giandomenico. Brown (in Fort Worth 1993, p. 309 n. 1) thinks this means that Cure bought the painting in Venice from Pagliano. However, Cure was heir to Edward Cheney, who bought his fabulous collection of drawings and *modelli* in Venice during visits in 1842 and 1852, and it is possible that the picture passed to Cure through Cheney. According to Waagen (1857, p. 173), Cheney owned nineteen oil sketches for ceilings. Twelve "designs" for ceilings were sold at Cheney's sale in 1885, but this one was not among them. See also Shapley 1979, pp. 447, 448 nn. 16, 17, and De Grazia and Garberson 1996, p. 282 n. 1.

THE SALETA OF THE PALACIO REAL

54a. The Apotheosis of the Spanish Monarchy
54b. The Apotheosis of the Spanish Monarchy

Tiepolo's arrival in Madrid in June 1762 to fresco the throne room of the royal palace was preceded by the departure of the brilliant Neapolitan artist Corrado Giaquinto, who had been employed in that city by Charles III's father, and by the arrival of Anton Raphael Mengs, who, like Tiepolo, had been invited to the court in 1761. Both Giaquinto and Mengs worked on the extensive decorations of the royal palace together with a number of Spanish painters, including Francisco Bayeu. Giaquinto frescoed the ceiling over the main staircase—a commission that would have brought out Tiepolo's best—and Mengs carried out work in other rooms. Tiepolo had anticipated finishing the fresco in the throne room in two years and then returning to Venice; once in Madrid, however, he must have seen that the palace offered the possibility of far more extensive employment, and on 7 August 1764 he wrote a Venetian correspondent that he was engaged on "molti soffitti" (many ceilings).[1] Whether he was referring to commissions in hand or, instead, was actively soliciting work through the production of *modelli* must remain a matter of speculation. In any event, he painted ceilings for two additional rooms, but a total of six oil sketches for four projects—including a particularly enchanting one for the ceiling of the queen's bedroom (fig. 119)—survive.[2] The two exhibited here are alternative *modelli* for the *saleta*, or small room, adjacent to the throne room (fig. 118). The program of the *saleta* was described in detail by Francisco José Fabre in a guide made for King Ferdinand VII in 1829.[3]

Not surprisingly, the *modelli* have many allegorical elements in common. Each shows, in the heavens, beneath a flapping canopy and accompanied by Minerva, Jupiter and his eagle with, to the side, a trumpeting figure of Fame. Below, in the center, crowned by a flying figure of Mercury, are the Spanish Monarchy and her lion with, in one picture, Neptune and Prudence (holding a snake), and, in the other, an old woman and a tower symbolizing Old Castile, the most eminent of Spain's provinces. Immediately under them are Mars and Venus, accompanied in one *modello* by the personification of Castile and in the other by Saturn-Time. In the lower left are Hercules (with a column symbolizing the Strait of Gibraltar, which separates Spain from Africa and the Atlantic Ocean from the Mediterranean) and figures representing the continents: Africa (wearing the elephant headdress prescribed by Cesare Ripa in his *Iconologia*), America (wearing feathers), and Europe (the female figure with a miniature temple), who is barely discernible in one sketch and highly prominent in the other. Asia may be personified by a fourth figure in one picture, but she is excluded from the other.

There are a host of differences between the secondary allegorical figures included in each work. For example, only one *modello* presents Merit and Justice next to the tower of Castile and shows Bacchus and Victory in the clouds behind the Spanish Monarchy. In the alternative sketch Fortitude (with her column) finds a place, and an American puma leaps out over the clouds. In one, Jupiter is seen against a blue sky, while in the other he is surrounded by a golden aureole. The most important iconographic shift, however, is the reduction of the role of Neptune, shown in one picture above the continents offering the riches of the sea to the Spanish Monarchy but overshadowed in the other by the prominence accorded Apollo, who advances proffering a scepter. The conceit behind the sculptural decoration of the facade of the royal palace was the enlightened, that is, Apolline, rule of Spain—the *Regia Solis*[4]—and Apollo plays a prominent part in the *saleta* ceiling fresco. If the *modelli* were done sequentially, it is the Apollo-based picture that must be the later proposal, since it is conceived around the one, crucial figure that the alternative sketch lacks.[5]

What is remarkable is not that two, alternative *modelli*, each with its own emphasis and compositional dynamics, should have been produced, but that the final ceiling should incorporate elements of both and, at the same time, introduce completely new features. Nothing could better demonstrate Tiepolo's inexhaustible ability to respond to the sometimes niggling demands of his patrons and the way his *modelli* were but a stage in his

54a. The Apotheosis of the Spanish Monarchy
Ca. 1764
81.6 × 66.4 cm (32⅛ × 26⅛ in.)
The Metropolitan Museum of Art, New York; Rogers Fund, 1937 (37.165.3)

†54b. The Apotheosis of the Spanish Monarchy
Ca. 1764
84 × 69 cm (33⅛ × 27⅛ in.)
The Metropolitan Museum of Art, New York; Gift of Mr. and Mrs. Charles Wrightsman, 1980 (1980.363)

PROVENANCE, 54a:
Guillaume Dubufe, Paris (until ca. 1900); Gimpel and Wildenstein, Paris (1901); Marquis de Biron, Paris and Geneva (1901–37)

REFERENCES:
Chennevières 1898, p. 111; Sack 1910, pp. 140, 209, 218, no. 492; Sánchez Cantón 1953, p. 17; Morassi 1955a, p. 150; Morassi 1962, pp. 21, 33; Pallucchini 1968, p. 132, no. 279d; Byam Shaw 1970, pp. 238–39; Fahy and Watson 1973, pp. 253–55; Zeri and Gardner 1973, pp. 253, 255; Levey 1986, pp. 263–64; Fort Worth 1993, pp. 310–12, no. 56; Gemin and Pedrocco 1993, pp. 200, 488, no. 518a

PROVENANCE, 54b:
Baron Ferdinand von Stumm-Holzhausen, Madrid and Holzhausen (by 1892?–1925); Van Diemen Gallery, Berlin; Jakob Goldschmidt, Berlin and New York (until 1937); I. Rosenbaum, Amsterdam (1937); Baroness Renée de Becker, Brussels and New York (1937–after 1955); Rosenberg and Stiebel, New York (after 1955–59); Edward Speelman, London (1959–60);

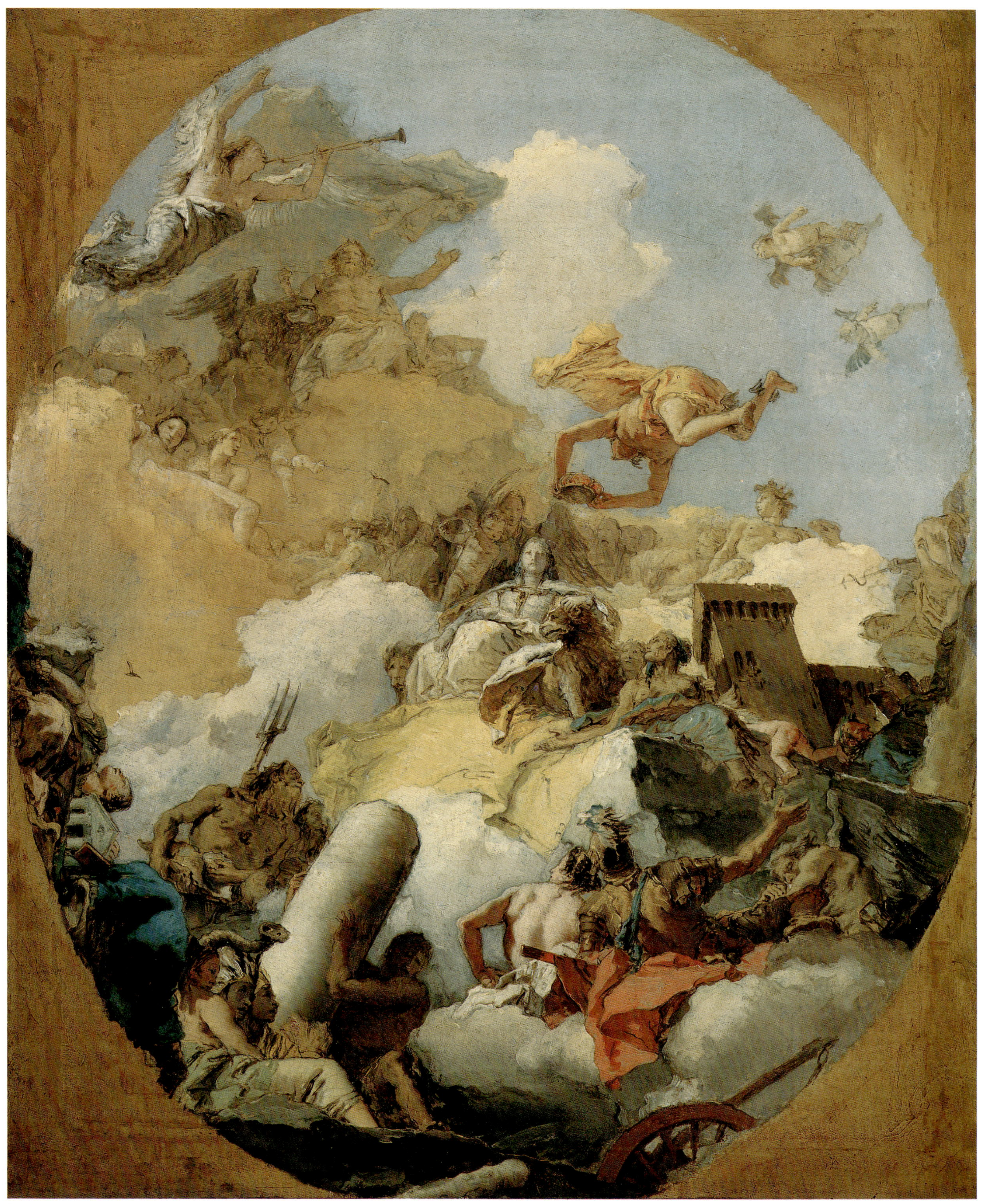

54a

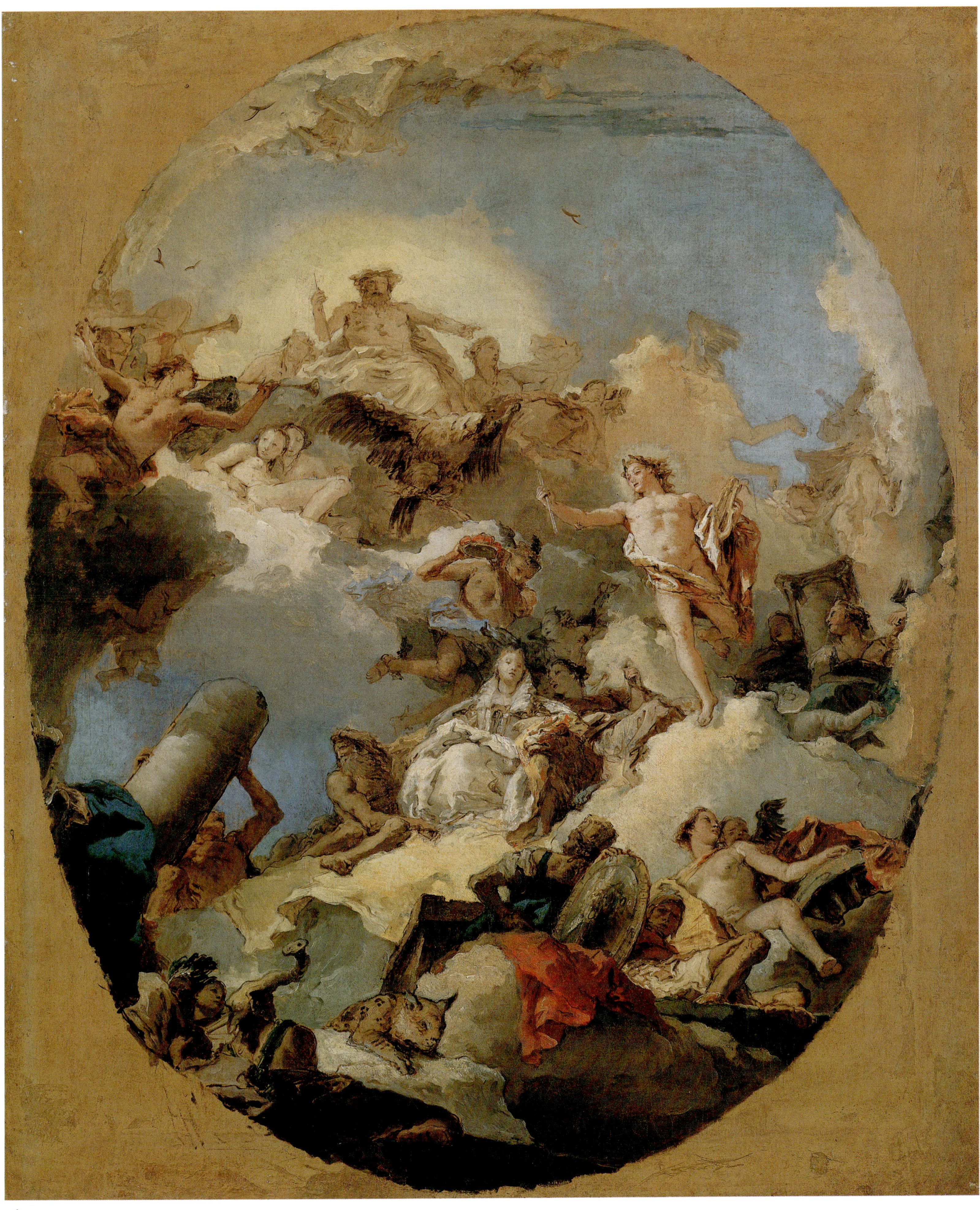

54b

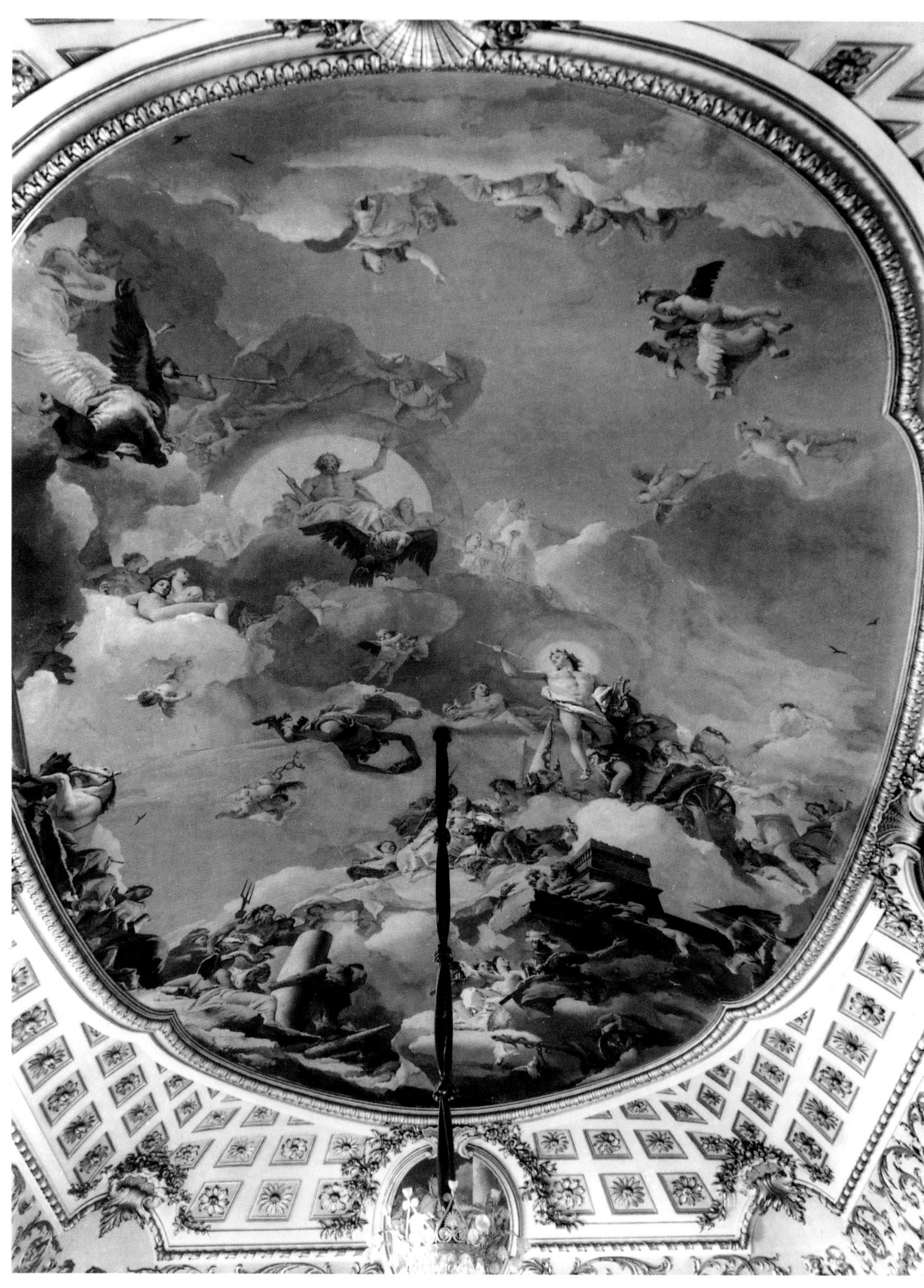

Fig. 118. *The Apotheosis of the Spanish Monarchy* (ceiling of *Saleta*). Fresco. Palacio Real, Madrid

Mr. and Mrs. Charles Wrightsman, New York (1960–80)

REFERENCES:

Morassi 1943, p. 48; Sánchez Cantón 1953, pp. 17–18; Morassi 1955a, p. 150; Morassi 1962, pp. 21, 33, 37; Pallucchini 1968, p. 132, no. 279d; Byam Shaw 1970, p. 239; Fahy and Watson 1973, pp. 248–56; Zeri and Gardner 1973, p. 59; Levey 1986, pp. 263–64; Fort Worth 1993, pp. 310–12; Gemin and Pedrocco 1993, pp. 200, 488, no. 518b

creative process, rather than fixed patterns he enlarged onto plaster surfaces.[6] Fortunately, the relative scale of figures in the *saleta* fresco was only half that in the *modello*, allowing Tiepolo plenty of room to maneuver. Not only was Apollo given pride of place, but there was also space for the chariot from which he leaps. The prominent roles accorded Neptune and Castile in the presumably earlier *modello* were retained, and Europe was given broader treatment. Mercury is shown in a pose that reverses that in one *modello*, while Jupiter and his eagle combine features from each sketch: the god is the benign figure of the one *modello*, and his eagle is the vigorously flying creature of the other. The poses of Fame and of a host of other figures are thought out anew. The mind at work is at once pragmatic, thrifty, and unfettered, and the result is Tiepolo's most brilliant scheme of decoration in the royal palace—one in which he deployed to the full his incomparable gifts as a narrative eulogizer: Jupiter, from his seat in Olympus, raises his hand to welcome into the empyrean the Spanish Monarchy, crowned by the gods' messenger, Mercury, guided by Apollo, and blessed by the wealth of Neptune.

KC

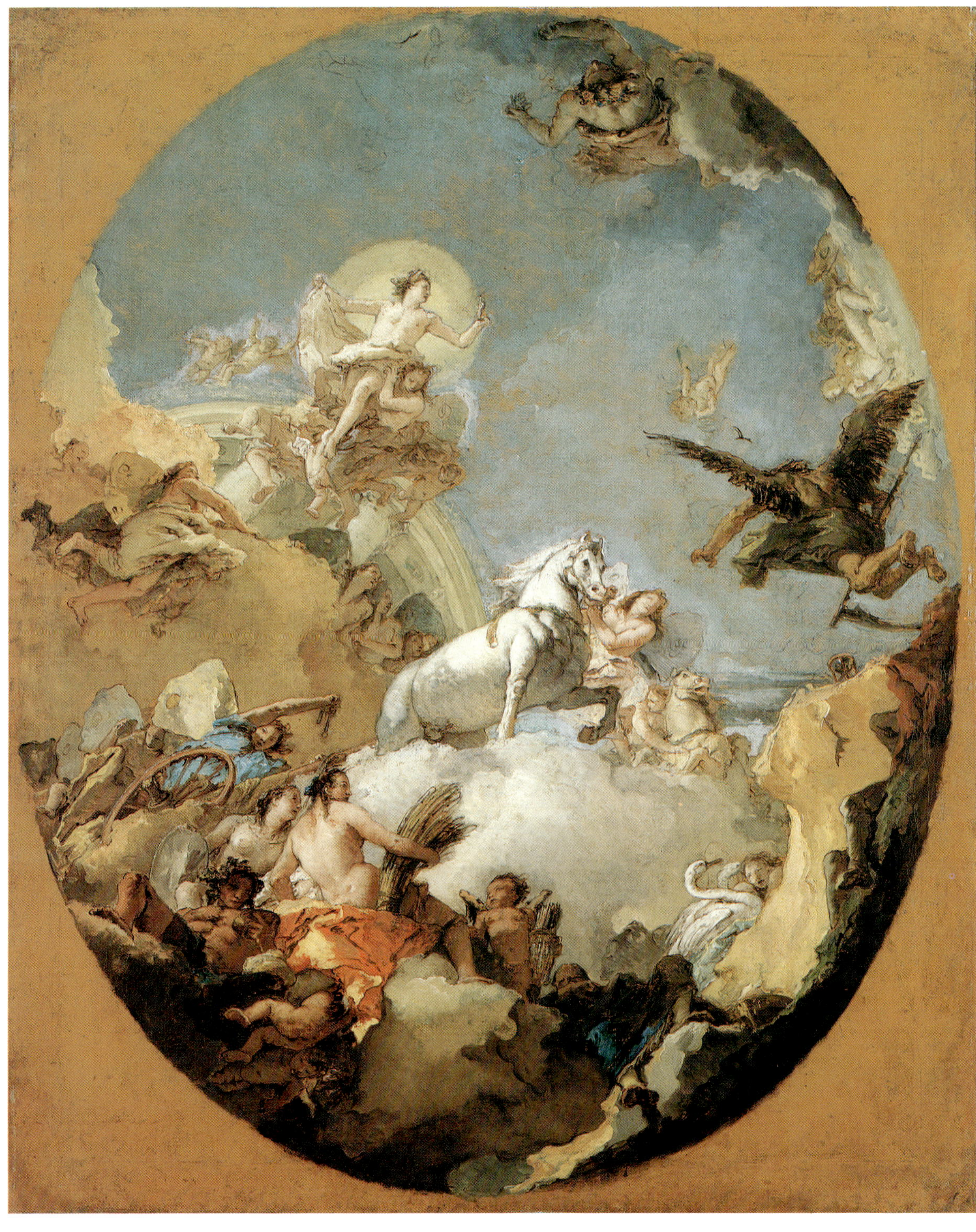

Fig. 119. *The Chariot of Aurora*. Oil on canvas. Private collection, New York

Notes

1. See Urbani de Gheltof 1879, pp. 24–25. Tiepolo requested that his correspondent—the son of a past patron—send along the cartoon for a particular ceiling, in which the subjects were of a type he was treating in the commissions he had in hand. Here we have a documented case of Tiepolo seeking drawings he could recycle for the Spanish ceilings.
2. Two, for the guardroom, are in the Museum of Fine Arts, Boston, and the Fogg Art Museum, Cambridge, Massachusetts; one, with Neptune and the winds, for an unspecified room, is in the Metropolitan Museum; the fourth, in a private collection in New York (fig. 119), shows the chariot of Aurora and has been associated only recently with a ceiling ultimately painted by Mengs in the queen's bedroom in 1763. See Whistler 1995b, p. 626.
3. Fabre 1829, pp. 521–22. Fabre summarized the program as follows: "un conjunto de cosas bizarras . . . que significasen el poder, grandeza, religión y otras cualidades de la monarquía española."
4. See Jones 1981, p. 220, with previous bibliography.
5. Brown (in Fort Worth 1993, p. 312) has proposed that Tiepolo painted them simultaneously, as alternative proposals to present to the king. This is possible and in some respects even likely. There is, however, no way of proving the matter one way or the other. Brown maintains that both sketches began as rectangular, not oval, compositions and that this supports her contention that they were painted simultaneously. The rectangular marks around the canvas that she notes appear to have been made by the stretchers and are irrelevant to the argument.
6. The attempt made to distinguish an oil sketch or a *bozzetto* from a *modello* seems to me fruitless in the case of Tiepolo.

55. Abraham Visited by Angels

55. Abraham Visited by Angels
Ca. 1765–70
67 × 40.5 cm (26⅜ × 16 in.)
Duquesa de Villahermosa, Pedrola

PROVENANCE:
Don Valentino Carderero, Madrid (before 1909); Duque de Villahermosa, Madrid and Pedrola (by 1909)

REFERENCES:
Molmenti 1909, p. 197; Sack 1910, p. 210; Morassi 1943, p. 39; Sánchez Cantón 1953, pp. 23, 36; Morassi 1962, p. 22; Pallucchini 1968, p. 134, no. 294; Knox in Stuttgart 1970, p. 142, no. 165; Knox 1980a, p. 266, no. M.438; Gemin and Pedrocco 1993, p. 499, no. 535

The story of Abraham visited, on the plains of Mamre, by three angels who announce that his aged wife, Sarah, will bear Isaac is told in Genesis 18.1–15. It was treated by Tiepolo in the 1720s in the Arcivescovado (Patriarchal Palace), Udine, and in an altarpiece dating from the last years of his life (Museo del Prado, Madrid). Aside from the pose of the angel farthest to the right, there are no direct compositional parallels between the altarpiece and this small canvas, which has all the characteristics of an independent painting rather than a *modello*. Nevertheless, the two works are obviously linked. Perhaps the larger one motivated a desire on the part of some patron for a smaller picture of the same subject, or perhaps Tiepolo simply felt moved to produce a smaller work for himself. That he would carry out a painting with no intention of sale may at first seem strange, but in fact we know that Tiepolo kept numerous *modelli* or *modello*-like pictures in his collection: even that of Saint Thecla (no. 51)—whose rare subject made it of little practical use as a model for repetition—was transported from Venice to Madrid, and it is not difficult to imagine Tiepolo adding to his repertory of paintings of this kind in the same way he assiduously gathered his drawings in albums. In any event, it is the small, sketchlike *Abraham Visited by Angels* rather than the altarpiece that is the more moving and original depiction, with greater attention given to the landscape setting—a common feature of Tiepolo's small, late works—and a more intense and personal note struck in the interpretation.

The Apolline beauty and proud bearing of the central angel, who strides forth in a pose that recalls one of Tiepolo's favorite classical points of reference, the *Apollo Belvedere*, contrast with the humility of the aged Abraham, who, according to the Bible, "bowed himself toward the ground." Abraham is shown in an act of complete self-abasement. The formulation is virtually identical to the one Tiepolo used for Gabriel in a contemporary depiction of the Annunciation (no. 56)—in terms not only of the pose but also of the corrugated piece of drapery that mimics the bent posture of the patriarch and the position of his raised hands. It is difficult to avoid the suspicion that the two works sprang from a fascination with this deeply expressive formal invention. Throughout his career Tiepolo was intrigued by the different effects that could be obtained by imaginatively utilizing the same pose, and it is no surprise that a beautiful chalk drawing of a figure in the precise attitude of Abraham-Gabriel exists (fig. 120).[1] The drawing evidently served for both pictures: the position of the hands is closer to that of Gabriel's in the Annunciation, while in its arrangement the drapery is similar to that of Abraham.

It cannot be said with certainty whether the *Abraham Visited by Angels* was intended as a pendant to the *Annunciation*, but this seems possible, especially given the fact that the events depicted are complementary: one standing for the founding of the Hebrew people, the other representing the beginning of the era of Christianity.

KC

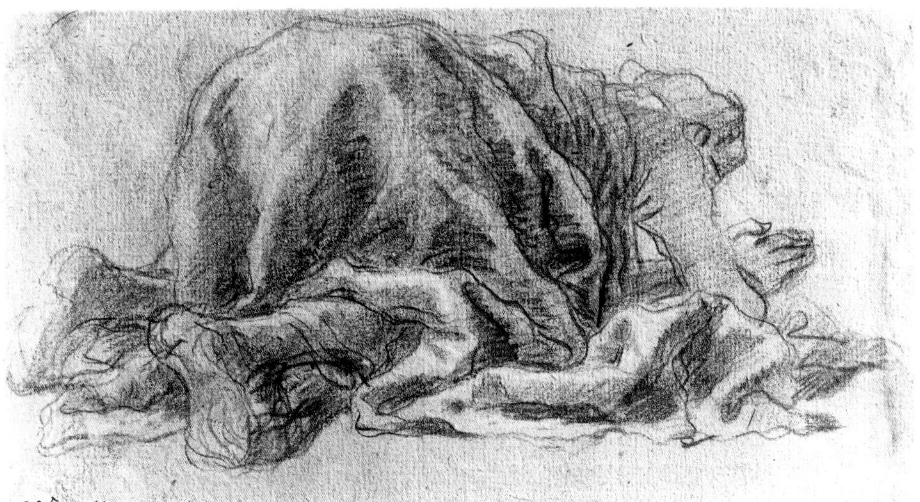

Fig. 120. *Study of a Prostrate Man*. Red chalk. Staatsgalerie Stuttgart

NOTE

1. Inv. no. 1436. See Hadeln 1928, p. 31, and Knox in Stuttgart 1970, p. 142, no. 165.

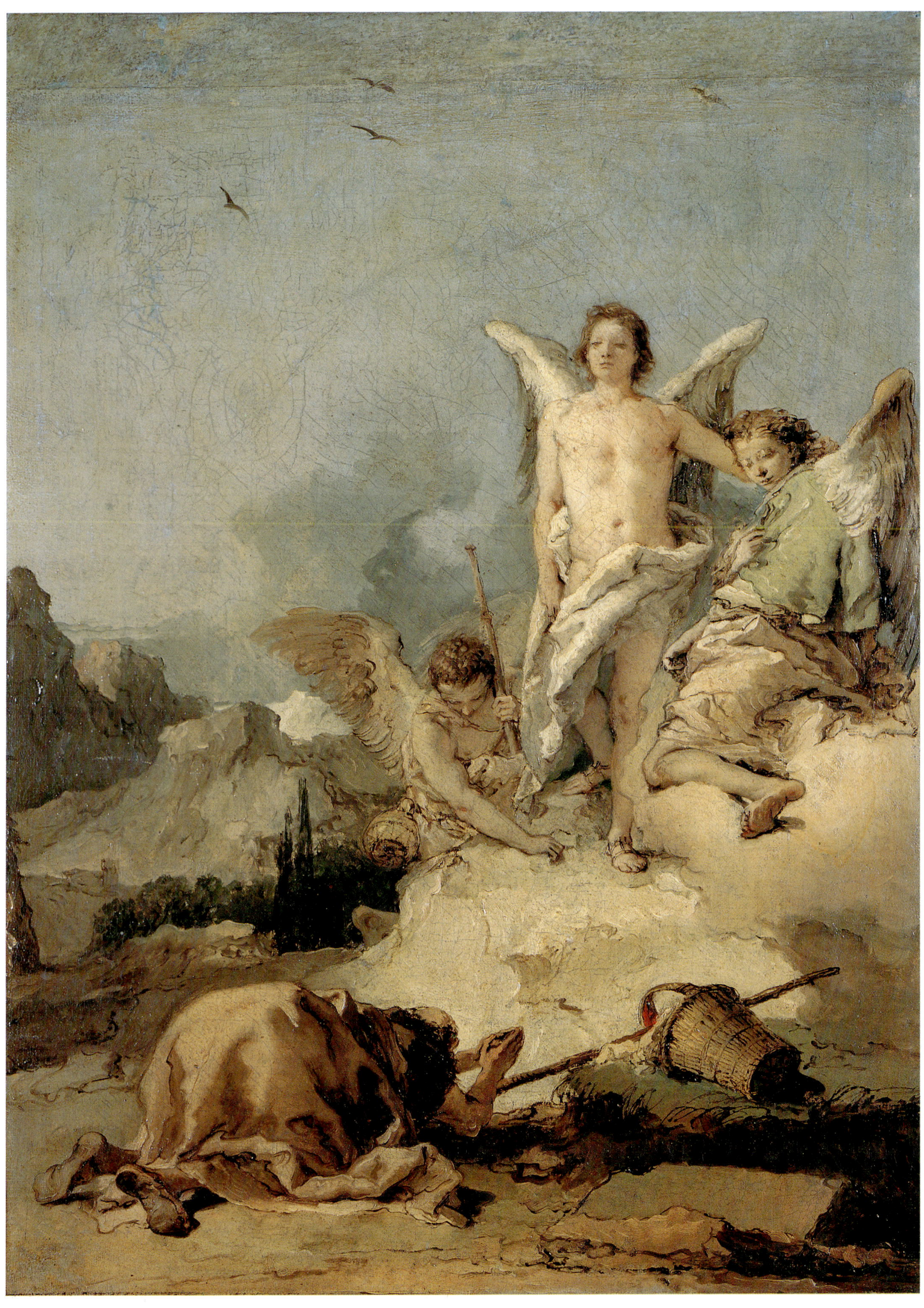

56. The Annunciation

56. The Annunciation
Ca. 1765–70
67 × 40.5 cm (26⅜ × 16 in.)
Duquesa de Villahermosa, Pedrola

PROVENANCE:
Don Valentino Carderero, Madrid (before 1909); Duque de Villahermosa, Madrid and Pedrola (by 1909)

REFERENCES:
Molmenti 1909, p. 197; Sack 1910, p. 210; Hadeln 1928, p. 31; Sánchez Cantón 1929, pp. 141–42; Sánchez Cantón 1953, pp. 24, 36; Morassi 1962, p. 22; Pallucchini 1968, p. 134, no. 295; Knox in Stuttgart 1970, p. 142, no. 165; Knox 1980a, p. 266, no. M.438; Gemin and Pedrocco 1993, p. 499, no. 536

This remarkable depiction of the Annunciation—at once elevated and intimate, grandiloquent and homely—is among the most poetic of the eight small canvases painted by Tiepolo during his eight-year residence in Madrid. Conceivably a pendant to *Abraham Visited by Angels* (no. 55), it was created independently of his four contemporary pictures on the theme of the Flight into Egypt (no. 57a–d), to which it nonetheless forms a narrative prelude. The moment when the archangel Gabriel entered the Virgin's house and announced to her that she would bear a son was one of the most familiar depicted in Christian art. Yet Tiepolo managed to bring to the theme a completely novel interpretation, in part by exploiting a vocabulary of contrasts. The Virgin is shown standing next to a prie-dieu at the back of a simple but spacious room, the beamed ceiling and tiled floor of which recede to different vanishing points. Her needlework lies in a basket on the floor, and a Spanish-style bench is pushed against the wall. A curtained opening allows a partial view into what must be the bedroom, although only a shelf with a dish on it is visible. Belying these spare, domestic surroundings, the Virgin—portrayed not as the demure handmaiden of the Lord but as an exalted member of the House of David—has assumed a statuesque posture expressive of benign, aristocratic dignity. A similar pose was employed by Tiepolo for the Virgin in the *Immaculate Conception* for S. Pascual Baylon, Aranjuez, commissioned in 1767 (no. 40a), a repetition that underscores his insistence throughout his career on the Virgin's elevated status. The windows of the chamber have blown open, and through them vaporous, incenselike clouds spill into the room and around the Virgin, adding a sacral touch, augmented by the three floating cherubs and by the luminous dove of the Holy Spirit, which, hovering above her, sends forth a beam of light. The angel Gabriel has evidently just entered, and he prostrates himself on the floor in an attitude of humility that recalls the ancient Byzantine ritual of *proskynesis*. It is a deeply expressive posture that Tiepolo repeated in *Abraham Visited by Angels*. This unprecedented depiction—so unlike the dramatic narratives of Tiepolo's earlier career—derives its effectiveness as a religious image from an approach that is strongly reminiscent of the procedures of seventeenth-century Bolognese classicism, and in particular those of Guido Reni, who also understood that figures and settings could, through emphasis on attitudes and traits, take on a didactically metaphoric character.[1] However, unlike Reni, Tiepolo insisted on picturesque details that suggest—sometimes paradoxically—the realm of everyday experience.

Virtually nothing is known about the circumstances surrounding the creation of this painting or its provenance prior to this century, and we are left to suppose that Tiepolo painted it for himself and that it was sold in Spain after his death by Giandomenico. Two intriguing questions are whether the *Abraham Visited by Angels* and this picture were produced as companions—both are from the same collection and both involve annunciatory scenes—and whether they are the two Tiepolo paintings of unspecified subjects listed in the 1812 inventory of Goya's collection.

KC

NOTE

1. On this aspect of Reni's vision, see Dempsey in Los Angeles 1988, pp. 101–18.

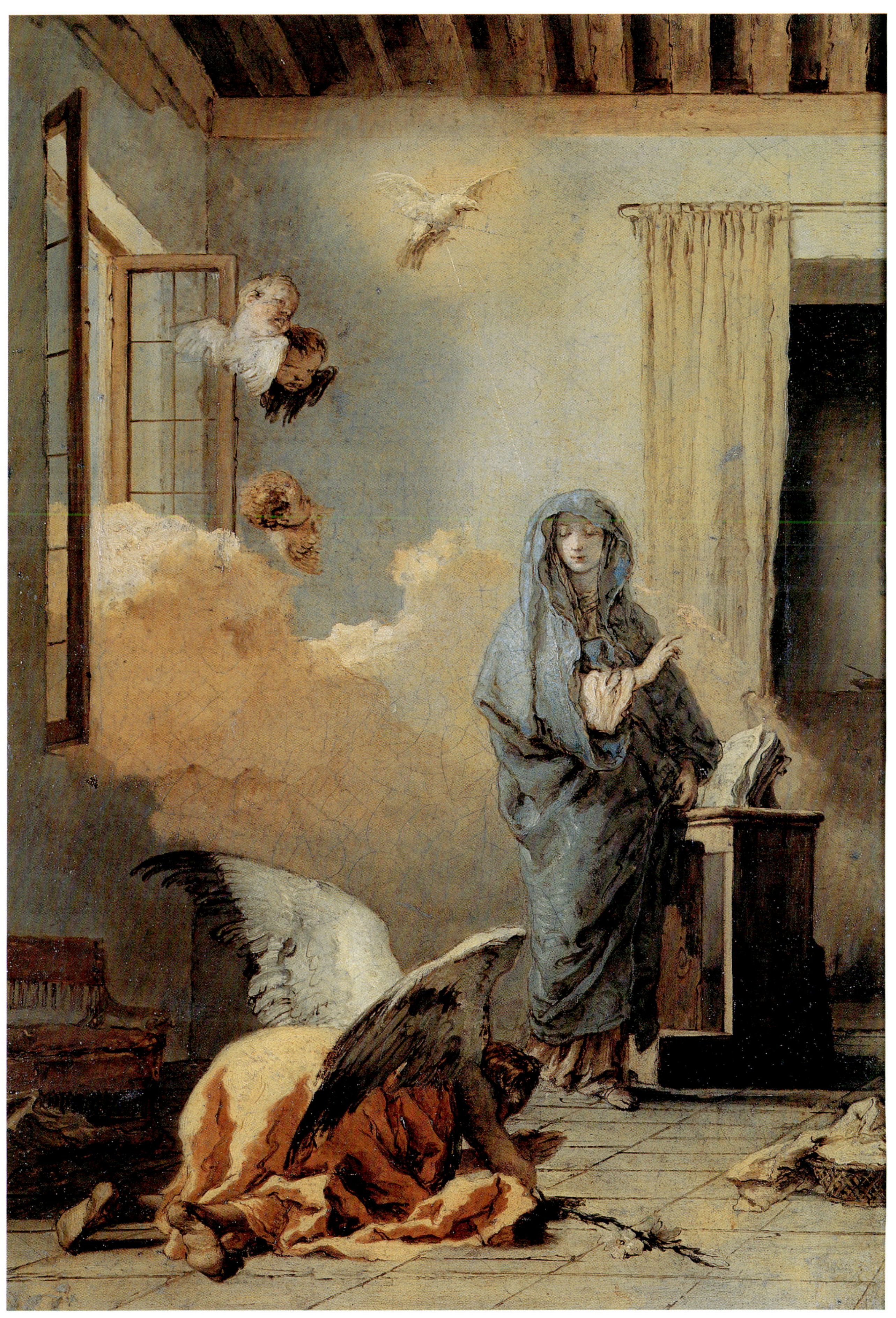

CAPRICCI ON THE FLIGHT INTO EGYPT

57a. Rest on the Flight into Egypt
57b. Rest on the Flight into Egypt
57c. The Flight into Egypt
57d. The Flight into Egypt

57a. Rest on the Flight into Egypt
Ca. 1767–70
60 × 45 cm (23⅝ × 17¾ in.)
Private collection

57b. Rest on the Flight into Egypt
Ca. 1767–70
55.5 × 41.5 cm (21⅞ × 16⅜ in.)
Staatsgalerie Stuttgart (3303)

57c. The Flight into Egypt
Ca. 1767–70
57 × 44 cm (22½ × 17⅜ in.)
Museu Nacional de Arte Antiga, Lisbon

†57d. The Flight into Egypt
Ca. 1767–70
59.4 × 40.8 cm (23⅜ × 16⅛ in.)
Private collection, New York

There is no external evidence that these four pictures, although related in size, date, and theme, were commissioned as a series. Indeed, it is just as likely that they were painted intermittently during the last years of Tiepolo's life either for individual collectors or for the artist's personal pleasure. When taken together with his related graphic work, they reflect in a remarkable fashion Tiepolo's unsurpassed ability to vary a subject endlessly, giving to each interpretation of it a special emphasis and character. In the preceding decade (perhaps even somewhat earlier) he had produced an album that contained at least seventy-five drawings on the theme of the Holy Family (see fig. 103) in which he explored the relationship of the figures with a fertile imagination that calls to mind Raphael and Rubens.[1] Another, more heterogeneous album included no fewer than six drawings of the Flight into Egypt, two of which were translated into etchings by Giandomenico between about 1745 and 1750; one of these shows the Holy Family in a barge punted by an angel.[2] The *Scherzi* contain two plates that might easily be mistaken for variations on the Flight into Egypt (no. 60d, i) and indicate that Tiepolo was fascinated with the purely formal properties of the theme to the degree that he adapted them to other subject matter. The inventive approach to the subject displayed by Giambattista finds a sort of climax in the independent series of twenty-four scenes of the Flight into Egypt that Giandomenico etched between 1750 and 1753 and dedicated to Prince-Bishop Greiffenclau at Würzburg. Although Giandomenico arranged the scenes to form a continuous narrative, the features of Saint Joseph vary, suggesting that the artist probably did not originally intend to produce such an ambitious, coherent sequence: the etchings took their cue, but not their tone or scope, from Giambattista's work. Titled *Idee pittoresche sopra la fugga in Egitto*, they are demonstrations of Giandomenico's inventive capacities and his ability to sustain interest in a subject lacking any inherent drama.[3] The notion of picturesque variations, or caprices (*capricci*), applies with even greater validity to Giambattista's four magical canvases, which do not describe a narrative sequence but explore the expressive and compositional variety of a seemingly conventional subject.

The literary sources for the theme are neither extensive nor important for an understanding of Tiepolo's pictures, for they reflect no interest whatever in the miracles told in the Apocrypha, the Golden Legend, the Meditations on the Life of Christ, or other popular devotional literature. Nor do they display any didactic intent. Rather, Tiepolo played on a rich pictorial tradition, to which Venetian and north Italian art had made a special contribution. Titian, Palma Vecchio, Lorenzo Lotto, and—perhaps most important for Tiepolo—Veronese had developed the related themes of the Holy Family in a landscape and the Flight into Egypt as a kind of religious counterpart to the fête champêtre, making it a sacred idyll or *poesia*, with the emphasis on mood and formal invention rather than iconography. In the seventeenth century the figures are sometimes little more than staffage in an arcadian landscape. One of the genre's most poetic innovations was the depiction of the Holy Family crossing a river—probably the Jordan or Nile—in a barge. Lodovico and Annibale Carracci were among the first to paint pictures of this imagined event, with obvious references to the canal-traversed plains of the Val Padana that they knew so well.[4] Subsequently, the river crossing was taken up by others, including Poussin (Cleveland Museum of Art; Dulwich Picture Gallery, London), Sebastien Bourdon (whose etchings Tiepolo owned), Sebastiano Ricci (Chatsworth) and Gasparo Diziani (S. Stefano, Venice). Tiepolo's earliest drawings of the theme seem to date from the 1730s.

In these four pictures Tiepolo has imagined the Holy Family resting on its journey through a rough terrain and crossing a river with the aid of an angel.

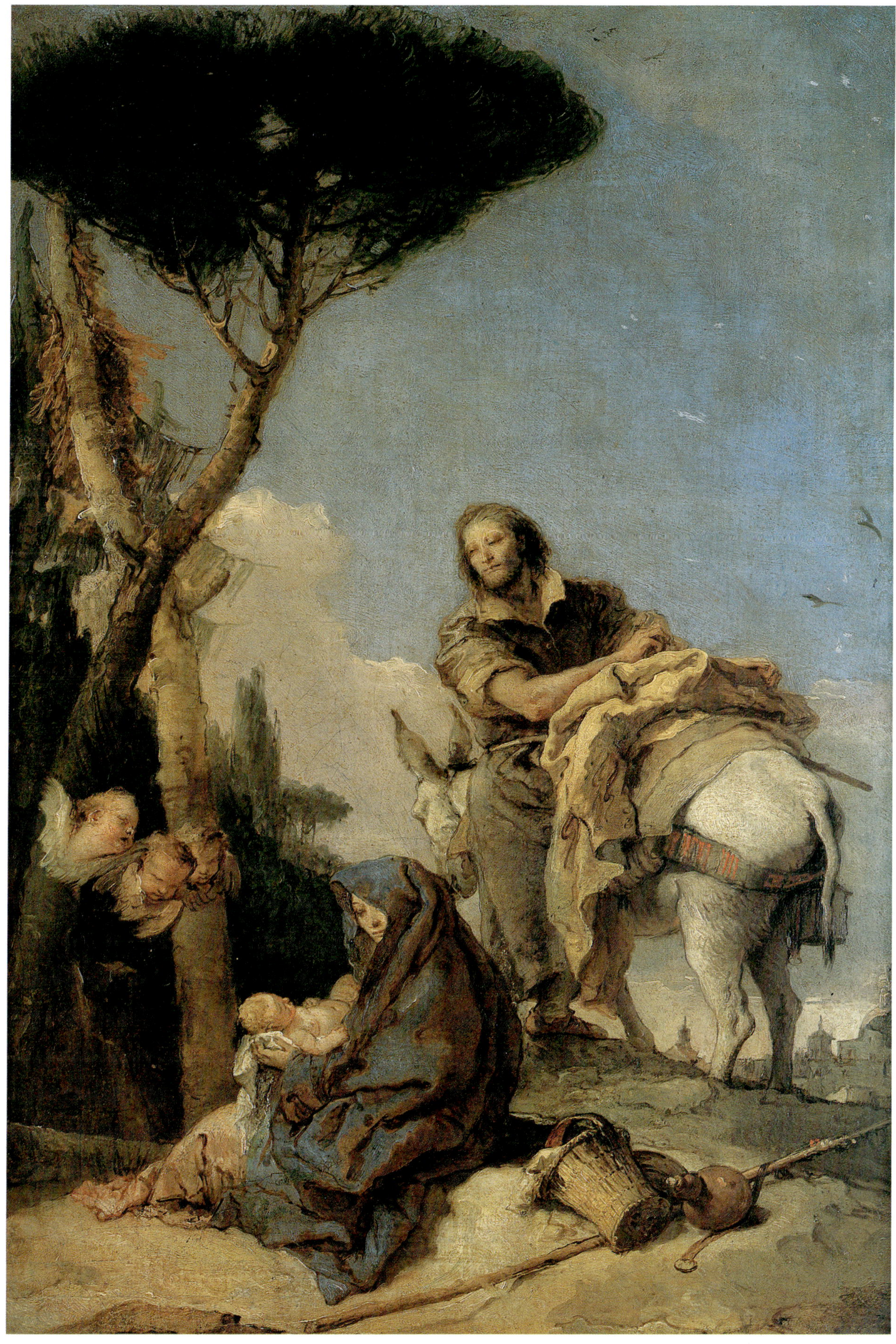

57a

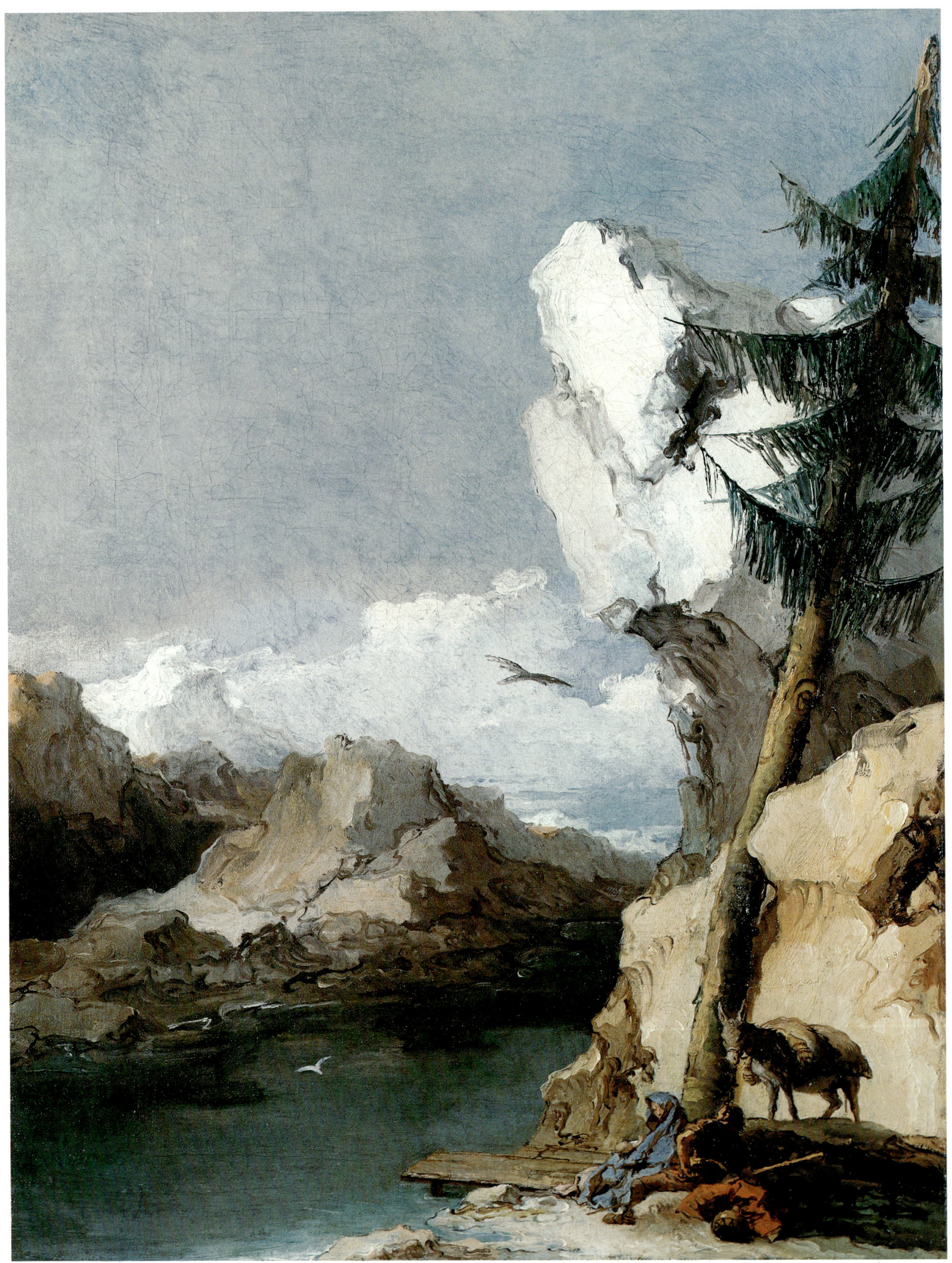

57b

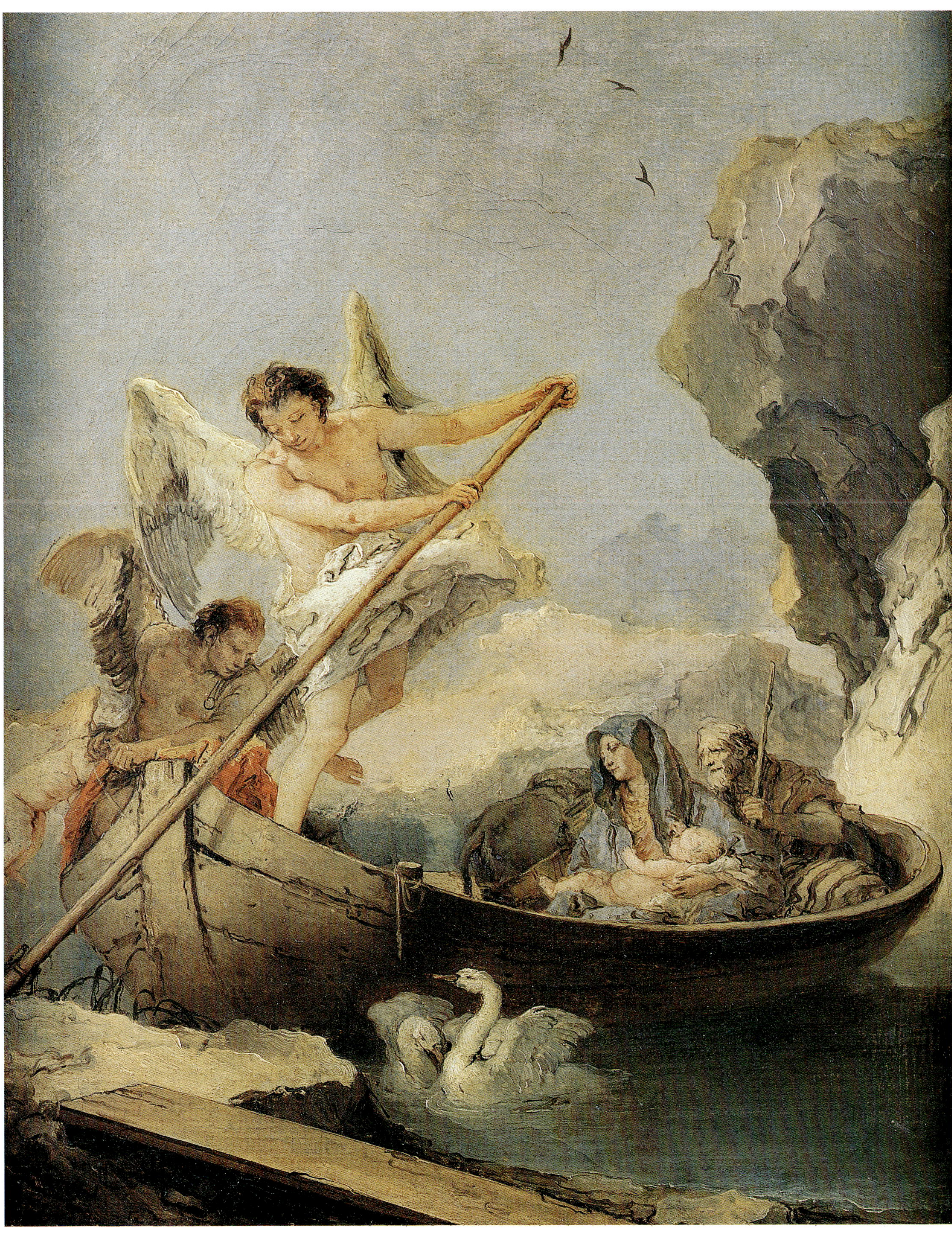

57c

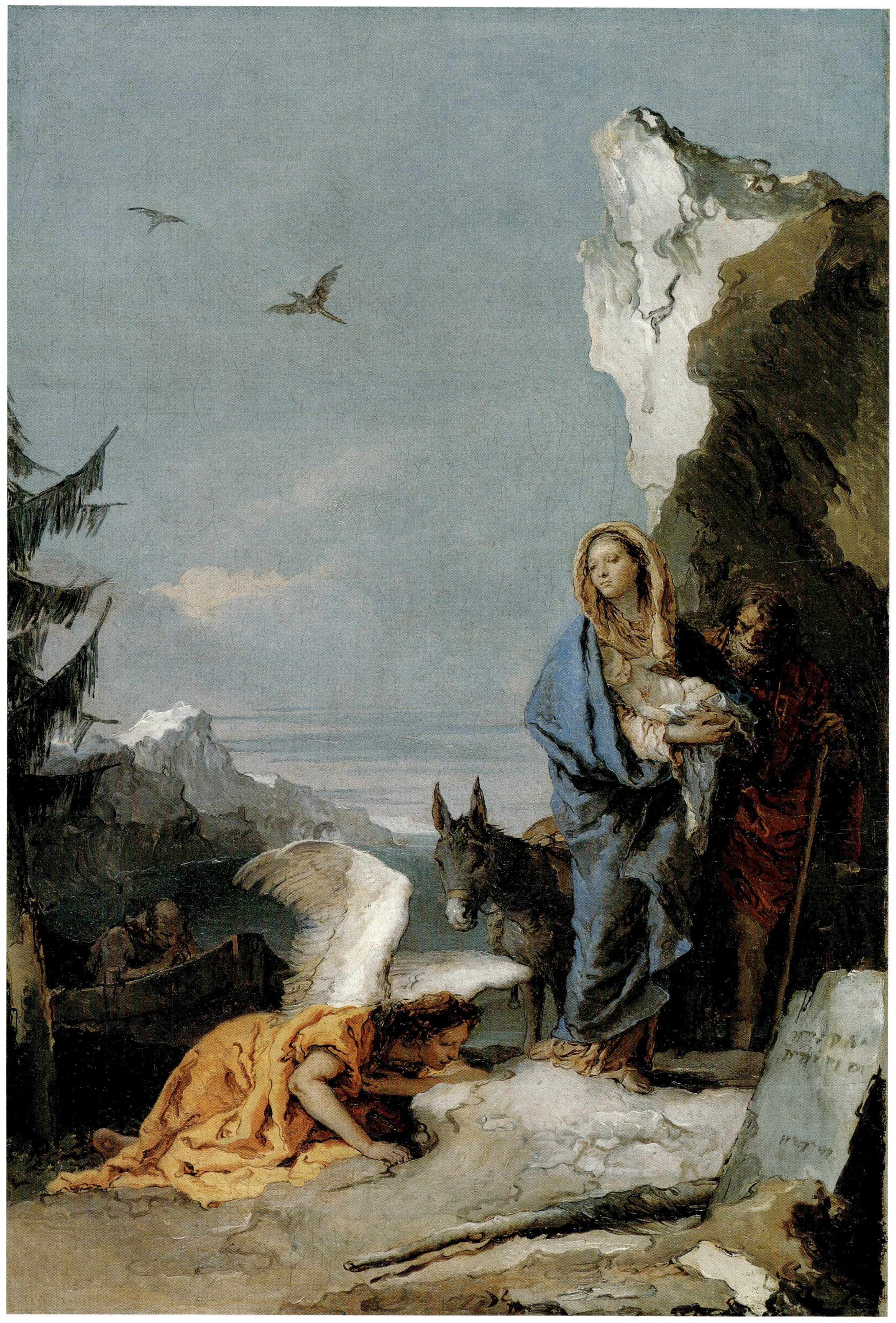

57d

In the New York painting the boatman and the angel pay homage to the Virgin and her Child after they have disembarked, the angel bowing to the ground and pressing one hand to his breast. In the Lisbon canvas the angels propel the boat. None of the paintings displays the domestic sweetness and anecdotal warmth of Giandomenico's etchings. Rather, they maintain a mood of meditative quiet and of sacral simplicity that gains poignancy from the imaginary landscape settings of barren hills, an occasional tree, and, in one case, a view of a city reminiscent of Madrid.[5] Of the group, the picture at Stuttgart is perhaps the most surprising, for it is conceived almost as a pure landscape. The diminutive figures of the Holy Family are shown seated beneath a scraggly pine, alone and as though marooned on the banks of a river. (Typically, Tiepolo presented the Virgin in a pose similar to that of her counterpart in one of the other canvases in the group [no. 57a].)[6] Tiepolo was a master at painting landscape backdrops for his compositions, and from his youth he made occasional landscape drawings—both imaginary and topographical—with a Rembrandt-like concision. But it is only in his late work that landscape is employed as more than an iconographic element (as in the altarpiece at Rampazzo [no. 39]) or a foil for the figures; beginning with the great altarpiece for the cathedral of Este (see no. 51), it becomes part of the poetic language—or, to appropriate the musical terminology dear to Tiepolo's greatest critic, Francesco Algarotti, the basso continuo to the figurative canto. Tiepolo's new interest in a fantastical landscape setting is apparent not only in these magical pictures of the Flight into Egypt but also in the deeply affective *modelli* for the altarpieces commissioned in 1767 for S. Pascual Baylon, especially the *Saint Francis Receiving the Stigmata* (no. 41b). Those *modelli* must be more or less contemporary with the present four canvases, with which they are so close in mood and handling; it is worth pointing out that except for the magnificent *Immaculate Conception* (no. 40b), the compositions gained nothing and lost much by their enlargement. It seems that this master of the monumental found in the intimacy and informality of the *modello* format the proper vehicle for his most personal ruminations.

Nothing is known about the circumstances surrounding the production of the Flight into Egypt pictures or any of Tiepolo's other small-scale works of their period. Only two of those under discussion here, the painting now at Stuttgart and that at Lisbon, have a shared provenance: when recorded early in this century, they belonged to a brother and sister of the Pinto Basto family.[7] The family owned at least three other small paintings by the master, but it has not been possible to ascertain how they came by them.

KC

Notes

1. This is the so-called Owen-Savile album, which Tiepolo left with a son when he departed for Madrid. The album was subsequently owned by Canova and came to public attention at the time of the sale of Edward Cheney's collection in 1885. For the provenance, see Knox and Byam Shaw 1987, p. 104.
2. This is the so-called Orloff album, for which see Knox 1961. For the etchings, see Rizzi 1971, nos. 65, 66.
3. For a general treatment of the etchings, see Russell in Washington, D.C., 1972. Moschini reported that Giandomenico executed the etchings in response to criticism that he was lacking in invention. See Byam Shaw 1962, p. 31. The story has, without much basis, been discredited, but this does not mean the etchings were not conceived as exercises in imaginative invention.
4. Malvasia (1841, vol. 1, p. 354) describes an overdoor by Lodovico portraying the Holy Family stepping out of a boat, and another painting (private collection, Bologna) depicts the Holy Family returning from Egypt in a boat at night. In one of the lunettes painted for Pietro Aldobrandini (Galleria Doria Pamphili, Rome), Annibale showed the Holy Family, viewed against a vast, panoramic landscape, after having disembarked from a boat.
5. See Brown in Fort Worth 1993, p. 134. The frequently stated idea that the mountainous landscapes allude to the Alps or the Pyrenees and that the theme is an expression of Tiepolo's feeling of estrangement and his desire to return to Venice is, in my estimation, an unnecessary romanticization.
6. Martini (1982, pp. 59, 511 n. 199) ascribes no. 57a here to Giandomenico rather than to Giambattista, but it should be pointed out that the painting has not been seen by scholars for decades.
7. See Fiocco 1940, p. 12.
8. In the literature the provenance of the Stuttgart picture is sometimes confused with that of no. 57c here.
9. In the literature the provenance of this picture is sometimes confused with that of no. 57b here.

PROVENANCE, 57a:
Godfrey Brauer, Nice; Prince Bobrinsky, Rome; Thomas Harris, London (1929); Princess Torre e Tasso, Bellagio

REFERENCES:
Morassi 1955a, p. 150; Voss 1957, p. 58; Morassi 1962, p. 3; Pallucchini 1968, p. 133, no. 291; Martini 1982, pp. 556–57 n. 383; Fort Worth 1993, p. 324; Gemin and Pedrocco 1993, p. 499, no. 534

PROVENANCE, 57b:
Alice Ferreira Pinto Basto, Lisbon (by 1915); (sale, Christie's, London, 11 April 1975, lot 6); private collection (until 1978)[8]

REFERENCES:
Fiocco 1940, p. 12; Morassi 1955a, p. 150; Voss 1957, pp. 56–57; Morassi 1962, p. 16; Gaya Nuño 1964, p. 91; Pallucchini 1968, p. 133, no. 293; Martini 1982, pp. 59, 511 n. 199; Levey 1986, pp. 269–70; Barcham 1992, p. 123; Fort Worth 1993, pp. 324–25, no. 62; Gemin and Pedrocco 1993, p. 498, no. 532; London 1994, p. 504, no. 131

PROVENANCE, 57c:
Don Eduardo Ferreira Pinto Basto, Quinta da Fonteireira (Lisbon) (by 1915); donated to Museu Nacional de Arte Antigua, Lisbon (1946)[9]

REFERENCES:
Sánchez Cantón 1929, p. 139; Fiocco 1940, p. 12; Morassi 1955a, p. 150; Morassi 1962, p. 16; Gaya Nuño 1964, p. 90; Pallucchini 1968, p. 133, no. 292; Fort Worth 1993, p. 324; Gemin and Pedrocco 1993, p. 497, no. 531

PROVENANCE, 57d:
Poltawa State Museum, Ukraine (before 1930); Mr. and Mrs. D. Birnbaum, Felden Lodge, Boxmoor, Hertfordshire (by 1938); private collection, Berlin and New York (by 1955); art market, London (1982); private collection, New York (from 1982)

REFERENCES:
Rotterdam 1938, no. 189; Fiocco 1940, p. 12; Morassi 1955a, p. 150; Morassi 1962, pp. 5, 16; Pallucchini 1968, p. 135, no. 290; Fort Worth 1993, p. 324; Gemin and Pedrocco 1993, p. 498, no. 533

MEDITATIONS ON THE PASSION OF CHRIST

58a. The Lamentation
58b. The Entombment

58a. The Lamentation
Ca. 1767–70
59 × 47 cm (23¼ × 18½ in.)
Private collection

58b. The Entombment
Ca. 1767–70
56.7 × 43.8 cm (22¼ × 17¼ in.)
Private collection

During his last years in Madrid, Tiepolo painted, in addition to the four compositions on the theme of the Flight into Egypt (no. 57a–d), at least two small pictures relating to the Passion of Christ, both of which are exhibited here. They treat sequential events and thus would be appropriate pendants, but we do not know if they were intended to be companions—or in fact anything else concerning their creation. Like the Flight into Egypt paintings, they are, in a real sense, religious *capricci* of a strikingly personal kind. The first shows the Virgin, Saint John, and a host of angels lamenting the dead Christ in the shadow of the three crosses of Calvary. The city view in the background is recognizably Madrid and reappears both in the *Rest on the Flight into Egypt* (no. 57a) and in the background of the S. Pascual Baylon altarpiece *Saint Joseph and the Christ Child*, commissioned in 1767. The most prominent angel is bent over in a pose similar to one used in another of the Flight into Egypt pictures (no. 57d). The recurring motifs serve to illuminate the degree to which Tiepolo worked imaginatively with a repertory of formal inventions and gestures to achieve dramatically different expressive ends.

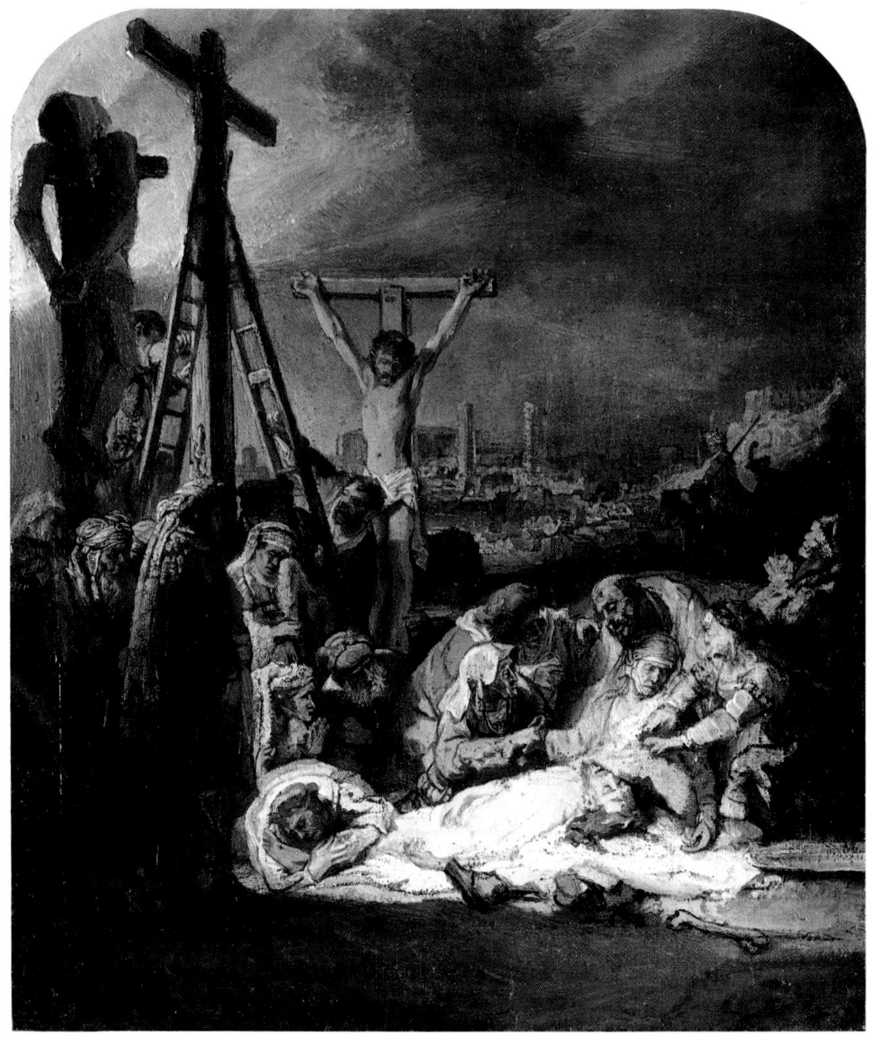

Fig. 121. Rembrandt van Rijn. *The Entombment*. Oil on canvas. The Trustees of The National Gallery, London

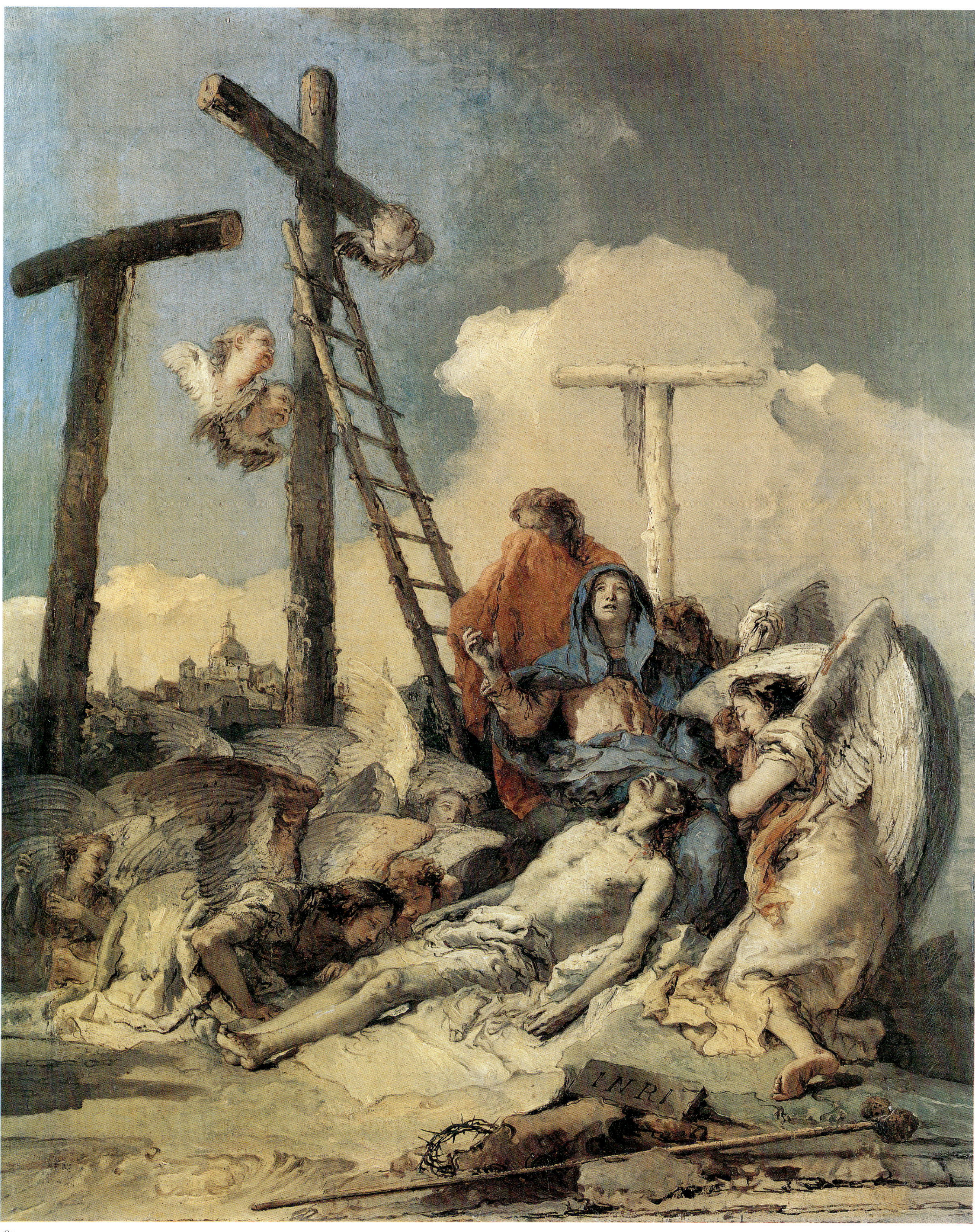

58a

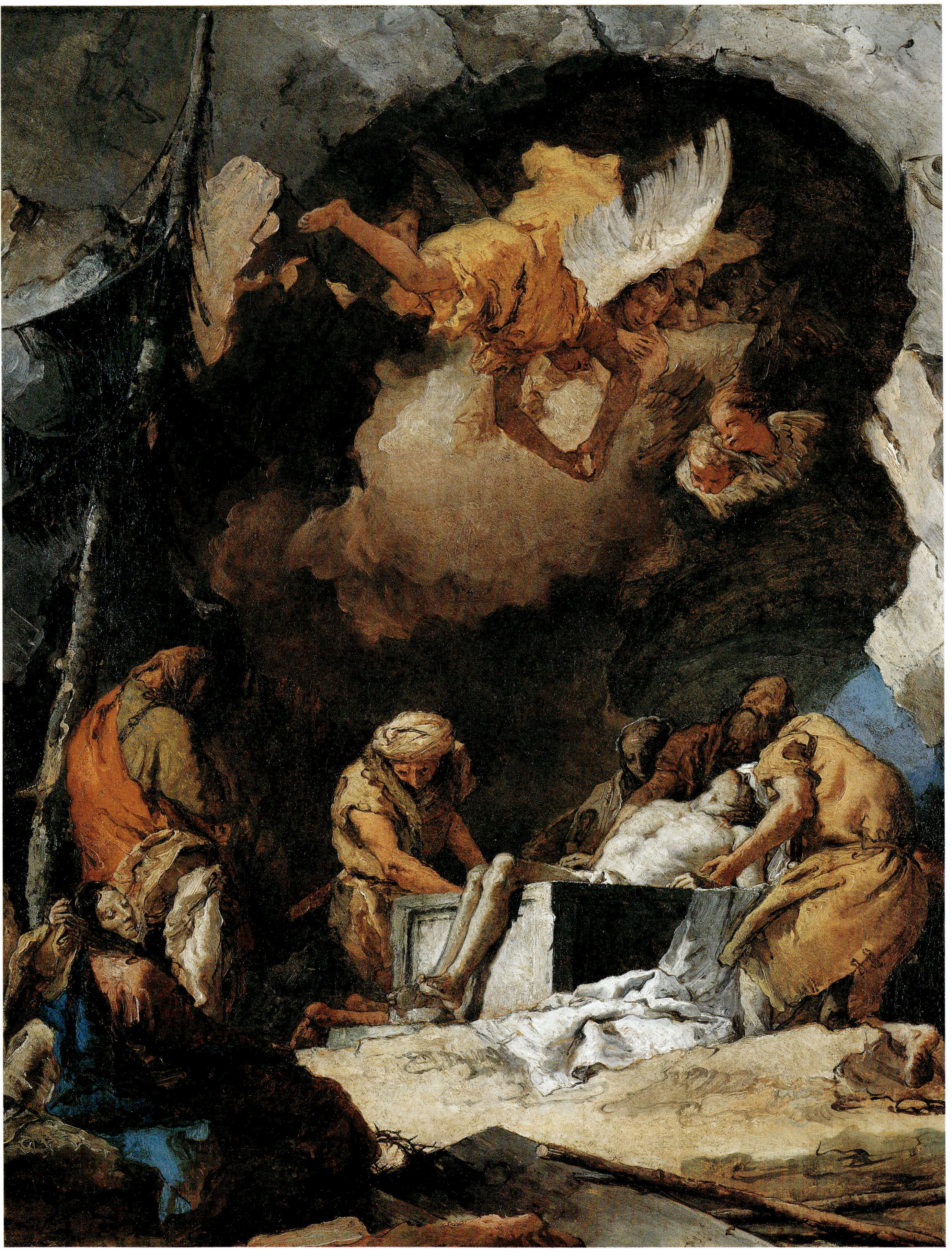

58b

Apart from its intrinsic beauty and intensity of feeling, the *Lamentation* is remarkable for its reworking of a compositional idea that seems to have originated in a small painting by Rembrandt (fig. 121) that was owned by Joseph Smith, British consul in Venice, and was, quite obviously, admired by Giambattista and his son Giandomenico. Rembrandt's picture certainly enjoyed considerable reputation: in 1738 a colored woodcut of it was made by John Baptist Jackson, a British artist resident in Venice with connections to Girolamo Zanetti. Giandomenico produced a number of painted variants and one drawn version of Rembrandt's composition; some of these were possibly based on designs by his father; none, however, attain the poignant eloquence of Giambattista's *Lamentation*.[1] In Tiepolo's canvas the three crosses, set at angles to one another and silhouetted against a distant city view, are taken over more or less directly from Rembrandt's painting and must be based on a fairly faithful drawing after it. But Tiepolo rejected the dark, monochromatic tonality of Rembrandt's picture and completely transformed the figurative content, giving it his own interpretation. Tiepolo's crosses are empty—forlorn emblems of despair against the blue sky—and the onlookers in Oriental garb and the holy women have departed, their places taken by a host of angels who, like a flock of doves, have settled around the pathetic body of Christ, their wings silently beating in the cool light of the evening. The Virgin is shown lifting her hands and head in an affective gesture of mourning, while Saint John covers his face with his cloak—a motif that unquestionably derives from a well-known engraving by Mantegna (Hind 2.1).[2] In the foreground the lance, crown of thorns, and superscription are laid out as if they were devotional objects for the viewer to contemplate. The tenderness and pathos—a combination without precedent in Tiepolo's work—are made even more intense in the related painting.

The second picture shows Christ's entombment. The alpinelike setting that plays so prominent a role in establishing the sense of strangeness and isolation in the Flight into Egypt paintings is here replaced by a cavernous, arched tomb chamber that dwarfs the figures, "shutting out any hint of sky or even air. Almost intolerable desolation is the mood."[3] A pitiful pine tree at the left sets off the grief-stricken group of Saint John, Mary Magdalen, and the Virgin, who has fallen back in a swoon, her drawn features turned toward the viewer. As in the *Lamentation*, a group of objects—in this instance the crown of thorns, the sarcophagus lid, and two poles evidently used to pry the sarcophagus open—is arranged in the foreground, near the Virgin's feet, and plays on the viewer's emotions with a hallucinatory insistence. Atypically for Tiepolo's work, the focus of the composition, illuminated by a shaft of light, is in the background. It would be difficult to imagine a more hauntingly moving scene than that enacted by the angular figures who struggle to place the broken body of Christ in the tomb. The sharp note of despair struck in this picture offers a revealing contrast to the calm melancholy of the Flight into Egypt paintings, and it is astonishingly out of tune with the effulgent brilliance of the decorative enterprises in the royal palace of Madrid—which Tiepolo had brought to conclusion just before he executed the *Lamentation*. This last comparison is hardly egregious, for the *di sotto-in-sù* pose of the angel who is viewed from the back and hovers over Christ's body is similar to one Tiepolo used for the figure of Mercury in his fresco for the *saleta* in the palace (fig. 118). There the pose is a tour-de-force decorative flourish. Here it sounds a piercing note of grief.

KC

Notes

1. For a discussion of the related pictures, see Robinson 1967, pp. 168–69, 180–87, with previous bibliography. These works have sometimes been ascribed to Giambattista but are now given to Giandomenico. Nonetheless, as Robinson notes, it is likely that Giambattista played some part in their design (see entry for no. 33). They comprise two paintings in the National Gallery, London (nos. 1333, 5589), and one in the Saint Louis Art Museum. Giandomenico's drawn variant of the painting (Musée du Louvre, Paris) formed part of an album made after his return from Madrid. The Rembrandt picture was certainly owned by Smith by 1738 and was acquired from him by George III in 1762. See MacLaren and Brown 1991, p. 326.
2. On this engraving, see especially Washington, D.C., 1973, p. 170, no. 70. The matter of the Mantegnesque origin of the motif is particularly interesting in that the engraving also employs as a background element the three empty crosses viewed at angles to one another. Rembrandt was an admirer and collector of Mantegna's graphic work and may well have taken his initial idea from this engraving or a related one sometimes ascribed to Mantegna (Hind 11b). Tiepolo also owned engravings by Mantegna. See the 1845 sale catalogue of the collection of Giandomenico, lot 14: Mantegne (André).—La sépulture.
3. Levey 1986, p. 269.
4. The information on the early provenance of the picture comes from Venice 1951. It is conceivable that Lenbach acquired it during his trip to Spain in 1867–68.

PROVENANCE, 58a:
Franz von Lenbach, Munich (before 1809);[4] Emden, Isole di Brissago, Switzerland; Hausmann collection, Zurich (by 1951)

REFERENCES:
Venice 1951, pp. 134–35, no. 95; Morassi 1955a, p. 39; Morassi 1962, p. 69; Robinson 1967, pp. 184–87; Pallucchini 1968, p. 133 n. 289; Levey 1986, p. 269; Gemin and Pedrocco 1993, p. 497, no. 503

PROVENANCE, 58b:
Don Eduardo Ferreira Pinto Basto, Quinta da Fonteireira (Lisbon) (by 1915)

REFERENCES:
Sánchez Cantón 1929, pp. 139–40; Fiocco 1940, pp. 11–12; Morassi 1955a, p. 39; Morassi 1962, p. 16; Gaya Nuño 1964, pp. 91, 312; Pallucchini 1968, p. 135, no. 300; Martini 1982, p. 59; Levey 1986, p. 269; Gemin and Pedrocco 1993, p. 500, no. 537; London 1994, p. 504, no. 132

THE CAPRICCI

59a. Figures in a Landscape with Ruins
59b. Soldiers and a Youth in a Landscape
59c. Soldier Seated on a Tomb, with Other Figures
59d. Standing Woman and Two Men, with an Obelisk
59e. Woman and Infant Satyr in a Landscape
59f. Sage and Two Figures
59g. Figures with a Burning Pyre of Bones
59h. Death Giving Audience
59i. Three Figures and a Snake
59j. Man with a Horse and Groom

59a–j. The Capricci
Ca. 1740–42
Etchings
The Metropolitan Museum of Art, New York; Harris Brisbane Dick Fund, 1932 (232.12.1)

59a. Figures in a Landscape with Ruins (DV 3)
142 × 180 mm (5⅝ × 7⅛ in.)
Signed on urn: Tiepolo

59b. Soldiers and a Youth in a Landscape (DV 4)
142 × 175 mm (5⅝ × 6⅞ in.)
Signed at left: Tiepolo

59c. Soldier Seated on a Tomb, with Other Figures (DV 5)
132 × 171 mm (5¼ × 6¾ in.)
Signed on tomb: Tiepolo

59d. Standing Woman and Two Men, with an Obelisk (DV 6)
137 × 176 mm (5⅜ × 7 in.)
Signed at lower left: Tiepolo

59e. Woman and Infant Satyr in a Landscape (DV 7)
141 × 175 mm (5⅝ × 6⅞ in.)
Signed at left: Tiepolo

59f. Sage and Two Figures (DV 8)
134 × 174 mm (5⅜ × 6⅞ in.)
Signed on tomb slab: Tiepolo

First published in 1743 as part of the third edition of Anton Maria Zanetti's celebrated compilation of chiaroscuro woodcuts after works by Parmigianino,[1] the *Capricci* affirm an aspect of Tiepolo's genius that, until then, had been known only to close acquaintances and collectors of his drawings. In 1785 they were published separately as *Vari capricci inventati, ed incisi dal celebre gio. Battista Tiepolo* (various caprices invented and etched by the celebrated G. B. Tiepolo) with a dedication to the wealthy collector Girolamo Manfrin. Just how they were viewed by contemporaries is well attested in a dedicatory letter Zanetti included as part of the fourth edition of the chiaroscuri (published in 1749) that he sent to the prince of Liechtenstein in 1751. In this letter Zanetti noted that in addition to his own work and examples by other artists, he had inserted prints "invented and etched by the hand of the renowned Giovanni Battista Tiepolo, which, being of a spirited and most piquant taste [*saporitissimo gusto*], are worthy of the highest esteem." This view was echoed by the collector-connoisseur Pierre-Jean Mariette, who remarked on Tiepolo's "rich and fertile genius. . . . [Moreover], his touch is very sprightly. It shines above all in his prints."[2]

There can be little doubt that Tiepolo turned to etching both because it offered greater scope for the witty, fantastical side of his imagination than did his formal commissions and because there existed a widespread demand for his inventions. This is affirmed by da Canal, who reported that Tiepolo's reputation as a draftsman was such that "albums were sent to distant countries" and, perhaps more to the point, that "printmakers sought to engrave his works and obtain his inventions and bizarre ideas."[3] Throughout his career he supplied designs for printmakers and publishers. Early on he had provided drawings of sixteenth-century paintings to serve as illustrations in Domenico Lovisa's *Il gran teatro delle pitture di Venezia*, and in 1724 he was invited by Scipione Maffei to make drawings of ancient sculpture for *Verona illustrata*, published in 1731–32. (The designs in the latter were engraved by Andrea Zucchi.) The printmaker Pietro Monaco included engravings after paintings and drawings by Tiepolo in his *Raccolta . . . di pitture della storia sacra* of 1739,[4] and Tiepolo was one of a number of artists who designed illustrations for an Italian edition of Milton's *Paradise Lost*. (His contribution for canto 10 of Milton's epic, showing Death and Sin in the form of a skeleton embracing a snake-entwined maiden, reveals a certain kinship with some of the *Capricci*.) Toward the end of his life, he designed a frontispiece in honor of Charles III of Spain for Paolantonio Paoli's book on the ruins of Paestum. It was in the years about 1740 that Tiepolo took up the etcher's needle himself, providing figures for the imaginary landscapes of Giuliano Giampiccoli (the landscapes were based on the work of Giampiccoli's deceased nephew Marco Ricci).[5] Tiepolo's subordinate role here may seem surprising for an artist of his ambition and success, but the very fact that he accepted it underscores the inquisitive, restless nature of his imagination. On a technical level, his work with Giampiccoli served as a proving ground for the *Capricci*.

The ten prints of the *Capricci* were published as a group, but they share no common theme and their order varies from edition to edition.[6] One shows a satyr family in a landscape; one a horse and rider with his groom; four depict an assortment of figures—some wearing exotic or military dress—involved in no readily specifiable action; in two a sage or sagelike individual holding a large book plays a prominent role; and two others seem to portray magical practices. The two scenes of sorcery have attracted the most attention, not least because necromancy became the dominant theme of Tiepolo's second and greatest series of etchings, the *Scherzi* (no. 60a–w).

It is difficult to say what precise meanings Tiepolo may have intended in the various *Capricci*. They are, above all, exercises in *bizzarria*. Paradoxically, one of the most surreal of them—showing a group of figures spellbound by the words of a seated skeleton reading from an open book while a pile of bones and other items burns on a raised altar or marble block—is actually the most straightforward: its subject is the confrontation of the living with Death, and it obviously draws on images of the triumph of Death and of the classical-pastoral theme of Death's presence even in Arcadia (*et in arcadia ego*). The sinister element that comes to the fore in the *Scherzi* is here scarcely hinted at, and the scrawny dog sniffing curiously at the unlikely apparition of the skeleton, the fur on its back standing on end, seems a product of Tiepolo's ironic sense of humor. Far more perplexing is the disjunctive combination of figures and setting that characterizes some of the other *Capricci*. In one an imposing woman in the shadow of a towering obelisk has placed a vase on a fragmentary cornice and stares enigmatically into the distance, apparently unaware of the two male figures seated on a nearby hillock. In another a rabbinical sage stands amid ancient ruins, also gazing toward the horizon and oblivious of the other individuals depicted, here a soldier and his companion—a Gypsy?—who gestures in his direction. Who, we might ask, is the armed youth, in still another print, resting one arm on a fanciful vase and balancing a book on his lap as he turns his head to engage the viewer—and what has he to do with the figures in exotic dress behind him, the bored youth looking at the barren earth, or the boys examining a piece of silver plate? Why, in the scene of a burning pyre of bones, is one character shown with chains around her arms, and what, in another print, is the significance of the sage who consults a book and of the staff with a snake wrapped around it? Concerning the *Capricci* Levey has written perceptively: "They are sophisticated assemblages of partly incongruous elements which have yet been fused together without dissonance or triviality. To press too hard the question of what they mean, in the sense of telling any particular narrative, is to miss the essential aspect of their capricious nature."[7] It was certainly as fantastic inventions that they were prized by collectors, none of whom commented on the subjects, and it is as *capricci* that they must be understood.

The term *capriccio*—like *fantasia* and *scherzo*—can be traced back to the sixteenth century. Initially it implied either an ignorance or a purposeful bending of conventional practice and rules and was as likely to denote censure as it was praise.[8] This changed in the course of the seventeenth century, as the imaginative faculties of artists came to be prized as much as academic conformity to classical precedent and convention—although the two were often seen as opposed to each other.[9] In musical practice the term *capriccio* implied the breaking of rules of composition and harmony for expressive effect; in his *Dictionnaire universel* of 1690, the French academic Antoine Furetière defined *capricci* as "pieces of music, poetry, or painting wherein the force of imagination has better success than observation of the rules of art." At about the same time the Florentine biographer of artists Filippo Baldinucci identified a *capriccio* as "one's own idea or invention: thus, done *a capriccio* or *di fantasia*, that is, of one's own idea or invention."[10] A clear notion of the freedom of imagination this concept encouraged and the pleasure it aimed to give can be gleaned by considering not only the works of art produced under its banner—from the prints of Jacques Callot and Stefano della Bella (which Tiepolo highly prized) to the extravagant keyboard works of Frescobaldi—but also the reactions of its Neoclassical critics at the end of the eighteenth century. Thus, Francesco Milizia, an admirer of Mengs, declared that the *capriccio* was based on a false notion of pleasure: "Attempting to please, the *capriccio* destroys pleasure. It is the sworn enemy of the fine arts and particularly of architecture. Thus, if an artist wishes truly to give pleasure, he should adhere to the principles of art and never ever leave them."[11] A key to the *capriccio* in music was variation on a theme coupled with virtuosity, traits certainly shared by Tiepolo's light-filled etchings.

Every author, beginning with Francesco Algarotti, has recognized the debt Tiepolo's prints owe to the examples of Castiglione (fig. 122) and Salvator Rosa (fig. 123)—not only in their technique but also in their imagery—especially in the case of those etchings evoking the ruined world of antiquity strewn with ox bones, discarded vases, and fragmentary sculpture. Perhaps not coincidentally, it was in the very years Tiepolo was at work on the *Capricci* that the heirs to Zaccaria Sagredo's stupendous collection, which included over 350 drawings by Castiglione and two celebrated paintings by Rosa, were discussing its sale; indeed, Tiepolo and Piazzetta compiled inventories of the collection in 1743. A preparatory drawing for the *Capriccio* of a man with a horse (Victoria and Albert Museum, London, D.1825.178-1885) suggests that Tiepolo took his point of departure from a sketch by Castiglione,[12] and a number of additional motifs in other *Capricci* could originate from Castiglione's drawings as easily as from his etchings. The depictions of seated soldiers were unmistakably inspired by Rosa's *Diverse Figures* of 1656–57, and the goat in the bucolic scene of a satyr family derives from an etching by Stefano della Bella. The graphic work of all three artists enjoyed enormous popularity in the

59g. Figures with a Burning Pyre of Bones (DV 9)
139 × 176 mm (5½ × 7 in.)
Signed at left: Tiepolo

59h. Death Giving Audience (DV 10)
141 × 178 mm (5⅝ × 7 in.)
Signed below dog: Tiepolo

59i. Three Figures and a Snake (DV 11)
133 × 172 mm (5¼ × 6¾ in.)
Signed above snake: Tiepolo

59j. Man with a Horse and Groom (DV 12)
140 × 179 mm (5½ × 7⅛ in.)
Signed on rock: Tiepolo

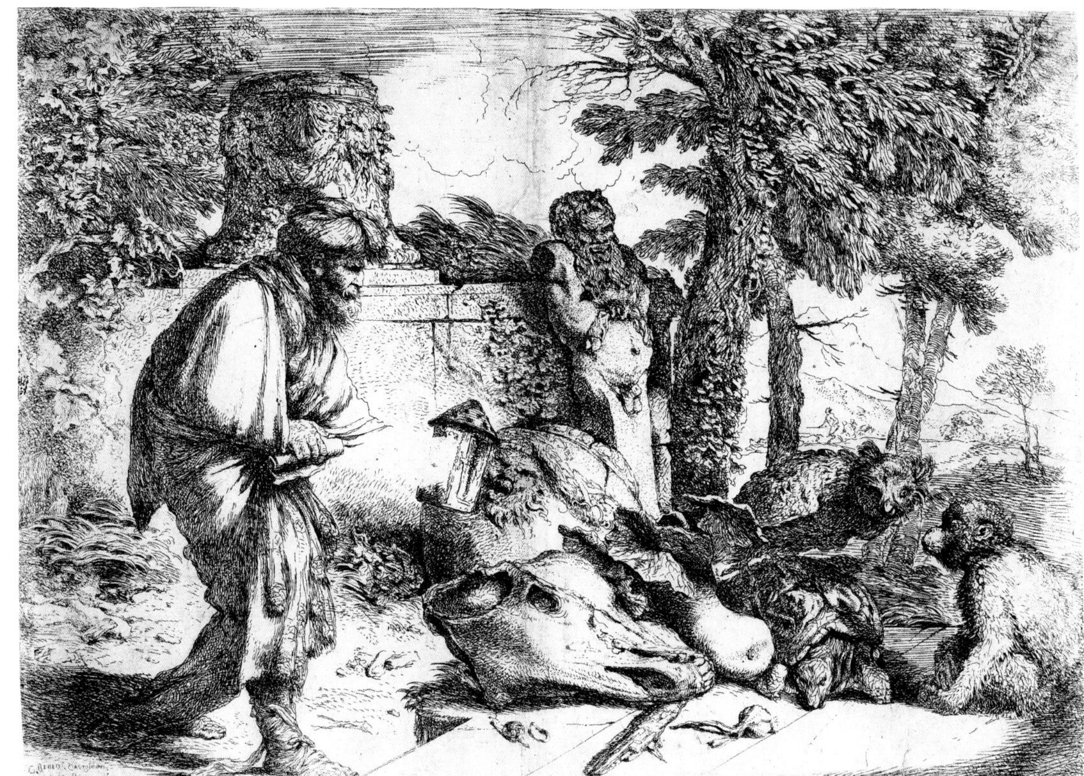

Fig. 122. Giovanni Benedetto Castiglione. *Diogenes in Search of an Honest Man*. Etching. The Metropolitan Museum of Art, New York; The Elisha Whittelsey Collection, the Elisha Whittelsey Fund, 1973 (1973.500.1)

REFERENCES:
Baudi di Vesme 1906, pp. 3–12; Molmenti 1909, pp. 226–34; Sack 1910, pp. 295–96; Thomas 1966, p. 262; Pignatti 1970, p. 306; Frerichs 1971a, pp. 239–40; Rizzi 1971, pp. 16–17, 84–103; Udine 1971, pp. 62–64, 82–86; Dempsey 1972; Russell in Washington, D.C., 1972, pp. 16–27, 40–49; Santifaller 1972, pp. 145–48; Knox 1975a, pp. 19–22; Ottawa 1976, pp. 14–17, 46–50; Succi in Gorizia 1983, pp. 359–64; Succi in Gorizia 1985, pp. 19–21, 24–25, 49–56; Levey 1986, pp. 99–102; Succi in Gorizia 1988, pp. 275–82; London 1995, p. 498, no. 111

eighteenth century: for example, the British consul in Venice, Joseph Smith, acquired many of the Sagredo Castigliones, and following his death they were purchased for the collection of George III; in addition Algarotti had wanted to buy some of the drawings for his patron.[13] Tiepolo fully expected his achievement to be measured against that of his predecessors. It might be added that one of the 1743 editions of Zanetti's *Raccolta* found its way to Dresden, probably either as a gift from Zanetti or as a purchase by Algarotti for Augustus of Saxony.

However enigmatic the *Capricci* may seem—and ambiguity is an intrinsic part of the genre to which they belong—their figures are stock Tiepolo types and at times seem almost to have wandered onto the copperplates from another context. It is as though the background figures from his oil paintings and frescoes—those detached bystanders in so many of his religious and secular compositions—had, like extras in some theatrical production, momentarily assumed the limelight in a plotless drama staged amid the clutter of the dilapidated props of a Roman pastoral play. The satyr family finds precise analogies with groups in two of the oval canvases painted as a subsidiary part of a roughly contemporary decorative series illustrating Tasso (no. 17 e, f), and it is in other elements of that same cycle that characters closely comparable to the soldier and sage can be seen. A preparatory drawing for the man seated on a tomb slab (Victoria and Albert Museum, London, D.1825.106-1885v) might, were it not for the print, be taken for a sketch for an individual in a ceiling decoration—one of those figures Tiepolo liked to pose on a cornice, gazing out at the viewer. Even the *Capriccio* portraying Death traces its origin to a more conventional subject. Four preliminary studies are known, and in the earliest of these (Victoria and Albert Museum, London, D.1825.219-1885r) a saint was shown performing a miracle in front of an upended tomb slab. Only on the reverse of the sheet did Death—looking like a hag in one of the Sagredo Castiglione drawings[14]—take the place of the slab and did a soldier pointing to her supplant the saint. The final composition was developed further in at least two additional sketches, again on the front and back of a single sheet (fig. 124). If the evolution of such scenes is followed, the *Capricci* can be understood less as a unified project than as an outgrowth of Tiepolo's fertile imagination, developing his own inventions as well as reacting to and transforming those of other artists.

KC

NOTES

1. The date of the *Capricci* and the matter of whether they preceded or followed the *Scherzi* (no. 60a–w) have been much discussed. Thanks to the publications of Santifaller and Succi, there is no longer any question that the *Capricci* were produced first and within the relatively narrow time frame of 1740 to 1742. The interested reader is directed to Succi's exhaustive treatment of the issues surrounding the date of the *Capricci*; the most complete discussion is in Gorizia 1985, and a summary appears in Gorizia 1988, pp. 275–82. Succi identifies four copies of the 1743 edition: in the Kupferstichkabinett, Dresden; the Museo Correr, Venice; The Metropolitan Museum of Art, New York; and one

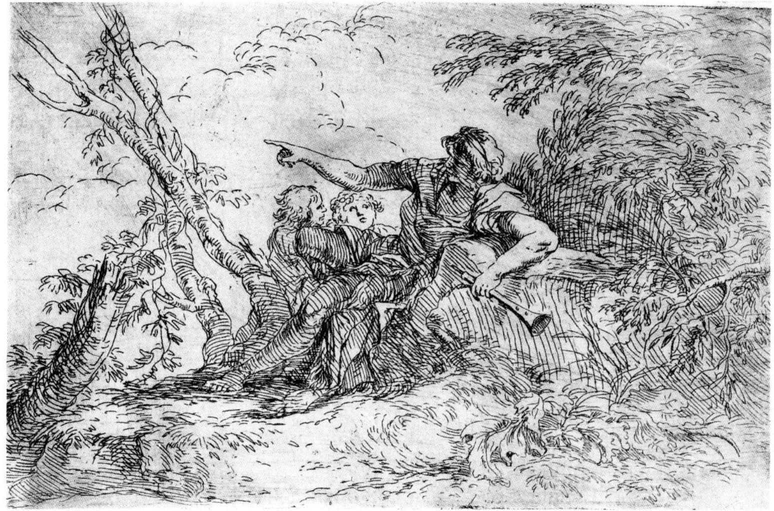

Fig. 123. Salvator Rosa. *Shepherd with a Flute and Two Other Figures*. Etching and drypoint. The Metropolitan Museum of Art, New York; The Elisha Whittelsey Collection, the Elisha Whittelsey Fund, 1953 (53.509.2)

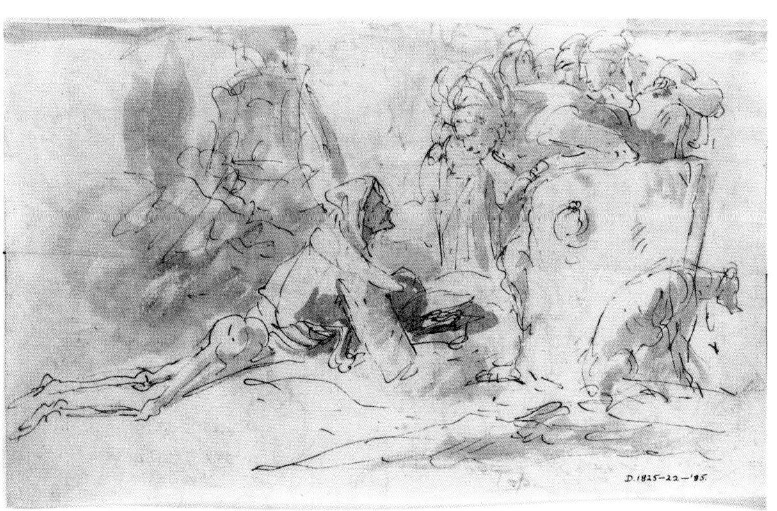

Fig. 124. *Death Giving Audience*, verso. Pen and ink and wash. Victoria and Albert Museum, London (D.1825.22-1885)

on the market in 1963. The reproductions here are taken from the Metropolitan's album.

2. Mariette (1774) 1858–59, p. 300: "une genie riche et fertile . . . . Sa touche est avec cela très spirituelle. Elle brille surtout dans ce qu'il a gravé."
3. Da Canal 1732 (1809 ed., p. XXXII).
4. See Knox 1965.
5. For the dating of Giampiccoli's etchings and an analysis of Tiepolo's involvement with them, see Succi in Gorizia 1985, pp. 21–25, 34–37. Succi calls attention to Algarotti's request that Tiepolo find time to paint figures in otherwise minor paintings by other artists. Tiepolo indulged Algarotti by participating in his friend's amateurish efforts at printmaking.
6. For a list of these variations, see Russell in Washington, D.C., 1972, p. 35.
7. Levey 1986, p. 102.
8. Vasari (1906, vol. 3, p. 462) praises the "strani capricci" that Filippino Lippi introduced in his work, noting his use of grotesque decoration as well as ancient vases, dress, armor, and other appurtenances. The decorative novelties introduced by Michelangelo in the sacristy at S. Lorenzo in Florence are characterized by Vasari (ibid., vol. 7, pp. 185, 193) as "alla grottesca piuttosto che a ragione o regola," and although he praises the histories, sibyls, and prophets of the Sistine Ceiling for their divine perfection, he lauds the figures representing the genealogy of Christ for their unprecedented variety in pose and attitude, "ed infinità di capricci straordinari e nuovi." Mere mention of Vasari's commendation of Raphael's specialist in grotesque ornament, Giovanni da Udine, for the "vaghissime e capricciose invenzioni, piene delle più varie e stravaganti cose che si possano imaginare (ibid., vol. 6, p. 553)" testifies to the association of the term with extravagant inventions and, in particular, with the imaginative genre of grotesque ornament. In his treatise of 1582, *Il discorso intorno alle imagini sacre e profane*, the Counter-Reformation cleric Gabriele Paleotti clearly links works done *a capriccio* with the monstrous censorious things born of the imagination rather than from nature (chaps. 36–42). His notion of *capricci*, like Vasari's, was closely tied to the fashion for grotesque ornament.
9. This opposition is clear from Giovanni Bellori's remark in his *Vite* (1672) contrasting Poussin's ordered manner of working to those who paint *a capriccio* and burn themselves out.
10. Baldinucci 1681, p. 28.
11. Milizia 1797, vol. 1, p. 145. Milizia was above all interested in architecture, but his views obviously apply also to painting. In the 1821 edition of his *Introduzione allo studio e vocabolario compendioso delle arti* this Neoclassical position had further hardened, and we read that "Dal capriccio deriva il gusto per le produzioni ripugnanti ai principi dell'arte, il quale non avendo alcuna solida base, non può sostenersi, nè durare lungamente."
12. The connection was first pointed out by Knox 1975a, p. 61, no. 111. It should, however, be noted that in Tiepolo's etching the figure wears a distinctive seventeenth-century, north European costume at variance with the garb of the turbaned individual in Castiglione's drawing. This raises the possibility that a northern print was his primary source.
13. See Blunt 1954, pp. 24–25, and Posse 1931, p. 43.
14. See Blunt 1954, no. 41.

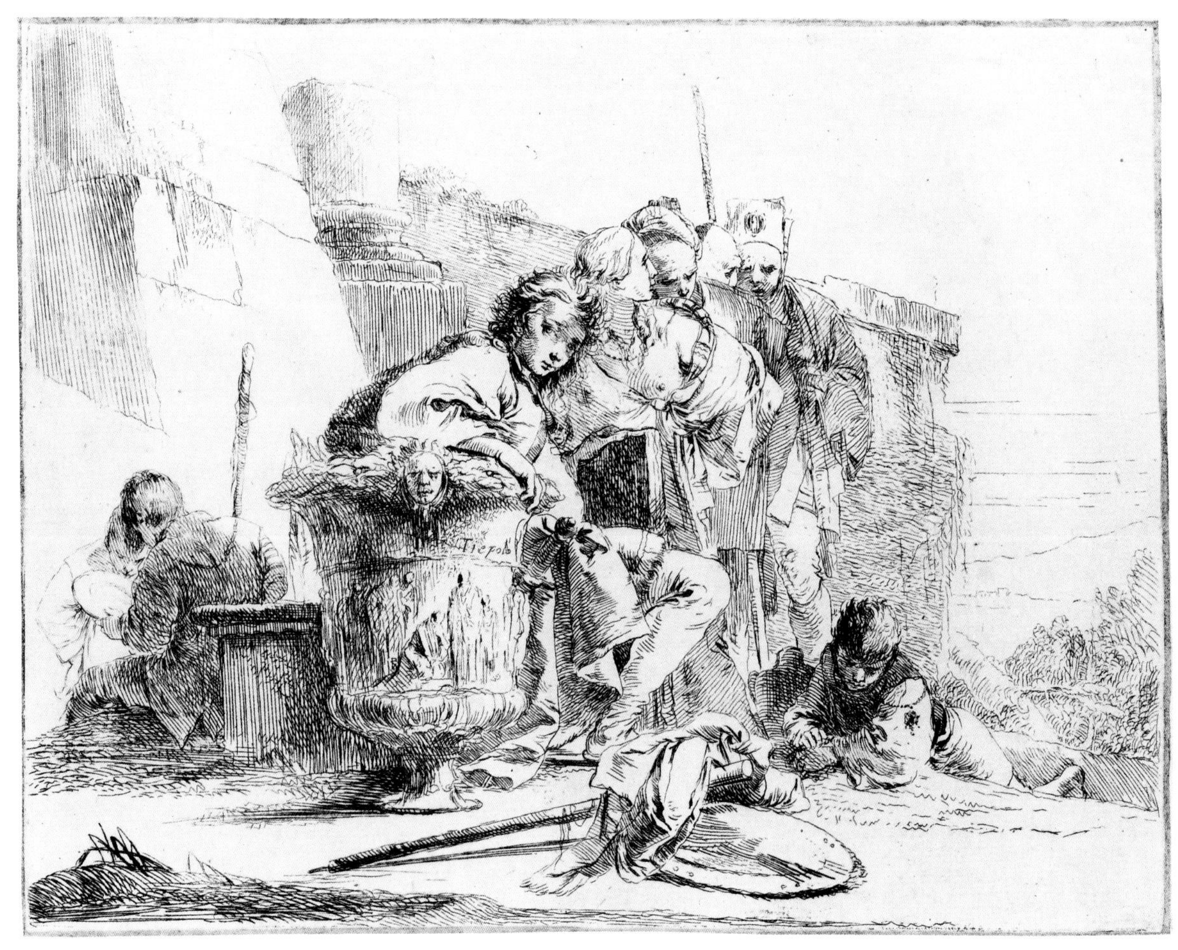

59a

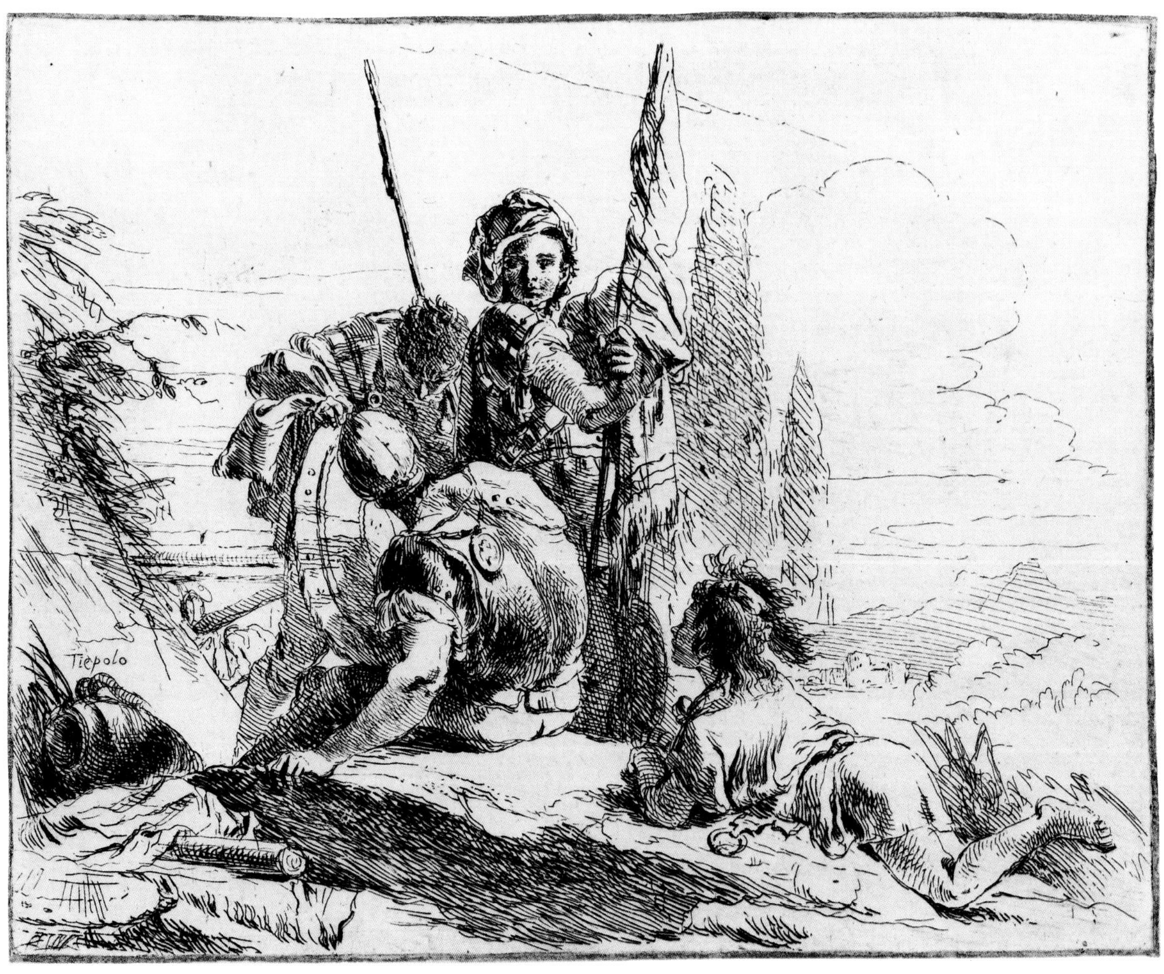

59b

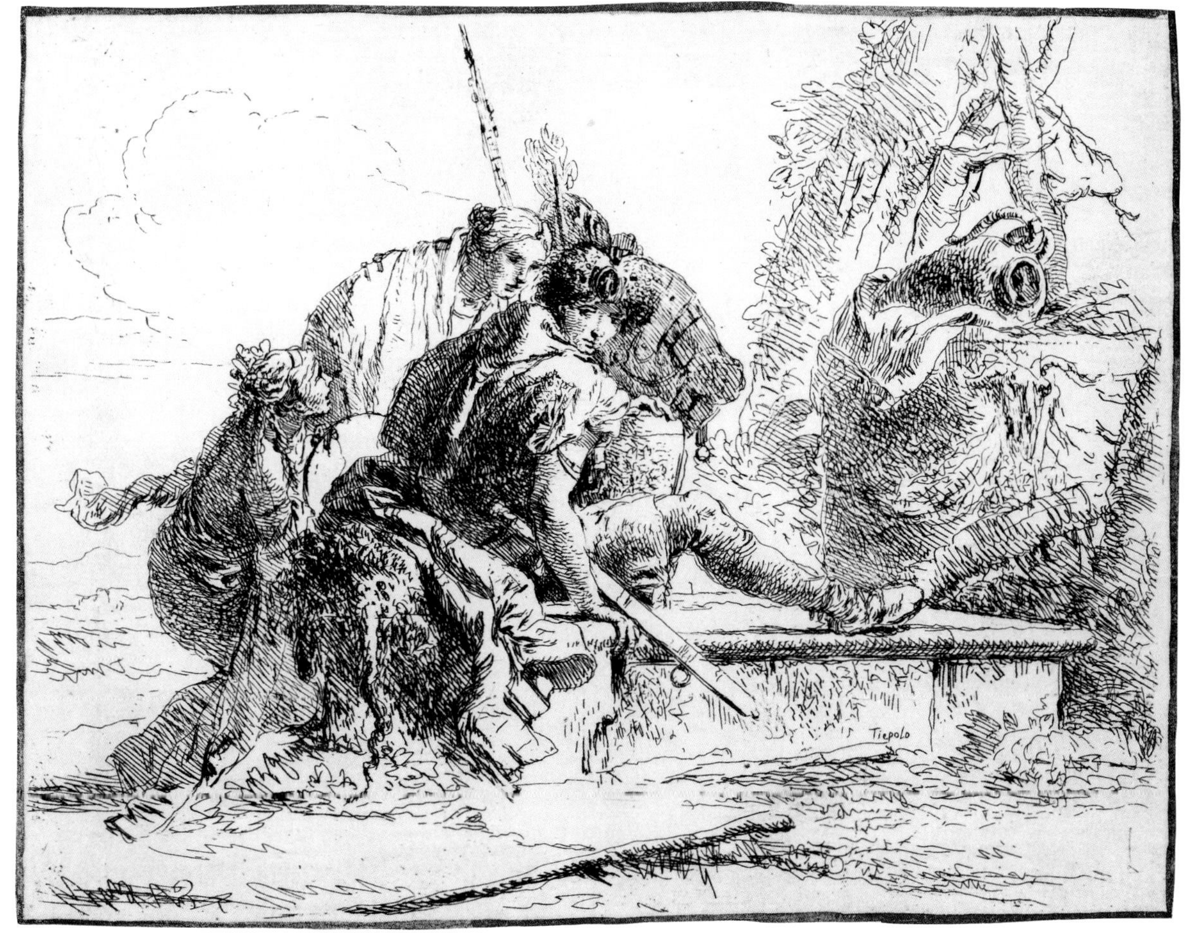

59c

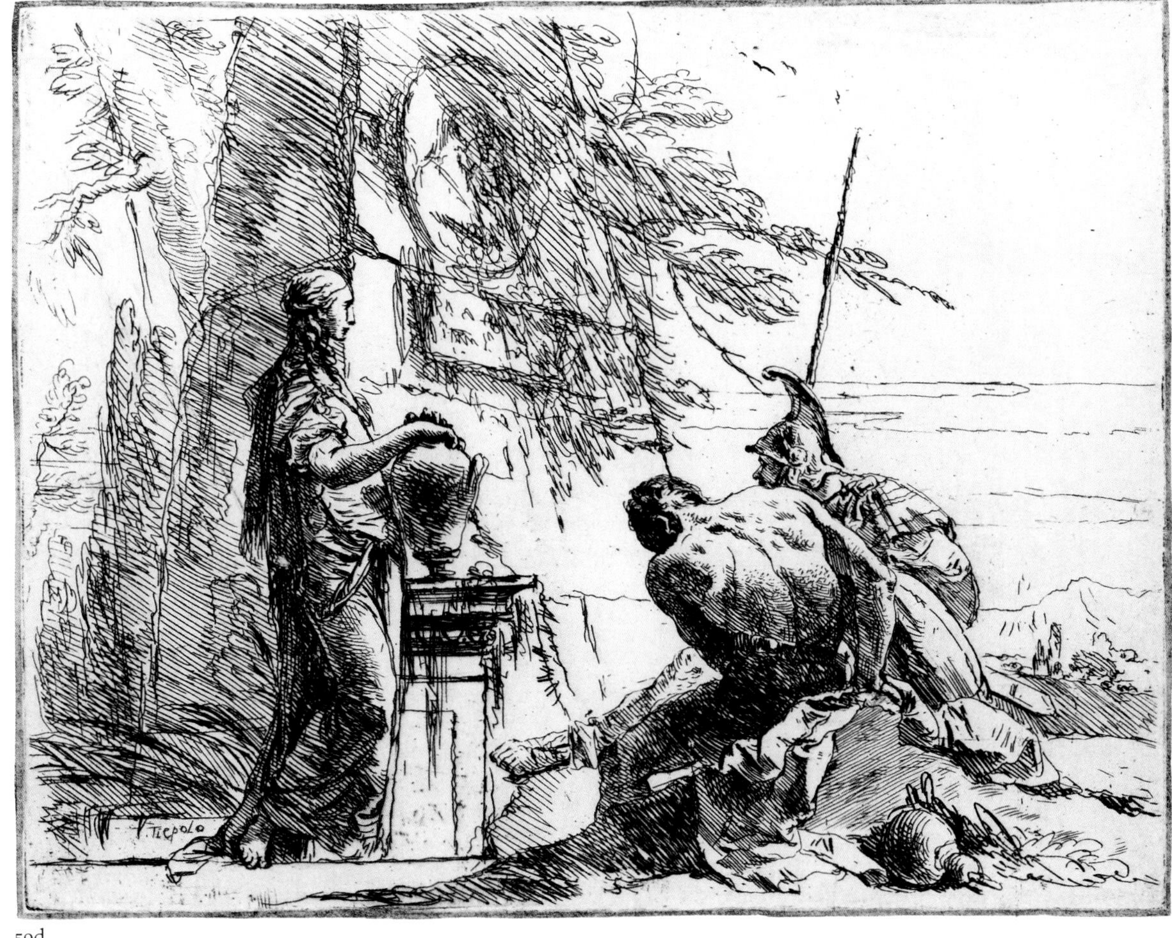

59d

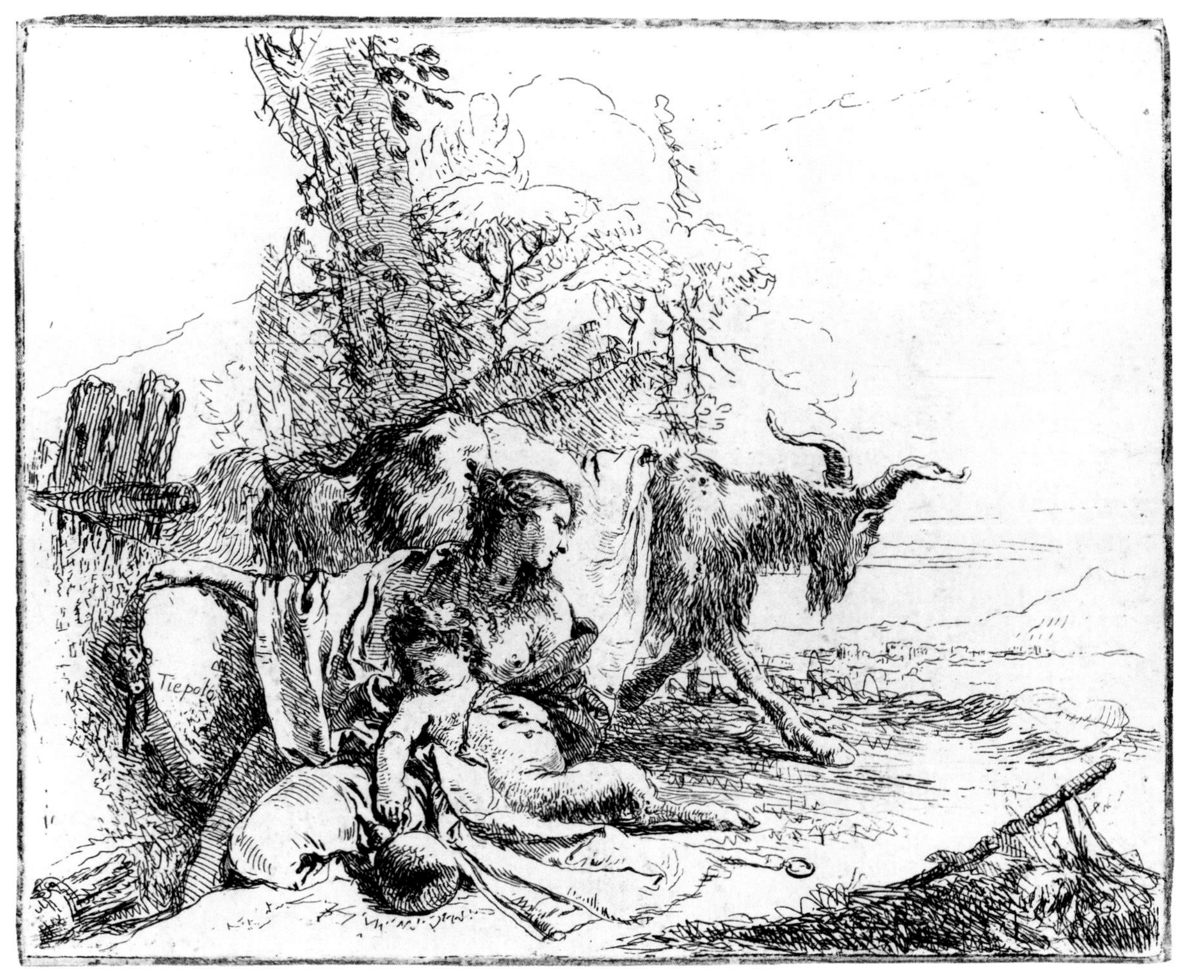

59e

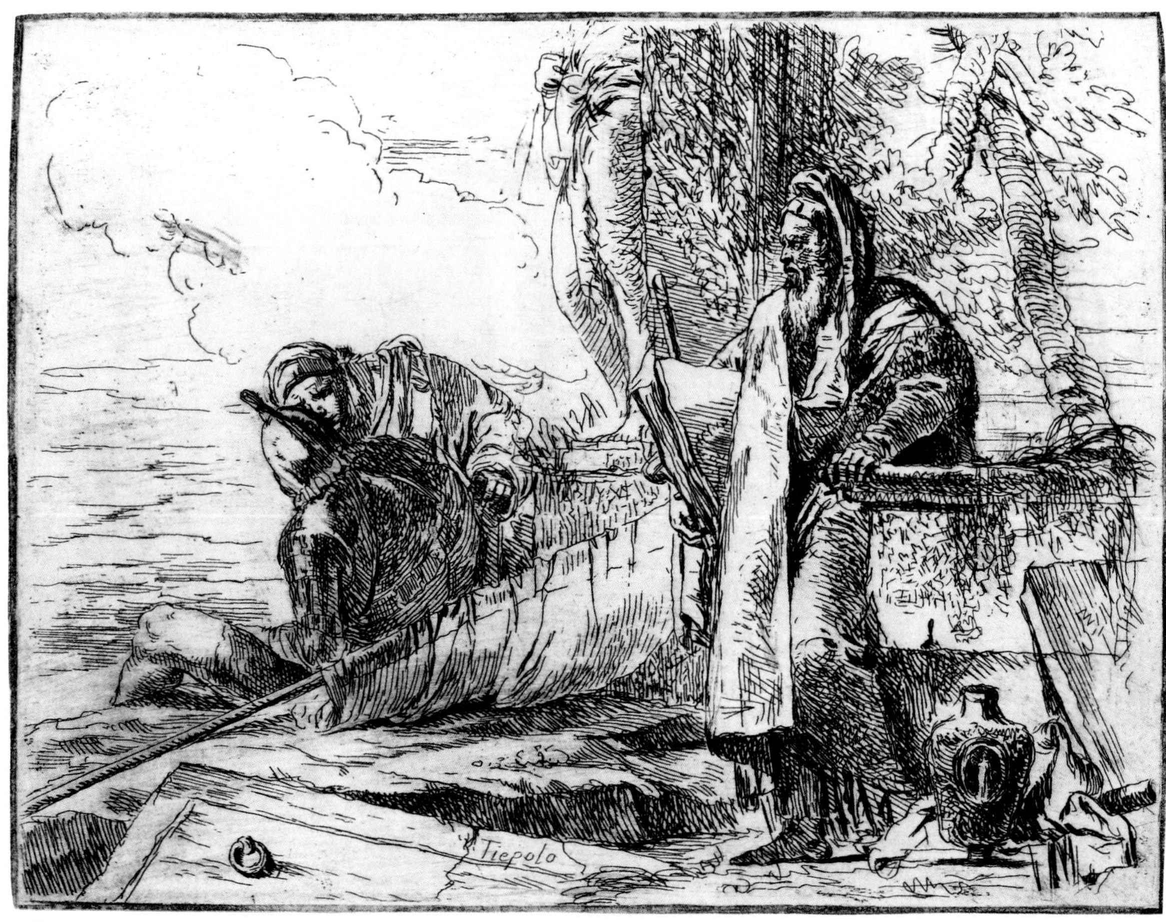

59f

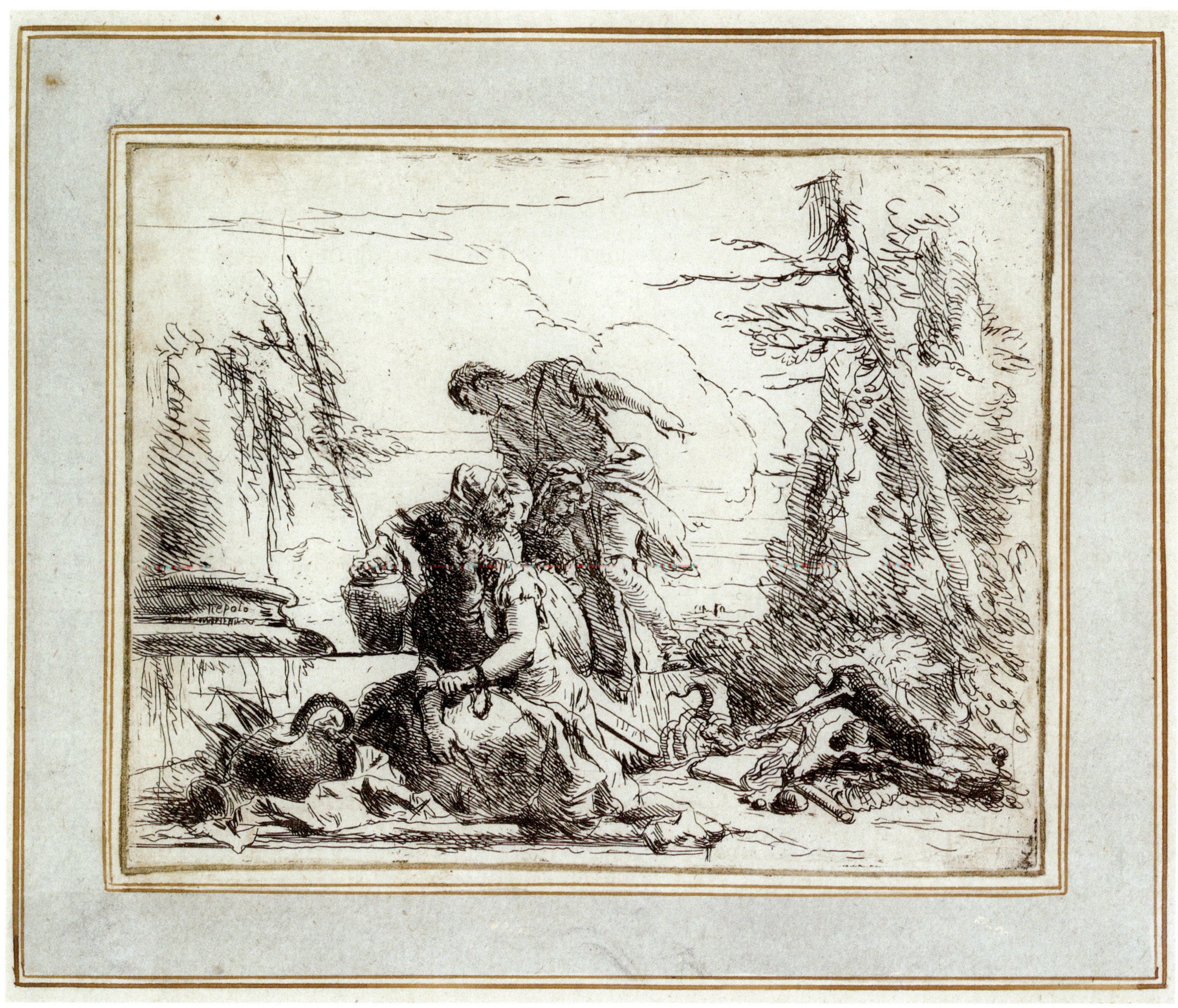

59g

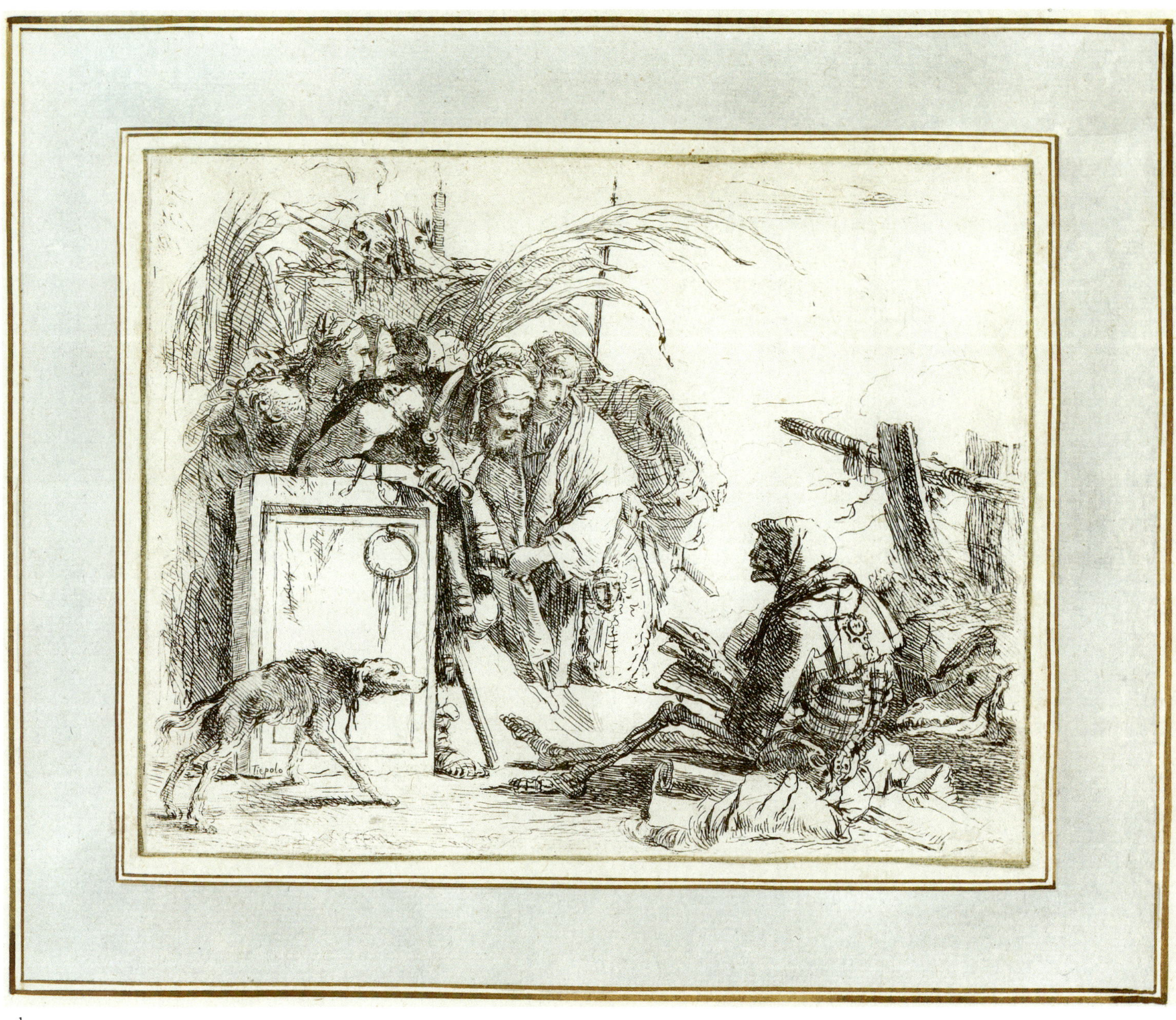

59h

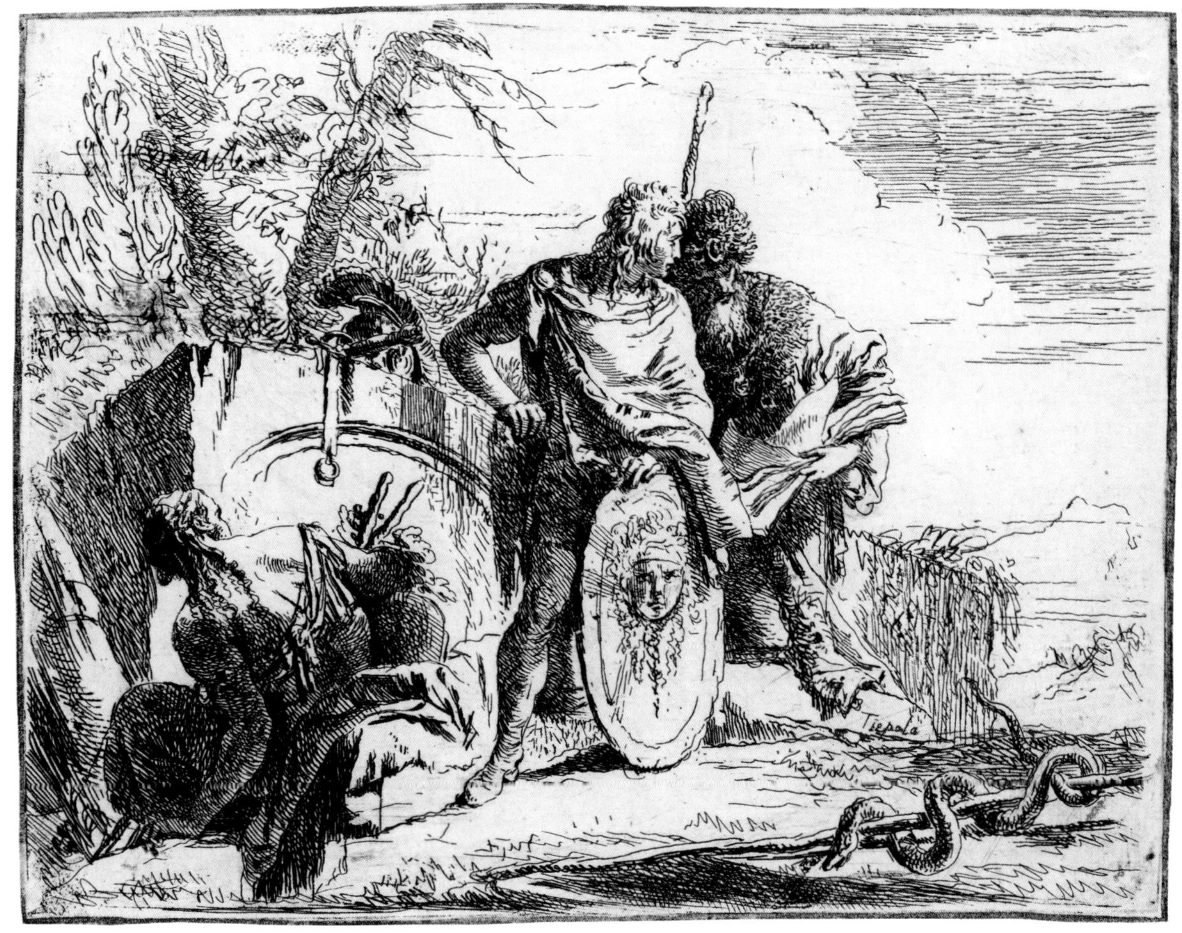

59i

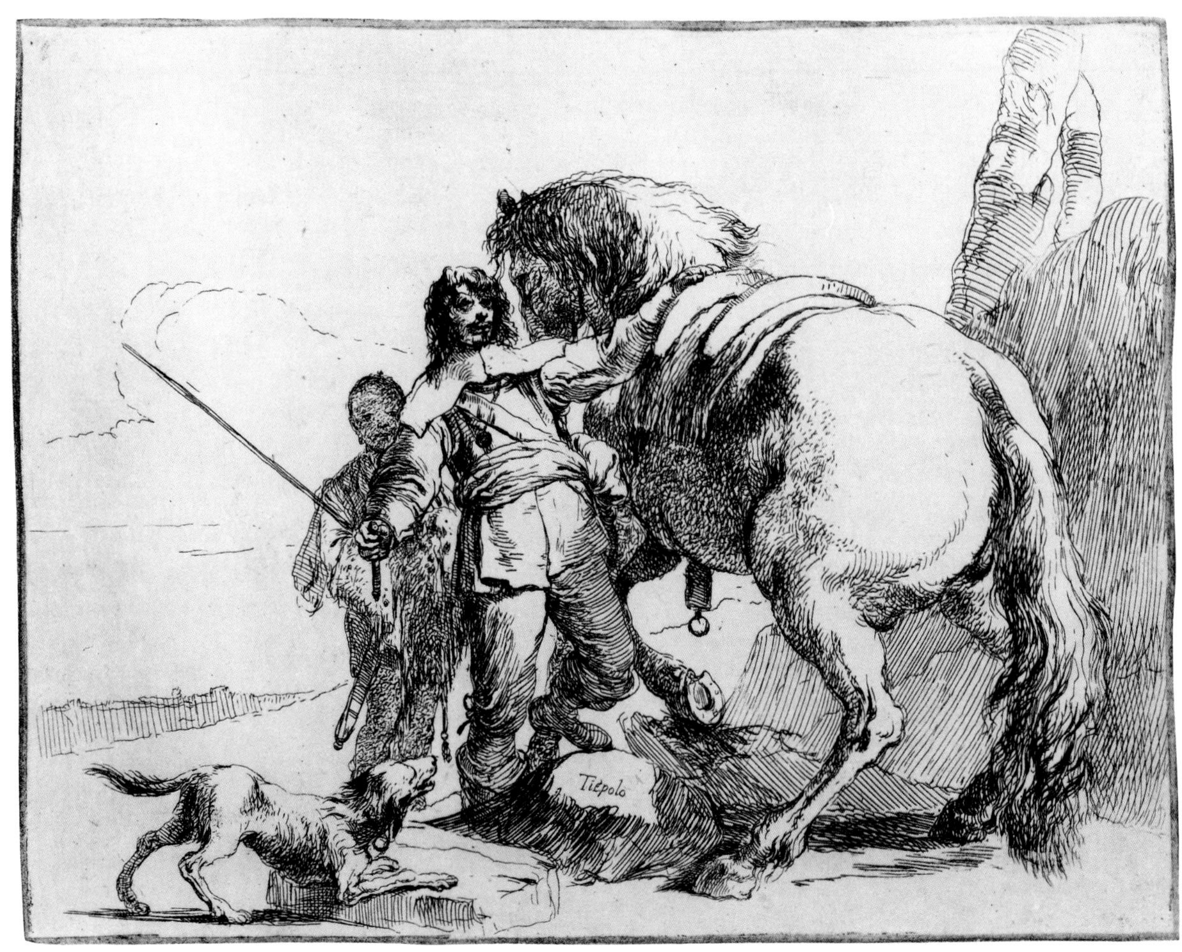

59j

THE SCHERZI DI FANTASIA

60a. Frontispiece
60b. A Satyr Family
60c. A Satyr Family
60d. Mother and Child and a Youth in a Landscape
60e. A Youth, Magus, and Monkey among Ancient Ruins
60f. Three Figures Observing a Snake
60g. Figures Observing a Snake
60h. A Seated Shepherd, Three Magi, and a Youth
60i. Family Reposing in a Landscape
60j. An Astrologer(?) and Other Figures
60k. An Astrologer(?) and His Assistants
60l. A Sorceress(?) Giving Audience
60m. A Bacchante, a Satyr, and a Nymph
60n. Punchinello Gives Counsel
60o. Two Figures with Their Horse and Groom
60p. A Scene of Necromancy
60q. A Scene of Necromancy
60r. A Scene of Necromancy
60s. A Scene of Necromancy
60t. Punchinello Observed
60u. Figures Gathered around an Ancient Altar
60v. Preparations for a Sacrifice
60w. An Astrologer(?)

60a–w. The Scherzi di Fantasia
Ca. 1743–57
Etchings
The Metropolitan Museum of Art, New York; Purchase, The Elisha Whittelsey Collection, The Elisha Whittelsey Fund; Dodge and Pfeiffer Funds; Joseph Pulitzer Bequest; Gift of Bertina Suida Manning and Robert L. Manning, 1976 (1976.537[1–24])

60a. Frontispiece (DV 13)
225 × 180 mm (8⅞ × 7⅛ in.)

60b. A Satyr Family (DV 23)
224 × 177 mm (8⅞ × 7 in.)
Signed in reverse, lower left: Tiepolo

60c. A Satyr Family (DV 22)
227 × 177 mm (9 × 7 in.)
Signed in reverse, lower left: Tiepolo

60d. Mother and Child and a Youth in a Landscape (DV 33)
224 × 176 mm (8⅞ × 7 in.)
Signed in reverse, lower center: Tiepolo

If the *Capricci* introduced Tiepolo as a printmaker to a wide audience of connoisseurs and collectors, the *Scherzi* secured him a reputation as one of the medium's most imaginative and accomplished practitioners. This is all the more impressive since Tiepolo adopted an uncharacteristically casual approach and was uninterested in exploring the possibilities of the medium. He made few changes as he worked and his technique was a simple one; several of the *Scherzi* suffered from defective biting and were left unfinished (in the most conspicuous example [60w] Tiepolo burnished out two heads but never got around to revising the composition). Invention and virtuosity, not technical innovation or fastidiousness, are the strengths of his etchings. Nonetheless, the *Scherzi*, with their luminous, textured surfaces—achieved by delicately inflected lines and flecks of the etching needle—display greater mastery than the *Capricci*, whose lines are penlike and scratchy.

A good deal of uncertainty still surrounds the date and circumstances of the production of the twenty-three *Scherzi*. Unlike the *Capricci*, they are not the result of a single burst of creative energy—Tiepolo seems to have taken more than a decade to produce them—and the plates were not handed over to a professional publisher for printing and distribution. They enjoyed wide commercial circulation only after Tiepolo's death, when Giandomenico issued them in various editions, numbered and with his father's untitled frontispiece inscribed with the name they have borne ever since.[1] However, well before their commercial printing various connoisseurs had secured the set—the one reproduced here is from an album in the Metropolitan Museum that was issued before the numbers and title were added by Giandomenico.[2] Perhaps in the 1750s Anton Maria Zanetti had pasted the series in a deluxe, bound album (National Gallery of Art, Washington, D.C., Rosenwald Collection),[3] and as early as 1757 the well-connected Parisian Pierre-Jean Mariette already owned nineteen and was in touch with Zanetti and Giandomenico in order to obtain the remaining four, which had been withheld to allow Giambattista to bring them to completion (eventually they were printed unfinished).[4] One of the etchings (60f) certainly existed by 1747, when it was copied by a German pupil of Tiepolo's,[5] and a strong case has been made for dating nineteen prior to 1750 and the four others to 1757–58.[6] That the prints were carried out in a number of campaigns is unquestionable: this is obvious from the differences in style as well as the various forms of signatures displayed. (They are here grouped according to types of signature.[7]) Tiepolo may have begun the *Scherzi* not long after he completed the *Capricci* and, after an initial, sustained effort, worked on them intermittently, as time allowed—while he was occupied with a flood of commissions before his departure for Würzburg.

It seems no less clear that as work on the project progressed, the focus of Tiepolo's interests shifted. In what is presented here as the earliest group of *Scherzi* (60b–g), the subjects range from the pastoral—bucolic satyr families or a mother and child taking rest with their donkey and exhausted dog, for example—to scenes with strange and mysterious content—such as the prints in which Orientals observe with fixed attention a snake that has emerged from a vessel or pile of classical debris. In a particularly enigmatic etching (60e) the two themes are combined: an ox and a classically draped youth appear to have stumbled on an ancient religious site and found, at the base of a circular altar, a bearded sage or priest with a leashed monkey. The single slightly dark note in this group is the persistent presence of an owl perched on a stand, a branch, or, in one case, on an altar. In the second group (60h–l) images involving Orientals and a snake assume greater prominence—even the male figure in the scene that calls to mind the Holy Family resting on its journey to Egypt (60i) wears an Orientalizing cap decorated with a medallion. Two of the sheets (60j, k) show a geographer or an astrologer with his globe and an open book, and it is in these that a distinctly sinister mood is introduced. In the remaining prints, in which the figures are treated with a new monumentality and the modeling is denser, there are still sunny moments—the etching of a bacchante with a satyr and a nymph in a vast landscape (60m) is the most conspicuous example—but the emphasis is increasingly on acts of necromancy: pyres of bones (60p, r) and, in one instance, a severed head (60s); rites at an altar near a tomb (60q); and a ritual that seems to involve the imminent sacrifice of a woman (60v). Even Punchinello, who makes two surprise appearances among these unlikely characters and props (60n, t), is not permitted a tranquil death: in one (60t) what is evidently his corpse is propped up against a tomb slab, as though to extract from the dead comic figure some buried secret (the hourglass and bone on a hillock and the pet owl next to the woman are particularly ominous).

Some of the exotic garb in these scenes is taken from Tiepolo's standard repertory and appears in many of his paintings, whether religious or mythological, as well as in his drawing albums of costumed figures (see fig. 102). This explains the general tendency to reject the notion that these prints, including the ones centered on necromancy, have specific subjects. Yet even *capricci* must play on some recognizable theme, and there is good reason to believe that in the *Scherzi* Tiepolo intended to evoke the ancient cultures of Egypt and Babylon and the magical-mystery cults associated with those civilizations.[8] Certainly witchcraft, as treated in the paintings of Salvator Rosa and the later *Caprichos* of Goya, plays little part in his subject matter.

Virtually all of the costumes pictured in the *Scherzi* also appear in Tiepolo's various treatments of the story of Antony and Cleopatra—indeed, the distinctive, blunt-tipped hat worn by one of the least appealing characters in the etchings (60g, h, j, l, t, v) is, astonishingly, sported by a musician playing the violin in the fresco of Cleopatra's banquet in Palazzo Labia, Venice (fig. 100). Tiepolo's canvas of the same subject painted for Augustus of Saxony (fig. 53) and admired by Algarotti included a sphinx and Egyptian statues that served to establish the proper setting.[9] The pyramid-like obelisks in a number of the *Scherzi* (60b, d, j, l, p, w) vaguely suggest Egypt or Assyria, and a closely similar obelisk functions as an attribute of Asia—or, more specifically, Palmyra—in the fresco on the ceiling over the stairwell in the Residenz, Würzburg. Palmyra's obelisk is accompanied by a stone block with a Greco-Oriental inscription and a snake entwined around a pole, while in a drawing related to the *Scherzi* (The Metropolitan Museum of Art, New York; Robert Lehman Collection), an obelisk is decorated with a pseudo-Egyptian head in a medallion.[10] We should remember that it was in the 1740s that Algarotti tried his hand at etching under Tiepolo's guidance, drawing Oriental heads, elaborate vases, and a herm like the one that appears on a sheet of the *Scherzi* (60g). Thus, to view Tiepolo's scenes as relating to Oriental and, more specifically, Egyptian-Chaldean religious-magical practices—perhaps inspired by Algarotti's own interests—is certainly reasonable.

The most convincing interpretation of the *Scherzi* advanced thus far is Dempsey's.[11] Noting the amulets worn by many of the figures and the devil set within rays of light that decorates a shield (60l), and emphasizing the key role played by snakes, he has suggested that the *Scherzi*—or at least those that have come to be considered representative of the whole series—concern Gnosticism, which originated on Egyptian soil, and, in particular, the snake-worshiping Ophites (*ophis* is Latin for serpent). As support for this interpretation, he has called attention to a drawing by Tiepolo in the Museo Civico, Trieste, of a crowd of figures watching, or rather worshiping, snakes.[12] Even allowing for the fact that similar decorative satanic heads appear in Tiepolo's frescoes, where they surely have no specific meaning—there is, for example, one ornamenting a vase in the *Family of Darius before Alexander* (Villa Cordellina, Montecchio Maggiore)—the context of the *Scherzi* endows them with a completely different effect.

60e. A Youth, Magus, and Monkey among Ancient Ruins (DV 30)
226 × 178 mm (9 × 7 in.)
Signed in reverse, lower right: Tiepolo

60f. Three Figures Observing a Snake (DV 25)
225 × 177 mm (8⅞ × 7 in.)
Signed in reverse, lower center: Tiepolo

60g. Figures Observing a Snake (DV 24)
225 × 175 mm (8⅞ × 6⅞ in.)
Signed in reverse, lower left: Tiepolo

60h. A Seated Shepherd, Three Magi, and a Youth (DV 28)
224 × 175 mm (8⅞ × 6⅞ in.)
Signed lower left: Tiepolo

60i. Family Reposing in a Landscape (DV 27)
222 × 175 mm (8¾ × 6⅞ in.)
Signed lower right: Tiepolo

60j. An Astrologer(?) and Other Figures (DV 26)
222 × 176 mm (8¾ × 7 in.)
Signed lower right: Tiepolo

60k. An Astrologer(?) and His Assistants (DV 34)
139 × 186 mm (5½ × 7⅜ in.)
Signed lower right: Tiepolo

60l. A Sorceress(?) Giving Audience (DV 15)
222 × 175 mm (8¾ × 6⅞ in.)
Signed lower left: Tiepolo

60m. A Bacchante, a Satyr, and a Nymph (DV 35)
133 × 200 mm (5¼ × 7⅞ in.)
Signed in reverse, lower left: BT.o

60n. Punchinello Gives Counsel (DV 21)
235 × 184 mm (9¼ × 7¼ in.)
Signed in reverse, lower right: BT.o

60o. Two Figures with Their Horse and Groom (DV 31)
220 × 180 mm (8¾ × 7⅛ in.)
Signed in reverse, lower left: BT.o

60p. A Scene of Necromancy (DV 19)
223 × 179 mm (8⅞ × 7⅛ in.)
Signed lower right: B.T.o

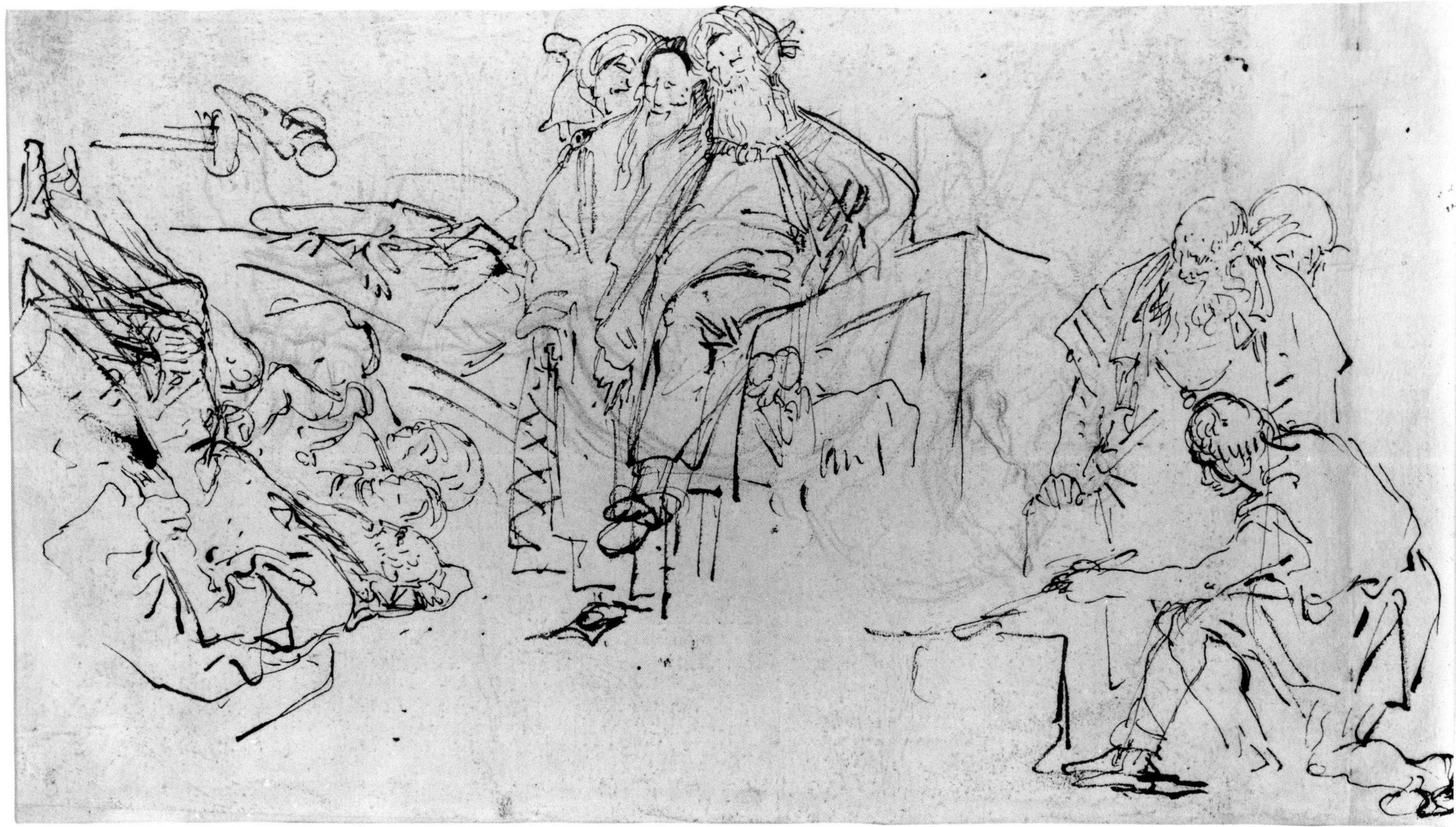

Fig. 125. *Three Sketches Related to the "Scherzi" Subjects.* Pen and ink over black chalk (?). Victoria and Albert Museum, London (D.1825.237-1885)

60q. A Scene of Necromancy (DV 14)
226 × 180 mm (9 × 7⅛ in.)
Signed lower right: B.T.o

60r. A Scene of Necromancy (DV 17)
226 × 179 mm (9 × 7⅛ in.)
Signed lower left and on altar: Tiepolo

60s. A Scene of Necromancy (DV 16)
227 × 187 mm (9 × 7⅜ in.)
Signed lower left: B Tiepolo

60t. Punchinello Observed (DV 29)
234 × 180 mm (9¼ × 7⅛ in.)
Signed lower right: B Tiepolo

60u. Figures Gathered around an Ancient Altar (DV 18)
222 × 180 mm (8¾ × 7⅛ in.)
Signed lower left: GB. Tiepolo

Moreover, Tiepolo's son Lorenzo made drawings on the theme that are clearly inspired by the *Scherzi* and intensify their occult-magical aspect.[13] The strongest indication of Tiepolo's intentions in the *Scherzi* is offered by the frontispiece, which shows a flock of nine owls—one perched on a dead tree, seven massed on an upright stone slab, and one, turned menacingly toward the viewer, on the ground. These are hardly the wise mascots of Minerva but are, instead, evil birds of the night—such as were later to be associated by Goya with the nightmares of his *Caprichos.* Prominently placed in the foreground are an egg and a head of garlic. The egg is a common fertility charm, garlic a well-known talisman against witchcraft or spells.

The fact that all early references to these prints viewed them as caprices and that Giandomenico considered them *scherzi*, or playful things, ought to warn against overinterpretation: magical practices evoked as much lighthearted curiosity in the eighteenth century as they do in the twentieth and provided literary as well as operatic material. The *Scherzi* might best be seen as highbrow caprices meant to titillate as well as give esoteric pleasure. In this they are decisively unlike Goya's *Caprichos*, with their scathing commentary on contemporary society. They are, first and foremost, exercises in the fantastic, and Goya must have admired their enigmatic allure. In them Tiepolo indulges as nowhere else his unquenchable love for the exotic and the ambiguous.

Just how closely both the *Capricci* and the *Scherzi* are bound up with Tiepolo's paintings is demonstrated by a sheet with studies of figures in Oriental dress (Martin von Wagner-Museum, Würzburg [7913]) that is certainly a preliminary sketch for the bystanders in the *Death of Hyacinth* (23); it seems to take as its point of departure one of the *Capricci* (59h) and to be working in the direction of some of the *Scherzi* (especially 60f or g).[14] Numerous drawings relating to the *Scherzi* survive (see figs. 91, 125).[15]

KC

Notes

1. All the earliest notices refer to the etchings as *capricci,* and it may have been to distinguish them from the earlier series published by Zanetti that Giandomenico renamed the set. For the various editions, see Succi in Gorizia 1985, pp. 58–62. The frontispiece has, without any foundation, occasionally been ascribed to Giandomenico.
2. Succi (in ibid., pp. 26–28) has noted that all twenty-three *Scherzi* are mentioned in Basan's *Dictionnaire des graveurs* of 1767 and are cited by Gori Gandellini in 1771. He also argues that nineteen were in limited circulation by 1750.
3. See Russell in Washington, D.C., 1972, pp. 13–16. The first volume contains Giambattista's *Capricci, Scherzi,* and print of Saint Joseph. The second has Giandomenico's two series, on the Passion and the Flight into Egypt. Fifteen of the *Scherzi* show hand corrections in pen and ink that Russell argues are Giambattista's. The corrections were never carried out, and it remains an open question whether the pen-and-ink additions were made by Giambattista, Giandomenico, or—equally likely—Zanetti. See note 4 below for Giandomenico's instructions to Mariette to fill in what he found lacking in the prints. I have examined an early impression of one of the prints, currently on the market, with sensitive pen-and-ink "corrections" that, to my mind, were added not by Tiepolo but by their owner.
4. See Frerichs 1971a, pp. 239–40. The correspondence is reprinted, translated, and discussed by Russell (in Washington, D.C., 1972, pp. 33–34). See Succi (in Gorizia 1985, pp. 26–28) for another, completely convincing appraisal. In a note of 29 December 1757 Zanetti informed Mariette that he could get only two of the three *Capricci* Mariette wanted—as one had been varnished for further work. A remark at the end of the note specifies the number as four, not three, prints (three *Scherzi* and the frontispiece). On 21 June 1758 Giandomenico wrote Mariette that the four *Capricci* had been consigned to Zanetti for delivery. He explained that the order had been delayed because the plates had all been varnished for finishing touches, noting also that he had removed the varnish and printed them, since Giambattista had done nothing to them. Mariette was encouraged to fill in whatever he found lacking—a remarkable commentary on Tiepolo's attitude toward the series and the pressure under which he was then working. From their appearance it is clear that the last four plates were never brought to the same level of perfection as the earlier ones.
5. The pupil was Martin Kuen, who studied with Tiepolo between 1746 and 1747. See Würzburg 1992, p. 56, no. A42.
6. See Succi in Gorizia 1985, pp. 26–28.
7. The relative chronology of the works within the series is far from established. For example, Russell (in Washington, D.C., 1972, p. 19) cautiously hypothesizes three groups; Succi (in Gorizia 1985, pp. 25–26) makes a detailed argument for six. Aside from Knox, no one has suggested that the signatures should be used as a primary means of ordering the etchings—perhaps because it seems too simple a criterion. However, the use of such widely divergent signatures on groups of prints surely implies something about their sequence. We know that the signatures on the *Capricci*—which are uniform—were added all at once, after they were finished and prior to their delivery to Zanetti. Thus, it seems likely that as Tiepolo finished groups of the *Scherzi,* he signed them en bloc. In one group (60b–g)—on stylistic grounds here judged the earliest—the extremely tentative signature is in reverse. In the very closely related prints proposed here to be the second group (60h–l), the same signature is in the correct sense—suggesting that, after printing the first batch, Tiepolo realized he had forgotten to make allowance for the reversal that occurs in printing. Then comes a less homogeneous group bearing monograms, some of which are backward (60m–o), some in the correct sense (60p, q). There follows an isolated print with the signature in block letters (60r); two with a careful signature adding the initial B (60s, t), and three—unquestionably the latest—with the full G B Tiepolo (60u–w); the frontispiece (60a) is not signed and was among the last executed. If the implications of this grouping are accepted, we can conclude that Tiepolo began the project with a burst of concentrated energy, completing half of the prints within a short period of time. He was then overwhelmed with work and was able to devote only occasional moments to them, eventually releasing etchings in an unfinished state. It stands to reason that Zanetti would have known of the project from its inception, and it was probably through him that his best clients learned of the prints and began to make inquiries about them.
8. François Menestrier noted (1694, p. 256) that "ces Images Mistericuses & Magiques, comme les nomme Lucain, nous sont venus des Egyptiens, peuples extraordinairement superstitieux, & premiers Auteurs de l'Idolatrie."
9. Draft of a letter of 1743–44 to Count Brühl. See Haskell 1958, p. 213.
10. The drawing is generally ascribed to Tiepolo and dated to the 1720s. Knox (in Knox and Byam Shaw 1987, p. 94) believes it more likely to be a pastiche after the *Scherzi.* The head on the medallion is similar to the statue in the background of a *Banquet of Cleopatra* (National Gallery of Victoria, Melbourne), which was painted with the advice of Algarotti. For the inscription in the Residenz, see Ashton 1978, pp. 116–19, and Büttner 1979, p. 167. Büttner notes the analogy with the *Scherzi* and identifies the man in the fresco holding a flaming lamp as a wise man or magus.
11. See Dempsey 1972.
12. Knox (1975a, p. 20) has cited as comparable Niccolò Nelli's proverb illustration of 1564 that shows a man holding a vase from which emerges a snake with the legend "Che se confida inquel ch'appar di fuora / Dentro vi trova il serpe ch'il devora." It is unlikely that Tiepolo's *Scherzi* have any direct relation to these homey proverbs.
13. See Thiem 1994, who fully discusses the Ophite content. She notes that at least some of Lorenzo's drawings were done in Würzburg, a fact that clearly has a bearing on the date of Tiepolo's prints.
14. See Knox in Cambridge 1970, p. 173, no. 190. The figure most closely related to *Capriccio* no. 59h is the one shown leaning over an undefined object.
15. See especially Knox 1975a, pp. 19–22. Like the *Scherzi,* the drawings show a range of styles, reinforcing the view that the etchings were carried out over an extended period of time. In some cases they also elucidate the way Tiepolo modulated the theme of the series. For example, the drawing related to print 60r (Victoria and Albert Museum, London, D.1825.85-1885) shows that Tiepolo initially considered putting the magus before an obelisk, which subsequently was abandoned in favor of the altar with a pile of bones on top of it.

60v. Preparations for a Sacrifice (DV 20)
228 × 171 mm (9 × 6¾ in.)
Signed lower left: GB. Tiepolo

60w. An Astrologer(?) (DV 32)
229 × 171 mm (9 × 6¾ in.)
Signed lower right: GB. Tiepolo

REFERENCES:
Baudi di Vesme 1906, pp. 13–35; Molmenti 1909, pp. 227–35; Sack 1910, pp. 292–94; Thomas 1966, pp. 261–63; Pignatti 1970; Frerichs 1971a, pp. 239–40; Rizzi 1971, pp. 11–16, 34–80; Udine 1971, pp. 62–64, 70–81; Dempsey 1972; Russell in Washington, D.C., 1972, pp. 14–27, 53–81; Santifaller 1972, pp. 148–51; Knox 1975a, pp. 19–22; Ottawa 1976, pp. 14–17, 28–36; Succi in Gorizia 1983, pp. 354–56, 364–81; Succi in Gorizia 1985, pp. 19–20, 25–28, 58–62, 126–73; Levey 1986, pp. 215–17; Succi in Gorizia 1988, pp. 293–301; Würzburg 1992, p. 156; London 1994, p. 499, no. 112; Thiem 1994, pp. 322–31

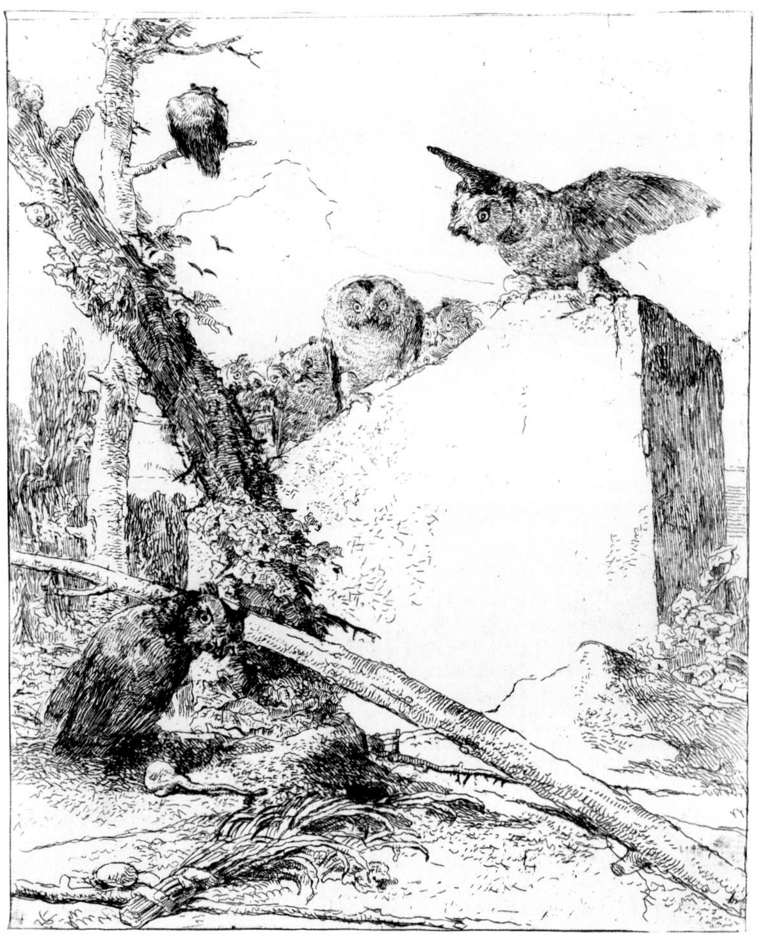
60 a

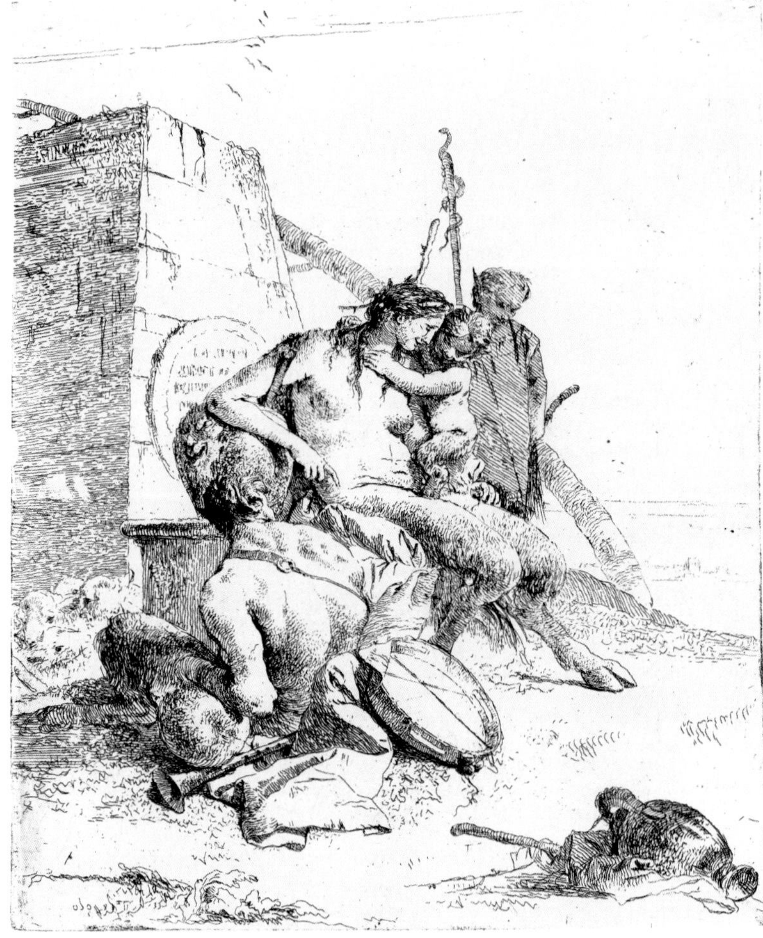
60 b

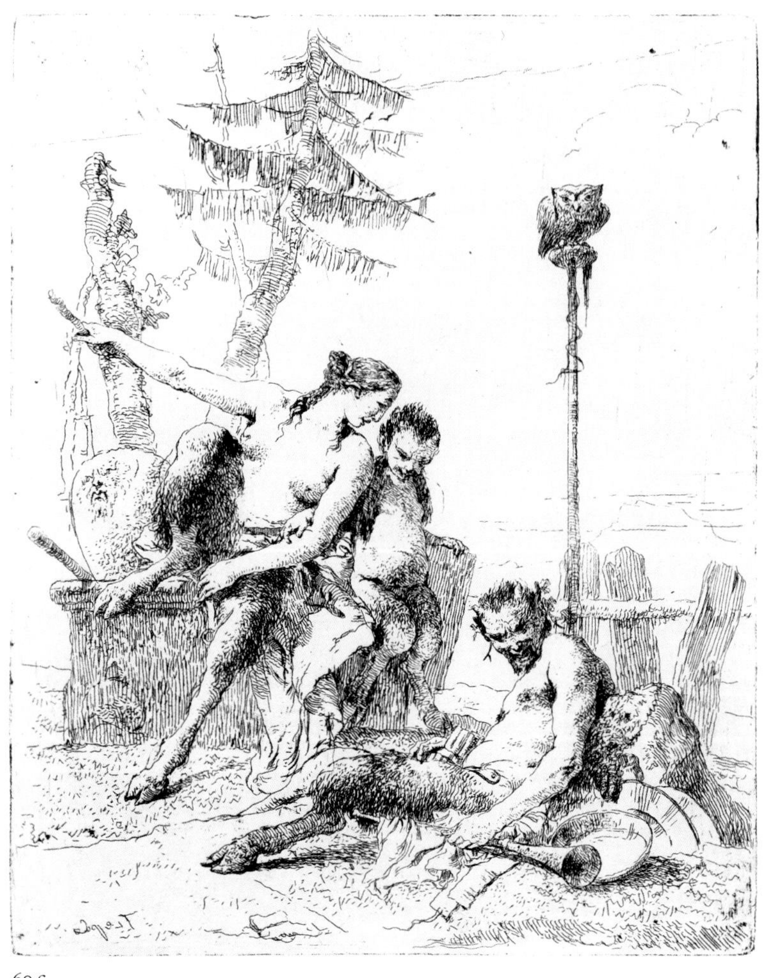
60 c

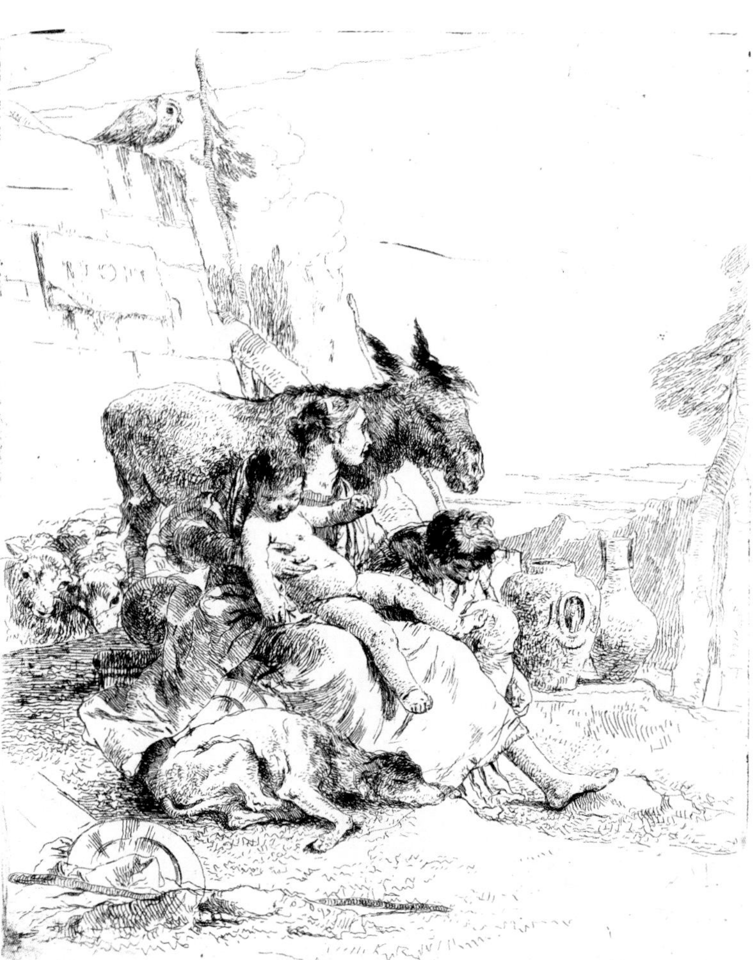
60 d

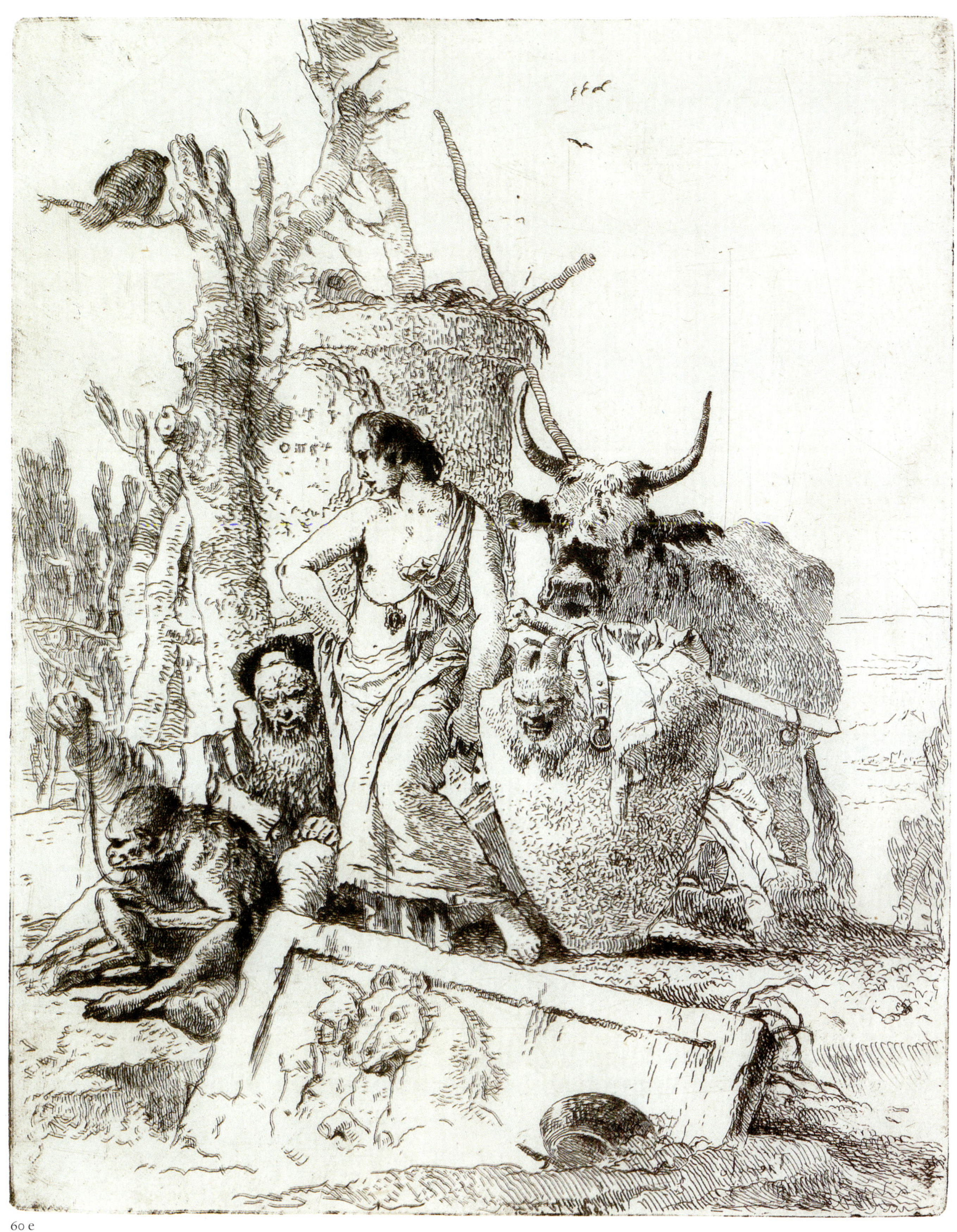

60 e

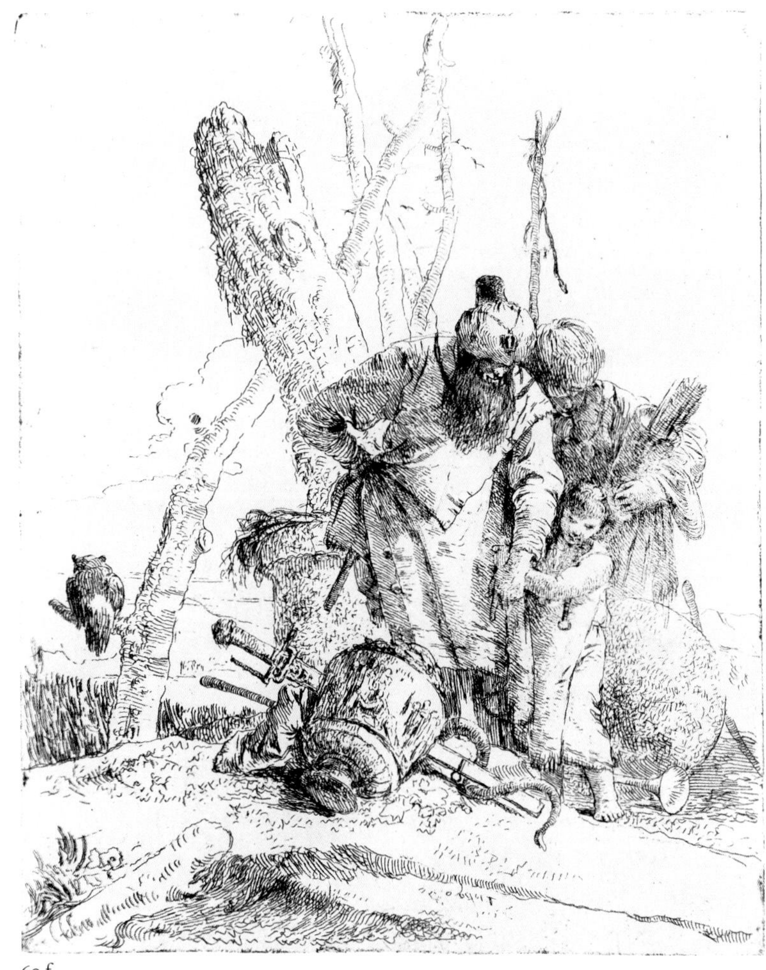
60 f

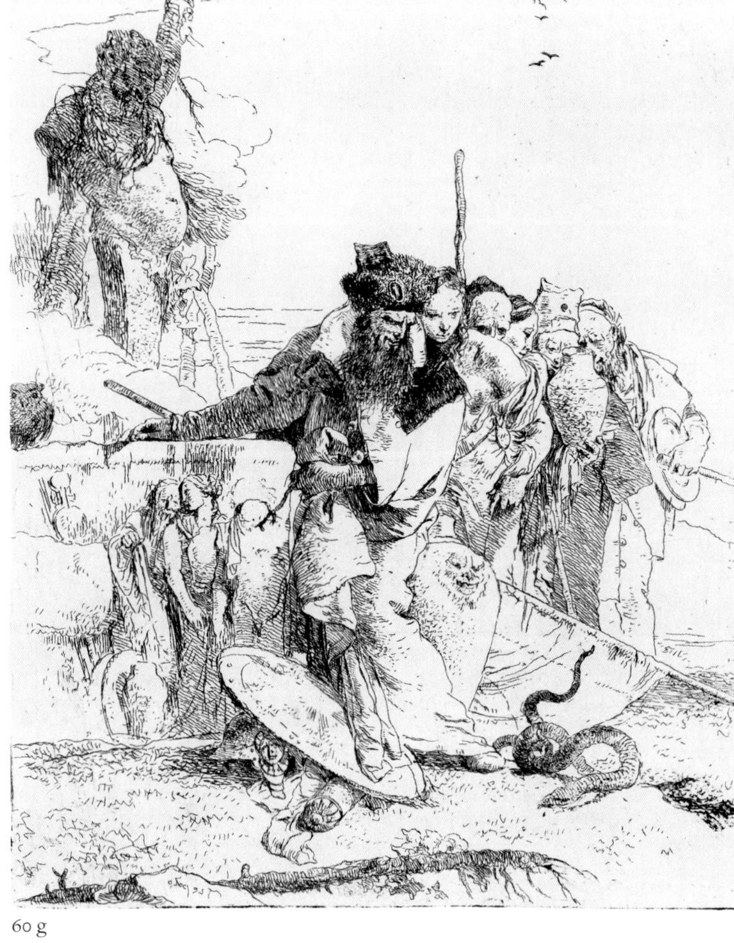
60 g

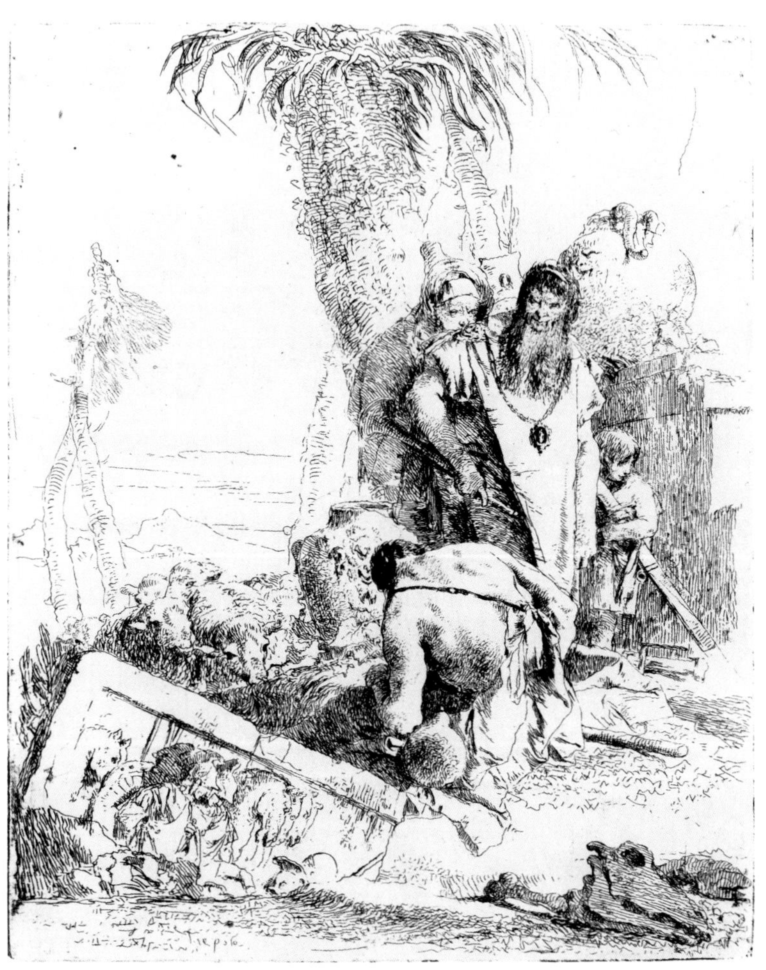
60 h

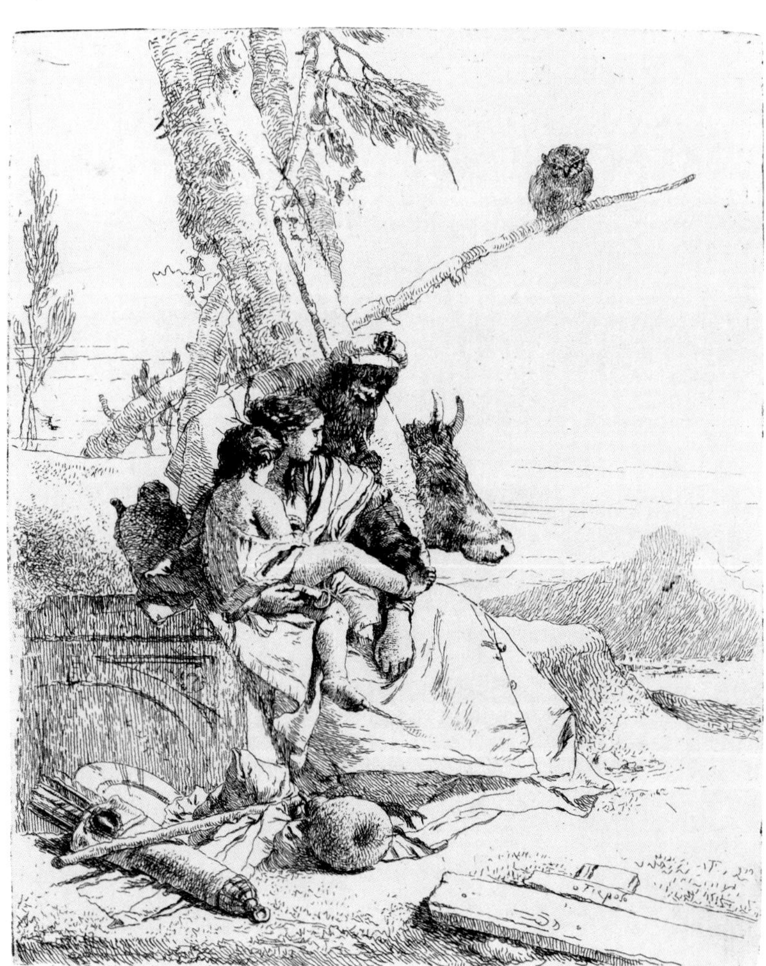
60 i

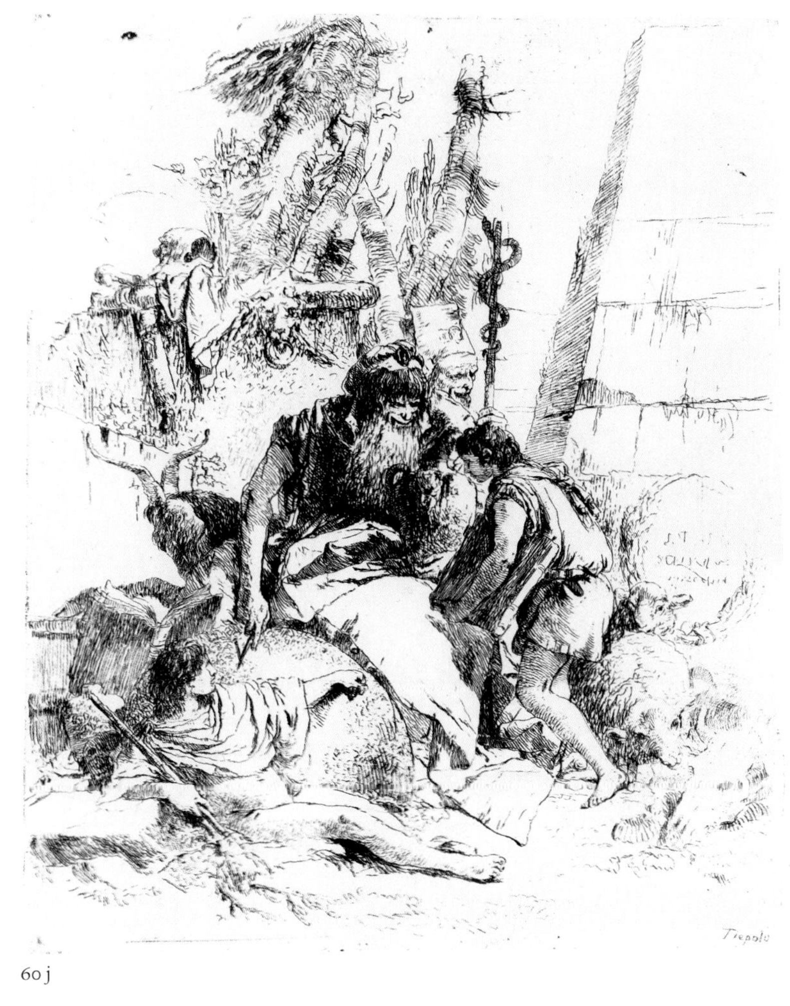

60j

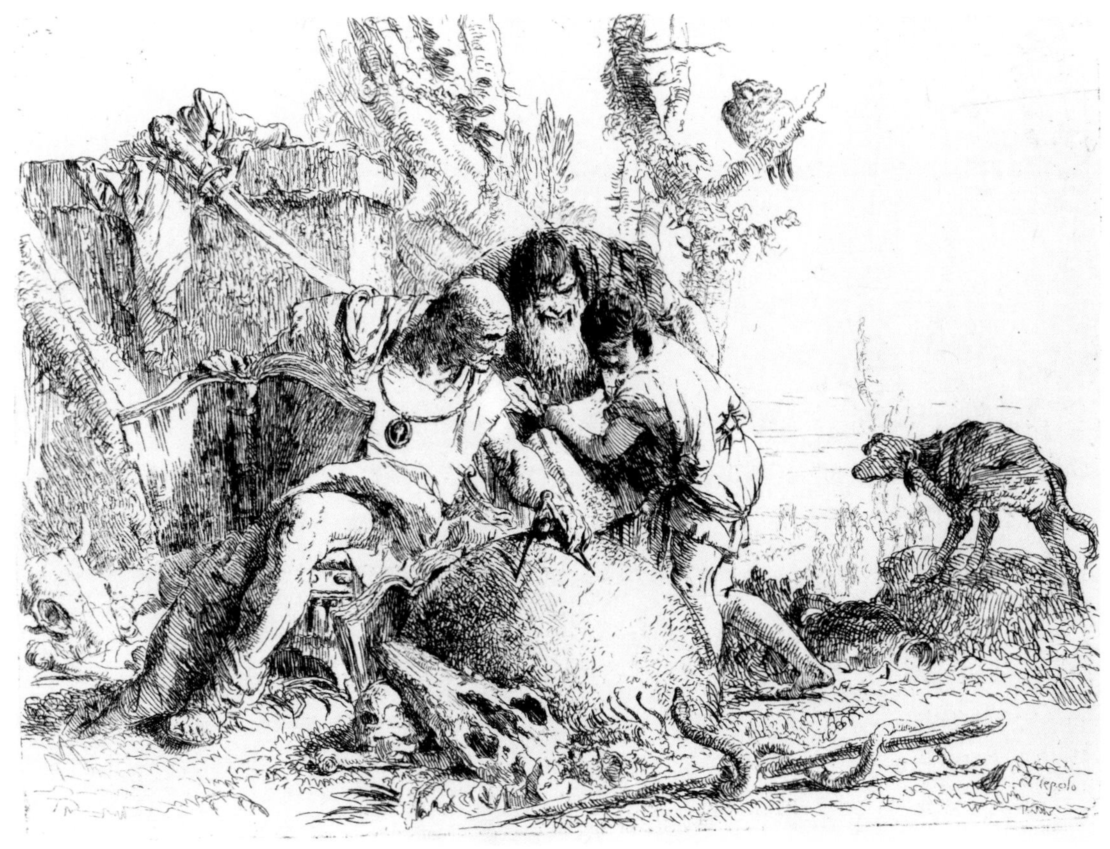

60k

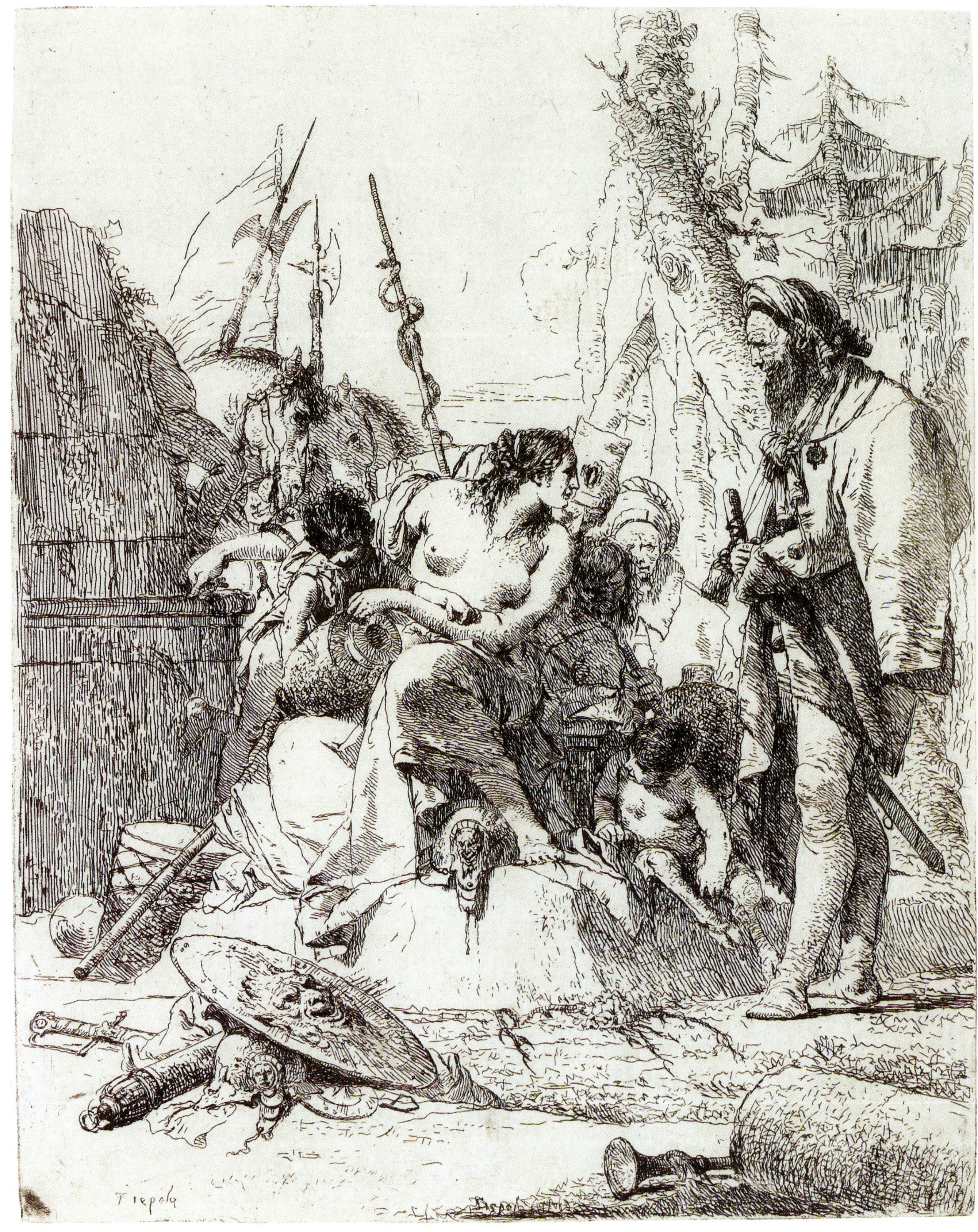

601

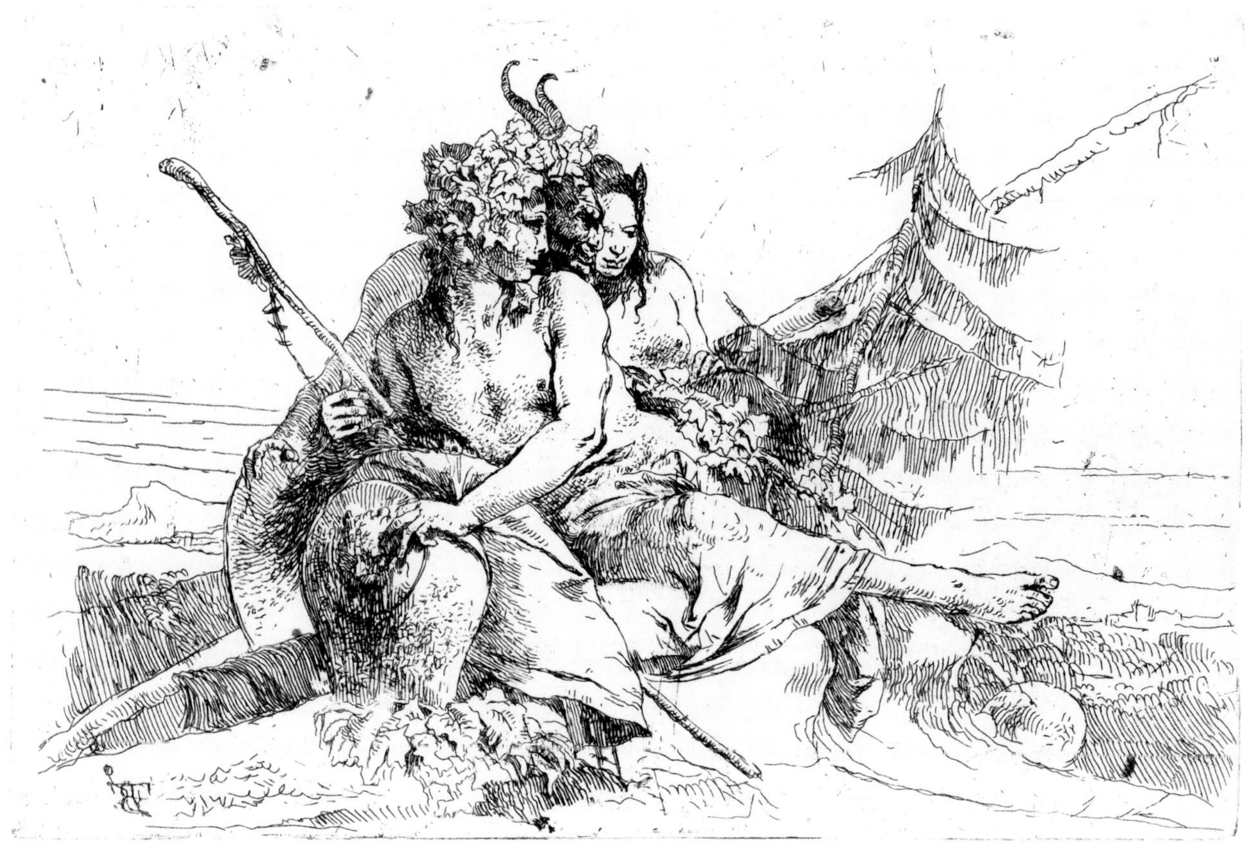

60 m

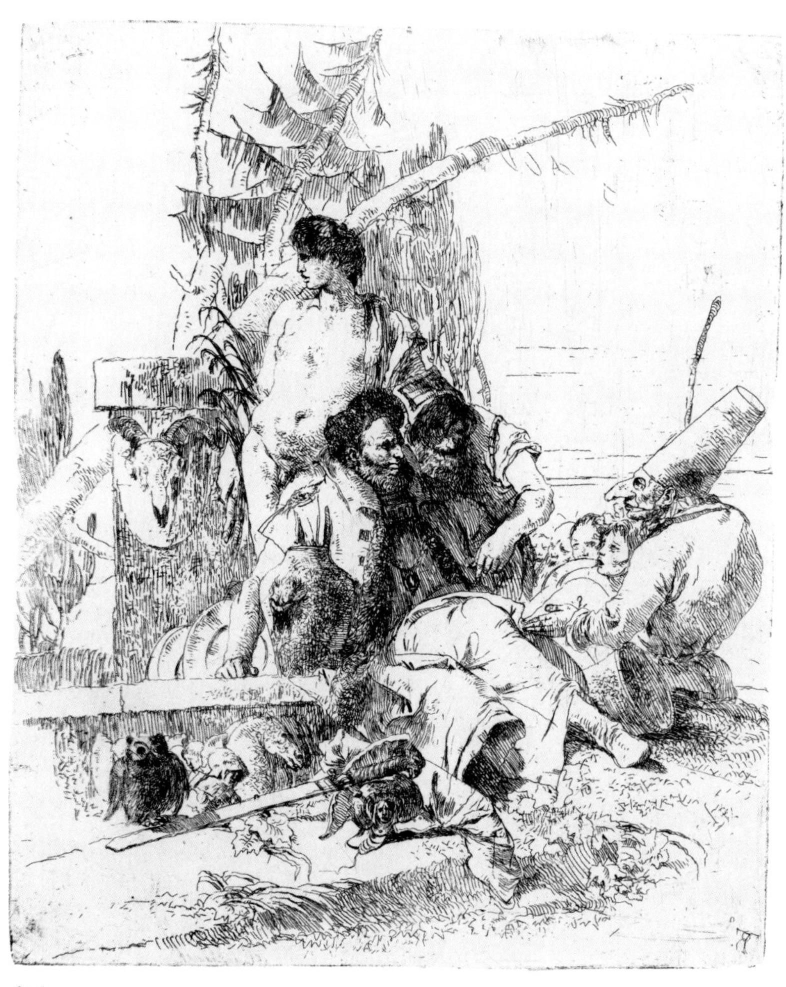

60 n

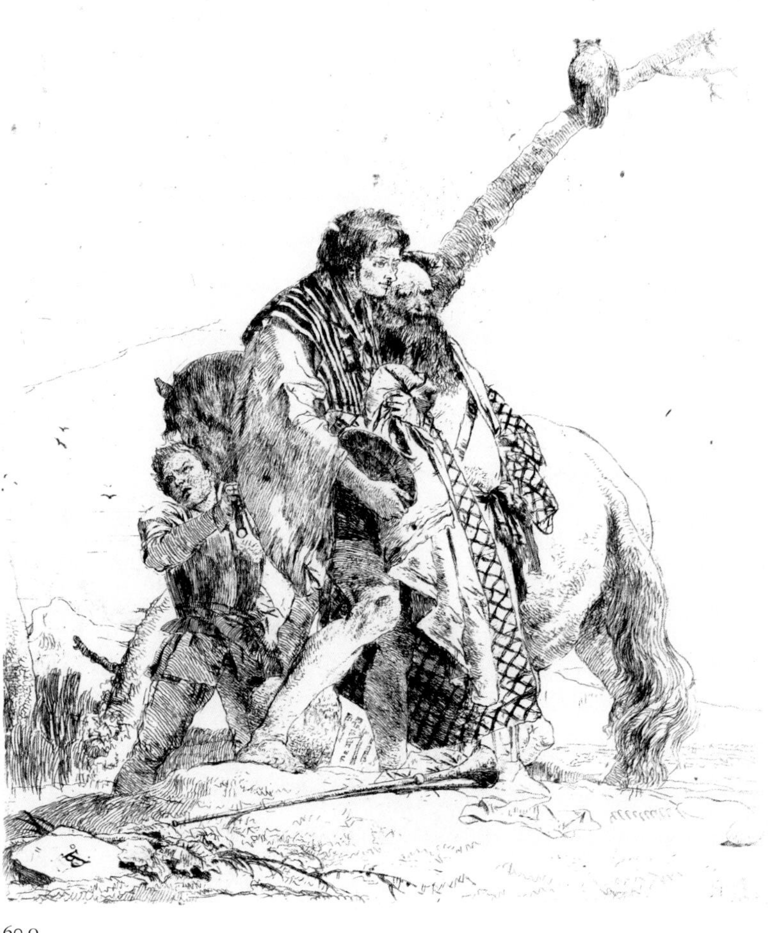

60 o

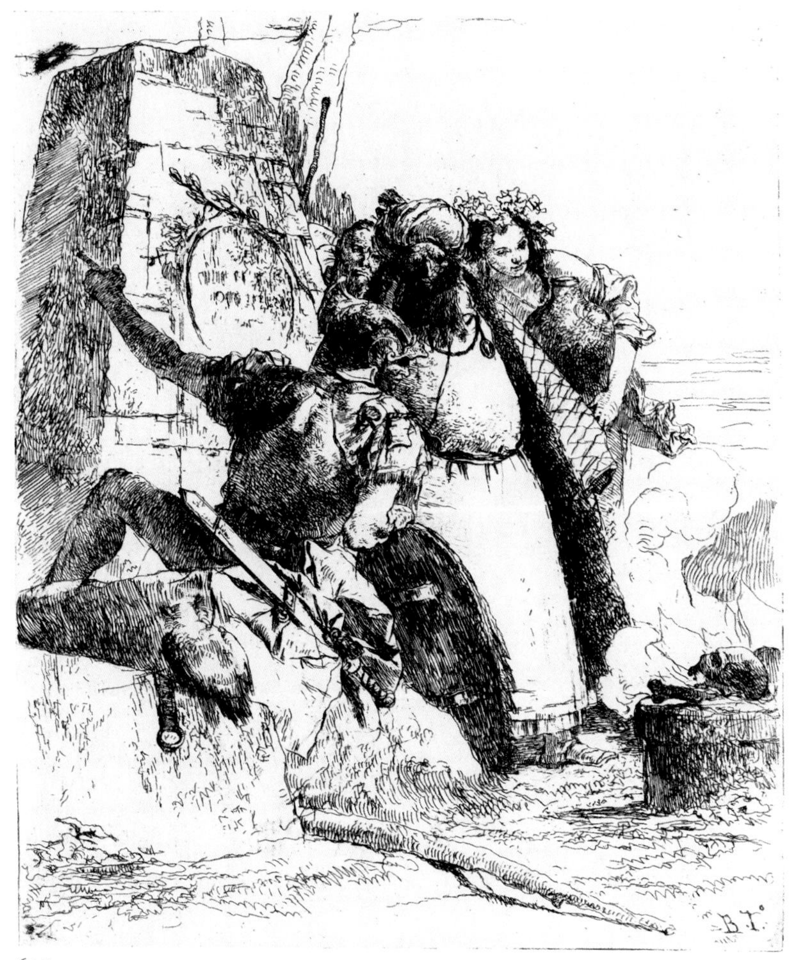

60 p

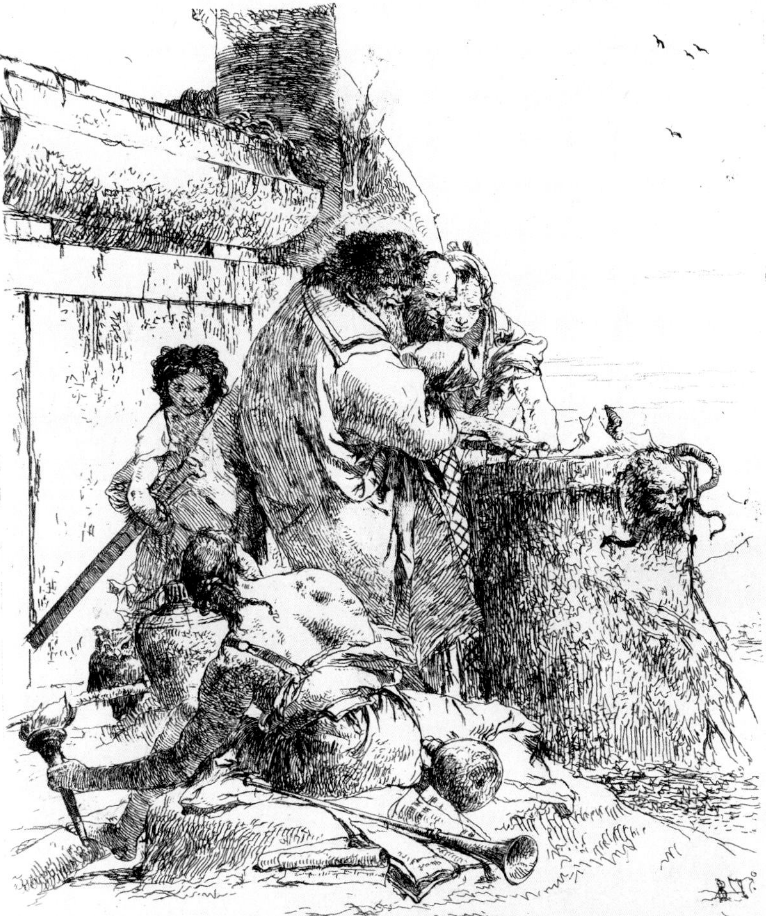

60 q

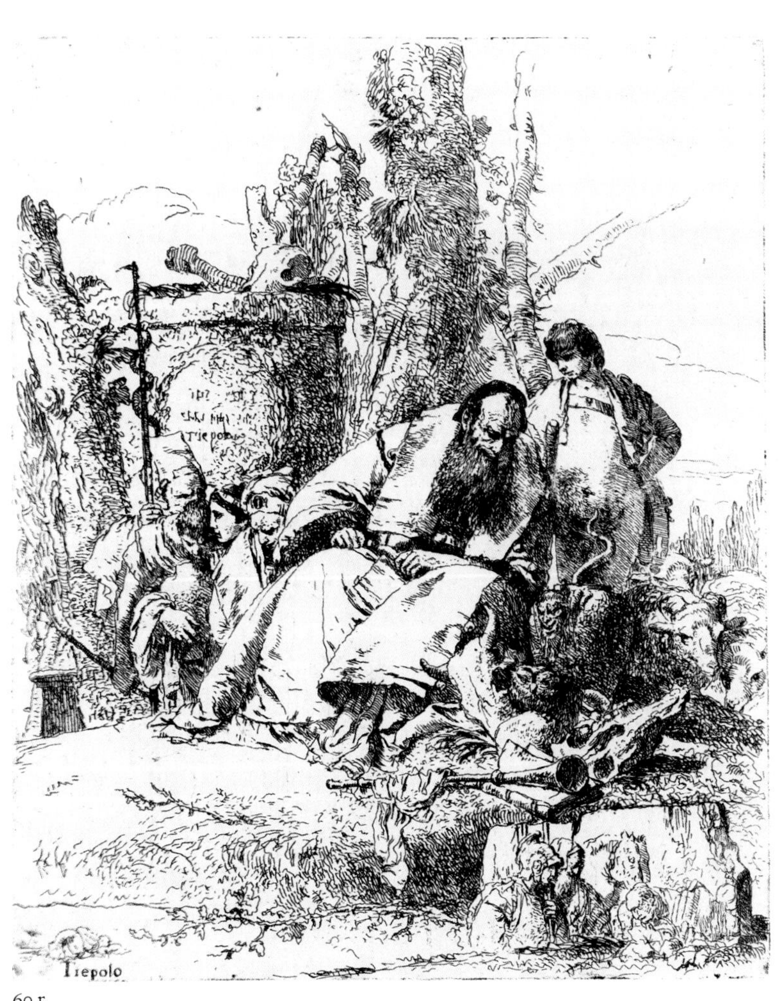

60 r

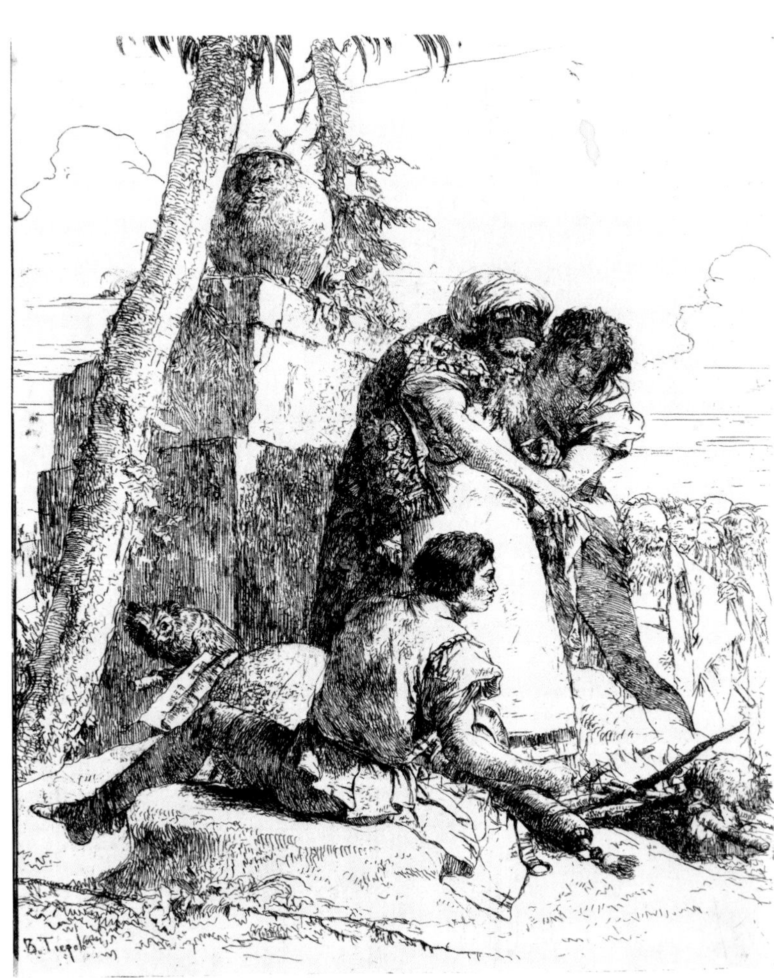

60 s

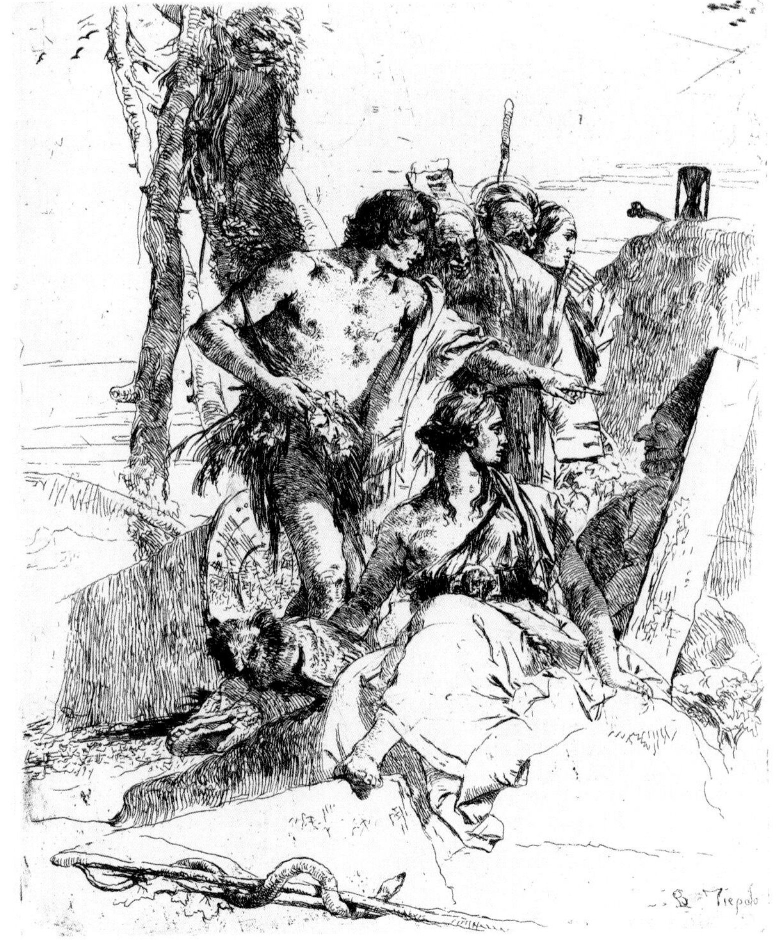

60 t

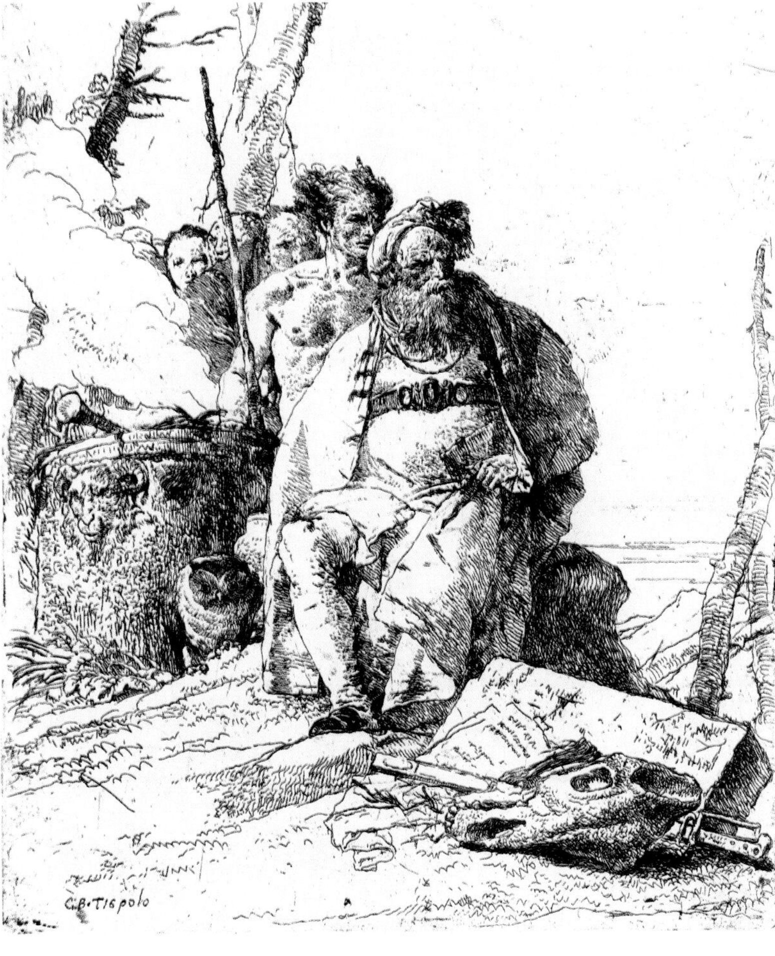

60 u

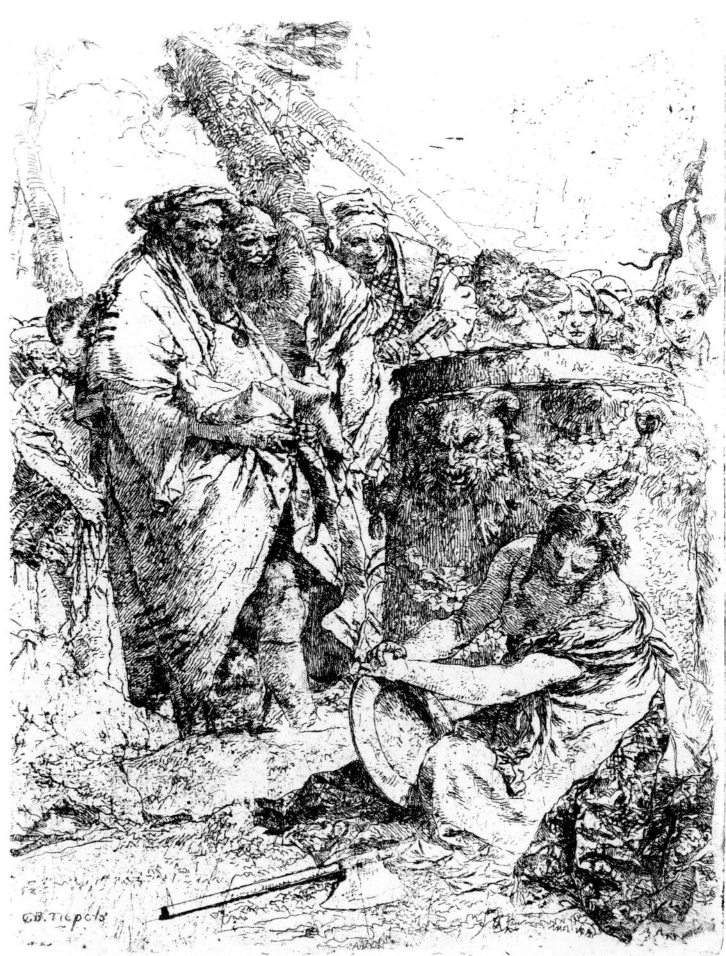

60 v

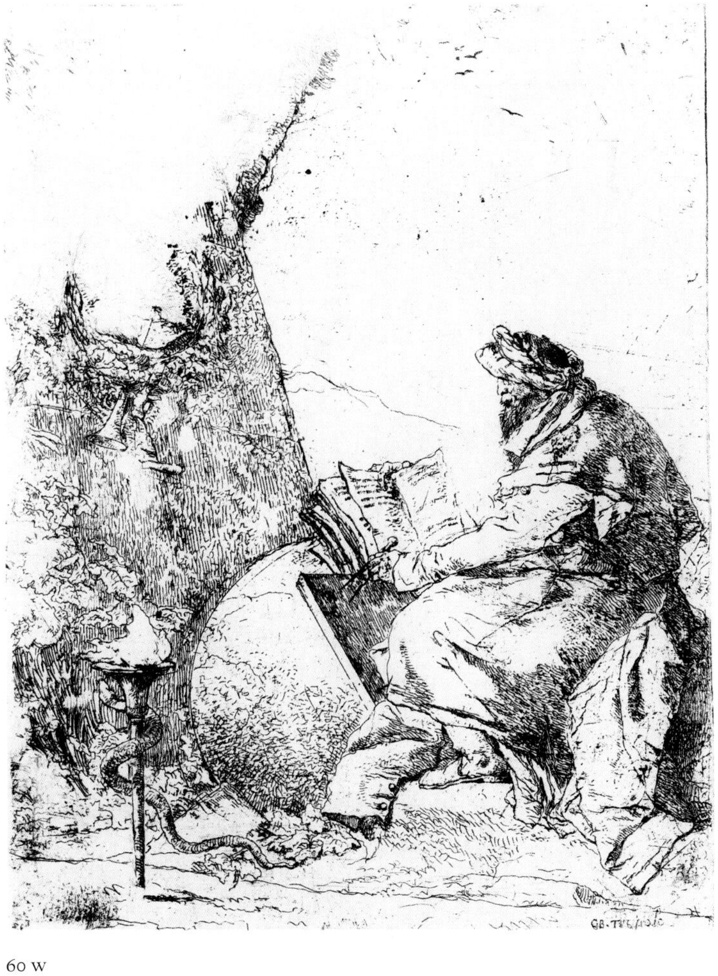

60 w

Bibliography

Acta Sanctorum
1863–1931 *Acta Sanctorum*. Edited by the Bollandist Fathers. 67 vols. in 69. Paris.

Aguirre, G. I. de
1725 *Considerazione per recitare sessantatre corone a nostra signora*. Trent.

Aikema, Bernard
1982 "Early Tiepolo Studies, 1: The Ospedaletto Problem." *Mitteilungen des Kunsthistorischen Institutes in Florenz* 26, pp. 339–82.
1986 "Nicolò Bambini e Giambattista Tiepolo nel Salone di Palazzo Sandi a Venezia." *Arte veneta* 40, pp. 167–71.
1987a "Le decorazioni di palazzo Barbaro-Curtis a Venezia fino alla metà del settecento." *Arte veneta* 41, pp. 147–53.
1987b "Quattro note su Giovanni Battista Tiepolo giovane." *Mitteilungen des Kunsthistorischen Institutes in Florenz* 31, pp. 441–54.
1994 "A Group of Drawings by Francesco Algarotti." *Apollo* 140 (September), pp. 58–64.
1995 "Carracci *redivivus*: Sull'importanza dell'arte Bolognese-Romana per gli inizi di Giambattista Tiepolo." In *Terzo incontro in ricordo di Michelangelo Muraro*, pp. 41–51. Sossano.

Aikema, Bernard, and Dulcia Meijers
1989 *Nel Regno dei Poveri: Arte e storia dei grandi ospedali veneziani in età moderna, 1474–1797*. Venice.

Albrizzi, Giovanni Battista
1740 *Forestiere illuminato intorno le cose più rare e curiose, antichi e moderne della città di Venezia, e dell'isole circonvicine. . . .* Venice.
1760 "Memorie intorno alla vita di Giambattista Piazzetta." In *Studi di pittura già disegnati da Giambattista Piazzetta. . . .* Venice.
1772 *Forestiero illuminato intorno le cose più rare e curiose, antiche e moderne della città di Venezia, e dell'isole circonvicine. . . .* Venice.

Alfonso de' Liguori
1750 *Le Glorie di Maria*. 1750. New ed., Bassano, 1828.

Algarotti, Francesco
1762 *Essai sur la peinture*. Facsimile ed., Geneva, 1972.
1763a *Saggio sopra l'accademia di Francia che è in Roma*. Livorno. Reprinted in *Saggi*, edited by Giovanni da Pozzo, pp. 1–27. Bari, 1963.
1763b *Saggio sopra la pittura*. Livorno. Preface dated 1762. Reprinted in *Saggi*, edited by Giovanni da Pozzo, pp. 53–144. Bari, 1963.
1763c *Saggio sopra l'opera in musica*. Pisa. Preface dated 1762. Reprinted in *Saggi*, edited by Giovanni da Pozzo, pp. 145–223. Bari, 1963.
1764–65 *Opere del Conte Algarotti. . . .* 9 vols. Livorno.
1784 *Opere del Conte Algarotti. . . .* Vol. 10. Cremona.
n.d. "Relazione storica de quadri acquistati dal Co: Francesco Algarotti per la Maestà del Rè di Polonia Elettor di Sassonia. . . ." Ms. Cicogna 3007, fasc. 122, Biblioteca del Museo Civico Correr, Venice.

Alpers, Svetlana
1971 *The Decoration of the Torre de la Parada*. London.

Alpers, Svetlana, and Michael Baxandall
1994 *Tiepolo and the Pictorial Intelligence*. New Haven.

Amerio Tardito, Rosalba
1975 "Su alcuni dipinti inediti." *Arte lombarda* 42/43, pp. 174–78.

Andersson, Ulrike
1984 "Giovanni Battista Tiepolo in der Villa Valmarana ai nani." Ph.D. dissertation, University of Munich.

Anguillara, Giovanni Andrea dell'
1669 *Le* Metamorfosi *d'Ovidio*. Venice.

Arslan, Wart
1932 "Gian Battista Tiepolo e G. M. Morlaiter ai Gesuati." *Rivista di Venezia* 11, pp. 19–26.
1934 *La Pinacoteca Civica di Vicenza*. Rome.
1935–36 "Studi sulla pittura del primo settecento veneziano." *Critica d'arte* 1, pp. 184–97, 238–50.

Art Institute
1961 *Paintings in the Art Institute of Chicago: A Catalogue of the Picture Collection*. Chicago.

Ashton, Mark
1978 "Allegory, Fact, and Meaning in Giambattista Tiepolo's Four Continents in Würzburg." *Art Bulletin* 60, pp. 109–25.

Askew, Pamela
1969 "The Angelic Consolation of St. Francis of Assisi in Post-Tridentine Italian Painting." *Journal of the Warburg and Courtauld Institutes* 32, pp. 280–306.

Augsburg
1991 *Mythos und bürgerliche Welt: Die Karl und Magdalene Haberstock-Stiftung. Gemälde und Zeichnungen*. Edited by Gode Kramer. Exh. cat. Augsburg: Städtische Kunstsammlungen Augsburg. Munich.

Aurnhammer, Achim
1994 *Torquato Tasso im deutschen Barock*. Tübingen.
1995 *Torquato Tasso in Deutschland: Seine Wirkung in Literatur, Kunst und Musik seit der Mitte des 18. Jahrhunderts*. Berlin.

Avena, Antonio
1937 *Il Museo di Castelvecchio a Verona*. Rome.

Baldinucci, Filippo
1681 *Vocabolario toscana dell'arte del disegno. . . .* Florence.

Ballarin, A., ed.
1982 *Pinacoteca di Vicenza*. Vicenza.

Baltrušaitis, Jurgis
1957 *Aberrations: Quatre essais sur la legende des formes*. Paris.

Barbaglia, Susanna
1981 *L'opera completa del Cellini*. Milan.
Barbieri, Franco
1962 *Il Museo Civico di Vicenza: Dipinti e scultura*. Vol. 2, *XVI al XVIII secolo*. Venice.
1987 *Vicenza, città di palazzi*. Milan.
Barcham, William L.
1979 "Giambattista Tiepolo's Ceiling for S. Maria di Nazareth in Venice: Legend, Traditions, and Devotions." *Art Bulletin* 61, pp. 430–47.
1983 "The Cappella Sagredo in San Francesco della Vigna." *Artibus et historiae* 7, pp. 101–24.
1984 "Costume in the Frescoes of Tiepolo and Eighteenth-Century Italian Opera." In *Opera and Vivaldi*, edited by M. Collins and E. Kirk, pp. 149–69. Austin.
1989 *The Religious Paintings of Giambattista Tiepolo: Piety and Tradition in Eighteenth-Century Venice*. Oxford.
1992 *Giambattista Tiepolo*. New York.
1993 "Il 'Trionfo di Flora' di Giambattista Tiepolo: Una Primavera per Dresda." *Arte veneta* 45, pp. 70–77.
Barrès, Maurice
1889 *Un homme libre*. Paris.
Bartoli, Francesco
1793 *Le pitture, sculture, ed architetture della città di Rovigo*. Venice.
Basan, François
1767 *Dictionnaire des graveurs anciens et moderns depuis l'origine de la graveur. . . .* 2 vols. Paris.
Bassi, Elena
1962 *L'architettura del sei e settecento a Venezia*. Naples.
1987 *Ville delle provincia di Venezia*. Milan.
Battilotti, Donatella
1990 "'Lusso plausibile' e senza 'frivolità': Un celebre avvocato, una villa, due palazzi." In Vicenza 1990, pp. 297–305.
Battisti, Eugenio
1960 "Postille documentarie su artisti italiani a Madrid e sulla collezione Maratta." *Arte antica e moderna*, no. 9, pp. 77–89.
Baudi di Vesme, Alessandro
1906 *Le peintre-graveur italien; ouvrage faisant suite au Peintre-graveur de Bartsch*. Milan.
Bauer, Hermann
1984 "Einige Bemerkungen zur Ölskizze im venezianischen settecento." In *Beiträge zur Geschichte der Ölskizze vom 16. bis 18. Jahrhundert*, pp. 89–92. Braunschweig.
Bean, Jacob, and William Griswold
1990 *Eighteenth Century Italian Drawings in The Metropolitan Museum of Art*. New York.
Bell, Daniel
1987 "Tiepolo's 'Betrothal': A Virtue in the History of Women." *Arte veneta* 41, pp. 159–62.
Bellina, Anna Laura, and Bruno Brizi
1985 "Il Melodramma." In *Storia della cultural veneta*, edited by Girolamo Arnaldi and M. Pastore Stocchi, vol. 5, part 1, *Il settecento*, pp. 337–400. Vicenza.
Bellori, Giovanni Pietro
1672 *Le vite de' pittori, scultori, e architetti moderni*. Rome. Reprint, edited by E. Borea, Turin, 1976.
Benedict XIII
1728 *Sermoni sopra il Purgatorio*. Padua.
Benesch, Otto
1957 "Tiepolo und die malerische Aufgabe des Freskos im Settecento." *Münchner Jahrbuch der bildenden Kunst*, ser. 3, 8, pp. 211–32.
Bennassuti, Giuseppe
1831 *Guida e compendio storico della città di Verona e cenni intorno alla sua provincia con tavole*. 2d ed. Verona.
Berenson, Bernard
1913 *Catalogue of a Collection of Paintings and Some Art Objects*. Vol. 1, *Italian Paintings*. Philadelphia.
Bergeret, Pierre Jacques Onésyme
1895 "Voyage d'Italie." *Bulletin et mémoires de la Société des Antiquaires de l'Ouest, 1894*, 17. Paris.
Bettinelli, Saverio
1769 "Dell'entusiasmo delle belle arti." In *Opere di Francesco Algarotti e di Saverio Bettinelli*, edited by Ettore Bonora. Milan, 1969.
Bettini, Sergio
1968–69 "La figura umana nella pittura veneziana del settecento." In *Atti dell'Istituto Veneto di Scienze, Lettere, ed Arti* 127.
Biadego, Giuseppe, ed.
1891 *Le vite dei pittori, scultori, e architetti veronesi*, by D. Zannandreis (d. 1836). Verona.
Bianchini, Giuseppe
1897 *La chiesa di Santa Maria dei Derelitti detta "l'Ospedaletto."* Verona and Padua.
Bianco, M. del
1951–52 "Documenti su due pale di Giambattista Tiepolo progettate per S. Marco a Roma." *Atti dell'Istituto Veneto di Scienze, Lettere, ed Arti* 110, pp. 283–90.
Biancolini, Giovanni Battista Giuseppe, and Giovanni Bragadino
1749 *Notizie storiche delle chiese di Verona raccolte da Giambattista Biancolini all'illustriss. e reverendiss. monsignor Giovanni Bragadino. . . .* 2 parts in 1 vol. Verona.
Biasutti, Guglielmo
1957 *I libri 'de scossi, e spessi' del Card. Danielo Delfino ultimo patriarca d'Aquileia (1734–62)*. Udine.
1958 *Guida turistico-artistica del Palazzo Arcivescovile di Udine*. Udine.
Bibliotheca Sanctorum
1961–69 *Bibliotheca Sanctorum*. 12 vols. Rome.
Biscaccia, Nicolò
1846 *L'Accademia dei Concordi in Rovigo: Illustrata da Nicolò Biscaccia*. Venice.
Blanc, Charles
1868 *Histoire des peintres de toutes les écoles: École vénitienne*. Paris.
Bloomington
1979 *Domenico Tiepolo's Punchinello Drawings*, by Marcia E. Vetrocq. Exh. cat. Bloomington: Indiana University Art Museum.
Blum, André S.
1928 *Histoire du costume: Les modes au XVIIe et au XVIIIe siècle*. Paris.

Blunt, Anthony
1954 *The Italian Drawings at Windsor Castle*. Vol. 12, *The Drawings of G. B. Castiglione and Stefano della Bella*. London.
1966 *The Paintings of Nicolas Poussin: Critical Catalogue*. London.

Bordeaux
1956 *De Tiepolo à Goya*, by Gilberte Martin-Méry. Exh. cat. Bordeaux: Galerie des Beaux-Arts.

Bordeaux, Jean-Luc
1974 "François Le Moyne's Painted Ceiling in the 'Salon d'Hercule' at Versailles: A Long Overdue Study." *Gazette des Beaux-Arts*, ser. 6, 83, pp. 301–18.

Borenius, Tancred
1932 "The Stefan von Auspitz Collection." *Burlington Magazine* 61, pp. 287–88.

Bortolan, Gino
1973 "Asterischi d'archivio per il '700 veneziano." *Notizie da Palazzo Albani* 2, no. 3, pp. 49–53.

Bortoluzzi, F.
1994 *Bernardo Ziliotti, 1716–1783: Incisor veneto del '700*. Borso del Grappa.

Boschini, Marco
1674 *Le ricche minere della pittura veneziana*. Venice.

Boselli, Camillo
1971 "Nuove fonti per la storia dell'arte. L'archivio dei conti Gambara presso la Civica Biblioteca Queriniana di Brescia: I. Il carteggio." *Memorie dell'Istituto Veneto di Scienze, Lettere, ed Arti*.

Bott, Gerhard
1963 "Giovanni Battista Tiepolo: Das Fresko im Treppenhaus der Würzburger Residenz." *Werkmonographien zur bildenden Kunst in Reclams Universal-Bibliothek* 92, pp. 140–64.

Bottari, Giovanni G., and Stefano Ticozzi
1822–25 *Raccolta di lettere sulla pittura, scultura, ed architettura scritte da' più celebri personaggi dei secoli XV, XVI, e XVII*. 8 vols. Milan. First published Rome, 1754–68.

Braham, Helen, comp.
1981 *The Princes Gate Collection*. London.

Brandolese, Pietro
1795a *Del genio dei Lendinaresi per la pittura*. Padua. Reprint, edited by Vittorio Sgarbi, Rovigo, 1990.
1795b *Pitture, sculture di Padova*. Padua.

Brejon de Lavergnée, Arnauld
1980 *Dijon, Musée Magnin: Catalogue des tableaux et dessins italiens (XVe–XIXe siècles)*. Inventaire des collections publiques françaises, 24. Paris.

Brigstocke, Hugh
1978 *Italian and Spanish Paintings in the National Gallery of Scotland*. Edinburgh.
1993 *Italian and Spanish Paintings in the National Gallery of Scotland*. 2d ed. Edinburgh.

Brown, Beverly
1988 "Paolo Veronese's *The Martyrdom and Last Communion of Saint Lucy*." *Venezia arti* 2, pp. 61–68.

Brunel, Georges
1991 *Tiepolo*. Mesnil-sur-l'Estrée.

Brunetti, Mario
1951 "Un eccezionale collegio peritale: Piazzetta, Tiepolo, Longhi." *Arte veneta* 5, pp. 158–60.

Buckley, C.
1955 "An Early Work by Giovanni Battista Tiepolo." *Wadsworth Atheneum Bulletin*, ser. 2, no. 54 (February), p. 1.

Burollet, Thérèse
1980 *Musée Cognacq-Jay*. Vol. 1, *Peintures et dessins*. Paris.

Burroughs, Bryson
1924 "A Masterpiece by Tiepolo." *Bulletin of The Metropolitan Museum of Art, New York* 19, pp. 14–16.

Butler's Lives of the Saints
1956 *Butler's Lives of the Saints*, by Alban Butler. Edited, revised, and supplemented by Herbert Thurston and Donald Attwater. 4 vols. New York.

Büttner, Frank
1979 "Die Sonne Frankens: Ikonographie des Freskos im Treppenhaus der Würzburger Residenz." *Münchner Jahrbuch der bildenden Kunst*, ser. 3, 30, pp. 159–86.
1980 *Giovanni Battista Tiepolo: Die Fresken in der Residenz zu Würzburg*. Würzburg.

Byam Shaw, James
1962 *The Drawings of Domenico Tiepolo*. London.
1970 "The Biron Collection of Venetian Eighteenth-Century Drawings at the Metropolitan Museum." *Metropolitan Museum Journal* 3, pp. 235–58.

Cacciaguerra, Bonsignore
1740 *Pie e divote meditazioni con la Celebre Meditazione di S. Luigi Gonzaga intorno a' SS. Angeli*. Padua.

Cadogan, Jean K., ed.
1991 *Wadsworth Atheneum Paintings, II: Italy and Spain, Fourteenth through Nineteenth Centuries*. Hartford.

Cailleux, Jean
[1972] "Tiepolo et Boucher (1696–1770)." In *Celebrazioni tiepoleschi: Atti del Congresso Internazionale di Studi sul Tiepolo [Udine, 25 September–1 October 1970]*, pp. 86–101. Milan, n.d.

Calvi, Felice
1885 *Famiglie notabili milanesi*. Vol. 4. Milan.

Cambridge, Mass.
1970 *Tiepolo, a Bicentenary Exhibition, 1770–1970: Drawings, Mainly from American Collections, by Giambattista Tiepolo and the Members of His Circle*, by George Knox. Exh. cat. Cambridge, Mass.: Fogg Art Museum, Harvard University.

Camon Aznar, José
1977 *La pintura española del siglo XVII*. Madrid.

Campbell, Lorne
1990 *Renaissance Portraits: European Portrait-Painting in the 14th, 15th, and 16th Centuries*. New Haven.

Campori, Giuseppe
1870 *Raccolta di cataloghi ed inventarii inediti di quadri, statue, disegni . . . dal secolo XV al secolo XIX*. Modena.

Cantalamessa, G.
1902 "La Galleria di Venezia." *Le gallerie nazionale italiane* 5, pp. 22–60.

Carboni, Giovanni Battista
1760 *Le pitture e sculture di Brescia*. Brescia.

Chennevières, Henry de
1896 "Les Tiepolo de l'Hôtel Édouard André." *Gazette des Beaux-Arts*, ser. 3, 15, pp. 121–30.
1898 *Les Tiepolo*. Paris.
Chiappini di Sorio, Ileana
1983 "Palazzo Pisani Moretta: Restauri e decorazioni (Angeli, Piazzetta, Tiepolo, Guarana)." *Notizie da Palazzo Albani* 12, no. 1–2, pp. 264–73.
Chicago
1938 *Loan Exhibition of Paintings, Drawings, and Prints by the Two Tiepolos, Giambattista and Giandomenico*, by [Daniel C. Rich]. Exh. cat. Chicago: Art Institute.
Cochin, Charles-Nicolas
1758 *Voyage d'Italie; ou, Recueil de notes sur les ouvrages de peinture et de sculpture, qu'on voit dans les principales villes d'Italie*. 3 vols. Paris. Facsimile reprint, edited by C. Michel, Rome, 1991.
Conisbee, Philip
1981 *Painting in Eighteenth Century France*. Oxford.
Conticella, Valentina
1996 Paper to be delivered at the Tiepolo conference, Venice, Fall 1996. Forthcoming.
Corner, Flaminio
1749 *Ecclesiae venetae, antiquis monumentis. . . .* 13 vols. Venice.
Coronelli, Vincenzo
1724 *Guida de' Forestieri Sacro-Profana per osservare il più ragguardevole nella città di Venezia*. Venice.
1741 *Nome, Cognome: Età de' Veneti patrizi*. Venice.
Coutts, Howard
1982 "A Ricci Pastiche or a Copy of a Lost Veronese?" *Arte veneta* 36, pp. 230–32.
Cropper, Elizabeth
1976 "On Beautiful Women, Parmigianino, *Petrarchismo*, and the Vernacular Style." *Art Bulletin* 58, pp. 374–94.
1986 "The Beauty of Woman: Problems in the Rhetoric of Renaissance Portraiture." In *Rewriting the Renaissance: The Discourses of Sexual Difference in Early Modern Europe*, edited by Margaret W. Ferguson, Maureen Quilligan, and Nancy Vickers, pp. 175–90. Chicago.
da Canal, Vincenzo
1732 *Vita di Gregorio Lazzarini*. Edited by Giovanni Antonio Moschini. Venice, 1809.
1810 "Della maniera del dipengere moderno." In *Mercurio filisofico letterario e poetico*, no. 3. Venice.
Dall'Acqua-Giusti, Antonio
1873 "L'Accademia e la Galleria di Venezia. Due Relazioni storiche per l'esposizione di Vienna del 1873: I. L'Accademia." *Atti della R. Accademia di Belle Arti in Venezia*, pp. 5–73.
Daniels, Jeffery
1976 *Sebastiano Ricci*. Hove.
da Persico, Giovanni Battista
1820 *Descrizione di Verona e della sua Provincia*. Verona.
Darmstadt
1965 *Visionen des Barock: Entwürfe aus der Sammlung Kurt Rossacher*. Exh. cat. Darmstadt: Hessisches Landesmuseum.
Dazzi, Manlio
1925 "Rovigo nel '700." *Cronache d'arte* 2, no. 1, pp. 68–76.
1951 "Schedà per il *Procuratore* di G. B. Tiepolo." *Arte veneta* 5, pp. 178–85.
Dazzi, Manlio, and Ettore Merkel
1979 *Catalogo della Pinacoteca della Fondazione Scientifica Querini Stampalia*. Vicenza.
De Grazia, Diane
1993 "Giambattista Tiepolo e la regina Zenobia." *Ca' de Sass* 123, pp. 2–7.
De Grazia, Diane, and Eric Garberson
1996 *The Collections of the National Gallery of Art, Systematic Catalogue: Italian Paintings of the Seventeenth and Eighteenth Century*. Washington, D.C.
De Logu, Giuseppe, and Guido Marinelli
1975–76 *Il ritratto nella pittura italiana*. 2 vols. Bergamo.
Deluca, Giannantonio
1760 *Orazione del Dolore che ne venne a San Giuseppe per la circoncisione di Gesù*. Venice.
Dempsey, Charles
1972 "Tiepolo Etchings at Washington." *Burlington Magazine* 114 (July), pp. 503–7.
Derschau, J. von
1916 "Irrige Zuschreibungen an Sebastiano Ricci." *Monatshefte für Kunstwissenschaft* 9, pp. 161–69.
1922 *Sebastiano Ricci: Ein Beitrag zu den Anfängen der venezianischen Rokokomalerei*. Heidelberg.
De Vito Battaglia, Silvia
1931 "Le opere di G. B. Tiepolo nella Chiesa dell'Ospedaletto a Venezia." *Rivista del Reale Istituto d'Archeologia e Storia dell'Arte* 3, pp. 189–206.
1934 "Precisazioni intorno agli Apostoli dell'Ospedaletto." *Rivista di Venezia* 13 (November), pp. 475–82.
Diderot, Denis
1765 "Observations sur le Salon de Peinture de 1765." In *Essais sur la peinture*. Paris, 1793.
Dodgson, Campbell
1917 "The Three Versions of Tiepolo's Phaëthon." *Burlington Magazine* 31, pp. 228–33.
Dolfin, N. H.
1924 *I Dolfin (Delfino): Patrizi veneziani nella storia di Venezia dall'anno 452 al 1923*. Milan.
Domenichini, Riccardo
1983–84 "Elementi per la ricostruzione dell'attività artistica di Gerolamo Mengozzi Colonna." *Civici Musei Veneziani d'Arte e di Storia: Bollettino* 28, pp. 41–49.
Donato, Maria Monica
1985 "Gli eroi romani tra storia ed 'exemplum': I primi cieli umanistici di Uomini Famosi." In *Memoria dell'antico nell'arte italiana*, edited by Salvatore Settis, vol. 2, pp. 97–152. Turin.
Ebert-Schifferer, Sybille
1992 "'Ma c'hanno da fare i precetti dell'oratore con quelli della pittura?': Reflections on Guercino's Narrative Structure." In *Guercino, Master Painter of the Baroque*, pp. 75–110. Exh. cat. Washington, D.C.: National Gallery.
Eitner, Lorenz, comp.
1970 *Neoclassicism and Romanticism, 1750–1850: Sources and Documents*. 2 vols. Englewood Cliffs, N.J.

Ellero, Giuseppe
1995 "Idillio all'Ospedaletto: Un documento d'archivio su Cecilia Guardi, futura sposa di Giovan Battista Tiepolo." *Arte/documento* 9.

Ewald, Gerhard
1965 *Johann Carl Loth, 1632–1698*. Amsterdam.

Fabre, Francisco José
1829 *Descripción de las allegorías pintadas en las bóvedas del Real Palacio de Madrid*. Madrid.

Fahy, Everett, and Francis Watson
1973 *The Wrightsman Collection*. Vol. 5, *Paintings, Drawings*. New York: The Metropolitan Museum of Art.

Fantelli, Pier Luigi, and Mauro Lucco
1985 *Catalogo della Pinacoteca della Accademia dei Concordi di Rovigo*. Vicenza.

Farr, Dennis, ed.
1987 *One Hundred Masterpieces from the Courtauld Collections: Bernardo Daddi to Ben Nicholson; European Paintings and Drawings from the 14th to the 20th Century*. London.

Fasolo, Giulio
1940 *Guida del Museo Civico di Vicenza*. Vicenza.

Fehl, Philipp P.
1979 "Farewell to Jokes: The Last *Capricci* of Giovanni Domenico Tiepolo and the Tradition of Irony in Venetian Painting." *Critical Inquiry* 5, pp. 761–91.
1992 *Decorum and Wit: The Poetry of Venetian Painting. Essays in the History of the Classical Tradition*. Vienna.

Ferino-Pagden, Sylvia, Wolfgang Prohaska, and Karl Schütz
1991 *Die Gemäldegalerie des Kunsthistorischen Museums in Wien: Verzeichnis der Gemälde*. Vienna.

Ferrara
1985 *Torquato Tasso tra letteratura, musica, teatro, e arti figurative*. Edited by Andrea Buzzoni. Exh. cat. Ferrara: Castello Estense.

Ferrari, Oreste, and Giuseppe Scavizzi
1966 *Luca Giordano*. 3 vols. Rome.
1992 *Luca Giordano: L'opera completa*. 2 vols. Naples.

Fiocco, Giuseppe
1925 *Palazzo Pesaro*. Venice.
1926 "Lorenzo Tiepolo." *Bolletino d'arte*, ser. 2, 5, no. 1 (July), pp. 17–28.
1929a "La pittura veneziana alla mostra del settecento." *Rivista della città di Venezia* 8, pp. 497–581.
1929b *La pittura veneziana del seicento e settecento*. Verona. Also published in English.
1931 "The Castiglioni Tiepolos at Vienna." *Burlington Magazine* 58 (April), pp. 168–74.
1932 "Due nuovi Tiepolo." *Dedalo* 12, pp. 470–76.
1938 "An Early Work by G. B. Tiepolo." *Art in America* 26 (October), pp. 147–57.
1940 *Pitture del settecento italiano in Portogallo*. Opere d'arte, 10. Rome.
1966 "Tiepolo e Fontebasso." *Bollettino dei Musei Civici Veneziani* 11, no. 1, pp. 1–9.

Fiorio, Maria Teresa, and Mercedes Garberi
1987 *La Pinacoteca del Castello Sforzesco*. Milan.

Florence
1922 *Mostra della pittura italiana del seicento e del settecento*, by Nello Tarchiani. Exh. cat. Florence: Palazzo Pitti.

Florio, Daniele
[1747] *Poetici componimenti per le gloriosissime nozze di S.S.E.E. il Sig. Giovanni Delfino e la Sig. Bianca Contarini*. Venice, n.d.

Florus, Lucius Annaeus
1929 *Epitome of Roman History*. Translated by E. S. Forster. London.

Fogolari, Gino
1908 "Ritrovamento di un dipinto di G. B. Tiepolo." *Bollettino d'arte* [2] (January), p. 115.
1913 *G. B. Tiepolo nel Veneto*. Milan.
1923 "Dipinti giovanili di G. B. Tiepolo: Nuovi acquisti e attribuzioni delle Gallerie dell'Accademia di Venezia." *Bollettino d'arte*, ser. 2, 3, pp. 49–64.
1931 "Il bozzetto del Tiepolo per il trasporto della Santa Casa di Loreto." *Bollettino d'arte*, ser. 3, 25, no. 1 (July), pp. 18–32.
1942 "Lettere inedite di G. B. Tiepolo." *Nuova antologia* 1 (September), pp. 32–37.

Fontana, G.
1967 *Venezia monumentale: I palazzi (1845–63)*. Edited by L. Moretti. Venice.

Fort Worth
1993 *Giambattista Tiepolo: Master of the Oil Sketch*, by Beverly L. Brown; with essays by Terisio Pignatti, Oreste Ferrari, Teresa Longyear. Exh. cat. Fort Worth: Kimbell Art Museum.

Franzoi, Umberto, and Dina Di Stefano
1976 *Le chiese di Venezia*. Venice.

Franzoi, Umberto, Terisio Pignatti, and Wolfgang Wolters
1990 *Il Palazzo Ducale di Venezia*. Treviso.

Franzoni, L.
1978 "Pietro Rotari e gli antichi marmi del Museo Trevisani." In Verona 1978.

Freeden, Max H. von, and Carl Lamb
1956 *Das Meisterwerk des Giovanni Battista Tiepolo: Die Fresken der Würzburger Residenz*. Munich.

Frerichs, Lina Christina
1971a "Mariette et les eaux-fortes des Tiepolo." *Gazette des Beaux-Arts*, ser. 6, 78, pp. 233–52.
1971b "Nouvelles sources pour la connaissance de l'activité incisoire de trois Tiepolo." *Nouvelles de l'estampe* 4, pp. 213–28.

Frizzoni, Gustavo
1902 "Illustrazione di alcune opere di Gian Batt. Tiepolo." *Emporium* 16, pp. 271–78.

Fröhlich-Bume, Lili
1932 "Die Sammlung Auspitz-Wien." *Pantheon* 10, pp. 399–400.
1937 "An Exhibition of Italian Baroque Painting." *Burlington Magazine* 71 (August), pp. 93–94.
1938 "Notes on Some Works by Giovanni Battista Tiepolo." *Burlington Magazine* 72 (February), pp. 82–87.
1958 "Sammlung Sir Joseph Robinson." *Weltkunst*, no. 16.

Fry, Roger
1933 "*Cleopatra's Feast* by G. B. Tiepolo." *Burlington Magazine* 63 (September), pp. 131–35.

Gabbrielli, Annamaria
1938 "L'Algarotti e la critica d'arte in Italia nel settecento." *Critica d'arte* 3, pp. 155–69.
Gaetani di Canossa, Isabella
1988 "Tre lettere inedite di Giambattista Tiepolo e altri documenti inediti su Palazzo Canossa." *Verona illustrata* 1, pp. 59–72.
Gallo, Rodolfo
1939 "Le aggiunte di Daniele Farsetti al libro 'Della pittura veneziana' di Antonmaria Zanetti." *Ateneo veneto*, pp. 253–54.
1945 *Una famiglia patrizia: I Pisani ed i Palazzi di S. Stefano e di Stra*. Venice.
Gambier, Madile
1990 "La piccola prostituzione tra sei e settecento." In Venice 1990, pp. 37–39.
Garas, Klára
1965 "Allegorie und Geschichte in der venezianischen Malerei des 18. Jahrhunderts." *Acta Historiae Artium* 11, pp. 275–302.
1968 *La peinture venitienne du XVIIIe siècle*. Budapest: Szépmüvészeti Múzeum. Also published in English as *Eighteenth Century Venetian Paintings*, Budapest, 1968.
1990 "Paolo Veronese—copie, falsi ed imitazioni nel settecento." In Meyer zur Capellen and Roeck 1990, pp. 65–71.
Gardner, Julian
1982 "The Louvre Stigmatization and the Problem of the Narrative Altarpiece." *Zeitschrift für Kunstgeschichte* 45, pp. 217–47.
Gasbarri, C.
1964 "S. Filippo Neri." In *Bibliotheca Sanctorum*, vol. 5, cols. 760–90. Rome.
Gaya Nuño, Juan A.
1964 *Pintura europea perdida por España, de Van Eyck a Tiépolo*. Madrid.
Gemin, Massimo
1990 "Le cortigiane di Venezia e i viaggiatori stranieri." In Venice 1990, pp. 73–79.
Gemin, Massimo, and Filippo Pedrocco
1993 *Giambattista Tiepolo: I dipinti, opera completa*. Venice.
Gerstenberg, Kurt
1952 "Tiepolos Weltbild in Würzburg und Madrid." *Zeitschrift für Kunstgeschichte* 15, pp. 143–62.
Glück, Gustav
1931 *Die Gemäldegalerie des Kunsthistorischen Museums in Wien*. 3d ed. Vienna.
Gnesotto, A.
1915–16 "Francisci Barbari de re uxoria liber." *Atti e memorie della R. Accademia di scienze, lettere, ed arti in Padova*, n.s., 32, pp. 1–107.
Godinez, Miguel
1738 *Practica della Teologia Mistica*. Venice.
Goering, Max
1936 *Italienische Malerei des siebzehnten und achtzehnten Jahrhunderts*. Berlin.
1939 "Tiepolo, Giovanni Battista." In *Allgemeines Lexikon der bildenden Künstler von der Antike bis zur Gegenwart, begründet von Ulrich Thieme und Felix Becker*, edited by Hans Vollmer, vol. 33, pp. 145–59. Leipzig.
1944 "Wenig bekannte und neu gefundene Werke von Giov. Batt. Tiepolo." *Pantheon* 32, pp. 97–110.
González-Palacios, Alvar
1972 "Mostra del Tiepolo." *Arte illustrata* 5, no. 47, pp. 85–87.
Gonzati, Bernardo
1852–53 *La Basilica di S. Antonio di Padova*. 2 vols. Padua.
Gori Gandellini, Giovanni
1771 *Notizie istoriche degl'intagliatori*. 3 vols. Siena.
Gorizia
1983 *Da Carlevarijs ai Tiepolo: Incisori veneti e friulani del settecento*. Edited by Dario Succi. Exh. cat. Gorizia: Musei Provinciale di Palazzo Attems; Venice: Museo Correr.
1985 *Giambattista Tiepolo: Il segno e l'enigma*. Edited by Dario Succi. Exh. cat. Gorizia: Castello di Gorizia.
1988 *Capricci veneziani del settecento*. Edited by Dario Succi. Exh. cat. Gorizia.
Gradenigo, Pietro
1942 "Notatori ed annali del N. H. Pietro Gradenigo, 1748–1774, ms. della B. N. M. e della B. M. C. di Venezia." In *Regia Deputazione di Storia Patri*, edited by Lina Livan. Venice.
Grigorieva, Irina S.
[1976] "Due disegni del Tiepolo già attribuiti a Sebastiano Ricci a Leningrado." In *Atti del Congresso Internazionale di Studi su Sebastiano Ricci e il Suo Tempo*, pp. 140–43. Milan.
Griseri, Andreina
1993 "Dell'interpretazione della natura: Da Juvarra all'Illuminismo." *Arte/documento* 7.
Hadeln, Detlev, Freiherr von
1928 *The Drawings of G. B. Tiepolo*. 2 vols. Florence.
Hagen, R. M., and R. Hagen
1985 "Giovanni Battista Tiepolo, *Der Tod des Hyazinth*: Tennis-Match mit Gott Apoll." *Art, das Kunstmagazin* 7, pp. 66–71.
Hamburger Kunsthalle
1966 *Katalog der alten Meister der Hamburger Kunsthalle*. 5th ed. Hamburg.
Hannegan, Barry
1983 "Antonio Zanchi and the Ceiling of the Salone of the Palazzo Barbaro Curtis." *Arte veneta* 37, pp. 201–5.
Hanon, A.
1953 "Sacré Coeur." In *Dictionnaire de spiritualité*, vol. 2, pp. 1023–46. Paris.
Haskell, Francis
1956 "Stefano Conti, Patron of Canaletto and Others." *Burlington Magazine* 98 (September), pp. 296–300.
1958 "Algarotti and Tiepolo's 'Banquet of Cleopatra.'" *Burlington Magazine* 100 (June), pp. 212–13.
1960 "Francesco Guardi as *Vedutista* and Some of His Patrons." *Journal of the Warburg and Courtauld Institutes* 23, pp. 256–76.
1963 *Patrons and Painters: A Study in the Relations Between Italian Art and Society in the Age of the Baroque*. London.
1967 "Tiepolo e gli artisti del secolo XIX." In *Sensibilità e razionalità nel settecento*, vol. 2. Florence.
1980 *Patrons and Painters: Art and Society in Baroque Italy*. 2d ed., revised. New Haven and London.
Haskell, Francis, and Michael Levey
1958 "Painters and Patrons at the Age of Rococo Exhibition, Munich." *Burlington Magazine* 100 (December), pp. 422–27.

Heckscher, W. S.
1974 "Petites Perceptions: An Account of *Sortes Warburgiane.*" *Journal of Medieval and Renaissance Studies* 4, pp. 101–34.
Hegemann, Hans Werner
1940 *Giovanni Battista Tiepolo*. Berlin.
Heine, Barbara
1974 "Tiepolos Dreifaltigkeitsbild in der Klosterkirche zu Nymphenburg." *Pantheon* 32, pp. 144–52.
Heinemann, Rudolf J.
1937 *Stiftung Sammlung Schloß Rohoncz*. Vols. 1–2. Lugano-Castagnola.
1971 *Sammlung Thyssen-Bornemisza*. Castagnola.
Held, Julius S.
1980 *The Oil Sketches of Peter Paul Rubens: A Critical Catalogue*. 2 vols. Princeton.
Hénard, Robert
1914 "Un tableau de Tiepolo retrouvé." *L'art et les artistes* 18, pp. 218–21.
Hermanin, Federico
1912 "Nuovi acquisti della Galleria Nazionale d'Arte Antica a Palazzo Corsini in Roma." *Bollettino d'arte* 6, pp. 369–82.
Honour, Hugh
1968 *Neo-Classicism*. London.
1980 *Neo-Classicism*. 2d ed., revised. New Haven.
Howard, Deborah
1986 "Giambattista Tiepolo's Frescoes for the Church of the Pietà in Venice." *Oxford Art Journal* 9, no. 1, pp. 11–28.
Ivanoff, Nicola
[**1972**] "La fortuna critica del Tiepolo nel settecento." In *Celebrazioni tiepolesche: Atti del Congresso Internazionale di Studi sul Tiepolo [Udine, 25 September–1 October 1970]*, pp. 51–52. Milan, n.d.
Jones, Leslie
1981 "Peace, Prosperity, and Politics in Tiepolo's *Glory of the Spanish Monarchy*." *Apollo* 114 (October), pp. 220–27.
Jongh, E. de
1968–69 "Erotica in vogelperspectief: De dubbelzinnigheid van een reeks 17de eeuwse genrevoorstellingen." *Simiolus* 3, pp. 22–74.
Joost-Gaugier, Christiane L.
1982 "The Early Beginnings of the Notion of 'Uomini Famosi' and the 'De Viris Illustribus' in Greco-Roman Literary Tradition." *Artibus et Historiae*, no. 6, pp. 97–115.
Joppi, U.
1894 *Contributo IV alla storia dell'arte nel Friuli*. Venice.
1889 "Di un quadro del Tiepolo nel Museo di Udine." *Pagine friulane* 9.
Jouin, Henry A.
1881 *Musée d'Angers: Peintures, sculptures, cartons, miniatures, gouaches, et dessins; collection Bodinier, collection Lenepveu, legs Robin; Musée David. . . .* Angers.
Kaley, D.
1980 *The Church of the Pietà*. Venice.
Karling, Sten I., comp.
1978 *The Stockholm University Collection of Paintings: Catalogue*. Translated by Patrick Smith. Stockholm.
Kay, George R., ed.
1965 *The Penguin Book of Italian Verse*. Reprint of 1958 ed. Baltimore.
Keith, L.
1994 "Giovanni Battista Tiepolo's *Saints Maximus and Oswald*: Conservation and Examination." *National Gallery Technical Bulletin* 15, pp. 37–41.
Kimbell, David
1994 *Italian Opera*. Cambridge.
King, M. L.
1976 "Caldiera and the Barbaros on Marriage and the Family: Humanist Reflections of Venetian Realities." *Journal of Medieval and Renaissance Studies* 6, no. 1, pp. 19–50.
Kiriaki, A. S.
1907 *La chiesa di Sta. Maria dei Derelitti della Casa di Ricovero. . . .* Venice.
Knorn, Nicola
1995 "Tiepolos 'Rinaldo und Armida'—Szenen in der Würzburger Residenz." *Pantheon* 53, pp. 93–107.
Knox, George
1957 Review of Freeden and Lamb 1956. *Burlington Magazine* 99 (April), p. 129.
1960 *Catalogue of the Tiepolo Drawings in the Victoria and Albert Museum*. London.
1961 "The Orloff Album of Tiepolo Drawings." *Burlington Magazine* 103 (June), pp. 269–75.
1964 "Drawings by Giambattista and Domenico Tiepolo at Princeton." *Record of the Art Museum, Princeton University* 23, pp. 2–28.
1965 "A Group of Tiepolo Drawings Owned and Engraved by Pietro Monaco." *Master Drawings* 3, pp. 389–97.
1966 Review of *Le acqueforti dei Tiepolo*, by Terisio Pignatti. *Burlington Magazine* 108 (November), pp. 584–86.
1968 "G. B. Tiepolo and the Ceiling of the Scalzi." *Burlington Magazine* 110, pp. 394–400.
1970 *Domenico Tiepolo: Raccolta di teste*. Milan.
1974 "Giambattista Tiepolo: Variations on the Theme of Anthony and Cleopatra." *Master Drawings* 12, pp. 378–90.
1975a *Catalogue of the Tiepolo Drawings in the Victoria and Albert Museum*. 2d ed., revised. London. First published 1960.
1975b "'Philosopher Portraits' by Giambattista, Domenico, and Lorenzo Tiepolo." *Burlington Magazine* 117 (March), pp. 147–55.
[**1976**] "Some Notes on Large Paintings Depicting Scenes from Antique History by Ricci, Piazzetta, Bambini, and Tiepolo." In *Atti del Congresso Internazionale di Studi su Sebastiano Ricci e il Suo Tempo*, pp. 96–105. Milan.
1978 "The Tasso Cycles of Giambattista Tiepolo and Gianantonio Guardi." *Museum Studies* 9, pp. 49–95.
1979 "Giambattista Tiepolo. Queen Zenobia and Ca' Zenobio: 'Una delle prime sue fatture.'" *Burlington Magazine* 121 (July), pp. 409–18.
1980a *Giambattista and Domenico Tiepolo: A Study and Catalogue Raisonné of the Chalk Drawings*. 2 vols. Oxford.
1980b "Anthony and Cleopatra in Russia: A Problem in the Editing of Tiepolo Drawings." In *Editing Illustrated Books: Papers Given at the Fifteenth Annual Conference on Editorial Problems, University of Toronto, 2–3 November 1979*, edited by W. Blissett, pp. 35–55. New York.

1991 "Tiepolo Triumphant: The Roman History Cycles of Ca' Dolfin, Venice." *Apollo* 134 (November), pp. 301–10.

1992 *Giambattista Piazzetta, 1682–1754*. Oxford.

1993 "Ca' Sandi: *La forza della eloquenza*." *Arte/documento* 7, pp. 135–45.

1996 "Giambattista Tiepolo in Baltimore: A Painting in Search of a Subject." *Apollo* 143 (June), pp. 15–17.

Knox, George, and James Byam Shaw

1987 *The Robert Lehman Collection, VI: Italian Eighteenth-Century Drawings*. New York.

Knox, Ronald A.

1950 *Enthusiasm, a Chapter in the History of Religion, with Special Reference to the XVII and XVIII Centuries*. New York.

Kossatz, Tilman

1996 "Quellen zum Würzburger Werk Giovanni Battista Tiepolos und seiner Söhne." In Würzburg 1996, vol. 2, pp. 165–81.

Kress Collection

1953 *The Samuel H. Kress Collection in the Isaac Delgado Museum of Art*. New Orleans.

Kunze, Irene, ed.

1931 *Die Gemäldegalerie*. Vol. 3, *Die italienischen Meister, 16. bis 18. Jahrhundert*. Berlin.

Lacombe, Jacques

1768 *Dizionario portatile delle Belle Arti. . . .* Venice.

Lanceni, Giovanni Battista

1733 *Verona illustrata*. Verona.

Lanzi, Luigi A.

1795–96 *Storia pittorica della Italia*. 2 vols. in 3. Bassano. Rev. ed., Florence, 1970.

Lee, Rensselaer W.

1961 "Armida's Abandonment: A Study in Tasso Iconography before 1700." In *De Artibus Opuscula: Essays in Honor of Erwin Panofsky*, pp. 335–49. New York.

1967 *Ut Pictura Poesis: The Humanistic Theory of Painting*. New York.

Lenz, Christian

1996 "Così felice, e giudizioso imitatore: Giambattista Tiepolo als Nachahmer Paolo Veroneses." In Würzburg 1996, vol. 2, pp. 63–69.

Leonardo da Porto Maurizio

1759 *Metodo pratico di fare il sacro esercizio della Via Crucis*. 2d ed. Rome.

Lépicié, François Bernard

1752 *Vies des premiers peintres du roi, depuis M. Le Brun, jusqu'à présent*. Paris.

Leroi, Paul

1876 "Italia sara de se." *L'art* 2, no. 4.

Lesure, François

1972 *L'Opéra classique français, XVIIe et XVIIIe siècles*. Geneva.

Levey, Michael

1955 "Tiepolo's 'Banquet of Cleopatra' at Melbourne." *Arte veneta* 9, pp. 199–203.

1957 "Tiepolo's Treatment of Classical Story at Villa Valmarana: A Study in Eighteenth-Century Iconography and Aesthetics." *Journal of the Warburg and Courtauld Institutes* 20, pp. 298–317.

1959 *Painting in XVIIIth-Century Venice*. London.

1960a "Count Seilern's Italian Pictures and Drawings." *Burlington Magazine* 102 (March), pp. 122–23.

1960b "Tiepolo and His Age." In *Art and Ideas in Eighteenth-Century Italy*, pp. 94–113. Rome.

1960c "Two Paintings by Tiepolo from the Algarotti Collection." *Burlington Magazine* 102 (June), pp. 250–57.

1961 "The Eighteenth-Century Italian Painting Exhibition at Paris: Some Corrections and Suggestions." *Burlington Magazine* 103 (April), pp. 139–43.

1963 Review of Morassi 1962. *Art Bulletin* 45, pp. 293–95.

1965 *Tiepolo's Banquet of Cleopatra*. Newcastle upon Tyne.

1966 *Rococo to Revolution: Major Trends in Eighteenth-Century Painting*. London.

1971 *The Seventeenth and Eighteenth Century Italian Schools*. National Gallery Catalogues. London.

1978 "Three Slight Revisions to Tiepolo Scholarship." *Arte veneta* 32, pp. 418–22.

1986 *Giambattista Tiepolo: His Life and Art*. New Haven. Also published in Italian as *Giambattista Tiepolo: La sua vita, la sua arte*, Milan, 1988. 2d printing with corrections, New Haven, 1994.

Levi D'Ancona, Mirella

1957 *The Iconography of the Immaculate Conception in the Middle Ages and Early Renaissance*. New York.

Lewis, Douglas

1979 *The Late Baroque Churches of Venice*. New York. Originally the author's Ph.D. dissertation, Yale University, New Haven, 1967.

1988 "Freemasonic Imagery in a Venetian Fresco Cycle of 1716." In *Hermeticism and the Renaissance: Intellectual History and the Occult in Early Modern Europe*, edited by I. Merkel and A. Debus, pp. 366–99. Washington, D.C.

Lippman, Edward

1992 *A History of Western Musical Aesthetics*. Lincoln, Neb.

Loche, Renée, and Marcel Roethlisberger

1978 *L'opera completa di Liotard*. Milan.

London

1961 *From Van Eyck to Tiepolo: An Exhibition of Pictures from the Thyssen-Bornemisza Collection, 'Villa Favorita,' Lugano-Castagnola*. 2 vols. Exh. cat. London: National Gallery.

1994 *The Glory of Venice: Art in the Eighteenth Century*. Edited by Jane Martineau and Andrew Robison. Exh. cat. London: Royal Academy of Arts.

1995 *The Age of Elegance: Paintings from the Rijksmuseum in Amsterdam, 1700–1800*, by Wiepke Loos, Guido Jansen, and Wouter Kloek. Exh. cat. London: National Gallery.

Longhi, Roberto

1946 *Viatico per cinque secoli di pittura veneziana*. Florence.

1961 *Scritti giovanili, 1912–1922*. 2 vols. Florence.

Lorenzetti, Giulio

1926 *Venezia e il suo estuario: Guida storico-artistica*. Venice. 2d ed., Rome, 1956.

1936 *Ca' Rezzonico*. Venice.

1942 *Das Jahrhundert Tiepolos*. Vienna.

1961 *Venice and Its Lagoon: Historical-Artistic Guide*. Rome.

Lorenzetti, Giulio, and Leo Planiscig
1934 *La collezione dei Conti Donà dalle Rose a Venezia*. Venice.
Los Angeles
1988 *Guido Reni, 1575–1642*. Exh. cat. Los Angeles: Los Angeles County Museum of Art.
Lugt, Frits
1953 *Répertoire des catalogue de ventes publiques. . . .* Vol. 2, *Deuxième période, 1826–1860*. The Hague.
MacLaren, Neil, and Christopher Brown
1991 *National Gallery Catalogues: The Dutch School, 1600–1900*. 2d ed., revised and expanded by Christopher Brown. 2 vols. London.
Maffei, Scipione
1731–32 *Verona illustrata. . . .* 4 vols. Verona.
Malvasia, Carlo C.
1841 *Felsina pittrice: Vite de' pittori bolognesi*. Edited by Giampietro Zanotti. 2 vols. Bologna. First published Bologna, 1678.
Manno, Antonio, and Sandro Sponza
1995 *Basilica dei Santi Giovanni e Paolo: Arte e devozione*. Venice.
Margel, N.
1914 *Catalogue des tableaux anciens des écoles italienne, espagnole, allemagne, flamande, et hollandaise composant la Galerie Crespi de Milan*. Paris.
Mariacher, Giovanni
1950 "Nota sulla pala di Rampazzo di G. B. Tiepolo." *Arte veneta* 4, pp. 153–54.
1959–60 "Per la datazione di un'opera perduta di Giambattista Tiepolo." *Arte veneta* 13–14, pp. 237–39.
Mariette, Pierre-Jean
1858–59 *Abecedario. . . .* Vol. 5. Edited by Ph. de Chennevières. Paris.
Marinelli, Sergio
1978 "Giambattista Tiepolo." In *La pittura a Verona tra sei e settecento*, edited by Licisco Magagnato. Verona.
1983 *Museum of Castelvecchio, Verona*. Venice.
Marini, G. F.
1907 *Veralanuova: Appunti di storia dell'arte*. Brescia.
Mariuz, Adriano
1971 *Giandomenico Tiepolo*. Venice.
1981 "La 'Magnifica Sala' di Palazzo Dolfin a Venezia: Gli affreschi di Nicolò Bambini e Antonio Felice Ferrari." *Arte veneta* 35, pp. 182–86.
1982 *L'opera completa del Piazzetta*. Milan.
1995 "Giambattista Tiepolo." In Venice 1995a, pp. 217–31.
Mariuz, Adriano, and Giuseppe Pavanello
1985 "I primi affreschi di Giambattista Tiepolo." *Arte veneta* 39, pp. 101–13.
1995 "Per la giovinezza di Giambattista Tiepolo: Un affresco e un disegno." *Arte veneto* 47, pp. 52–61.
Martini, Egidio
1964 *La pittura veneziana del settecento*. Venice.
1974 "I ritratti di Ca' Cornaro di G. B. Tiepolo giovane." *Notizie da Palazzo Albani* 3, no. 1, pp. 30–35.
1982 *La pittura del settecento veneto*. Udine.
1992 *Pittura veneta e altra italiana dal XV al XIX secolo*. Rimini.
Matilla Tascon, Antonio
1960 "Documentos del archivo del Ministerio de Hacienda relativos a pintores de cámara, y de las fábricas de tapices y porcelana, siglo XVIII." *Rivista de archivos, bibliotecas, y museos* 68, pp. 199–270.
Mayer, A.
1935 "Dos bocetas de Juan Bautista Tiépolo." *Revista española de arte* 4, pp. 300–309.
Mazzariol, Giuseppe, and Terisio Pignatti
1951 *Itinerario tiepolesco*. Venice.
McComb, Arthur K.
1934 *The Baroque Painters of Italy: An Introductory Historical Survey*. Cambridge, Mass.
Menegozzo, Rita
1990 *Nobili e Tiepolo a Vicenza: L'artista e i committenti*. Vicenza.
Menestrier, Claude François
1694 *La philosophie des images énigmatiques. . . .* Lyons.
Metastasio, Pietro A. D. B.
1857 *Opere*. Vol. 1. Trieste.
Meyer zur Capellen, Jürg, and Bernd Roeck, eds.
1990 *Paolo Veronese: Fortuna critica und künstlerisches Nachleben*. Sigmaringen.
Michelessi, Domenico
1770 *Memorie intorno alla vita ed agli scritti del conte Francesco Algarotti*. Venice.
Milan
1992 *Giambattista Tiepolo: Uno straordinario capolavoro commissionato nel 1748 per il Palazzo Dolfin Manin a Rialto*, by Dario Succi. Exh. cat. Milan: Gabinetto Salamon.
Milizia, Francesco
1797 *Dizionario delle belle arti del disegno. . . .* Bassano.
1821 *Introduzione allo studio delle arti del disegno e vocabolario compendioso delle arti*. 2 vols. Milan.
Minneapolis
1995 *Treasures of Venice: Paintings from the Museum of Fine Arts, Budapest*. Edited by George Keyes, István Barkóczi, and Jane Satkowski, with essays by Klára Garas, George Keyes, and Philip Sohm. Exh. cat. Minneapolis: Minneapolis Institute of Arts.
Mirano
1988 *I Tiepolo: Virtuosismo ed ironia*. Edited by Dario Succi. Exh. cat. Mirano: Barchessa Villa XXV Aprile.
Modern, Heinrich
1902 *Giovanni Battista Tiepolo, eine Studie*. Vienna.
Modigliani, Ettore
1933 "Dipinti noti o malnoti di Giambattista Tiepolo." *Dedalo* 13, pp. 129–47.
Molmenti, Pompeo G.
1880 *Les fresques de Tiepolo dans la Villa Valmarana*. Venice.
1909 *G. B. Tiepolo: La sua vita e le sue opere*. Milan.
1911 *Tiepolo, la vie et l'oeuvre du peintre*. Translated by H. L. de Péréra. Paris.
Monaco, Pietro
1743 *Raccolta di cinquantacinque storie sacre incise in altrettanti rame*. Venice.
1763 *Raccolta di centodidici stampe di pitture della storia sacra, I–II*. Venice.

Montagu, Jennifer
1994 *The Expression of the Passions: The Origin and Influence of Charles Le Brun's "Conférence sur l'expression générale et particulière."* New Haven. Originally the author's Ph.D. dissertation, Warburg Institute, London, 1959.
Montecuccoli degli Erri, Federico
1990 "Almorò Pisani, un patrizio dilettante di incisione." *Bollettino dei Musei Civici Veneziani d'Arte e di Storia*, n.s., 34, pp. 41–62.
n.d. *Giambattista Tiepolo e la sua famiglia—nuove pagine di vita privata*. Ateneo veneto. Venice. Forthcoming.
Montesquieu, C. L. de
1757 "Goût." In *Encyclopédie; ou, Dictionnaire raisonné des sciences, des arts, et des métiers, par une société de gens de lettres; mis en ordre et publié par M. Diderot. . . ,* vol. 7. Paris.
Morassi, Antonio
1934 "The Young Tiepolo," parts 1, 2. *Burlington Magazine* 64 (February), pp. 86–92 (March), pp. 127–33.
1935 "More about the Young Tiepolo." *Burlington Magazine* 67 (October), pp. 143–49.
1937 "An Unknown Early Work by Giambattista Tiepolo." *Burlington Magazine* 70 (February), p. 53.
1941–42 "Novità e precisazioni sul Tiepolo." *Le arti* 4, pp. 87–97, 259–67.
1943 *Tiepolo*. Bergamo.
1949 "Settecento inedito." *Arte veneta* 3, pp. 70–84.
1950 *Tiepolo*. [2d ed.] Bergamo.
1952 "Settecento inedito." *Arte veneta* 6, pp. 85–98.
1955a *G. B. Tiepolo, His Life and Work*. London.
1955b "Some 'Modelli' and Other Unpublished Works by Tiepolo." *Burlington Magazine* 97 (January), pp. 4–12.
1958 "Giambattista Tiepolo's 'Girl with a Lute' and the Clarification of Some Points in the Work of Domenico Tiepolo." *Art Quarterly* 31, no. 2, pp. 177–86.
1962 *A Complete Catalogue of the Paintings of G. B. Tiepolo, Including Pictures by His Pupils and Followers Wrongly Attributed to Him*. London.
1964 "Un nouveau Tiepolo pour la National Gallery de Londres." *Connaissance des arts*, no. 150 (August), pp. 32–39.
1971 "A 'Scuola del Nudo' by Tiepolo." *Master Drawings* 9, pp. 43–50.
1973 *Guardi*. Venice.
Moretti, Lino
1973 "La data degli apostoli della chiesa di San Stae." *Arte veneta* 27, pp. 318–20.
1984–85 "Notizie e appunti su G. B. Piazzetta: Alcuni piazzetteschi e G. B. Tiepolo." *Atti dell'Istituto Veneto di Scienze, Lettere, e Arti* 143, pp. 359–95.
Moschetti, Andrea
1928 *I danni ai monumenti e alle opere d'arte delle Venezie nella Guerra Mondiale, MCMXV–MCMXVIII*. Venice.
Moschini, Giovanni Antonio
1806–8 *Della letteratura veneziana del secolo XVIII fino à nostri giorni*. 4 vols. Venice.
1815 *Guida per la città di Venezia all'amico delle belle arti*. 2 vols. Venice.
Moschini, Vittorio
1931 *La pittura italiana del settecento*. Florence.
1963 "Un'opera di Girolamo Mengozzi Colonna a Sant'Agnese." *Arte veneta* 17, p. 200.
Moschini Marconi, Sandra
1970 *Gallerie dell'Accademia di Venezia*. Vol. 3, *Opere d'arte dei secoli XVII, XVIII, XIX*. Rome.
Mras, George P.
1956 "Some Drawings by G. B. Tiepolo." *Record of the Art Museum, Princeton University* 15, no. 2, pp. 39–59.
Muller, Priscilla E.
1977 "Francisco Bayeu, Tiepolo, and the Trinitarian Dome Frescoes of the Colegiata at La Granja." *Pantheon* 35, pp. 20–28.
Munich
1958 *Europäisches Rokoko*. Exh. cat. Munich: Residenz.
Munro, Hugh A. J.
1865 *A Complete Catalogue of the Paintings, Water-Colour Drawings, Drawings, and Prints, in the Collection of the Late Hugh Andrew Johnstone Munro . . . at the Time of His Death. . . .* London.
Muraro, Michelangelo
1960 "L'Olympe de Tiepolo." *Gazette des Beaux-Arts*, ser. 6, 55, pp. 19–34.
[1976] "Giovanni Battista Tiepolo tra Ricci e Piazzetta." In *Atti del Congresso Internazionale di Studi su Sebastiano Ricci e il Suo Tempo*, pp. 59–65. Venice.
Muratori, Lodovico Antonio
1706 *Della perfetta poesia italiana. . . .* 2 vols. Modena.
Murray, Peter
1980 *Dulwich Picture Gallery: A Catalogue*. London.
Museo del Prado
1990 *Museo del Prado, inventario general de pinturas: I, La colección real*. Madrid.
Nagler, Alois M.
1959 *A Source Book in Theatrical History*. New York. First published 1952.
National Gallery of Art
1941 *Preliminary Catalogue of Paintings and Sculpture*. Washington, D.C.
Nepi Scirè, Giovanna
1991 *Treasures of Venetian Painting: The Gallerie dell'Accademia*. London.
Nepi Scirè, Giovanna, and Francesco Valcanover
1985 *Gallerie dell'Accademia di Venezia*. Milan.
New Grove Dictionary of Music
1980 *The New Grove Dictionary of Music and Musicians*. Edited by Stanley Sadie. 20 vols. London.
New York
1938 *Tiepolo and His Contemporaries*, by Harry B. Wehle. New York: The Metropolitan Museum of Art.
1970 *Masterpieces of Fifty Centuries*. Exh. cat. New York: The Metropolitan Museum of Art.
1971 *The Eighteenth Century in Italy*, by Jacob Bean and Felice Stampfle. Drawings from New York Collections, 3. Exh. cat. New York: The Metropolitan Museum of Art.

1992 *Jusepe de Ribéra, 1591–1652*, by Alfonso E. Pérez Sánchez and Nicola Spinosa. Exh. cat. New York: The Metropolitan Museum of Art.

1993 *Splendid Legacy: The Havemeyer Collection*. Exh. cat. New York: The Metropolitan Museum of Art.

Nicoletti, G.

1890 "Lista di nomi d'artisti. . . ." *Ateneo veneto*, November–December.

Niero, Antonio

1963 *La Scuola Grande dei Carmini*. Venice. 2d ed., revised, Venice, 1991.

1976–77 "Giambattista Tiepolo alla Scuola dei Carmini: Precisazioni d'archivio." *Atti dell'Istituto Veneto di Scienze, Lettere, ed Arti* 135, pp. 373–91.

1979 *Tre artisti per un tempio: S. Maria del Rosario-Gesuati*. Padua.

1982 "Alcuni aspetti del Quietismo veneziano." In *Problemi di storia della Chiesa nei secoli XVII–XVIII*, pp. 223–49. Naples.

Niero, Antonio, and Filippo Pedrocco

1994 *Chiesa dei Gesuati: Arte e devozione*. Venice.

Nugent, Margherita

1925 *Alla mostra della pittura italiana del '600 e del '700*. San Casciano.

Oddasso, A. C.

1963 "S. Caterina Benincasa." In *Bibliotheca Sanctorum*, vol. 3, cols. 996–1044. Rome.

Officium Beatae Mariae Virginis

1772 *Officium Beatae Mariae Virginis*. Rome.

Ojetti, Ugo

1927 *Il ritratto italiano dal Caravaggio al Tiepolo*. Florence: Palazzo Vecchio.

Olivato, Loredana

1973 "Storia di un'avventura edilizia a Venezia tra il seicento e il settecento: Palazzo Cornaro della Regina." *Antichità viva* 12, no. 3, pp. 27–49.

Olsen, Harald

1961 *Italian Paintings and Sculpture in Denmark*. Copenhagen.

Ottawa

1976 *Etchings by the Tiepolos: Domenico Tiepolo's Collection of the Family Etchings*, by George Knox and Elaine Dee. Exh. cat. Ottawa: National Gallery of Canada.

Ovid

1967 *Metamorphoses*. Translated by Mary M. Innes. Baltimore.

Pagiaro, S.

1983 *Il Tiepolo a Verolanuova*. Brescia.

Palazzo Accoramboni

1897 *Catalogue de peinture, sculptures, et archéologie au Palais Accoramboni*. Rome.

Paleotti, Gabriele

1582 *Il discorso intorno alle imagini sacre e profane*. Bologna.

Pallucchini, Anna

1968 *L'opera completa di Giambattista Tiepolo*. Milan.

1971 "Nota tiepolesca." In *Studi di storia dell'arte in onore di Antonio Morassi*, pp. 303–7. Venice.

Pallucchini, Rodolfo

1934a *L'arte di Giovanni Battista Piazzetta*. Bologna.

1934b "Sempre a proposito del Polazzo." *Rivista di Venezia* 13 (November), pp. 483–86.

1935–36 "Profilo di Federico Bencovich." *Critica d'arte* 1, pp. 205–20.

1944 "Nota per Giambattista Tiepolo." *Emporium* 22, pp. 3–18.

1945 *Gli affreschi di Giambattista e Giandomenico Tiepolo alla Villa Valmarana di Vicenza*. Bergamo.

1947 *Trésors de l'art vénitien*. Milan.

1960 *La pittura veneziana del settecento*. Venice.

1961 *Die venezianische Malerei des 18. Jahrhunderts*. Munich.

1971 "Il settecento veneziano all'Orangerie." *Arte veneta* 15, pp. 323–33.

1978 *Gli affreschi nelle ville venete dal seicento all'ottocento*. 2 vols. Venice.

1983 "Il 'Modelletto' della pala camerte di Giambattista Tiepolo." *Notizie da Palazzo Albani* 12, no. 1–2, pp. 261–63.

1984 "Un Tiepolo in più, un Bencovich in meno." In *Studi in onore di Giulio Carlo Argan*, vol. 1, pp. 367–70. Rome.

1995 *La pittura nel Veneto*. Vol. 1, *Il settecento*. Milan.

Paoletti, Ermolao

1839 *Il fiore di Venezia*. Vol. 2. Venice.

Paris

1952 *Tiepolo et Guardi*, by Jean Cailleux. Exh. cat. Paris: Galerie Cailleux.

1971 *Vénise au dix-huitième siècle: Peintures, dessins, et gravures des collections françaises*. Exh. cat. Paris: Musée de l'Orangerie.

1974 *Giambattista Tiepolo, 1696–1770, Domenico Tiepolo, 1727–1804, Lorenzo Tiepolo, 1736–1776: Peintures, dessins, pastels*. Exh. cat. Paris: Galerie Cailleux.

1982 *Le portrait en Italie au siècle de Tiepolo*, by Marco Chiarini. Exh. cat. Paris: Musée du Petit Palais.

Patrignani, Giuseppe

1709 *Il divoto di San Giuseppe*. Venice.

Pavanello, Giuseppe

1979 "Un progetto di Girolamo Mengozzi Colonna per Giambattista Tiepolo: La 'Salla per il N.H. Vizenzo Pisani alla Mira.'" *Bollettino dei Musei Civici Veneziani* 24, pp. 52–59.

Pedrocco, Filippo

1982 "I Labia di San Geremia." In Pignatti, Pedrocco, and Martinelli Pedrocco 1982, pp. 9–54.

1985 "Giambattista Tiepolo: Illustratore di libri." In Gorizia 1985, pp. 64–76.

1989–90 "L'Oratorio del Crocifisso nella chiesa di San Polo." *Arte veneta* 43, pp. 108–15.

1990 "Iconografia delle cortigiane di Venezia." In Venice 1990, pp. 81–93.

1995 "La Scuola dei Carmini." In Venice 1995a, pp. 505–11.

Pedrocco, Filippo, and Federico Montecuccoli degli Erri

1992 *Antonio Guardi*. Milan.

Pepper, Stephen

1983 "'Bacchus and Ariadne' in the Los Angeles County Museum: The 'Scherzo' as Artistic Mode." *Burlington Magazine* 125 (February), pp. 68–74.

Pérez Sánchez, Alfonso

1977 "Nueva documentación para un Tiépolo problemático." *Archivo español de arte* 50, pp. 75–80.

Perkins, F. Mason

1905 "Pitture italiane nella raccolta Johnson a Filadelfia." *Rassegna d'arte* 5, no. 9 (September), pp. 129–35.

Philadelphia
1971 *Giovanni Benedetto Castiglione, Master Draughtsman of the Italian Baroque*, by Ann Percy. Exh. cat. Philadelphia: Philadelphia Museum of Art.

Pigler, Andor
1974 *Barockthemen: Eine Auswahl von Verzeichnissen zur Ikonographie des 17. und 18. Jahrhunderts*. 2d ed. 3 vols. Budapest.

Pignatti, Terisio
1950 "I ritratti settecenteschi della Querini-Stampalia." *Bollettino d'arte*, ser. 4, 35, pp. 216–18.
1951 *Tiepolo*. Verona.
1960 *Il Museo Correr di Venezia: Dipinti del XVII e XVIII secolo*. Venice.
[1966] *I disegni veneziani del settecento*. Rome, n.d.
1970 "In margine alla mostra delle acqueforti dei Tiepolo a Udine." *Arte veneta* 24, pp. 305–10.
1976 *Veronese*. 2 vols. Venice.
1990 "Pintura." In Franzoi, Pignatti, and Wolters 1990, pp. 227–363.
1991 *Veronese: Catalogo completo dei dipinti*. Florence.

Pignatti, Terisio, Filippo Pedrocco, and Elisabetta Martinelli Pedrocco
1982 *Palazzo Labia a Venezia*. Turin.

Piles, Roger de
1715 *Abrégé de la vie des peintres, avec des réflexions sur leurs ouvrages, et un traité du peintre parfait. . . .* 2d ed., revised. Paris.

Pilo, Giuseppe M.
1961 *Canaletto*. Utrecht.
1981a "L'esordio veneziano di Nicola Grassi." *Notizie da Palazzo Albani* 10, no. 2, pp. 67–73.
1981b "Nicolas Régnier e lo 'Spedale di San Giovanni e Paolo' a Venezia." *Antichità viva* 20, no. 1, pp. 7–14.
1982 "Presenze di Nicola Grassi all'Ospedaletto." *Il Noncello* 54.
1983 "L'incisione venete e friulana del settecento." In Gorizia 1983, pp. 13–28.
[1985] *La chiesa dello "Spedaletto" in Venezia*. Venice, n.d.

Pinetti, Angelo
1931 *Inventario della provincia di Bergamo*. Rome.

Plato
1930–35 *The Republic*. Translated by Paul Shorey. 2 vols. London.

Polazzo, Marco
1990 *Antonio Balestra, pittore veronese del settecento*. Verona.

Pope-Hennessy, John
1985 *Cellini*. London.

Porcella, Antonio
1941 "Tiepolo e i Tiepoleschi." *L'arte* 44 (December).

Posner, Donald
1984 *Antoine Watteau*. Ithaca.

Posse, Hans
1931 "Die Briefe des Grafen Francesco Algarotti an den sächsischen Hof und seine Bilderkäufe für die Dresdner Gemäldegalerie, 1743–1747." *Jahrbuch der Preuszischen Kunstsammlungen* 52 (Beiheft), pp. 1–73.

Pozzi, F.
1903 *Bibliografia per servire alla storia della Basilica e Monastero di S. Giustina*. Padua.

Pradella, G.
1979–80 "La decorazione pittorica di Ca' Dolfin." Thesis, Università degli Studi di Venezia.

Precerutti Garberi, Mercedes
1958 "Di alcuni dipinti perduti del Tiepolo." *Commentari* 9, pp. 110–23.
1964 "Segnalazioni tiepolesche." *Commentari* 15, pp. 246–61.
1968 *Affreschi settecenteschi delle ville venete*. Milan. Also published in English, London, 1971.

Puglisi, C.
1983 "A Study of the Bolognese-Roman Painter Francesco Albani." Ph.D. dissertation, New York University.

Puppi, Lionello
1968a "Carlo Cordellina committente d'artisti." *Arte veneta* 22, pp. 212–16.
1968b "I 'Nani' di Villa Valmarana a Vicenza." *Antichità viva* 7, no. 2, pp. 34–46.
[1972] "I Tiepolo 'decoratori' e l'architettura" and "Una lettera sconosciuta di Giambattista Tiepolo." In *Celebrazioni tiepoleschi: Atti del Congresso Internazionale di Studi sul Tiepolo [Udine, 25 September–1 October 1970]*, pp. 53–55, 131–33. Milan, n.d.

Raimondi, A.
1952 "Il Tiepolo a Bergamo nella Cappella Colleoni." *L'eco di Bergamo*, 26 November.

Raleigh
1994 *A Gift to America: Masterpieces of European Painting from the Samuel H. Kress Collection*, by Chiyo Ishikawa et al. Exh. cat. Raleigh: North Carolina Museum of Art.

Ravoux-Rallo, Elisabeth
1984 *La femme à Venise au temps de Casanova*. Paris.

Reitlinger, Gerald
1961 *The Economics of Taste*. Vol. 1, *The Rise and Fall of Picture Prices, 1760–1960*. London.

Renner, M.
1995 "Giovanni Battista Tiepolo und Adam Friedrich Graf von Seinsheim." *Würzburger Diözesangeschichtsblätter* 57, pp. 345–56.

Riccoboni, Luigi
1728 *Histoire du théatre italien. . . .* Paris.

Richardson, Edgar P.
1957–58 "An Unrecorded Painting by Tiepolo." *Bulletin of the Detroit Institute of Arts* 37, no. 4, pp. 80–81.

Richter, Jean Paul, and John C. L. Sparkes
1880 *Catalogue of the Pictures in the Dulwich College Gallery, with Biographical Notices of the Painters*. [2d ed.] London.

Ridolfi, Carlo
1648 *Le maraviglie dell'arte; ouero, Le vite de gl'illvstri pittori veneti, e dello stato. . . .* 2 vols. in 1. Venice.

Ripa, Cesare
1603 *Iconologia*. Edited by Piero Buscaroli. Rome. New ed., Milan, 1992.

Rizzi, Aldo
1967 *Storia dell'arte in Friuli: Il settecento*. Udine.
1971 *The Etchings of the Tiepolos*. London. Also published in Italian as *L'opera grafica dei Tiepolo: Le acqueforti*.
1988 "Un modelletto del Tiepolo." *Pantheon* 46, pp. 103–5.
1990 *Giambattista Tiepolo: Disegni dai Civici Musei di Storia e Arte di Trieste*. Milan.

Robertson, Giles
1949 "Tiepolo's and Veronese's *Finding of Moses*." *Burlington Magazine* 91 (April), pp. 99–101.

Robinson, Franklin W.
1967 "Rembrandt's Influence in Eighteenth Century Venice." *Nederlands Kunsthistorisch Jaarboek* 18, pp. 167–96.

Robison, A.
1974 "The Albrizzi-Piazzetta Tasso." *Non Solus* 1, pp. 1–12.

Roettgen, Steffi
1996 "Francesco Algarotti in Preußen und Sachsen und—in Würzburg?" In Würzburg 1996, vol. 2, pp. 46–53.

Romagnolo, Antonio
1981 *La Pinacoteca dell'Accademia dei Concordi*. Rovigo.

Romagnolo, T.
1975 *La Pinacoteca dell'Accademia dei Concordi: Profilo storico*. Rovigo.

Romanelli, Giandomenico, and Filippo Pedrocco
1986 *Ca' Rezzonico*. Milan.

Rome
1941 *Mostra di pittura veneziana del settecento*, by Alessandro Morandotti. Rome: Palazzo Massimo alle Colonne.
1989 *I premiati dell'Accademia, 1682–1754*. Edited by Angela Cipriani. Exh. cat. Rome: Accademia Nazionale di San Luca.
1995 *La regola e la fama: San Filippo Neri e l'arte*. Exh. cat. Rome: Museo Nazionale di Palazzo Venezia.

Rosenberg, Pierre, and Barbara Brejon de Lavergnée, eds.
1986 *Saint-Non, Fragonard. Panopticon Italiano: Un diario di viaggio ritrovato, 1759–1761*. Rome.

Rossetti, Giovanni Battista
1765 *Descrizione delle pitture, sculture, ed architetture di Padova*. 2 vols. Padua.

Rotterdam
1938 *Meesterwerken uit vier eeuwen, 1400–1800*. Exh. cat. Rotterdam: Museum Boymans.
1983 *Schilderkunst uit de eerste hand: Olieverfschetsen van Tintoretto tot Goya*, by J. Giltay. Exh. cat. Rotterdam: Museum Boymans-van Beuningen.

Ruffo, Vincenzo
1917 *La Galleria Ruffo in Messina nel secolo XVII*. 3 vols. Rome.

Ruggeri, Ugo
1972 "Le collezioni pittoriche rodigine." In *L'Accademia dei Concordi di Rovigo*, pp. 29–112. Vicenza.

Ruskin, John
1884 *St. Mark's Rest*. London.

Saccardo, M.
1977 "Nell'antica chiesa dell'Araceli la 'mano' dell'architetto Guarini." *Vicenza* 2 (March–April).
1981 *Notizie d'arte e di artisti vicentini*. Vicenza.

Sack, Eduard
1910 *Giambattista und Domenico Tiepolo: Ihr Leben und ihre Werke: Ein Beitrag zur Kunstgeschichte des achtzehnten Jahrhunderts*. Hamburg.

Saint Petersburg
1910 *Les anciennes écoles de peinture dans les palais et collections privées russes representées à l'exposition organisée à St.-Petersbourg en 1909 par la revue d'art ancien "Starye gody,"* by E. de Liphart et al. Exh. cat. Brussels.
1973 *Pittura italiana del settecento*, by Eugenio Riccomini. Exh. cat. Saint Petersburg: Hermitage.

Salas, Xavier de
1968–69 "Inventario: Pinturas elegidas para el Principe de la paz. . . ." *Arte español* 17, no. 1, pp. 29–33.

Salerno, Luigi
1988 *I dipinti del Guercino*. Rome.

Saltillo, Marques del
1952 "Goya en Madrid: Su familia y allegados." *Miscelánea madrileña, historica y artistica* 1.

Sánchez Cantón, Francisco J.
1916 *Los pintores de cámara de los reyes de España*. Madrid.
1927 "Los Tiépolos de Aranjuez." *Archivo español de arte y arqueología* 3, pp. 1–17.
1929 "Bocetos y dibujos de Tiépolo." *Archivo español de arte y arqueología* 5, pp. 137–43.
1942 *Catálogo de los cuadros, Museo del Prado*. Madrid.
1952 *Catálogo de los cuadros, Museo del Prado*. Madrid.
1953 *J. B. Tiepolo en España*. Madrid.
1963 *Museo del Prado: Catálogo de las pinturas*. Madrid.

Sani, Bernardina
1988 *Rosalba Carriera*. Turin.

Santangelo, Antonino
1935–36 "Un capolavoro del Tiepolo e altri inediti del Fontebasso." *Critica d'arte* 1, pp. 48–50.

Santifaller, M.
1972 "Carl Heinrich von Heinecken e le acqueforti di Giambattista Tiepolo." *Arte veneta* 26, pp. 145–53.

Saragossa
1990 *El settecento veneciano: Aspectos de la pintura veneciana del siglo XVIII*. Exh. cat. Saragossa: Palacio de la Lonja.

Scaramelli, Giovanni Battista
1754 *Il Direttorio Mistica*. Venice.

Scharf, Alfred
1958 "The Robinson Collection." *Burlington Magazine* 100 (September), pp. 299–304.

Scherbachova, M.
1941 *Tiepolo's Pictures of the Venice Dolfino Palace at the Hermitage Museum*. Leningrad.

Schiavo, Remo
1975 *La Villa Cordellina Lombardi di Montecchio Maggiore*. Vol. 1. Vicenza.
1989 *Giovanni Battista Tiepolo alla Villa Cordellina di Montecchio Maggiore/Giovanni Battista Tiepolo at the Villa Cordellina in Montecchio Maggiore*. Vicenza.
1990 "La ritrovata quadreria di Carlo Cordellina." In Vicenza 1990, pp. 334–49.

Schulz, Juergen
1968 *Venetian Painted Ceilings of the Renaissance*. Berkeley and Los Angeles.

Seilern, Antoine von
1969 *Italian Paintings and Drawings at 56 Princes Gate: Addenda*. Vol. 5. London.

Serra, Luigi
1914 *Catalogo delle R. Gallerie di Venezia*. Venice.

Sgarbi, Vittorio, ed.
1990 *Del genio de' Lendinaresi per la pittura: Pietro Brandolese*. Rovigo.
Sgarbi, Vittorio, Vittorio Veller, and Mauro Cova
1986 *Palazzo dei Conti Valle: Annotazioni per un tesoro ritrovato*. Vicenza.
Shapley, Fern Rusk
1973 *Paintings from the Samuel H. Kress Foundation: Italian School, XVI–XVIII Century*. 3 vols. London.
1974 "Tiepolo's Zenobia Cycle." In *Hortus Imaginum: Essays in Western Art*, pp. 193ff. Lawrence, Kans.
1979 *Catalogue of the Italian Paintings*. 2 vols. Washington, D.C.: National Gallery of Art.
Shipp, Horace
1958 "Treasures of the Robinson Collection: Some Problems of Attribution." *Apollo* 68 (August), pp. 39–43.
Siddons, Henry
1822 *Practical Illustrations of Rhetorical Gesture and Action, Adapted to the English Drama; from a Work on the Subject by M. Engel*. 2d ed. London.
Simon, Erika
1971 "Sol, Virtus, und Veritas im Würzburger Treppenhausfresko des Giovanni Battista Tiepolo." *Pantheon* 29, pp. 483–96.
Sirèn, Osvald
1902 *Dessins et tableaux de la Renaissance italienne dans les collections de Suède*. Stockholm.
Sohm, Philip L.
1983 "Unknown Epithalamia as Sources for G. B. Tiepolo's Iconography and Style." *Arte veneta* 37, pp. 138–50.
1984 "Giambattista Tiepolo at the Palazzo Archinto in Milan." *Arte lombarda*, n.s., 68–69, pp. 70–78.
1990 "The Critical Reception of Paolo Veronese in Eighteenth-Century Italy: The Example of Giambattista Tiepolo as Veronese Redivivus." In Meyer zur Capellen and Roeck 1990, pp. 87–107.
Soravia, Giambattista
1822 *Le chiese di Venezia*. Venice.
Spear, Richard E.
1982 *Domenichino*. 2 vols. New Haven.
Sponza, Sandro
1986 "La decorazione pittorica della chiesa dell'Ospedaletto terminata con la pala eseguita in occasione della beatificazione di San Girolamo." In *San Girolamo Miani e Venezia: Nel V centenario della nascita*, pp. 38–61. Venice.
1986–87 "Della decorazione pittorica della chiesa dell'Ospedaletto ed il problema della prima attività di Giambattista Tiepolo." *Atti dell'Istituto Veneto di Scienze, lettere, ed arti* 145, pp. 213–34.
Statens Museum for Kunst
1946 *Katalog over aeldre malerier*. Copenhagen.
1951 *Royal Museum of Fine Arts: Catalogue of Old Foreign Paintings*. Copenhagen.
Stuttgart
1970 *Tiepolo: Zeichnungen von Giambattista, Domenico, und Lorenzo Tiepolo aus der Graphischen Sammlung der Staatsgalerie Stuttgart, aus württembergischem Privatbesitz und dem Martin von Wagner Museum der Universität Würzburg (Stuttgarter Galerieverein e. V. Graphische Sammlung Staatsgalerie Stuttgart)*, by George Knox, with Christel Thiem. Exh. cat. Stuttgart: Graphische Sammlung der Staatsgalerie Stuttgart. Also published in English, 1971.
Suida, William E.
1930 "Die Werke des Cav. Giuseppe Petrini von Carona." *Indicateur d'antiquités suisses*, pp. 269–80.
Sweeny, Barbara
1966 *John G. Johnson Collection: Catalogue of Italian Paintings*. Philadelphia.
Tasso, Torquato
1581 *La Gerusalemme liberata*. Edited by P. Nardi. Verona, 1973.
Temanza, Tommaso
1963 *Zibaldon di memorie storiche*. Edited by Nicola Ivanoff. Venice.
Teresa d'Ávila
1755 *Le opere nuovamente tradotte*. Venice.
Thiem, Christel
1993 "Lorenzo Tiepolos Position innerhalb der Künstlerfamilie Tiepolo." *Pantheon* 51, pp. 138–50.
1994 "Lorenzo Tiepolo as a Draftsman." *Master Drawings* 32, pp. 315–50.
Thomas, Hylton A.
1966 Review of Knox 1960. *Art Bulletin* 48, pp. 261–63.
1969 "Tasso and Tiepolo in Chicago." *Museum Studies* 4, pp. 27–48.
Tiozzo, Clauco B.
1986 "Giambattista Tiepolo a Ca' Pisani di Stra." *Notizie di Palazzo Albani* 15, no. 1, pp. 54–67.
Toffanin, Giuseppe
1988 *Cento chiese padovane scomparse*. Padua.
Tornézy, A., ed.
1895 "Bergeret et Fragonard: Journal inédit d'un voyage en Italie, 1773–1774." *Bulletin et mémoires de la Société des Antiquaires de l'Ouest, 1894*, 17. Paris.
Toronto
1980 *An Album of Eighteenth Century Venetian Operatic Caricatures Formerly in the Collection of Count Algarotti*, by Edward Croft-Murray. Exh. cat. Toronto: Art Gallery of Ontario.
Trecca, Giuseppe
1912 *Catalogo della Pinacoteca Comunale di Verona*. Bergamo.
Treffers, Bert
1988 "Il Francesco Hartford del Caravaggio e la spiritualità francescana alla fine del XVI. sec." *Mitteilungen des Kunsthistorischen Institutes in Florenz* 32, pp. 145–72.
Trieste
1988 *Giambattista Tiepolo: Disegni dai Civici Musei di Storia e Arte di Trieste*, by Aldo Rizzi. Exh. cat. Trieste: Civico Museo Sartorio.
Udine
1971 *Mostra del Tiepolo*, by Aldo Rizzi. 2 vols. Exh. cat. Udine: Villa Manin di Passariano.
Uhde-Bernays, Hermann
1913 "Ein unbekanntes Porträt Tiepolos." *Der Cicerone* 5, pp. 15–17.
Urbana
1962 *Seventeenth and Eighteenth Century Paintings from the University of Notre Dame*, by Dwight Miller. Exh. cat. Urbana: Krannert Art Museum.
Urbani de Gheltof, Giuseppe M.
1879 *Tiepolo e la sua famiglia; note e documenti inediti*. Venice.
1880 "Tiepolo in Ispagna." *Bulletino d'arti . . . e curiosità veneziane* 3, nos. 3–4, pp. 170–85.

1895 *Guida storico-artistico della Scuola di S. Giovanni Evangelista in Venezia*. Venice.

Valcanover, Francesco

1956 "Il ritratto veneto da Tiziano al Tiepolo a Varsavia." *Arte veneta* 10, pp. 240–44.

1958 "I veneti e la Mostra del Rococò europeo." *Arte veneta* 12, pp. 255–57.

1962 *La Pinacoteca dell'Accademia dei Concordi*. Venice.

Vale, G., and U. Masotti

1932 *La Chiesa della Purità: Notizie storiche*. Udine.

Vasari, Giorgio

1906 *Le vite de' più eccellenti pittori, scultori, ed architettori, con nuove annotazioni e commenti di Gaetano Milanesi*. 9 vols. Florence. First published 1568.

Vecchi, Alberto

1967 *Correnti religiosi nel sei-settecento Veneto*. Venice.

Vecellio, Cesare

1590 *Degli abiti antichi et moderni di diuerse parti del mondo, libri due*. Venice.

Venice

1929 *Mostra del settecento italiano*. Exh. cat. Venice.

1946 *I Capolavori dei musei veneti*, by Rodolfo Pallucchini. Exh. cat. Venice.

1951 *Mostra del Tiepolo: Catalogo ufficiale*, by Giulio Lorenzetti. Exh. cat. Venice

1969a *Caricature di Anton Maria Zanetti*, by Alessandro Bettagno. Exh. cat. Venice: Fondazione Giorgio Cini.

1969b *Dal Ricci al Tiepolo: I pittori di figura del settecento a Venezia*, by Pietro Zampetti. Exh. cat. Venice: Palazzo Ducale.

1979 *Tiepolo: Tecnica e immaginazione*, by George Knox. Exh. cat. Venice: Palazzo Ducale.

1983 *G. B. Piazzetta: Disegni, incisioni, libri, manoscritti*. Introduction by George Knox. Exh. cat. Venice: Fondazione Giorgio Cini.

1990 *Le cortegiane di Venezia: Dal trecento al settecento*. Exh. cat. Venice: Casinò Municipale, Ca' Vendramin Calergi.

1993 *Pietro Longhi*, by Adriano Mariuz, Giuseppe Pavanello, and Giandomenico Romanelli. Exh. cat. Venice: Museo Correr.

1995a *Splendori del settecento veneziano*. Edited by Giovanna Nepi Scirè and Giandomenico Romanelli. Exh. cat. Venice: Museo del Settecento Veneziano-Ca' Rezzonico, Galleria dell'Accademia, Palazzo Mocenigo.

1995b *Torquato Tasso e la Repubblica Veneta*. Edited by Giovanni da Pozzo. Exh. cat. Venice: Biblioteca Nazionale Marciana.

Venturi, Adolfo

1900 *La Galleria Crespi in Milano: Note e raffronti*. Milan.

Venturi, Lionello

1933 *Italian Paintings in America*. Vol. 3, *Sixteenth to Eighteenth Century*. New York.

Verona

1978 *La pittura a Verona tra sei e settecento*. Edited by Licisco Magagnato. Exh. cat. Verona: Museo di Castelvecchio.

Vicenza

1990 *I Tiepolo e il settecento vicentino*. Edited by Fernando Rigon et al. Exh. cat. Vicenza: Villa Cordellina, Palazzo della Ragione, and Palazzo Leoni Montanari.

1993 *Restituzione '93: Opere restaurate*. Exh. cat. Vicenza: Palazzo Leoni Montanari.

Vigni, Giorgio

1951 *Tiepolo*. Milan.

1972 *Disegni del Tiepolo*. Trieste.

Vivian, Frances

1971 *Il console Smith, mercante e collezionista*. Translated by Marisa Padoan. Vicenza.

Voss, Hermann

1922 "Über Tiepolos Jugendentwicklung." *Kunst und Künstler* 20, pp. 423–33.

1957 "Die Flucht nach Aegypten." *Saggi e memorie di storia dell'arte* 1, pp. 25–61.

Waagen, Gustav F.

1854 *Treasures of Art in Great Britain. . . .* Translated by Lady Eastlake. 3 vols. London.

1857 *Galleries and Cabinets of Art in Great Britain, Forming a Supplementary Volume to the* Treasures of Art in Great Britain, *Being an Account of More than Forty Collections of Paintings, Drawings, Sculptures, Mss., &c. &c., Visited in 1854 and 1856, and Now for the First Time Described*. London.

Washington, D.C.

1972 *Rare Etchings by Giovanni Battista and Giovanni Domenico Tiepolo*, by H. Diane Russell. Exh. cat. Washington, D.C.: National Gallery of Art.

1973 *Early Italian Engravings from the National Gallery of Art*, by Jay A. Levenson, Konrad Oberhuber, and Jacquelyn L. Sheehan. Exh. cat. Washington, D.C.: National Gallery of Art.

1983 *Piazzetta: A Tercentenary Exhibition of Drawings, Prints, and Books*, by George Knox. Exh. cat. Washington, D.C.: National Gallery of Art.

1984 *Watteau, 1684–1721*, by Margaret M. Grasselli and Pierre Rosenberg. Exh. cat. Washington, D.C.: National Gallery of Art.

1985 *Collection for a King: Old Master Paintings from the Dulwich Picture Gallery*. Exh. cat. Washington, D.C.: National Gallery of Art.

1988 *The Art of Paolo Veronese, 1528–1588*, by William R. Rearick. Exh. cat. Washington, D.C.: National Gallery of Art.

Watson, Francis J. B.

1952 "Reflections on the Tiepolo Exhibition." *Burlington Magazine* 94 (February), pp. 40–44.

1955 Review of Morassi 1955a. *Connoisseur* 136 (December), pp. 212–15.

1963 Review of Morassi 1962. *Apollo* 77 (March), pp. 244–48.

Wehle, Harry B.

1940 *The Metropolitan Museum of Art: A Catalogue of Italian, Spanish, and Byzantine Paintings*. New York.

Wethey, Harold E.

1969–75 *The Paintings of Titian*. 3 vols. London.

Whistler, Catherine

1984 "Giambattista Tiepolo in Spain: The Late Religious Paintings." Ph.D. dissertation, University College Dublin, National University of Ireland.

1985a "G. B. Tiepolo and Charles III: The Church of S. Pascual Baylon at Aranjuez." *Apollo* 121 (May), pp. 321–37.

1985b "A *Modello* for Tiepolo's Final Commission: The *Allegory of the Immaculate Conception*." *Apollo* 121 (March), pp. 172–73.
1985c "Tiepolo's St. Patrick Altarpiece." *Irish Arts Review* 2, pp. 32–35.
1986 "G. B. Tiepolo at the Court of Charles III." *Burlington Magazine* 128 (March), pp. 199–203.
1993 Review of Fort Worth 1993. *Burlington Magazine* 135 (December), pp. 857–59.
1994 "Wheels within Wheels: Some Exchanges between the Tiepolos." *Apollo* 140 (September), pp. 40–44.
1995a "Domenico Tiepolo e i suoi contemporanei." In Venice 1995a, pp. 371–81.
1995b Review of Gemin and Pedrocco 1993. *Burlington Magazine* 137 (September), pp. 625–27.

White, Christopher, and Karel G. Boon
1970 *Rembrandt's Etchings, an Illustrated Critical Catalogue*. 2 vols. Amsterdam.

Willis, Fred C.
1913 "Ein unbekanntes Porträt Tiepolos." *Der Cicerone* 5, pp. 139–40.

Winckelmann, Johann J.
1755 *Gedanken über die Nachahmung der griechischen Werke in der Malerey und Bildhauerkunst*. Dresden.
1756 *Gedanken über die Nachahmung der griechischen Werke in der Malerey und Bildhauerkunst*. 2d ed. Dresden.
1763 *Abhandlung von der Fähigkeit der Empfindung des Schönen in der Kunst und dem Unterrichte in derselben*. . . . Dresden.

Wolters, Wolfgang
1987 *Storia e politica nei dipinti di Palazzo Ducale: Aspetti dell'autocelebrazione della Repubblica di Venezia nel cinquecento*. Venice. Translated by Benedetta Heinemann Campana from *Der Bilderschmuck des Dogenpalastes*, Stuttgart, 1983.

Wright, Christopher
1985 *Poussin Paintings: A Catalogue Raisonné*. London.

Würzburg
1992 *Vorbild Tiepolo: Die Zeichnungen des Franz Martin Kuen aus dem Museum Weissenhorn*, by Matthias Kunze et al. Kataloge des Museums Weissenhorn: Heimat und Museumsverein Weissenhorn, vol. 3. Exh. cat. Würzburg, Augsburg, Rothenburg, and Weissenhorn.
1996 *Der Himmel auf Erden: Tiepolo in Würzburg*. Edited by Peter O. Krückmann. 2 vols. Exh. cat. Würzburg: Residenz.

Wynne, Michael
1986 *Later Italian Paintings in the National Gallery of Ireland: The Seventeenth, Eighteenth, and Nineteenth Centuries*. Dublin.

Zafran, Eric M.
1984 *European Art in the High Museum*. Atlanta.

Zampetti, Pietro
1964 "Una sconosciuta pala di G. B. Tiepolo." *Arte veneta* 18, pp. 119–22.

Zanetti, Anton Maria
1733 *Descrizione di tutte le pubbliche pitture della città di Venezia e isole circonvicine*. . . . Venice.
1771 *Della pittura veneziana e delle opere pubbliche de' veneziani maestri, libri V*. Venice.

Zanotto, Francesco
1837 *Storia della pittura veneziana*. Venice. First published 1834.
1856 *Pinacoteca di Valentino Benfatto veneziana*. Venice.

Zava Boccazzi, Franca
1974 "Per il catalogo di Giambattista Pittoni: Proposte e inediti." *Arte veneta* 28, pp. 179–204.
1976 "La documentazione archivistica delle tele settecentesche nel coro del Duomo di Bergamo." *Arte veneta* 30, pp. 233–39.
1979 *Pittoni: L'opera completa*. Venice.

Zeri, Federico
1976 *Italian Paintings in the Walters Art Gallery*. 2 vols. Baltimore.

Zeri, Federico, with Elizabeth Gardner
1973 *Italian Paintings: A Catalogue of the Collection of The Metropolitan Museum of Art*. [Vol. 2], *Venetian School*. New York.

Ziliotti, Bernardo
1775–79 "Osservazioni sopra la pittura e sopra i più celebri pittori d'Italia." Ms., Biblioteca del Museo Civico, Bassano del Grappa.

Zucchini, T.
1784 *Nuova cronaca veneta*. . . . Venice.

General Index

NOTE: Tiepolo's works are listed separately in an index arranged by subject and an index arranged by location.
Italic page references indicate illustrations.

Index of Works Arranged by Subject

NOTE: Works by Tiepolo cited in the catalogue are listed alphabetically by title, under the following headings: *Religious*, with the subdivisions *Old Testament* and *New Testament, Saints, and Devotional Themes*; and *Secular*, subdivided into *History, Genre and Portraiture, Allegory and Mythology*, and *Poetic Themes*. Works belonging to cycles are grouped within these categories under the church or palace for which they were commissioned. See also the Index of Works Arranged by Location. Unless otherwise noted, works are oil on canvas.

Italic page references indicate illustrations.

RELIGIOUS

Old Testament

New Testament, Saints, and Devotional Themes

SECULAR

History

Index of Works Arranged by Location

NOTE: Works by Tiepolo cited in the catalogue are listed alphabetically under the city in which they are located. See also the Index of Works Arranged by Subject. Unless otherwise noted, works are oil on canvas.

Italic page references indicate illustrations.

Photograph Credits

Photographs were supplied by the owners of the works and are reproduced by permission of the owners, except as indicated in the following additional credits.

Archivo Mas, Madrid: fig. 118
Archivo Oronoz, Madrid: fig. 117
Jörg P. Anders: no. 38; figs. 55, 56, 79, 80, 106
Musée d'Angers (Pierre David): frontis., p. 274; no. 52
© 1990 The Art Institute of Chicago, All Rights Reserved: no. 17a
© 1994 The Art Institute of Chicago, All Rights Reserved: no. 17c,d, detail no. 17b
© 1996 The Art Institute of Chicago, All Rights Reserved: no. 17b, detail no. 17b
Copyright Osvaldo Böhm: frontis., p. 28; nos. 1, 2a,b, 5, 6a,b, 13, 20, 24, 25a,b, 27–29, 31, 35, 36a, 46, 48a; figs. 4, 15–18, 22, 27–29, 43, 46, 63–70, 81, 92, 100, 111, 113, 115, 116
Bulloz: figs. 5, 11, 108
Richard Carafelli: no. 45b
Stefano and Elio Ciol: figs. 3, 23–26, 62
Museo Civico Torino Archivio Fotografico: fig. 99
A. C. Cooper Ltd., London: no. 30b
Antoni E. Dolinski, Sierra Madre, California: no. 17f,g
Fotoarchiv Tiroler Landesmuseum Ferdinandeum: fig. 93
Foto Saporetti, Milan: no. 36b
Fototecnica, Vicenza: frontis., p. 14; nos. 9a,b, 18, 39; figs. 9, 30, 38, 40, 42, 44, 45, 82, 98
Scott Hyde: fig. 101
© 1996 Copyright by Kunsthaus Zürich, All Rights Reserved: no. 58a
Bernard Lehn Fotografie, Fotodesign, Munich: frontis., p. 104; no. 22a,b
David A. Loggie: fig. 14
Paulo Manusardi Fotografo, Milan: no. 57a
A. Szenczi Maria: fig. 77
Adriano Mariuz: fig. 1
Brian Merrett, Musée des Beaux Arts, Montreal/Montreal Museum of Fine Arts: no. 11; fig. 2
Stanley Moss and Company, Inc., Riverdale-on-Hudson, New York: no. 42
Wolf-Christian von der Mülbe: frontis., p. 18; figs. 6, 37, 39, 95, 112
The Photograph Studio, The Metropolitan Museum of Art, New York, Katherine Dahab, Oi-Cheong Lee, Bruce Schwarz, Eileen Travell: frontis., pp. 2, 36; no. 12e, detail no. 12e, no. 12f, detail no. 12f, nos. 12g, 59a–j, 60a–w; figs. 12, 14, 78, 86, 87, 96, 119, 123
© Photothèque des Musées de la Ville de Paris/Cliché Andreani. By SPADEM: no. 19
Antonia Reeve Photography, Edinburgh: 16a
Réunion des Musées Nationaux, France: figs. 10, 13, 36, 72
Soprintendenza B. S. A. di Milano: fig. 19
Studio Fotografico Luca Carra', Milan: no. 8
Copyright Umberto Tomba, Verona: no. 10
Elke Walford Fotowerkstatt, Hamburger Kunsthalle: no. 33; fig. 71
Westend Color: no. 47a
Graydon Wood, 1993: no. 26
Fotoflash di Elisabetta Zennaro: fig. 107